# FORD

# LINCOLN COUPES AND SEDANS 1988-00 REPAIR MANUAL

CHILTON'S

Covers all U.S. and Canadian models of Lincoln Continental, Mark VII, Mark VIII and Town Car

by Joseph D'Orazio, A.S.E.

CHILTON Automotive Books

PUBLISHED BY HAYNES NORTH AMERICA, Inc.

Haynes ®

APA AUTOMOTIVE PARTS & ACCESSORIES ASSOCIATION MEMBER

Manufactured in USA

ISBN 0-8019-9314-8
Library of Congress Catalog Card No. 00-132-508
1234567890 9876543210

**Haynes Publishing Group**
Sparkford Nr Yeovil
Somerset BA22 7JJ England

**Haynes North America, Inc**
861 Lawrence Drive
Newbury Park
California 91320 USA

ABCDE
F

**10K3**

# Contents


**1 GENERAL INFORMATION AND MAINTENANCE**

- 1-2 HOW TO USE THIS BOOK
- 1-3 TOOLS AND EQUIPMENT
- 1-6 SERVICING YOUR VEHICLE SAFELY
- 1-7 FASTENERS, MEASUREMENTS AND CONVERSIONS
- 1-11 SERIAL NUMBER IDENTIFICATION
- 1-13 ROUTINE MAINTENANCE
- 1-33 FLUIDS AND LUBRICANTS
- 1-45 JUMP STARTING A DEAD BATTERY
- 1-46 JACKING

**2 ENGINE ELECTRICAL**

- 2-2 DISTRIBUTOR IGNITION
- 2-6 DISTRIBUTORLESS IGNITION SYSTEM
- 2-8 FIRING ORDERS
- 2-8 CHARGING SYSTEM
- 2-10 STARTING SYSTEM
- 2-10 SENDING UNITS AND SENSORS

**3 ENGINE AND ENGINE OVERHAUL**

- 3-2 ENGINE MECHANICAL
- 3-42 EXHAUST SYSTEM
- 3-43 ENGINE RECONDITIONING

**4 DRIVEABILITY AND EMISSION CONTROLS**

- 4-2 EMISSION CONTROLS
- 4-6 ELECTRONIC ENGINE CONTROLS
- 4-14 COMPONENT LOCATIONS
- 4-17 TROUBLE CODES—EEC IV SYSTEM
- 4-21 TROUBLE CODES—EEC V SYSTEM (OBD-II)
- 4-27 VACUUM DIAGRAMS

**5 FUEL SYSTEM**

- 5-2 BASIC FUEL SYSTEM DIAGNOSIS
- 5-2 FUEL LINES AND FITTINGS
- 5-4 GASOLINE FUEL INJECTION SYSTEM
- 5-11 FUEL TANK

**6 CHASSIS ELECTRICAL**

- 6-2 UNDERSTANDING AND TROUBLESHOOTING ELECTRICAL SYSTEMS
- 6-7 BATTERY CABLES
- 6-7 AIR BAG (SUPPLEMENTAL RESTRAINT SYSTEM)
- 6-9 HEATING AND AIR CONDITIONING
- 6-15 CRUISE CONTROL
- 6-16 ENTERTAINMENT SYSTEMS
- 6-19 WINDSHIELD WIPERS AND WASHERS
- 6-21 INSTRUMENTS AND SWITCHES
- 6-23 LIGHTING
- 6-29 CIRCUIT PROTECTION
- 6-41 WIRING DIAGRAMS

# Contents


7-2 AUTOMATIC TRANSMISSION
7-4 AUTOMATIC TRANSAXLE
7-9 DRIVELINE

DRIVE TRAIN 7

8-2 WHEELS
8-4 FRONT SUSPENSION
8-12 REAR SUSPENSION
8-18 STEERING

SUSPENSION AND STEERING 8

9-2 BRAKE OPERATING SYSTEM
9-5 DISC BRAKES
9-10 DRUM BRAKES
9-15 PARKING BRAKE
9-16 ANTI-LOCK BRAKE SYSTEM

BRAKES 9

10-2 EXTERIOR
10-6 INTERIOR

BODY AND TRIM 10

11-2 TROUBLESHOOTING INDEX
11-6 DIAGNOSTIC PROCEDURES

TROUBLESHOOTING 11

11-25 GLOSSARY

GLOSSARY

11-29 MASTER INDEX

MASTER INDEX

## SAFETY NOTICE

Proper service and repair procedures are vital to the safe, reliable operation of all motor vehicles, as well as the personal safety of those performing repairs. This manual outlines procedures for servicing and repairing vehicles using safe, effective methods. The procedures contain many NOTES, CAUTIONS and WARNINGS which should be followed, along with standard procedures to eliminate the possibility of personal injury or improper service which could damage the vehicle or compromise its safety.

It is important to note that repair procedures and techniques, tools and parts for servicing motor vehicles, as well as the skill and experience of the individual performing the work vary widely. It is not possible to anticipate all of the conceivable ways or conditions under which vehicles may be serviced, or to provide cautions as to all possible hazards that may result. Standard and accepted safety precautions and equipment should be used when handling toxic or flammable fluids, and safety goggles or other protection should be used during cutting, grinding, chiseling, prying, or any other process that can cause material removal or projectiles.

Some procedures require the use of tools specially designed for a specific purpose. Before substituting another tool or procedure, you must be completely satisfied that neither your personal safety, nor the performance of the vehicle will be endangered.

Although information in this manual is based on industry sources and is complete as possible at the time of publication, the possibility exists that some car manufacturers made later changes which could not be included here. While striving for total accuracy, the authors or publishers cannot assume responsibility for any errors, changes or omissions that may occur in the compilation of this data.

## PART NUMBERS

Part numbers listed in this reference are not recommendations by Haynes North America, Inc. for any product brand name. They are references that can be used with interchange manuals and aftermarket supplier catalogs to locate each brand supplier's discrete part number.

## SPECIAL TOOLS

Special tools are recommended by the vehicle manufacturer to perform their specific job. Use has been kept to a minimum, but where absolutely necessary, they are referred to in the text by the part number of the tool manufacturer. These tools can be purchased, under the appropriate part number, from your local dealer or regional distributor, or an equivalent tool can be purchased locally from a tool supplier or parts outlet. Before substituting any tool for the one recommended, read the SAFETY NOTICE at the top of this page.

## ACKNOWLEDGMENTS

This publication contains material that is reproduced and distributed under a license from Ford Motor Company. No further reproduction or distribution of the Ford Motor Company material is allowed without the express written permission from Ford Motor Company.

**HOW TO USE THIS BOOK 1-2**
WHERE TO BEGIN 1-2
AVOIDING TROUBLE 1-2
MAINTENANCE OR REPAIR? 1-2
AVOIDING THE MOST COMMON MISTAKES 1-2
**TOOLS AND EQUIPMENT 1-3**
SPECIAL TOOLS 1-4
**SERVICING YOUR VEHICLE SAFELY 1-6**
DO'S 1-6
DON'TS 1-6
**FASTENERS, MEASUREMENTS AND CONVERSIONS 1-7**
BOLTS, NUTS AND OTHER THREADED RETAINERS 1-7
TORQUE 1-7
TORQUE WRENCHES 1-8
TORQUE ANGLE METERS 1-10
STANDARD AND METRIC MEASUREMENTS 1-10
**SERIAL NUMBER IDENTIFICATION 1-11**
VEHICLE IDENTIFICATION PLATE 1-11
ENGINE NUMBER 1-11
TRANSMISSION/TRANSAXLE NUMBER 1-11
DRIVE AXLE 1-11
**ROUTINE MAINTENANCE 1-13**
AIR CLEANER 1-16
REMOVAL & INSTALLATION 1-16
FUEL FILTER 1-16
REMOVAL & INSTALLATION 1-16
PCV VALVE 1-18
REMOVAL & INSTALLATION 1-18
EVAPORATIVE CANISTER 1-18
SERVICING 1-18
BATTERY 1-18
PRECAUTIONS 1-18
GENERAL MAINTENANCE 1-18
BATTERY FLUID 1-18
CABLES 1-19
CHARGING 1-20
REPLACEMENT 1-20
BELTS 1-20
INSPECTION 1-20
ADJUSTING 1-20
REMOVAL AND INSTALLATION 1-21
HOSES 1-21
INSPECTION 1-21
REMOVAL & INSTALLATION 1-22
CV-BOOTS 1-22
INSPECTION 1-22
SPARK PLUGS 1-22
SPARK PLUG HEAT RANGE 1-23
REMOVAL & INSTALLATION 1-23
INSPECTION & GAPPING 1-24
SPARK PLUG WIRES 1-26
TESTING 1-26
REMOVAL & INSTALLATION 1-26
DISTRIBUTOR CAP AND ROTOR 1-27
REMOVAL AND INSTALLATION 1-27
INSPECTION 1-27
IGNITION TIMING 1-27
INSPECTION &ADJUSTMENT 1-28
VALVE LASH 1-28
ADJUSTMENT 1-28
IDLE SPEED AND MIXTURE ADJUSTMENTS 1-28
ADJUSTMENT 1-28
AIR CONDITIONING SYSTEM 1-29
SYSTEM SERVICE & REPAIR 1-29
PREVENTIVE MAINTENANCE 1-30
SYSTEM INSPECTION 1-30
WINDSHIELD WIPERS 1-30
ELEMENT (REFILL) CARE & REPLACEMENT 1-30
TIRES AND WHEELS 1-30
TIRE ROTATION 1-31
TIRE DESIGN 1-31
TIRE STORAGE 1-31
INFLATION & INSPECTION 1-31
**FLUIDS AND LUBRICANTS 1-33**
FLUID DISPOSAL 1-33
FUEL AND ENGINE OIL RECOMMENDATIONS 1-33
FUEL 1-33
OIL 1-33
ENGINE 1-33
OIL LEVEL CHECK 1-33
CHANGING OIL & FILTER 1-34
AUTOMATIC TRANSAXLE 1-36
FLUID RECOMMENDATIONS 1-36
LEVEL CHECK 1-37
AUTOMATIC TRANSMISSIONS 1-37
FLUID RECOMMENDATIONS 1-37
PAN & FILTER SERVICE 1-37
DRIVE AXLE 1-38
FLUID RECOMMENDATIONS 1-38
LEVEL CHECK 1-39
DRAIN AND REFILL 1-39
COOLING SYSTEM 1-40
FLUID RECOMMENDATION 1-40
LEVEL CHECK 1-40
TESTING FOR LEAKS 1-40
DRAIN & REFILL 1-41
FLUSHING & CLEANING THE SYSTEM 1-42
MASTER CYLINDER 1-42
FLUID RECOMMENDATION 1-42
FLUID LEVEL 1-42
POWER STEERING PUMP 1-43
FLUID RECOMMENDATION 1-43
LEVEL CHECK 1-43
CHASSIS GREASING 1-43
WHEEL BEARINGS 1-43
REPACKING 1-43
**JUMP STARTING A DEAD BATTERY 1-45**
JUMP STARTING PRECAUTIONS 1-45
JUMP STARTING PROCEDURE 1-45
**JACKING 1-46**
JACKING PRECAUTIONS 1-46
**COMPONENT LOCATIONS**
UNDERHOOD COMPONENT LOCATIONS—3.8L ENGINE 1-13
UNDERHOOD COMPONENT LOCATIONS—4.6L ENGINE 1-14
UNDERHOOD COMPONENT LOCATIONS—5.0L ENGINE 1-15
**SPECIFICATIONS CHARTS**
LINCOLN VEHICLE IDENTIFICATION CHART 1-11
ENGINE IDENTIFICATION AND SPECIFICATIONS 1-12
GASOLINE ENGINE TUNE-UP SPECIFICATIONS 1-29
MANUFACTURER RECOMMENDED NORMAL MAINTENANCE INTERVALS 1-46
MANUFACTURER RECOMMENDED SEVERE MAINTENANCE INTERVALS 1-47
CAPACITIES 1-48

# 1

# GENERAL INFORMATION AND MAINTENANCE

HOW TO USE THIS BOOK 1-2
TOOLS AND EQUIPMENT 1-3
SERVICING YOUR VEHICLE SAFELY 1-6
FASTENERS, MEASUREMENTS AND CONVERSIONS 1-7
SERIAL NUMBER IDENTIFICATION 1-11
ROUTINE MAINTENANCE 1-13
FLUIDS AND LUBRICANTS 1-33
JUMP STARTING A DEAD BATTERY 1-45
JACKING 1-46

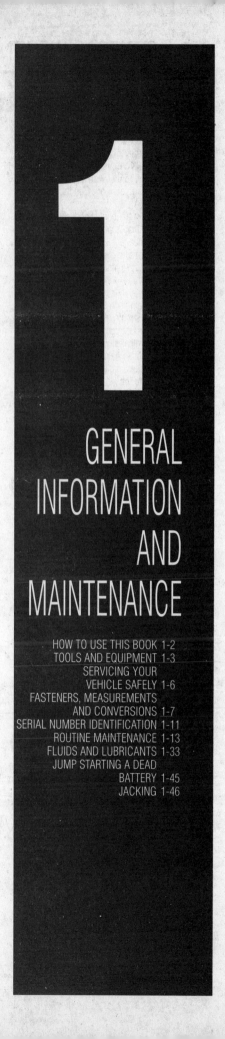

## HOW TO USE THIS BOOK

Chilton's Total Car Care manual for the 1988 to 2000 Lincoln Town Car, 1988 to 2000 Lincoln Continental, the 1988 to 1992 Mark VII, and the 1993 to 1998 MARK VIII, is intended to help you learn more about the inner workings of your vehicle while saving you money on its upkeep and operation.

The beginning of the book will likely be referred to the most, since that is where you will find information for maintenance and tune-up. The other sections deal with the more complex systems of your vehicle. Operating systems from engine through brakes are covered to the extent that the average do-it-yourselfer becomes mechanically involved. This book will not explain such things as rebuilding a differential for the simple reason that the expertise required and the investment in special tools make this task uneconomical. It will, however, give you detailed instructions to help you change your own brake pads and shoes, replace spark plugs, and perform many more jobs that can save you money, give you personal satisfaction and help you avoid expensive problems.

A secondary purpose of this book is a reference for owners who want to understand their vehicle and/or their mechanics. In this case, no tools at all are required.

### Where to Begin

Before removing any bolts, read the entire procedure. This will give you the overall view of what tools and supplies will be required. There is nothing more frustrating than having to walk to the bus stop on Monday morning because you were short one bolt on Sunday afternoon. So read ahead and plan. Each operation should be approached logically and all procedures thoroughly understood before attempting any work.

All sections contain adjustments, maintenance, removal and installation procedures, and in some cases, repair or overhaul procedures. When repair is not considered practical, we tell you how to remove the part and then how to install the new or rebuilt replacement. In this way, you at least save labor costs. "Backyard" repair of some components is just not practical.

### Avoiding Trouble

Many procedures in this book require you to "label and disconnect . . . " a group of lines hoses or wires. Don't be lulled into thinking you can remember where everything goes—you won't. If you hook up vacuum or fuel lines incorrectly, the vehicle may run poorly, if at all. If you hook up electrical wiring incorrectly, you may instantly learn a very expensive lesson.

You don't need to know the official or engineering name for each hose or line. A piece of masking tape on the hose and a piece on its fitting will allow you to assign your own label such as the letter A or a short name. As long as you remember your own code, the lines can be reconnected by matching similar letters or names. Do remember that tape will dissolve in gasoline or other fluids; if a component is to be washed or cleaned, use another method of identification. A permanent felt-tipped marker or a metal scribe can be very handy for marking metal parts. Remove any tape or paper labels after assembly.

### Maintenance or Repair?

It's necessary to mention the difference between maintenance and repair. Maintenance includes routine inspections, adjustments, and replacement of parts which show signs of normal wear. Maintenance compensates for wear or deterioration. Repair implies that something has broken or is not working. A need for repair is often caused by lack of maintenance. Example: draining and refilling the automatic transmission fluid is maintenance recommended by the manufacturer at specific mileage intervals. Failure to do this can shorten the life of the transmission/transaxle, requiring very expensive repairs. While no maintenance program can prevent items from breaking or wearing out, a general rule can be stated: MAINTENANCE IS CHEAPER THAN REPAIR.

Two basic mechanic's rules should be mentioned here. First, whenever the left side of the vehicle or engine is referred to, it is meant to specify the driver's side. Conversely, the right side of the vehicle means the passenger's side. Second, screws and bolts are removed by turning counterclockwise and tightened by turning clockwise unless specifically noted.

Safety is always the most important rule. Constantly be aware of the dangers involved in working on an automobile and take the proper precautions. See the information in this section regarding SERVICING YOUR VEHICLE SAFELY and the SAFETY NOTICE on the acknowledgment page.

### Avoiding the Most Common Mistakes

Pay attention to the instructions provided. There are 3 common mistakes in mechanical work:

1. Incorrect order of assembly, disassembly or adjustment. When taking something apart or putting it together, performing steps in the wrong order usually just costs you extra time; however, it CAN break something. Read the entire procedure before beginning disassembly. Perform everything in the order in which the instructions say you should, even if you can't immediately see a reason for it. When you're taking apart something that is very intricate, you might want to draw a picture of how it looks when assembled at one point in order to make sure you get everything back in its proper position. We will supply exploded views whenever possible. When making adjustments, perform them in the proper order. One adjustment possibly will affect another.
2. Overtorquing (or undertorquing). While it is more common for overtorquing to cause damage, undertorquing may allow a fastener to vibrate loose causing serious damage. Especially when dealing with aluminum parts, pay attention to torque specifications and utilize a torque wrench in assembly. If a torque figure is not available, remember that if you are using the right tool to perform the job, you will probably not have to strain yourself to get a fastener tight enough. The pitch of most threads is so slight that the tension you put on the wrench will be multiplied many times in actual force on what you are tightening. A good example of how critical torque is can be seen in the case of spark plug installation, especially where you are putting the plug into an aluminum cylinder head. Too little torque can fail to crush the gasket, causing leakage of combustion gases and consequent overheating of the plug and engine parts. Too much torque can damage the threads or distort the plug, changing the spark gap.

   There are many commercial products available for ensuring that fasteners won't come loose, even if they are not torqued just right (a very common brand is Loctite•). If you're worried about getting something together tight enough to hold, but loose enough to avoid mechanical damage during assembly, one of these products might offer substantial insurance. Before choosing a threadlocking compound, read the label on the package and make sure the product is compatible with the materials, fluids, etc. involved.
3. Crossthreading. This occurs when a part such as a bolt is screwed into a nut or casting at the wrong angle and forced. Crossthreading is more likely to occur if access is difficult. It helps to clean and lubricate fasteners, then to start threading the bolt, spark plug, etc. with your fingers. If you encounter resistance, unscrew the part and start over again at a different angle until it can be inserted and turned several times without much effort. Keep in mind that many parts, especially spark plugs, have tapered threads, so that gentle turning will automatically bring the part you're threading to the proper angle. Don't put a wrench on the part until it's been tightened a couple of turns by hand. If you suddenly encounter resistance, and the part has not seated fully, don't force it. Pull it back out to make sure it's clean and threading properly.

Be sure to take your time and be patient, and always plan. Allow yourself ample time to perform repairs and maintenance. You may find maintaining your car a satisfying and enjoyable experience.

## TOOLS AND EQUIPMENT

**See Figures 1 thru 15**

Naturally, without the proper tools and equipment it is impossible to properly service your vehicle. It would also be virtually impossible to catalog every tool that you would need to perform all of the operations in this book. Of course, It would be unwise for the amateur to rush out and buy an expensive set of tools on the theory that he/she may need one or more of them at some time.

The best approach is to proceed slowly, gathering a good quality set of those tools that are used most frequently. Don't be misled by the low cost of bargain tools. It is far better to spend a little more for better quality. Forged wrenches, 6 or 12-point sockets and fine tooth ratchets are by far preferable to their less expensive counterparts. As any good mechanic can tell you, there are few worse experiences than trying to work on a vehicle with bad tools. Your monetary savings will be far outweighed by frustration and mangled knuckles.

Begin accumulating those tools that are used most frequently: those associated with routine maintenance and tune-up. In addition to the normal assortment of screwdrivers and pliers, you should have the following tools:

- Wrenches/sockets and combination open end/box end wrenches in sizes from 1/8–3/4 in. or 3–19mm, as well as a 13/16 in. or 5/8 in. spark plug socket (depending on plug type).

**➡If possible, buy various length socket drive extensions. Universal-joint and wobble extensions can be extremely useful, but be careful when using them, as they can change the amount of torque applied to the socket.**

- Jackstands for support.
- Oil filter wrench.
- Spout or funnel for pouring fluids.
- Grease gun for chassis lubrication (unless your vehicle is not equipped with any grease fit-

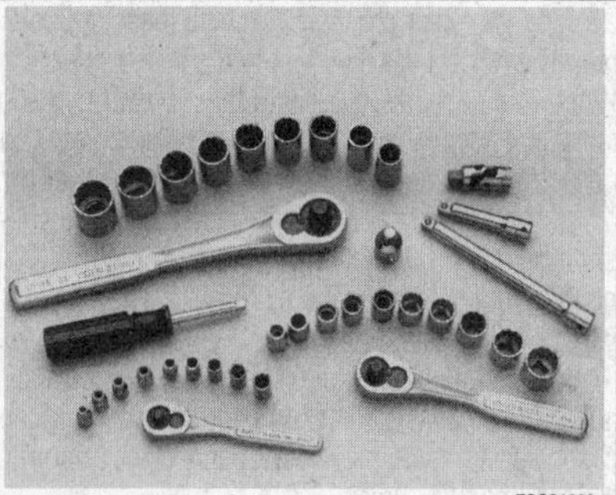

TCCS1200

**Fig. 1 All but the most basic procedures will require an assortment of ratchets and sockets**

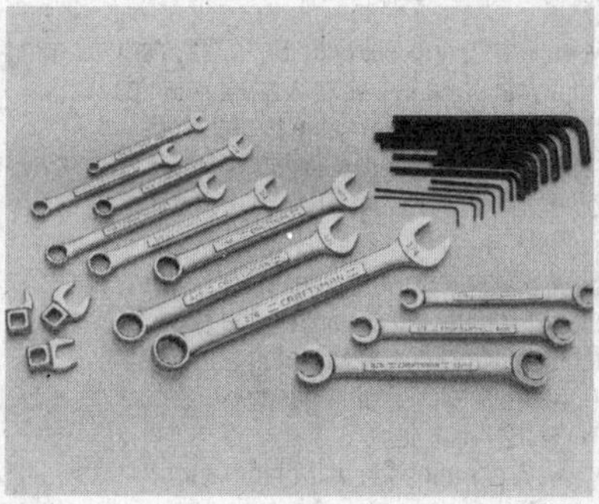

TCCS1201

**Fig. 2 In addition to ratchets, a good set of wrenches and hex keys will be necessary**

TCCS1202

**Fig. 3 A hydraulic floor jack and a set of jackstands are essential for lifting and supporting the vehicle**

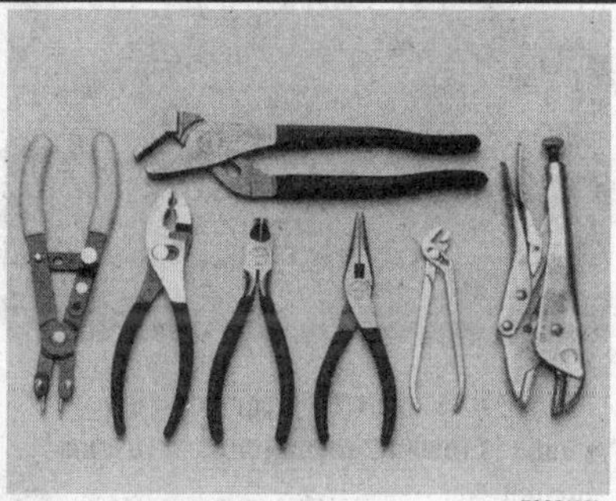

TCCS1203

**Fig. 4 An assortment of pliers, grippers and cutters will be handy for old rusted parts and stripped bolt heads**

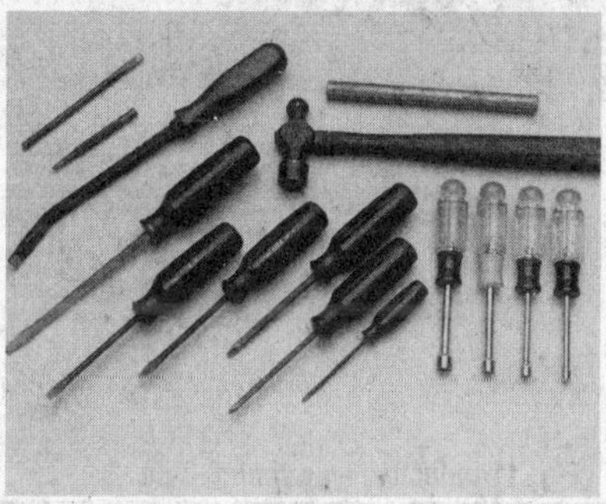

TCCS1204

**Fig. 5 Various drivers, chisels and prybars are great tools to have in your toolbox**

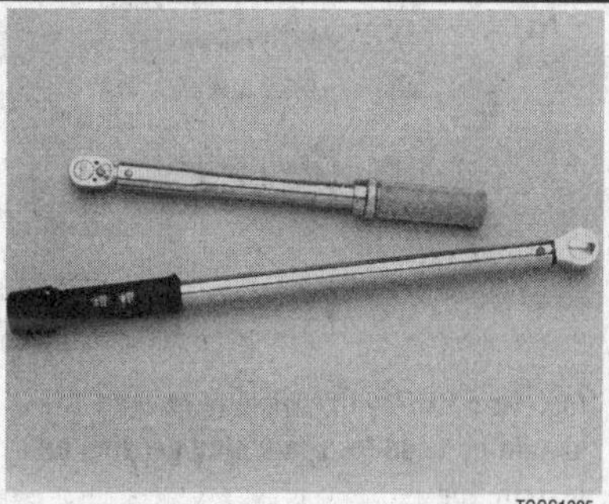

TCCS1205

**Fig. 6 Many repairs will require the use of a torque wrench to assure the components are properly fastened**

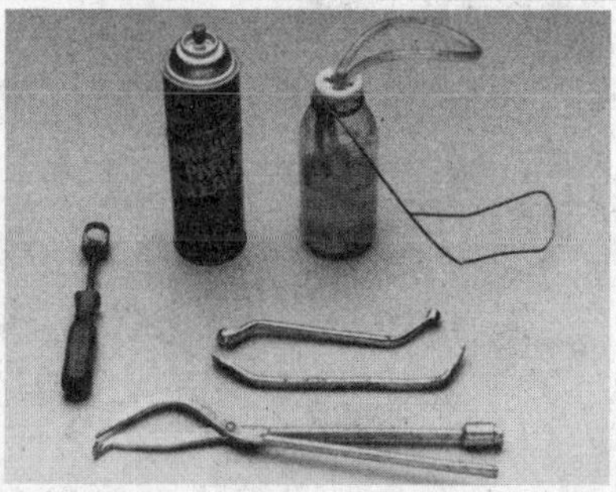

TCCS1209

**Fig. 7 Although not always necessary, using specialized brake tools will save time**

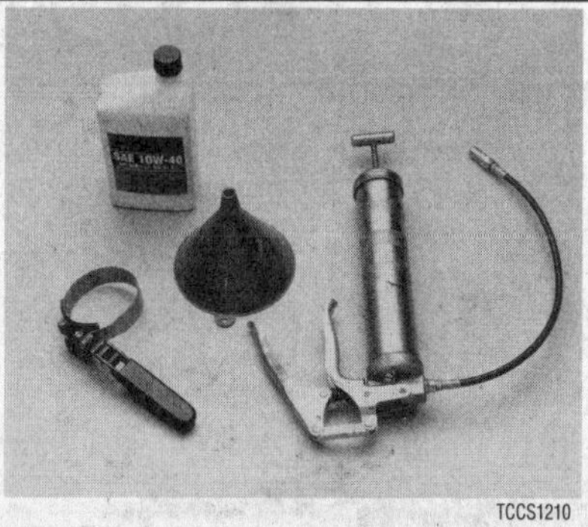

TCCS1210

**Fig. 8 A few inexpensive lubrication tools will make maintenance easier**

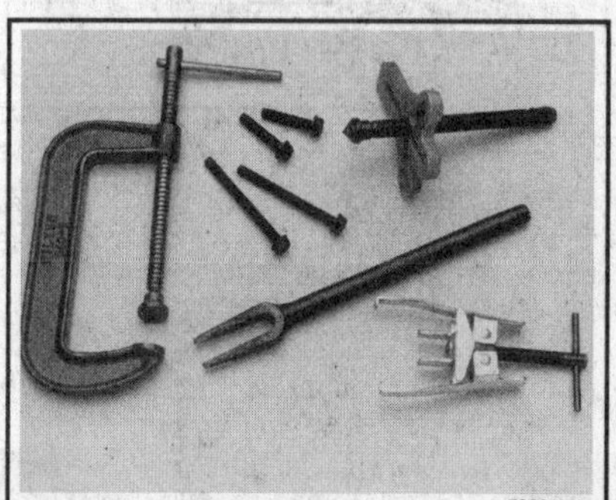

TCCS1211

**Fig. 9 Various pullers, clamps and separator tools are needed for many larger, more complicated repairs**

tings—for details, please refer to information on Fluids and Lubricants, later in this section).

- Hydrometer for checking the battery (unless equipped with a sealed, maintenance-free battery).
- A container for draining oil and other fluids.
- Rags for wiping up the inevitable mess.

In addition to the above items there are several others that are not absolutely necessary, but handy to have around. These include Oil Dry® (or an equivalent oil absorbent gravel—such as cat litter) and the usual supply of lubricants, antifreeze and fluids, although these can be purchased as needed. This is a basic list for routine maintenance, but only your personal needs and desire can accurately determine your list of tools.

After performing a few projects on the vehicle, you'll be amazed at the other tools and non-tools on your workbench. Some useful household items are: a large turkey baster or siphon, empty coffee cans and ice trays (to store parts), ball of twine, electrical tape for wiring, small rolls of colored tape for tagging lines or hoses, markers and pens, a note pad, golf tees (for plugging vacuum lines), metal coat hangers or a roll of mechanic's wire (to hold things out of the way), dental pick or similar long, pointed probe, a strong magnet, and a small mirror (to see into recesses and under manifolds).

A more advanced set of tools, suitable for tune-up work, can be drawn up easily. While the tools are slightly more sophisticated, they need not be outrageously expensive. There are several inexpensive tach/dwell meters on the market that are every bit as good for the average mechanic as a professional model. Just be sure that it goes to a least 1200–1500 rpm on the tach scale and that it works on 4, 6 and 8-cylinder engines. The key to these purchases is to make them with an eye towards adaptability and wide range. A basic list of tune-up tools could include:

- Tach/dwell meter.
- Spark plug wrench and gapping tool.
- Feeler gauges for valve adjustment.
- Timing light.

The choice of a timing light should be made carefully. A light which works on the DC current supplied by the vehicle's battery is the best choice; it should have a xenon tube for brightness. On any vehicle with an electronic ignition system, a timing light with an inductive pickup that clamps around the No. 1 spark plug cable is preferred.

In addition to these basic tools, there are several other tools and gauges you may find useful. These include:

- Compression gauge. The screw-in type is slower to use, but eliminates the possibility of a faulty reading due to escaping pressure.
- Manifold vacuum gauge.
- 12V test light.
- A combination volt/ohmmeter
- Induction Ammeter. This is used for determining whether or not there is current in a wire. These are handy for use if a wire is broken somewhere in a wiring harness.

As a final note, you will probably find a torque wrench necessary for all but the most basic work. The beam type models are perfectly adequate, although the newer click types (breakaway) are easier to use. The click type torque wrenches tend to be more expensive. Also keep in mind that all types of torque wrenches should be periodically checked and/or recalibrated. You will have to decide for yourself which better fits your pocketbook, and purpose.

## Special Tools

Normally, the use of special factory tools is avoided for repair procedures, since these are not readily available for the do-it-yourself mechanic. When it is possible to perform the job with more commonly available tools, it will be pointed out, but occasionally, a special tool was designed to perform a specific function and should be used. Before substituting another tool, you should be convinced that neither your safety nor the performance of the vehicle will be compromised.

Special tools can usually be purchased from an automotive parts store or from your dealer. In some cases special tools may be available directly from the tool manufacturer.

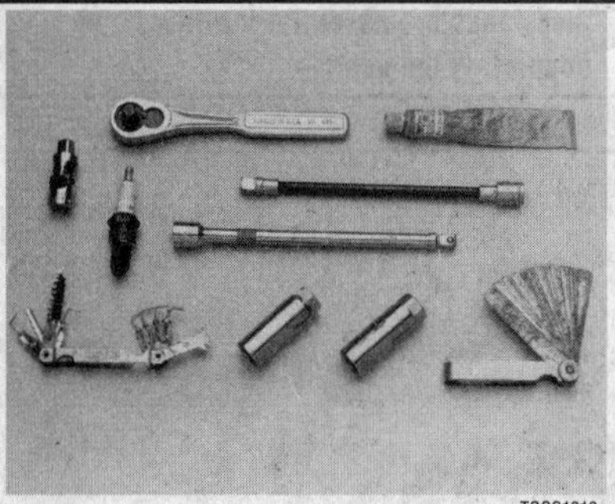

TCCS1212

**Fig. 10 A variety of tools and gauges should be used for spark plug gapping and installation**

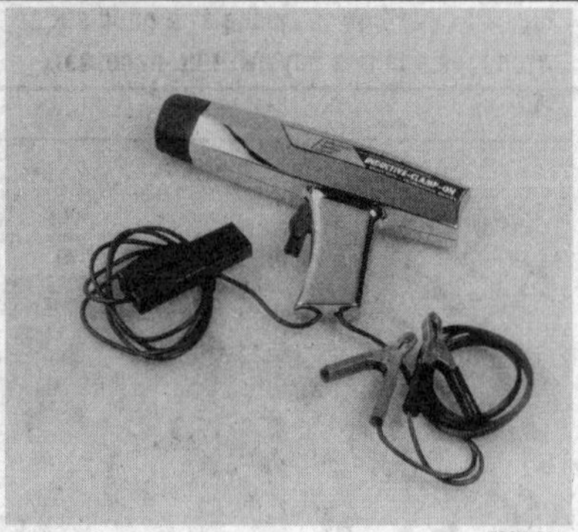

TCCX1P01

**Fig. 11 Inductive type timing light**

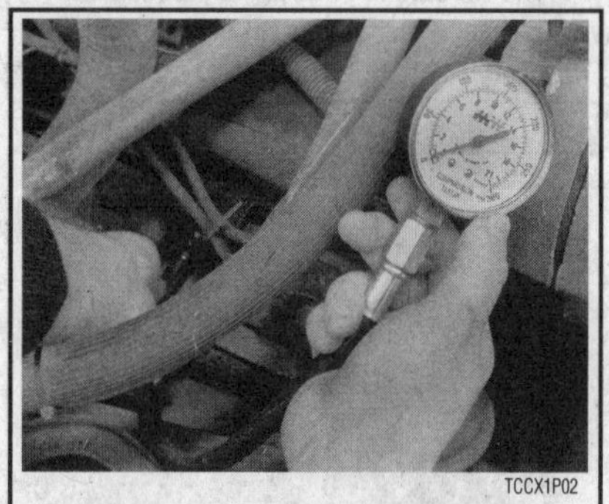

TCCX1P02

**Fig. 12 A screw-in type compression gauge is recommended for compression testing**

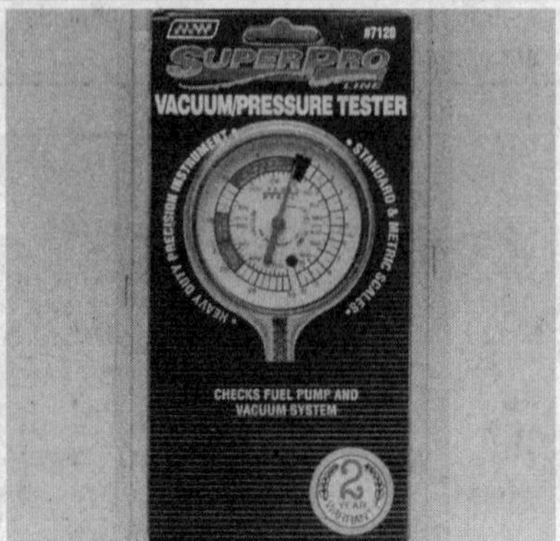


TCCX1P03

**Fig. 13 A vacuum/pressure tester is necessary for many testing procedures**

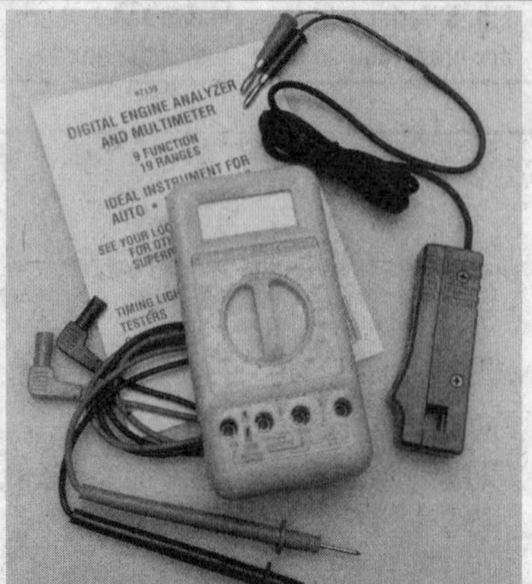


TCCX1P06

**Fig. 14 Most modern automotive multimeters incorporate many helpful features**

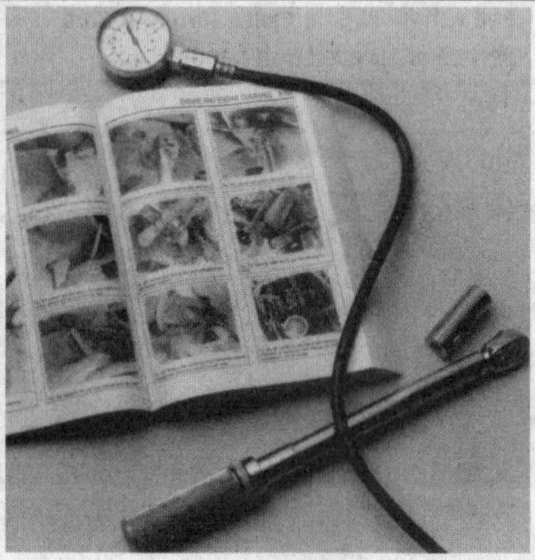

TCCS1213

**Fig. 15 Proper information is vital, so always have a Chilton Total Car Care manual handy**

# DIAGNOSTIC TEST EQUIPMENT

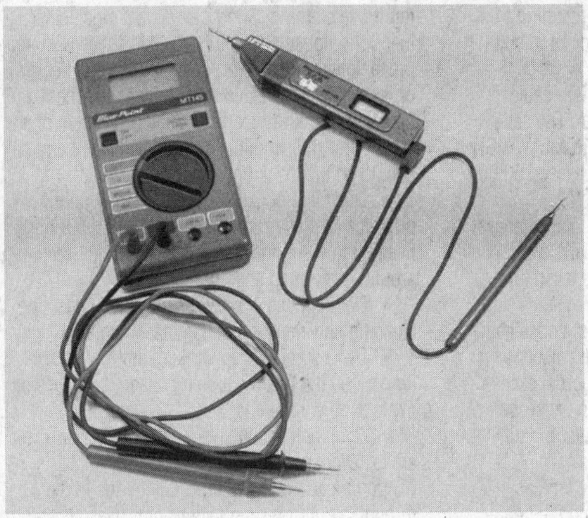

**Digital multimeters** come in a variety of styles and are a "must-have" for any serious home mechanic. Digital multimeters measure voltage (volts), resistance (ohms) and sometimes current (amperes). These versatile tools are used for checking all types of electrical or electronic components

Modern vehicles equipped with computer-controlled fuel, emission and ignition systems require modern electronic tools to diagnose problems. Many of these tools are designed solely for the professional mechanic and are too costly and difficult to use for the average do-it-yourselfer. However, various automotive aftermarket companies have introduced products that address the needs of the average home mechanic, providing sophisticated information at affordable cost. Consult your local auto parts store to determine what is available for your vehicle.

**Trouble code tools** allow the home mechanic to extract the "fault code" number from an on-board computer that has sensed a problem (usually indicated by a Check Engine light). Armed with this code, the home mechanic can focus attention on a suspect system or component

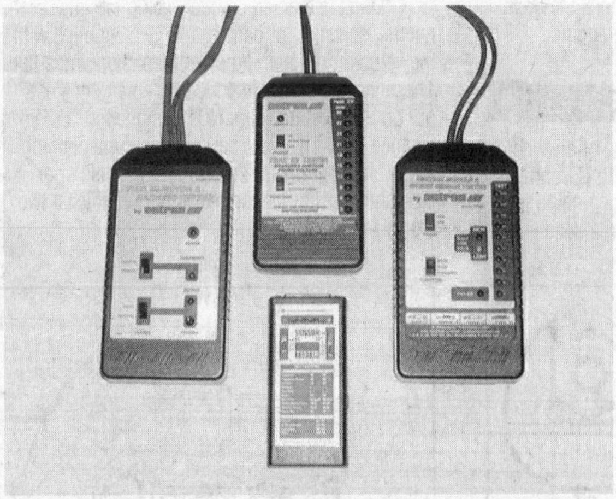

**Sensor testers** perform specific checks on many of the sensors and actuators used on today's computer-controlled vehicles. These testers can check sensors both on or off the vehicle, as well as test the accompanying electrical circuits

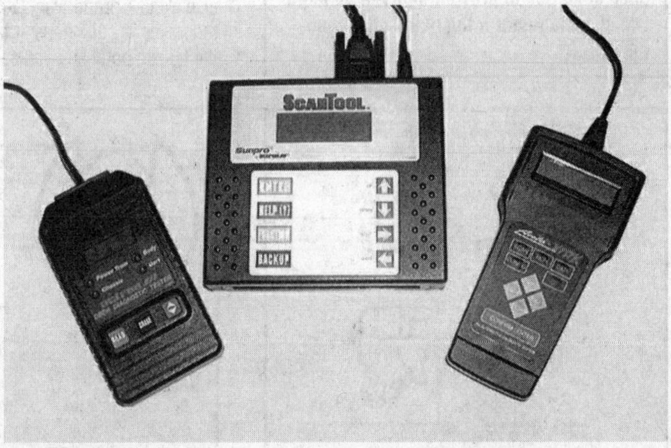


**Hand-held scanners** represent the most sophisticated of all do-it-yourself diagnostic tools. These tools do more than just access computer codes like the code readers above; they provide the user with an actual interface into the vehicle's computer. Comprehensive data on specific makes and models will come with the tool, either built-in or as a separate cartridge

## SERVICING YOUR VEHICLE SAFELY

➧ **See Figures 16, 17, 18 and 19**

It is virtually impossible to anticipate all of the hazards involved with automotive maintenance and service, but care and common sense will prevent most accidents.

The rules of safety for mechanics range from "don't smoke around gasoline," to "use the proper tool(s) for the job." The trick to avoiding injuries is to develop safe work habits and to take every possible precaution.

### Do's

- Do keep a fire extinguisher and first aid kit handy.
- Do wear safety glasses or goggles when cutting, drilling, grinding or prying, even if you have 20–20 vision. If you wear glasses for the sake of vision, wear safety goggles over your regular glasses.
- Do shield your eyes whenever you work around the battery. Batteries contain sulfuric acid. In case of contact with the eyes or skin, flush the area with water or a mixture of water and baking soda, then seek immediate medical attention.
- Do use safety stands (jackstands) for any undervehicle service. Jacks are for raising vehicles; jackstands are for making sure the vehicle stays raised until you want it to come down. Whenever the vehicle is raised, block the wheels remaining on the ground and set the parking brake.
- Do use adequate ventilation when working with any chemicals or hazardous materials. Like carbon monoxide, the asbestos dust resulting from some brake lining wear can be hazardous in sufficient quantities.
- Do disconnect the negative battery cable when working on the electrical system. The secondary ignition system contains EXTREMELY HIGH VOLTAGE. In some cases it can even exceed 50,000 volts.
- Do follow manufacturer's directions whenever working with potentially hazardous materials. Most chemicals and fluids are poisonous if taken internally.
- Do properly maintain your tools. Loose hammerheads, mushroomed punches and chisels, frayed or poorly grounded electrical cords, excessively worn screwdrivers, spread wrenches (open end), cracked sockets, slipping ratchets, or faulty droplight sockets can cause accidents.
- Likewise, keep your tools clean; a greasy wrench can slip off a bolt head, ruining the bolt and often harming your knuckles in the process.
- Do use the proper size and type of tool for the job at hand. Do select a wrench or socket that fits the nut or bolt. The wrench or socket should sit straight, not cocked.
- Do, when possible, pull on a wrench handle rather than push on it, and adjust your stance to prevent a fall.
- Do be sure that adjustable wrenches are tightly closed on the nut or bolt and pulled so that the force is on the side of the fixed jaw.
- Do strike squarely with a hammer; avoid glancing blows.
- Do set the parking brake and block the drive wheels if the work requires a running engine.

### Don'ts

- Don't run the engine in a garage or anywhere else without proper ventilation—EVER! Carbon monoxide is poisonous; it takes a long time to leave the human body and you can build up a deadly supply of it in your system by simply breathing in a little every day. You may not realize you are slowly poisoning yourself. Always use power vents, windows, fans and/or open the garage door.
- Don't work around moving parts while wearing loose clothing. Short sleeves are much safer than long, loose sleeves. Hard-toed shoes with neoprene soles protect your toes and give a better grip on slippery surfaces. Jewelry such as watches, fancy belt buckles, beads or body adornment of any kind is not safe working around a vehicle. Long hair should be tied back under a hat or cap.
- Don't use pockets for toolboxes. A fall or bump can drive a screwdriver deep into your body. Even a rag hanging from your back pocket can wrap around a spinning shaft or fan.
- Don't smoke when working around gasoline, cleaning solvent or other flammable material.
- Don't smoke when working around the battery. When the battery is being charged, it gives off explosive hydrogen gas.
- Don't use gasoline to wash your hands; there are excellent soaps available. Gasoline contains dangerous additives which can enter the body through a cut or through your pores. Gasoline also removes all the natural oils from the skin so that bone dry hands will suck up oil and grease.
- Don't service the air conditioning system unless you are equipped with the necessary tools and training. When liquid or compressed gas refrigerant is released to atmospheric pressure it will absorb heat from whatever it contacts. This will chill or freeze anything it touches.
- Don't use screwdrivers for anything other than driving screws! A screwdriver used as an prying tool can snap when you least expect it, causing injuries. At the very least, you'll ruin a good screwdriver.
- Don't use an emergency jack (that little ratchet, scissors, or pantograph jack supplied with the vehicle) for anything other than changing a flat! These jacks are only intended for emergency use out on the road; they are NOT designed as a maintenance tool. If you are serious about maintaining your vehicle yourself, invest in a hydraulic floor jack of at least a 1½ ton capacity, and at least two sturdy jackstands.

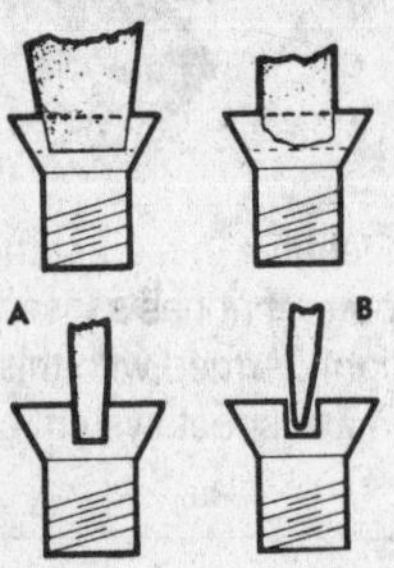

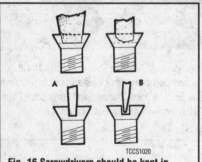

**Fig. 16 Screwdrivers should be kept in good condition to prevent injury or damage which could result if the blade slips from the screw**

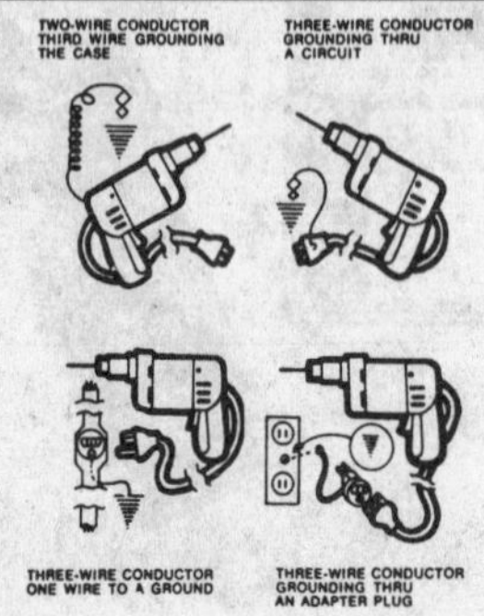


**Fig. 17 Power tools should always be properly grounded**

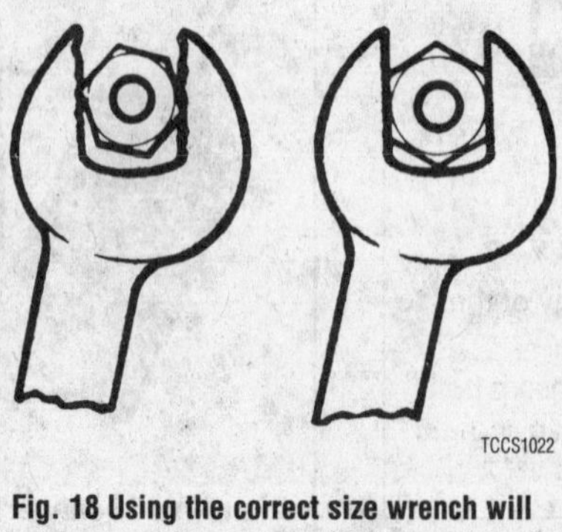


**Fig. 18 Using the correct size wrench will help prevent the possibility of rounding off a nut**

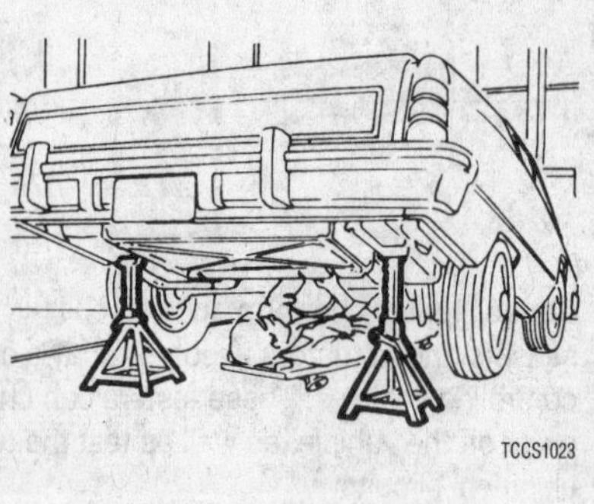


**Fig. 19 NEVER work under a vehicle unless it is supported using safety stands (jackstands)**

# FASTENERS, MEASUREMENTS AND CONVERSIONS

## Bolts, Nuts and Other Threaded Retainers

**See Figures 20, 21, 22 and 23**

Although there are a great variety of fasteners found in the modern car or truck, the most commonly used retainer is the threaded fastener (nuts, bolts, screws, studs, etc.). Most threaded retainers may be reused, provided that they are not damaged in use or during the repair. Some retainers (such as stretch bolts or torque prevailing nuts) are designed to deform when tightened or in use and should not be reinstalled.

Whenever possible, we will note any special retainers which should be replaced during a procedure. But you should always inspect the condition of a retainer when it is removed and replace any that show signs of damage. Check all threads for rust or corrosion which can increase the torque necessary to achieve the desired clamp load for which that fastener was originally selected. Additionally, be sure that the driver surface of the fastener has not been compromised by rounding or other damage. In some cases a driver surface may become only partially rounded, allowing the driver to catch in only one direction. In many of these occurrences, a fastener may be installed and tightened, but the driver would not be able to grip and loosen the fastener again. (This could lead to frustration down the line should that component ever need to be disassembled again).

If you must replace a fastener, whether due to design or damage, you must ALWAYS be sure to use the proper replacement. In all cases, a retainer of the same design, material and strength should be used. Markings on the heads of most bolts will help determine the proper strength of the fastener. The same material, thread and pitch must be selected to assure proper installation and safe operation of the vehicle afterwards.

Thread gauges are available to help measure a bolt or stud's thread. Most automotive and hardware stores keep gauges available to help you select the proper size. In a pinch, you can use another nut or bolt for a thread gauge. If the bolt you are replacing is not too badly damaged, you can select a match by finding another bolt that will thread in its place. If you find a nut which threads properly onto the damaged bolt, then use that nut to help select the replacement bolt. If however, the bolt you are replacing is so badly damaged (broken or drilled out) that its threads cannot be used as a gauge, you might start by looking for another bolt (from the same assembly or a similar location on your vehicle) which will thread into the damaged bolt's mounting. If so, the other bolt can be used to select a nut; the nut can then be used to select the replacement bolt.

In all cases, be absolutely sure you have selected the proper replacement. Don't be shy, you can always ask the store clerk for help.

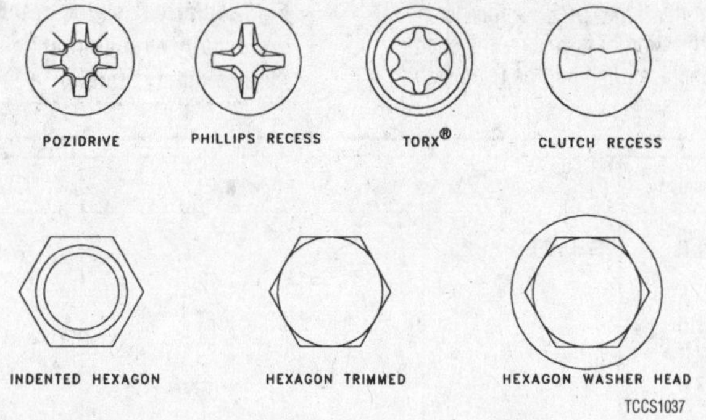


**Fig. 20 Here are a few of the most common screw/bolt driver styles**

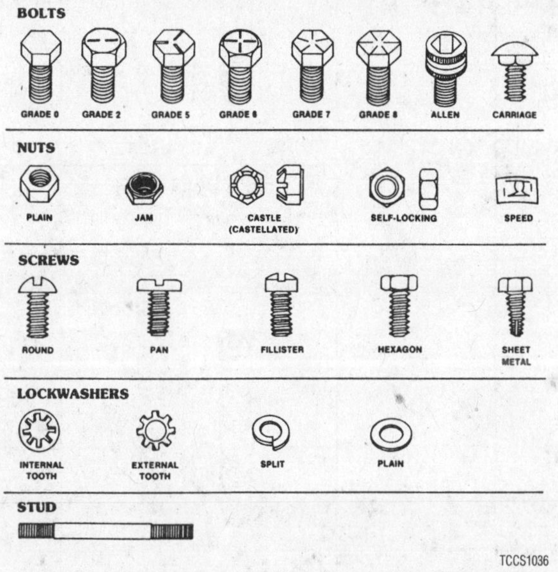


**Fig. 21 There are many different types of threaded retainers found on vehicles**

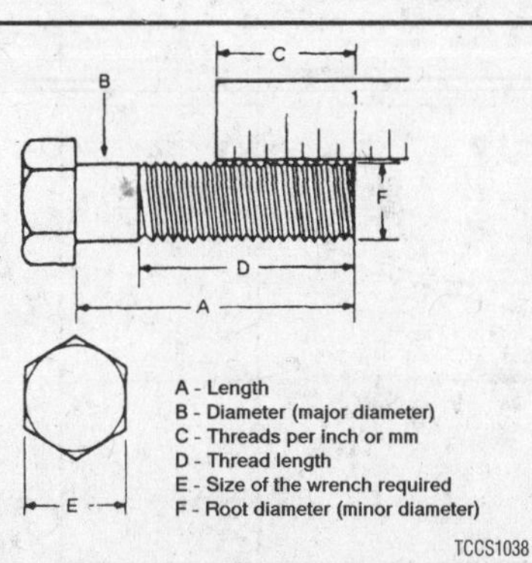


**Fig. 22 Threaded retainer sizes are determined using these measurements**

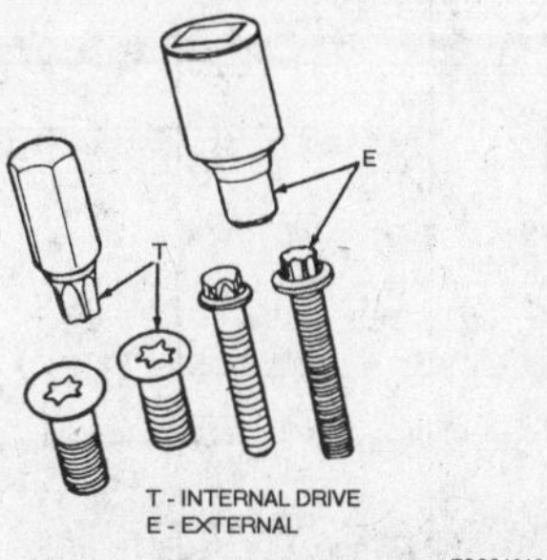


**Fig. 23 Special fasteners such as these Torx® head bolts are used by manufacturers to discourage people from working on vehicles without the proper tools**

**** WARNING**

**Be aware that when you find a bolt with damaged threads, you may also find the nut or drilled hole it was threaded into has also been damaged. If this is the case, you may have to drill and tap the hole, replace the nut or otherwise repair the threads. NEVER try to force a replacement bolt to fit into the damaged threads.**

## Torque

Torque is defined as the measurement of resistance to turning or rotating. It tends to twist a body about an axis of rotation. A common example of this would be tightening a threaded retainer such as a nut, bolt or screw. Measuring torque is one of the most common ways to help assure that a threaded retainer has been properly fastened.

When tightening a threaded fastener, torque is applied in three distinct areas, the head, the bearing surface and the clamp load. About 50 percent of the measured torque is used in overcoming bearing friction. This is the friction between the bearing surface of the bolt head, screw head or nut face and the base material or washer (the surface on which the fastener is rotating). Approximately 40 percent of the applied torque is used in overcoming thread friction. This leaves only about 10 percent of the applied torque to develop a useful clamp load (the force which holds a joint together). This means that friction can account for as much as 90 percent of the applied torque on a fastener.

## TORQUE WRENCHES

**➧ See Figures 24, 25 and 26**

In most applications, a torque wrench can be used to assure proper installation of a fastener. Torque wrenches come in various designs and most automotive supply stores will carry a variety to suit your needs. A torque wrench should be used any time we supply a specific torque value for a fastener. A torque wrench can also be used if you are following the general guidelines in the accompanying charts. Keep in mind that because there is no worldwide standardization of fasteners, the charts are a general guideline and should be used with

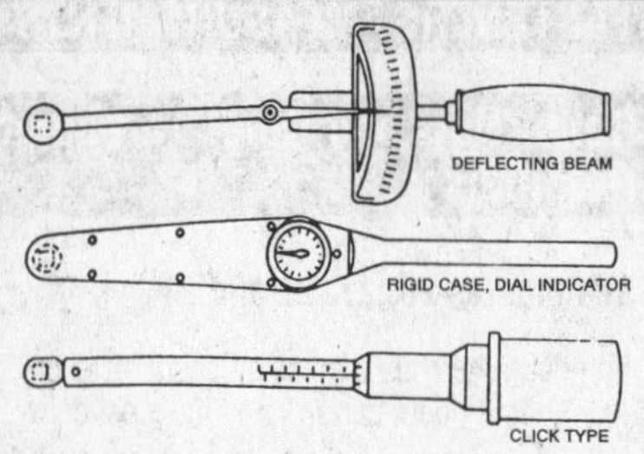


**Fig. 24 Various styles of torque wrenches are usually available at your local automotive supply store**

| | Mark | Class | | Mark | Class |
|---|---|---|---|---|---|
| Hexagon head bolt | Bolt head No. 4— 5— 6— 7— 8— 9— 10— 11— | 4T 5T 6T 7T 8T 9T 10T 11T | Stud bolt | No mark | 4T |
| | No mark | 4T | | | |
| Hexagon flange bolt w/ washer hexagon bolt | No mark | 4T | | Grooved | 6T |
| Hexagon head bolt | Two protruding lines | 5T | | | |
| Hexagon flange bolt w/ washer hexagon bolt | Two protruding lines | 6T | Welded bolt | | 4T |
| Hexagon head bolt | Three protruding lines | 7T | | | |
| Hexagon head bolt | Four protruding lines | 8T | | | |

TCCS1240

**Fig. 25 Determining bolt strength of metric fasteners—NOTE: this is a typical bolt marking system, but there is not a worldwide standard**

| Class | Diameter mm | Pitch mm | Specified torque | | | | | |
|---|---|---|---|---|---|---|---|---|
| | | | Hexagon head bolt | | | Hexagon flange bolt | | |
| | | | N·m | kgf·cm | ft·lbf | N·m | kgf·cm | ft·lbf |
| 4T | 6 | 1 | 5 | 55 | 48 in.·lbf | 6 | 60 | 52 in.·lbf |
| | 8 | 1.25 | 12.5 | 130 | 9 | 14 | 145 | 10 |
| | 10 | 1.25 | 26 | 260 | 19 | 29 | 290 | 21 |
| | 12 | 1.25 | 47 | 480 | 35 | 53 | 540 | 39 |
| | 14 | 1.5 | 74 | 760 | 55 | 84 | 850 | 61 |
| | 16 | 1.5 | 115 | 1,150 | 83 | — | — | — |
| 5T | 6 | 1 | 6.5 | 65 | 56 in.·lbf | 7.5 | 75 | 65 in.·lbf |
| | 8 | 1.25 | 15.5 | 160 | 12 | 17.5 | 175 | 13 |
| | 10 | 1.25 | 32 | 330 | 24 | 36 | 360 | 26 |
| | 12 | 1.25 | 59 | 600 | 43 | 65 | 670 | 48 |
| | 14 | 1.5 | 91 | 930 | 67 | 100 | 1,050 | 76 |
| | 16 | 1.5 | 140 | 1,400 | 101 | — | — | — |
| 6T | 6 | 1 | 8 | 80 | 69 in.·lbf | 9 | 90 | 78 in.·lbf |
| | 8 | 1.25 | 19 | 195 | 14 | 21 | 210 | 15 |
| | 10 | 1.25 | 39 | 400 | 29 | 44 | 440 | 32 |
| | 12 | 1.25 | 71 | 730 | 53 | 80 | 810 | 59 |
| | 14 | 1.5 | 110 | 1,100 | 80 | 125 | 1,250 | 90 |
| | 16 | 1.5 | 170 | 1,750 | 127 | — | — | — |
| 7T | 6 | 1 | 10.5 | 110 | 8 | 12 | 120 | 9 |
| | 8 | 1.25 | 25 | 260 | 19 | 28 | 290 | 21 |
| | 10 | 1.25 | 52 | 530 | 38 | 58 | 590 | 43 |
| | 12 | 1.25 | 95 | 970 | 70 | 105 | 1,050 | 76 |
| | 14 | 1.5 | 145 | 1,500 | 108 | 165 | 1,700 | 123 |
| | 16 | 1.5 | 230 | 2,300 | 166 | — | — | — |
| 8T | 8 | 1.25 | 29 | 300 | 22 | 33 | 330 | 24 |
| | 10 | 1.25 | 61 | 620 | 45 | 68 | 690 | 50 |
| | 12 | 1.25 | 110 | 1,100 | 80 | 120 | 1,250 | 90 |
| 9T | 8 | 1.25 | 34 | 340 | 25 | 37 | 380 | 27 |
| | 10 | 1.25 | 70 | 710 | 51 | 78 | 790 | 57 |
| | 12 | 1.25 | 125 | 1,300 | 94 | 140 | 1,450 | 105 |
| 10T | 8 | 1.25 | 38 | 390 | 28 | 42 | 430 | 31 |
| | 10 | 1.25 | 78 | 800 | 58 | 88 | 890 | 64 |
| | 12 | 1.25 | 140 | 1,450 | 105 | 155 | 1,600 | 116 |
| 11T | 8 | 1.25 | 42 | 430 | 31 | 47 | 480 | 35 |
| | 10 | 1.25 | 87 | 890 | 64 | 97 | 990 | 72 |
| | 12 | 1.25 | 155 | 1,600 | 116 | 175 | 1,800 | 130 |

TCCS1241

**Fig. 26 Typical bolt torques for metric fasteners—WARNING: use only as a guide**

caution. Again, the general rule of "if you are using the right tool for the job, you should not have to strain to tighten a fastener" applies here.

### Beam Type

➧ See Figure 27

The beam type torque wrench is one of the most popular types. It consists of a pointer attached to the head that runs the length of the flexible beam (shaft) to a scale located near the handle. As the wrench is pulled, the beam bends and the pointer indicates the torque using the scale.

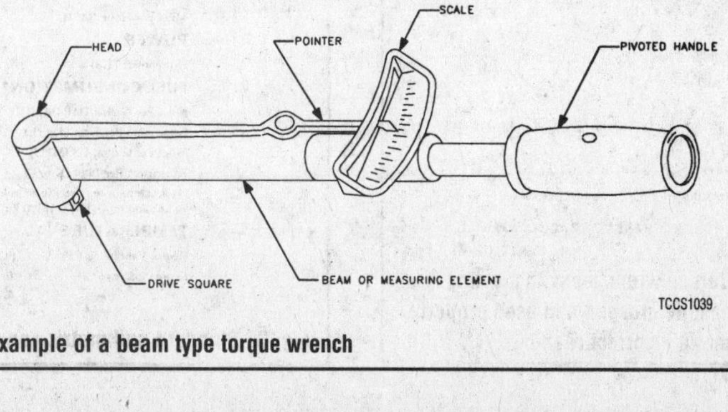


**Fig. 27 Example of a beam type torque wrench**

### Click (Breakaway) Type

➧ See Figure 28

Another popular design of torque wrench is the click type. To use the click type wrench you pre-adjust it to a torque setting. Once the torque is reached, the wrench has a reflex signaling feature that causes a momentary breakaway of the torque wrench body, sending an impulse to the operator's hand.

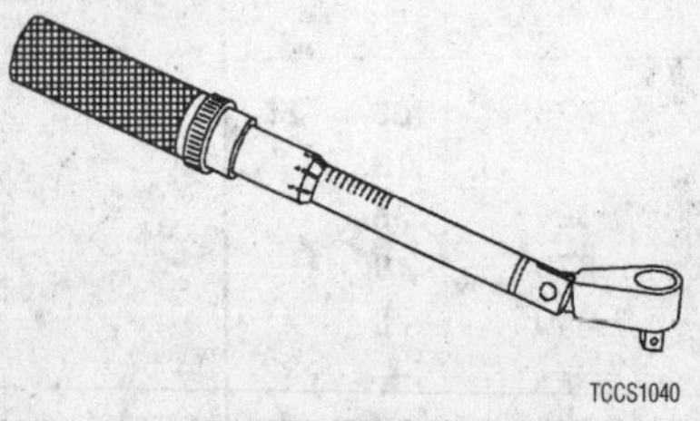


**Fig. 28 A click type or breakaway torque wrench—note that this one has a pivoting head**

### Pivot Head Type

➧ See Figures 28 and 29

Some torque wrenches (usually of the click type) may be equipped with a pivot head that can allow it to be used in areas of limited access. BUT, it must be used properly. To hold a pivot head wrench, grasp the handle lightly, and as you pull on the handle, it should be floated on the pivot point. If the handle comes in contact with the yoke extension during the process of pulling, there is a very good chance the torque readings will be inaccurate because this could alter the wrench loading point. The design of the handle is usually such as to make it inconvenient to deliberately misuse the wrench.

**➡It should be mentioned that the use of any U-joint, wobble or extension will have an effect on the torque readings, no matter what type of wrench you are using. For the most accurate readings, install the socket directly on the wrench driver. If necessary, straight extensions (which hold a socket directly under the wrench driver) will have the least effect on the torque reading. Avoid any extension that alters the length of the wrench from the handle to the head/driving point (such as a crow's foot). U-joint or wobble extensions can greatly affect the readings; avoid their use at all times.**

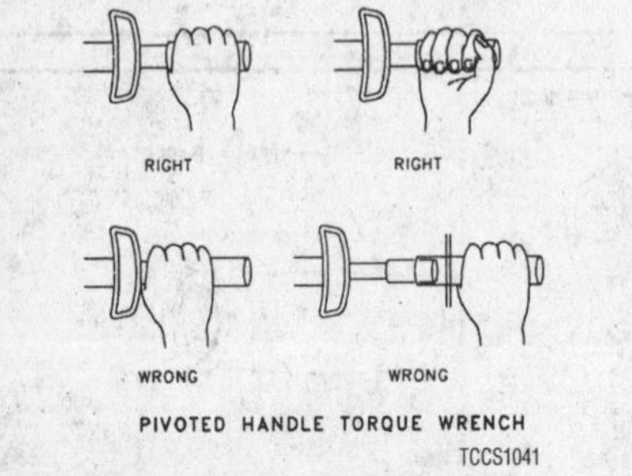


**Fig. 29 Torque wrenches with pivoting heads must be grasped and used properly to prevent an incorrect reading**

### Rigid Case (Direct Reading)

➧ See Figure 30

A rigid case or direct reading torque wrench is equipped with a dial indicator to show torque values. One advantage of these wrenches is that they can be held at any position on the wrench without affecting accuracy. These wrenches are often preferred because they tend to be compact, easy to read and have a great degree of accuracy.

## TORQUE ANGLE METERS

➧ See Figure 31

Because the frictional characteristics of each fastener or threaded hole will vary, clamp loads, which are based strictly on torque, will vary as well. In most applications, this variance is not significant enough to cause worry. But, in certain applications, a manufacturer's engineers may determine that more precise clamp loads are necessary (such is the case with many aluminum cylinder heads). In these cases, a torque angle method of installation would be specified. When installing fasteners which are torque angle tightened, a predetermined seating torque and standard torque wrench are usually used first to remove any compliance from the joint. The fastener is then tightened the specified additional portion of a turn measured in degrees. A torque angle gauge (mechanical protractor) is used for these applications.

# Standard and Metric Measurements

➧ See Figure 32

Throughout this manual, specifications are given to help you determine the condition of various com-

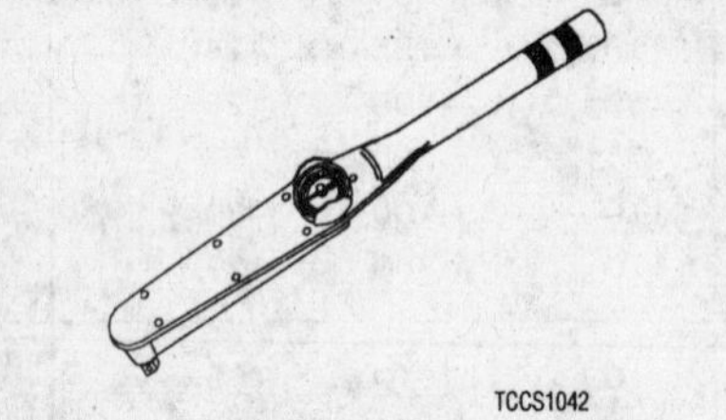


**Fig. 30 The rigid case (direct reading) torque wrench uses a dial indicator to show torque**

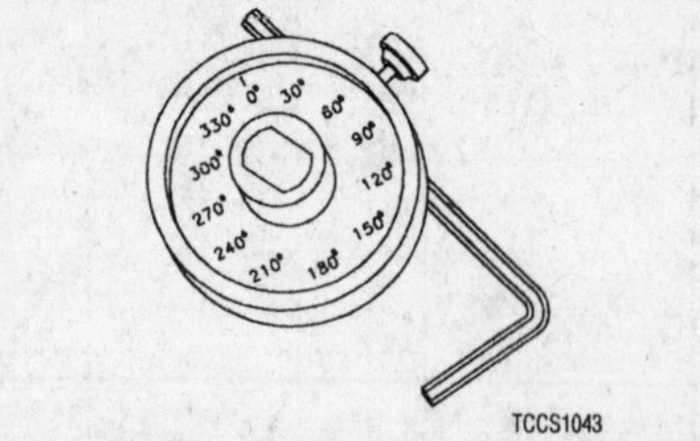


**Fig. 31 Some specifications require the use of a torque angle meter (mechanical protractor)**

**CONVERSION FACTORS**

| | | | | |
|---|---|---|---|---|
| **LENGTH–DISTANCE** | | | | |
| Inches (in.) | x 25.4 | = Millimeters (mm) | x .0394 | = Inches |
| Feet (ft.) | x .305 | = Meters (m) | x 3.281 | = Feet |
| Miles | x 1.609 | = Kilometers (km) | x .0621 | = Miles |
| **VOLUME** | | | | |
| Cubic Inches (in3) | x 16.387 | = Cubic Centimeters | x .061 | = in3 |
| IMP Pints (IMP pt.) | x .568 | = Liters (L) | x 1.76 | = IMP pt. |
| IMP Quarts (IMP qt.) | x 1.137 | = Liters (L) | x .88 | = IMP qt. |
| IMP Gallons (IMP gal.) | x 4.546 | = Liters (L) | x .22 | = IMP gal. |
| IMP Quarts (IMP qt.) | x 1.201 | = US Quarts (US qt.) | x .833 | = IMP qt. |
| IMP Gallons (IMP gal.) | x 1.201 | = US Gallons (US gal.) | x .833 | = IMP gal. |
| Fl. Ounces | x 29.573 | = Milliliters | x .034 | = Ounces |
| US Pints (US pt.) | x .473 | = Liters (L) | x 2.113 | = Pints |
| US Quarts (US qt.) | x .946 | = Liters (L) | x 1.057 | = Quarts |
| US Gallons (US gal.) | x 3.785 | = Liters (L) | x .264 | = Gallons |
| **MASS–WEIGHT** | | | | |
| Ounces (oz.) | x 28.35 | = Grams (g) | x .035 | = Ounces |
| Pounds (lb.) | x .454 | = Kilograms (kg) | x 2.205 | = Pounds |
| **PRESSURE** | | | | |
| Pounds Per Sq. In. (psi) | x 6.895 | = Kilopascals (kPa) | x .145 | = psi |
| Inches of Mercury (Hg) | x .4912 | = psi | x 2.036 | = Hg |
| Inches of Mercury (Hg) | x 3.377 | = Kilopascals (kPa) | x .2961 | = Hg |
| Inches of Water ($H_2O$) | x .07355 | = Inches of Mercury | x 13.783 | = $H_2O$ |
| Inches of Water ($H_2O$) | x .03613 | = psi | x 27.684 | = $H_2O$ |
| Inches of Water ($H_2O$) | x .248 | = Kilopascals (kPa) | x 4.026 | = $H_2O$ |
| **TORQUE** | | | | |
| Pounds–Force Inches (in–lb) | x .113 | = Newton Meters (N·m) | x 8.85 | = in–lb |
| Pounds–Force Feet (ft–lb) | x 1.356 | = Newton Meters (N·m) | x .738 | = ft–lb |
| **VELOCITY** | | | | |
| Miles Per Hour (MPH) | x 1.609 | = Kilometers Per Hour (KPH) | x .621 | = MPH |
| **POWER** | | | | |
| Horsepower (Hp) | x .745 | = Kilowatts | x 1.34 | = Horsepower |
| **FUEL CONSUMPTION*** | | | | |
| Miles Per Gallon IMP (MPG) | x .354 | = Kilometers Per Liter (Km/L) | | |
| Kilometers Per Liter (Km/L) | x 2.352 | = IMP MPG | | |
| Miles Per Gallon US (MPG) | x .425 | = Kilometers Per Liter (Km/L) | | |
| Kilometers Per Liter (Km/L) | x 2.352 | = US MPG | | |

*It is common to covert from miles per gallon (mpg) to liters/100 kilometers (1/100 km), where mpg (IMP) x 1/100 km = 282 and mpg (US) x 1/100 km = 235.

| | |
|---|---|
| **TEMPERATURE** | |
| Degree Fahrenheit (°F) | = (°C x 1.8) + 32 |
| Degree Celsius (°C) | = (°F – 32) x .56 |

TCCS1044

**Fig. 32 Standard and metric conversion factors chart**

ponents on your vehicle, or to assist you in their installation. Some of the most common measurements include length (in. or cm/mm), torque (ft. lbs., inch lbs. or Nm) and pressure (psi, in. Hg, kPa or mm Hg). In most cases, we strive to provide the proper measurement as determined by the manufacturer's engineers.

Though, in some cases, that value may not be conveniently measured with what is available in your toolbox. Luckily, many of the measuring devices which are available today will have two scales so the Standard or Metric measurements may easily be taken. If any of the various measuring tools which are available to you do not contain the same scale as listed in the specifications, use the accompanying conversion factors to determine the proper value.

The conversion factor chart is used by taking the given specification and multiplying it by the necessary conversion factor. For instance, looking at the first line, if you have a measurement in inches such as "free-play should be 2 in." but your ruler reads only in millimeters, multiply 2 in. by the conversion factor of 25.4 to get the metric equivalent of 50.8mm. Likewise, if the specification was given only in a Metric measurement, for example in Newton Meters (Nm), then look at the center column first. If the measurement is 100 Nm, multiply it by the conversion factor of 0.738 to get 73.8 ft. lbs.

## SERIAL NUMBER IDENTIFICATION

The official vehicle identification number is stamped onto a metal tab fastened to the instrument panel and visible through the driver's side of the windshield from the outside. The vehicle identification number contains 17 digits. The VIN is used for title and registration purposes and indicates the vehicle manufacturer, country of origin, type of restraint system, assembly line, series, body type, engine, model year, and consecutive unit number. It is important for servicing and ordering parts to be certain of the vehicle and engine identification.

### Vehicle Identification Plate

The Vehicle Identification Number (VIN) is stamped on a metal plate that is fastened to the instrument panel adjacent to the windshield. It can be seen by looking through the lower corner of the windshield on the driver's side.

The VIN is a 17-digit combination of numbers and letters. The first three digits represent the world manufacturer identifier. Using the example in the figure, the number and letter combination 2FA signifies Ford Motor Company of Canada, Ltd. The fourth digit indicates the type of passenger restraint system; in the example, the letter C stands for active belts and a driver's side air bag. The fifth digit is a constant, the letter P signifying passenger car. The sixth and seventh digits indicate the body style. The eighth digit is the engine code: F for the 5.0L engine, or in this case W for the 4.6L engine. The ninth digit is a check digit for all vehicles. The 10th digit indicates the model year: K for 1989, L for 1990, M for 1991, N for 1992, P for 1993, R for 1994 and so on. The 11th digit is the assembly plant code, the letter X represents St. Thomas, Ontario, Canada. The 12th through 17th digits indicate the production sequence number.

The Vehicle Certification Label is attached to the left front door lock panel. The upper half of the label contains the name of the manufacturer, month and year of manufacture, Gross Vehicle Weight Rating (GVWR), Gross Axle Weight Rating (GAWR), and the certification statement. The lower half of the label contains the VIN and a series of codes indicating exterior color, body type, interior trim type and color, radio type, sun roof type (if any), as well as axle, transmission, spring, district and special order codes.

### Engine Number

➧ **See Figure 33**

The engine identification code is located in the VIN at the 8th digit. The VIN can be found on the Vehicle Certification Label and on the VIN plate attached to the instrument panel. See the Engine Identification chart for engine VIN codes.

**Fig. 33 Sample engine code information label**

There is also an engine code information label located on the engine. This label contains the engine calibration number, engine build date and engine plant code. On the 3.8L and 5.0L engines, the label is located on the side of the right rocker arm cover. On the 4.6L engine, the label is located on the front of the engine.

### Transmission/Transaxle Number

➧ **See Figures 34 and 35**

The transmission identification code can be found in the space marked TR on the Vehicle Certification Label. There is also an identification tag located on the transmission case which contains the transmission model code, build date code, serial number and assembly part number prefix and suffix.

All 1989–92½ vehicles are equipped with a 4-speed Automatic Overdrive (AOD) transmission. Beginning in February 1992, an electronically controlled Automatic Overdrive (AODE) transmission replaced the AOD transmission.

### Drive Axle

The Plant Code on the axle identification tag is the official service identifier. The axle identification tag is located under the cover-to-carrier bolt in the 12 o'clock position. The Plant Code for a particular axle assembly will not be duplicated.

## LINCOLN VEHICLE IDENTIFICATION CHART

**Engine Code**

| Code | Liters | Cu. In. (cc) | Cyl. | Fuel Sys. | Eng. Mfg. |
|---|---|---|---|---|---|
| E | 5.0-HO | 302 (4943) | 8 | SFI | Ford |
| F | 5.0 | 302 (4943) | 8 | SFI | Ford |
| W | 4.6 | 281 (4593) | 8 | SFI | Ford |
| 4 | 3.8 | 232 (3802) | 6 | MFI | Ford |
| V | 4.6 | 281 (4593) | 8 | SFI | Ford |

SFI - Sequential Fuel Injection

MFI - Multi-port Fuel Injection

**Model Year**

| Code | Year |
|---|---|
| H | 1988 |
| K | 1989 |
| M | 1991 |
| N | 1992 |
| P | 1993 |
| R | 1994 |
| S | 1995 |
| T | 1996 |
| V | 1997 |
| W | 1998 |
| X | 1999 |
| Y | 2000 |

93141C01

## ENGINE IDENTIFICATION AND SPECIFICATIONS

| Year | Model | Engine ID/VIN | Engine Displacement Liters (cc) | No. of Cyl. | Engine Type | Fuel System Type | Net Horsepower @ rpm | Net Torque @ rpm (ft. lbs.) | Bore x Stroke (in.) | Com-pression Ratio | Oil Pressure @ rpm |
|---|---|---|---|---|---|---|---|---|---|---|---|
| 1988 | Town car | F | 5.0 (4943) | 8 | OHV | SFI | ① | ② | 4.00 X 3.00 | 8.9:1 | 40-60@2000 |
| | Mark VII | E | 5.0 HO (4943) | 8 | OHV | SFI | 225@4200 | 300@3200 | 4.00 X 3.00 | 9.0:1 | 40-60@2000 |
| | Continental | 4 | 3.8 (3802) | 6 | OHV | SFI | 140@3800 | 215@2400 | 3.81 X 3.39 | 9.0:1 | 40-60@2500 |
| 1989 | Town car | F | 5.0 (4943) | 8 | OHV | SFI | ① | ② | 4.00 X 3.00 | 8.9:1 | 40-60@2000 |
| | Mark VII | E | 5.0 HO (4943) | 8 | OHV | SFI | 225@4200 | 300@3200 | 4.00 X 3.00 | 9.0:1 | 40-60@2000 |
| | Continental | 4 | 3.8 (3802) | 6 | OHV | SFI | 140@3800 | 215@2400 | 3.81 X 3.39 | 9.0:1 | 40-60@2500 |
| 1990 | Town car | F | 5.0 (4943) | 8 | OHV | SFI | ① | ② | 4.00 X 3.00 | 8.9:1 | 40-60@2000 |
| | Mark VII | E | 5.0 HO (4943) | 8 | OHV | SFI | 225@4200 | 300@3200 | 4.00 X 3.00 | 9.0:1 | 40-60@2000 |
| | Continental | 4 | 3.8 (3802) | 6 | OHV | SFI | 140@3800 | 215@2400 | 3.81 X 3.39 | 9.0:1 | 40-60@2500 |
| 1991 | Town car | W | 4.6 (4593) | 8 | SOHC | SFI | ③ | ④ | 3.55 X 3.54 | 9.0:1 | 20-45@1500 |
| | Mark VII | E | 5.0 HO (4943) | 8 | OHV | SFI | 225@4200 | 300@3200 | 4.00 X 3.00 | 9.0:1 | 40-60@2000 |
| | Continental | 4 | 3.8 (3802) | 6 | OHV | SFI | 140@3800 | 215@2400 | 3.81 X 3.39 | 9.0:1 | 40-60@2500 |
| 1992 | Town car | W | 4.6 (4593) | 8 | SOHC | SFI | ③ | ④ | 3.55 X 3.54 | 9.0:1 | 20-45@1500 |
| | Mark VII | E | 5.0 HO (4943) | 8 | OHV | SFI | 225@4200 | 300@3200 | 4.00 X 3.00 | 9.0:1 | 40-60@2000 |
| | Continental | 4 | 3.8 (3802) | 6 | OHV | SFI | 140@3800 | 215@2400 | 3.81 X 3.39 | 9.0:1 | 40-60@2500 |
| 1993 | Town car | W | 4.6 (4593) | 8 | SOHC | SFI | ③ | ④ | 3.55 X 3.54 | 9.0:1 | 20-45@1500 |
| | Mark VIII | V | 4.6 (4593) | 8 | DOHC | SFI | 280@5500 | 285@4500 | 3.55 X 3.54 | 9.8:1 | 33@2000 |
| | Continental | 4 | 3.8 (3802) | 6 | OHV | SFI | 140@3800 | 215@2400 | 3.81 X 3.39 | 9.0:1 | 40-60@2500 |
| 1994 | Town car | W | 4.6 (4593) | 8 | SOHC | SFI | ③ | ④ | 3.55 X 3.54 | 9.0:1 | 20-45@1500 |
| | Mark VIII | V | 4.6 (4593) | 8 | DOHC | SFI | 280@5500 | 285@4500 | 3.55 X 3.54 | 9.8:1 | 33@2000 |
| | Continental | 4 | 3.8 (3802) | 6 | OHV | SFI | 140@3800 | 215@2400 | 3.81 X 3.39 | 9.0:1 | 40-60@2500 |
| 1995 | Town car | W | 4.6 (4593) | 8 | SOHC | SFI | ③ | ④ | 3.55 X 3.54 | 9.0:1 | 20-45@1500 |
| | Mark VIII | V | 4.6 (4593) | 8 | DOHC | SFI | 280@5500 | 285@4500 | 3.55 X 3.54 | 9.8:1 | 33@2000 |
| | Continental | V | 4.6 (4593) | 8 | DOHC | SFI | 260@5750 | 265@4750 | 3.55 X 3.54 | 9.8:1 | 33@1500 |
| 1996 | Town car | W | 4.6 (4593) | 8 | SOHC | SFI | ③ | ④ | 3.55 X 3.54 | 9.0:1 | 20-45@1500 |
| | Mark VIII | V | 4.6 (4593) | 8 | DOHC | SFI | 280@5500 | 285@4500 | 3.55 X 3.54 | 9.8:1 | 33@2000 |
| | Continental | V | 4.6 (4593) | 8 | DOHC | SFI | 260@5750 | 265@4750 | 3.55 X 3.54 | 9.8:1 | 33@1500 |
| 1997 | Town car | W | 4.6 (4593) | 8 | SOHC | SFI | ③ | ④ | 3.55 X 3.54 | 9.0:1 | 20-45@1500 |
| | Mark VIII | V | 4.6 (4593) | 8 | DOHC | SFI | 280@5500 | 285@4500 | 3.55 X 3.54 | 9.8:1 | 33@2000 |
| | Continental | V | 4.6 (4593) | 8 | DOHC | SFI | 260@5750 | 265@4750 | 3.55 X 3.54 | 9.8:1 | 33@1500 |
| 1998 | Town car | W | 4.6 (4593) | 8 | SOHC | SFI | ③ | ④ | 3.55 X 3.54 | 9.0:1 | 20-45@1500 |
| | Continental | V | 4.6 (4593) | 8 | DOHC | SFI | 260@5750 | 265@4750 | 3.55 X 3.54 | 9.8:1 | 33@1500 |
| 1999 | Town car | W | 4.6 (4593) | 8 | SOHC | SFI | ③ | ④ | 3.55 X 3.54 | 9.0:1 | 20-45@1500 |
| | Continental | V | 4.6 (4593) | 8 | DOHC | SFI | 260@5750 | 265@4750 | 3.55 X 3.54 | 9.8:1 | 33@1500 |
| 2000 | Town car | W | 4.6 (4593) | 8 | SOHC | SFI | ③ | ④ | 3.55 X 3.54 | 9.0:1 | 20-45@1500 |
| | Continental | V | 4.6 (4593) | 8 | DOHC | SFI | 260@5750 | 265@4750 | 3.55 X 3.54 | 9.8:1 | 33@1500 |

SFI - Sequential Fuel Injection
SOHC - Single Overhead Camshaft
DOHC - Dual Overhead Camshaft
① Single exhaust: 150@3200
Double exhaust: 160@3400
② Single exhaust: 270@2000
Double exhaust: 280@2200
③ Single exhaust: 190@4200
Double exhaust: 210@4600
④ Single exhaust: 260@3200
Double exhaust: 270@3400

93141C02

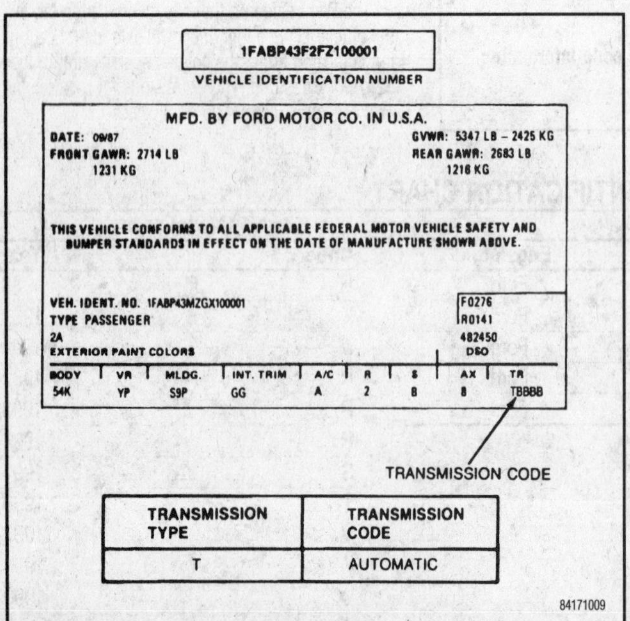


**Fig. 34 This tag gives pertinent information about transmissions. In addition, the tag identifies paint color**

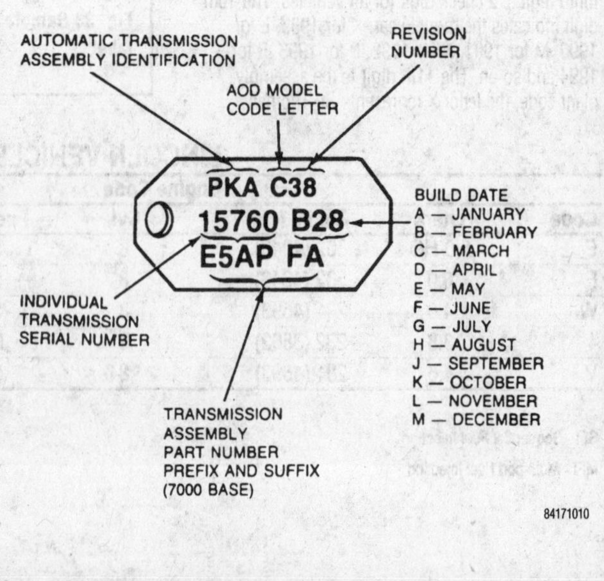


**Fig. 35 This transmission identification tag gives necessary information for ordering internal parts**

**UNDERHOOD COMPONENT MAINTENANCE LOCATIONS—3.8L ENGINE**

1. Battery
2. Air Cleaner
3. Radiator hose
4. Master cylinder
5. Transaxle dipstick
6. PCV valve
7. Spark plug wires
8. Accessory drive (Serpentine belt)
9. Coolant tank
10. Windshield washer fluid reservoir
11. Radiator cap
12. Power steering fill cap
13. Oil fill cap
14. Oil dipstick
15. Spark plugs (3 on each side)

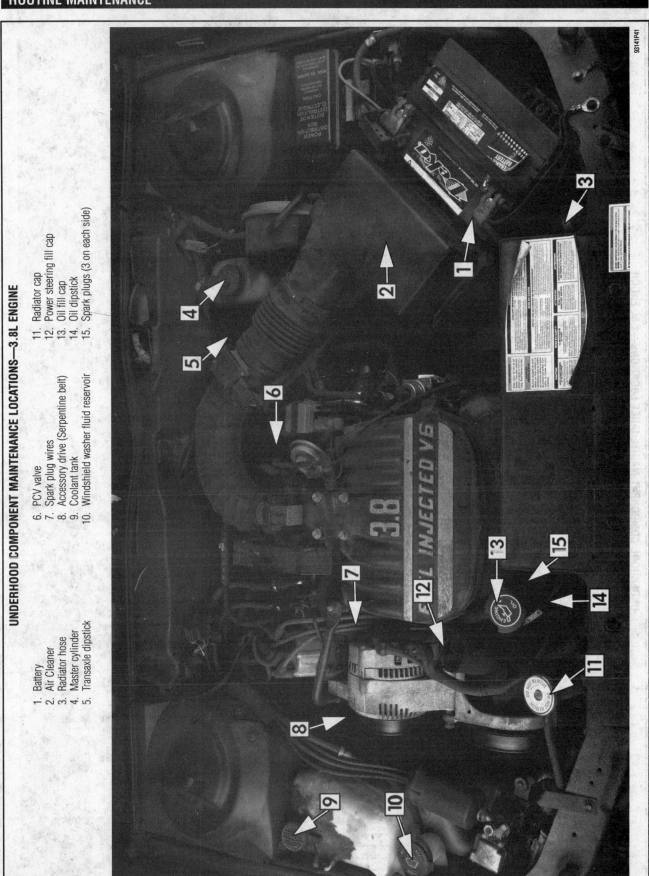

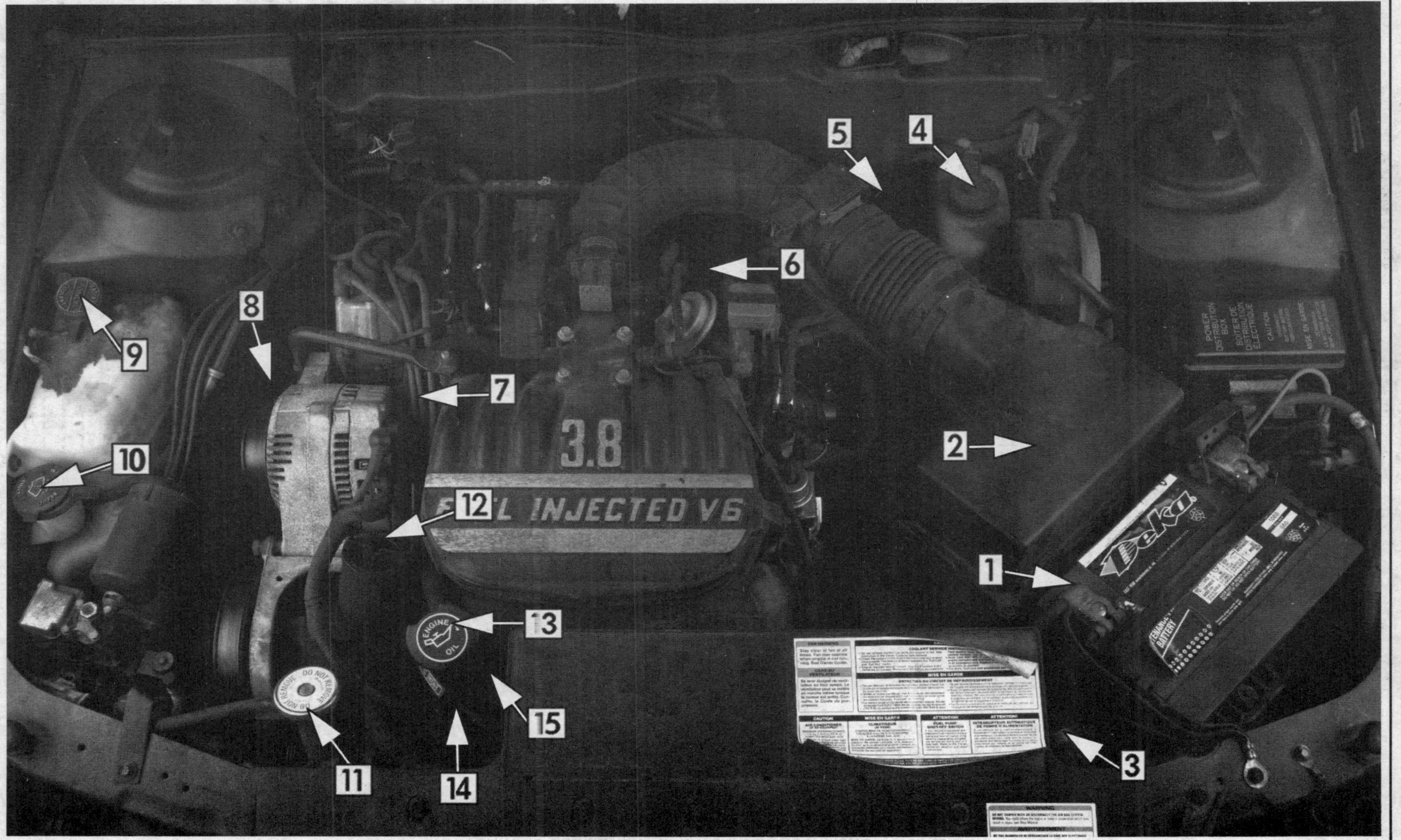


93141P41

**UNDERHOOD COMPONENT MAINTENANCE LOCATIONS—4.6L ENGINE**

1. Battery
2. Air Cleaner
3. Radiator hose (Upper)
4. Master cylinder
5. Transmission dipstick
6. PCV valve
7. Spark plug wires
8. Accessory drive (Serpentine belt)
9. Coolant tank
10. Windshield washer fluid reservoir
11. Radiator cap
12. Power steering fill cap
13. Oil fill cap
14. Oil dipstick
15. Spark plugs (4 on each side)

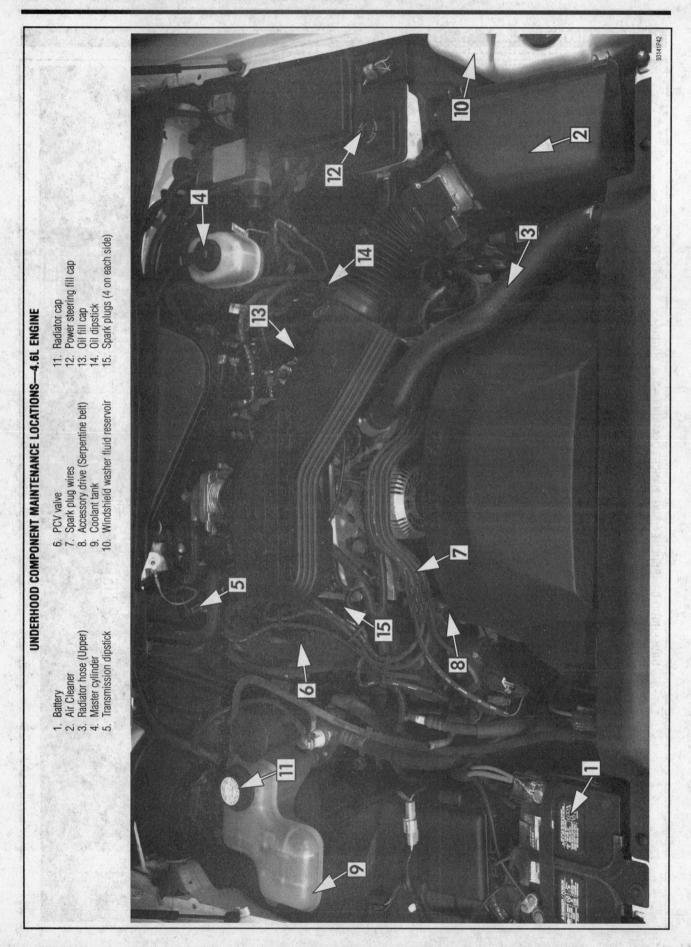

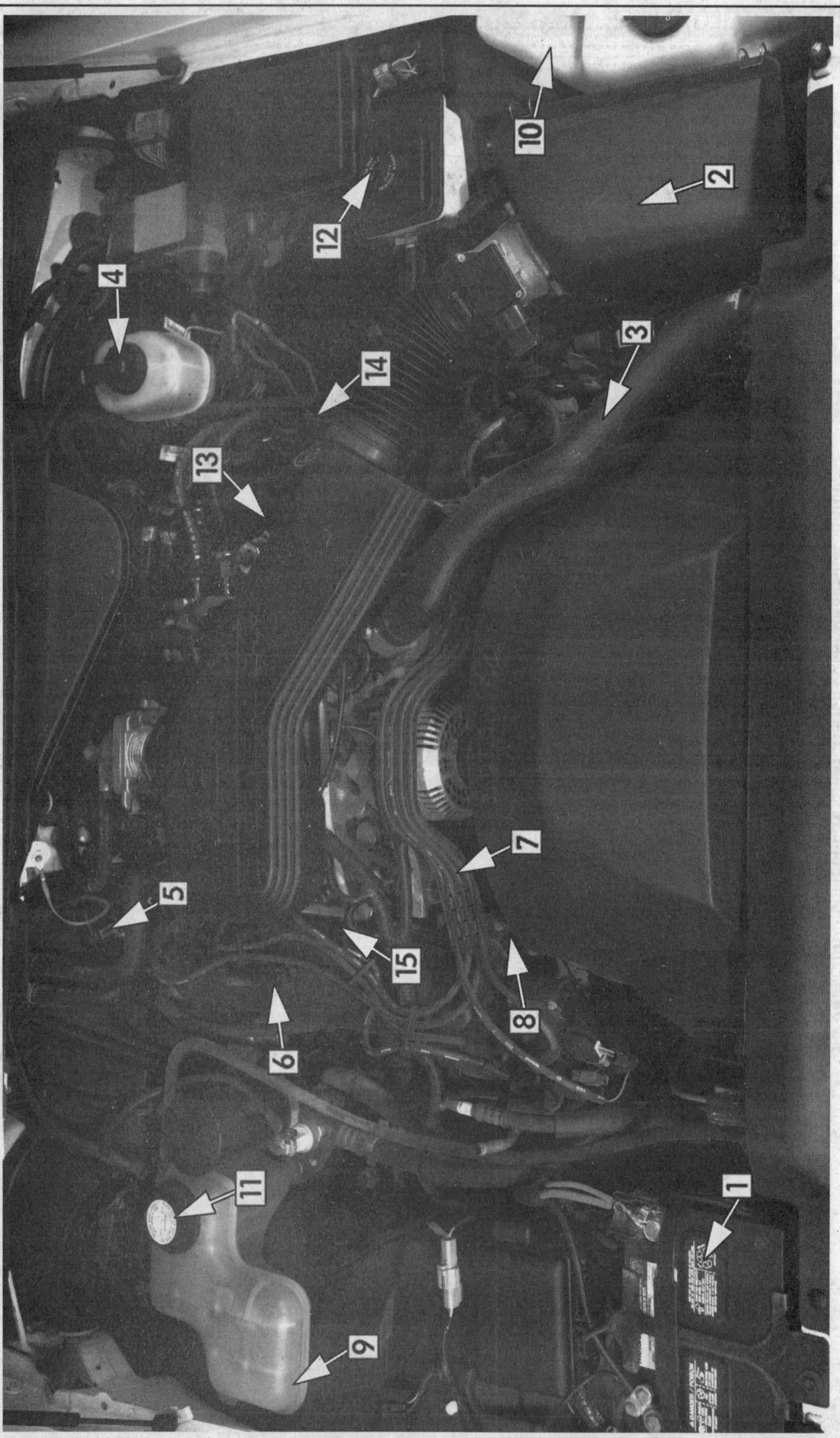

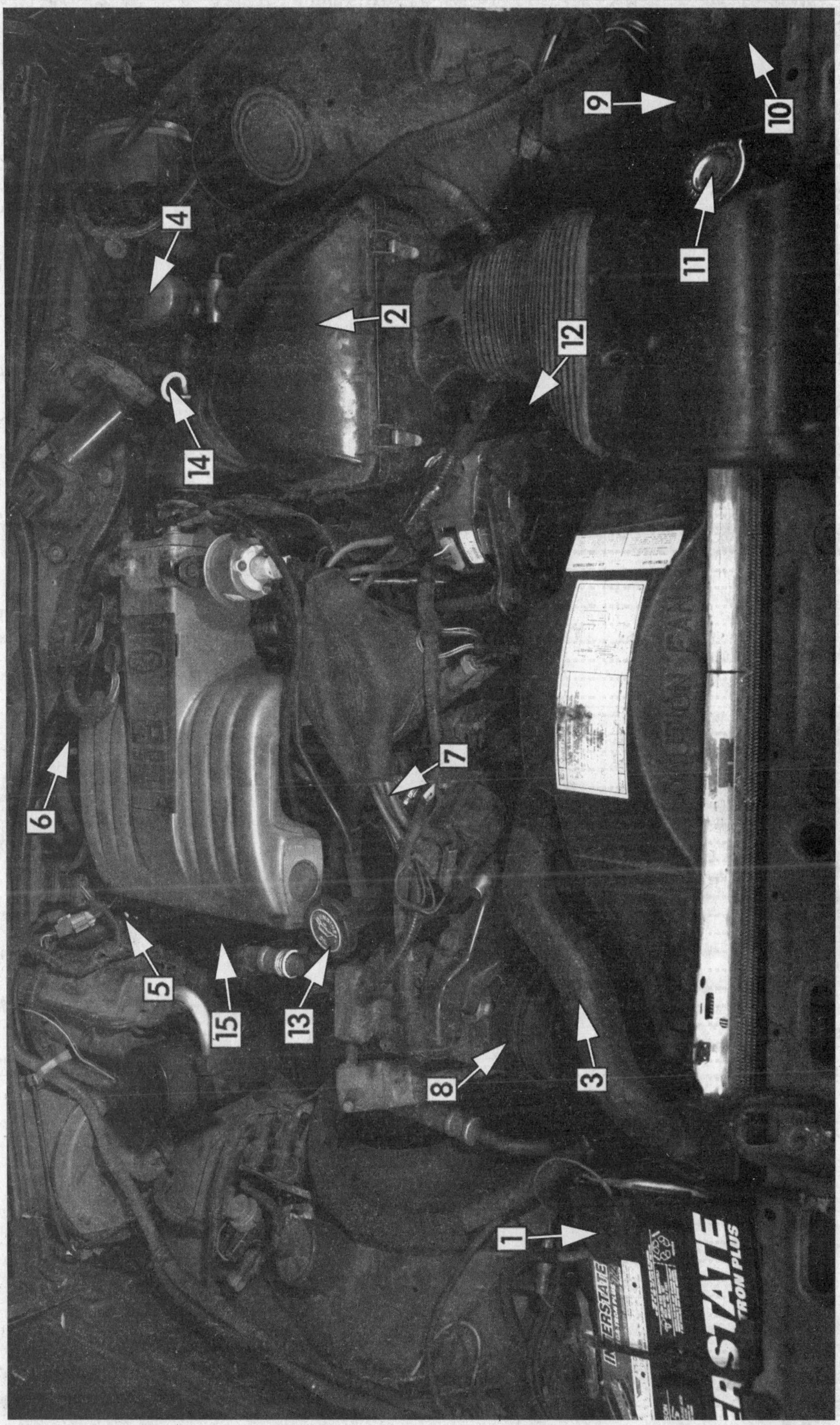


93141P43

**UNDERHOOD COMPONENT MAINTENANCE LOCATIONS—5.0L ENGINE**

1. Battery
2. Air Cleaner
3. Radiator hose (Upper)
4. Master cylinder
5. Transmission dipstick
6. PCV valve
7. Spark plug wires
8. Accessory drive (Serpentine belt)
9. Coolant tank
10. Windshield washer fluid reservoir
11. Radiator cap
12. Power steering fill cap
13. Oil fill cap
14. Oil dipstick
15. Spark plugs (4 on each side)

Proper maintenance and tune-up is the key to long and trouble-free vehicle life, and the work can yield its own rewards. Studies have shown that a properly tuned and maintained vehicle can achieve better gas mileage than an out-of-tune vehicle. As a conscientious owner and driver, set aside a Saturday morning, say once a month, to check or replace items which could cause major problems later. Keep your own personal log to jot down which services you performed, how much the parts cost you, the date, and the exact odometer reading at the time. Keep all receipts for such items as engine oil and filters, so that they may be referred to in case of related problems or to determine operating expenses. As a do-it-yourselfer, these receipts are the only proof you have that the required maintenance was performed. In the event of a warranty problem, these receipts will be invaluable.

The literature provided with your vehicle when it was originally delivered includes the factory recommended maintenance schedule. If you no longer have this literature, replacement copies are usually available from the dealer. A maintenance schedule is provided later in this section, in case you do not have the factory literature.

## Air Cleaner

If an engine maintenance procedure requires the temporary removal of the air cleaner, remove it; otherwise, never run the engine without it. The air filter should be replaced every 30,000 miles (50,000 km) under normal driving conditions.

### REMOVAL & INSTALLATION

**See Figures 36, 37, 38, 39 and 40**

Locate the air cleaner in the engine compartment. Inspect the flexible air intake ducting for cracks and tears. If the ducting is torn it should be replaced.

The air cleaner element may be replaced easily.

1. Disengage the fasteners securing the top of the air cleaner.

**Some fasteners are clips, some are screws, depending on the vehicle configuration.**

2. Carefully pull the air filter cover back to expose the element.
3. Remove the air filter element.
4. Wipe out the housing with a clean rag.

**To install:**

5. Position the air filter element in the housing, make sure it seats properly.
6. Install the air cleaner cover.
7. Install the air cleaner fasteners, and tighten as necessary.

## Fuel Filter

**CAUTION**

**Observe all applicable safety precautions when working around fuel. Whenever servicing the fuel system, always work in a well ventilated area. Do not allow fuel spray or vapors to be exposed to a spark or open flame. Keep a dry chemical fire extinguisher near the work area. Always keep fuel in a container specifically designed for fuel storage; also, always properly seal fuel containers to avoid the possibility of fire or explosion.**

The purpose of the in-line fuel filter is to provide filtration to protect the small metering orifices of the injector nozzles. The filter is located downstream of the electric fuel pump and is mounted on the underbody. The fuel filter is a one-piece construction that cannot be cleaned. If it becomes clogged, it must be replaced.

### REMOVAL & INSTALLATION

**See Figures 41 thru 49**

**CAUTION**

**Never smoke when working around gasoline! Avoid all sources of sparks or ignition. Gasoline vapors are EXTREMELY volatile!**

**CAUTION**

**Fuel supply lines on fuel injected vehicles will remain pressurized for some time after the engine is shut off. Fuel pressure must be relieved before servicing the fuel system.**

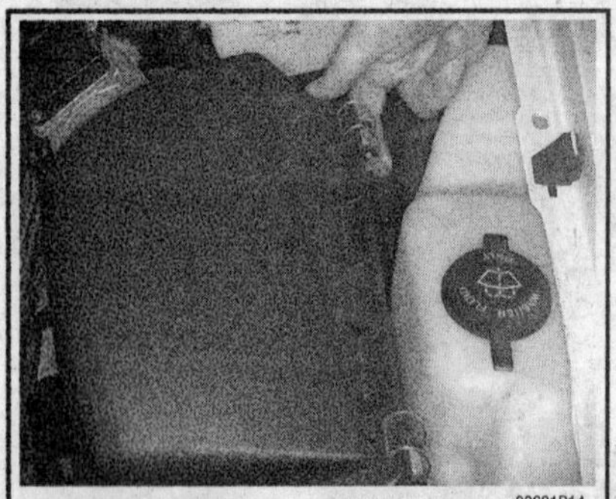

89601P14

**Fig. 36 Releasing the spring clips to remove the air cleaner cover—4.6L engine**

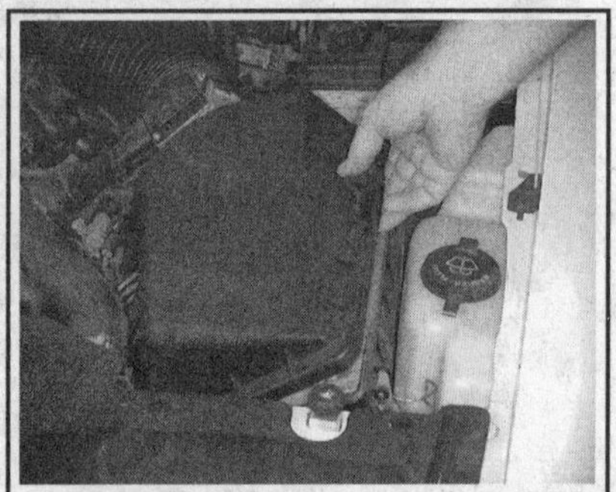

89601P15

**Fig. 37 Lift the lid to access the spring clips and . . .**

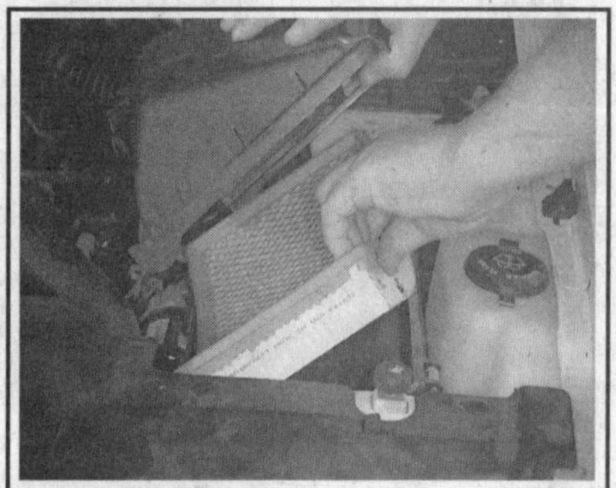

89601P16

**Fig. 38 . . . remove the air cleaner element—4.6L engine**

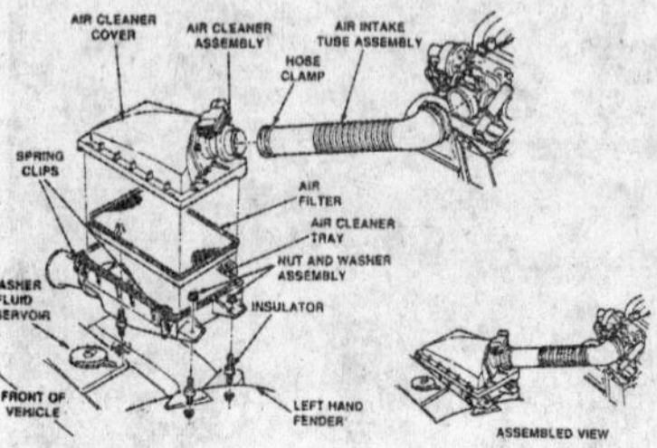


84171020

**Fig. 39 Air cleaner assembly—5.0L engine**

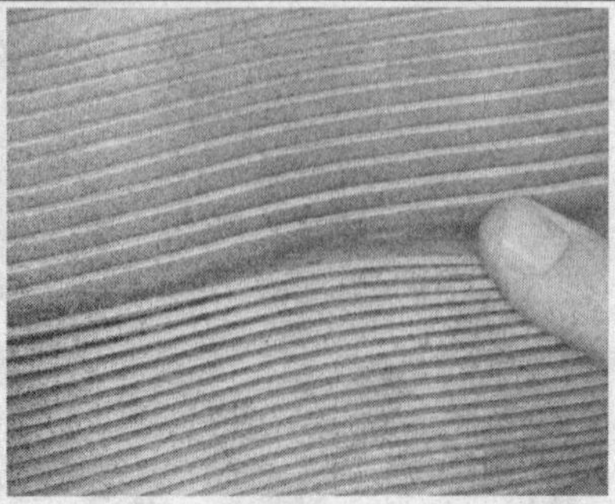

89601P19

**Fig. 40 Spread the air cleaner element to inspect it for dirt and contamination**

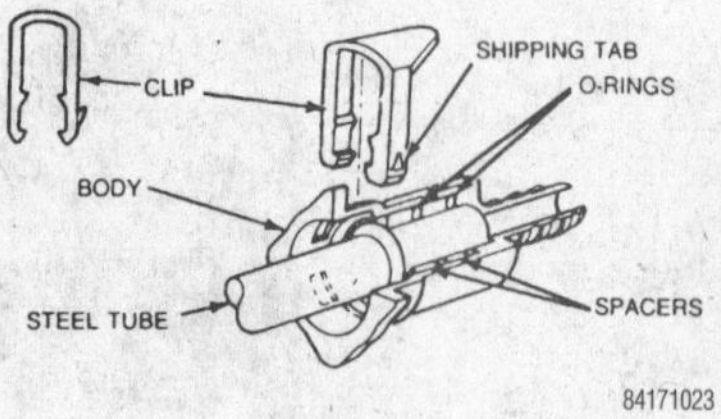


84171023

**Fig. 41 Hairpin clip push connect fitting**

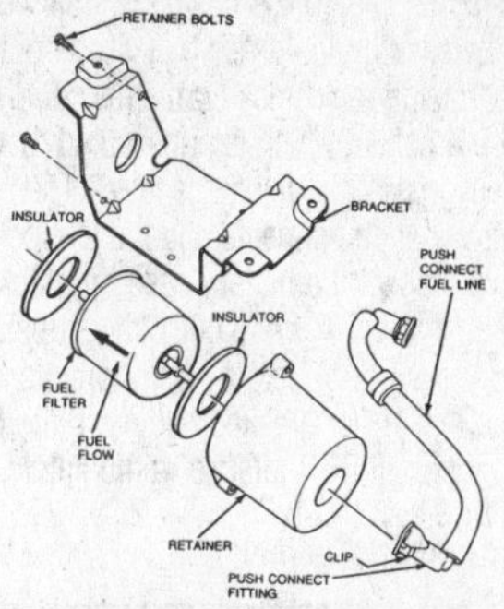


84171024

**Fig. 42 In-line fuel filter assembly—1989–91 vehicles**

84171025

**Fig. 43 In-line fuel filter location—1992–up vehicles**

89601P82

**Fig. 44 The fuel filter is located under the vehicle, along the frame rail on the passenger side —1992–98 vehicles**

89601P83

**Fig. 45 Release the clips holding the fuel lines to the filter by gently prying them from the line. A cotter pin puller works very well for this**

89601P84

**Fig. 46 After the clip's tangs are released, remove the clip from the line**

89601P85

**Fig. 47 After the clip is removed, slide the line off the filter**

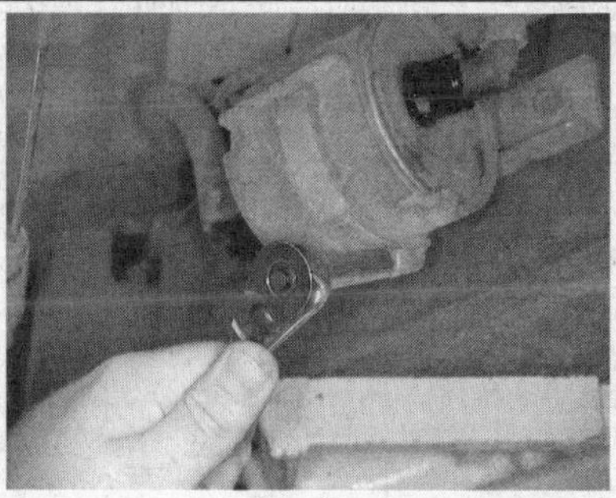

89601P86

**Fig. 48 Loosen the clamp around the filter and . . .**

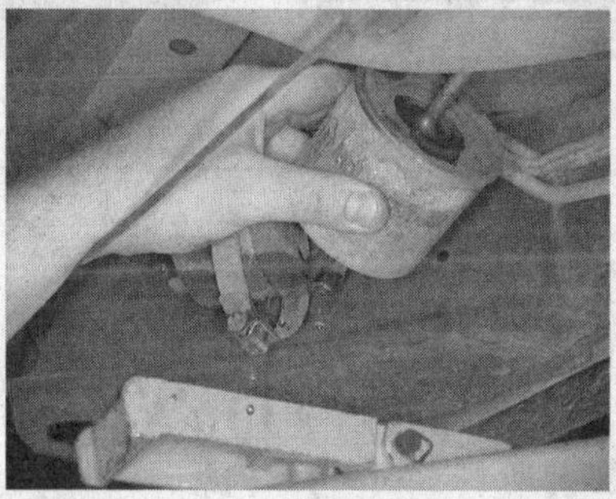

89601P87

**Fig. 49 . . . remove the filter by sliding it out of the clamp**

1. To replace the in-line fuel filter.
2. Disconnect the negative battery cable.
3. Relieve the fuel system pressure as follows:
   a. Remove the fuel tank cap to relieve the pressure in the fuel tank.
   b. Remove the cap from the Schrader valve located on the fuel injection supply manifold.
4. Connect the pressure gauge tool, to the fuel pressure relief valve (Schrader).
5. Open the manual valve on the pressure gauge tool to relieve the fuel system pressure.
6. Drain the fuel through the drain tube into a suitable container.
7. Raise and safely support the rear of the vehicle securely on jackstands.
8. Locate the fuel filter mounted on the right side inner frame rail near the wheel.
9. It will be necessary to remove the white hair-pin clips that lock the filter in place.
10. First, bend the shipping tab downward so that it will clear the body.
11. Next, using no tools, spread the two clip legs about (⅛) each to disengage the body and push the legs into the fitting.
12. Complete removal is accomplished by lightly pulling from the triangular end of the clip and working it clear of the tube and fitting.

**➡Do not use hand tools to complete this operation.**

   a. Grasp the fitting and pull in an axial (twisting) direction to remove the fitting from the filter. Be careful on 90 ° elbow connectors, as excessive side loading could break the connector body.
   b. After disassembly, inspect the inside of the fitting for any internal parts such as O-rings and spacers that may have been dislodged from the fitting. Replace any damaged connector.

13. On 1988–91 Town Cars, remove the filter retainer bolts and remove the filter and retainer from the mounting bracket. Remove the filter from the retainer. Note that the direction of the flow arrow points to the open end of the retainer. Remove the rubber insulator rings.
14. On 1992–up vehicles, loosen the filter retaining clamp and remove the fuel filter. Note the direction of the flow arrow on the filter, so the replacement filter can be reinstalled in the same position.

**➡Fuel will empty from the fuel filter. Have a suitable container ready to accept it.**

**To install:**

**➡Do not re-use the hair-pin clips, new clips are supplied with a new filter.**

15. Install the hairpin clip push connect fittings at both ends of the fuel filter as follows:
   a. Install a new connector if damage was found. Insert a new clip into any 2 adjacent open-

ings with the triangular portion pointing away from the fitting opening. Install the clip until the legs of the clip are locked on the outside of the body. Piloting with an index finger is necessary.

16. On 1992–up vehicles, install the fuel filter with the flow arrow facing the proper direction and tighten the filter retaining clamp.

17. On 1988–91 Town Cars, install the rubber insulator rings on the new filter (replace the insulator rings if the filter moves freely after the retainer is installed). Install the filter into the retainer with the flow arrow pointing out the open end of the retainer. Install the retainer on the bracket and tighten the mounting bolts to 27–44 inch lbs. (3–5 Nm).

a. Before installing the fitting on the filter, wipe the filter end with a clean cloth. Inspect the inside of the fitting to make sure it is free of dirt and/or obstructions.

b. Align the fitting and filter axially and push the fitting onto the filter end. When the fitting is engaged, a definite click will be heard. Pull on the fitting to make sure it is fully engaged.

18. Lower the vehicle and connect the negative battery cable.

19. Cycle the key (on-off, on-off,) at two second intervals. Do this three or four times, and check for leaks, before starting the vehicle.

## PCV Valve

The crankcase ventilation system (PCV) must be operating correctly to provide complete scavenging of the crankcase vapors. Fresh air is supplied to the crankcase after passing through the air filter, mixed with the internal exhaust gases, passed through the PCV valve and into the intake manifold.

The PCV system should be checked at every oil change and serviced every 30,000 miles.

**** WARNING**

**Never operate an engine without a PCV valve or a ventilation system, for it can become damaged.**

### REMOVAL & INSTALLATION

**See Figures 50, 51 and 52**

1. Locate the PCV valve — usually located either in the valve cover (3.8L or 4.6L engine) or in the intake manifold (5.0L engine).

2. Disconnect the crankcase ventilation tube from the positive crankcase ventilation valve.

3. Remove the PCV valve from the PCV valve grommet.

**To install:**

4. Install the PCV valve into the grommet.

5. Connect the ventilation tube to the PCV valve.

## Evaporative Canister

### SERVICING

**See Figure 53**

The evaporative canister requires no periodic servicing. However, a careful inspection of the canister and hoses should be made frequently. Replace damaged components as required.

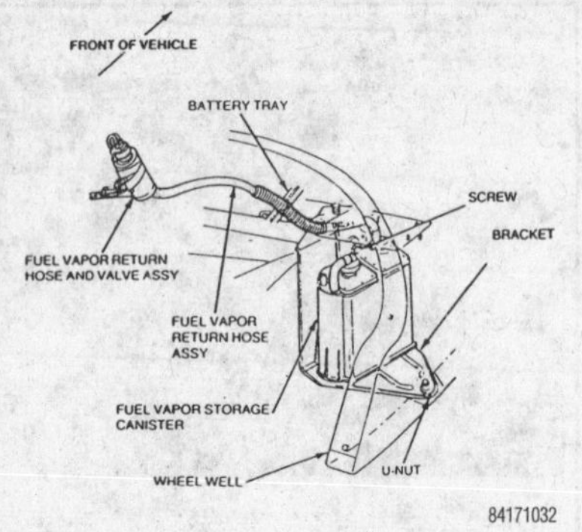


**Fig. 53 Evaporative canister location—5.0L engine equipped vehicles**

## Battery

### PRECAUTIONS

Always use caution when working on or near the battery. Never allow a tool to bridge the gap between the negative and positive battery terminals. Also, be careful not to allow a tool to provide a ground between the positive cable/terminal and any metal component on the vehicle. Either of these conditions will cause a short circuit, leading to sparks and possible personal injury.

Do not smoke or all open flames/sparks near a battery; the gases contained in the battery are very explosive and, if ignited, could cause severe injury or death.

All batteries, regardless of type, should be carefully secured by a battery hold-down device. If not, the terminals or casing may crack from stress during vehicle operation. A battery which is not secured may allow acid to leak, making it discharge faster. The acid can also eat away at components under the hood.

Always inspect the battery case for cracks, leakage and corrosion. A white corrosive substance on the battery case or on nearby components would indicate a leaking or cracked battery. If the battery is cracked, it should be replaced immediately.

### GENERAL MAINTENANCE

Always keep the battery cables and terminals free of corrosion. Check and clean these components about once a year.

Keep the top of the battery clean, as a film of dirt can help discharge a battery that is not used for long periods. A solution of baking soda and water may be used for cleaning, but be careful to flush this off with clear water. DO NOT let any of the solution into the filler holes. Baking soda neutralizes battery acid and will de-activate a battery cell.

Batteries in vehicles which are not operated on a regular basis can fall victim to parasitic loads (small current drains which are constantly drawing current from the battery). Normal parasitic loads may drain a battery on a vehicle that is in storage and not used for 6–8 weeks. Vehicles that have additional accessories such as a phone or an alarm system may discharge a battery sooner. If the vehicle is to be stored for longer periods in a secure area and the alarm system is not necessary, the negative battery cable should be disconnected to protect the battery.

Remember that constantly deep cycling a battery (completely discharging and recharging it) will shorten battery life.

### BATTERY FLUID

**See Figure 54**

Check the battery electrolyte level at least once a month, or more often in hot weather or during periods of extended vehicle operation. On non-sealed batteries, the level can be checked either through the case (if translucent) or by removing the cell caps. The electrolyte level in each cell should be kept filled to the split ring inside each cell, or the line marked on the outside of the case.

If the level is low, add only distilled water through the opening until the level is correct. Each cell must be checked and filled individually. Dis-

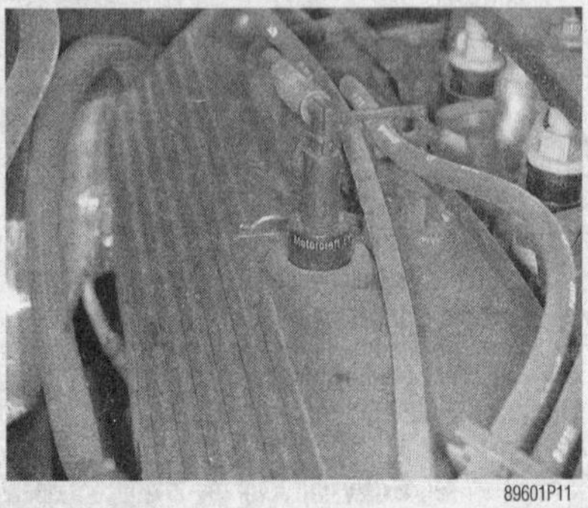

89601P11

**Fig. 50 The PCV valve is located in the passenger side valve cover—4.6L engine**

89601P12

**Fig. 51 Grasp the valve and gently remove it from the grommet in the valve cover**

89601P13

**Fig. 52 Remove the valve from the hose by carefully twisting it out**

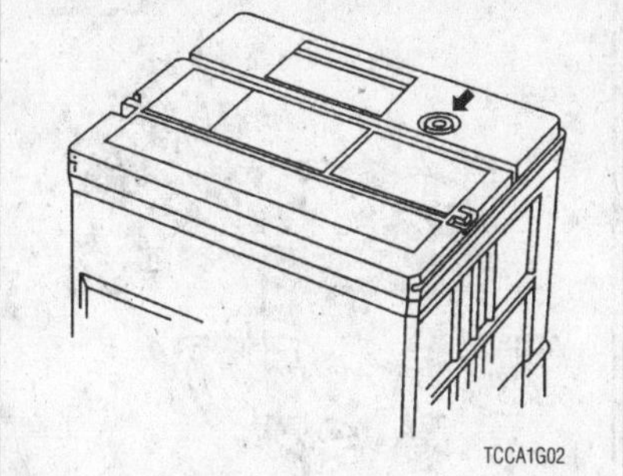


**Fig. 54 Maintenance-free batteries usually contain a built-in hydrometer to check fluid level**

tilled water should be used, because the chemicals and minerals found in most drinking water are harmful to the battery and could significantly shorten its life.

If water is added in freezing weather, the vehicle should be driven several miles to allow the water to mix with the electrolyte. Otherwise, the battery could freeze.

Although some maintenance-free batteries have removable cell caps, the electrolyte condition and level on all sealed maintenance-free batteries must be checked using the built-in hydrometer "eye." The exact type of eye will vary. But, most battery manufacturers, apply a sticker to the battery itself explaining the readings.

➡**Although the readings from built-in hydrometers will vary, a green eye usually indicates a properly charged battery with sufficient fluid level. A dark eye is normally an indicator of a battery with sufficient fluid, but which is low in charge. A light or yellow eye usually indicates that electrolyte has dropped below the necessary level. In this last case, sealed batteries with an insufficient electrolyte must usually be discarded.**

### Checking the Specific Gravity

**See Figures 55, 56 and 57**

A hydrometer is required to check the specific gravity on all batteries that are not maintenance-free. On batteries that are maintenance-free, the specific gravity is checked by observing the built-in hydrometer "eye" on the top of the battery case.

**CAUTION**

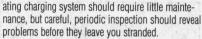

**Battery electrolyte contains sulfuric acid. If you should splash any on your skin or in your eyes, flush the affected area with plenty of clear water. If it lands in your eyes, get medical help immediately.**

The fluid (sulfuric acid solution) contained in the battery cells will tell you many things about the condition of the battery. Because the cell plates must be kept submerged below the fluid level in order to operate, the fluid level is extremely important. And, because the specific gravity of the acid is an indication of electrical charge, testing the fluid can be an aid in determining if the battery must be replaced. A battery in a vehicle with a properly operating charging system should require little maintenance, but careful, periodic inspection should reveal problems before they leave you stranded.

At least once a year, check the specific gravity of the battery. It should be between 1.20 and 1.26 on the gravity scale. Most auto stores carry a variety of inexpensive battery hydrometers. These can be used on any non-sealed battery to test the specific gravity in each cell.

The battery testing hydrometer has a squeeze bulb at one end and a nozzle at the other. Battery electrolyte is sucked into the hydrometer until the float is lifted from its seat. The specific gravity is then read by noting the position of the float. If gravity is low in one or more cells, the battery should be slowly charged and checked again to see if the gravity has come up. Generally, if after charging, the specific gravity between any two cells varies more than 50 points (0.50), the battery should be replaced, as it can no longer produce sufficient voltage to guarantee proper operation.

## CABLES

**See Figures 58, 59, 60 and 61**

Once a year (or as necessary), the battery terminals and the cable clamps should be cleaned. Loosen the clamps and remove the cables, negative cable first. On top post batteries, the use of a puller specially made for this purpose is recommended. These are inexpensive and available in most parts stores. Side terminal battery cables are secured with a small bolt.

Clean the cable clamps and the battery terminal with a wire brush, until all corrosion, grease, etc., is

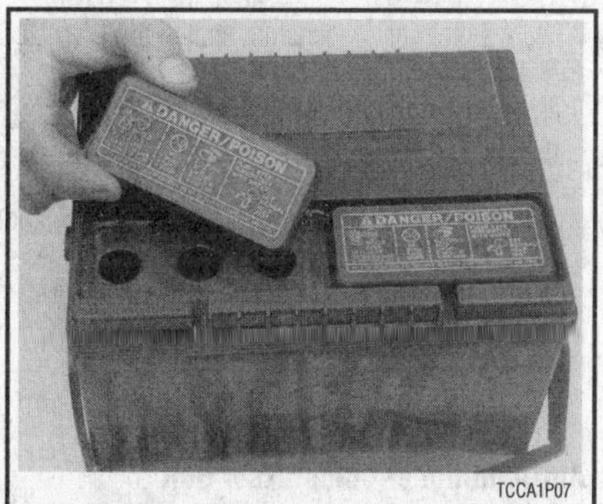


**Fig. 55 On non-sealed batteries, the fluid level can be checked by removing the cell caps**

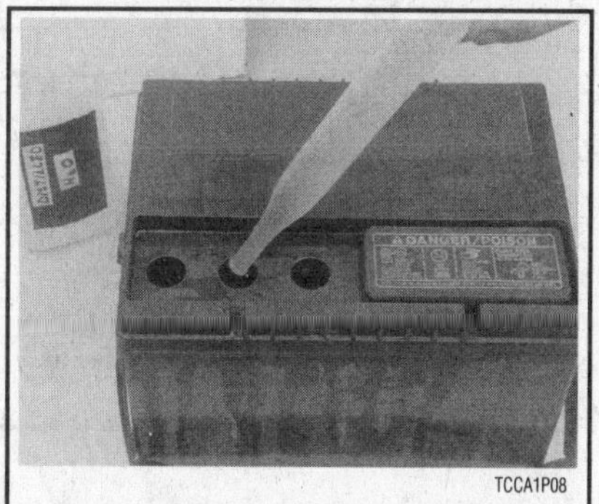


**Fig. 56 If the fluid level is low, add only distilled water until the level is correct**

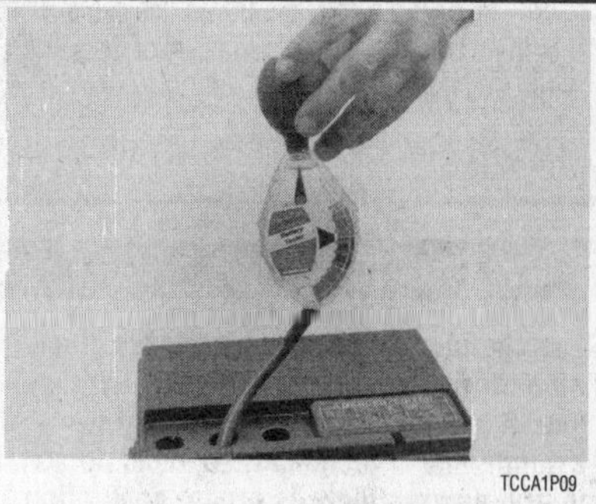


**Fig. 57 Check the specific gravity of the battery's electrolyte with a hydrometer**

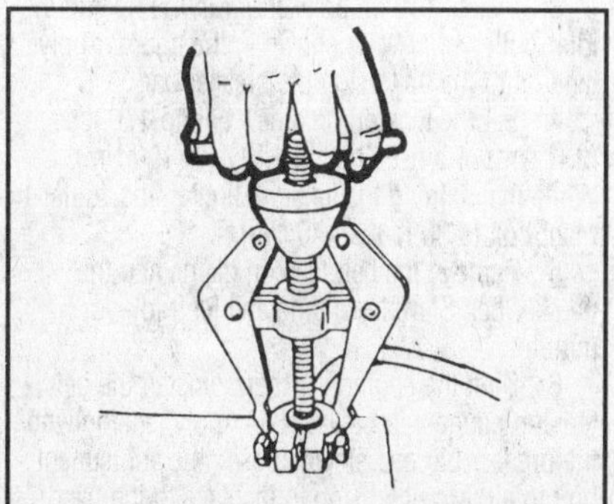


**Fig. 58 A special tool is available to pull the clamp from the post**

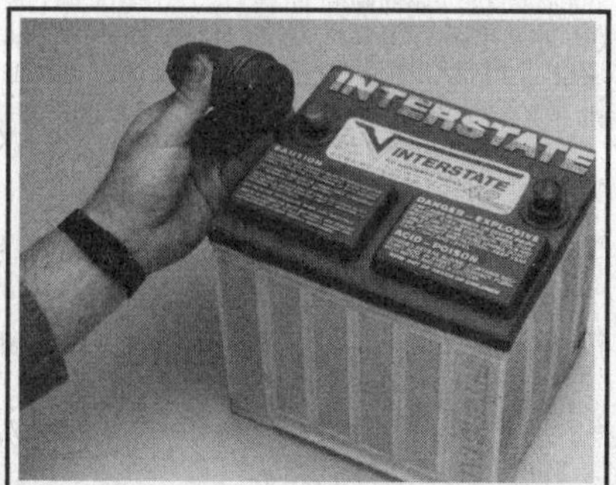


**Fig. 59 The underside of this special battery tool has a wire brush to clean post terminals**

**Fig. 60 Place the tool over the battery posts and twist to clean until the metal is shiny**

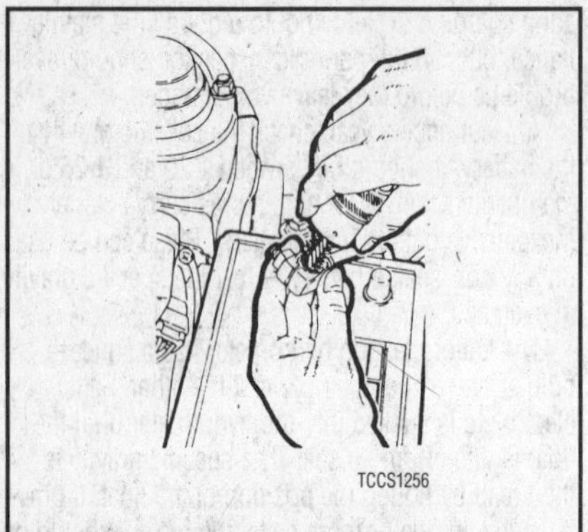


**Fig. 61 The cable ends should be cleaned as well**

removed and the metal is shiny. It is especially important to clean the inside of the clamp thoroughly (an old knife is useful here), since a small deposit of oxidation there will prevent a sound connection and inhibit starting or charging. Special tools are available for cleaning these parts, one type for conventional top post batteries and another type for side terminal batteries. It is also a good idea to apply some dielectric grease to the terminal, as this will aid in the prevention of corrosion.

After the clamps and terminals are clean, reinstall the cables, negative cable last; DO NOT hammer the clamps onto battery posts. Tighten the clamps securely, but do not distort them. Give the clamps and terminals a thin external coating of grease after installation, to retard corrosion.

Check the cables at the same time that the terminals are cleaned. If the cable insulation is cracked or broken, or if the ends are frayed, the cable should be replaced with a new cable of the same length and gauge.

### CHARGING

**CAUTION**

**The chemical reaction which takes place in all batteries generates explosive hydrogen gas. A spark can cause the battery to explode and splash acid. To avoid personal injury, be sure there is proper ventilation and take appropriate fire safety precautions when working with or near a battery.**

A battery should be charged at a slow rate to keep the plates inside from getting too hot. However, if some maintenance-free batteries are allowed to discharge until they are almost "dead," they may have to be charged at a high rate to bring them back to "life." Always follow the charger manufacturer's instructions on charging the battery.

### REPLACEMENT

When it becomes necessary to replace the battery, select one with an amperage rating equal to or greater than the battery originally installed. Deterioration and just plain aging of the battery cables, starter motor, and associated wires makes the battery's job harder in successive years. This makes it prudent to install a new battery with a greater capacity than the old.

## Belts

### INSPECTION

▶ **See Figures 62 and 63**

The belts, which drive the engine accessories such as the alternator, the air pump, power steering pump, air conditioning compressor and water pump, are of serpentine belt design. Older style belts show wear and damage readily, since their basic design was a belt with a rubber casing. As the casing wore, cracks and fibers were readily apparent. Newer design, caseless belts do not show wear as readily, and many untrained people cannot distinguish between a good, serviceable belt and one that is worn to the point of failure. It is a good idea, therefore, to visually inspect the belt regularly and replace it, routinely, every two to three years.

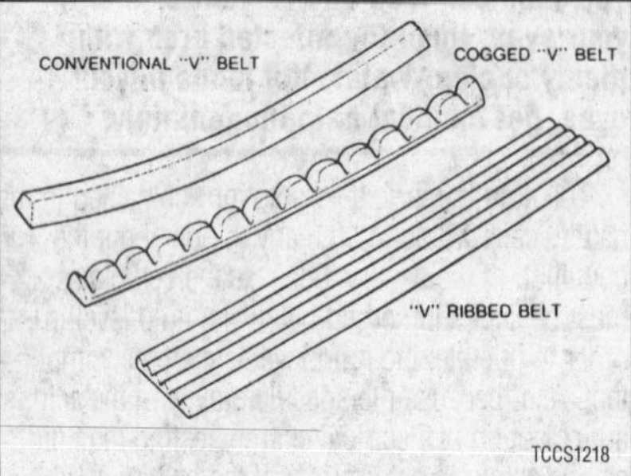


**Fig. 62 Typically, there are three types of belts found on today's vehicles**

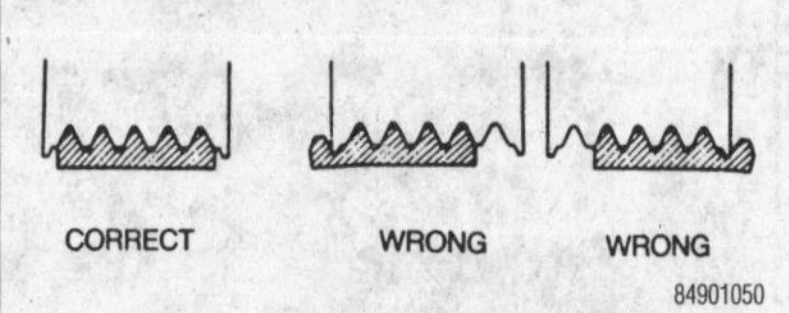


**Fig. 63 On serpentine belts, the ribs of the belt should be positioned in the pulley as shown**

### ADJUSTING

Vehicles are equipped with V-ribbed (serpentine) accessory drive belts. To ensure maximum life, the replacement belt should be of the same type as the original. This system is equipped with an automatic belt tensioner that will maintain the correct tension on the belt and should not require any tension adjustment for the life of the belt. A worn belt can result in slippage, which may cause a noise concern or improper accessory operation.

Automatic tensioners do not have to be removed to remove a drive belt. To remove a drive belt, rotate the tensioner away from the belt.

#### Alternator Belt

▶ **See Figures 64 and 65**

1. Loosen the alternator pivot and adjustment bolts.
2. Position a suitable belt tension gauge at the point indicated in the figure. Install an open end wrench over the alternator adjustment boss, then apply tension to the belt, using the wrench.

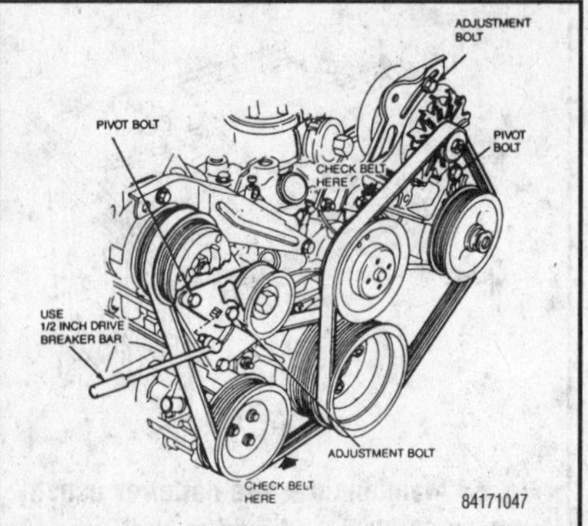


**Fig. 64 Alternator and air conditioner belt tension adjustment—5.0L**

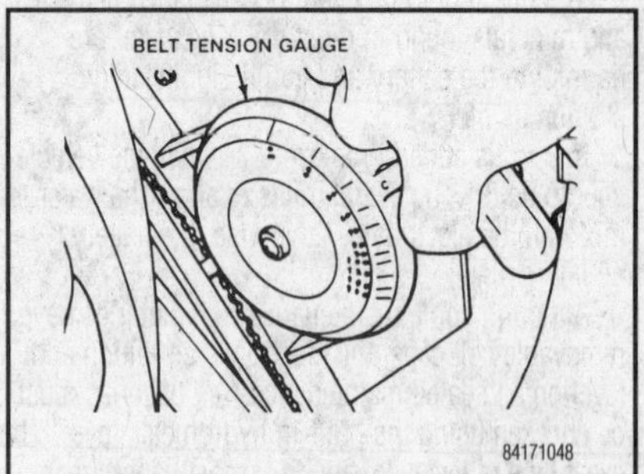


**Fig. 65 Belt tension gauge**

3. Set the tension on a new belt to 170 ft. lbs. (231 Nm) or a used belt to 140 ft. lbs. (190 Nm). While maintaining the tension, tighten the alternator adjustment bolt to 29 ft. lbs. (39 Nm).
4. Remove the belt tension gauge, start the engine and let it idle for 5 minutes.
5. Shut off the engine and install the tension gauge. Apply tension with the open end wrench and slowly loosen the adjustment bolt to allow belt tension to increase to the used belt specification, 140 lbs. Tighten the adjustment bolt to 29 ft. lbs. (39 Nm).
6. Tighten the pivot bolt to 50 ft. lbs. (68 Nm).

#### Air Conditioner Compressor Belt

1. Loosen the idler pulley bracket adjustment and pivot bolts.
2. Position a suitable belt tension gauge at the point indicated in the figure.
3. Install a ½ in. breaker bar in the hole in the idler pulley bracket as shown in the figure. Apply tension to the belt using the breaker bar.
4. Set the tension on a new belt to 170 lbs. (231 Nm) or a used belt to 140 lbs. (190 Nm). While maintaining the tension, tighten the adjustment bolt to 30 ft. lbs. (40 Nm).
5. Remove the belt tension gauge and the breaker bar. Start the engine and let it idle for 5 minutes.
6. Shut the engine off, then reinstall the belt tension gauge and breaker bar. Apply tension with the breaker bar and slowly loosen the adjustment bolt to allow belt tension to increase to the used belt specification, 140 ft. lbs. (190 Nm). Tighten the adjustment bolt to 30 ft. lbs. (40 Nm).
7. Tighten the pivot bolt to 50 ft. lbs. (68 Nm).

#### Serpentine Belt

On some applications, a single belt is used to drive all of the engine accessories formerly driven by multiple drive belts. The single belt is referred to a serpentine belt. All the belt driven accessories are rigidly mounted with belt tension maintained by a spring-loaded tensioner. Because of the belt tensioner, no adjustment is necessary.

On other applications, a dual belt system is employed. Although the belts are still of a serpentine belt design, they must be adjusted to the proper tension manually. When making this adjustment, allow about ½ inch deflection when pushing on the longest run of the belt.

Cracks on the rib side of a drive belt are considered acceptable. If the drive belt has chunks missing from the ribs, if two or more adjacent ribs have lost sections, or if the missing chunks are creating a noise, vibrations, or harshness condition, replace the drive belt.

### REMOVAL AND INSTALLATION

#### Continental With The 3.8L Engine

1. Insert a ½inch flex handle in the square hole in the tensioner. The tensioner has a square hole cast into the rear of the tensioner body directly behind the pulley. Rotate the tensioner clockwise and remove the belt from the pulleys.

**➡As an alternate method, a 16mm socket can be placed on the tensioner pulley bolt and rotated clockwise to remove the belt.**

**To install:**

2. Following the schematic on the decal under the hood, loop the drive belt over all the pulleys except the alternator pulley.
3. With the belt installed properly on all except the alternator pulley, rotate the tensioner as described above and install the belt on the alternator pulley. Ensure that all the V-grooves make proper contact with the pulleys.

#### Continental And Mark VIII With The 4.6L Engine

**⁂ WARNING**

**Do not allow the drive belt tensioner to snap back as damage to the drive belt tensioner or personal injury could result.**

1. Rotate the drive belt tensioner clockwise with a breaker bar installed in the ⅜ inch square hole in the drive belt tensioner.
2. Lift the drive belt over the idler pulley flange and remove the drive belt.

**To install:**

3. Following the schematic on the decal under the hood, position the belt over the pulleys, except the idler pulley.
4. Rotate the tensioner as described above and install the belt on the idler. Ensure that all the V-grooves make proper contact with the pulleys.

#### Town Car With The 4.6L Engine

➧ See Figures 66 and 67

1. Install a breaker bar in the ½ in. square hole in the automatic tensioner arm.

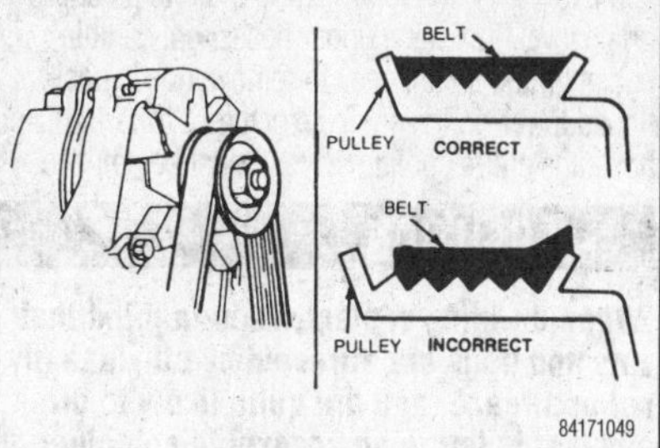


**Fig. 66 Make sure the belt makes proper contact with the pulley grooves**

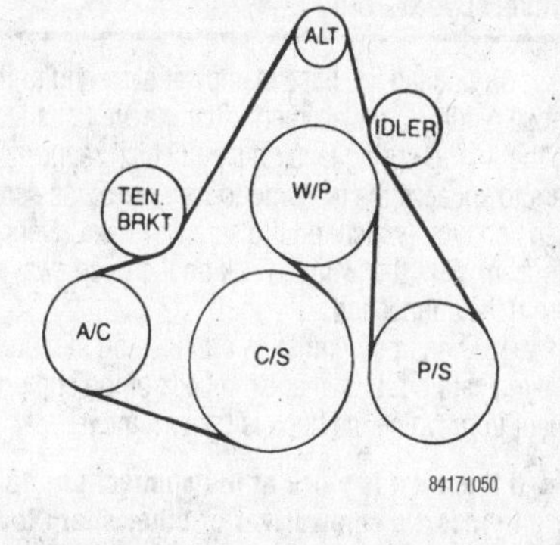


**Fig. 67 Accessory drive belt routing—4.6L engine**

2. Rotate the tensioner away from the belt with the breaker bar.
3. Lift the old belt over the alternator pulley flange and remove it.

**To install:**

4. Position the new belt over all the pulleys, except the alternator pulley, rotate the tensioner as described above and install the belt on the alternator pulley. Refer to the belt routing illustration on the sticker located at the front of the engine compartment. Ensure that all the V-grooves and all the ribs on the belt properly contact the grooves on the pulleys.
5. Rotate the tensioner toward the belt and remove the breaker bar.

#### Town Car And Mark VII With The 5.0L Engine

##### *ALTERNATOR BELT*

1. Loosen the alternator adjustment and pivot bolts.
2. Rotate the alternator towards the engine until the belt is slack enough to remove from the pulleys.

**To install:**

3. Install the belt over the pulleys. Make sure the ribs on the belt properly contact the grooves on the pulleys.
4. Adjust the belt tension as described earlier in this Section.

##### *AIR CONDITIONER COMPRESSOR BELT*

1. Remove the alternator belt.
2. Loosen the idler bracket adjustment and pivot bolts.
3. Rotate the idler bracket away from the belt until the belt is slack enough to remove from the pulleys.

**To install:**

4. Install the belt over the pulleys. Make sure the ribs on the belt properly contact the grooves on the pulleys.
5. Adjust the belt tension as described earlier in this Section.
6. Install the alternator belt and adjust the tension.

## Hoses

### INSPECTION

➧ See Figures 68, 69, 70 and 71

Upper and lower radiator hoses, along with the heater hoses, should be checked for deterioration,

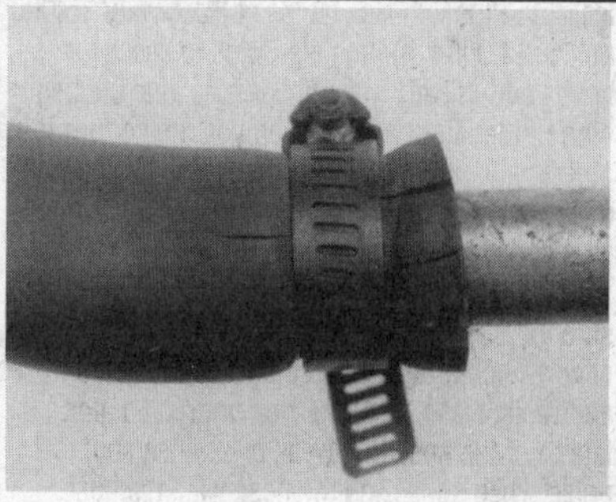

TCCS1219

**Fig. 68 The cracks developing along this hose are a result of age-related hardening**

TCCS1220

**Fig. 69 A hose clamp that is too tight can cause older hoses to separate and tear on either side of the clamp**

TCCS1221

**Fig. 70 A soft spongy hose (identifiable by the swollen section) will eventually burst and should be replaced**

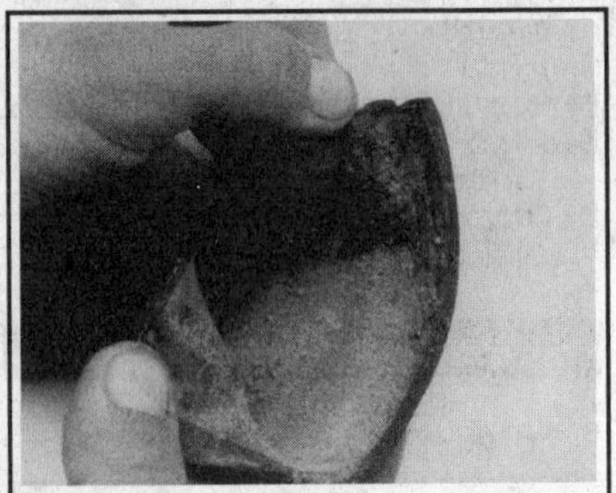

TCCS1222

**Fig. 71 Hoses are likely to deteriorate from the inside if the cooling system is not periodically flushed**

leaks and loose hose clamps at least every 15,000 miles (24,000 km). It is also wise to check the hoses periodically in early spring and at the beginning of the fall or winter when you are performing other maintenance. A quick visual inspection could discover a weakened hose, which might leave you stranded if it remains faulty.

Whenever you are checking the hoses, make sure the engine and cooling system are cold. Visually inspect for cracking, rotting or collapsed hoses, and replace as necessary. Run your hand along the length of the hose. If a weak or swollen spot is noted when squeezing the hose wall, the hose should be replaced.

### REMOVAL & INSTALLATION

1. Remove the radiator pressure cap.

**✱✱ CAUTION**

**Never remove the pressure cap while the engine is running, or personal injury from scalding hot coolant or steam may result. If possible, wait until the engine has cooled to remove the pressure cap. If this is not possible, wrap a thick cloth around the pressure cap and turn it slowly to the stop. Step back while the pressure is released from the cooling system. When you are sure all the pressure has been released, use the cloth to turn and remove the cap.**

2. Position a clean container under the radiator and/or engine draincock or plug, then open the drain and allow the cooling system to drain to an appropriate level. For some upper hoses, only a little coolant must be drained. To remove hoses positioned lower on the engine, such as a lower radiator hose, the entire cooling system must be emptied.

**✱✱ CAUTION**

**When draining coolant, keep in mind that cats and dogs are attracted by ethylene glycol antifreeze, and are quite likely to drink any that is left in an uncovered container or in puddles on the ground. This will prove fatal in sufficient quantity. Always drain coolant into a sealable container. Coolant may be reused unless it is contaminated or several years old.**

3. Loosen the hose clamps at each end of the hose requiring replacement. Clamps are usually either of the spring tension type (which require pliers to squeeze the tabs and loosen) or of the screw tension type (which require screw or hex drivers to loosen). Pull the clamps back on the hose away from the connection.
4. Twist, pull and slide the hose off the fitting, taking care not to damage the neck of the component from which the hose is being removed.

**➡ If the hose is stuck at the connection, do not try to insert a screwdriver or other sharp tool under the hose end in an effort to free it, as the connection and/or hose may become damaged. Heater connections especially may be easily damaged by such a procedure. If the hose is to be replaced, use a single-edged razor blade or suitable cutting edge, to make a slice along the portion of the hose that is stuck on the connection, perpendicular to the end of the hose. Do not cut too deeply, damage to the connection could result. The hose can then be peeled from the connection and discarded.**

5. Clean both hose mounting connections. Inspect the condition of the hose clamps and replace them, if necessary.

**To install:**

6. Dip the ends of the new hose into clean engine coolant to ease installation.
7. Slide the clamps over the replacement hose, then slide the hose ends over the connections into position.
8. Position and secure the clamps at least 1/4 in. (6.35mm) from the ends of the hose. Make sure they are located beyond the raised bead of the connector.
9. Close the radiator or engine drains and properly refill the cooling system with the clean drained engine coolant or a suitable mixture of ethylene glycol coolant and water. Be sure to maintain a 50/50 mix as a minimum in the system.
10. If available, install a pressure tester and check for leaks. If a pressure tester is not available, run the engine until normal operating temperature is reached (allowing the system to naturally pressurize), then check for leaks.

**✱✱ CAUTION**

**If you are checking for leaks with the system at normal operating temperature, BE EXTREMELY CAREFUL not to touch any moving or hot engine parts. Once temperature has been reached, shut the engine OFF, and check for leaks around the hose fittings and connections that were removed earlier.**

## CV-Boots

### INSPECTION

**➧ See Figures 72 and 73**

The CV (Constant Velocity) boots should be checked for damage each time the oil is changed and any other time the vehicle is raised for service. These boots keep water, grime, dirt and other damaging matter from entering the CV-joints. Any of these could cause early CV-joint failure that can be expensive to repair. Heavy grease thrown around the inside of the front wheel(s) and on the brake caliper/drum can be an indication of a torn boot. Thoroughly check the boots for missing clamps and tears. If the boot is damaged, it should be replaced immediately. Please refer to Section 7 for procedures.

## Spark Plugs

**➧ See Figures 74 and 75**

A typical spark plug consists of a metal shell surrounding a ceramic insulator. A metal electrode extends downward through the center of the insulator and protrudes a small distance. Located at the end of the plug and attached to the side of the outer metal shell is the side electrode. The side electrode

TCCS1011

**Fig. 72 CV-boots must be inspected periodically for damage**

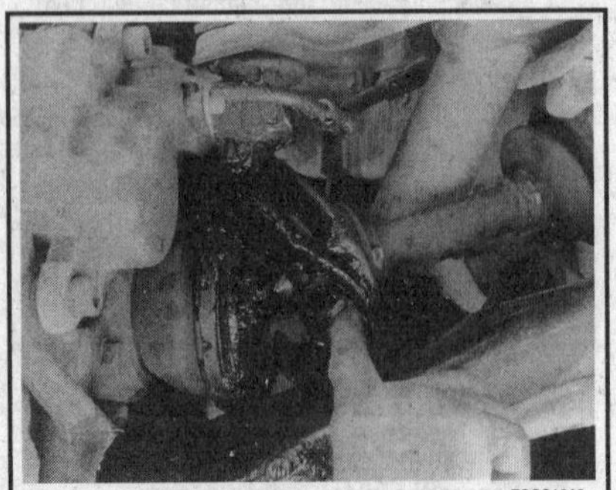

TCCS1010

**Fig. 73 A torn boot should be replaced immediately**

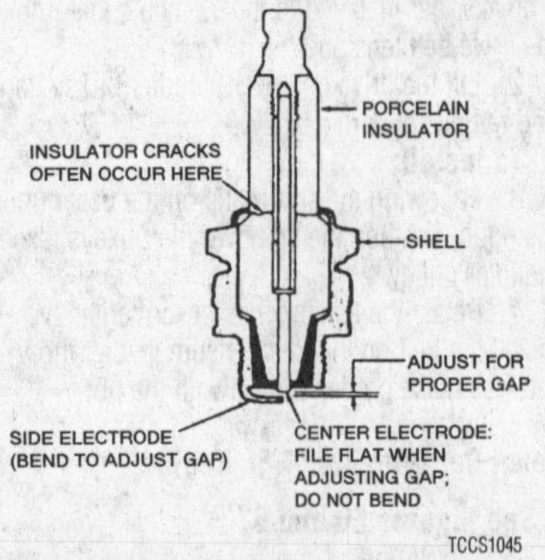


TCCS1045

**Fig. 74 Cross-section of a spark plug**

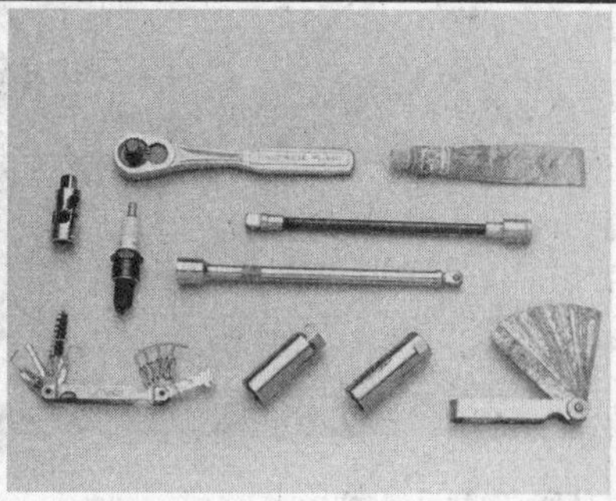
TCCS1212

Fig. 75 A variety of tools and gauges are needed for spark plug service

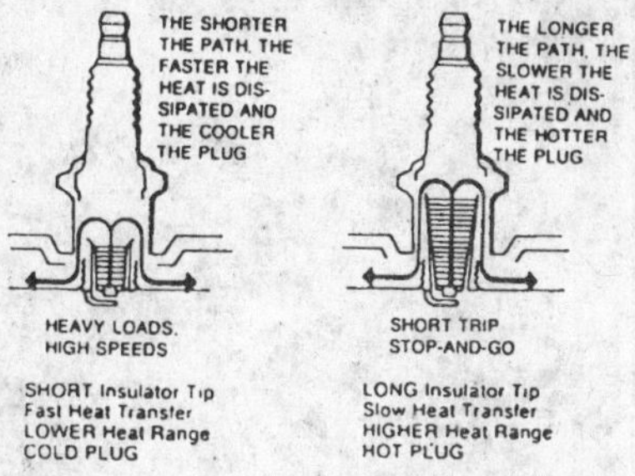

TCCS1046

Fig. 76 Spark plug heat range

89601P95

Fig. 77 Grasp the plug wire and carefully twist the wire to release the retainer from the spark plug. If the plug wire is stubborn, a pair of special removal pliers is recommended to remove the wires from the plugs

bends in at a 90° angle so that its tip is just past and parallel to the tip of the center electrode. The distance between these two electrodes (measured in thousandths of an inch or hundredths of a millimeter) is called the spark plug gap.

The spark plug does not produce a spark, but instead provides a gap across which the current can arc. The coil produces anywhere from 20,000 to 50,000 volts (depending on the type and application) which travels through the wires to the spark plugs. The current passes along the center electrode and jumps the gap to the side electrode, and in doing so, ignites the air/fuel mixture in the combustion chamber.

## SPARK PLUG HEAT RANGE

**▶ See Figure 76**

Spark plug heat range is the ability of the plug to dissipate heat. The longer the insulator (or the farther it extends into the engine), the hotter the plug will operate; the shorter the insulator (the closer the electrode is to the block's cooling passages) the cooler it will operate. A plug that absorbs little heat and remains too cool will quickly accumulate deposits of oil and carbon since it is not hot enough to burn them off. This leads to plug fouling and consequently to misfiring. A plug that absorbs too much heat will have no deposits but, due to the excessive heat, the electrodes will burn away quickly and might possibly lead to preignition or other ignition problems. Preignition takes place when plug tips get so hot that they glow sufficiently to ignite the air/fuel mixture before the actual spark occurs. This early ignition will usually cause a pinging during low speeds and heavy loads.

The general rule of thumb for choosing the correct heat range when picking a spark plug is: if most of your driving is long distance, high speed travel, use a colder plug; if most of your driving is stop and go, use a hotter plug. Original equipment plugs are generally a good compromise between the 2 styles and most people never have the need to change their plugs from the factory-recommended heat range.

## REMOVAL & INSTALLATION

**▶ See Figures 77 thru 84**

A set of standard spark plugs usually requires replacement after about 30,000 miles (32,000–48,000 km), depending on your style of driving. In normal operation plug gap increases about 0.001 in. (0.025mm) for every 2500 miles (4000 km). As the gap increases, the voltage requirement of the plug also increases. It requires a greater voltage to jump the wider gap and about two to three times as much voltage to fire the plug at high speeds than at idle. The improved air/fuel ratio control of modern fuel injection combined with the higher voltage output of modern ignition systems will often allow an engine to run significantly longer on a set of standard spark plugs, but keep in mind that efficiency will drop as the gap widens (along with fuel economy and power).

When you're removing spark plugs, work on one at a time. Don't start by removing the plug wires all at once, because, unless you number them, they may become mixed up. Take a minute before you begin and number the wires with tape.

1. Disconnect the negative battery cable, and if the vehicle has been run recently, allow the engine to thoroughly cool.
2. On some applications, it may be necessary to remove the air cleaner assembly.
3. Carefully twist the spark plug wire boot ½ turn to loosen it, then pull upward and remove the boot from the plug. Be sure to pull on the boot and not on the wire, otherwise the connector located inside the boot may become separated.
4. Using compressed air, blow any water or debris from the spark plug well to assure that no harmful contaminants are allowed to enter the combustion chamber when the spark plug is removed. If compressed air is not available, use a rag or a brush to clean the area.

**➡Remove the spark plugs when the engine is cold, if possible, to prevent damage to the threads. If removal of the plugs is difficult, apply a few drops of penetrating oil or silicone spray to the area around the base of the plug, and allow it a few minutes to work.**

5. Using a spark plug socket that is equipped with a rubber insert to properly hold the plug, turn the spark plug counterclockwise to loosen and remove the spark plug from the bore.

**To install:**

6. Inspect the spark plug boot for tears or damage. If a damaged boot is found, the spark plug wire must be replaced.
7. Using a wire feeler gauge, check and adjust

91191P45

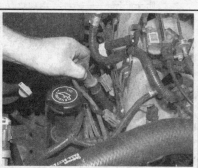

Fig. 78 Carefully remove the plug wire from the cylinder head

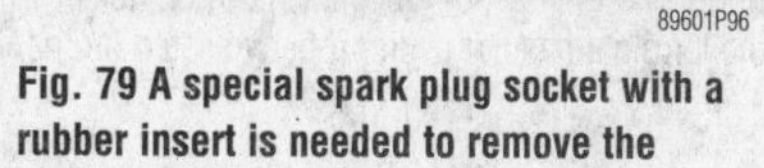
89601P96

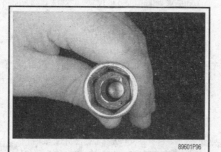

Fig. 79 A special spark plug socket with a rubber insert is needed to remove the spark plugs. Typically the spark plugs on engines covered by this manual require a ⅝ socket

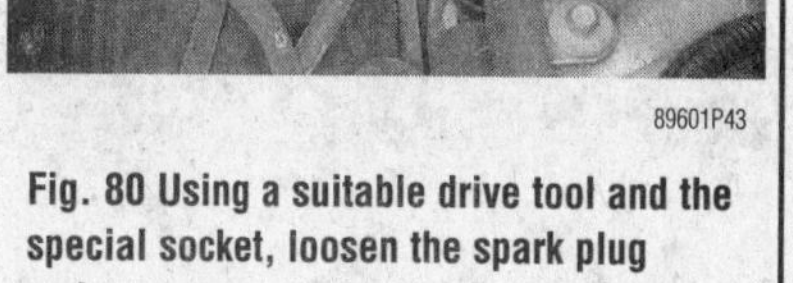
89601P43

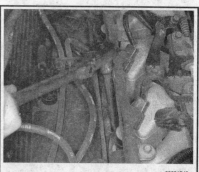

Fig. 80 Using a suitable drive tool and the special socket, loosen the spark plug and . . .

89601P42

Fig. 81 . . . remove the spark plug from the engine

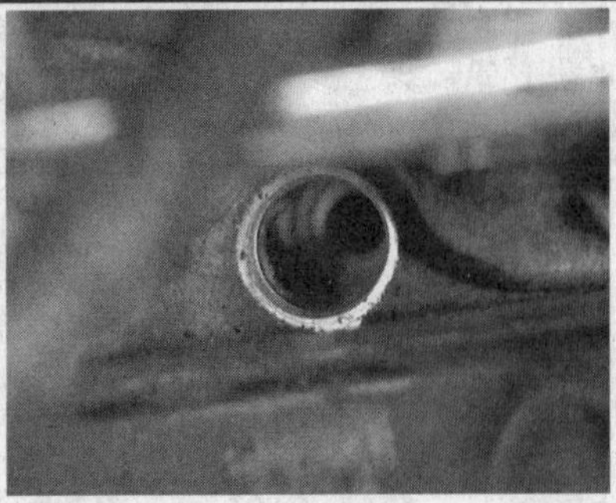
91191P49

Fig. 82 Clean out the spark plug bore and threads before installing the new spark plug

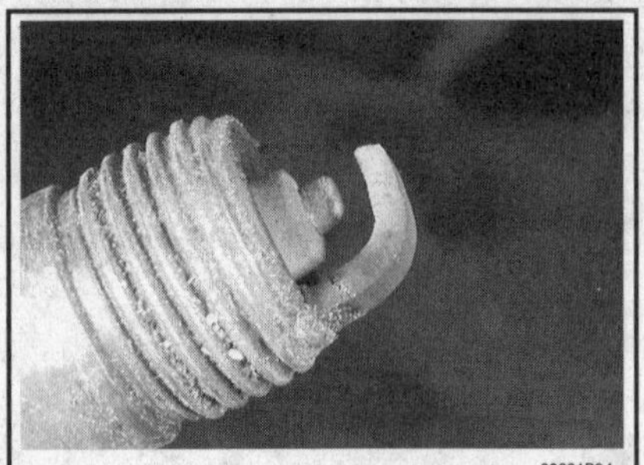
89601P34

Fig. 83 An inspection of the old spark plugs will give a general idea of the condition of the motor, compare the spark plugs to the chart in this section

89601P33

Fig. 84 A piece of fuel line or a small hose is useful in installing the spark plugs to avoid stripping the threads

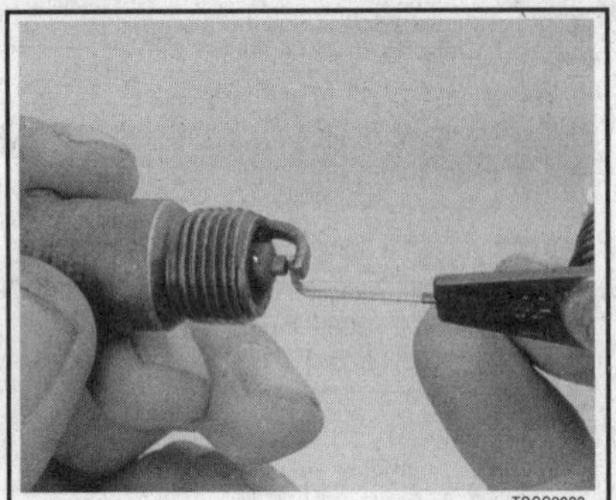
TCCS2903

Fig. 85 Checking the spark plug gap with a feeler gauge

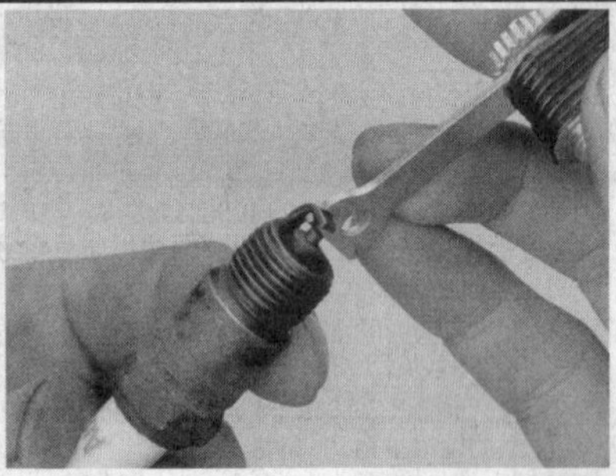
TCCS2904

Fig. 86 Adjusting the spark plug gap

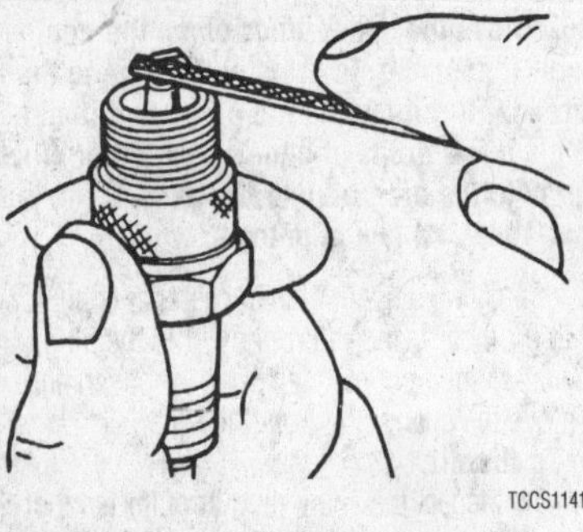
TCCS1141

Fig. 87 If the standard plug is in good condition, the electrode may be filed flat—WARNING: do not file platinum plugs

the spark plug gap. When using a gauge, the proper size should pass between the electrodes with a slight drag. The next larger size should not be able to pass while the next smaller size should pass freely.

8. Carefully thread the plug into the bore by hand. If resistance is felt before the plug is almost completely threaded, back the plug out and begin threading again. In small, hard to reach areas, an old spark plug wire and boot could be used as a threading tool. The boot will hold the plug while you twist the end of the wire and the wire is supple enough to twist before it would allow the plug to crossthread.

**⁂ WARNING**

**Do not use the spark plug socket to thread the plugs. Always carefully thread the plug by hand or using an old plug wire, or vacuum line, to prevent the possibility of crossthreading and damaging the cylinder head bore.**

9. Carefully tighten the spark plug. These engine applications use a tapered seat plug.

10. Apply a small amount of silicone dielectric compound to the end of the spark plug. This assures no water will enter and no corrosion will develop. It will also aid in removal of the boot when the time comes.

Use special care when reinstalling spark plug boots, to assure that the metal terminal within the boot is fully seated on the spark plug terminal and that the boot has not moved on the wire. If boot to wire movement has occurred, the boot will give a false visual impression of being fully seated. A good check to assure that boots have been properly assembled is to push sideways on the installed boots. If they have been correctly installed, a stiff boot, with only slight looseness, will be noted. If the terminal has not been properly seated on the sparkplug, only the resistance of the rubber boot will be felt when pushing sideways.

## INSPECTION & GAPPING

**See Figures 85, 86, 87 and 88**

Check the plugs for deposits and wear. If they are not going to be replaced, clean the plugs thoroughly. Remember that any kind of deposit will decrease the efficiency of the plug. Plugs can be cleaned on a spark plug cleaning machine, which can sometimes be found in service stations, or you can do an acceptable job of cleaning with a stiff brush. If the plugs are cleaned, the electrodes must be filed flat. Use an ignition points file, not an emery board or the like, which will leave deposits. The electrodes must be filed perfectly flat with sharp edges; rounded edges reduce the spark plug voltage by as much as 50%.

Check spark plug gap before installation. The ground electrode (the L-shaped one connected to the body of the plug) must be parallel to the center electrode and the specified size wire gauge (please refer to the Tune-Up Specifications chart for details) must pass between the electrodes with a slight drag.

➡**NEVER adjust the gap on a used platinum type spark plug.**

Always check the gap on new plugs as they are not always set correctly at the factory. Do not use a

**A normally worn** spark plug should have light tan or gray deposits on the firing tip.

**A carbon fouled** plug, identified by soft, sooty, black deposits, may indicate an improperly tuned vehicle. Check the air cleaner, ignition components and engine control system.

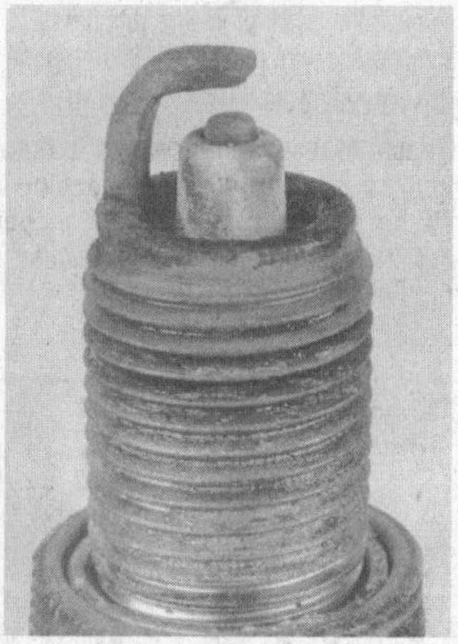

This spark plug has been **left in the engine too long,** as evidenced by the extreme gap- Plugs with such an extreme gap can cause misfiring and stumbling accompanied by a noticeable lack of power.

**An oil fouled** spark plug indicates an engine with worn poston rings and/or bad valve seals allowing excessive oil to enter the chamber.

**A physically damaged** spark plug may be evidence of severe detonation in that cylinder. Watch that cylinder carefully between services, as a continued detonation will not only damage the plug, but could also damage the engine.

**A bridged or almost bridged** spark plug, identified by a build-up between the electrodes caused by excessive carbon or oil build-up on the plug.

TCCA1P40

**Fig. 88 Inspect the spark plug to determine engine running conditions**

flat feeler gauge when measuring the gap on a used plug, because the reading may be inaccurate. A round-wire type gapping tool is the best way to check the gap. The correct gauge should pass through the electrode gap with a slight drag. If you're in doubt, try one size smaller and one larger. The smaller gauge should go through easily, while the larger one shouldn't go through at all. Wire gapping tools usually have a bending tool attached. Use that to adjust the side electrode until the proper distance is obtained. Absolutely never attempt to bend the center electrode. Also, be careful not to bend the side electrode too far or too often as it may weaken and break off within the engine, requiring removal of the cylinder head to retrieve it.

## Spark Plug Wires

### TESTING

➧ **See Figures 89 and 90**

Visually inspect the spark plug wires for burns, cuts, or breaks in the insulation. Check the spark plug boots and the nipples on the distributor cap and/or coil(s). Replace any damaged wiring. If no physical damage is obvious, the wires can be checked with an ohmmeter for excessive resistance and continuity.

At every tune-up/inspection, visually check the spark plug cables for burns cuts, or breaks in the insulation. Check the boots and the nipples on the distributor cap and/or coil. Replace any damaged wiring.

Every 50,000 miles (80,000 Km) or 60 months, the resistance of the wires should be checked with an ohmmeter. Wires with excessive resistance will cause misfiring, and may make the engine difficult to start in damp weather.

To check resistance, disconnect plug wires (do only one at a time) from the spark plug and distributor cap or coil pack.

- Connect one lead of an ohmmeter to the spark plug side of the wire (make sure to contact the metal clip inside the boot).
- Attach the other lead of the ohmmeter to the distributor (coil pack) side of the wire. Again, make sure you contact the metal clip.
- Spark plug wire resistance is a function of length, the longer the wire the greater the resistance. You should replace any wire with a resistance over 7k ohms per foot.
- Spraying the secondary ignition wires with a light mist of water may help locate an intermittent problem. Ignition components will arc to ground when a secondary ignition component is faulty.

**➡Whenever the high-tension wires are removed from the plugs, coil, or distributor, silicone grease must be applied to the boot before reconnection. Coat the entire interior surface with Ford silicone grease D7AZ-19A331-A or its equivalent.**

### REMOVAL & INSTALLATION

➧ **See Figures 91 thru 96**

When it becomes necessary to replace spark plug wires, because of age or breakage, it is recommended that you purchase a wire set for your specific engine model. These wire sets are precut to the proper length, and already have the boots installed.

**✲✲ WARNING**

**Use care when removing spark plug wire boots from spark plugs. Grasp the wire by the rubber boot. Twist and pull the boot and wire from the spark plug. Never pull on the plug wire directly, or it may become separated from the connector inside the boot.**

1. Twist the boot ½- turn before trying to pull the boot off. Pull only on the boot, pulling on the wire could cause separation or breakage.
2. On 3.8L and 5.0L applications, disconnect the spark plug wire from the distributor cap in the same manner as the wire was disconnected from the spark plug. On the 4.6L engine, squeeze the locking tabs and twist the boot, while pulling upward from the coil.
3. Remove the necessary wire retainer clips and separators and remove the spark plug wire.
4. Disconnect the battery negative cable.
5. Remove the air cleaner assembly.
6. Remove the spark plug wire retainers.
7. Replace one wire at a time. Match the length of the old wires to new, to ease installation.

**➡Make a note of the wire placement to the cap (or coil pack) and routing to the engine so as to maintain correct firing order and proper clearances to engine parts that could cause damage to the wiring.**

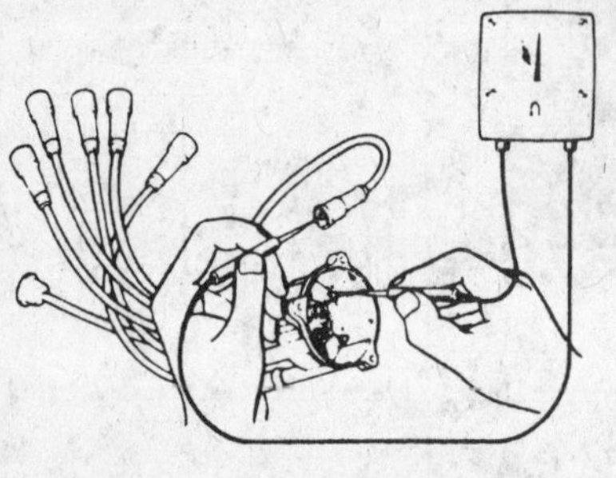

TCCS1008

**Fig. 89 Checking plug wire resistance through the distributor cap with an ohmmeter**

TCCS1009

**Fig. 90 Checking individual plug wire resistance with a digital ohmmeter**

91191P44

**Fig. 91 Grasp the plug wire and carefully twist the wire to release the retainer from the spark plug**

91191PA7

**Fig. 92 If the plug wire is stubborn, a pair of special removal pliers is recommended to remove the wires from the plugs**

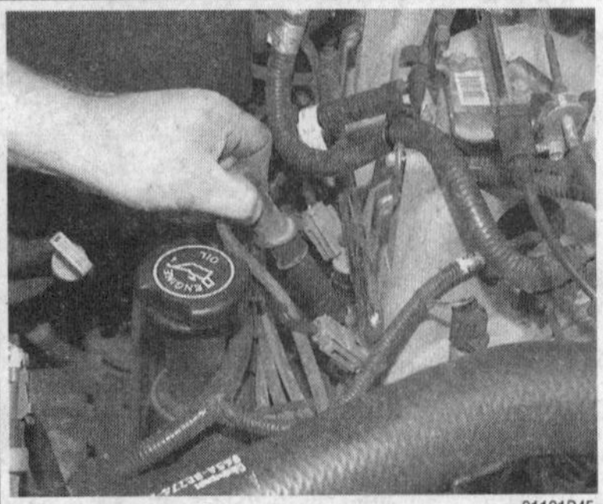

91191P45

**Fig. 93 Carefully remove the plug wire from the cylinder head**

91191PA6

**Fig. 94 Remove the plug wires from the ignition coil by squeezing the retaining tabs and carefully lifting the wires up**

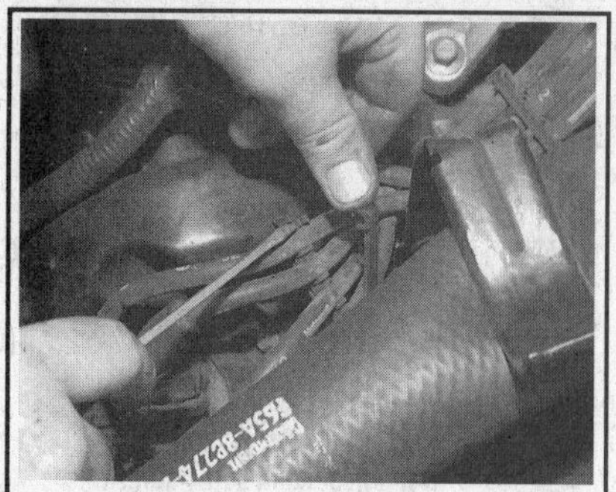

91191PA8

**Fig. 95 Disconnect the plug wire retaining clips from the wires and . . .**

91191PA9

**Fig. 96 . . . remove the plug wires from the engine**

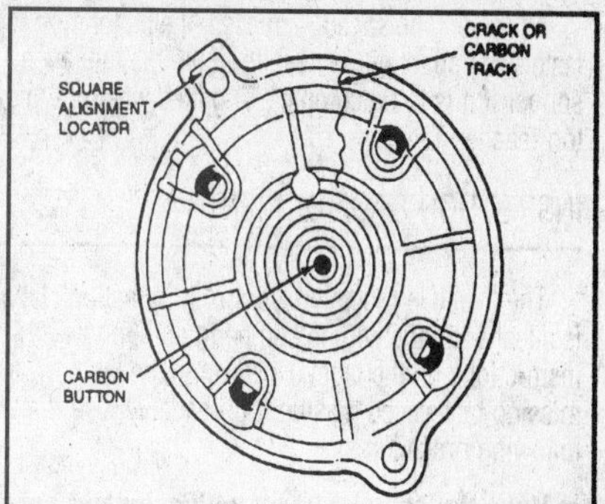


90951G22

**Fig. 97 Inspection points for the distributor cap**

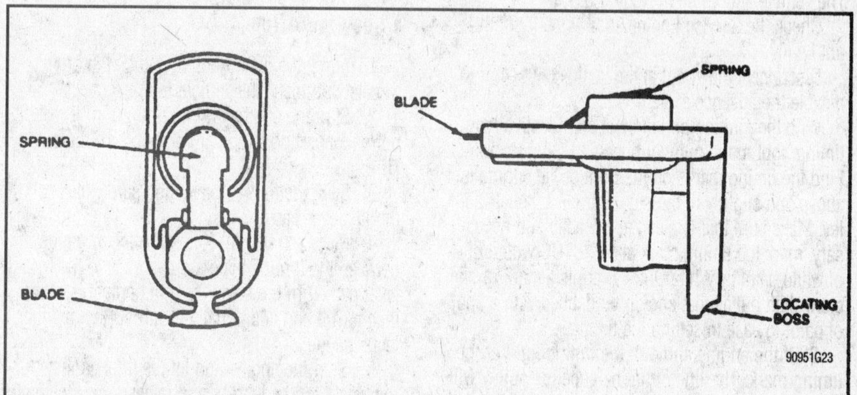


90951G23

**Fig. 98 Inspection points for the distributor rotor**

**To install:**

**Ensure that, when replacing plug wires, the wires are routed correctly and through the proper retainers. Failure to route the wires properly can lead to radio ignition noise and crossfiring of the plugs, or shorting of the leads to ground.**

8. Coat the spark plug terminal end (or inside of the plug boot) with dielectric compound, install the boot onto the spark plug. Make sure it "clicks" on.

**⁂ WARNING**

**On the 4.6L engine, it is critical to vehicle operation that the spark plug wires be properly installed at the spark plugs and ignition coils. If one spark plug wire is not properly installed, both spark plugs connected to that ignition coil may not fire under load.**

9. Route the wire through the necessary retainer clips and separators.
10. Route the wires along the engine, keeping the proper clearances.
11. Install the wire to the proper distributor cap or ignition coil terminal, making sure the boot is firmly seated. On the 4.6L engine, make sure the coil boot locking tabs are engaged. Keep the proper firing order.

**➡On the 4.6L engine, the spark plug boot must be positioned 45 degrees from crankshaft centerline (outboard and forward) to make sure the boot seal is fully seated.**

12. Install spark plug wire retainers.
13. Install air cleaner assembly.

## Distributor Cap and Rotor

### REMOVAL AND INSTALLATION

1. Disconnect the negative battery cable.
2. Remove the rubber cap cover (if equipped), from the distributor cap.
3. Remove the secondary wiring (spark plug wires) if a new cap is being installed.

**➡Record wire placement at each wire location in order to maintain the correct firing order.**

4. On the 3.8L engine, remove the two retaining screws in the cap to disengage it from the distributor housing.
5. On the 5.0L engine, unsnap the retaining clips holding the cap to the distributor housing.
6. Remove the cap, this exposes the ignition rotor.
7. Note the position of the rotor before removal.

**To install:**

8. To install the rotor, align it to the distributor shaft.
9. Seat the distributor cap onto the distributor housing, making sure to align the cap properly.
10. Install the cap screws carefully to hold the cap in place; or snap the retaining clips onto the distributor cap.
11. Install the negative battery cable.

### INSPECTION

**▶ See Figures 97 and 98**

A physical inspection of the distributor cap and rotor should be done at the same time as the plug wires are being checked. When inspecting the distributor cap, check for obvious signs of damage, such as a broken tower, crack in the body of the cap, or external carbon tracks . When checking on the inside of the cap, use a bright light to illuminate the inner surface. Check for charred or eroded terminals, inspect for carbon tracks that go from terminal to terminal or run to the bottom of the cap. Look for a worn or damaged rotor button (center electrode). Also, take a close look at the inside terminals for metal to metal contact. Damaged or cut terminals could mean a rotor or cap that was not properly installed; or it could mean that the distributor housing has worn beyond its limits and the shaft is wobbling when it rotates, or that the distributor shaft is bent.

## Ignition Timing

Ignition timing is the measurement, in degrees of crankshaft rotation, of the point at which the spark plugs fire in each of the cylinders. It is measured in degrees before or after Top Dead Center (TDC) of the compression stroke.

Ideally, the air/fuel mixture in the cylinder will be ignited by the spark plug just as the piston passes TDC of the compression stroke. If this happens, the piston will be beginning the power stroke just as the compressed and ignited air/fuel mixture starts to expand. The expansion of the air/fuel mixture then forces the piston down on the power stroke and turns the crankshaft.

Because it takes a fraction of a second for the spark plug to ignite the mixture in the cylinder, the spark plug must fire a little before the piston reaches TDC. Otherwise, the mixture will not be completely ignited as the piston passes TDC and the full power of the explosion will not be used by the engine.

The timing measurement is given in degrees of crankshaft rotation before the piston reaches TDC (BTDC, or Before Top Dead Center). If the setting for the ignition timing is 10 BTDC, each spark plug must fire 10 degrees before each piston reaches TDC. This only holds true, however, when the engine is at idle speed.

As the engine speed increases, the pistons go faster. The spark plugs have to ignite the fuel even sooner if it is to be completely ignited when the piston reaches TDC.

### INSPECTION &ADJUSTMENT

The "Vehicle Emission Control Information" label is attached in the engine compartment. Follow all instructions on the label. However, if the label is missing or defaced making it unreadable, use the following procedures:

**➡Make timing adjustment with engine at normal operating temperature and the air conditioning system, if so equipped, turned off.**

Set the parking brake and block the drive wheels. The vehicle should be in Neutral or Park.

Check the Service Engine soon light. It should not be lit.

Disconnect the spout at the in-line connector to disable the advance system.

With the ignition off, connect an inductive type timing light to the number one spark plug lead. Find the timing marks on the front of the engine just above and slightly to the side of the crankshaft pulley. Make sure this is clean and readable. If necessary, mark the timing mark at 10° BTDC with a dot of white paint or White Out®. There is a mark on the crankshaft pulley that should be dabbed with a spot of paint to ease in setting the timing.

Start the engine and aim the timing light at the timing mark. The line of the balancer or pulley will line up at the timing mark. If a change is necessary, loosen the distributor hold-down clamp bolt at the base of the distributor slightly. While observing the mark with the timing light, slightly rotate the distributor until the line indicates the correct timing. Tighten the hold-down bolt to 25 ft. lbs. (34 Nm)

Turn off the engine and remove the timing light.

On the 4.6L engine, the base ignition timing is set from the factory at 10 degrees BTDC and is not adjustable.

## Valve Lash

### ADJUSTMENT

Adjustment of the hydraulic lash adjusters or hydraulic lifters is neither possible nor necessary.

## Idle Speed and Mixture Adjustments

### ADJUSTMENT

#### 1988 Continental

1. Apply the parking brake, block the drive wheels and place the vehicle in **P** (AT) or **N** (MT).
2. Start the engine and let it run until it reaches normal operating temperature, then turn the engine **OFF**.
3. Connect an inductive tachometer, then start the engine and run it at 2,500 rpm for 30 seconds.
4. Allow the engine idle to stabilize, then place the automatic transaxle in **P** or the manual transaxle in neutral.
5. Adjust the engine idle rpm to the specification shown on the vehicle emission calibration label by turning the throttle stop screw.
6. After the idle speed is within specification, repeat Steps 3–6 to ensure that the adjustment is correct.
7. Turn the engine **OFF**, then disconnect the test equipment and unblock the wheels.

#### 1989–90 Continental

➧ See Figure 100

1. Apply the parking brake, block the drive wheels, and place the vehicle in **P**.
2. Start the engine and let it run until it reaches normal operating temperature, then turn the engine **OFF**.
3. Back the throttle plate stop screw clear off the throttle lever pad.
4. Place a 0.010 in. (0.25mm) feeler gauge between the throttle plate stop screw and the throttle lever pad. Turn the screw in until contact is made, then turn it and additional 1½ turns. Remove the feeler gauge.
5. Start the engine and let the idle stabilize for 2 minutes. Lightly depress and release the accelerator, then let the engine idle.

#### 1991–94 Continental

➧ See Figure 99

1. Hook-up the appropriate scan tool (Super star tester or equivalent). Initiate Key On Engine Off (KOEO) test. Repair any hard faults that are recorded.
2. Activate the engine running tests.
3. After the DTC (Diagnostic Trouble Code) slow codes output is completed, unlatch and within 4 seconds latch the STI (Self-Test-Input) button.
4. A single pulse code indicates the entry mode, then observe the Self-Test Output (STO) of the STAR Tester.
5. A constant tone, solid light or "STO LO" readout means the base idle rpm is within range. To exit the test, unlatch the STI button, then wait four seconds for reinitialization (after 10 minutes it will exit by itself).
6. A beeping tone, flashing light, or "STO LO" readout at (8Hz) indicates the TP sensor is out of range due to over adjustment; some adjustment may be required.
7. A beeping tone, flashing light, or "STO LO" readout at (4Hz) indicates the base idle rpm is too fast, adjustment is required.
8. A beeping tone, flashing light, or "STO LO" readout at (1Hz) indicates the base idle rpm is too slow, adjustment will be required.
9. If the rpm is out of specification, turn the air trim screw until conditions for "base idle is within range" are met.

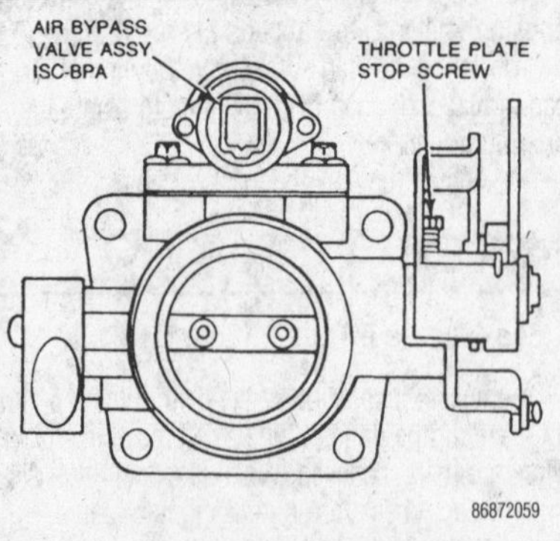


**Fig. 99 Throttle plate stop screw—3.8L engine**

**➡A sealant/coating covers the throttle bore and throttle plate which makes the throttle body airflow tolerant to engine intake sludge accumulation. These throttle body assemblies must not be cleaned and have a yellow/black attention decal advising not to clean.**

#### 4.6L Engines

The traditional idle air adjustment procedure is not used on 4.6L engine applications.

During idle, the throttle body assembly provides a set amount of air flow to the engine through the idle air trim screw passage or throttle plate idle air orifice and the PCV valve. The IAC valve assembly provides additional air when commanded by the Powertrain Control Module (PCM) to maintain the proper engine idle speed under varying conditions. The IAC valve assembly mounts directly to the throttle body assembly in most applications. Idle speed is controlled by the PCM and cannot be adjusted.

#### 5.0L Engines

1. Apply the parking brake, block the drive wheels, and place the vehicle in **P**.
2. Start the engine and let it run until it reaches normal operating temperature, then turn the engine **OFF**.
3. Back the throttle plate stop screw clear off the throttle lever pad.
4. Place a 0.010 in. (0.25mm) feeler gauge between the throttle plate stop screw and the throttle lever pad. Turn the screw in until contact is made, then turn it and additional 1½ turns for the 5.0L Hi Output engine, and 1⅞ for the base engine. Remove the feeler gauge.
5. Shut the engine off and disconnect battery for 5 minutes.
6. Start the engine and let the idle stabilize for 2 minutes. Lightly depress and release the accelerator, then let the engine idle.

## GASOLINE ENGINE TUNE-UP SPECIFICATIONS

| Year | Engine ID/VIN | Engine Displacement Liters (cc) | Spark Plugs Gap (in.) | Ignition Timing (deg.) MT | Ignition Timing (deg.) AT | Fuel Pump (psi) | Idle Speed (rpm) MT | Idle Speed (rpm) AT | Valve Clearance In. | Valve Clearance Ex. |
|---|---|---|---|---|---|---|---|---|---|---|
| 1988 | E | 5.0 HO (4993) | 0.044 in. | - | 10B | 35-40 ① | - | 700 | HYD | HYD |
| | 4 | 3.8 (3802) | 0.044 in. | - | 10B | 35-40 ① | - | 550 | HYD | HYD |
| | F | 5.0 (4993) | 0.044 in. | - | 10B | 35-40 ① | - | ③ | HYD | HYD |
| 1989 | E | 5.0 HO (4993) | 0.044 in. | - | 10B | 35-40 ① | - | 700 | HYD | HYD |
| | 4 | 3.8 (3802) | 0.044 in. | - | 10B | 35-40 ① | - | 550 | HYD | HYD |
| | F | 5.0 (4993) | 0.044 in. | - | 10B | 35-40 ① | - | ③ | HYD | HYD |
| 1990 | E | 5.0 HO (4993) | 0.054 in. | - | 10B | 35-40 ① | - | 700 | HYD | HYD |
| | 4 | 3.8 (3802) | 0.054 in. | - | 10B | 35-40 ① | - | 550 | HYD | HYD |
| | F | 5.0 (4993) | 0.054 in. | - | 10B | 35-40 ① | - | ③ | HYD | HYD |
| 1991 | E | 5.0 HO (4993) | 0.054 in. | - | 10B | 35-40 ① | - | 700 | HYD | HYD |
| | 4 | 3.8 (3802) | 0.054 in. | - | 10B | 35-40 ① | - | 550 | HYD | HYD |
| | W | 4.6 (4593) | 0.054 in. | - | 10B | 35-40 ① | - | ③ | HYD | HYD |
| 1992 | E | 5.0 HO (4993) | 0.054 in. | - | 10B | 35-40 ① | - | 700 | HYD | HYD |
| | 4 | 3.8 (3802) | 0.054 in. | - | 10B | 35-40 ① | - | 550 | HYD | HYD |
| | W | 4.6 (4593) | 0.054 in. | - | 10B | 35-40 ① | - | ③ | HYD | HYD |
| 1993 | V | 4.6 (4593) | 0.054 in. | - | 10B | 35-40 ① | - | ③ | HYD | HYD |
| | 4 | 3.8 (3802) | 0.054 in. | - | 10B | 35-40 ① | - | 550 | HYD | HYD |
| | W | 4.6 (4593) | 0.054 in. | - | 10B | 35-40 ① | - | ③ | HYD | HYD |
| 1994 | V | 4.6 (4593) | 0.054 in. | - | 10B | 30-45 ① | - | ③ | HYD | HYD |
| | 4 | 3.8 (3802) | 0.054 in. | - | 10B | 30-45 ① | - | 550 | HYD | HYD |
| | W | 4.6 (4593) | 0.054 in. | - | 10B | 30-45 ① | - | ③ | HYD | HYD |
| 1995 | V | 4.6 (4593) | 0.054 in. | - | 10B | 30-45 ① | - | ③ | HYD | HYD |
| | W | 4.6 (4593) | 0.054 in. | - | 10B | 30-45 ① | - | ③ | HYD | HYD |
| 1996 | V | 4.6 (4593) | 0.054 in. | - | 10B | 30-45 ① | - | ③ | HYD | HYD |
| | W | 4.6 (4593) | 0.054 in. | - | 10B | 30-45 ① | - | ③ | HYD | HYD |
| 1997 | W | 4.6 (4593) | 0.054 in. | - | 10B | 30-45 ① | - | ③ | HYD | HYD |
| | 9 | 4.6 (4593) | 0.054 in. | - | 10B | 30-45 ① | - | ③ | HYD | HYD |
| 1998 | W | 4.6 (4593) | 0.054 in. | - | 10B | 30-45 ① | - | ③ | HYD | HYD |
| | 9 | 4.6 (4593) | 0.054 in. | - | 10B | 30-45 ① | - | ③ | HYD | HYD |
| 1999 | W | 4.6 (4593) | 0.054 in. | - | 10B | 30-45 ① | - | ③ | HYD | HYD |
| | 9 | 4.6 (4593) | 0.054 in. | - | 10B | 30-45 ① | - | ③ | HYD | HYD |
| 2000 | W | 4.6 (4593) | 0.054 in. | - | 10B | 30-45 ① | - | ③ | HYD | HYD |
| | 9 | 4.6 (4593) | 0.054 in. | - | 10B | 30-45 ① | - | ③ | HYD | HYD |

NOTE: The Vehicle Emission Control Information label often reflects specification changes made during production. The label figures must be used if they differ from those in this chart.

HYD - Hydraulic

① Fuel pressure with engine running, pressure regulator vacuum hose connected

② Before Top Dead Center

③ Refer to Vehicle Emission Control Information label

93141C03

## Air Conditioning System

### SYSTEM SERVICE & REPAIR

**➡It is recommended that the A/C system be serviced by an EPA Section 609 certified automotive technician utilizing a refrigerant recovery/recycling machine.**

The do-it-yourselfer should not service his/her own vehicle's A/C system for many reasons, including legal concerns, personal injury, environmental damage and cost.

According to the U.S. Clean Air Act, it is a federal crime to service or repair (involving the refrigerant) a Motor Vehicle Air Conditioning (MVAC) system for money without being EPA certified. It is also illegal to vent R-12 and R-134a refrigerants into the atmosphere. State and/or local laws may be more strict than the federal regulations, so be sure to check with your state and/or local authorities for further information.

**➡Federal law dictates that a fine of up to $25,000 may be levied on people convicted of venting refrigerant into the atmosphere.**

When servicing an A/C system you run the risk of handling or coming in contact with refrigerant, which may result in skin or eye irritation or frostbite. Although low in toxicity (due to chemical stability), inhalation of concentrated refrigerant fumes is dangerous and can result in death; cases of fatal cardiac arrhythmia have been reported in people accidentally subjected to high levels of refrigerant. Some early symptoms include loss of concentration and drowsiness.

**➡Generally, the limit for exposure is lower for R-134a than it is for R-12. Exceptional care must be practiced when handling R-134a.**

Also, some refrigerants can decompose at high temperatures (near gas heaters or open flame), which may result in hydrofluoric acid, hydrochloric acid and phosgene (a fatal nerve gas).

It is usually more economically feasible to have a certified MVAC automotive technician perform A/C system service on your vehicle.

### R-12 Refrigerant Conversion

If your vehicle still uses R-12 refrigerant, one way to save A/C system costs down the road is to investigate the possibility of having your system converted to R-134a. The older R-12 systems can be easily converted to R-134a refrigerant by a certified automotive technician by installing a few new components and changing the system oil.

The cost of R-12 is steadily rising and will continue to increase, because it is no longer imported or manufactured in the United States. Therefore, it is often possible to have an R-12 system converted to R-134a and recharged for less than it would cost to just charge the system with R-12.

If you are interested in having your system converted, contact local automotive service stations for more details and information.

### PREVENTIVE MAINTENANCE

Although the A/C system should not be serviced by the do-it-yourselfer, preventive maintenance should be practiced to help maintain the efficiency of the vehicle's A/C system. Be sure to perform the following:

- The easiest and most important preventive maintenance for your A/C system is to be sure that it is used on a regular basis. Running the system for five minutes each month (no matter what the season) will help ensure that the seals and all internal components remain lubricated.

**➡Some vehicles automatically operate the A/C system compressor whenever the windshield defroster is activated. Therefore, the A/C system would not need to be operated each month if the defroster was used.**

- In order to prevent heater core freeze-up during A/C operation, it is necessary to maintain proper antifreeze protection. Be sure to properly maintain the engine cooling system.
- Any obstruction of or damage to the condenser configuration will restrict air flow which is essential to its efficient operation. Keep this unit clean and in proper physical shape.

**➡Bug screens which are mounted in front of the condenser (unless they are original equipment) are regarded as obstructions.**

- The condensation drain tube expels any water which accumulates on the bottom of the evaporator housing into the engine compartment. If this tube is obstructed, the air conditioning performance can be restricted and condensation buildup can spill over onto the vehicle's floor.

### SYSTEM INSPECTION

Although the A/C system should not be serviced by the do-it-yourselfer, system inspections should be performed to help maintain the efficiency of the vehicle's A/C system. Be sure to perform the following:

The easiest and often most important check for the air conditioning system consists of a visual inspection of the system components. Visually inspect the system for refrigerant leaks, damaged compressor clutch, abnormal compressor drive belt tension and/or condition, plugged evaporator drain tube, blocked condenser fins, disconnected or broken wires, blown fuses, corroded connections and poor insulation.

A refrigerant leak will usually appear as an oily residue at the leakage point in the system. The oily residue soon picks up dust or dirt particles from the surrounding air and appears greasy. Through time, this will build up and appear to be a heavy dirt impregnated grease.

For a thorough visual and operational inspection, check the following:

- Check the surface of the radiator and condenser for dirt, leaves or other material which might block air flow.
- Check for kinks in hoses and lines. Check the system for leaks.
- Make sure the drive belt is properly tensioned. During operation, make sure the belt is free of noise or slippage.
- Make sure the blower motor operates at all appropriate positions, then check for distribution of the air from all outlets.

**➡Remember that in high humidity, air discharged from the vents may not feel as cold as expected, even if the system is working properly. This is because moisture in humid air retains heat more effectively than dry air, thereby making humid air more difficult to cool.**

## Windshield Wipers

### ELEMENT (REFILL) CARE & REPLACEMENT

**➧ See Figures 100, 101 and 102**

For maximum effectiveness and longest element life, the windshield and wiper blades should be kept clean. Dirt, tree sap, road tar and so on will cause streaking, smearing and blade deterioration if left on the glass. It is advisable to wash the windshield carefully with a commercial glass cleaner at least once a month. Wipe off the rubber blades with the wet rag afterwards. Do not attempt to move wipers across the windshield by hand; damage to the motor and drive mechanism will result.

To inspect and/or replace the wiper blade elements, place the wiper switch in the **LOW** speed position and the ignition switch in the **ACC** position. When the wiper blades are approximately vertical on the windshield, turn the ignition switch to **OFF**.

Examine the wiper blade elements. If they are found to be cracked, broken or torn, they should be replaced immediately. Replacement intervals will vary with usage, although ozone deterioration usually limits element life to about one year. If the wiper pattern is smeared or streaked, or if the blade chatters across the glass, the elements should be replaced. It is easiest and most sensible to replace the elements in pairs.

If your vehicle is equipped with aftermarket blades, there are several different types of refills and your vehicle might have any kind. Aftermarket blades and arms rarely use the exact same type blade or refill as the original equipment.

Regardless of the type of refill used, be sure to follow the part manufacturer's instructions closely. Make sure that all of the frame jaws are engaged as the refill is pushed into place and locked. If the metal blade holder and frame are allowed to touch the glass during wiper operation, the glass will be scratched.

## Tires and Wheels

Common sense and good driving habits will afford maximum tire life. Fast starts, sudden stops and hard cornering are hard on tires and will

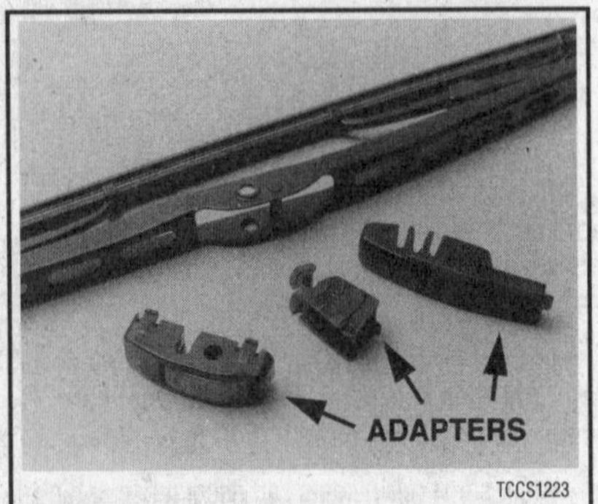


TCCS1223

**Fig. 100 Most aftermarket blades are available with multiple adapters to fit different vehicles**

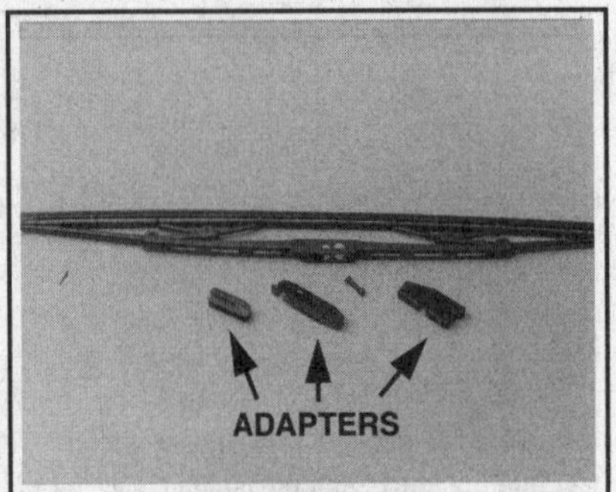


TCCS1224

**Fig. 101 Choose a blade which will fit your vehicle, and that will be readily available next time you need blades**

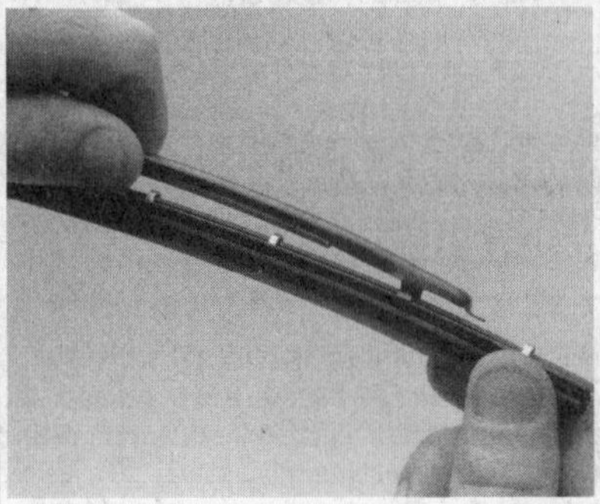

TCCS1231

**Fig. 102 When installed, be certain the blade is fully inserted into the backing**

shorten their useful life span. Make sure that you don't overload the vehicle or run with incorrect pressure in the tires. Both of these practices will increase tread wear.

**➡ For optimum tire life, keep the tires properly inflated, rotate them often and have the wheel alignment checked periodically.**

Inspect your tires frequently. Be especially careful to watch for bubbles in the tread or sidewall, deep cuts or underinflation. Replace any tires with bubbles in the sidewall. If cuts are so deep that they penetrate to the cords, discard the tire. Any cut in the sidewall of a radial tire renders it unsafe. Also, look for uneven tread wear patterns that may indicate the front end is out of alignment or that the tires are out of balance.

Most tires today have a service description branded on the side wall after the tire size. This service description consists of two parts: the load index and the speed symbol. The load index is a number usually between 75 and 115, which defines the tire's load capacity at maximum inflation. Higher numbers mean greater load capacity. The speed symbol is a letter usually between P and Z, which defines the speed capability of the tire. In the past, this letter might have been part of the tire size.

## TIRE ROTATION

**See Figures 103 and 104**

Tires must be rotated periodically to equalize wear patterns that vary with a tire's position on the vehicle. Tires will also wear in an uneven way as the front steering/suspension system wears to the point where the alignment should be reset.

Rotating the tires will ensure maximum life for the tires as a set, so you will not have to discard a tire early due to wear on only part of the tread. Regular rotation is required to equalize wear.

When rotating "unidirectional tires," make sure that they always roll in the same direction. This means that a tire used on the left side of the vehicle must not be switched to the right side and vice-versa. Such tires should only be rotated front-to-rear or rear-to-front, while always remaining on the same side of the vehicle. These tires are marked on the sidewall as to the direction of rotation; observe the marks when reinstalling the tire(s).

## TIRE DESIGN

**See Figure 105**

For maximum satisfaction, tires should be used in sets of four. Mixing of different types (radial, bias-belted, fiberglass belted) must be avoided. In most cases, the vehicle manufacturer has designated a type of tire on which the vehicle will perform best. Your first choice when replacing tires should be to use the same type of tire that the manufacturer recommends.

When radial tires are used, tire sizes and wheel diameters should be selected to maintain ground clearance and tire load capacity equivalent to the original specified tire. Radial tires should always be used in sets of four.

**➡Changing the tire size or wheel diameter from the original factory installed component could cause speedometer error and driveability concerns.**

**CAUTION**

**Radial tires should never be used on only the front axle.**

When selecting tires, pay attention to the original size as marked on the tire. Most tires are described using an industry size code sometimes referred to as P-Metric. This allows the exact identification of the tire specifications, regardless of the manufacturer. If selecting a different tire size or brand, remember to check the installed tire for any sign of interference with the body or suspension while the vehicle is stopping, turning sharply or heavily loaded.

### Snow Tires

Good radial tires can produce a big advantage in slippery weather, but in snow, a street radial tire does not have sufficient tread to provide traction and control. The small grooves of a street tire quickly pack with snow and the tire behaves like a billiard ball on a marble floor. The more open, chunky tread of a snow tire will self-clean as the tire turns, providing much better grip on snowy surfaces.

To satisfy municipalities requiring snow tires during weather emergencies, most snow tires carry either an M + S designation after the tire size stamped on the sidewall, or the designation "all-season." In general, no change in tire size is necessary when buying snow tires.

Most manufacturers strongly recommend the use of four snow tires on their vehicles for reasons of stability. If snow tires are fitted only to the drive wheels, the opposite end of the vehicle may become very unstable when braking or turning on slippery surfaces. This instability can lead to unpleasant endings if the driver can't counteract the slide in time.

Note that snow tires, whether 2 or 4, will affect vehicle handling in all non-snow situations. The stiffer, heavier snow tires will noticeably change the turning and braking characteristics of the vehicle. Once the snow tires are installed, you must relearn the behavior of the vehicle and drive accordingly.

**➡ Consider buying extra wheels on which to mount the snow tires. Once done, the "snow wheels" can be installed and removed as needed. This eliminates the potential damage to tires or wheels from seasonal removal and installation. Even if your vehicle has styled wheels, see if inexpensive steel wheels are available. Although the look of the vehicle will change, the expensive wheels will be protected from salt, curb hits and pothole damage.**

## TIRE STORAGE

If they are mounted on wheels, store the tires at proper inflation pressure. All tires should be kept in a cool, dry place. If they are stored in the garage or basement, do not let them stand on a concrete floor; set them on strips of wood, a mat or a large stack of newspaper. Keeping them away from direct moisture is of paramount importance. Tires should not be stored upright, but in a flat position.

## INFLATION & INSPECTION

**See Figures 106 thru 113**

The importance of proper tire inflation cannot be overemphasized. A tire employs air as part of its structure. It is designed around the supporting strength of the air at a specified pressure. For this reason, improper inflation drastically reduces the

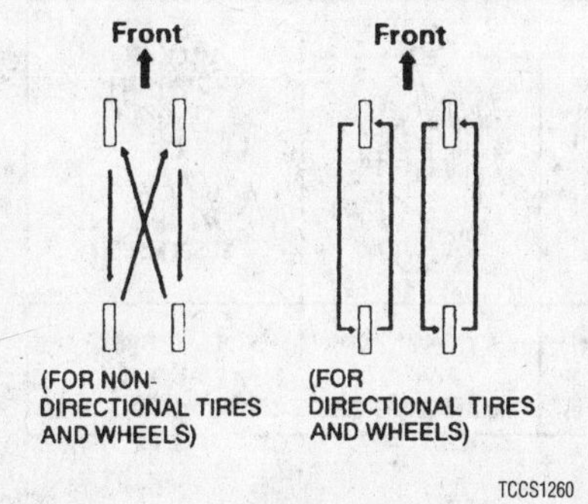


**Fig. 103 Compact spare tires must NEVER be used in the rotation pattern**

**Fig. 104 Unidirectional tires are identifiable by sidewall arrows and/or the word "rotation"**

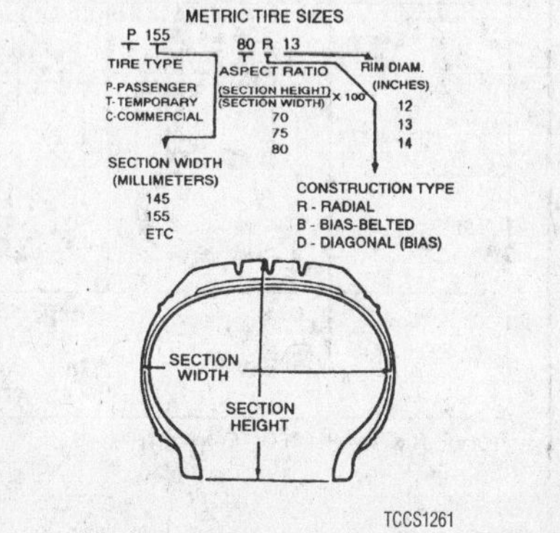


**Fig. 105 P-Metric tire coding**

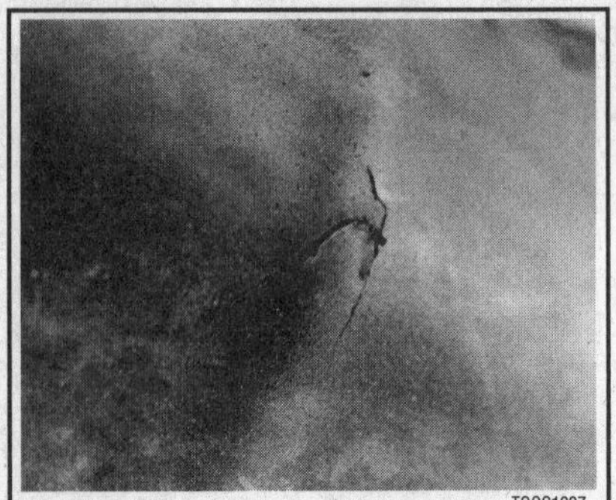

TCCS1097

**Fig. 106 Tires should be checked frequently for any sign of puncture or damage**

TCCS1095

**Fig. 107 Tires with deep cuts, or cuts which bulge, should be replaced immediately**

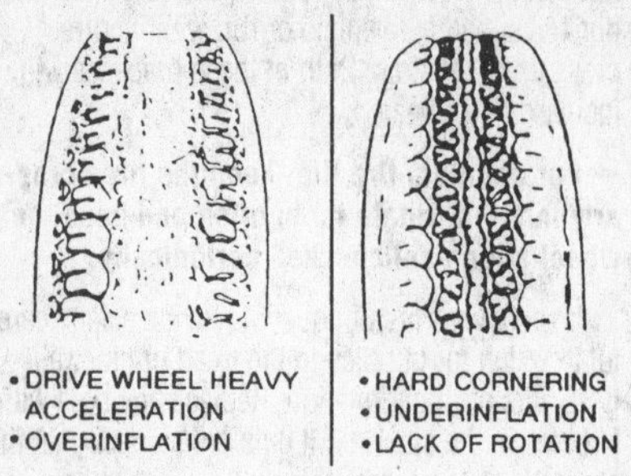


TCCS1262

**Fig. 108 Examples of inflation-related tire wear patterns**

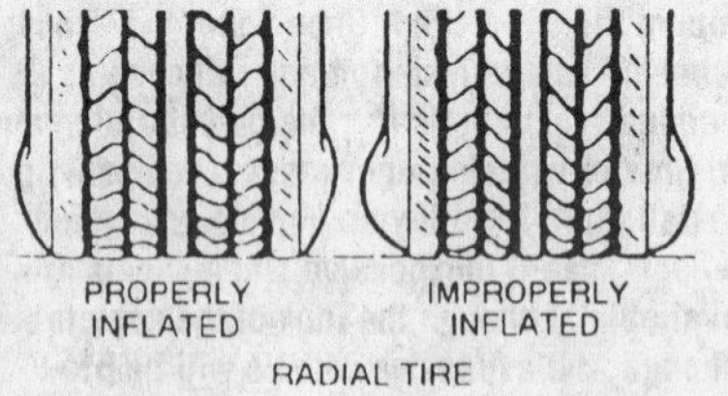


TCCS1263

**Fig. 109 Radial tires have a characteristic sidewall bulge; don't try to measure pressure by looking at the tire. Use a quality air pressure gauge**

tire's ability to perform as intended. A tire will lose some air in day-to-day use; having to add a few pounds of air periodically is not necessarily a sign of a leaking tire.

Two items should be a permanent fixture in every glove compartment: an accurate tire pressure gauge and a tread depth gauge. Check the tire pressure (including the spare) regularly with a pocket type gauge. Too often, the gauge on the end of the air hose at your corner garage is not accurate because it suffers too much abuse. Always check tire pressure when the tires are cold, as pressure increases with temperature. If you must move the vehicle to check the tire inflation, do not drive more than a mile before checking. A cold tire is generally one that has not been driven for more than three hours.

A plate or sticker is normally provided somewhere in the vehicle (door post, hood, trunk or trunk lid)

This shows the proper pressure for the tires. Never counteract excessive pressure build-up by bleeding off air pressure (letting some air out). This will cause the tire to run hotter and wear quicker.

**CAUTION**

**Never exceed the maximum tire pressure embossed on the tire! This is the pressure to be used when the tire is at maximum loading, but it is rarely the correct pressure for everyday driving. Consult the owner's manual or the tire pressure sticker for the correct tire pressure.**

Once you've maintained the correct tire pressures for several weeks, you'll be familiar with the vehicle's braking and handling personality. Slight adjustments in tire pressures can fine-tune these characteristics, but never change the cold pressure specification by more than 2 psi. A slightly softer tire pressure will give a softer ride but also yield lower fuel mileage. A slightly harder tire will give crisper dry road handling but can cause skidding on wet surfaces. Unless you're fully attuned to the vehicle, stick to the recommended inflation pressures.

All tires made since 1968 have built-in tread wear indicator bars that show up as ½ in. (13mm) wide smooth bands across the tire when 1⁄16 in. (1.5mm) of tread remains. The appearance of tread wear indicators means that the tires should be replaced. In fact, many states have laws prohibiting the use of tires with less than this amount of tread.

When replacing tires, only the size, load range

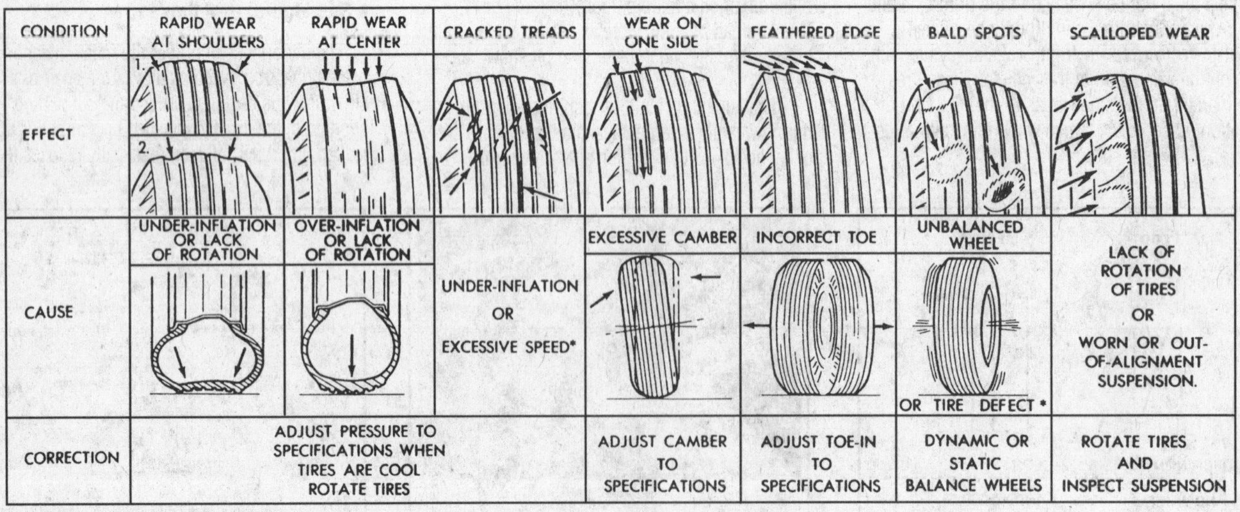

| CONDITION | RAPID WEAR AT SHOULDERS | RAPID WEAR AT CENTER | CRACKED TREADS | WEAR ON ONE SIDE | FEATHERED EDGE | BALD SPOTS | SCALLOPED WEAR |
|---|---|---|---|---|---|---|---|
| EFFECT | 1. / 2. | | | | | | |
| CAUSE | UNDER-INFLATION OR LACK OF ROTATION | OVER-INFLATION OR LACK OF ROTATION | UNDER-INFLATION OR EXCESSIVE SPEED* | EXCESSIVE CAMBER | INCORRECT TOE | UNBALANCED WHEEL OR TIRE DEFECT* | LACK OF ROTATION OF TIRES OR WORN OR OUT-OF-ALIGNMENT SUSPENSION. |
| CORRECTION | ADJUST PRESSURE TO SPECIFICATIONS WHEN TIRES ARE COOL ROTATE TIRES | | | ADJUST CAMBER TO SPECIFICATIONS | ADJUST TOE-IN TO SPECIFICATIONS | DYNAMIC OR STATIC BALANCE WHEELS | ROTATE TIRES AND INSPECT SUSPENSION |

*HAVE TIRE INSPECTED FOR FURTHER USE.

TCCS1267

**Fig. 110 Common tire wear patterns and causes**

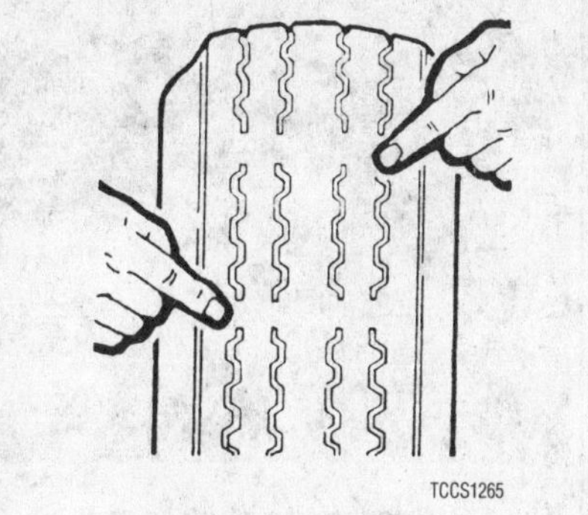


**Fig. 111 Tread wear indicators will appear when the tire is worn**

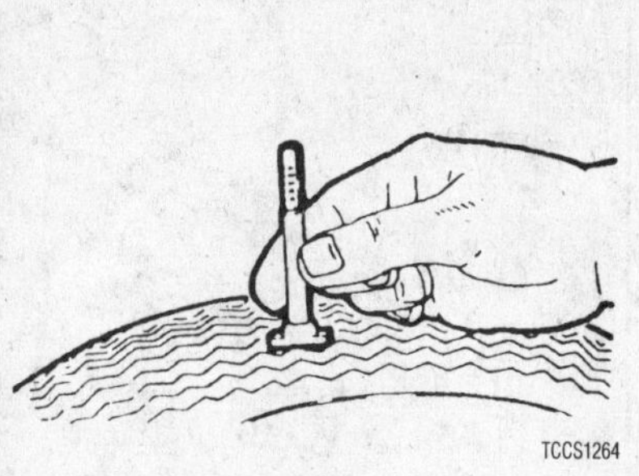


**Fig. 112 Accurate tread depth indicators are inexpensive and handy**

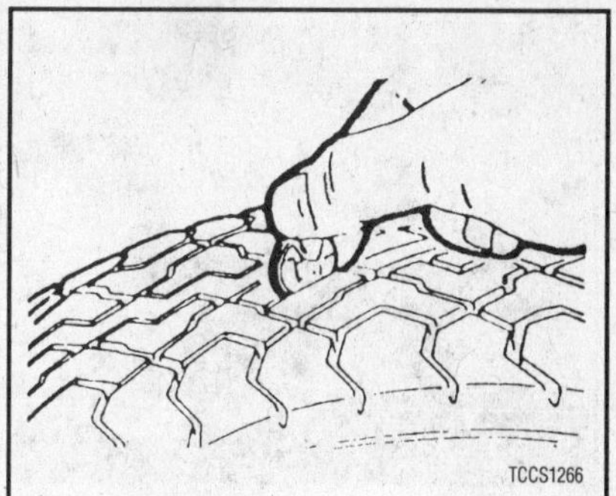


**Fig. 113 A penny works well for a quick check of tread depth**

and construction as were originally installed on the vehicle are recommended.

You can check your own tread depth with an inexpensive gauge or by using a Lincoln head penny. Slip the Lincoln penny (with Lincoln's head upside-down) into several treads grooves. If you can see the top of Lincoln's head in 2 adjacent grooves, the tire has less than 1/16 in. (1.5mm) tread left and should be replaced. You can measure snow tires in the same manner by using the "tails" side of the Lincoln penny. If you can see the top of the Lincoln memorial, it's time to replace the snow tire(s).

# FLUIDS AND LUBRICANTS

## Fluid Disposal

Used fluids such as engine oil, transmission fluid, antifreeze and brake fluid are hazardous wastes and must be disposed of properly. Before draining any fluids, consult with your local authorities; in many areas, waste oil, antifreeze, etc. is being accepted as a part of recycling programs. A number of service stations and auto parts stores are also accepting waste fluids for recycling.

Be sure of the recycling center's policies before draining any fluids, as many will not accept different fluids that have been mixed together.

## Fuel and Engine Oil Recommendations

### FUEL

The engine is designed to operate on unleaded gasoline ONLY and is essential for the proper operation of the emission control system. The use of unleaded fuel will reduce spark plug fouling, exhaust system corrosion and engine oil deterioration.

In most parts of the United States, fuel with an octane rating of 87 should be used unless otherwise specified by the vehicle manufacturer for performance reasons. Using fuels with a lower octane may decrease engine performance, increase emissions and engine wear.

In some areas, fuel consisting of a blend of alcohol may be used; this blend of gasoline and alcohol is known as gasohol. When using gasohol, never use blends exceeding 10% ethanol or 5% methanol.

➡**The use of fuel with excessive amounts of alcohol may jeopardize the new car warranties.**

### OIL

**▶ See Figure 114**

Use only oil that has the API (American Petroleum Institute) designation "SJ," "SJ/CC" or "SJ/CD."

Since the viscosity (thickness) of the engine oil affects fuel economy, it is recommended to select oil with reference to the outside temperature. For satisfactory lubrication, use lower viscosity oil for colder temperatures and higher viscosity oil for warmer temperatures.

For maximum fuel economy, look for an oil that carries the words "Energy Conserving II" in the API symbol. This means that the oil contains friction-reducing additives that help reduce the amount of fuel burned to overcome engine friction.

The Society of Automotive Engineers (SAE) viscosity rating indicates an oil's ability to flow at a given temperature. The number designation indicates the thickness or "weight" of the oil. SAE 5-weight oil is thin light oil; it allows the engine to crank over easily even when it is very cold, and quickly provides lubrication for all parts of the engine. However, as the engine temperature increases, the 5-weight oil becomes too thin, resulting in metal-to-metal contact and damage to internal engine parts. Heavier SAE 50-weight oil can lubricate and protect internal engine parts even under extremely high operating temperatures. However, it would not be able to flow quickly enough to provide internal engine protection during cold weather start-up, one of the most critical periods for lubrication protection in an engine.

The answer to the temperature extremes problem is the multi-grade or multi-viscosity oil. Multi-viscosity oils carry multiple number designations, such as SAE 5W-30 oil that has the flow characteristics of the thin 5 weight oil in cold weather, providing rapid lubrication and allowing easy engine cranking. When the engine warms up, the oil acts like a straight 30 weight oil providing internal engine protection under higher temperatures.

**Fig. 114 Look for the API oil identification label when choosing your engine oil**

## Engine

### OIL LEVEL CHECK

**▶ See Figures 115 thru 122**

Every time you stop for fuel, check the engine oil as follows:

1. Make sure the vehicle is parked on level ground.
2. When checking the oil level it is best for the engine to be at normal operating temperature, although checking the oil immediately after stopping will lead to a false reading. Wait a few minutes after turning off the engine to allow the oil to drain back into the crankcase.
3. Open the hood and locate the dipstick that will be on either the right or left side depending

91191P15

**Fig. 115 Grasp the engine oil dipstick and . . .**

91191P16

**Fig. 116 . . . pull the dipstick out of the tube**

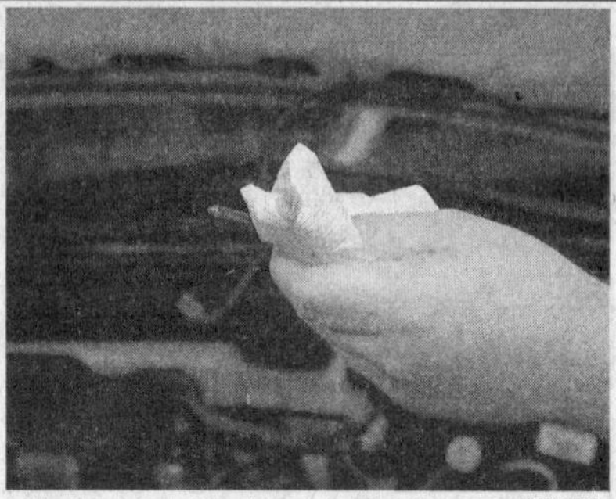

91191P17

**Fig. 117 Wipe the dipstick clean and replace it into the tube to inspect the oil level**

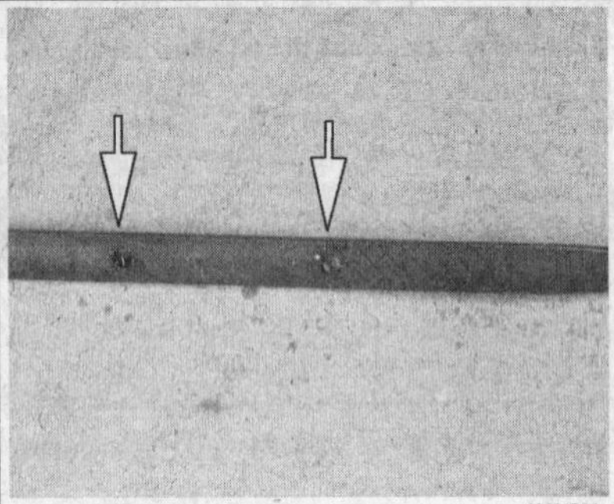

89601P54

**Fig. 118 Ensure that the oil level is between the MIN and MAX lines**

89601P10

**Fig. 119 To remove the oil fill cap, grasp the cap and turn it counter-clockwise until . . .**

91191P11

**Fig. 120 . . . the cap unscrews from the valve cover. Be sure to place the oil cap in a safe place so as not to lose it**

89601P07

**Fig. 121 Place a funnel directly into the oil fill port and . . .**

89601P08

**Fig. 122 . . . pour oil into the engine**

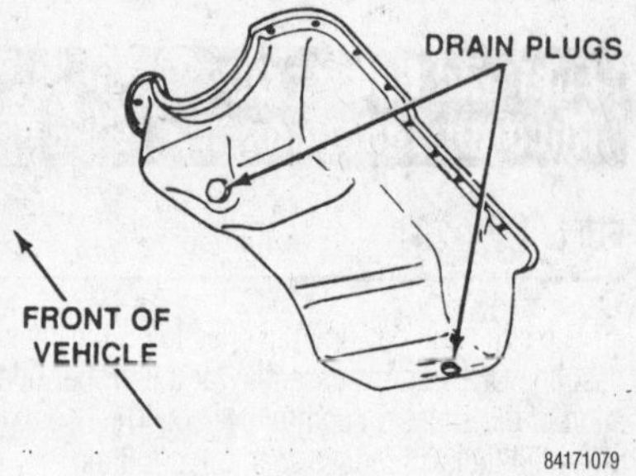


84171079

**Fig. 123 The oil pans on the 5.0L engine have two drain plugs**

upon your particular engine. Pull the dipstick from its tube, wipe it clean and then reinsert it.

4. Pull the dipstick out again and, holding it horizontally, read the oil level. The oil should be between the "FULL" and "ADD" marks on the dipstick. If the oil is below the "ADD" mark, add oil of the proper viscosity through the capped opening in the top of the cylinder head cover.

5. Replace the dipstick and check the oil level again after adding any oil. Be careful not to overfill the crankcase. Approximately 1 quart of oil will raise the level from the "ADD" mark to the "FULL" mark. Excess oil will generally be consumed at an accelerated rate.

## CHANGING OIL & FILTER

**See Figures 123 thru 144**

The oil is to be changed every 7,500 miles (12,500 km) or 12 months, which ever occurs first. Under normal conditions, change the filter at first oil change and then at every oil change. We recommend that the oil filter be changed every time the oil is changed. As much as a quart of dirty oil remains in the old filter. For a few dollars, it is a small expense for extended engine life.

If driving under such conditions, such as: dusty areas, trailer towing, idling for long periods of time, low speed operation, or when operating with temperatures below freezing or driving short distances (under 4 miles), change the oil and filter every 3,000 miles (5,000 km) or 3 months.

1. Run the engine until it reaches normal operating temperature.

2. Usually a run to the parts store to pick up the oil and filter will get the engine hot enough.

3. Apply the parking brake and block the rear wheels.

4. Disable the Computer controlled air suspension (where applicable).

5. Raise the vehicle and support it on jack

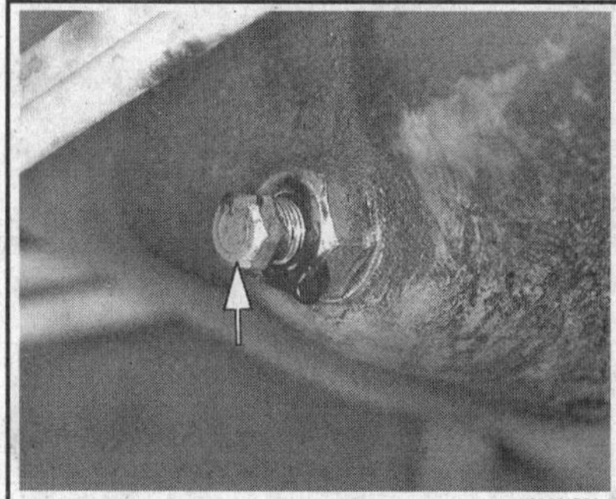

93141P01

Fig. 124 If the drain plug is stripped beyond repair, this drain bolt and sealing nut may help

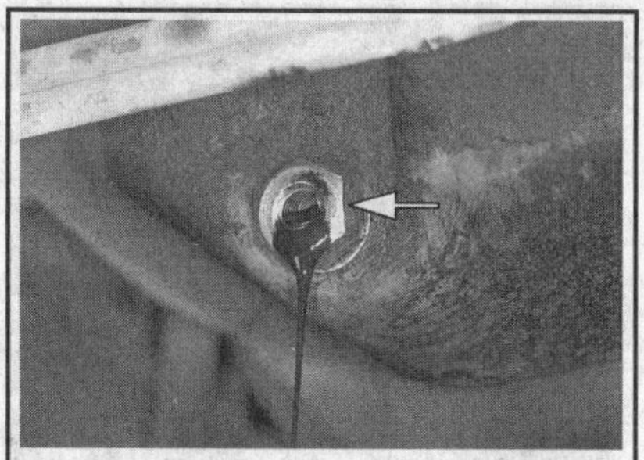

93141P02

Fig. 125 Install the sealing nut tight and leave it. Then just remove the drain bolt to change the oil. Do not overtighten the bolt

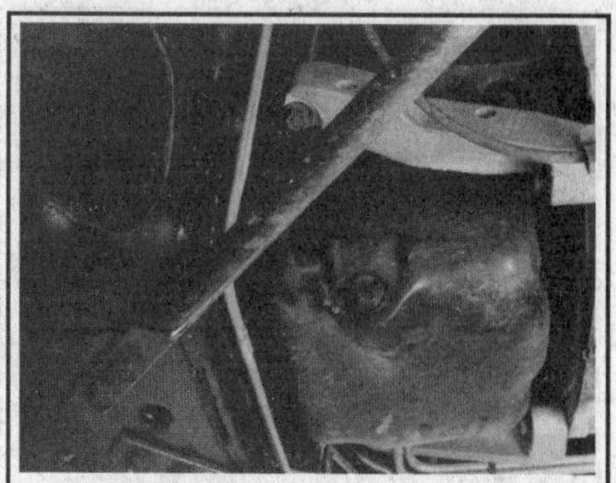

84171080

Fig. 126 Oil pan drain plug location on the 4.6L engine

84171083

Fig. 127 Oil filter location shown for a 4.6L engine

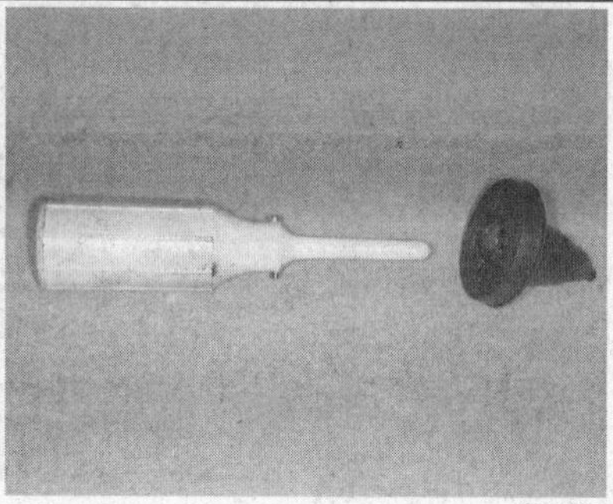

93141P05

Fig. 128 If an oversized pan bolt has stripped, this tool may be your last chance

93141P06

Fig. 129 Push the rubber stopper onto the tool and lock it onto the tabs by giving it a half-twist

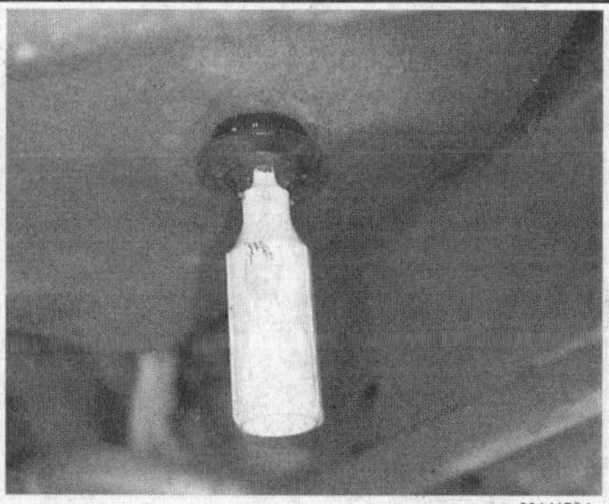

93141P04

Fig. 130 Push the stopper and tool into the oil pan drain hole until it is up tight against the pan

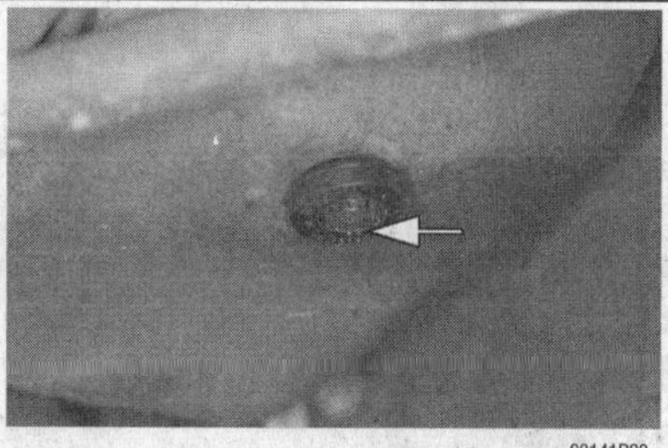

93141P03

Fig. 131 Give the tool a half-twist and remove it. The rubber stopper is now secured in the drain hole of the oil pan. Put the remover/installer tool in a safe place. You will need it for the next oil change

93141P30

Fig. 132 Oil drain plug location—3.8L engine Continental

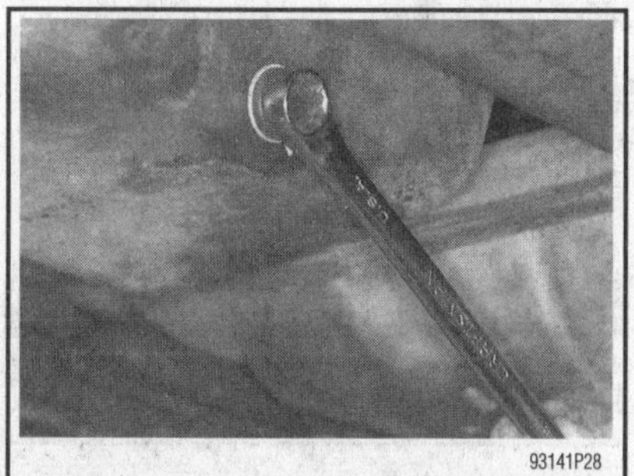

93141P28

Fig. 133 Use a box end wrench on the drain plug to prevent rounding of the bolt. Typically the drain plug requires a 16mm wrench

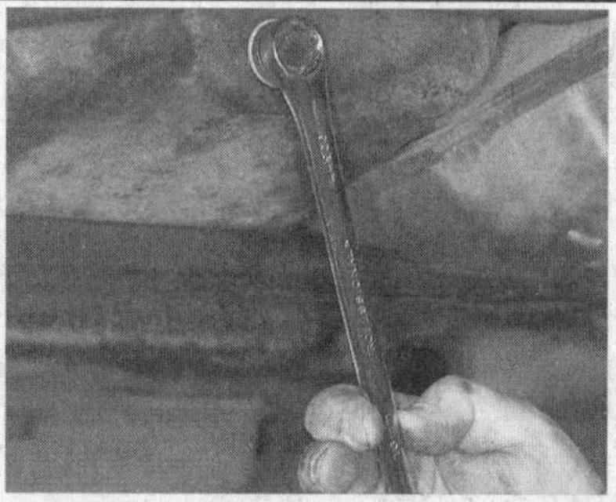

93141P27

Fig. 134 Loosen the drain plug using a wrench until . . .

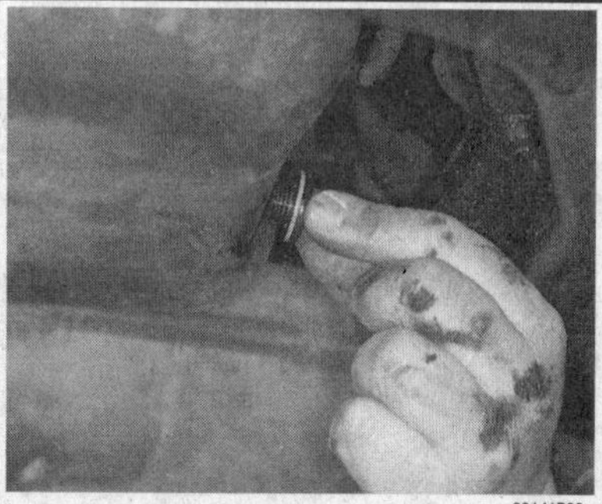

93141P26

Fig. 135 . . . you can remove it by hand

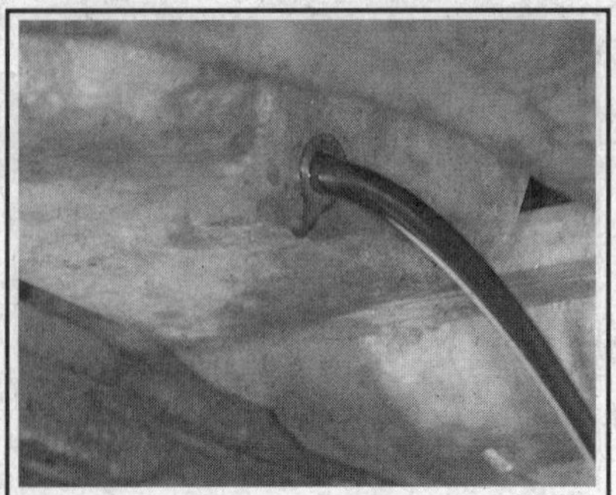
93141P25

**Fig. 136 Let the oil drain into a catch pan**

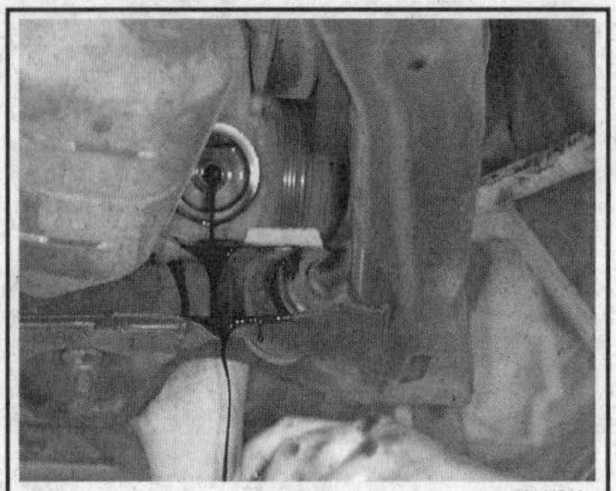
93141P32

**Fig. 137 When you remove the oil filter on the 3.8L Continental, the residual oil drains into the subframe**

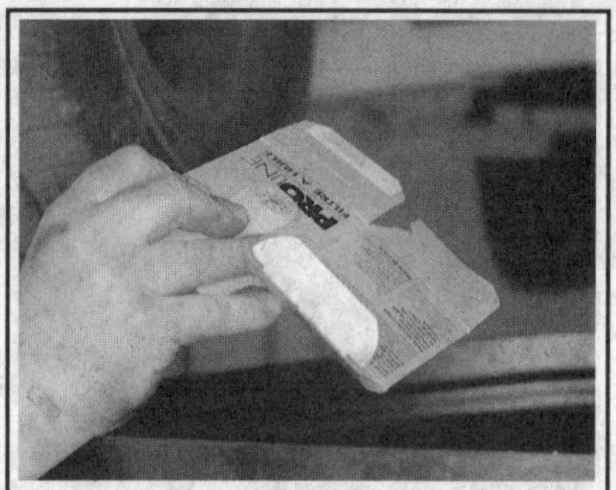
93141P24

**Fig. 138 Using the box, the new oil filter came in . . .**

93141P29

**Fig. 139 . . . slide it under the filter before you take it off**

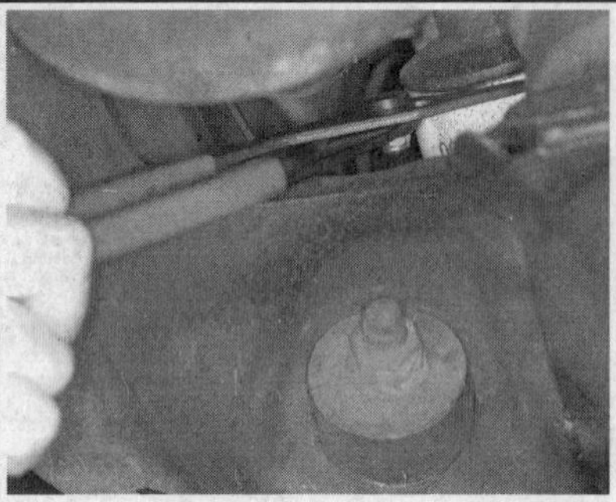
93141P33

**Fig. 140 A pliers type oil filter wrench fits in front of the subframe and . . .**

93141P34

**Fig. 141 . . . allows a good grip on the filter**

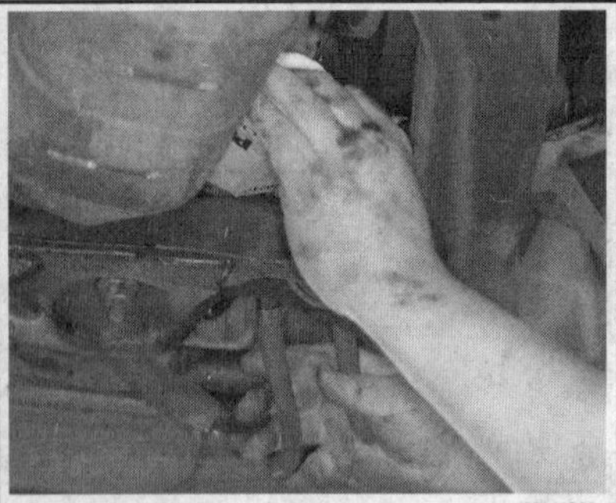
93141P23

**Fig. 142 Removing the oil filter allows the residual oil to drain . . .**

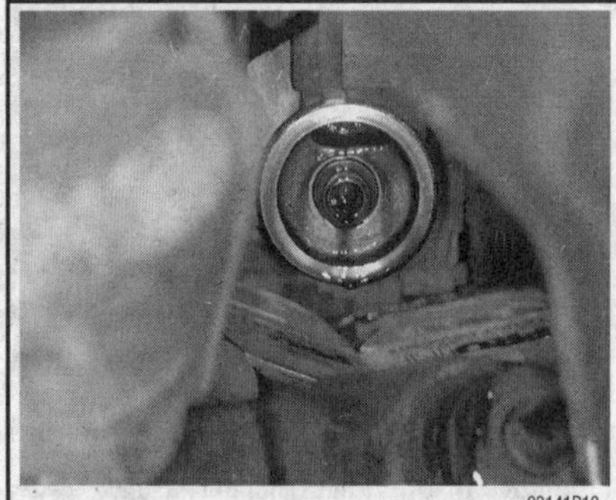
93141P10

**Fig. 143 . . . without draining into the subframe**

TCCS1901

**Fig. 144 Before installing a new oil filter, lightly coat the rubber gasket with clean oil**

stands. Slide a six-quart (minimum) drain pan under the oil pan drain plug.

6. Loosen the drain plug with a socket or box wrench. Push in on the plug as you turn in so no oil escapes until the plug is completely removed.

7. Remove the oil pan plug and drain the dirty oil into a catch pan. Vehicles with a 5.0L engine have two drain plugs. The front one will drain about a quart. The rear drain plug will drain the rest of the oil. Both must be removed. Allow the oil to drain into the pan. Be careful, if the engine is at operating temperature, the oil is hot enough to burn you.

8. Clean the drain plug and check it carefully; if the threads are stripped, replace it with a new one and a new gasket. If the gasket is cracked or damaged, replace it. Slide the oil drain pan under the oil filter.

9. Using the right size oil filter wrench, remove the oil filter by turning it counter-clockwise. Wrap a rag around it (to protect you from the hot oil), unscrew it the rest of the way, and place it in the oil catch pan.

10. Ensure that the old oil filter gasket is not stuck on the cylinder block or oil filter adapter. Using a clean rag, wipe the filter-mounting surface.

**To install:**

11. When installing the oil filter, spread a small amount of clean oil on the sealing gasket on the new filter and tighten the filter only hand tight. Install the oil pan plug and torque to no more than 20 ft. lbs. (27 Nm).

12. Make sure the plug is tight in the pan, but do not overtighten.

13. Slide the oil drain pan out from under the vehicle, and lower the vehicle to the ground.

14. Remove the oil filler cap from the rocker arm cover and place a funnel in the oil filler hole. Fill the crankcase with the quantity of oil specified in the capacity chart at the end of this section.

15. Remove the funnel, install the oil cap, and wipe away any spilled oil.

16. Start the engine, and inspect for oil leaks.

## Automatic Transaxle

### FLUID RECOMMENDATIONS

Motorcraft Mercon ATF (Automatic Transmission Fluid) XT-2-QDX or equivalent Mercon ATF fluid (Dexron Mercon III) is the only fluids recommend for use in the automatic transaxles of the vehicles in this book.

## LEVEL CHECK

See Figures 145 and 146

Check the automatic transaxle fluid level at least every 15,000 miles or 12 months. The dipstick can be found on the left (driver) side of the engine compartment. The fluid level should be checked only when the transaxle is hot (normal operating temperature). The transaxle is considered hot after about 20 miles of highway driving.

1. Start the engine, set the parking brake, and put the transaxle selector lever in the **P** position.
2. Move the selector lever through all the positions and return to the PARK position. DO NOT TURN OFF THE ENGINE DURING THE FLUID LEVEL CHECK.
3. Remove the dipstick, wipe it clean and then reinsert it firmly. Be sure that it has been pushed all the way in. Remove the dipstick again and check the fluid level while holding it horizontally. With the engine running, the fluid level should be in the cross-hatched area.
4. If the fluid level is below the crosshatched area (engine hot), add MERCON®III automatic transaxle fluid through the dipstick tube. This is easily done with the aid of a funnel. Check the level often as you are filling the transaxle. Be extremely careful not to overfill it. Overfilling will cause slippage, seal damage and overheating. Approximately 1 pint of ATF will raise the fluid level into the cross-hatched area.

The fluid on the dipstick should always be a bright red color. If it is discolored (brown or black), or smells burnt, serious transaxle troubles, probably due to overheating, should be suspected. A qualified technician should inspect the transaxle to determine the cause of the burnt fluid.

# Automatic Transmissions

## FLUID RECOMMENDATIONS

Motorcraft Mercon ATF (Automatic Transmission Fluid) XT-2-QDX or equivalent Mercon ATF fluid (Dexron Mercon III) is the only fluids recommend for use in the automatic transmissions of the vehicles in this book.

## PAN & FILTER SERVICE

See Figures 147 thru 159

The fluid should be changed according to the schedule in the Maintenance Intervals chart. If the car is normally used in severe service, such as stop and start driving, trailer towing, or the like, the interval should be halved. If the car is driven under especially nasty conditions, such as in heavy city traffic where the temperature normally reaches 90°F (32°C), or in very hilly or mountainous areas, or in police, taxi, or delivery service, the fluid should be changed according to the severe service schedule.

**➡To drain the automatic transmission fluid, the fluid pan must be removed.**

1. Raise and safely support the vehicle.
2. Place a drain pan underneath the transmission pan, then remove the pan attaching bolts except on the four corners of the pan.
3. Loosen the four attaching bolts on the corners approximately four turns each, but do not remove them.
4. Very carefully pry the pan loose on one corner. You can use a small prybar for this if you work CAREFULLY. Do not distort the pan flange, or score the mating surface of the transmission case. You'll be very sorry later if you do. As the pan is pried loose, all of the fluid is going to come pouring out.
5. Carefully break the other corners loose until fluid is flowing steadily from the entire pan.

**➡If the drained fluid is discolored (brown or black), thick, or smells burnt, serious transmission troubles, probably due to overheating, should be suspected. Your car's transmission should be inspected by a reliable transmission specialist to determine the problem.**

6. After the fluid is down flowing, remove one corner bolt and attempt to drain any remaining fluid. Remove the remaining bolts and remove the pan and gasket.

**➡On some later models, the transmission pan gasket is reusable, do no throw it away.**

7. Clean the pan and the magnets with solvent and allow them to air dry. If you use a rag to wipe out the pan, you risk leaving bits of lint behind, which will clog the dinky hydraulic passages in the transmission.
8. Remove and discard the filter and the O-ring seal if applicable.

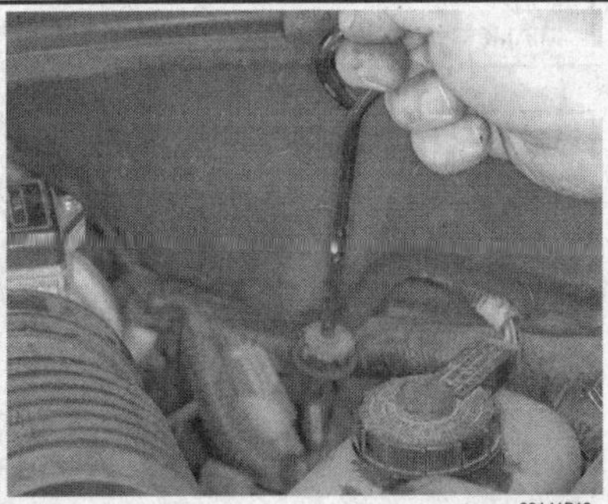

93141P13

**Fig. 145 Automatic Transmission dipstick location—Continentals**

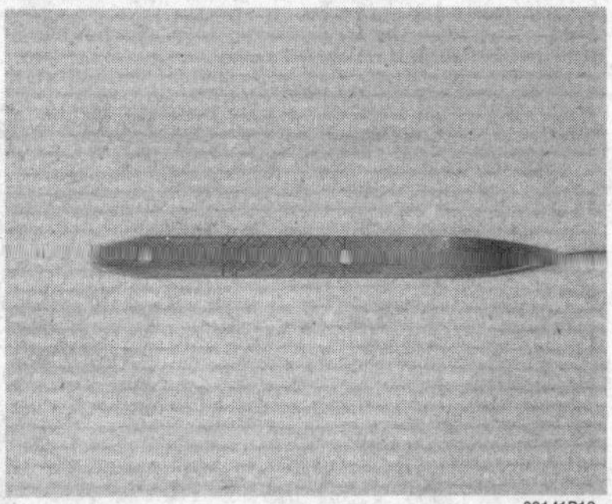

93141P12

**Fig. 146 The dipstick is easy to read and well marked. Do not add if level is in the crosshatch area**

89601P58

**Fig. 147 The transmission pan is held to the transmission case by retaining bolts. Typically the retaining bolts require a 10mm socket**

89601P59

**Fig. 148 Remove the retaining bolts on the transmission pan except . . .**

89601P61

**Fig. 149 . . . for the bolts on the four corners of the pan**

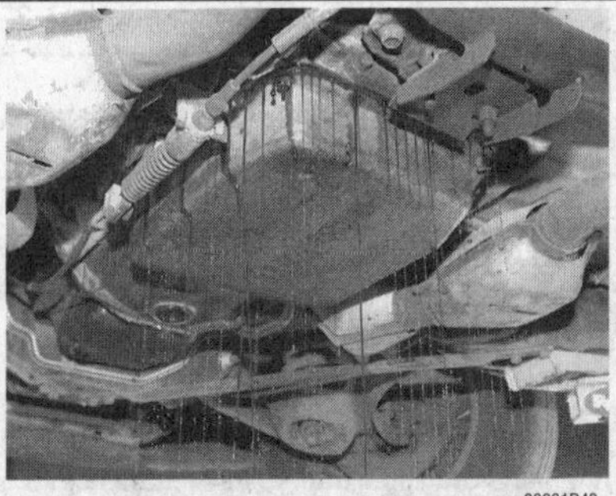

89601P40

**Fig. 150 Slowly loosen the four corner bolts and lower the pan. As the pan is lowered, fluid will begin to pour out**

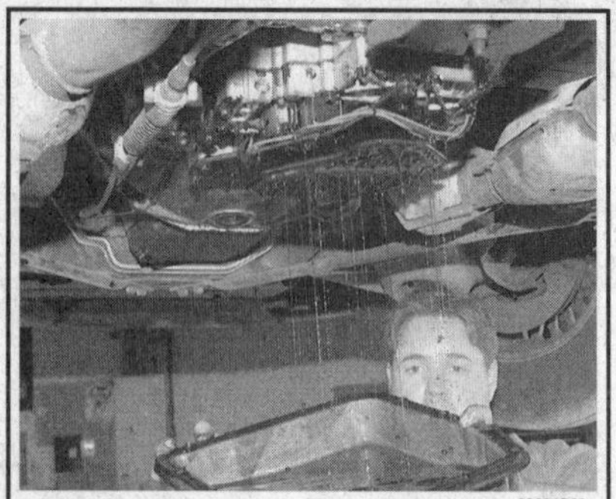

89601P62

**Fig. 151 After the fluid is drained out, remove the pan from the transmission**

91191P87

**Fig. 152 Remove the transmission filter by gently pulling it out of the valve body**

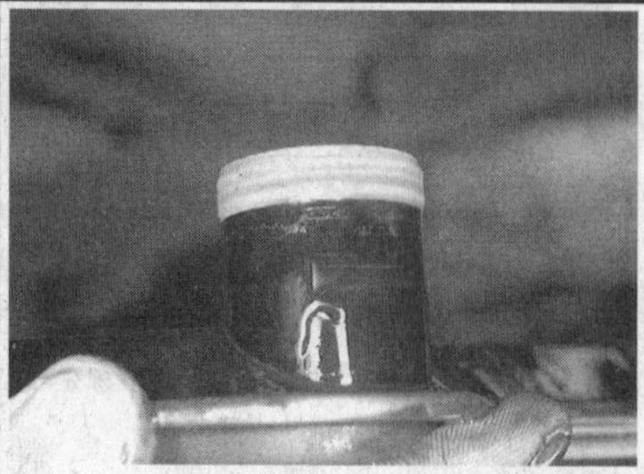

89601P68

**Fig. 153 Make sure that the O-ring on the filter nipple is removed from the valve body, typically it will stay on the filter nipple**

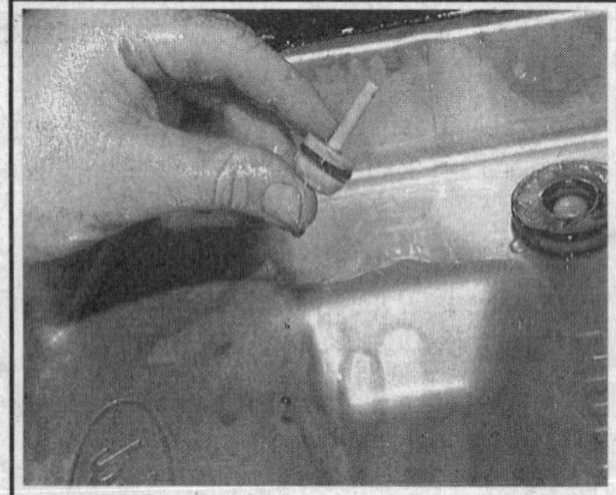

91191P85

**Fig. 154 If you happen to find this piece in your transmission pan upon removal, don't panic, it is a dipstick tube plug that is knocked out on the assembly line while the vehicle is being built**

89601P64

**Fig. 155 Remove the transmission pan gasket from the pan and place it in a safe place, if the gasket is reusable as this one is**

89601P65

**Fig. 156 Remove the transmission pan magnets from the pan and . . .**

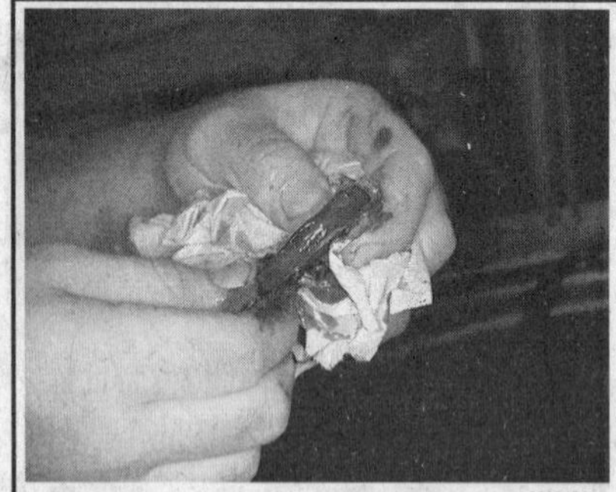

89601P66

**Fig. 157 . . . wipe the magnets clean before installing them back into the pan**

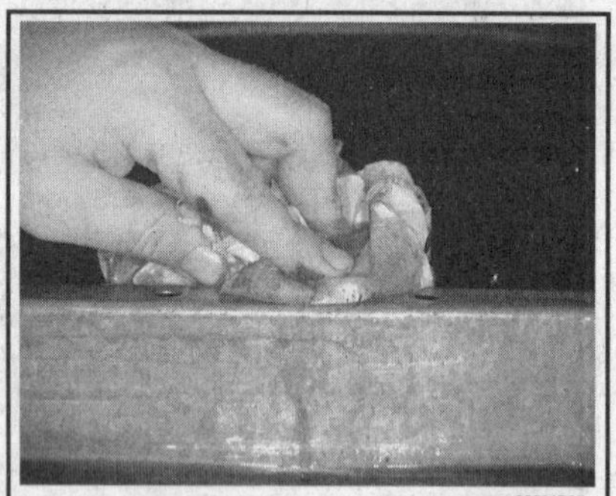

89601P67

**Fig. 158 Thoroughly clean the mating surfaces of the pan and . . .**

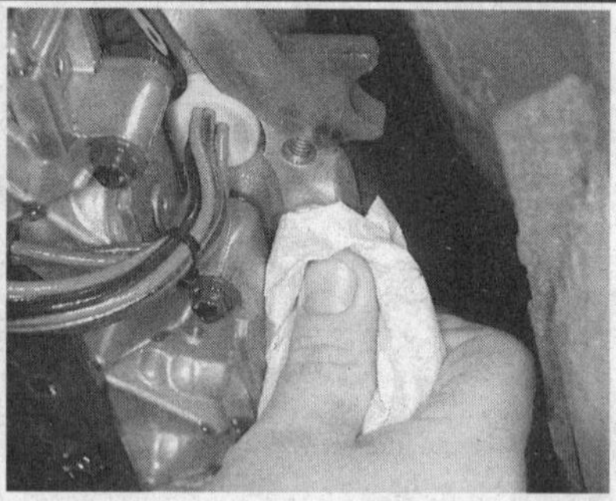

89601P63

**Fig. 159 . . . the transmission case before installing the gasket and pan onto the case**

**➡On some models, the filter may be retained by bolts, remove the bolts and the filter from the valve body.**

**To install:**

9. Install a new filter and O-ring, if applicable.
10. If the filter is retained by bolts, tighten the bolts to 80–120 inch lbs. (9–14 Nm).

**➡If removed from the pan, make sure the magnets are repositioned back into the pan.**

11. Position the gasket on the pan, then install the pan. Tighten the bolts evenly and in rotation to 10 ft. lbs. (13 Nm.). Do not overtighten.
12. Lower the vehicle.
13. Add the recommended automatic transmission fluid to the transmission through the dipstick tube. You will need a long necked funnel, or a funnel and tube to do this. A quick check of the capacities chart later in this Section will reveal the capacity of the transmission in your vehicle. On a first fill after removing the pan and filter, this number should cut into a ⅓ and checked on the dipstick before refilling.
14. With the transmission in **P**, put on the parking brake, block the front wheels, start the engine and let it idle. DO NOT RACE THE ENGINE. DO NOT MOVE THE LEVER THROUGH ITS RANGES.
15. With the lever in Park, check the fluid level. If it's OK, take the car out for a short drive, park on a level surface, and check the level again, as outlined earlier in this section. Add more fluid if necessary. Be careful not to overfill, which will cause foaming and fluid loss.

## Drive Axle

### FLUID RECOMMENDATIONS

All conventional axles use Premium Rear Axle Lubricant XY–80W90–QL or –KL or equivalent, meeting Ford specification WSP–M2C 197–A. For

Traction-Lok equipped vehicles, add 5 oz. (118 ml) of Ford Friction Modifier or equivalent meeting Ford Specifications.

## LEVEL CHECK

**See Figures 160, 161, 162, 163 and 164**

Checking the differential fluid level is generally unnecessary unless a leak is suspected.

1. Raise and safely support the vehicle on jackstands.
2. Remove the oil fill plug from the differential housing. The hex drive on a 3/8 in. drive ratchet, breaker bar or extension works well on some applications.
3. Insert a finger into the fill hole; be careful as the threads can be sharp. The oil level should be about 1/4 in. below the bottom of the fill hole with the axle in normal running position.
4. If the oil level feels low, add oil through the fill hole. Most hypoid gear oil comes in squeeze bottles equipped with small fill nozzles, designed for this purpose.
5. When the oil level is correct, install the oil fill plug and tighten to 15–30 ft. lbs. (20–41 Nm).

## DRAIN AND REFILL

**See Figures 165 thru 171**

The differential should be drained and refilled every 100,000 miles or if the axle has been submerged in water.

1. Raise and safely support the vehicle on jackstands.
2. Clean all dirt from the area of the differential cover.
3. Position a drain pan under the differential.
4. Remove all but 2 cover retaining bolts and allow the fluid to drain from the differential. Once the fluid has drained, remove the remaining bolts to free the cover.
5. Thoroughly clean the differential cover. Cover the differential carrier with a clean rag to prevent axle contamination, then clean all the old sealant from the machined surface of the differential housing.
6. Make sure the machined surfaces of the cover and differential are clean and free of oil. Apply a 1/4 in. wide bead of silicone sealer around the cir-

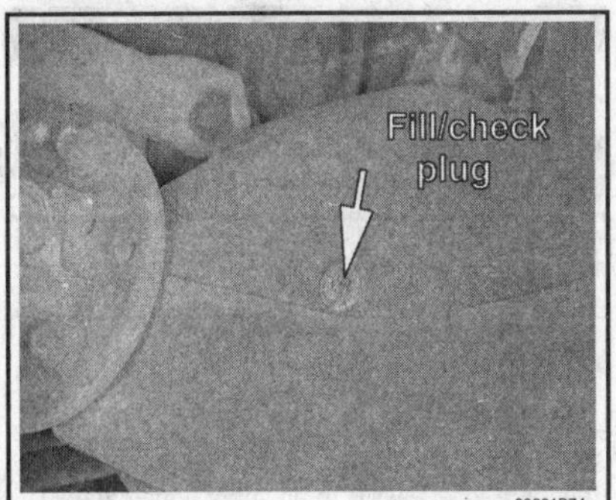

89601P74

**Fig. 160 The check/fill plug location—rear axle**

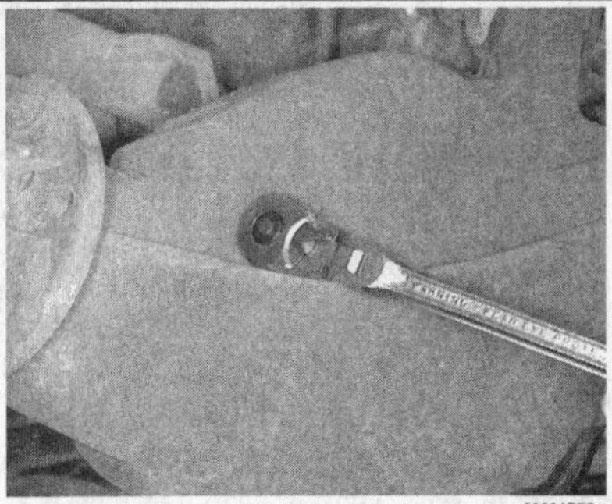
89601P75

**Fig. 161 Loosen the check/fill plug with a 3/8 drive tool and . . .**

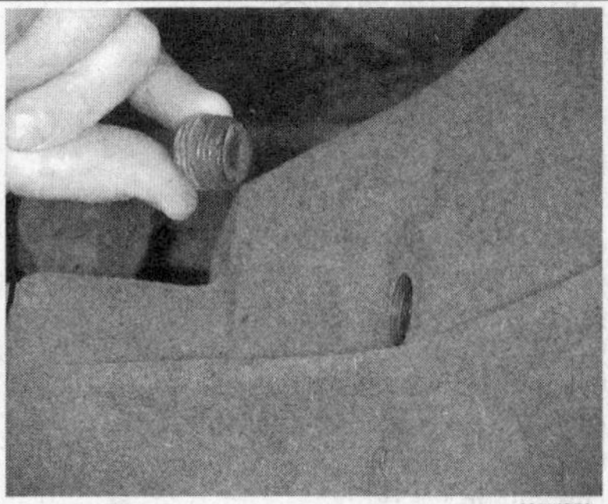
89601P76

**Fig. 162 . . . remove the check/fill plug**

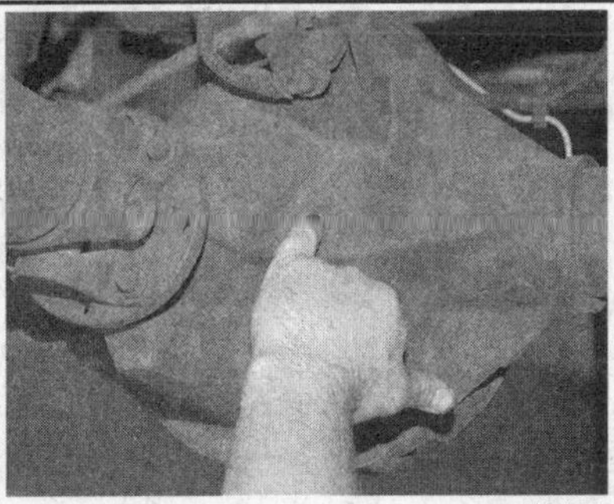
91191P75

**Fig. 163 Check the fluid level by placing a finger into the hole—rear axle**

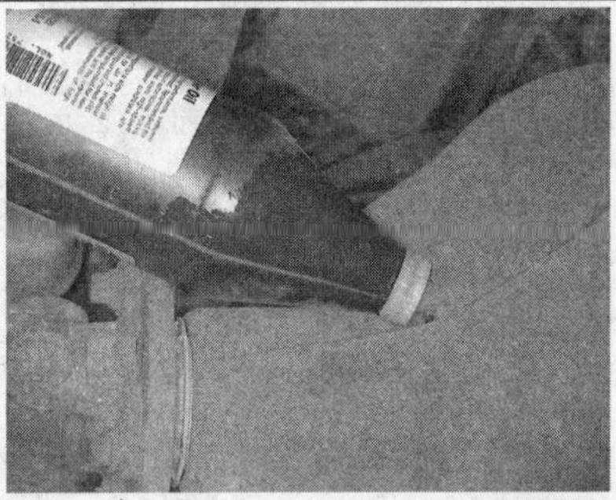
89601P77

**Fig. 164 Add the proper lubricant into the differential through the check/fill plug location**

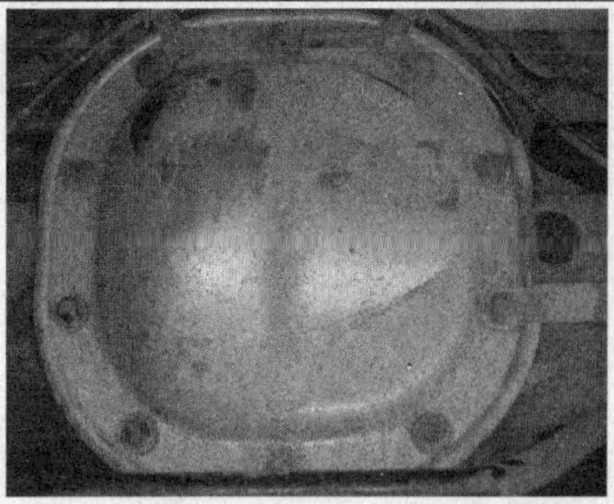
89601P69

**Fig. 165 Remove the axle cover retaining bolts**

89601P71

**Fig. 166 After the cover bolts are removed, carefully pry the cover loose so that fluid begins to drain out the bottom**

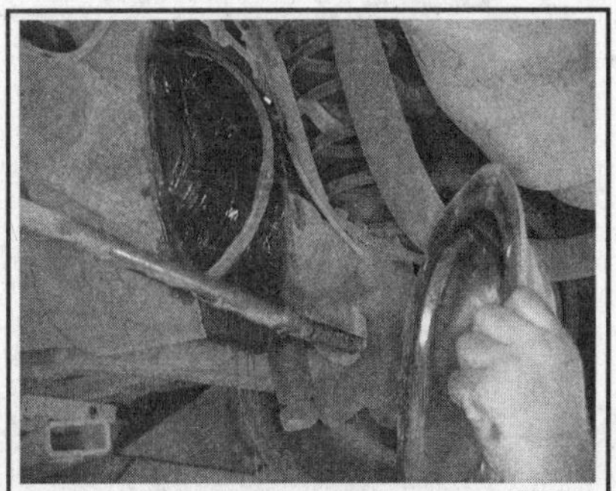
89601P73

**Fig. 167 After most of the fluid has drained out, remove the cover from the axle**

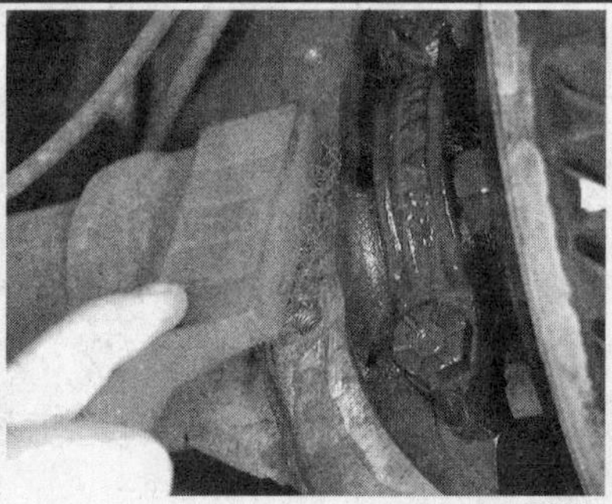
89601P80

**Fig. 168 Thoroughly clean the axle housing and . . .**

89601P78

Fig. 169 . . .cover mating surfaces using a brush or other suitable tool

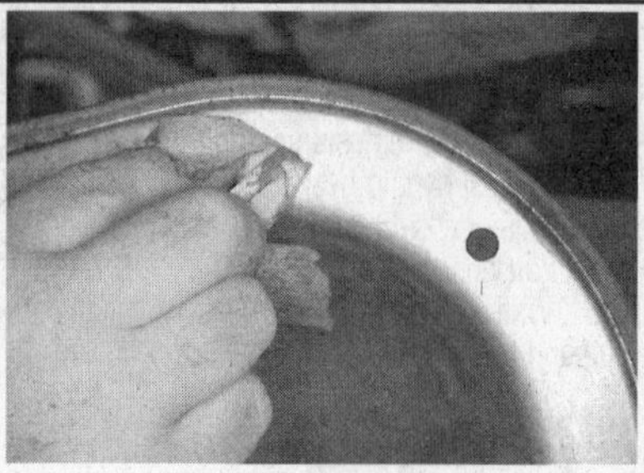

89601P79

Fig. 170 Wipe the cover mating surface using a cloth or other rag and a suitable solvent to remove any contaminants on the surface

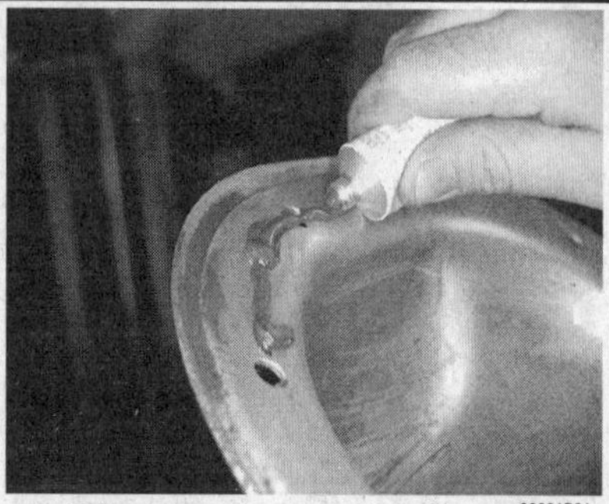

89601P81

Fig. 171 Apply a bead of silicone to the cover mating surface before installing the cover onto the rear axle

cumference of the cover, going inside the bolt holes.

7. Install the cover with the retaining bolts. Tighten the bolts, evenly, to 25–35 ft. lbs. (34–47 Nm) in a crisscross pattern.

8. Remove the oil fill plug and add the required amount of hypoid gear oil through the oil fill hole. Refer to the Capacities chart at the end of this Section.

**➡If equipped with Traction-Lok differential, 4 oz. of friction modifier additive C8AZ–19B546–A or equivalent, must be included in the refill.**

9. Install the oil fill plug and tighten to 15–30 ft. lbs. (20–41 Nm). Lower the vehicle.

10. Road test the vehicle to warm the fluid. Check for leaks.

## Cooling System

### FLUID RECOMMENDATION

**▶ See Figures 172 and 173**

The cooling system was designed to maintain engine temperature at an efficient level during all engine-operating conditions.

When adding or changing the fluid in the system, be sure to maintain a 50/50 mixture of high quality ethylene glycol antifreeze and water in the cooling system. Use only antifreeze that is SAFE FOR USE WITH AN ALUMINUM RADIATOR.

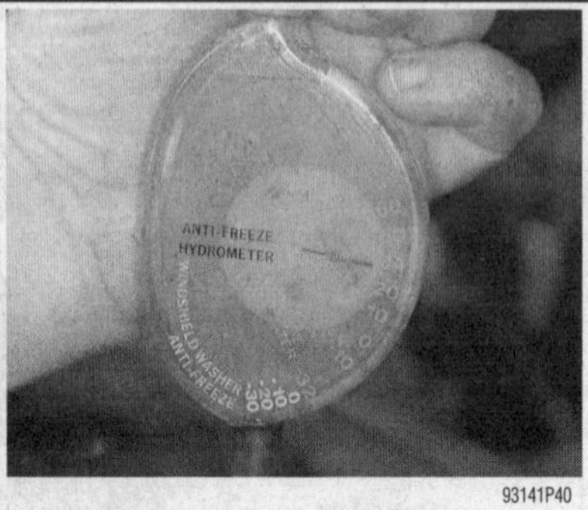


93141P40

Fig. 172 Testing the concentration level of the cooling system (-34°F)

A 50/50 mixture of ethylene glycol and water will provide the following protection:

- Freezing protection down to -34°F (-37°C).
- Boiling protection up to 265°F (129°C), with an operating pressure cap.
- Help keep the proper engine operating temperature
- Help protect against rust and corrosion
- Allow the sensors and switches to operate as designed

**➡ DO not use a solution stronger than 70% antifreeze. Pure antifreeze will freeze at -8°F (-22°C).**

### LEVEL CHECK

Check the coolant level in the recovery bottle or surge tank. The fluid level may be checked by observing the fluid level marks of the recovery tank. With the engine cold, the level should be at the FULL COLD or between the HOT and ADD level. When the engine is at normal operating temperatures, the coolant level should be at the HOT level. Only add coolant to bring the system to the proper level.

**✲✲ CAUTION**

**Should it he necessary to remove the radiator cap, make sure that the system has had time to cool, reducing the internal pressure.**

### TESTING FOR LEAKS

**▶ See Figures 174 thru 180**

If a the fluid level of your cooling system is constantly low, the chances of a leak are probable. There are several ways to go about finding the source of your leak.

The first way should be a visual inspection. During the visual inspection, look around the entire engine area including the radiator and the heater hoses. The interior of the car should be inspected behind the glove box and passenger side floorboard area, and check the carpet for any signs of moisture. The smartest way to go about finding a leak visually is to first inspect any and all joints in the system such as where the radiator hoses connect to the radiator and the engine. Another thing to look for is white crusty stains that are signs of a leak where the coolant has already dried.

If a visual inspection cannot find the cause of

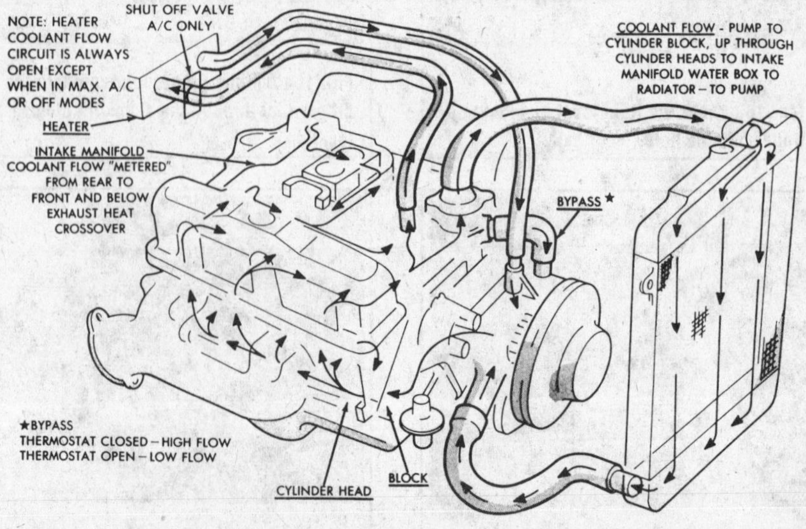


TCCS1082

Fig. 173 Cutaway view of a typical cooling system flow

93141P16

**Fig. 174 Maximum pressure for the cooling system is printed right on the cap**

93141P08

**Fig. 175 Check the seal on the cap to make sure it seals**

93141P36

**Fig. 176 The pressure tester adapter. . .**

93141P35

**Fig. 177 . . . allows you to pressure test the radiator cap. . .**

93141P38

**Fig. 178 . . . and read the static pressure for the cap**

93141P37

**Fig. 179 Pressure testing the coolant system**

93141P39

**Fig. 180 Reading the pressure. On this system, the cooling system holds pressure**

your leak, a pressure test is a logical and extremely helpful way to find a leak. A pressure tester will be needed to perform this and if one is not available they can be purchased or even rented at many auto parts stores. The pressure tester usually has a standard size radiator cap adapter on the pressure port, however, other adapters are available based on the size of the vehicle's radiator neck or recovery tank depending on where the pressure tester connects. when pressurizing the cooling system, make sure you do not exceed the pressure rating of the system, which can be found on the top of the radiator cap, however, if you have and aftermarket or replacement cap that does not have the rating on it, 16psi is a standard to use but some cars are higher. Overpressurizing the system can cause a rupture in a hose or worse in the radiator or heater core and possibly cause an injury or a burn if the coolant is hot. Overpressurizing is normally controlled by the radiator cap which has a vent valve in it which is opened when the system reaches it's maximum pressure rating. To pressure test the system:

**➡The pressure test should be performed with the engine OFF.**

1. Remove the radiator or recovery tank cap.
2. Using the proper adapter, insert it onto the opening and connect the pressure tester,
3. Begin pressurizing the system by pumping the pressure tester and watching the gauge, when the maximum pressure is reached, stop.
4. Watch the gauge slowly and see if the pressure on the gauge drops, if it does, a leak is definitely present.
5. If the pressure stayed somewhat stable, visually inspect the system for leaks. If the pressure dropped, repressurize the system and then visually inspect the system.
6. If no signs of a leak are noticed visually, pressurize the system to the maximum pressure rating of the system and leave the pressure tester connected for about 30 minutes. Return after 30 minutes and verify the pressure on the gauge, if the pressure dropped more than 20%, a leak definitely exists, if the pressure drop is less than 20%, the system is most likely okay.

Another way coolant is lost is by a internal engine leak, causing the oil to be contaminated or the coolant to be burned in the process of combustion and sent out the exhaust. To check for oil contamination, remove the dipstick and check the condition of the oil in the oil pan. If the oil is murky and has a white or beige "milkshake" look to it, the coolant is contaminating the oil through an internal leak and the engine must be torn down to find the leak. If the oil appears okay, the coolant can be burned and going out the tailpipe. A quick test for this is a cloud of white smoke appearing from the tailpipe, especially on start-up. On cold days, the white smoke will appear, this is due to condensation and the outside temperature, not a coolant leak. If the "smoke test" does not verify the situation, removing the spark plugs one at a time and checking the electrodes for a green or white tint can verify an internal coolant leak and identify which cylinder(s) is the culprit and aiding your search for the cause of the leak. If the spark plugs appear okay, another method is to use a gas analyzer or emissions tester, or one of several hand-held tools that most professional shops possess. This tools are used to check the cooling system for the presence of Hydrocarbons (HC's) in the coolant.

## DRAIN & REFILL

**➧ See Figures 181, 182 and 183**

Ensure that the engine is completely cool prior to starting this service.

**✲✲ CAUTION**

**Never open, service or drain the radiator or cooling system when hot; serious burns can occur from the steam and hot coolant. Also, when draining engine coolant, keep in mind that cats and dogs are attracted to ethylene glycol antifreeze and could drink any that is**

89601P38

**Fig. 181 On later models, it might be necessary to remove the air deflector**

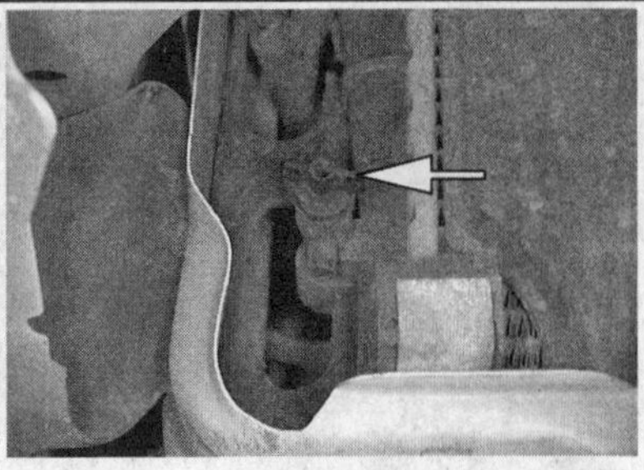

89601P56

**Fig. 182 The radiator petcock (drain) is typically located on the driver's side of the radiator, on the side tank. It is accessible from underneath the vehicle**

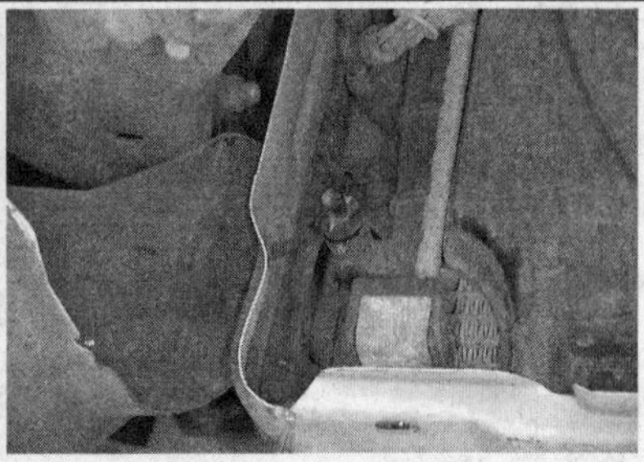

89601P57

**Fig. 183 Make sure you have a drain pan in place before you open the drain because coolant will immediately begin to flow out**

**left in an uncovered container or in puddles on the ground. This will prove fatal in sufficient quantities. Always drain coolant into a sealable container. Coolant should be reused unless it is contaminated or is several years old.**

1. Remove the recovery tank or radiator cap.
2. Raise and support the vehicle.
3. Remove the front air deflector, if necessary.
4. Place a drain pan of sufficient capacity under the radiator and open the petcock (drain) on the radiator.

**➡Plastic petcocks easily bind. Before opening a plastic radiator petcock, spray it with some penetrating lubricant.**

5. Drain the cooling system completely.
6. Close the petcock.
7. Remove the drain pan.
8. If removed, install the air deflector.
9. Lower the vehicle.
10. Determine the capacity of the cooling system, then properly refill the system at the recovery tank or radiator opening with a 50/50 mixture of fresh coolant and distilled water until it reaches the **FULL COLD** line on the recovery tank or the radiator is full.
11. Leave the recovery tank or radiator cap off to aid in bleeding the system.
12. Start the engine and allow it to idle until the thermostat opens (the upper radiator hose will become hot). The coolant level should go down, this is normal as the system bleeds the air pockets out of the system.
13. Refill the system with coolant to the proper level.
14. Turn the engine **OFF** and check for leaks.

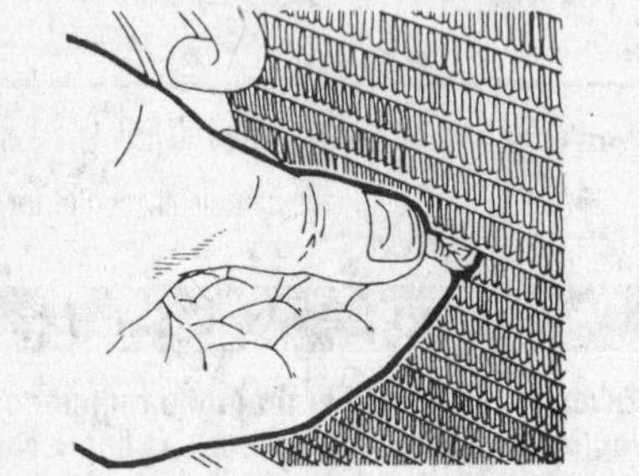

TCCS1081

**Fig. 184 Periodically remove all debris from the radiator fins**

## FLUSHING & CLEANING THE SYSTEM

**See Figure 184**

1. Drain the cooling system completely as described earlier.
2. Close the petcock and fill the system with a cooling system flush (clean water may also be used, but is not as efficient).
3. Idle the engine until the upper radiator hose gets hot.
4. Allow the engine to cool completely and drain the system again.
5. Repeat this process until the drained water is clear and free of scale.
6. Flush the recovery tank with water and leave empty.

**✲✲ CAUTION**

**Never open, service or drain the radiator or cooling system when hot; serious burns can occur from the steam and hot coolant. Also, when draining engine coolant, keep in mind that cats and dogs are attracted to ethylene glycol antifreeze and could drink any that is left in an uncovered container or in puddles on the ground. This will prove fatal in sufficient quantities. Always drain coolant into a sealable container. Coolant should be reused unless it is contaminated or is several years old.**

89601P45

**Fig. 185 The brake fluid level should not be above the MAX line on the side of the reservoir**

7. Fill and bleed the cooling system as described earlier.

# Master Cylinder

## FLUID RECOMMENDATION

When adding or replacing the brake fluid, always use a top quality fluid, such as DOT-3. DO NOT allow the brake fluid container or master cylinder reservoir to remain open for long periods; brake fluid absorbs moisture from the air, reducing its effectiveness and causing corrosion in the lines.

## FLUID LEVEL

**See Figures 185, 186, 187 and 188**

The master cylinder—located in the left rear section of the engine compartment—consists of an aluminum body and a reservoir with minimum fill indicators. The fluid level of the reservoirs should be kept near the top of the observation windows.

**➡Avoid spilling brake fluid on any of the vehicles painted surfaces, wiring cables or electrical connectors. Brake fluid will damage paint and electrical connections. If any fluid is spilled on the vehicle, flush the area with water to lessen the damage.**

Any sudden decrease in the fluid level indicates a possible leak in the system and should be checked out immediately.

89601P46

**Fig. 186 Wipe the master cylinder reservoir clean before . . .**

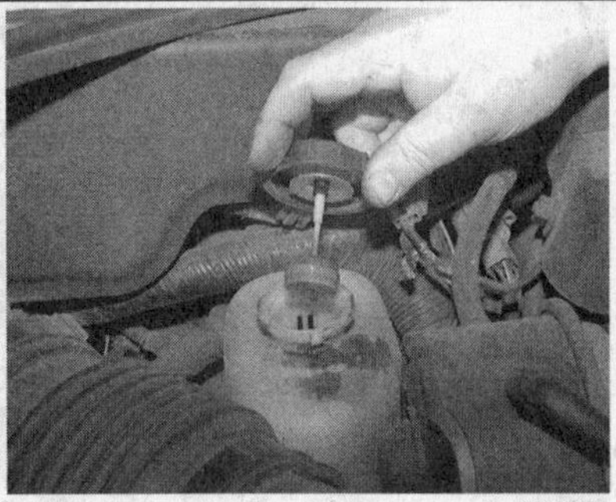

93141P22

Fig. 187 . . . removing the reservoir cap

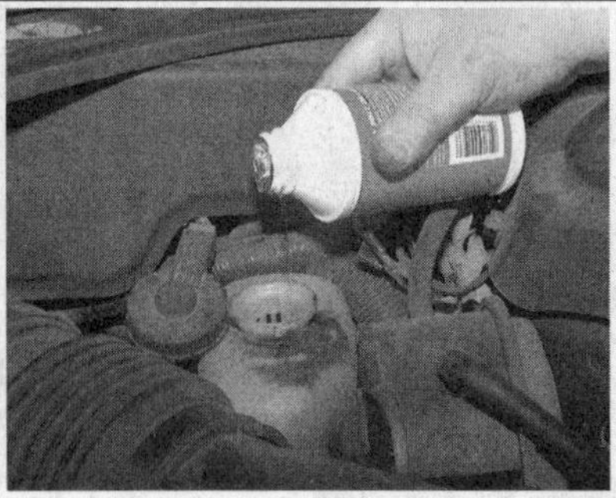

93141P21

Fig. 188 Pour brake fluid from a sealed container directly into the reservoir

89601P49

Fig. 189 Power steering fluid reservoir—typical

## Power Steering Pump

### FLUID RECOMMENDATION

When filling or replacing the fluid of the power steering pump reservoir, use power steering fluid only. E6AZ–19582–AA or equivalent power steering fluid is recommended.

### LEVEL CHECK

➧ **See Figures 189, 190 and 191**

Power steering fluid level should be checked at least once every 12 months or 7,500 miles. To prevent possible overfilling, check the fluid level only when the fluid has warmed to operating temperatures and the wheels are turned straight ahead. If the level is low, fill the pump reservoir until the fluid level measures "full" on the reservoir dipstick. Low fluid level usually produces a moaning sound as the wheels are turned (especially when standing still or parking) and increases steering wheel effort.

## Chassis Greasing

➧ **See Figures 192, 193, 194 and 195**

➡**Note: Not all models have grease fittings that can be lubricated.**

Chassis greasing can be performed with a pressurized grease gun or by using a hand-operated grease gun. Wipe the grease fittings clean before greasing in order to prevent the possibility of forcing any dirt into the component. Do not over grease the components; because damage may occur to the grease seals.

## Wheel Bearings

### REPACKING

#### 1988–90

***TOWN CAR AND MARK VII***

➧ **See Figures 196, 197, 198, 199 and 200**

1. Raise and safely support the front of the vehicle securely on jackstands.
2. Remove the wheel and tire assembly and the disc brake caliper. Suspend the caliper, do not let it hang from the brake hose.

93141P19

Fig. 190 Notice the location and size of the power steering reservoir cap—Continental

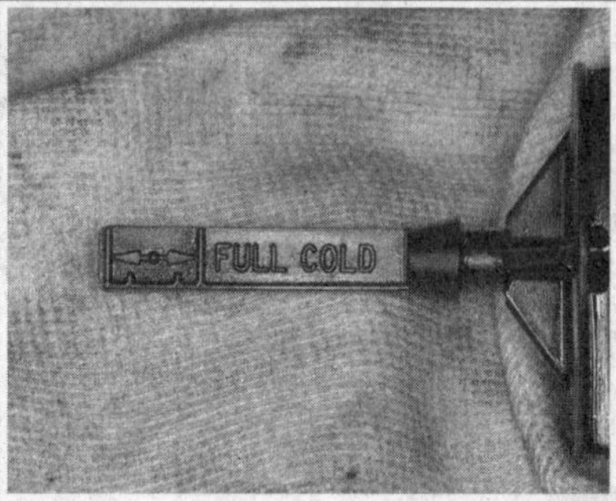


93141P17

Fig. 191 The cap has a built in dipstick. It clearly shows where the fluid level should be

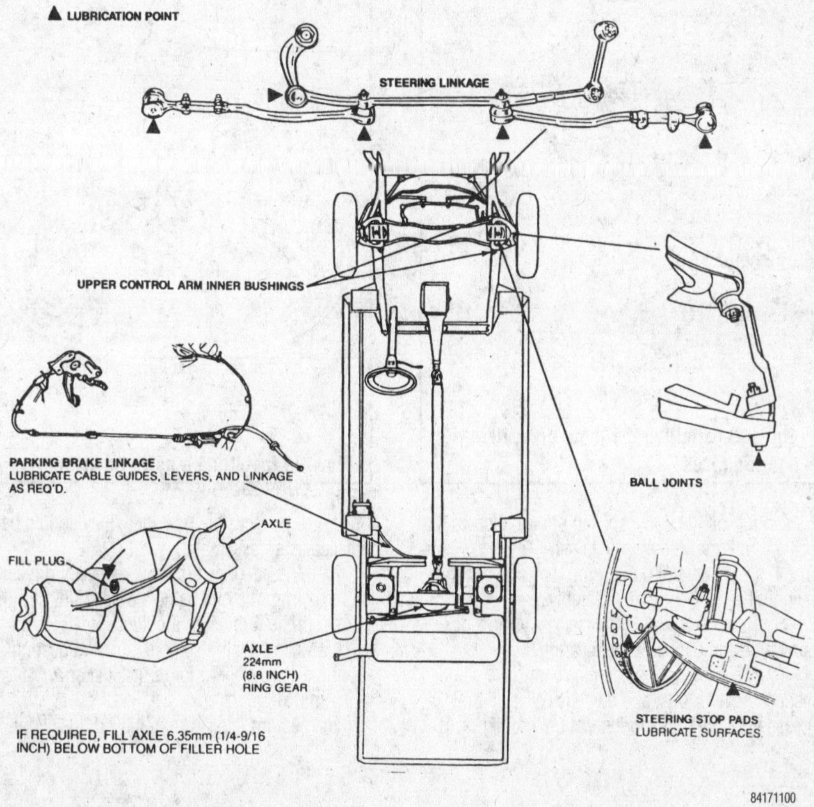


84171100

Fig. 192 Chassis lubrication points

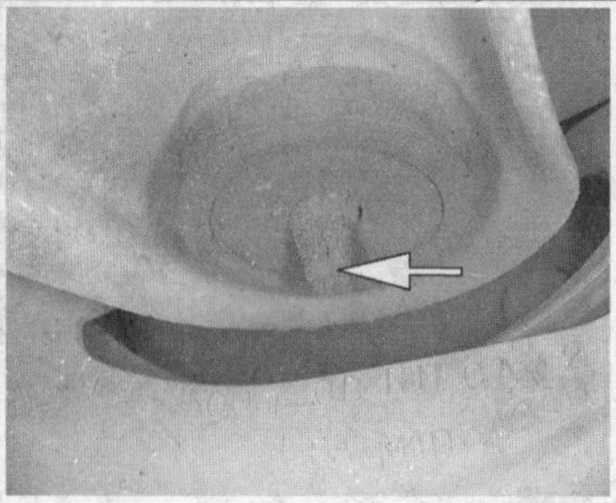

89601P92

Fig. 193 Any greasable item will have a Zerk® fitting located on it such as this lower ball joint

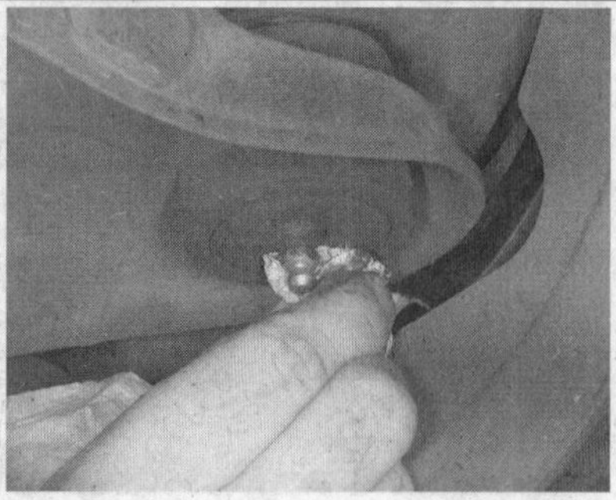

89601P93

Fig. 194 Wipe any road grime or old grease off of the fitting before inserting new grease

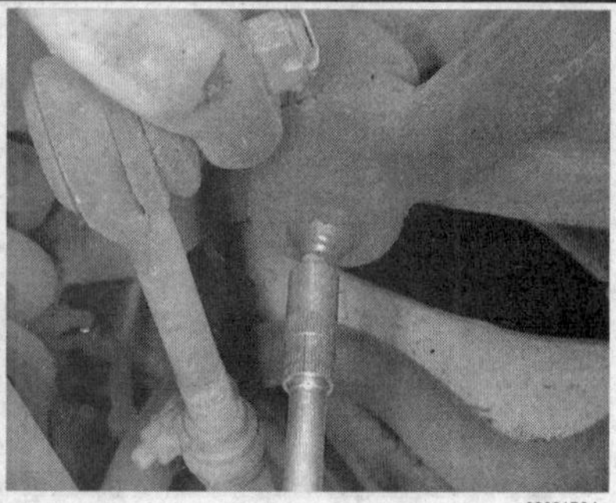

89601P94

Fig. 195 Place the grease gun nozzle on the fitting and squeeze 2-3 pumps into the fitting

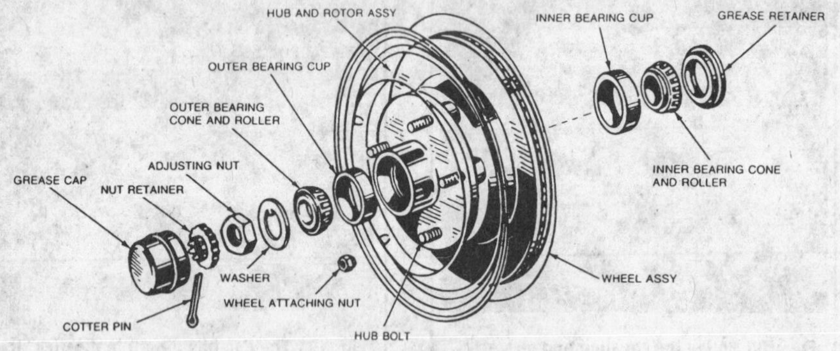


84171101

Fig. 196 Front wheel bearing assembly –1988–89

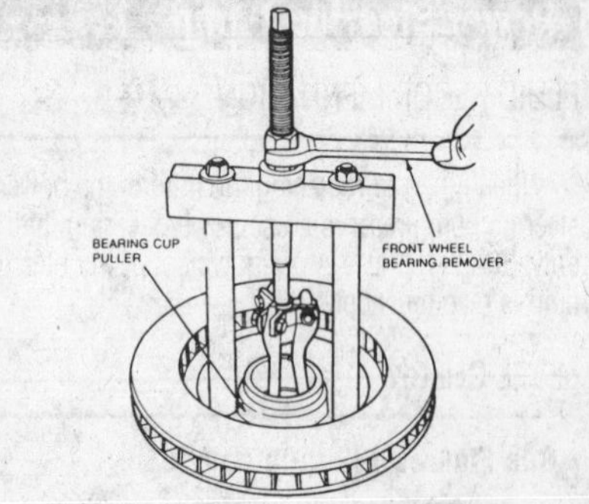


84171102

Fig. 197 Removing the inner bearing race using a puller

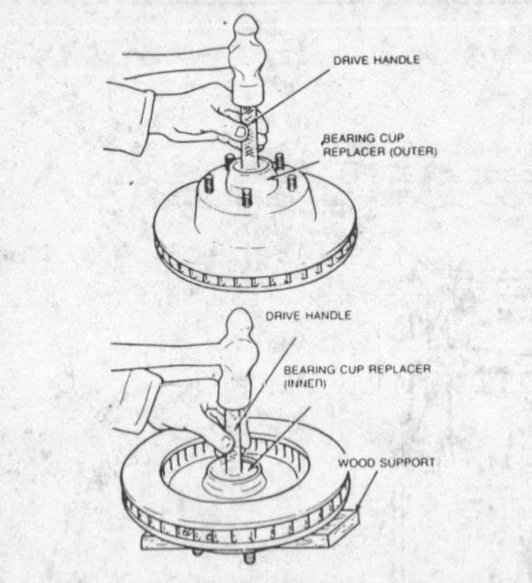


84171103

Fig. 198 Installing the inner and outer bearing races

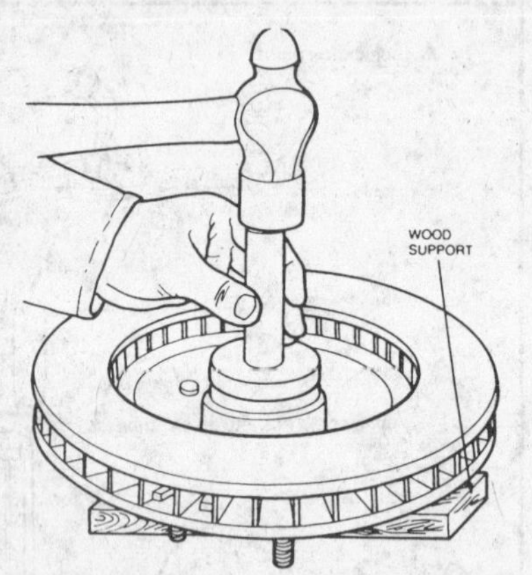


84171104

Fig. 199 Installing a new grease seal

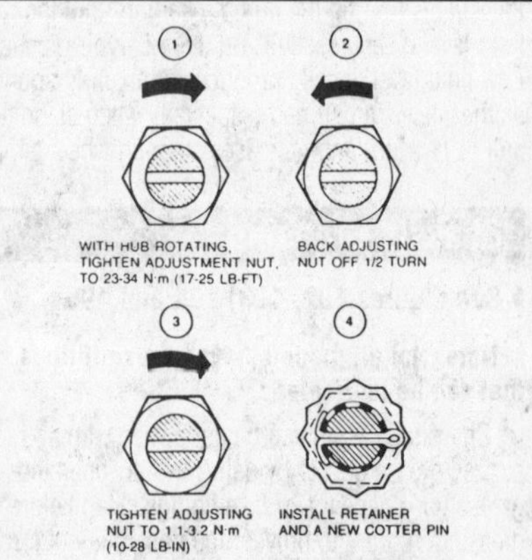


841171105

Fig. 200 Wheel bearing adjustment procedure

3. Pry off the dust cap. Tap out and discard the cotter pin. Remove the nut retainer.

4. Being careful not to drop the outer bearing, pull off the rotor and hub assembly.

5. Remove the inner grease seal using a pry-bar. Remove the inner wheel bearing.

6. Clean the wheel bearings with solvent and inspect them for pits, and damage. Wipe all the old grease from the hub and inspect the bearing races. If bearings or races are damaged, they should be replaced as an assembly.

7. If the bearings are to be replaced, drive out the races from the hub using a brass drift, or pull them from the hub using a puller.

8. Make sure the spindle, hub and bearing assemblies are clean prior to installation.

**To install:**

If the bearing races were removed, install new ones using a suitable bearing race installer. Pack the bearings with high-temperature wheel bearing grease using a bearing packer. If a packer is not available, work as much grease as possible between the rollers and cages using your hands.

9. Coat the inner surface of the hub and bearing races with grease.

10. Install the inner bearing in the hub. Using a seal installer, install a new grease seal into

the hub. Lubricate the lip of the seal with grease.

a. Loosen the adjusting nut 3 turns and rock the wheel in and out a few times to release the brake pads from the rotor.

b. While rotating the wheel and hub assembly, tighten the adjusting nut to 17–25 ft. lbs. (23–34 Nm).

c. Back off the adjusting nut½turn, then retighten to 10–28 inch lbs. (1.1–3.2 Nm).

d. Install the nut retainer and a new cotter pin. Replace the grease cap.

11. Lower the vehicle. Before driving the vehicle, pump the brake pedal several times to restore normal brake pedal travel.

**1990–00**

***TOWN CAR AND MARK***

The front wheel bearings are a sealed hub design, are lubed for life, and require no maintenance. The bearings are preset and cannot be adjusted. For bearing hub removal and installation, see Section 8.

## JUMP STARTING A DEAD BATTERY

**See Figure 201**

Whenever a vehicle is jump started, precautions must be followed in order to prevent the possibility of personal injury. Remember that batteries contain a small amount of explosive hydrogen gas that is a by-product of battery charging. Sparks should always be avoided when working around batteries, especially when attaching jumper cables. To minimize the possibility of accidental sparks, follow the procedure carefully.

**** CAUTION**

**NEVER hook the batteries up in a series circuit or the entire electrical system will go up in smoke, including the starter!**

Vehicles equipped with a diesel engine may utilize two 12 volt batteries. If so, the batteries are connected in a parallel circuit (positive terminal to positive terminal, negative terminal to negative terminal). Hooking the batteries up in parallel circuit increases battery cranking power without increasing total battery voltage output. Output remains at 12 volts. On the other hand, hooking two 12 volt batteries up in a series circuit (positive terminal to negative terminal, positive terminal to negative terminal) increases total battery output to 24 volts (12 volts plus 12 volts).

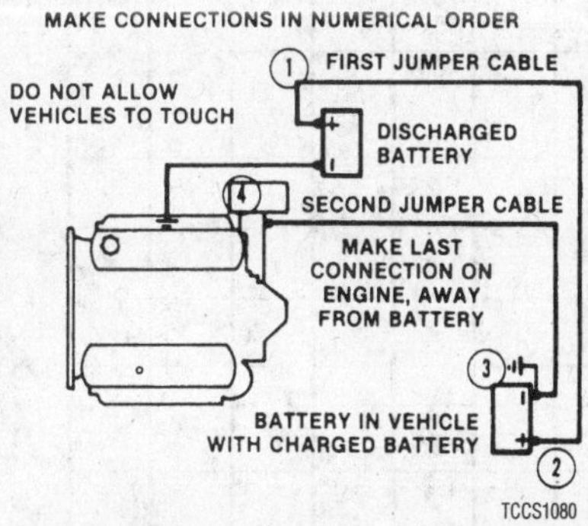


**Fig. 201 Connect the jumper cables to the batteries and engine in the order shown**

### Jump Starting Precautions

- Be sure that both batteries are of the same voltage. Vehicles covered by this manual and most vehicles on the road today utilize a 12 volt charging system.
- Be sure that both batteries are of the same polarity (have the same terminal, in most cases NEGATIVE grounded).
- Be sure that the vehicles are not touching or a short could occur.
- On serviceable batteries, be sure the vent cap holes are not obstructed.
- Do not smoke or allow sparks anywhere near the batteries.
- In cold weather, make sure the battery electrolyte is not frozen. This can occur more readily in a battery that has been in a state of discharge.
- Do not allow electrolyte to contact your skin or clothing.

**** CAUTION**

**Make certain that the ignition key, in the vehicle with the dead battery, is in the OFF position. Connecting cables to vehicles with on-board computers will result in computer destruction if the key is not in the OFF position. Turn the heater blower motor on the high speed setting.**

### Jump Starting Procedure

1. Make sure that the voltages of the 2 batteries are the same. Most batteries and charging systems are of the 12 volt variety.
2. Pull the jumping vehicle (with the good battery) into a position so the jumper cables can reach the dead battery and that vehicle's engine. Make sure that the vehicles do NOT touch.
3. Place the transmissions of both vehicles in **Neutral** (MT) or **P** (AT), as applicable, then firmly set their parking brakes.

**➡If necessary for safety reasons, the hazard lights on both vehicles may be operated throughout the entire procedure without significantly increasing the difficulty of jumping the dead battery.**

4. Turn all lights and accessories OFF on both vehicles. Make sure the ignition switches on both vehicles are turned to the **OFF** position.
5. Cover the battery cell caps with a rag, but do not cover the terminals.
6. Make sure the terminals on both batteries are clean and free of corrosion or proper electrical connection will be impeded. If necessary, clean the battery terminals before proceeding.
7. Identify the positive (+) and negative (-) terminals on both batteries.
8. Connect the first jumper cable to the positive (+) terminal of the dead battery, then connect the other end of that cable to the positive (+) terminal of the booster (good) battery.
9. Connect one end of the other jumper cable to the negative (-) terminal on the booster battery and the final cable clamp to an engine bolt head, alternator bracket or other solid, metallic point on the engine with the dead battery. Try to pick a ground on the engine that is positioned away from the battery in order to minimize the possibility of the 2 clamps touching should one loosen during the procedure. DO NOT connect this clamp to the negative (-) terminal of the bad battery.

**** CAUTION**

**Be very careful to keep the jumper cables away from moving parts (cooling fan, belts, etc.) on both engines.**

10. Check to make sure that the cables are routed away from any moving parts, then start the donor vehicle's engine. Run the engine at moderate speed for several minutes to allow the dead battery a chance to receive some initial charge.
11. With the donor vehicle's engine still running slightly above idle, try to start the vehicle with the dead battery. Crank the engine for no more than 10 seconds at a time and let the starter cool for at least 20 seconds between tries. If the vehicle does not start in 3 tries, it is likely that something else is also wrong or that the battery needs additional time to charge.
12. Once the vehicle is started, allow it to run at idle for a few seconds to make sure that it is operating properly.
13. Turn ON the headlights, heater blower and, if equipped, the rear defroster of both vehicles in order to reduce the severity of voltage spikes and subsequent risk of damage to the vehicles' electrical systems when the cables are disconnected. This step is especially important to any vehicle equipped with computer control modules.
14. Carefully disconnect the cables in the reverse order of connection. Start with the negative cable that is attached to the engine ground, then the negative cable on the donor battery. Disconnect the positive cable from the donor battery and finally, disconnect the positive cable from the formerly dead battery. Be careful when disconnecting the cables from the positive terminals not to allow the alligator clips to touch any metal on either vehicle or a short and sparks will occur.

## JACKING

Your vehicle was supplied with a jack for emergency road repairs. This jack is fine for changing a flat tire or other short-term procedures not requiring you to go beneath the vehicle. If it is used in an emergency, carefully follow the instruction provided either with the jack or in your owner's manual. Do not attempt to use the jack on any portions of the vehicle other than specified by the vehicle manufacturer. Always block the diagonally opposite wheel when using a jack.

A more convenient way of jacking is the use of a garage or floor jack. You may use the floor jack on either side of he front of the vehicle by positioning the jack on the frame. However, it is usually easier to raise the front of the vehicle at the front crossmember.

At the rear of the vehicle, the jack can be positioned under the rear axle housing tubes, between the suspension arm brackets and the differential housing. Do not raise the rear of the vehicle using the differential housing as a lift point.

### Jacking Precautions

**⁂ WARNING**

**On vehicles equipped with air suspension, the electrical power supply to the air suspension system must be shut off before jacking the vehicle. This can be accomplished by disconnecting the battery or turning off the power switch located in the luggage compartment, usually on the LH side (Continental and Mark). The suspension switch is located on the right side of the trunk in Town Cars. Failure to do so may result in unexpected inflation or deflation of the air springs that may result in shifting of the vehicle during these operations.**

The following safety points cannot be overemphasized:

- Always block the opposite wheels or wheels to keep the vehicle from rolling off the jack.
- When raising the front of the vehicle, firmly apply the parking brake.
- When the drive wheels are to remain on the ground, leave the vehicle in park to help prevent it from rolling.

**⁂ CAUTION**

**Never use cinder blocks or stacks of wood to support the vehicle, even if you're only going to be under it for a few minutes. Never crawl under the vehicle when it is supported only by the tire-changing jack or other floor jack.**

- Always use jackstands to support the vehicle when you are working underneath. Place the stands beneath the vehicle's jacking brackets. Before climbing underneath, rock the vehicle a bit to make sure it is firmly supported.

Small hydraulic (bottle jack), screw or scissors jacks are satisfactory for raising the vehicle. Drive-on trestles or ramps are also a handy and safe way to both raise and support the vehicle. Be careful though, some ramps may be too steep to drive your vehicle onto without scraping the front bottom panels. Never support on any suspension member (unless specifically instructed to do so by a repair manual).

- Never place the jack under the radiator, engine or transmission components, severe and extensive damage will result when he jack is raised. Additionally, never jack under the floorpan or bodywork.

**MANUFACTURER RECOMMENDED NORMAL MAINTENANCE INTERVALS**

VEHICLE MAINTENANCE INTERVAL

| | Miles (x1000) | 5 | 10 | 15 | 20 | 25 | 30 | 35 | 40 | 45 | 50 | 55 | 60 | 65 | 70 | 75 | 80 |
|---|---|---|---|---|---|---|---|---|---|---|---|---|---|---|---|---|---|
| | km (x1000) | 8 | 16 | 24 | 32 | 40 | 48 | 56 | 64 | 72 | 80 | 88 | 96 | 104 | 112 | 121 | 128 |
| Component | Type of Service | | | | | | | | | | | | | | | | |
| Engine oil and filter | Replace | ✓ | ✓ | ✓ | ✓ | ✓ | ✓ | ✓ | ✓ | ✓ | ✓ | ✓ | ✓ | ✓ | ✓ | ✓ | ✓ |
| Tires | Rotate | ✓ | | ✓ | | ✓ | | ✓ | | ✓ | | ✓ | | ✓ | | ✓ | |
| Air cleaner | Replace | | | | | | ✓ | | | | | | ✓ | | | | |
| Spark plugs ① | Replace | | | | | | | | | | | | ✓ | | | | |
| Drive belt | Inspect | | | | | | | | | | | | ✓ | | | | |
| Cooling system | Inspect | | | ✓ | | | ✓ | | | ✓ | | | ✓ | | | ✓ | |
| Coolant | Replace | | | | | | | ✓ | | | | | | | ✓ | | |
| PCV valve | Replace | | | | | | | | | | | | ✓ | | | | |
| Automatic transmission fluid and filter | Replace | | | | | | ✓ | | | | | | ✓ | | | | |
| Exhaust heat shields | Inspect | | | | | | ✓ | | | | | | ✓ | | | | |
| Brake linings and drums | Inspect | | ✓ | | ✓ | | ✓ | | ✓ | | ✓ | | ✓ | | ✓ | | ✓ |
| Brake pads and rotors | Inspect | | ✓ | | ✓ | | ✓ | | ✓ | | ✓ | | ✓ | | ✓ | | ✓ |
| Fuel filter | Replace | | | | | | ✓ | | | | | | ✓ | | | | |
| Lubricate suspension | Inspect | | ✓ | | ✓ | | ✓ | | ✓ | | ✓ | | ✓ | | ✓ | | ✓ |
| Brake line hoses and connections | Inspect | | | | | | ✓ | | | | | | ✓ | | | | |
| Front suspension | Inspect | | | | | | ✓ | | | | | | ✓ | | | | |
| Bolts and nuts on chassis body | Inspect | | | | | | ✓ | | | | | | ✓ | | | | |
| Steering linkage operation | Inspect | | | | | | ✓ | | | | | | ✓ | | | | |

Perform maintenance at the same intervals for mileage beyond that on this chart

Follow the normal service interval schedule if the vehicle is driven in the following conditions:

The vehicle is driven more than 10 miles on a daily basis

The vehicle is not used in the following conditions:

towing a trailer or using a car-top carrier

operating in severe dust conditions

extensive idling such as a police car, taxi, or delivery service

short trips of less than 10 miles when outside temperatures remain below 0°F (-18°C)

① Except on the 4.6L engines. Replace every 100,000 miles on the 4.6L engines.

93141C04

## MANUFACTURER RECOMMENDED SEVERE MAINTENANCE INTERVALS

| | | VEHICLE MAINTENANCE INTERVAL | | | | | | | | | | | | | | | | | | | |
|---|---|---|---|---|---|---|---|---|---|---|---|---|---|---|---|---|---|---|---|---|---|
| | Miles (x1000) | 3 | 6 | 9 | 12 | 15 | 18 | 21 | 24 | 27 | 30 | 33 | 36 | 39 | 42 | 45 | 48 | 51 | 54 | 57 | 60 |
| | km (x1000) | 5 | 10 | 15 | 20 | 25 | 30 | 35 | 40 | 45 | 50 | 55 | 60 | 65 | 70 | 75 | 80 | 85 | 90 | 95 | 100 |
| Component | Type of Service | | | | | | | | | | | | | | | | | | | | |
| Engine oil and filter | Replace | ✓ | ✓ | ✓ | ✓ | ✓ | ✓ | ✓ | ✓ | ✓ | ✓ | ✓ | ✓ | ✓ | ✓ | ✓ | ✓ | ✓ | ✓ | ✓ | ✓ |
| Tires | Rotate | | ✓ | | ✓ | | ✓ | | ✓ | | ✓ | | ✓ | | ✓ | | ✓ | | ✓ | | ✓ |
| Air cleaner | Replace | | | | | | | | | | ✓ | | | | | | | | | | ✓ |
| Spark plugs ① | Replace | | | | | | | | | | | | | | | | | | | | ✓ |
| Drive belt | Inspect | | | | | | | | | | | | | | | | | | | | ✓ |
| Cooling system | Inspect | | | | | ✓ | | | | | ✓ | | | | | ✓ | | | | | ✓ |
| Coolant | Replace | | | | | | | | | | | | | | | | ✓ | | | | |
| PCV valve | Replace | | | | | | | | | | | | | | | | | | | | ✓ |
| Automatic transmission fluid & filter | Replace | | | | | | | ✓ | | | | | | | ✓ | | | | | | |
| Exhaust heat shields | Inspect | | | | | | | | | | ✓ | | | | | | | | | | ✓ |
| Brake linings and drums | Inspect | | | ✓ | | | ✓ | | | ✓ | | | ✓ | | | ✓ | | | ✓ | | |
| Brake pads and rotors | Inspect | | | ✓ | | | ✓ | | | ✓ | | | ✓ | | | ✓ | | | ✓ | | |
| Fuel filter | Replace | | | | | ✓ | | | | | ✓ | | | | | | | | | | |
| Lubricate suspension | Inspect | | | | | ✓ | | | | | ✓ | | | | | ✓ | | | | | ✓ |
| Brake line hoses and connections | Inspect | | | | | ✓ | | | | | ✓ | | | | | ✓ | | | | | ✓ |
| Front suspension | Inspect | | | | | ✓ | | | | | ✓ | | | | | ✓ | | | | | ✓ |
| Bolts and nuts on chassis body | Inspect | | | | | ✓ | | | | | ✓ | | | | | ✓ | | | | | ✓ |
| Steering linkage operation | Inspect | | | | | ✓ | | | | | ✓ | | | | | ✓ | | | | | ✓ |

Perform maintenance at the same intervals for mileage beyond that on this chart

Follow the severe service interval schedule if the vehicle is driven in the following conditions:

towing a trailer or using a car-top carrier

operating in severe dust conditions

extensive idling such as a police car, taxi, or delivery service

short trips of less than 10 miles when outside temperatures remain below 0°F (-18°C)

① Except on the 4.6L engines. Replace every 100,000 miles on the 4.6L engines.

93141C05

## CAPACITIES

| Year | Model | Engine Displacement Liters (cc) | Engine ID/VIN | Engine Oil with Filter (qts.) | Automatic Transmission (pts.) | Rear Drive Axle (pts.) | Fuel Tank (gal.) | Cooling System (qts.) |
|---|---|---|---|---|---|---|---|---|
| 1988 | Town car | 5.0 (4943) | F | 5.0 | 24.6 | 3.8 | 22.1 | 14.1 |
| | Mark VII | 5.0 HO (4943) | E | 5.0 | 24.6 | 3.8 | 22.3 | 14.1 |
| | Continental | 3.8 (3802) | 4 | 4.5 | 26.2 | ① | 18.6 | 11.1 |
| 1989 | Town car | 5.0 (4943) | F | 5.0 | 24.6 | 3.8 | 22.3 | 14.1 |
| | Mark VII | 5.0 HO (4943) | E | 5.0 | 24.6 | 3.8 | 22.1 | 14.1 |
| | Continental | 3.8 (3802) | 4 | 4.5 | 26.2 | ① | 18.6 | 12.1 |
| 1990 | Town car | 5.0 (4943) | F | 5.0 | 24.6 | 3.8 | 18.0 | 14.1 |
| | Mark VII | 5.0 HO (4943) | E | 5.0 | 24.6 | 3.8 | 20.0 | 14.1 |
| | Continental | 3.8 (3802) | 4 | 4.5 | 25.6 | ① | 18.6 | 12.1 |
| 1991 | Town car | 4.6 (4593) | W | 5.0 | 24.6 | 3.8 | 20.0 | 14.1 |
| | Mark VII | 5.0 HO (4943) | E | 5.0 | 24.6 | 3.8 | 20.0 | 14.1 |
| | Continental | 3.8 (3802) | 4 | 4.5 | 25.6 | ① | 18.6 | 12.1 |
| 1992 | Town car | 4.6 (4593) | W | 5.0 | 24.6 | 3.8 | 20.0 | 14.1 |
| | Mark VII | 5.0 HO (4943) | E | 5.0 | 24.6 | 3.8 | 20.0 | 14.1 |
| | Continental | 3.8 (3802) | 4 | 4.5 | 25.6 | ① | 18.6 | 12.1 |
| 1993 | Town car | 4.6 (4593) | W | 5.0 | 24.6 | 4.1 | 20.0 | 14.1 |
| | Mark VIII | 4.6 (4593) | V | 6 | 24.6 | 3.0 | 18.0 | 14.1 |
| | Continental | 3.8 (3802) | 4 | 4.5 | 25.6 | ① | 18.4 | 11.1 |
| 1994 | Town car | 4.6 (4593) | W | 5.0 | 24.6 | 4.1 | 20.0 | 14.1 |
| | Mark VIII | 4.6 (4593) | V | 6 | 25 | 3.0 | 18.0 | 16.0 |
| | Continental | 3.8 (3802) | 4 | 4.5 | 27.4 ③ | ① | 18.4 | 12.1 |
| 1995 | Town car | 4.6 (4593) | W | 5.0 | 24.6 | 4.1 | 20.0 | 14.1 |
| | Mark VIII | 4.6 (4593) | V | 6 | 25 | 3.0 | 18.0 | 16 |
| | Continental | 4.6 (4593) | V | 6 | 27.4 ③ | ① | 18.4 | 14.3 |
| 1996 | Town car | 4.6 (4593) | W | 5.0 | 27.2 | ② | 20.0 | 14.1 |
| | Mark VIII | 4.6 (4593) | V | 6 | 25.6 | 3.0 | 18.0 | 16.0 |
| | Continental | 4.6 (4593) | V | 6 | 27.4 ③ | 3.0 | 17.8 | 14.3 |
| 1997 | Town car | 4.6 (4593) | W | 5.0 | 27.2 | ② | 20.0 | 14.1 |
| | Mark VIII | 4.6 (4593) | V | 6 | 25.6 | 3.0 | 18.0 | 16.0 |
| | Continental | 4.6 (4593) | V | 6 | 27.4 ③ | 3.0 | 17.8 | 14.3 |
| 1998 | Town car | 4.6 (4593) | W | 5.0 | 27.2 | ② | 20.0 | 14.1 |
| | Mark VIII | 4.6 (4593) | V | 6 | 25.6 | 3.0 | 18.0 | 16.0 |
| | Continental | 4.6 (4593) | V | 6 | 27.4 ③ | 3.0 | 17.8 | 14.3 |
| 1999 | Town car | 4.6 (4593) | W | 5.0 | 27.2 | ② | 20.0 | 14.1 |
| | Continental | 4.6 (4593) | V | 6 | 27.4 ③ | 3.0 | 17.8 | 14.3 |
| 2000 | Town car | 4.6 (4593) | W | 5.0 | 27.2 | ② | 20.0 | 14.1 |
| | Continental | 4.6 (4593) | V | 6 | 27.4 ③ | 3.0 | 17.8 | 14.3 |

NOTE: All capacities are approximate. Add fluid gradually and ensure a proper fluid level is obtained.

① Included in the transaxle capacity

② 7.50" axle: 3.0 pts.
8.80" axle: 3.25 pts.

③ Includes torque converter.

93141C06

**DISTRIBUTOR IGNITION 2-2**
GENERAL INFORMATION 2-2
THICK FILM INTEGRATED (TFI-IV) IGNITION SYSTEM 2-2
DIAGNOSIS AND TESTING 2-2
SECONDARY SPARK TEST 2-2
CYLINDER DROP TEST 2-3
ADJUSTMENTS 2-3
IGNITION COIL 2-3
TESTING 2-3
REMOVAL & INSTALLATION 2-4
IGNITION MODULE 2-4
REMOVAL & INSTALLATION 2-4
DISTRIBUTOR 2-5
REMOVAL & INSTALLATION 2-5
**DISTRIBUTORLESS IGNITION SYSTEM 2-6**
GENERAL INFORMATION 2-6
ELECTRONIC DISTRIBUTORLESS IGNITION SYSTEM (EDIS) 2-6
OBD II—EEC V 2-6
DIAGNOSIS AND TESTING 2-6
ADJUSTMENTS 2-6
IGNITION COIL PACK 2-6
TESTING 2-6
REMOVAL & INSTALLATION 2-6
IGNITION MODULE 2-7
REMOVAL & INSTALLATION 2-7
CRANKSHAFT AND CAMSHAFT POSITION SENSORS 2-8
**FIRING ORDERS 2-8**
**CHARGING SYSTEM 2-8**
ALTERNATOR PRECAUTIONS 2-8
ALTERNATOR 2-8
TESTING 2-8
REMOVAL & INSTALLATION 2-9
REGULATOR 2-9
REMOVAL & INSTALLATION 2-9
**STARTING SYSTEM 2-10**
STARTER 2-10
TESTING 2-10
REMOVAL & INSTALLATION 2-10
SOLENOID/RELAY REPLACEMENT 2-10
**SENDING UNITS AND SENSORS 2-10**
SENDING UNITS AND SENSORS 2-10
COOLANT TEMPERATURE SENSOR 2-10
TESTING 2-10
REMOVAL & INSTALLATION 2-10
OIL PRESSURE SENDER/SWITCH 2-11
TESTING 2-11
REMOVAL & INSTALLATION 2-11
LOW OIL LEVEL SENSOR 2-11
TESTING 2-11
REMOVAL & INSTALLATION 2-11
ELECTRIC FAN SWITCH 2-12
TESTING 2-12
REMOVAL & INSTALLATION 2-12


# 2

# ENGINE ELECTRICAL


DISTRIBUTOR IGNITION 2-2
DISTRIBUTORLESS IGNITION SYSTEM 2-6
FIRING ORDERS 2-8
CHARGING SYSTEM 2-8
STARTING SYSTEM 2-10
SENDING UNITS AND SENSORS 2-10

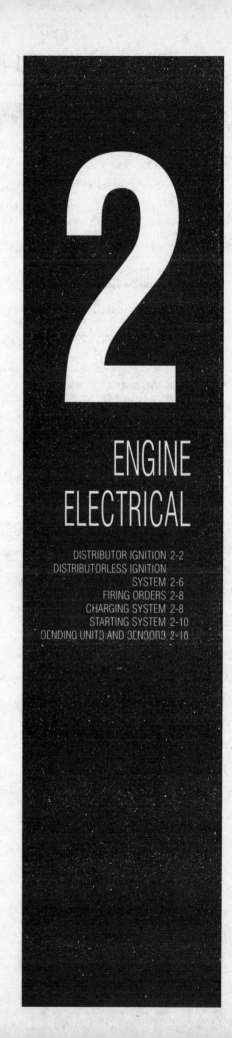

# DISTRIBUTOR IGNITION

**➡For information on understanding electricity and troubleshooting electrical circuits, please refer to Section 6 of this manual.**

Distributors are used in the Town Car with a 5.0L engine up until the 1991 model year. The Mark VII employed a distributor until the end of the model run in 1992. The 3.8L Continental also incorporated the TFI-IV ignition system and the use of a distributor until 1994.

## General Information

### THICK FILM INTEGRATED (TFI-IV) IGNITION SYSTEM

**➧ See Figures 1, 2, 3, 4 and 5**

The Thick Film Integrated (TFI-IV) ignition system uses a camshaft driven distributor with no centrifugal or vacuum advance. The distributor has a diecast base, incorporating a Hall effect stator assembly. The TFI-IV system module is mounted on the distributor base, it has 6 pins and uses an E-Core ignition coil, named after the shape of the laminations making up the core.

The TFI-IV module supplies voltage to the Profile Ignition Pick-up (PIP) sensor, which sends the crankshaft position information to the TFI-IV module. The TFI-IV module then sends this information to the EEC-IV module, which determines the spark timing and sends an electronic signal to the TFI-IV ignition module to turn off the coil and produce a spark to fire the spark plug.

The operation of the universal distributor is accomplished through the Hall effect stator assembly, causing the ignition coil to be switched off and on by the EEC-IV computer and TFI-IV modules. The vane switch is an encapsulated package consisting of a Hall sensor on one side and a permanent magnet on the other side.

A rotary vane cup, made of ferrous metal, is used to trigger the Hall effect switch. When the window of the vane cup is between the magnet and the Hall effect device, a magnetic flux field is completed from the magnet through the Hall effect device back to the magnet. As the vane passes through the opening, the flux lines are shunted through the vane and back to the magnet. A voltage is produced while the vane passes through the opening. When the vane clears the opening, the window causes the signal to go to 0 volts. The signal is then used by the EEC-IV system for crankshaft position sensing and the computation of the desired spark advance based on the engine demand and calibration. The voltage distribution is accomplished through a conventional rotor, cap and ignition wires.

## Diagnosis and Testing

### SECONDARY SPARK TEST

**➧ See Figures 6, 7, 8 and 9**

The best way to perform this procedure is to use a spark tester (available at most automotive parts stores). Three types of spark testers are commonly available. The Neon Bulb type is connected to the spark plug wire and flashes with each ignition pulse. The Air Gap type must be adjusted to the individual spark plug gap specified for the engine. The last type of spark plug tester looks like a spark plug with a grounding clip on the side, but there is no side electrode for the spark to jump to. The last two types of testers allows the user to not only detect the presence of spark, but also the intensity (orange/yellow is weak, blue is strong).

1. Disconnect a spark plug wire at the spark plug end.
2. Connect the plug wire to the spark tester and ground the tester to an appropriate location on the engine.
3. Crank the engine and check for spark at the tester.
4. If spark exists at the tester, the ignition system is functioning properly.
5. If spark does not exist at the spark plug wire,

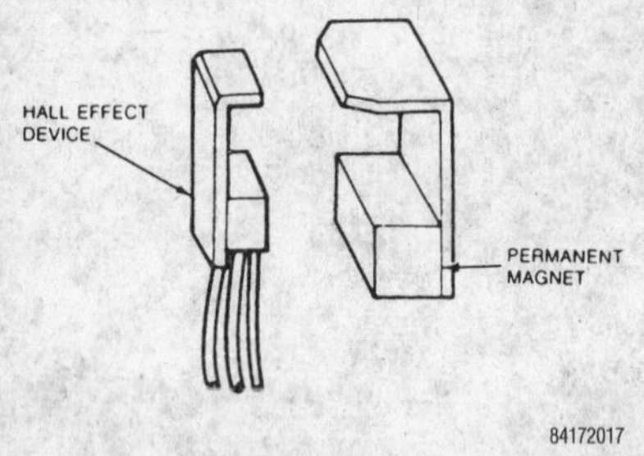


**Fig. 1 Hall effect vane switch assembly**

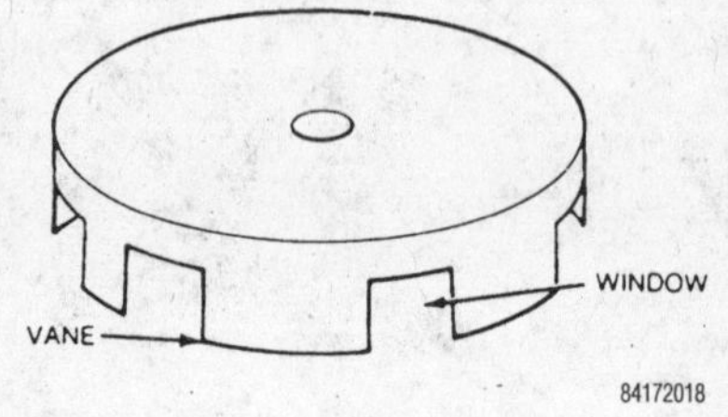


**Fig. 2 Rotary vane cup**

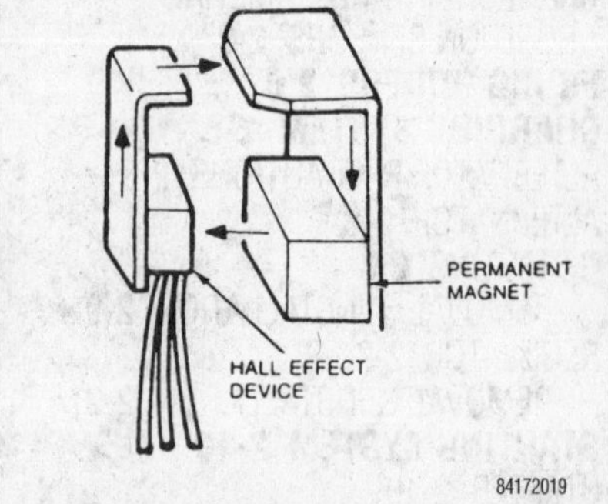


**Fig. 3 Hall effect response to vane cup window**

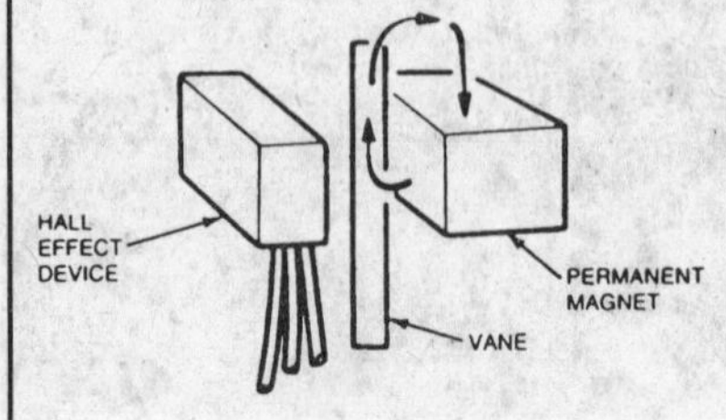


**Fig. 4 Hall effect response to vane**

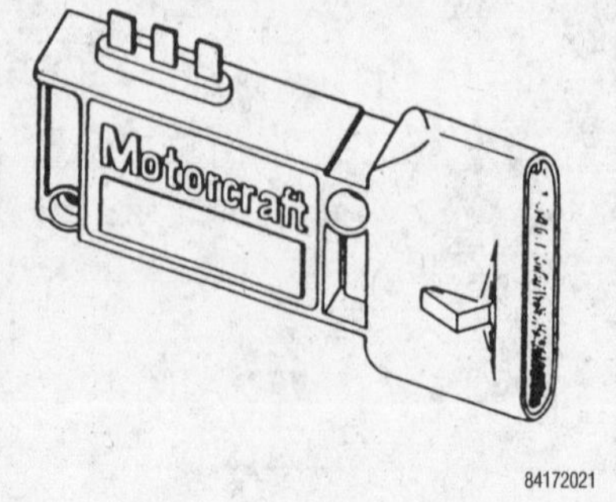


**Fig. 5 TFI-IV module**

**Fig. 6 This spark tester looks just like a spark plug, attach the clip to ground and crank the engine to check for spark**

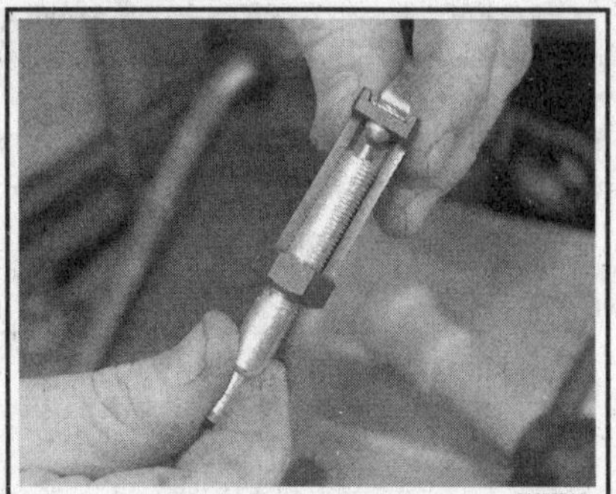

91052P11

**Fig. 7 This spark tester has an adjustable air-gap for measuring spark strength and testing different voltage ignition systems**

perform diagnosis of the ignition system using individual component diagnosis procedures.

### CYLINDER DROP TEST

**See Figures 10, 11 and 12**

The cylinder drop test is performed when an engine misfire is evident. This test helps determine which cylinder is not contributing the proper power. The easiest way to perform this test is to remove the plug wires one at a time from the cylinders with the engine running.

1. Place the transmission in **P**, engage the emergency brake, and start the engine and let it idle.
2. Using a spark plug wire removing tool, preferably, the plier type, carefully remove the boot from one of the cylinders.

91052P12

**Fig. 8 Attach the clip to ground and crank the engine to check for spark**

**CAUTION**

**Make sure your body is free from touching any part of the car which is metal. The secondary voltage in the ignition system is high and although it cannot kill you, it will shock you and it does hurt.**

3. The engine will sputter, run worse, and possibly nearly stall. If this happens reinstall the plug wire and move to the next cylinder. If the engine runs no differently, or the difference is minimal, shut the engine off and inspect the spark plug wire, spark plug, and if necessary, perform component diagnostics as covered in this section. Perform the test on all cylinders to verify which cylinders are suspect.

91052P13

**Fig. 9 This spark tester is the easiest to use just place it on a plug wire and the spark voltage is detected and the bulb on the top will flash with each pulse**

## Adjustments

The only adjustment available on the TFI-IV system is the timing. Refer to Section 1 for Timing inspection and adjustment.

## Ignition Coil

### TESTING

#### Primary Coil

**See Figures 13, 14 and 15**

The first check of the primary ignition coil is to verify that there is battery voltage at the **BATT** ter-

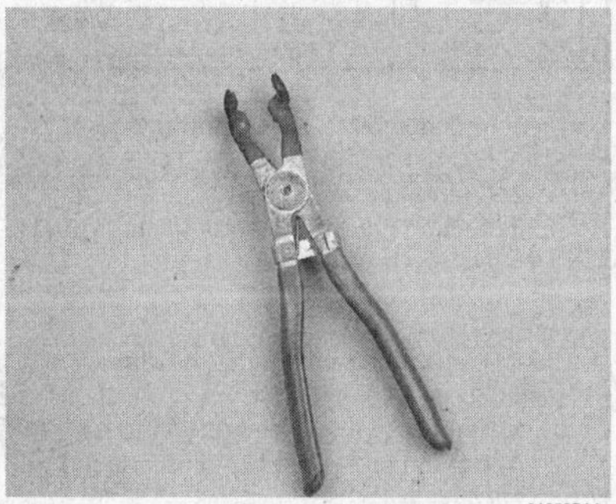

91052P14

**Fig. 10 These pliers are insulated and help protect the user from shock as well as the plug wires from being damaged**

91052P15

**Fig. 11 To perform the cylinder drop test, remove one wire at a time and . . .**

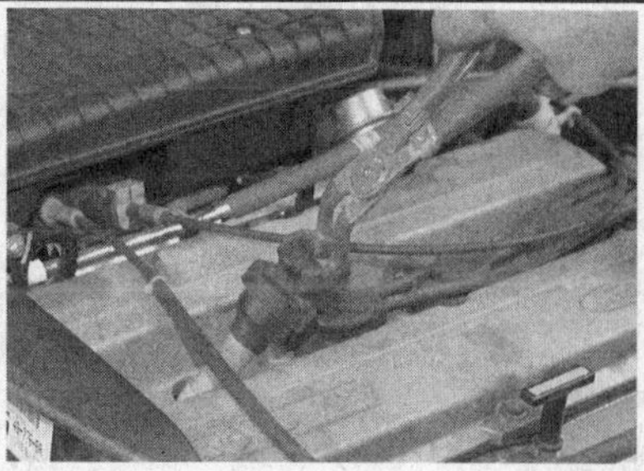

91052P16

**Fig. 12 . . . note the idle speed and idle characteristics of the engine. The cylinder(s) with the least drop is the non-contributing cylinder(s)**

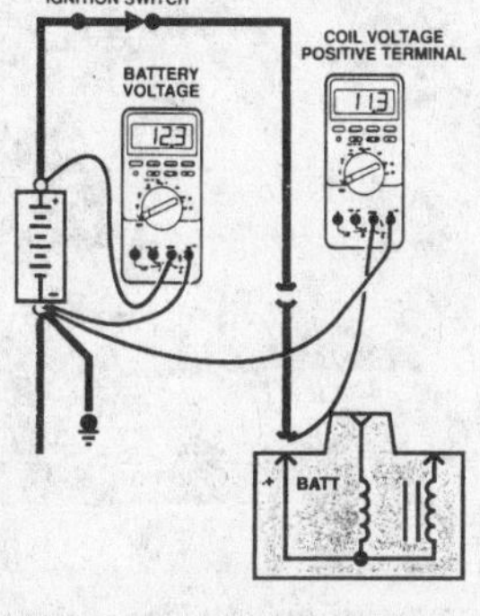


91192G01

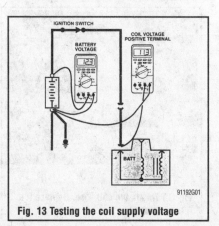

**Fig. 13 Testing the coil supply voltage**

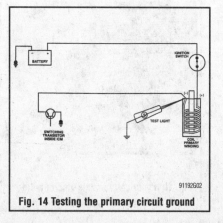

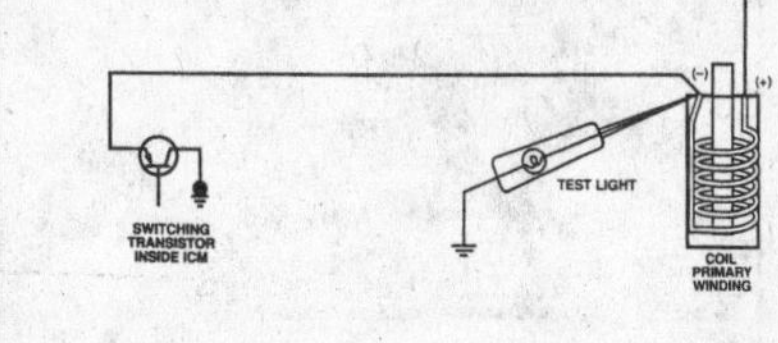


91192G02

**Fig. 14 Testing the primary circuit ground**

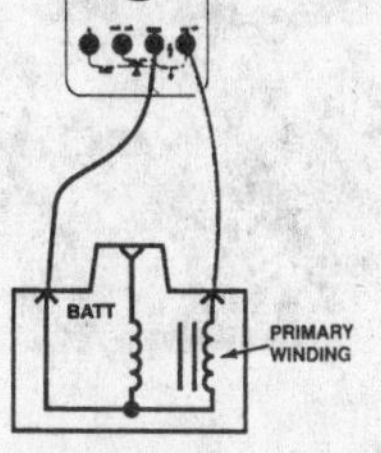

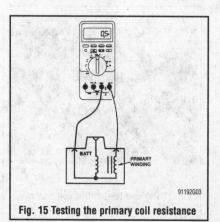

91192G03

**Fig. 15 Testing the primary coil resistance**

minal on the coil. A DVOM is recommended to test for voltage. Turn the ignition switch to the **RUN** position and connect the negative lead of the DVOM to a ground or the negative post/cable clamp on the battery. Connect the other lead of the DVOM to the **BATT** terminal on the coil. The voltage measured should be within 1 volt of the battery voltage as measure across the posts of the battery.

After verifying there is battery voltage present, the next check is to verify the operation of the coil primary ground which is received at the coil from the ICM (Ignition Control Module). This check is accomplished using a test lamp and connecting the lead of the test lamp to the ground or the battery negative post/cable clamp. Connect the test lamp to the ground side of the coil (the connection opposite the **BATT** terminal on the coil on the other side of the coil tower) and crank the engine. The light should blink on and off repeatedly as long as the engine cranks or runs. If the light does not blink the problem is either in the ICM or the **PIP** signal generated by the sensor inside the distributor.

The final check of the primary coil is to check the resistance of the coil. This is accomplished by using a DVOM and probing the **BATT** terminal and the coil ground terminal. Measure the resistance between the two terminals. If the resistance is between 0.3 and 1.0 ohm, the primary ignition coil is within specifications. If the reading differs from this specification, replace the coil and retest.

**Secondary Windings**

**➧ See Figure 16**

The coil secondary resistance is the final check of the ignition coil. Use a DVOM to measure the resistance between the **BATT** terminal to the high voltage terminal of the ignition coil. If the reading is between 6,500–11,500 ohms, the ignition coil is OK. If the reading is less than 6,500 or more than 11,500 ohms, replace the ignition coil. If the secondary windings are within specifications and the primary circuit also tests within specifications, inspect and test the spark plug wires and the spark plugs, refer to Section 1.

REMOVAL & INSTALLAIION

**➧ See Figures 17, 18, 19 and 20**

1. Disconnect the negative battery cable.
2. Disengage the TFI-IV harness or the engine control sensor wiring connector from the ignition coil, as applicable.
3. On the 3.8L engine, disengage the engine control wiring connector from the radio ignition interference capacitor.
4. Remove the ignition coil retaining screws and the ignition coil and radio interference capacitor (if equipped) from the ignition coil mounting bracket.
5. Remove the ignition coil cover from the ignition coil by releasing the locking tabs on both sides of the cover, then remove the ignition coil.

**To install:**

6. Install the ignition coil, then attach ignition coil cover, making sure the cover is firmly in place.
7. If removed, connect the ignition coil and radio interference capacitor, then install the ignition coil retaining screws. Tighten the retaining screws to 25–35 inch lbs. (3–4 Nm).
8. Connect the coil wire, then engage any electrical connectors that were removed.
9. Connect the negative battery cable.

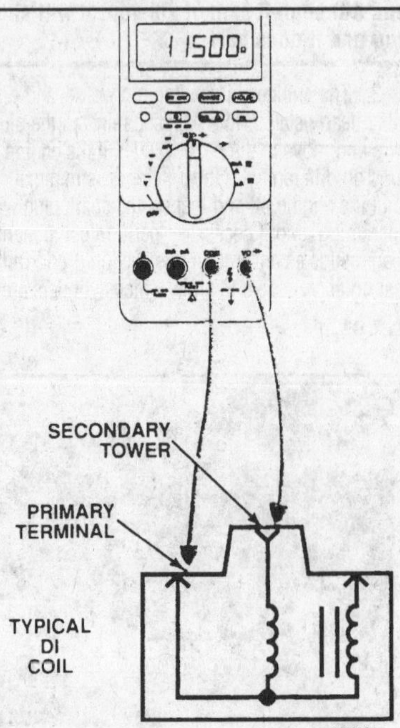


**Fig. 16 Testing the coil secondary resistance**

## Ignition Module

**➡In earlier models, the ICM was referred to as the TFI-IV Ignition Module; the name was later changed to Ignition Control Module (ICM).**

REMOVAL & INSTALLATION

**➧ See Figures 21 and 22**

1. Disconnect the negative battery cable.
2. Remove the screws attaching the cowl vent screen to the top of the cowl.

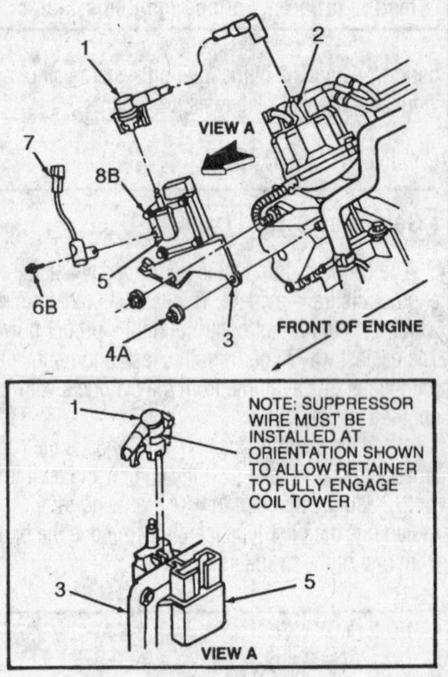


1 Ignition coil to distributor high tension wiring
2 Distributor cap
3 Ignition coil mounting bracket
4A Nut (2 req'd)
5 Ignition coil
6B Screw
7 Radio ignition interference capacitor
8B Screw (4 req'd)
A Tighten to 40-50 Nm (30-41 lb.ft.)
B Tighten to 2.8-4.0 Nm (25-35 lb.in.)

86872032

**Fig. 17 Ignition coil and related components—late model 3.8L shown**

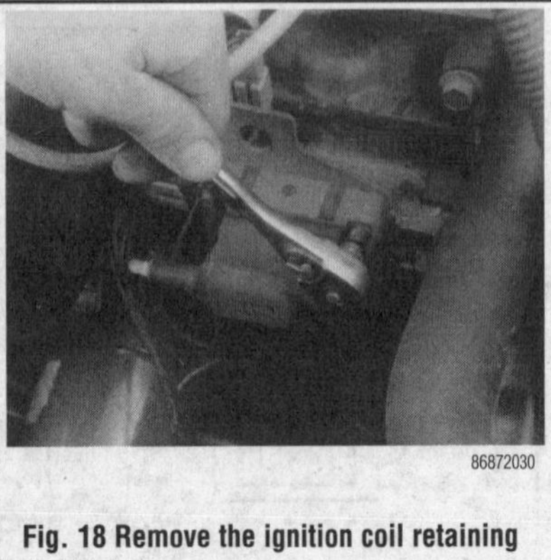

86872030

**Fig. 18 Remove the ignition coil retaining screws**

93142P26

**Fig. 19 If your coil has this kind of build-up, it needs a good cleaning**

93144P18

**Fig. 20 This is the coil wire. Replace it if it looks like this**

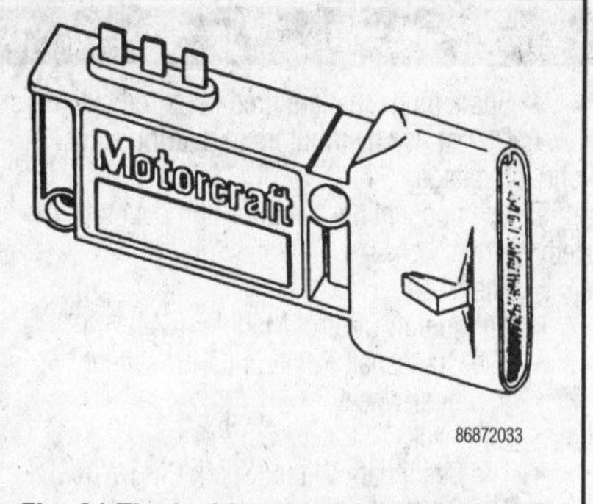


**Fig. 21 The ignition control module (or TFI ignition module, as applicable), is located on the distributor—5.0L engines**

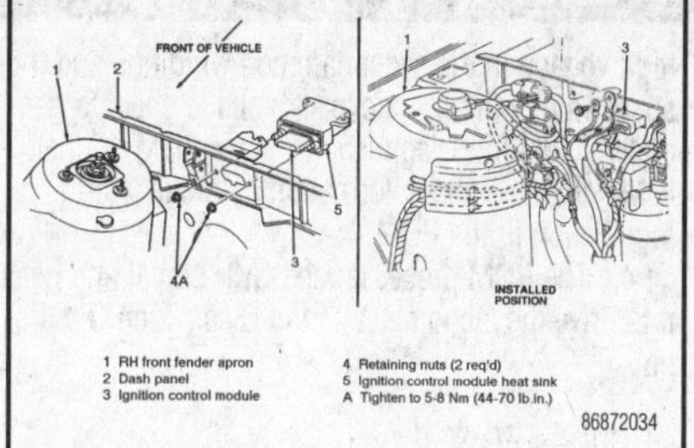


**Fig. 22 Location of the ignition control module—3.8L engines only**

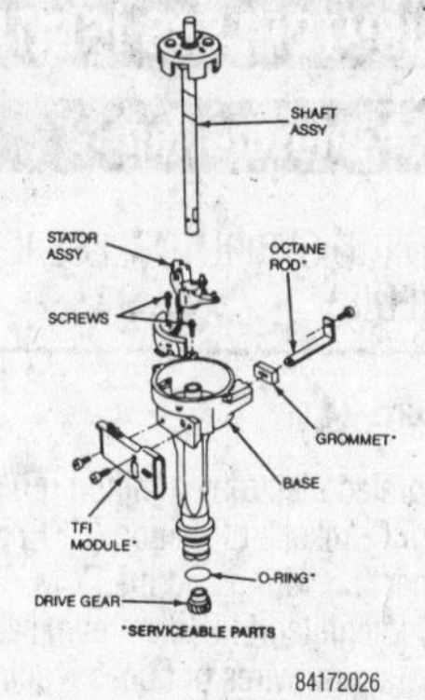

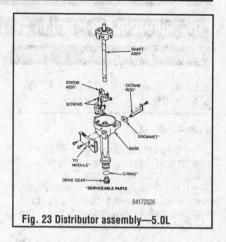

**Fig. 23 Distributor assembly—5.0L**

3. Separate the engine compartment cowl seal strip from the cowl vent screen and the cowl dash extension panel in the area of the ignition control module.

4. Lift the cowl vent screen off to allow access to the ignition control module/TFI module assembly.

**➡The connector latch is underneath the ICM/TFI shroud. Press upward to unlatch.**

5. Disengage the engine control sensor wiring connector from the ICM or TFI, as applicable.

**➡The ignition control module and heatsink are mounted with the heatsink fins pointed downward.**

6. Remove the two retaining nuts attaching the ICM/TFI and heatsink to the dash panel, then remove the ICM/TFI and the heatsink.

7. Remove the two module retaining screws, then remove the ICM or TFI from the heatsink.

8. While holding the module connector shroud with one hand, pull the seal off the other end of the module.

**To install:**

9. Coat the metal base of the ICM or TFI module uniformly with a thin film of Silicone Dielectric Compound D7AZ-19A331-A or equivalent.

10. Place the module onto the heatsink. Install the retaining screws, then tighten them to 15–35 inch lbs. (1.7–4.0 Nm).

11. Push the seal over the module connector shroud and heatsink studs with the metal part toward the heatsink.

12. Insert the module and heatsink into the cowl dash extension panel enough to have the mounting studs protrude into the engine compartment side.

13. Hand-tighten the retaining nuts to 44–70 inch lbs. (5–8 Nm).

14. Engage the engine control sensor wiring connector to the module.

15. Install the cowl vent screen and retaining screws, then install the engine compartment cowl panel and seal strip.

16. Connect the negative battery cable.

## Distributor

### REMOVAL & INSTALLATION

**▶ See Figure 23**

1. Bring the engine to TDC on the number 1 cylinder.

2. Disconnect the negative battery cable.

3. Mark the position of the No. 1 cylinder wire tower onto the distributor base.

**➡This reference is necessary in case the engine is disturbed while the distributor is removed.**

4. Remove the distributor cap and position the cap and ignition wires to the side. Disconnect the wiring harness plug from the distributor connector.

5. Scribe a mark on the distributor body to indicate the position of the rotor tip. Scribe a mark on the outside base of the distributor housing and the engine block to indicate the position of the distributor in the engine.

6. Remove the hold-down bolt and clamp located at the base of the distributor. Remove the distributor from the engine. Note the direction the rotor tip points as it moves from the No. 1 position when the drive gear disengages. For reinstallation purposes, the rotor should be at this point to insure proper gear mesh and timing.

7. Cover the distributor opening in the engine to prevent the entry of dirt or foreign material.

8. Avoid turning the engine, if possible, while the distributor is removed. If the engine is disturbed, the No. 1 cylinder piston will have to be brought to Top Dead Center (TDC) on the compression stroke before the distributor is installed.

**➡Before installing, visually inspect the distributor. The drive gear should be free of nicks, cracks and excessive wear. The distributor drive shaft should move freely, without binding. If equipped with an O-ring, it should fit tightly and be free of cuts.**

#### Timing Not Disturbed

1. Position the distributor in the engine, aligning the rotor and distributors housing with the marks that were made during removal. If the distributor does not fully seat in the engine block or timing cover, it may be because the distributor is not engaging properly with the oil pump intermediate shaft. Remove the distributor and, using a screwdriver or similar tool, turn the intermediate shaft until the distributor will seat properly.

2. Install the hold-down clamp and bolt. Snug the mounting bolt so the distributor can be turned for ignition timing purposes.

3. Install the distributor cap and connect the distributor to the wiring harness.

4. Connect the negative battery cable. Check and, if necessary, set the ignition timing. Tighten the distributor hold-down clamp bolt to 17–25 ft. lbs. (23–34 Nm). Recheck the ignition timing after tightening the bolt.

#### Timing Disturbed (Engine Rotated)

1. Disconnect the No. 1 cylinder spark plug wire and remove the No. 1 cylinder spark plug.

2. Place a finger over the spark plug hole and crank the engine slowly until compression is felt.

3. Align the TDC mark on the crankshaft pulley with the pointer on the timing cover. This places the piston in No. 1 cylinder at TDC on the compression stroke.

4. Turn the distributor shaft until the rotor points to the distributor cap No. 1 spark plug tower.

5. Install the distributor in the engine, aligning the rotor and distributor housing with the marks that were made during removal. If the distributor does not fully seat in the engine block or timing cover, it may be because the distributor is not engaging properly with the oil pump intermediate shaft. Remove the distributor and, using a screwdriver or similar tool, turn the intermediate shaft until the distributor will seat properly.

6. Install the hold-down clamp and bolt. Snug the mounting bolt so the distributor can be turned for ignition timing purposes.

7. Install the No. 1 cylinder spark plug and connect the spark plug wire. Install the distributor cap and connect the distributor to the wiring harness.

8. Connect the negative battery cable and set the ignition timing.

9. After the timing has been set, tighten the distributor hold-down clamp bolt to 17–25 ft. lbs. (23–34 Nm). Recheck the ignition timing after tightening the bolt.

# DISTRIBUTORLESS IGNITION SYSTEM

## General Information

### ELECTRONIC DISTRIBUTORLESS IGNITION SYSTEM (EDIS)

**➧ See Figure 24**

The Integrated Electronic Ignition (EI) system consists of a Crankshaft Position (CKP) Sensor, coil packs, connecting wiring and the PCM. The Coil On Plug (COP) Integrated EI System eliminates the need for spark plug wires but does require input from the Camshaft Position (CMP) Sensor. Operation of the components is as follows:

**➡Electronic Ignition engine timing is entirely controlled by the PCM. Electronic Ignition engine timing is NOT adjustable. Do not attempt to check base timing. You will receive false readings.**

1. The CKP Sensor is used to indicate crankshaft position and speed by sensing a missing tooth on a pulse wheel mounted to the crankshaft. The CMP Sensor is used by the COP Integrated EI System to identify top dead center of compression of cylinder #1 to synchronizer the firing of the individual coils.
2. The PCM uses the CKP signal to calculate a spark target and then fires the coil packs to that target. The PCM uses the CMP sensor on COP Integrated EI System to identify top dead center of the compression of cylinder #1 to synchronizer the firing of the individual coils.
3. The coils and coil packs receive their signal from the PCM to fire at a calculated spark target. Each coil within the pack fires two spark plugs at the same time. The plugs are paired so that as one fires during the compression stroke the other fires during the exhaust stroke. The next time the coil is fired the situation is reversed. The COP system fires only one spark plug per coil and only on the compression stroke.

The PCM acts as an electronic switch to ground in the coil primary circuit. When the switch is closed, battery power applied to the coil primary circuit builds a magnetic field around the primary coil;. When the switch opens, the power is interrupted and the primary field collapses inducing the high voltage in the secondary coil windings and the spark plug is fired. A kickback voltage spike to generate an Ignition Diagnostic Monitor (IDM) signal. IDM communicates information by pulse width modulation in the PCM.

4. The PCM processes the CKP signal and uses it to drive the tachometer as the Clean Tach Out signal.

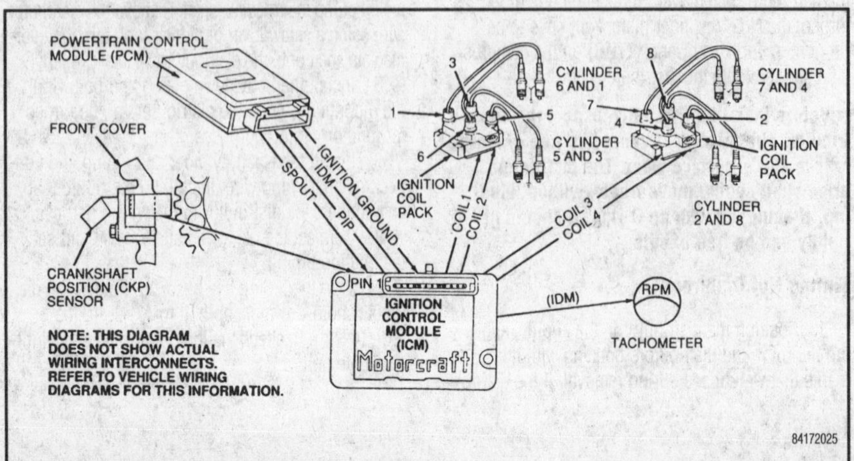


**Fig. 24 Electronic Distributorless Ignition System**

### OBD II—EEC V

The clean air act of 1990 requires that all vehicles sold in the United States meet On-Board Diagnostic (OBD)II requirements by the 1996 model year. Ford's fifth generation of electronic engine control systems, known as EEC V, is designed to meet OBD II requirements. The primary difference between EEC IV and EEC V are the monitors. EEC IV monitors are designed to detect system and component failure. EEC V monitors are designed to monitor the efficiency of engine and emission systems. The Malfunction Indicator Lamp (MIL) illuminates if the vehicle emissions exceed 1.5 times the allowable standard based on federal test procedures. If any single component or strategy failure permits emissions to exceed this level, the MIL illuminates to alert the operator and a Diagnostic Trouble Code (DTC) will be stored the Powertrain Control Module (PCM).

Lincoln vehicles produced by Ford in North America could come equipped (depending on the year) with either of two types of ignition systems. A (DI) distributor ignition (discussed earlier in this section), or an (EI) electronic ignition. EI systems are Distributorless. They contain multiple coils, known as coil packs. Secondary voltage is delivered directly from the coils to the spark plugs via spark plug wires. This ignition system also uses the EEC system to control spark timing.

There are two types of EI ignition systems:

- Low data rate
- High data rate

The vehicles discussed here use a high data rate system, on the 4.6L engine.

There are many similarities between the EI—low data rate and high data rate ignition systems. Both systems have the following similar features:

- Coil packs that contain multiple coils
- Spark plugs that are fired in paired cylinders
- Do not use distributors to distribute secondary voltage.

The components in the EI—high data rate system include:

- The PCM
- An Ignition Control Module (ICM)
- The Crankshaft Position (CKP) sensor
- A Trigger wheel
- Coil packs
- The Secondary Wires (Spark Plug Wires)
- The Spark plugs

## Diagnosis and Testing

Refer to Diagnosis and Testing under Distributor Ignition in this section.

## Adjustments

All adjustments in the ignition system are controlled by the Powertrain Control Module (PCM) for optimum performance. No adjustments are possible.

## Ignition Coil Pack

### TESTING

#### Primary Winding Resistance

**➧ See Figure 25**

1. Turn the ignition **OFF**.
2. Disconnect the negative battery cable.
3. Disconnect the wiring harness from the ignition coil.
4. Check for dirt, corrosion or damage on the terminals and repair as necessary.
5. Measure coil primary resistance between ignition coil pin 2 (B+) and pins 1 (coil 2), 2 (coil 3) and 3 (coil 1).
6. Resistance should be 0.3–1.0 ohms. If resistance is out of specifications, replace the coil pack. If resistance is within specifications, proceed to secondary windings testing.

#### Secondary Winding Resistance

**➧ See Figure 26**

1. Measure coil secondary resistance between the corresponding spark plug wire towers on the coil.
   - Coil 1—cylinders 1 and 6
   - Coil 2—cylinders 3 and 5
   - Coil 3—cylinders 4 and 7
   - Coil 4—cylinders 2 and 8
2. Resistance should be 12.8–13.1 kilohms. If secondary resistance is not within specification, replace the coil pack.

### REMOVAL & INSTALLATION

**➧ See Figures 27, 28, 29 and 30**

**➡Two ignition coil packs are used, one for each bank of cylinders. This procedure is for removing 1 ignition coil pack, but the procedure remains the same for either side.**

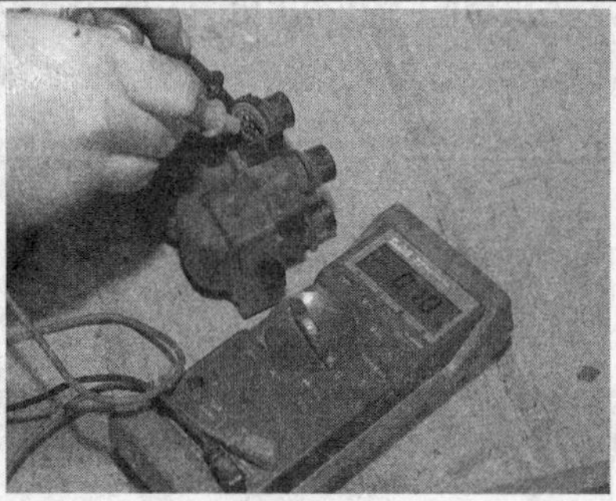

91192P07

Fig. 25 Testing the primary ignition coil resistance–4.6L engine

91192P03

Fig. 26 Testing the secondary ignition coil resistance–4.6L engine

91192P02

Fig. 27 Remove the ignition wires from the coil pack by squeezing the retaining tabs and carefully lifting up

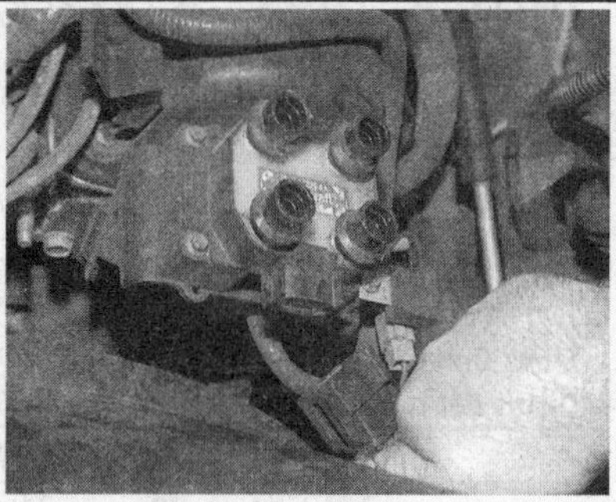

91192P04

Fig. 28 Detach the connector for the coil pack

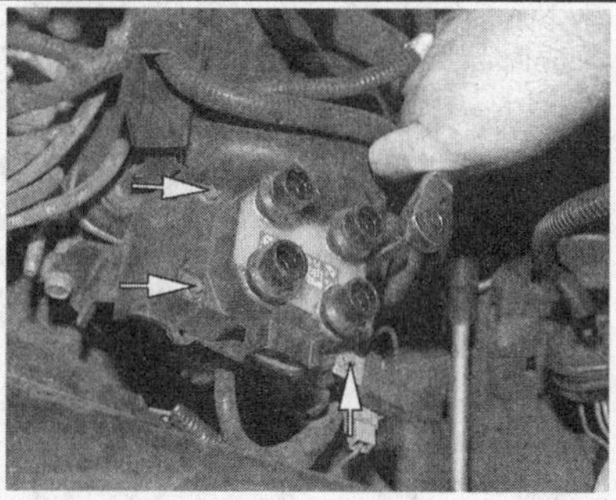

91192P05

Fig. 29 Remove the four coil pack retaining screws and . . .

91192P06

Fig. 30 . . . remove the coil pack from the bracket

1. Disconnect the negative battery cable.
2. Detach the ignition coil and radio ignition interference capacitor electrical harness connectors.
3. Tag the ignition wires and note their location on the coil pack before removing. Remove the ignition wires by squeezing the locking tabs to release the coil boot retainers and twisting while pulling upward.
4. Remove 4 ignition coil retaining screws and remove the ignition coil and radio capacitor.
5. If replacing the ignition coil, save the radio capacitor for installation on the new ignition coil.

**To install:**

6. Place the ignition coil and radio capacitor on the mounting bracket.
7. Install 4 retaining screws and tighten to 40–61 inch lbs. (5–7 Nm).
8. Install the ignition wires to their proper terminals on the ignition coil. Apply silicone dielectric compound to the ignition wire boots prior to installation.
9. Connect the electrical harness connectors to the ignition coil and the radio ignition interference capacitor.
10. Connect the negative battery cable.
11. Road test the vehicle and check for proper engine operation.

## Ignition Module

### REMOVAL & INSTALLATION

**➧ See Figures 31, 32 and 33**

1. Disconnect the negative battery cable.
2. Remove the module retaining screws and remove the module from the fender.

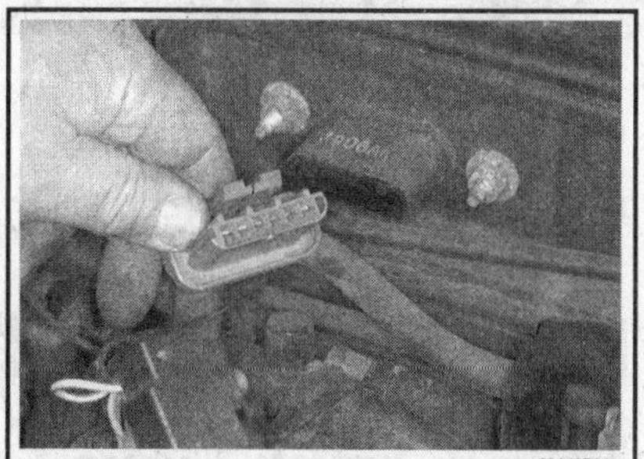

93142P21

Fig. 31 Detach the electrical connectors at the module by pushing in on the connector finger ends while grasping the connector body and pulling away from the module

93142P20

Fig. 32 Remove the module retaining screws and . . .

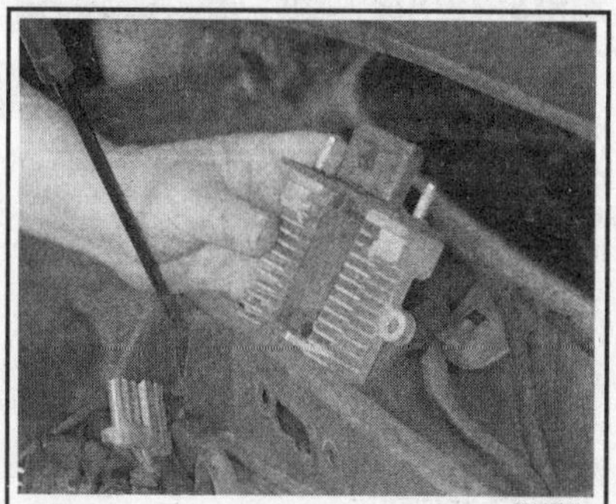

93144P03

Fig. 33 . . . remove the module from the fender

3. Detach the electrical connector at the module by pushing in on the connector finger ends while grasping the connector body and pulling away from the module.

**To install:**

4. Attach the electrical connector to the module by pushing until the connector fingers are locked over the locking wedge feature on the module.
5. Install the module and the retaining screws. Tighten the screws to 24–35 inch lbs. (3–4 Nm).

**➡Locking the connector is important to ensure sealing of the connector/module interface.**

6. Connect the negative battery cable.

## Crankshaft and Camshaft Position Sensors

For procedures on the position sensors, please refer to Section 4 in this manual.

# FIRING ORDERS

**See Figures 34, 35, 36a and 36b**

**➡To avoid confusion, remove, and tag the spark plug wires one at a time, for replacement**

If a distributor is not keyed for installation with only one orientation, it could have been removed previously and rewired. The resultant wiring would hold the correct firing order, but could change the relative placement of the plug towers in relation to the engine. For this reason, it is imperative that you label all wires before disconnecting any of them. Also, before removal, compare the current wiring with the accompanying illustrations. If the current wiring does not match, make notes in your book to reflect how your engine is wired.

On the 3.8L and 5.0L engine's ignition system, the distributor is driven off the camshaft and uses no centrifugal or vacuum advance. The distributor operates by using a Hall effect vane switch assembly, causing the ignition coil to be switched on and off by the EEC-IV and TFI-IV modules.

The 4.6L engine uses no distributor. The ignition system is the EDIS system, which consists of a crankshaft sensor, ignition module ignition coil pack, the spark angle portion of the Powertrain Control Module (PCM), and the related wiring. The EDIS eliminates the need for a distributor by using multiple ignition coils.

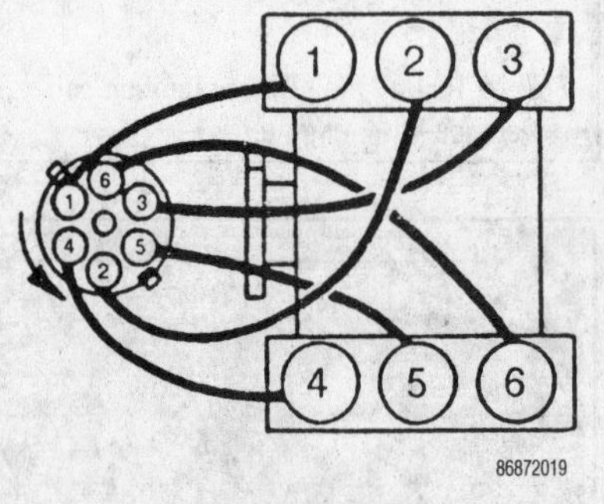


**Fig. 34 3.8L Engine**
**Firing Order 1-4-2-5-3-6**
**Distributor rotation: Counterclockwise**

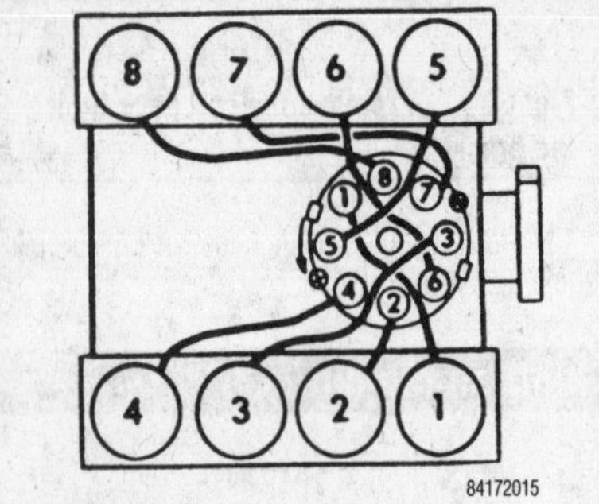


**Fig. 35 5.0L Engine**
**Firing Order 1-5-4-2-6-3-7-8**
**Distributor rotation: Counterclockwise**

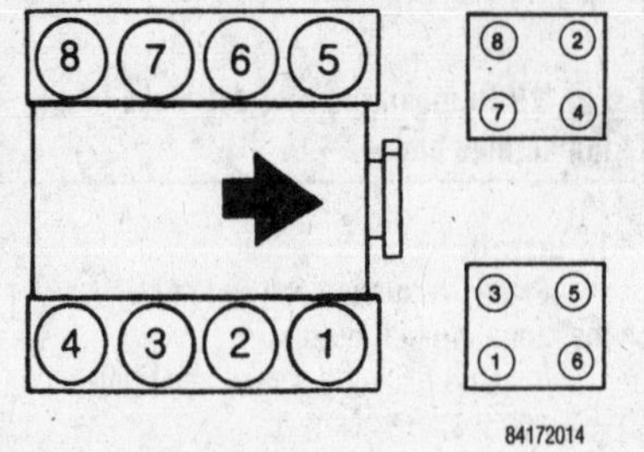


**Fig. 36a 4.6L Engine**
**Firing Order 1-3-7-2-6-5-4-8**
**Distributorless ignition system - all except 1995 through 1997 Continental**

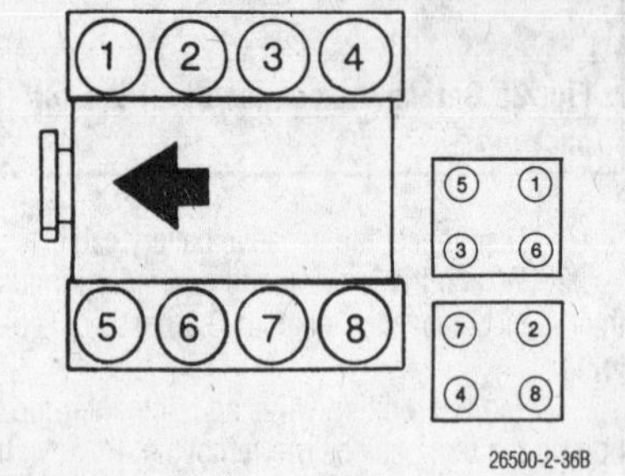


**Fig. 36b 4.6L Engine**
**Firing Order 1-3-7-2-6-5-4-8**
**Distributorless ignition system - 1995 through 1997 Continentals**

# CHARGING SYSTEM

## Alternator precautions

Several precautions must be observed when performing work on the alternator equipment.

- If the battery is removed for any reason, make sure that it is reconnected with the correct polarity. Reversing the battery connections may result in damage to the one-way rectifiers.
- Never operate the alternator with the main circuit broken. Make sure that the battery, alternator, and regulator leads are not disconnected while the engine is running.
- Never attempt to polarize an alternator.
- When charging a battery that is installed in the vehicle, disconnect the negative battery cable.
- When utilizing a booster battery as a starting aid, always connect it in parallel; positive to positive, and negative to negative.
- When arc (electric) welding is to be performed on any part of the vehicle, disconnect the negative battery cable and alternator leads.
- Never unplug the PCM while the engine is running or with the ignition in the ON position. Severe and expensive damage may result within the sold state equipment.

## Alternator

### Testing

#### Voltage test

1. Make sure the engine is OFF, and turn the headlights on for 15–20 seconds to remove any surface charge from the battery.
2. Using a DVOM set to volts DC, probe across the battery terminals.
3. Measure the battery voltage.
4. Write down the voltage reading and proceed to the next test.

#### No-Load test

1. Connect a tachometer to the engine.

**CAUTION:**

**Ensure that the transmission is in PARK and the emergency brake is set. Blocking a wheel is optional and an added safety measure.**

2. Turn off all electrical loads (radio, blower motor, wipers, etc.).
3. Start the engine and increase engine speed to approximately 1500 rpm.
4. Measure the voltage reading at the battery with the engine holding a steady 1500 rpm. Voltage

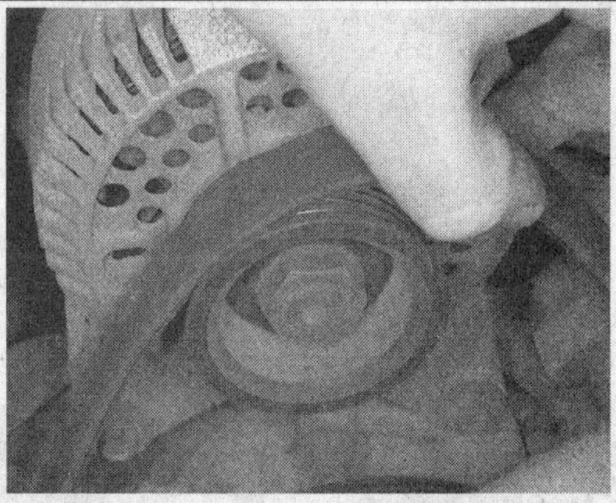
89602P01

Fig. 37 Rotate the tensioner and remove the belt from around the alternator pulley

89602P02

Fig. 38 Detach the 2 connectors from the alternator

89602P03

Fig. 39 Slide the boot up to access the battery cable on the rear of the alternator

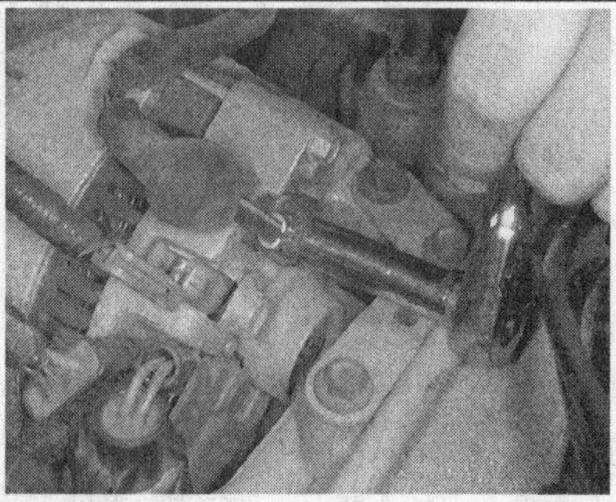
89602P04

Fig. 40 Remove the nut retaining the battery cable and . . .

89602P05

Fig. 41 . . . remove the battery cable from the post on the rear of the alternator

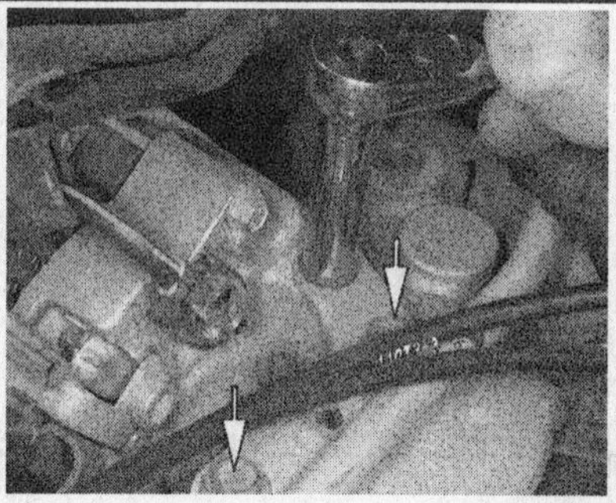
89602P06

Fig. 42 Remove the three alternator rear mounting bolts

89602P07

Fig. 43 Remove the two front alternator mounting bolts

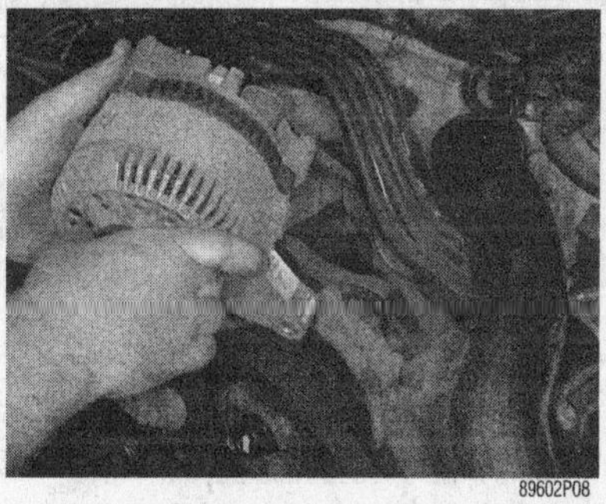
89602P08

Fig. 44 Remove the alternator from the engine by carefully lifting it up and out of the engine compartment

should have raised at least 0.5 volts, but no more than 2.5 volts.

5. If the voltage does not go up more than 0.5 volts, the alternator is not charging. If the voltage goes up more than 2.5 volts, the alternator is overcharging.

**➡Usually under and overcharging is caused by a defective alternator, or its related parts (regulator), and replacement will fix the problem. However, faulty wiring and other problems can cause the charging system to malfunction. Further testing, which is not covered by this book, will reveal the exact component failure. Many automotive parts stores have alternator bench testers available for use by customers. An alternator bench test is the most definitive way to determine the condition of your alternator.**

6. If the voltage is within specifications, proceed to the next test.

### Load test

1. With the engine running, turn on the blower motor and the high beams (or other electrical accessories to place a load on the charging system).
2. Increase and hold engine speed to 2000 rpm.
3. Measure the voltage reading at the battery.
4. The voltage should increase at least 0.5 volts from the voltage test. If the voltage does not meet specifications, the charging system is malfunctioning.

**➡Usually under and overcharging is caused by a defective alternator, or its related parts (regulator), and replacement will fix the problem. However, faulty wiring and other problems can cause the charging system to malfunction. Further testing, which is not covered by this book, will reveal the exact component failure. Many automotive parts stores have alternator bench testers available for use by customers. An alternator bench test is the most definitive way to determine the condition of your alternator.**

## Removal & Installation

**➧ See Figures 37 thru 44**

1. Disconnect the negative battery cable.
2. Tag and disconnect the wiring connectors from the rear (or side) of the alternator. To disconnect push-on type terminals, depress the lock tab and pull straight off.
3. On 3.8L and 4.6L engines, rotate the automatic tensioner away from the drive belt and disengage the drive belt from the alternator pulley. Remove the alternator brace.
4. On 3.8L engines, remove the alternator pivot bolts, top and bottom and remove the alternator.
5. On 5.0L engines, loosen the alternator pivot bolt and remove the adjusting bolt. Disengage the drive belt from the alternator pulley.
6. On 3.8L and 5.0L engines, remove the alternator pivot bolt and the alternator. On 4.6L engines, removal the alternator mounting bolts and remove the alternator.

7. Installation is the reverse of the removal procedure. On 4.6L engines, tighten the alternator mounting bolts to 15–22 ft. lbs. (20–30 Nm) and the alternator brace bolts to 70–106 inch lbs. (8–12 Nm). In addition, on 5.0L engines, adjust the drive belt tension (refer to Section 1).

## Regulator

### Removal & Installation

**External regulator only**

1. Disconnect the negative battery cable.
2. Disconnect the wiring harness from the regulator.
3. Remove the regulator retaining screws and the regulator.
4. Installation is the reverse of the removal procedure.

# STARTING SYSTEM

## Starter

### Testing

**Voltage drop test**

**➡The battery must be in good condition and fully charged prior to performing this test.**

1. Disable the ignition system by unplugging the primary (low voltage) wires from the coil pack. Verify that the vehicle will not start.
2. Connect a voltmeter between the positive terminal of the battery and the starter B+ circuit.

84173025

**Fig. 45 View of the starter motor—4.6L engine**

3. Turn the ignition key to the START position and note the voltage on the meter.
4. If the voltage reads 0.5 volts or more, there is high resistance in the starter cables or the cable ground, repair as necessary. If the voltage reading is ok, proceed to the next step.
5. Connect a voltmeter between the positive terminal of the battery and the starter M circuit.
6. Turn the ignition key to the START position and note the voltage on the meter.
7. If voltage reads 0.5 volts or more, there is high resistance in the starter. Repair or replace the starter as necessary.

**➡Many automotive parts stores have starter bench testers available for use by customers. A starter bench test is the most definitive way to determine the condition of your starter.**

### Removal & Installation

**See Figure 45**

1. Disconnect the negative battery cable.
2. Raise the vehicle and support is safely.
3. Disconnect the starter cable form the starter. If equipped with starter-mounted solenoid, disconnect the push-on connector from the solenoid.

**➡To disconnect the hard-shell connector from the solenoid S terminal, grasp the plastic shell and pull off; do not pull on the wire. Pull straight off to prevent damage.**

4. Remove the starter bolts and the starter.

**➡Some 3.8L applications have a starter mounting stud that is used for engine ground. Ensure this connection is tight when replacing a starter.**

**To install:**

5. Position the starter to the engine and tighten the mounting bolts to 15–20 ft. lbs. (20–27 Nm).
6. Reconnect the electrical leads. Connect the negative battery cable.

### Solenoid/relay replacement

**Starter mounted solenoid**

1. Disconnect the negative battery cable.
2. Remove the starter.
3. Remove the positive brush connector from the solenoid M terminal.
4. Remove the solenoid retaining screws and remove the solenoid.
5. Attach the solenoid plunger rod to the slot in the lever and tighten the solenoid retaining screws to 45–54 inch lbs. (5–6 Nm).
6. Attach the positive brush connector to the solenoid M terminal and tighten the retaining nut to 80–120 inch lbs. (9–14 Nm).
7. Install the starter and connect the negative battery terminal.

**Relay**

1. Disconnect the negative battery cable.
2. Label and disconnect the wires from the relay.
3. Remove the relay retaining bolts and remove the relay.
4. Installation is the reverse of the removal procedure.

# SENDING UNITS AND SENSORS

This section describes the operating principles of sending units, warning lights and gauges. Sensors, which provide information to the Powertrain Control Module (PCM), are covered in Section 4 of this manual.

## Sending units and sensors

Instrument panels contain a number of indicating devices (gauges and warning lights). These devices are composed of two separate components. One is the sending unit, mounted on the engine or other remote part of the vehicle, and the other is the actual gauge or light in the instrument panel.

Several types of sending units exist, however most can be characterized as being either a pressure type or a resistance type. Pressure type sending units convert liquid pressure into an electrical signal that is sent to the gauge. Resistance type sending units are most often used to measure temperature and use variable resistance to control the current flow back top the indicating device. Both types of sending units are connected in series by a wire to the battery (through the ignition switch). When the ignition is turned ON, current flows from the battery through the indicating device and on to the sending unit.

## Coolant Temperature Sensor

### Testing

**✲✲ CAUTION:**

**Never open, service, or drain the radiator or cooling system when hot; serious burns can occur from the steam and hot coolant. In addition, when draining engine coolant, keep in mind that cats and dogs are attracted to ethylene glycol antifreeze and could drink any that is left in an uncovered container or in puddles on the ground. This will prove fatal in sufficient quantities.**

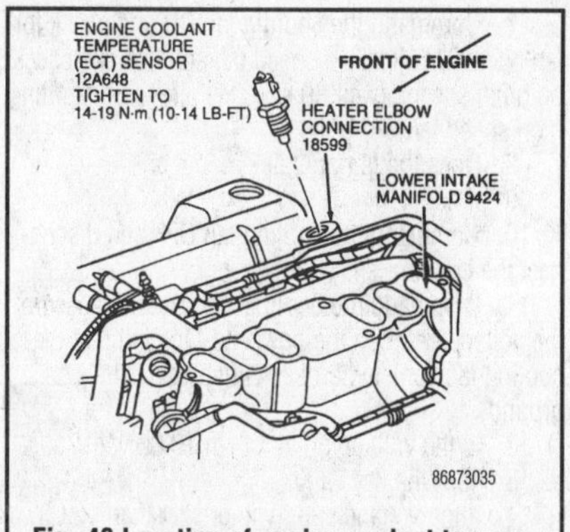


**Fig. 46 Location of engine coolant temperature sensor—3.8L engine**

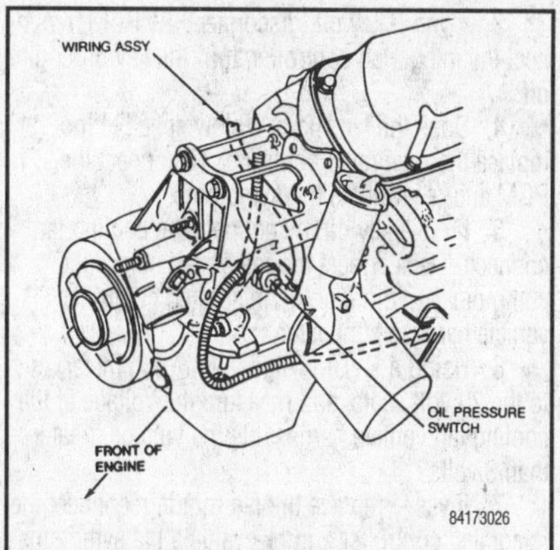


**Fig. 47 Oil pressure switch—5.0L**

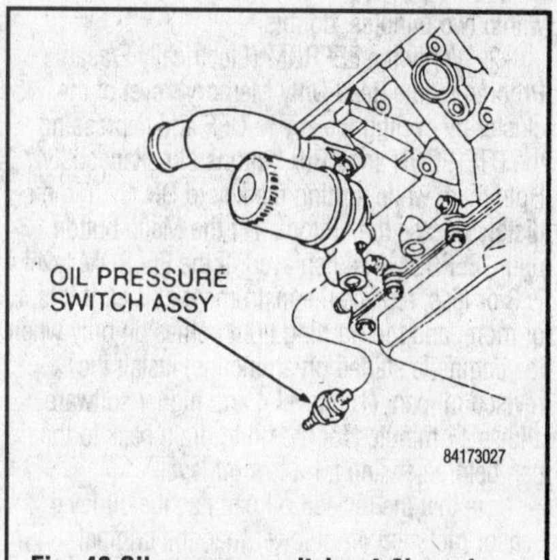


**Fig. 48 Oil pressure switch—4.6L engine**

**Always drain coolant into a sealable container. Coolant should be reused unless it is contaminated or it is several years old.**

The sending unit is located in a water jacket or coolant passage near the thermostat.

1. Check the appropriate fuse before attempting any other diagnostics.
2. Make sure the cooling system is full and free of any trapped air.
3. Tape a mechanic's thermometer to the radiator return hose (upper hose) securely.
4. Disconnect the sending unit electrical harness.
5. Using and ohmmeter, check the resistance between the sending unit terminals.
6. Resistance should be high (58K ohms) with engine coolant cold 50–degrees F (10-degrees C) and low (2.8K ohms) with engine coolant hot 194-degrees F (90-degrees C).

➡**It is best to check resistance with the engine cool, then start the engine, and watch the resistance change as the engine warms.**

7.If resistance does not drop as engine temperature rises, the sending unit is faulty.

### Removal & Installation

▶ **See Figure 46**

1. Disconnect the negative battery cable.
2. Drain the cooling system into a suitable container.
3. Disconnect the electrical connector at the temperature sender/switch.
4. Remove the temperature sender/switch.

**To install:**

5. Apply pipe sealant or Teflon tape to the threads of the new sender/switch.
6. Install the temperature sender/switch and connect the electrical connector.
7. Connect the negative battery cable. Fill the cooling system.
8. Run the engine and check for leaks.

## Oil pressure sender/switch

### Testing

1. Test and verify the engine oil pressure. See Section 3 for more information. If no or insufficient pressure exists, oil pressure problem exists and gauge and sensor are operational, repair oil pressure problem.
2. Check the appropriate fuse before attempting any other diagnostics.
3. Unplug the sensor electrical harness.
4. Using an ohmmeter, check continuity between the sensor terminals.
5. With the engine stopped, continuity should not exist.

➡**The switch inside the oil pressure sensor opens at 6 psi or less of pressure.**

6. With the engine running, continuity should exist.
7. If continuity does not exist as stated, the sensor is faulty.

### Removal & Installation

▶ **See Figures 47 and 48**

**✲✲ WARNING:**

**The pressure switch used with the oil pressure warning light is not interchangeable with the sending unit used with the oil pressure gauge. If the incorrect part is installed, the oil pressure indicating system will be inoperative and the sending unit or gauge will be damaged.**

1. Disconnect the negative battery cable.
2. Disconnect the electrical connector and remove the oil pressure sender/switch.

**To install:**

3. Apply pipe sealant to the threads of the new sender/switch.
4. Install the oil pressure sender/switch and tighten to 9–11 ft. lbs. (12–16 Nm).
5. Connect the electrical connector to the sender/switch and connect the negative battery cable.
6. Run the engine and check for leaks and proper operation.

## Low Oil Level Sensor

### Testing

With the oil at the FULL mark on the dipstick and the engine oil warm to ensure that the oil drains properly from the oil sensor, turn the ignition switch to the RUN position and start the engine. The warning indicator should come on briefly in START for a bulb to prove-out, then go out. Turn the engine off. Drain 2 quarts of oil from the engine. Wait for five minutes, then restart the engine. The warning indicator should come on and stay on.

**Sensor test**

Connect the positive lead of a DVOM to the sensor terminal and the negative lead to the sensor housing. With the sensor submerged in oil (engine full), the meter should read "open." Resistance should be greater than 100,000 ohms. With the sensor out of oil (oil drained), the resistance should be less than 1000 ohms.

➡**The sensor must be horizontal when this test is conducted.**

### Removal & Installation

▶ **See Figure 49**

➡**It is possible for the low oil level warning light to come on in a 1995-96 Continental built through 4/15/96 when it is started while parked on an incline. Ford says this is caused by too-sensitive instrument cluster software and/or the location of the oil level sensor in the oil pan. The fix is to install either a revised instrument cluster or a revised oil pan with the sensor mounted in a different spot.**

1. Here is the procedure: first obviously, make sure the oil level is okay. Then, if the light comes on only after the engine is shut off and restarted

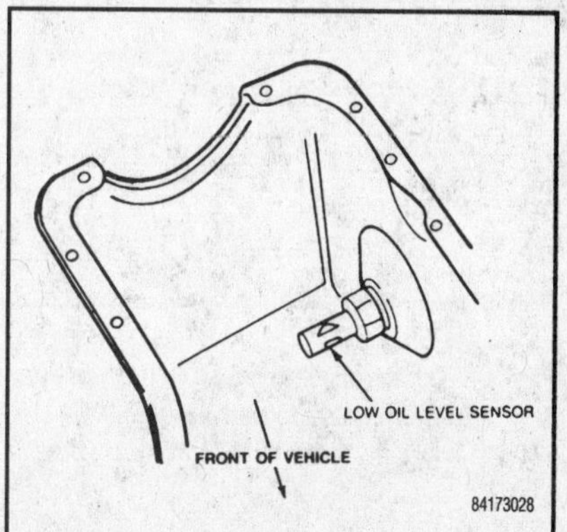


**Fig. 49 Low oil level sensor—4.6L engine**

within two minutes, do this:

2. Verify the EEPROM (Electrically Erasable Programmable Read Only Memory) level of the cluster by cycling the key to OFF and depressing the DTE/ECON and TRIP buttons simultaneously. Hold them while turning the key to ON, then immediately release the buttons. Hit the Menu button until "EEPROM" is displayed. If the EEPROM level is 3 or less, replace the instrument cluster. If it is 4 or more, and the warning light comes on only when the engine is started on an incline, install the revised oil pan. (The level 4 and higher software allows 11 minutes for the oil to drain back to the pan before sensing for a low oil level.)

Note that the revised oil pan has the oil level sensor mounted 4mm lower than the original design and therefore is less susceptible to indicate a low oil level when parked on an incline.

3. Disconnect the negative battery cable.
4. Raise and safely support the vehicle.
5. Drain at least 2 quarts of oil from the engine into a suitable container.
6. Disconnect the electrical connector from the sensor.
7. Remove the sensor using a 1 in. socket or wrench.

**To install:**

8. Install the sensor and tighten to 15–25 ft. lbs. (20–34 Nm).
9. Connect the electrical connector.
10. Tighten the oil pan drain plug to 8-12 ft. lbs. (11–16 Nm) on 4.6L engines or 15–25 ft. lbs. (20–34 Nm) on 5.0L engines.
11. Lower the vehicle.
12. Add oil to the proper level.
13. Connect the negative battery cable, start the engine and check for leaks.

## Electric fan switch

### Testing

#### 3.8L engines

Checking cooling fan operation with an integrated controller.

1. Make sure the ignition key is turned off. Disconnect the integrated controller.
2. Jump pin 3 to pin 2 at the integrated controller harness connector. Does fan run?
3. If yes—key off, disconnect the PCM, reconnect the integrated controller, turn the key on/engine off.
4. Does the fan run at a slow speed? If no-replace the integrated controller. Reconnect the PCM and re-evaluate the symptoms.
5. If no—key off, disconnect the cooling fan connector. Disconnect the integrated controller. Jump pin 3 to pin 6 at the integrated controller vehicle harness connector.
6. Using a DVOM (digital volt/ohm meter), set to the 20 volt scale, and measure the voltage at the cooling fan vehicle harness. Is the voltage greater than 8 volts?
7. If yes—replace the fan motor, reconnect the integrated controller and re-evaluate the symptoms.
8. If no—key off. Disconnect the cooling fan and the integrated controller. Jump pin 3 to pin 6 at the integrated controller vehicle harness connector. With a DVOM on a 20 volt scale, measure the voltage at the cooling fan harness connector, positive side and the battery negative post. Is the voltage greater than 8 volts?
9. If yes—service the open in the ground circuit to the fan. Reconnect all the components and re-evaluate the symptoms.
10. If no—service the open in the power-to-fan circuit from pin 6 and pin 7 of the integrated controller harness connector the cooling fan harness connector. Reconnect all the components and re-evaluate the symptoms.

#### 4.6L engines

The Variable Control Relay Module (VCRM) controls

- The cooling fan motor operation and speed.
- The A/C clutch operation.
- Other non-A/C functions.
- It also increases and decreases the cooling fan motor speed as necessary, depending on the refrigerant system high-side pressure.
- Turns off the A/C clutch circuit OFF if the high-side pressure exceeds 425 psi.

1. To begin testing, perform the PCM quick test.
2. Service any codes.
3. Check for a binding/seized cooling fan.
4. Connect scan tool.
5. Turn the Key-on Engine off (KOEO).
6. Access the output test mode on the scan tool.
7. Command the cooling fan ON and check for fan operation - for two speed fan applications check both fan speeds (wait 30 seconds after commanding high speed fan on).
8. Does the fan operate?
9. If no?
10. Command the cooling fan OFF and disconnect the cooling fan.
11. Command the cooling fan ON and measure the voltage between the power-to-fan circuit at the cooling fan vehicle harness connector and chassis ground.
12. Is the voltage greater than 10.00 volts?
13. Turn the key OFF.
14. If the voltage supply is greater than 10.00 volts (source voltage) than power is being supplied to the fan.
15. Disconnect the scan tool from the Data Link Connector (DLC).
16. Measure the resistance between the ground circuit at the cooling fan vehicle harness connector and the chassis ground.
17. If resistance is less than 5 ohms, replace the fan motor.
18. If not, service the open ground circuit; reconnect all components, verify proper operation.

### Removal & Installation

#### 3.8L engines

1. Remove the radiator upper sight shield.
2. Disconnect the engine control sensor wiring from the CCRM electrical connector
3. Remove the retaining bolts and constant control relay module (CCRM) from its mount on the radiator support.
4. Installation is the reversal of the removal procedure.

#### 4.6L engines

1. Remove the radiator upper sight shield.
2 Disconnect the electrical connector.
3. Remove the variable control relay module (VCRM) retainer bracket nuts, located on the radiator support and remove the VCRM.
4. To install the VCRM, reverse the removal procedures. Tighten the VCRM bracket retainer nuts to 36 in. lbs. (4 Nm).

**ENGINE MECHANICAL 3-2**
ENGINE 3-4
REMOVAL & INSTALLATION 3-4
ROCKER ARM (VALVE) COVER 3-8
REMOVAL & INSTALLATION 3-8
ROCKER ARMS/ROLLER FOLLOWERS 3-10
REMOVAL & INSTALLATION 3-10
THERMOSTAT 3-10
REMOVAL & INSTALLATION 3-10
INTAKE MANIFOLD 3-11
REMOVAL & INSTALLATION 3-11
EXHAUST MANIFOLD 3-16
REMOVAL & INSTALLATION 3-16
RADIATOR 3-18
REMOVAL & INSTALLATION 3-18
ENGINE FAN 3-20
REMOVAL & INSTALLATION 3-20
WATER PUMP 3-21
REMOVAL & INSTALLATION 3-21
CYLINDER HEAD 3-24
REMOVAL & INSTALLATION 3-24
OIL PAN 3-29
REMOVAL & INSTALLATION 3-29
OIL PUMP 3-31
REMOVAL & INSTALLATION 3-31
CRANKSHAFT DAMPER 3-32
REMOVAL & INSTALLATION 3-32
TIMING CHAIN COVER 3-34
REMOVAL & INSTALLATION 3-34
REMOVAL & INSTALLATION 3-35
TIMING CHAIN AND GEARS 3-35
REMOVAL & INSTALLATION 3-35
CAMSHAFT, BEARINGS AND LIFTERS 3-38
REMOVAL & INSTALLATION 3-38
INSPECTION 3-39
BALANCE SHAFT 3-40
REMOVAL & INSTALLATION 3-40
REAR MAIN SEAL 3-40
REMOVAL & INSTALLATION 3-40
FLYWHEEL/FLEXPLATE 3-41
REMOVAL & INSTALLATION 3-41
**EXHAUST SYSTEM 3-42**
INSPECTION 3-42
REPLACEMENT 3-42
**ENGINE RECONDITIONING 3-43**
DETERMINING ENGINE CONDITION 3-43
COMPRESSION TEST 3-43
BUY OR REBUILD? 3-44
ENGINE OVERHAUL TIPS 3-44
TOOLS 3-44
OVERHAUL TIPS 3-44
CLEANING 3-44
REPAIRING DAMAGED THREADS 3-45
ENGINE PREPARATION 3-46
CYLINDER HEAD 3-46
DISASSEMBLY 3-46
INSPECTION 3-48
REFINISHING & REPAIRING 3-49
ASSEMBLY 3-50
ENGINE BLOCK 3-51
GENERAL INFORMATION 3-51
DISASSEMBLY 3-51
INSPECTION 3-52
REFINISHING 3-53
ASSEMBLY 3-53
ENGINE START-UP AND BREAK-IN 3-56
STARTING THE ENGINE 3-56
BREAKING IT IN 3-56
KEEP IT MAINTAINED 3-56
**SPECIFICATIONS CHARTS**
ENGINE MECHANICAL SPECIFICATIONS 3-2
TORQUE SPECIFICATIONS 3-57

# 3

# ENGINE AND ENGINE OVERHAUL

ENGINE MECHANICAL 3-2
EXHAUST SYSTEM 3-42
ENGINE RECONDITIONING 3-43

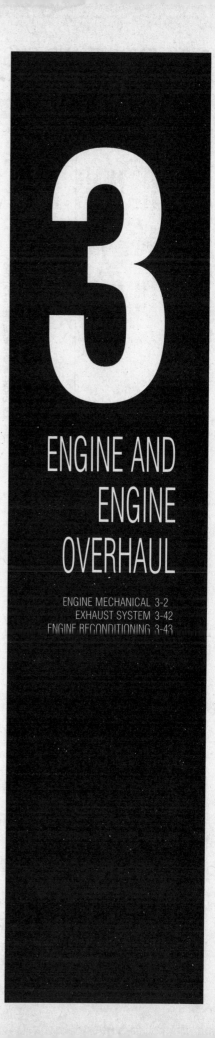

## ENGINE MECHANICAL

### 3.8L ENGINE MECHANICAL SPECIFICATIONS

| Description | English Specifications | Metric Specifications |
|---|---|---|
| **General Information** | | |
| Type | 90° V Iron Block, Liquid Cooled, Overhead Valve | |
| Displacement | 232 cid | 3.8L (3802cc) |
| Number of cylinders | 6 | |
| Bore | 3.81in | 96.8mm |
| Stroke | 3.39in | 86.0mm |
| Compression ratio | 9.0:1 | |
| Firing order | 1-4-2-5-3-6 | |
| Oil pressure | 40-60 psi @2500rpm | |
| **Cylinder Head and Valve Train** | | |
| Valve-to-valve guide clearance | 0.0007-0.0027in. | 0.018-0.068mm |
| Valve clearance-intake valve | 0.001-0.0028in. | 0.026-0.071mm |
| Valve clearance-exhaust valve | 0.0015-0.0033in. | 0.038-0.083mm |
| Combustion Chamber volume (cc) | 61.48-64.48 | |
| Valve guide bore diameter (ICD) | 0.3443-0.3433in. | 8.745-8.720mm |
| Intake | 1.8532-18542in. | 47.072-47.097mm |
| Exhaust | 1.5645in. | 39.739mm |
| Head gasket surface flatness | 0.007 in. | 0.018mm |
| Head face surface finish | 15 microns (max.) | |
| Valve head diameter | | |
| Intake | 1.78in. | 45.3mm |
| Exhaust | 1.46in. | 37.1mm |
| Valve face run-out limit | | |
| Intake | 0.002in. | 0.05mm |
| Exhaust | 0.002in. | 0.05mm |
| Valve face angle | 45.8 degrees | |
| Valve stem diameter | | |
| Intake | 0.3423-0.3415in. | 8.694-8.674mm |
| Exhaust | 0.3418-0.3410in. | 8.682-8.662mm |
| Valve spring compression | | |
| Valve Open | 220 lbs. @ 1.18 in. | 979 Nm @ 30.0mm |
| Valve Closed | 85 lbs. @ 1.65 in. | 378 Nm @ 41.9mm |
| Free length | 1.97 in. | 50.0mm |
| Pressure lost @ specific height | 10% Force Loss @ Specified Length | |
| Rocker Arm | | |
| Ratio | 1.73:1 | |
| Valve Tappet-Hydraulic | | |
| Diameter | 0.8740-.8745in. | 22.200-22.212mm |
| Clearance to Bore | 0.0007-0.0027in. | 0.018-0.068mm |
| **Camshaft** | | |
| Lobe lift | | |
| Intake | 0.245in. | 6.22mm |
| Exhaust | 0.259in. | 6.57mm |
| Theoretical valve maximum lift | | |
| Intake | 0.424in | 10.67mm |
| Exhaust | 0.448in. | 11.37mm |
| End-play service limit | 0.001-0.006in. | 0.025-0.150mm |
| Bearing journal diameter | 2.0515-2.0505in. | 52.108-52.082mm |
| Camshaft bearing runout limit | 0.002in. | 0.05mm |
| **Cylinder Block** | | |
| Cylinder bore diameter | 3.81in. | 98.80mm |
| Piston selection | | |
| Red | 3.8110-3.8122in. | 96.799-96.830mm |
| Blue | 3.8122-3.8134in. | 96.830-96.860mm |
| Yellow | 3.8134-3.8146in. | 96.860-96.891mm |
| Piston-to-cylinder bore clearance | 0.0009-0.0027in. | 0.022-0.069mm |
| Surface Finish (RMS) | 0.45-0.96 | |
| Out-of-round limit | 0.001in. | 0.025mm |
| Taper limit (max.) | 0.002in. | 0.050mnm |
| Main bearing bore diameter | 2.712-2.713 | 68.885-68.905mm |
| **Crankshaft** | | |
| Main bearing journal diameter | 2.5190-2.5198in. | 63.983-64.003mm |
| Out-of-Round Limit | 0.0003in. | 0.008mm |
| Maximum @ 45° | 0.006in. | 0.015mm |
| Taper Limit | 0.003in. | 0.008mm |
| Journal Runout Limit | 0.002in. | 0.05mm |
| **Connecting Rod** | | |
| Connecting rod bearing | | |
| Connecting rod bearing journal diameter | 2.3103-2.3111in. | 58.682-58.702mm |
| Clearance-to-crankshaft | 0.0047-0.0114in. | 0.11-0.29mm |
| Connecting rod piston pin bore diameter | 0.9096-0.9112in. | 23.105-23.145mm |
| Crankshaft bearing bore diameter | 2.4266-2.4274in. | 61.635-61.655mm |

93143C01

### 3.8L ENGINE MECHANICAL SPECIFICATIONS

| Description | English Specifications | Metric Specifications |
|---|---|---|
| **Pistons** | | |
| Piston-to-bore clearance | 0.0009-0.0027in. | 0.022-0.069mm |
| Piston bore diameter | Piston Required | |
| Ring groove width | | |
| Upper compression ring | 0.0610-0.0602in | 1.550-1.530mm |
| Lower compression ring | 0.0610-0.0602in | 1.550-1.530mm |
| Oil control ring | 0.1587-0.1596in. | 4.030-4.055mm |
| Ring width | | |
| Upper compression ring | 0.0575-0.0587in. | 1.460-1.490mm |
| Lower compression ring | 0.0576-0.0587in. | 1.463-1.490mm |
| Oil control ring | Side seal -Snug fit | |
| Piston pin length | 3.012-3.039in. | 76.5-77.2mm |
| Piston pin diameter | 0.9119 -0.09124in. | 23.162-23.175mm |
| Pin-to-piston clearance | 0.0002-0.0005in. | 0.005-0.012mm |
| **Lubrication System** | | |
| Oil pump type | Gerotor | |
| Oil Pump Gear Backlash | 0.008-0.012in. | 0.02-0.03mm |
| Relief Valve Spring Tension | 17.1-15.2 lbs. @ 1.20in. | 76.2-67.6 N @ 30.5mm |
| Relief Valve to Bore Clearance | 0.0029-0.0017in. | 0.073-0.043mm |
| Driver Shaft to Housing Clearance | 0.0030-0.0015in. | 0.076-0.038mm |

### 4.6L ENGINE MECHANICAL SPECIFICATIONS

| Description | English Specifications | Metric Specifications |
|---|---|---|
| **General Information** | | |
| Type | Liquid Cooled, Overhead Camshaft | |
| Displacement | 281 cid | 4.6L |
| Number of cylinders | 8 | |
| Bore | 3.55 in. | 90.2mm |
| Stroke | 3.54 in. | 90.0mm |
| Compression ratio | 9.0:1 | |
| Firing order | 1-3-7-2-6-5-4-8 | |
| Oil Pressure | 20-45 psi @ 1500 RPM (engine hot) | |
| **Cylinder Head and Valve Train** | | |
| Valve guide bore diameter | 0.3443-0.3433 in. | 8.745-8.720 |
| Valve seat width | | |
| Intake | 0.074-0.083 in. | 1.9-2.1mm |
| Exhaust | 0.074-0.083 in. | 1.9-2.1mm |
| Valve seat angle | 45 degrees | |
| Valve seat run-out | 0.00094 in. | 0.025mm |
| Valve stem-to-guide clearance | | |
| Intake | 0.00078-0.00272 in. | 0.020-0.069mm |
| Exhaust | 0.018-0.0037 in. | 0.046-0.095mm |
| Valve guide inner diameter | 0.2773-0.2762 in. | 7.044-7.015mm |
| Valve head diameter | | |
| Intake | 1.75 in. | 44.5mm |
| Exhaust | 1.34 in. | 34.0mm |
| Valve face run-out limit | 0.001 in. | 0.05mm |
| Valve face angle | 45.5 degrees | |
| Valve stem diameter | | |
| Intake | 0.275-0.2746 in. | 6.995-6.975mm |
| Exhaust | 0.274-0.2736 in. | 6.970-6.949mm |
| Free length | | |
| Intake | 1.976 in. | 50.2mm |
| Exhaust | 1.976 in. | 50.2mm |
| Valve spring assembled length | 1.566-1.637 in. | 39.8-41.6mm |
| Rocker arm ratio | 1.75:1 | |
| Valve tappet diameter | 0.63-0.629 in. | 16.0-15.98mm |
| Valve tappet-to-bore clearance | 0.00071-0.00272 in. | 0.018-0.069mm |
| Valve tappet service limit | 0.00063 in. | 0.016mm |
| Valve tappet leakdown rate | 5-25 seconds | |
| Valve tappet collapsed tappet gap (desired) | 0.0335-0.0177 in. | 0.85-0.45mm |
| **Camshaft** | | |
| Lobe lift | | |
| Intake | 0.2594 in. | 6.59mm |
| Exhaust | 0.2594 in. | 6.59mm |
| Lobe wear limit (all) | 0.005 in. | 0.127mm |
| Theoretical valve lift @ zero lash (all) | 0.472 in. | 12.0mm |
| End-play | 0.00098-0.0065 in. | 0.025-0.165mm |
| End-play wear limit | 0.0075 in. | 0.190mm |
| Bearing-to-journal clearance | 0.00098-0.003 in. | 0.025-0.076mm |
| Bearing-to-journal clearance service limit | 0.0048 in. | 0.121mm |
| Journal diameter | 1.061-1.060 in. | 26.962-26.936mm |

93143C02

## 4.6L ENGINE MECHANICAL SPECIFICATIONS

| Description | English Specifications | Metric Specifications |
|---|---|---|
| **Camshaft (cont'd)** | | |
| Bearing journal inside diameter | 1.063-1.0625 in. | 27.0[illegible]2-26.987mm |
| Run-out | 0.002 in. | [illegible].05mm |
| **Cylinder Block** | | |
| Cylinder bore diameter | | |
| Out-of-round | 0.0006 in. | [illegible].015mm |
| Out-of-round (service limit) | 0.00079 in. | [illegible].020mm |
| Taper limit | 0.00023 in. | .006mm |
| Main bearing bore | 2.85-2.851 in. | 72.4[illegible]2-72.422mm |
| **Crankshaft** | | |
| Main bearing journal diameter | 2.65-2.657 in. | 67.4[illegible]3-67.503mm |
| Main bearing journal taper | 0.0007 in. | [illegible].02mm |
| Main bearing journal run-out | 0.002 in. | [illegible].05mm |
| Main bearing-to-crankshaft clearance | 0.0011-0.0026 in. | 0.0[illegible]7-0.065mm |
| Bearing wall thickness | 0.075-0.076 in. | 1.9[illegible]0-1.928mm |
| Connecting rod bearing journal diameter | 2.087-2.867 in. | 52.9[illegible]8-53.003mm |
| Crankshaft free end-play | 0.130-0.301 in. | 0.0[illegible]51-0.012mm |
| Crankshaft runout-to-rear face of the block | 0.002 in. | [illegible].05mm |
| **Connecting Rod** | | |
| Connecting rod bearing-to-crankshaft clearance | 0.001-0.0027 in. | 0.0[illegible]7-0.069mm |
| Connecting rod bearing wall thickness | 0.096-0.0965 in. | 2.4[illegible]4-2.452mm |
| Connecting rod main bearing bore diameter | 2.234-2.24 in. | 56.7[illegible]6-56.876mm |
| Connecting rod length (center-to-center) | 5.93 in. | 50.7mm |
| Connecting rod-to-crank side clearance (standard) | 0.0006-0.0177 in. | 0.[illegible]15-0.45mm |
| Connecting rod-to-crank side clearance (maximum) | 0.02 in. | 0.5mm |
| Connecting rod main bearing journal taper | 0.0005 in. | .015 mm |
| **Pistons** | | |
| Piston diameter | | |
| Coded red | 3.550-3.551 in. | 90.[illegible]7-90.197mm |
| Coded blue | 3.5507-3.5515 in. | 90.[illegible]0-90.210mm |
| Coded yellow | 3.5513-3.5521 in. | 90.[illegible]3-90.223mm |
| Piston-to-bore clearance | 0.0005-0.001 in. | 0.0[illegible]2-0.026mm |
| Piston pin bore diameter | 0.864-0.865 in. | 21.[illegible]9-21.979mm |
| Piston pin bore length | 2.44-2.443 in. | 61[illegible]3-62.05mm |
| Piston pin-to-rod clearance | 0.0006-0.00157 in. | 0.0[illegible]5-0.040mm |
| Piston pin-to-piston clearance | 0.0002-0.0004 in. | 0.0[illegible]5-0.010mm |
| Piston ring side clearance | | |
| Upper compression ring | 0.0016-0.0035 in. | 0.0[illegible]0-0.090mm |
| Lower compression ring | 0.0012-0.0031 in. | 0.0[illegible]0-0.080mm |
| Oil control ring | 0.05 in. | 1.25mm |
| Piston ring groove width | | |
| Upper compression ring | 0.060-0.0610 in. | 1.[illegible]0-1.550mm |
| Lower compression ring | 0.060-0.0602 in. | 1.[illegible]0-1.530mm |
| Oil control ring | 0.2750-0.2844 in. | 6.[illegible]6-7.224mm |
| Piston ring gap | | |
| Upper compression ring | 0.01-0.02 in. | 0[illegible]23-0.49mm |
| Lower compression ring | 0.01-0.02 in. | 0[illegible]23-0.49mm |
| Oil control ring | 0.006-0.026 in. | 0[illegible]15-0.66mm |
| **Oil Pump** | | |
| Oil pump gear radial clearance (idler and drive) | 0.0055-0.002 in. | 0.[illegible]25-0.050mm |
| Oil pump gear end height (extends below the housing) | 0.0033-0.0004 in. | 0.[illegible]35-0.010mm |

93143C03

## 5.0L ENGINE MECHANICAL SPECIFICATIONS

| Description | English Specifications | Metri[illegible] Specifications |
|---|---|---|
| **General Information** | | |
| Type | 90° V8 Overhead Valve Engin[illegible] | |
| Displacement | 302 cu. in. | 5[illegible]L (4949cc) |
| Number of Cylinders | 8 | |
| Bore | 4.00 in. | 101.6mm |
| Stroke | 3.00 in. | 76.2mm |
| Compression ratio | 8.9:1 | |
| Firing order | 1-5-4-2-6-3-7-8 | |
| Oil Pressure | 40-60 psi @ 2000 RPM (engine h[illegible]t) | |
| **Cylinder head** | | |
| Cylinder head-to-engine block surface warpage | 0.003 in. (0.0762mm) in a 6.0 in. (152.4[illegible]m) span | |
| Valve seat width | | |
| Intake valves | 0.060-0.080 in. | 1.[illegible]24-2.032mm |
| Exhaust valve | 0.060-0.080 in. | 1.[illegible]24-2.032mm |
| Valve seat angle—Intake and exhaust valves | 45° | |
| Valve guide bore diameter—Intake and exhaust valves | 0.3433-0.3443 | 8.[illegible]20-8.745mm |

## 5.0L ENGINE MECHANICAL SPECIFICATIONS

| Description | English Specifications | Metric Specifications |
|---|---|---|
| **Valves, valve springs and camshaft** | | |
| Camshaft journal diameter | | |
| No. 1 | 2.0815 in. | 52.8701mm |
| No. 2 | 2.0665 in. | 52.4891mm |
| No. 3 | 2.0515 in. | 52.1081mm |
| No. 4 | 2.0365 in. | 51.7271mm |
| No. 5 | 2.0215 in. | 51.3461mm |
| Camshaft-to-bearing clearance | 0.001-0.003 in. | 0.0254-0.0762mm |
| Camshaft thrust clearance | 0.007 in. max | 0.1778mm max |
| Camshaft lobe lift | | |
| Intake valve | 0.2637 in. | 6.69798mm |
| Exhaust valve | 0.2801 in. | 7.11454mm |
| Camshaft runout | 0.005 in. max | 0.127mm |
| Valve stem diameter | | |
| Intake valves | 0.3415-0.3423 in. | 8.6741-8.6944mm |
| Exhaust valves | 0.3410-0.3418 in. | 8.6614-8.6817mm |
| Valve guide-to-valve stem clearance | | |
| Intake valves | 0.0010-0.0027 in. | 0.0254-0.0686mm |
| Exhaust valves | 0.0015-0.0032 in. | 0.0381-0.08128mm |
| Valve face angle limit | 44° | |
| Valve head diameter | | |
| Intake valve | 1.837-1.847 in. | 46.660-46.914mm |
| Exhaust valve | 1.536-1.546 in. | 39.01-39.27mm |
| Valve head radial runout | 0.002 in. | 0.0508mm |
| Valve spring free length (approximate) | 1.84 in. | 46.7mm |
| Intake valve spring | 2.06 in. | 52.324mm |
| Exhaust valve spring | 1.88 in. | 47.752mm |
| Valve spring preload | | |
| Intake valve spring | 74-82 lbs. @ 1.78 in. | 33.6-37.2kg @ 45.21mm |
| Exhaust valve spring | 76-84 lbs. @ 1.60 in. | 34.5-38.1kg @ 40.64mm |
| Valve spring installed height | | |
| Intake valve spring | 1.75-1.81 in. | 44.45-45.974mm |
| Exhaust valve spring | 1.58-1.64 in. | 40.132-41.656mm |
| Valve spring out-of-square | 0.078 in. | 1.9812mm |
| Rocker arm ratio | 1.62:1 | |
| **Engine block** | | |
| Engine block-to-cylinder head surface warpage | 0.003 in. (0.0762mm) in a 6.0 in. (152.4mm) span | |
| Standard cylinder bore | 4.0000-4.0012 in. | 101.6-101.6305mm |
| Cylinder bore out-of-round and taper | 0.0015/0.010 in. | 0.0381/0.254mm |
| Cylinder bore-to-piston clearance | 0.0012-0.0020 in. | 0.0305-0.0508mm |
| **Pistons** | | |
| Standard piston diameter | 3.9987-3.9993 in. | 101.567-101.5822mm |
| Piston ring groove width | | |
| Top compression ring | 0.0602-0.0612 in. | 1.530-1.555mm |
| Second compression ring | 0.0602-0.0612 in. | 1.530-1.555mm |
| Oil control ring | 0.1587-0.1596 in. | 4.030-4.055mm |
| Piston pin diameter | 0.9121-0.9122 in. | 23.1673-23.1699mm |
| **Piston rings** | | |
| Thickness | | |
| Top compression ring | 0.0575-0.0587 in. | 1.460-1.490mm |
| Second compression ring | 0.0575-0.0587 in. | 1.460-1.490mm |
| Oil Control ring | Side seal -Snug fit | |
| Side clearance | | |
| Top compression ring | 0.0013-0.0033 in. | 0.0330-0.0838mm |
| Second compression ring | 0.0013-0.0033 in. | 0.0330-0.0838mm |
| End-gap | | |
| Top compression ring | 0.010-0.020 in. | 0.25-0.50mm |
| Second compression ring | 0.018-0.028 in. | 0.4572-0.7112mm |
| Oil ring | 0.010-0.040 in. | 0.25-1.016mm |
| **Crankshaft and connecting rods** | | |
| Crankshaft main journal diameter | 2.2482-2.2490 in. | 57.1043-57.1246mm |
| Main bearing-to-journal clearance (oil clearance) | 0.0008-0.0026 in. | 0.0203-0.06604mm |
| Crankshaft journal out-of-round and taper | 0.0006 in. | 0.01524mm |
| Crankshaft thrust play | 0.004-0.008 in. | 0.1016-0.2032mm |
| Crankshaft runout | 0.002 in. | 0.050mm |
| Connecting rod journal diameter | 2.1228-2.1236 in. | 53.9191-53.9191mm |
| Connecting rod journal out-of-round and taper | 0.0006 in. | 0.01524mm |
| Connecting rod journal-to-connecting rod clearance | 0.0007-0.0024 in. | 0.01778-0.06096mm |
| Connecting rod small end bore inside diameter | 0.9097-0.9112 in. | 23.1064-23.1445mm |
| Connecting rod big end side clearance | 0.010-0.020 in. | 0.254-0.508mm |
| Connecting rod twist | 0.015 in. | 0.381mm |
| Connecting rod bend | 0.012 in. | 0.3048mm |

93143C04

## Engine

In the process of removing the engine, you will come across a number of steps which call for the removal of a separate component or system, such as "disconnect the exhaust system" or "remove the radiator." In most instances, a detailed removal procedure can be found elsewhere in this manual.

It is virtually impossible to list each individual wire and hose which must be disconnected, simply because so many different model and engine combinations have been manufactured. Careful observation and common sense are the best possible approaches to any repair procedure.

Removal and installation of the engine can be made easier if you follow these basic points:

- If you have to drain any of the fluids, use a suitable container.
- Always tag any wires or hoses and, if possible, the components they came from before disconnecting them.
- Because there are so many bolts and fasteners involved, It is wise to store, and label the retainers from components separately in marked containers, jars, or coffee cans. This will prevent confusion during installation.
- After unbolting the transmission or transaxle, always make sure it is properly supported.
- If it is necessary to disconnect the air conditioning system, have this service performed by a qualified technician using a recovery/recycling station. If the system does not have to be disconnected, unbolt the compressor and set it aside.
- When unbolting the engine mounts, always make sure the engine is properly supported. When removing the engine, make sure that any lifting devices are properly attached to the engine. It is recommended that if your engine is supplied with lifting hooks, your lifting apparatus be attached to them.
- Lift the engine from its compartment slowly, checking that no hoses, wires, or other components are still connected.
- After the engine is clear of the compartment, place it on an engine stand or workbench.
- After the engine has been removed, you can perform a partial or full teardown of the engine using the procedures outlined in this manual.

**➡Label all wiring, vacuum hoses, fuel lines, etc. before disconnecting them; making installation much easier. Be sure to disable the air suspension systems where applicable.**

**➡If your vehicle is equipped with air conditioning, refer to Section 1 for information regarding the implications of servicing your A/C system yourself. Only an MVAC-trained, EPA-certified, automotive technician should service the A/C system or its components.**

**** CAUTION**

**Never open, service, or drain the radiator or cooling system when hot; serious burns can occur from the steam and hot coolant. In addition, when draining engine coolant, keep in mind that cats and dogs are attracted to ethylene glycol antifreeze and could drink any that is left in an uncovered container or in puddles on the ground. This will prove fatal in sufficient quantities. Always drain coolant into a sealable container. Coolant should be reused unless it is contaminated or is several years old.**

**** CAUTION**

**Observe all applicable safety precautions when working around fuel. Whenever servicing the fuel system, always work in a well-ventilated area. Do not allow fuel spray or vapors to be exposed to a spark or open flame. Keep a dry chemical fire extinguisher near the work area. Always keep fuel in a container specifically designed for fuel storage; also, always properly seal fuel containers to avoid the possibility of fire or explosion.**

### REMOVAL & INSTALLATION

#### 3.8L Engine

**See Figures 1 thru 8**

**➡If your vehicle is equipped with air conditioning, refer to Section 1 for information regarding the implications of servicing your A/C system yourself. Only an MVAC-trained, EPA-certified, automotive technician should service the A/C system or its components. Turn off or disable the air suspension system.**

1. Drain the cooling system, then disconnect the negative battery cable.
2. Properly relieve the fuel system pressure.

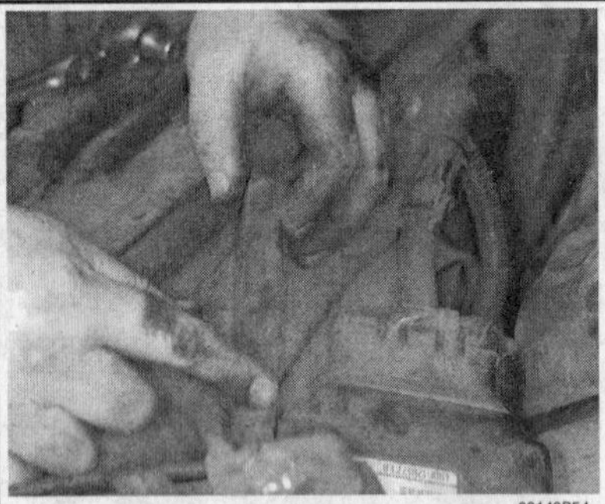
93143P54

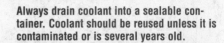

**Fig. 1 Pointing to the IRCM, partially hidden under the radiator frame near the battery**

93143P42

**Fig. 2 One screw at the base of the air cleaner holds the entire assembly in place**

93143P41

**Fig. 3 Lifting the air cleaner assembly out as an assembly**

93143P55

**Fig. 4 The fan shroud and fan comes out as an assembly**

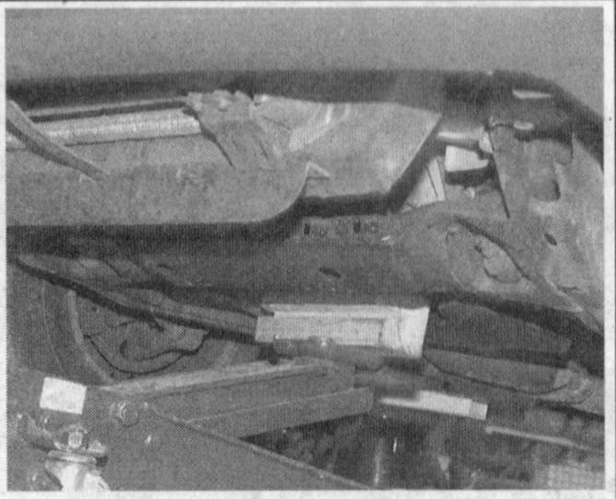
93143P13

**Fig. 5 Be sure to use a block of wood to protect the bottom of the engine**

93143P12

**Fig. 6 With the engine slightly raised the water pump pulley is removable**

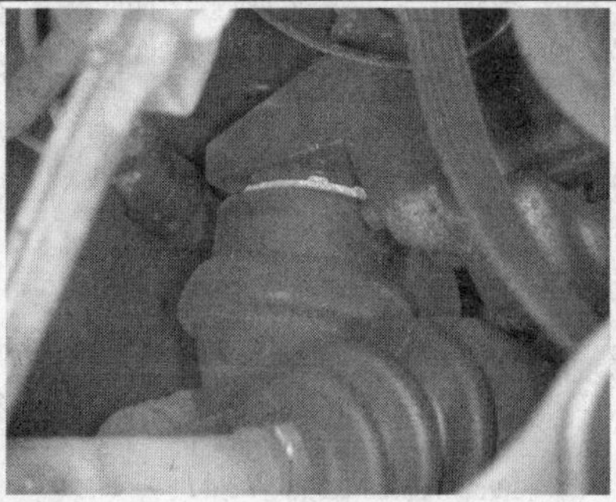

93143P17

**Fig. 7 Flex sockets are a big help here. Only remove the lower nut to remove the engine**

93143P19

**Fig. 8 Just remove the lower nut to pull the engine. Once the engine is out you can easily get the top bolt on the motor mount**

For details, please refer to the procedure located in Section 5 of this manual.

3. Disengage the underhood light wiring connector. Matchmark the position of the hood hinges, then remove the hood.
4. Remove the oil level indicator tube.
5. Disconnect the alternator-to-voltage regulator wiring assembly if equipped.
6. Remove the radiator upper sight shield.
7. Remove the Integrated Relay Controller Module (IRCM) and the bracket retaining bolts, then position the IRCM and bracket out of the way.
8. Remove the air cleaner assembly.
9. Disconnect the cooling fan motor and the front center radiator primary-crash-sensor wire connectors, if equipped.
10. Remove the cooling fan motor/fan blade and fan shroud assembly.
11. Remove the upper radiator hose.
12. Disconnect and plug the transaxle oil cooler inlet and outlet tubes to prevent dirt and grease from entering the tubes. Disconnect the heater hoses.
13. Disconnect the power steering pressure hose assembly.
14. Disconnect the engine control sensor wiring from the A/C clutch field coil. Discharge the A/C system using the proper equipment, then disconnect the compressor-to-condenser discharge line.
15. Remove the radiator coolant recovery reservoir assembly. Remove the wiring shield from the throttle body.
16. Remove the accelerator cable-mounting bracket.
17. Disconnect the fuel supply and return lines.
18. Disconnect the power steering pump pressure hose from the bracket.
19. Disconnect the fuel charging wiring from the engine control sensor wiring assembly.
20. Identify, tag, and disconnect all necessary vacuum hoses.
21. Disconnect the ground wire assembly. Remove the air cleaner outlet tube.
22. Disconnect one end of the throttle control valve cable. Detach the bulkhead electrical connector and transaxle pressure switches.
23. Remove the transaxle support assembly retaining bolts, then remove the transaxle support assembly from the vehicle.
24. Raise and safely support the vehicle. Remove the wheel and tire assemblies.
25. Position a drain pan under the car's oil pan, then drain the engine oil and remove the filter. Move the drain pan out of the way.
26. Disconnect the heated oxygen sensor.
27. Loosen and remove the drive belt. Remove the crankshaft pulley and drive belt tensioner assemblies.
28. Remove the starter motor. For details, please refer to the procedure located earlier in this section.
29. Remove the dual converter Y-pipe retaining bolts, then remove the Y-pipe.
30. Remove the left and right front engine support (motor mount) insulator-to-front subframe retaining nuts.
31. If equipped, remove the engine rear cover, then remove the converter-to-flywheel nuts.
32. Disconnect the engine control sensor wiring from the low oil level sensor. Remove the crankshaft pulley and damper assembly.
33. Disconnect the lower radiator hose.
34. Remove the engine-to-transaxle bolts and partially lower the vehicle. Remove the front wheel and tire assemblies.
35. Unfasten the water pump pulley retaining bolts.
36. Remove the distributor cap and position aside, then pull out the distributor rotor.
37. Remove the radiator.
38. Unfasten the exhaust manifold bolt lock retaining bolts. Remove the thermactor air pump retaining bolts and the thermactor air pump.
39. Disconnect the engine control sensor wiring from the oil pressure sensor.
40. Install Engine Lifting Eyes, then position, and install suitable engine lifting equipment.
41. Position a suitable jack under the transaxle and raise the transaxle slightly, then remove the water pump pulley.
42. Carefully remove the engine from the vehicle.

**To install:**

➡**Lightly oil all bolt and stud threads before installation, except those specifying special sealant.**

43. Position the engine assembly in the vehicle.
44. Install the engine-to-transaxle bolts, then remove the jack from under the transaxle, and remove the engine lifting equipment. Remove the engine lifting eyes. Place all lifting equipment aside and out of the way.
45. Tighten the engine-to-transaxle bolts to 41–50 ft. lbs. (55–68 Nm).
46. Engage the engine control sensor wiring to the oil pressure sensor.
47. Install the air conditioning compressor and tighten the retaining bolts to 30–45 ft. lbs. (41–61 Nm). Connect the compressor-to-condenser discharge line.
48. Connect the A/C clutch field coil to the engine control sensor wiring.
49. Fasten the heater hoses and the fuel supply and return hoses, then connect the vacuum hoses.
50. Connect the engine control module wiring assembly.
51. Attach the transaxle oil cooler inlet and outlet tubes.
52. Install the radiator assembly.
53. Partially raise and safely support the vehicle.
54. Install the converter-to-flywheel nuts/bolts and tighten to 20–34 ft. lbs. (27–46 Nm).
55. Install the left and right front engine supports, then install the engine rear plate.
56. Install the starter motor. For details, please refer to the procedure located earlier in this section.
57. Connect the lower radiator hose.
58. Install the drive belt-tensioner assembly and the crankshaft pulley and vibration damper assembly. Tighten the crankshaft pulley retaining bolts to 20–28 ft. lbs. (27–38 Nm).
59. Install the dual converter Y-pipe, then connect the engine control sensor wiring to the heated exhaust gas oxygen sensor.
60. Install the oil filter, and then connect the engine control sensor wiring to the low oil level sensor.
61. Carefully lower the vehicle.
62. Position the thermactor air supply pump and install the retaining bolts.
63. Connect the vacuum pump and install the exhaust air supply pump pulley assembly.
64. Install the wiring shield.
65. Install the distributor cap and rotor.
66. Install the radiator reservoir /coolant recovery assembly, upper radiator hose, and water pump pulley.
67. Connect the alternator-to-voltage regulator wiring assembly, then fasten the fuel charging wiring to the engine control sensor wiring.
68. Connect the wiring assembly ground.
69. Install the accelerator cable-mounting bracket.
70. Connect the power steering pressure hose assembly and the power steering return hose.
71. Install the cooling fan motor/fan blade and the fan shroud assembly.
72. Connect the cooling fan motor and the front center radiator primary crash-sensor wire connectors.
73. Install the IRCM relay and bracket. Make sure to tighten the retainers securely.
74. Install the drive belts.
75. Position and install the engine and transaxle support assembly.
76. Install the radiator upper sight shield.
77. Partially raise and safely support the vehicle. Install the wheel and tire assemblies, then tighten the lug nuts to 85–105 ft. lbs. (115–142 Nm).
78. Carefully lower the vehicle.
79. Install the hood, using the aligning marks made during removal, and connect the negative battery cable.

80. Fill the cooling system with the proper type and quantity of coolant. Fill the crankcase with the proper type and viscosity of motor oil to the required level.

81. Have a MVAC certified evacuate, pressure test and recharge the A/C system, using the proper equipment.

82. Start the engine and check for leaks.

### 4.6L Engine except Continental

**See Figures 9 thru 14**

1. Disconnect the negative, then the positive battery cable. Drain the crankcase and the cooling system into suitable containers.

**If your vehicle is equipped with air conditioning, refer to Section 1 for information regarding the implications of servicing your A/C system yourself. Only an MVAC-trained, EPA-certified, automotive technician should service the A/C system or its components.**

2. Properly relieve the fuel system pressure.
3. Drain and recycle the engine coolant.
4. Relieve the fuel system pressure and disconnect the fuel lines; refer to Section 5. Discharge the air conditioning system; refer to Section 1.
5. Mark the position of the hood on the hinges and remove the hood.
6. Remove the cooling fan, shroud, and radiator.
7. Remove the wiper module and support bracket. Remove the air inlet tube.
8. Remove the 42-pin connector from the retaining bracket on the brake vacuum booster. Disconnect the 42-pin connector and transmission harness connector and position aside.
9. Disconnect the accelerator and cruise control cables. Disconnect the throttle valve cable.
10. Disconnect the electrical connector and vacuum hose from the purge solenoid. Disconnect the power supply from the power distribution box and starter relay.
11. Disconnect the vacuum supply hose from the throttle body adapter vacuum port. Disconnect the heater hoses.
12. Disconnect the alternator harness from the fender apron and junction block. Disconnect the air conditioning hoses from the compressor.
13. Disconnect the Electronic Variable Orifice (EVO) sensor connector from the power steering pump and disconnect the body ground strap from the dash panel.
14. Raise and safely support the vehicle.
15. Disconnect the exhaust system from the exhaust manifolds and support with wire hung from the crossmember.
16. Remove the retaining nut from the transmission line bracket and remove the 3 bolts and stud retaining the engine to the transmission knee braces.
17. Remove the starter. Remove the 4 bolts retaining the power steering pump to the engine block and position aside.
18. Remove the plug from the engine block to access the torque converter retaining nuts. Rotate the crankshaft until each of the 4 nuts is accessible and remove the nuts. Matchmark the converter and flexplate with a dab of paint to ease installation.
19. Remove the 6 transmission-to-engine retaining bolts. Remove the engine mount through bolts, 2 on the left mount and 1 on the right mount.
20. Lower the vehicle. Support the transmission with a floor jack and remove the bolt retaining the right engine mount to the lower engine bracket.
21. Install an engine-lifting bracket to the left cylinder head on the front and the right cylinder head on the rear. Connect suitable engine lifting equipment to the lifting brackets.
22. Raise the engine slightly and carefully separate the engine from the transmission.
23. Carefully lift the engine out of the engine compartment and position on a workstand. Remove the engine lifting equipment.

**To install:**

24. Install the engine lifting brackets to the left cylinder head on the front and the right cylinder head on the rear. Connect the engine lifting equipment to the brackets and remove the engine from the workstand.
25. Carefully lower the engine into the engine compartment. Start the converter pilot into the flexplate and align the paint marks on the flexplate and torque converter. Make sure the studs on the torque converter align with the holes in the flexplate.
26. Fully engage the engine to the transmission and lower onto the mounts. Remove the engine lifting equipment and brackets. Install the bolt retaining the right engine mount to the frame.
27. Raise and safely support the vehicle. Install the 6 engine-to-transmission bolts and tighten to 30–44 ft. lbs. (40–60 Nm).
28. Install the engine mount through bolts and tighten to 15–22 ft. lbs. (20–30 Nm). Install the 4

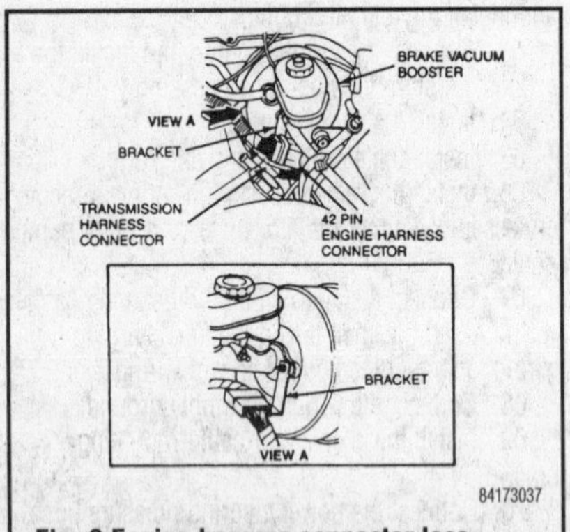


**Fig. 9 Engine harness connector location—4.6L engine**

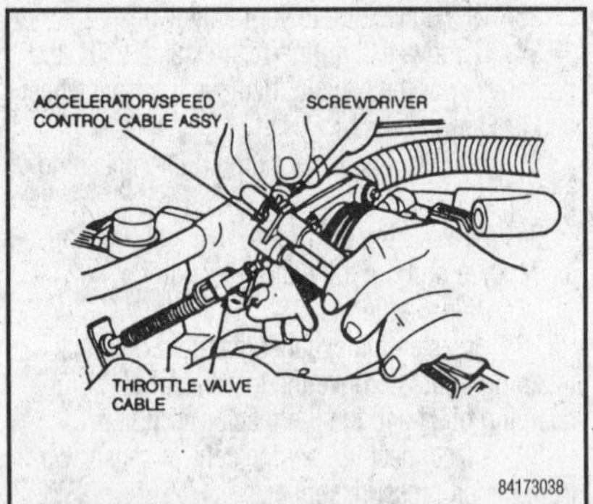


**Fig. 10 Disconnecting the accelerator/cruise control cables—4.6L engine**

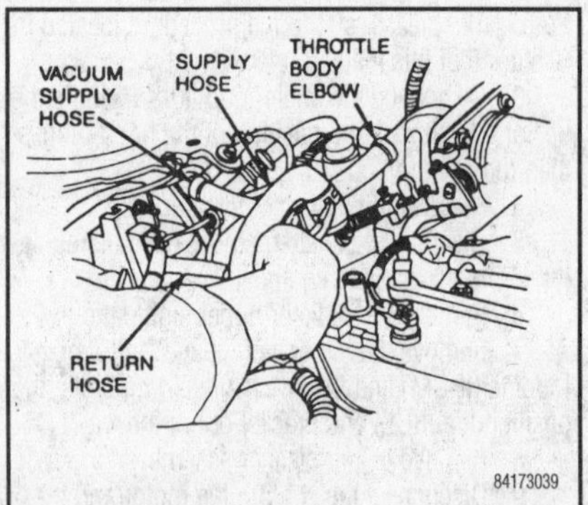


**Fig. 11 Disconnecting the vacuum supply hose—4.6L engine**

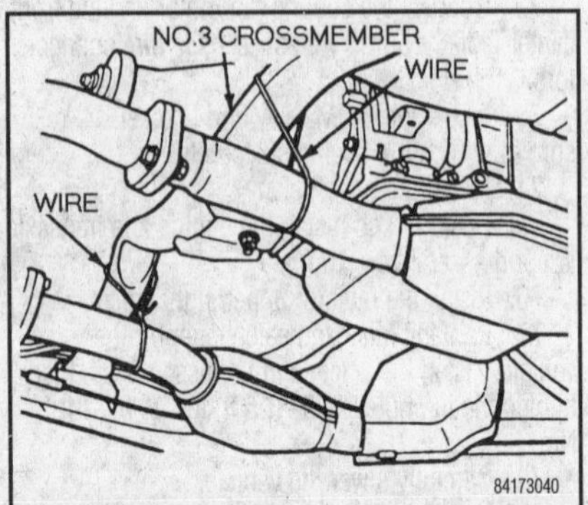


**Fig. 12 Hang the exhaust system from the crossmember with wire**

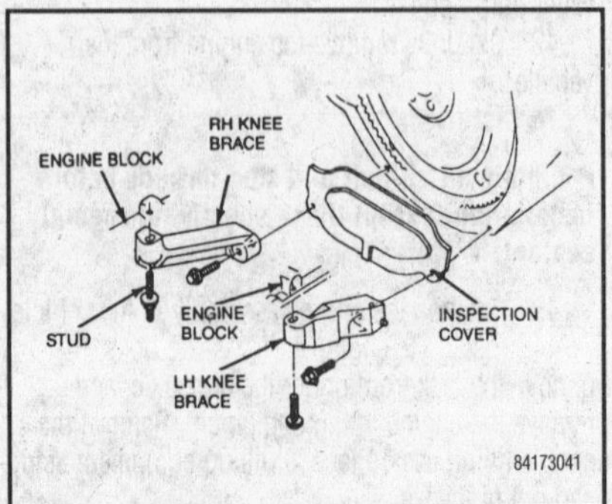


**Fig. 13 Engine-to-transmission knee braces—4.6L engine**

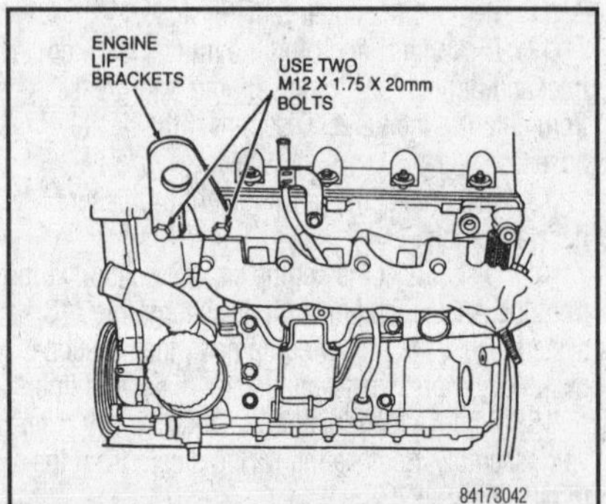


**Fig. 14 Install an engine-lifting bracket at the front of the left cylinder head—4.6L engine**

torque converter retaining nuts and tighten to 22–25 ft. lbs. (20–30 Nm). Install the plug into the access hole in the engine block.

29. Position the power steering pump on the engine block and install the 4 retaining nuts. Tighten to 15–22 ft. lbs. (20–30 Nm). Install the starter.

30. Position the engine to transmission braces and install the 3 bolts and 1 stud. Tighten the bolts and stud to 18–31 ft. lbs. (25–43 Nm).

31. Position the transmission line bracket to the knee brace stud and install the retaining nut. Tighten to 15–22 ft. lbs. (20–30 Nm).

32. Cut the wire and position the exhaust system to the manifolds. Install the 4 nuts and tighten to 20–30 ft. lbs. (27–41 Nm).

**➡Make sure the exhaust system clears the No. 3 crossmember. Adjust as necessary.**

33. Lower the vehicle and connect the EVO sensor.

34. Connect the air conditioner lines to the compressor. Connect the alternator harness from the fender apron and junction block.

35. Connect the heater hoses and connect the vacuum supply hose to the throttle body adapter vacuum port.

36. Connect the power supply to the power distribution box and starter relay. Connect the electrical connector and vacuum hose to the purge solenoid.

37. Connect and if necessary, adjust the throttle valve cable. Connect the accelerator and cruise control cables.

38. Connect the 42-pin engine harness connector and transmission harness connector. Install the 42-pin connector to the retaining bracket on the brake vacuum booster.

39. Install the wiper module and support bracket. Connect the fuel lines.

40. Install the radiator, cooling fan and shroud. Install the air inlet tube.

41. Fill the crankcase with the proper type and quantity of engine oil. Fill the cooling system.

42. Install the hood, aligning the marks that were made during removal. Connect the battery cables.

43. Start the engine and bring to operating temperature. Check for leaks. Check all fluid levels.

44. Have a MVAC certified evacuate and charge the air conditioning system.

45. Road test the vehicle.

### 4.6L Engine Continental

**➡The Front Wheel Drive 4.6L Engine has to be removed with the transaxle intact mounted onto the sub-frame as an assembly. It requires the use of a hoist and a special lifting platform to lower the assembly from the body.**

**➡Your vehicle is equipped with air conditioning, refer to Section 1 for information regarding the implications of servicing your A/C system yourself. Only an MVAC-trained, EPA-certified, automotive technician should service the A/C system or its components.**

1. Disconnect the negative battery cable.

2. Disconnect the steering coupling at the pinch bolt joint inside the passenger compartment

3. Remove the engine appearance cover retainers and remove the engine appearance cover from the vehicle.

4. Disconnect the engine control sensor wiring from the intake air temperature sensor and the crankcase ventilation tube from the air cleaner outlet tube.

Loosen the clamps on the air cleaner outlet tube to the engine air cleaner and the throttle body. Remove the air cleaner outlet tube.

5. Drain and recycle the engine coolant.

6. Properly relieve the fuel system pressure.

7. Disconnect the fuel tubes from the fuel injection supply manifold.

8. Disconnect the chassis vacuum supply hose at the connection on the intake manifold. Position the hose out of the way.

9. Remove the ground straps from the dash panel.

10. Disconnect the engine control sensor wiring from the powertrain control module and position the engine control sensor wiring out of the way.

11. Remove the connectors for the engine control sensor wiring from the retaining bracket on the power brake booster. Disconnect the engine control sensor wiring at the two connectors

12. Disconnect the engine control sensor wiring from the mass air flow sensor, and the wiring from the evaporative emission canister purge valve.

13. Disconnect the evaporative emission hose at the crankcase vent connector and position it out of the way.

14. Remove the shield and disconnect the throttle and speed control cables from the throttle body and from the cable bracket. Move them out of the way.

15. Disconnect the manual lever control at the transmission range sensor.

16. Remove and disconnect the connectors from the engine control sensors wiring bracket from the top of the transaxle

17. Disconnect the main emission vacuum control connector at the connection near the fan shroud

18. Disconnect the oil cooler inlet tube from the transaxle. Remove the dipstick.

19. Disconnect the heater hoses and upper radiator hose.

20. Remove the power steering return hose and drain the reservoir.

21. Disconnect the wiring harness from the generator, and remove the retaining clip.

22. Partially raise the vehicle on a hoist, and remove the front tire assemblies

23. Disconnect the ride height sensors, if equipped, from the lower suspension arms.

24. Remove the stabilizer bar links from the front stabilizer bar.

25. Separate the RH and LH front suspension lower arms from the knuckles at the ball-joints.

26. Separate the tie rod ends from the steering knuckles.

27. Remove the RH and LH front axle wheel hub retainers from the halfshaft ends, and remove the halfshafts from the front wheel knuckle.

28. Raise the vehicle and remove the splash shield from the radiator support and from the front sub-frame.

29. Drain the engine oil.

30. Remove the dual converter Y pipe.

31. Disconnect the power steering pressure hose from the cooler connection and position it out of the way. Be sure to catch any fluid that may leak from the hose.

32. Disconnect the lower radiator hose at the thermostat housing and remove the lower hose.

33. Disconnect the starter wiring and remove the starter.

34. Disconnect the lower oil cooler from the transaxle.

35. Disconnect the retaining clips and the A/C compressor lines.

36. Support the front sub-frame, (engine and transaxle assembly), using a suitable powertrain lift.

37. Remove the front sub-frame retaining bolts, and lower the engine transaxle and front sub-frame from the vehicle.

38. Disconnect the power steering pressure hose from the power steering pump.

39. Install the necessary engine lifting brackets to the engine, and using a suitable crane, support the engine and transaxle assembly.

40. Remove the front engine support insulator, rear engine support insulator, (motor mounts) and the engine and transmission support.

41. Lift the engine and transaxle from the front sub-frame.

42. Lower the engine and transaxle support the transaxle on a level, stationary surface. Remove the transaxle-to-cylinder block mounting bolts and separate the engine from the transaxle assembly.

**To install:**

Installation is the reversal of the removal procedures

### 5.0L Engine

1. Disconnect the negative, then the positive battery cable. Drain the crankcase and the cooling system into suitable containers.

2. Drain and recycle the engine coolant.

3. Properly relieve the fuel system pressure.

**➡If your vehicle is equipped with air conditioning, refer to Section 1 for information regarding the implications of servicing your A/C system yourself. Only an MVAC-trained, EPA-certified, automotive technician should service the A/C system or its components.**

**CAUTION**

**Never open, service, or drain the radiator or cooling system when hot; serious burns can occur from the steam and hot coolant. In addition, when draining engine coolant, keep in mind that cats and dogs are attracted to ethylene glycol antifreeze and could drink any that is left in an uncovered container or in puddles on the ground. This will prove fatal in sufficient quantities. Always drain coolant into a sealable container. Coolant should be reused unless it is contaminated or is several years old.**

4. Mark the position of the hood on the hinges and remove the hood. Disconnect the battery ground cables from the cylinder block.

5. Remove the air intake duct and the air cleaner.

6. Disconnect the upper radiator hose from the thermostat housing and the lower hose from the water pump. Disconnect the oil cooler lines from the radiator.

7. Remove the bolts attaching the radiator fan shroud to the radiator. Remove the radiator. Remove the fan, belt pulley, and shroud.

8. Remove the alternator bolts and position the alternator aside.

9. Disconnect the oil pressure sending unit wire from the sending unit. Disconnect the fuel lines; refer to Section 5.

10. Disconnect the accelerator cable from the throttle body. Disconnect the throttle valve rod/cable. Disconnect the cruise control cable, if equipped.

11. Disconnect the throttle valve vacuum line from the intake manifold, if equipped. Disconnect the transmission filler tube bracket from the cylinder block.

12. Disconnect the air conditioning lines and electrical connectors at the compressor; refer to Section 6. Plug the lines and the compressor fittings to prevent the entrance of dirt and moisture.

13. Disconnect the power steering pump bracket from the cylinder head. Remove the drive belt. Position the power steering pump aside in a position that will prevent the fluid from leaking.

14. Disconnect the power brake vacuum line from the intake manifold.

15. Disconnect the heater hoses from the heater tubes. Disconnect the electrical connector from the coolant temperature-sending unit.

16. Remove the transmission-to-engine upper bolts.

17. Disconnect the wiring harness at the two 10-pin connectors.

18. Raise and safely support the vehicle. Disconnect the starter cable from the starter and remove the starter.

19. Disconnect the muffler inlet pipes from the exhaust manifolds. Disconnect the engine mounts from the chassis. Disconnect the downstream thermactor tubing and check valve from the right exhaust manifold stud, if equipped.

20. Disconnect the transmission cooler lines from the retainer and remove the transmission inspection cover..

21. Match mark the converter and flywheel with a dab of paint to ease installation. Disconnect the flywheel from the converter and secure the converter assembly in the transmission. Remove the remaining transmission-to-engine bolts.

22. Lower the vehicle and then support the transmission. Attach suitable engine lifting equipment and hoist the engine.

23. Raise the engine slightly and carefully pull it from the transmission. Carefully lift the engine out of the engine compartment. Avoid bending or damaging the rear cover plate or other components. Install the engine on a workstand.

**To install:**

24. Attach the engine lifting equipment and remove the engine from the workstand.

25. Lower the engine carefully into the engine compartment. Make sure the exhaust manifolds are properly aligned with the muffler inlet pipes.

26. Start the converter pilot into the crankshaft. Align the paint mark on the flywheel to the paint mark on the torque converter.

27. Install the transmission upper bolts, making sure the dowels in the cylinder block engage the transmission.

28. Install the engine mount-to-chassis attaching fasteners and remove the engine lifting equipment.

29. Raise and safely support the vehicle. Connect both muffler inlet pipes to the exhaust manifolds. Install the starter and connect the starter cable.

30. Remove the retainer holding the torque converter in the transmission. Attach the converter to the flywheel. Install the converter housing inspection cover and install the remaining transmission attaching bolts.

31. Remove the support from the transmission and lower the vehicle.

32. Connect the wiring harness at the two 10-pin connectors.

33. Connect the coolant temperature sending unit wire and connect the heater hoses. Connect the wiring to the metal heater tubes and the engine coolant temperature, air charge temperature and oxygen sensors.

34. Connect the transmission filler tube bracket. Connect the manual shift rod and the retracting spring. Connect the throttle valve vacuum line, if equipped.

35. Connect the accelerator cable and throttle valve cable. Connect the cruise control cable, if equipped.

36. Connect the fuel lines and the oil pressure sending unit wire.

37. Install the pulley, water pump belt and fan/clutch assembly.

38. Position the alternator bracket and install the alternator bolts. Connect the alternator and ground cables. Adjust the drive belt tension.

39. Unplug and connect the refrigerant lines and connect the electrical connector to the compressor.

40. Install the power steering drive belt and power steering pump bracket. Connect the power brake vacuum line.

41. Place the shroud over the fan and install the radiator. Connect the radiator hoses and the transmission oil cooler lines. Position the shroud and install the bolts.

42. Connect the heater hoses to the heater tubes. Fill the cooling system. Fill the crankcase with the proper type and quantity of engine oil. Adjust the transmission throttle linkage.

43. Connect the positive and then the negative battery cables. Start the engine and bring to normal operating temperature. Check for leaks. Check all fluid levels.

44. Install the air intake duct assembly. Install the hood, aligning the marks that were made during removal.

45. Have a MVAC certified evacuate and charge the air conditioning system.

46. Road test the vehicle.

## Rocker Arm (Valve) Cover

### REMOVAL & INSTALLATION

#### 3.8L Engine

**See Figures 15, 16, 17, 18 and 19**

1. Disconnect the negative battery cable.

2. Tag and disconnect the ignition wires from the spark plugs.

3. Remove the ignition wire separators from the valve cover retaining bolt studs.

4. If the left cover is being removed, remove the upper intake manifold. For details, please refer to the procedure located later in this section.

5. If the right cover is being removed, position the air cleaner assembly aside and remove the PCV valve.

6. If the left cover is being removed, removing the oil filler cap is not necessary.

7. Remove the rocker arm/valve cover mounting bolts, then remove the cover.

**To install:**

8. Lightly oil all bolt and stud bolt threads, then, using solvent, clean the cylinder head and valve cover sealing surface to remove all gasket material and dirt.

9. Position a new rocker arm/valve cover gasket on the cylinder head, then install the retaining bolts. Make sure to note the position of the ignition wire separator stud bolts, then tighten the retaining bolts to 80–106 inch lbs. (9–12 Nm).

10. If removed, install the upper intake manifold. For details, please refer to the procedure located later in this section.

11. If the left cover is being installed, install the oil filler cap.

93143P84

**Fig. 15 Removing the upper intake manifold to access the left side rocker cover**

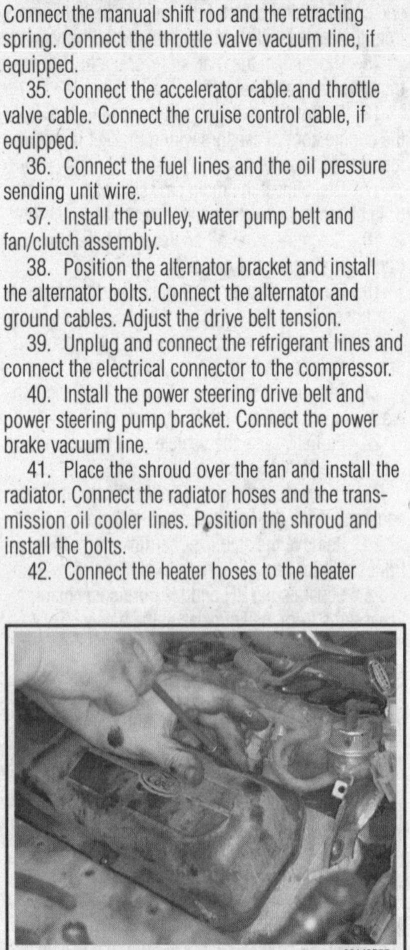

93143P57

**Fig. 16 Remove the 5 fasteners holding the rocker cover in place**

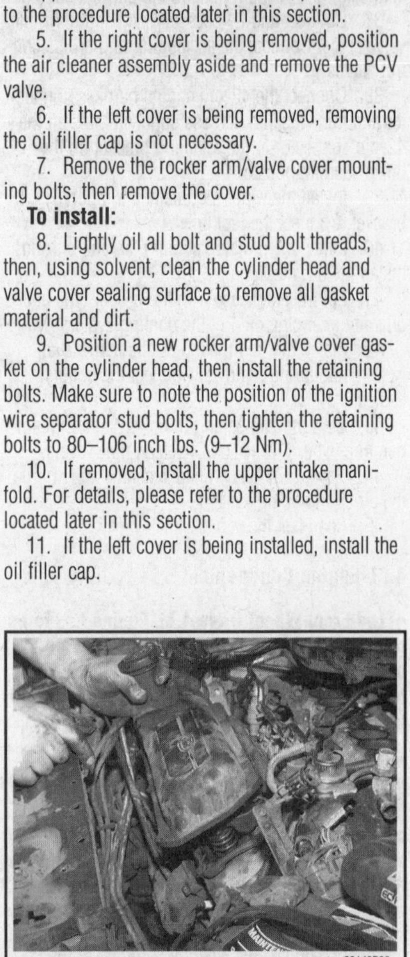

93143P86

**Fig. 17 Lift the rocker cover straight up to clear the valve train, be careful with the ignition wires**

93143P58

**Fig. 18 Remove the rocker cover to expose the upper valve train; removing the oil filler cap is not necessary**

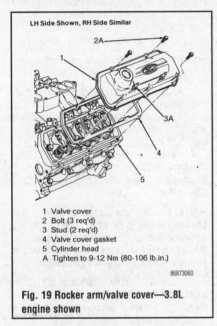

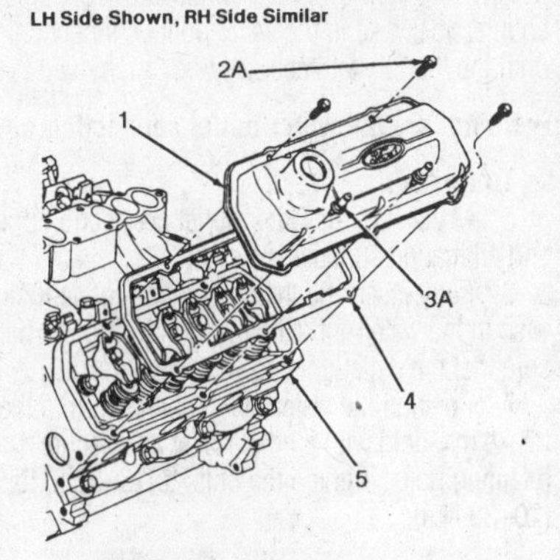


1 Valve cover
2 Bolt (3 req'd)
3 Stud (2 req'd)
4 Valve cover gasket
5 Cylinder head
A Tighten to 9-12 Nm (80-106 lb.in.)

86873060

**Fig. 19 Rocker arm/valve cover—3.8L engine shown**

12. If the right cover is being installed, install the PCV valve, then the air cleaner.

13. Install the ignition wire separators, then connect the ignition wires to the spark plugs as tagged during removal.

14. Connect the negative battery cable, then start the engine, and check for oil leaks.

### 4.6L Engine

➧ **See Figure 20**

1. Disconnect the negative battery cable.
2. Remove the right valve cover as follows:
   a. Disconnect the positive battery cable at the battery and at the power distribution box. Remove the retaining bolt from the positive battery cable bracket located on the side of the right cylinder head.
   b. Disconnect the crankshaft position sensor, air conditioning compressor clutch and canister purge solenoid connectors. Position the harness out of the way.
   c. Disconnect the vent hose from the purge solenoid and position the positive battery cable out of the way.
   d. Disconnect the spark plug wires from the spark plugs. Remove the spark plug wire brackets from the camshaft cover studs and position the wires out of the way.
   e. Remove the PCV valve from the valve cover grommet and position out of the way.
   f. Remove the bolts and stud bolts (note their positions for reassembly) and remove the valve cover.
3. Remove the left valve cover as follows:
   a. Remove the air inlet tube. Relieve the fuel system pressure and disconnect the fuel lines; refer to Section 5.
   b. Raise and safely support the vehicle.
   c. Disconnect the Electronic Variable Orifice (EVO) sensor and oil pressure-sending unit and position the harness out of the way. Lower the vehicle.
   d. Remove the 42-pin engine harness connector from the retaining bracket on the brake vacuum booster. Disconnect and position out of the way.
   e. Remove the windshield wiper module.
   f. Disconnect the spark plug wires from the spark plugs. Remove the spark plug wire brackets from the studs and position the wires out of the way.
   g. Remove the bolts and stud bolts (noting their position for reassembly) and remove the valve cover.

**To install:**

4. Clean the sealing surfaces of the valve covers and cylinder heads. Apply silicone sealer to the places where the front engine cover meets the cylinder head.
5. Attach new gaskets to the valve covers, using suitable sealant. Install the covers with the bolts and stud bolts and tighten to 6.0–8.8 ft. lbs. (8–12 Nm).
6. When installing the right valve cover, proceed as follows:
   a. Install the PCV into the valve cover grommet.
   b. Install the spark plug wire brackets on the studs and connect the wires to the spark plugs.
   c. Position the harness and connect the canister purge solenoid, air conditioning compressor clutch and crankshaft position sensor.
   d. Position the positive battery cable harness on the right cylinder head. Install the bolt retaining the cable bracket to the cylinder head.

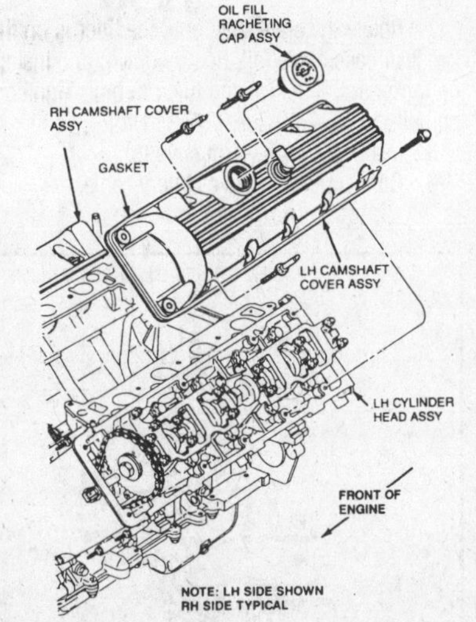


84173047

**Fig. 20 Valve cover installation—4.6L engine**

   e. Connect the positive battery cable at the power distribution box and the battery.
7. When installing the left valve cover, proceed as follows:
   a. Install the spark plug wire brackets on the studs and connect the wires to the spark plugs.
   b. Install the windshield wiper module.
   c. Connect the 42-pin connector and transmission harness connector. Install the connector on the retaining bracket.
   d. Raise and safely support the vehicle. Position and connect the EVO sensor and oil pressure sending unit harness.
   e. Lower the vehicle. Connect the fuel lines.
8. Connect the negative battery cable. Start the engine and check for leaks.

### 5.0L Engine

1. Disconnect the negative battery cable.
2. Before removing the right rocker arm cover, disconnect the PCV closure tube from the oil fill standpipe at the rocker cover.
3. Remove the thermactor bypass valve and air supply hoses as necessary to provide clearance.
4. Disconnect the spark plug wires from the spark plugs. Remove the wires and bracket assembly from the rocker arm cover attaching stud and position the wires out of the way.
5. Remove the upper intake manifold as follows:
   a. Tag and disconnect the electrical connectors at the air bypass valve, throttle position sensor, and EGR position sensor.
   b. Disconnect the throttle and transmission linkage at the throttle body. Remove the cable bracket from the intake manifold and position the bracket and cables aside.
   c. Tag and disconnect the vacuum lines from the vacuum tree, EGR valve, fuel pressure regulator, and evaporative canister.
   d. Disconnect the PCV hose from the fitting on the rear of the upper manifold and disconnect the PCV vent closure tube at the throttle body.
   e. Remove the 2 EGR coolant lines from the EGR spacer.
   f. Remove the upper intake manifold cover plate.
   g. Remove the 6 retaining bolts and remove the upper intake manifold.
6. Remove the attaching bolts and remove the rocker arm covers.

**To install:**

7. Clean all gasket mating surfaces of the rocker arm covers and cylinder heads.
8. Attach new rocker arm cover gaskets to the rocker arm covers, using suitable sealant. Install the rocker arm covers and tighten the bolts to 10–13 ft. lbs. (14–18 Nm), wait 2 minutes and tighten again to the same specification.
9. Install the crankcase ventilation tube in the right cover.
10. Install the upper intake manifold in the reverse order of removal. Use a new gasket and tighten the retaining bolts to 12–18 ft. lbs. (16–24 Nm).
11. Install the spark plug wires and bracket assembly on the rocker cover attaching stud. Connect the spark plug wires.
12. Install the air cleaner and intake duct assembly. Install the thermactor bypass valve and air supply hoses, if required.
13. Connect the negative battery cable, start the engine, and check for leaks.

## Rocker Arms/Roller Followers

### REMOVAL & INSTALLATION

#### 3.8L Engine

1. Disconnect the negative battery cable.
2. Remove the rocker arm/valve cover(s). For details, please refer to the procedure located earlier in this section.
3. Remove the rocker arm bolt, fulcrum, and rocker arm. Keep all parts in order so they can be reinstalled in their original positions.

**To install:**

4. Lubricated all rocker arms with an Engine Assembly Lubricant.

**➡Rocker arm seats must be fully seated in the cylinder head, and pushrods must be seated in the rocker arm sockets before final tightening, or engine damage may occur.**

5. For each valve, rotate the crankshaft until the valve lifter rests on the heel (base circle) of the camshaft lobe. Position the rocker arm(s) over the push rods, then install the rocker arm seats. Tighten the rocker arm seat retaining bolts to 44 inch lbs. (5 Nm).
6. Final tightening of the rocker arm retaining bolt(s) is to 19–25 ft. lbs. (25–35 Nm). For final tightening, the camshaft may be in any position.
7. Clean the rocker arm cover and cylinder head mating surfaces of old gasket material and dirt.
8. Install the rocker arm/valve cover(s). For details, please refer to the procedure located earlier in this section.
9. Connect the negative battery cable.

#### 4.6L Engine

**➧ See Figure 21**

1. Disconnect the negative battery cable.
2. Remove the valve cover(s).
3. Position the piston of the cylinder being serviced at the bottom of its stroke and position the camshaft lobe on the base circle.
4. Install a valve spring spacer tool, between the spring coils to prevent valve seal damage.

**WARNING**

**If the valve spring spacer tool is not used, the retainer will hit the valve stem seal and damage the seal.**

5. Install a valve spring compressor tool, under the camshaft and on top of the valve spring retainer.
6. Compress the valve spring and remove the roller follower. Remove the valve spring compressor and spacer.
7. Repeat Steps 3–;6 for each roller follower to be removed. Inspect the roller follower(s) for wear and/or damage and replace, as necessary.

**To install:**

8. Apply engine oil or assembly lubricant to the valve stem tip and roller follower contact surfaces.
9. Install a valve spring spacer tool, between the spring coils. Compress the valve spring using a valve spring compressor tool, and install the roller follower.

**➡The piston must be at the bottom of its stroke and the camshaft at the base circle.**

10. Remove the valve spring compressor and spacer.
11. Repeat Steps 8–10 for each roller follower to be installed.
12. Install the valve cover(s). Connect the negative battery cable.

#### 5.0L Engine

**➧ See Figure 22**

1. Disconnect the negative battery cable.
2. Remove the rocker arm cover(s). Use the procedures given earlier in this section.
3. Remove the rocker arm fulcrum bolt, fulcrum seat, and rocker arm. Keep all rocker arm assemblies together. Identify each assembly so it may be reinstalled in its original position.
4. Inspect the rocker arm and fulcrum seat contact surfaces for wear and/or damage. Also, check the rocker arm for wear on the valve stem tip contact surface and the pushrod socket. Replace complete rocker arm assemblies, as necessary.
5. Inspect the pushrod end and the valve stem tip. Replace pushrods, as necessary. If the valve stem tip is worn, the cylinder head must be removed to replace or machine the valve.

**To install:**

6. Apply engine oil or assembly lubricant to the valve stem tip and pushrod end. Also, apply lubricant to the rocker arm and fulcrum seat contact surfaces.
7. Rotate the crankshaft until the lifter is on the camshaft base circle (all the way down) and install the rocker, fulcrum seat and fulcrum bolt. Tighten the bolts to 18–25 ft. lbs. (24–34 Nm).
8. Install the rocker arm cover(s).
9. Connect the negative battery cable.

## Thermostat

### REMOVAL & INSTALLATION

#### 3.8L Engine

**➧ See Figure 23**

1. Disconnect the negative battery cable.
2. Place a suitable drain pan below the radiator.
3. Carefully remove the radiator cap, then connect a ⅜ in. (9.5mm) hose to the drain tube, then open the draincock. Drain the radiator to a level below the water outlet connection, then close the draincock.
4. Loosen the upper radiator hose clamp at the radiator, then remove the water outlet connection retaining bolts and lift the water outlet clear of the engine. Note the position of the thermostat in the water outlet. Remove the thermostat by rotating it counterclockwise in the water outlet connection until the thermostat becomes free to remove.

**➡Do not pry the water outlet connection off.**

**To install:**

5. Make sure the water outlet connection pocket and all mating surfaces are clean.
6. Fully insert the thermostat and rotate it clockwise in the water outlet connection to secure; be sure that the pellet goes toward the block.
7. Position the water outlet connection to the intake manifold with a new gasket and secure the retaining bolts. Tighten the bolts to 15–22 ft. lbs. (20–30 Nm).

**➡Make sure the hose clamps are beyond the bead and placed in the center of the clamping surface of the connection. Any worn hose clamps must be replaced with a new clamp to ensure proper sealing at the connection.**

8. Position the upper radiator hose to the radiator. Position the clamps between the alignment marks on both ends of the upper radiator hose, then slide the hose on the connections. Tighten the screw clamps to 20–30 inch lbs. (2.2–3.4 Nm).
9. Refill the cooling system. Connect the negative battery cable. Start the engine and check for leaks. Check the coolant level and add as required.

#### 4.6L Engine

**➧ See Figures 24**

1. Drain the cooling system to a level below the thermostat.

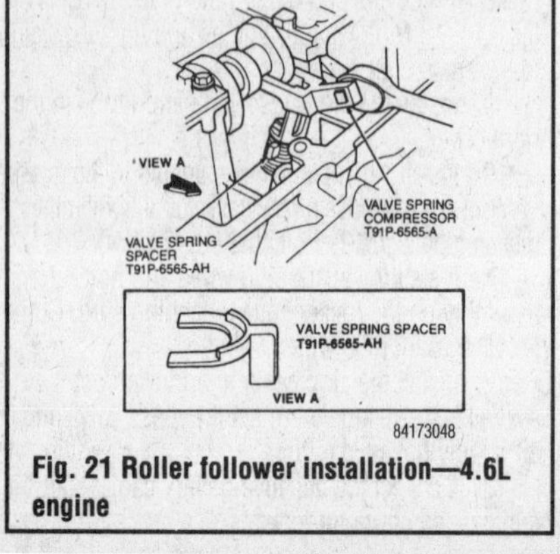


**Fig. 21 Roller follower installation—4.6L engine**

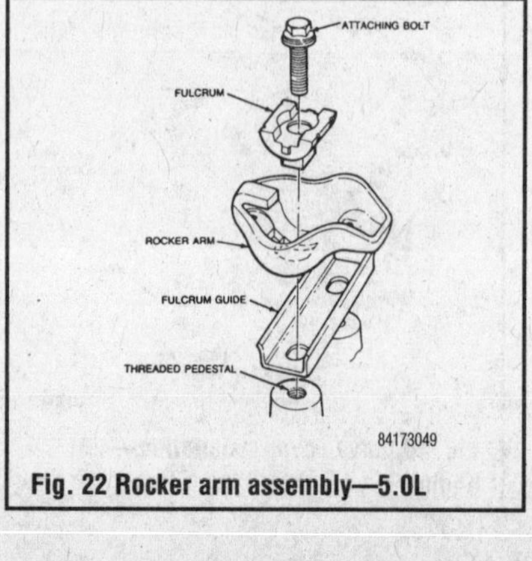


**Fig. 22 Rocker arm assembly—5.0L**

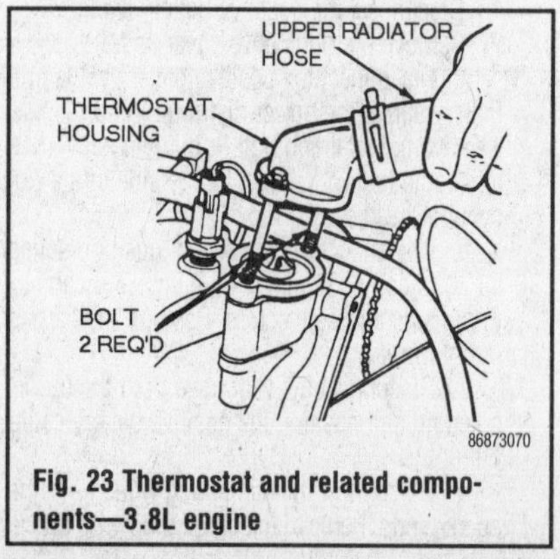


**Fig. 23 Thermostat and related components—3.8L engine**

**⁂ CAUTION**

**Never open, service, or drain the radiator or cooling system when hot; serious burns can occur from the steam and hot coolant. In addition, when draining engine coolant, keep in mind that cats and dogs are attracted to ethylene glycol antifreeze and could drink any that is left in an uncovered container or in puddles on the ground. This will prove fatal in sufficient quantities. Always drain coolant into a sealable container. Coolant should be reused unless it is contaminated or is several years old.**

2. Disconnect the upper radiator hose at the thermostat housing.
3. Remove the two thermostat-housing retaining bolts and remove the thermostat housing.
4. Remove the thermostat and O-ring seal. Inspect the O-ring for damage and replace, as necessary.

**To install:**

5. Make sure all mating surfaces are clean.
6. Install the thermostat, O-ring, and thermostat housing. Make sure the thermostat is positioned as shown in the figure.
7. Install and alternately tighten the thermostat housing retaining bolts to 15–22 ft. lbs. (20–30 Nm). Connect the upper radiator hose.
8. Fill the cooling system as described in Section 1. Check for leaks.

### 5.0L Engines

**▶ See Figures 25 and 26**

1. Drain the cooling system to a level below the thermostat.

**⁂ CAUTION**

**Never open, service, or drain the radiator or cooling system when hot; serious burns can occur from the steam and hot coolant. In addition, when draining engine coolant, keep in mind that cats and dogs are attracted to ethylene glycol antifreeze and could drink any that is left in an uncovered container or in puddles on the ground. This will prove fatal in sufficient quantities. Always drain coolant into a sealable container. Coolant should be reused unless it is contaminated or is several years old.**

2. Disconnect the upper radiator hose and the bypass hose at the thermostat housing.
3. To gain access to the thermostat housing: Mark the location of the distributor, loosen the hold-down clamp and rotate the distributor; or remove the distributor cap and rotor.
4. Remove the thermostat housing retaining bolts and the housing and gasket. Remove the thermostat from the housing.

**To install:**

5. Clean the gasket mating surfaces. Position a new gasket on the thermostat housing.
6. Install the thermostat in the housing, rotating slightly to lock the thermostat in place on the flats cast into the housing. Install the housing on the manifold and tighten the bolts to 12–18 ft. lbs. (16–24 Nm).

**➡If the thermostat has a bleeder valve, the thermostat should be positioned with the bleeder valve as close to the 12 o'clock position as possible when viewed from the front of the engine.**

7. Install the distributor cap and rotor, or reposition the distributor for correct ignition timing, as necessary. Tighten the hold-down bolt to 18–26 ft. lbs. (24–35 Nm).
8. Connect the bypass hose and the upper radiator hose to the thermostat housing. Fill the cooling system as described in Section 1.
9. Check for leaks.

## Intake Manifold

### REMOVAL & INSTALLATION

### 3.8L Engine

**▶ See Figures 27 thru 48**

1. Disconnect the negative battery cable, then properly drain the cooling system.
2. Remove the air cleaner assembly including the air intake duct tube.

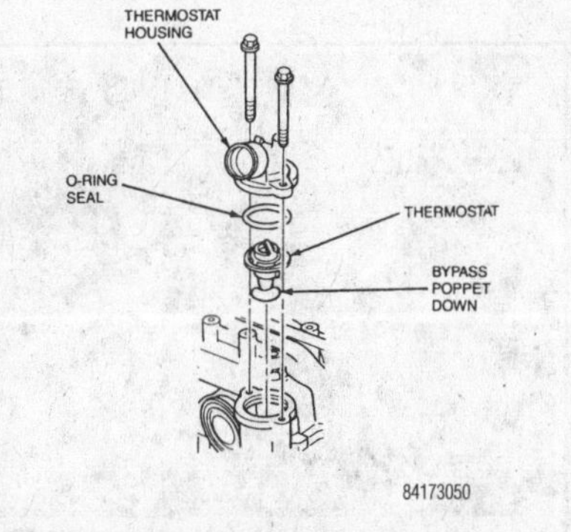


**Fig. 24 Thermostat installation—4.6L engine**

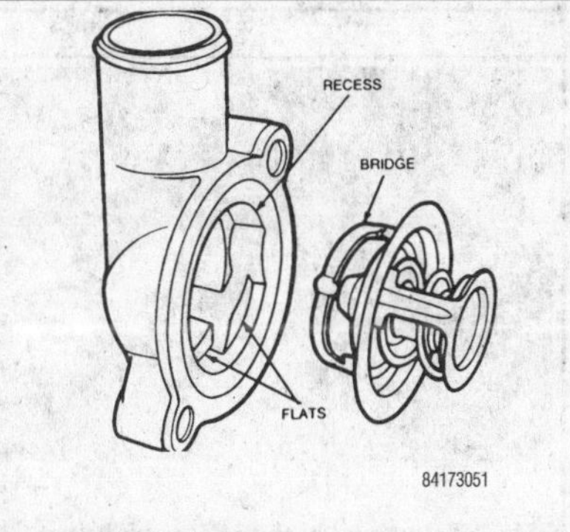


**Fig. 25 Thermostat installation—5.0L engines**

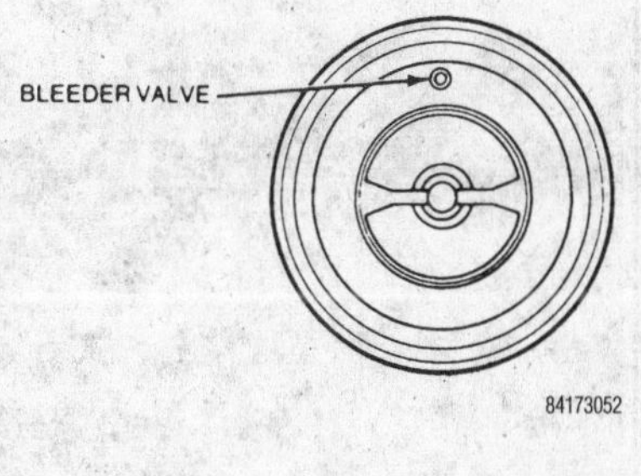


**Fig. 26 Thermostat bleeder valve location**

**Fig. 27 Remove the linkage cover at the intake manifold**

**Fig. 28 Remove the linkage from the throttle**

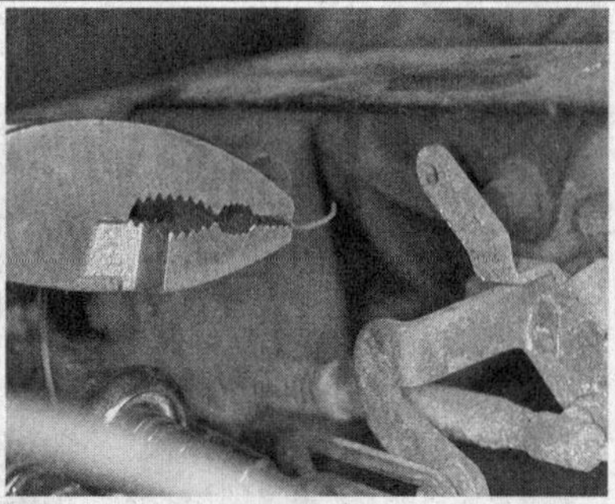


**Fig. 29 Using a pliers to disconnect the accelerator return spring**

93143P87

**Fig. 30 Removing the vacuum lines at the intake manifold**

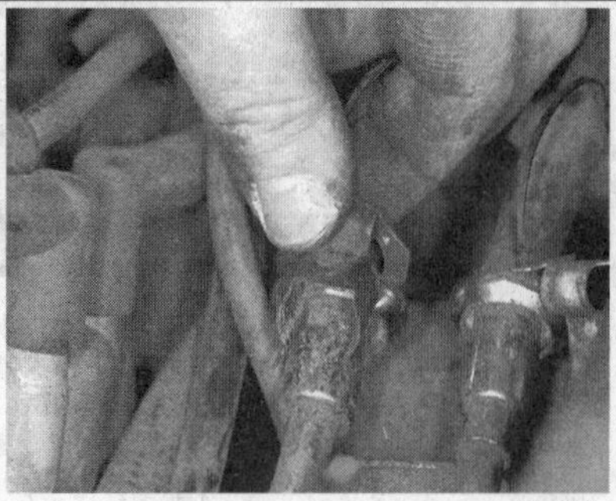
93143P48

**Fig. 31 Remove the fuel line locks by just pulling them off**

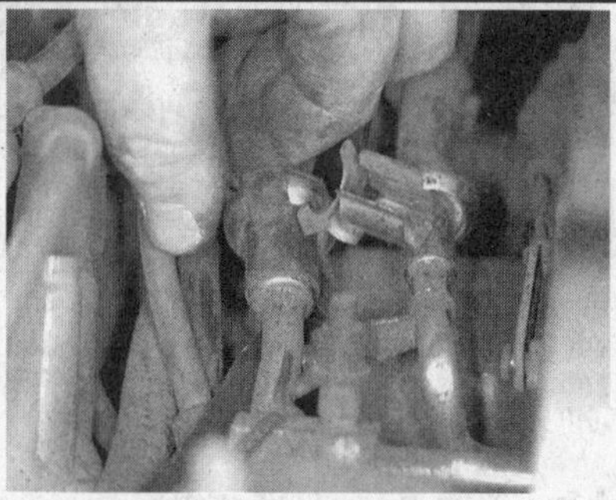
93143P49

**Fig. 32 There is a lock on each line and the fuel lines are different diameters. The smaller is the return**

93143P47

**Fig. 33 Install the special tool into the fuel line to separate the connector**

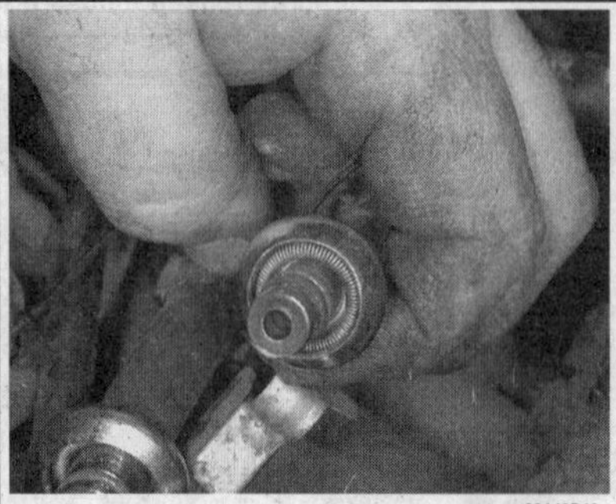
93143P46

**Fig. 34 The special tool must engage the spring to release the fuel line**

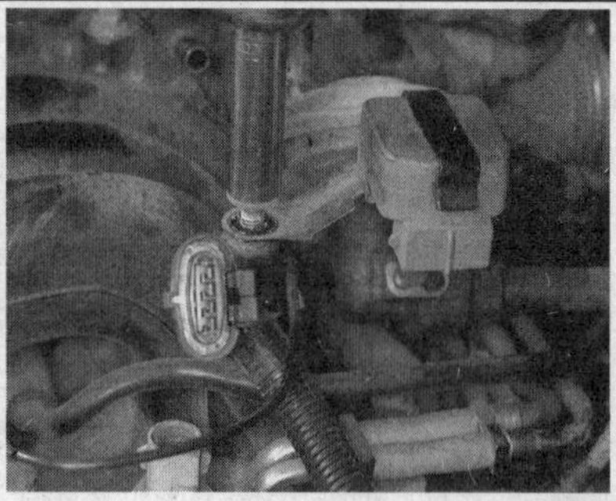
93143P36

**Fig. 35 Disconnecting and removing the PFE sensor**

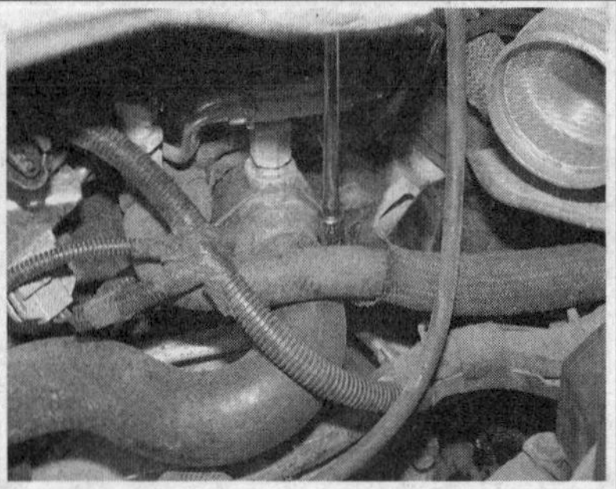
93143P40

**Fig. 36 The upper hose connects to the thermostat housing. It is easier to get to once the air cleaner has been removed**

93143P81

**Fig. 37 Removal of the EGR valve is not necessary in this procedure. Disconnect the EGR tube when not removing the EGR valve from the manifold**

93143P63

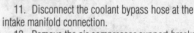

**Fig. 38 This wiring retainer bracket is easier to access with the alternator removed**

93143P53

**Fig. 39 Lifting the upper air intake manifold off the engine**

3. Disconnect the accelerator cable return spring at the throttle body assembly.
4. Disconnect the transaxle linkage at the upper intake manifold.
5. Remove the attaching bolts from the accelerator cable mounting bracket, then position the cables aside.
6. Tag and disconnect the vacuum lines from the fuel pressure regulator and the intake manifold
7. Disconnect the fuel lines at the injector fuel rail assembly.
8. Disengage any necessary electrical connectors.
9. Remove the drive belt. For details regarding this procedure, please refer to Section 1 of this manual.
10. Disconnect the radiator hose at the thermostat housing connection.
11. Disconnect the coolant bypass hose at the intake manifold connection.
12. Remove the air compressor support bracket. Remove the alternator mounting brace.
13. Disconnect the PCV lines. Disconnect the crankcase ventilation hoses located on the upper intake manifold.
14. Remove the throttle body assembly and remove the EGR valve assembly from the upper intake manifold, if necessary. For details regarding throttle body removal, please refer to Section 5 of this manual.
15. Remove the attaching nut, then remove the wiring retainer bracket located at the left front of the intake manifold and set aside with the ignition wires.
16. Remove the upper intake manifold attaching

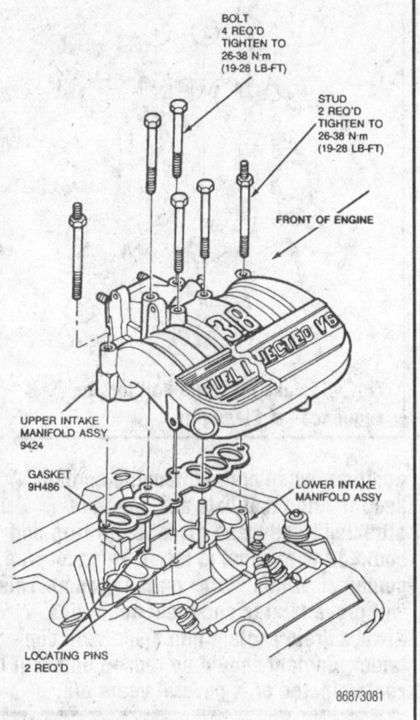


**Fig. 40 Upper intake manifold assembly—3.8L engine**

bolts/studs. Remove the upper intake manifold and gasket.

17. Remove the injectors and fuel injection supply manifold assembly.

18. Remove the heater water outlet hose.

**➡When removing the intake manifold retainers keep them in order so they can be installed in their original positions.**

19. Remove the lower intake manifold attaching bolts/studs, then remove the lower intake manifold. Remove the manifold side gaskets and end seals. Discard and replace with new gaskets and end seals.

**➡The manifold is sealed at each end with RTV-type sealer. To break the seal, it may be necessary to pry on the front of the manifold with a small or medium pry bar. If it is necessary to pry on the manifold, use care to prevent damage to the machined surfaces.**

**To install:**

**➡When installing the upper and/or lower intake manifold(s), ALWAYS use a new gasket.**

20. Lightly oil all attaching bolt and stud threads before installation.

**➡When using silicone rubber sealer, assembly must occur within 15 minutes after sealer application. After this time, the sealer may start to set-up and its sealing effectiveness may be reduced. The lower intake manifold, cylinder head and cylinder block mating surfaces should be clean and free of oil and gasket material. Use a suitable solvent to clean these surfaces.**

21. Apply Gasket Adhesive to each cylinder head mating surface. Press the new intake manifold gaskets into place, using locating pins as necessary to aid in assembly alignment.

22. Apply a ⅛ in. (3–4mm) bead of silicone sealer at each corner where the cylinder head joins the cylinder block.

23. Install the front and rear intake manifold end seals.

24. Carefully lower the intake manifold into position onto the cylinder block and between the cylinder heads. Use locating pins as necessary to guide the manifold.

25. Install the retaining bolts and stud bolts in their original locations.

26. For vehicles through 1991, torque the retaining bolts in numerical sequence to the following specifications in 3 steps:

a. Step 1: 8 ft. lbs. (11 Nm)
b. Step 2: 15 ft. lbs. (20 Nm)
c. Step 3: 24 ft. lbs. (32 Nm)

27. For 1992–94 vehicles torque the retaining bolts in numerical sequence to the following specifications in 2 steps:

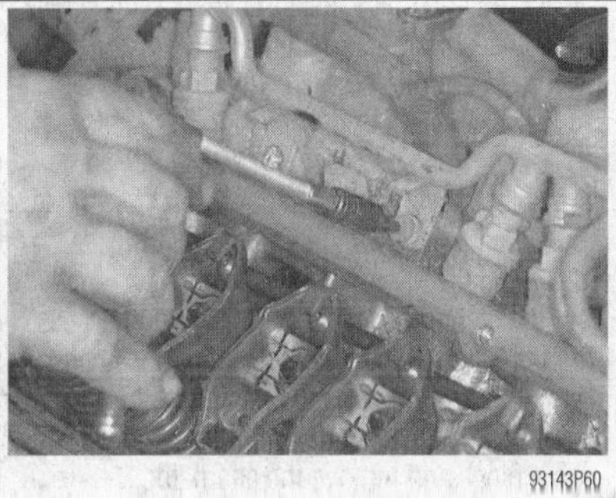


**Fig. 41 Remove the 2 retaining Torx® screws on each side of the manifold to . . .**

**Fig. 42 . . . Release the fuel injection rail. Carefully pull the injector out of the manifold, leaving it connected to the rail**

**Fig. 43 Breaking loose the intake manifold bolts**

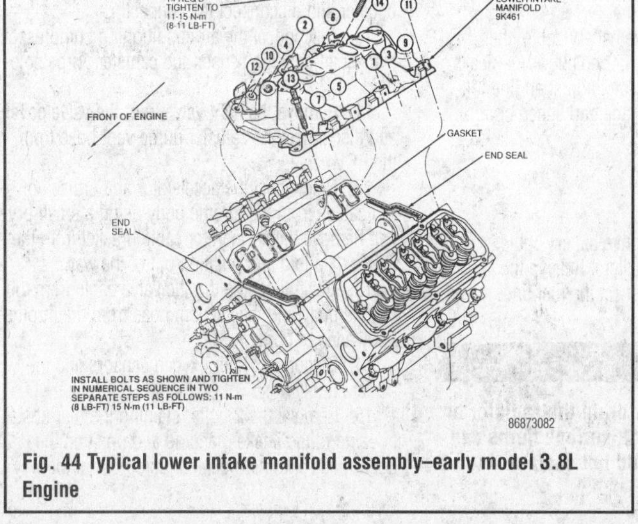


**Fig. 44 Typical lower intake manifold assembly–early model 3.8L Engine**

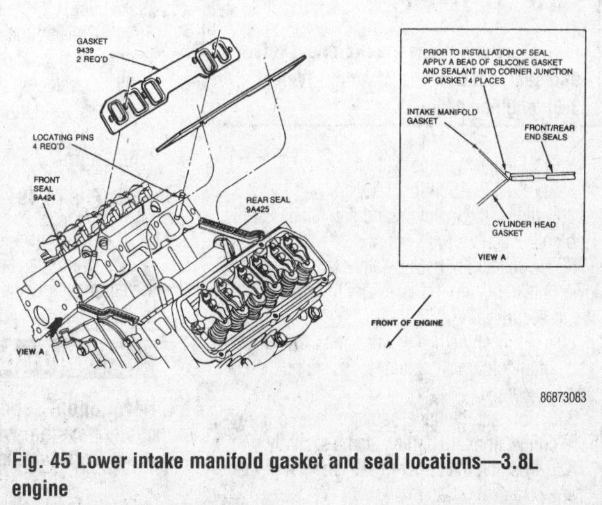


**Fig. 45 Lower intake manifold gasket and seal locations—3.8L engine**

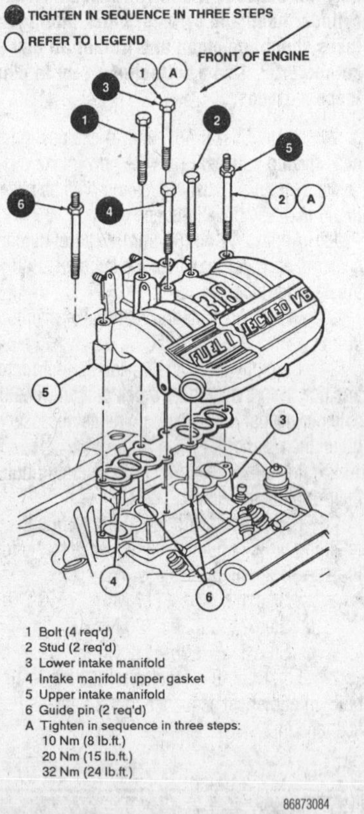


**Fig. 46 Upper intake manifold assembly. Typical 3.8L engine shown**

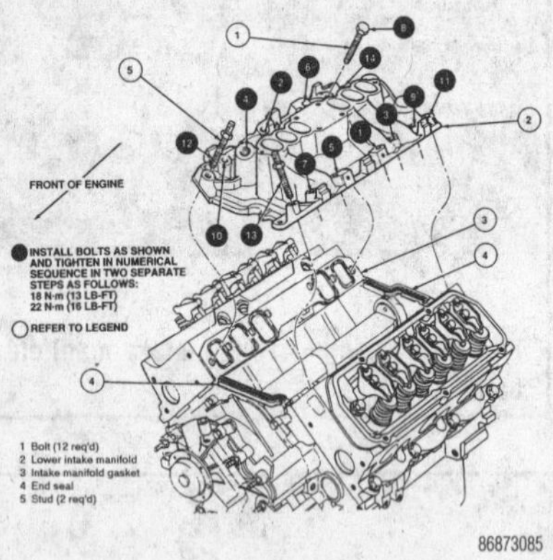


**Fig. 47 Lower intake manifold, gasket, and seal location—later model Typical 3.8L engine shown**

a. Step 1: 8 ft. lbs. (11 Nm)
b. Step 2: 15 ft. lbs. (20 Nm)

28. Install the injectors and fuel rail assembly. Tighten the screws to 6–8 ft. lbs. (8–11 Nm).
29. Connect the heater water outlet tube to the lower intake manifold. Make sure to fasten the hose clamp securely.
30. Connect the heater water hose to the lower intake manifold, making sure to fasten the hose clamp securely.
31. Connect the upper radiator hose to the water hose connection and tighten clamp securely.
32. Position the upper intake gasket and manifold on top of the lower intake. Use locating pins to secure position of gasket between manifolds.

**Fig. 48 Using a small pry bar to separate the intake manifold**

33. Install bolts and studs in their original locations. Tighten the four center bolts, then tighten the end bolts. Tighten the bolts in numerical sequence to the following specifications in two steps:
    a. Step 1: 13 ft. lbs. (18 Nm)
    b. Step 2: 16 ft. lbs. (22 Nm)
34. Install the EGR valve assembly on the manifold if removed earlier. Tighten the attaching bolt to 15–22 ft. lbs. (20–30 Nm).
35. Install the throttle body if removed earlier. Cross-tighten the retaining nuts to 15–22 ft. lbs. (20–30 Nm).
36. Connect the rear crankcase ventilation hoses at the PCV valve and the upper intake manifold
37. Engage all electrical connectors and vacuum hoses.
38. Connect the fuel line(s) at injector fuel rail assembly.
39. Position the accelerator cable mounting bracket, then install and tighten the retaining bolts to 15–22 ft. lbs. (20–30 Nm).Install the return spring.
40. Connect the transaxle linkage at the upper intake manifold.
41. Install the alternator mounting brace, then install the drive belt. For drive belt installation procedures, please refer to Section 1 of this manual.
42. Fill the cooling system to the proper level with the specified coolant.
43. Install the air cleaner assembly and air intake duct.
44. Connect the negative battery cable, then start the engine, and check for coolant or fuel leaks.
45. Check and, if necessary, adjust engine idle speed, transaxle throttle linkage and speed control.

### 4.6L Engine

**See Figure 49**

1. Disconnect the negative battery cable.
2. Drain the cooling system. Relieve the fuel system pressure and disconnect the fuel lines; refer to Section 5.

**** CAUTION**

**Never open, service, or drain the radiator or cooling system when hot; serious burns can occur from the steam and hot coolant. In addition, when draining engine coolant, keep in mind that cats and dogs are attracted to ethylene glycol antifreeze and could drink any that is left in an uncovered container or in puddles on the ground. This will prove fatal in sufficient quantities. Always drain coolant into a sealable container. Coolant should be reused unless it is contaminated or is several years old.**

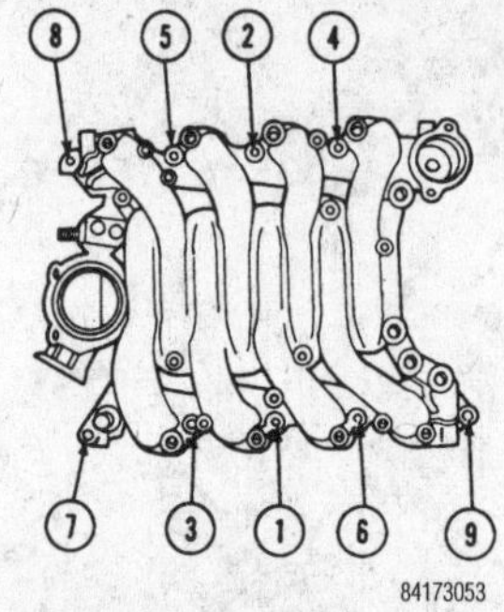


**Fig. 49 Intake manifold bolt torque sequence—4.6L engine**

3. Remove the wiper module and the air inlet tube. Release the belt tensioner and remove the accessory drive belt.
4. Tag and disconnect the spark plug wires from the spark plugs. Disconnect the spark plug wire brackets from the valve cover studs.
5. Disconnect both of the ignition coils and the CID sensor. Tag and disconnect all spark plug wires from both ignition coils. Remove the 2 bolts retaining the spark plug wire tray to the coil brackets and remove the spark plug wire assembly.
6. Disconnect the alternator wiring harness from the junction block at the fender apron and alternator. Remove the bolts retaining the alternator brace to the intake manifold and the alternator to the engine block and remove the alternator.
7. Raise and safely support the vehicle. Disconnect the oil sending unit and EVO harness sensor and position the wiring harness out of the way.
8. Disconnect the EGR tube from the right exhaust manifold and lower the vehicle.
9. Remove the 42-pin engine harness connector from the retaining bracket on the vacuum brake booster and disconnect the connector.
10. Disconnect the air conditioning compressor, crankshaft position sensor and canister purge solenoid.
11. Remove the PCV valve from the valve cover and disconnect the canister purge vent hose from the PCV valve.
12. Disconnect the accelerator and cruise control cables from the throttle body using a small prybar. Remove the accelerator cable bracket from the intake manifold and position out of the way.
13. Disconnect the throttle valve cable from the throttle body and the vacuum hose from the throttle-body adapter port.
14. Disconnect both oxygen sensors and the heater supply hose.
15. Remove the 2 bolts retaining the thermostat housing to the intake manifold and position the upper hose and thermostat housing out of the way.

**➡The 2 thermostat housing bolts also retain the intake manifold.**

16. Remove the bolts retaining the intake manifold to the cylinder heads and remove the intake manifold. Remove and discard the gaskets.

**To install:**

17. Clean all gasket-mating surfaces. Position new intake manifold gaskets on the cylinder heads. Make sure the alignment tabs on the gaskets are aligned with the holes in the cylinder heads.
18. Install the intake manifold and the retaining bolts. Tighten the bolts, in sequence, to 15–22 ft. lbs. (20–30 Nm).
19. Inspect and replace the O-ring seal on the thermostat housing. Position the housing and upper hose and install the 2 bolts. Tighten to 15–22 ft. lbs. (20–30 Nm).
20. Connect the heater supply hose and connect both oxygen sensors.
21. Connect the vacuum hose to the throttle-body adapter port. Connect and, if necessary, adjust the throttle valve cable.
22. Install the accelerator cable bracket on the intake manifold and connect the accelerator and cruise control cables to the throttle body.
23. Install the PCV valve in the valve cover and connect the canister purge solenoid vent hose. Connect the air conditioning compressor, crankshaft position sensor and canister purge solenoid.
24. Connect the 42-pin engine harness connector. Install the connector on the retaining bracket on the vacuum brake booster.
25. Raise and safely support the vehicle. Connect the EGR tube to the right exhaust manifold and tighten the line nut to 26–33 ft. lbs. (35–45 Nm).
26. Connect the EVO sensor and oil-sending unit. Lower the vehicle.
27. Position the alternator and install the retaining bolts. Tighten to 15–22 ft. lbs. (20–30 Nm). Install the 2 bolts retaining the alternator brace to the intake manifold and tighten to 6–9 ft. lbs. (8–12 Nm).
28. Connect the alternator wiring harness to the alternator, right-hand fender apron and junction block.
29. Position the spark plug wire assembly on the engine and install the 2 bolts retaining the spark plug wire tray to the coil brackets. Tighten the bolts to 6.0–8.8 ft. lbs. (8–12 Nm).
30. Connect the spark plug wires to the ignition coils in their proper positions. Connect the spark plug wires to the spark plugs.
31. Connect the spark plug wire brackets on the valve cover studs. Connect both ignition coils and CID sensor.
32. Install the accessory drive belt and the air inlet tube. Install the wiper module and connect the fuel lines.
33. Fill the cooling system. Connect the negative battery cable, start the engine, and bring to normal operating temperature. Check for leaks.

### 5.0L Engine

**➧ See Figures 50, 51, 52 and 53**

1. Disconnect the negative battery cable.
2. Drain the cooling system. Relieve the fuel system pressure; refer to Section 5.

**⁂ CAUTION**

**Never open, service, or drain the radiator or cooling system when hot; serious burns can occur from the steam and hot coolant. In addition, when draining engine coolant, keep in mind that cats and dogs are attracted to ethylene glycol antifreeze and could drink any that is left in an uncovered container or in puddles on the ground. This will prove fatal in sufficient quantities. Always drain coolant into a sealable container. Coolant should be reused unless it is contaminated or is several years old.**

3. Disconnect the accelerator cable and cruise control linkage, if equipped, from the throttle body. Disconnect the throttle valve cable, if equipped. Label and disconnect the vacuum lines at the intake manifold fitting.
4. Label and disconnect the spark plug wires from the spark plugs. Remove the wires and bracket assembly from the rocker arm cover attaching stud. Remove the distributor cap and wires assembly.
5. Disconnect the fuel lines (see Section 5) and the distributor wiring connector. Mark the position of the rotor on the distributor housing and the position of the distributor housing in the block. Remove the hold-down bolt and remove the distributor.
6. Disconnect the upper radiator hose at the thermostat housing and the water temperature sending unit wire at the sending unit. Disconnect the heater hose from the intake manifold and disconnect the 2 throttle body cooler hoses.
7. Disconnect the water pump bypass hose from the thermostat housing. Label and disconnect the connectors from the engine coolant temperature, air charge temperature, throttle position and EGR sensors and the idle speed control solenoid. Disconnect the injector wire connections and the fuel charging assembly wiring.
8. Remove the PCV valve from the grommet at the rear of the lower intake manifold. Disconnect the fuel evaporative purge hose from the plastic connector at the front of the upper intake manifold.
9. Remove the upper intake manifold cover plate and upper intake bolts. Remove the upper intake manifold.
10. Remove the heater tube assembly from the lower intake manifold studs. Remove the alternator and air conditioner braces from the intake studs. Disconnect the heater hose from the lower intake manifold.
11. Remove the lower intake manifold retaining bolts and remove the lower intake manifold.

**➡If it is necessary to pry the intake manifold away from the cylinder heads, be careful to avoid damaging the gasket sealing surfaces.**

**To install:**

12. Clean all gasket-mating surfaces. Apply a ⅛ in. bead of silicone sealer to the points where the cylinder block rails meet the cylinder heads.

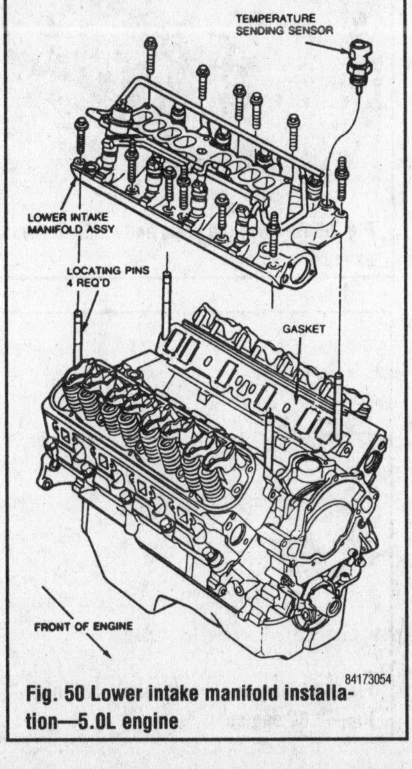


**Fig. 50 Lower intake manifold installation—5.0L engine**

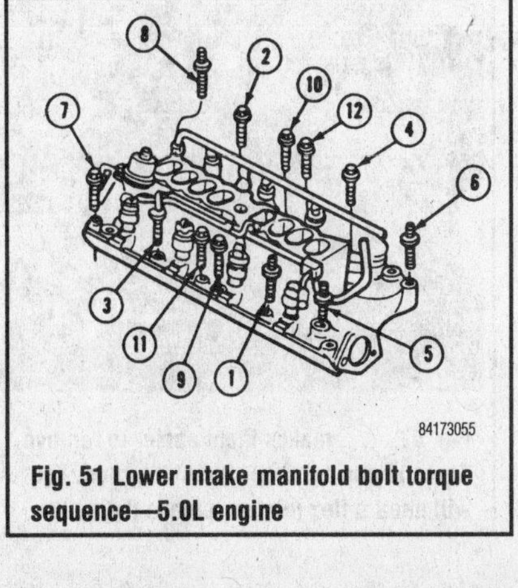


**Fig. 51 Lower intake manifold bolt torque sequence—5.0L engine**

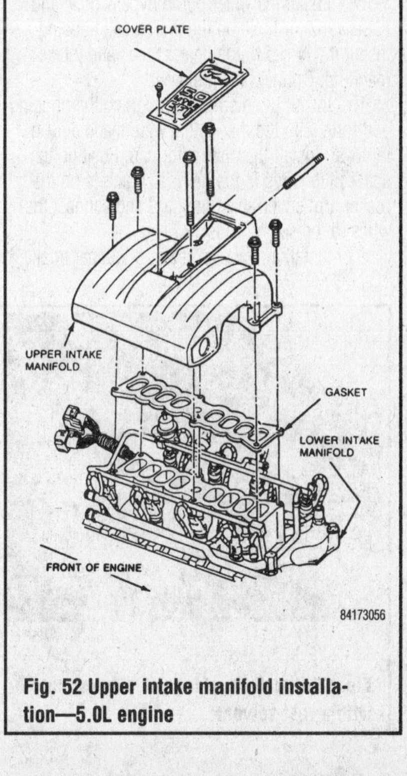


**Fig. 52 Upper intake manifold installation—5.0L engine**

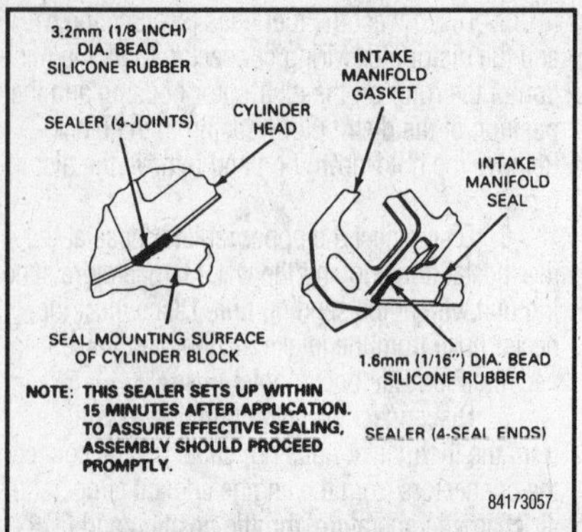


**Fig. 53 Apply sealer as shown during intake manifold installation—5.0L engines**

13. Position new seals on the cylinder block and new gaskets on the cylinder heads with the gaskets interlocked with the seal tabs. Make sure the holes in the gaskets are aligned with the holes in the cylinder heads.
14. Apply a 3⁄16 in. bead of sealer to the outer end of each intake manifold seal for the full width of the seal.
15. Using guide pins to ease installation, carefully lower the intake manifold into position on the cylinder block and cylinder heads.

**➡After the intake manifold is in place, run a finger around the seal area to make sure the seals are in place. If the seals are not in place, remove the intake manifold and position the seals.**

16. Make sure the holes in the manifold gaskets and the manifold are in alignment. Remove the guide pins. Install the intake manifold attaching bolts and tighten, in sequence, to 23–25 ft. lbs. (31–34 Nm).
17. If required, install the heater tube assembly to the lower intake manifold studs.
18. Install the water pump bypass hose and upper radiator hose on the thermostat housing. Install the hoses to the heater tubes and intake manifold. Connect the fuel lines.
19. Install the distributor, aligning the housing and rotor with the marks that were made during removal. Install the distributor cap. Position the spark plug wires in the harness brackets on the rocker arm cover-attaching stud and connect the wires to the spark plugs.
20. Install a new gasket and the upper intake manifold. Tighten the bolts to 12–18 ft. lbs. (16–24 Nm). Install the cover plate and connect the crankcase vent tube.
21. Connect the accelerator, throttle valve cable and cruise control cable, if equipped, to the throttle body. Connect the electrical connectors and vacuum lines to their proper locations.
22. Connect the coolant hoses to the EGR spacer. Fill the cooling system.
23. Connect the negative battery cable, start the engine, and check for leaks. Check the ignition timing.
24. Operate the engine at fast idle. When engine temperatures have stabilized, tighten the intake manifold bolts to 23–25 ft. lbs. (31–34 Nm).
25. Connect the air intake duct and the crankcase vent hose.

## Exhaust Manifold

### REMOVAL & INSTALLATION

#### 3.8L Engine

##### *LEFT SIDE*

**▸ See Figures 54, 55, 56, 57 and 58**

1. Disconnect the negative battery cable. and the stud. Matchmark the stud and hole
2. Remove the oil level dipstick tube support bracket.
3. Tag and disconnect the spark plug wires.
4. Raise and safely support the vehicle.
5. Remove the exhaust manifold-to-exhaust pipe attaching nuts.
6. Lower the vehicle.
7. Remove the exhaust manifold retaining bolts, then remove the exhaust manifold from the vehicle.

**To install:**

8. Lightly oil all bolt and stud threads before installation. Clean the exhaust manifold, cylinder head and Y-pipe mating surfaces.
9. Position the exhaust manifold on the cylinder head. Install the lower front bolt on the No. 5 cylinder as a pilot bolt.

**➡A slight warping in the exhaust manifold may cause a misalignment between the bolt-holes in the head and the manifold. Elongate the holes in the exhaust manifold as necessary to correct the misalignment, if apparent. Do not elongate the pilot hole, the lower front bolt on No. 5 cylinder.**

10. Install the remaining exhaust manifold retaining bolts, then tighten the bolts 15–22 ft. lbs. (20–30 Nm).
11. Raise and safely support the vehicle.
12. Connect the dual converter Y-pipe to the exhaust manifold. Tighten the attaching nuts to 16–24 ft. lbs. (21–32 Nm).
13. Carefully lower the vehicle.
14. Connect the spark plug wires as tagged during removal.
15. Install the oil level dipstick tube support bracket-attaching nut. Tighten to 15–22 ft. lbs. (20–30 Nm).
16. Connect the negative battery cable, then start the engine, and check for exhaust leaks.

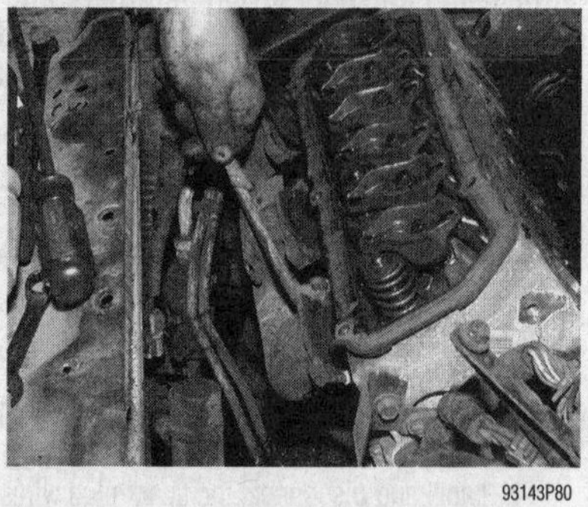


**Fig. 54 Remove the nut holding the dipstick tube support bracket and the stud. Matchmark the stud and hole**

**Fig. 55 Remove the bolts and studs to the exhaust manifold**

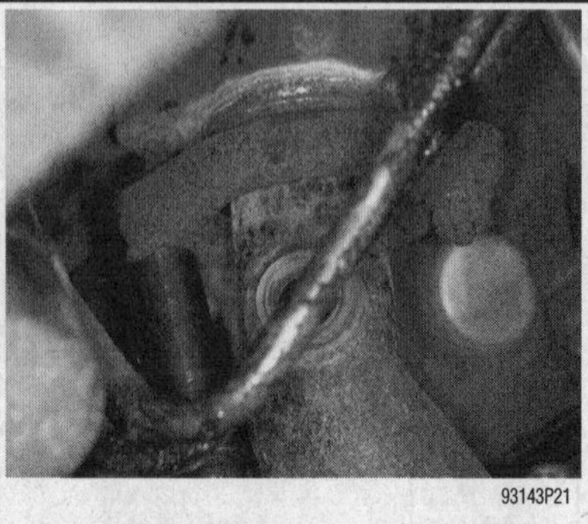


**Fig. 56 Usually soaking the exhaust nuts with a rust solvent . . .**

**Fig. 57 . . . makes them easier to remove. There is one on each side of the pipe. You will need a flex joint to remove them**

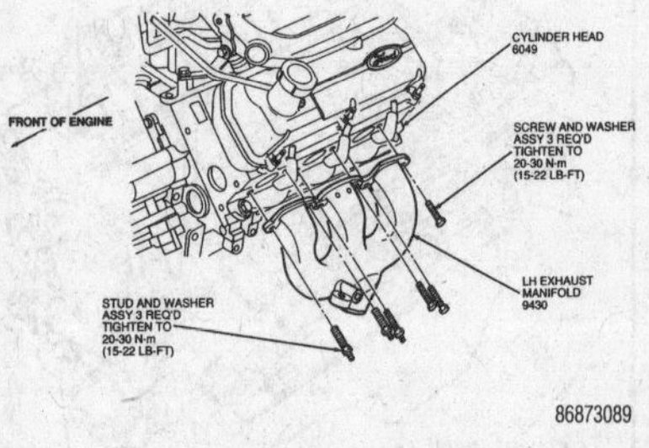


**Fig. 58 Left side exhaust manifold mounting—3.8L engine**

### *RIGHT SIDE*

**➧ See Figure 59**

1. Disconnect the negative battery cable.
2. Remove the air cleaner and the air cleaner outlet tube assembly.
3. Tag and disconnect the ignition wire from the ignition coil, then tag and disconnect the wires from the spark plugs. Remove the spark plugs.
4. Disconnect the EGR valve-to-exhaust manifold tube.
5. Raise and safely support the vehicle.
6. Remove the transaxle dipstick tube.
7. Remove the exhaust manifold-to-exhaust pipe attaching nuts.
8. Carefully lower the vehicle.
9. Remove the exhaust manifold retaining bolts, them remove the exhaust manifold from the vehicle.

**To install:**

10. Lightly oil all bolt and stud threads before installation. Clean the exhaust manifold, cylinder head and Y-pipe mating surfaces.
11. Position the inner half of the heat shroud, if equipped, and exhaust manifold on cylinder head. Start two retaining bolts to align the manifold with the cylinder head. Install the remaining retaining bolts and tighten to 15–22 ft. lbs. (20–30 Nm). Do not overtorque the retainers, it may cause exhaust leaks.

**➡A slight warping in the exhaust manifold may cause a misalignment between the bolt-holes in the cylinder head and exhaust manifold. Elongate the holes in the exhaust manifold as necessary to correct the misalignment. Do not elongate the pilot hole (the lower rear bolt hole on the No. 2 cylinder).**

12. Raise and safely support the vehicle.
13. Connect the dual converter Y-pipe to the exhaust manifold. Tighten the retaining nuts to 16–24 ft. lbs. (22–33 Nm).
14. Install the transaxle dipstick tube, and then carefully lower the vehicle.
15. If equipped, install the outer heat shroud, then tighten the retaining screws to 50–70 inch lbs. (6–8 Nm).
16. Install the spark plugs. Connect the ignition wires to their respective spark plugs, then connect the ignition wire to the coil.
17. Apply special heat-resistant anti-seize compound to the threads and connect the EGR valve-to-exhaust manifold tube.
18. Install the air cleaner. Install the air cleaner outlet tube assembly.
19. Connect the negative battery cable, then start the engine, and check for exhaust leaks. Check the transaxle fluid.

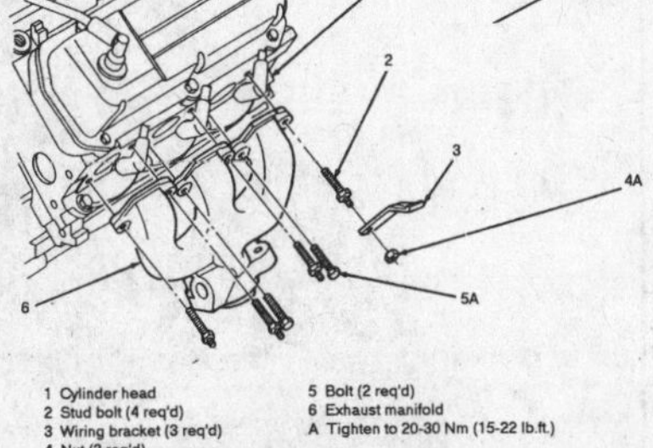


86873090

**Fig. 59 Right side exhaust manifold mounting—3.8L engine**

### 4.6l Engine except Continental

**➧ See Figure 60**

1. Disconnect the battery cables, negative cable first. Remove the air inlet tube.
2. Drain the cooling system and remove the cooling fan and shroud. Relieve the fuel system pressure and disconnect the fuel lines; refer to Section 5.

**✻✻ CAUTION**

**Never open, service, or drain the radiator or cooling system when hot; serious burns can occur from the steam and hot coolant. In addition, when draining engine coolant, keep in mind that cats and dogs are attracted to ethylene glycol antifreeze and could drink any that is left in an uncovered container or in puddles on the ground. This will prove fatal in sufficient quantities. Always drain coolant into a sealable container. Coolant should be reused unless it is contaminated or is several years old.**

3. Remove the upper radiator hose. Remove the wiper module and support bracket.
4. Discharge the air conditioning system; refer to Section 1. Disconnect and plug the compressor outlet hose at the compressor and remove the bolt retaining the hose assembly to the right coil bracket. Cap the compressor opening.
5. Remove the 42-pin engine harness connector from the retaining bracket on the brake vacuum booster. Disconnect the connector.
6. Disconnect the throttle valve cable from the throttle body. Disconnect the heater outlet hose.
7. Remove the nut retaining the ground strap to the right cylinder head. Remove the upper stud and lower bolt retaining the heater outlet hose to the right cylinder head and position out of the way.
8. Remove the blower motor resistor and remove the bolt retaining the right engine mount to the lower engine bracket. Disconnect both oxygen sensors.
9. Raise and safely support the vehicle. Remove the engine mount through bolts.

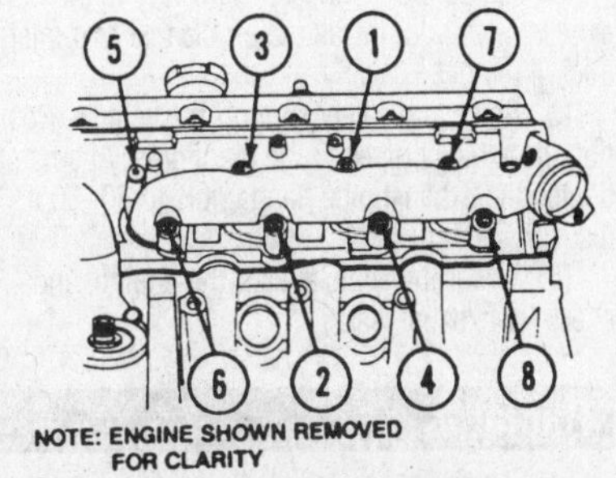


84173060

**Fig. 60 Exhaust manifold bolt torque sequence—4.6L engine**

10. Remove the EGR tube line nut from the right exhaust manifold.
11. Disconnect the exhaust pipes from the manifolds. Lower the exhaust system and hang it from the crossmember with wire.
12. To remove the left exhaust manifold, remove the engine mount from the engine block and remove the 8 bolts retaining the exhaust manifold.
13. Position a jack and a block of wood under the oil pan, rearward of the oil drain hole. Raise the engine approximately 4 in. (100 mm).
14. Remove the 8 bolts retaining the right exhaust manifold and remove the manifold.

**To install:**

15. If the exhaust manifolds are being replaced, transfer the oxygen sensors and tighten to 27–33 ft. lbs. (37–45 Nm). On the right manifold, transfer the EGR tube connector and tighten to 33–48 ft. lbs. (45–65 Nm).
16. Clean the mating surfaces of the exhaust manifolds and cylinder heads.
17. Position the exhaust manifolds to the cylinder heads and install the retaining bolts. Tighten, in sequence, to 15–22 ft. lbs. (20–30 Nm).
18. Position and connect the EGR valve and tube assembly to the exhaust manifold. Tighten the line nut to 26–33 ft. lbs. (35–45 Nm).
19. Install the left engine mount and tighten the bolts to 15–22 ft. lbs. (20–30 Nm). Lower the engine onto the mounts and remove the jack. Install the engine mount through bolts and tighten to 15–22 ft. lbs. (20–30 Nm).
20. Cut the wire and position the exhaust system. Tighten the nuts to 20–30 ft. lbs. (27–41 Nm).

**➡Make sure the exhaust system clears the No. 3 crossmember. Adjust as necessary.**

21. Lower the vehicle. Connect both oxygen sensors and install the bolt retaining the right engine mount to the frame. Tighten to 15–22 ft. lbs. (20–30 Nm).
22. Install the blower motor resistor. Position the heater outlet hoses. Install the upper stud and lower bolt and tighten to 15–22 ft. lbs. (20–30 Nm). Install the ground strap onto the stud and tighten the nut to 15–22 ft. lbs. (20–30 Nm).
23. Connect the heater outlet hose. Connect and if necessary, adjust the throttle valve cable.
24. Connect the 42-pin connector and transmission harness connector. Install the connector to the retaining bracket on the brake vacuum booster.
25. Connect the air conditioning compressor outlet hose to the compressor and install the bolt retaining the hose assembly to the right coil bracket.
26. Install the upper radiator hose and connect the fuel lines. Install the wiper module and retaining bracket.
27. Install the cooling fan and shroud. Fill the cooling system.
28. Install the air inlet tube. Connect the battery cables, start the engine, and check for leaks.
29. Have a MVAC certified tech evacuate and charge the air conditioning system.

### 4.6L Engine Continental

### *LEFT-HAND SIDE*

1. Disable the air suspension.
2. Disconnect the negative battery cable.
3. Raise and safely support the vehicle securely on a hoist.

4. Remove the splash shield form the lower radiator support and the front sub-frame.
5. Remove the dual converter Y pipe.
6. Loosen the retaining nut and remove the LH secondary air injection manifold tube from the LH exhaust manifold.
7. Remove the eight exhaust manifold-to-cylinder head retaining nuts.
8. remove the LH exhaust manifold and exhaust manifold gaskets.

**To install:**

9. Clean the mating surfaces of the exhaust manifold and the cylinder head.
10. Install the new exhaust manifold gasket on the LH cylinder head. Lightly press the exhaust manifold gasket over the exhaust manifold-positioning studs.
11. Install the LH exhaust manifold and install the eight retaining nuts. Tighten the retaining nuts in sequence to 13-16 ft. lbs. (18-22 Nm)
12. Connect the LH secondary air injection manifold tube to the LH exhaust manifold. Tighten the nut for the LH secondary air injection manifold tube to the LH exhaust manifold to 25-34 ft. lbs. (34-46Nm)
13. Install the dual converter Y pipe.
14. Install the splash shield to front sub-frame and lower radiator support. Tighten the retaining screws securely.
15. Lower the vehicle and connect the negative battery cable.
16. Check the exhaust system for leaks. Turn on the air suspension

***RIGHT-HAND SIDE***

1. Disable the air suspension.
2. Disconnect the negative battery cable.
3. Raise and safely support the vehicle securely on a hoist.
4. Disconnect the heated oxygen sensors at the wiring connectors.
5. Remove the dual converter Y pipe.
6. Remove the exhaust connector retaining bolts and exhaust connector and muffler inlet pipe gasket from the RH exhaust manifold
7. Remove the EGR valve to exhaust manifold tube from the EGR valve tube to manifold connector using a 22 mm crowfoot wrench.
8. Loosen the retaining nut and remove the RH secondary air injection manifold tube from the RH exhaust manifold.
9. Remove the eight exhaust manifold-to-cylinder head retaining nuts.
10. Remove the RH exhaust manifold from the RH cylinder head by gaining access through the RH wheel opening area.
11. Remove the exhaust manifold gasket from the RH cylinder head Discard the exhaust manifold gasket.

**To install:**

12. Clean the mating surfaces of exhaust manifold and cylinder head.
13. If removed, install the EGR valve tube to manifold connector to the RH exhaust manifold. Tighten the EGR valve tube to manifold connector to 33-48 ft. lbs.. (45-65 Nm)
14. Position the new exhaust manifold gasket and the exhaust manifold onto the cylinder head. Install the eight retaining nuts. Tighten in sequence to 13-16 ft. lbs. (18-22 Nm)
15. Connect the RH secondary air injection manifold tube to the RH exhaust manifold. Tighten the nut for the RH secondary air injection manifold tube to the RH exhaust manifold to 25-34 ft. lbs.(34-46 Nm)
16. Connect the EGR valve to exhaust manifold tube to the EGR valve to exhaust manifold tube to the EGR valve tube to manifold connector. Tighten the nut to 30-33 ft. lbs. (40-45 Nm)
17. Install the exhaust connector with a new muffler inlet-pipe-gasket and retaining bolts to the RH exhaust manifold. Tighten the retaining bolts in two steps.
 a. Tighten the bolts in sequence to 13-17 ft. lbs. (17-23 Nm).
 b. Tighten the bolts in sequence to 30-40 ft. lbs. (41-54 Nm)
18. Install the dual converter Y pipe, and connect the heated oxygen sensors the wiring harness connectors.
19. Lower the vehicle and connect the negative battery cable.
20. Check the exhaust system for leaks. Turn on the air suspension.

### 5.0L Engine

1. Disconnect the negative battery cable.
2. Remove the thermactor hardware from the right exhaust manifold.
3. Remove the air cleaner and inlet duct, if necessary.
4. Tag and disconnect the spark plug wires. Remove the spark plugs.
5. Disconnect the engine oil dipstick tube from the exhaust manifold stud.
6. Raise and safely support the vehicle. Disconnect the exhaust pipes from the exhaust manifolds.
7. Remove the engine oil dipstick tube by carefully tapping upward on the tube. Disconnect the oxygen sensor connector.
8. Lower the vehicle.
9. Remove the attaching bolts and washers and remove the exhaust manifolds.

**To install:**

10. Clean the manifold, cylinder head, and exhaust pipe mating surfaces.
11. Position the manifolds on the cylinder heads and install the mounting bolts and washers. Working from the center to the ends, tighten the bolts to 18–24 ft. lbs. (24–32 Nm).
12. Install the engine oil dipstick tube. Connect the oxygen sensor connector.
13. Install the spark plugs and connect the spark plug wires.
14. Install the thermactor hardware to the right exhaust manifold. Install the air cleaner and inlet duct, if removed.
15. Raise and safely support the vehicle. Position the exhaust pipes to the manifolds. Alternately tighten the exhaust pipe flange nuts to 20–30 ft. lbs. (27–41 Nm).
16. Lower the vehicle, start the engine, and check for exhaust leaks.

## Radiator

**CAUTION**

**Never open, service, or drain the radiator or cooling system when hot; serious burns can occur from the steam and hot coolant. In addition, when draining engine coolant, keep in mind that cats and dogs are attracted to ethylene glycol antifreeze and could drink any that is left in an uncovered container or in puddles on the ground. This will prove fatal in sufficient quantities. Always drain coolant into a sealable container. Coolant should be reused unless it is contaminated or is several years old.**

### REMOVAL & INSTALLATION

#### 1988–94 Continental

➧ See Figures 61, 62, 63 and 64

1. Disconnect the negative battery cable.
2. Loosen the radiator cap.
3. Drain the cooling system by opening the draincock located at the lower rear corner of the radiator inlet tank.
4. Detach the rubber overflow tube from the radiator.
5. Remove 2 upper shroud-retaining screws and lift the shroud out of the lower retaining clip(s).
6. Disconnect the electric cooling fan motor wires and remove the fan and shroud assembly.
7. Loosen the upper and lower hose clamps at the radiator and remove the hoses from the radiator tank connectors.
8. If equipped with an automatic transaxle, disconnect the transmission oil cooling lines from the transmission oil cooler radiator fittings using a disconnect tool
9. Remove 2 hex nuts from the right radiator support bracket and 2 screws from the left radiator support bracket and remove the brackets. For 1993–94, remove the two hex nuts from the right hand radiator support bracket, then remove the two retaining nuts from the left hand radiator support bracket, then remove both brackets.
10. Tilt the radiator rearward approximately 1 in. (25mm) and lift it directly upward, clear of the radiator support.
11. If the lower or upper radiator hose it to be replaced, loosen the clamp at the engine end and, using a twisting motion, slip the hose off the connections.
12. Remove the radiator lower support rubber pads, if pad replacement is necessary.

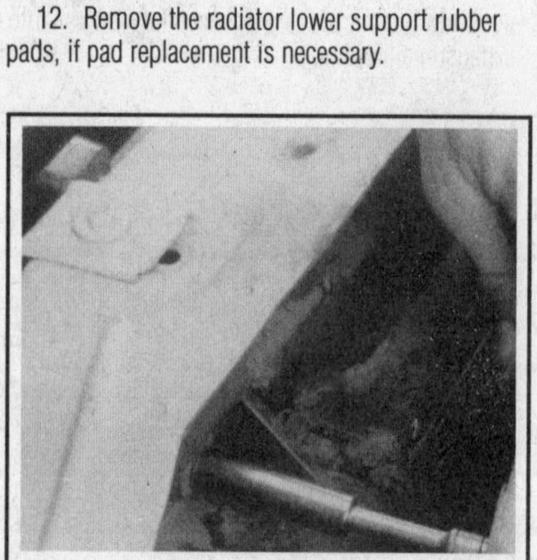

86873092

Fig. 61 Remove the radiator retaining bolts/screws

86873093

**Fig. 62 Lift the radiator upward, then remove it from the engine**

**To install:**

13. Position the radiator lower support rubber pads to the lower support, if removed.

**➡Make sure the hose clamps are beyond the bead and placed in the center of the clamping surface of the connection. Any worn clamp must be replaced with a new clamp to ensure proper sealing at the connection.**

14. If the lower or upper hose has been replaced, position the hose on the engine with the index arrow in-line with the mark on the fitting at the engine. Tighten the screw clamps to 20–30 inch lbs. (2.5–3.4 Nm).
15. Position the radiator into the engine compartment, and to the radiator support. Insert the molded pins at the bottom of each tank through slotted holes in the lower support rubber pads.
16. Inspect the radiator nylon tank upper mounting bushings for damage. Replace if damaged.
17. If the outlet tank pin bracket must be replaced, remove the two retaining bolts. Position the bracket on the outlet tank, then install the two retaining bolts and tighten to 6.6–9.6 ft. lbs. (9–13 Nm).
18. Install the two upper retaining bolts to attach the radiator to the radiator support. Tighten the bolts to 13–20 ft. lbs. (17–27 Nm).
19. For vehicles through 1992, equipped with the 3.8L engine, position the right hand support bracket onto the radiator and over the two studs on the radiator support.
20. Position the left-hand support bracket over the radiator and the radiator support. Align the holes in the bracket with the corresponding holes in the radiator support and secure with the two retaining screws. Tighten the screws to 9–17 ft. lbs. (12–24 Nm).
21. On the 1993–94 3.8L engines, position the left and right hand support bracket over the radiator and radiator support. Align the holes in the bracket with the corresponding holes in the radiator support and secure with the two retaining screws. Tighten the screws to 9–17 ft. lbs. (12–24 Nm).
22. If applicable, secure the right hand support bracket to the radiator support with two hex nuts, then tighten the nuts to 8.7–17.7 ft. lbs. (11.8–24 Nm).
23. Install the radiator upper and lower hoses to the radiator. Position the hose on the radiator connector so that the index arrow on the hose is in line with the mark on the connector. Position the clamps between the alignment marks on both ends of the hose, then slide the hose on the connections. Tighten the clamps to 20–30 inch lbs. (2.3–3.4 Nm.
24. On vehicles equipped with automatic transaxles, connect the oil cooler lines using Pipe Sealant with Teflon® or equivalent oil resistant sealer if necessary.
25. Install the fan and shroud assembly by connecting the motor wiring and positioning it on the lower retainer clips. Attach the top of the shroud to the radiator with the two screws and washer assemblies, and nuts. Tighten to 35 inch lbs. (4 Nm).
26. Attach the rubber overflow tube to the radiator filler neck.
27. Connect the negative battery cable.
28. Install a 50/50 mixture of clean water and fresh antifreeze, then run the engine for 15 minutes. Check the coolant level and bring it to within 1½ in. (30mm) of the radiator filler neck.

**1995–00 Continental**

**✲✲ CAUTION**

**Never open, service, or drain the radiator or cooling system when hot; serious burns can occur from the steam and hot coolant. In addition, when draining engine coolant, keep in mind that cats and dogs are attracted to ethylene glycol antifreeze and could drink any that is left in an uncovered container or in puddles on the ground. This will prove fatal in sufficient quantities. Always drain coolant into a sealable container. Coolant should be reused unless it is contaminated or is several years old.**

1. Drain and recycle the engine coolant.
2. Disconnect the negative battery cable.
3. Remove the engine air cleaner
4. Remove the upper radiator host from the water bypass tube.
5. Remove the radiator overflow hose from the radiator and the fan shroud.

**➡Loosen the transmission oil cooler tubes whole holding the radiator connector with a back-up wrench.**

6. Remove the transmission oil cooler tube from the oil cooler inlet fitting.
7. Remove the nuts retaining the A/C condenser core to the radiator.
8. Disconnect engine control sensor wiring from the cooling fan motors and the CCRM.
9. Raise the vehicle on a hoist. Remove the splash shield from lower radiator support and the front sub-frame.
10. Remove the lower radiator hose from the radiator
11. Remove the retaining screws for power steering/transaxle oil cooler and position the cooler aside.
12. Support the fan shroud, radiator and A/C condenser core with a suitable jack stand. Remove the lower radiator support. Position the jack stand

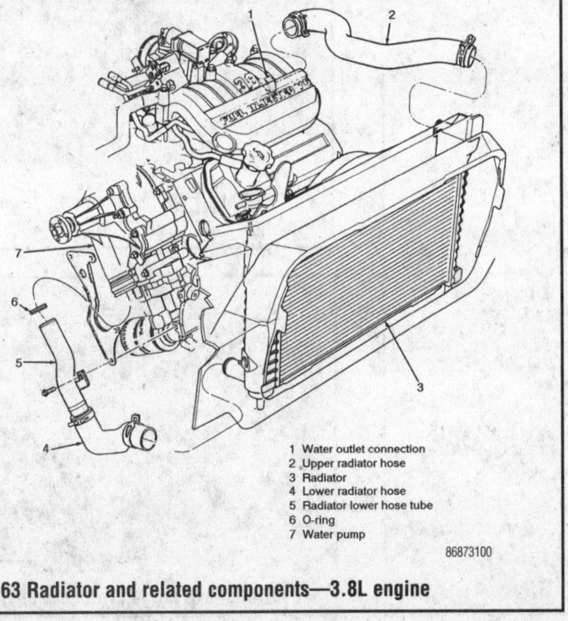

86873100

**Fig. 63 Radiator and related components—3.8L engine**

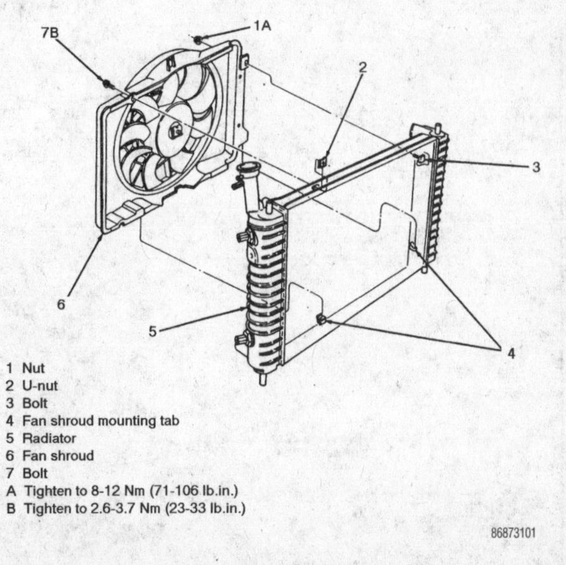

86873101

**Fig. 64 Radiator and fan retainer locations—3.8L engine**

aside and carefully remove the radiator and the fan shroud .

13. Remove the two retaining bolts for the fan shroud at the top of the radiator and remove the fan shroud from the radiator

14. Remove the upper radiator hose from the radiator.

**To install:**

15. To install, reverse the removal procedures.

### 4.6L/5.0L Engines (Except Continental)

**See Figures 65, 66 and 67**

1. Disconnect the upper, lower and coolant reservoir hoses at the radiator.
2. Disconnect the fluid cooler lines at the radiator, use a backup wrench to hold the radiator fitting while loosening the fluid cooler lines.
3. Remove the 2 upper fan shroud retaining bolts at the radiator support, lift the fan shroud sufficiently to disengage the lower retaining clips and lay the shroud back over the fan.
4. Remove the radiator upper support retaining bolts and remove the supports. Lift the radiator from the vehicle.

**To install:**

5. If a new radiator is to be installed, transfer the petcock from the old radiator to the new one. Remove the fluid cooler line fittings from the old radiator and install them on the new one, using an oil resistant sealer.
6. Position the radiator assembly into the vehicle. Install the upper supports and the retaining bolts. Connect the fluid cooler lines.
7. Place the fan shroud into the clips on the lower radiator support and install the 2 upper shroud-retaining bolts. Position the shroud to maintain approximately 1 in. (25mm) clearance between the fan blades and the shroud.
8. Connect the radiator hoses. Close the radiator petcock. Fill the cooling system as explained in Section 1.
9. Start the engine and bring to operating temperature. Check for coolant and transmission fluid leaks.
10. Check the coolant and transmission fluid levels.

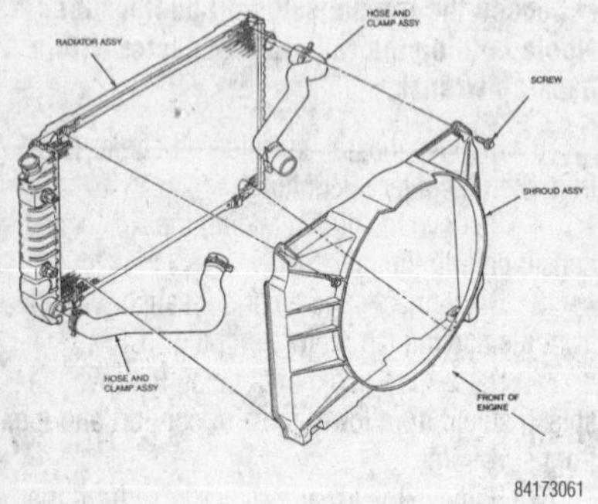


Fig. 65 Radiator and related components—5.0L Engines

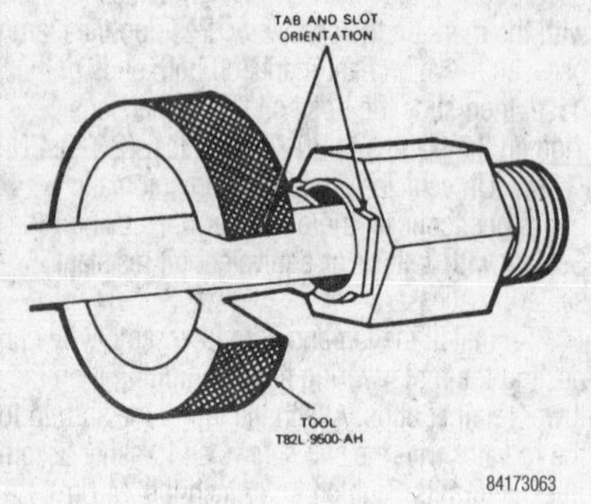


Fig. 67 Transmission fluid cooler line quick connect/disconnect tool

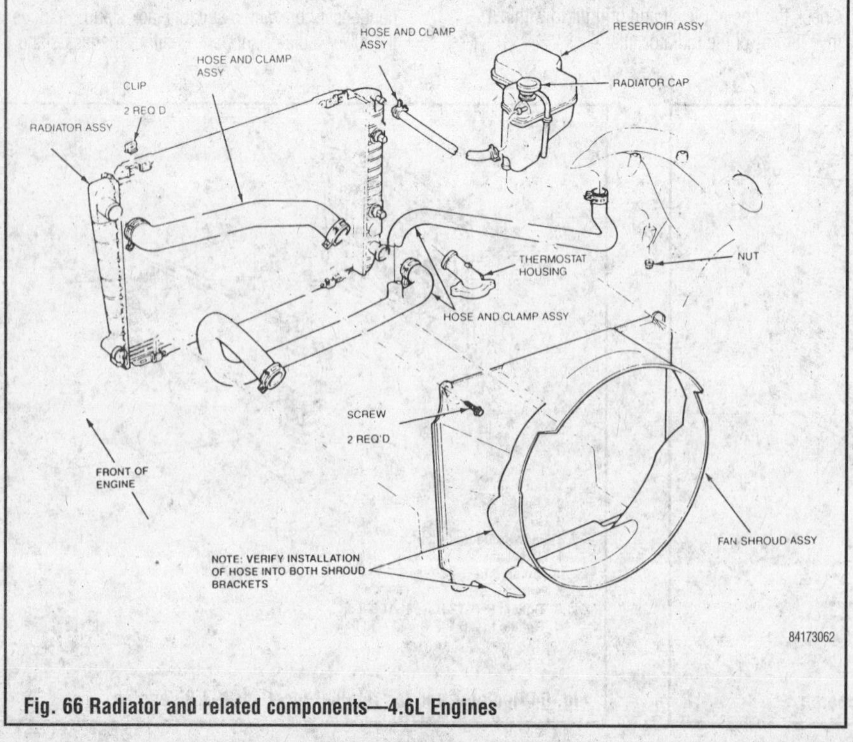


Fig. 66 Radiator and related components—4.6L Engines

## Engine Fan

### REMOVAL & INSTALLATION

#### 3.8L Engines

**See Figures 68, 69, 70, 71 and 72**

1. Disconnect the negative battery cable.
2. Remove the radiator upper sight shield.
3. Disengage the electrical connector, then remove the integrated relay control/constant control relay module assembly located on the radiator support.
4. Disconnect the fan electrical connector.
5. If necessary, remove the air bag crash sensor.
6. Unbolt the fan/shroud assembly from the radiator and remove.
7. Remove the retainer and the fan from the motor shaft and unbolt the fan motor from the shroud.
8. Installation is the reverse of the removal pro-

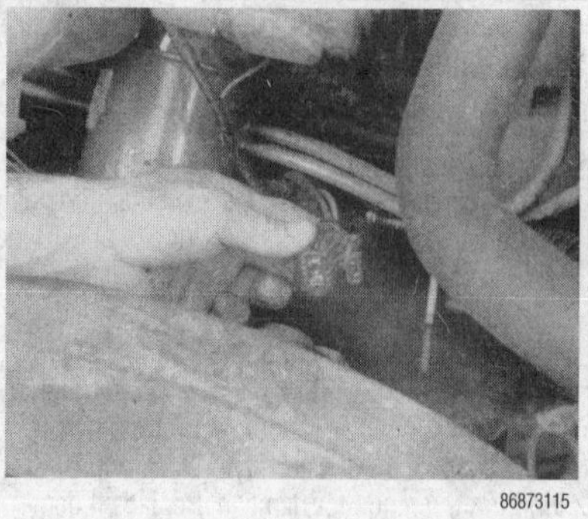


Fig. 68 Disengage the fan electrical connector

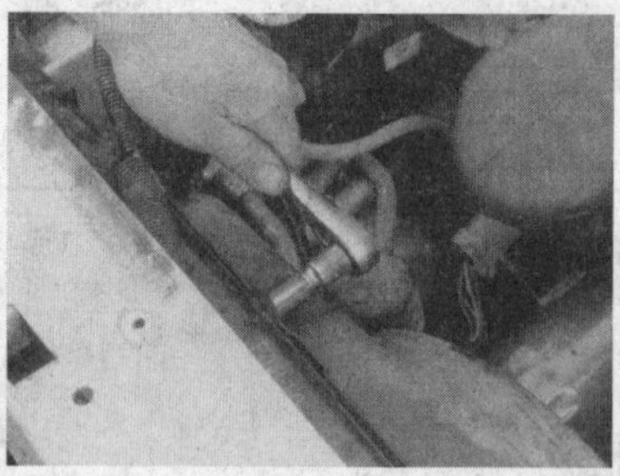


Fig. 69 Unbolt the fan assembly from the radiator

Fig. 70 Remove the fan from the engine

93143P56

**Fig. 71 Slide the fan as an assembly up and away from the radiator. Be careful not to dislodge the mounting stud on the left side**

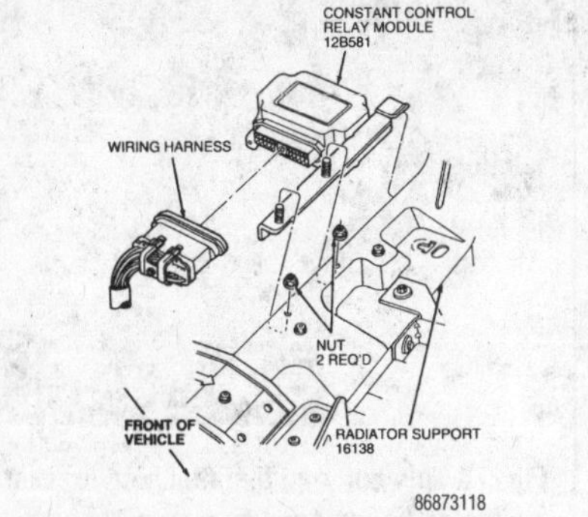


86873118

**Fig. 72 Constant control relay module location—3.8L engines**

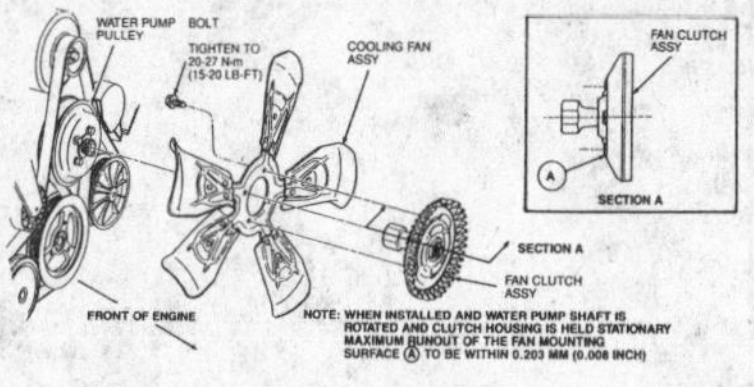


84173064

**Fig. 73 Fan and fan clutch assembly—4.6L engine**

cedures. Tighten the fan shroud retaining bolt to 23–33 inch lbs. (3–4 Nm). Tighten the fan shroud retaining nut to 71–106 inch lbs. (8–12 Nm).

#### 4.6L Engine

**See Figure 73**

1. Loosen the fan clutch-mounting shaft from the water pump hub.
2. Loosen the fan shroud from its radiator mounting and remove the lower hose from the shroud.
3. Lift the fan and clutch assembly and the fan shroud from the vehicle.
4. If necessary, remove the fan-to-fan clutch retaining bolts and separate the fan from the fan clutch.

**CAUTION**

**Closely examine the fan for cracks or separation, to avoid the possibility of personal injury or vehicle damage.**

**To install:**

5. Assemble the fan and fan clutch. Tighten the retaining bolts to 15–20 ft. lbs. (20–27 Nm).
6. Install the fan and clutch assembly and the fan shroud. Mount the fan clutch shaft to the water pump hub and tighten to 37–46 ft. lbs. (50–62 Nm).
7. Slip the shroud into the lower mounting clips and install the shroud retaining screws.

#### 5.0L Engines

1. Loosen the fan clutch-to-water pump hub retaining bolts.
2. If necessary, remove the drive belt from the water pump pulley.
3. Remove the fan shroud upper retaining screws. Lift the shroud to disengage it from the lower retaining clips.
4. Remove the fan clutch-to-water pump hub bolts and remove the fan and clutch assembly and the fan shroud.
5. If necessary, remove the fan-to-fan clutch retaining bolts and separate the fan from the fan clutch.

**CAUTION**

**Closely examine the fan for cracks or separation, to avoid the possibility of personal injury or vehicle damage.**

**To install:**

6. Assemble the fan and fan clutch. Tighten the retaining bolts evenly and alternately to 12–18 ft. lbs. (16–24 Nm).
7. Install the fan and clutch assembly and the fan shroud.
8. Install the fan clutch-to-water pump hub bolts.
9. Slip the shroud into the lower mounting clips and install the shroud retaining screws.
10. If removed, install the water pump drive pulley and adjust the belt tension; refer to Section 1.
11. Tighten the fan clutch-to-water pump hub bolts evenly and alternately to 15–22 ft. lbs. (20–27 Nm). Recheck the belt tension.

## Water Pump

### REMOVAL & INSTALLATION

#### 3.8L Engine

**See Figures 74 thru 90**

1. Disconnect the negative battery cable.
2. Drain and recycle the engine coolant.

**CAUTION**

**Never open, service, or drain the radiator or cooling system when hot; serious burns can occur from the steam and hot coolant. In addition, when draining engine coolant, keep in mind that cats and dogs are attracted to ethylene glycol antifreeze and could drink any that is left in an uncovered container or in puddles on the ground. This will prove fatal in sufficient quantities. Always drain coolant into a sealable container. Coolant should be reused unless it is contaminated or is several years old.**

3. Remove the drive belt.
4. Remove the two nuts and bolt retaining the drive belt tensioner to the engine.
5. Disconnect the heater hose at the water pump. Remove the lower hose.

93143P27

**Fig. 74 It is best to leave the belt in place while breaking loose the mounting bolts on the radiator pulley**

93143P15

**Fig. 75 The water pump pulley does not clear the space between the water pump and the frame**

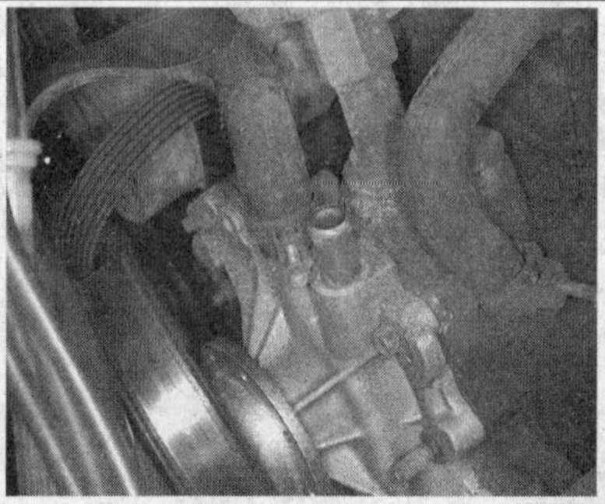

93143P31

**Fig. 76 Moving the pulley around to gain clearance to the water pump bolts does not always work**

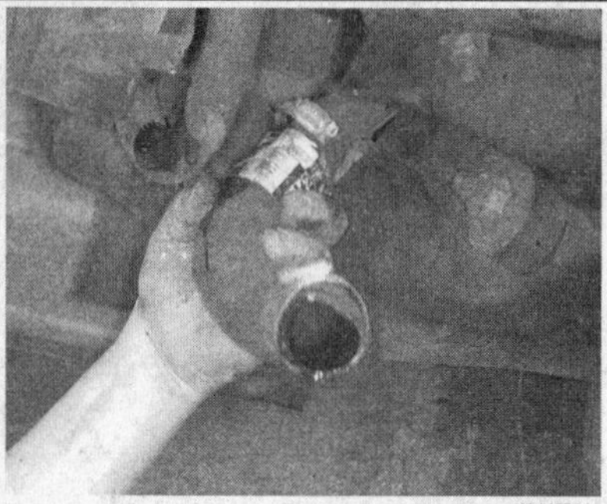

93143P14

Fig. 77 Removing the lower hose

93143P26

Fig. 78 This bolt and the attaching bracket must also be removed to access the water pump. Be sure to get the right one, they are difficult to see

93143P28

Fig. 79 Remove the nut holding the top of this support bar . . .

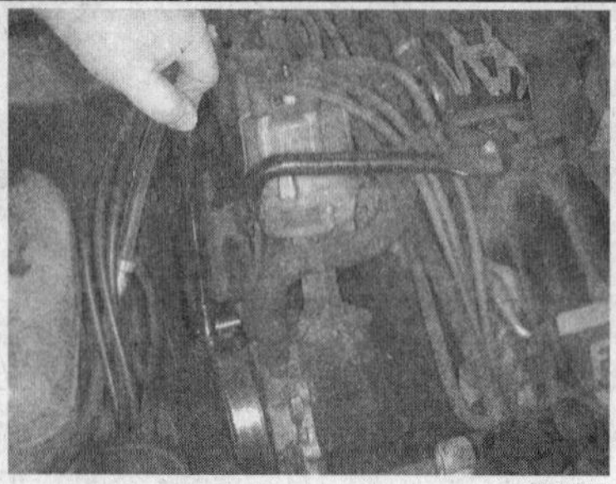

93143P29

Fig. 80 . . . and the bottom mounted nut to get the support bar out of the way, and give you access to the water pump bolts

93143P91

Fig. 81 Loosen the bottom nut on the front motor mount; remove it if necessary

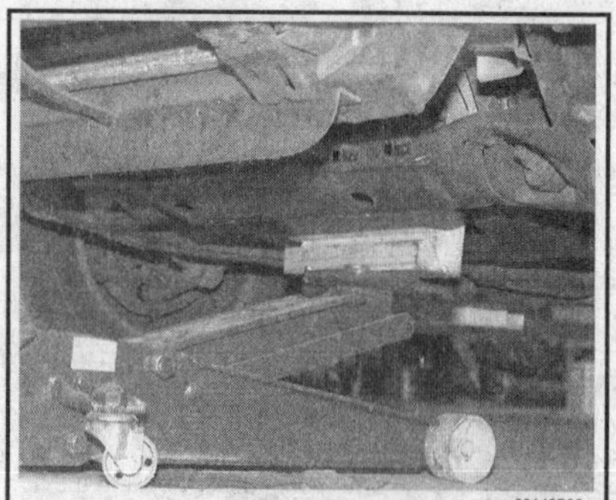

93143P90

Fig. 82 Place a piece of wood on the jack to protect the oil pan and jack up the engine about 4 or 5 inches

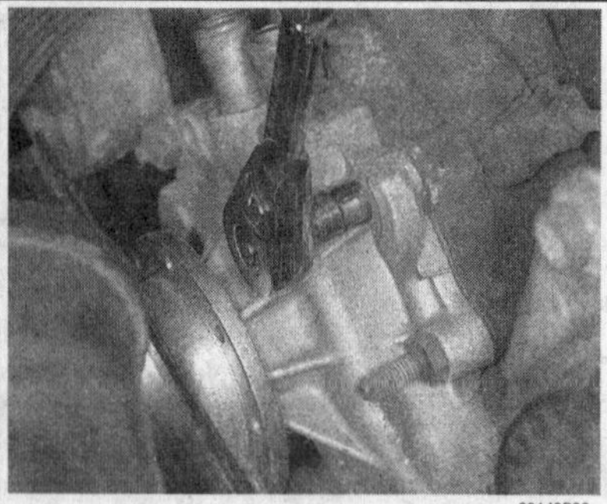

93143P30

Fig. 83 There are two different size bolts holding the water pump to the block

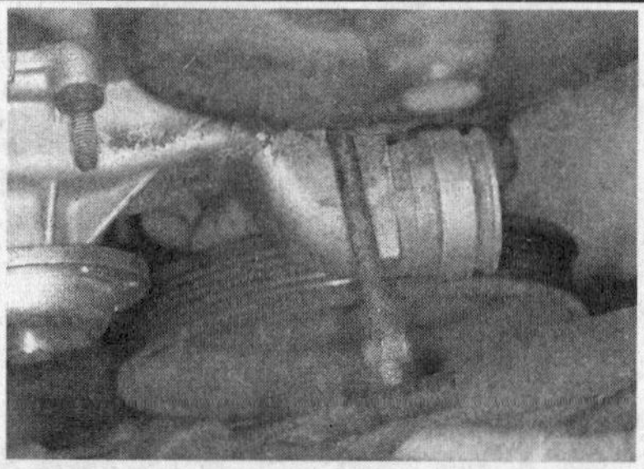

93143P10

Fig. 84 This long bolt has to be removed to remove the water pump. You will have to lift the engine slightly to slide the bolt out freely

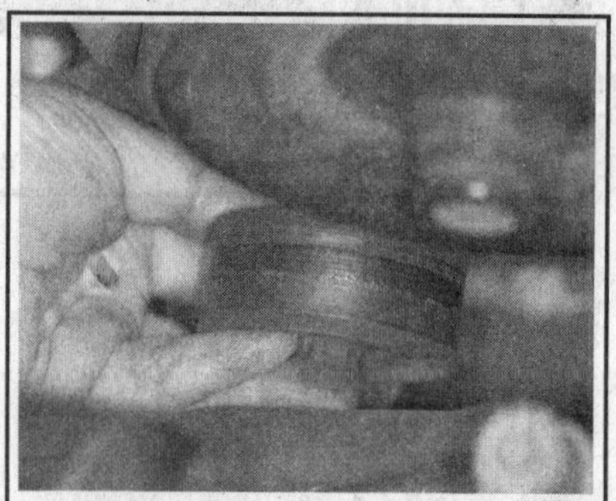

93143P89

Fig. 85 Retaining the idler pulley on this engine is the single bolt through the center

93143P24

Fig. 86 If the idler pulley on your car looks like this, replace it. Replace the serpentine belt along with it

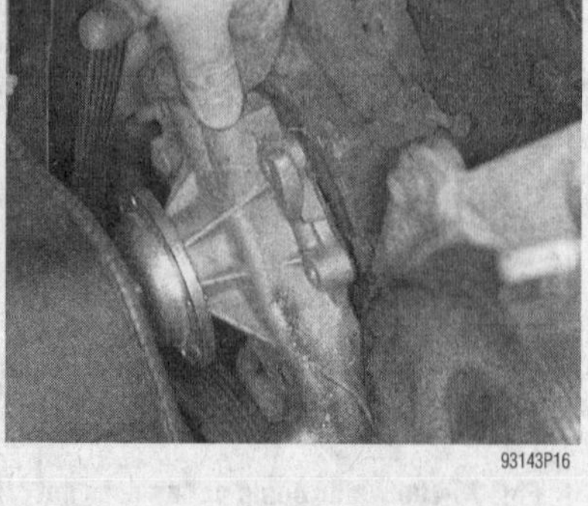

93143P16

Fig. 87 Pull the water pump away from the engine block

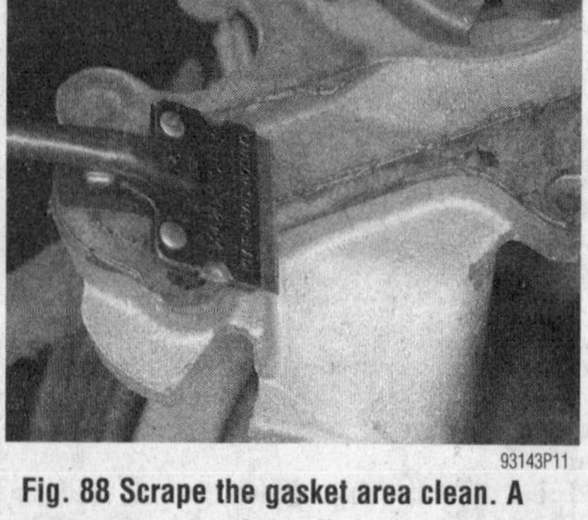

93143P11

Fig. 88 Scrape the gasket area clean. A razor scraper works well, but use it carefully

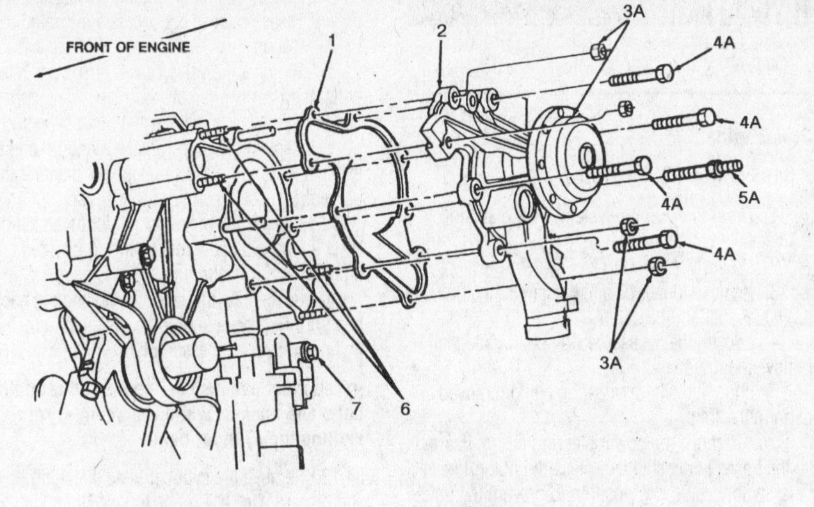

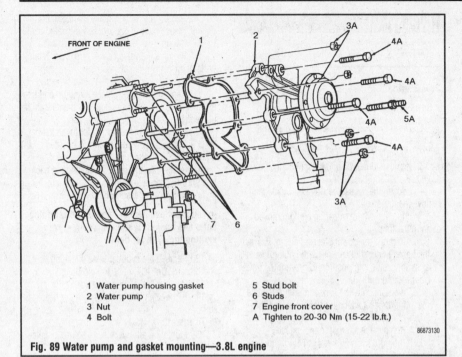

**Fig. 89 Water pump and gasket mounting—3.8L engine**

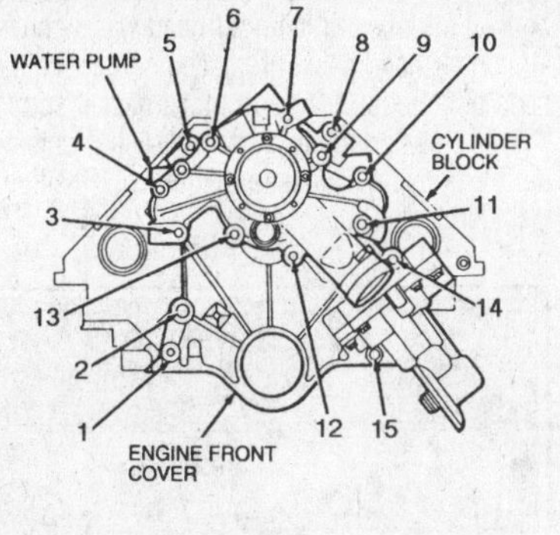


| Reference Number | Part Number | Size | Part Name |
|---|---|---|---|
| 1 | N805112 | M8 x 1.25 x 98.0 | Stud |
| 2 | N805112 | M8 x 1.25 x 98.0 | Stud |
| 3 | N805757 | M8 x 1.25 x 131.0 | Stud |
| 4 | N805757 | M8 x 1.25 x 131.0 | Stud |
| 5 | N605787 | M8 x 1.25 x 25.0 | Bolt |
| 6 | N605908 | M8 x 1.25 x 35.0 | Bolt |
| 7 | N605908 | M8 x 1.25 x 35.0 | Bolt |
| 8 | N605787 | M8 x 1.25 x 25.0 | Bolt |
| 9 | N804756 | M8 x 1.25 x 61.5 | Stud Bolt |
| 10 | N805275 | M8 x 1.25 x 141.0 | Stud |
| 11 | N804757 | M8 x 1.25 x 131.0 | Stud |
| 12 | N605908 | M8 x 1.25 x 35.0 | Bolt |
| 13 | N605908 | M8 x 1.25 x 35.0 | Bolt |
| 14 | N804839 | M8 x 1.25 x 105.0 | Bolt |
| 15 | N804841 | M8 x 1.25 x 20.0 | Cap Screw |

86873131

**Fig. 90 3.8L engine water pump retaining bolt locations. Since two bolt lengths are used, install the bolts as shown to prevent possible damage to the engine**

6. Remove the four water pump pulley bolts. The pulley will remain loose on the hub because there is insufficient room between the inner fender and the water pump, restricting removal from the vehicle.
7. Remove the water pump-to-engine retaining bolts, then lift the water pump and pulley assembly out of the vehicle.

**To install:**

8. Lightly oil all bolt and stud threads before installation except those that require sealant. Thoroughly clean, the water pump and front cover gasket contact surfaces.
9. Position the new water pump gasket on the pump-sealing surface using Gasket Adhesive.
10. With the water pump pulley positioned on the water pump hub, position the water pump on the engine front cover, then install the retaining bolts. Tighten the retaining bolts to 15–22 ft. lbs. (20–30 Nm).

**➡There are two different lengths of bolts used to retain the water pump. Install the bolts as shown in the accompanying figure or damage to the engine may occur.**

11. Install the water pump pulley bolts, then tighten the bolts to 16 ft. lbs. (21 Nm).
12. Connect the heater water hose to the water pump.
13. Install the drive belt tensioner to the engine front cover, then install the drive belt.
14. Connect the negative battery cable, then fill the cooling system with a 50/50 mixture of approved coolant and water. Start and run the engine until in reaches normal operating temperatures, then check for leaks and check the coolant level.

### 4.6L Engine

**See Figure 91**

1. Disconnect the negative battery cable.
2. Drain the cooling system, remove the cooling fan and the shroud.

**CAUTION**

**Never open, service, or drain the radiator or cooling system when hot; serious burns can occur from the steam and hot coolant. In addition, when draining engine coolant, keep in mind that cats and dogs are attracted to ethylene glycol antifreeze and could drink any that is left in an uncovered container or in puddles on the ground. This will prove fatal in sufficient quantities. Always drain coolant into a sealable container. Coolant should be reused unless it is contaminated or is several years old.**

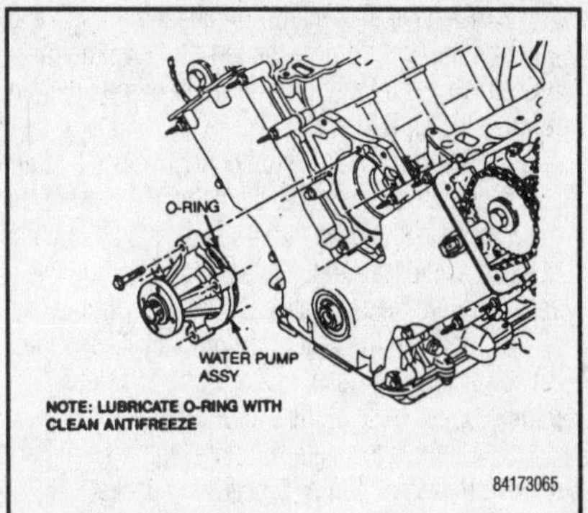


**Fig. 91 Water pump installation—4.6L engine**

3. Release the belt tensioner and remove the accessory drive belt.
4. Remove the 4 bolts retaining the water pump pulley to the water pump and remove the pulley.
5. Remove the 4 bolts retaining the water pump to the engine assembly and remove the water pump.

**To install:**

6. Clean the sealing surfaces of the water pump and engine block.
7. Lubricate a new O-ring seal with clean antifreeze and install on the water pump.
8. Install the water pump and tighten the retaining bolts to 15–22 ft. lbs. (20–30 Nm).
9. Install the water pump pulley and tighten the retaining bolts to 15–22 ft. lbs. (20–30 Nm).
10. Install the accessory drive belt; refer to Section 1.
11. Install the cooling fan and shroud. Connect the negative battery cable and fill the cooling system as explained in Section 1.
12. Run the engine and check for leaks.

### 5.0L Engines

1. Disconnect the negative battery cable.
2. Drain the cooling system. Remove the air inlet tube.

**CAUTION**

**Never open, service, or drain the radiator or cooling system when hot; serious burns can occur from the steam and hot coolant. In addition, when draining engine coolant, keep in mind that cats and dogs are attracted to ethylene glycol antifreeze and could drink any that is left in an uncovered container or in puddles on the ground. This will prove fatal in sufficient quantities. Always drain coolant into a sealable container. Coolant should be reused unless it is contaminated or is several years old.**

3. Remove the fan shroud attaching bolts and position the shroud over the fan. Remove the fan and clutch assembly from the water pump shaft and remove the shroud.

4. Remove the air conditioner drive belt and idler pulley bracket. Remove the alternator and power steering drive belts. Remove the power steering pump and position aside, leaving the hoses attached. Remove all accessory brackets that attach to the water pump.

5. Remove the water pump pulley. Disconnect the lower radiator hose, heater hose and water pump bypass hose at the water pump.

6. Remove the water pump attaching bolts and remove the water pump. Discard the gasket.

**To install:**

7. Clean all old gasket material from the timing cover and water pump.

8. Apply a suitable waterproof sealing compound to both sides of a new gasket and install the gasket on the timing cover.

9. Install the water pump and tighten the mounting bolts to 12–18 ft. lbs. (16–24 Nm).

10. Connect the hoses and accessory brackets to the water pump. Install the pulley on the water pump shaft.

11. Install the power steering pump and air conditioner idler pulley bracket. Install the accessory drive belts.

12. Install the fan and fan clutch assembly and the fan shroud.

13. Adjust the accessory drive belt tension; refer to Section 1.

14. Connect the negative battery cable and fill the cooling system, as explained in Section 1.

15. Run the engine and check for leaks.

## Cylinder Head

### REMOVAL & INSTALLATION

#### 3.8L Engine

➧ See Figures 92 thru 106

1. Drain the cooling system, then disconnect the negative battery cable.

2. Properly relieve the fuel system pressure.

3. Remove the air cleaner assembly including air intake duct and heat tube.

4. Loosen the accessory drive belt idler, then remove the drive belt.

5. If the left cylinder head is being removed, perform the following:

a. Remove the power steering pump. Leave the hoses connected and place the pump/bracket assembly aside in a position to prevent the fluid from leaking out.

b. If equipped with air conditioning, remove mounting bracket attaching bolts. Leaving the hoses connected, position the compressor aside.

c. Remove the alternator and bracket.

6. If the right cylinder head is being removed, perform the following:

a. Disconnect the thermactor air control valve or bypass valve hose assembly at the air pump.

b. If equipped, disconnect the thermactor tube support bracket from the rear of cylinder head.

c. Remove the accessory drive idler pulley.

d. Remove the PCV valve.

7. Remove the upper intake manifold. For details, please refer to the procedure located earlier in this section.

8. Remove the valve/rocker arm cover retaining bolts, then remove the covers.

9. Remove the injector fuel rail assembly.

10. Remove the lower intake manifold and the exhaust manifold(s). For details, please refer to the procedure located earlier in this section.

11. Loosen the rocker arm fulcrum attaching bolts enough to allow rocker arm to be lifted off the pushrod and rotate to one side. Remove the pushrods. Identify and label the position of each pushrod. Pushrods should be installed in their original position during assembly.

**➡You must use new cylinder head retaining bolts and gaskets when replacing or reinstalling the cylinder head!**

12. Remove the cylinder head attaching bolts and discard. Do NOT reuse the old bolts.

13. Remove the cylinder head(s).

14. Remove and discard old cylinder head gasket(s).

**To install:**

15. Lightly oil all bolt threads before installation.

16. Clean cylinder head, intake manifold, valve rocker arm cover, and cylinder head gasket contact surfaces. If cylinder head was removed for a cylinder head gasket replacement, check flatness of cylinder head and block gasket surfaces.

17. Position the new head gasket(s) onto cylinder block using dowels for alignment. Position cylinder head(s) onto block.

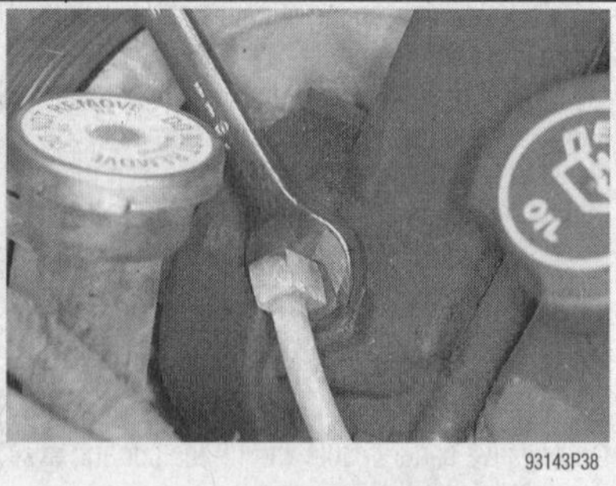

93143P38

**Fig. 92 If you are removing the head to replace the head gasket, remove the pressure and return lines for power steering and leave the pump attached**

93143P34

**Fig. 93 Loosening the 4 center bolts (long) holding the intake manifold in place**

93143P32

**Fig. 94 Removing the studs on the outer flanges of the upper intake manifold**

93143P83

**Fig. 95 This fuel rail comes off in one piece, but has 2 different spots with flex hoses**

93143P74

**Fig. 96 Removing the lower mounted head bolts. Notice the exhaust manifold has been removed**

93143P79

**Fig. 97 Removing the fulcrum to allow clearance to the head bolts**

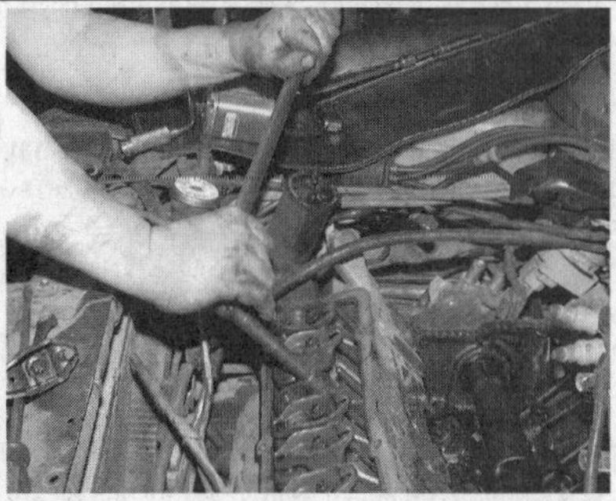

93143P78

Fig. 98 Breaking loose the head bolts with a ½ inch breaker

93143P77

Fig. 99 Removing the head bolts after breaking them loose

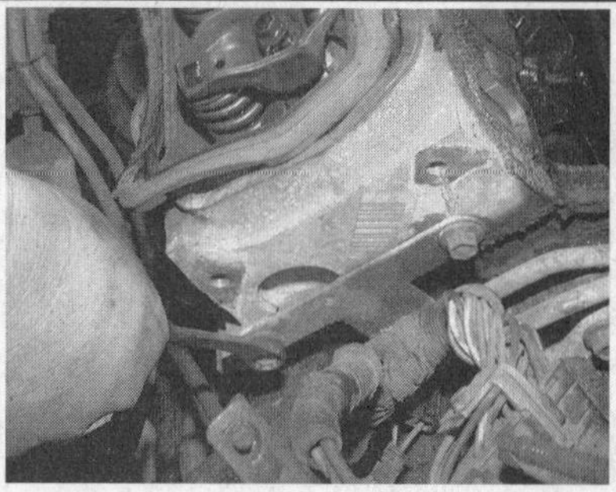

93143P73

Fig. 100 Don't forget the bolts and connectors on the back side of the head. The head won't come off unless you remove them

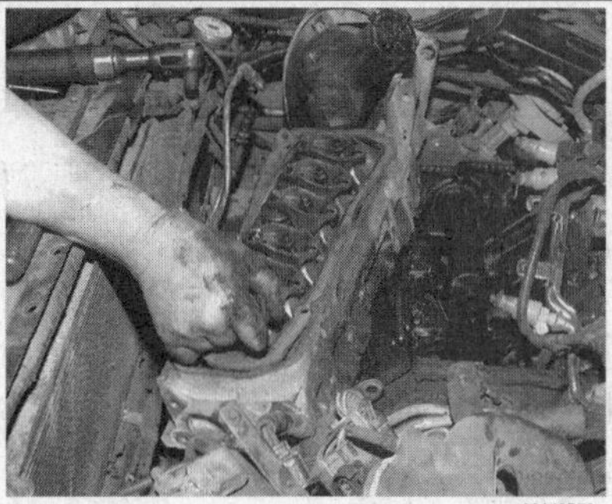

93143P70

Fig. 101 Lifting the head off the block, the power steering pump is intact

93143P69

Fig. 102 With the head removed, inspect and compare the combustion chambers for any differences in appearance

93143P66

Fig. 103 Inspect the head gasket for any breaks or tears

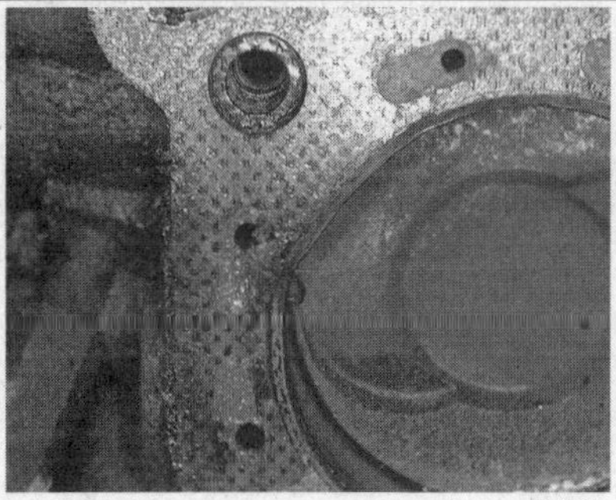

93143P65

Fig. 104 Check the cooling passages to make sure they are open

18. Apply a thin coating of pipe sealant with Teflon® to the threads of the short cylinder head bolts, nearest to the exhaust manifold. Do not apply sealant to the long bolts. Install the cylinder head bolts.

**➡Always use new cylinder head bolts to ensure a leak-tight assembly. Torque retention with used bolts can vary, which may result in coolant or compression leakage at the cylinder head mating surface area.**

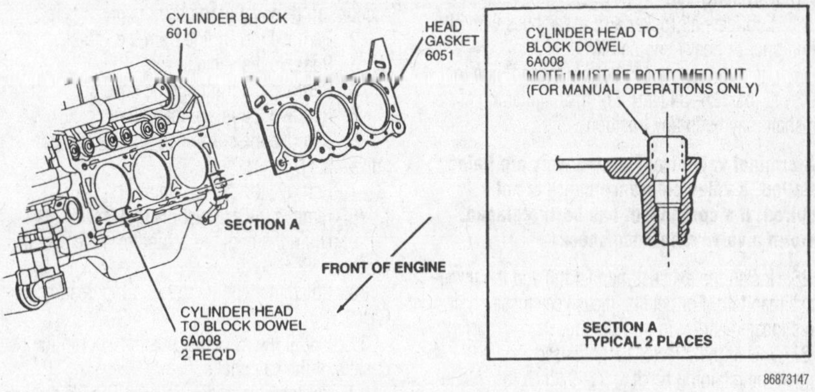


86873147

Fig. 105 When replacing or reinstalling the head, ALWAYS use new gasket(s) and bolts to avoid possible coolant and/or compression leaks which could result in engine damage

19. For vehicles through 1994, tighten the cylinder head attaching bolts, in sequence, to the following specifications:

- Step 1:37 ft. lbs. (50 Nm)
- Step 2:45 ft. lbs. (60 Nm)
- Step 3:52 ft. lbs. (70 Nm)

20. For vehicles through 1992, retighten the cylinder head bolts, in sequence, one at a time in the following manner:

a. Long cylinder head bolts: Loosen the bolts and back them out 2–3 turns. Retighten to 11–18 ft. lbs. (15–25 Nm). Then tighten the bolt an additional 85–105° and go to the next bolt in sequence.

b. Short cylinder head bolts: Loosen the bolts and back them out 2–3 turns. Retighten to 11–18 ft. lbs. (15–25 Nm). Then tighten the bolt an additional 65–85°.

21. For 1993–94 vehicles, retighten the cylinder head bolts, in sequence, one at a time in the following manner:

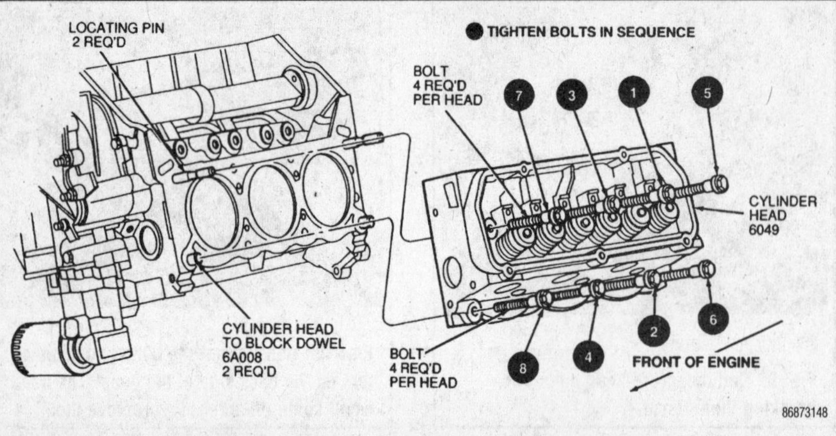


**Fig. 106 Cylinder head bolt tightening sequence—3.8L engine**

a. Long cylinder head bolts: Loosen the bolts and back them out 2–3 turns. Retighten to 11–18 ft. lbs. (15–25 Nm). Then tighten the bolt an additional 85–95° and go to the next bolt in sequence.

b. Short cylinder head bolts: Loosen the bolt and back them out 2–3 turns. Retighten to 7–15 ft. lbs. (10–20 Nm). Then tighten the bolt an additional 85–95°.

**➡When cylinder head attaching bolts have been tightened using the above procedures, it is not necessary to retighten bolts after extended engine operation. However, bolts can be checked for tightness if desired.**

22. Dip each pushrod end in oil conditioner or heavy engine oil, then install the pushrods in their original position.

23. For each valve, rotate crankshaft until the tappet rests on the heel (base circle) of the camshaft lobe. Torque the fulcrum attaching bolts to 44 inch lbs. (5 Nm) maximum.

24. Lubricate all rocker arm assemblies with oil conditioner or heavy engine oil.

25. Tighten the fulcrum bolts a second time to 19–25 ft. lbs. (26–34 Nm). For final tightening, camshaft may be in any position.

**➡If original valve train components are being installed, a valve clearance check is not required. If a component has been replaced, perform a valve clearance check.**

26. Install the exhaust manifold(s) and the lower intake manifold. For details, please see these procedures located earlier in this section.

27. Install the injector fuel rail assembly. Tighten the retaining bolts to 71–97 inch lbs. (8–11 Nm).

28. Position the rocker arm/valve cover(s) and new gasket on cylinder head and install attaching bolts. Note location of spark plug wire routing clip stud bolts. Tighten attaching bolts to 80–106 inch lbs. (9–12 Nm).

29. Install the upper intake manifold, then connect the ignition wires to the spark plugs.

30. If the left cylinder head is being installed, perform the following: install oil fill cap, compressor mounting and support brackets, power steering pump mounting and support brackets and the alternator/support bracket.

31. If the right cylinder head is being installed, perform the following: install the PCV valve, alternator bracket, thermactor pump and pump pulley, accessory drive idler, thermactor air control valve or air bypass valve hose.

32. Install the accessory drive belt. Attach the thermactor tube(s) support bracket to the rear of the cylinder head. Tighten the attaching bolts to 30–40 ft. lbs. (40–55 Nm).

33. Install the air cleaner assembly, including the air intake duct and heat tube.

34. Connect the negative battery cable and fill the cooling system.

35. Start the engine and check for leaks.

### 4.6L Engine FWD

1. To remove the head on a 4.6L engine that is a front-wheel drive, it is first necessary to remove the engine from the vehicle. Since an explanation on how to remove the engine has already been given in this section and a detailed account of how to disassemble the head follows this, an abbreviated account on removal of the head is given here.
2. Remove the engine from the vehicle.
3. Remove the valve covers.
4. Remove the front engine covers.
5. Remove the intake manifold.
6. Remove the crankshaft position sensor pulse wheel.
7. Remove the rocker arms.
8. remove the exhaust manifolds.
9. Drain the engine coolant from the cylinder block.
10. Rotate the engine to No. 1 top dead center (TDC).
11. Install the camshaft position tool in the rear D-slots of the camshafts.
12. Remove the bolts retaining The RH and LH primary timing chain tensioners to the cylinder heads and remove the timing chain tensioners.
13. Remove the LH and RH primary timing chains, timing chain tensioner arms, and timing chain guides. Do not loosen the camshaft-timing sprocket retaining bolts.
14. Remove the outlet heater water hose retaining bolts from the rear of the RH cylinder head.
15. Using the reverse of the torque sequence, loosen and remove the 10 cylinder head bolts.
16. The cylinder head bolts are torque to yield and must be replaced. Do not re-use the old head bolts. Discard them.
17. Remove the heads. Remove the head gaskets.

**➡The cylinder heads must not be set on the head face if the valves are open. Damage may occur to the valves.**

### 4.6L Engine RWD

**➧ See Figures 107 thru 116**

1. Disconnect the negative battery cable.
2. Drain the cooling system and remove the cooling fan and shroud.
3. Relieve the fuel system pressure and disconnect the fuel lines; refer to Section 5.
4. Remove the air inlet tube and the wiper module. Release the belt tensioner and remove the accessory drive belt.
5. Tag and disconnect the spark plug wires from the spark plugs. Disconnect the spark plug wire brackets from the valve cover studs and remove the 2 bolts retaining the spark plug wire tray to the coil brackets.
6. Remove the bolt retaining the air conditioner high-pressure line to the right coil bracket. Disconnect both ignition coils and CID sensor.
7. Remove the nuts retaining the coil brackets to the front cover. Slide the ignition coil brackets and spark plug wire assembly off the mounting studs and remove from the vehicle.
8. Remove the water pump pulley. Disconnect the alternator wiring harness from the junction block, fender apron, and alternator. Disconnect the bolts retaining the alternator to the intake manifold and engine block and remove the alternator.
9. Disconnect the positive battery cable at the power distribution box. Remove the retaining bolt from the positive battery cable bracket located on the side of the right cylinder head.
10. Disconnect the vent hose from the canister purge solenoid and position the positive battery cable out of the way. Disconnect the canister purge solenoid vent hose from the PCV valve and remove the PCV valve from the valve cover.
11. Remove the 42-pin engine harness connector from the retaining bracket on the brake vacuum booster, disconnect, and position out of the way.
12. Disconnect the crankshaft position sensor, air conditioning compressor clutch and canister purge solenoid connectors.
13. Raise and safely support the vehicle.
14. Remove the bolts retaining the power steering pump to the engine block and front cover. The

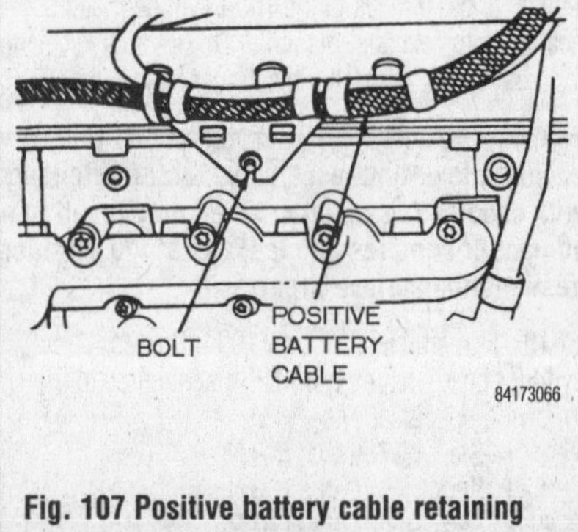


**Fig. 107 Positive battery cable retaining bolt location—4.6L engine**

front lower bolt on the power steering pump will not come all the way out. Wire the power steering pump out of the way.

15. Remove the 4 bolts retaining the oil pan to the front cover. Remove the crankshaft damper retaining bolt and remove the damper, using a suitable puller.

16. Disconnect the Electronic Variable Orifice (EVO) sensor and oil-sending unit. Position the EVO sensor and oil pressure sending unit harness out of the way.

17. Disconnect the EGR tube from the right exhaust manifold. Disconnect the exhaust pipes from the exhaust manifolds. Lower the exhaust pipes and hang with wire from the crossmember.

18. Remove the bolt retaining the starter wiring harness to the rear of the right cylinder head. Lower the vehicle.

19. Remove the bolts and the stud bolts retaining the valve covers to the cylinder heads and then remove the covers.

20. Disconnect the accelerator, cruise control and throttle valve cables. Remove the accelerator cable bracket from the intake manifold and position out of the way.

21. Disconnect the vacuum hose from the throttle body elbow vacuum port, both oxygen sensors and the heater supply hose.

22. Remove the 2 bolts retaining the thermostat housing to the intake manifold and position the upper hose and thermostat housing out of the way.

**➡The two thermostat housing bolts also retain the intake manifold.**

23. Remove the 9 bolts retaining the intake manifold to the cylinder heads and remove the intake manifold and gaskets.

24. Remove the 7 stud bolts and 4 bolts retaining the front cover to the engine and remove the front cover.

25. Remove the timing chains; refer to the procedure in this Section.

26. Remove the 10 bolts retaining the left cylinder head to the engine block and remove the head.

**➡The lower rear bolt cannot be removed due to interference with the brake vacuum booster. Use a rubber band to hold the bolt away from the engine block.**

27. Remove the ground strap, 1 stud, and 1 bolt retaining the heater return line to the right cylinder head.

28. Remove the 10 bolts retaining the right cylinder head to the engine block and remove the head.

**➡The lower rear bolt cannot be removed due to interference with the evaporator housing. Use a rubber band to hold the bolt away from the engine block.**

29. Clean all gasket-mating surfaces. Check the cylinder head and engine block for flatness. Check the cylinder head for scratches near the coolant passage and combustion chamber that could provide leak paths.

**To install:**

30. Rotate the crankshaft counterclockwise 45 degrees. The crankshaft keyway should be at the 9 o'clock position viewed from the front of the engine. This ensures that all pistons are below the top of the engine block deck face.

31. Rotate the camshaft to a stable position where the valves do not extend below the head face.

32. Position new head gaskets on the engine block. Install the lower rear bolts on both cylinder heads and retain with rubber bands as explained during the removal procedure.

**➡New cylinder head bolts must be used whenever the cylinder head is removed and reinstalled. The cylinder head bolts are a torque-to-yield design and cannot be reused.**

33. Position the cylinder heads on the engine block dowels, being careful not to score the surface of the head face. Apply clean oil to the head bolts, remove the rubber band from the lower rear bolt and install all bolts hand-tight.

34. Tighten the head bolts as follows:

a. Tighten the bolts, in sequence, to 25–30 ft. lbs. (35–45 Nm).

b. Rotate each bolt, in sequence, 85–95 degrees.

c. Rotate each bolt, in sequence, an additional 85–95 degrees.

35. Position the heater return hose and install the 2 bolts. Rotate the camshafts using the flats matched at the center of the camshaft until both are in time. Install cam positioning tools T91P–6256–A or equivalent, on the flats of the camshafts to keep them from rotating.

36. Rotate the crankshaft clockwise 45 degrees to position the crankshaft at TDC on No. 1 cylinder.

**➡The crankshaft must only be rotated in the clockwise direction and only as far as TDC.**

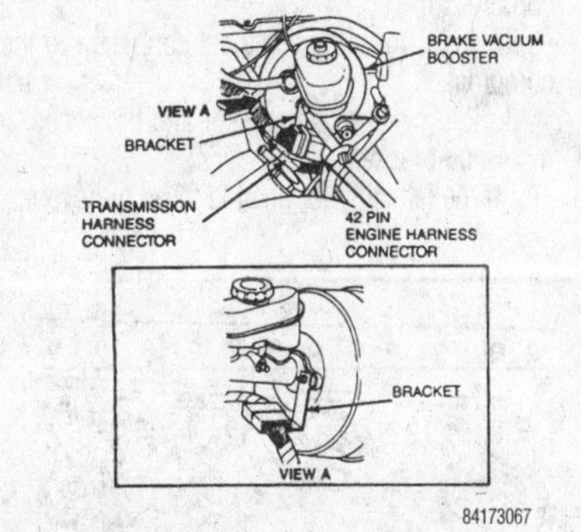


**Fig. 108 Engine harness connector location—4.6L engine**

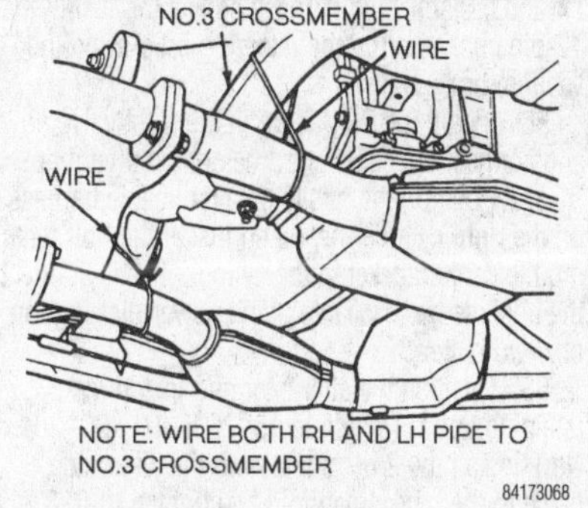


**Fig. 109 Hang the exhaust system from the crossmember with wire**

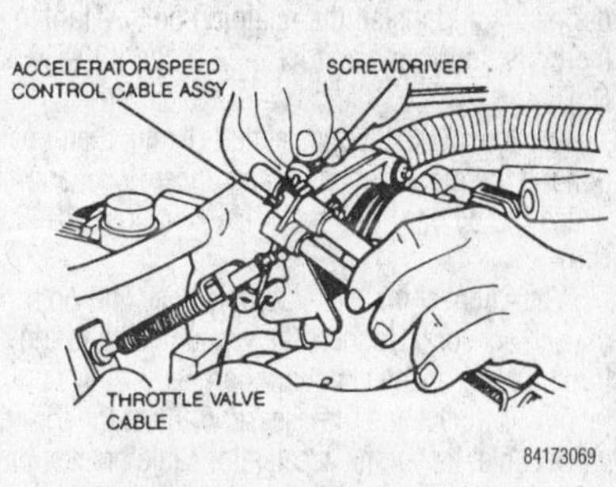


**Fig. 110 Disconnecting the accelerator/cruise control cables—4.6L engine**

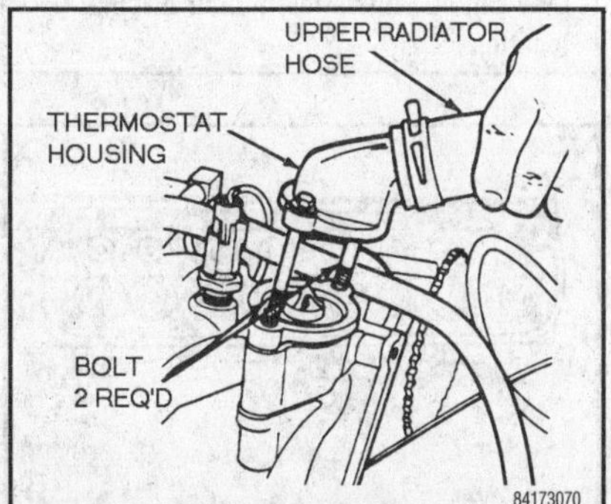


**Fig. 111 Remove the thermostat housing with the radiator hose attached—4.6L engine**

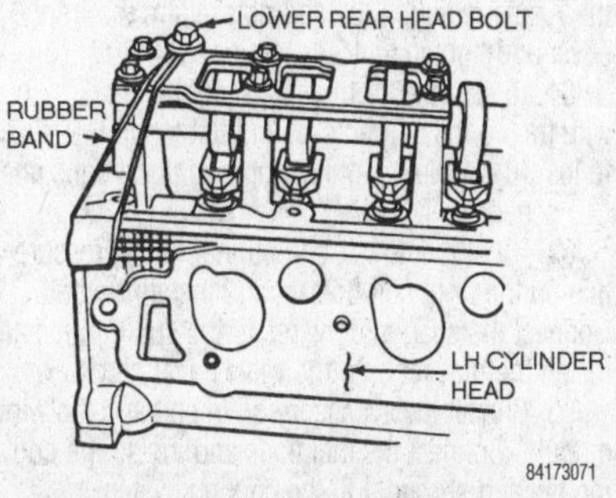


**Fig. 112 Hold the lower rear bolt on the left cylinder head with a rubber band—4.6L engine**

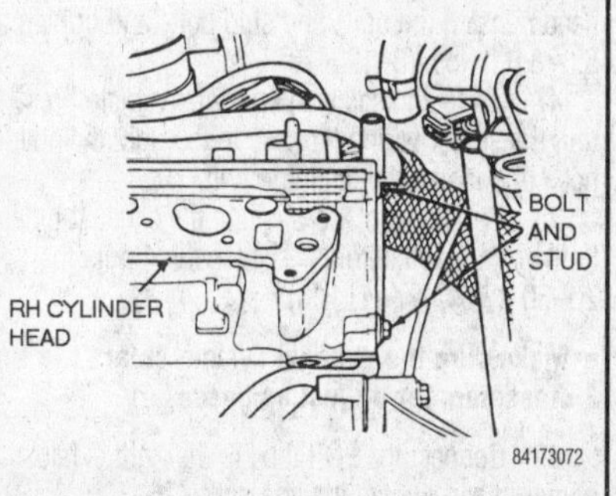


**Fig. 113 Heater return line retaining bolt and stud location—4.6L engine**

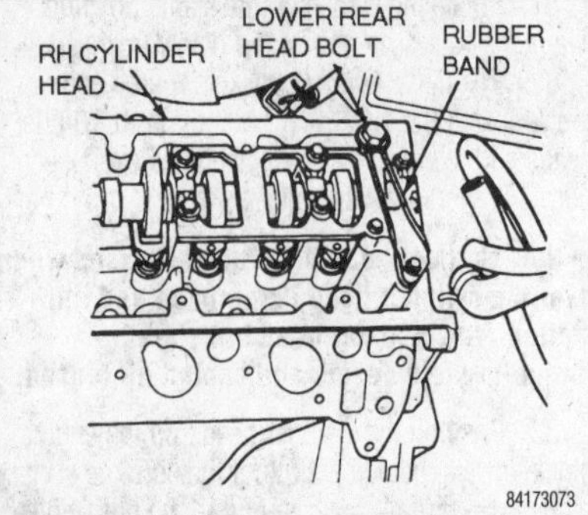


**Fig. 114 Hold the lower rear bolt on the right cylinder head with a rubber band—4.6L engine**

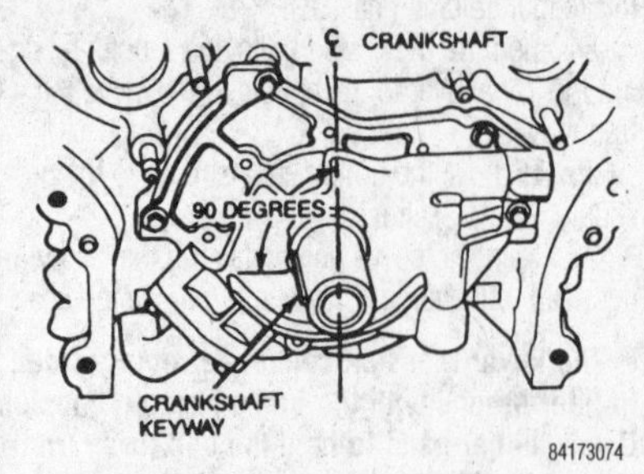


**Fig. 115 Position the crankshaft as shown before installing the cylinder heads—4.6L engine**

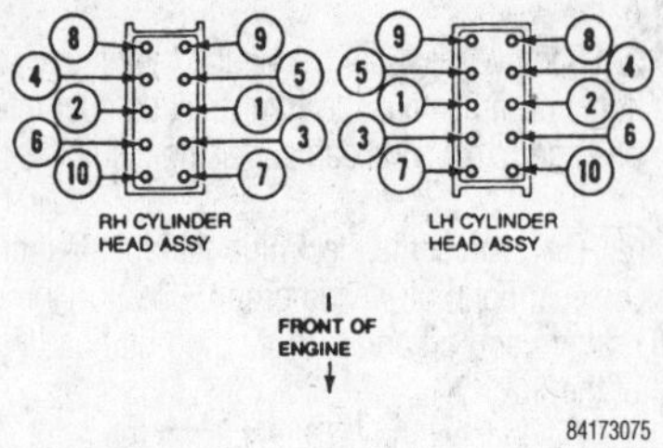


**Fig. 116 Cylinder head bolt torque sequence—4.6L engine**

37. Install the timing chains according to the procedure in this Section.
38. Install a new front cover seal and gasket. Apply silicone sealer to the lower corners of the cover where it meets the junction of the oil pan and cylinder block and to the points where the cover contacts the junction of the cylinder block and cylinder head.
39. Install the front cover and the stud bolts and bolts. Tighten to 15–22 ft. lbs. (20–30 Nm).
40. Position new intake manifold gaskets on the cylinder heads. Make sure the alignment tabs on the gaskets are aligned with the holes in the cylinder heads.

**➡Before installing the intake manifold, inspect it for nicks and cuts that could provide leak paths.**

41. Position the intake manifold on the cylinder heads and install the retaining bolts. Tighten the bolts, in sequence, to 15–22 ft. lbs. (20–30 Nm).
42. Install the thermostat and O-ring, then position the thermostat housing and upper hose, and install the 2 bolts. Tighten to 15–22 ft. lbs. (20–30 Nm).
43. Connect the heater supply hose and both oxygen sensors. Connect the vacuum hose to the throttle body adapter vacuum port.
44. Connect and, if necessary, adjust the throttle valve cable. Install the accelerator cable bracket on the intake manifold and connect the accelerator and cruise control cables to the throttle body.
45. Apply silicone sealer to both places where the front cover meets the cylinder head. Install new gaskets on the valve covers.
46. Install the valve covers on the cylinder heads. Install the bolts and stud bolts and tighten to 6.0–8.8 ft. lbs. (8–12 Nm).
47. Raise and safely support the vehicle. Position the starter wiring harness to the right cylinder head and install the retaining bolt.
48. Cut the wire and position the exhaust pipes to the exhaust manifolds. Tighten the 4 nuts to 20–30 ft. lbs. (27–41 Nm).

**➡Make sure the exhaust system clears the No. 3 crossmember. Adjust as necessary.**

49. Connect the EGR tube to the right exhaust manifold and tighten the line nut to 26–33 ft. lbs. (35–45 Nm). Connect the EVO sensor and oil-sending unit.
50. Apply a small amount of silicone sealer in the rear of the keyway on the damper. Position the damper on the crankshaft, making sure the crankshaft key and keyway are aligned.
51. Using damper installer T74P–6316–B or equivalent, install the crankshaft damper. Install the damper bolt and washer and tighten to 114–121 ft. lbs. (155–165 Nm).
52. Install the 4 bolts retaining the oil pan to the front cover and tighten to 15–22 ft. lbs. (20–30 Nm).
53. Position the power steering pump on the engine and install the 4 retaining bolts. Tighten to 15–22 ft. lbs. (20–30 Nm). Lower the vehicle.
54. Connect the air conditioning compressor, crankshaft position sensor and canister purge solenoid.
55. Connect the 42-pin engine harness connector and transmission harness connector. Install the 42-pin connector on the retaining bracket on the vacuum brake booster.
56. Install the PCV valve in the right valve cover and connect the canister purge solenoid vent hose.
57. Position the positive battery cable harness on the right cylinder head and install the bolt retaining the cable bracket to the cylinder head. Connect the positive battery cable at the power distribution box and battery.
58. Position the alternator and install the 2 retaining bolts. Tighten to 15–22 ft. lbs. (20–30 Nm). Install the 2 bolts retaining the alternator brace to the intake manifold and tighten to 6–8 ft. lbs. (8–12 Nm).
59. Install the water pump pulley and tighten the bolts to 15–22 ft. lbs. (20–30 Nm).
60. Position the ignition coil brackets and spark plug wire assembly onto the mounting studs. Install the 7 nuts retaining the coil brackets to the front cover and tighten to 15–22 ft. lbs. (20–30 Nm).
61. Install the 2 bolts retaining the spark plug wire tray to the coil bracket and tighten to 6.0–8.8 ft. lbs. (8–12 Nm). Connect both ignition coils and CID sensor.
62. Position the air conditioner high-pressure line on the right coil bracket and install the bolt. Connect the spark plug wires to the spark plugs and install the bracket onto the valve cover studs.
63. Install the accessory drive belt and the wiper module. Connect the fuel lines and install the cooling fan and shroud. Fill the cooling system.
64. Install the air inlet tube and connect the negative battery cable. Start the engine and bring to normal operating temperature. Check for leaks. Check all fluid levels.

## 5.0L Engines

**➧ See Figures 117 and 118**

1. Disconnect the negative battery cable.
2. Relieve the fuel system pressure; refer to Section 5. Drain the cooling system.
3. On 5.0L engine, remove the upper and lower intake manifold and throttle body assembly.
4. If the air conditioning compressor is in the way of a cylinder head that is to be removed, proceed as follows:
   a. Discharge the air conditioning system; refer to Section 1.
   b. Disconnect and plug the refrigerant lines at the compressor. Cap the openings on the compressor.
   c. Disconnect the electrical connector to the compressor.
   d. Remove the compressor and the necessary mounting brackets.
5. If the left cylinder head is to be removed,

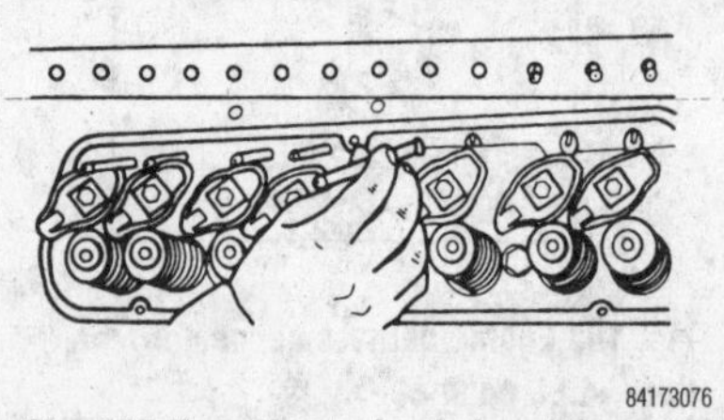


**Fig. 117 Keep the pushrods in order so they can be reinstalled in their original locations**

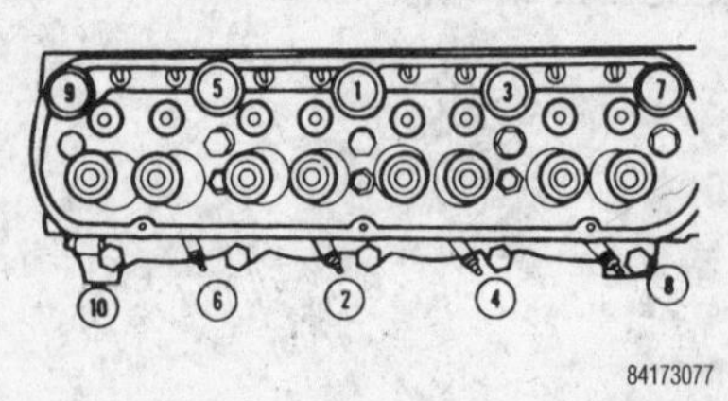


**Fig. 118 Cylinder head bolt torque sequence—5.0L engines**

disconnect the power steering pump bracket from the cylinder head and remove the drive belt from the pump pulley. Position the pump out of the way in a position that will prevent the oil from draining out.

6. Disconnect the oil level dipstick tube bracket from the exhaust manifold stud, if necessary.

7. If the right cylinder head is to be removed, on some vehicles it is necessary to disconnect the alternator-mounting bracket from the cylinder head.

8. Remove the thermactor crossover tube from the rear of the cylinder heads. If equipped, remove the fuel line from the clip at the front of the right cylinder head.

9. Raise and safely support the vehicle. Disconnect the exhaust manifolds from the muffler inlet pipes. Lower the vehicle.

10. Loosen the rocker arm fulcrum bolts so the rocker arms can be rotated to the side. Remove the pushrods in sequence so they may be installed in their original positions.

11. Remove the cylinder head attaching bolts and the cylinder heads. If necessary, remove the exhaust manifolds to gain access to the lower bolts. Remove and discard the head gaskets.

12. Clean all gasket-mating surfaces. Check the flatness of the cylinder head using a straightedge and a feeler gauge. The cylinder head must not be warped any more than 0.003 in. in any 6.0 in. span; 0.006 in. overall. Machine as necessary.

**To install:**

13. Position the new cylinder head gasket over the dowels on the block. Position the cylinder heads on the block and install the attaching bolts.

14. On 5.0L engine, tighten the bolts, in sequence, in 2 steps, first to 55–65 ft. lbs. (75–88 Nm), then to 65–72 ft. lbs. (88–97 Nm). On 5.8L engine, tighten the bolts, in sequence, in 3 steps, first to 85 ft. lbs. (116 Nm), then to 95 ft. lbs. (129 Nm), and finally to 105–112 ft. lbs. (142–152 Nm).

**➡When the cylinder head bolts have been tightened following this procedure, it is not necessary to retighten the bolts after extended operation.**

15. If removed, install the exhaust manifolds. Tighten the retaining bolts to 18–24 ft. lbs. (24–32 Nm).

16. Clean the pushrods, making sure the oil passages are clean. Check the ends of the pushrods for wear. Visually check the pushrods for straightness or check for runout using a dial indicator. Replace pushrods, as necessary.

17. Apply suitable grease to the ends of the pushrods and install them in their original positions. Position the rocker arms over the pushrods and the valves.

18. Before tightening each fulcrum bolt, bring the lifter for the fulcrum bolt to be tightened onto the base circle of the camshaft by rotating the engine. When the lifter is on the base circle of the camshaft, tighten the fulcrum bolt to 18–25 ft. lbs. (24–34 Nm).

**➡If all the original valve train parts are reinstalled, a valve clearance check is not necessary. If any valve train components are replaced, a valve clearance check must be performed.**

19. Install new gaskets on the rocker arm covers and install the covers onto the cylinder heads.

20. Raise and safely support the vehicle. Connect the exhaust manifolds to the muffler inlet pipes. Lower the vehicle.

21. If necessary, install the air conditioning compressor and brackets. Connect the refrigerant lines and electrical connector to the compressor.

22. If necessary, install the alternator bracket.

23. If the left cylinder head was removed, install the power steering pump.

24. Install the drive belts. Install the thermactor tube at the rear of the cylinder heads.

25. Install the intake manifold. Fill and bleed the cooling system.

26. Connect the negative battery cable, start the engine, and bring to normal operating temperature. Check for leaks. Check all fluid levels.

27. If necessary, have a MVAC certified tech evacuate and charge the air conditioning system.

## Oil Pan

### REMOVAL & INSTALLATION

#### 3.8L Engine

**➧ See Figure 119**

1. Disconnect the negative battery cable.
2. Raise and safely support the vehicle.
3. Drain the oil pan, then remove the oil filter. Position the drain pan out of the way.
4. Remove the dual converter Y-pipe assembly.
5. Remove the starter motor. For details, please refer to the procedure located earlier in this section.
6. Remove the engine rear plate/converter housing cover.
7. Remove the retaining bolts and remove the oil pan.

**To install:**

8. Clean the gasket surfaces on cylinder block and the oil pan.

9. Trial fit oil pan to cylinder block. Ensure that enough clearance has been provided to allow the oil pan to be installed without sealant being scraped off when pan is positioned under the engine.

10. Apply a bead of silicone sealer to the oil pan flange. Also apply a bead of sealer to the front cover/cylinder block joint and fill the grooves on both sides of the rear main seal cap.

**➡When using silicone rubber sealer, assembly must occur within 15 minutes after sealer application. After this time, the sealer may start to harden and its sealing effectiveness may be reduced.**

11. Install the oil pan and secure to the block with the attaching screws. Tighten the screws to 7–9 ft. lbs. (9–12 Nm).

12. Install a new oil filter.

13. Install the engine rear plate/converter housing cover.

14. Install the starter motor. For details, please refer to the procedure located earlier in this section.

15. Install the Y-pipe converter assembly, then carefully lower the vehicle.

16. Fill the crankcase with the correct viscosity and amount of oil, then connect the negative battery cable.

17. Start the engine and check for leaks.

#### 4.6L Engine

**➧ See Figures 120, 121 and 122**

1. Disconnect the battery cables, negative cable first, and remove the air inlet tube.

2. Relieve the fuel system pressure and disconnect the fuel lines; refer to Section 5. Drain the

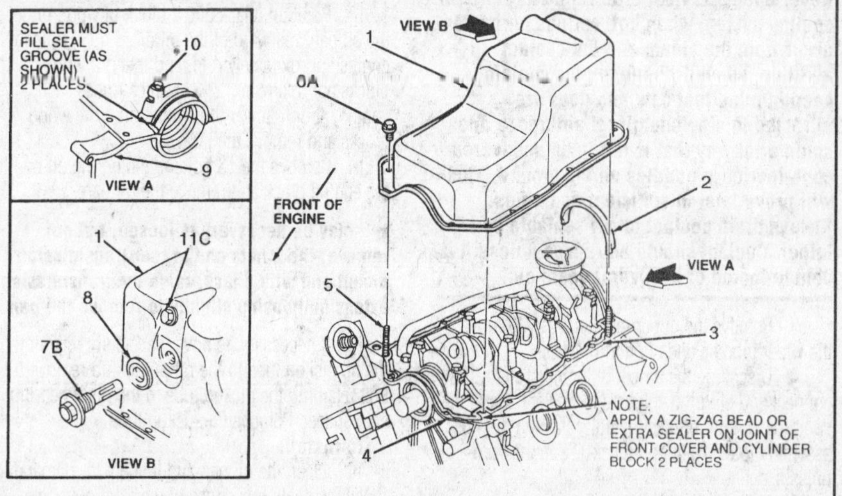


1 Oil pan
2 Oil pan rear seal
3 Silicone gasket and sealant
4 Engine front cover
5 Guide pin ( 2 req'd)
6 Bolt (18 req'd)
7 Low oil level sensor
8 Low oil level sensor washer
9 Cylinder block
10 Rear cap
11 Oil pan drain plug
A Tighten to 9-12 Nm (80-106 lb.in.)
B Tighten to 25-34 Nm (18-25 lb.ft.)
C Tighten to 20-34 Nm (15-25 lb.ft.)

86873161

**Fig. 119 Exploded view of the oil pan assembly—3.8L engine**

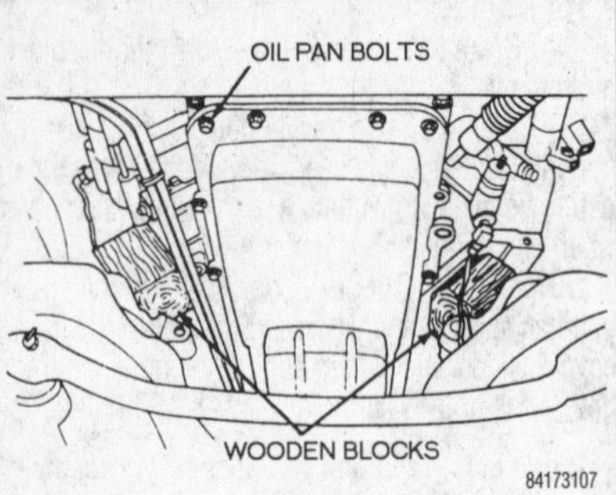


**Fig. 120 Position of wood blocks under the engine mounts—4.6L engine**

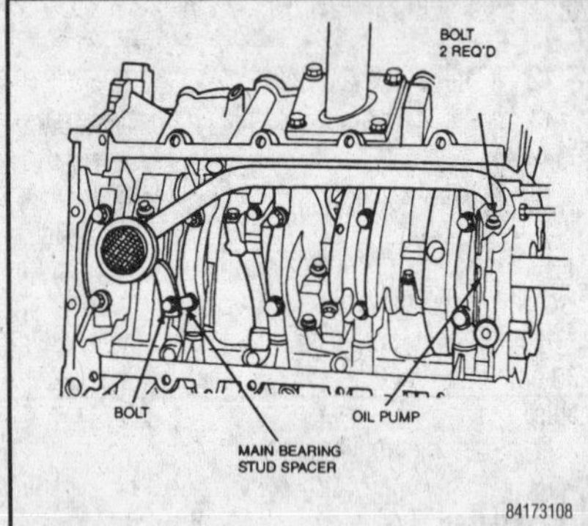


**Fig. 121 Oil pump pickup tube—4.6L engine**

cooling system and remove the cooling fan and shroud.

**CAUTION**

**Never open, service, or drain the radiator or cooling system when hot; serious burns can occur from the steam and hot coolant. In addition, when draining engine coolant, keep in mind that cats and dogs are attracted to ethylene glycol antifreeze and could drink any that is left in an uncovered container or in puddles on the ground. This will prove fatal in sufficient quantities. Always drain coolant into a sealable container. Coolant should be reused unless it is contaminated or is several years old.**

3. Remove the upper radiator hose. Remove the wiper module and support bracket.
4. Discharge the air conditioning system. Disconnect and plug the compressor outlet hose at the compressor and remove the bolt retaining the hose assembly to the right coil bracket. Cap the compressor outlet.
5. Remove the 42-pin engine harness connector from the retaining bracket on the brake vacuum booster and disconnect the connector and transmission harness connector.
6. Disconnect the throttle valve cable from the throttle body and disconnect the heater outlet hose.
7. Remove the nut retaining the ground strap to the right cylinder head. Remove the upper stud and loosen the lower bolt retaining the heater outlet hose to the right cylinder head and position out of the way.

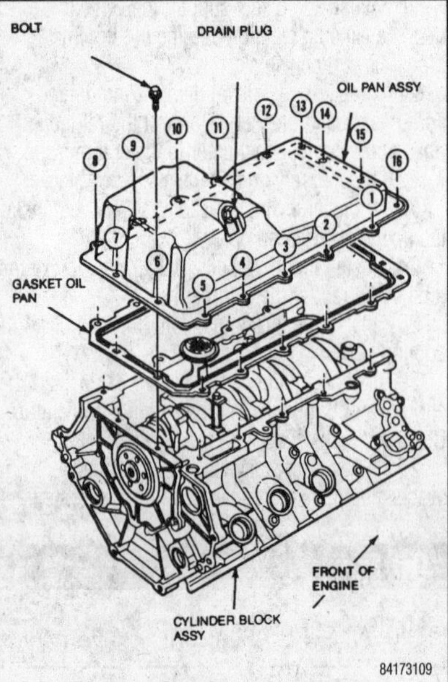


**Fig. 122 Oil pan bolt torque sequence—4.6L engine**

8. Remove the blower motor resistor. Remove the bolt retaining the right engine mount to the lower engine bracket.
9. Disconnect the vacuum hoses from the EGR valve and tube. Remove the 2 bolts retaining the EGR valve to the intake manifold.
10. Raise and safely support the vehicle. Drain the crankcase and remove the engine mount through bolts.
11. Remove the EGR tube line nut from the right exhaust manifold and remove the EGR valve and tube assembly.
12. Disconnect the exhaust from the exhaust manifolds. Lower the exhaust system and support it with wire from the crossmember.
13. Position a jack and a block of wood under the oil pan, rearward of the oil drain hole. Raise the engine approximately 4 in. and insert 2 wood blocks approximately 2½ in. thick under each engine mount. Lower the engine onto the wood blocks and remove the jack.
14. Remove the 16 bolts retaining the oil pan to the engine block and remove the oil pan.

**➡It may be necessary to loosen, but not remove, the 2 nuts on the rear transmission mount and with a jack, raise the transmission extension housing slightly to remove the pan.**

15. If necessary, remove the 2 bolts retaining the oil pickup tube to the oil pump and remove the bolt retaining the pickup tube to the main bearing stud spacer. Remove the pickup tube.

**To install:**

16. Clean the oil pan and inspect for damage. Clean the sealing surfaces of the front cover and engine block. Clean and inspect the oil pickup tube and replace the O-ring.
17. If removed, position the oil pickup tube on the oil pump and hand start the 2 bolts. Install the bolt retaining the pickup tube to the main bearing stud spacer hand tight.
18. Tighten the pickup tube-to-oil pump bolts to 6.0–8.8 ft. lbs. (8–12 Nm), then tighten the pickup tube-to-main bearing stud spacer bolt to 15–22 ft. lbs. (20–30 Nm).
19. Position a new gasket on the oil pan. Apply silicone sealer to where the front cover meets the cylinder block and rear seal retainer meets the cylinder block. Position the oil pan on the engine and install the bolts. Tighten the bolts, in sequence, to 15–22 ft. lbs. (20–30 Nm).
20. Position the jack and wood block under the oil pan, rearward of the oil drain hole, and raise the engine enough to remove the wood blocks. Lower the engine and remove the jack.
21. Install the engine mount through bolts and tighten to 15–22 ft. lbs. (20–30 Nm).
22. Position the EGR valve and tube assembly in the vehicle and connect to the exhaust manifold. Tighten the line nut to 26–33 ft. lbs. (35–45 Nm).

**➡Loosen the line nut at the EGR valve prior to installing the assembly into the vehicle. This will allow enough movement to align the EGR valve retaining bolts.**

23. Cut the wire and position the exhaust system to the manifolds. Install the 4 nuts and tighten to 20–30 ft. lbs. (27–41 Nm). Make sure the exhaust system clears the crossmember. Adjust as necessary.
24. Install a new oil filter and lower the vehicle.
25. Install the bolt retaining the right engine mount to the lower engine bracket. Tighten to 15–22 ft. lbs. (20–30 Nm).
26. Install a new gasket on the EGR valve and position on the intake manifold. Install the 2 bolts retaining the EGR valve to the intake manifold and tighten to 15–22 ft. lbs. (20–30 Nm). Tighten the EGR tube line nut at the EGR valve to 26–33 ft. lbs. (35–45 Nm). Connect the vacuum hoses to the EGR valve and tube.
27. Install the blower motor resistor. Position the heater outlet hose, install the upper stud and tighten the upper and lower bolts to 15–22 ft. lbs. (20–30 Nm). Install the ground strap on the stud and tighten to 15–22 ft. lbs. (20–30 Nm).
28. Connect the heater outlet hose and the throttle valve cable. If necessary, adjust the throttle valve cable.
29. Connect the 42-pin connector and transmission harness connector. Install the harness connector on the brake vacuum booster.
30. Connect the air conditioning compressor outlet hose to the compressor and install the bolt retaining the hose to the right coil bracket.
31. Install the upper radiator hose and connect the fuel lines. Install the wiper module and retaining bracket.
32. Install the cooling fan and shroud and fill the cooling system. Fill the crankcase with the proper type and quantity of engine oil.
33. Connect the negative battery cable and install the air inlet tube. Start the engine and check for leaks.
34. Have a MVAC certified evacuate and recharge the air conditioning system.

### 5.0L Engines

**➧ See Figure 123**

1. Disconnect the negative battery cable. Relieve the fuel system pressure; refer to Section 5.
2. Disconnect the accelerator and throttle valve cables at the throttle body or carburetor.
3. Remove the fan shroud attaching bolts, positioning the fan shroud back over the fan. Remove the dipstick and tube assembly.

4. Disconnect the wiper motor electrical connector and remove the wiper motor. Disconnect the windshield washer hose and remove the wiper motor mounting cover.

5. Remove the thermactor air dump tube-retaining clamp on 5.0L engine. Remove the thermactor crossover tube at the rear of the vehicle.

6. Raise and safely support the vehicle. Drain the crankcase. Remove the filler tube from the oil pan and drain the transmission.

7. Disconnect the starter cable and remove the starter. Disconnect the fuel line.

8. Disconnect the exhaust system from the manifolds. Remove the oxygen sensors from the exhaust manifolds.

9. Remove the thermactor secondary air tube to torque converter housing clamps. Remove the converter inspection cover.

10. Disconnect the exhaust pipes to the catalytic converter outlet. Remove the catalytic converter secondary air tube; and the inlet pipes to the exhaust manifold.

11. Loosen the rear engine mount attaching nuts and remove the engine mount through bolts. Remove the shift crossover bolts at the transmission.

12. Remove the brake line retainer from the front crossmember and disconnect the transmission kick-down rod.

13. Position a jack and wood block under the engine and raise the engine as high as it will go. Place wood blocks between the engine mounts and the chassis brackets, lower the engine, and remove the jack.

14. Remove the oil pan retaining bolts and lower the oil pan. Remove the 2 bolts retaining the oil pump pickup tube and screen to the oil pump and the nut from the main bearing cap stud. Allow the pickup tube to drop into the oil pan.

15. Rotate the crankshaft, as required, for clearance and remove the oil pan from the vehicle.

**To install:**

16. Clean the oil pan and the gasket mating surfaces. Clean the oil pump pickup tube and screen assembly.

17. Install a new oil filter. Position a new oil pan gasket on the cylinder block. Place the oil pickup tube and screen in the oil pan and position the oil pan on the crossmember.

18. Install the pickup tube and screen with a new gasket. Install the bolts and tighten to 12–18 ft. lbs. (16–24 Nm). Position the oil pan and install the retaining bolts. Tighten to 7–10 ft. lbs. (9–14 Nm).

19. Position the jack and wood block under the engine and raise the engine enough to remove the wood blocks. Lower the engine and remove the jack. Install the engine mount through bolts and tighten to 33–46 ft. lbs. (45–62 Nm).

20. Connect the fuel lines. Install the converter inspection cover. Tighten the rear mount attaching nuts to 35–50 ft. lbs. (48–68 Nm).

21. Install the shift crossover. Position the catalytic converters, secondary air tube and inlet pipes to the exhaust manifold and then install the retaining nuts.

22. Install the catalytic converter outlet attaching bolts and install the secondary air tube on the converter housing. Install the starter and connect the starter cable.

23. Install the oxygen sensors and lower the vehicle. Install the dipstick and tube. Install the thermactor air dump valve to exhaust manifold clamp.

24. Connect the windshield wiper hose and install the wiper motor mounting plate. Install the wiper motor.

25. Position the shroud and install the retaining bolts. Install the thermactor tube to the rear of the engine. Install the air cleaner assembly and air ducts.

26. Fill the crankcase with the proper type and quantity of engine oil. Fill the transmission with the proper type and quantity of transmission fluid.

27. Connect the negative battery cable. Start the engine and check for leaks.

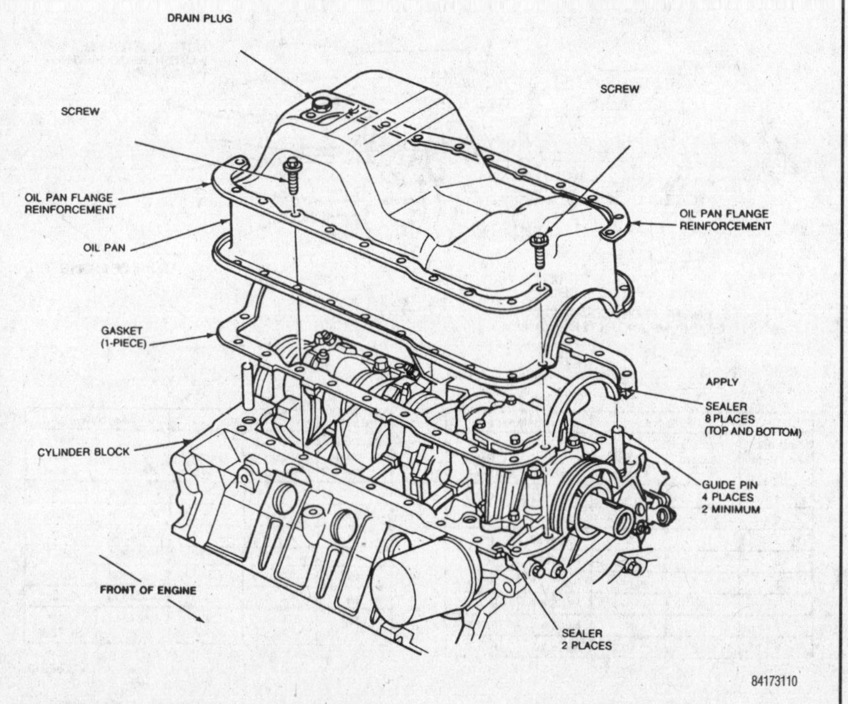


**Fig. 123 Oil pan installation—5.0L engines**

## Oil Pump

### REMOVAL & INSTALLATION

#### 3.8L Engine

**➡The oil pump, oil pressure relief valve and drive intermediate shaft are contained in the front cover assembly.**

1. Disconnect the negative battery cable.

2. If necessary for access, remove the oil filter.

3. Remove the oil pump and filter body-to-engine front cover retaining bolts, them remove the oil pump and filter body from the engine front cover.

4. Inspect the oil pump body seal, oil pump and filter body, and engine front cover for distortion. Replace damaged components as necessary.

**To install:**

5. Position the oil pump and filter body on the engine front cover, then install the retaining bolts.

6. Tighten the four large engine front cover retaining bolts to 17–23 ft. lbs. (23–32 Nm), then tighten the remaining retaining bolts to 6–8 ft. lbs. (8–11 Nm).

7. If removed, install the oil filter, then connect the negative battery cable.

#### 4.6L Engine

➧ See Figure 124

1. Disconnect the negative battery cable.

2. Remove the valve covers, timing chain cover, and oil pan. Refer to the procedures in this Section.

3. Remove the timing chains according to the procedure in this Section.

4. Remove the 4 bolts retaining the oil pump to the cylinder block and remove the pump.

5. Remove the 2 bolts retaining the oil pickup tube to the oil pump and remove the bolt retaining the oil pickup tube to the main bearing stud spacer. Remove the pickup tube.

**To install:**

6. Clean the oil pickup tube and replace the O-ring.

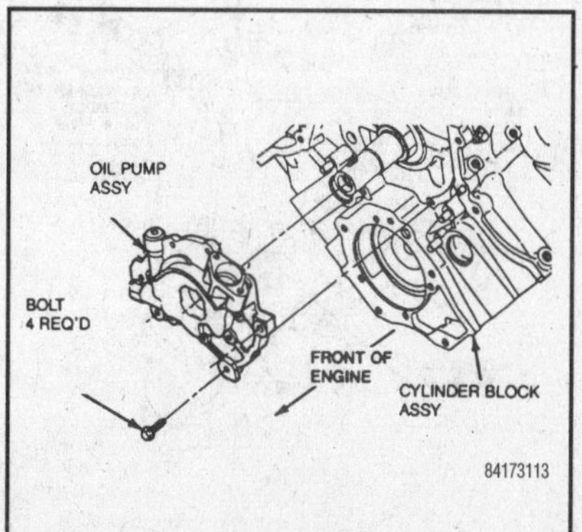


**Fig. 124 Oil pump installation—4.6L engine**

7. Position the tube on the oil pump and hand-start the 2 bolts. Install the bolt retaining the pickup tube to the main bearing stud spacer hand tight.

8. Tighten the pickup tube-to-oil pump bolts to 6.0–8.8 ft. lbs. (8–12 Nm). Tighten the pickup tube to main bearing stud spacer bolt to 15–22 ft. lbs. (20–30 Nm).

9. Rotate the inner rotor of the oil pump to align with the flats on the crankshaft and install the oil pump flush with the cylinder block. Install the 4 retaining bolts and tighten to 6.0–8.8 ft. lbs. (8–12 Nm).

10. Install a new oil filter. Install the timing chains.

11. Install the oil pan, front cover and camshaft covers.

12. Fill the crankcase with the proper type and quantity of engine oil. Connect the negative battery cable, start the engine, and check for leaks.

### 5.0L Engines

**See Figure 125**

1. Disconnect the negative battery cable. Remove the oil pan; see the procedure in this Section.

2. Remove the oil pump inlet tube and screen assembly.

3. Remove the oil pump attaching bolts and gasket. Remove the oil pump intermediate shaft.

**To install:**

4. Prime the oil pump by filling either the inlet or outlet ports with engine oil and rotating the pump shaft to distribute the oil within the pump body.

5. Position the intermediate driveshaft into the distributor socket. With the shaft firmly seated in the distributor socket, the stop on the shaft should touch the roof of the crankcase. Remove the shaft and position the stop, as necessary.

6. Position a new gasket on the pump body, insert the intermediate shaft into the oil pump, and install the pump and shaft as an assembly.

**Do not attempt to force the pump into position if it will not seat readily. The driveshaft hex may be misaligned with the distributor shaft. To align, rotate the intermediate shaft into a new position.**

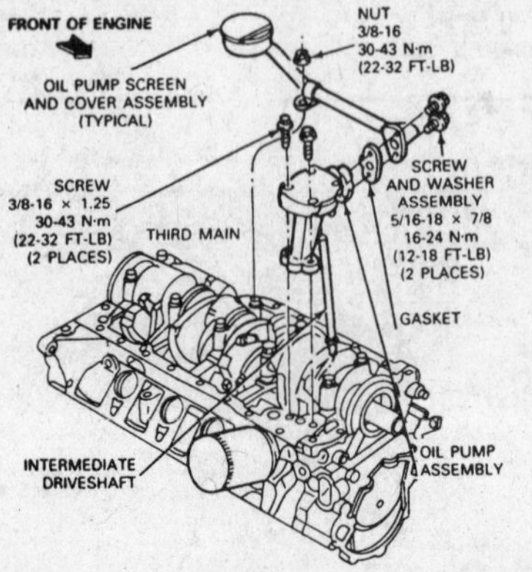


**Fig. 125 Oil pump installation—5.0L engines**

7. Tighten the oil pump attaching bolts to 22–32 ft. lbs. (30–43 Nm).

8. Clean and install the oil pump inlet tube and screen assembly.

9. Install the oil pan and the remaining components in the reverse order of removal. Start the engine and check for leaks.

## Crankshaft Damper

### REMOVAL & INSTALLATION

#### 3.8L Engine

**See Figure 126**

1. Disconnect the negative battery cable. Properly drain the cooling system and the engine oil.

2. Remove the air cleaner assembly and air intake duct.

3. If necessary, remove the fan shroud attaching screws and bolts, then remove the fan/clutch assembly and shroud.

4. Loosen the accessory drive belt idler. Remove the drive belt and water pump pulley.

5. Remove the power steering pump-mounting bracket attaching bolts. Leaving the hoses connected, place the pump/bracket assembly in a position that will prevent the loss of power steering fluid.

6. If equipped with air conditioning, remove the compressor front support bracket. Leave the compressor in place.

7. Disconnect coolant bypass and heater hoses at the water pump. Disconnect the radiator upper hose at the thermostat housing.

8. Disconnect the coil wire from the distributor cap, then remove the cap with the secondary wires still attached. Remove the distributor-retaining clamp and lift distributor out of the front cover.

9. Raise and safely support the vehicle.

10. Remove the crankshaft damper and pulley.

**If the crankshaft pulley and vibration damper have to be separated, mark the damper and pulley so they may be reassembled in the same relative position. This is important as the damper and pulley are initially balanced as a unit. If the crankshaft damper is being replaced, check if the original damper has balance pins installed. If so, new balance pins must be installed on the new damper in the same position as the original damper. The crankshaft pulley must also be installed in the original installation position.**

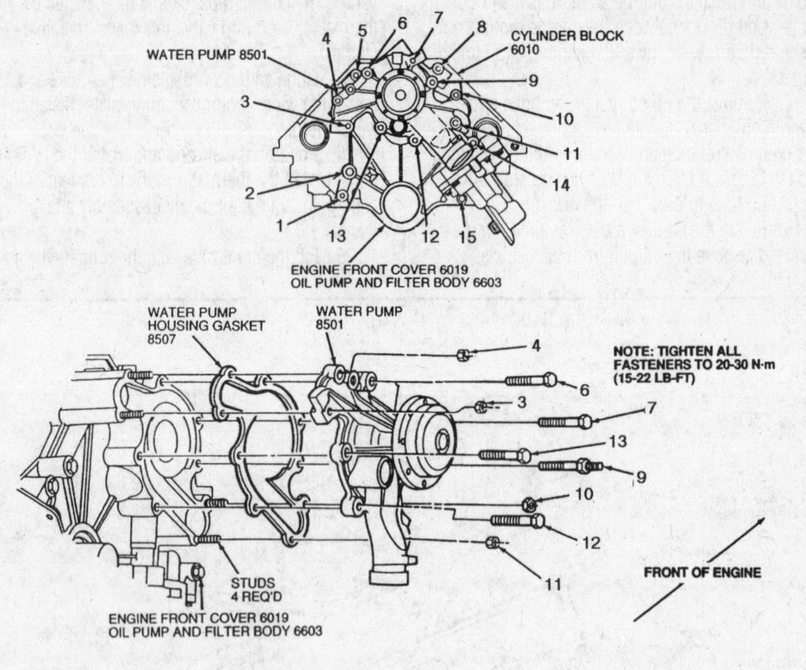


| Fastener And Hole No. | Hole No. | | Fasteners | |
|---|---|---|---|---|
| | Water Pump | Front Cover | Part No. | Part Name |
| 1 | | 4 | N805112 | STUD |
| 2 | | 2 | N805112 | STUD |
| 3 | 2 | 9 | N804758 | NUT |
| 4 | 1 | 8 | N804758 | NUT |
| 5 | | 10 | N605787 | BOLT |
| 6 | 9 | 15 | N605908 | BOLT |
| 7 | 8 | 16 | N605908 | BOLT |
| 8 | | 11 | N605787 | BOLT |

| Fastener And Hole No. | Hole No. | | Fasteners | |
|---|---|---|---|---|
| | Water Pump | Front Cover | Part No. | Part Name |
| 9 | 7 | 17 | N804756 | STUD |
| 10 | 6 | 1 | N804758 | NUT |
| 11 | 5 | 7 | N804758 | NUT |
| 12 | 4 | 13 | N605908 | BOLT |
| 13 | 3 | 14 | N605908 | BOLT |
| 14 | | 6 | N804839 | BOLT |
| 15 | | 5 | N804841 | CAP SCREW |

86873170

**Fig. 126 Timing/engine front cover mounting—3.8L engine**

11. Remove the oil filter, then disconnect the radiator lower hose at the water pump.
12. Remove the oil pan. For details, please refer to the procedure located earlier in this section.
13. Lower the vehicle.
14. Remove the front cover attaching bolts.

**➡Do not overlook the cover-attaching bolt located behind the oil filter adapter. The front cover will break if pried upon and not all of the attaching bolts are removed.**

15. Remove the ignition-timing indicator.
16. Remove the front cover and water pump as an assembly. Remove the cover gasket and discard.

**➡The front cover houses the oil pump. If a new front cover is to be installed, remove the water pump and oil pump from the old front cover.**

**To install:**

17. Lightly oil all bolt and stud threads before installation. Clean all gasket surfaces on the front cover, cylinder block, and fuel pump. If reusing the front cover, replace crankshaft front oil seal.
18. If a new front cover is to be installed, complete the following:
    a. Install the oil pump gears.
    b. Clean the water pump gasket surface. Position a new water pump gasket on the front cover and install the water pump. Install the pump attaching bolts and tighten to 15–22 ft. lbs. (20–30 Nm).
19. Install the distributor drive gear.
20. Lubricate the crankshaft front oil seal with clean engine oil.
21. Position a new cover gasket on the cylinder block and install the front cover/water pump assembly using dowels for proper alignment. A suitable contact adhesive is recommended to hold the gasket in position while the front cover is installed.
22. Position and install the ignition-timing indicator.
23. Install the front cover attaching bolts. Apply Loctite® or equivalent, to the threads of the bolt installed below the oil filter housing prior to installation. This bolt is to be installed and tightened last. Tighten all bolts to 15–22 ft. lbs. (20–30 Nm).
24. Raise the vehicle and support safely.
25. Install the oil pan. Connect the radiator lower hose. Install a new oil filter.
26. Coat the crankshaft damper sealing surface with clean engine oil.
27. Position the crankshaft pulley key in the crankshaft keyway.
28. Install the damper with damper washer and attaching bolt. Tighten the bolt to 103–132 ft. lbs. (140–179 Nm).
29. Install the crankshaft pulley and tighten the attaching bolts 19–28 ft. lbs. (26–38 Nm).
30. Lower the vehicle.
31. Connect the coolant bypass hose.
32. Install the distributor with rotor pointing at No. 1 distributor cap tower. Install the distributor cap and coil wire.
33. Connect the radiator upper hose at thermostat housing.
34. Connect the heater hose.
35. If equipped with air conditioning, install compressor and mounting brackets.
36. Install the power steering pump and mounting brackets.
37. Position the accessory drive belt over the pulleys.
38. Install the water pump pulley. Position the accessory drive belt over water pump pulley and tighten the belt.
39. Connect the negative battery cable. Fill the crankcase and cooling system to the proper level.
40. Install the air cleaner assembly and air intake duct.
41. Start the engine and check for leaks.
42. Check the ignition timing and adjust as required.

### 4.6L Engine

**➧ See Figures 127, 128 and 129**

1. Disconnect the negative battery cable.
2. Release the belt tensioner and remove the accessory drive belt.
3. Raise and safely support the vehicle.
4. Remove the crankshaft damper retaining bolt and washer. Remove the damper using a suitable puller.

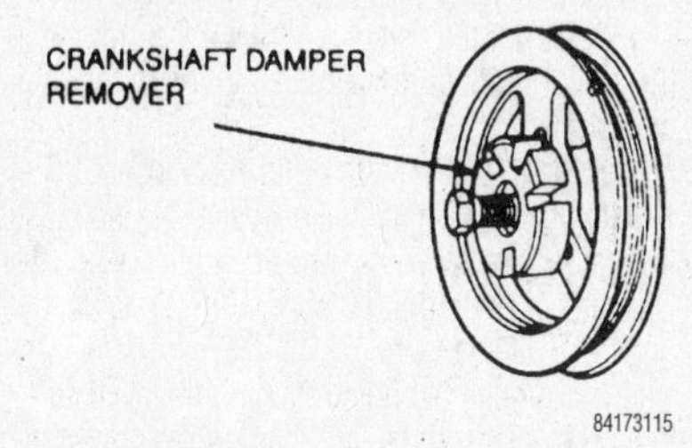


**Fig. 127 Crankshaft damper puller installed on 4.6L engine crankshaft damper**

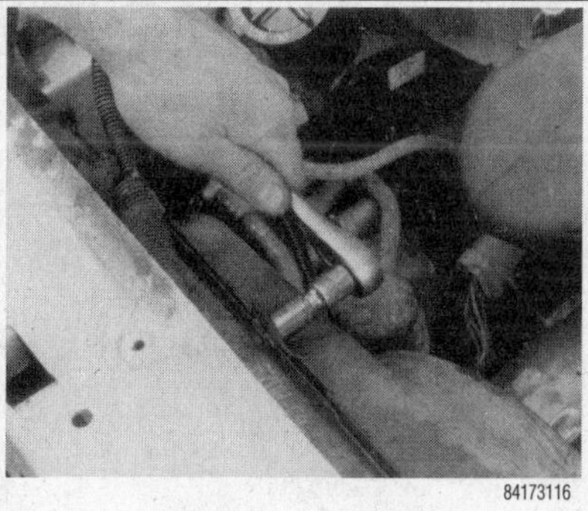


**Fig. 128 Apply silicone sealer to the damper keyway as shown—4.6L engine**

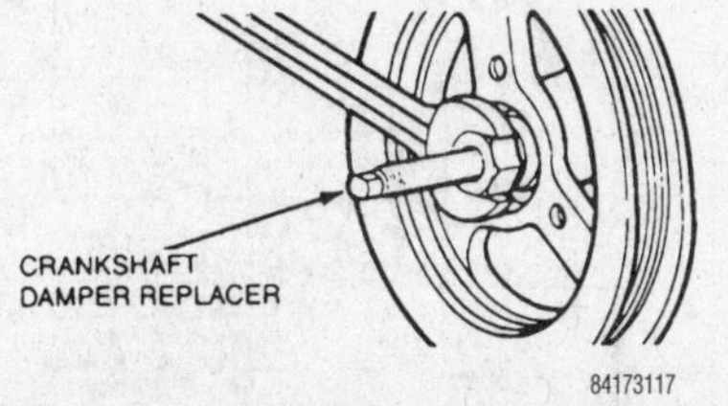


**Fig. 129 Installing the crankshaft damper with the proper installation tool—4.6L engine**

**To install:**

5. Apply clean engine oil to the sealing surface of the damper. Apply a small amount of silicone sealer to the rear of the damper keyway. Using a damper installer, install the crankshaft damper. Be sure the key on the crankshaft aligns with the keyway in the damper.

**⁂ WARNING**

**Do not drive the damper onto the crankshaft with a hammer; damage to the crankshaft and/or thrust bearings may result. Always use a crankshaft damper installation tool.**

6. Install the crankshaft damper retaining bolt and washer and tighten to 114–121 ft. lbs. (155–165 Nm).
7. Lower the vehicle and install the accessory drive belt.
8. Connect the negative battery cable, start the engine, and check for leaks.

### 5.0L Engines

**➧ See Figures 130 and 131**

1. Disconnect the negative battery cable.
2. Remove the fan shroud and position it back over the fan. Remove the fan/clutch assembly and shroud.
3. Remove the accessory drive belts.
4. Remove the crankshaft pulley from the damper and remove the damper retaining bolt. Remove the damper using a suitable puller.

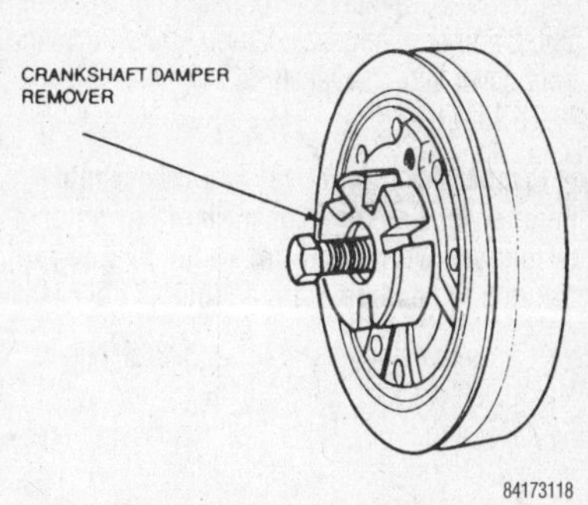


**Fig. 130 Crankshaft damper puller installed on 5.0L engine crankshaft damper**

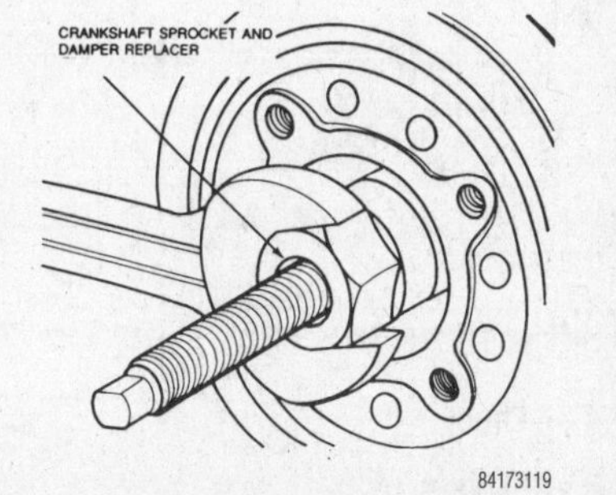


**Fig. 131 Installing the crankshaft damper with the proper installation tool—5.0L engines**

**To install:**

5. Apply clean engine oil to the sealing surface of the damper. Apply a small amount of silicone sealer to the damper keyway. Line up the crankshaft damper keyway with the crankshaft key and install the damper using a damper installation tool.

**⁂ WARNING**

**Do not drive the damper onto the crankshaft with a hammer; damage to the crankshaft and/or thrust bearings may result. Always use a crankshaft damper installation tool.**

6. Install the damper retaining bolt and tighten to 70–90 ft. lbs. (95–122 Nm).
7. Install the remaining components in the reverse order of their removal.

## Timing Chain Cover

### REMOVAL & INSTALLATION

#### 3.8L Engine

1. Disconnect the negative battery cable.
2. Loosen the accessory drive belt idler.
3. Raise the vehicle and support safely.
4. Disengage the accessory drive belt and remove crankshaft pulley.
5. Remove the crankshaft/vibration damper using a Crankshaft Damper Remover and a Vibration Damper Remover Adapter, or equivalent suitable removal tools.
6. Remove the seal from the front cover with a suitable prying tool. Use care to prevent damage to front cover and crankshaft.

**To install:**

**➡Inspect the front cover and crankshaft damper for damage, nicks, burrs or other roughness which may cause the seal to fail. Service or replace components as necessary.**

7. Lubricate the seal lip with clean engine oil and install the seal using Damper/Front Cover Seal Replacer and Front Cover Seal Replacer or equivalent suitable seal installers.
8. Lubricate the seal surface on the damper with clean engine oil. Install damper and pulley assembly. Install the damper attaching bolt and tighten to 103–132 ft. lbs. (140–179 Nm).
9. Position the crankshaft pulley and install the retaining bolts. Tighten to 19–28 ft. lbs. (26–38 Nm).
10. Position accessory drive belt over crankshaft pulley.
11. Lower the vehicle.
12. Check accessory drive belt for proper routing and engagement in the pulleys. Adjust the drive belt tension.
13. Connect the negative battery cable. Start the engine and check for leaks.

#### 4.6L Engine

➧ See Figure 132

**➡To replace the seal in the front cover (timing chain cover), it will be necessary to obtain special tools. A power steering plump pulley remover and replacer will be necessary; it is also necessary to use a crankshaft damper remover and replacer to effectively complete this job**

1. Disconnect the negative battery cable.
2. Remove the windshield wiper module assembly, if necessary.
3. Remove the engine appearance cover, if applicable.
4. Remove the air cleaner outlet tube and the engine air intake resonator, where necessary..
5. Remove the cooling fan and shroud. Loosen the water pump pulley bolts, remove the accessory drive belt, and remove the water pump pulley.
6. Raise and safely support the vehicle.
7. Remove the bolts retaining the power steering pump to the engine block and cylinder front cover. The lower front bolt on the power steering pump will not come all the way out. Wire the power steering pump out of the way.
8. Remove the four bolts retaining the oil pan to the front cover. Remove the crankshaft damper retaining bolt and washer. Remove the damper using a puller.
9. Lower the vehicle. Remove the bolt retaining the air conditioner high-pressure line to the right coil bracket.
10. Remove the front bolts and loosen the remaining bolts on the valve covers. Using plastic wedges or similar tools, prop up both valve covers. Disconnect both ignition coils and Camshaft Identification (CID) sensor.
11. Remove the nuts retaining the right coil bracket to the front cover. Position the power steering hose out of the way.
12. Remove the nuts retaining the left coil bracket to the front cover. Slide both coil brackets and spark plug wires off the mounting studs and lay the assembly on top of the engine.
13. Disconnect the crankshaft position sensor. Remove the seven stud bolts and four bolts retaining the front cover to the engine and remove the front cover.

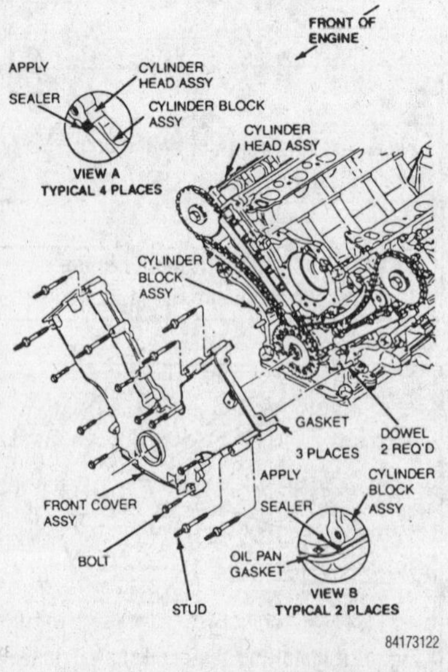


**Fig. 132 Timing chain cover installation—4.6L engine**

**To install:**

14. Inspect and replace the front cover seal as necessary and clean the sealing surfaces of the cylinder block. Apply silicone sealer to the oil pan where it meets the cylinder block and to the points where the cylinder head meets the cylinder block.
15. Install the front cover and the attaching studs and bolts. Tighten to 15–22 ft. lbs. (20–30 Nm). Connect the crankshaft position sensor.
16. Position the coil brackets and spark plug wires as an assembly onto the mounting studs. Position the power steering hose and install the nuts retaining the coil brackets to the front cover. Tighten the nuts to 15–22 ft. lbs. (20–30 Nm). Connect both ignition coils and CID sensor.
17. Remove the plastic wedges holding up the valve covers. Apply silicone sealer where the front cover meets the cylinder head and make sure the valve cover gaskets are properly positioned. Install the front retaining bolts into the valve cover and tighten the bolts to 6.0–8.8 ft. lbs. (8–12 Nm).
18. Position the air conditioner high-pressure line on the right coil bracket and install the bolt. Raise and safely support the vehicle.
19. Apply a small amount of silicone sealer in the rear of the keyway in the damper. Position the damper on the crankshaft and install, using a suitable installation tool. Install the damper bolt and washer and tighten to 114–121 ft. lbs. (155–165 Nm).
20. Install the four bolts retaining the oil pan to the front cover. Tighten to 15–22 ft. lbs. (20–30 Nm).
21. Position the power steering pump on the engine and install the 4 retaining bolts. Tighten to 15–22 ft. lbs. (20–30 Nm). Lower the vehicle.
22. Install the water pump pulley with the four bolts. Tighten to 15–22 ft. lbs. (20–30 Nm). Install the accessory drive belt and the cooling fan and shroud.
23. Connect the negative battery cable, start the engine and check for leaks.

#### 5.0L Engines

➧ See Figure 133

1. Disconnect the negative battery cable.
2. Drain the cooling system. Remove the air inlet tube.

**⁂ CAUTION**

**Never open, service, or drain the radiator or cooling system when hot; serious burns can occur from the steam and hot coolant. In addition, when draining engine coolant, keep in mind that cats and dogs are attracted to ethylene glycol antifreeze and could drink any that is left in an uncovered container or in puddles on the ground. This will prove fatal in sufficient quantities. Always drain coolant into a sealable container. Coolant should be reused unless it is contaminated or is several years old.**

3. Remove the fan shroud attaching bolts and position the shroud over the fan. Remove the fan and clutch assembly from the water pump shaft and remove the shroud.
4. Remove the air conditioner drive belt and idler pulley bracket. Remove the alternator and power steering drive belts. Remove the power steering pump and position aside, leaving the hoses

attached. Remove all accessory brackets that attach to the water pump.

5. Remove the water pump pulley. Disconnect the lower radiator hose, heater hose and water pump bypass hose at the water pump.

6. Remove the crankshaft pulley from the crankshaft vibration damper. Remove the damper attaching bolt and washer and remove the damper using a puller.

7. Remove the fuel line from the clip on the front cover, if equipped.

8. Remove the oil pan-to-front cover attaching bolts. Use a thin blade knife to cut the oil pan gasket flush with the cylinder block face prior to separating the cover from the cylinder block.

9. Remove the cylinder front cover and water pump as an assembly.

➡**Cover the front oil pan opening while the cover assembly is off to prevent foreign material from entering the pan.**

**To install:**

10. If a new front cover is to be installed, remove the water pump from the old front cover and install it on the new front cover.

11. Clean all gasket-mating surfaces. Pry the old oil seal from the front cover and install a new one, using a seal installer.

12. Coat the gasket surface of the oil pan with sealer, cut, position the required sections of a new gasket on the oil pan, and apply silicone sealer at the corners. Apply sealer to a new front cover gasket and install on the block.

13. Position the front cover on the cylinder block. Use care to avoid seal damage or gasket misalignment. It may be necessary to force the cover downward to slightly compress the pan gasket. Use a front cover aligner tool to assist the operation.

14. Coat the threads of the front cover attaching screws with pipe sealant and install. While pushing in on the alignment tool, tighten the oil pan to cover attaching screws to 9–11 ft. lbs. (12–15 Nm).

15. Tighten the front cover to cylinder block attaching bolts to 15–18 ft. lbs. (20–24 Nm). Remove the alignment tool.

16. Apply multi-purpose grease to the sealing surface of the vibration damper. Apply silicone sealer to the keyway of the vibration damper.

17. Line up the vibration damper keyway with the crankshaft key and install the damper using a suitable installation tool. Tighten the retaining bolt to 70–90 ft. lbs. (95–122 Nm). Install the crankshaft pulley.

18. Install the remaining components in the reverse order of their removal.

19. Fill the crankcase with the proper type and quantity of engine oil. Fill the cooling system.

20. Connect the negative battery cable, start the engine and check for leaks.

### REMOVAL & INSTALLATION

#### 5.0L engines

➧ **See Figures 134 and 135**

1. Remove the crankshaft damper as described in this Section.

2. Use a suitable seal removal tool to remove the seal from the cover. Be careful not to damage the crankshaft or the seal bore in the timing chain cover.

**To install:**

3. Lubricate the seal bore in the front cover and the seal lip with clean engine oil.

4. Install the new seal using a suitable seal installation tool. Make sure the seal is installed evenly and straight.

5. Install the crankshaft damper. Be sure to lubricate the sealing surface of the damper with clean engine oil prior to installation.

6. Start the engine and check for leaks.

## Timing Chain and Gears

### REMOVAL & INSTALLATION

#### 3.8L Engine

➧ **See Figures 136, 137 and 138**

1. Disconnect the negative battery cable. Drain the cooling system and crankcase.

2. Remove the timing chain/engine front cover and water pump as an assembly. For details, please refer to the timing chain cover procedure located earlier in this section.

3. Remove the camshaft sprocket bolt and washer from end of the camshaft.

4. Remove the distributor drive gear.

5. Remove the camshaft sprocket, crankshaft sprocket, and timing chain.

➡**If the crankshaft sprocket is difficult to remove, carefully pry to sprocket off the shaft using a pair of large prybars positioned on both sides of the crankshaft sprocket.**

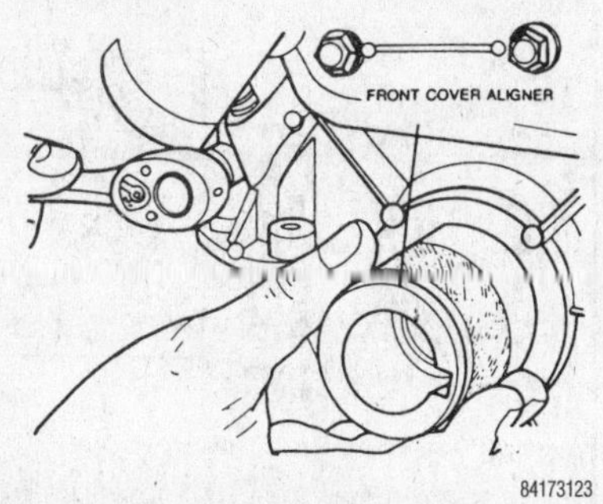


**Fig. 133 Positioning the front cover aligner tool—5.0L engines**

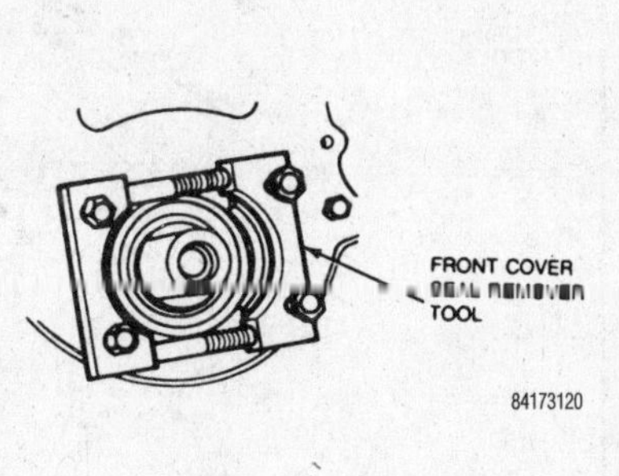


**Fig. 134 Removing the timing chain cover seal—5.0L engines**

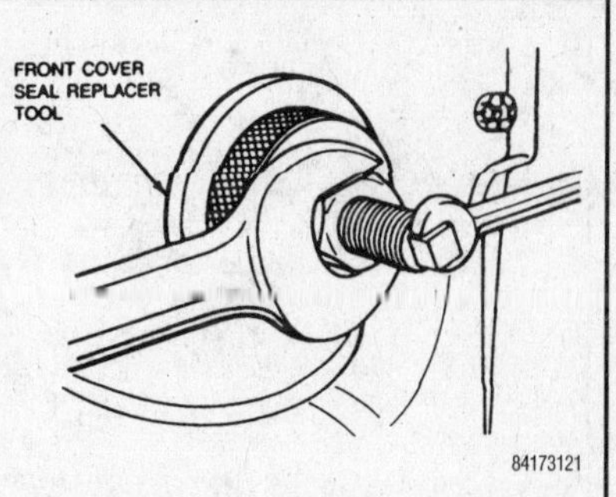


**Fig. 135 Installing the timing chain cover seal**

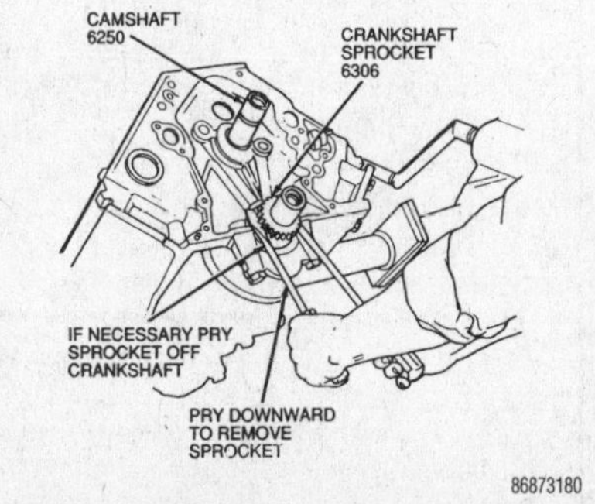


**Fig. 136 If difficulty is encountered removing the crankshaft sprocket, use 2 prybars to carefully pry if off the shaft**

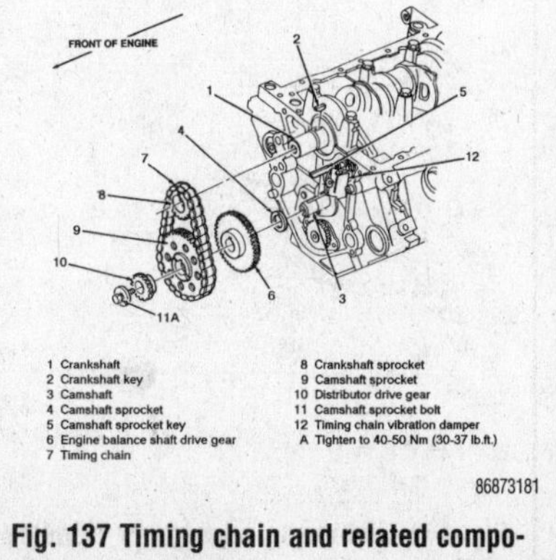


**Fig. 137 Timing chain and related components—3.8L engine**

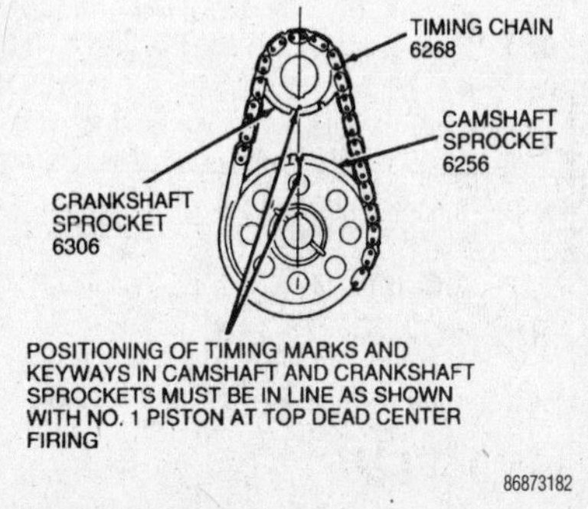


**Fig. 138 Position of the timing marks when the No. 1 piston is at TDC**

6. Remove the chain tensioner assembly from the front of the cylinder block. This is accomplished by pulling back on the ratcheting mechanism and installing a pin through the hole in the bracket to relieve tension.

**➡The front cover houses the oil pump. If a new front cover is to be installed, remove the water pump and oil pump from the old front cover.**

**To install:**

7. Lightly oil all bolt and stud threads before installation. Clean all gasket surfaces on the front cover, cylinder block, and fuel pump. If reusing the front cover, replace crankshaft front oil seal.

8. If a new front cover is to be installed, complete the following:

a. Install the oil pump gears.

b. Clean the water pump gasket surface. Position a new water pump gasket on the front cover and install water pump. Install the pump attaching bolts and tighten to 15–22 ft. lbs. (20–30 Nm).

9. Rotate the crankshaft as necessary to position piston No. 1 at TDC and the crankshaft keyway at the 12 o' clock position.

10. Install the tensioner assembly. Make sure the ratcheting mechanism is in the retracted position with the pin pointing outward from the hole in the bracket assembly. Tighten the retaining bolts to 6–10 ft. lbs. (8–14 Nm).

11. Lubricate timing chain with clean engine oil. Install the camshaft sprocket, crankshaft sprocket, and timing chain.

12. Remove the pin from the tensioner/vibration damper assembly to load the timing chain vibration damper arm against the timing chain. Make certain the timing marks are positioned across from each other.

13. Install the distributor drive gear.

14. Install the camshaft sprocket washer and bolt at the end of the camshaft, then tighten to 30–37 ft. lbs. (41–50 Nm).

15. Install the timing chain/engine front cover, using a new gasket. For details regarding this procedure, please refer to timing chain cover removal and installation earlier in this section.

16. Connect battery ground cable. Start the engine and check for leaks.

### 4.6L Engine

**▶ See Figures 139 thru 147**

**➡This is not a free wheeling engine. If it has "jumped time," there will be damage to the valves and/or pistons and will require the removal of the cylinder heads.**

**⁂ WARNING**

**The camshafts and/or crankshaft must never be rotated when the cylinder heads are installed and the timing chain is removed. Failure to heed this warning will result in valve and/or piston damage.**

1. Disconnect the negative battery cable.

2. Remove the valve covers and the timing chain front cover.

3. Remove the crankshaft position sensor tooth wheel.

4. Rotate the engine to set the No. 1 piston at TDC on the compression stroke.

5. Install cam positioning, on the flats of the camshaft. This will prevent accidental rotation of the camshafts.

6. Remove the 2 bolts retaining the right tensioner to the cylinder head and remove the tensioner. Remove the right tensioner arm.

7. Remove the 2 bolts retaining the right chain guide to the cylinder head and remove the chain guide. Remove the right chain and right crankshaft sprocket. If necessary, remove the right camshaft sprocket retaining bolt, washer, sprocket, and spacer.

**➡Cam positioning tools must be installed on the camshaft to prevent the camshaft from rotating.**

8. Remove the 2 bolts retaining the left tensioner to the cylinder head and remove the tensioner. Remove the left tensioner arm.

9. Remove the 2 bolts retaining the left chain guide to the cylinder head and remove the chain guide. Remove the left chain and left crankshaft sprocket. If necessary, remove the left camshaft sprocket retaining bolt, washer, sprocket, and spacer.

**➡Cam positioning tools, must be installed on the camshaft to prevent the camshaft from rotating.**

10. Inspect the friction material on the tensioner arms and chain guides. If worn or damaged, remove and clean the oil pan and replace the oil pickup tube.

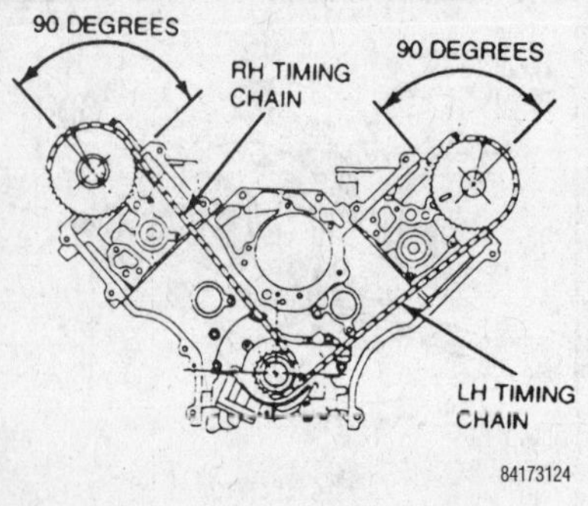


**Fig. 139 Engine positioned for timing chain removal (No. 1 TDC)—4.6L engine**

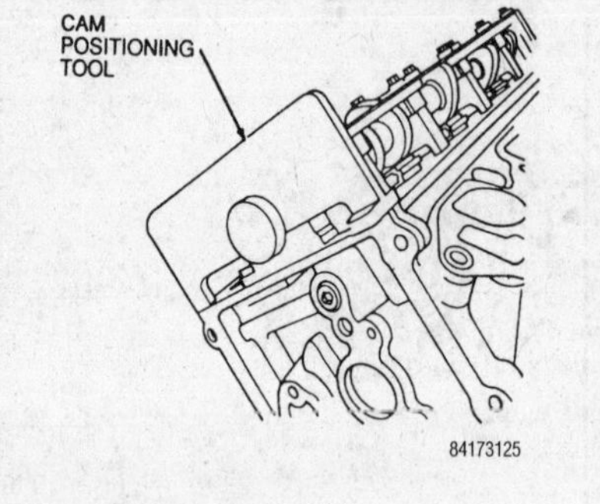


**Fig. 140 Camshaft positioning tool installed—4.6L engine**

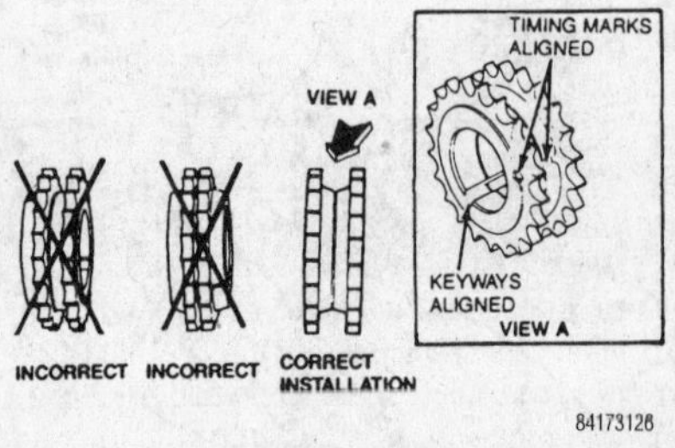


**Fig. 141 Crankshaft sprocket positioning—4.6L engine**

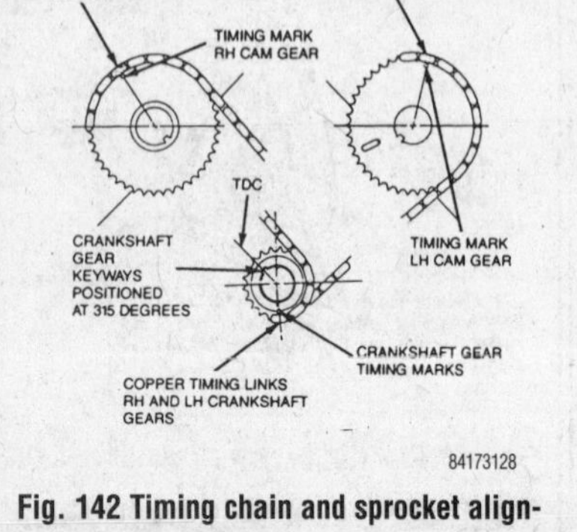


**Fig. 142 Timing chain and sprocket alignment—4.6L engine**

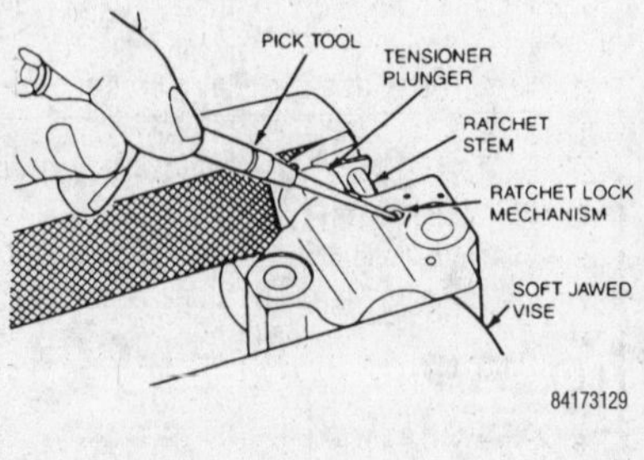


**Fig. 143 Timing chain tensioner bleeding procedure—4.6L engine**

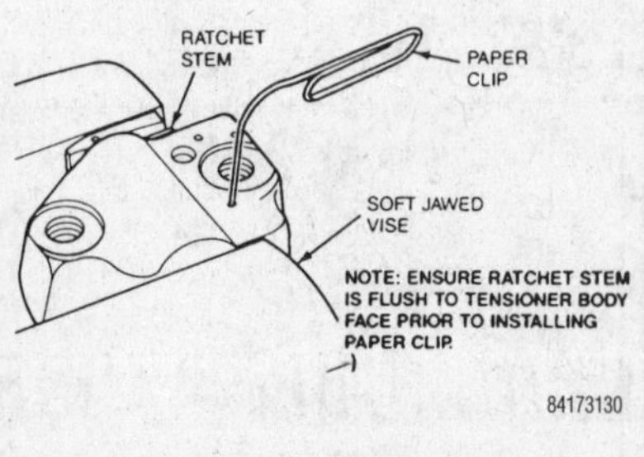


**Fig. 144 Timing chain tensioner locking procedure—4.6L engine**

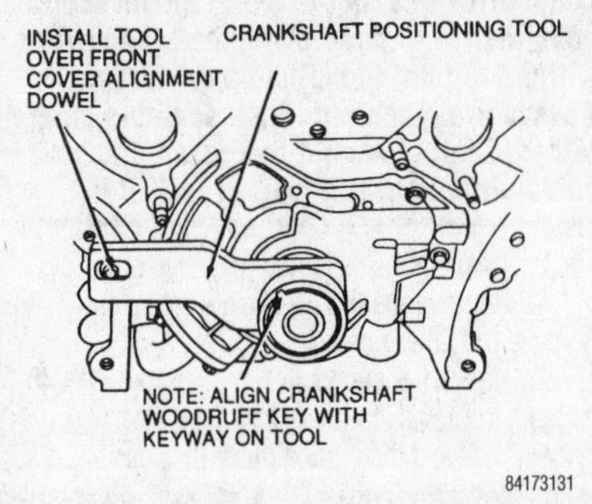


**Fig. 145 Crankshaft positioning tool installation—4.6L engine**

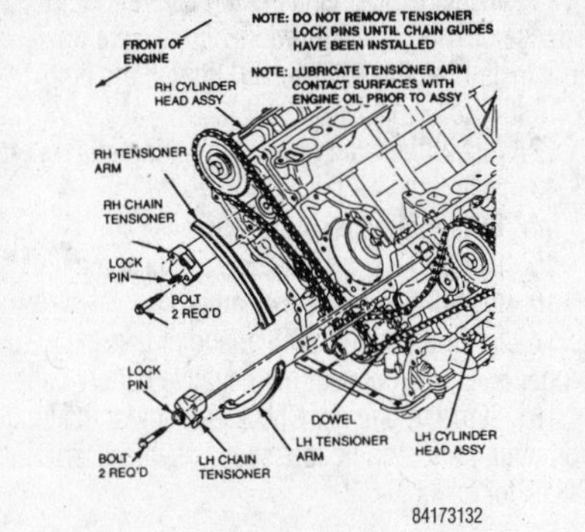


**Fig. 146 Timing chain tensioner and tensioner arm installation—4.6L engine**

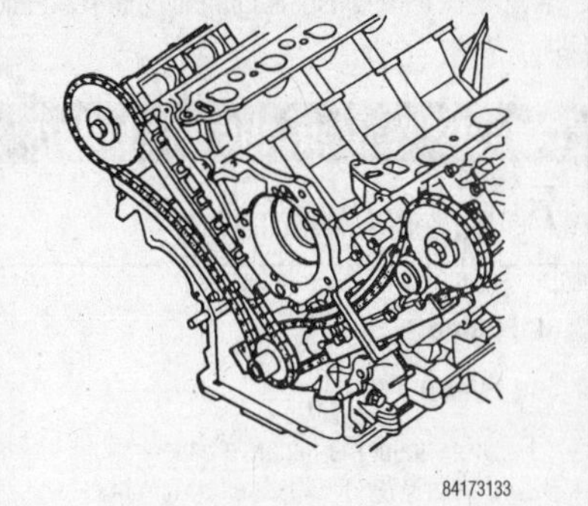


**Fig. 147 Removing slack from the timing chain with a C-clamp—4.6L engine**

**WARNING**

**Do not rotate the crankshaft and/or camshafts.**

**To install:**

11. Make sure cam positioning tools, are installed on the camshafts to prevent them from rotating.

12. If removed, position the camshaft spacers and sprockets on the camshafts and install the washers and retaining bolts. Do not tighten at this time.

13. Install the left crankshaft sprocket with the tapered part of the sprocket facing away from the engine block.

**➡The crankshaft sprockets are identical. They may only be installed 1 way, with the tapered part of the sprocket facing each other.**

14. Install the left timing chain on the camshaft and crankshaft sprockets. Make sure the copper links of the chain line up with the timing marks of the sprockets.

**➡If the copper links of the timing chain are not visible, pull the chain taught until the opposite sides of the chain contact one another and lay it on a flat surface. Mark the links at each end of the chain and use them in place of the copper links.**

15. Install the right crankshaft sprocket with the tapered part of the sprocket facing the left crankshaft sprocket.

16. Install the right timing chain on the camshaft and crankshaft sprockets. Make sure the copper links of the chain line up with the timing marks of the sprockets.

17. It is necessary to bleed the timing chain tensioners before installation. Proceed as follows:

a. Position the timing chain tensioner in a soft-jawed vice.

b. Using a small pick or similar tool, hold the ratchet lock mechanism away from the ratchet stem and slowly compress the tensioner plunger by rotating the vise handle.

**WARNING**

**The tensioner must be compressed slowly or damage to the internal seals will result.**

c. Once the tensioner plunger bottoms in the tensioner bore, continue to hold the ratchet lock mechanism and push down on the ratchet stem until flush with the tensioner face.

d. While holding the ratchet stem flush to the tensioner face, release the ratchet lock mechanism and install a paper clip or similar tool in the tensioner body to lock the tensioner in the collapsed position.

e. The paperclip must not be removed until the timing chain, tensioner, tensioner arm and timing chain guide is completely installed on the engine.

18. Install the right and left timing chain tensioners and secure with 2 bolts on each. Tighten the bolts to 15–22 ft. lbs. (20–30 Nm).

19. On 1993 and later vehicles, install a crankshaft positioning tool, over the crankshaft and front cover alignment dowel, to position the crankshaft.

20. Lubricate the tensioner arm contact surfaces with engine oil and install the right and left tensioner arms on their dowels.

21. Install the right and left timing chain guides and secure with 2 bolts on each. Tighten the bolts to 6–9 ft. lbs. (8–12 Nm).

22. Position a suitable C-clamp around the tensioner arm and chain guide, to remove all slack from the chain.

23. Remove the paper clips from the timing chain tensioners and make sure all timing marks are aligned.

24. Using a camshaft positioning tool, align the camshaft, tighten the camshaft sprocket-to-camshaft bolt to 81–95 ft. lbs. (110–130 Nm).

25. On 1993 and later vehicles, position a suitable dial indicator in the No. 1 cylinder spark plug hole. Check that the camshaft is at maximum lift for the intake valve when the piston is at 114° after TDC. If it is not, loosen the camshaft sprocket bolt and repeat Steps 18–22.

26. Remove the camshaft and crankshaft positioning tools.

27. Installation of the remaining components is the reverse of removal.

28. Connect the negative battery cable, start the engine and check for leaks and proper operation.

### 5.0L Engines

**➧ See Figure 148**

1. Disconnect the negative battery cable and drain the cooling system.

**CAUTION**

**Never open, service, or drain the radiator or cooling system when hot; serious burns can occur from the steam and hot coolant. In addition, when draining engine coolant, keep in mind that cats and dogs are attracted to ethylene glycol antifreeze and could drink any that is left in an uncovered container or in puddles on the ground. This will prove fatal in sufficient quantities. Always drain coolant into a sealable container. Coolant should be reused unless it is contaminated or is several years old.**

2. Remove the timing chain front cover.

3. Rotate the crankshaft until the timing marks on the sprockets are aligned.

4. Remove the camshaft retaining bolt, washer, and eccentric. Slide both sprockets and the timing chain forward and remove them as an assembly.

**To install:**

5. Position the sprockets and timing chain on the camshaft and crankshaft simultaneously. Make sure the timing marks on the sprockets are aligned.

6. Install the washer, eccentric, and camshaft sprocket-retaining bolt. Tighten the bolt to 40–45 ft. lbs. (54–61 Nm).

7. Install the timing chain front cover and remaining components.

8. Fill the cooling system. Connect the negative battery cable, start the engine, and check for leaks.

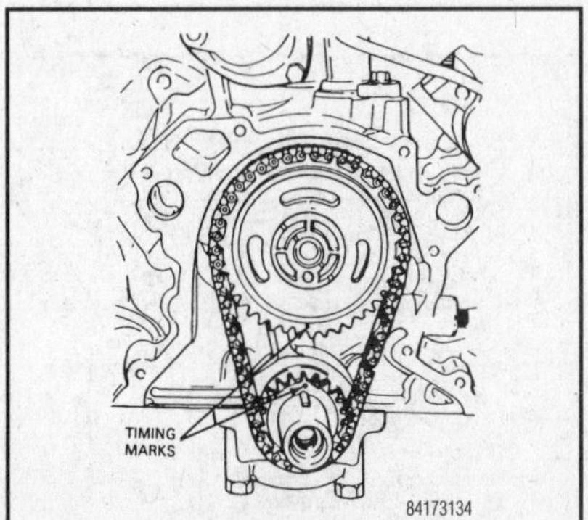


**Fig. 148 Timing sprocket alignment—5.0L engines**

9. Check and adjust the ignition timing and idle speed, as necessary.

## Camshaft, Bearings and Lifters

### REMOVAL & INSTALLATION

#### 3.8L Engine

**➧ See Figure 149**

1. Disconnect the negative battery cable.
2. Properly relieve the fuel system pressure.
3. Drain the cooling system and crankcase.
4. Remove the engine from the vehicle and position in a suitable holding fixture.
5. Remove the intake manifold.
6. Remove the rocker arm covers, rocker arms, pushrods, and lifters.
7. Remove the oil pan.
8. Remove the front cover and timing chain.
9. Remove the thrust plate. Remove the camshaft through the front of the engine, being careful not to damage bearing surfaces.

**To install:**

10. Lightly oil all attaching bolts and studs threads before installation. Lubricate the cam lobes, thrust plate and bearing surfaces with suitable heavy engine oil.
11. Install the camshaft being careful not to damage bearing surfaces while sliding into position. Install the thrust plate and tighten the bolts to 6–10 ft. lbs. (8–14 Nm).
12. Install the front cover and timing chain.
13. Install the oil pan.
14. Install the lifters.
15. Install the upper and lower intake manifolds.
16. Install the engine assembly.
17. Fill the cooling system and crankcase to the proper level and connect the negative battery cable.
18. Start the engine. Check and adjust the ignition timing and engine idle speed as necessary. Check for leaks.

#### 4.6L Engine

**➧ See Figures 150 thru 155**

1. Disconnect the negative battery cable and drain the cooling system. Relieve the fuel system pressure as described in Section 5.

**⁂ CAUTION**

**Never open, service, or drain the radiator or cooling system when hot; serious burns can occur from the steam and hot coolant. In addition, when draining engine coolant, keep in mind that cats and dogs are attracted to ethylene glycol antifreeze and could drink any that is left in an uncovered container or in puddles on the ground. This will prove fatal in sufficient quantities. Always drain coolant into a sealable container. Coolant should be reused unless it is contaminated or is several years old.**

2. Remove the right and left valve covers.
3. Remove the timing chain front cover. Remove the timing chains.
4. Rotate the crankshaft counterclockwise 45 degrees from TDC to make sure all pistons are below the top of the engine block deck face.

**⁂ WARNING**

**The crankshaft must be in this position before rotating the camshafts or damage to the pistons and/or valve train will result.**

5. Install a valve spring compressor tool, under the camshaft and on top of the valve spring retainer.

**➡A special valve spring spacer tool must be installed between the spring coils and the camshaft must be at the base circle before compressing the valve spring.**

6. Compress the valve spring far enough to remove the roller follower. Repeat Steps 5 and 6 until all roller followers are removed.
7. Remove the bolts retaining the camshaft cap cluster assemblies to the cylinder heads. Tap upward on the camshaft caps at points near the upper bearing halves and gradually lift the camshaft clusters from the cylinder heads.
8. Remove the camshafts straight upward to avoid bearing damage.

**To install:**

9. Apply heavy engine oil to the camshaft journals and lobes. Position the camshafts on the cylinder heads.
10. Install and seat the camshaft cap cluster assemblies. Hand start the bolts.
11. Tighten the camshaft cluster retaining bolts in sequence to 6.0–8.8 ft. lbs. (8–12 Nm).

**➡Each camshaft cap cluster assembly is tightened individually.**

12. Loosen the camshaft cap cluster retaining bolts approximately 2 turns or until the heads of the bolts are free. Retighten all bolts, in sequence, to 6.0–8.8 ft. lbs. (8–12 Nm).

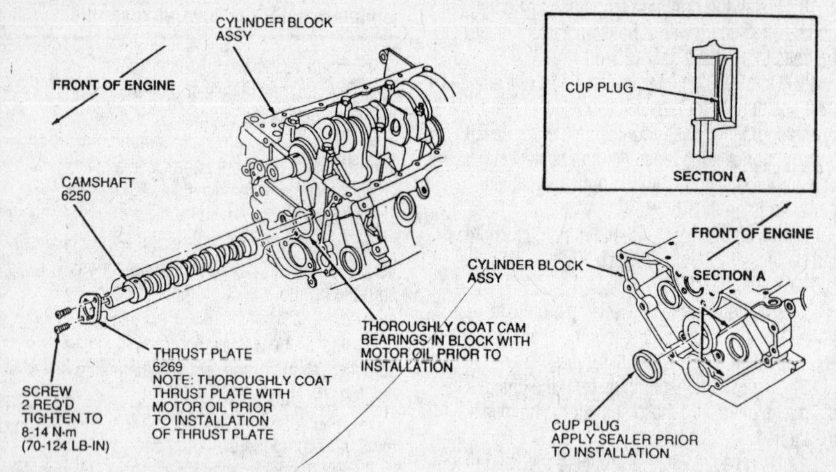


**Fig. 149 Remove the camshaft through the front of the engine, but be careful not to damage the bearing surfaces**

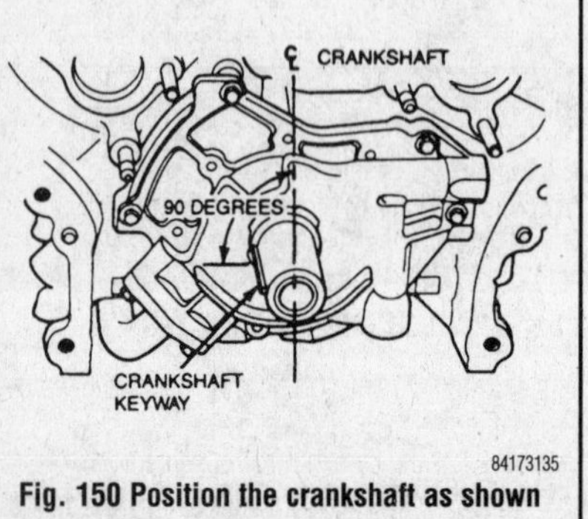


**Fig. 150 Position the crankshaft as shown before rotating the camshafts—4.6L engine**

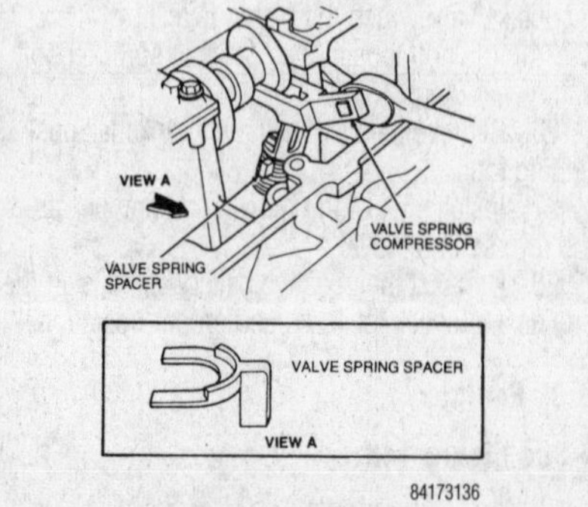


**Fig. 151 Compressing the valve spring—4.6L engine**

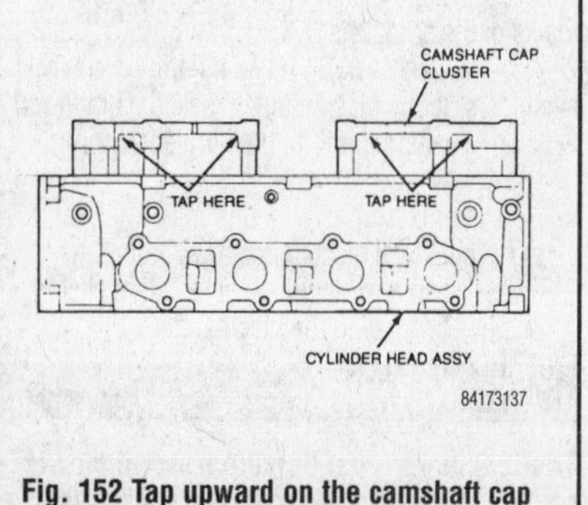


**Fig. 152 Tap upward on the camshaft cap cluster assemblies at the points shown—4.6L engine**

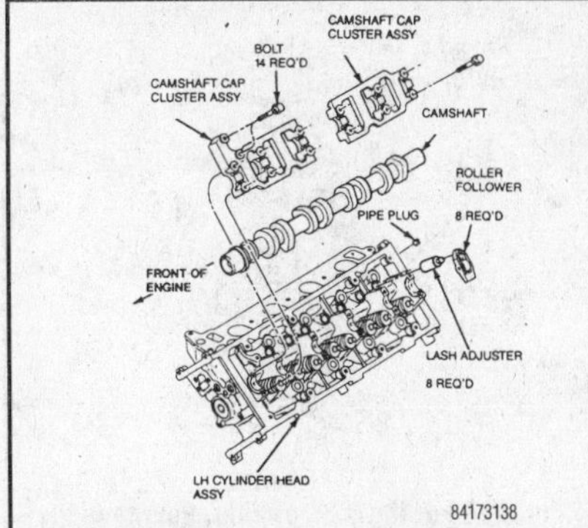


**Fig. 153 Camshaft and related components—4.6L engine**

➡**The camshafts should turn freely with a slight drag.**

13. Check camshaft endplay as follows:
   a. Install a suitable dial indicator on the front of the engine. Position it so the indicator foot is resting on the camshaft sprocket bolt or the front of the camshaft.
   b. Push the camshaft toward the rear of the engine and zero the dial indicator.
   c. Pull the camshaft forward and release it. Compare the dial indicator reading with specification.
   d. If endplay is too tight, check for binding or foreign material in the camshaft thrust bearing. If endplay is excessive, check for worn camshaft thrust plate and replace the cylinder head, as required.
   e. Remove the dial indicator.
14. If necessary, install the cam positioning tools, on the flats of the camshafts and install the spacers and camshaft sprockets. Install the bolts and washers and tighten to 81–95 ft. lbs. (110–130 Nm).
15. Install a valve spring compressor, under the camshaft and on top of the valve spring retainer.

➡**The valve spring spacer tool, must be installed between the spring coils and the camshaft must be at the base circle before compressing the valve spring.**

16. Compress the valve spring far enough to install the roller followers.
17. Repeat Steps 15 and 16 until all roller followers are installed.
18. Rotate the crankshaft clockwise 45 degrees to position the crankshaft at TDC.

➡**The crankshaft must only be rotated in the clockwise direction and only as far as TDC.**

19. Install the timing chains and install the timing chain front cover. Install the valve covers.
20. Install the remaining components in the reverse order of removal.
21. Connect the negative battery cable. Start the engine and check for leaks.

### 5.0L Engines

➧ **See Figures 156 and 157**

1. Disconnect the negative battery cable and drain the cooling system.

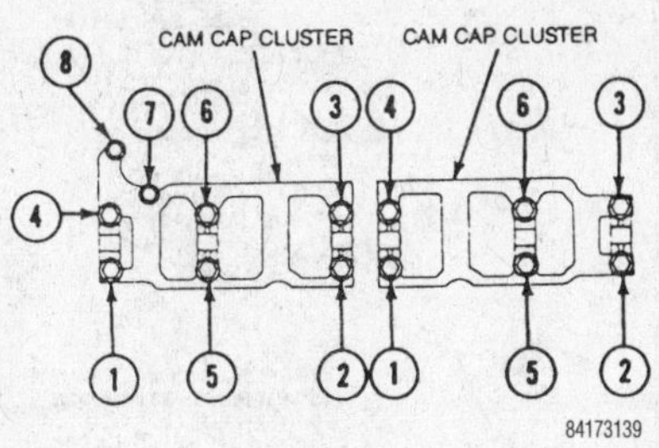


**Fig. 154 Camshaft cap cluster retaining bolt torque sequence—4.6L engine**

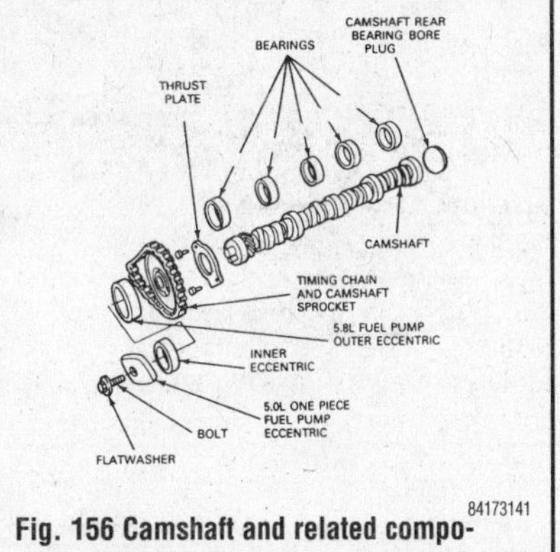


**Fig. 156 Camshaft and related components—5.0L engines**

**⁂ CAUTION**

**Never open, service, or drain the radiator or cooling system when hot; serious burns can occur from the steam and hot coolant. In addition, when draining engine coolant, keep in mind that cats and dogs are attracted to ethylene glycol antifreeze and could drink any that is left in an uncovered container or in puddles on the ground. This will prove fatal in sufficient quantities. Always drain coolant into a sealable container. Coolant should be reused unless it is contaminated or is several years old.**

2. Relieve the fuel system pressure as described in Section 5. Discharge the air conditioning system.
3. Remove the radiator and air conditioner condenser.
4. Remove the grille.
5. Remove the intake manifold and the lifters.
6. Remove the timing chain front cover, the timing chain and camshaft sprocket.
7. Check the camshaft endplay as follows:
   a. Position a dial indicator on the front of the engine, with the indicator foot resting on the end of the camshaft.
   b. Push the camshaft toward the rear of the engine and set the indicator pointer to 0.
   c. Pull the camshaft forward and release it. Check the dial indicator reading.
   d. If endplay exceeds specification, replace the thrust plate.

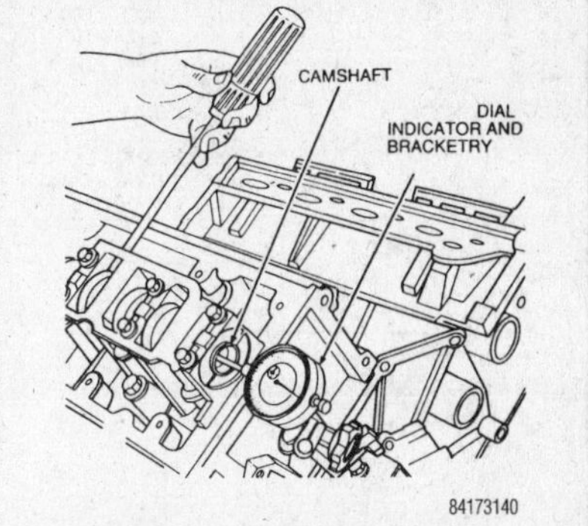


**Fig. 155 Checking camshaft end-play—4.6L engine**

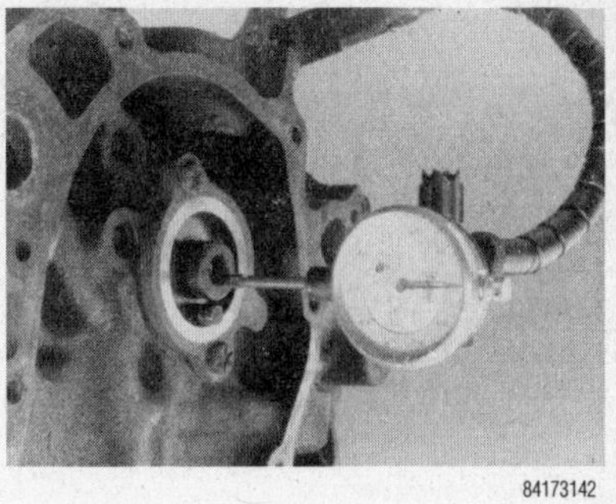


**Fig. 157 Checking camshaft end-play—5.0L engines**

   e. Recheck the endplay with the new thrust plate installed. If endplay is still excessive, check the camshaft and rear camshaft bore plug.
8. Remove the thrust plate. Remove the camshaft, being careful not to damage the bearing surfaces.

**To install:**

9. Lubricate the cam lobes and journals with heavy engine oil. Install the camshaft, being careful not to damage the bearing surfaces while sliding into position.
10. Install the thrust plate. Tighten the bolts to 9–12 ft. lbs. (12–16 Nm).
11. Install the timing chain and sprockets. Install the engine front cover.
12. Install the lifters and the intake manifolds.
13. Install the grille and the air conditioner condenser.
14. Install the radiator. Fill the cooling system.
15. Connect the negative battery cable. Start the engine and check for leaks.
16. Have a MVAC certified tech evacuate and recharge the air conditioning system.

## INSPECTION

➧ **See Figure 158**

1. Clean the camshaft in solvent and allow it to dry.
2. Inspect the camshaft for obvious signs of wear: scores, nicks, or pits on the journals or lobes. Light scuffs or nicks can be removed with oil stone.

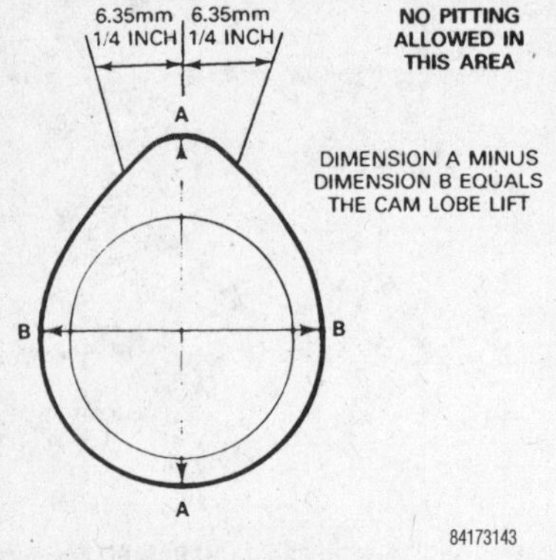


Fig. 158 Measuring lobe height

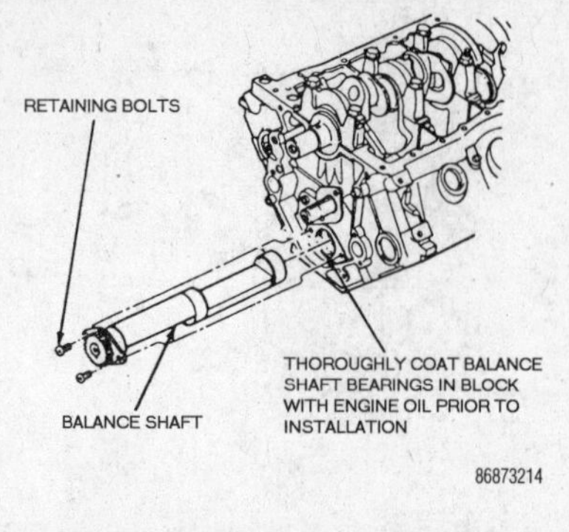


Fig. 159 Balance shaft assembly and related components—3.8L engine

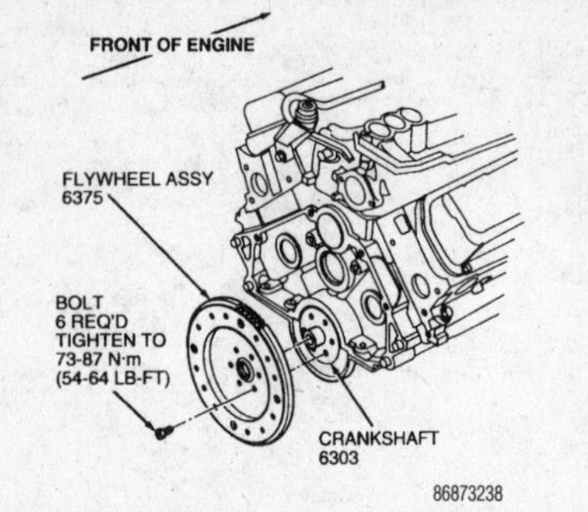


Fig. 160 For the 3.8L engine, you have to remove the flywheel to access the rear main oil seal

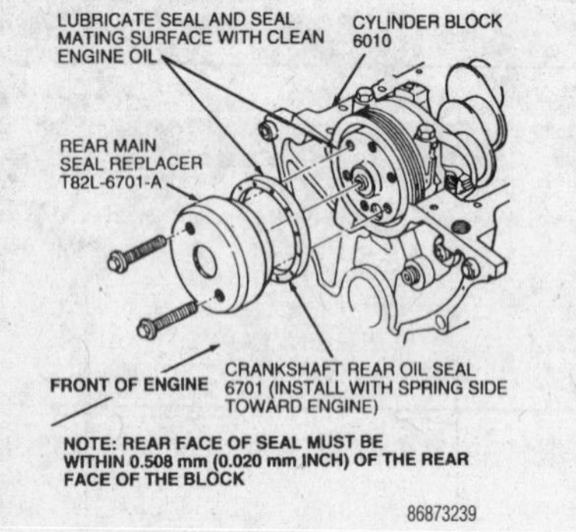


Fig. 161 Exploded view of installing the rear main oil seal—3.8L engine

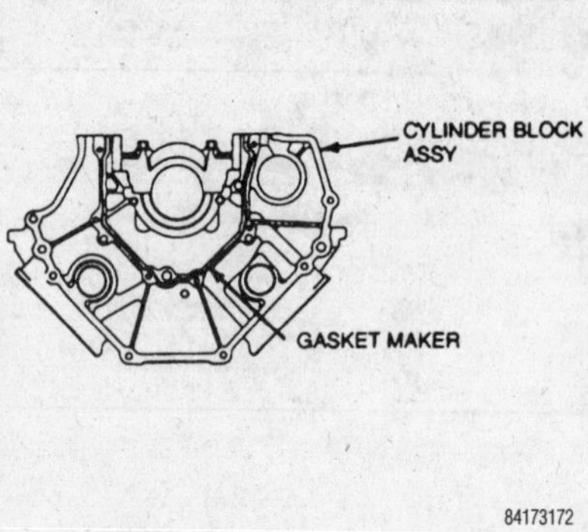


Fig. 162 Apply gasket maker to the cylinder block as shown—4.6L engine

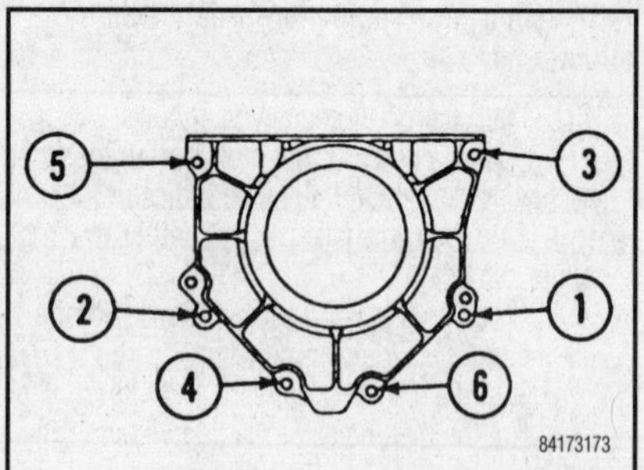


Fig. 163 Rear main seal retainer bolt torque sequence—4.6L engine

**➡Lobe pitting except in the area shown in the figure will not hurt the operation of the camshaft; do not replace the camshaft because of pitting unless the pitting has occurred in the lobe lift area.**

3. Using a micrometer, measure the diameter of the journals and compare to specifications. Replace the camshaft if any journals are not within specification.
4. Measure the camshaft lobes at the major (A–A) and minor (B–B) diameters, using a micrometer. The difference in readings is the lobe height. Compare your measurements with the lobe height specifications. Replace the camshaft if any lobe heights are not within specification.

## Balance Shaft

### REMOVAL & INSTALLATION

#### 3.8L Engine

**➧ See Figure 159**

1. Remove the engine from the vehicle.
2. Remove the intake manifolds.
3. Remove the oil pan.
4. Remove the front cover and timing chain and camshaft sprocket.
5. Remove the balance shaft drive gear and spacer.
6. Remove the balance shaft gear, thrust plate and shaft assembly.

**To install:**

7. Thoroughly coat the balance shaft bearings in the block with engine oil.
8. Install the balance shaft gear.
9. Install the balance shaft, thrust plate and gear, then tighten the retaining bolts to 6–10 ft. lbs. (8–14 Nm).
10. Install the timing chain and camshaft sprocket.
11. Install the oil pan.
12. Install the timing cover.
13. Install the intake manifolds.
14. Install the engine in the vehicle.

## Rear Main Seal

### REMOVAL & INSTALLATION

#### 3.8L Engine

**➧ See Figures 160 and 161**

1. Disconnect the negative battery cable.
2. Raise and safely support the vehicle.
3. Remove the transaxle. For details, please refer to the procedure located in Section 7 of this manual.
4. Remove the flywheel and the rear cover plate, if necessary.
5. Using a sharp awl, punch one hole into the crankshaft rear oil seal metal surface between the seal lip and the cylinder block.
6. Screw in the threaded end of Jet Plug Remover or an equivalent seal removing tool, then use the tool to remove the seal.

**➡Use caution to avoid damaging the oil seal surface.**

**To install:**

7. Inspect the crankshaft seal area for any damage that may cause the seal to leak. If damage is evident, service or replace the crankshaft as necessary.
8. Coat the crankshaft seal area and the lip with engine oil.
9. Using a Rear Crankshaft Seal Replacement tool, or an appropriate seal installer tool, install the seal. Tighten the bolts of the seal installer tool evenly so the seal is straight and seats without misalignment.
10. Install the flywheel. Tighten attaching bolts to 54–64 ft. lbs. (73–87 Nm).
11. Install rear cover plate, if necessary.
12. Install the transaxle and connect the negative battery cable.

#### 4.6L Engine

**➧ See Figures 162 and 163**

**➡The Front Wheel Drive 4.6L Engine has to be removed with the transaxle intact mounted onto the sub-frame as an assembly. It requires the use of a hoist and a special lifting platform to lower the assembly from the body**

1. Disconnect the negative battery cable.
2. Remove the transmission; refer to Section 7.

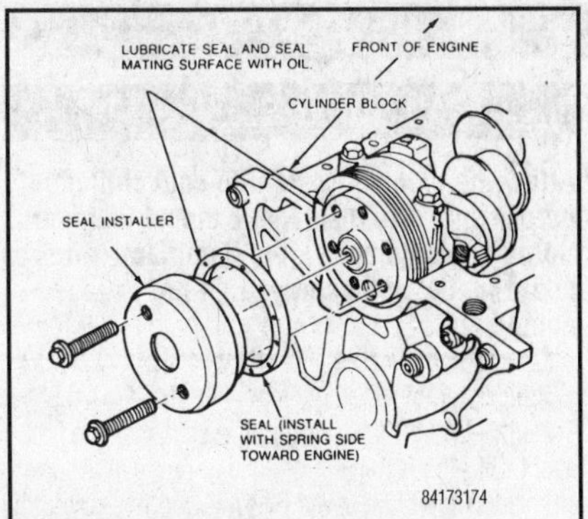


**Fig. 164 Rear main seal installation—5.0L engines shown**

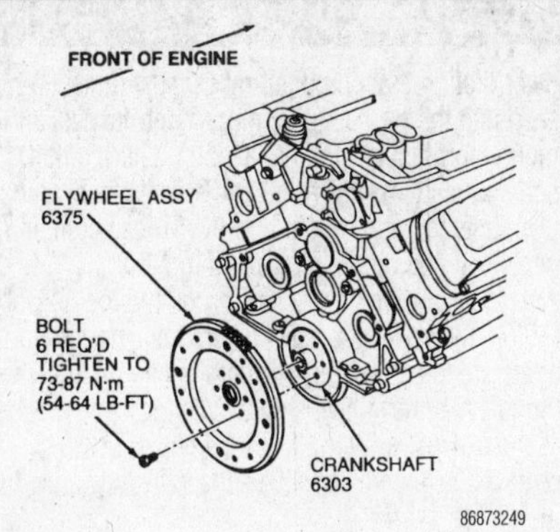


**Fig. 165 Flywheel mounting—3.8L engine**

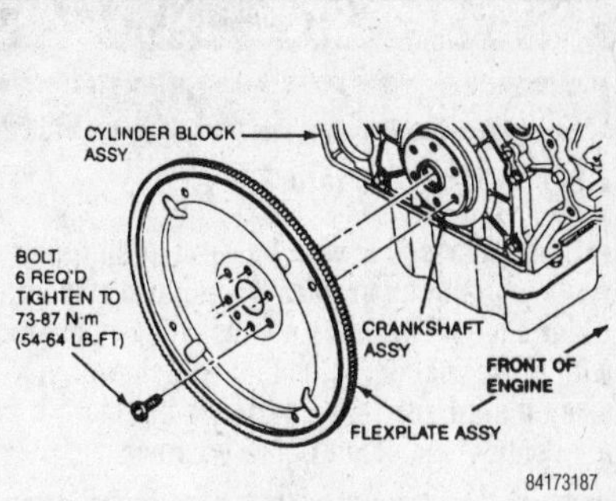


**Fig. 166 Flexplate installation—4.6L engine**

3. Remove the flexplate from the crankshaft.
4. Remove the rear main seal retainer from the cylinder block.
5. Securely support the seal retainer and remove the seal, using a sharp pick.

**To install:**

6. Clean and inspect the retainer and retainer-to-cylinder block mating surfaces.
7. Apply a 0.060 in. (1.5mm) continuous bead of a suitable gasket maker to the cylinder block.
8. Install the seal retainer and tighten the bolts, in sequence, to 6.0–8.8 ft. lbs. (8–12 Nm).
9. Install the new rear main seal using rear main seal installer T82L–6701–A and adapter T91P–6701–A or equivalents.
10. Install the flexplate and tighten the bolts, in a crisscross pattern, to 54–64 ft. lbs. (73–87 Nm).
11. Install the transmission and lower the vehicle.
12. Connect the negative battery cable, start the engine and check for leaks.

### 5.0L Engines

**See Figure 164**

1. Disconnect the negative battery cable.
2. Remove the transmission; refer to Section 7.
3. Remove the flexplate from the crankshaft.
4. Punch 2 holes in the crankshaft rear oil seal on opposite sides of the crankshaft, just above the bearing cap to cylinder block split line. Install a sheet metal screw in each of the holes or use a small slide hammer and pry the crankshaft rear main oil seal from the block.

**Use extreme caution not to scratch the crankshaft oil seal surface.**

**To install:**

5. Clean the oil seal recess in the cylinder block and main bearing cap.
6. Coat the seal and all of the seal mounting surfaces with oil. Position the seal on rear main seal installer or an equivalent seal installer, and position the tool and seal to the rear of the engine.
7. Alternate bolt tightening to seat the seal properly. The rear face of the seal must be within 0.005 in. (0.127mm) of the rear face of the block.
8. Install the flexplate. Apply pipe sealant to the flexplate bolt threads, then tighten them, in a crisscross pattern, to 75–85 ft. lbs. (102–115 Nm).
9. Install the transmission and lower the vehicle.
10. Connect the negative battery cable, start the engine and check for leaks.

## Flywheel/Flexplate

### REMOVAL & INSTALLATION

### 3.8L Engine

**See Figure 165**

1. Remove the transaxle from the vehicle.
2. Remove the flywheel/flexplate attaching bolts and the flywheel.

**To install:**

**All major rotating components including the flexplate/flywheel are individually balance to zero. Engine assembly balancing is not required. Balance weights should not be installed on new flywheels.**

3. Install the rear cover plate, if removed.
4. Position the flywheel on the crankshaft and install the attaching bolts. Tighten the attaching bolts to 54–64 ft. lbs. (73–87 Nm), using the standard cross-tightening sequence
5. Install the transaxle.

### 4.6L & 5.0L Engines

**See Figures 166 and 167**

1. Disconnect the negative battery cable.
2. Remove the transmission; refer to Section 7.

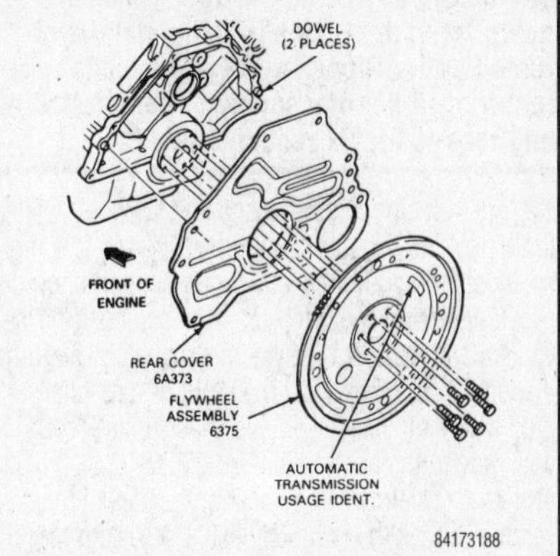


**Fig. 167 Flexplate installation—5.0L engines**

3. Remove the retaining bolts and remove the flexplate from the crankshaft.
4. Inspect the flexplate for cracks or other damage. Check the ring gear for worn, chipped or cracked teeth. If the teeth are damaged, the entire flexplate must be replaced.

**To install:**

5. Make sure the crankshaft flange and flexplate mating surfaces are clean.
6. Position the flexplate on the crankshaft and install the retaining bolts.

**On 5.0L engines, apply suitable pipe sealant to the flexplate bolt threads before installation.**

7. On 4.6L engine, tighten the flexplate retaining bolts, in a crisscross pattern, to 54–64 ft. lbs. (73–87 Nm).
8. On 5.0L engines, tighten the flexplate retaining bolts, in a crisscross pattern, to 75–85 ft. lbs. (102–115 Nm).
9. Install the transmission and lower the vehicle. Connect the negative battery cable.

# EXHAUST SYSTEM

## Inspection

➧ See Figures 168 thru 174

**➡Safety glasses should be worn at all times when working on or near the exhaust system. Older exhaust systems will usually be covered with loose rust particles that will shower you when disturbed. These particles are more than a nuisance and could injure your eye.**

### ✳✳ CAUTION

**DO NOT perform exhaust repairs or inspection with the engine or exhaust hot. Allow the system to cool completely before attempting any work. Exhaust systems are noted for sharp edges, flaking metal and rusted bolts. Gloves and eye protection are required. A healthy supply of penetrating oil and rags is highly recommended.**

Your vehicle must be raised and supported safely to inspect the exhaust system properly. By placing 4 safety stands under the vehicle for support should provide enough room for you to slide under the vehicle and inspect the system completely. Start the inspection at the exhaust manifold or turbocharger pipe where the header pipe is attached and work your way to the back of the vehicle. On dual exhaust systems, remember to inspect both sides of the vehicle. Check the complete exhaust system for open seams, holes loose connections, or other deterioration that could permit exhaust fumes to seep into the passenger compartment. Inspect all mounting brackets and hangers for deterioration, some models may have rubber O-rings that can be overstretched and non-supportive. These components will need to be replaced if found. It has always been a practice to use a pointed tool to poke up into the exhaust system where the deterioration spots are to see whether or not they crumble. Some models may have heat shield covering certain parts of the exhaust system , it will be necessary to remove these shields to have the exhaust visible for inspection also.

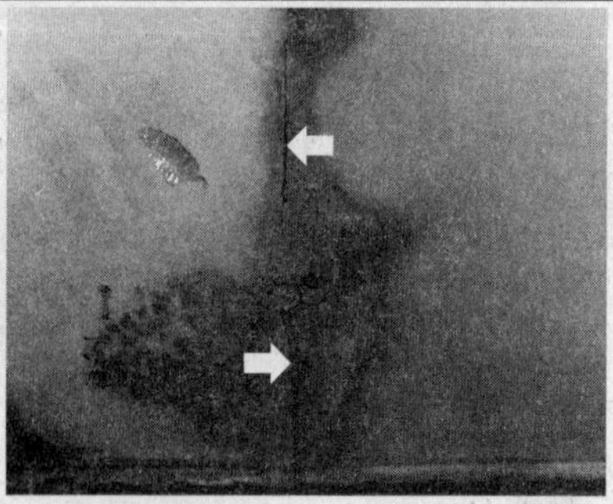

TCCA3P73

**Fig. 168 Cracks in the muffler are a guaranteed leak**

## REPLACEMENT

➧ See Figure 175

There are two types of exhaust systems. One is the flange type where the component ends are attached with bolts and a gasket in-between. The other exhaust system is the slip joint type. These components slip into one another using clamps to retain them together.

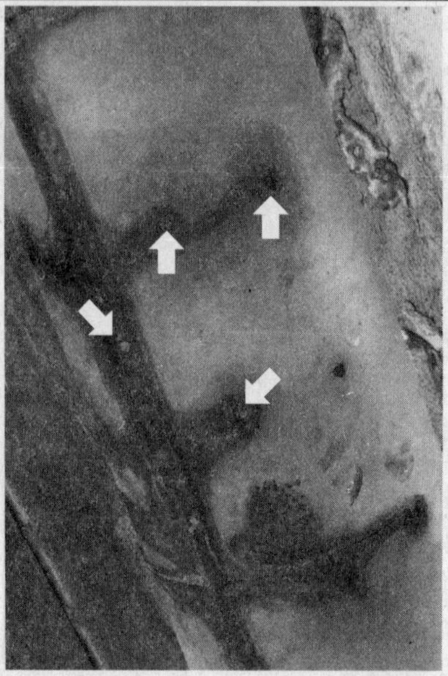

TCCA3P74

**Fig. 169 Check the muffler for rotted spot welds and seams**

### ✳✳ CAUTION

**Allow the exhaust system to cool sufficiently before spraying a solvent exhaust fasteners. Some solvents are highly flammable and could ignite when sprayed on hot exhaust components.**

Before removing any component of the exhaust system, ALWAYS squirt a liquid rust-dissolving agent onto the fasteners for ease of removal. A lot of knuckle skin will be saved by following this rule. It may even be wise to spray the fasteners and allow them to sit overnight.

### Flange Type

➧ See Figure 176

### ✳✳ CAUTION

**Do NOT perform exhaust repairs or inspection with the engine or exhaust hot. Allow the system to cool completely before attempting any work. Exhaust systems are noted for sharp edges, flaking metal and rusted bolts. Gloves and eye protection are required. A healthy supply of penetrating oil and rags is highly recommended. Never spray liquid rust dissolving agent onto a hot exhaust component.**

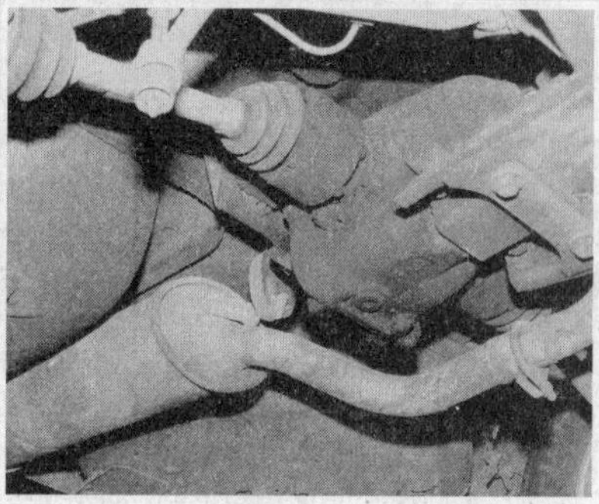

TCCA3P77

**Fig. 170 Make sure the exhaust components are not contacting the body or suspension**

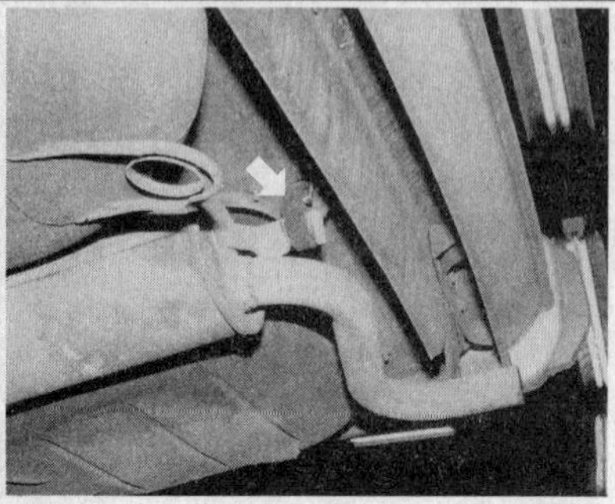

TCCA3P78

**Fig. 171 Check for overstretched or torn exhaust hangers**

TCCA3P75

**Fig. 172 Example of a badly deteriorated exhaust pipe**

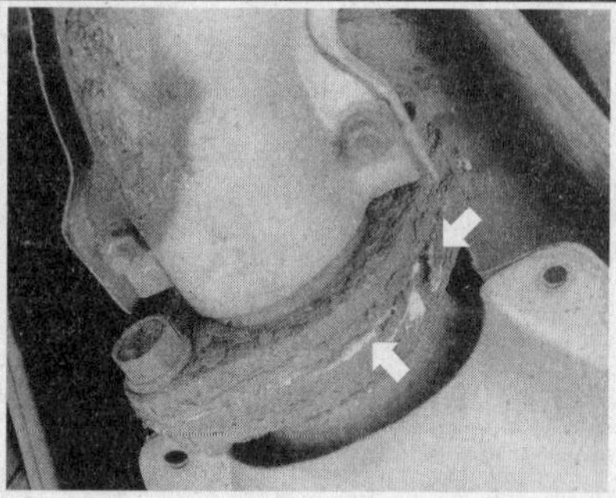

TCCA3P71

**Fig. 173 Inspect flanges for gaskets that have deteriorated and need replacement**

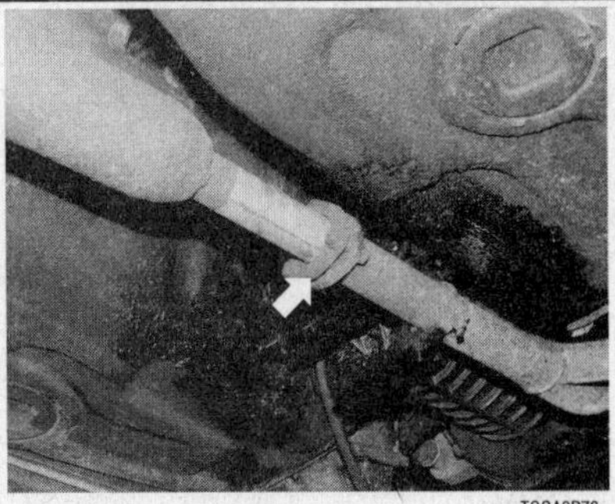

TCCA3P76

**Fig. 174 Some systems, like this one, use large O-rings (doughnuts) in between the flanges**

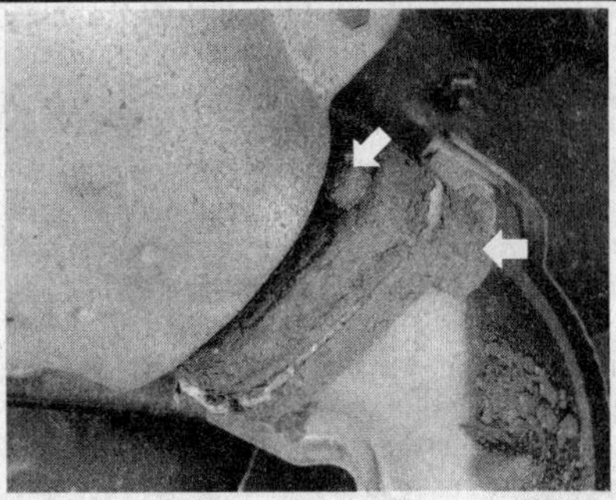

TCCA3P70

**Fig. 175 Nuts and bolts will be extremely difficult to remove when deteriorated with rust**

TCCA3P72

**Fig. 176 Example of a flange type exhaust system joint**

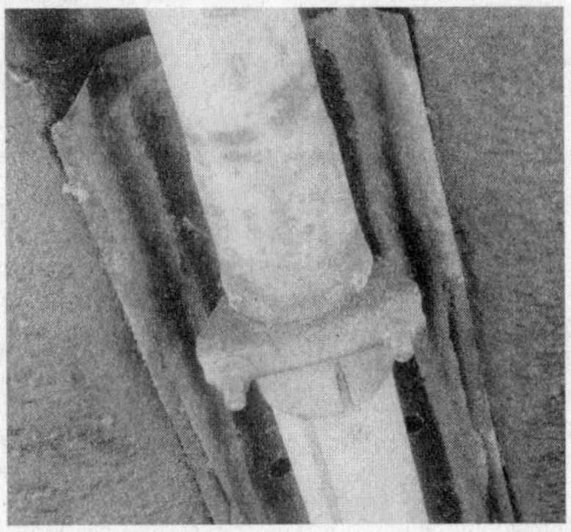

TCCA3P79

**Fig. 177 Example of a common slip joint type system**

Before removing any component on a flange type system, ALWAYS squirt a liquid rust-dissolving agent onto the fasteners for ease of removal. Start by unbolting the exhaust piece at both ends (if required). When unbolting the headpipe from the manifold, make sure that the bolts are free before trying to remove them. if you snap a stud in the exhaust manifold, the stud will have to be removed with a bolt extractor, which often means removal of the manifold itself. Next, disconnect the component from the mounting; slight twisting and turning may be required to remove the component completely from the vehicle. You may need to tap on the component with a rubber mallet to loosen the component. If all else fails, use a hacksaw to separate the parts. An oxy-acetylene cutting torch may be faster but the sparks are DANGEROUS near the fuel tank, and at the very least, accidents could happen, resulting in damage to the under-car parts, not to mention yourself.

### Slip Joint Type

**▶ See Figure 177**

Before removing any component on the slip joint type exhaust system, ALWAYS squirt a liquid rust-dissolving agent onto the fasteners for ease of removal. Start by unbolting the exhaust piece at both ends (if required). When unbolting the headpipe from the manifold, make sure that the bolts are free before trying to remove them. if you snap a stud in the exhaust manifold, the stud will have to be removed with a bolt extractor, which often means removal of the manifold itself. Next, remove the mounting U-bolts from around the exhaust pipe you are extracting from the vehicle. Don't be surprised if the U-bolts break while removing the nuts. Loosen the exhaust pipe from any mounting brackets retaining it to the floor pan and separate the components.

# ENGINE RECONDITIONING

## Determining Engine Condition

Anything that generates heat and/or friction will eventually burn or wear out (for example, a light bulb generates heat, therefore its life span is limited). With this in mind, a running engine generates tremendous amounts of both; friction is encountered by the moving and rotating parts inside the engine and heat is created by friction and combustion of the fuel. However, the engine has systems designed to help reduce the effects of heat and friction and provide added longevity. The oiling system reduces the amount of friction encountered by the moving parts inside the engine, while the cooling system reduces heat created by friction and combustion. If either system is not maintained, a breakdown will be inevitable. Therefore, you can see how regular maintenance can affect the service life of your vehicle. If you do not drain, flush and refill your cooling system at the proper intervals, deposits will begin to accumulate in the radiator, thereby reducing the amount of heat it can extract from the coolant. The same applies to your oil and filter; if it is not changed often enough it becomes laden with contaminates and is unable to properly lubricate the engine. This increases friction and wear.

There are a number of methods for evaluating the condition of your engine. A compression test can reveal the condition of your pistons, piston rings, cylinder bores, head gasket(s), valves and valve seats. An oil pressure test can warn you of possible engine bearing, or oil pump failures. Excessive oil consumption, evidence of oil in the engine air intake area and/or bluish smoke from the tailpipe may indicate worn piston rings, worn valve guides and/or valve seals. Generally, an engine that uses no more than one quart of oil every 1000 miles is in good condition. Engines that use one quart of oil or more in less than 1000 miles should first be checked for oil leaks. If any oil leaks are present, have them fixed before determining how much oil is consumed by the engine, especially if blue smoke is not visible at the tailpipe.

### COMPRESSION TEST

**▶ See Figure 178**

A noticeable lack of engine power, excessive oil consumption and/or poor fuel mileage measured over an extended period are all indicators of internal engine wear. Worn piston rings, scored or worn cylinder bores, blown head gaskets, sticking or burnt valves, and worn valve seats are all possible culprits. A check of the compression of each cylinder will help locate the problem.

**➡A screw-in type compression gauge is more accurate than the type you simply hold against the spark plug hole. Although it takes slightly longer to use, it's worth the effort to obtain a more accurate reading.**

1. Make sure that the proper amount and viscosity of engine oil is in the crankcase, then ensure the battery is fully charged.
2. Warm-up the engine too normal operating temperature, then shut the engine **OFF**.
3. Disable the ignition system.
4. Label and disconnect all of the spark plug wires from the plugs.
5. Thoroughly clean the cylinder head area around the spark plug ports, then remove the spark plugs.
6. Set the throttle plate to the fully open (wide-

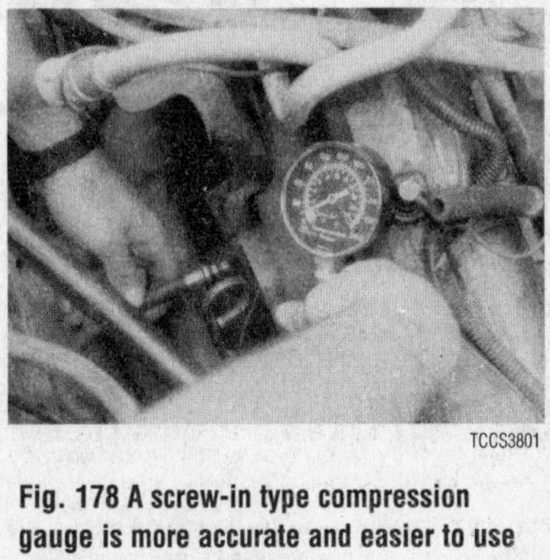

TCCS3801

**Fig. 178 A screw-in type compression gauge is more accurate and easier to use without an assistant**

open throttle) position. You can block the accelerator linkage open for this, or you can have an assistant fully depress the accelerator pedal.

7. Install a screw-in type compression gauge into the No. 1 spark plug hole until the fitting is snug.

**✲✲ WARNING**

**Be careful not to crossthread the spark plug hole.**

8. According to the tool manufacturer's instructions, connect a remote starting switch to the starting circuit.

9. With the ignition switch in the **OFF** position, use the remote starting switch to crank the engine through at least five compression strokes (approximately 5 seconds of cranking) and record the highest reading on the gauge.

10. Repeat the test on each cylinder, cranking the engine approximately the same number of compression strokes and/or time as the first.

11. Compare the highest readings from each cylinder to that of the others. The indicated compression pressures are considered within specifications if the lowest reading cylinder is within 75 percent of the pressure recorded for the highest reading cylinder. For example, if your highest reading cylinder pressure was 150 psi (1034 kPa), then 75 percent of that would be 113 psi (779 kPa). Therefore, the lowest reading cylinder should be no less than 113 psi (779 kPa).

12. If a cylinder exhibits an unusually low compression reading, pour a tablespoon of clean engine oil into the cylinder through the spark plug hole and repeat the compression test. If the compression rises after adding oil, it means that the cylinder's piston rings and/or cylinder bore are damaged or worn. If the pressure remains low, the valves may not be seating properly (a valve job is needed), or the head gasket may be blown near that cylinder. If compression in any two adjacent cylinders is low, and if the addition of oil doesn't help raise compression, there is leakage past the head gasket. Oil and coolant in the combustion chamber, combined with blue or constant white smoke from the tailpipe, are symptoms of this problem. However, don't be alarmed by the normal white smoke emitted from the tailpipe during engine warm-up or from cold weather driving. There may be evidence of water droplets on the engine dipstick and/or oil droplets in the cooling system if a head gasket is blown.

## Buy or Rebuild?

Now that you have determined that your engine is worn out, you must make some decisions. The question of whether or not an engine is worth rebuilding is largely a subjective matter and one of personal worth. Is the engine a popular one, or is it an obsolete model? Are parts available? Will it get acceptable gas mileage once it is rebuilt? Is the car it's being put into worth keeping? Would it be less expensive to buy a new engine, have your engine rebuilt by a pro, rebuild it yourself or buy a used engine from a salvage yard? On the other hand, would it be simpler and less expensive to buy another car? If you have considered all these matters and more, and have still decided to rebuild the engine, then it is time to decide how you will rebuild it.

**➡The editors at Chilton feel that most engine machining should be performed by a professional machine shop. Don't think of it as wasting money, rather, as an assurance that the job has been done right the first time. There are many expensive and specialized tools required to perform such tasks as boring and honing an engine block or having a valve job done on a cylinder head. Even inspecting the parts requires expensive micrometers and gauges to properly measure wear and clearances. In addition, a machine shop can deliver to you clean, and ready to assemble parts, saving you time and aggravation. Your maximum savings will come from performing the removal, disassembly, assembly and installation of the engine and purchasing or renting only the tools required to perform the above tasks. Depending on the particular circumstances, you may save 40 to 60 percent of the cost doing these yourself.**

A complete rebuild or overhaul of an engine involves replacing all of the moving parts (pistons, rods, crankshaft, camshaft, etc.) with new ones and machining the non-moving wearing surfaces of the block and heads. Unfortunately, this may not be cost effective. For instance, your crankshaft may have been damaged or worn, but it can be machined undersize for a minimal fee.

So, as you can see, you can replace everything inside the engine, but, it is wiser to replace only those parts which are really needed, and, if possible, repair the more expensive ones. Later in this section, we will break the engine down into its two main components: the cylinder head and the engine block. We will discuss each component, and the recommended parts to replace during a rebuild on each.

## Engine Overhaul Tips

Most engine overhaul procedures are standard. In addition to specific parts replacement procedures and specifications for your individual engine, this section is also a guide to acceptable rebuilding procedures. Examples of standard rebuilding practice are given and should be used along with specific details concerning your particular engine.

Competent and accurate machine shop services will ensure maximum performance, reliability and engine life. In most instances it is more profitable for the do-it-yourself mechanic to remove, clean and inspect the component, buy the necessary parts and deliver these to a shop for actual machine work.

Much of the assembly work (crankshaft, bearings, piston rods, and other components) is well within the scope of the do-it-yourself mechanic's tools and abilities. You will have to decide for yourself the depth of involvement you desire in an engine repair or rebuild.

### TOOLS

The tools required for an engine overhaul or parts replacement will depend on the depth of your involvement. With a few exceptions, they will be the tools found in a mechanic's tool kit (see Section 1 of this manual). More in-depth work will require some or all of the following:

- A dial indicator (reading in thousandths) mounted on a universal base
- Micrometers and telescope gauges
- Jaw and screw-type pullers
- Scraper
- Valve spring compressor
- Ring groove cleaner
- Piston ring expander and compressor
- Ridge reamer
- Cylinder hone or glaze breaker
- Plastigage®
- Engine stand

The use of most of these tools is illustrated in this section. Many can be rented for a one-time use from a local parts jobber or tool supply house specializing in automotive work.

Occasionally, the use of special tools is called for. See the information on Special Tools and the Safety Notice in the front of this book before substituting another tool.

### OVERHAUL TIPS

Aluminum has become extremely popular for use in engines, due to its low weight. Observe the following precautions when handling aluminum parts:

- Never hot tank aluminum parts (the caustic hot tank solution will eat the aluminum.
- Remove all aluminum parts (identification tag, etc.) from engine parts prior to the tanking.
- Always coat threads lightly with engine oil or anti-seize compounds before installation, to prevent seizure.
- Never overtighten bolts or spark plugs especially in aluminum threads.

When assembling the engine, any parts that will be exposed to frictional contact must be prelubed to provide lubrication at initial start-up. Any product specifically formulated for this purpose can be used, but engine oil is not recommended as a prelube in most cases.

When semi-permanent (locked, but removable) installation of bolts or nuts is desired, threads should be cleaned and coated with Loctite• or another similar, commercial non-hardening sealant.

### CLEANING

**➧ See Figures 179, 180, 181 and 182**

Before the engine and its components are inspected, they must be thoroughly cleaned. You will need to remove any engine varnish, oil sludge and/or carbon deposits from all of the components to insure an accurate inspection. A crack in the engine block or cylinder head can easily become overlooked if hidden by a layer of sludge or carbon.

Most of the cleaning process can be carried out with common hand tools and readily available solvents or solutions. Carbon deposits can be chipped away using a hammer and a hard wooden chisel. Old gasket material and varnish or sludge can usually be removed using a scraper and/or cleaning solvent. Extremely stubborn deposits may require the use of a power drill with a wire brush. If using a wire brush, use extreme care around any critical machined surfaces (such as the gasket surfaces, bearing saddles, cylinder bores, etc.). USE OF A WIRE BRUSH IS NOT RECOMMENDED ON ANY ALUMINUM COMPONENTS. Always follow any safety recommendations given by the manufacturer of the tool and/or solvent. You should always wear eye protection during any cleaning process involving scraping, chipping or spraying of solvents.

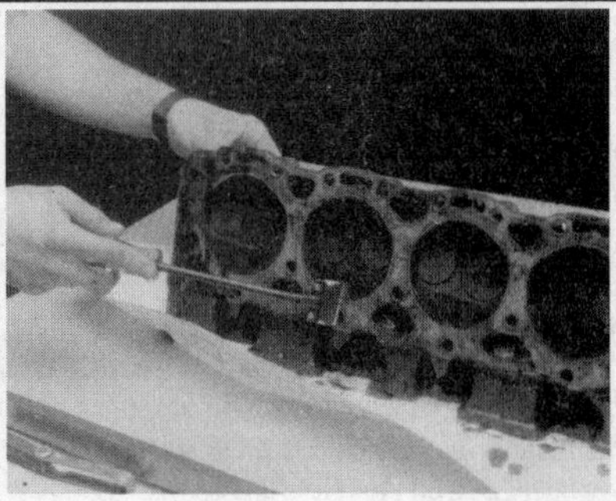

TCCS3132

Fig. 179 Use a gasket scraper to remove the old gasket material from the mating surfaces

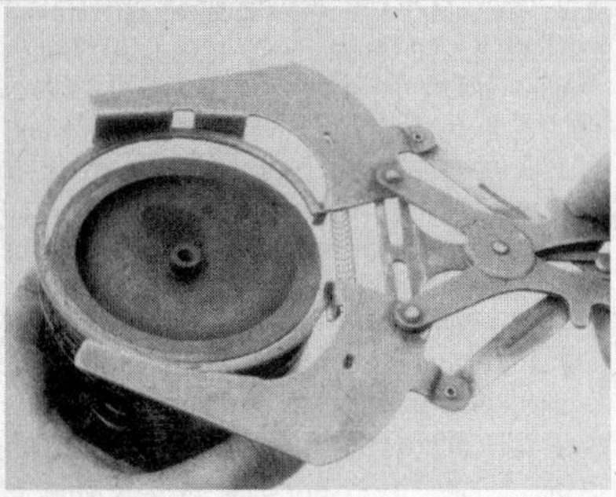

TCCS3211

Fig. 180 Use a ring expander tool to remove the piston rings

TCCS3208

Fig. 181 Clean the piston ring grooves using a ring groove cleaner tool, or . . .

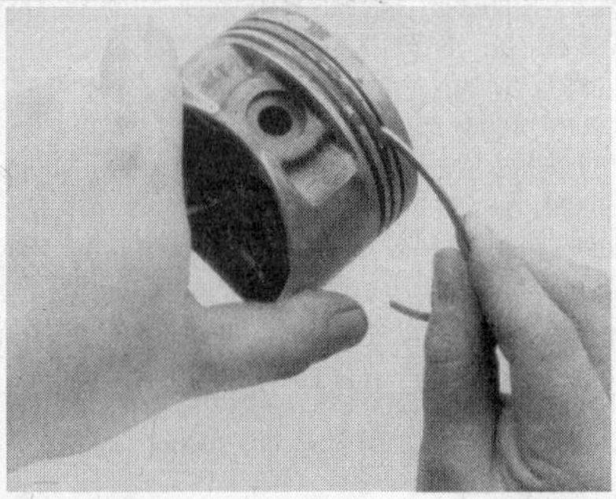

TCCS3911

Fig. 182 . . . use a piece of an old ring to clean the grooves. Be careful, the ring can be quite sharp

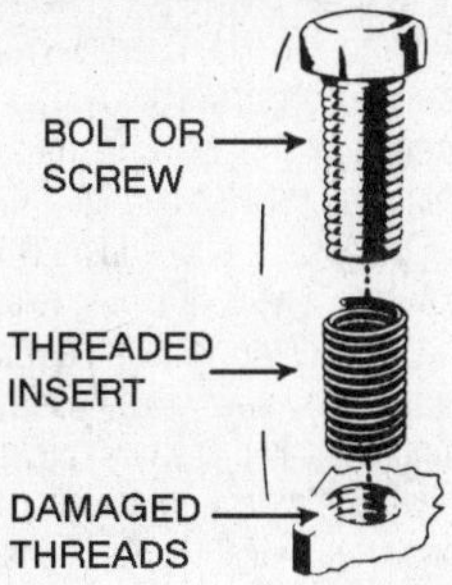


TCCS3039

Fig. 183 Damaged bolt hole threads can be replaced with thread repair inserts

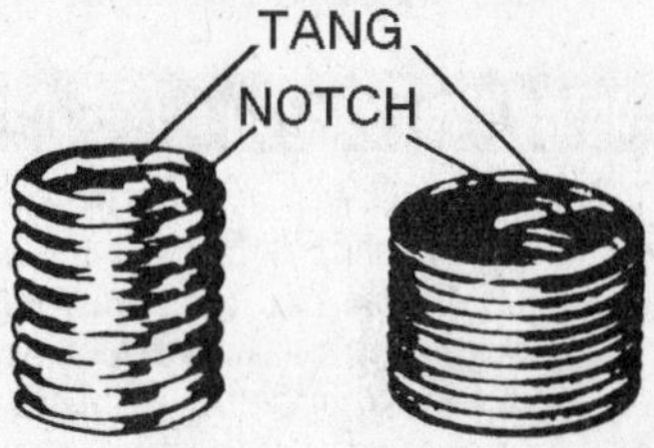


TCCS3040

Fig. 184 Standard thread repair insert (left), and spark plug thread insert

An alternative to the mess and hassle of cleaning the parts yourself is to drop them off at a local garage or machine shop. They will, more than likely, have the necessary equipment to properly clean all of the parts for a nominal fee.

**CAUTION**

**Always wear eye protection during any cleaning process involving scraping, chipping or spraying of solvents.**

Remove any oil galley plugs, freeze plugs and/or pressed-in bearings and carefully wash and degrease all of the engine components including the fasteners and bolts. Small parts such as the valves, springs, etc., should be placed in a metal basket and allowed to soak. Use pipe cleaner type brushes, and clean all passageways in the components. Use a ring expander and remove the rings from the pistons. Clean the piston ring grooves with a special tool or a piece of broken ring. Scrape the carbon off the top of the piston. You should never use a wire brush on the pistons. After preparing all of the piston assemblies in this manner, wash and degrease them again.

**WARNING**

**Use extreme care when cleaning around the cylinder head valve seats. A mistake or slip may cost you a new seat.**

When cleaning the cylinder head, remove carbon from the combustion chamber with the valves installed. This will avoid damaging the valve seats.

## REPAIRING DAMAGED THREADS

**See Figures 183, 184, 185, 186 and 187**

Several methods of repairing damaged threads are available. Heli-Coil® (shown here), Keenserts® and Microdot® are among the most widely used. All involve basically the same principle—drilling out stripped threads, tapping the hole and installing a prewound insert—making welding, plugging and oversize fasteners unnecessary.

Two types of thread repair inserts are usually supplied: a standard type for most inch coarse, inch fine, metric course and metric fine thread sizes and

TCCS3041

Fig. 185 Drill out the damaged threads with the specified size bit. Be sure to drill completely through the hole or to the bottom of a blind hole

TCCS3042

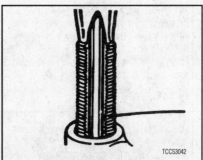

Fig. 186 Using the kit, tap the hole in order to receive the thread insert. Keep the tap well oiled and back it out frequently to avoid clogging the threads

TCCS3043

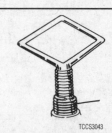

Fig. 187 Screw the insert onto the installer tool until the tang engages the slot. Thread the insert into the hole until it is $\frac{1}{4}$–$\frac{1}{2}$ turn below the top surface, then remove the tool and break off the tang using a punch

a spark lug type to fit most spark plug port sizes. Consult the individual tool manufacturer's catalog to determine exact applications. Typical thread repair kits will contain a selection of prewound threaded inserts, a tap (corresponding to the outside diameter threads of the insert) and an installation tool. Spark plug inserts usually differ because they require a tap equipped with pilot threads and a combined reamer/tap section. Most manufacturers also supply blister-packed thread repair inserts separately in addition to a master kit containing a variety of taps and inserts plus installation tools.

Before attempting to repair a threaded hole, remove any snapped, broken or damaged bolts or studs. Penetrating oil can be used to free frozen threads. The offending item can usually be removed with locking pliers or using a screw/stud extractor. After the hole is clear, the thread can be repaired, as shown in the series of accompanying illustrations and in the kit manufacturer's instructions.

## Engine Preparation

To properly rebuild an engine, you must first remove it from the vehicle, then disassemble and diagnose it. Ideally you should place your engine on an engine stand. This affords you the best access to the engine components. Follow the manufacturer's directions for using the stand with your particular engine. Remove the flywheel or flexplate before installing the engine to the stand.

Now that you have the engine on a stand, and assuming that you have drained the oil and coolant from the engine, it's time to strip it of all but the necessary components. Before you start disassembling the engine, you may want to take a moment to draw some pictures, or fabricate some labels or containers to mark the locations of various components and the bolts and/or studs which fasten them. Modern day engines use a lot of little brackets and clips which hold wiring harnesses and such, and these holders are often mounted on studs and/or bolts that can be easily mixed up. The manufacturer spent a lot of time and money designing your vehicle, and they wouldn't have wasted any of it by haphazardly placing brackets, clips or fasteners on the vehicle. If it's present when you disassemble it, put it back when you assemble, you will regret not remembering that little bracket which holds a wire harness out of the path of a rotating part.

You should begin by unbolting any accessories still attached to the engine, such as the water pump, power steering pump, alternator, etc. Then, unfasten any manifolds (intake or exhaust) which were not removed during the engine removal procedure. Finally, remove any covers remaining on the engine such as the rocker arm, front or timing cover and oil pan. Some front covers may require the vibration damper and/or crank pulley to be removed beforehand. The idea is to reduce the engine to the bare necessities (cylinder head(s), valve train, engine block, crankshaft, pistons and connecting rods), plus any other `in block' components such as oil pumps, balance shafts and auxiliary shafts.

Finally, remove the cylinder head(s) from the engine block and carefully place on a bench. Disassembly instructions for each component follow later in this section.

## Cylinder Head

There are two basic types of cylinder heads used on today's automobiles: the Overhead Valve (OHV) and the Overhead Camshaft (OHC). The latter can also be broken down into two subgroups: the Single Overhead Camshaft (SOHC) and the Dual Overhead Camshaft (DOHC). Generally, if there is only a single camshaft on a head, it is just referred to as an OHC head. In addition, an engine with an OHV cylinder head is also known as a pushrod engine.

Most cylinder heads these days are made of an aluminum alloy due to its light weight, durability and heat transfer qualities. However, cast iron was the material of choice in the past, and is still used on many vehicles today. Whether made from aluminum or iron, all cylinder heads have valves and seats. Some use two valves per cylinder, while the more hi-tech engines will utilize a multi-valve configuration using 3, 4 and even 5 valves per cylinder. When the valve contacts the seat, it does so on precision machined surfaces, which seals the combustion chamber. All cylinder heads have a valve guide for each valve. The guide centers the valve to the seat and allows it to move up and down within it. The clearance between the valve and guide can be critical. Too much clearance and the engine may consume oil, lose vacuum and/or damage the seat. Too little, and the valve can stick in the guide causing the engine to run poorly if at all, and possibly causing severe damage. The last component all cylinder heads have are valve springs. The spring holds the valve against its seat. It also returns the valve to this position when the valve has been opened by the valve train or camshaft. The spring is fastened to the valve by a retainer and valve locks (sometimes called keepers). Aluminum heads will also have a valve spring shim to keep the spring from wearing away the aluminum.

An ideal method of rebuilding the cylinder head would involve replacing all of the valves, guides, seats, springs, etc. with new ones. However, depending on how the engine was maintained, often this is not necessary. A major cause of valve, guide and seat wear is an improperly tuned engine. An engine that is running too rich, will often wash the lubricating oil out of the guide with gasoline, causing it to wear rapidly. Conversely, an engine which is running too lean will place higher combustion temperatures on the valves and seats allowing them to wear or even burn. Springs fall victim to the driving habits of the individual. A driver who often runs the engine rpm to the redline will wear out or break the springs faster then one that stays well below it. Unfortunately, mileage takes it toll on all of the parts. Generally, the valves, guides, springs and seats in a cylinder head can be machined and re-used, saving you money. However, if a valve is burnt, it may be wise to replace all of the valves, since they were all operating in the same environment. The same goes for any other component on the cylinder head. Think of it as an insurance policy against future problems related to that component.

Unfortunately, the only way to find out which components need replacing, is to disassemble and carefully check each piece. After the cylinder head(s) are disassembled, thoroughly clean all of the components.

### DISASSEMBLY

#### 3.8L and 5.0L Engines

**See Figures 188 thru 193**

Before disassembling the cylinder head, you may want to fabricate some containers to hold the various parts, as some of them can be quite small (such as keepers) and easily lost. Also keeping yourself and the components organized will aid in assembly and reduce confusion. Where possible, try to maintain a components original location; this is especially important if there is not going to be any machine work performed on the components.

1. If you haven't already removed the rocker arms and/or shafts, do so now.
2. Position the head so that the springs are easily accessed.
3. Use a valve spring compressor tool, and relieve spring tension from the retainer.

TCCS3137

**Fig. 188 When removing an OHV valve spring, use a compressor tool to relieve the tension from the retainer**

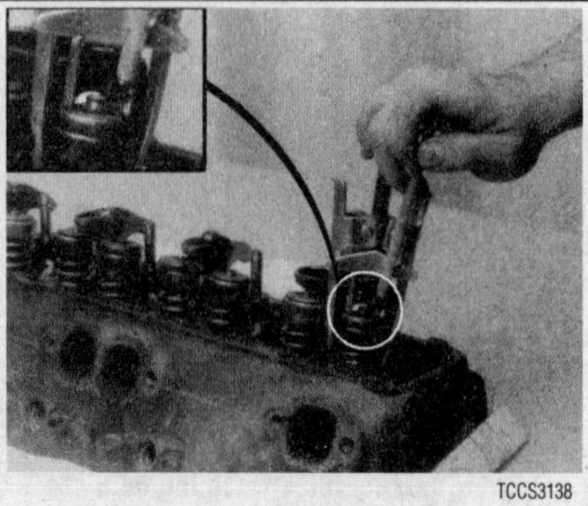
TCCS3138

**Fig. 189 A small magnet will help in removal of the valve locks**

TCCS3139

**Fig. 190 Be careful not to lose the small valve locks (keepers)**

TCCS3140

Fig. 191 Remove the valve seal from the valve stem—O-ring type seal shown

TCCS3252

Fig. 192 Removing an umbrella/positive type seal

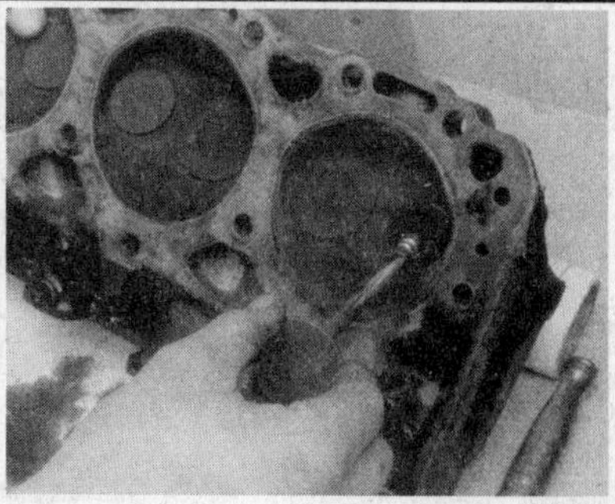
TCCS3141

Fig. 193 Invert the cylinder head and withdraw the valve from the valve guide bore

**➡Due to engine varnish, the retainer may stick to the valve locks. A gentle tap with a hammer may help to break it loose.**

4. Remove the valve locks from the valve tip and/or retainer. A small magnet may help in removing the locks.
5. Lift the valve spring, tool and all, off of the valve stem.
6. If equipped, remove the valve seal. If the seal is difficult to remove with the valve in place, try removing the valve first, then the seal. Follow the steps below for valve removal.
7. Position the head to allow access for withdrawing the valve.

**➡Cylinder heads that have seen a lot of miles and/or abuse may have mushroomed the valve lock grove and/or tip, causing difficulty in removal of the valve. If this has happened, use a metal file to carefully remove the high spots around the lock grooves and/or tip. Only file it enough to allow removal.**

8. Remove the valve from the cylinder head.
9. If equipped, remove the valve spring shim. A small magnetic tool or screwdriver will aid in removal.
10. Repeat Steps 3 though 9 until all of the valves have been removed.

### 4.6L Engine Heads

**➧ See Figures 194 thru 198**

Whether it is a single or dual overhead camshaft cylinder head, the disassembly procedure is relatively unchanged. One aspect to pay attention to is careful labeling of the parts on the dual camshaft cylinder head. There will be an intake camshaft and followers as well as an exhaust camshaft and followers and they must be labeled as such. In some cases, the components are identical and could easily be installed incorrectly. DO NOT MIX THEM UP! Determining which is which is very simple; the intake camshaft and components are on the same side of the head as was the intake manifold. Conversely, the exhaust camshaft and components are on the same side of the head as was the exhaust manifold.

Most cylinder heads with cup type camshaft followers will have the valve spring, retainer and locks recessed within the follower's bore. You will need a C-clamp style valve spring compressor tool, an OHC spring removal tool (or equivalent) and a small magnet to disassemble the head.

1. If not already removed, remove the camshaft(s) and/or followers. Mark their positions for assembly.
2. Position the cylinder head to allow use of a C-clamp style valve spring compressor tool.

**➡It is preferred to position the cylinder head gasket surface facing you with the valve springs facing the opposite direction and the head laying horizontal.**

3. With the OHC spring removal adapter tool positioned inside of the follower bore, compress the valve spring using the C-clamp style valve spring compressor.
4. Remove the valve locks. A small magnetic tool or screwdriver will aid in removal.
5. Release the compressor tool and remove the spring assembly.
6. Withdraw the valve from the cylinder head.
7. If equipped, remove the valve seal.

**➡Special valve seal removal tools are available. Regular or needlenose type pliers, if used with care, will work just as well. If using ordinary pliers, be sure not to damage the follower bore. The follower and its bore are machined to close tolerances and any damage to the bore will effect this relationship.**

8. If equipped, remove the valve spring shim. A small magnetic tool or screwdriver will aid in removal.
9. Repeat Steps 3 through 8 until all of the valves have been removed.

TCCA3P54

Fig. 194 Exploded view of a valve, seal, spring, retainer and locks from an OHC cylinder head

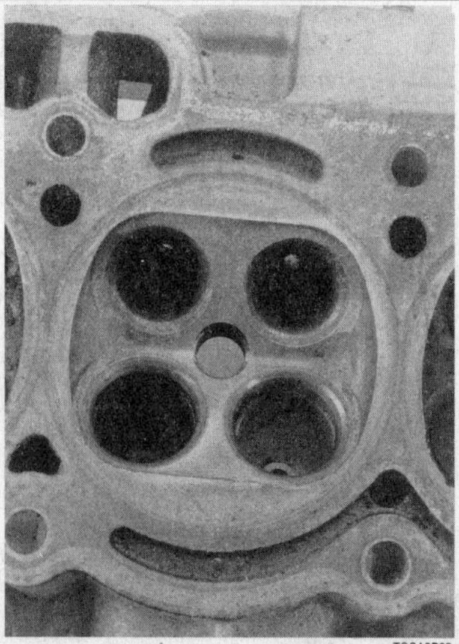
TCCA3P62

Fig. 195 Example of a multi-valve cylinder head. Note how it has 2 intake and 2 exhaust valve ports

TCCA3P51

Fig. 196 C-clamp type spring compressor and an OHC spring removal tool (center) for cup type followers

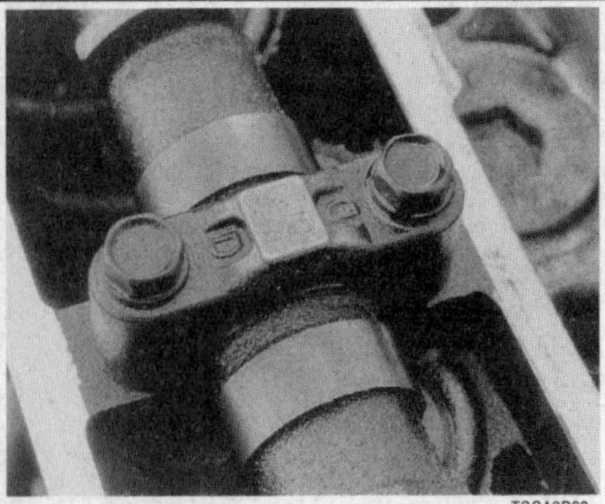

TCCA3P63

**Fig. 197 Most cup type follower cylinder heads retain the camshaft using bolt-on bearing caps**

TCCA3P65

**Fig. 198 Position the OHC spring tool in the follower bore, then compress the spring with a C-clamp type tool**

## INSPECTION

Now that all of the cylinder head components are clean, it's time to inspect them for wear and/or damage. To accurately inspect them, you will need some specialized tools:

- A 0–1 in. micrometer for the valves
- A dial indicator or inside diameter gauge for the valve guides
- A spring pressure test gauge

If you do not have access to the proper tools, you may want to bring the components to a shop that does.

### Valves

➧ See Figures 199 and 200

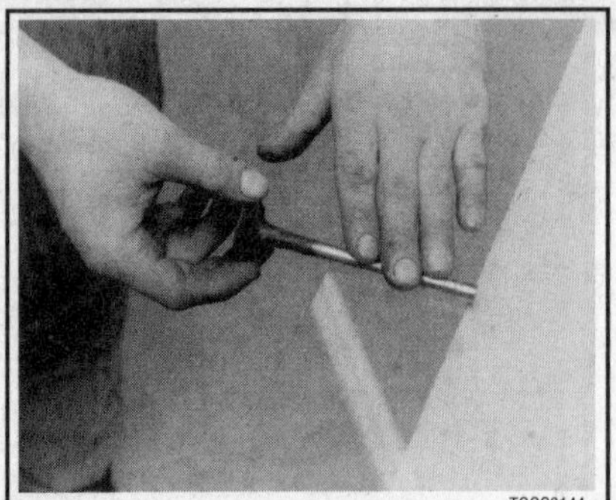

TCCS3144

**Fig. 199 Valve stems may be rolled on a flat surface to check for bends**

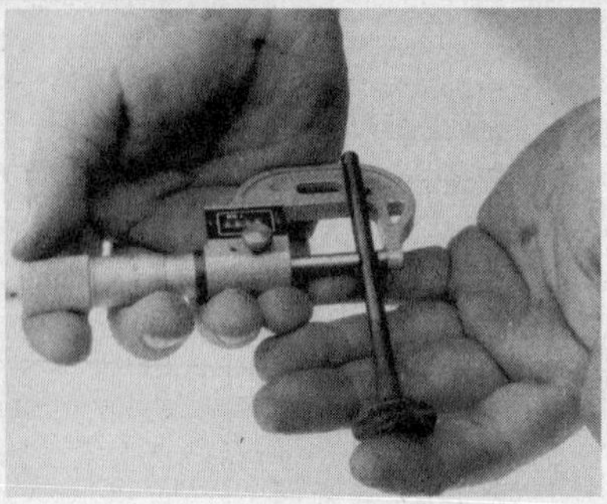

TCCS3910

**Fig. 200 Use a micrometer to check the valve stem diameter**

The first thing to inspect are the valve heads. Look closely at the head, margin and face for any cracks, excessive wear or burning. The margin is the best place to look for burning. It should have a squared edge with an even width all around the diameter. When a valve burns, the margin will look melted and the edges rounded. Also inspect the valve head for any signs of tulipping. This will show as a lifting of the edges or dishing in the center of the head and will usually not occur to all of the valves. All of the heads should look the same, any that seem dished more than others are probably bad. Next, inspect the valve lock grooves and valve tips. Check for any burrs around the lock grooves, especially if you had to file them to remove the valve. Valve tips should appear flat, although slight rounding with high mileage engines is normal. Slightly worn valve tips will need to be machined flat. Last, measure the valve stem diameter with the micrometer. Measure the area that rides within the guide, especially towards the tip where most of the wear occurs. Take several measurements along its length and compare them to each other. Wear should be even along the length with little to no taper. If no minimum diameter is given in the specifications, then the stem should not read more than 0.001 in. (0.025mm) below the unworn area of the valve stem. Any valves that fail these inspections should be replaced.

### Springs, Retainers and Valve Locks

➧ See Figures 201 and 202

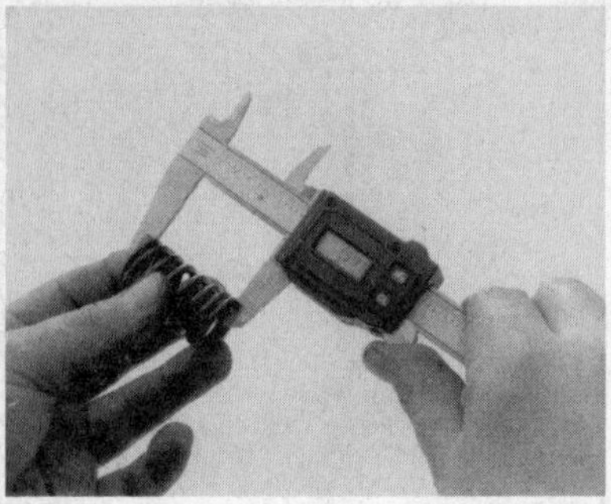

TCCS3907

**Fig. 201 Use a caliper to check the valve spring free-length**

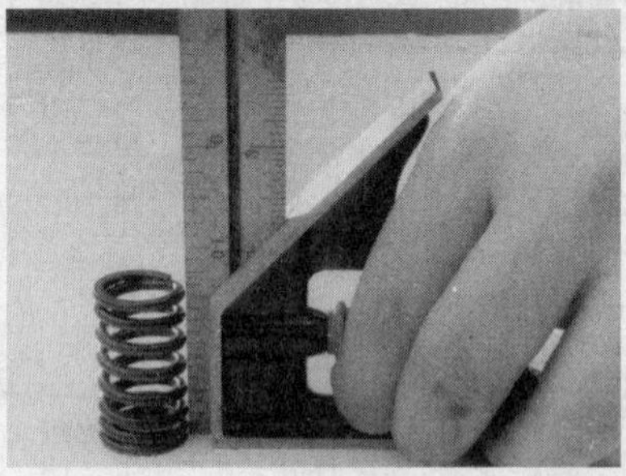

TCCS3908

**Fig. 202 Check the valve spring for squareness on a flat surface; a carpenter's square can be used**

The first thing to check is the most obvious, broken springs. Next check the free length and squareness of each spring. If applicable, insure to distinguish between intake and exhaust springs. Use a ruler and/or carpenter's square to measure the length. A carpenter's square should be used to check the springs for squareness. If a spring pressure test gauge is available, check each springs rating and compare to the specifications chart. Check the readings against the specifications given. Any springs that fail these inspections should be replaced.

The spring retainers rarely need replacing, however they should still be checked as a precaution. Inspect the spring mating surface and the valve lock retention area for any signs of excessive wear. Also check for any signs of cracking. Replace any retainers that are questionable.

Valve locks should be inspected for excessive wear on the outside contact area as well as on the inner notched surface. Any locks which appear worn or broken and its respective valve should be replaced.

### Cylinder Head

There are several things to check on the cylinder head: valve guides, seats, cylinder head surface flatness, cracks and physical damage.

#### *VALVE GUIDES*

➧ See Figure 203

Now that you know the valves are good, you can use them to check the guides, although a new valve, if available, is preferred. Before you measure anything, look at the guides carefully and inspect them for any cracks, chips or breakage. Also if the guide is a removable style (as in most aluminum heads), check them for any looseness or evidence of movement. All of the guides should appear to be at the same height from the spring seat. If any seem lower (or higher) from another, the guide has moved. Mount a dial indicator onto the spring side of the cylinder head. Lightly oil the valve stem and insert it into the cylinder head. Position the dial indicator against the valve stem near the tip and zero the gauge. Grasp the valve stem and wiggle towards and away from the dial indicator and observe the readings. Mount the dial indicator 90 degrees from the initial point and zero the gauge and again take a reading. Compare the two readings for a out of round condition. Check the readings against the specifications given. An Inside Diameter (I.D.) gauge designed for valve guides will give you an accurate valve guide bore measurement. If the I.D. gauge is used, compare the readings with the specifications given. Any guides that fail these inspections should be replaced or machined.

#### VALVE SEATS

A visual inspection of the valve seats should show a slightly worn and pitted surface where the valve face contacts the seat. Inspect the seat carefully for severe pitting or cracks. Also, a seat that is badly worn will be recessed into the cylinder head. A severely worn or recessed seat may need to be replaced. All cracked seats must be replaced. A seat concentricity gauge, if available, should be used to check the seat run-out. If run-out exceeds specifications the seat must be machined (if no specification is given use 0.002 in. or 0.051mm).

#### CYLINDER HEAD SURFACE FLATNESS

**See Figures 204 and 205**

After you have cleaned the gasket surface of the cylinder head of any old gasket material, check the head for flatness.

Place a straightedge across the gasket surface. Using feeler gauges, determine the clearance at the center of the straightedge and across the cylinder head at several points. Check along the centerline and diagonally on the head surface. If the warpage exceeds 0.003 in. (0.076mm) within a 6.0 in. (15.2cm) span, or 0.006 in. (0.152mm) over the total length of the head, the cylinder head must be resurfaced. After resurfacing the heads of a V-type engine, the intake manifold flange surface should be checked, and if necessary, milled proportionally to allow for the change in its mounting position.

#### CRACKS AND PHYSICAL DAMAGE

Generally, cracks are limited to the combustion chamber, however, it is not uncommon for the head to crack in a spark plug hole, port, outside of the head or in the valve spring/rocker arm area. The first area to inspect is always the hottest: the exhaust seat/port area.

A visual inspection should be performed, but just because you don't see a crack does not mean it is not there. Some more reliable methods for inspecting for cracks include Magnaflux®, a magnetic process or Zyglo®, a dye penetrant. Magnaflux® is used only on ferrous metal (cast iron) heads. Zyglo® uses a spray on fluorescent mixture along with a black light to reveal the cracks. It is strongly recommended to have your cylinder head checked professionally for cracks, especially if the engine was known to have overheated and/or leaked or consumed coolant. Contact a local shop for availability and pricing of these services.

Physical damage is usually very evident. For example, a broken mounting ear from dropping the head or a bent or broken stud and/or bolt. All of these defects should be fixed or, if unrepairable, the head should be replaced.

### Camshaft and Followers

Inspect the camshaft(s) and followers as described earlier in this section.

## REFINISHING & REPAIRING

Many of the procedures given for refinishing and repairing the cylinder head components must be performed by a machine shop. Certain steps, if the inspected part is not worn, can be performed yourself inexpensively. However, you spent a lot of time and effort so far, why risk trying to save a couple bucks if you might have to do it all over again?

### Valves

Any valves that were not replaced should be refaced and the tips ground flat. Unless you have access to a valve grinding machine, this should be done by a machine shop. If the valves are in extremely good condition, as well as the valve seats and guides, they may be lapped in without performing machine work.

It is a recommended practice to lap the valves even after machine work has been performed and/or new valves have been purchased. This insures a positive seal between the valve and seat.

#### LAPPING THE VALVES

**➡Before lapping the valves to the seats, read the rest of the cylinder head section to insure that any related parts are in acceptable enough condition to continue.**

**➡Before any valve seat machining and/or lapping can be performed, the guides must be within factory recommended specifications.**

1. Invert the cylinder head.
2. Lightly lubricate the valve stems and insert them into the cylinder head in their numbered order.
3. Raise the valve from the seat and apply a small amount of fine lapping compound to the seat.
4. Moisten the suction head of a hand-lapping tool and attach it to the head of the valve.
5. Rotate the tool between the palms of both hands, changing the position of the valve on the valve seat and lifting the tool often to prevent grooving.
6. Lap the valve until a smooth, polished circle is evident on the valve and seat.
7. Remove the tool and the valve. Wipe away all traces of the grinding compound and store the valve to maintain its lapped location.

**** WARNING**

**Do not get the valves out of order after they have been lapped. They must be put back with the same valve seat with which they were lapped.**

### Springs, Retainers and Valve Locks

There is no repair or refinishing possible with the springs, retainers and valve locks. If they are found to be worn or defective, they must be replaced with new (or known good) parts.

### Cylinder Head

Most refinishing procedures dealing with the cylinder head must be performed by a machine shop. Read the sections below and review your inspection data to determine whether or not machining is necessary.

TCCS3142

**Fig. 203 A dial gauge may be used to check valve stem-to-guide clearance; read the gauge while moving the valve stem**

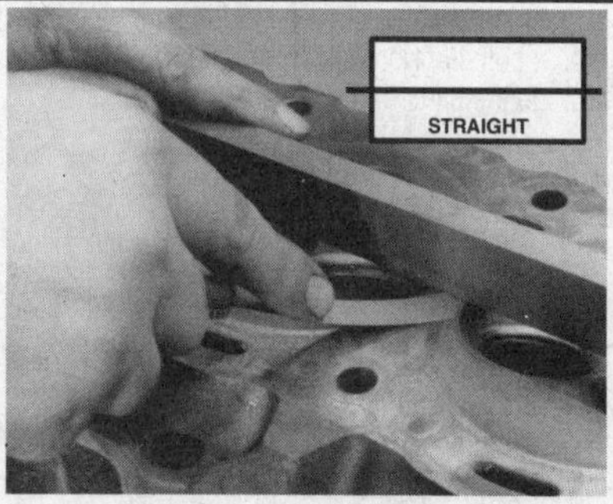

TCCS3919

**Fig. 204 Check the head for flatness across the center of the head surface using a straightedge and feeler gauge**

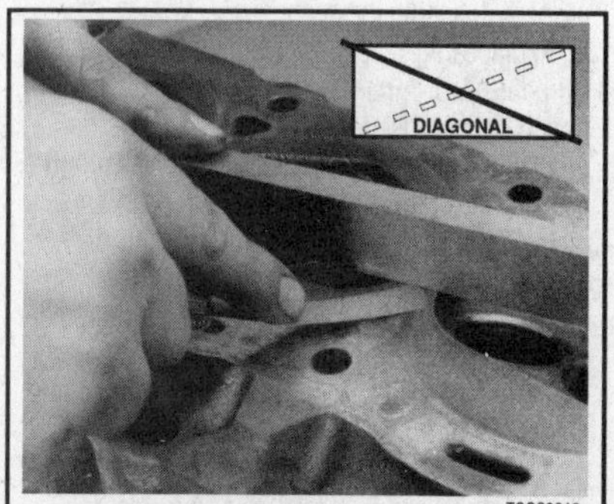

TCCS3918

**Fig. 205 Checks should also be made along both diagonals of the head surface**

### *VALVE GUIDE*

**➡If any machining or replacements are made to the valve guides, the seats must be machined.**

Unless the valve guides need machining or replacing, the only service to perform is to thoroughly clean them of any dirt or oil residue.

There are only two types of valve guides used on automobile engines: the replaceable-type (all aluminum heads) and the cast-in integral-type (most cast iron heads). There are four recommended methods for repairing worn guides.

- Knurling
- Inserts
- Reaming oversize
- Replacing

Knurling is a process in which metal is displaced and raised, thereby reducing clearance, giving a true center, and providing oil control. It is the least expensive way of repairing the valve guides. However, it is not necessarily the best, and in some cases, a knurled valve guide will not stand up for more than a short time. It requires a special knurlizer and precision reaming tools to obtain proper clearances. It would not be cost effective to purchase these tools, unless you plan on rebuilding several of the same cylinder head.

Installing a guide insert involves machining the guide to accept a bronze insert. One style is the coil-type which is installed into a threaded guide. Another is the thin-walled insert where the guide is reamed oversize to accept a split-sleeve insert. After the insert is installed, a special tool is then run through the guide to expand the insert, locking it to the guide. The insert is then reamed to the standard size for proper valve clearance.

Reaming for oversize valves restores normal clearances and provides a true valve seat. Most cast-in type guides can be reamed to accept an valve with an oversize stem. The cost factor for this can become quite high as you will need to purchase the reamer and new, oversize stem valves for all guides which were reamed. Oversizes are generally 0.003 to 0.030 in. (0.076 to 0.762mm), with 0.015 in. (0.381mm) being the most common.

To replace cast-in type valve guides, they must be drilled out, then reamed to accept replacement guides. This must be done on a fixture which will allow centering and leveling off of the original valve seat or guide, otherwise a serious guide-to-seat misalignment may occur making it impossible to properly machine the seat.

Replaceable-type guides are pressed into the cylinder head. A hammer and a stepped drift or punch may be used to install and remove the guides. Before removing the guides, measure the protrusion on the spring side of the head and record it for installation. Use the stepped drift to hammer out the old guide from the combustion chamber side of the head. When installing, determine whether or not the guide also seals a water jacket in the head, and if it does, use the recommended sealing agent. If there is no water jacket, grease the valve guide and its bore. Use the stepped drift, and hammer the new guide into the cylinder head from the spring side of the cylinder head. A stack of washers the same thickness as the measured protrusion may help the installation process.

### *VALVE SEATS*

**➡Before any valve seat machining can be performed, the guides must be within factory recommended specifications.**

**➡If any machining or replacements were made to the valve guides, the seats must be machined.**

If the seats are in good condition, the valves can be lapped to the seats, and the cylinder head assembled. See the valves section for instructions on lapping.

If the valve seats are worn, cracked or damaged, they must be serviced by a machine shop. The valve seat must be perfectly centered to the valve guide, which requires very accurate machining.

### *CYLINDER HEAD SURFACE*

If the cylinder head is warped, it must be machined flat. If the warpage is extremely severe, the head may need to be replaced. In some instances, it may be possible to straighten a warped head enough to allow machining. In either case, contact a professional machine shop for service.

**➡Any OHC cylinder head that shows excessive warpage should have the camshaft bearing journals align bored after the cylinder head has been resurfaced.**

**WARNING**

**Failure to align bore the camshaft bearing journals could result in severe engine damage including but not limited to: valve and piston damage, connecting rod damage, camshaft and/or crankshaft breakage.**

### *CRACKS AND PHYSICAL DAMAGE*

Certain cracks can be repaired in both cast iron and aluminum heads. For cast iron, a tapered threaded insert is installed along the length of the crack. Aluminum can also use the tapered inserts, however welding is the preferred method. Some physical damage can be repaired through brazing or welding. Contact a machine shop to get expert advice for your particular dilemma.

## ASSEMBLY

The first step for any assembly job is to have a clean area in which to work. Next, thoroughly clean all of the parts and components that are to be assembled. Finally, place all of the components onto a suitable work space and, if necessary, arrange the parts to their respective positions.

### 3.8L and 5.0L Engines

1. Lightly lubricate the valve stems and insert all of the valves into the cylinder head. If possible, maintain their original locations.
2. If equipped, install any valve spring shims that were removed.
3. If equipped, install the new valve seals, keeping the following in mind:
   - If the valve seal presses over the guide, lightly lubricate the outer guide surfaces.
   - If the seal is an O-ring type, it is installed just after compressing the spring but before the valve locks.
4. Place the valve spring and retainer over the stem.
5. Position the spring compressor tool and compress the spring.
6. Assemble the valve locks to the stem.
7. Relieve the spring pressure slowly and insure that neither valve lock becomes dislodged by the retainer.
8. Remove the spring compressor tool.
9. Repeat Steps 2 through 8 until all of the springs have been installed.

### 4.6L Engines

➧ See Figure 206

### *CUP TYPE CAMSHAFT FOLLOWERS*

To install the springs, retainers and valve locks on heads which have these components recessed into the camshaft follower's bore, you will need a small screwdriver-type tool, some clean white grease and a lot of patience. You will also need the C-clamp style spring compressor and the OHC tool used to disassemble the head.

1. Lightly lubricate the valve stems and insert all of the valves into the cylinder head. If possible, maintain their original locations.
2. If equipped, install any valve spring shims which were removed.
3. If equipped, install the new valve seals, keeping the following in mind:
   - If the valve seal presses over the guide, lightly lubricate the outer guide surfaces.
   - If the seal is an O-ring type, it is installed just after compressing the spring but before the valve locks.
4. Place the valve spring and retainer over the stem.
5. Position the spring compressor and the OHC tool, then compress the spring.
6. Using a small screwdriver as a spatula, fill the valve stem side of the lock with white grease. Use the excess grease on the screwdriver to fasten the lock to the driver.
7. Carefully install the valve lock, which is stuck to the end of the screwdriver, to the valve stem then press on it with the screwdriver until the grease squeezes out. The valve lock should now be stuck to the stem.
8. Repeat Steps 6 and 7 for the remaining valve lock.
9. Relieve the spring pressure slowly and insure that neither valve lock becomes dislodged by the retainer.

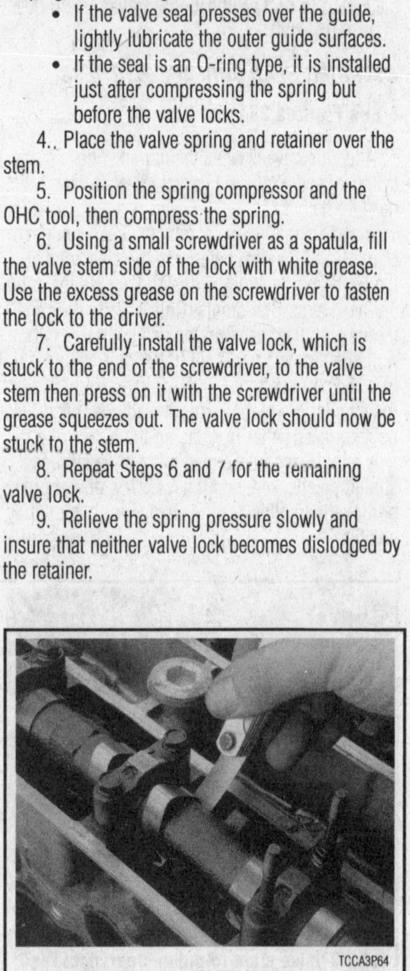

TCCA3P64

**Fig. 206 Once assembled, check the valve clearance and correct as needed**

10. Remove the spring compressor tool.
11. Repeat Steps 2 through 10 until all of the springs have been installed.
12. Install the followers, camshaft(s) and any other components that were removed for disassembly.

## Engine Block

### GENERAL INFORMATION

A thorough overhaul or rebuild of an engine block would include replacing the pistons, rings, bearings, timing belt/chain assembly and oil pump. For OHV engines also include a new camshaft and lifters. The block would then have the cylinders bored and honed oversize (or if using removable cylinder sleeves, new sleeves installed) and the crankshaft would be cut undersize to provide new wearing surfaces and perfect clearances. However, your particular engine may not have everything worn out. What if only the piston rings have worn out and the clearances on everything else are still within factory specifications? Well, you could just replace the rings and put it back together, but this would be a very rare example. Chances are, if one component in your engine is worn, other components are sure to follow, and soon. At the very least, you should always replace the rings, bearings and oil pump. This is what is commonly called a "freshen up".

#### Cylinder Ridge Removal

Because the top piston ring does not travel to the very top of the cylinder, a ridge is built up between the end of the travel and the top of the cylinder bore.

Pushing the piston and connecting rod assembly past the ridge can be difficult, and damage to the piston ring lands could occur. If the ridge is not removed before installing a new piston or not removed at all, piston ring breakage and piston damage may occur.

**➡It is always recommended that you remove any cylinder ridges before removing the piston and connecting rod assemblies. If you know that new pistons are going to be installed and the engine block will be bored oversize, you may be able to forego this step. However, some ridges may actually prevent the assemblies from being removed, necessitating its removal.**

There are several different types of ridge reamers on the market, none of which are inexpensive. Unless a great deal of engine rebuilding is anticipated, borrow or rent a reamer.

1. Turn the crankshaft until the piston is at the bottom of its travel.
2. Cover the head of the piston with a rag.
3. Follow the tool manufacturers instructions and cut away the ridge, exercising extreme care to avoid cutting too deeply.
4. Remove the ridge reamer, the rag and as many of the cuttings as possible. Continue until all of the cylinder ridges have been removed.

### DISASSEMBLY

**➧ See Figures 207 and 208**

The engine disassembly instructions following assume that you have the engine mounted on an engine stand. If not, it is easiest to disassemble the engine on a bench or the floor with it resting on the bell housing or transmission mounting surface. You must be able to access the connecting rod fasteners and turn the crankshaft during disassembly. Also, all engine covers (timing, front, side, oil pan, whatever) should have already been removed. Engines which are seized or locked up may not be able to be completely disassembled, and a core (salvage yard) engine should be purchased.

#### 3.8L and 5.0L Engines

If not done during the cylinder head removal, remove the pushrods and lifters, keeping them in order for assembly. Remove the timing gears and/or timing chain assembly, then remove the oil pump drive assembly and withdraw the camshaft from the engine block. Remove the oil pick-up and pump assembly. If equipped, remove any balance or auxiliary shafts. If necessary, remove the cylinder ridge from the top of the bore. See the cylinder ridge removal procedure earlier in this section.

#### 4.6L Engines

If not done during the cylinder head removal, remove the timing chain/belt and/or gear/sprocket assembly. Remove the oil pick-up and pump assembly and, if necessary, the pump drive. If equipped, remove any balance or auxiliary shafts. If necessary, remove the cylinder ridge from the top of the bore. See the cylinder ridge removal procedure earlier in this section.

#### All Engines

Rotate the engine over so that the crankshaft is exposed. Use a number punch or scribe and mark each connecting rod with its respective cylinder number. The cylinder closest to the front of the engine is always number 1. However, depending on the engine placement, the front of the engine could either be the flywheel or damper/pulley end. Generally the front of the engine faces the front of the vehicle. Use a number punch or scribe and also mark the main bearing caps from front to rear with the front most cap being number 1 (if there are five caps, mark them 1 through 5, front to rear).

**⁂ WARNING**

**Take special care when pushing the connecting rod up from the crankshaft because the sharp threads of the rod bolts/studs will score the crankshaft journal. Insure that special plastic caps are installed over them, or cut two pieces of rubber hose to do the same.**

Again, rotate the engine, this time to position the number one cylinder bore (head surface) up. Turn the crankshaft until the number one piston is at the bottom of its travel, this should allow the maximum access to its connecting rod. Remove the number one connecting rods fasteners and cap and place two lengths of rubber hose over the rod bolts/studs to protect the crankshaft from damage. Using a sturdy wooden dowel and a hammer, push the connecting rod up about 1 in. (25mm) from the crankshaft and remove the upper bearing insert. Continue pushing or tapping the connecting rod up until the piston rings are out of the cylinder bore. Remove the piston and rod by hand, put the upper half of the bearing insert back into the rod, install the cap with its bearing insert installed, and hand-tighten the cap fasteners. If the parts are kept in order in this manner, they will not get lost and you will be able to tell which bearings came form what cylinder if any problems are discovered and diagnosis is

TCCS3803

**Fig. 207 Place rubber hose over the connecting rod studs to protect the crankshaft and cylinder bores from damage**

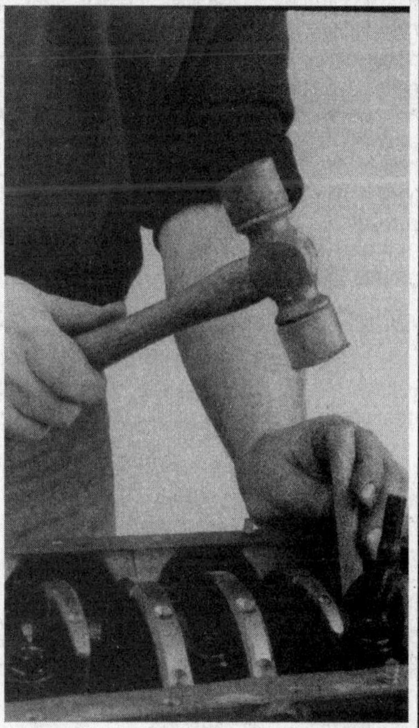

TCCS3804

**Fig. 208 Carefully tap the piston out of the bore using a wooden dowel**

necessary. Remove all the other piston assemblies in the same manner. On V-style engines, remove all of the pistons from one bank, then reposition the engine with the other cylinder bank head surface up, and remove that banks piston assemblies.

The only remaining component in the engine block should now be the crankshaft. Loosen the main bearing caps evenly until the fasteners can be turned by hand, then remove them and the caps. Remove the crankshaft from the engine block. Thoroughly clean all of the components.

## INSPECTION

Now that the engine block and all of its components are clean, it's time to inspect them for wear and/or damage. To accurately inspect them, you will need some specialized tools:

- Two or three separate micrometers to measure the pistons and crankshaft journals
- A dial indicator
- Telescoping gauges for the cylinder bores
- A rod alignment fixture to check for bent connecting rods

If you do not have access to the proper tools, you may want to bring the components to a shop that does.

Generally, you shouldn't expect cracks in the engine block or its components unless it was known to leak, consume or mix engine fluids, it was severely overheated, or there was evidence of bad bearings and/or crankshaft damage. A visual inspection should be performed on all of the components, but just because you don't see a crack does not mean it is not there. Some more reliable methods for inspecting for cracks include Magnaflux®, a magnetic process or Zyglo®, a dye penetrant. Magnaflux® is used only on ferrous metal (cast iron). Zyglo® uses a spray on fluorescent mixture along with a black light to reveal the cracks. It is strongly recommended to have your engine block checked professionally for cracks, especially if the engine was known to have overheated and/or leaked or consumed coolant. Contact a local shop for availability and pricing of these services.

### Engine Block

#### *ENGINE BLOCK BEARING ALIGNMENT*

Remove the main bearing caps and, if still installed, the main bearing inserts. Inspect all of the main bearing saddles and caps for damage, burrs or high spots. If damage is found, and it is caused from a spun main bearing, the block will need to be align-bored or, if severe enough, replacement. Any burrs or high spots should be carefully removed with a metal file.

Place a straightedge on the bearing saddles, in the engine block, along the centerline of the crankshaft. If any clearance exists between the straightedge and the saddles, the block must be align-bored.

Align-boring consists of machining the main bearing saddles and caps by means of a flycutter that runs through the bearing saddles.

#### *DECK FLATNESS*

The top of the engine block where the cylinder head mounts is called the deck. Insure that the deck surface is clean of dirt, carbon deposits and old gasket material. Place a straightedge across the surface of the deck along its centerline and, using feeler gauges, check the clearance along several points. Repeat the checking procedure with the straightedge placed along both diagonals of the deck surface. If the reading exceeds 0.003 in. (0.076mm) within a 6.0 in. (15.2cm) span, or 0.006 in. (0.152mm) over the total length of the deck, it must be machined.

#### *CYLINDER BORES*

➧ See Figure 209

The cylinder bores house the pistons and are slightly larger than the pistons themselves. A common piston-to-bore clearance is 0.0015–0.0025 in. (0.0381mm–0.0635mm). Inspect and measure the cylinder bores. The bore should be checked for out-of-roundness, taper and size. The results of this inspection will determine whether the cylinder can be used in its existing size and condition, or a rebore to the next oversize is required (or in the case of removable sleeves, have replacements installed).

The amount of cylinder wall wear is always greater at the top of the cylinder than at the bottom. This wear is known as taper. Any cylinder that has a taper of 0.0012 in. (0.305mm) or more, must be rebored. Measurements are taken at a number of positions in each cylinder: at the top, middle and bottom and at two points at each position; that is, at a point 90 degrees from the crankshaft centerline, as well as a point parallel to the crankshaft centerline. The measurements are made with either a special dial indicator or a telescopic gauge and micrometer. If the necessary precision tools to check the bore are not available, take the block to a machine shop and have them mike it. Also if you don't have the tools to check the cylinder bores, chances are you will not have the necessary devices to check the pistons, connecting rods and crankshaft. Take these components with you and save yourself an extra trip.

For our procedures, we will use a telescopic gauge and a micrometer. You will need one of each, with a measuring range which covers your cylinder bore size.

1. Position the telescopic gauge in the cylinder bore, loosen the gauges lock and allow it to expand.

**➡Your first two readings will be at the top of the cylinder bore, then proceed to the middle and finally the bottom, making a total of six measurements.**

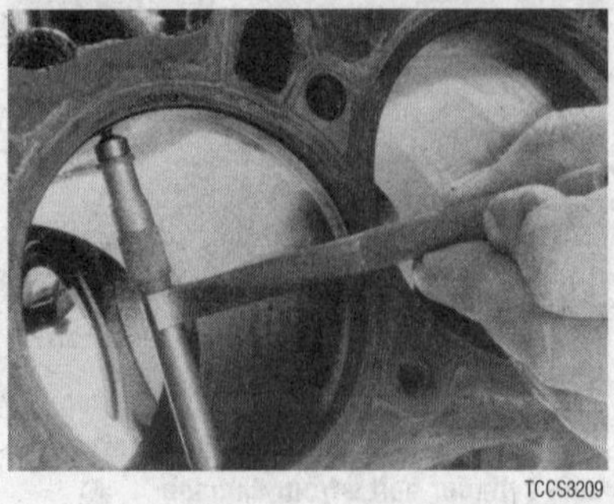

TCCS3209

**Fig. 209 Use a telescoping gauge to measure the cylinder bore diameter—take several readings within the same bore**

2. Hold the gauge square in the bore, 90 degrees from the crankshaft centerline, and gently tighten the lock. Tilt the gauge back to remove it from the bore.
3. Measure the gauge with the micrometer and record the reading.
4. Again, hold the gauge square in the bore, this time parallel to the crankshaft centerline, and gently tighten the lock. Again, you will tilt the gauge back to remove it from the bore.
5. Measure the gauge with the micrometer and record this reading. The difference between these two readings is the out-of-round measurement of the cylinder.
6. Repeat steps 1 through 5, each time going to the next lower position, until you reach the bottom of the cylinder. Then go to the next cylinder, and continue until all of the cylinders have been measured.

The difference between these measurements will tell you all about the wear in your cylinders. The measurements which were taken 90 degrees from the crankshaft centerline will always reflect the most wear. That is because at this position is where the engine power presses the piston against the cylinder bore the hardest. This is known as thrust wear. Take your top, 90 degree measurement and compare it to your bottom, 90 degree measurement. The difference between them is the taper. When you measure your pistons, you will compare these readings to your piston sizes and determine piston-to-wall clearance.

### Crankshaft

Inspect the crankshaft for visible signs of wear or damage. All of the journals should be perfectly round and smooth. Slight scores are normal for a used crankshaft, but you should hardly feel them with your fingernail. When measuring the crankshaft with a micrometer, you will take readings at the front and rear of each journal, then turn the micrometer 90 degrees and take two more readings, front and rear. The difference between the front-to-rear readings is the journal taper and the first-to-90 degree reading is the out-of-round measurement. Generally, there should be no taper or out-of-roundness found, however, up to 0.0005 in. (0.0127mm) for either can be overlooked. Also, the readings should fall within the factory specifications for journal diameters.

If the crankshaft journals fall within specifications, it is recommended that it be polished before being returned to service. Polishing the crankshaft insures that any minor burrs or high spots are smoothed, thereby reducing the chance of scoring the new bearings.

### Pistons and Connecting Rods

#### *PISTONS*

➧ See Figure 210

The piston should be visually inspected for any signs of cracking or burning (caused by hot spots or detonation), and scuffing or excessive wear on the skirts. The wrist pin attaches the piston to the connecting rod. The piston should move freely on the wrist pin, both sliding and pivoting. Grasp the connecting rod securely, or mount it in a vise, and try to rock the piston back and forth along the centerline of the wrist pin.

TCCS3210

Fig. 210 Measure the piston's outer diameter, perpendicular to the wrist pin, with a micrometer

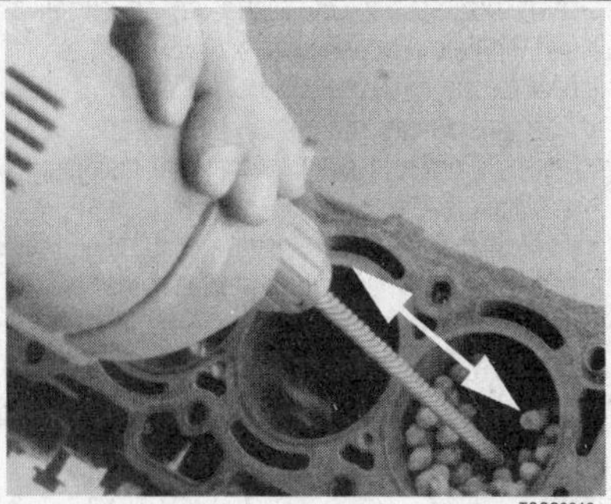
TCCS3913

Fig. 211 Use a ball type cylinder hone to remove any glaze and provide a new surface for seating the piston rings

TCCS3814

Fig. 212 Most pistons are marked to indicate positioning in the engine (usually a mark means the side facing the front)

There should not be any excessive play evident between the piston and the pin. If there are C-clips retaining the pin in the piston then you have wrist pin bushings in the rods. There should not be any excessive play between the wrist pin and the rod bushing. Normal clearance for the wrist pin is approx. 0.001–0.002 in. (0.025mm–0.051mm).

Use a micrometer and measure the diameter of the piston, perpendicular to the wrist pin, on the skirt. Compare the reading to its original cylinder measurement obtained earlier. The difference between the two readings is the piston-to-wall clearance. If the clearance is within specifications, the piston may be used as is. If the piston is out of specification, but the bore is not, you will need a new piston. If both are out of specification, you will need the cylinder rebored and oversize pistons installed. Generally if two or more pistons/bores are out of specification, it is best to rebore the entire block and purchase a complete set of oversize pistons.

### *CONNECTING RODS*

You should have the connecting rod checked for straightness at a machine shop. If the connecting rod is bent, it will unevenly wear the bearing and piston, as well as place greater stress on these components. Any bent or twisted connecting rods must be replaced. If the rods are straight and the wrist pin clearance is within specifications, then only the bearing end of the rod need be checked. Place the connecting rod into a vice, with the bearing inserts in place, install the cap to the rod and torque the fasteners to specifications. Use a telescoping gauge and carefully measure the inside diameter of the bearings. Compare this reading to the rods original crankshaft journal diameter measurement. The difference is the oil clearance. If the oil clearance is not within specifications, install new bearings in the rod and take another measurement. If the clearance is still out of specifications, and the crankshaft is not, the rod will need to be reconditioned by a machine shop.

**➡You can also use Plastigage® to check the bearing clearances. The assembling section has complete instructions on its use.**

### Camshaft

Inspect the camshaft and lifters/followers as described earlier in this section.

### Bearings

All of the engine bearings should be visually inspected for wear and/or damage. The bearing should look evenly worn all around with no deep scores or pits. If the bearing is severely worn, scored, pitted or heat blued, then the bearing, and the components that use it, should be brought to a machine shop for inspection. Full-circle bearings (used on most camshafts, auxiliary shafts, balance shafts, etc.) require specialized tools for removal and installation, and should be brought to a machine shop for service.

### Oil Pump

**➡The oil pump is responsible for providing constant lubrication to the whole engine and so it is recommended that a new oil pump be installed when rebuilding the engine.**

Completely disassemble the oil pump and thoroughly clean all of the components. Inspect the oil pump gears and housing for wear and/or damage. Insure that the pressure relief valve operates properly and there is no binding or sticking due to varnish or debris. If all of the parts are in proper working condition, lubricate the gears and relief valve, and assemble the pump.

## REFINISHING

**➧ See Figure 211**

Almost all engine block refinishing must be performed by a machine shop. If the cylinders are not to be rebored, then the cylinder glaze can be removed with a ball hone. When removing cylinder glaze with a ball hone, use a light or penetrating type oil to lubricate the hone. Do not allow the hone to run dry as this may cause excessive scoring of the cylinder bores and wear on the hone. If new pistons are required, they will need to be installed to the connecting rods. This should be performed by a machine shop as the pistons must be installed in the correct relationship to the rod or engine damage can occur.

### Pistons and Connecting Rods

**➧ See Figure 212**

Only pistons with the wrist pin retained by C-clips are serviceable by the home-mechanic. Press fit pistons require special presses and/or heaters to remove/install the connecting rod and should only be performed by a machine shop.

All pistons will have a mark indicating the direction to the front of the engine and the must be installed into the engine in that manner. Usually it is a notch or arrow on the top of the piston, or it may be the letter F cast or stamped into the piston.

### *C-CLIP TYPE PISTONS*

1. Note the location of the forward mark on the piston and mark the connecting rod in relation.
2. Remove the C-clips from the piston and withdraw the wrist pin.

**➡Varnish build-up or C-clip groove burrs may increase the difficulty of removing the wrist pin. If necessary, use a punch or drift to carefully tap the wrist pin out.**

3. Insure that the wrist pin bushing in the connecting rod is usable, and lubricate it with assembly lube.
4. Remove the wrist pin from the new piston and lubricate the pin bores on the piston.
5. Align the forward marks on the piston and the connecting rod and install the wrist pin.
6. The new C-clips will have a flat and a rounded side to them. Install both C-clips with the flat side facing out.
7. Repeat all of the steps for each piston being replaced.

## ASSEMBLY

Before you begin assembling the engine, first give yourself a clean, dirt free work area. Next, clean every engine component again. The key to a good assembly is cleanliness.

Mount the engine block into the engine stand and wash it one last time using water and detergent (dishwashing detergent works well). While washing it, scrub the cylinder bores with a soft bristle brush and thoroughly clean all of the oil passages. Completely dry the engine and spray the entire assembly down with an anti-rust solution such as WD-40® or similar product. Take a clean lint-free rag and wipe up any excess anti-rust solution from the bores, bearing saddles, etc. Repeat the final cleaning process on the crankshaft. Replace any freeze or oil galley plugs which were removed during disassembly.

### Crankshaft

➧ See Figures 213, 214, 215 and 216

1. Remove the main bearing inserts from the block and bearing caps.
2. If the crankshaft main bearing journals have been refinished to a definite undersize, install the correct undersize bearing. Be sure that the bearing inserts and bearing bores are clean. Foreign material under inserts will distort bearing and cause failure.
3. Place the upper main bearing inserts in bores with tang in slot.

**➡The oil holes in the bearing inserts must be aligned with the oil holes in the cylinder block.**

4. Install the lower main bearing inserts in bearing caps.
5. Clean the mating surfaces of block and rear main bearing cap.
6. Carefully lower the crankshaft into place. Be careful not to damage bearing surfaces.
7. Check the clearance of each main bearing by using the following procedure:
   a. Place a piece of Plastigage® or its equivalent, on bearing surface across full width of bearing cap and about 1/4 in. off center.
   b. Install cap and tighten bolts to specifications. Do not turn crankshaft while Plastigage® is in place.
   c. Remove the cap. Using the supplied Plastigage® scale, check width of Plastigage® at widest point to get maximum clearance. Difference between readings is taper of journal.
   d. If clearance exceeds specified limits, try a 0.001 in. or 0.002 in. undersize bearing in combination with the standard bearing. Bearing clearance must be within specified limits. If standard and 0.002 in. undersize bearing does not bring clearance within desired limits, refinish crankshaft journal, then install undersize bearings.
8. Install the rear main seal.
9. After the bearings have been fitted, apply a light coat of engine oil to the journals and bearings. Install the rear main bearing cap. Install all bearing caps except the thrust bearing cap. Be sure that main bearing caps are installed in original locations. Tighten the bearing cap bolts to specifications.
10. Install the thrust bearing cap with bolts finger-tight.
11. Pry the crankshaft forward against the thrust surface of upper half of bearing.
12. Hold the crankshaft forward and pry the thrust bearing cap to the rear. This aligns the thrust surfaces of both halves of the bearing.
13. Retain the forward pressure on the crankshaft. Tighten the cap bolts to specifications.
14. Measure the crankshaft end-play as follows:
   a. Mount a dial gauge to the engine block and position the tip of the gauge to read from the crankshaft end.
   b. Carefully pry the crankshaft toward the rear of the engine and hold it there while you zero the gauge.
   c. Carefully pry the crankshaft toward the front of the engine and read the gauge.
   d. Confirm that the reading is within specifications. If not, install a new thrust bearing and repeat the procedure. If the reading is still out of

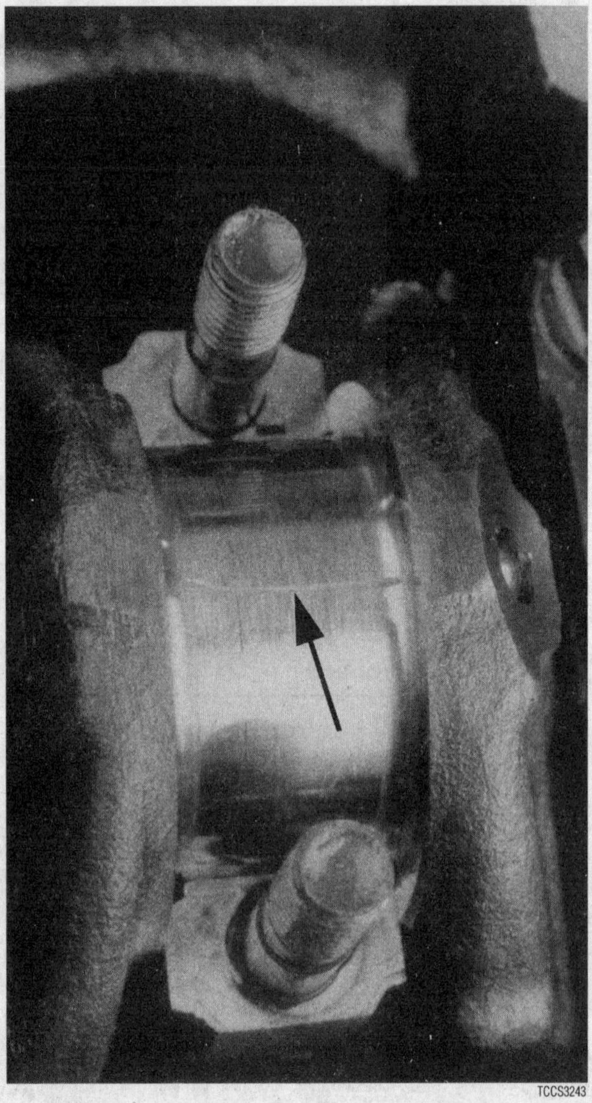
TCCS3243

Fig. 213 Apply a strip of gauging material to the bearing journal, then install and torque the cap

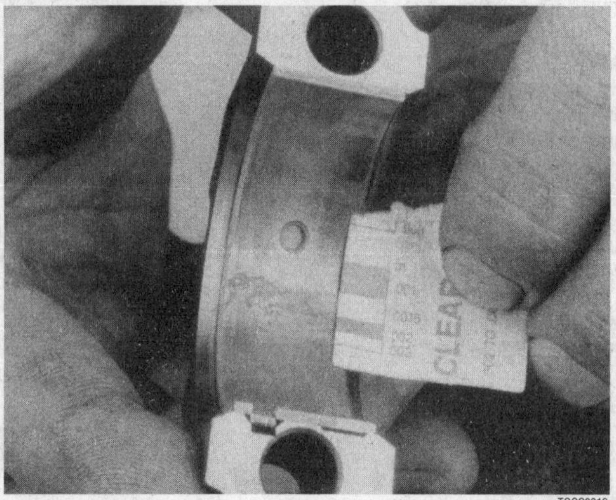
TCCS3912

Fig. 214 After the cap is removed again, use the scale supplied with the gauging material to check the clearance

TCCS3805

Fig. 215 A dial gauge may be used to check crankshaft end-play

**Fig. 216 Carefully pry the crankshaft back and forth while reading the dial gauge for end-play**

**Fig. 217 Checking the piston ring-to-ring groove side clearance using the ring and a feeler gauge**

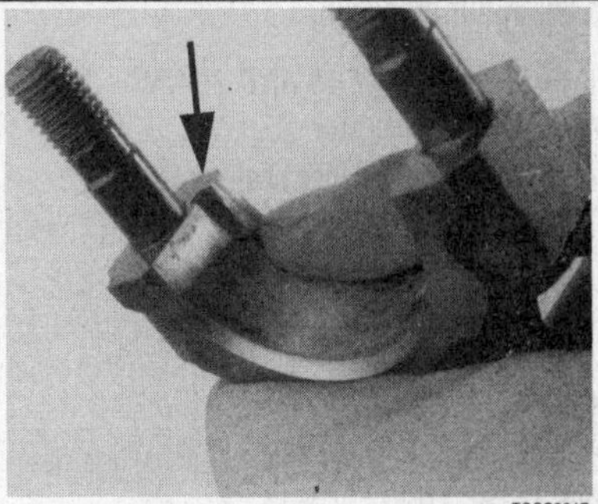


**Fig. 218 The notch on the side of the bearing cap matches the tang on the bearing insert**

specifications with a new bearing, have a machine shop inspect the thrust surfaces of the crankshaft, and if possible, repair it.

15. Rotate the crankshaft so as to position the first rod journal to the bottom of its stroke.

### Pistons and Connecting Rods

**➧ See Figures 217, 218, 219 and 220**

1. Before installing the piston/connecting rod assembly, oil the pistons, piston rings and the cylinder walls with light engine oil. Install connecting rod bolt protectors or rubber hose onto the connecting rod bolts/studs. Also perform the following:
   a. Select the proper ring set for the size cylinder bore.
   b. Position the ring in the bore in which it is going to be used.
   c. Push the ring down into the bore area where normal ring wear is not encountered.
   d. Use the head of the piston to position the ring in the bore so that the ring is square with the cylinder wall. Use caution to avoid damage to the ring or cylinder bore.
   e. Measure the gap between the ends of the ring with a feeler gauge. Ring gap in a worn cylinder is normally greater than specification. If the ring gap is greater than the specified limits, try an oversize ring set.
   f. Check the ring side clearance of the compression rings with a feeler gauge inserted between the ring and its lower land according to specification. The gauge should slide freely around the entire ring circumference without binding. Any wear that occurs will form a step at the inner portion of the lower land. If the lower lands have high steps, the piston should be replaced.
2. Unless new pistons are installed, be sure to install the pistons in the cylinders from which they were removed. The numbers on the connecting rod and bearing cap must be on the same side when installed in the cylinder bore. If a connecting rod is ever transposed from one engine or cylinder to another, new bearings should be fitted and the connecting rod should be numbered to correspond with the new cylinder number. The notch on the piston head goes toward the front of the engine.
3. Install all of the rod bearing inserts into the rods and caps.
4. Install the rings to the pistons. Install the oil control ring first, then the second compression ring and finally the top compression ring. Use a piston ring expander tool to aid in installation and to help reduce the chance of breakage.
5. Make sure the ring gaps are properly spaced around the circumference of the piston. Fit a piston ring compressor around the piston and slide the piston and connecting rod assembly down into the cylinder bore, pushing it in with the wooden hammer handle. Push the piston down until it is only slightly below the top of the cylinder bore. Guide the connecting rod onto the crankshaft bearing journal carefully, to avoid damaging the crankshaft.
6. Check the bearing clearance of all the rod bearings, fitting them to the crankshaft bearing journals. Follow the procedure in the crankshaft installation above.
7. After the bearings have been fitted, apply a light coating of assembly oil to the journals and bearings.
8. Turn the crankshaft until the appropriate bearing journal is at the bottom of its stroke, then push the piston assembly all the way down until the connecting rod bearing seats on the crankshaft journal. Be careful not to allow the bearing cap screws to strike the crankshaft bearing journals and damage them.
9. After the piston and connecting rod assemblies have been installed, check the connecting rod side clearance on each crankshaft journal.
10. Prime and install the oil pump and the oil pump intake tube.

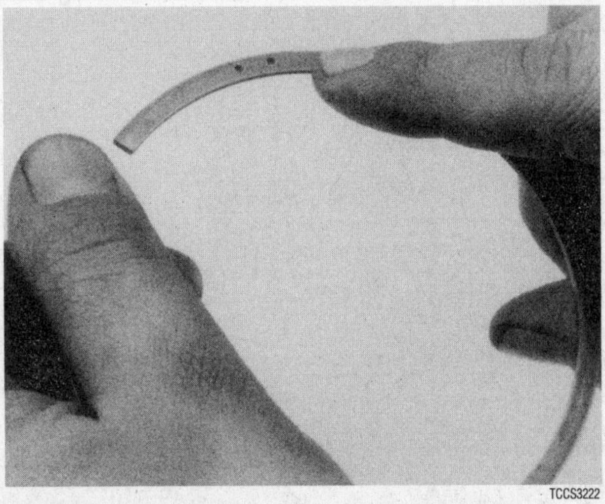


**Fig. 219 Most rings are marked to show which side of the ring should face up when installed to the piston**

**Fig. 220 Install the piston and rod assembly into the block using a ring compressor and the handle of a hammer**

### 3.8L and 5.0L Engines

#### *CAMSHAFT, LIFTERS AND TIMING ASSEMBLY*

1. Install the balance shaft on the 3.8L engine.
2. Install the camshaft.
3. Install the lifters/followers into their bores.
4. Install the timing gears/chain assembly.

#### *CYLINDER HEAD(S)*

1. Install the cylinder head(s) using new gaskets.
2. Assemble the rest of the valve train (pushrods and rocker arms and/or shafts).

### 4.6L Engines

#### *CYLINDER HEAD(S)*

1. Install the cylinder head(s) using new gaskets.
2. Install the timing sprockets/gears and the belt/chain assemblies.

### Engine Covers and Components

Install the timing cover(s) and oil pan. Refer to your notes and drawings made prior to disassembly and install all of the components that were removed. Install the engine into the vehicle.

## Engine Start-up and Break-in

### STARTING THE ENGINE

Now that the engine is installed and every wire and hose is properly connected, go back and double check that all coolant and vacuum hoses are connected. Check that your oil drain plug is installed and properly tightened. If not already done, install a new oil filter onto the engine. Fill the crankcase with the proper amount and grade of engine oil. Fill the cooling system with a 50/50 mixture of coolant/water.

1. Connect the vehicle battery.
2. Start the engine. Keep your eye on your oil pressure indicator; if it does not indicate oil pressure within 10 seconds of starting, turn the vehicle off.

**WARNING**

**Damage to the engine can result if it is allowed to run with no oil pressure. Check the engine oil level to make sure that it is full. Check for any leaks and if found, repair the leaks before continuing. If there is still no indication of oil pressure, you may need to prime the system.**

3. Confirm that there are no fluid leaks (oil or other).
4. Allow the engine to reach normal operating temperature (the upper radiator hose will be hot to the touch).
5. At this point you can perform any necessary checks or adjustments, such as checking the ignition timing.
6. Install any remaining components or body panels which were removed.

### BREAKING IT IN

Make the first miles on the new engine, easy ones. Vary the speed but do not accelerate hard. Most importantly, do not lug the engine, and avoid sustained high speeds until at least 100 miles. Check the engine oil and coolant levels frequently. Expect the engine to use a little oil until the rings seat. Change the oil and filter at 500 miles, 1500 miles, then every 3000 miles past that.

### KEEP IT MAINTAINED

Now that you have just gone through all of that hard work, keep yourself from doing it all over again by thoroughly maintaining it. Not that you may not have maintained it before, heck you could have had one to two hundred thousand miles on it before doing this. However, you may have bought the vehicle used, and the previous owner did not keep up on maintenance. Which is why you just went through all of that hard work. See?

## 3.8L ENGINE TORQUE SPECIFICATIONS

| Components | English | Metric |
|---|---|---|
| Accelerator cable mounting bracket | 15-22 ft. lbs. | 20-30 Nm |
| Balance shaft thrust blate bolt | 70-124 in. lbs. | 8-14 Nm |
| Camshaft sprocket bolts | 30-36 ft. lbs. | 40-50 Nm |
| Camshaft thrust plate | 6-10 lb.ft. | 8-14 Nm |
| Connecting rod nuts | 31-36 lbs. | 41-49 Nm |
| Crankshaft main bearing cap bolts | 65-81 ft. lbs. | 88-110 Nm |
| Crankshaft damper and pulley to crankshaft bolts | 103-132 ft. lbs. | 140-180 Nm |
| Crankshaft pulley to damper bolt | 19-28 ft. lbs. | 26-38 Nm |
| Cylinder head bolts. ① | | |
| 1st step | 37 ft. lbs. | 50 Nm |
| 2nd step | 45 ft. lbs. | 60 Nm |
| 3rd step | 52 lb ft. | 70 Nm |
| 4th step | 59 lb ft. | 80 Nm |
| Engine front cover-to-cylinder block bolts | 15-22 ft. lbs. | 20-30 Nm |
| EGR valve-to-intake manifold bolts | 15-22 ft. lbs. | 20-30 Nm |
| Exhaust manifold bolt | 15-22 ft. lbs. | 20-30 Nm |
| Exhaust pipe to manifold nuts | 16-24 ft. lbs. | 21-32 Nm |
| Engine oil dipstick tube bolt | 15-22 ft. lbs. | 20-30 Nm |
| Engine-to-automatic transaxle bolts | 40-50 ft. lbs. | 55-68 Nm |
| Wire support bracket retaining nuts | 15-22 ft. lbs. | 20-30 Nm |
| Flywheel bolts | | |
| Automatic transaxle | 54-64 ft. lbs. | 73-87 Nm |
| Upper intake manifold | 19-28 ft. lbs. | 26-38 Nm |
| Intake manifold-to-cylinder head retaining bolts | | |
| Tighten in two steps | | |
| (a) | 8 ft. lbs | 11 Nm |
| (b) | 11 ft. lbs. | 15 Nm |
| Oil pan bolts | 80-106 inch lbs. | 9-12 Nm |
| Oil pan drain plug | 15-25 ft. lbs. | 20-34 Nm |
| Low oil level sensor | 18-25 ft. lbs. | 25-34 Nm |
| Oil pressure sender-to-engine front cover | 12-18 ft. lbs. | 16-24 Nm |
| Power steering pump bolts | 30-45 ft. lbs. | 41-61 Nm |
| Spark plugs | 6-10 ft. lbs. | 7-14 Nm |
| Thermostat water outlet bolts | 15-22 ft. lbs. | 20-30 Nm |
| Throttle body retaining nuts | 15-22 ft. lbs. | 20-30 Nm |
| Transaxle mount retaining nuts | 50-70 ft. lbs | 68-95 Nm |
| Rocker arm fulcrum-to-cylinder head | | |
| Tighten in two steps | | |
| (a) | 8 ft. lbs. | 11 Nm |
| (b) | 11 ft. lbs. | 15 Nm |
| Valve cover bolts | 80-106 inch lbs.. | 9-12 Nm |
| Water pump bolts | 15-22 ft. lbs. | 20-30 Nm |
| Water pump pulley bolts | 12-18 ft. lbs. | 16-24 Nm |

## 4.6L ENGINE TORQUE SPECIFICATIONS

| Components | English Specifications | Metric Specifications |
|---|---|---|
| A/C compressor bolts | 15-22 ft. lbs. | 20-30 Nm |
| Alternator bolts | 34 ft. lbs. | 47 Nm |
| Camshaft journal cap bolts ① | 71-106 inch lbs. | 8-12 Nm |
| Camshaft position sensor retaining screw | 71-106 inch lbs. | 8-12 Nm |
| Camshaft rear oil seal retainer bolts | 71-106 inch lbs. | 8-12 Nm |

93143C05

## 4.6L ENGINE TORQUE SPECIFICATIONS

| Components | English Specifications | Metric Specifications |
|---|---|---|
| Step 2 | Tighten the bolts an additional 85-95° | |
| Crankshaft position sensor retaining screw | 71-106 inch lbs. | 8-12 Nm |
| Crankshaft pulley bolt | | |
| Step 1 | 89 ft. lbs. | 120 Nm |
| Step 2 | Loosen the bolt one full turn | |
| Step 3 | 35-39 ft. lbs. | 47-53 Nm |
| Step 4 | Tighten the bolts an additional 85-95° | |
| Cylinder head bolts ① | | |
| Step 1 | 27-32 ft. lbs. | 37-43 Nm |
| Step 2 | Tighten the bolts an additional 85-95° | |
| Step 3 | Loosen the bolts 85-95° | |
| Step 4 | 27-32 ft. lbs. | 37-43 Nm |
| Step 5 | Tighten the bolts an additional 85-95° | |
| Step 6 | Tighten the bolts an additional 85-95° | |
| EGR valve | 15-22 ft. lbs. | 20-30 Nm |
| EGR valve-to-exhaust manifold tube nut | 26-33 ft. lbs. | 35-45 Nm |
| Engine lifting eye bolts | 29-40 ft. lbs. | 40-55 Nm |
| Engine oil dipstick tube bolt | 71-106 inch lbs. | 8-12 Nm |
| Engine-to-transaxle bolts | 25-34 ft. lbs. | 34-46 Nm |
| Exhaust manifold heat shield bolts | 71-106 inch lbs. | 8-12 Nm |
| Exhaust manifold nuts ① | 13-16 ft. lbs. | 17-21 Nm |
| Flywheel bolts | 54-64 ft. lbs. | 73-87 Nm |
| Front engine support isolator nuts and bolt | 50-68 ft. lbs. | 67-93 Nm |
| Lower cylinder block ① | ② | |
| Lower intake manifold bolts ① | 71-106 inch lbs. | 8-12 Nm |
| Lower radiator support | 71-97 inch lbs. | 8-11 Nm |
| Oil pan baffle nuts | 15-22 ft. lbs. | 20-30 Nm |
| Oil pan bolts ① | 15-22 ft. lbs. | 20-30 Nm |
| Oil pan drain plug | 16-22 ft. lbs. | 22-30 Nm |
| Oil pan-to-transaxle bolts | 25-34 ft. lbs. | 34-46 Nm |
| Oil pressure sender | 9-12 ft. lbs. | 12-16 Nm |
| Oil pump bolts ① | 71-106 inch lbs. | 8-12 Nm |
| Oil pump screen cover and tube bolts | 71-106 inch lbs. | 8-12 Nm |
| Oil pump screen cover and tube support-main bearing retaining nut | 15-22 ft. lbs. | 20-30 Nm |
| Oil separator bolt | 71-106 inch lbs. | 8-12 Nm |
| Power steering pump bolts | 15-22 ft. lbs. | 20-30 Nm |
| Spark plugs | 7-15 ft. lbs. | 9-20 Nm |
| Spark plug cover bolts | 62 inch lbs. | 7 Nm |
| Splash shield assembly | 62-97 inch lbs. | 7-11 Nm |
| Thermostat water outlet | 15-22 ft. lbs. | 20-30 Nm |
| Throttle body bolts | 71-106 inch lbs. | 8-12 Nm |
| Timing chain guide retaining bolts | 15-22 ft. lbs. | 20-30 Nm |
| Timing chain tensioner retaining bolts | 15-22 ft. lbs. | 20-30 Nm |
| Timing cover bolts ① | 15-22 ft. lbs. | 20-30 Nm |
| Torque converter inspection cover bolt | 28-38 ft. lbs. | 38-51 Nm |
| Transaxle oil cooler line bolts | 71-106 inch lbs. | 8-12 Nm |
| Water crossover bolts | 71-106 inch lbs. | 8-12 Nm |
| Water pump-to-housing bolts | 16-18 ft. lbs. | 22-25 Nm |
| Water pump housing-to-cylinder head bolts | | |
| Step 1 | 11-13 ft. lbs. | 15-18 Nm |
| Step 2 | Tighten the bolts an additional 85-95° | |

## 5.0L ENGINE TORQUE SPECIFICATIONS

| Components | English Specifications | Metric Specifications |
|---|---|---|
| Belt driven engine fan | | |
| Fan-to-fan clutch bolts | 12-18 ft. lbs. | 16-25 Nm |
| Fan clutch shaft-to-water pump | 15-22 ft. lbs. | 20-30 Nm |

93143C06

## 5.0L ENGINE TORQUE SPECIFICATIONS

| Components | English Specifications | Metric Specifications |
|---|---|---|
| Camshaft | | |
| Thrust plate bolts | 9-12 ft. lbs. | 12-16 Nm |
| Connecting rod nuts | 19-24 ft. lbs. | 26-32 Nm |
| Crankshaft damper retaining bolt | 70-90 ft. lbs. | 95-122 Nm |
| Crankshaft main bearing bolts | 60-70 ft. lbs. | 81-95 Nm |
| Cylinder head bolts | ① | ① |
| EGR tube-to-valve/manifold nut | 26-33 ft. lbs. | 35-45 Nm |
| EGR valve-to-manifold bolts | 15-22 ft. lbs. | 20-30 Nm |
| Electric cooling fan retaining screws | 27-53 inch lbs. | 3-6 Nm |
| Engine mounts | | |
| Through-bolts | 80 ft. lbs. | 108 Nm |
| Nuts | 70 ft. lbs. | 95 Nm |
| Engine-to-transmission retaining bolts | 50 ft. lbs. | 68 Nm |
| Exhaust manifold retaining bolts | 18-24 ft. lbs. | 24-32 Nm |
| Exhaust manifold-to-exhaust pipe/catalytic converter bolts | 20-30 ft. lbs. | 27-41 Nm |
| Flywheel/flexplate retaining bolts | 75-85 ft. lbs. | 103-115 Nm |
| Intake manifold retaining bolts | | |
| Lower intake | 23-25 ft. lbs. | 31-34 Nm |
| Upper Intake | 12-18 ft. lbs. | 16-25 Nm |
| Oil pan retaining bolts | 7-10 ft. lbs. | 9-14 Nm |
| Oil pump pickup tube and screen retaining bolts | 12-18 ft. lbs. | 16-25 Nm |
| Oil pump retaining bolts | 22-32 ft. lbs. | 30-43 Nm |
| Rocker arm retaining bolts | 18-25 ft. lbs. | 25-34 Nm |
| Thermostat housing retaining bolts | 12-18 ft. lbs. | 16-24 Nm |
| Timing cover retaining bolts | | |
| Oil pan-to-timing cover retaining bolts | 9-11 ft. lbs. | 12-15 Nm |
| Timing cover-to-engine block retaining bolts | 15-18 ft. lbs. | 20-24 Nm |
| Torque converter retaining nuts | 30 ft. lbs. | 41 Nm |
| Valve cover retaining bolts | 10-13 ft. lbs. | 14-18 Nm |
| Water pump bolts | 18 ft. lbs. | 25 Nm |
| Water pump pulley-to-water pump bolts | 12-18 ft. lbs. | 16-25 Nm |

VCT: Variable Cam Timing

① Refer to the procedure for the tightening sequence

② Step 1: Tighten the bolts in sequence to 26-44 inch lbs. (3-5 Nm)

Step 2: Push the crankshaft rearward and seat the thrust washer

Step 3: Tighten fasteners 1-8 to 16-21 ft. lbs. (22-28 Nm)

Step 4: Tighten fasteners 9-16 to 27-32 ft. lbs. (37-43 Nm)

Step 5: Rotate fasteners 1-16 an additional 85-95 degrees

Step 6: Tighten fasteners 17-22 to 15-22 ft. lbs. (20-30 Nm)

# 4

# DRIVEABILITY AND EMISSIONS CONTROLS


**EMISSION CONTROLS 4-2**
POSITIVE CRANKCASE VENTILATION SYSTEM 4-2
OPERATION 4-2
TESTING 4-2
REMOVAL & INSTALLATION 4-2
EVAPORATIVE EMISSION CONTROLS 4-2
OPERATION 4-2
REMOVAL & INSTALLATION 4-3
EXHAUST GAS RECIRCULATION SYSTEM 4-3
OPERATION 4-3
COMPONENT TESTING 4-4
REMOVAL & INSTALLATION 4-4
**ELECTRONIC ENGINE CONTROLS 4-6**
POWERTRAIN CONTROL MODULE (PCM) 4-6
OPERATION 4-6
OXYGEN SENSOR 4-6
OPERATION 4-6
TESTING 4-7
REMOVAL & INSTALLATION 4-7
IDLE AIR CONTROL VALVE 4-8
OPERATION 4-8
TESTING 4-8
REMOVAL & INSTALLATION 4-8
ENGINE COOLANT TEMPERATURE (ECT) SENSOR 4-8
OPERATION 4-8
TESTING 4-8
REMOVAL & INSTALLATION 4-9
INTAKE AIR TEMPERATURE SENSOR 4-10
OPERATION 4-10
TESTING 4-10
REMOVAL & INSTALLATION 4-10
MASS AIRFLOW SENSOR 4-10
OPERATION 4-10
TESTING 4-11
REMOVAL & INSTALLATION 4-11
MANIFOLD AIR PRESSURE (MAP) SENSOR 4-11
OPERATION 4-11
TESTING 4-11
REMOVAL & INSTALLATION 4-12
THROTTLE POSITION SENSOR 4-12
OPERATION 4-12
TESTING 4-12
REMOVAL & INSTALLATION 4-12
CAMSHAFT POSITION SENSOR 4-12
TESTING 4-12
REMOVAL & INSTALLATION 4-12
CRANKSHAFT POSITION SENSOR 4-13
OPERATION 4-13
TESTING 4-13
REMOVAL & INSTALLATION 4-13
**COMPONENT LOCATIONS 4-14**
**TROUBLE CODES —EEC-IV SYSTEM 4-17**
GENERAL INFORMATION 4-17
FAILURE MODE EFFECTS MANAGEMENT (FMEM) 4-17
HARDWARE LIMITED OPERATION STRATEGY (HLOS) 4-17
DIAGNOSTIC LINK CONNECTOR 4-17
HAND-HELD SCAN TOOLS 4-17
ELECTRICAL TOOLS 4-17
READING CODES 4-18
VISUAL INSPECTION 4-18
ELECTRONIC TESTING 4-18
CLEARING CODES 4-21
CONTINUOUS MEMORY CODES 4-21
KEEP ALIVE MEMORY 4-21
**TROUBLE CODES —EEC-V SYSTEM (OBD-II) 4-21**
GENERAL INFORMATION 4-21
MALFUNCTION INDICATOR LAMP 4-22
DATA LINK CONNECTOR 4-22
ELECTRICAL TOOLS 4-22
READING CODES 4-22
CLEARING CODES 4-22
CONTINUOUS MEMORY CODES 4-22
KEEP ALIVE MEMORY 4-22
EEC-V DIAGNOSTIC TROUBLE CODES (DTC'S) 4-22
**VACUUM DIAGRAMS 4-27**
**COMPONENT LOCATIONS**
COMMON EMISSIONS AND ELECTRONIC ENGINE CONTROL COMPONENT LOCATIONS—3.8L ENGINE 4-14
COMMON EMISSIONS AND ELECTRONIC ENGINE CONTROL COMPONENT LOCATIONS—4.6L ENGINE 4-15
COMMON EMISSIONS AND ELECTRONIC ENGINE CONTROL COMPONENT LOCATIONS—5.0L ENGINE 4-16



EMISSION CONTROLS 4-2
ELECTRONIC ENGINE CONTROLS 4-6
COMPONENT LOCATIONS 4-14
TROUBLE CODES—EEC IV SYSTEM 4-17
TROUBLE CODES—EEC V SYSTEM (OBD-II) 4-21
VACUUM DIAGRAMS 4-27

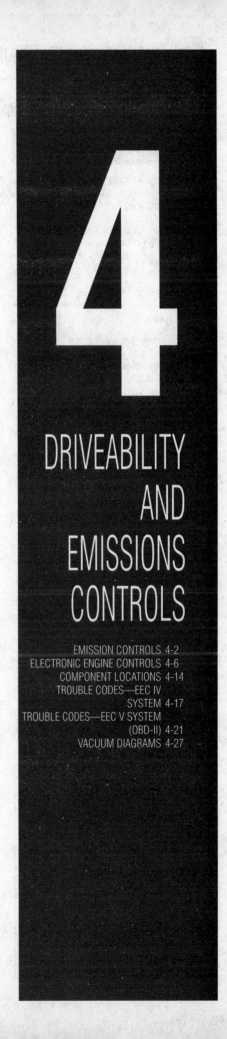

# EMISSION CONTROLS

## Positive Crankcase Ventilation System

The Positive Crankcase Ventilation (PCV) system is used on all vehicles covered by this manual. The PCV system vents harmful combustion blow-by fumes from the engine crankcase into the engine air intake for burning with the fuel and air mixture. The PCV system maximizes oil cleanliness by venting moisture and corrosive fumes from the crankcase.

### OPERATION

**➧ See Figure 1**

Your car is equipped with a closed Positive Crankcase Ventilation (PCV) system. The PCV system vents crankcase gases into the engine air intake where they are burned with the air/fuel mixture. The PCV system keeps pollutants from being released into the atmosphere, and also helps to keep the engine oil clean, by ridding the crankcase of moisture and corrosive fumes. The PCV system consists of the PCV valve, a closed oil fill cap and the various connecting hoses.

The PCV system recycles crankcase gases as follows: When the engine is running, clean filtered air is drawn into the crankcase through the intake air filter. As the air passes through the crankcase, it picks up the combustion gases and carries them out of the crankcase, up through the PCV valve and into the intake manifold. After they enter the intake manifold, they are drawn into the combustion chamber and burned.

The most critical component of the PCV system is the PCV valve. The PCV valve regulates the amount of ventilating air and blow-by gas to the intake manifold and also prevents backfire from traveling into the crankcase, avoiding the explosion of crankcase gases. At low engine speeds, the PCV valve is partially closed, limiting the flow of gases into the intake manifold. As engine speed increases, the valve opens to admit greater quantities of gases into the intake manifold.

If the PCV valve becomes blocked or plugged, crankcase gases will not be able to escape by the normal route. Since these gases are under pressure, they will seek an alternate route, which is usually an oil seal or gasket. As the gases escape, an oil leak will be created.

Besides causing oil leaks, a clogged PCV valve will also allow gases to remain in the crankcase for an extended period, promoting the formation of sludge in the engine.

### TESTING

1. Visually inspect the PCV valve hose and the fresh air supply hose and their attaching nipples or grommets for splits, cuts, damage, clogging, or restrictions. Repair or replace, as necessary.
2. If the hoses pass inspection, remove the PCV valve from its mounting grommet. Shake the PCV valve and listen or feel for the rattle of the valve plunger within the valve body. If the valve plunger does not rattle, the PCV valve must be cleaned or replaced. If the valve plunger rattles, the PCV valve is okay; reinstall it.
3. Start the engine and bring it to normal operating temperature. Remove the fresh air supply hose from the air cleaner or air outlet tube. Place a stiff piece of paper over the hose end and wait 1 minute. If vacuum holds the paper in place, the system is okay.
4. On the 4.6L engine, the PCV system is connected with the evaporative emission system. If the paper is not held in place, disconnect the evaporative hose, cap the connector and retest. If vacuum now holds the paper in place, the problem is in the evaporative emission system.
5. If the paper is not held by vacuum, check the fresh air and PCV hoses for leaks or loose connections. Also, check for a loose fitting oil fill cap or loose dipstick. Correct as required until vacuum can be felt at the end of the supply hose.

**➡If air pressure and oil or sludge is present at the end of the fresh air supply hose, the engine has excessive blow-by and cylinder bore or piston ring wear.**

### REMOVAL & INSTALLATION

Refer to Section 1 for removal and installation of the PCV valve.

## Evaporative Emission Controls

### OPERATION

The evaporative emission control system prevents the escape of fuel vapors to the atmosphere under hot soak and engine off conditions by storing the vapors in a carbon canister. Then, with the engine warm and running, the system controls the purging of stored vapors from the canister to the engine, where they are efficiently burned.

Evaporative emission control components consist of the carbon canister, purge valve(s), vapor valve, rollover vent valve, check valve and the necessary lines. All vehicles may not share all components.

#### OBD-II EVAP System Monitor

Some of the models covered in this manual have added system components due to the EVAP system monitor incorporated in the OBD-II engine control system. A pressure sensor is mounted on the fuel tank which measures pressure inside the tank, and a purge flow sensor measures the flow of the gases from the canister into the engine. The purge valve is now called the Vapor Management Valve (VMV). It performs the same functions as the purge valve, however it looks slightly different. A canister vent solenoid is mounted on the canister, taking the place of the vent cap, providing a source of fresh air to the canister.

The PCM can store trouble codes for EVAP system performance, a list of the codes is provided later in this section. Normal testing procedure can be used, see EVAP System Component Testing in this Section.

#### Carbon Canister

**➧ See Figure 2**

The carbon canister contains vapor absorbent material to facilitate the storage of fuel vapors. Fuel vapors flow from the fuel tank to the canister, where they are stored until purged to the engine for burning.

#### Purge Control Valve

**➧ See Figure 3**

The purge valves control the flow of fuel vapor from the carbon canister to the engine. Purge

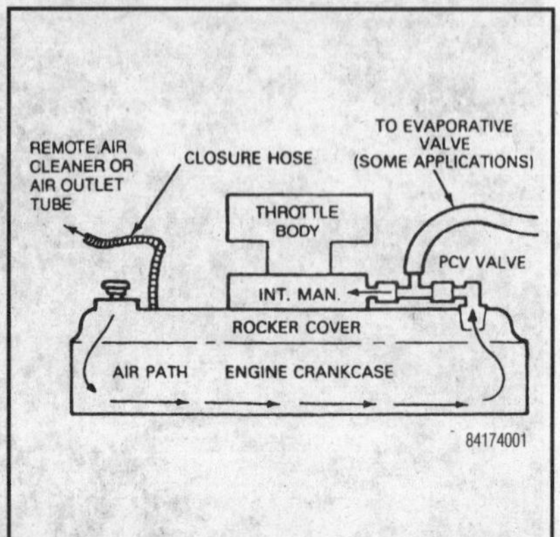


**Fig. 1 PCV system functional diagram**

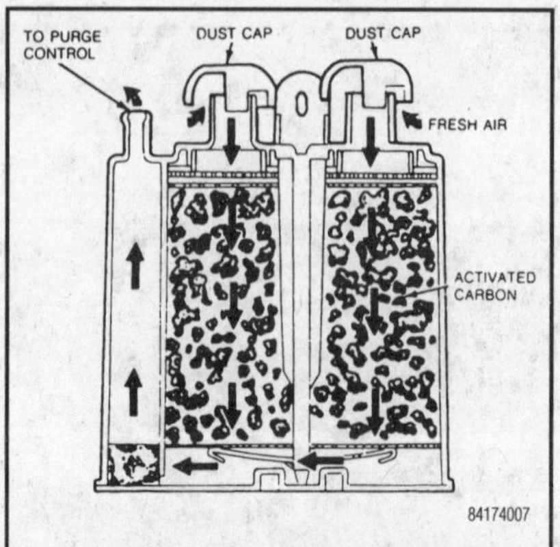


**Fig. 2 Cross-section of a carbon canister**

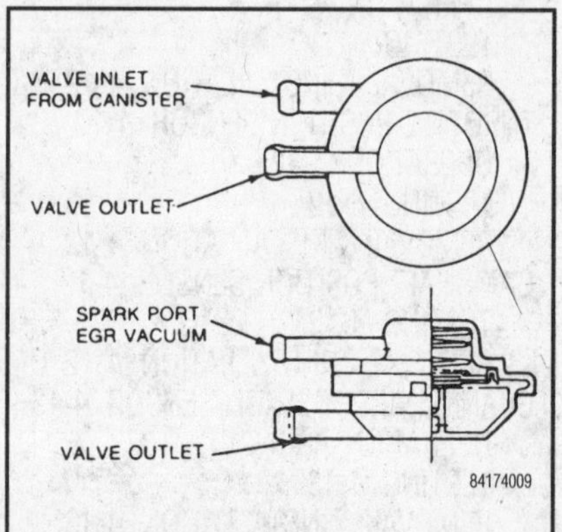


**Fig. 3 Purge control valve**

valves are either vacuum or electrically controlled. When electrically controlled, a purge valve is known as a purge solenoid. A vehicle may be equipped with a vacuum purge valve or purge solenoid or a combination of the two. Purging occurs when the engine is at operating temperature and off idle.

**Fuel Tank Vapor Orifice and Roll over Valve Assembly**

**▶ See Figure 4**

Fuel vapor in the fuel tank is vented to the carbon canister through the vapor valve assembly. The valve is mounted in a rubber grommet at a central location in the upper surface of the fuel tank. A vapor space between the fuel level and the tank upper surface is combined with a small orifice and float shut-off valve in the vapor valve assembly to prevent liquid fuel from passing to the carbon canister. The vapor space also allows for thermal expansion of the fuel. The vapor valve incorporates the rollover valve. In the event of a vehicle rollover, the valve blocks the vapor line automatically to prevent fuel leakage.

The check valve is located in the fuel filler cap or on the underside of the vehicle. Its function is to protect the fuel tank from heat build-up rupture and cool-down collapse by allowing air to pass in or out of the tank to equalize pressure. On cool-down, air enters either at the carbon canister vent or at the check valve.

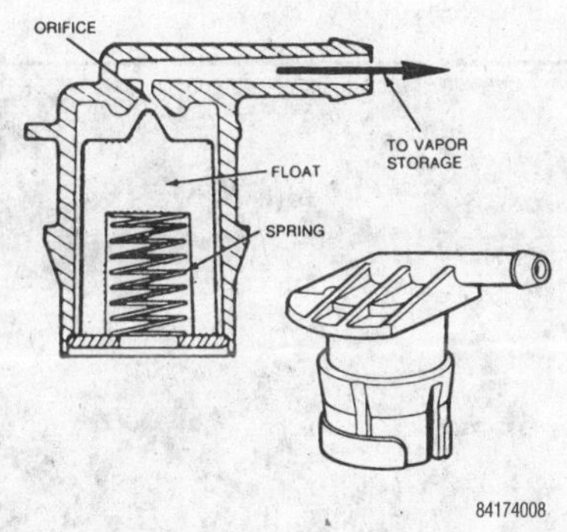


**Fig. 4 Fuel tank vapor orifice and roll over valve assembly**

**Purge Solenoid Valve**

**▶ See Figure 5**

The purge solenoid valve is in-line with the carbon canister and controls the flow of fuel vapors out of the canister. It is normally closed. When the engine is shut off, the vapors from the fuel tank flow into the canister. After the engine is started, the solenoid is engaged and opens, purging the vapors into the engine. With the valve open, vapors from the fuel tank are routed directly into the engine.

**Pressure/Vacuum Relief Fuel Cap**

The fuel cap contains an integral pressure and vacuum relief valve. The vacuum valve acts to allow air into the fuel tank to replace the fuel as it is used, while preventing vapors from escaping the tank

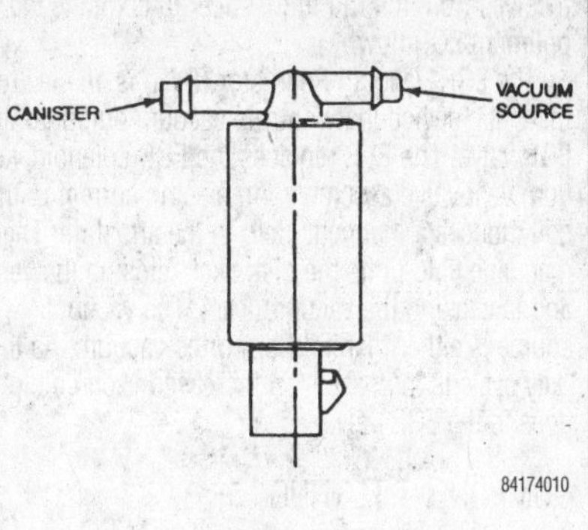


**Fig. 5 Purge solenoid valve**

through the atmosphere. The vacuum relief valve opens after a vacuum of −0.5 psi. The pressure valve acts as a backup pressure relief valve in the event the normal venting system is overcome by excessive generation of internal pressure or restriction of the normal venting system. The pressure relief range is 1.6–2.1 psi. Fill cap damage or contamination that stops the pressure vacuum valve from working may result in deformation of the fuel tank.

## REMOVAL & INSTALLATION

**Carbon Canister**

1. Disconnect the negative battery cable.
2. Label and disconnect the vapor hoses from the carbon canister.
3. Remove the canister attaching screws and remove the canister.
4. Installation is the reverse of the removal procedure.

**Fuel Tank Vapor Orifice and Roll over Valve Assembly**

1. Disconnect the negative battery cable.
2. Remove the fuel tank as described in Section 5.
3. Remove the vapor orifice and roll over valve assembly from the fuel tank.
4. Installation is the reverse of the removal procedure.

**Purge Control Valve**

1. Disconnect the negative battery cable.
2. Label and disconnect the hoses from the purge control valve.
3. Remove the purge control valve.
4. Installation is the reverse of the removal procedure.

**Purge Solenoid Valve**

1. Disconnect the negative battery cable.
2. Label and disconnect the hoses from the purge solenoid valve.
3. Disconnect the electrical connector from the valve.
4. Remove the purge solenoid valve.
5. Installation is the reverse of the removal procedure.

# Exhaust Gas Recirculation System

## OPERATION

**▶ See Figures 6, 7, 8 and 9**

The Exhaust Gas Recirculation (EGR) system is designed to reintroduce exhaust gas into the combustion cycle, thereby lowering combustion temperatures and reducing the formation of nitrous oxide. This is accomplished by the use of an EGR valve that opens under specific engine operating conditions, to admit a small amount of exhaust gas into the intake manifold, below the throttle plate. The exhaust gas mixes with the incoming air charge and displaces a portion of the oxygen in the air/fuel mixture entering the combustion chamber. The exhaust gas does not support combustion, but it takes up volume, the net effect is to lower the temperature of the combustion chamber. There are a few different EGR systems used.

The most commonly used system is the Pressure Feedback Electronic (PFE) system. The PFE is a subsonic closed loop EGR system that controls EGR flow rate by monitoring the pressure drop across a remotely located sharp-edged orifice. The system uses a pressure transducer as the feedback device and controlled pressure is varied by valve modulation using vacuum output of the EGR Vacuum Regulator (EVR) solenoid. With the PFE system, the EGR valve only serves as a pressure regulator rather than a flow-metering device.

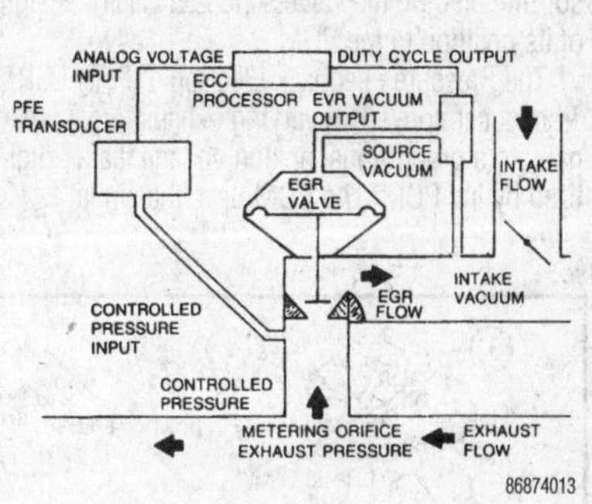


**Fig. 6 Pressure Feedback Electronic (PFE) EGR system schematic**

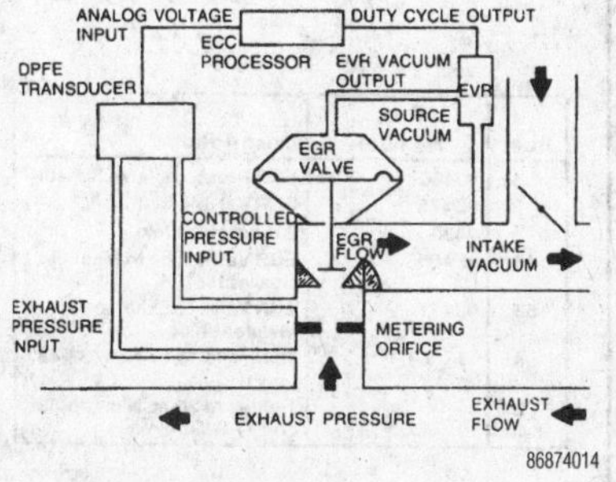


**Fig. 7 Differential Pressure Feedback Electronic (DPFE) EGR system schematic**

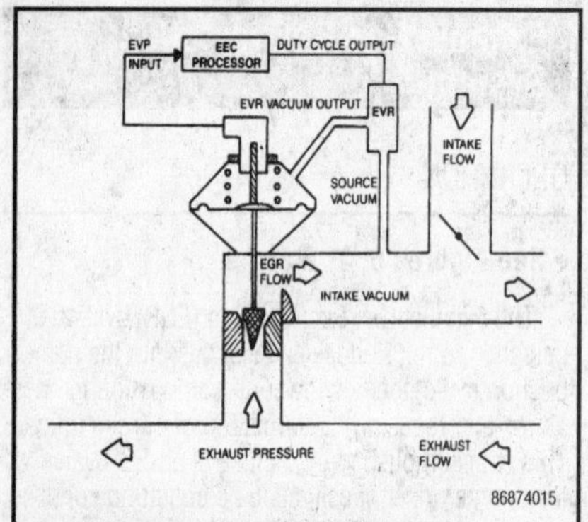


86874015

**Fig. 8 Electronic EGR (EEGR) system schematic**

The Differential Pressure Feedback Electronic (DPFE) EGR system operates in the same manner except it directly monitors the pressure drop across the metering orifice. This allows for a more accurate assessment of EGR flow requirements.

The Electronic EGR (EEGR) valve system is used on some vehicles equipped with the 5.0L engine. An electronic EGR valve is required in EEC systems where EGR flow is controlled according to computer demands by means of an EGR Valve Position (EVP) sensor attached to the valve. The valve is operated by a vacuum signal from the electronic vacuum regulator that actuates the valve diaphragm. As supply vacuum overcomes the spring load, the diaphragm is actuated. This lifts the pintle off of its seat allowing exhaust gas to recirculate. The amount of flow is proportional to the pintle position. The EVP sensor mounted on the valve sends an electrical signal of its position to the PCM.

The Pressure Feedback Electronic (PFE) EGR Transducer converts a varying exhaust pressure signal into a proportional analog voltage that is digitized by the PCM. The PCM uses the signal

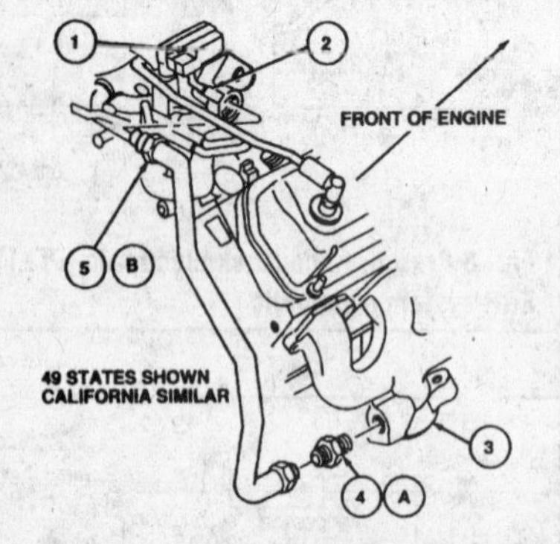


| Item | Part Number | Description |
|---|---|---|
| 1 | 9J460 | EGR Pressure Valve Sensor |
| 2 | 9D475 | EGR Valve |
| 3 | 9430 | Exhaust Manifold |
| 4A | 9F485 | EGR Valve Tube to Manifold Connector |
| 5B | 9D477 | EGR Valve to Exhaust Manifold Tube |
| A | | Tighten to 45-65 N·m (33-48 Lb-Ft) |
| B | | Tighten to 35-45 N·m (26-33 Lb-Ft) |

86874026

**Fig. 9 View of the EGR system components—late model 3.8L engine shown**

received from the PFE transducer to compute the optimum EGR flow.

The EGR Vacuum Regulator (EVR) is an electromagnetic device that controls vacuum output to the EGR valve. The EVR replaces the EGR solenoid vacuum vent valve assembly. An electric current in the coil induces a magnetic field in the armature. The magnetic field pulls the disk back, closing the vent and increasing the vacuum level. The vacuum source is either manifold or ported vacuum. As the duty cycle is increased, an increased vacuum signal goes to the EGR valve.

## COMPONENT TESTING

**➡Many of the following testing procedures require the use of a breakout box tool for EEC systems diagnosis. SUPER STAR II tester or NEW GENERATION STAR (NGS) tester or equivalent scan tools.**

### DPFE Sensor

1. Disconnect the pressure hoses at the DPFE sensor.
2. Connect a hand vacuum pump to the downstream pickup marked **REF** on the sensor.
3. Using a multimeter, backprobe the SIG RTN circuit at the DPFE connector.
4. With the ignition **ON**, signal voltage should be 0.20–0.70 volts.
5. Apply 8–9 in. Hg of vacuum to the sensor. Voltage should be greater than 4 volts.
6. Quickly release the vacuum from the sensor. Voltage should drop to less than 1 volt in 3 seconds.
7. If the sensor does not respond as specified, check the power and ground circuits.
8. If power and ground circuits are functional, the sensor is faulty.

### EGR Valve Control Solenoid

1. Remove the EVR solenoid.
2. Attempt to lightly blow air into the EVR solenoid.
   a. If air blows through the solenoid, replace the solenoid with a new one.
   b. If air does not pass freely through the solenoid, continue with the test.
3. Apply battery voltage (approximately 12 volts) and a ground to the EVR solenoid electrical terminals. Attempt to lightly blow air, once again, through the solenoid.
   a. If air does not pass through the solenoid, replace the solenoid with a new one.
   b. If air does not flow through the solenoid, the solenoid is OK.
4. If the solenoid is functional but the problem still exists, check the power and ground circuits.

### EGR Valve

1. Install a tachometer on the engine, following the manufacturer's instructions.
2. Detach the engine wiring harness connector from the Idle Air Control (IAC) solenoid.
3. Disconnect and plug the vacuum supply hose from the EGR valve.
4. Start the engine, then apply the parking brake, block the rear wheels and position the transmission in Neutral.
5. Observe and note the idle speed.

**➡If the engine will not idle with the IAC solenoid disconnected, provide an air bypass to the engine by slightly opening the throttle plate or by creating an intake vacuum leak. Do not allow the idle speed to exceed typical idle rpm.**

6. Using a hand-held vacuum pump, slowly apply 5–10 in. Hg (17–34 kPa) of vacuum to the EGR valve nipple.
   a. If the idle speed drops more than 100 rpm with the vacuum applied and returns to normal after the vacuum is removed, the EGR valve is OK.
   b. If the idle speed does not drop more than 100 rpm with the vacuum applied and return to normal after the vacuum is removed, inspect the EGR valve for a blockage; clean it if a blockage is found. Replace the EGR valve if no blockage is found, or if cleaning the valve does not remedy the malfunction.

## REMOVAL & INSTALLATION

### DPFE Sensor

➧ See Figures 10, 11, 12, 13 and 14

1. Disconnect the negative battery cable.
2. Label and disconnect the wiring harness from the DPFE sensor.
3. Label and disconnect the vacuum hoses.
4. Remove the mounting screws and remove the DPFE sensor.

**To install:**

5. Position the DPFE sensor and tighten the mounting screws.

91194P37

**Fig. 10 Detach the connector for the DPFE sensor**

91194P38

**Fig. 11 Matchmark and remove the vacuum hoses for the DPFE sensor and . . .**

91194P39

**Fig. 12 . . . remove the retaining nuts from the DPFE sensor and . . .**

91194P40

**Fig. 13 . . . remove the DPFE sensor from the intake manifold**

93144P07

**Fig. 14 Location of PFE sensor. Also note the EGR valve behind it. Lubricating the fasteners before removal**

6. Attach all necessary hoses and wiring to the sensor.
7. Connect the negative battery cable.

## EGR Valve Control Solenoid

**➧ See Figures 15, 16, 17, 18 and 19**

1. Disconnect the negative battery cable.
2. Label and detach the vacuum hoses from the EVR solenoid.
3. Detach the electrical connector from the solenoid.
4. Remove the retaining hardware, and remove the solenoid.

**To install:**

5. Position the solenoid and install the retaining hardware.
6. Attach the main emission vacuum control connector and the wiring harness connector to the EVR solenoid.
7. Connect the negative battery cable.

## EGR Valve

### *3.8L ENGINE*

1. Disconnect the negative battery cable.
2. Detach the vacuum line(s) and/or electrical connector(s) from the EGR valve.
3. Remove the mounting bolts, then remove the EGR valve. Remove all old gasket material.

**To install:**

4. Using a new gasket, install the EGR valve, then secure using the retaining bolts.
5. Attach any vacuum lines or electrical connectors disengaged during removal.
6. Connect the negative battery cable.

### *4.6L ENGINE*

**➧ See Figures 20 thru 27**

1. Disconnect the negative battery cable.
2. Remove the vacuum hose from the EGR valve.
3. On the 4.6L engine, remove the nut and the brake booster bracket.
4. Disconnect the EGR valve-to-exhaust manifold tube from the EGR valve.
5. Remove the EGR valve mounting bolts, then separate the valve from the intake manifold.
6. Remove and discard the old EGR valve gas-

91194P32

**Fig. 15 Detach the connector for the EVR solenoid**

91194P33

**Fig. 16 Match mark the vacuum hoses for the EVR solenoid and . . .**

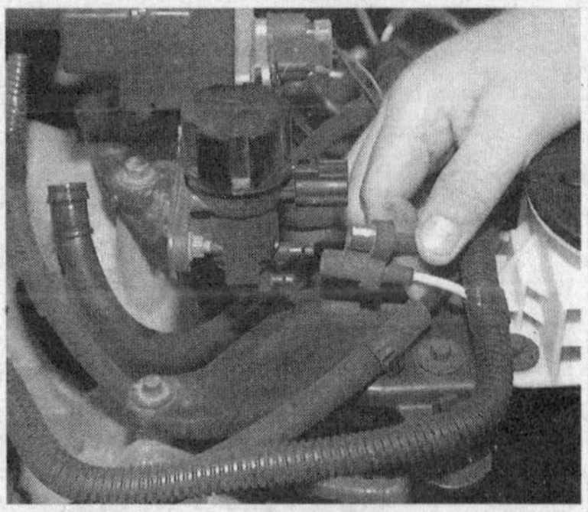
91194P34

**Fig. 17 . . . remove the vacuum hoses from the EVR solenoid**

91194P35

**Fig. 18 Remove the retaining nut for the solenoid and . . .**

91194P36

**Fig. 19 . . . remove the solenoid from the intake manifold**

91194P44

**Fig. 20 Remove the vacuum hose from the EGR valve**

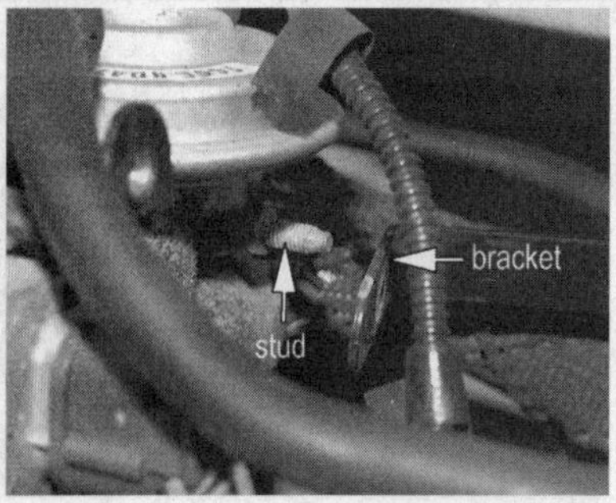


91194P41

**Fig. 21 On the 4.6L engine, remove the nut and the brake booster bracket from the EGR mounting stud**

91194P42

**Fig. 22 Using a suitable size wrench, loosen the EGR valve-to-exhaust manifold tube and . . .**

91194P43

**Fig. 23 . . . remove the tube from the EGR valve**

91194P45

**Fig. 24 Remove the EGR valve mounting bolts and . . .**

91194P46

**Fig. 25 . . . remove the EGR valve from the intake manifold**

91194P47

**Fig. 26 Remove the EGR valve gasket and . . .**

91194P48

**Fig. 27 . . . thoroughly clean the EGR valve mounting surface**

ket, and clean the gasket mating surfaces on the valve and the intake manifold.

**To install:**

7. Install the EGR valve, along with a new gasket, on the intake manifold, then install and tighten the mounting bolts.
8. Connect the EGR valve-to-exhaust manifold tube to the valve, then tighten the tube nut to 25–35 ft. lbs. (34–47 Nm).
9. Connect the vacuum hose to the EGR valve.
10. On the 4.6L engine install the brake booster bracket and the retaining nut.
11. Connect the negative battery cable.

### *5.0L ENGINE*

1. Disconnect the negative battery cable.
2. Remove the air cleaner outlet tube.
3. Detach the EVP sensor connector.
4. Disconnect the EGR valve-to-exhaust manifold tube from the EGR valve.
5. Remove the vacuum hose from the EGR valve.
6. Remove the EGR valve mounting bolts, then separate the valve from the intake manifold.
7. Remove and discard the old EGR valve gasket, and clean the gasket mating surfaces on the valve and the intake manifold.

**To install:**

**➡If replacing the EGR valve, transfer the EVP sensor onto the new valve.**

8. Install the EGR valve, along with a new gasket, on the upper intake manifold, then install and tighten the mounting bolts.
9. Connect the EGR valve-to-exhaust manifold tube to the valve, then tighten the tube nut to 25–35 ft. lbs. (34–47 Nm).
10. Connect the vacuum hose to the EGR valve.
11. Attach the EVP sensor connector.
12. Install the air cleaner outlet tube.
13. Connect the negative battery cable.

# ELECTRONIC ENGINE CONTROLS

## Powertrain Control Module (PCM)

### OPERATION

The Powertrain Control Module (PCM) performs many functions on your vehicle. The module accepts information from various engine sensors and computes the required fuel flow rate necessary to maintain the correct amount of air/fuel ratio throughout the entire engine operational range.

Based on the information that is received and programmed into the PCM's memory, the PCM generates output signals to control relays, actuators and solenoids. The PCM also sends out a command to the fuel injectors that meters the appropriate quantity of fuel. The module automatically senses and compensates for any changes in altitude when driving your vehicle.

## Oxygen Sensor

### OPERATION

**See Figure 28**

The oxygen (O2) sensor is a device that produces an electrical voltage when exposed to the oxygen present in the exhaust gases. The sensor is mounted in the exhaust system, usually in the manifold or a boss located on the down pipe before the catalyst. Most of the oxygen sensors used on the sophisticated systems of today are heated internally for faster reaction when the engine is started cold. The oxygen sensor produces a voltage within zero and one volt. When there is a large amount of oxygen present (lean mixture), the sensor produces a low voltage (less than 0.4v). When there is a lesser amount present (rich mixture) it produces a higher voltage (0.6 –1.0v). The stoichiometric or correct air to fuel ratio will fluctuate between 0.4 and 0.6v. By monitoring the oxygen content and converting it to electrical voltage, the sensor acts as a rich-lean switch. The voltage is transmitted to the PCM.

Some models have two or more sensors, before the catalyst and after. This is done for a catalyst efficiency monitor that is a part of the OBD-II engine controls that are on all models from the 1995 model year on. The sensor before the catalyst measures the exhaust emissions right out of the engine, and sends the signal to the PCM about the state of the mixture as previously talked about. The second sensor reports the difference in the emissions after the exhaust gases have gone through the catalyst. This sensor reports to the PCM the amount of emissions reduction the catalyst is performing.

The oxygen sensor will not work until a predetermined temperature is reached, until this time the PCM is running in OPEN LOOP operation. OPEN LOOP means that the PCM has not yet begun to correct the air-to-fuel ratio by reading the oxygen sensor. After the engine comes to operating temperature, the PCM will monitor the oxygen sensor and correct the air/fuel ratio from the readings of the sensor. This is known as CLOSED LOOP operation.

A heated oxygen sensor (HO2S) has a heating element that keeps the sensor at proper operating temperature during all operating modes. Maintaining correct sensor temperature at all times allows the system to enter CLOSED LOOP operation sooner.

In CLOSED LOOP operation the PCM monitors the sensor input (along with other inputs) and adjusts the injector pulse width accordingly. During OPEN LOOP operation, the PCM ignores the sensor input and adjusts the injector pulse to a preprogrammed value based on other inputs.

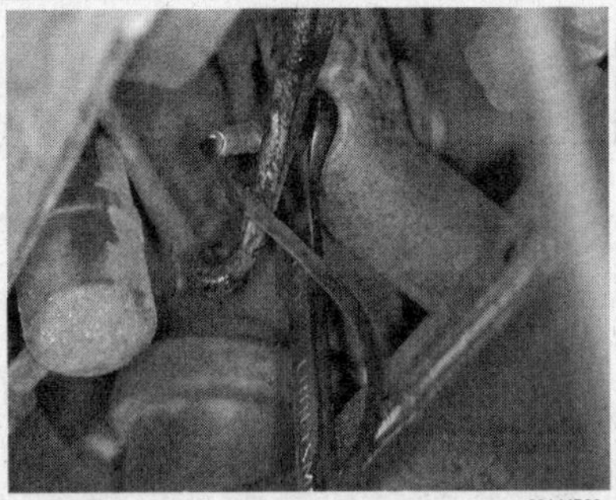

93144P20

**Fig. 28 This is the location of the HO2 sensor on the 3.8L Continental—easilly accessible**

### TESTING

**See Figure 29**

**WARNING**

**Do not pierce the wires when testing this sensor; this can lead to wiring harness damage. Backprobe the connector to properly read the voltage of the HO2S.**

1. Warm the engine to normal operating temperature.
2. Turn the engine **OFF**. Disconnect the HO2S.
3. Connect a voltmeter, and engine running, measure the voltage on the DC scale between terminals **HO2S** and **SIG RTN** (GND) of the oxygen sensor connector. Voltage should fluctuate between 0.01 –1.0 volts. If voltage fluctuation is slow or voltage is not within specification, the sensor may be faulty.

### REMOVAL & INSTALLATION

**See Figures 30 thru 36**

**An oxygen sensor socket/wrench is available from Ford or aftermarket manufacturers to ease the removal and installation of the oxygen sensor(s). If one is not available, an open-end wrench can be used.**

**WARNING**

**The sensor uses a permanently attached pigtail and connector. This pigtail should**

91054P13

**Fig. 29 The HO2S can be monitored with an appropriate and Data-stream capable scan tool**

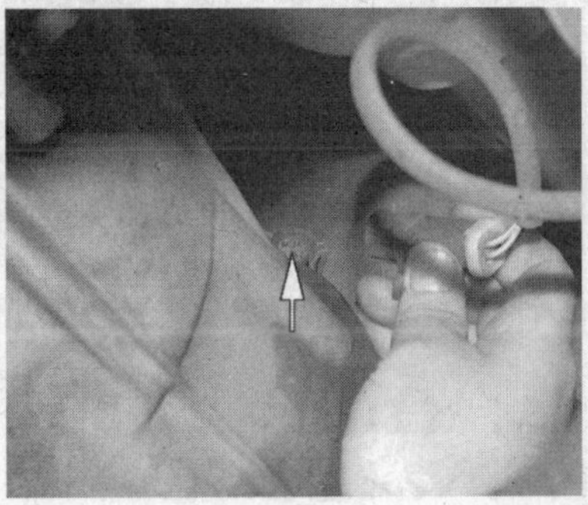

91194P20

**Fig. 30 Detach the connector for the HO2S sensor**

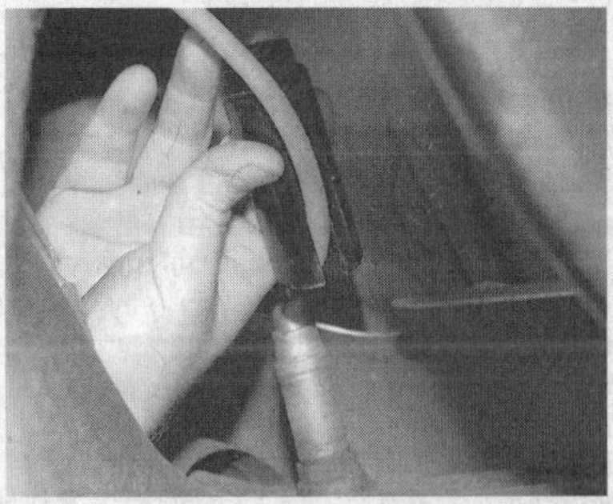

91194P23

**Fig. 31 A special socket is available to remove the HO2S sensor that contains a slot for the wire harness to slide out of**

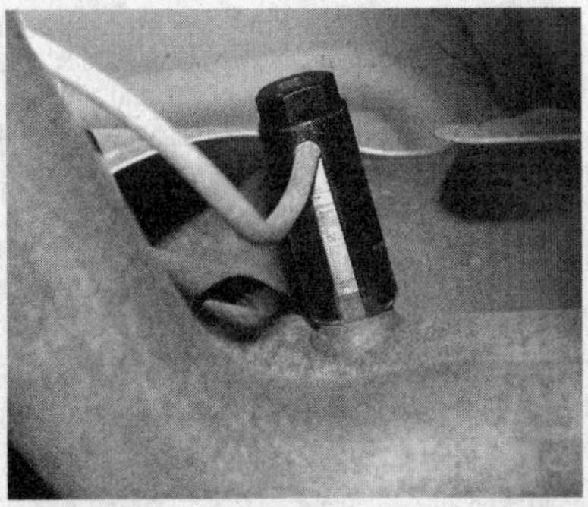

91194P22

**Fig. 32 Place the socket onto the sensor and . . .**

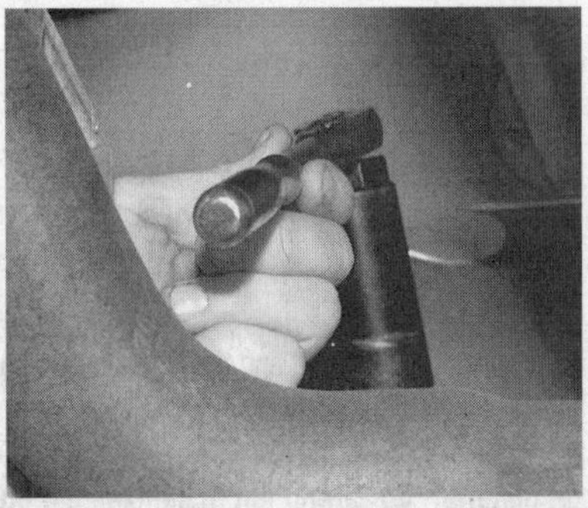

91194P21

**Fig. 33 loosen the sensor using a suitable drive tool**

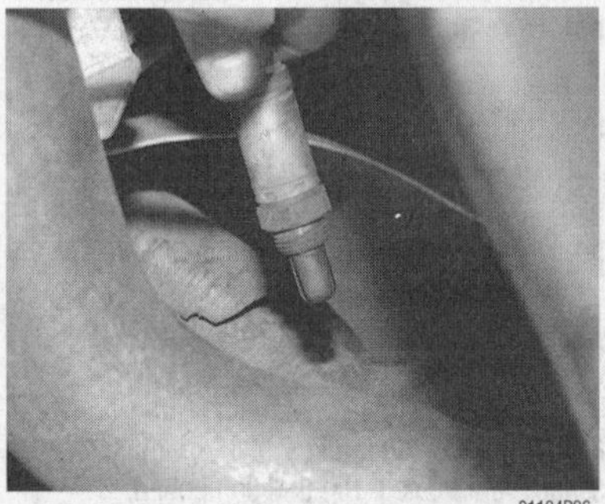

91194P26

**Fig. 34 After the sensor is sufficiently loose using the drive tool, remove the sensor from the exhaust pipe by hand**

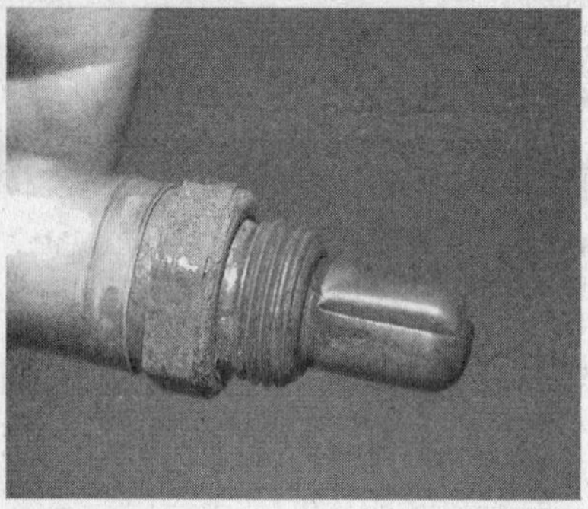

91194P25

**Fig. 35 Inspect the sensor tip for any signs of build-up or damage**

93144P19

**Fig. 36 Coat the threads of the sensor with a suitable anti-seize compound before installation**

**not be removed from the sensor. Damage or removal of the pigtail or connector will affect the proper operation of the sensor. Keep the electrical connector and louvered end of the sensor clean and free of grease. NEVER use cleaning solvents of any type on the sensor! The oxygen sensor may be difficult to remove when the temperature of the engine is below 120°F (49°C). Excessive force may damage the threads in the exhaust manifold or exhaust pipe.**

1. Disconnect the negative battery cable.
2. Raise and support the vehicle.
3. Unplug the electrical connector and any attaching hardware.

**➡Lubricate the sensor with penetrating oil before removal.**

4. Remove the sensor using an appropriate tool. Special oxygen sensor sockets are available to remove the sensor and can be purchased at many parts stores or where automotive tools are sold. The proper size wrench can be used, most sensors are ⅞ inch or 22mm sizes.
5. A 22mm crows foot works very well.

**To install:**

6. Coat the threads of the sensor with a suitable anti-seize compound before installation. New sensors are treated with this compound.
7. Install the sensor and tighten it. Use care in making sure the silicone boot is in the correct position to avoid melting it during operation.
8. Attach the electrical connector.
9. Lower the vehicle.
10. Connect the negative battery cable.

## Idle Air Control Valve

### OPERATION

The Idle Air Control (IAC) valve adjusts the engine idle speed. The valve is located on the throttle body. The valve is controlled by a duty cycle signal from the PCM and allows air to bypass the throttle plate in order to maintain the proper idle speed.

### TESTING

**➧ See Figure 37**

1. Turn the ignition switch to the **OFF** position.
2. Disconnect the wiring harness from the IAC valve.
3. Measure the resistance between the terminals of the valve.

**➡Due to the diode in the solenoid, place the ohmmeter positive lead on the VPWR terminal and the negative lead on the ISC terminal.**

4. Resistance should be 7–13 ohms.
5. If resistance is not within specification, the valve may be faulty.

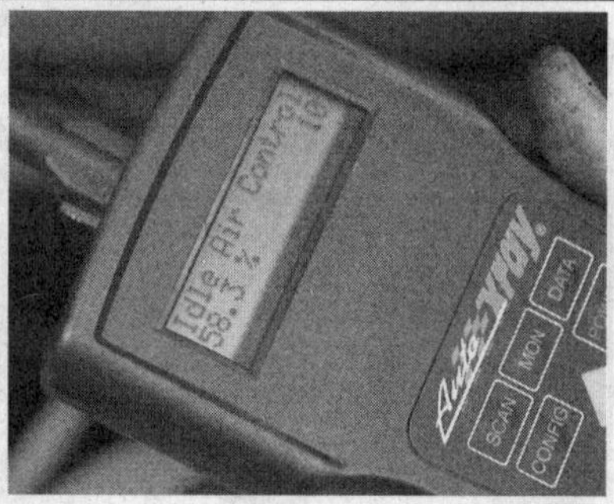

91054P12

**Fig. 37 The IAC can be monitored with an appropriate and Data-stream capable scan tool**

### REMOVAL & INSTALLATION

**➧ See Figures 38 and 39**

1. Disconnect the negative battery cable.
2. Detach the IAC solenoid connector.
3. Remove the two retaining bolts and remove the IAC solenoid and gasket from the throttle body.
4. Installation is the reverse of the removal procedure. Use a new gasket and tighten the retaining bolts to 71–97 inch lbs. (8–11 Nm).

**➡If scraping is necessary to remove old gasket material, be careful not to damage the IAC solenoid or the throttle body gasket surfaces or drop material into the throttle body.**

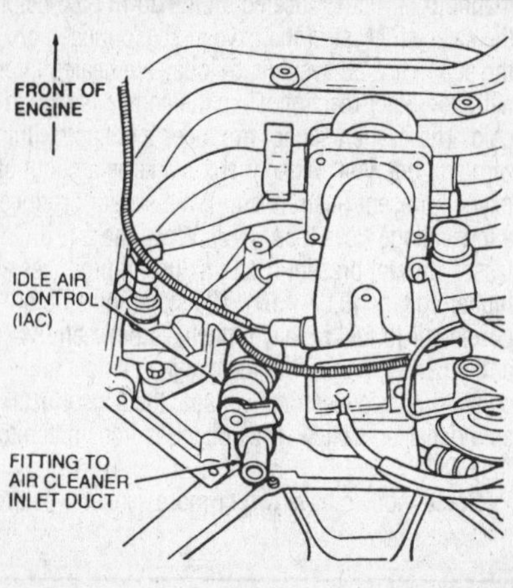


84174028

**Fig. 38 IAC solenoid location—4.6L engine**

93143P08

**Fig. 39 This is an IAC valve off of a 5.0L engine**

## Engine Coolant Temperature (ECT) Sensor

### OPERATION

The Engine Coolant Temperature (ECT) sensor resistance changes in response to engine coolant temperature. The sensor resistance decreases as the coolant temperature increases, and increases as the coolant temperature decreases. This provides a reference signal to the PCM, which indicates engine coolant temperature. The signal sent to the PCM by the ECT sensor helps the PCM to determine spark advance, EGR flow rate, air/fuel ratio, and engine temperature. The ECT is a two-wire sensor, a 5-volt reference signal is sent to the sensor and the signal return is based upon the change in the measured resistance due to temperature.

### TESTING

**➧ See Figures 40, 41 and 42**

1. Disconnect the engine wiring harness from the ECT sensor.
2. Connect an ohmmeter between the ECT sensor terminals.

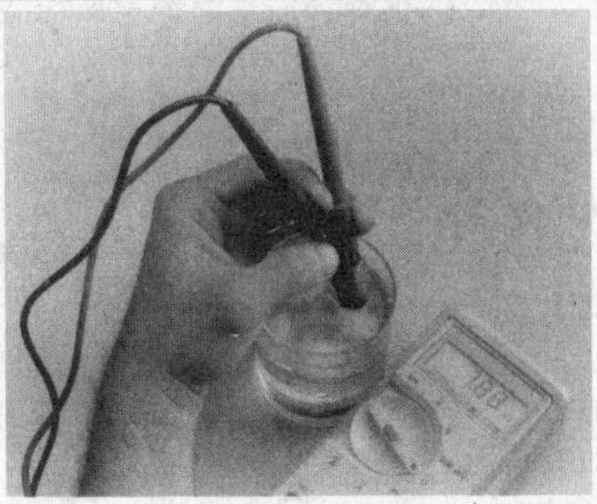

TCCS4P02

**Fig. 40 Another method of testing the ECT is to submerge it in cold or hot water and check resistance**

| Temperature | | Engine Coolant/Intake Air Temperature Sensor Values |
|---|---|---|
| °F | °C | Resistance (K ohms) |
| 248 | 120 | 1.18 |
| 230 | 110 | 1.55 |
| 212 | 100 | 2.07 |
| 194 | 90 | 2.80 |
| 176 | 80 | 3.84 |
| 158 | 70 | 5.37 |
| 140 | 60 | 7.70 |
| 122 | 50 | 10.97 |
| 104 | 40 | 16.15 |
| 86 | 30 | 24.27 |
| 68 | 20 | 37.30 |
| 50 | 10 | 58.75 |

89694G23

**Fig. 41 ECT resistance-to-temperature specifications**

91194P14

**Fig. 42 Test the ECT resistance across the two sensor terminals**

3. With the engine cold and the ignition switch in the **OFF** position, measure and note the ECT sensor resistance.
4. Connect the engine wiring harness to the sensor.
5. Start the engine and allow the engine to reach normal operating temperature.
6. Once the engine has reached normal operating temperature, turn the engine **OFF**.
7. Again, disconnect the engine wiring harness from the ECT sensor.
8. Measure and note the ECT sensor resistance with the engine hot.
9. Compare the cold and hot ECT sensor resistance measurements with the accompanying chart.
10. If readings do not approximate those in the chart, the sensor may be faulty.

## REMOVAL & INSTALLATION

**See Figures 43 thru 48**

1. Disconnect the negative battery cable.
2. Drain and recycle the engine coolant.

**CAUTION**

**Never open, service, or drain the radiator or cooling system when hot; serious burns can occur from the steam and hot coolant. In addition, when draining engine coolant, keep in mind that cats and dogs are attracted to ethylene glycol antifreeze and could drink any that is left in an uncovered container or in puddles on the ground. This**

89604P21

**Fig. 43 Detach the connector for the ECT sensor and . . .**

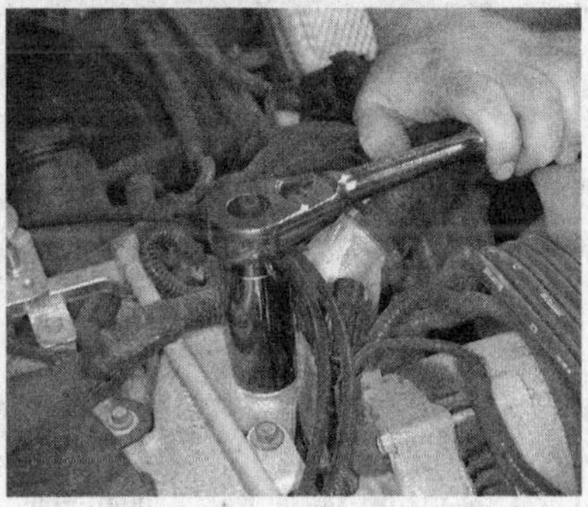

89604P22

**Fig. 44 . . . and loosen the sensor using a suitable socket or other drive tool**

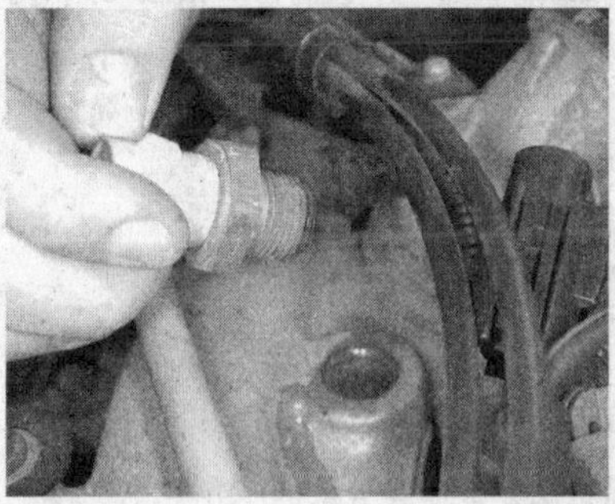

89604P23

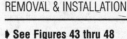

**Fig. 45 Once the sensor is sufficiently loose, remove the sensor from the intake manifold by hand**

91054P36

**Fig. 46 Use a quality thread sealant to . . .**

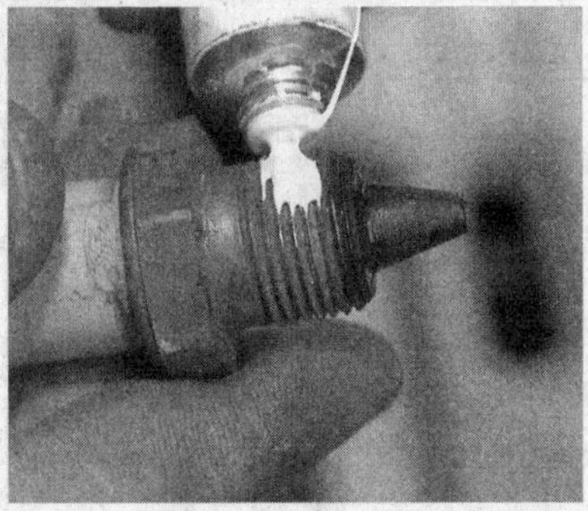

91054P37

**Fig. 47 . . . coat the threads of the ECT sensor before installation**

89604P24

**Fig. 48 The ECT sensor must be tightened with a torque wrench to specifications**

**will prove fatal in sufficient quantities. Always drain coolant into a sealable container. Coolant should be reused unless it is contaminated or is several years old.**

3. Remove the air cleaner outlet tube if necessary.
4. Detach the ECT sensor connector.
5. Remove the ECT sensor from the intake manifold.

**To install:**

6. Coat the sensor threads with Teflon® sealant.
7. Thread the sensor into position and tighten to 6–8 ft. lbs. (8–13 Nm).
8. Attach the ECT sensor connector.
9. Install the air cleaner outlet tube.
10. Connect the negative battery cable.
11. Refill the engine cooling system.
12. Start the engine and check for coolant leaks.
13. Bleed the cooling system.

## Intake Air Temperature Sensor

### OPERATION

➧ See Figure 49

The Intake Air Temperature (IAT) sensor determines the air temperature inside the intake manifold. Resistance changes in response to the ambient air temperature. The sensor has a negative temperature coefficient. As the temperature of the sensor rises the resistance across the sensor decreases. This provides a signal to the PCM indicating the temperature of the incoming air charge. This sensor helps the PCM to determine spark timing and air/fuel ratio. Information from this sensor is added to the pressure sensor information to calculate the air mass being sent to the cylinders. The IAT is a two-wire sensor, a 5-volt reference signal is sent to the sensor and the signal return is based upon the change in the measured resistance due to temperature.

### TESTING

➧ See Figures 50 and 51

1. Turn the ignition switch **OFF**.
2. Disconnect the wiring harness from the IAT sensor.
3. Measure the resistance between the sensor terminals.
4. Compare the resistance reading with the accompanying chart.
5. If the resistance is not within specification, the IAT may be faulty.
6. Connect the wiring harness to the sensor.

### REMOVAL & INSTALLATION

#### 1988–95 Models

1. Disconnect the negative battery cable.
2. Detach the electrical connector from the IAT sensor.
3. Using a suitable socket and drive tool, remove the IAT sensor from the air inlet.
4. On the 5.0L engine Lincoln models, the IAT sensor is located in the intake manifold

**To install:**

5. Coat the sensor threads with Teflon® sealant.
6. Thread the sensor into position and tighten it to 6–8 ft. lbs. (8–13 Nm)..
7. Attach the electrical connector to the IAT sensor.
8. Connect the negative battery cable.

#### 1996–00 Models

1. Disconnect the negative battery cable.
2. Detach the electrical connector from the IAT sensor.
3. Turn the sensor 90° counterclockwise and remove the IAT sensor from the air cleaner lid.
4. Remove the sensor O-ring and inspect it. Replace as necessary.

**To install:**

5. The installation is the reverse of the removal.

## Mass Airflow Sensor

### OPERATION

➧ See Figure 52

The Mass Air Flow (MAF) sensor directly measures the mass of air being drawn into the engine. The sensor output is used to calculate injector pulse width. The MAF sensor is what is referred to as a "hot-wire sensor". The sensor uses a thin platinum wire filament, wound on a ceramic bobbin and coated with glass, that is heated to 200°C (417°F) above the ambient air temperature and subjected to the intake airflow stream. A "cold-wire" is used inside the MAF sensor to determine the ambient air temperature.

Battery voltage from the EEC power relay, and a reference signal and a ground signal from the PCM are supplied to the MAF sensor. The sensor returns a signal proportionate to the current flow required keeping the "hot-wire" at the required temperature. The increased airflow across the "hot-wire" acts as a cooling fan, lowering the resistance and requiring more current to maintain the temperature of the wire. The voltage in the circuit measures the increased current. As current increases, voltage increases. As the airflow increases the signal return voltage of a normally operating MAF sensor will increase.

89604P14

**Fig. 49 The tip of the IAT sensor has an exposed thermistor that changes the resistance of the sensor based upon the force of the air rushing past it**

91054P09

**Fig. 50 The IAT sensor can be monitored with an appropriate and Data-stream capable scan tool**

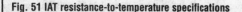

| Temperature | | Engine Coolant/Intake Air Temperature Sensor Values |
|---|---|---|
| °F | °C | Resistance (K ohms) |
| 248 | 120 | 1.18 |
| 230 | 110 | 1.55 |
| 212 | 100 | 2.07 |
| 194 | 90 | 2.80 |
| 176 | 80 | 3.84 |
| 158 | 70 | 5.37 |
| 140 | 60 | 7.70 |
| 122 | 50 | 10.97 |
| 104 | 40 | 16.15 |
| 86 | 30 | 24.27 |
| 68 | 20 | 37.30 |
| 50 | 10 | 58.75 |

89694G23

**Fig. 51 IAT resistance-to-temperature specifications**

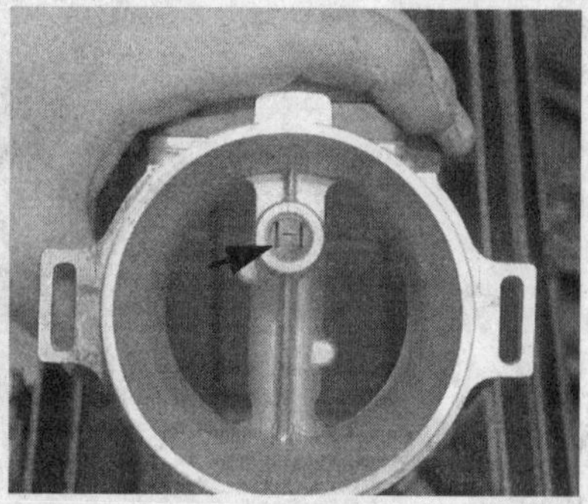

91054P45

**Fig. 52 The exposed "hot wire" of the MAF sensor**

### TESTING

See Figure 53

1. Using a multimeter, check for voltage by backprobing the MAF sensor connector.
2. With the key **ON**, and the engine **OFF**, verify that there is at least 10.5 volts between the VPWR and GND terminals of the MAF sensor connector. If voltage is not within specification, check power and ground circuits and repair as necessary.
3. With the key **ON**, and the engine **ON**, verify that there is at least 4.5 volts between the SIG and GND terminals of the MAF sensor connector. If voltage is not within specification, check power and ground circuits and repair as necessary.
4. With the key **ON**, and the engine **ON**, check voltage between GND and SIG RTN terminals. Voltage should be approximately 0.34–1.96 volts. If voltage is not within specification, the sensor may be faulty.

93144P08

**Fig. 53 Unplugging the sensor connector below the MAF sensor, for testing purposes**

### REMOVAL & INSTALLATION

1. Disconnect the negative battery cable.
2. Remove the air intake tube from the MAF sensor and the throttle body.
3. Detach the connector from the MAF sensor.
4. Remove the four sensor retaining screws and remove the sensor.
5. Remove the sensor gasket.

**To install:**

6. Installation is the reverse of removal.

## Manifold Air Pressure (MAP) Sensor

### OPERATION

The most important information for measuring engine fuel requirements comes from the pressure sensor. Using the pressure and temperature data, the PCM calculates the intake air mass. It is connected to the engine intake manifold through a hose and takes readings of the absolute pressure. A piezoelectric crystal changes a voltage input to a frequency output, which reflects the pressure in the intake manifold.

Atmospheric pressure is measured when the engine is started and when driving fully loaded, then the pressure sensor information is adjusted accordingly.

The Manifold Absolute Pressure (MAP) sensor was used on the 3.8L & the 5.0L engines, until it was replaced by the Mass Air Flow (MAF). The MAP sensor operates as a pressure-sensing disc. It does not generate a voltage; instead its output is a frequency change. The sensor changes frequency according to intake manifold vacuum; as vacuum increases sensor frequency increases. This gives the Powertrain Control Module (PCM) information on engine load. The PCM uses the MAP sensor signal to help determine spark advance, EGR flow and air/fuel ratio.

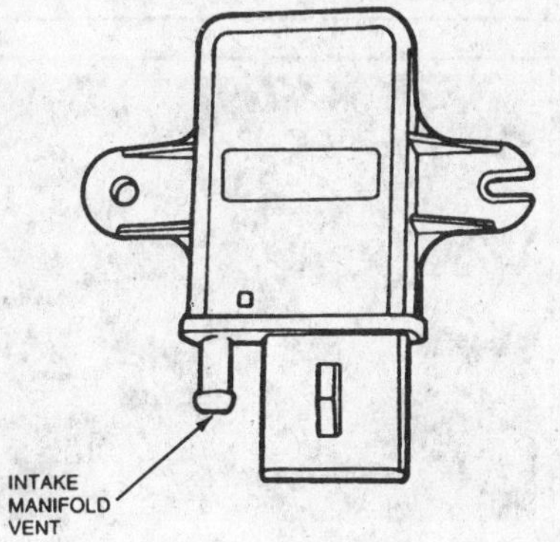


84174020

**Fig. 54 Manifold Absolute Pressure Sensor**

### TESTING

See Figures 54, 55 and 56

**Unusually high or low barometric pressures can generate a false DTC for the MAP sensor. If no driveability symptoms accompany the MAP code, do not replace it.**

1. Connect a MAP/BARO tester to the sensor connector and sensor harness connector. With ignition **ON** and engine **OFF**, use DVOM to measure voltage across tester terminals. If the tester's 4-6V indicator is ON, the reference voltage input to the sensor is okay.

**The green light on the tester indicates that the VREF circuit is okay, 4–6 volts. A red light or no light indicates the VREF is either too low or too high.**

| Approximate Altitude (Ft.) | Voltage Output (±.04 Volts) |
|---|---|
| 0 | 1.59 |
| 1000 | 1.56 |
| 2000 | 1.53 |
| 3000 | 1.50 |
| 4000 | 1.47 |
| 5000 | 1.44 |
| 6000 | 1.41 |
| 7000 | 1.39 |

84174023

**Fig. 55 MAP sensor altitude/voltage output relationship**

**MAP Sensor Graph**

NOTE: **MAP sensor output frequency versus manifold vacuum data is based on 30.0 in-Hg barometric pressure.**

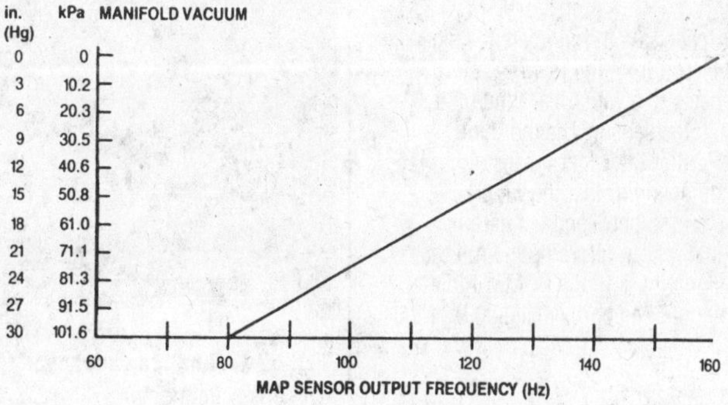


**MAP Sensor Data**

| Manifold Vacuum | | Frequency |
|---|---|---|
| in-Hg | kPa | Hz |
| 0 | 0 | 159 |
| 3 | 10.2 | 150 |
| 6 | 20.3 | 141 |
| 9 | 30.5 | 133 |
| 12 | 40.6 | 125 |
| 15 | 50.8 | 117 |
| 18 | 61.0 | 109 |
| 21 | 71.1 | 102 |
| 24 | 81.3 | 95 |
| 27 | 91.5 | 88 |
| 30 | 101.6 | 80 |

84174022

**Fig. 56 MAP sensor frequency data**

2. Measure the reference signal of the MAP sensor. If the DVOM voltage reading is as indicated in the table, the sensor is okay.
   a. Turn the ignition **OFF**.
   b. Disconnect the vacuum hose from the MAP sensor and connect a vacuum pump in its place.
   c. Apply 18 in. Hg of vacuum to the MAP sensor.
   d. If the MAP sensor holds vacuum, it is okay. If the MAP sensor does not hold vacuum, it must be replaced.

### REMOVAL & INSTALLATION

1. Disconnect the negative battery cable.
2. Detach the electrical connector and the vacuum line from the sensor.
3. Remove the sensor mounting bolts and remove the sensor.
4. Installation is the reverse of the removal procedure.

## Throttle Position Sensor

### OPERATION

The Throttle Position (TP) sensor is a potentiometer that provides a signal to the PCM that is directly proportional to the throttle plates position. The TP sensor is mounted on the side of the throttle body and is connected to the throttle plate shaft. The TP sensor monitors the throttle plate's movement and position, and transmits an appropriate electrical signal to the PCM. The PCM uses these signals to adjust the air/fuel mixture, spark timing, and EGR operation according to engine load at idle, part throttle, or full throttle. The TP sensor is not adjustable.

The TP sensor receives a 5-volt reference signal and a ground circuit from the PCM. A return signal circuit connects to a wiper that runs on a resistor internally in the sensor. The more the throttle opens the further the wiper moves along the resistor. At wide open throttle, the wiper essentially creates a loop between the reference signal and the signal return, returning the full, or nearly full 5 volt signal back to the PCM. At idle the signal return should be approximately 0.9 volts.

### TESTING

See Figures 57, 58, 59 and 60

1. With the engine **OFF** and the ignition **ON**, check the voltage at the signal return circuit of the TP sensor by carefully backprobing the connector using a DVOM.
2. Voltage should be between 0.2 and 1.4 volts at idle.
3. Slowly move the throttle pulley to the wide-open throttle (WOT) position and watch the voltage on the DVOM. The voltage should slowly rise to slightly less than 4.8v at Wide Open Throttle (WOT).
4. If no voltage is present, check the wiring harness for supply voltage (5.0v) and ground (0.3v or less), by referring to your corresponding wiring guide. If supply voltage and ground are present, but

91194P53

**Fig. 57 Testing the TP sensor signal return voltage at idle**

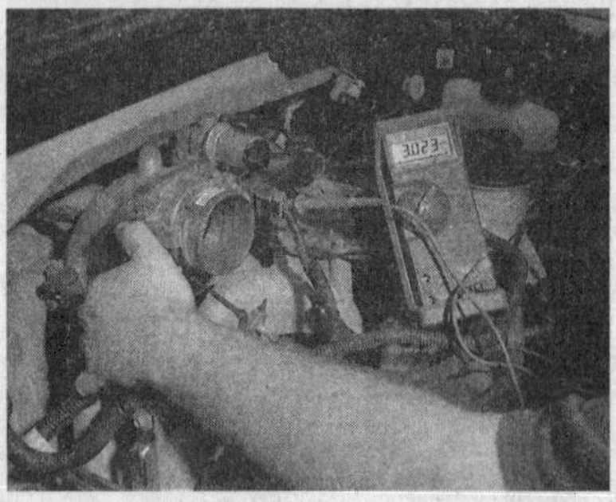

91194P55

**Fig. 58 Test the operation of the TP sensor by gently opening the throttle while observing the signal return voltage. The voltage should move smoothly according to the amount the throttle is opened**

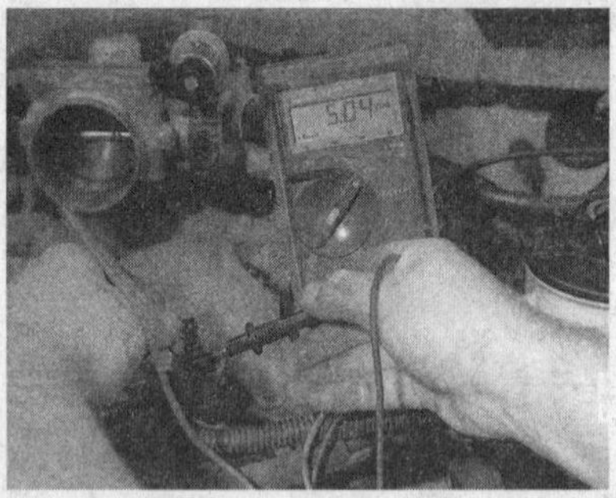

91194P52

**Fig. 59 Testing the supply voltage at the TP sensor connector**

91054P11

**Fig. 60 The TP sensor can be monitored with an appropriate and Data-stream capable scan tool**

no output voltage from TP, replace the TP sensor. If supply voltage and ground do not meet specifications, make necessary repairs to the harness or PCM.

### REMOVAL & INSTALLATION

1. Disconnect the negative battery cable.

**➡On a 4.6L engine, it may be necessary to remove the throttle cover from the engine.**

2. Disconnect the wiring harness from the TP sensor.
3. Remove the two sensor mounting screws, then pull the TP sensor off of the throttle shaft.

**To install:**

4. Carefully slide the rotary tangs on the sensor into position over the throttle shaft, then rotate the sensor clockwise to the installed position..

**CAUTION**

**Failure to install the TP sensor in this manner may result in sensor damage or high idle speeds.**

**➡The TP sensor is not adjustable.**

5. Install and tighten the sensor mounting screws to 27 inch lbs. (3 Nm).
6. Connect the wiring harness to the sensor.
7. If removed, install the throttle cover.
8. Connect the negative battery cable.

## Camshaft Position Sensor

**➡The Camshaft Position Sensor (CMP) is only outfitted on the 4.6L engine.**

The camshaft position sensor (CMP) is a variable reluctance sensor that is triggered by a high point on the left-hand exhaust camshaft sprocket. The CMP sends a signal relating camshaft position back to the PCM and that signal is used by the PCM to check engine timing.

### TESTING

1. Check voltage between the camshaft position sensor terminals PWR GND and CID.
2. With engine running, voltage should be greater than 0.1 volt AC and vary with engine speed.
3. If voltage is not within specification, check for proper voltage at the VPWR terminal.
4. If VPWR voltage is greater than 10.5 volts, sensor may be faulty.

### REMOVAL & INSTALLATION

#### 4.6L Engine

See Figures 61, 62 and 63

1. Disconnect the negative battery cable.
2. Detach the electrical connector for the CMP sensor.
3. Remove the CMP sensor retaining bolt(s) and remove the CMP sensor from the front cover.

**To Install:**

4. Installation is the reverse of removal.

91194P57

**Fig. 61 Detach the connector for the CMP sensor and . . .**

91194P58

**Fig. 62 . . . remove the bolt retaining the CMP sensor to the front cover and . . .**

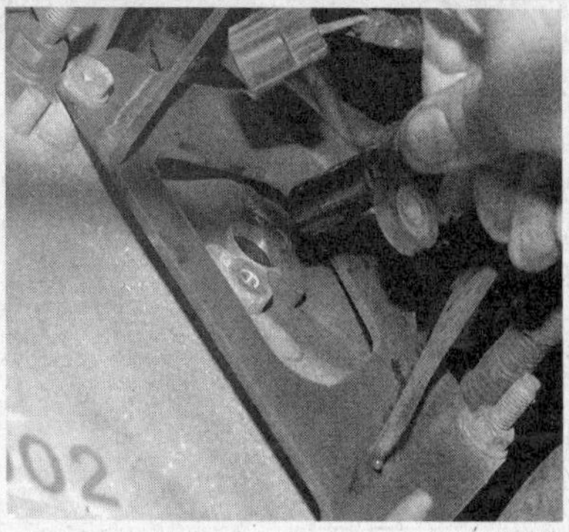
91194P59

**Fig. 63 . . . remove the sensor**

## Crankshaft Position Sensor

### OPERATION

**➧ See Figure 64**

The Crankshaft Position (CKP) sensor is a variable reluctance sensor that uses a trigger wheel to induce voltage. The CKP sensor is a fixed magnetic sensor mounted to the engine block and monitors the trigger or "pulse" wheel that is attached to the crank pulley/damper. As the pulse wheel rotates by the CKP sensor, teeth on the pulse wheel induce voltage inside the sensor through magnetism. The pulse wheel has a missing tooth that changes the reading of the sensor. This is used for the Cylinder Identification (CID) function to properly monitor and adjust engine timing by locating the number 1 cylinder. The voltage created by the CKP sensor is alternating current (A/C). This voltage reading is sent to the PCM, it is used to determine engine RPM, engine timing, and is used to fire the ignition coils.

### TESTING

1. Measure the voltage between the sensor CKP sensor terminals by backprobing the sensor connector.

**➡If the connector cannot be backprobed, fabricate or purchase a test harness.**

2. Sensor voltage should be more than 0.1 volt AC with the engine running and should vary with engine RPM.
3. If voltage is not within specification, the sensor may be faulty.

### REMOVAL & INSTALLATION

**➧ See Figure 65**

1. Disconnect the negative battery cable.
2. Remove the accessory drive belt from the engine.
3. Raise and safely support the vehicle.
4. Remove the A/C compressor mounting bolts, but do not disconnect the A/C lines. Remove and support the compressor out of the way.
5. Detach the electrical connector for the CKP sensor.
6. Remove the CKP sensor retaining bolts and remove the CKP sensor.

**To install:**

7. Installation is the reverse of removal.

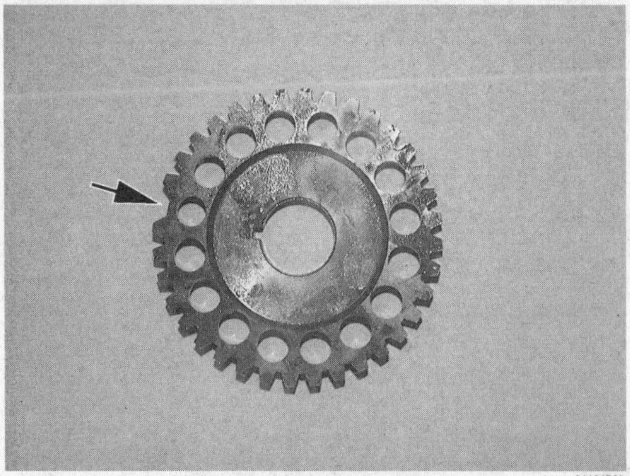
91194P63

**Fig. 64 The CKP sensor trigger wheel rides on the front of the crankshaft. The missing tooth creates a fluctuation of voltage in the sensor**

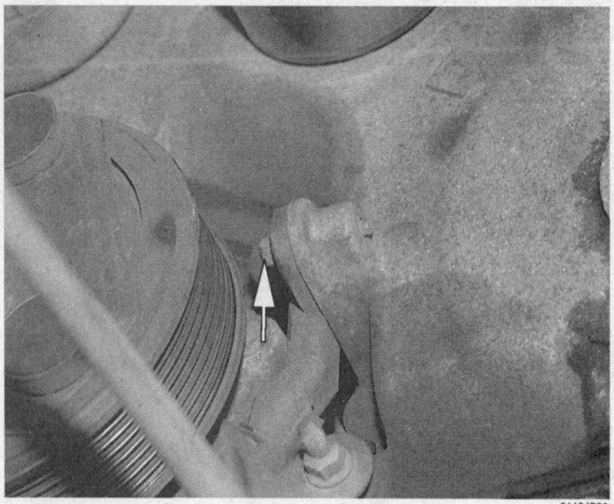
91194P56

**Fig. 65 Remove the retaining bolt for the CKP sensor and remove the sensor from the front cover**

## COMPONENT LOCATIONS

**COMMON EMISSIONS AND ELECTRONIC ENGINE CONTROL COMPONENT LOCATIONS—3.8L ENGINE**

1. VECI decal
2. ICRM control (under sight shield)
3. Fuel pressure regulator
4. ECT (Engine Coolant Temperature) sensor
5. EGR (Exhaust Gas Recirculation) valve
6. PFE (Pressure Feedback Exhaust) sensor
7. MAF (Mass Air Flow) sensor
8. TP (Throttle Position) sensor
9. IAC (Idle Air Control) valve
10. Fuel injector (6 total)
11. Scan tool (VIP test) connector
12. TFI (Ignition) module

**COMMON EMISSIONS AND ELECTRONIC ENGINE CONTROL COMPONENT LOCATIONS—4.6L ENGINE**

1. Fuel pressure regulator
2. ECT (Engine Coolant Temperature) sensor
3. EGR (Exhaust Gas Recirculation) valve
4. DPFE (Delta Pressure Feedback Exhaust) sensor
5. MAF (Mass Air Flow) sensor
6. TP (Throttle Position) sensor
7. IAC (Idle Air Control) valve
8. Fuel injector (8 total)
9. Scan tool (VIP test) connector
10. EDIS (Electronic Distributorless Ignition) module
11. Anti-lock brake test connector

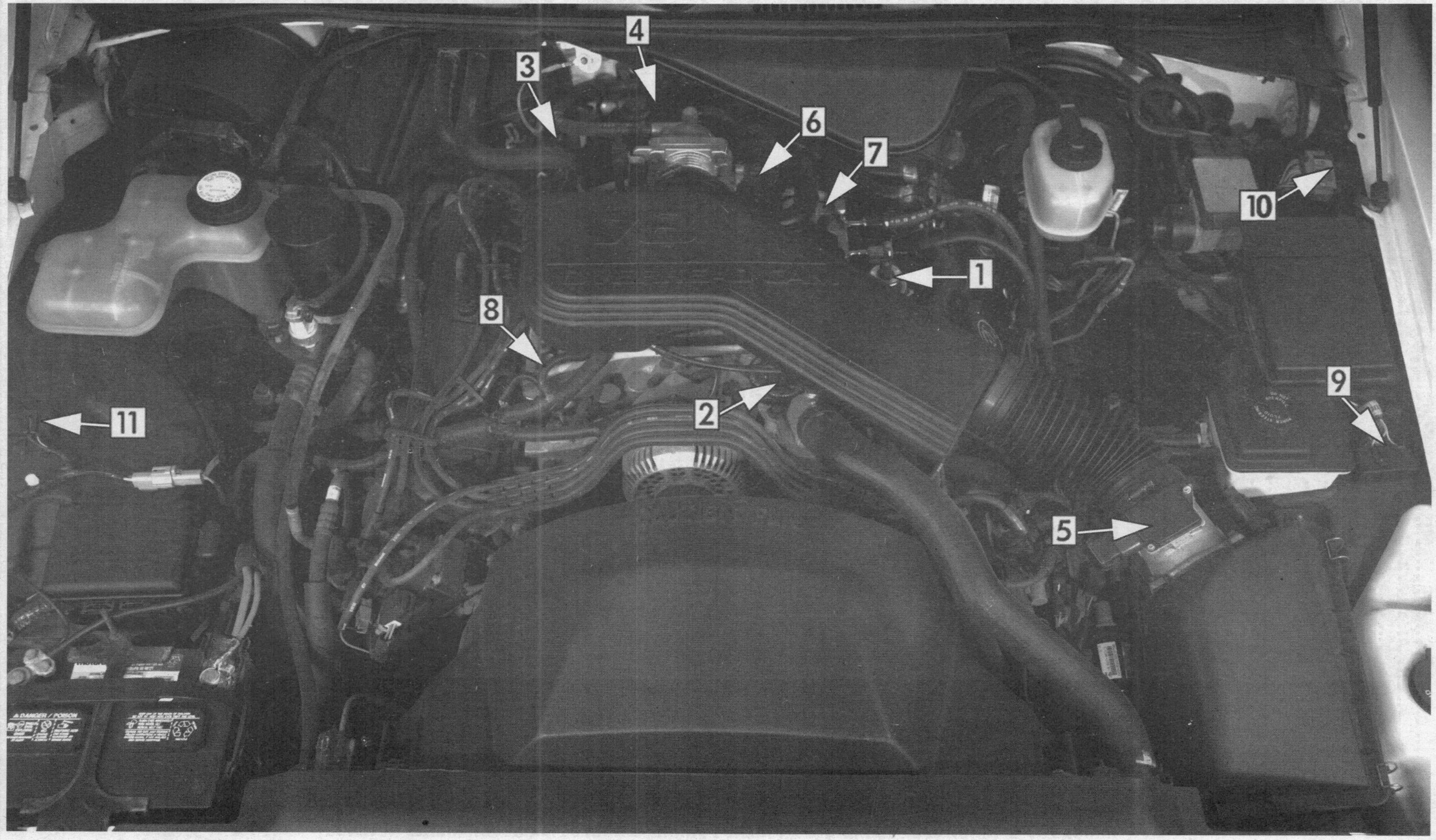


93144P23

**COMMON EMISSIONS AND ELECTRONIC ENGINE CONTROL COMPONENT LOCATIONS—5.0L ENGINE**

1. VECI decal
2. Fuel pressure regulator
3. ECT (Engine Coolant Temperature) sensor
4. EGR (Exhaust Gas Recirculation) valve
5. EVP (Electronic Valve Position) sensor
6. TP (Throttle Position) sensor
7. IAC (Idle Air Control) vale
8. Fuel injectors (8 total)
9. Scan tool (VIP test) connector
10. TFI (Ignition) module
11. Thermactor pump
12. EVR (Electronic Vacuum Regulator)

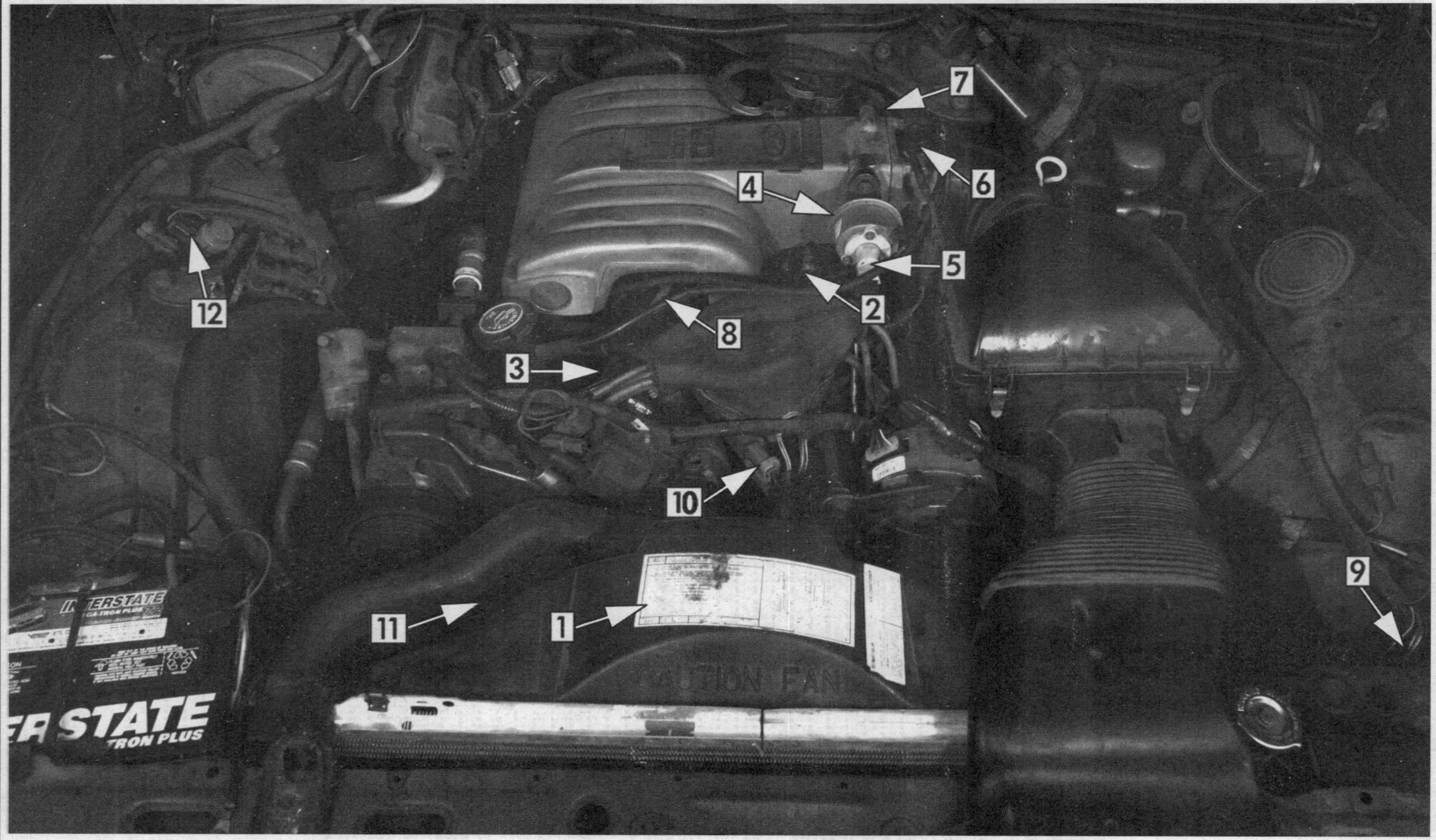


93144P24

# TROUBLE CODES —EEC-IV SYSTEM

## General Information

The Powertrain Control Module (PCM) is devoted to monitoring both input and output functions within the system. This ability forms the core of the self-diagnostic system. If a problem is detected within a circuit, the controller will recognize the fault, assign it an identification code, and store the code in a memory section. Depending on the year and model, the fault code(s) may be represented by two or three-digit numbers. The stored code(s) may be retrieved during diagnosis.

While the EEC-IV system is capable of recognizing many internal faults, certain faults will not be recognized. Because the computer system sees only electrical signals, it cannot sense or react to mechanical or vacuum faults affecting engine operation. Some of these faults may affect another component which will set a code. For example, the PCM monitors the output signal to the fuel injectors, but cannot detect a partially clogged injector. As long as the output driver responds correctly, the computer will read the system as functioning correctly. However, the improper flow of fuel may result in a lean mixture. This would, in turn, be detected by the oxygen sensor and noticed as a constantly lean signal by the PCM. Once the signal falls outside the pre-programmed limits, the engine control assembly would notice the fault and set an identification code.

### FAILURE MODE EFFECTS MANAGEMENT (FMEM)

The PCM contains back-up programs that allow the engine to operate if a sensor signal is lost. If sensor input is seen to be out of range —either high or low —the FMEM program is used. The processor substitutes a fixed value for the missing sensor signal. The engine will continue to operate, although performance and driveability may be noticeably reduced. This function of the controller is sometimes referred to as the limp-in or fail-safe mode. If the missing sensor signal is restored, the FMEM system immediately returns the system to normal operation. The dashboard-warning lamp will be lit when FMEM is in effect.

### HARDWARE LIMITED OPERATION STRATEGY (HLOS)

This mode is only used if the fault is too extreme for the FMEM circuit to handle. In this mode, the processor has ceased all computation and control; the entire system is run on fixed values. The vehicle may be operated but performance and driveability will be greatly reduced. The fixed or default settings provide minimal calibration, allowing the vehicle to be carefully driven in for service. The dashboard-warning lamp will be lit when HLOS is engaged. Codes cannot be read while the system is operating in this mode.

## Diagnostic Link Connector

With the advent of OBD-II, the Federal Government has mandated the location of the DLC (Data Link Connector) .The Data Link Connector is located in the passenger compartment. It is attached to the instrument panel and accessible from the driver's seat.

The DLC is rectangular in design and capable of allowing access to 16 terminals. The connector has keying features that allow easy connection. The test equipment and the DLC have a latching feature to ensure a good mated connection. The Scan tool uses the DLC as a pathway to communicate with the on board computer system.

If the DLC is not located under the dash, the vehicle is using OBD-I. This is a slightly different management system in its operation and diagnosis. Look for DLC under the hood near the left front headlight on the Town Car and Mark VII, near the right side firewall on the Continental.

### HAND-HELD SCAN TOOLS

**➧ See Figures 66, 67, 68 and 69**

Although stored codes may be read through the flashing of the CHECK ENGINE or SERVICE ENGINE SOON lamp, the use of hand-held scan tools such as Ford's Self-Test Automatic Readout (STAR) tester or the second generation SUPER STAR II tester or their equivalent is highly recommended. There are many manufacturers of these tools; the purchaser must be certain that the tool is proper for the intended use.

The scan tool allows any stored faults to be read from the engine controller memory. Use of the scan tool provides additional data during troubleshooting, but does not eliminate the use of the charts. The scan tool makes collecting information easier, but an operator familiar with the system must correctly interpret the data.

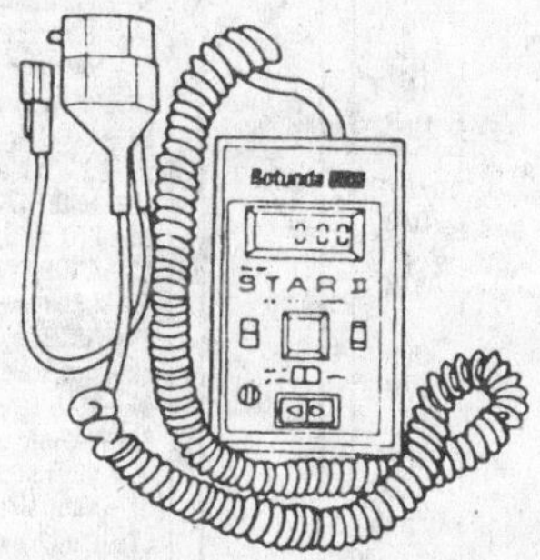


84924047

**Fig. 66 Super Star II tester —Ford Motor Co.**

TCCS4P11

**Fig. 67 Inexpensive scan tools, such as this Auto Xray ®, are available to interface with your Ford vehicle**

91054P14

**Fig. 68 An economically friendly alternative is this Code Scanner® from SunPro. They are purchased according to manufacturer and are available at many parts stores**

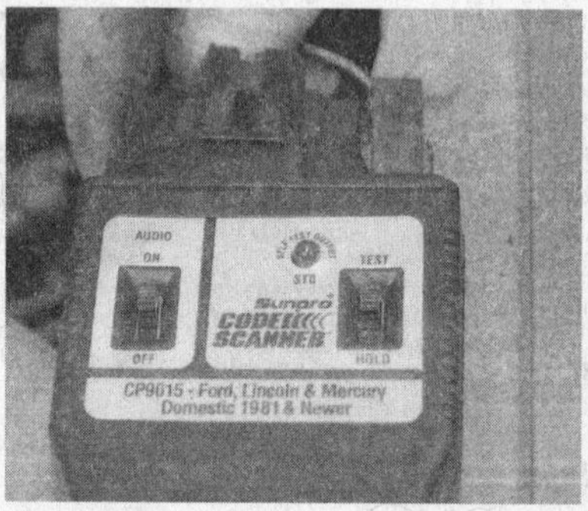


91054P16

**Fig. 69 The Code Scanner® from SunPro has no LCD display, just a LED that will flash out the codes and an audible buzzer to alert that the test is in progress**

### ELECTRICAL TOOLS

The most commonly required electrical diagnostic tool is the digital multimeter; also known as a Digital Volt Ohmmeter (DVOM), which permits voltage, resistance (ohms) and amperage to be read by one instrument.

The multimeter must be a high impedance unit, with 10 megaohms of impedance in the voltmeter. This type of meter will not place an additional load on the circuit it is testing; this is extremely important in low voltage circuits. The multimeter must be of high quality in all respects. It should be handled carefully and protected from impact or damage. Replace the batteries frequently in the unit.

Additionally, an analog (needle type) voltmeter may be used to read stored fault codes if the STAR tester is not available. The codes are transmitted as visible needle sweeps on the face of the instrument.

Nearly all the diagnostic procedures will require

the use of a Breakout Box, a device that connects into the EEC-IV harness and provides testing ports for the 60 wires in the harness. Direct testing of the harness connectors at the terminals or by backprobing is not recommended; damage to the wiring and terminals are almost certain to occur.

Other necessary tools include a quality tachometer with inductive (clip-on) pickup, a fuel pressure gauge with system adapters and a vacuum gauge with an auxiliary source of vacuum.

## Reading Codes

Diagnosis of a driveability problem requires attention to detail and following the diagnostic procedures in the correct order. Resist the temptation to begin extensive testing before completing the preliminary diagnostic steps. The preliminary or visual inspection must be completed in detail before diagnosis begins. In many cases this will shorten diagnostic time and often cure the problem without electronic testing.

### VISUAL INSPECTION

This is possibly the most critical step of diagnosis. A detailed examination of all connectors, wiring and vacuum hoses can often lead to a repair without further diagnosis. Performance of this step relies on the skill of the technician performing it; a careful inspector will check the undersides of hoses as well as the integrity of hard-to-reach hoses blocked by the air cleaner or other components. Wiring should be checked carefully for any sign of strain, burning, crimping or terminal pull-out from a connector.

Checking connectors at components or in harnesses is required; usually, pushing them together will reveal a loose fit. Pay particular attention to ground circuits, making sure they are not loose or corroded. Remember to inspect connectors and hose fittings at components not mounted on the engine, such as the evaporative canister or relays mounted on the fender aprons. Any component or wiring near a fluid leak or spillage should be given extra attention during inspection.

Additionally, inspect maintenance items such as belt condition and tension, battery charge and condition and the radiator cap carefully. Any of these very simple items may affect the system enough to set a fault.

### ELECTRONIC TESTING

If a code was set before a problem self-corrected (such as a momentarily loose connector), the code will be erased if the problem does not reoccur within 80 warm-up cycles. Codes will be output and displayed as numbers on the hand-held scan tool, such as 23. If the codes are being read on an analog voltmeter, the needle sweeps indicate the code digits. code 23 will appear as two needle pulses (sweeps) then, after a 1.6 second pause, the needle will pulse (sweep) three times.

| Service Codes | Quick Test Mode |
|---|---|
| 11—System pass | O/R/C |
| 12—Rpm unable to reach upper test limit | R |
| 13—DC motor movement not detected | O |
| 13—Rpm unable to achieve lower test limit | R |
| 13—DC motor did follow dashpot | C |
| 14—PIP circuit failure | C |
| 15—ECA read only memory test failed | O |
| 15—ECA keep alive memory test failed | C |
| 16—Idle rpm high with ISC off | R |
| 16—Idle too low to perform EGO test | R |
| 17—Idle rpm low with ISC off | R |
| 18—SPOUT circuit open or spark angle word failure | R |
| 18—IDM circuit failure or SPOUT circuit grounded | C |
| 19—Failure in ECA internal voltage | O |
| 19—CID circuit failure | C |
| 19—Rpm dropped too low in ISC off test | R |
| 19—Rpm for EGR test not achieved | R |
| 21—ECT out of self-test range | O/R |
| 22—BP sensor out of self-test range | O/C |
| 22—BP or MAP out of self-test range | O/R/C |
| 23—TP out of self-test range | O/R |
| 23—TP out of self-test range | O/R/C |
| 24—ACT sensor out of self-test range | O/R |
| 25—Knock not sensed during dynamic test | R |
| 26—VAF/MAF out of self-test range | O/R |
| 28—VAT out of self-test range | O/R |
| 29—Insufficient input from vehicle speed sensor | C |
| 31—PFE, EVP or EVR circuit below minimum voltage | O/R/C |
| 32—EPT circuit voltage low (PFE) | R/C |
| 32—EVP voltage below closed limit | O/R/C |
| 32—EGR not controlling | R |
| 33—EGR valve opening not detected | R/C |
| 33—EGR not closing fully | R |
| 34—Defective PFE sensor or voltage out of range | O |
| 34—EPT sensor voltage high (PFE) | R/C |
| 34—EVP voltage above closed limit | O/R/C |
| 34—EGR opening not detected | R |
| 35—PFE or EVP circuit above maximum voltage | O/R/C |
| 35—Rpm too low to perform EGR test | R |
| 38—Idle tracking switch circuit open | C |
| 39—AXOD lock up failed | C |
| 41—HEGO sensor circuit indicates system lean | R |
| 41—No HEGO switching detected | R |
| 42—HEGO sensor circuit indicates system rich | R |
| 42—No HEGO switching detected—reads rich | C |
| 43—HEGO lean at wide open throttle | C |
| 44—Thermactor air system inoperative—ride side | R |
| 45—Thermactor air upstream during self-test | R |
| 45—Coil 1 primary circuit failure | C |
| 46—Thermactor air not bypassed during self-test | R |
| 46—Coil 2 primary circuit failure | C |
| 47—Measured airflow low at base idle | R |
| 48—Coil 3 primary circuit failure | C |
| 48—Measured airflow high at base idle | R |
| 49—SPOUT signal defaulted to 10°BTDC or SPOUT open | C |
| 51—ECT/ACT reads −40°F or circuit open | O/C |
| 52—Power steering pressure switch circuit open | O |
| 52—Power steering pressure switch always open or closed | R |

93144G04

**EEC-IV trouble codes—(1 of 3)**

| Service Codes | Quick Test Mode |
|---|---|
| 53—TP circuit above maximum voltage | O/C |
| 54—ACT sensor circuit open | O/C |
| 55—Keypower circuit open | R |
| 56—VAF or MAF circuit above maximum voltage | O/C |
| 56—MAF circuit above maximum voltage | O/R/C |
| 57—Octane adjust service pin in use | O |
| 57—AXOD neutral pressure switch circuit failed open | C |
| 58—Idle tracking switch circuit open | O |
| 58—Idle tracking switch closed/circuit grounded | R |
| 58—VAT reads −40°F or circuit open | O/C |
| 59—Idle adjust service pin in use | O |
| 59—AXOD 4/3 pressure switch circuit failed open | C |
| 59—Low speed fuel pump circuit open—Battery to ECA | O/C |
| 59—AXOD 4/3 pressure switch failed closed | O |
| 61—ECT reads 254°F or circuit grounded | O/C |
| 62—AXOD 4/3 or 3/2 pressure switch circuit grounded | O |
| 63—TP circuit below minimum voltage | O/C |
| 64—ACT sensor input below test minimum or grounded | O/C |
| 65—Never went to closed loop fuel control | C |
| 66—MAF sensor input below minimum voltage | C |
| 66—VAF sensor below minimum voltage | O/C |
| 66—MAF circuit below minimum voltage | R/C |
| 67—Neutral/drive switch open or A/C on | O |
| 67—Clutch switch circuit failure | C |
| 67—Neutral/drive switch open or A/C on | O/R |
| 68—Idle tracking switch closed or circuit grounded | O |
| 68—Idle tracking switch circuit open | R |
| 68—AXOD transmission temperature switch failed open | O/R/C |
| 68—VAT reads 254°F or circuit grounded | O/C |
| 69—AXOD 3/2 pressure switch circuit failed closed | O |
| 69—AXOD 3/4 pressure switch circiut failed open | C |
| 70—ECA DATA communications link circuit failure | C |
| 71—Software re-initialization detected | C |
| 71—Idle tracking switch shorted to ground | C |
| 71—Cluster control assembly circuit failed | C |
| 72—Insufficient MAF/MAP change during dynamic test | R |
| 72—Power interrupt or re-initialization detected | C |
| 72—Message center control assembly circuit failed | C |
| 73—Insufficient throttle position change | O |
| 73—Insufficient TP change during dynamic test | R |
| 74—Brake on/off switch failure or not actuated | R |
| 75—Brake on/off switch circuit closed or ECA input open | R |
| 76—Insufficient VAF change during dynamic test | R |
| 77—No WOT seen in self-test or operator error | R |
| 79—A/C or defrost on during self-test | O |

93144G05

**EEC-IV trouble codes —(2 of 3)**

| Service Codes | Quick Test Mode |
|---|---|
| 81—IAS circuit failure | O |
| 81—Air management 2 circuit failure | O |
| 82—Air management 1 circuit failure | O |
| 82—Supercharger bypass circuit failure | O |
| 83—High speed electro drive fan circuit failure | O |
| 83—Low speed fuel pump circuit failure | O/C |
| 84—EGR vacuum solenoid circuit failure | O |
| 84—EGR vacuum regulator circuit failure | O/R |
| 85—Canister purge circuit failure | O/R |
| 85—Canister purge solenoid circuit failure | O |
| 85—Adaptive fuel lean limit reached | C |
| 86—3-4 shift solenoid circuit failure | O |
| 86—Adaptive fuel rich limit reached | C |
| 87—Fuel pump primary circuit failure | O/C |
| 87—Fuel pump primary circuit failure | O/C/R |
| 87—Fuel pump primary circuit failure | O |
| 88—Electro drive fan circuit failure | O |
| 89—Converter clutch override circuit failure | O |
| 89—Lock-up solenoid circuit failure | O |
| 91—HEGO sensor indicates system lean | R |
| 91—No HEGO switching detected | C |
| 92—HEGO sensor indicates system rich | R |
| 93—TP sensor input low at maximum motor travel | O |
| 94—Thermactor air system inoperative-left side | R |
| 95—Fuel pump secondary circuit failure—ECA to ground | O/C |
| 96—Fuel pump secondary circuit failure—Battery to ECA | O/C |
| 96—High speed fuel pump circuit open | O/C |
| 98—Hard fault present | R |
| 99—EEC has not learned to control idle: ignore codes 12 & 13 | R |

No Codes: Cannot begin self-test or cannot transmit codes
Codes Not Listed: Do not apply to vehicle being tested
O—Key on, engine off test
R—Key on, engine running test
C—Continuous memory
① Front HEGO
② Right HEGO
③ Left HEGO
④ Rear HEGO

93144G06

**EEC-IV trouble codes —(3 of 3)**

### Key On Engine Off (KOEO) Test

**See Figures 70 thru 76**

1. Connect the scan tool to the self-test connectors. Make certain the test button is unlatched or up.
2. Start the engine and run it until normal operating temperature is reached.
3. Turn the engine **OFF** for 10 seconds.
4. Activate the test button on the STAR tester.
5. Turn the ignition switch **ON** but do not start the engine.
6. The KOEO codes will be transmitted. Six to nine seconds after the last KOEO code, a single separator pulse will be transmitted. Six to nine seconds after this pulse, the codes from the Continuous Memory will be transmitted.
7. Record all service codes displayed. Do not depress the throttle on gasoline engines during the test.

### Key On Engine Running (KOER) Test

**See Figures 66, 75, and 77**

84924042

1. Make certain the self-test button is released or de-activated on the STAR tester.
2. Start the engine and run it at 2000 rpm for two minutes. This action warms up the oxygen sensor.
3. Turn the ignition switch **OFF** for 10 seconds.
4. Activate or latch the self-test button on the scan tool.
5. Start the engine. The engine identification

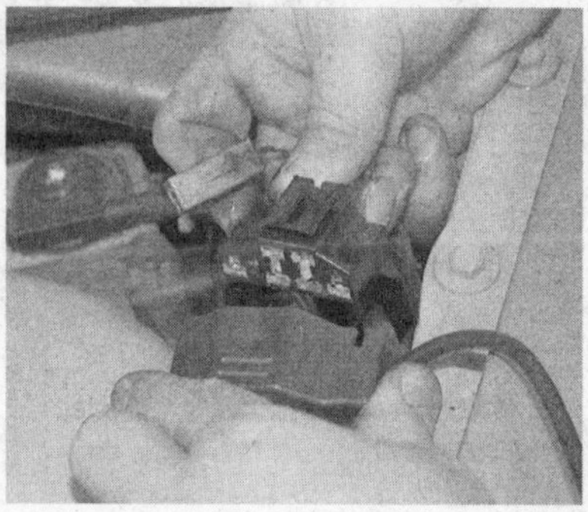

91054P04

**Fig. 70 Connect the scan tool to the DLC connector**

91054P05

**Fig. 71 The scan tool menu will be displayed, follow the instructions included with the scan tool**

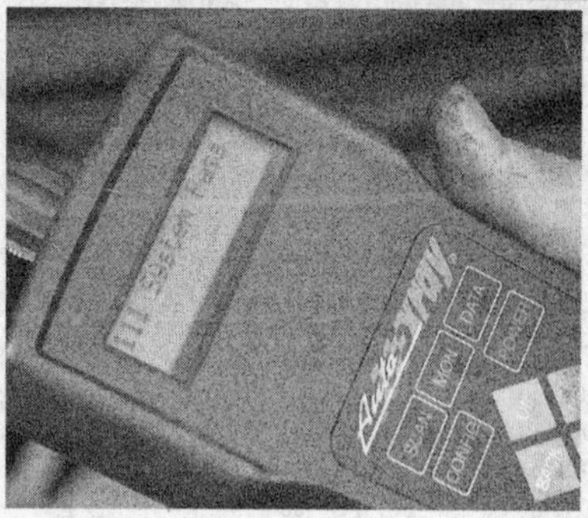

91054P08

**Fig. 72 This PCM had no DTC's stored and passed the KOEO**

91054P06

**Fig. 73 This PCM had a DTC 113 stored. Most scan tools will give a code definition on-screen as the Auto X-ray shown here informs what code 113 is for— the IAT sensor**

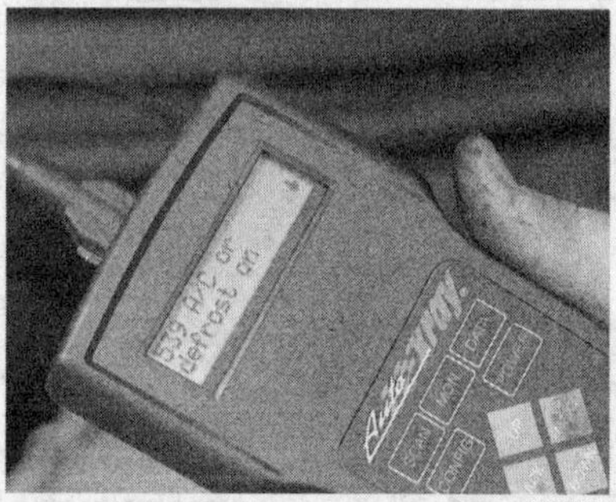

91054P07

**Fig. 74 If the A/C or Blower motor is left on, a code 539 will be tripped. Turn the A/C or blower motor off and retest**

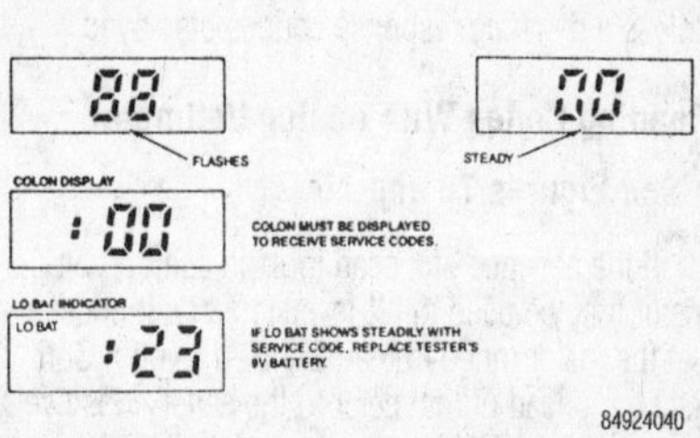


84924040

**Fig. 75 STAR tester displays; note that the colon must be present before codes can be received**

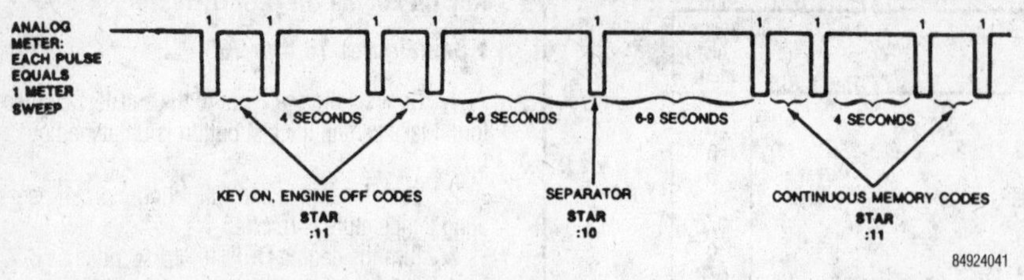


**Fig. 76 Code transmission during KOEO test. Note that the continuous memory codes are transmitted after a pause and a separator pulse**

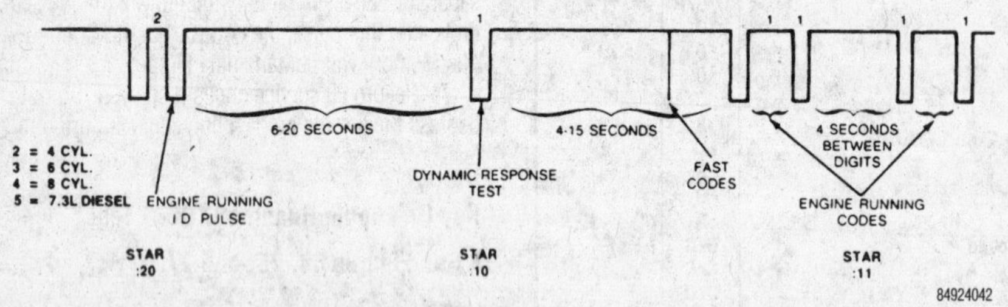


**Fig. 77 Code transmission during KOER testing begins with the engine identification pulse and may include a dynamic response prompt**

code will be transmitted. This is a single digit number representing ½ the number of cylinders in a gasoline engine. On the STAR tester, this number may appear with a zero, such as 20 = 2. The code is used to confirm that the correct processor is installed and that the self-test has begun.

6. If the vehicle is equipped with a Brake On/Off (BOO) switch, the brake pedal must be depressed and released after the ID code is transmitted.

7. If the vehicle is equipped with a Power Steering Pressure Switch (PSPS), the steering wheel must be turned at least ½ turn and released within 2 seconds after the engine ID code is transmitted.

8. Certain Ford vehicles will display a Dynamic Response code 6 –20 seconds after the engine ID code. This will appear as one pulse on a meter or as a 10 on the STAR tester. When this code appears, briefly take the engine to wide-open throttle. This allows the system to test the throttle position, MAF and MAP sensors.

9. All relevant codes will be displayed and should be recorded. Remember that the codes refer only to faults present during this test cycle. Codes stored in Continuous Memory are not displayed in this test mode.

10. Do not depress the throttle during testing unless a dynamic response code is displayed.

### Reading Codes With Analog Voltmeter

**▶ See Figures 78 and 79**

In the absence of a scan tool, an analog voltmeter may be used to retrieve stored fault codes. Set the meter range to read DC 0 –15 volts. Connect the + lead of the meter to the battery positive terminal and connect the -; lead of the meter to the self-test output pin of the diagnostic connector.

Follow the directions given previously for performing the KOEO and KOER tests. To activate the tests, use a jumper wire to connect the signal return pin on the diagnostic connector to the self-test input connector. The self-test input line is the separate wire and connector with or near the diagnostic connector.

The codes will be transmitted as groups of needle sweeps. This method may be used to read either 2 or 3-digit codes. The Continuous Memory codes are separated from the KOEO codes by 6 seconds, a single sweep and another 6-second delay.

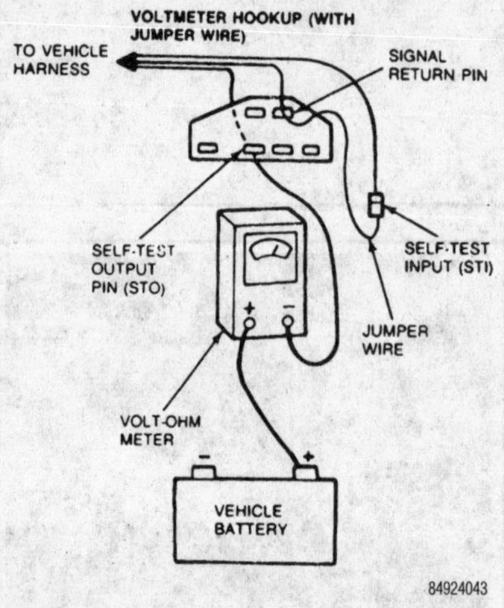


**Fig. 78 Correct hookup to read codes with a voltmeter**

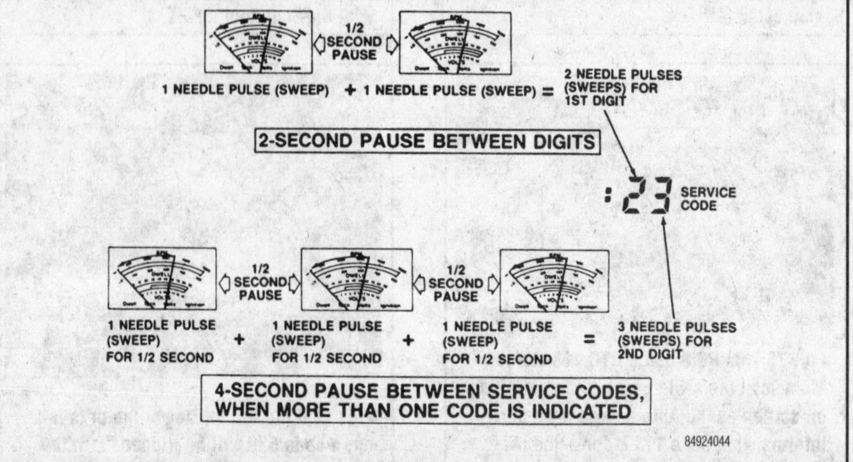


**Fig. 79 Code display patterns on an analog voltmeter**

### Malfunction Indicator Lamp Method

**▶ See Figures 80 and 81**

The Malfunction Indicator Lamp (MIL) on the dashboard may also be used to retrieve the stored codes. This method displays only the stored codes and does not allow any system investigation. It should only be used in field conditions where a quick check of stored codes is needed.

Follow the directions given previously for performing the scan tool procedure. To activate the tests, use a jumper wire to connect the signal return pin on the diagnostic connector to the Self-Test Input (STI) connector. The self-test input line is the separate wire and connector with or near the diagnostic connector.

Codes are transmitted by place value with a pause between the digits; for example, code 32 would be sent as 3 flashes, a pause and 2 flashes. A slightly longer pause divides codes from each other. Be ready to count and record codes; the only way to repeat a code is to recycle the system. This method may be used to read either 2 or 3-digit codes. The Continuous Memory codes are separated from the other codes by 6 seconds, a single flash and another 6-second delay.

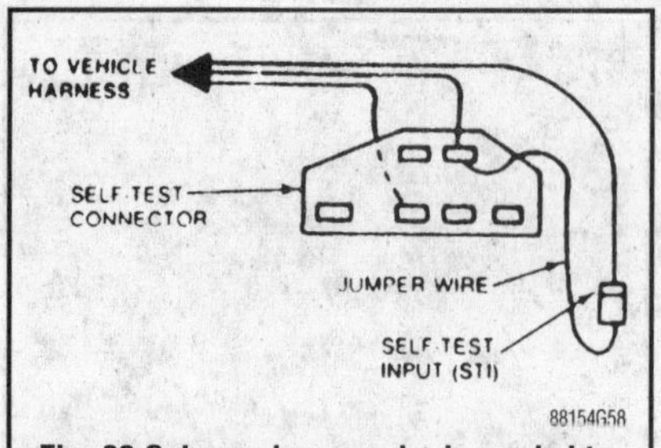


**Fig. 80 Only one jumper wire is needed to read codes through the MIL or the message center**

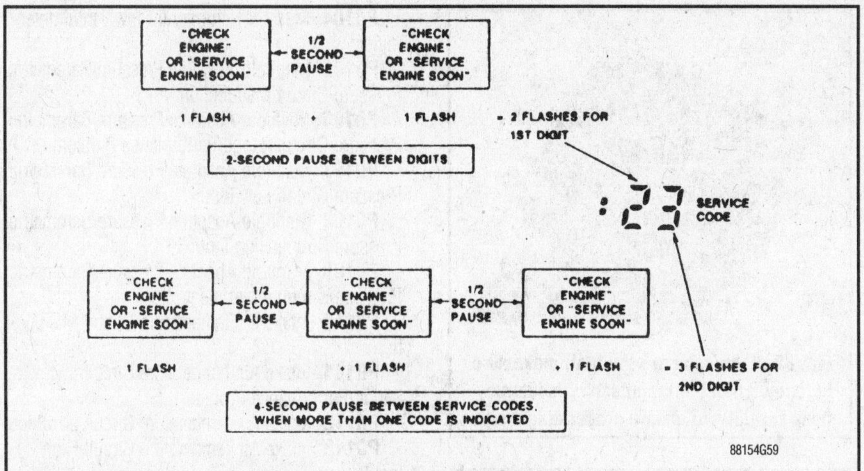


**Fig. 81 Code display pattern using the dashboard warning lamp**

### Other Test Modes

#### *CONTINUOUS MONITOR OR WIGGLE TEST*

Once entered, this mode allows the operator to attempt to recreate intermittent faults by wiggling or tapping components, wiring or connectors. The test may be performed during either KOEO or KOER procedures. The test requires the use of either an analog voltmeter or a hand-held scan tool.

To enter the continuous monitor mode during KOEO testing, turn the ignition switch **ON** . Activate the test, wait 10 seconds, then deactivate, and reactivate the test; the system will enter the continuous monitor mode. Tap, move, or wiggle the harness, component or connector suspected of causing the problem; if a fault is detected, the code will store in the memory. When the fault occurs, the dash-warning lamp will illuminate, the STAR tester will light a red indicator (and possibly beep) and the analog meter needle will sweep once.

To enter this mode in the KOER test:

1. Start the engine and run it at 2000 rpm for two minutes. This action warms up the oxygen sensor.
2. Turn the ignition switch **OFF** for 10 seconds.
3. Start the engine.
4. Activate the test, wait 10 seconds, then deactivate, and reactivate the test; the system will enter the continuous monitor mode.
5. Tap, move, or wiggle the harness, component or connector suspected of causing the problem; if a fault is detected, the code will store in the memory.
6. When the fault occurs, the dash-warning lamp will illuminate, the STAR tester will light a red indicator (and possibly beep) and the analog meter needle will sweep once.

#### *OUTPUT STATE CHECK*

This testing mode allows the operator to energize and de-energize most of the outputs controlled by the EEC-IV system. Many of the outputs may be checked at the component by listening for a click or feeling the item move or engage by a hand placed on the case. To enter this check:

1. Enter the KOEO test mode.
2. When all codes have been transmitted, depress the accelerator all the way to the floor and release it.
3. The output actuators are now all ON. Depressing the throttle pedal to the floor again switches the all the actuator outputs OFF.
4. This test may be performed as often as necessary, switching between ON and OFF by depressing the throttle.
5. Exit the test by turning the ignition switch **OFF** , detaching the jumper at the diagnostic connector or releasing the test button on the scan tool.

### Clearing Codes

#### CONTINUOUS MEMORY CODES

These codes are retained in memory for 40 warm-up cycles. To clear the codes for purposes of testing or confirming repair, perform the code reading procedure. When the fault codes begin to be displayed, de-activate the test either by disconnecting the jumper wire (if using a meter, MIL or message center) or by releasing the test button on the hand scanner. Stopping the test during code transmission will erase the Continuous Memory. Do not disconnect the negative battery cable to clear these codes; the Keep Alive memory will be cleared and a new code, 19, will be stored for loss of PCM power.

#### KEEP ALIVE MEMORY

The Keep Alive Memory (KAM) contains the adaptive factors used by the processor to compensate for component tolerances and wear. It should not be routinely cleared during diagnosis. If an emission related part is replaced during repair, the KAM must be cleared. Failure to clear the KAM may cause severe driveability problems since the correction factor for the old component will be applied to the new component.

To clear the Keep Alive Memory, disconnect the negative battery cable for at least 5 minutes. After the memory is cleared and the battery reconnected, the vehicle must be driven at least 10 miles (16 km) so that the processor may relearn the needed correction factors. The distance to be driven depends on the engine and vehicle, but all drives should include steady-throttle cruise on open roads. Certain driveability problems may be noted during the drive because the adaptive factors are not yet functioning.

## TROUBLE CODES —EEC-V SYSTEM (OBD-II)

### General Information

The Powertrain Control Module (PCM) is given responsibility for the operation of the emission control devices, cooling fans, ignition and advance and in some cases, automatic transmission functions. Because the EEC-V oversees both the ignition timing and the fuel injection operation, a precise air/fuel ratio will be maintained under all operating conditions. The PCM is a microprocessor or small computer that receives electrical inputs from several sensors, switches, and relays on and around the engine.

Based on combinations of these inputs, the PCM controls various output devices concerned with engine operation and emissions. The control module relies on the signals to form a correct picture of current vehicle operation. If any of the input signals is incorrect, the PCM reacts to whatever picture is painted for it. For example, if the coolant temperature sensor is inaccurate and reads too low, the PCM may see a picture of the engine never warming up. Consequently, the engine settings will be maintained as if the engine were cold. Because so many inputs can affect one output, correct diagnostic procedures are essential on these systems.

One part of the PCM is devoted to monitoring both input and output functions within the system. This ability forms the core of the self-diagnostic system. If a problem is detected within a circuit, the control module will recognize the fault, assign it an Diagnostic Trouble Code (DTC), and store the code in memory. The stored code(s) may be retrieved during diagnosis.

While the EEC-V system is capable of recognizing many internal faults, certain faults will not be recognized. Because the control module sees only electrical signals, it cannot sense or react to mechanical or vacuum faults affecting engine operation. Some of these faults may affect another component which will set a code. For example, the PCM monitors the output signal to the fuel injectors, but cannot detect a partially clogged injector. As long as the output driver responds correctly, the computer will read the system as functioning correctly. However, the improper flow of fuel may result in a lean mixture. This would, in turn, be detected by the oxygen sensor and noticed as a constantly lean signal by the PCM. Once the signal falls outside the pre-programmed limits, the control module would notice the fault and set an trouble code.

Additionally, the EEC-V system employs adaptive fuel logic. This process is used to compensate for normal wear and variability within the fuel system. Once the engine enters steady-state operation, the control module watches the oxygen sensor signal for a bias or tendency to run slightly rich or lean. If such a bias is detected, the adaptive logic corrects the fuel delivery to bring the air/fuel mixture towards a centered or 14.7:1 ratio. This compensating shift is stored in a non-volatile memory which is retained by battery power even with the ignition switched **OFF**. The correction factor is then available the next time the vehicle is operated.

## Malfunction Indicator Lamp

The Malfunction Indicator Lamp (MIL) is located on the instrument panel. The lamp is connected to the PCM and will alert the driver to certain malfunctions within the EEC-V system. When the lamp is illuminated, the PCM has detected a fault and stored a DTC in memory.

The light will stay illuminated as long as the fault is present. Should the fault self-correct, the MIL will extinguish but the stored code will remain in memory.

Under normal operating conditions, the MIL should illuminate briefly when the ignition key is turned **ON**. This is commonly known as a prove-out. As soon as the PCM receives a signal that the engine is cranking, the lamp should extinguish. The lamp should remain extinguished during the normal operating cycle.

## Data Link Connector

The Data Link Connector (DLC) may be found in the following location:

- Under the driver's side dashboard, near the steering column.

The DLC is rectangular in design and capable of allowing access to 16 terminals. The connector has keying features that allow easy connection. The test equipment and the DLC have a latching feature to ensure a good mated connection.

### ELECTRICAL TOOLS

The most commonly required electrical diagnostic tool is the Digital Multimeter, allowing voltage, resistance, and amperage to be read by one instrument.

The multimeter must be a high impedance unit, with 10 megaohms of impedance in the voltmeter. This type of meter will not place an additional load on the circuit it is testing; this is extremely important in low voltage circuits. The multimeter must be of high quality in all respects. It should be handled carefully and protected from impact or damage. Replace the batteries frequently in the unit.

## Reading Codes

**See Figure 82**

The EEC-V equipped engines utilize On Board Diagnostic II (OBD-II) DTC's, which are alphanumeric (they use letters and numbers). The letters in the OBD-II DTC's make it highly difficult to convey the codes through the use of anything but a scan tool. Therefore, to read the codes on these vehicles it is necessary to utilize an OBD-II compatible scan tool.

Since each manufacturers scan tool is different, please follow the manufacturer's instructions for connecting the tool and obtaining code information.

TCCS4P08

**Fig. 82 When using a scan tool, make sure to follow all of the manufacturer's instructions carefully to ensure proper diagnosis**

## Clearing Codes

### CONTINUOUS MEMORY CODES

These codes are retained in memory for 40 warm-up cycles. To clear the codes for the purposes of testing or confirming repair, perform the code reading procedure. When the fault codes begin to be displayed, de-activate the test by either disconnecting the jumper wire (meter, MIL or message center) or releasing the test button on the hand scanner. Stopping the test during code transmission will erase the Continuous Memory. Do not disconnect the negative battery cable to clear these codes; the Keep Alive memory will be cleared and a new code, 19, will be stored for loss of PCM power.

### KEEP ALIVE MEMORY

The Keep Alive Memory (KAM) contains the adaptive factors used by the processor to compensate for component tolerances and wear. It should not be routinely cleared during diagnosis. If an emissions related part is replaced during repair, the KAM must be cleared. Failure to clear the KAM may cause severe driveability problems since the correction factor for the old component will be applied to the new component.

To clear the Keep Alive Memory, disconnect the negative battery cable for at least 5 minutes. After the memory is cleared and the battery reconnected, the vehicle must be driven at least 10 miles so that the processor may relearn the needed correction factors. The distance to be driven depends on the engine and vehicle, but all drives should include steady-throttle cruise on open roads. Certain driveability problems may be noted during the drive because the adaptive factors are not yet functioning.

## EEC-V Diagnostic Trouble Codes (DTC's)

**P0000** No Failures
**P0100** Mass or Volume Air Flow Circuit Malfunction
**P0101** Mass or Volume Air Flow Circuit Range/Performance Problem
**P0102** Mass or Volume Air Flow Circuit Low Input
**P0103** Mass or Volume Air Flow Circuit High Input
**P0104** Mass or Volume Air Flow Circuit Intermittent
**P0105** Manifold Absolute Pressure/Barometric Pressure Circuit Malfunction
**P0106** Manifold Absolute Pressure/Barometric Pressure Circuit Range/Performance Problem
**P0107** Manifold Absolute Pressure/Barometric Pressure Circuit Low Input
**P0108** Manifold Absolute Pressure/Barometric Pressure Circuit High Input
**P0109** Manifold Absolute Pressure/Barometric Pressure Circuit Intermittent
**P0110** Intake Air Temperature Circuit Malfunction
**P0111** Intake Air Temperature Circuit Range/Performance Problem
**P0112** Intake Air Temperature Circuit Low Input
**P0113** Intake Air Temperature Circuit High Input
**P0114** Intake Air Temperature Circuit Intermittent
**P0115** Engine Coolant Temperature Circuit Malfunction
**P0116** Engine Coolant Temperature Circuit Range/Performance Problem
**P0117** Engine Coolant Temperature Circuit Low Input
**P0118** Engine Coolant Temperature Circuit High Input
**P0119** Engine Coolant Temperature Circuit Intermittent
**P0120** Throttle/Pedal Position Sensor/Switch "A" Circuit Malfunction
**P0121** Throttle/Pedal Position Sensor/Switch "A" Circuit Range/Performance Problem
**P0122** Throttle/Pedal Position Sensor/Switch "A" Circuit Low Input
**P0123** Throttle/Pedal Position Sensor/Switch "A" Circuit High Input
**P0124** Throttle/Pedal Position Sensor/Switch "A" Circuit Intermittent
**P0125** Insufficient Coolant Temperature For Closed Loop Fuel Control
**P0126** Insufficient Coolant Temperature For Stable Operation
**P0130** O2 Circuit Malfunction (Bank 1 Sensor 1)
**P0131** O2 Sensor Circuit Low Voltage (Bank 1 Sensor 1)
**P0132** O2 Sensor Circuit High Voltage (Bank 1 Sensor 1)
**P0133** O2 Sensor Circuit Slow Response (Bank 1 Sensor 1)
**P0134** O2 Sensor Circuit No Activity Detected (Bank 1 Sensor 1)
**P0135** O2 Sensor Heater Circuit Malfunction (Bank 1 Sensor 1)
**P0136** O2 Sensor Circuit Malfunction (Bank 1 Sensor 2)
**P0137** O2 Sensor Circuit Low Voltage (Bank 1 Sensor 2)
**P0138** O2 Sensor Circuit High Voltage (Bank 1 Sensor 2)
**P0139** O2 Sensor Circuit Slow Response (Bank 1 Sensor 2)
**P0140** O2 Sensor Circuit No Activity Detected (Bank 1 Sensor 2)
**P0141** O2 Sensor Heater Circuit Malfunction (Bank 1 Sensor 2)
**P0142** O2 Sensor Circuit Malfunction (Bank 1 Sensor 3)
**P0143** O2 Sensor Circuit Low Voltage (Bank 1 Sensor 3)

**P0144** O2 Sensor Circuit High Voltage (Bank 1 Sensor 3)
**P0145** O2 Sensor Circuit Slow Response (Bank 1 Sensor 3)
**P0146** O2 Sensor Circuit No Activity Detected (Bank 1 Sensor 3)
**P0147** O2 Sensor Heater Circuit Malfunction (Bank 1 Sensor 3)
**P0150** O2 Sensor Circuit Malfunction (Bank 2 Sensor 1)
**P0151** O2 Sensor Circuit Low Voltage (Bank 2 Sensor 1)
**P0152** O2 Sensor Circuit High Voltage (Bank 2 Sensor 1)
**P0153** O2 Sensor Circuit Slow Response (Bank 2 Sensor 1)
**P0154** O2 Sensor Circuit No Activity Detected (Bank 2 Sensor 1)
**P0155** O2 Sensor Heater Circuit Malfunction (Bank 2 Sensor 1)
**P0156** O2 Sensor Circuit Malfunction (Bank 2 Sensor 2)
**P0157** O2 Sensor Circuit Low Voltage (Bank 2 Sensor 2)
**P0158** O2 Sensor Circuit High Voltage (Bank 2 Sensor 2)
**P0159** O2 Sensor Circuit Slow Response (Bank 2 Sensor 2)
**P0160** O2 Sensor Circuit No Activity Detected (Bank 2 Sensor 2)
**P0161** O2 Sensor Heater Circuit Malfunction (Bank 2 Sensor 2)
**P0162** O2 Sensor Circuit Malfunction (Bank 2 Sensor 3)
**P0163** O2 Sensor Circuit Low Voltage (Bank 2 Sensor 3)
**P0164** O2 Sensor Circuit High Voltage (Bank 2 Sensor 3)
**P0165** O2 Sensor Circuit Slow Response (Bank 2 Sensor 3)
**P0166** O2 Sensor Circuit No Activity Detected (Bank 2 Sensor 3)
**P0167** O2 Sensor Heater Circuit Malfunction (Bank 2 Sensor 3)
**P0170** Fuel Trim Malfunction (Bank 1)
**P0171** System Too Lean (Bank 1)
**P0172** System Too Rich (Bank 1)
**P0173** Fuel Trim Malfunction (Bank 2)
**P0174** System Too Lean (Bank 2)
**P0175** System Too Rich (Bank 2)
**P0180** Fuel Temperature Sensor "A" Circuit Malfunction
**P0181** Fuel Temperature Sensor "A" Circuit Range/Performance
**P0182** Fuel Temperature Sensor "A" Circuit Low Input
**P0183** Fuel Temperature Sensor "A" Circuit High Input
**P0184** Fuel Temperature Sensor "A" Circuit Intermittent
**P0185** Fuel Temperature Sensor "B" Circuit Malfunction
**P0186** Fuel Temperature Sensor "B" Circuit Range/Performance
**P0187** Fuel Temperature Sensor "B" Circuit Low Input
**P0188** Fuel Temperature Sensor "B" Circuit High Input
**P0189** Fuel Temperature Sensor "B" Circuit Intermittent
**P0190** Fuel Rail Pressure Sensor Circuit Malfunction
**P0191** Fuel Rail Pressure Sensor Circuit Range/Performance
**P0192** Fuel Rail Pressure Sensor Circuit Low Input
**P0193** Fuel Rail Pressure Sensor Circuit High Input
**P0194** Fuel Rail Pressure Sensor Circuit Intermittent
**P0200** Injector Circuit Malfunction
**P0201** Injector Circuit Malfunction —Cylinder 1
**P0202** Injector Circuit Malfunction —Cylinder 2
**P0203** Injector Circuit Malfunction —Cylinder 3
**P0204** Injector Circuit Malfunction —Cylinder 4
**P0205** Injector Circuit Malfunction —Cylinder 5
**P0206** Injector Circuit Malfunction —Cylinder 6
**P0207** Injector Circuit Malfunction —Cylinder 7
**P0208** Injector Circuit Malfunction —Cylinder 8
**P0215** Engine Shutoff Solenoid Malfunction
**P0217** Engine Over Temperature Condition
**P0218** Transmission Over Temperature Condition
**P0219** Engine Over Speed Condition
**P0220** Throttle/Pedal Position Sensor/Switch "B" Circuit Malfunction
**P0221** Throttle/Pedal Position Sensor/Switch "B" Circuit Range/Performance Problem
**P0222** Throttle/Pedal Position Sensor/Switch "B" Circuit Low Input
**P0223** Throttle/Pedal Position Sensor/Switch "B" Circuit High Input
**P0224** Throttle/Pedal Position Sensor/Switch "B" Circuit Intermittent
**P0225** Throttle/Pedal Position Sensor/Switch "C" Circuit Malfunction
**P0226** Throttle/Pedal Position Sensor/Switch "C" Circuit Range/Performance Problem
**P0227** Throttle/Pedal Position Sensor/Switch "C" Circuit Low Input
**P0228** Throttle/Pedal Position Sensor/Switch "C" Circuit High Input
**P0229** Throttle/Pedal Position Sensor/Switch "C" Circuit Intermittent
**P0230** Fuel Pump Primary Circuit Malfunction
**P0231** Fuel Pump Secondary Circuit Low
**P0232** Fuel Pump Secondary Circuit High
**P0233** Fuel Pump Secondary Circuit Intermittent
**P0261** Cylinder 1 Injector Circuit Low
**P0262** Cylinder 1 Injector Circuit High
**P0263** Cylinder 1 Contribution/Balance Fault
**P0264** Cylinder 2 Injector Circuit Low
**P0265** Cylinder 2 Injector Circuit High
**P0266** Cylinder 2 Contribution/Balance Fault
**P0267** Cylinder 3 Injector Circuit Low
**P0268** Cylinder 3 Injector Circuit High
**P0269** Cylinder 3 Contribution/Balance Fault
**P0270** Cylinder 4 Injector Circuit Low
**P0271** Cylinder 4 Injector Circuit High
**P0272** Cylinder 4 Contribution/Balance Fault
**P0273** Cylinder 5 Injector Circuit Low
**P0274** Cylinder 5 Injector Circuit High
**P0275** Cylinder 5 Contribution/Balance Fault
**P0276** Cylinder 6 Injector Circuit Low
**P0277** Cylinder 6 Injector Circuit High
**P0278** Cylinder 6 Contribution/Balance Fault
**P0279** Cylinder 7 Injector Circuit Low
**P0280** Cylinder 7 Injector Circuit High
**P0281** Cylinder 7 Contribution/Balance Fault
**P0282** Cylinder 8 Injector Circuit Low
**P0283** Cylinder 8 Injector Circuit High
**P0284** Cylinder 8 Contribution/Balance Fault
**P0300** Random/Multiple Cylinder Misfire Detected
**P0301** Cylinder 1 —Misfire Detected
**P0302** Cylinder 2 —Misfire Detected
**P0303** Cylinder 3 —Misfire Detected
**P0304** Cylinder 4 —Misfire Detected
**P0305** Cylinder 5 —Misfire Detected
**P0306** Cylinder 6 —Misfire Detected
**P0307** Cylinder 7 —Misfire Detected
**P0308** Cylinder 8 —Misfire Detected
**P0320** Ignition/Distributor Engine Speed Input Circuit Malfunction
**P0321** Ignition/Distributor Engine Speed Input Circuit Range/Performance
**P0322** Ignition/Distributor Engine Speed Input Circuit No Signal
**P0323** Ignition/Distributor Engine Speed Input Circuit Intermittent
**P0325** Knock Sensor 1 —Circuit Malfunction (Bank 1 or Single Sensor)
**P0326** Knock Sensor 1 —Circuit Range/Performance (Bank 1 or Single Sensor)
**P0327** Knock Sensor 1 —Circuit Low Input (Bank 1 or Single Sensor)
**P0328** Knock Sensor 1 —Circuit High Input (Bank 1 or Single Sensor)
**P0329** Knock Sensor 1 —Circuit Input Intermittent (Bank 1 or Single Sensor)
**P0330** Knock Sensor 2 —Circuit Malfunction (Bank 2)
**P0331** Knock Sensor 2 —Circuit Range/Performance (Bank 2)
**P0332** Knock Sensor 2 —Circuit Low Input (Bank 2)
**P0333** Knock Sensor 2 —Circuit High Input (Bank 2)
**P0334** Knock Sensor 2 —Circuit Input Intermittent (Bank 2)
**P0335** Crankshaft Position Sensor "A" Circuit Malfunction
**P0336** Crankshaft Position Sensor "A" Circuit Range/Performance
**P0337** Crankshaft Position Sensor "A" Circuit Low Input
**P0338** Crankshaft Position Sensor "A" Circuit High Input
**P0339** Crankshaft Position Sensor "A" Circuit Intermittent
**P0340** Camshaft Position Sensor Circuit Malfunction
**P0341** Camshaft Position Sensor Circuit Range/Performance
**P0342** Camshaft Position Sensor Circuit Low Input
**P0343** Camshaft Position Sensor Circuit High Input
**P0344** Camshaft Position Sensor Circuit Intermittent
**P0350** Ignition Coil Primary/Secondary Circuit Malfunction
**P0351** Ignition Coil "A" Primary/Secondary Circuit Malfunction
**P0352** Ignition Coil "B" Primary/Secondary Circuit Malfunction
**P0353** Ignition Coil "C" Primary/Secondary Circuit Malfunction
**P0354** Ignition Coil "D" Primary/Secondary Circuit Malfunction

**P0355** Ignition Coil "E" Primary/Secondary Circuit Malfunction
**P0356** Ignition Coil "F" Primary/Secondary Circuit Malfunction
**P0357** Ignition Coil "G" Primary/Secondary Circuit Malfunction
**P0358** Ignition Coil "H" Primary/Secondary Circuit Malfunction
**P0359** Ignition Coil "I" Primary/Secondary Circuit Malfunction
**P0360** Ignition Coil "J" Primary/Secondary Circuit Malfunction
**P0361** Ignition Coil "K" Primary/Secondary Circuit Malfunction
**P0362** Ignition Coil "L" Primary/Secondary Circuit Malfunction
**P0370** Timing Reference High Resolution Signal "A" Malfunction
**P0371** Timing Reference High Resolution Signal "A" Too Many Pulses
**P0372** Timing Reference High Resolution Signal "A" Too Few Pulses
**P0373** Timing Reference High Resolution Signal "A" Intermittent/Erratic Pulses
**P0374** Timing Reference High Resolution Signal "A" No Pulses
**P0375** Timing Reference High Resolution Signal "B" Malfunction
**P0376** Timing Reference High Resolution Signal "B" Too Many Pulses
**P0377** Timing Reference High Resolution Signal "B" Too Few Pulses
**P0378** Timing Reference High Resolution Signal "B" Intermittent/Erratic Pulses
**P0379** Timing Reference High Resolution Signal "B" No Pulses
**P0385** Crankshaft Position Sensor "B" Circuit Malfunction
**P0386** Crankshaft Position Sensor "B" Circuit Range/Performance
**P0387** Crankshaft Position Sensor "B" Circuit Low Input
**P0388** Crankshaft Position Sensor "B" Circuit High Input
**P0389** Crankshaft Position Sensor "B" Circuit Intermittent
**P0400** Exhaust Gas Recirculation Flow Malfunction
**P0401** Exhaust Gas Recirculation Flow Insufficient Detected
**P0402** Exhaust Gas Recirculation Flow Excessive Detected
**P0403** Exhaust Gas Recirculation Circuit Malfunction
**P0404** Exhaust Gas Recirculation Circuit Range/Performance
**P0405** Exhaust Gas Recirculation Sensor "A" Circuit Low
**P0406** Exhaust Gas Recirculation Sensor "A" Circuit High
**P0407** Exhaust Gas Recirculation Sensor "B" Circuit Low
**P0408** Exhaust Gas Recirculation Sensor "B" Circuit High
**P0410** Secondary Air Injection System Malfunction
**P0411** Secondary Air Injection System Incorrect Flow Detected
**P0412** Secondary Air Injection System Switching Valve "A" Circuit Malfunction
**P0413** Secondary Air Injection System Switching Valve "A" Circuit Open
**P0414** Secondary Air Injection System Switching Valve "A" Circuit Shorted
**P0415** Secondary Air Injection System Switching Valve "B" Circuit Malfunction
**P0416** Secondary Air Injection System Switching Valve "B" Circuit Open
**P0417** Secondary Air Injection System Switching Valve "B" Circuit Shorted
**P0418** Secondary Air Injection System Relay "A" Circuit Malfunction
**P0419** Secondary Air Injection System Relay "B" Circuit Malfunction
**P0420** Catalyst System Efficiency Below Threshold (Bank 1)
**P0421** Warm Up Catalyst Efficiency Below Threshold (Bank 1)
**P0422** Main Catalyst Efficiency Below Threshold (Bank 1)
**P0423** Heated Catalyst Efficiency Below Threshold (Bank 1)
**P0424** Heated Catalyst Temperature Below Threshold (Bank 1)
**P0430** Catalyst System Efficiency Below Threshold (Bank 2)
**P0431** Warm Up Catalyst Efficiency Below Threshold (Bank 2)
**P0432** Main Catalyst Efficiency Below Threshold (Bank 2)
**P0433** Heated Catalyst Efficiency Below Threshold (Bank 2)
**P0434** Heated Catalyst Temperature Below Threshold (Bank 2)
**P0440** Evaporative Emission Control System Malfunction
**P0441** Evaporative Emission Control System Incorrect Purge Flow
**P0442** Evaporative Emission Control System Leak Detected (Small Leak)
**P0443** Evaporative Emission Control System Purge Control Valve Circuit Malfunction
**P0444** Evaporative Emission Control System Purge Control Valve Circuit Open
**P0445** Evaporative Emission Control System Purge Control Valve Circuit Shorted
**P0446** Evaporative Emission Control System Vent Control Circuit Malfunction
**P0447** Evaporative Emission Control System Vent Control Circuit Open
**P0448** Evaporative Emission Control System Vent Control Circuit Shorted
**P0449** Evaporative Emission Control System Vent Valve/Solenoid Circuit Malfunction
**P0450** Evaporative Emission Control System Pressure Sensor Malfunction
**P0451** Evaporative Emission Control System Pressure Sensor Range/Performance
**P0452** Evaporative Emission Control System Pressure Sensor Low Input
**P0453** Evaporative Emission Control System Pressure Sensor High Input
**P0454** Evaporative Emission Control System Pressure Sensor Intermittent
**P0455** Evaporative Emission Control System Leak Detected (Gross Leak)
**P0460** Fuel Level Sensor Circuit Malfunction
**P0461** Fuel Level Sensor Circuit Range/Performance
**P0462** Fuel Level Sensor Circuit Low Input
**P0463** Fuel Level Sensor Circuit High Input
**P0464** Fuel Level Sensor Circuit Intermittent
**P0465** Purge Flow Sensor Circuit Malfunction
**P0466** Purge Flow Sensor Circuit Range/Performance
**P0467** Purge Flow Sensor Circuit Low Input
**P0468** Purge Flow Sensor Circuit High Input
**P0469** Purge Flow Sensor Circuit Intermittent
**P0480** Cooling Fan 1 Control Circuit Malfunction
**P0481** Cooling Fan 2 Control Circuit Malfunction
**P0482** Cooling Fan 3 Control Circuit Malfunction
**P0483** Cooling Fan Rationality Check Malfunction
**P0484** Cooling Fan Circuit Over Current
**P0485** Cooling Fan Power/Ground Circuit Malfunction
**P0500** Vehicle Speed Sensor Malfunction
**P0501** Vehicle Speed Sensor Range/Performance
**P0502** Vehicle Speed Sensor Circuit Low Input
**P0503** Vehicle Speed Sensor Intermittent/Erratic/High
**P0505** Idle Control System Malfunction
**P0506** Idle Control System RPM Lower Than Expected
**P0507** Idle Control System RPM Higher Than Expected
**P0510** Closed Throttle Position Switch Malfunction
**P0530** A/C Refrigerant Pressure Sensor Circuit Malfunction
**P0531** A/C Refrigerant Pressure Sensor Circuit Range/Performance
**P0532** A/C Refrigerant Pressure Sensor Circuit Low Input
**P0533** A/C Refrigerant Pressure Sensor Circuit High Input
**P0534** A/C Refrigerant Charge Loss
**P0550** Power Steering Pressure Sensor Circuit Malfunction
**P0551** Power Steering Pressure Sensor Circuit Range/Performance
**P0552** Power Steering Pressure Sensor Circuit Low Input
**P0553** Power Steering Pressure Sensor Circuit High Input
**P0554** Power Steering Pressure Sensor Circuit Intermittent
**P0560** System Voltage Malfunction
**P0561** System Voltage Unstable
**P0562** System Voltage Low
**P0563** System Voltage High
**P0565** Cruise Control On Signal Malfunction
**P0566** Cruise Control Off Signal Malfunction
**P0567** Cruise Control Resume Signal Malfunction
**P0568** Cruise Control Set Signal Malfunction
**P0569** Cruise Control Coast Signal Malfunction
**P0570** Cruise Control Accel Signal Malfunction
**P0571** Cruise Control/Brake Switch "A" Circuit Malfunction
**P0572** Cruise Control/Brake Switch "A" Circuit Low
**P0573** Cruise Control/Brake Switch "A" Circuit High
**P0574 Through P0580** Reserved for Cruise Codes

**P0600** Serial Communication Link Malfunction
**P0601** Internal Control Module Memory Check Sum Error
**P0602** Control Module Programming Error
**P0603** Internal Control Module Keep Alive Memory (KAM) Error
**P0604** Internal Control Module Random Access Memory (RAM) Error
**P0605** Internal Control Module Read Only Memory (ROM) Error
**P0606** PCM Processor Fault
**P0608** Control Module VSS Output "A" Malfunction
**P0609** Control Module VSS Output "B" Malfunction
**P0620** Generator Control Circuit Malfunction
**P0621** Generator Lamp "L" Control Circuit Malfunction
**P0622** Generator Field "F" Control Circuit Malfunction
**P0650** Malfunction Indicator Lamp (MIL) Control Circuit Malfunction
**P0654** Engine RPM Output Circuit Malfunction
**P0655** Engine Hot Lamp Output Control Circuit Malfunction
**P0656** Fuel Level Output Circuit Malfunction
**P0700** Transmission Control System Malfunction
**P0701** Transmission Control System Range/Performance
**P0702** Transmission Control System Electrical
**P0703** Torque Converter/Brake Switch "B" Circuit Malfunction
**P0704** Clutch Switch Input Circuit Malfunction
**P0705** Transmission Range Sensor Circuit Malfunction (PRNDL Input)
**P0706** Transmission Range Sensor Circuit Range/Performance
**P0707** Transmission Range Sensor Circuit Low Input
**P0708** Transmission Range Sensor Circuit High Input
**P0709** Transmission Range Sensor Circuit Intermittent
**P0710** Transmission Fluid Temperature Sensor Circuit Malfunction
**P0711** Transmission Fluid Temperature Sensor Circuit Range/Performance
**P0712** Transmission Fluid Temperature Sensor Circuit Low Input
**P0713** Transmission Fluid Temperature Sensor Circuit High Input
**P0714** Transmission Fluid Temperature Sensor Circuit Intermittent
**P0715** Input/Turbine Speed Sensor Circuit Malfunction
**P0716** Input/Turbine Speed Sensor Circuit Range/Performance
**P0717** Input/Turbine Speed Sensor Circuit No Signal
**P0718** Input/Turbine Speed Sensor Circuit Intermittent
**P0719** Torque Converter/Brake Switch "B" Circuit Low
**P0720** Output Speed Sensor Circuit Malfunction
**P0721** Output Speed Sensor Circuit Range/Performance
**P0722** Output Speed Sensor Circuit No Signal
**P0723** Output Speed Sensor Circuit Intermittent
**P0724** Torque Converter/Brake Switch "B" Circuit High
**P0725** Engine Speed Input Circuit Malfunction
**P0726** Engine Speed Input Circuit Range/Performance
**P0727** Engine Speed Input Circuit No Signal
**P0728** Engine Speed Input Circuit Intermittent
**P0730** Incorrect Gear Ratio
**P0731** Gear 1 Incorrect Ratio
**P0732** Gear 2 Incorrect Ratio
**P0733** Gear 3 Incorrect Ratio
**P0734** Gear 4 Incorrect Ratio
**P0735** Gear 5 Incorrect Ratio
**P0736** Reverse Incorrect Ratio
**P0740** Torque Converter Clutch Circuit Malfunction
**P0741** Torque Converter Clutch Circuit Performance or Stuck Off
**P0742** Torque Converter Clutch Circuit Stuck On
**P0743** Torque Converter Clutch Circuit Electrical
**P0744** Torque Converter Clutch Circuit Intermittent
**P0745** Pressure Control Solenoid Malfunction
**P0746** Pressure Control Solenoid Performance or Stuck Off
**P0747** Pressure Control Solenoid Stuck On
**P0748** Pressure Control Solenoid Electrical
**P0749** Pressure Control Solenoid Intermittent
**P0750** Shift Solenoid "A" Malfunction
**P0751** Shift Solenoid "A" Performance or Stuck Off
**P0752** Shift Solenoid "A" Stuck On
**P0753** Shift Solenoid "A" Electrical
**P0754** Shift Solenoid "A" Intermittent
**P0755** Shift Solenoid "B" Malfunction
**P0756** Shift Solenoid "B" Performance or Stuck Oft
**P0757** Shift Solenoid "B" Stuck On
**P0758** Shift Solenoid "B" Electrical
**P0759** Shift Solenoid "B" Intermittent
**P0760** Shift Solenoid "C" Malfunction
**P0761** Shift Solenoid "C" Performance Or Stuck Oft
**P0762** Shift Solenoid "C" Stuck On
**P0763** Shift Solenoid "C" Electrical
**P0764** Shift Solenoid "C" Intermittent
**P0765** Shift Solenoid "D" Malfunction
**P0766** Shift Solenoid "D" Performance Or Stuck Oft
**P0767** Shift Solenoid "D" Stuck On
**P0768** Shift Solenoid "D" Electrical
**P0769** Shift Solenoid "D" Intermittent
**P0770** Shift Solenoid "E" Malfunction
**P0771** Shift Solenoid "E" Performance Or Stuck Oft
**P0772** Shift Solenoid "E" Stuck On
**P0773** Shift Solenoid "E" Electrical
**P0774** Shift Solenoid "E" Intermittent
**P0780** Shift Malfunction
**P0781** 1 –2 Shift Malfunction
**P0782** 2 –3 Shift Malfunction
**P0783** 3 –4 Shift Malfunction
**P0784** 4 –5 Shift Malfunction
**P0785** Shift/Timing Solenoid Malfunction
**P0786** Shift/Timing Solenoid Range/Performance
**P0787** Shift/Timing Solenoid Low
**P0788** Shift/Timing Solenoid High
**P0789** Shift/Timing Solenoid Intermittent
**P0790** Normal/Performance Switch Circuit Malfunction
**P0801** Reverse Inhibit Control Circuit Malfunction
**P0803** 1–4 Upshift (Skip Shift) Solenoid Control Circuit Malfunction
**P0804** 1–4 Upshift (Skip Shift) Lamp Control Circuit Malfunction
**P1000** OBD II Monitor Testing Not Complete More Driving Required
**P1001** Key On Engine Running (KOER) Self-Test Not Able To Complete, KOER Aborted
**P1100** Mass Air Flow (MAF) Sensor Intermittent
**P1101** Mass Air Flow (MAF) Sensor Out Of Self-Test Range
**P1111** System Pass 49 State
**P1112** Intake Air Temperature (IAT) Sensor Intermittent
**P1116** Engine Coolant Temperature (ECT) Sensor Out Of Self-Test Range
**P1117** Engine Coolant Temperature (ECT) Sensor Intermittent
**P1120** Throttle Position (TP) Sensor Out Of Range (Low)
**P1121** Throttle Position (TP) Sensor Inconsistent With MAF Sensor
**P1124** Throttle Position (TP) Sensor Out Of Self-Test Range
**P1125** Throttle Position (TP) Sensor Circuit Intermittent
**P1127** Exhaust Not Warm Enough, Downstream Heated Oxygen Sensors ($HO_2S$) Not Tested
**P1128** Upstream Heated Oxygen Sensors ($HO_2S$) Swapped From Bank To Bank
**P1129** Downstream Heated Oxygen Sensors ($HO_2S$) Swapped From Bank To Bank
**P1130** Lack Of Upstream Heated Oxygen Sensor ($HO_2S$ 11) Switch, Adaptive Fuel At Limit (Bank #1)
**P1131** Lack Of Upstream Heated Oxygen Sensor ($HO_2S$ 11) Switch, Sensor Indicates Lean (Bank #1)
**P1132** Lack Of Upstream Heated Oxygen Sensor ($HO_2S$ 11) Switch, Sensor Indicates Rich (Bank#1)
**P1137** Lack Of Downstream Heated Oxygen Sensor ($HO_2S$ 12) Switch, Sensor Indicates Lean (Bank#1)
**P1138** Lack Of Downstream Heated Oxygen Sensor ($HO_2S$ 12) Switch, Sensor Indicates Rich (Bank#1)
**P1150** Lack Of Upstream Heated Oxygen Sensor ($HO_2S$ 21) Switch, Adaptive Fuel At Limit (Bank #2)
**P1151** Lack Of Upstream Heated Oxygen Sensor ($HO_2S$ 21) Switch, Sensor Indicates Lean (Bank#2)
**P1152** Lack Of Upstream Heated Oxygen Sensor ($HO_2S$ 21) Switch, Sensor Indicates Rich (Bank #2)
**P1157** Lack Of Downstream Heated Oxygen Sensor ($HO_2S$ 22) Switch, Sensor Indicates Lean (Bank #2)
**P1158** Lack Of Downstream Heated Oxygen Sensor ($HO_2S$ 22) Switch, Sensor Indicates Rich (Bank#2)
**P1169** ($HO_2S$ 12) Signal Remained Unchanged For More Than 20 Seconds After Closed Loop
**P1170** ($HO_2S$ 11) Signal Remained Unchanged For More Than 20 Seconds After Closed Loop

**P1173** Feedback A/F Mixture Control ($HO_2S$ 21) Signal Remained Unchanged For More Than 20 Seconds After Closed Loop

**P1195** Barometric (BARO) Pressure Sensor Circuit Malfunction (Signal Is From EGR Boost Sensor)

**P1196** Starter Switch Circuit Malfunction

**P1218** Cylinder Identification (CID) Stuck High

**P1219** Cylinder Identification (CID) Stuck Low

**P1220** Series Throttle Control Malfunction (Traction Control System)

**P1224** Throttle Position Sensor "B" (TP-B) Out Of Self-Test Range (Traction Control System)

**P1230** Fuel Pump Low Speed Malfunction

**P1231** Fuel Pump Secondary Circuit Low With High Speed Pump On

**P1232** Low Speed Fuel Pump Primary Circuit Malfunction

**P1233** Fuel Pump Driver Module Off-line (MIL DTC)

**P1234** Fuel Pump Driver Module Disabled Or Off-line (No MIL)

**P1235** Fuel Pump Control Out Of Range (MIL DTC)

**P1236** Fuel Pump Control Out Of Range (No MIL)

**P1237** Fuel Pump Secondary Circuit Malfunction (MIL DTC)

**P1238** Fuel Pump Secondary Circuit Malfunction (No DMIL)

**P1260** THEFT Detected —Engine Disabled

**P1261** High To Low Side Short —Cylinder #1 (Indicates Low side Circuit Is Shorted To B+ Or To The High Side Between The IDM And The Injector)

**P1262** High To Low Side Short —Cylinder #2 (Indicates Low side Circuit Is Shorted To B+ Or To The High Side Between The IDM And The Injector)

**P1263** High To Low Side Short —Cylinder #3 (Indicates Low side Circuit Is Shorted To B+ Or To The High Side Between The IDM And The Injector)

**P1264** High To Low Side Short —Cylinder #4 (Indicates Low side Circuit Is Shorted To B+ Or To The High Side Between The IDM And The Injector)

**P1265** High To Low Side Short —Cylinder #5 (Indicates Low side Circuit Is Shorted To B+ Or To The High Side Between The IDM And The Injector)

**P1266** High To Low Side Short —Cylinder #6 (Indicates Low side Circuit Is Shorted To B+ Or To The High Side Between The IDM And The Injector)

**P1267** High To Low Side Short —Cylinder #7 (Indicates Low side Circuit Is Shorted To B+ Or To The High Side Between The IDM And The Injector)

**P1268** High To Low Side Short —Cylinder #8 (Indicates Low side Circuit Is Shorted To B+ Or To The High Side Between The IDM And The Injector)

**P1270** Engine RPM Or Vehicle Speed Limiter Reached

**P1271** High To Low Side Open —Cylinder #1 (Indicates A High To Low Side Open Between The Injector And The IDM)

**P1272** High To Low Side Open —Cylinder #2 (Indicates A High To Low Side Open Between The Injector And The IDM)

**P1273** High To Low Side Open —Cylinder #3 (Indicates A High To Low Side Open Between The Injector And The IDM)

**P1274** High To Low Side Open —Cylinder #4 (Indicates A High To Low Side Open Between The Injector And The IDM)

**P1275** High To Low Side Open —Cylinder #5 (Indicates A High To Low Side Open Between The Injector And The IDM)

**P1276** High To Low Side Open —Cylinder #6 (Indicates A High To Low Side Open Between The Injector And The IDM)

**P1277** High To Low Side Open —Cylinder #7 (Indicates A High To Low Side Open Between The Injector And The IDM)

**P1278** High To Low Side Open —Cylinder #8 (Indicates A High To Low Side Open Between The Injector And The IDM)

**P1285** Cylinder Head Temperature (CHT) Over Temperature Sensed

**P1288** Cylinder Head Temperature (CHT) Sensor Out Of Self-Test Range

**P1289** Cylinder Head Temperature (CHT) Sensor Circuit Low Input

**P1290** Cylinder Head Temperature (CHT) Sensor Circuit High Input

**P1299** Engine Over Temperature Condition

**P1309** Misfire Detection Monitor Is Not Enabled

**P1320** Distributor Signal Interrupt

**P1336** Crankshaft Position Sensor (Gear)

**P1345** No Camshaft Position Sensor Signal

**P1351** Ignition Diagnostic Monitor (IDM) Circuit Input Malfunction

**P1351** Indicates Ignition System Malfunction

**P1352** Indicates Ignition System Malfunction

**P1353** Indicates Ignition System Malfunction

**P1354** Indicates Ignition System Malfunction

**P1355** Indicates Ignition System Malfunction

**P1356** PIPs Occurred While IDM Pulse width Indicates Engine Not Turning

**P1357** Ignition Diagnostic Monitor (IDM) Pulse width Not Defined

**P1358** Ignition Diagnostic Monitor (IDM) Signal Out Of Self-Test Range

**P1359** Spark Output Circuit Malfunction

**P1364** Spark Output Circuit Malfunction

**P1390** Octane Adjust (OCT ADJ) Out Of Self-Test Range

**P1397** System Voltage Out Of Self Test Range

**P1400** Differential Pressure Feedback EGR (DPFE) Sensor Circuit Low Voltage Detected

**P1401** Differential Pressure Feedback EGR (DPFE) Sensor Circuit High Voltage Detected/EGR Temperature Sensor

**P1402** EGR Valve Position Sensor Open Or Short

**P1403** Differential Pressure Feedback EGR (DPFE) Sensor Hoses Reversed

**P1405** Differential Pressure Feedback EGR (DPFE) Sensor Upstream Hose Off Or Plugged

**P1406** Differential Pressure Feedback EGR (DPFE) Sensor Downstream Hose Off Or Plugged

**P1407** Exhaust Gas Recirculation (EGR) No Flow Detected (Valve Stuck Closed Or Inoperative)

**P1408** Exhaust Gas Recirculation (EGR) Flow Out Of Self-Test Range

**P1409** Electronic Vacuum Regulator (EVR) Control Circuit Malfunction

**P1410** Check That Fuel Pressure Regulator Control Solenoid And The EGR Check Solenoid Connectors Are Not Swapped

**P1411** Secondary Air Injection System Incorrect Downstream Flow Detected

**P1413** Secondary Air Injection System Monitor Circuit Low Voltage

**P1414** Secondary Air Injection System Monitor Circuit High Voltage

**P1442** Evaporative Emission Control System Small Leak Detected

**P1443** Evaporative Emission Control System —Vacuum System, Purge Control Solenoid Or Purge Control Valve Malfunction

**P1444** Purge Flow Sensor (PFS) Circuit Low Input

**P1445** Purge Flow Sensor (PFS) Circuit High Input

**P1449** Evaporative Emission Control System Unable To Hold Vacuum

**P1450** Unable To Bleed Up Fuel Tank Vacuum

**P1455** Evaporative Emission Control System Control Leak Detected (Gross Leak)

**P1460** Wide Open Throttle Air Conditioning Cut-Off Circuit Malfunction

**P1461** Air Conditioning Pressure (ACP) Sensor Circuit Low Input

**P1462** Air Conditioning Pressure (ACP) Sensor Circuit High Input

**P1463** Air Conditioning Pressure (ACP) Sensor Insufficient Pressure Change

**P1464** Air Conditioning (A/C) Demand Out Of Self-Test Range/A/C On During KOER Or CCT Test

**P1469** Low Air Conditioning Cycling Period

**P1473** Fan Secondary High, With Fan(s) Off

**P1474** Low Fan Control Primary Circuit Malfunction

**P1479** High Fan Control Primary Circuit Malfunction

**P1480** Fan Secondary Low, With Low Fan On

**P1481** Fan Secondary Low, With High Fan On

**P1483** Power To Fan Circuit Over current

**P1484** Open Power/Ground To Variable Load Control Module (VLCM)

**P1485** EGR Control Solenoid Open Or Short

**P1486** EGR Vent Solenoid Open Or Short

**P1487** EGR Boost Check Solenoid Open Or Short

**P1500** Vehicle Speed Sensor (VSS) Circuit Intermittent

**P1501** Vehicle Speed Sensor (VSS) Out Of Self-Test Range/Vehicle Moved During Test

**P1502** Invalid Self Test —Auxiliary Powertrain Control Module (APCM) Functioning

**P1504** Idle Air Control (IAC) Circuit Malfunction

**P1505** Idle Air Control (IAC) System At Adaptive Clip

**P1506** Idle Air Control (IAC) Overspeed Error

**P1507** Idle Air Control (IAC) Underspeed Error

**P1512** Intake Manifold Runner Control (IMRC) Malfunction (Bank#1 Stuck Closed)

**P1513** Intake Manifold Runner Control (IMRC) Malfunction (Bank#2 Stuck Closed)

**P1516** Intake Manifold Runner Control (IMRC) Input Error (Bank #1)

**P1517** Intake Manifold Runner Control (IMRC) Input Error (Bank #2)

**P1518** Intake Manifold Runner Control (IMRC) Malfunction (Stuck Open)

**P1519** Intake Manifold Runner Control (IMRC) Malfunction (Stuck Closed)

**P1520** Intake Manifold Runner Control (IMRC) Circuit Malfunction

**P1521** Variable Resonance Induction System (VRIS) Solenoid #1 Open Or Short

**P1522** Variable Resonance Induction System (VRIS) Solenoid#2 Open Or Short

**P1523** High Speed Inlet Air (HSIA) Solenoid Open Or Short

**P1530** Air Condition (A/C) Clutch Circuit Malfunction
**P1531** Invalid Test —Accelerator Pedal Movement
**P1536** Parking Brake Applied Failure
**P1537** Intake Manifold Runner Control (IMRC) Malfunction (Bank#1 Stuck Open)
**P1538** Intake Manifold Runner Control (IMRC) Malfunction (Bank#2 Stuck Open)
**P1539** Power To Air Condition (A/C) Clutch Circuit Overcurrent
**P1549** Problem In Intake Manifold Tuning (IMT) Valve System
**P1550** Power Steering Pressure (PSP) Sensor Out Of Self-Test Range
**P1601** Serial Communication Error
**P1605** Powertrain Control Module (PCM) —Keep Alive Memory (KAM) Test Error
**P1608** PCM Internal Circuit Malfunction
**P1609** PCM Internal Circuit Malfunction (2.5L Only)
**P1625** B+ Supply To Variable Load Control Module (VLCM) Fan Circuit Malfunction
**P1626** B+ Supply To Variable Load Control Module (VLCM) Air Conditioning (A/C) Circuit
**P1650** Power Steering Pressure (PSP) Switch Out Of Self-Test Range
**P1651** Power Steering Pressure (PSP) Switch Input Malfunction
**P1660** Output Circuit Check Signal High
**P1661** Output Circuit Check Signal Low
**P1663** Fuel Delivery Command Signal (FDCS) Circuit Failure
**P1667** Cylinder Identification (CID) Circuit Failure
**P1668** PCM —IDM Diagnostic Communication Error
**P1670** EF Feedback Signal Not Detected
**P1701** Reverse Engagement Error
**P1703** Brake On/Off (BOO) Switch Out Of Self-Test Range
**P1704** Digital Transmission Range (TR) Sensor Failed To Transition State
**P1705** Transmission Range (TR) Sensor Out Of Self-Test Range
**P1705** Park Neutral Position (PNP) Problem
**P1706** High Vehicle Speed In Park
**P1709** Park Or Neutral Position (PNP) Switch Out Of Self-Test Range
**P1711** Transmission Fluid Temperature (TFT) Sensor Out Of Self-Test Range
**P1714** Shift Solenoid "A" Inductive Signature Malfunction
**P1715** Shift Solenoid "B" Inductive Signature Malfunction
**P1716** Transmission Malfunction
**P1717** Transmission Malfunction
**P1719** Transmission Malfunction
**P1720** Vehicle Speed Sensor (VSS) Circuit Malfunction
**P1727** Coast Clutch Solenoid Inductive Signature Malfunction
**P1728** Transmission Slip Error —Converter Clutch Failed
**P1731** Improper 1 –2 Shift
**P1732** Improper 2 –3 Shift
**P1733** Improper 3 –4 Shift
**P1734** Improper 4 –5 Shift
**P1740** Torque Converter Clutch (TCC) Inductive Signature Malfunction
**P1741** Torque Converter Clutch (TCC) Control Error
**P1742** Torque Converter Clutch (TCC) Solenoid Failed On (Turns On MIL)
**P1743** Torque Converter Clutch (TCC) Solenoid Failed On (Turns On TCIL)
**P1744** Torque Converter Clutch (TCC) System Mechanically Stuck In Off Position
**P1746** Electronic Pressure Control (EPC) Solenoid Open Circuit (Low Input)
**P1747** Electronic Pressure Control (EPC) Solenoid Short Circuit (High Input)
**P1748** Electronic Pressure Control (EPC) Malfunction
**P1749** Electronic Pressure Control (EPC) Solenoid Failed Low
**P1751** Shift Solenoid#1 (SS1) Performance
**P1754** Coast Clutch Solenoid (CCS) Circuit Malfunction
**P1756** Shift Solenoid#2 (SS2) Performance
**P1760** Overrun Clutch SN
**P1761** Shift Solenoid #(SS2) Performance
**P1762** Transmission Malfunction
**P1765** 3 –2 Timing Solenoid Malfunction (2.5L Only)
**P1779** TCIL Circuit Malfunction
**P1780** Transmission Control Switch (TCS) Circuit Out Of Self-Test Range
**P1783** Transmission Over Temperature Condition
**P1784** Transmission Malfunction
**P1785** Transmission Malfunction
**P1786** Transmission Malfunction
**P1787** Transmission Malfunction
**P1788** 3 –2 Timing/Coast Clutch Solenoid (3 –2/CCS) Circuit Open
**P1789** 3 –2 Timing/Coast Clutch Solenoid (3 –2/CCS) Circuit Shorted
**P1792** Idle (IDL) Switch (Closed Throttle Position Switch) Malfunction
**P1794** Loss Of Battery Voltage Input
**P1797** Neutral Switch Circuit Malfunction
**P1900** Cooling Fan
**U1021** SCP Indicating The Lack Of Air Conditioning (A/C) Clutch Status Response
**U1039** Vehicle Speed Signal (VSS) Missing Or Incorrect
**U1051** Brake Switch Signal Missing Or Incorrect
**U1073** SCP Indicating The Lack Of Engine Coolant Fan Status Response
**U1131** SCP Indicating The Lack Of Fuel Pump Status Response
**U1135** SCP Indicating The Ignition Switch Signal Missing Or Incorrect
**U1256** SCP Indicating A Communications Error
**U1451** Lack Of Response From Passive Anti-Theft System (PATS) Module —Engine Disabled

## VACUUM DIAGRAMS

Following are vacuum diagrams for most of the engine and emissions package combinations covered by this manual. Because vacuum circuits will vary based on various engine and vehicle options, always refer first to the vehicle emission control information label, if present. Should the label be missing, or should vehicle be equipped with a different engine from the vehicle's original equipment, refer to the diagrams below for the same or similar configuration.

If you wish to obtain a replacement emissions label, most manufacturers make the labels available for purchase. The labels can usually be ordered from a local dealer.

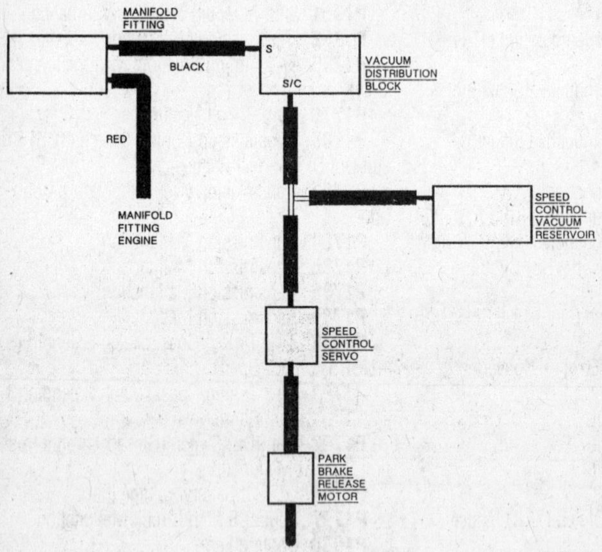


Fig. 83 1988–1990 Continental typical vacuum diagram—3.8L engine

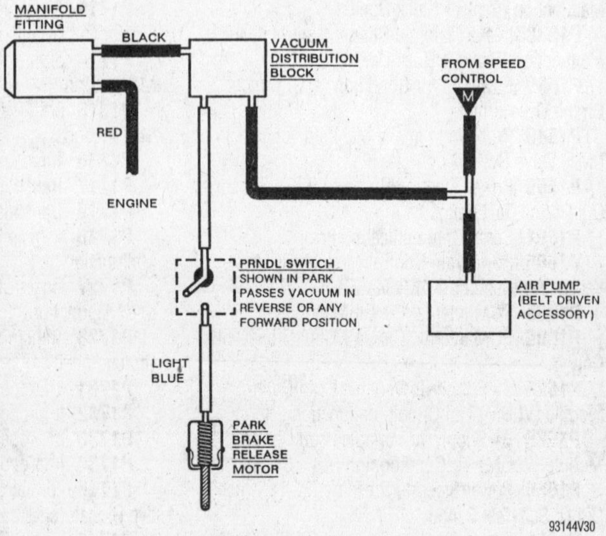


Fig. 84 1988–1990 Mark VII typical vacuum diagram—5.0L engine

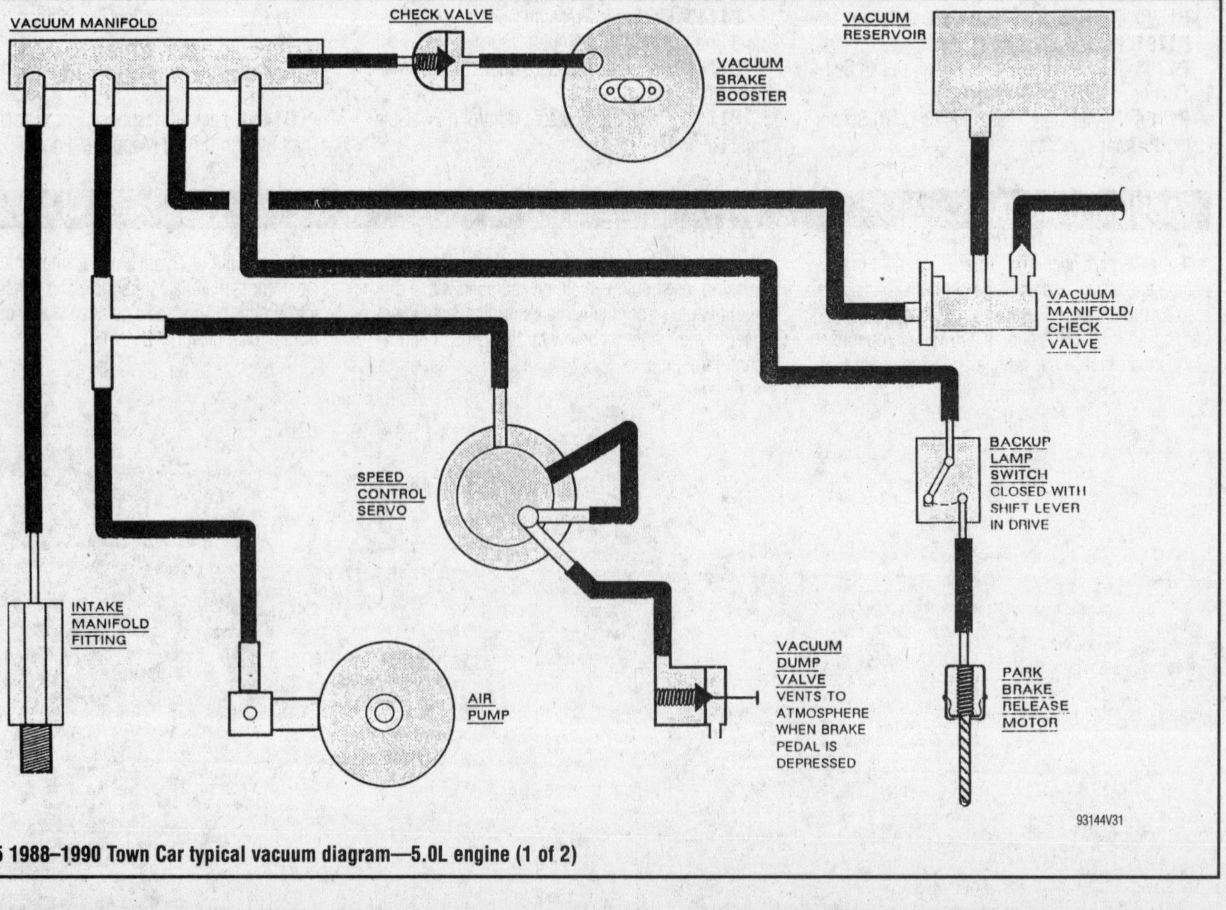


Fig. 85 1988–1990 Town Car typical vacuum diagram—5.0L engine (1 of 2)

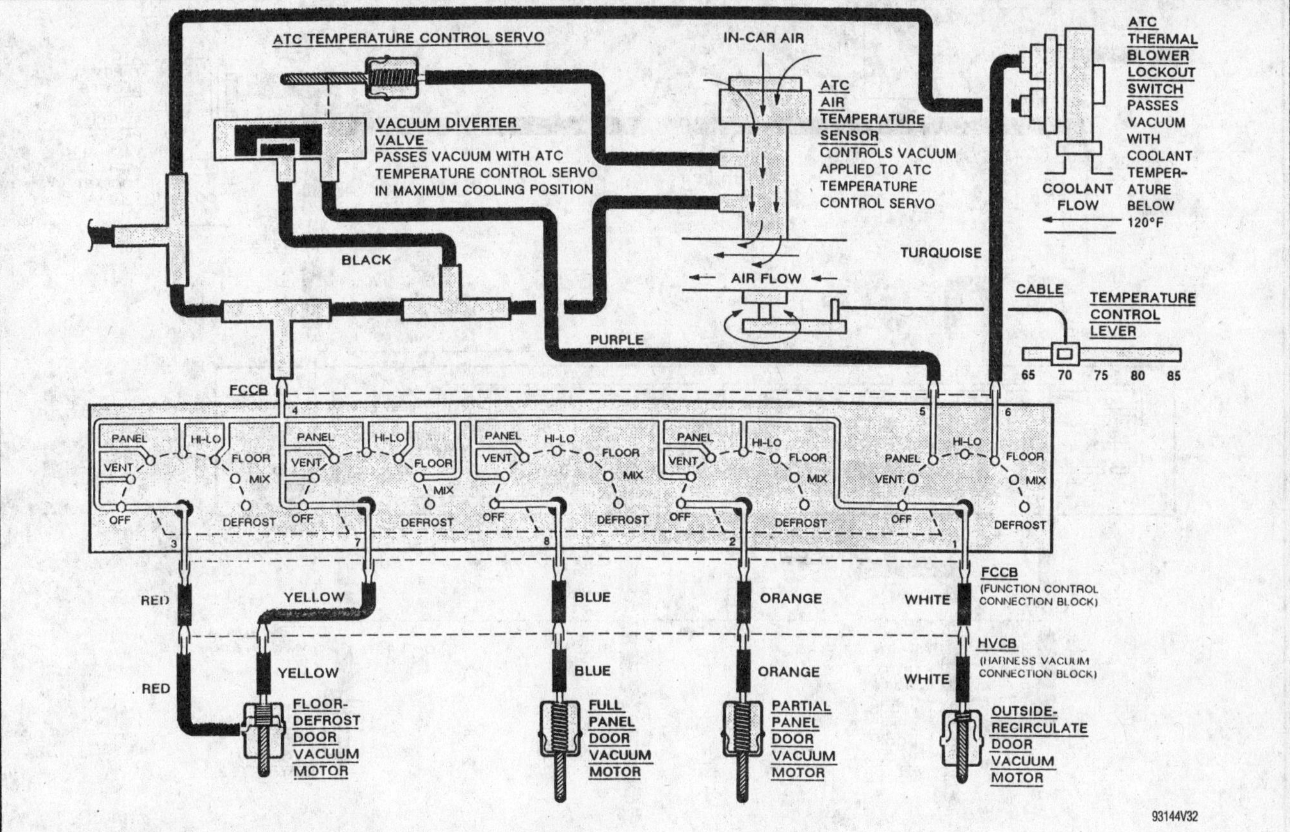


**Fig. 86 1988–1990 Town Car typical vacuum diagram—5.0L engine (2 of 2)**

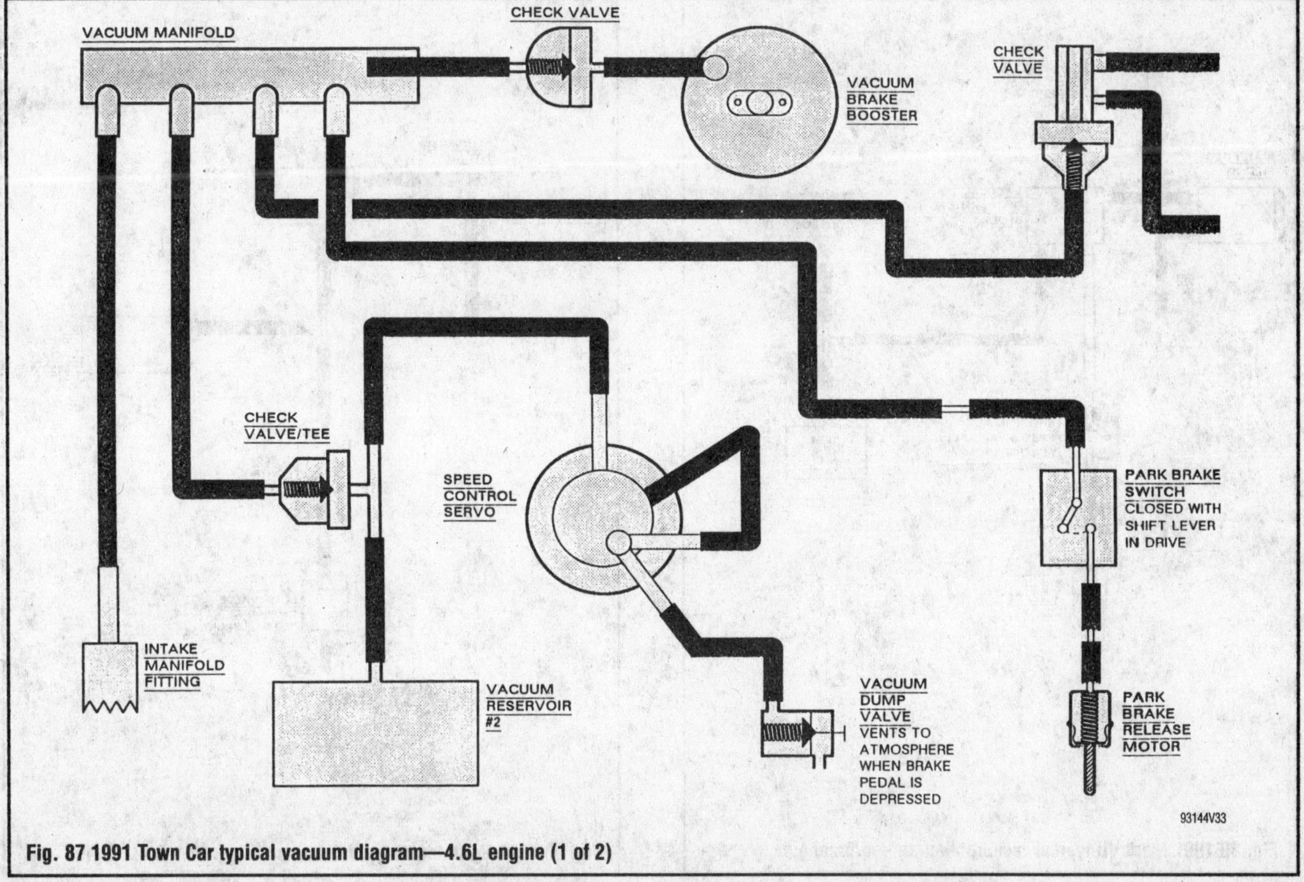


**Fig. 87 1991 Town Car typical vacuum diagram—4.6L engine (1 of 2)**

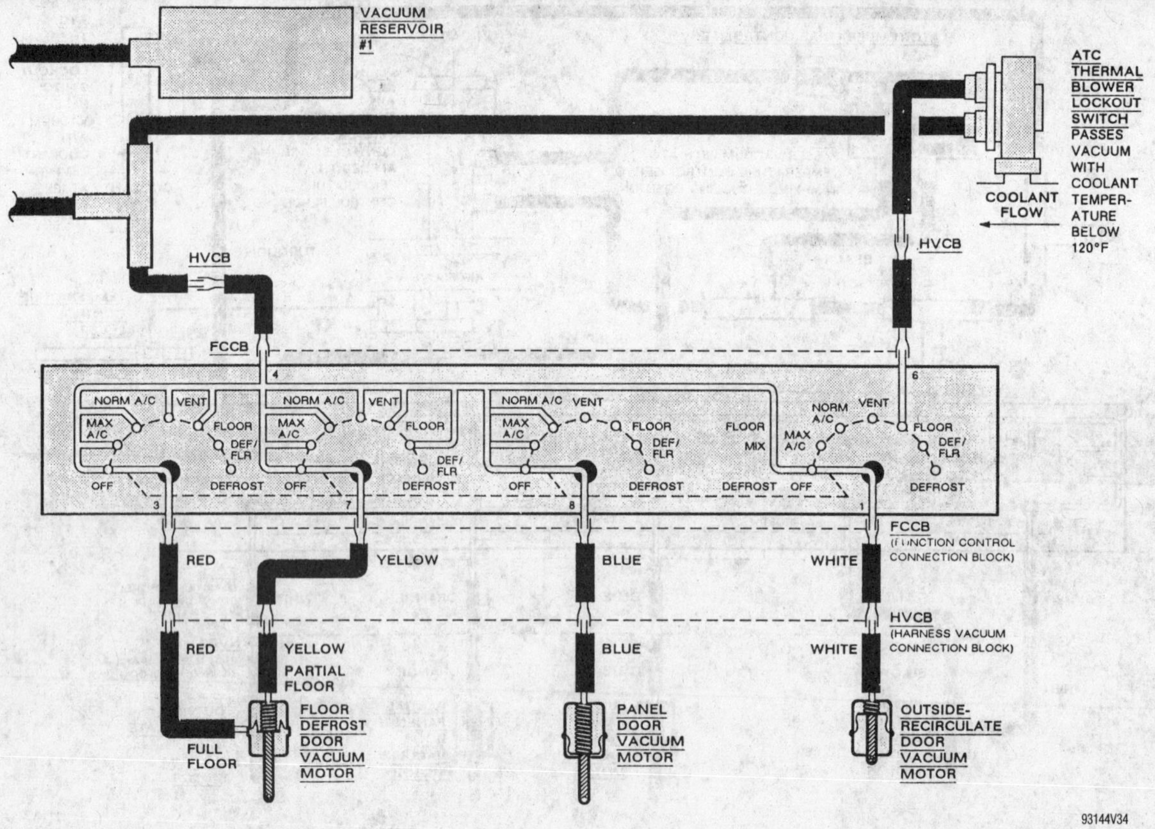


**Fig. 88 1991 Town Car typical vacuum diagram—4.6L engine (2 of 2)**

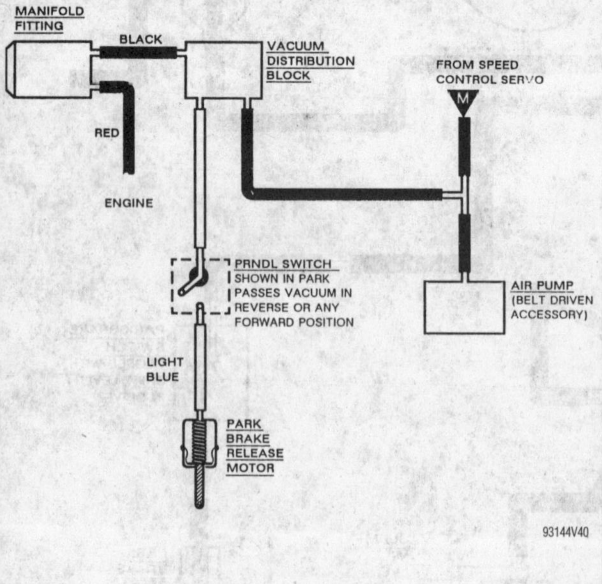


**Fig. 89 1991 Mark VII typical vacuum diagram—5.0L engine**

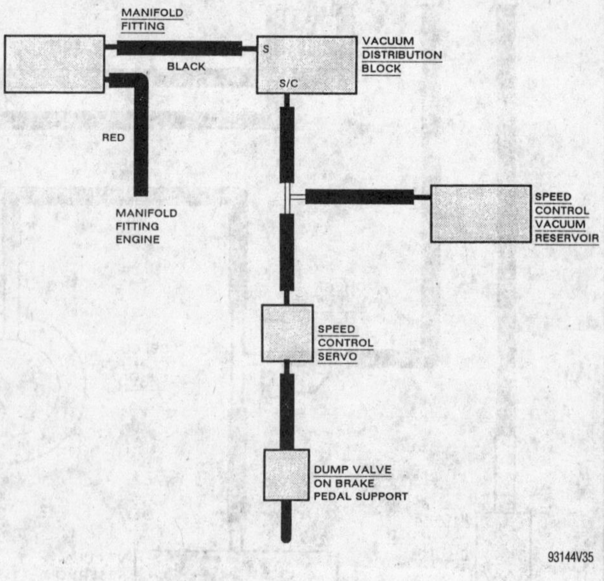


**Fig. 90 1992 Continental typical vacuum diagram—3.8L engine**

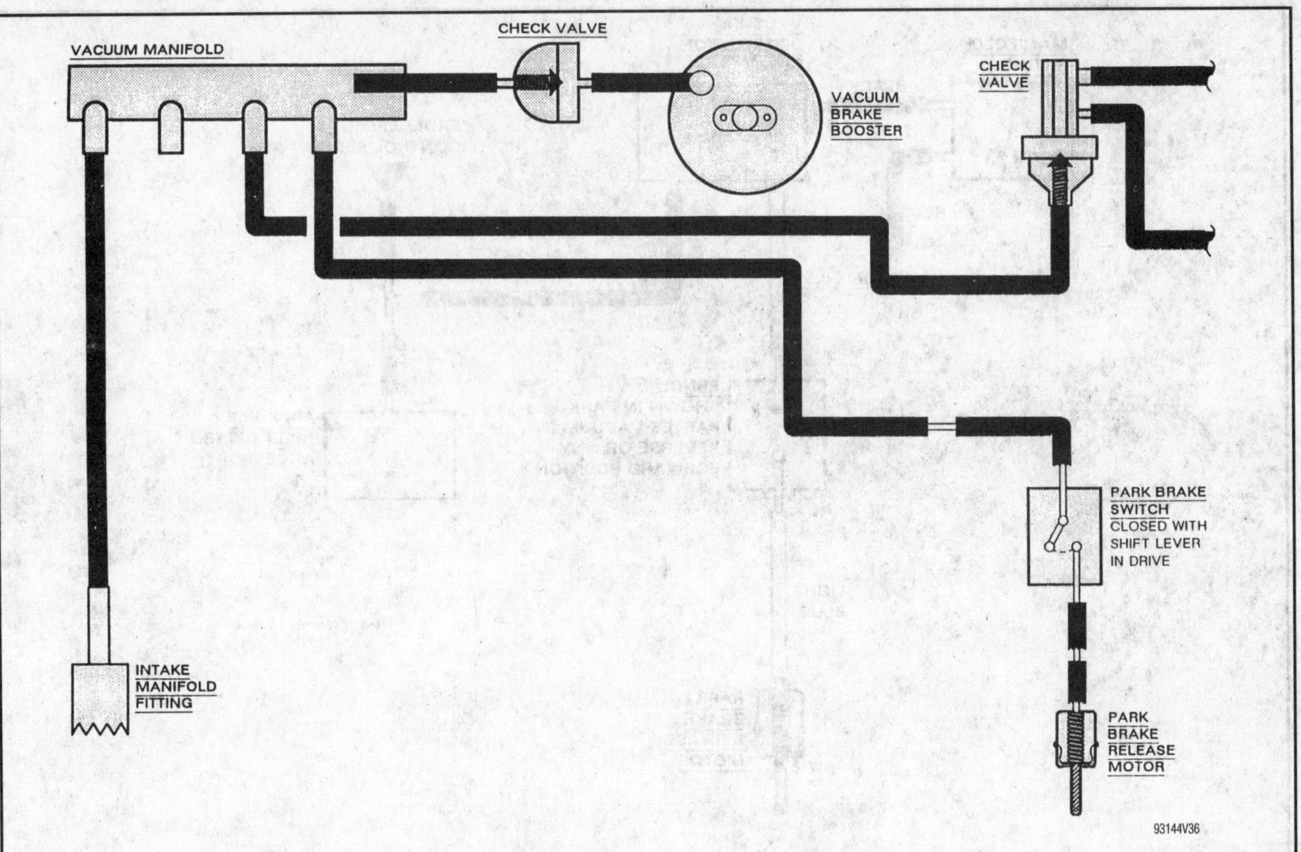


**Fig. 91 1992 Town Car typical vacuum diagram—4.6L engine (1 of 2)**

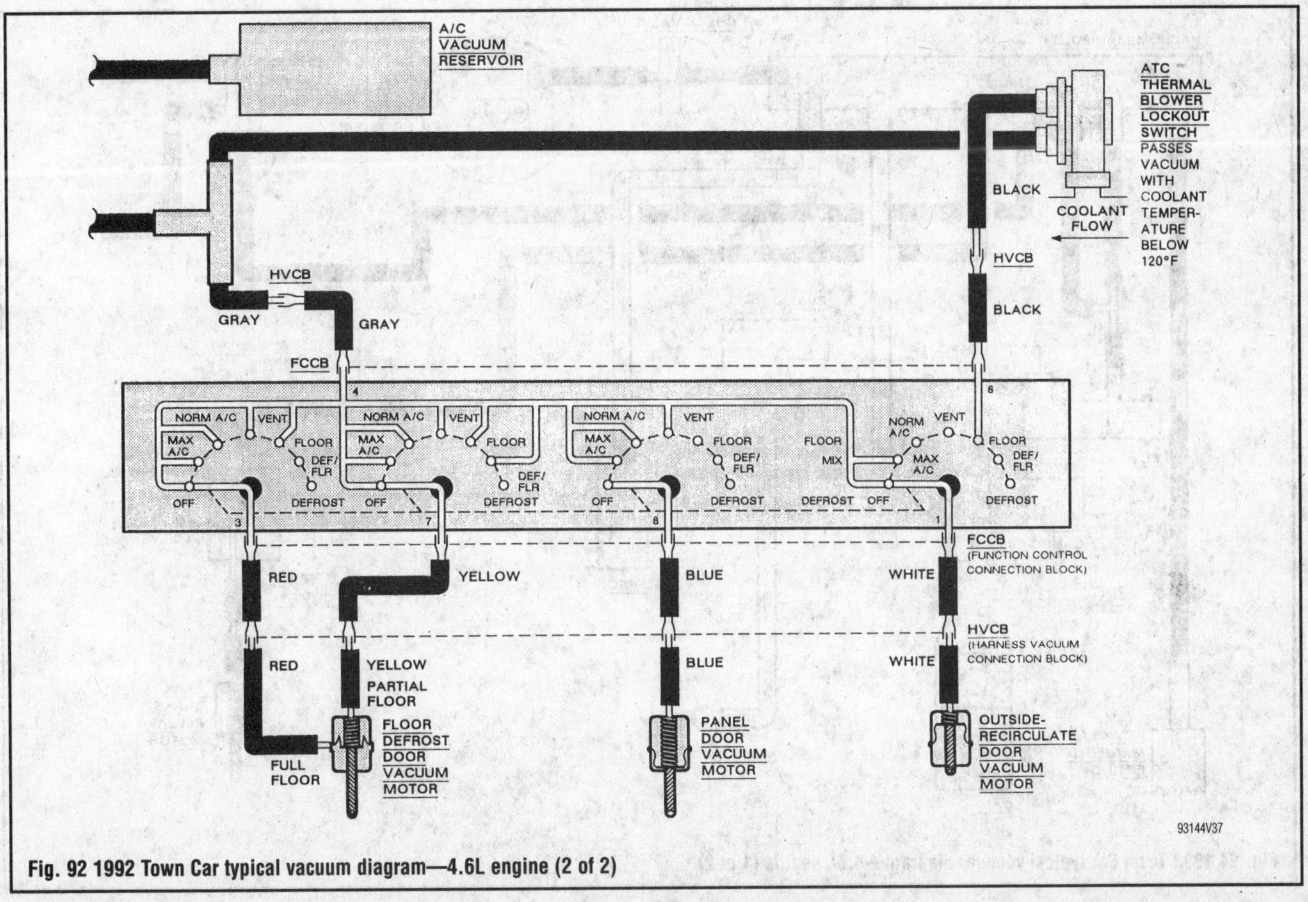


**Fig. 92 1992 Town Car typical vacuum diagram—4.6L engine (2 of 2)**

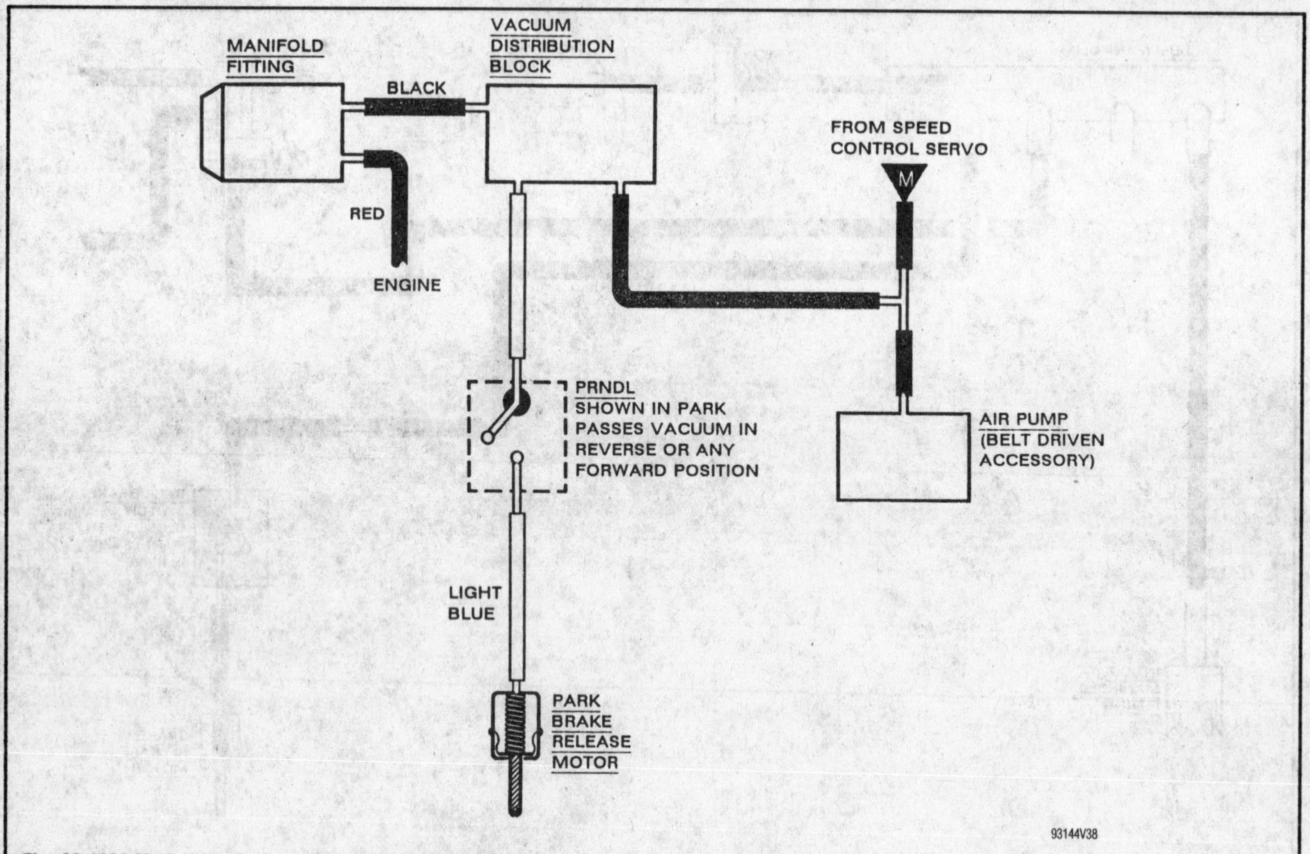


**Fig. 93 1992 Mark VII typical vacuum diagram—5.0L engine**

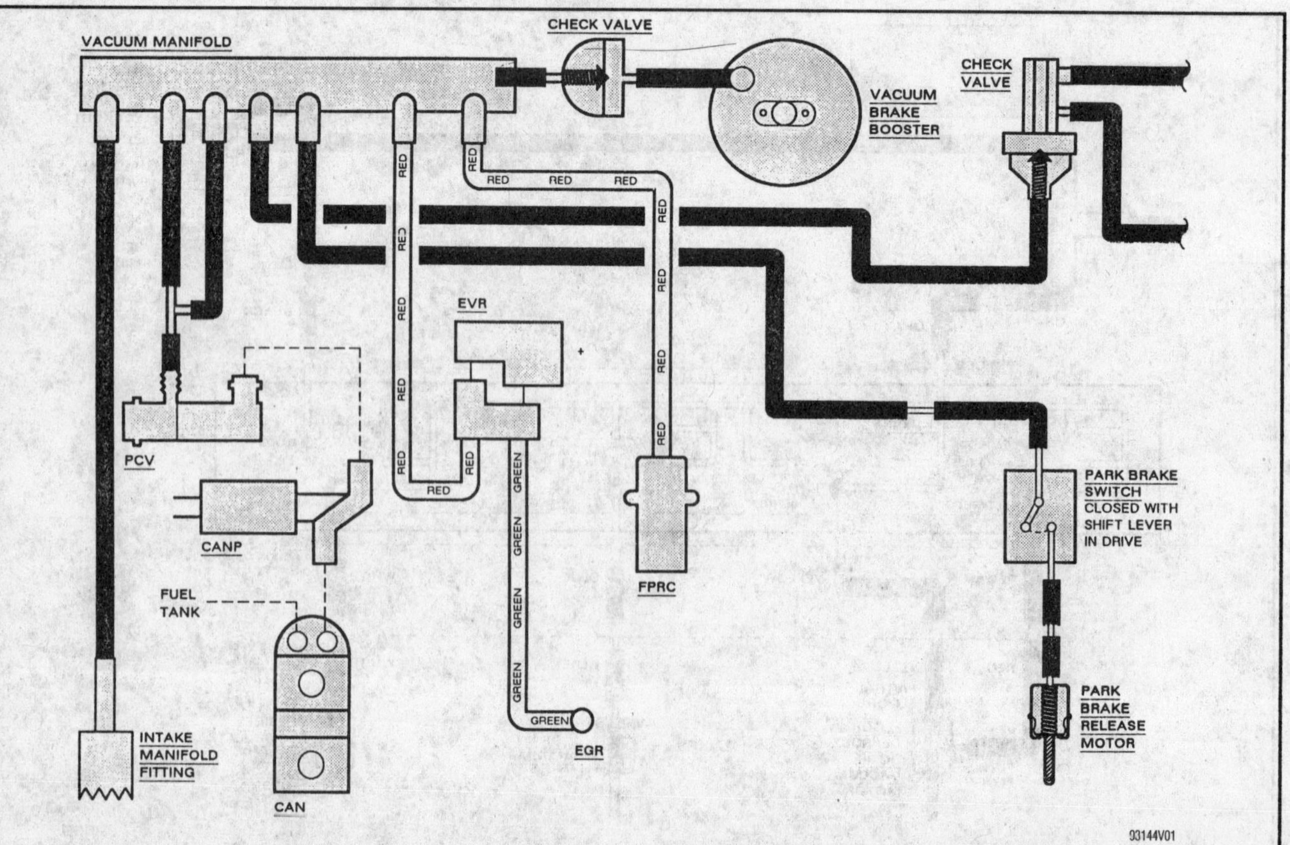


**Fig. 94 1993 Town Car typical vacuum diagram—4.6L engine (1 of 2)**

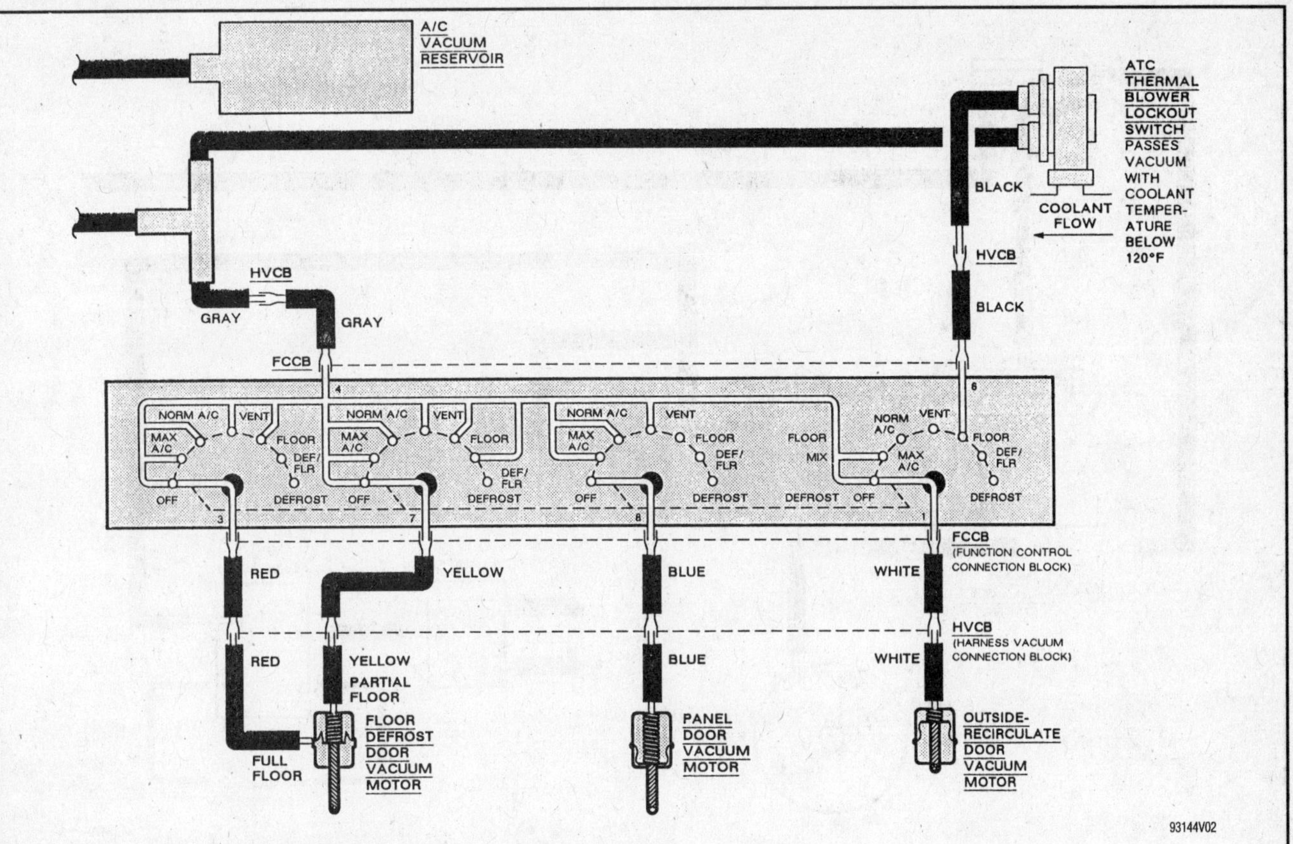


Fig. 95 1993 Town Car typical vacuum diagram—4.6L engine (2 of 2)

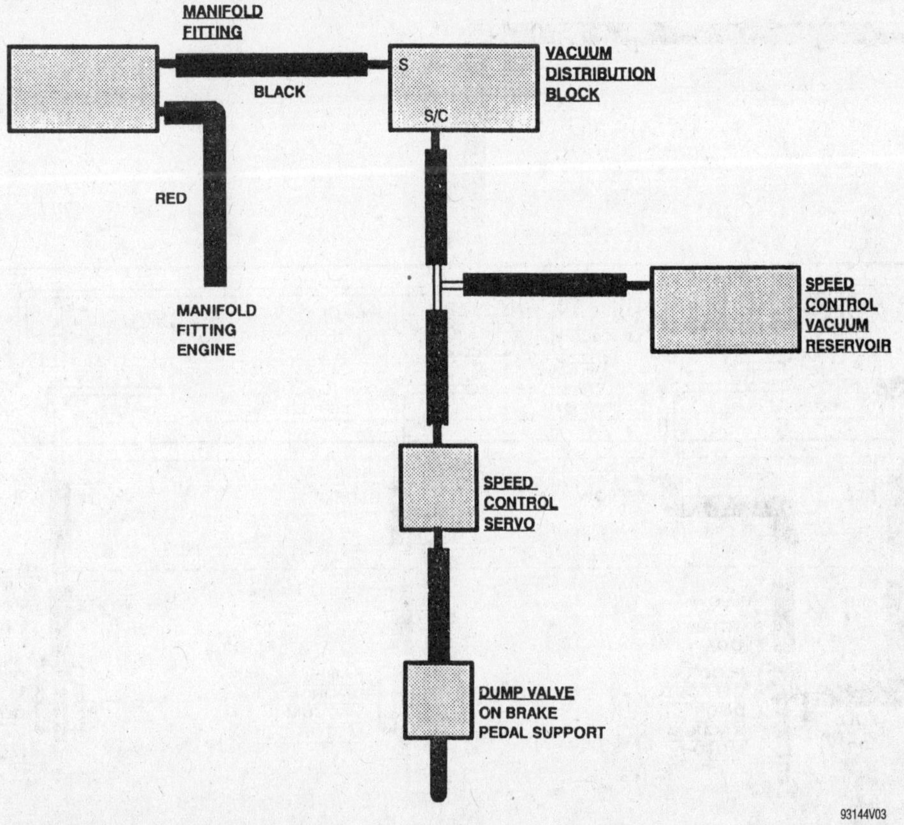


Fig. 96 1993 Continental typical vacuum diagram—3.8L engine

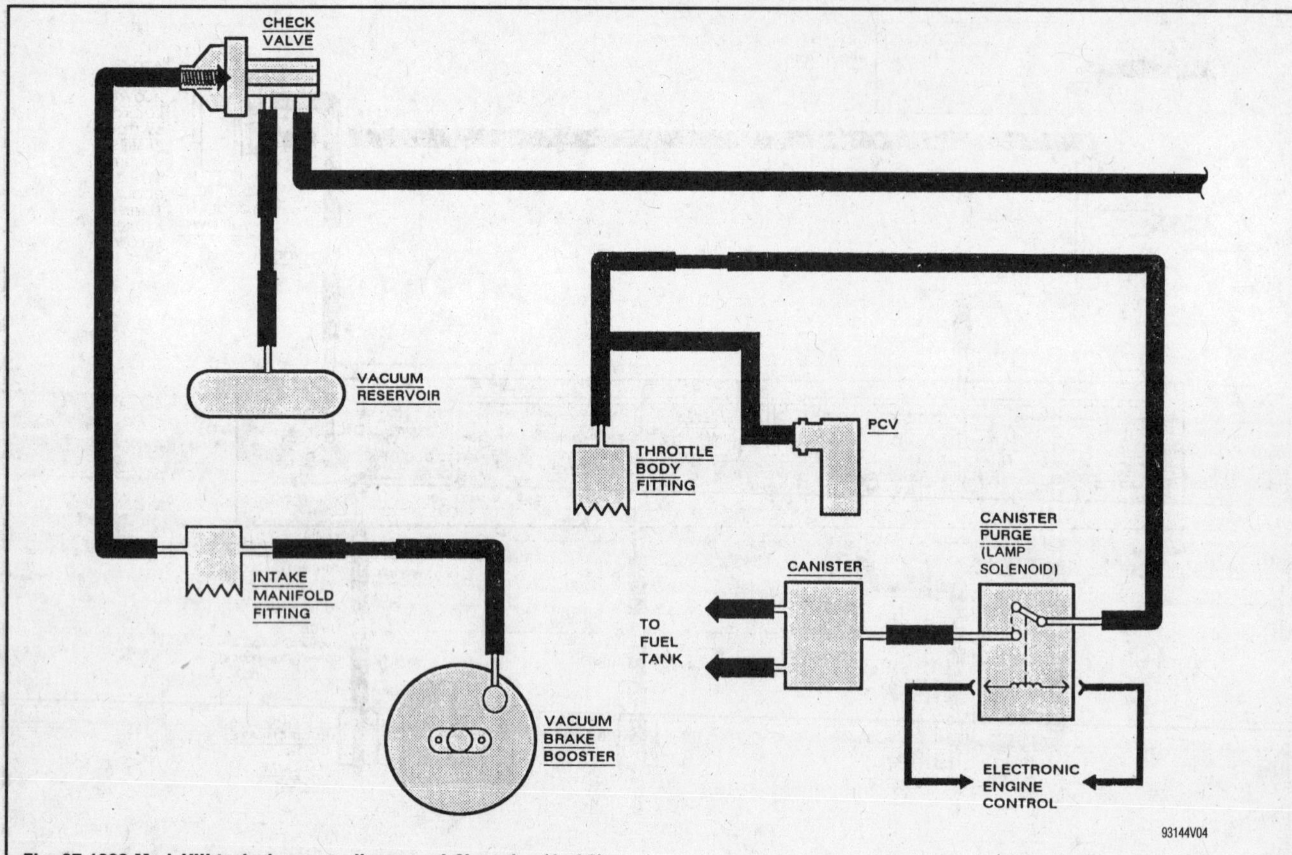


Fig. 97 1993 Mark VIII typical vacuum diagram—4.6L engine (1 of 2)

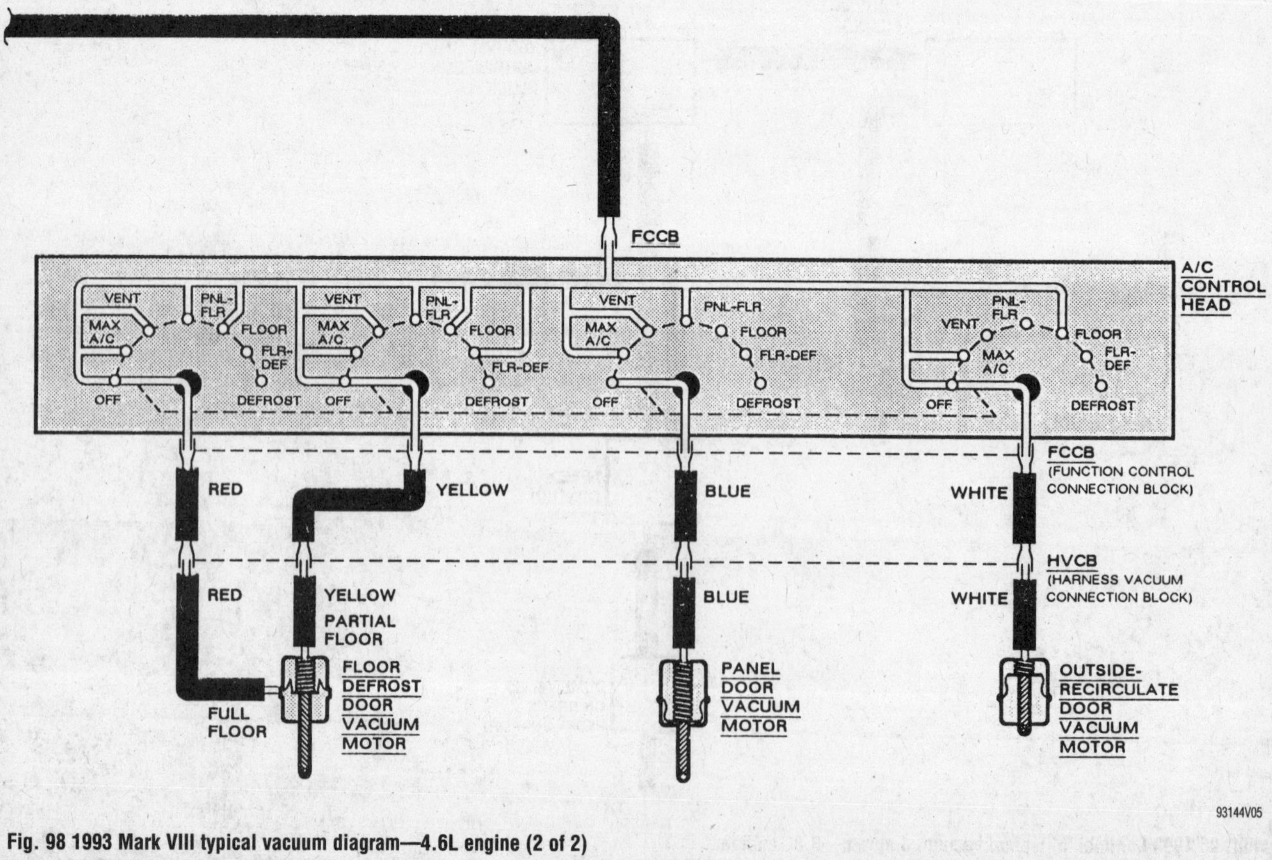


Fig. 98 1993 Mark VIII typical vacuum diagram—4.6L engine (2 of 2)

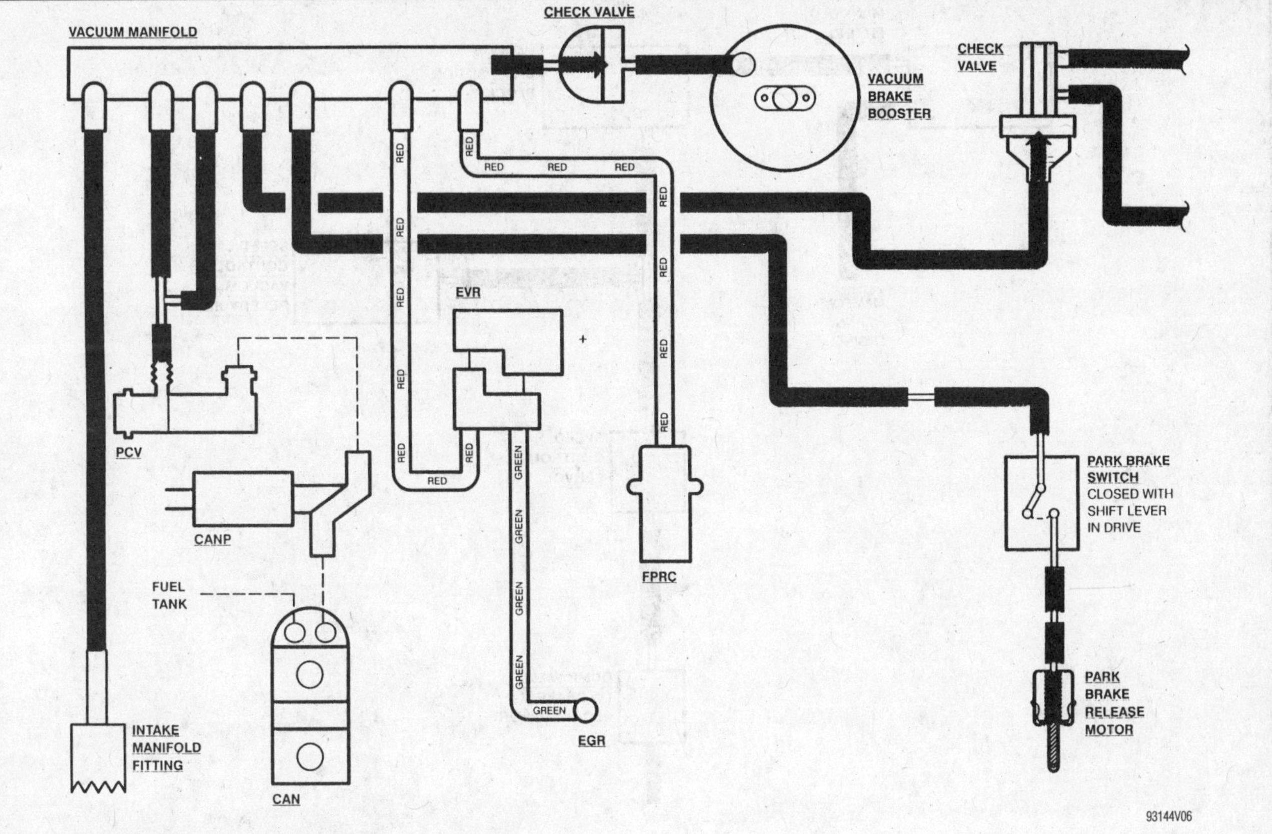

Fig. 99 1994 Town Car typical vacuum diagram—4.6L engine (1 of 2)

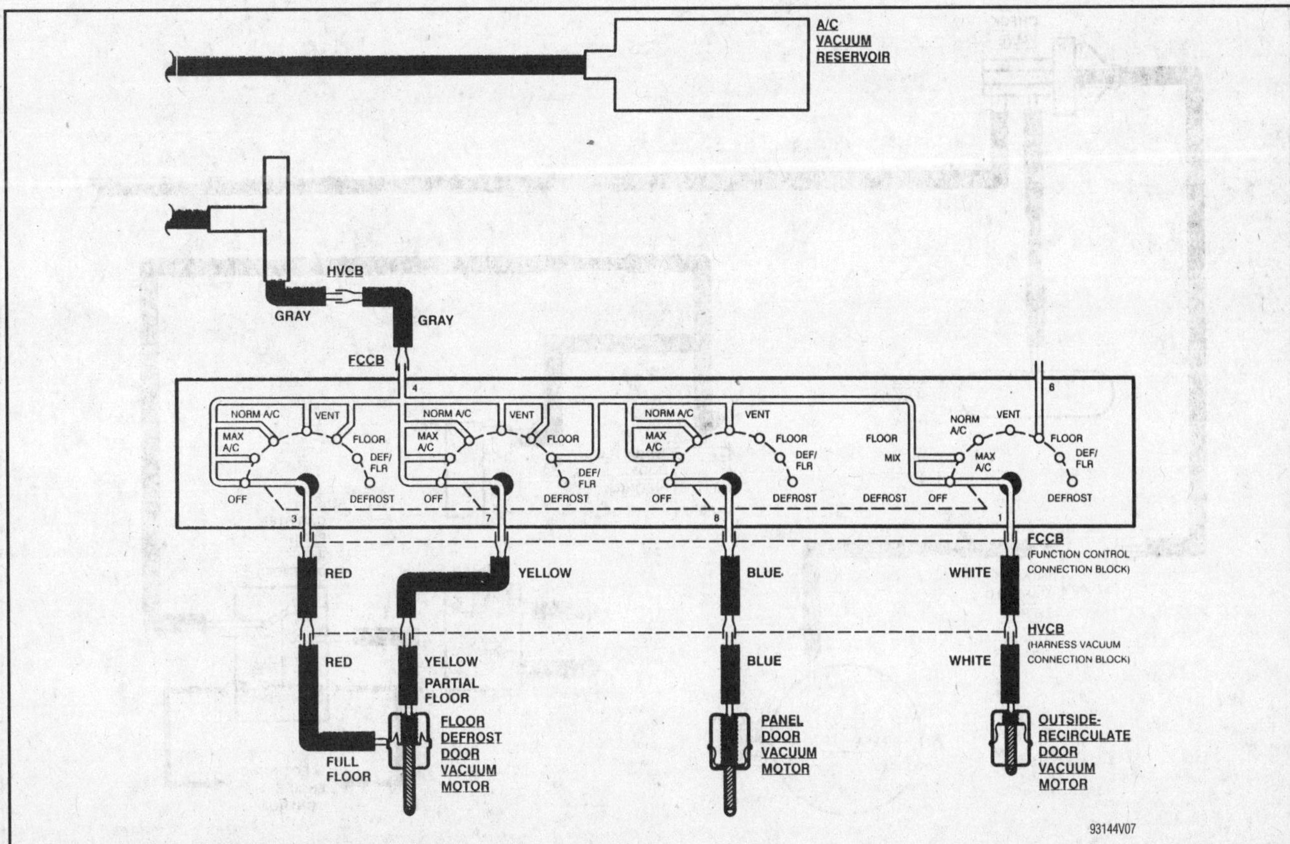

Fig. 100 1994 Town Car typical vacuum diagram—4.6L engine (2 of 2)

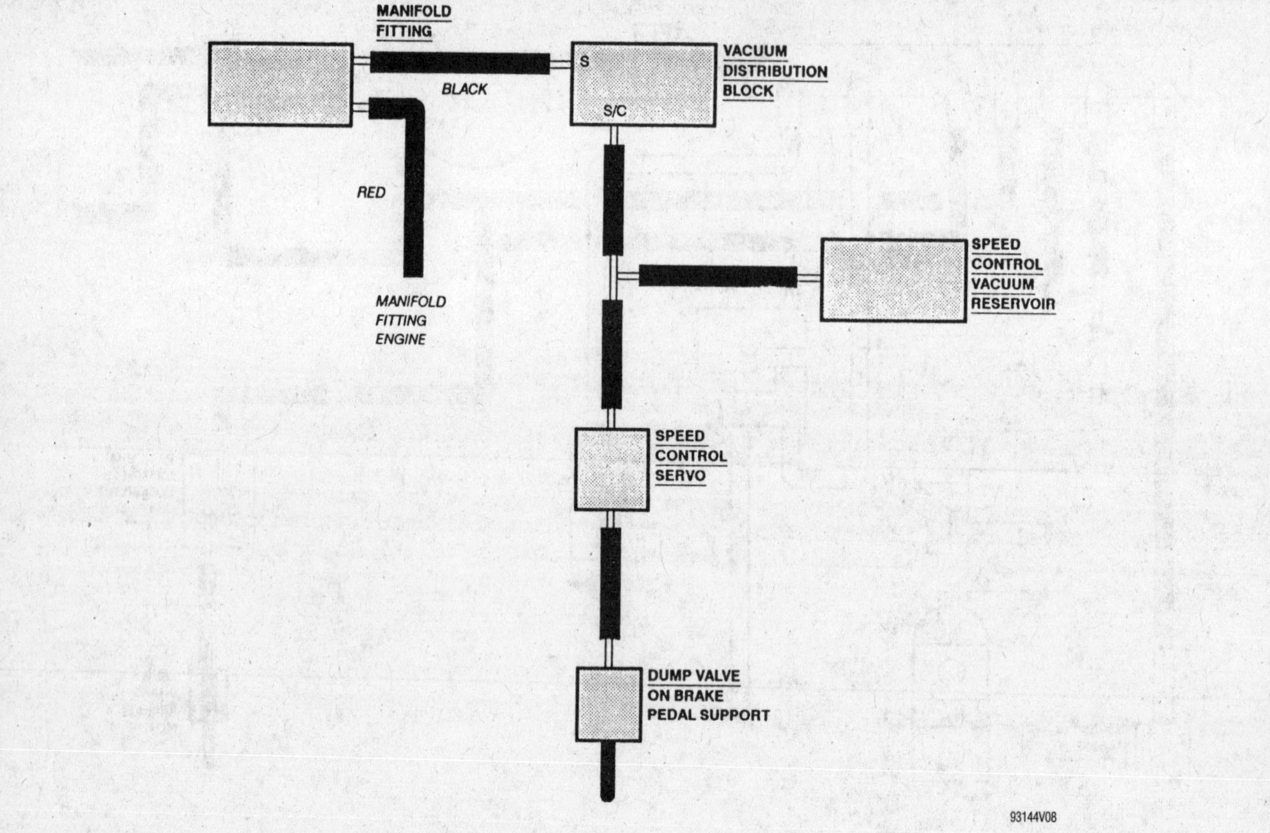


Fig. 101 1994 Continental typical vacuum diagram—3.8L engine

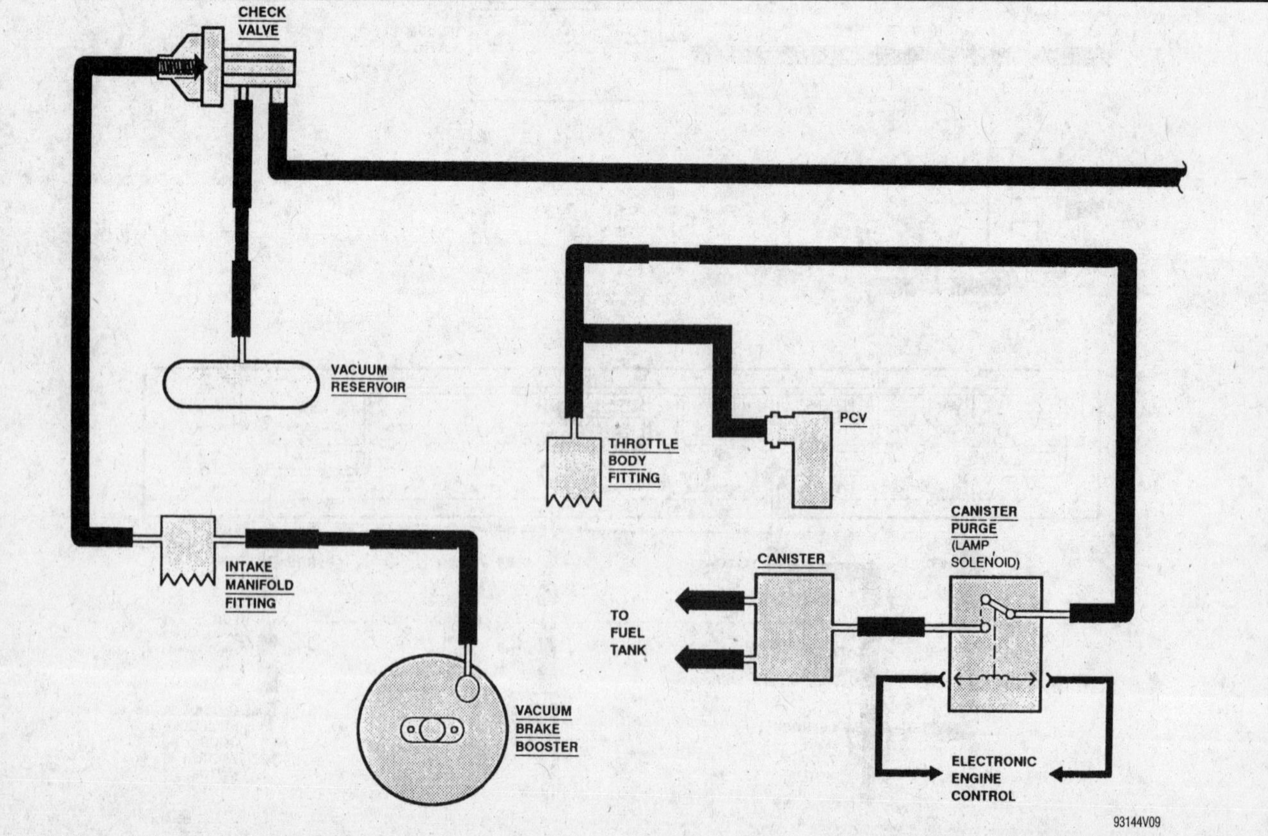


Fig. 102 1994 Mark VIII typical vacuum diagram—4.6L engine (1 of 3)

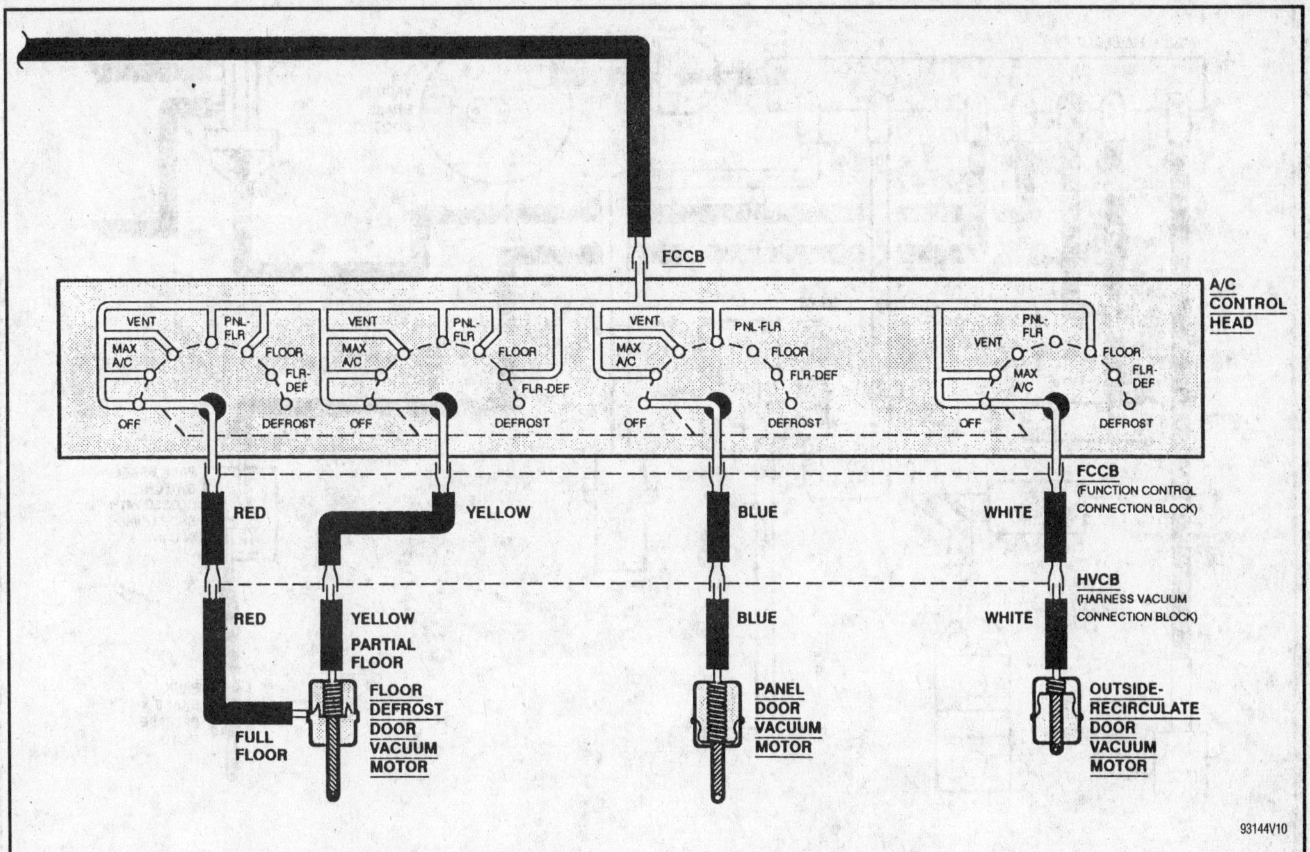


Fig. 103 1994 Mark VIII typical vacuum diagram—4.6L engine (2 of 3)

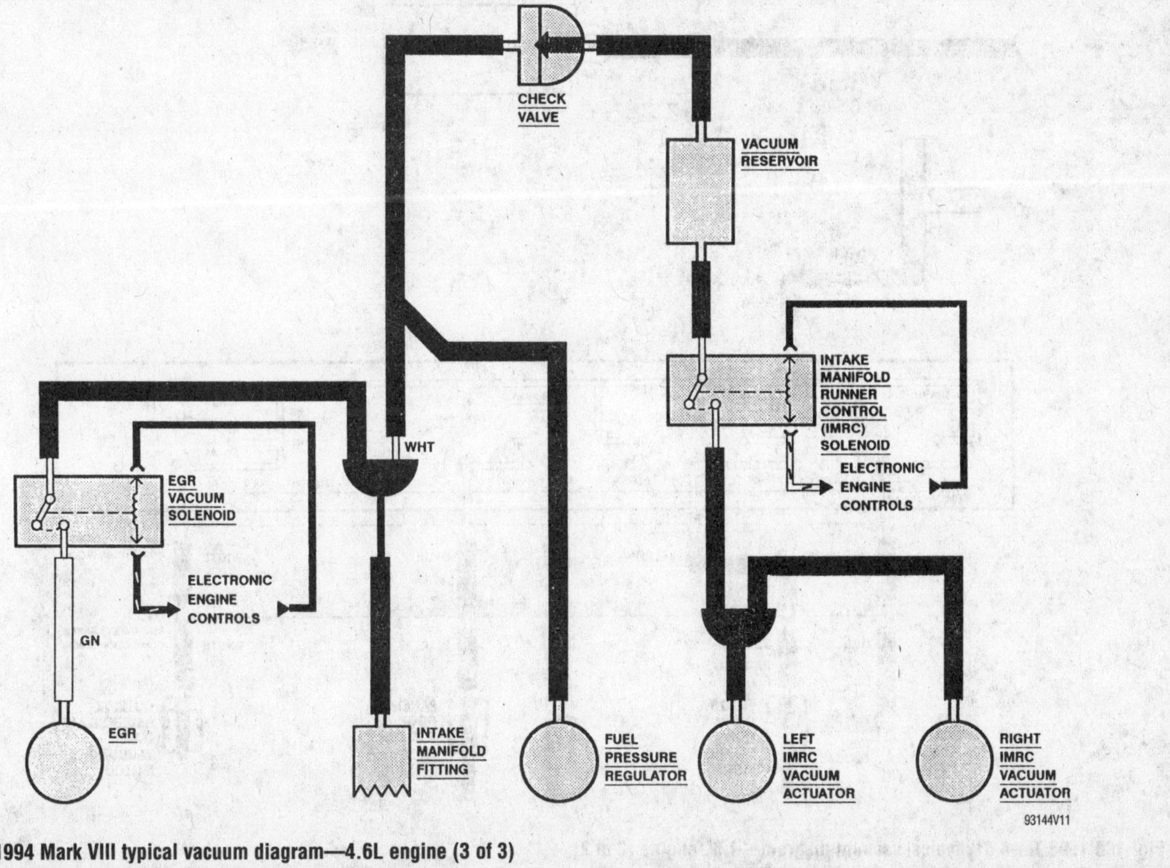


Fig. 104 1994 Mark VIII typical vacuum diagram—4.6L engine (3 of 3)

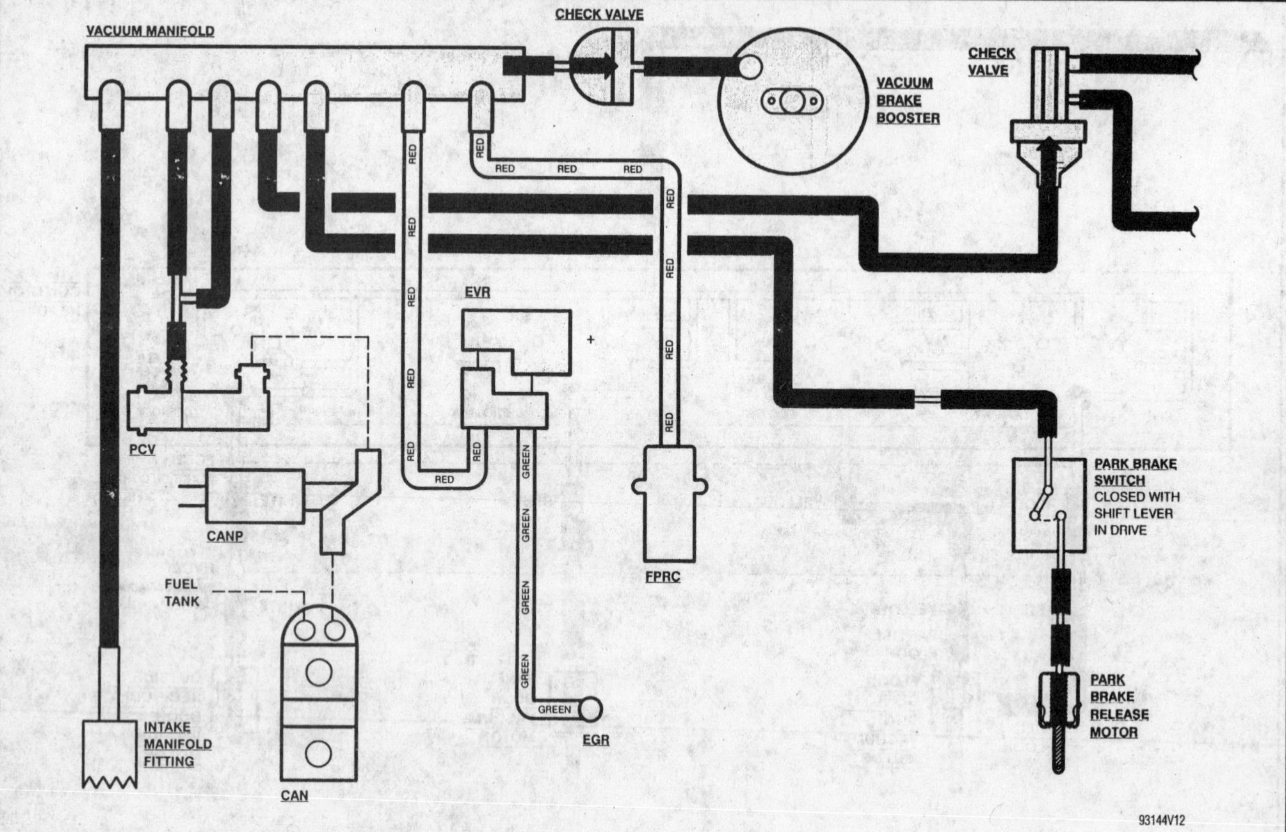


Fig. 105 1995 Town Car typical vacuum diagram—4.6L engine (1 of 2)

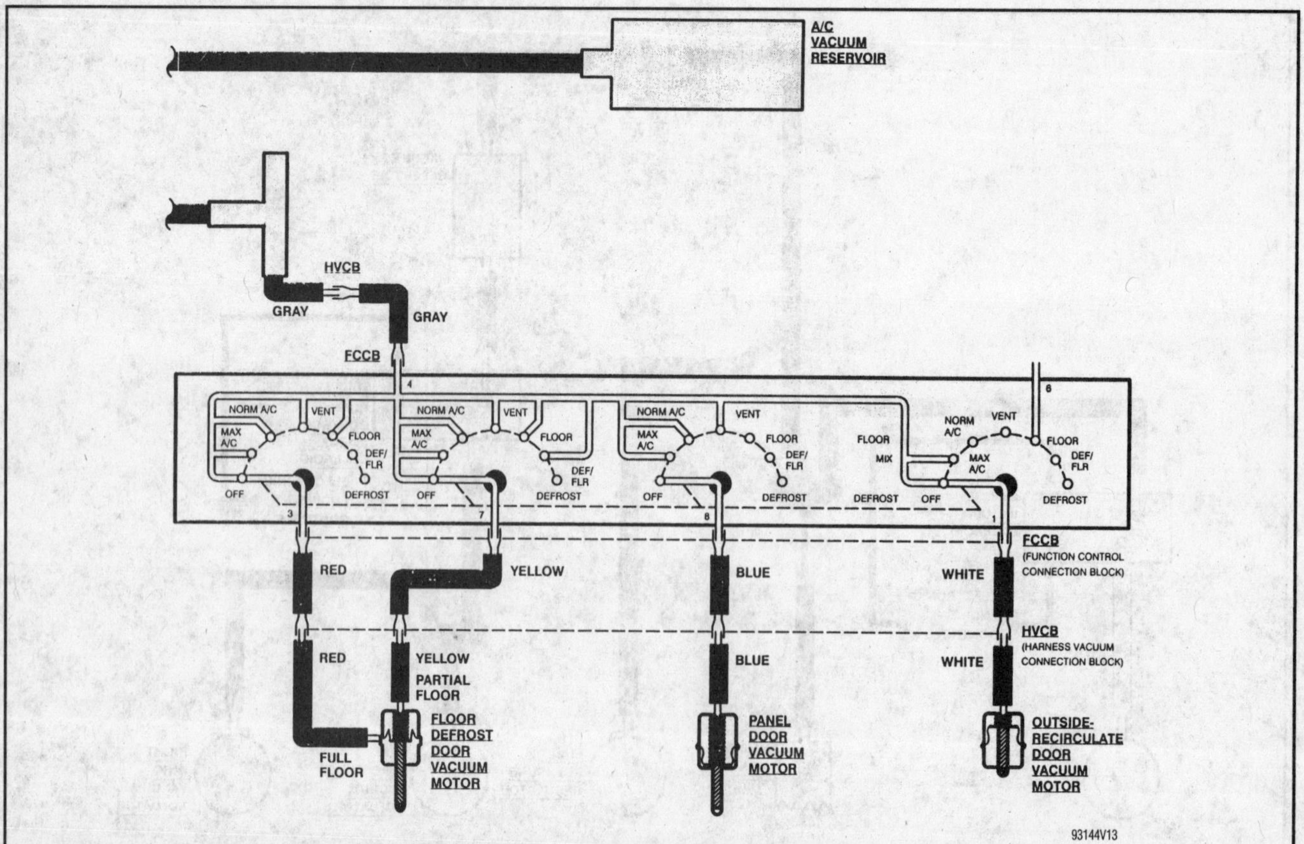


Fig. 106 1995 Town Car typical vacuum diagram—4.6L engine (2 of 2)

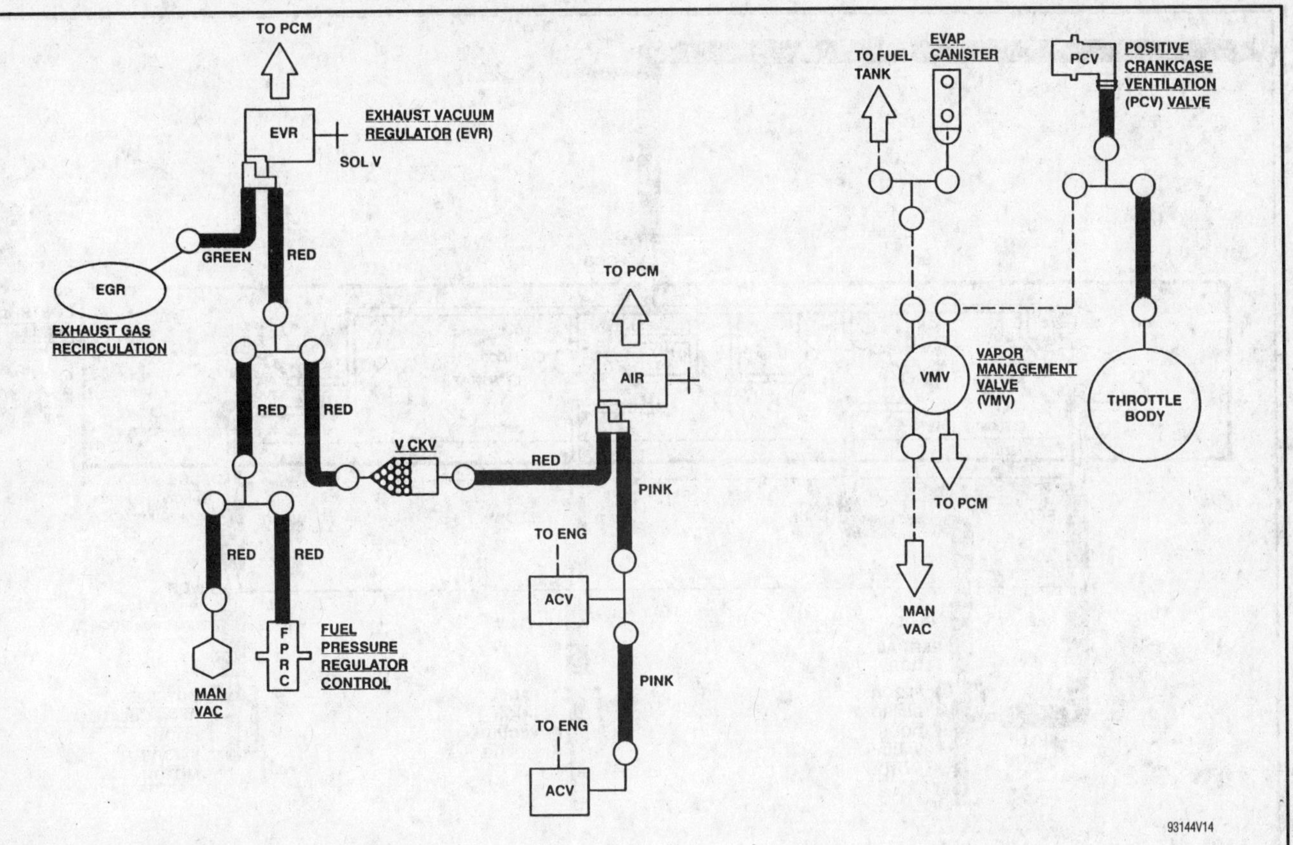


Fig. 107 1995 Continental typical vacuum diagram—4.6L engine

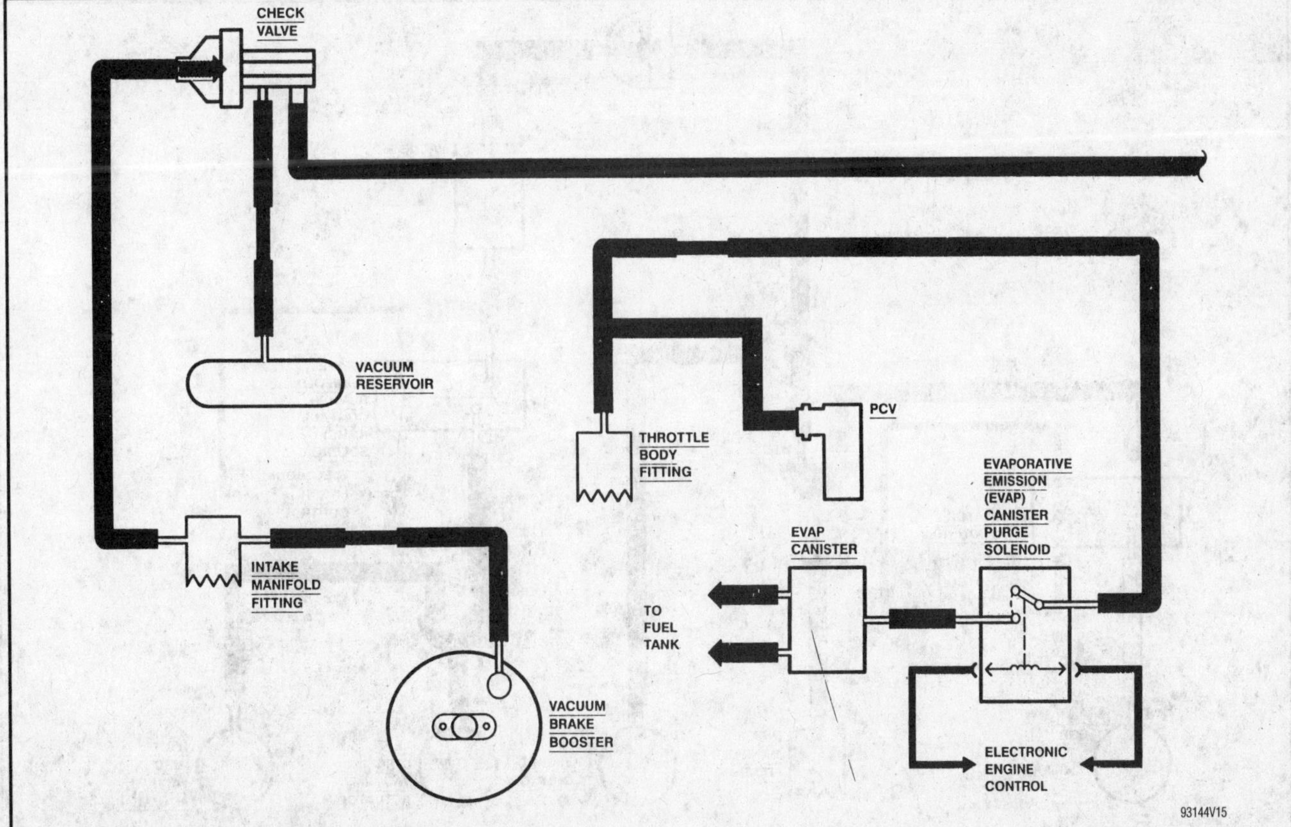


Fig. 108 1995 Mark VIII typical vacuum diagram—4.6L engine (1 of 3)

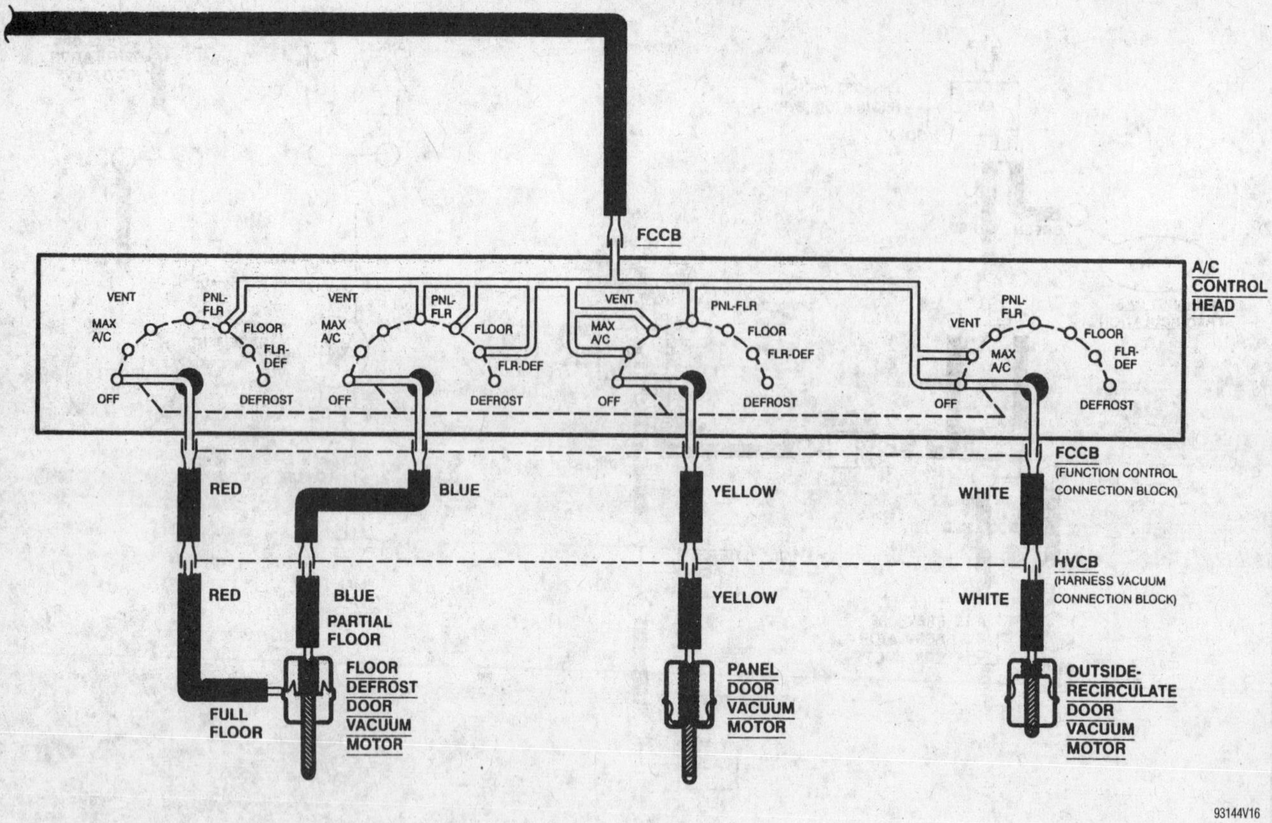


Fig. 109 1995 Mark VIII typical vacuum diagram—4.6L engine (2 of 3)

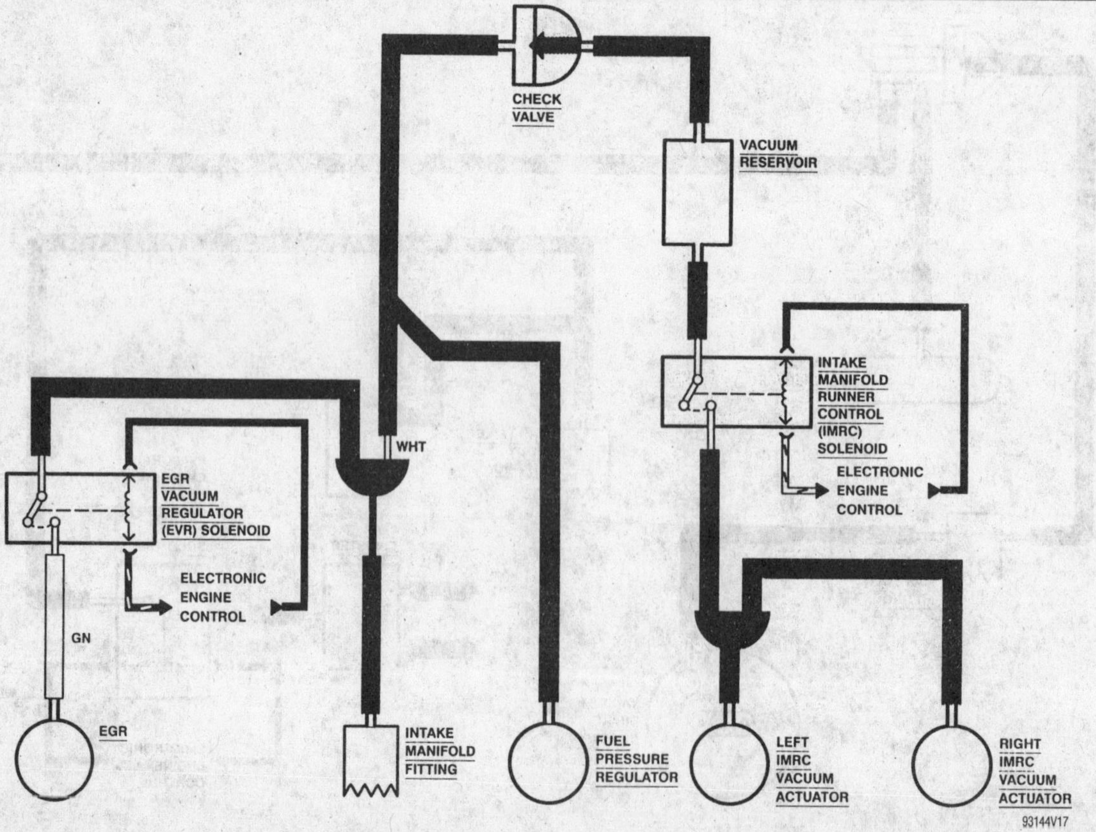


Fig. 110 1995 Mark VIII typical vacuum diagram—4.6L engine (3 of 3)

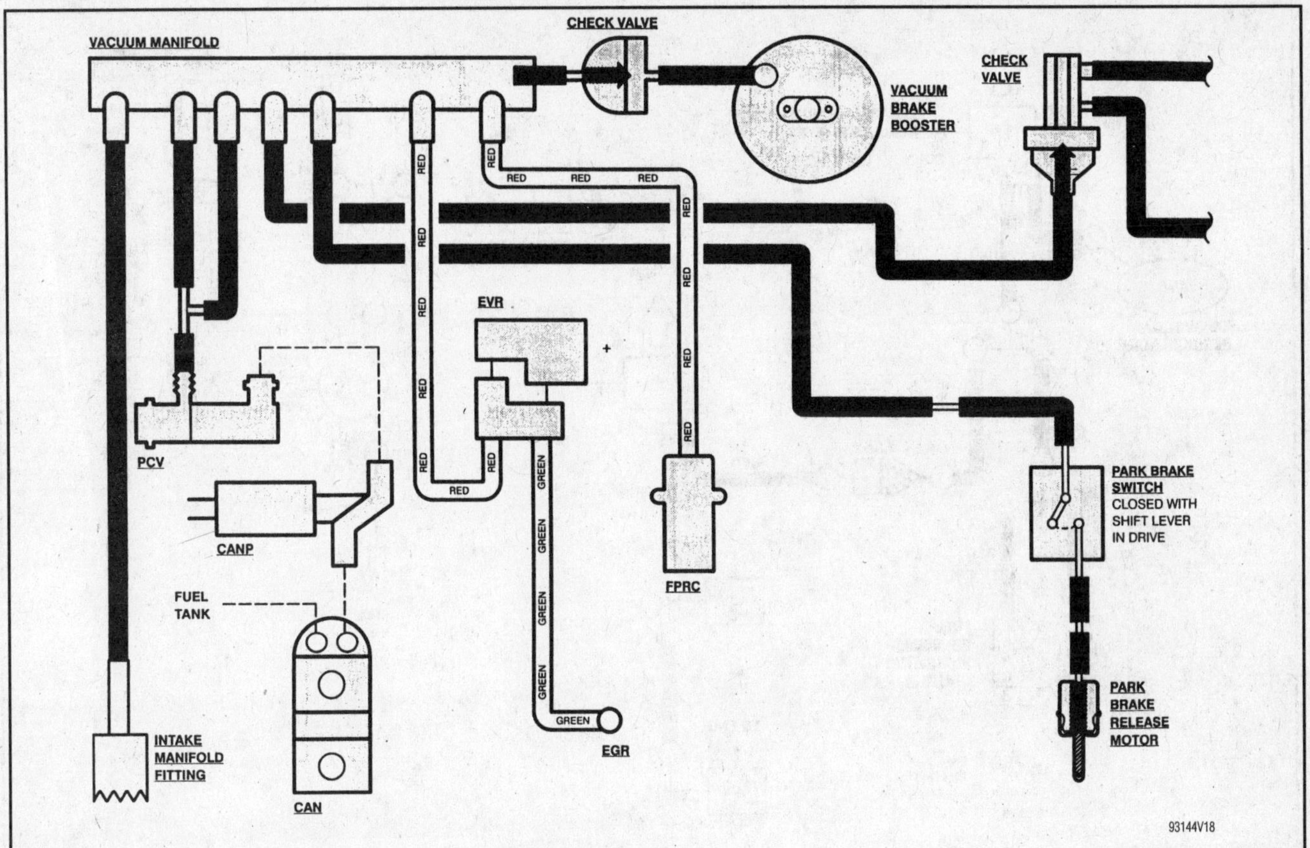


Fig. 111 1996 Town Car typical vacuum diagram—4.6L engine (1 of 2)

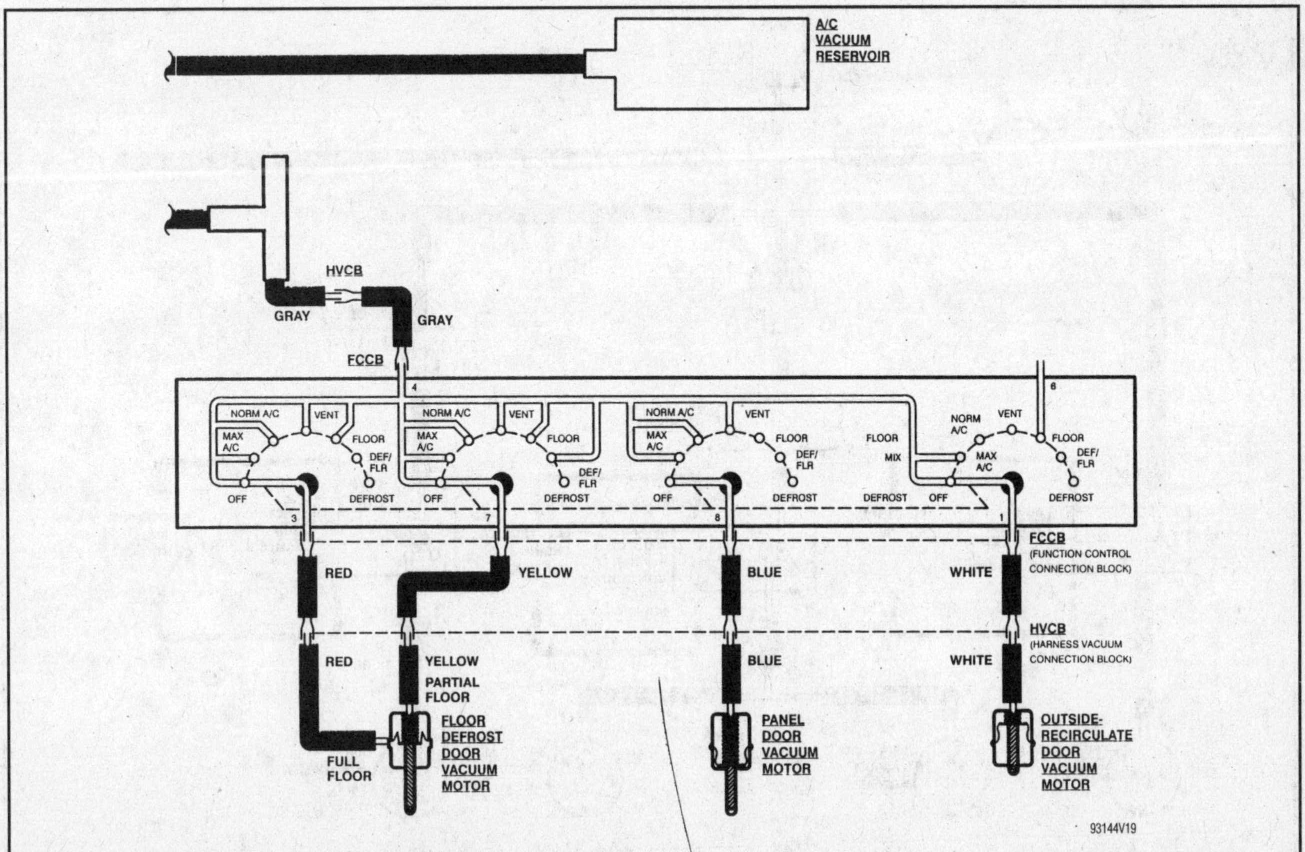


Fig. 112 1996 Town Car typical vacuum diagram—4.6L engine (2 of 2)

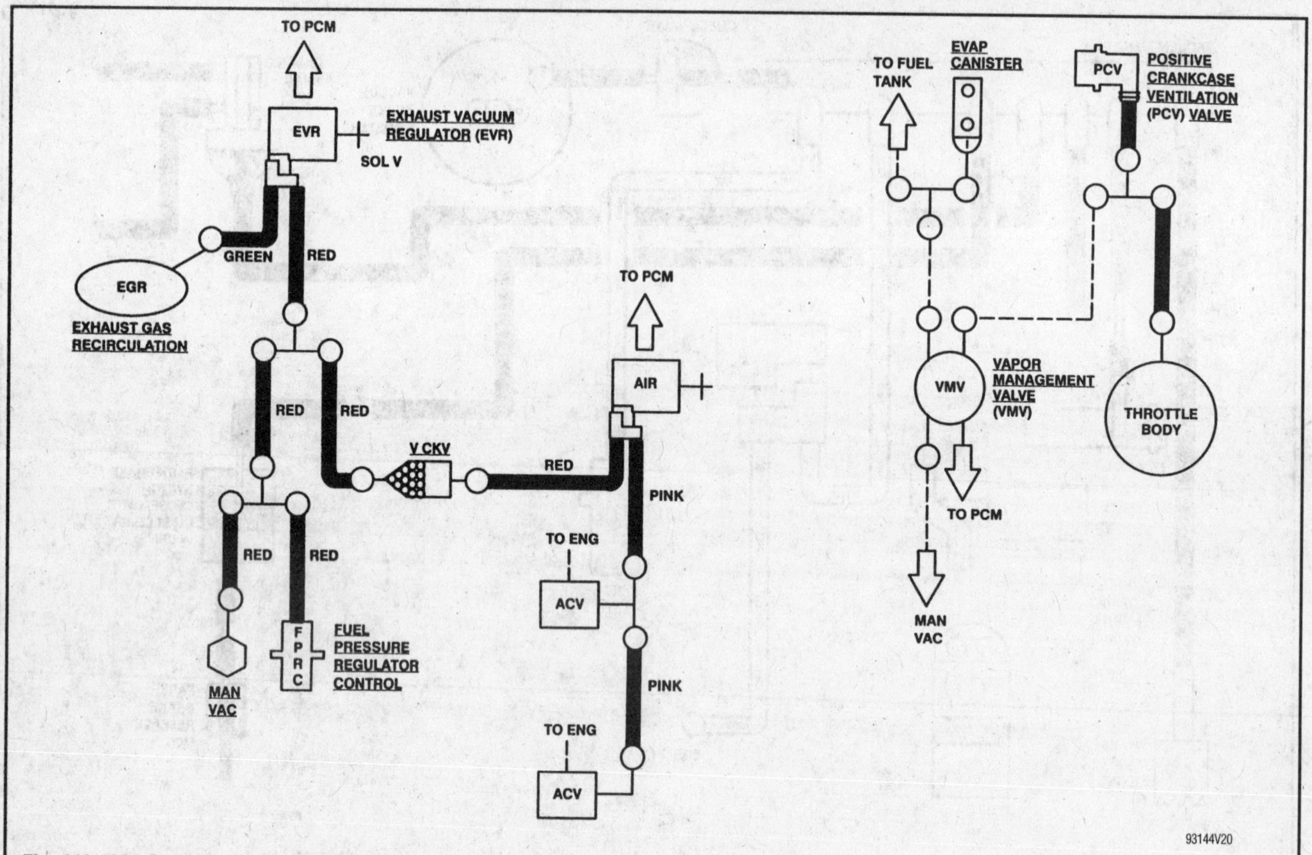


Fig. 113 1996 Continental typical vacuum diagram—4.6L engine

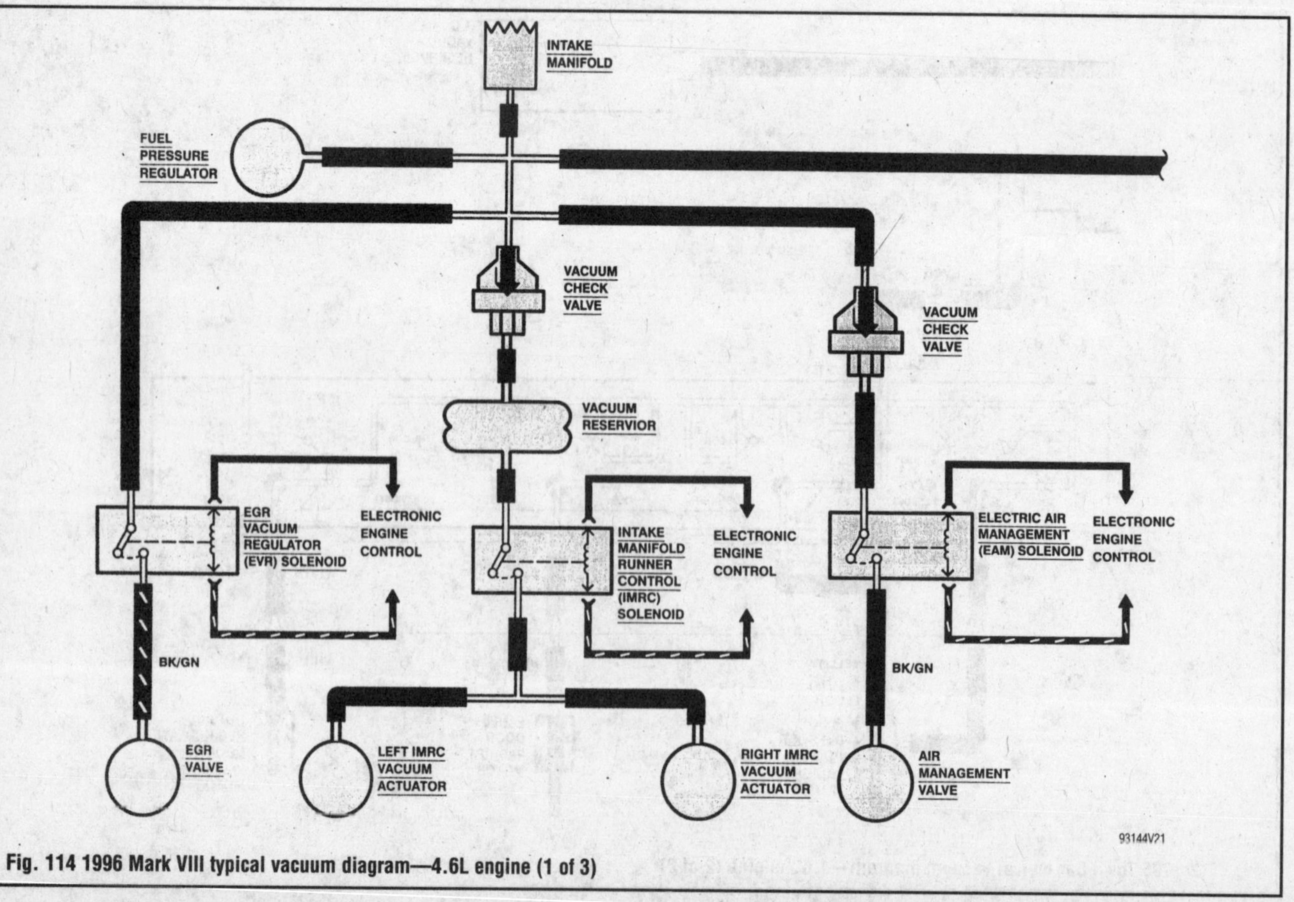


Fig. 114 1996 Mark VIII typical vacuum diagram—4.6L engine (1 of 3)

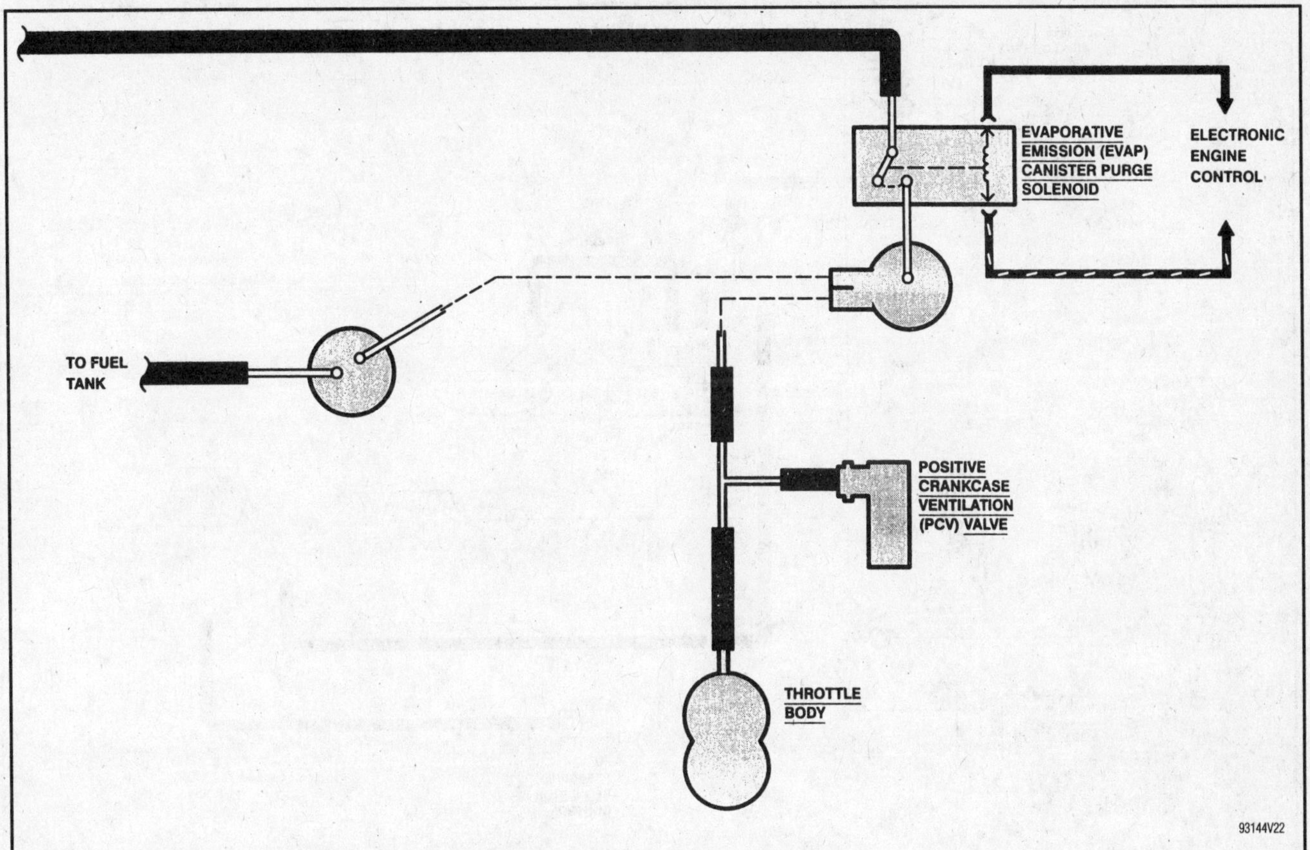


Fig. 115 1996 Mark VIII typical vacuum diagram—4.6L engine (2 of 3)

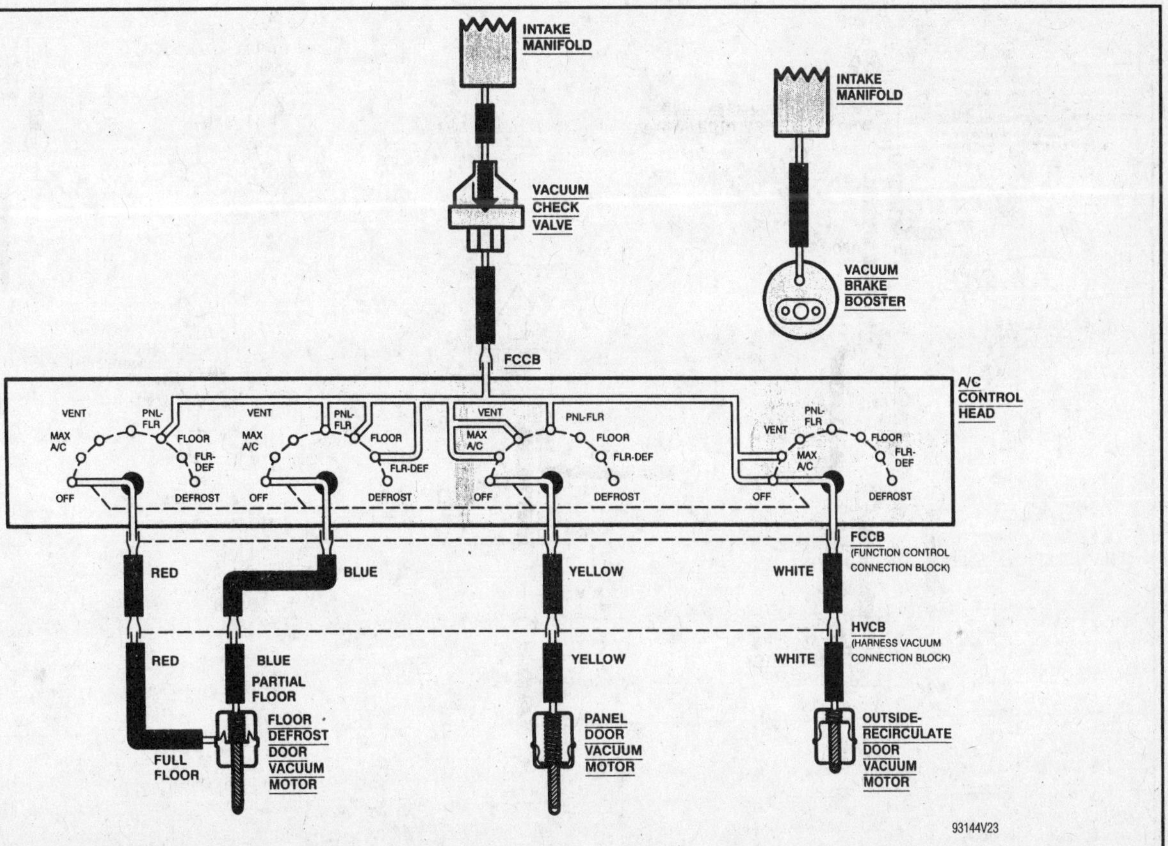


Fig. 116 1996 Mark VIII typical vacuum diagram—4.6L engine (3 of 3)

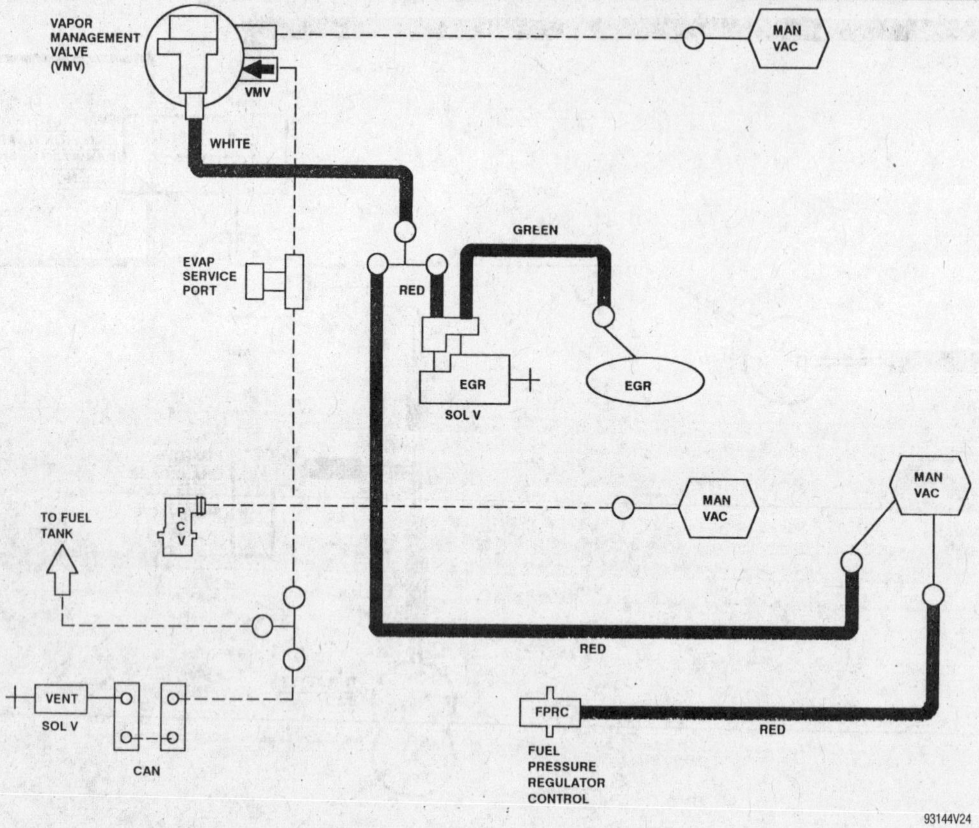


Fig. 117 1997 Town Car typical vacuum diagram—4.6L engine

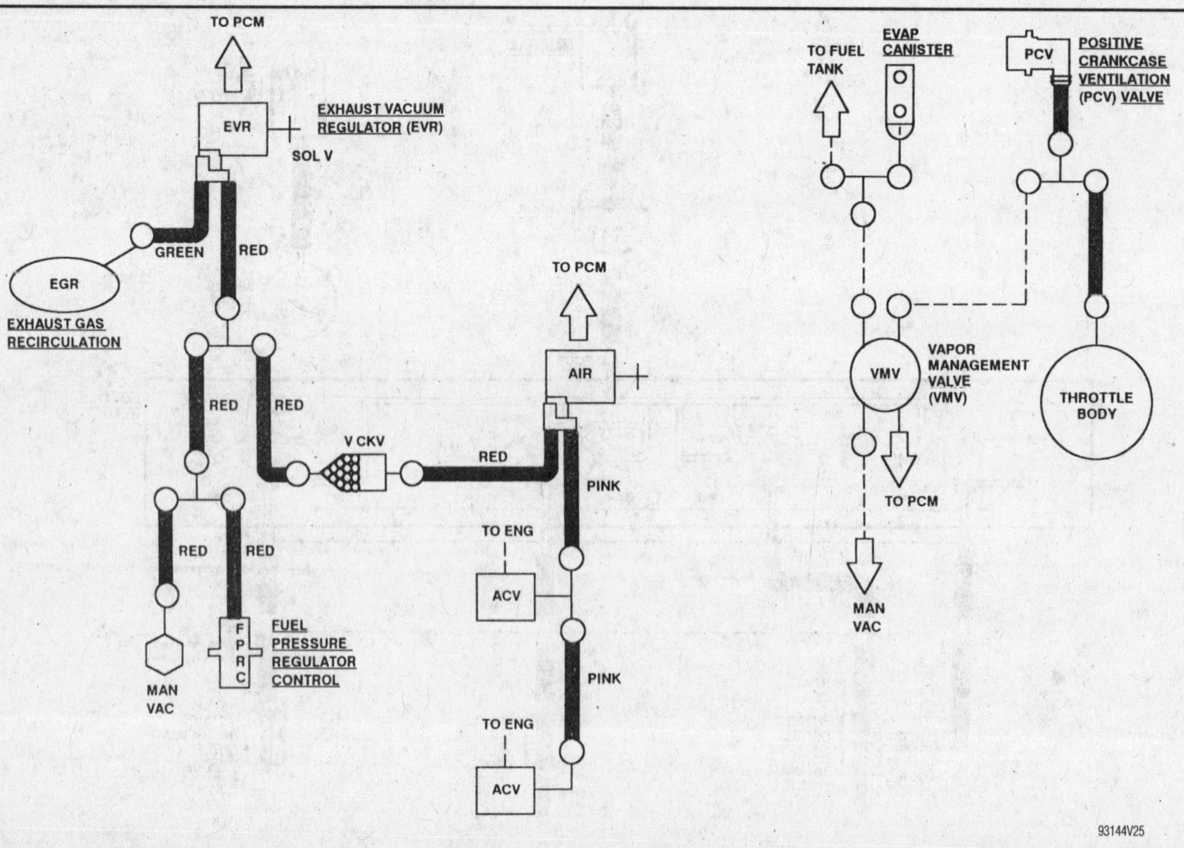


Fig. 118 1997 Continental typical vacuum diagram—4.6L engine

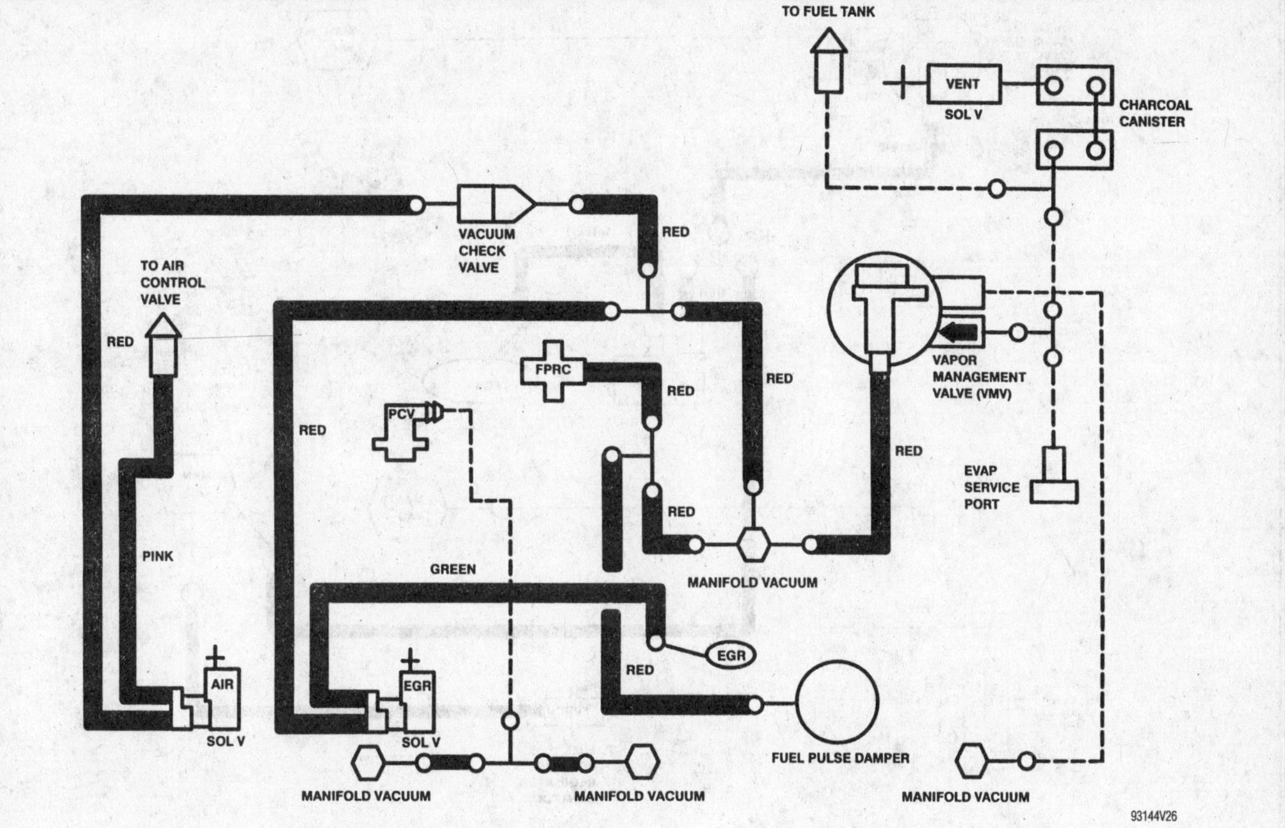

Fig. 119 1997 Mark VIII typical vacuum diagram—4.6L engine

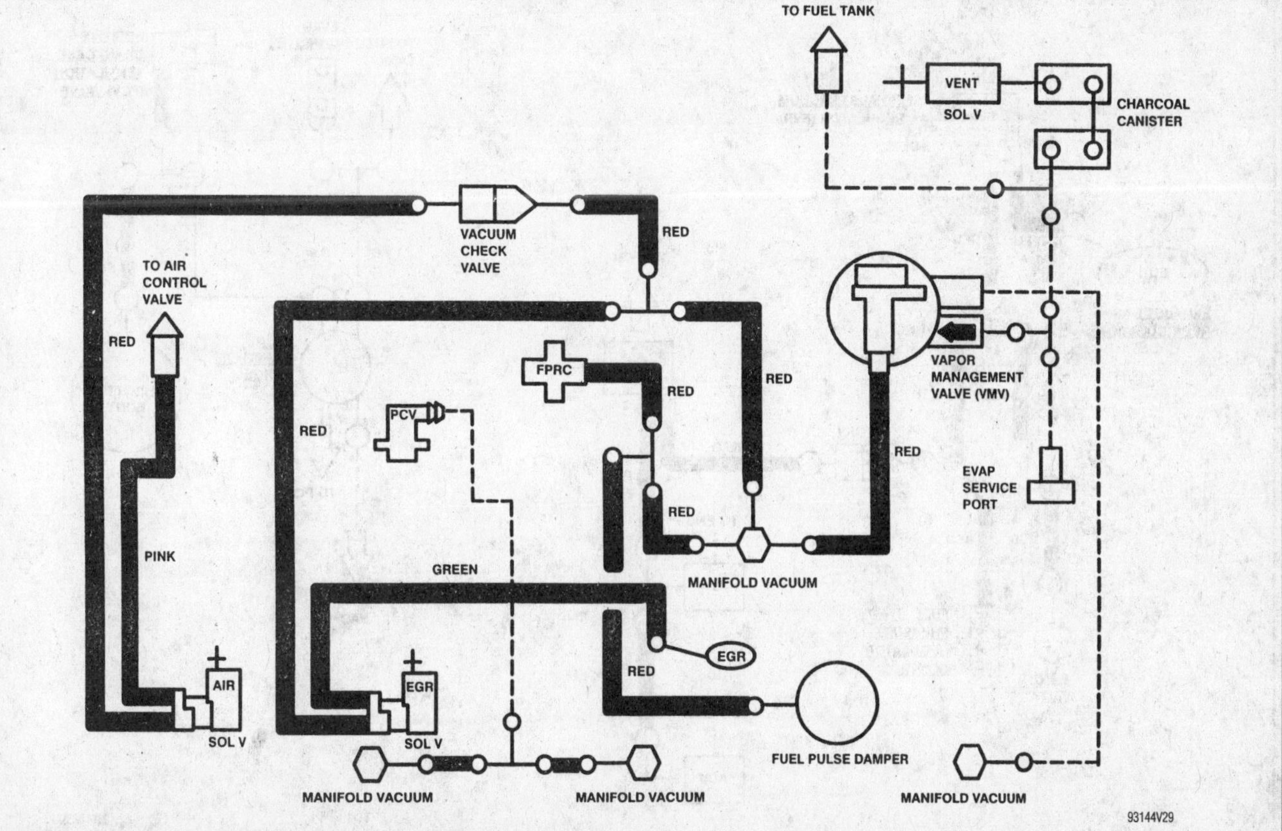

Fig. 120 1998 Mark VIII typical vacuum diagram—4.6L engine

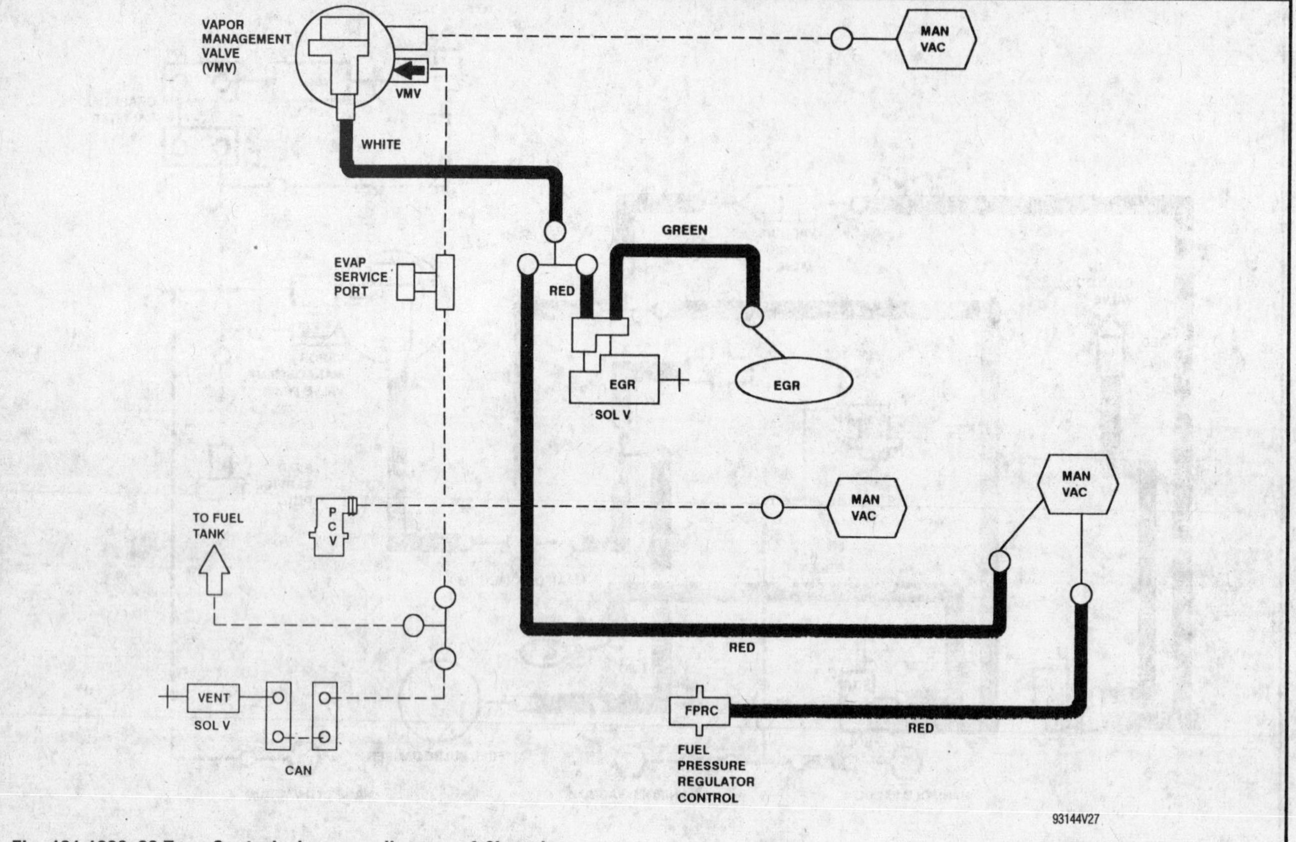


Fig. 121 1998–00 Town Car typical vacuum diagram—4.6L engine

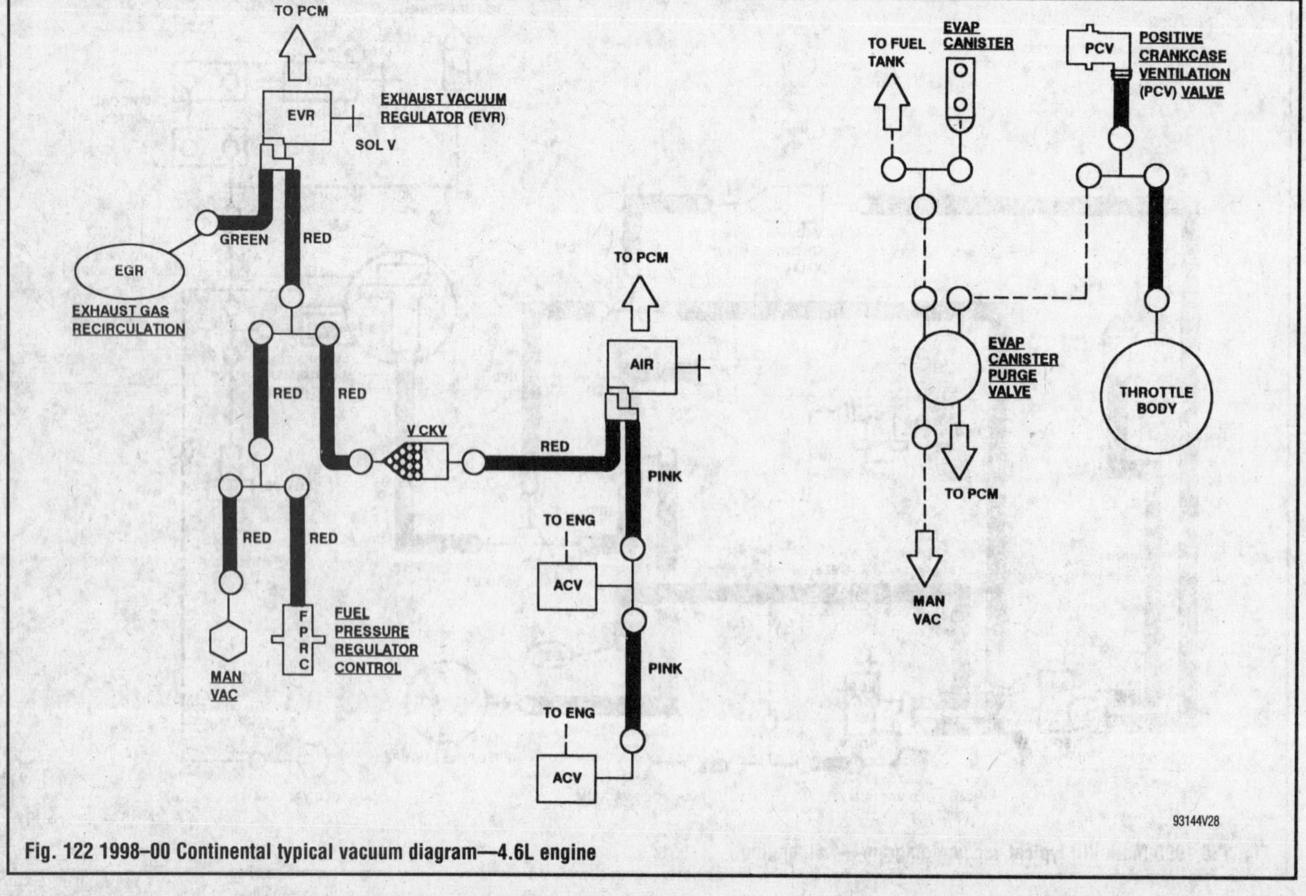


Fig. 122 1998–00 Continental typical vacuum diagram—4.6L engine

**BASIC FUEL SYSTEM DIAGNOSIS 5-2**
**FUEL LINES AND FITTINGS 5-2**
HAIRPIN CLIP FITTING 5-2
REMOVAL & INSTALLATION 5-2
DUCKBILL CLIP FITTING 5-2
REMOVAL & INSTALLATION 5-2
SPRING LOCK COUPLING 5-2
REMOVAL & INSTALLATION 5-2
**GASOLINE FUEL INJECTION SYSTEM 5-4**
GENERAL INFORMATION 5-4
FUEL SYSTEM SERVICE PRECAUTIONS 5-5
RELIEVING FUEL SYSTEM PRESSURE 5-5
FUEL PUMP 5-5
TESTING 5-5
REMOVAL & INSTALLATION 5-5
THROTTLE BODY 5-5
REMOVAL & INSTALLATION 5-5
FUEL RAIL AND FUEL INJECTOR(S) 5-7
REMOVAL & INSTALLATION 5-7
TESTING 5-9
FUEL PRESSURE REGULATOR 5-10
REMOVAL & INSTALLATION 5-10
PRESSURE RELIEF VALVE 5-11
REMOVAL & INSTALLATION 5-11
**FUEL TANK 5-11**
TANK ASSEMBLY 5-11
REMOVAL & INSTALLATION 5-11
ELECTRIC FUEL PUMP 5-11
REMOVAL & INSTALLATION 5-11

# 5

# FUEL SYSTEM

BASIC FUEL SYSTEM DIAGNOSIS 5-2
BASIC FUEL LINES AND FITTINGS 5-2
GASOLINE FUEL INJECTION SYSTEM 5-4
FUEL TANK 5-11

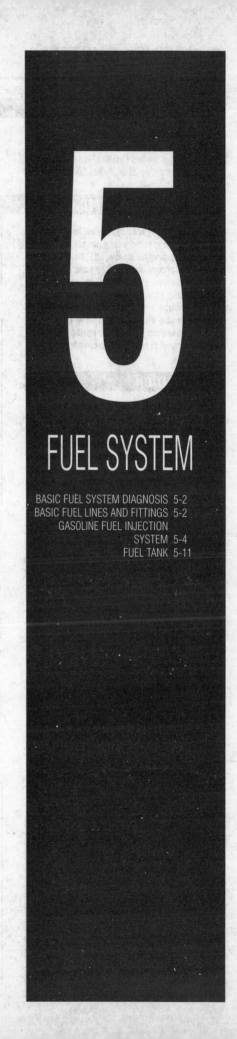

## BASIC FUEL SYSTEM DIAGNOSIS

When there is a problem starting or driving a vehicle, two of the most important checks involve the ignition and the fuel systems. The questions most mechanics attempt to answer first, "is there spark?" and "is there fuel?" will often lead to solving most basic problems. For ignition system diagnosis and testing, please refer to the information on engine electrical components and ignition systems found earlier in this manual. If the ignition system checks out (there is spark), then you must determine if the fuel system is operating properly (is there fuel?).

## FUEL LINES AND FITTINGS

**➡Quick-connect (push type) fuel line fittings must be disconnected using proper procedure or the fitting may be damaged. There are two types of retainers used on the push connect fittings. Line sizes of ⅜ and 5/16 in. diameter use a hairpin clip retainer. The ¼ in. diameter line connectors use a duck-bill clip retainer. In addition, some engines use spring-lock connections, secured by a garter spring, which require a special fuel line disconnect tool for removal.**

### ⁂ CAUTION

**Observe all applicable safety precautions when working around fuel. Whenever servicing the fuel system, always work in a well ventilated area. Do not allow fuel spray or vapors to come in contact with a spark or open flame. Keep a dry chemical fire extinguisher near the work area. Always keep fuel in a container specifically designed for fuel storage; also, always properly seal fuel containers to avoid the possibility of fire or explosion.**

### Hairpin Clip Fitting

REMOVAL & INSTALLATION

**➧ See Figures 1 and 2**

1. Clean all dirt and grease from the fitting. Spread the two clip legs about ⅛ in. (3mm) each to disengage from the fitting and pull the clip outward from the fitting. Use finger pressure only; do not use any tools.
2. Grasp the fitting and hose assembly and pull away from the steel line. Twist the fitting and hose assembly slightly while pulling, if the assembly sticks.
3. Inspect the hairpin clip for damage, replacing the clip if necessary. Reinstall the clip in position on the fitting.

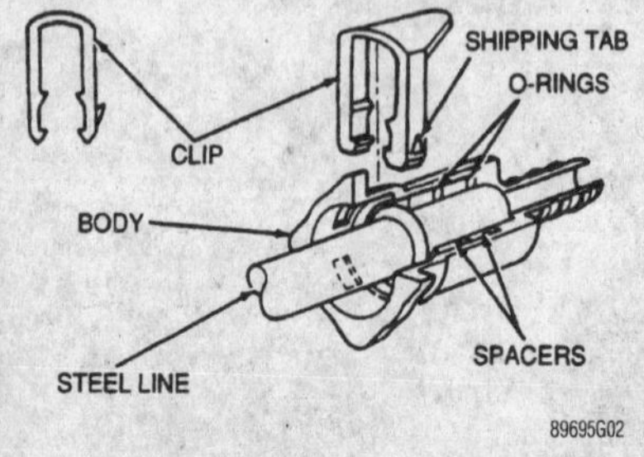


**Fig. 1 Cutaway view of the hairpin clip fitting**

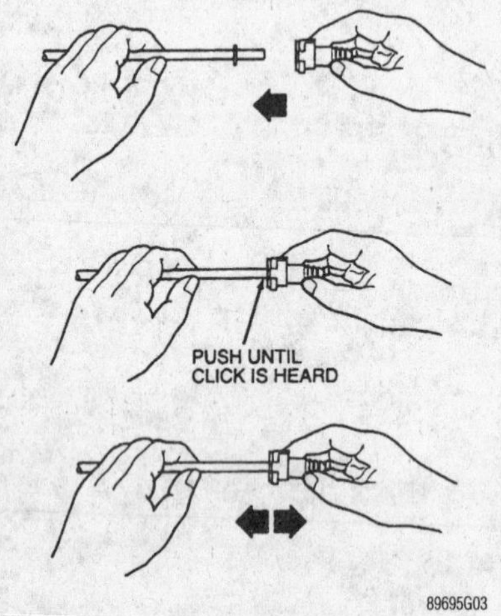


**Fig. 2 When assembling the fitting, push the pipe into the fitting until a click is heard**

4. Inspect the fitting and inside of the connector to ensure freedom from dirt or obstruction. Install the fitting into the connector and push together. A click will be heard when the hairpin snaps into the proper connection. Pull on the line to insure full engagement.

### Duckbill Clip Fitting

REMOVAL & INSTALLATION

**➧ See Figure 3**

1. A special tool is available from Ford and other manufacturers for removing the retaining clips. Use Ford Tool T90T-9550-B or C or equivalent. If the tool is not on hand, go onto step 2. Align the slot on the push connector disconnect tool with either tab on the retaining clip. Pull the line from the connector.
2. If the special clip tool is not available, use a pair of narrow 6-inch slip-jaw pliers with a jaw width of 0.2 in (5mm) or less. Align the jaws of the pliers with the openings of the fitting case and compress the part of the retaining clip that engages the case. Compressing the retaining clip will release the fitting, which may be pulled from the connector. Both sides of the clip must be compressed at the same time to disengage.
3. Inspect the retaining clip, fitting end and connector. Replace the clip if any damage is apparent.
4. Push the line into the steel connector until a click is heard, indicating the clip is in place. Pull on the line to check engagement.

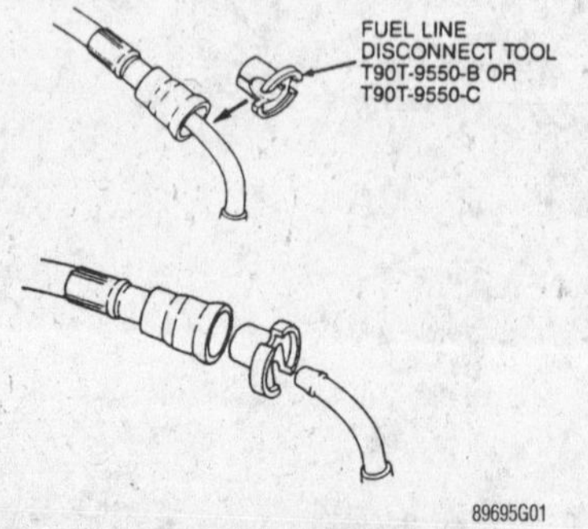


**Fig. 3 A fuel line disconnect tool is required to properly separate a duckbill clip fitting**

### Spring Lock Coupling

REMOVAL & INSTALLATION

**➧ See Figures 4 thru 14**

The spring lock coupling is held together by a garter spring inside a circular cage. When the cou-

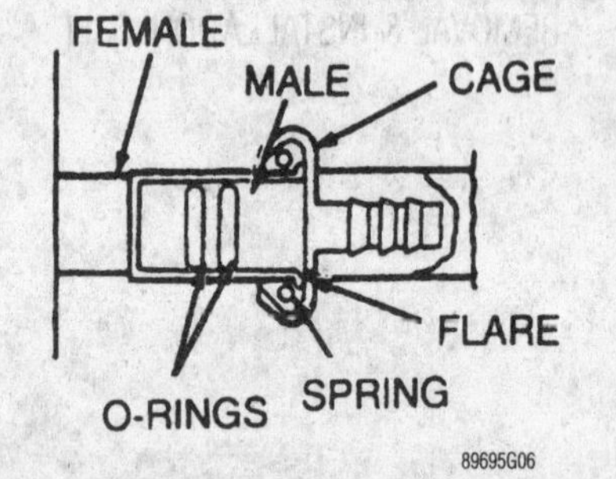


**Fig. 4 Cutaway view of a spring lock coupling**

**Fig. 5 Remove the safety clip from the fuel lines, the clip is attached to a small wire that keeps it from getting lost**

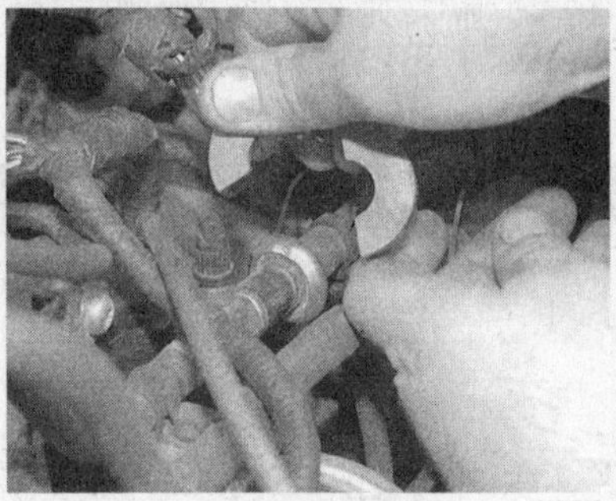

91055P23

Fig. 6 This type of removal tool has a hinged center section that allows you to fit it around the fuel line

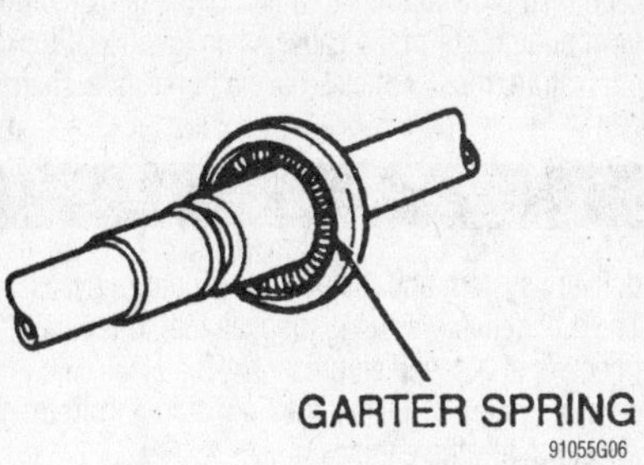


91055G06

Fig. 7 The garter spring is located inside the fitting and holds the fitting together

91055P24

Fig. 8 Slide the tool back to unseat the garter spring on the fitting, and pull back on the fuel line to separate them

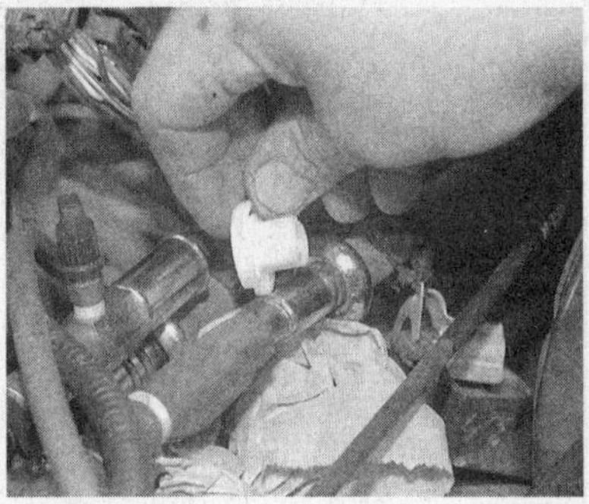

91055P25

Fig. 9 This type of removal tool snaps over the line

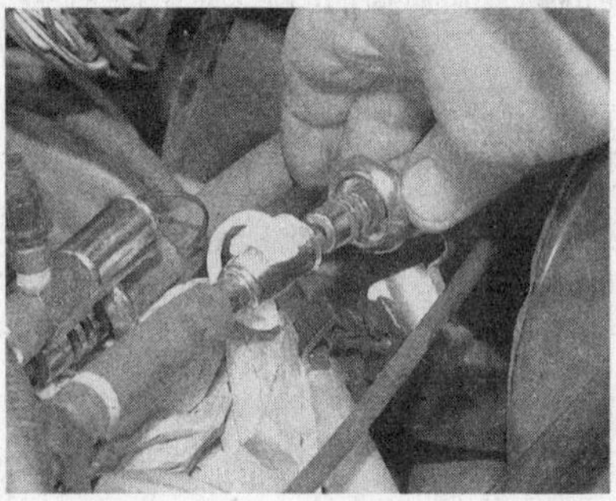

91055P26

Fig. 10 Slide the tool back to unseat the garter spring on the fitting, and pull back on the fuel line to separate them

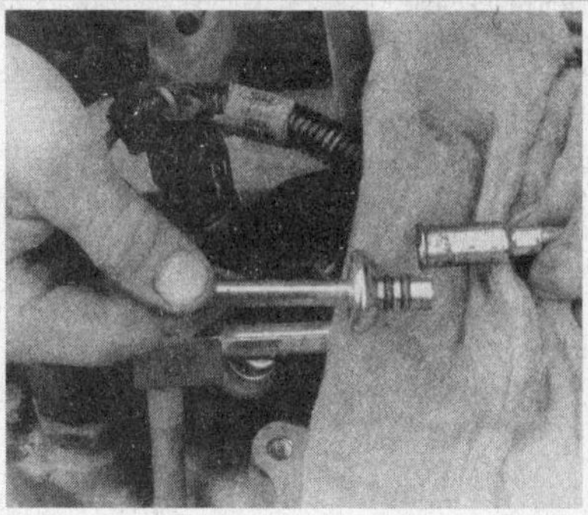

88155P48

Fig. 11 Be sure to check the O-rings for damage; replace them if necessary

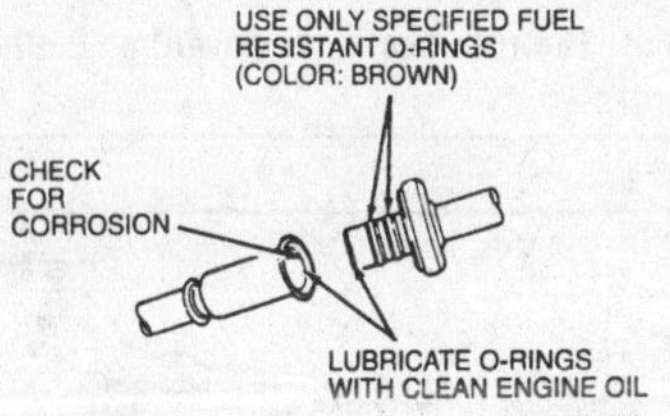


91055G05

Fig. 12 The O-rings should be replaced if necessary with the specific ones used for the fuel system, a non-specific O-ring could leak

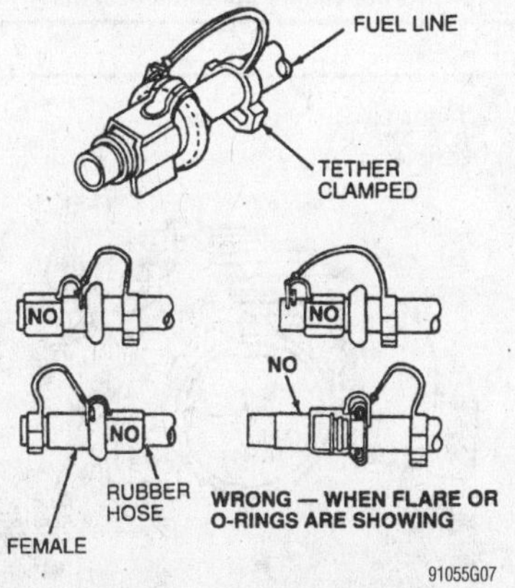


91055G07

Fig. 13 The fitting should be inspected after assembly

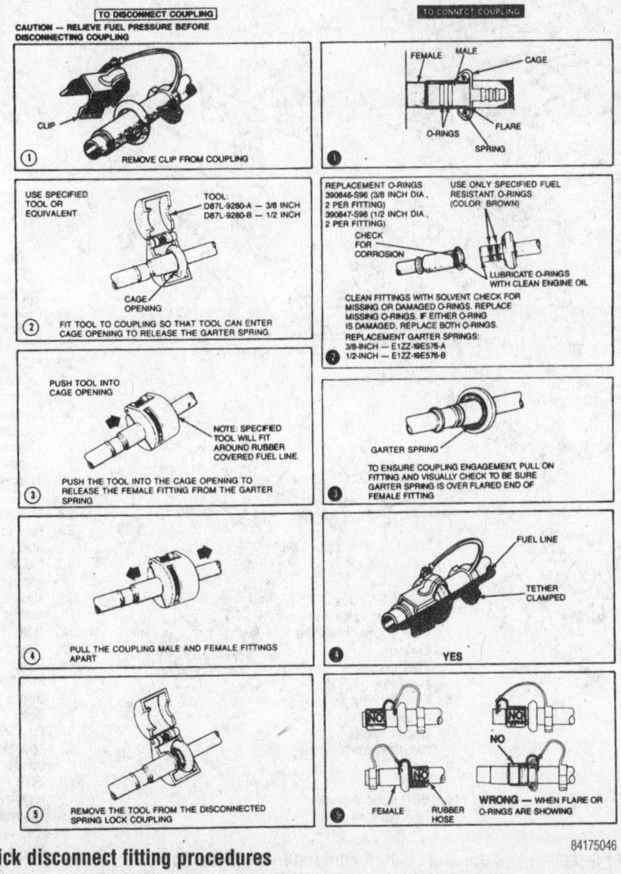


84175046

Fig. 14 Quick disconnect fitting procedures

pling is connected together, the flared end of the female fitting slips behind the garter spring inside the cage of the male fitting. The garter spring and cage then prevent the flared end of the female fitting from pulling out of the cage. As an additional locking feature, most vehicles have a horseshoe-shaped retaining clip that improves the retaining reliability of the spring lock coupling.

# GASOLINE FUEL INJECTION SYSTEM

## General Information

▸ See Figures 15, 16, 17 and 18

The Electronic Fuel Injection (EFI) system was used 1988–94 3.8L engines. The EFI fuel system includes a high pressure (30–45 psi/209–310 kPa) tank-mounted electric fuel pump, throttle body, fuel charging manifold, pressure regulator, fuel filter, and both solid and flexible fuel lines. The fuel charging manifold includes six electronically controlled fuel injectors, each mounted directly above an intake port in the lower intake manifold. The Electronic Engine Control (EEC-IV) computer outputs a command to the fuel injectors to meter the appropriate quantity of fuel.

All vehicles with the 4.6L and 5.0L engines are equipped with a Sequential Electronic Fuel Injection (SEFI) system. In this system, fuel is metered into each intake port in sequence with the engine firing order, according to engine demand, through fuel injectors mounted on a tuned intake manifold. The SEFI system consists of two subsystems, the fuel delivery system and the electronic control system. The fuel delivery system supplies fuel to the fuel injectors at a specified pressure. The electronic control system regulates the flow of fuel from the injectors into the engine.

The fuel delivery system consists of an electric fuel pump, fuel filters, fuel supply manifold (fuel rail), fuel pressure regulator and fuel injectors. The electric fuel pump, mounted in the fuel tank, draws fuel through a filter screen attached to the fuel pump/sending unit assembly. Fuel is pumped through a frame mounted fuel filter, to the engine compartment, and into the fuel supply manifold. The fuel supply manifold supplies fuel directly to the injectors. A constant fuel pressure to the injectors is maintained by the fuel pressure regulator. The fuel pressure regulator is mounted on the fuel supply manifold, downstream from the fuel injectors. The excess fuel supplied by the fuel pump but not required by the engine, passes through the regulator and returns to the fuel tank through the fuel return line. The fuel injectors spray a metered quantity of fuel into the intake air stream when they are

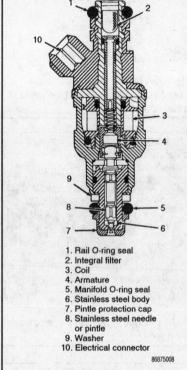

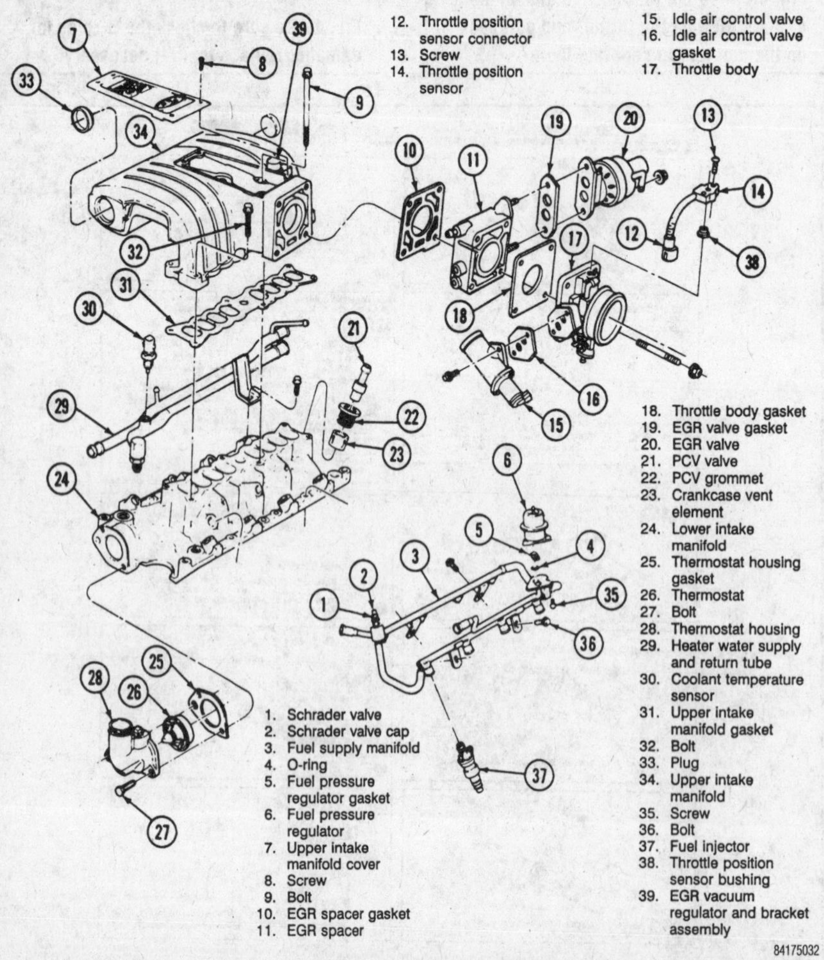


**Fig. 15 Fuel injection system and related components—5.0L engine**

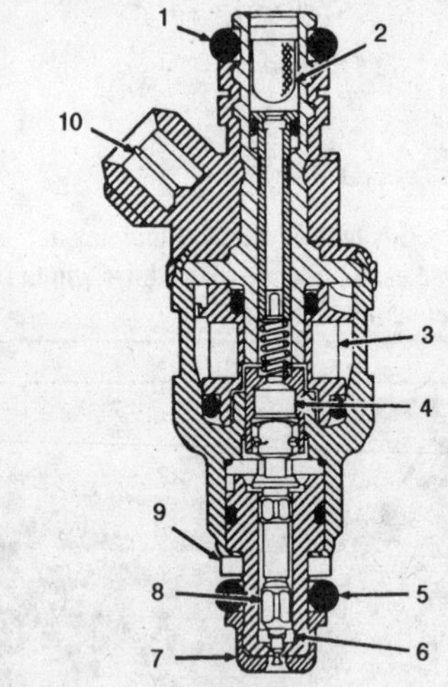


**Fig. 16 Cross-sectional view of an EFI fuel injector**

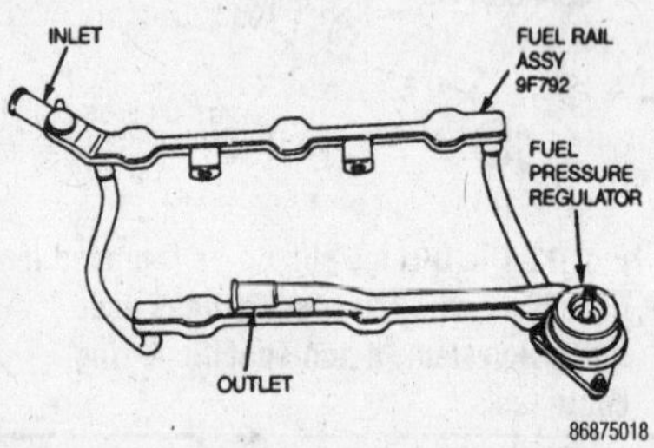


**Fig. 17 Fuel supply manifold assembly**

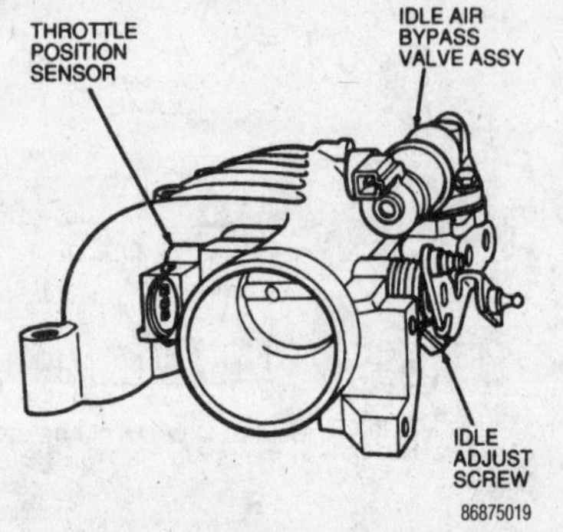


**Fig. 18 Throttle position sensor and idle air bypass valve location on the throttle body**

energized. The quantity of fuel is determined by the electronic control system.

Air entering the engine is monitored by speed, pressure and temperature sensors. The outputs of these sensors are processed by the Powertrain Control Module (PCM). The PCM computes the required fuel flow rate and determines the needed injector pulse width (injector "on" time) and sends a signal to the injector to meter the exact quantity of fuel. Each fuel injector is energized once every other crankshaft revolution, in sequence with the ignition firing order.

**➡For description and testing of electronic control system components, see Section 4.**

### FUEL SYSTEM SERVICE PRECAUTIONS

Safety is the most important factor when performing not only fuel system maintenance, but any type of maintenance. Failure to conduct maintenance and repairs in a safe manner may result in serious personal injury or death. Work on a vehicle's fuel system components can be accomplished safely and effectively by adhering to the following rules and guidelines.

- To avoid the possibility of fire and personal injury, always disconnect the negative battery cable unless the repair or test procedure requires that battery voltage by applied.
- Always relieve the fuel system pressure prior to detaching any fuel system component (injector, fuel rail, pressure regulator, etc.) fitting or fuel line connection. Exercise extreme caution whenever relieving fuel system pressure to avoid exposing skin, face and eyes to fuel spray. Please be advised that fuel under pressure may penetrate the skin or any part of the body that it contacts.
- Always place a shop towel or cloth around the fitting or connection prior to loosening to absorb any excess fuel due to spillage. Ensure that all fuel spillage is quickly remove from engine surfaces. Ensure that all fuel-soaked cloths or towels are deposited into a flame-proof waste container with a lid.
- Always keep a dry chemical (Class B) fire extinguisher near the work area.
- Do not allow fuel spray or fuel vapors to come into contact with a spark or open flame.
- Always use a second wrench when loosening or tightening fuel line connections fittings. This will prevent unnecessary stress and torsion to fuel piping. Always follow the proper torque specifications.
- Always replace worn fuel fitting O-rings with new ones. Do not substitute fuel hose where rigid pipe is installed.

## Relieving Fuel System Pressure

**⁂ CAUTION**

**Fuel supply lines on fuel injected vehicles will remain pressurized for some time after the engine is shut off. Fuel pressure must be relieved before servicing the fuel system.**

1. Disconnect the negative battery cable.
2. Remove the fuel tank cap to relieve the pressure in the fuel tank.
3. Remove the cap from the Schrader valve located on the fuel supply manifold.
4. Attach fuel pressure gauge T80L–9974–A or equivalent, to the Schrader valve and drain the fuel through the drain tube into a suitable container.
5. After the fuel system pressure is relieved, remove the fuel pressure gauge and install the cap on the Schrader valve.

## Fuel Pump

### TESTING

**➧ See Figure 19**

**⁂ CAUTION**

**Observe all applicable safety precautions when working around fuel. Whenever servicing the fuel system, always work in a well ventilated area. Do not allow fuel spray or vapors to come in contact with a spark or open flame. Keep a dry chemical fire extinguisher near the work area. Always keep fuel in a container specifically designed for fuel storage; also, always properly seal fuel containers to avoid the possibility of fire or explosion.**

1. Check all hoses and lines for kinks and leaking. Repair as necessary.
2. Check all electrical connections for looseness and corrosion. Repair as necessary.
3. Turn the ignition key from the **OFF** position to the **RUN** position several times (do not start the engine) and verify that the pump runs briefly each time, (you will here a low humming sound from the fuel tank).

**➡Check that the inertia switch is reset before diagnosing power supply problems to the fuel pump.**

The use of a scan tool is required to perform these tests.

4. Turn the ignition key **OFF**.
5. Connect a suitable fuel pressure gauge to the fuel test port (Schrader valve) on the fuel rail.
6. Connect the scan tool and turn the ignition key **ON** but do not start the engine.
7. Following the scan tool manufacturer's instructions, enter the output test mode and run the fuel pump to obtain the maximum fuel pressure.

**Fig. 19 The fuel pressure test port is located on the fuel rail, under the protective cap**

8. The fuel pressure should be between 30–45 psi (210–310 kPa).
9. If the fuel pressure is within specification the pump is working properly. If not, continue with the test.
10. Check the pump ground connection and service as necessary.
11. Turn the ignition key **ON**.
12. Using the scan tool, enter output test mode and turn on the fuel pump circuit.
13. Using a Digital Volt Ohmmeter (DVOM), check for voltage (approximately 10.5 volts) at the fuel pump electrical connector.
14. If the pump is getting a good voltage supply, the ground connection is good and the fuel pressure is not within specification, then replace the pump.

### REMOVAL & INSTALLATION

See fuel pump under fuel tank in this section.

## Throttle Body

### REMOVAL & INSTALLATION

**3.8L Engine**

***UPPER INTAKE MANIFOLD AND THROTTLE BODY***

**➧ See Figure 20**

1. Disconnect the negative battery cable.
2. Disengage the electrical connectors at the idle air bypass valve, throttle position sensor and the EGR position sensor.
3. Disconnect the throttle linkage at the throttle ball and transmission linkage from the throttle body. Remove the two retaining bolts securing the bracket to the intake manifold, then position the bracket with the cables out of the way.
4. Disengage the upper intake manifold vacuum fitting connections by disconnecting all of the vacuum lines to the vacuum tree, EGR valve and fuel pressure regulator.

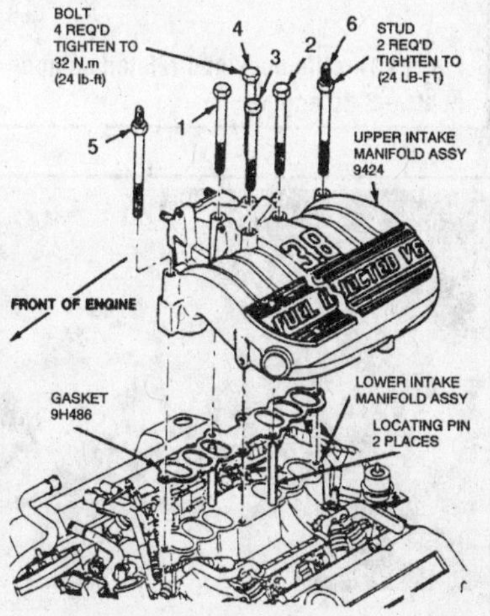


**Fig. 20 Upper intake manifold mounting—3.8L engine**

5. Disconnect the PCV system by removing the hose from the fitting on the rear of the upper manifold.

6. Remove the nut retaining the EGR transducer to the upper intake manifold. Loosen the EGR tube at the exhaust manifold, then disconnect at the EGR valve.

7. Remove the two bolts retaining the EGR valve to the upper intake manifold, then remove the EGR valve and the EGR transducer as an assembly.

8. Remove the two canister purge lines from the fittings on the throttle body.

9. Remove the six upper intake manifold retaining bolts.

10. Remove the two retaining bolts on the front and rear edges of the upper intake manifold where the manifold support brackets are located.

11. Remove the nut retaining the alternator bracket to the upper intake manifold, then remove the two bolts retaining the alternator bracket to the water pump and alternator.

12. Remove the upper intake and throttle body as an assembly from the lower intake manifold.

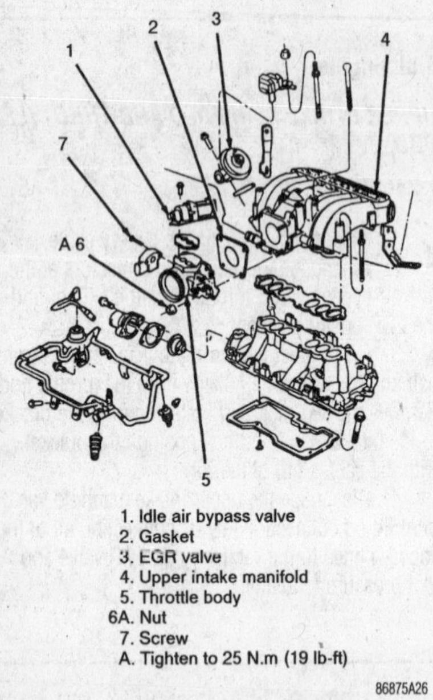

86875A26

**Fig. 21 Throttle body and related components—3.8L engine**

**To install:**

13. Clean and inspect the mating surfaces of the lower and upper intake manifold.

14. Position a new gasket on the lower intake manifold mounting surface. Using alignment studs will make the job easier.

15. Install the upper intake manifold and throttle body assembly to the lower intake manifold. If alignment studs are not used, make sure the gasket stays in place.

16. Install the four center retaining bolts and two studs to the upper manifold and tighten to 8 ft. lbs. (10 Nm). Repeat, in sequence, in two steps:

a. Step 1: 15 ft. lbs. (20 Nm).

b. Step 2: 24 ft. lbs. (32 Nm).

17. Install the two bolts retaining the manifold support brackets to the upper manifold, then tighten to 19 ft. lbs. (25 Nm).

18. Position the alternator bracket, then install the two retaining bolts to the water pump and alternator. Install the alternator bracket to the upper intake manifold retaining nut, then tighten to 19 ft. lbs. (26 Nm).

19. Connect the EGR valve to the EGR tube, making sure that the tube is properly seated in the EGR valve. Connect the EGR valve to the upper manifold, then tighten to 19 ft. lbs. (26 Nm).

20. Install the canister purge lines to the fittings on the throttle body.

21. Connect the PCV hose to the rear of the upper manifold.

22. Connect the vacuum lines to the vacuum tree, EGR valve, and fuel pressure regulator.

23. Position the throttle linkage bracket with cables to the upper intake manifold. Install the two retaining bolts, then tighten them to 13 ft. lbs. (17 Nm). Connect the throttle cable and the transaxle cable to the throttle body.

24. Engage the air bypass valve, TP sensor and EGR position sensor electrical connectors.

**➡If the lower intake manifold was removed, fill and bleed the cooling system.**

### *AIR INTAKE THROTTLE BODY*

**➧ See Figure 21**

1. Disconnect the negative battery cable.

2. Disengage the TP sensor and air bypass valve electrical connectors.

3. Remove the four throttle body retaining bolts. Remove the throttle body assembly, then remove and discard the gasket between the throttle body and the upper intake manifold.

4. If scraping is necessary, be careful not to damage the air bypass valve or throttle body gasket surfaces. Also, do not allow gasket material to drop into the throttle body.

**To install:**

5. Install the throttle body using a new gasket on the four studs of the upper intake manifold. Tighten the retaining nuts to 19 ft. lbs. (26 Nm).

6. Engage the throttle position sensor and the idle air bypass valve.

7. Connect the negative battery cable.

#### 4.6L Engine

**➧ See Figures 22 thru 29**

1. Disconnect the negative battery cable.

2. Remove the air cleaner outlet tube from the throttle body.

91195P01

**Fig. 22 Detach the TP sensor connector**

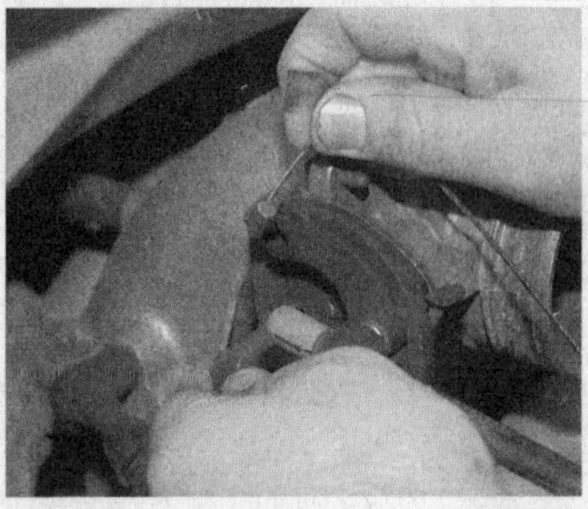
91195P02

**Fig. 23 Disconnect the accelerator cable from the throttle lever**

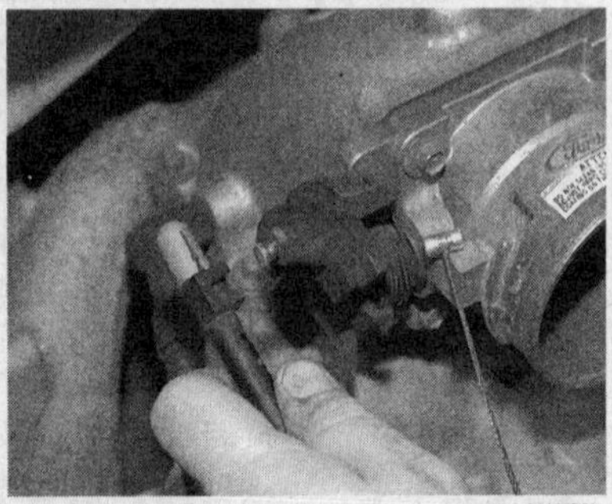
91195P03

**Fig. 24 If equipped with speed control, disconnect the speed control actuator from the throttle lever**

91195P04

**Fig. 25 Disconnect the accelerator return spring from the throttle body**

89605P14

**Fig. 26 Remove the four retaining bolts and . . .**

**Fig. 27 . . . remove the throttle body from the intake manifold**

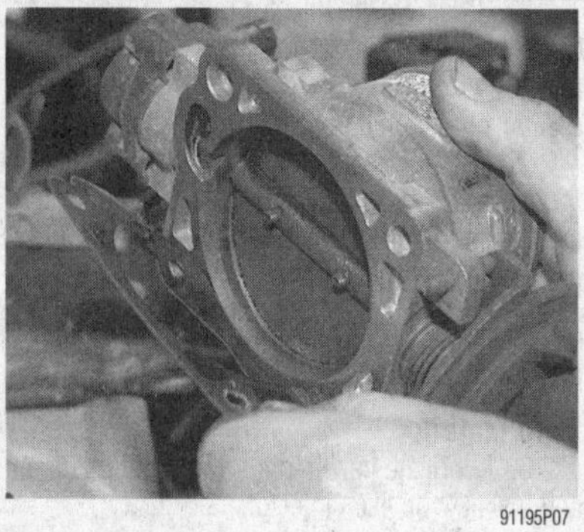


**Fig. 28 Remove and discard the gasket from the throttle body**

**Fig. 29 Thoroughly clean the throttle body mating surfaces**

3. Disconnect the throttle position sensor and throttle linkage at the throttle lever.
4. Remove the 4 throttle body mounting bolts.
5. Carefully separate the throttle body from the intake manifold adapter.
6. Remove and discard the gasket between the throttle body adapter.

**To install:**

7. Clean all gasket mating surfaces, being careful not to damage them or allow material to drop into the manifold.
8. Install the throttle body, a new gasket and the 4 mounting bolts. Tighten the bolts to 6–8.5 ft. lbs. (8–11.5 Nm).
9. Connect the throttle position sensor and the throttle linkage.
10. Install the air cleaner outlet tube.
11. Connect the negative battery cable.

### 5.0L Engine

**➧ See Figure 30**

1. Disconnect the negative battery cable.
2. Remove the air cleaner outlet tube from the throttle body.
3. Detach the throttle position sensor and idle air control valve connectors.
4. Remove the PCV vent closure hose at the throttle body.
5. Remove the 4 throttle body mounting nuts.

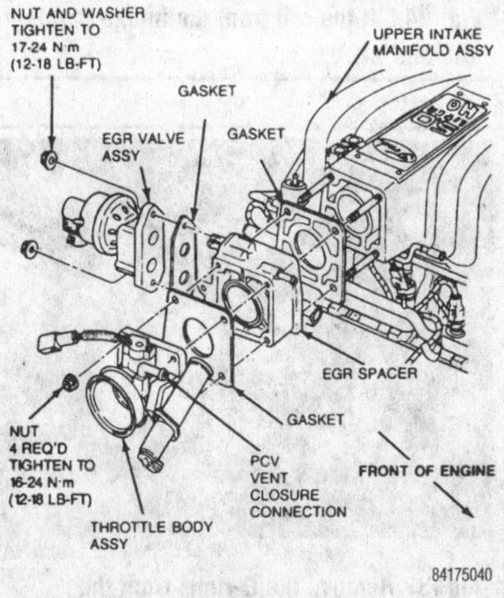


**Fig. 30 Throttle body installation—5.0L engine**

6. Carefully separate the throttle body from the EGR spacer and intake manifold.
7. Remove and discard the gasket between the throttle body and EGR spacer.

**To install:**

8. Clean all gasket mating surfaces, being careful not to damage them or allow material to drop into the manifold.
9. Install the throttle body with a new gasket on the 4 studs of the EGR spacer. Install the nuts and tighten to 12–18 ft. lbs. (16–24 Nm).
10. Connect the PCV vent closure hose.
11. Connect the throttle position sensor and idle air control valve connectors.
12. Install the air cleaner outlet tube.
13. Connect the negative battery cable.

## Fuel Rail and Fuel Injector(s)

### REMOVAL & INSTALLATION

### 3.8L Engine

**➧ See Figures 31**

1. Disconnect the negative battery cable.
2. Remove the fuel cap at the tank to release the fuel tank pressure.
3. Properly relieve the pressure from the fuel system. For details, please refer to the procedure located earlier in this section.
4. Remove the upper intake manifold and the fuel supply manifold as follows:
   a. Disengage the electrical connectors at the air bypass valve, TP sensor, and EGR position sensor.
   b. Disconnect the throttle linkage at the throttle ball and the transmission linkage from the throttle body. Remove the 2 bolts securing the bracket to the intake manifold and position the bracket with the cables aside.
   c. Disconnect the upper intake manifold vacuum fitting connections by disconnecting all vacuum lines to the vacuum tree, EGR valve and pressure regulator.
   d. Disconnect the PCV hose and remove the nut retaining the EGR transducer to the upper intake manifold.
   e. Loosen the EGR tube at the exhaust manifold, then disconnect at the EGR valve.
   f. Remove 2 bolts retaining the EGR valve to the upper intake manifold, then remove the EGR valve and EGR transducer as an assembly.
   g. Remove the 2 canister purge lines from the fittings on the throttle body, then remove the 6 upper intake manifold retaining bolts.
   h. Remove 2 retaining bolts on the front and rear edges of the upper intake manifold where the manifold support brackets are located.
   i. Remove the nut retaining the alternator bracket to the upper intake manifold and the 2 bolts retaining the alternator bracket to the water pump and alternator.
   j. Remove the upper intake manifold and throttle body as an assembly.
   k. Disconnect the fuel supply and return lines from the fuel rail assembly.
   l. Remove the fuel rail assembly retaining bolts, carefully disengage the fuel rail from the fuel injectors, and then remove the fuel rail.
5. Remove the injector retaining clips.
6. Remove the electrical connectors from the fuel injectors.
7. To remove the injector, pull it up while gently rocking it from side-to-side.
8. Inspect the injector O-rings, pintle protection cap (plastic hat) and washer for deterioration and replace, as required.

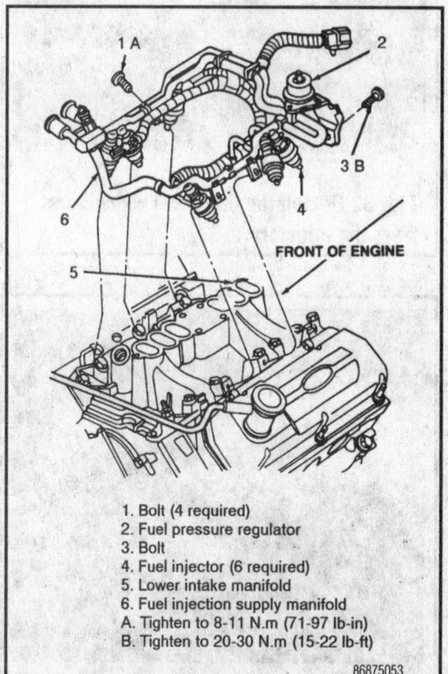


**Fig. 31 Fuel injection supply manifold and related components—3.8L SEFI engine**

**To install:**

9. Lubricate new engine O-rings with engine oil and install 2 on each injector.
10. Install the injectors, using a light, twisting, pushing motion to install them.
11. Reconnect the injector retaining clips.
12. Install the fuel rail assembly.
13. Install the electrical harness connectors to the injectors.
14. Install the upper intake manifold by reversing the removal procedure.
15. Install the fuel cap at the tank.
16. Connect the negative battery cable.
17. Turn the ignition switch from ON to OFF position several times without starting the engine to check for fuel leaks.

### 4.6L Engine

➧ See Figures 32 thru 37

1. Disconnect the negative battery cable.
2. Remove the fuel tank cap and relieve the fuel system pressure, as explained in this Section.
3. Disconnect the vacuum line at the pressure regulator.
4. Disconnect the fuel lines from the fuel rail.
5. Detach the electrical connectors from the injectors.
6. Remove the fuel rail assembly retaining bolts.
7. Carefully disengage the fuel rail from the fuel injectors and remove the fuel rail.

**➡It may be easier to remove the injectors with the fuel rail as an assembly.**

8. Grasping the injector body, pull while gently rocking the injector from side-to-side to remove the injector from the fuel rail or intake manifold.
9. Inspect the pintle protection cap and washer for signs of deterioration. Replace the complete injector, as required. If the cap is missing, look for it in the intake manifold.

**➡The pintle protection cap is not available as a separate part.**

**To install:**

10. Lubricate new O-rings with light grade oil and install 2 on each injector.

**➡Never use silicone grease as it will clog the injectors.**

11. Install the injectors using a light, twisting, pushing motion.
12. Install the fuel rail, pushing it down to ensure all injector O-rings are fully seated in the fuel rail cups and intake manifold.
13. Install the retaining bolts while holding the fuel rail down and tighten to 71–106 inch lbs. (8–12 Nm).
14. Connect the fuel lines to the fuel rail and the vacuum line to the pressure regulator.
15. With the injector wiring disconnected, connect the negative battery cable and turn the ignition switch to the **RUN** position to allow the fuel pump to pressurize the system.
16. Check for fuel leaks.
17. Disconnect the negative battery cable.
18. Connect the electrical connectors to the fuel injectors.
19. Connect the negative battery cable and start the engine. Let it idle for 2 minutes.
20. Turn the engine **OFF** and check for leaks.

### 5.0L Engine

➧ See Figure 38

1. Disconnect the negative battery cable.
2. Remove the fuel tank cap and relieve the fuel system pressure, as explained in this Section.
3. Partially drain the cooling system into a suitable container.

**⁂ CAUTION**

**When draining the coolant, keep in mind that cats and dogs are attracted by the ethylene glycol antifreeze, and are quite likely to drink any that is left in an uncovered container or in puddles on the ground. This will prove fatal in sufficient quantity. Always drain the coolant into a sealable container. Coolant should be reused unless it is contaminated or several years old.**

4. Label and detach the electrical connectors at the idle air control valve, throttle position sensor and EGR sensor.
5. Disconnect the throttle linkage at the throttle ball and transmission linkage from the throttle body. Remove the 2 bolts securing the bracket to the intake manifold and position the bracket with the cables aside.
6. Label and disconnect the upper intake manifold vacuum fitting connections by disconnecting

89605P04

**Fig. 32 Detach the electrical connectors from the injectors**

89605P05

**Fig. 33 Remove the fuel rail assembly retaining bolts. There are two on each side of the engine**

89605P06

**Fig. 34 Lift the rail from the intake manifold and . . .**

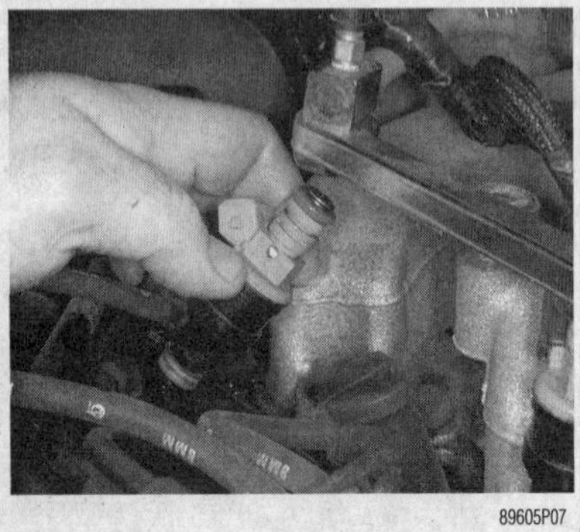

89605P07

**Fig. 35 . . . remove the injectors by gently puling them out of the rail**

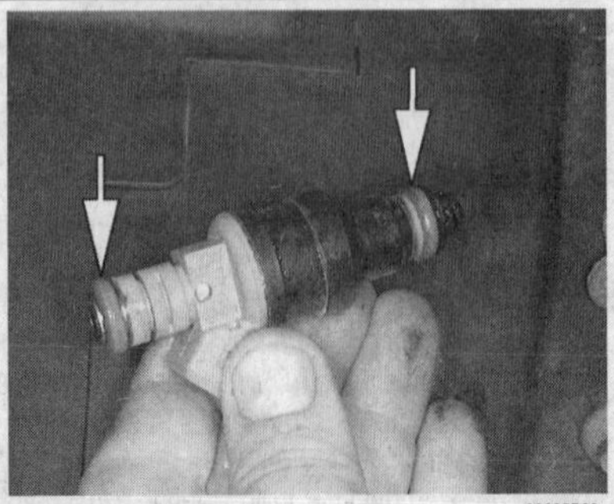

89605P09

**Fig. 36 Replace the injector O-rings before installing the injectors back into the engine**

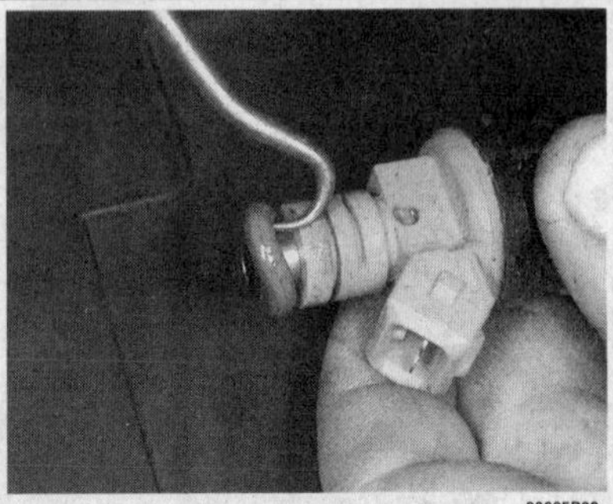

89605P08

**Fig. 37 Remove the O-rings from the injectors using a small pick or other suitable tool**

all vacuum lines to the vacuum tree, EGR valve, fuel pressure regulator and evaporative canister.

7. Disconnect the PCV hose from the fitting on the rear of the upper manifold and disconnect the PCV vent closure tube at the throttle body.

8. Remove the 2 EGR coolant lines from the fittings on the EGR spacer.

9. Remove the 6 upper intake manifold retaining bolts.

10. Remove the upper intake and throttle body as an assembly from the lower intake manifold.

11. Disconnect the fuel lines from the fuel rail.

12. Remove the 4 fuel rail assembly retaining bolts.

13. Detach the electrical connectors from the injectors.

14. Carefully disengage the fuel rail from the fuel injectors.

**➡It may be easier to remove the injectors with the fuel rail as an assembly.**

15. Grasping the injector body, pull up while gently rocking the injector from side-to-side to remove the injector from the fuel rail or intake manifold.

16. Inspect the pintle protection cap and washer for signs of deterioration. Replace the complete injector, as required. If the cap is missing, look for it in the intake manifold.

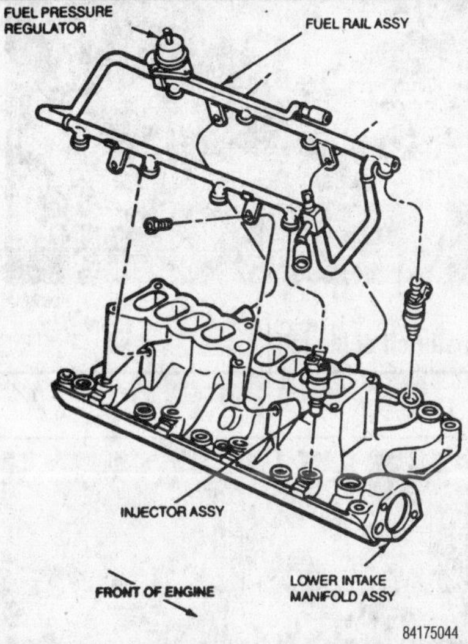


**Fig. 38 Fuel rail (fuel supply manifold)—5.0L engine**

**➡The pintle protection cap is not available as a separate part.**

**To install:**

17. Lubricate new O-rings with light grade oil and install 2 on each injector.

**➡Never use silicone grease as it will clog the injectors.**

18. Install the injectors using a light, twisting, pushing motion.

19. Install the fuel rail, pushing it down to ensure all the injector O-rings are fully seated in the fuel rail cups and intake manifold.

20. Install the retaining bolts while holding the fuel rail down and tighten to 71–106 inch lbs. (8–12 Nm).

21. Connect the fuel lines to the fuel rail.

22. With the injector wiring disconnected, connect the negative battery cable and turn the ignition switch to the **RUN** position to allow the fuel pump to pressurize the system.

23. Check for fuel leaks.

24. Disconnect the negative battery cable.

25. Connect the electrical connectors to the injectors.

26. Install the upper intake manifold and throttle body assembly by reversing the removal procedure. Use a new gasket and tighten the retaining bolts to 12–18 ft. lbs. (16–24 Nm).

27. Refill the cooling system and connect the negative battery cable.

28. Start the engine and let it idle for 2 minutes. Turn the engine **OFF** and check for leaks.

## TESTING

The easiest way to test the operation of the fuel injectors is to listen for a clicking sound coming from the injectors while the engine is running. This is accomplished using a mechanic's stethoscope, or a long screwdriver. Place the end of the stethoscope or the screwdriver (tip end, not handle) onto the body of the injector. Place the ear pieces of the stethoscope in your ears, or if using a screwdriver, place your ear on top of the handle. An audible clicking noise should be heard; this is the solenoid operating. If the injector makes this noise, the injector driver circuit and computer are operating as designed. Continue testing all the injectors this way.

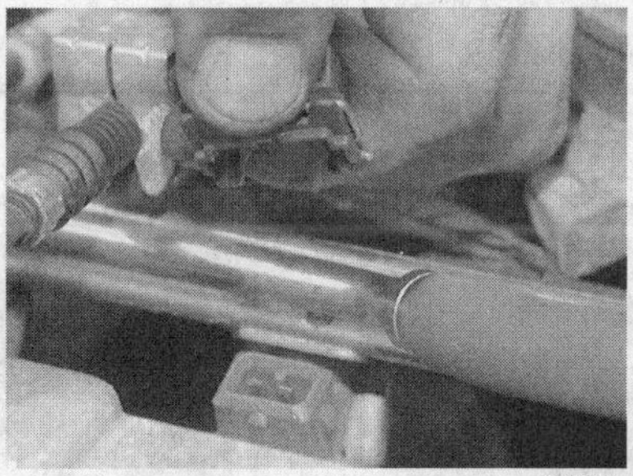


**Fig. 39 Unplug the fuel injector connector**

**⁂ CAUTION**

**Be extremely careful while working on an operating engine, make sure you have no dangling jewelry, loose clothing, power tool cords or other items that might get caught in a moving part of the engine.**

### All Injectors Clicking

If all the injectors are clicking, but you have determined that the fuel system is the cause of your driveability problem, continue diagnostics. Make sure that you have checked fuel pump pressure as outlined earlier in this section. An easy way to determine a weak or unproductive cylinder is a cylinder drop test. This is accomplished by removing one spark plug wire at a time, and seeing which cylinder causes the least difference in the idle. The one that causes the least change is the weak cylinder.

If the injectors were all clicking and the ignition system is functioning properly, remove the injector of the suspect cylinder and bench test it. This is accomplished by checking for a spray pattern from the injector itself. Install a fuel supply line to the injector (or rail if the injector is left attached to the rail) and momentarily apply 12 volts DC and a ground to the injector itself; a visible fuel spray should appear. If no spray is achieved, replace the injector and check the running condition of the engine.

### One or More Injectors Are Not Clicking

**➧ See Figures 39, 40, 41 and 42**

If one or more injectors are found to be not operating, testing the injector driver circuit and computer can be accomplished using a "noid" light. First, with the engine not running and the ignition key in the **OFF**position, remove the connector from

**Fig. 40 Probe the two terminals of a fuel injector to check it's resistance**

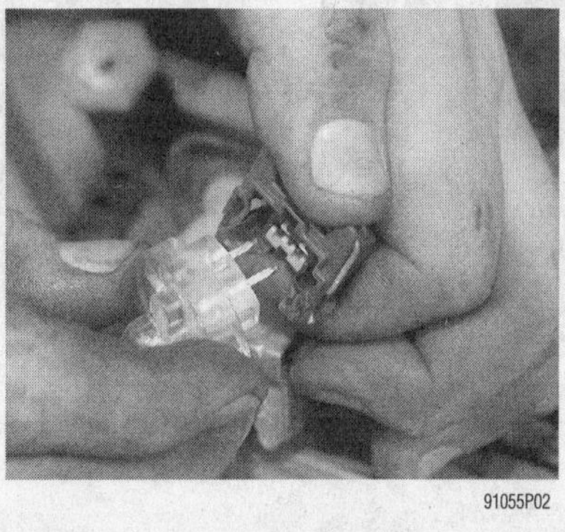


**Fig. 41 Plug the correct "noid" light directly into the injector harness connector**

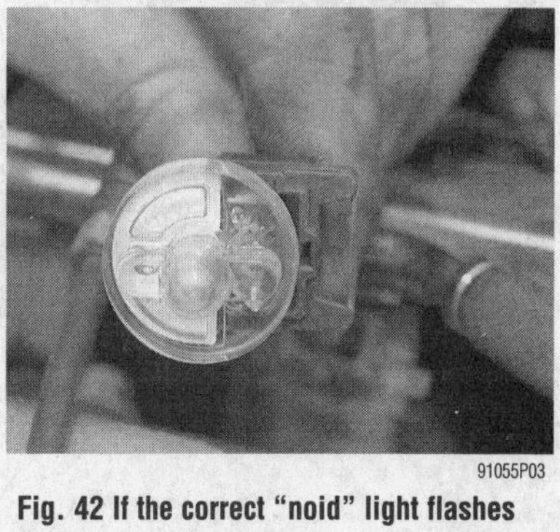


**Fig. 42 If the correct "noid" light flashes while the engine is running, the injector driver circuit inside the PCM is working**

the injector you plan to test, then plug the "noid" light tool into the injector connector. Start the engine and the "noid" light should flash, signaling that the injector driver circuit is working. If the "noid" light flashes, but the injector does not click when plugged in, test the injector's resistance. resistance should be between 11–18 ohms.

If the "noid" light does not flash, the injector driver circuit is faulty. Disconnect the negative battery cable. Unplug the "noid" light from the injector connector and also unplug the PCM. Check the harness between the appropriate pins on the harness side of the PCM connector and the injector connector. Resistance should be less than 5.0 ohms; if not, repair the circuit. If resistance is within specifications, the injector driver inside the PCM is faulty and replacement of the PCM will be necessary.

## Fuel Pressure Regulator

### REMOVAL & INSTALLATION

**See Figures 43, 44, 45 and 46**

1. Disconnect the negative battery cable.
2. Remove the fuel tank cap and relieve the fuel system pressure, as explained in this section.
3. Disconnect the vacuum line at the pressure regulator.
4. Remove and discard the 3 Allen head screws retaining the regulator housing.
5. Remove the pressure regulator, gasket and O-ring.
6. If scraping is necessary to remove old gasket material, be careful not to damage the pressure regulator or fuel supply manifold gasket surfaces.

**To install:**

7. Lubricate a new fuel pressure regulator O-ring with clean engine oil.

**Never use silicone grease as it will clog the injectors.**

8. Make sure the pressure regulator and fuel supply manifold gasket mating surfaces are clean.
9. Install the new O-ring and new gasket on the pressure regulator.
10. Install the fuel pressure regulator on the fuel supply manifold. Install new Allen screws and tighten to 27–40 inch lbs. (3–4.5 Nm).
11. Connect the vacuum line to the pressure regulator.

89605P10

**Fig. 43 Remove the vacuum hose from the pressure regulator**

89605P12

**Fig. 45 . . . lift the regulator off of the rail**

89605P11

**Fig. 44 Remove the pressure regulator retaining screws and . . .**

89605P13

**Fig. 46 Replace the O-ring on the bottom of the fuel pressure regulator**

12. Connect the negative battery cable and turn the ignition switch to the **RUN** position to allow the fuel pump to pressurize the system.
13. Check for fuel leaks.
14. Start the engine and let it idle for 2 minutes. Turn the engine **OFF** and check for leaks.

## Pressure Relief Valve

### REMOVAL & INSTALLATION

➧ **See Figure 47**

1. Disconnect the negative battery cable.
2. Properly relieve the fuel system pressure.
3. Remove the air cleaner outlet tube(s).

89605P03

**Fig. 47 The fuel pressure relief valve is located on the fuel rail, under the protective cap**

4. Remove any necessary components to access the pressure relief valve.
5. Remove the cap from the pressure relief valve.
6. Remove the pressure relief valve from the fuel rail using the proper size socket and drive tool.

**To install:**

7. The installation is the reverse of the removal.

# FUEL TANK

## Tank Assembly

### REMOVAL & INSTALLATION

1. Disable the air suspension, if equipped.
2. Disconnect the negative battery cable and relieve the fuel system pressure.
3. Siphon or pump as much fuel as possible out through the fuel filler pipe.

**➡Fuel injected vehicles have reservoirs inside the fuel tank to maintain fuel near the fuel pickup during cornering and under low fuel operating conditions. These reservoirs could block siphon tubes or hoses from reaching the bottom of the fuel tank. Repeated attempts using different hose orientations can overcome this obstacle.**

4. Raise and safely support the vehicle.
5. If equipped with a metal retainer that fastens the filler pipe to the fuel tank, remove the screw attaching the retainer to the fuel tank flange.
6. Detach the fuel lines and the electrical connector to the fuel tank sending unit. On some vehicles, these are inaccessible on top of the tank. In these cases they must be disconnected with the tank partially removed.
7. Place a safety support under the fuel tank and remove the bolts or nuts from the fuel tank straps. Allow the straps to swing out of the way.
8. Partially remove the tank and detach the fuel lines and electrical connector from the sending unit, if not detached previously.
9. Remove the tank from the vehicle.

**To install:**

10. Raise the fuel tank into position in the vehicle. Connect the fuel lines and sending unit electrical connector if it is necessary to connect them before the tank is in the final installed position.
11. Lubricate the fuel filler pipe with water base tire mounting lubricant and install the tank onto the filler pipe, then bring the tank into final position. Be careful not to deform the tank.
12. Bring the fuel tank straps around the tank and start the retaining nut or bolt. Align the tank with the straps. If equipped, make sure the fuel tank shields are installed with the straps and are positioned correctly on the tank.
13. Check the hoses and wiring mounted on the tank top to make sure they are correctly routed and will not be pinched between the tank and body.
14. Tighten the fuel tank strap retaining nuts or bolts to 20–30 ft. lbs. (28–40 Nm).
15. If not already connected, connect the fuel hoses and lines which were detached. Make sure the fuel supply, fuel return, if present, and vapor vent connections are made correctly. If not already connected, connect the sending unit electrical connector.
16. Lower the vehicle.
17. Replace the fuel that was drained from the tank.
18. Check all connections for leaks.

## Electric Fuel Pump

### REMOVAL & INSTALLATION

➧ **See Figures 48, 49 and 50**

**✲✲ CAUTION**

**Fuel injection systems remain under pressure, even after the engine has been turned OFF. The fuel system pressure must be relieved before disconnecting any fuel lines. Failure to do so may result in fire and/or personal injury.**

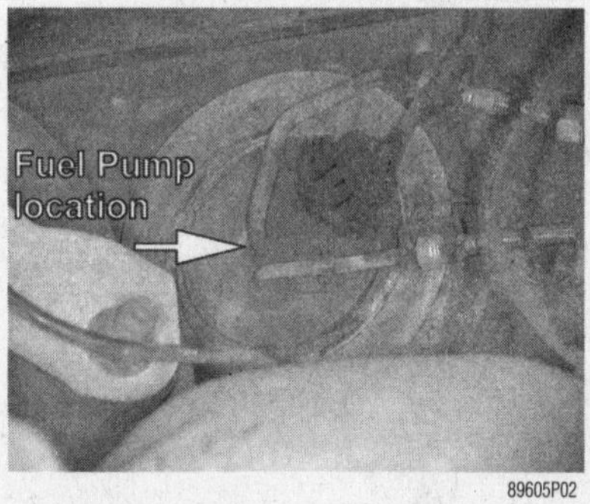


89605P02

**Fig. 48 The fuel pump is located in the fuel tank. On some models it can be viewed from the side as shown here**

1. If equipped with air suspension, the air suspension switch, located on a side panel of the trunk compartment, must be turned to the **OFF** position before raising the vehicle.
2. Disconnect the negative battery cable.
3. Relieve fuel system pressure using the recommended procedure.
4. Raise and safely support the vehicle.
5. Remove the fuel tank from the vehicle and place on a suitable work bench.
6. Remove any dirt that has accumulated around the fuel pump retaining flange so it will not enter the tank during pump removal and installation.
7. On 1988–94 models, turn the fuel pump locking ring counterclockwise and remove the locking ring.
8. On 1995–00 models, remove the retaining bolts around the perimeter of the fuel pump module.
9. Remove the fuel pump/sending unit assembly. Remove and discard the seal ring.

**To install:**

10. Clean the fuel pump mounting flange, fuel tank mounting surface and seal ring groove.
11. Apply a light coating of grease on a new seal ring to hold it in place during assembly and install it in the seal ring groove.
12. Install the fuel pump/sending unit assembly carefully to ensure the filter is not damaged. Make sure the locating keys are in the keyways and the seal ring remains in the groove.
13. Hold the pump assembly in place and install the locking ring finger-tight. Make sure all the locking tabs are under the tank lock ring tabs.

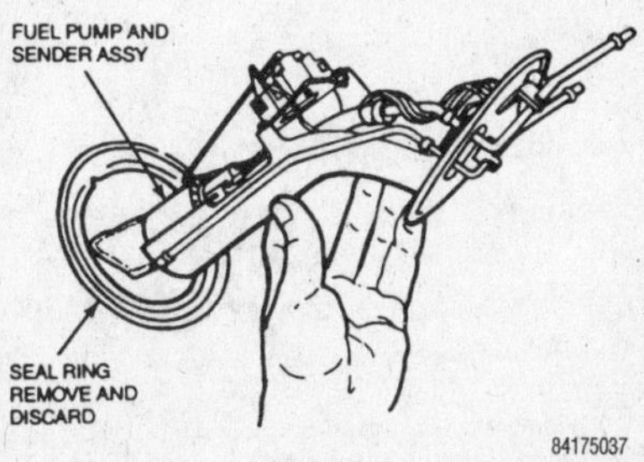


84175037

**Fig. 49 Electric fuel pump removal**

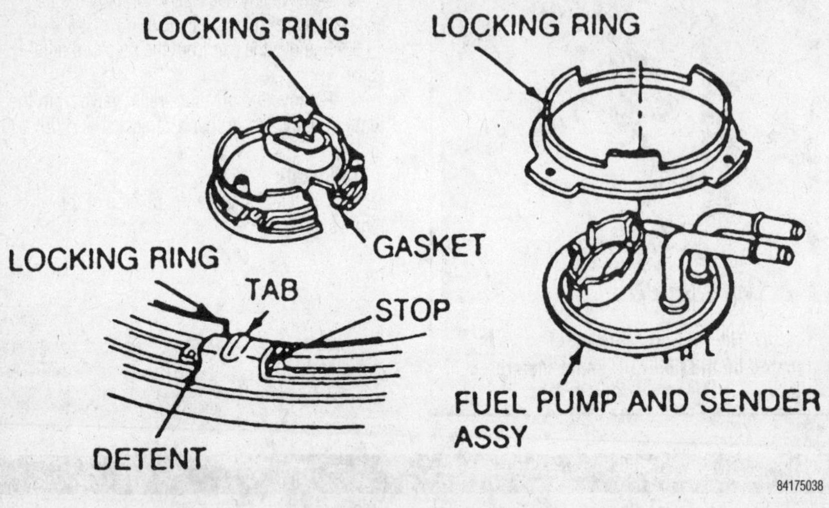


Fig. 50 Fuel pump locking ring installation

14. Rotate the locking ring clockwise until the ring is against the stops.
15. Install the fuel tank into the vehicle.
16. Lower the vehicle.
17. If equipped with air suspension, turn the air suspension switch to the **ON** position.
18. Add a minimum of 10 gallons of fuel to the tank and check for leaks.
19. Reconnect the negative battery cable.
20. Turn the ignition switch to the **RUN** position several times to pressurize the fuel system. Check for fuel leaks and correct as necessary.
21. Start the engine and check for leaks.
22. Road test the vehicle and check for proper operation.

**UNDERSTANDING AND TROUBLESHOOTING ELECTRICAL SYSTEMS 6-2**
BASIC ELECTRICAL THEORY 6-2
HOW DOES ELECTRICITY WORK: THE WATER ANALOGY 6-2
OHM'S LAW 6-2
ELECTRICAL COMPONENTS 6-2
POWER SOURCE 6-2
GROUND 6-3
PROTECTIVE DEVICES 6-3
SWITCHES & RELAYS 6-3
LOAD 6-3
WIRING & HARNESSES 6-4
CONNECTORS 6-4
TEST EQUIPMENT 6-4
JUMPER WIRES 6-4
TEST LIGHTS 6-5
MULTIMETERS 6-5
TROUBLESHOOTING ELECTRICAL SYSTEMS 6-5
TESTING 6-6
OPEN CIRCUITS 6-6
SHORT CIRCUITS 6-6
VOLTAGE 6-6
VOLTAGE DROP 6-6
RESISTANCE 6-6
WIRE AND CONNECTOR REPAIR 6-7
**BATTERY CABLES 6-7**
DISCONNECTING THE CABLES 6-7
**AIR BAG (SUPPLEMENTAL RESTRAINT SYSTEM) 6-7**
GENERAL INFORMATION 6-7
SERVICE PRECAUTIONS 6-7
DISARMING THE SYSTEM 6-8
ARMING THE SYSTEM 6-9
**HEATING AND AIR CONDITIONING 6-9**
BLOWER MOTOR 6-9
REMOVAL & INSTALLATION 6-9
HEATER CORE 6-11
REMOVAL & INSTALLATION 6-11
AIR CONDITIONING COMPONENTS 6-15
REMOVAL & INSTALLATION 6-15
**CRUISE CONTROL 6-15**
**ENTERTAINMENT SYSTEMS 6-16**
RADIO RECEIVER/AMPLIFIER/TAPE PLAYER/CD PLAYER 6-16
REMOVAL & INSTALLATION 6-16
SPEAKERS 6-17
REMOVAL & INSTALLATION 6-17
**WINDSHIELD WIPERS AND WASHERS 6-19**
WINDSHIELD WIPER BLADE AND ARM 6-19
REMOVAL & INSTALLATION 6-19
WINDSHIELD WIPER MOTOR 6-20
REMOVAL & INSTALLATION 6-20
**INSTRUMENTS AND SWITCHES 6-21**
INSTRUMENT CLUSTER 6-21
REMOVAL & INSTALLATION 6-21
GAUGES 6-23
REMOVAL & INSTALLATION 6-23
**LIGHTING 6-23**
HEADLIGHTS 6-23
REMOVAL & INSTALLATION 6-23
AIMING THE HEADLIGHTS 6-24
SIGNAL AND MARKER LIGHTS 6-25
REMOVAL & INSTALLATION 6-25
**CIRCUIT PROTECTION 6-29**
FUSES 6-29
REPLACEMENT 6-29
FUSIBLE LINKS 6-29
REPLACEMENT 6-30
CIRCUIT BREAKERS 6-31
FLASHERS 6-31
**WIRING DIAGRAMS 6-41**
**TROUBLESHOOTING CHARTS**
CRUISE CONTROL TROUBLESHOOTING 6-15

# 6

# CHASSIS ELECTRICAL

UNDERSTANDING AND TROUBLESHOOTING ELECTRICAL SYSTEMS 6-2
BATTERY CABLES 6-7
AIR BAG (SUPPLEMENTAL RESTRAINT SYSTEM) 6-7
HEATING AND AIR CONDITIONING 6-9
CRUISE CONTROL 6-15
ENTERTAINMENT SYSTEMS 6-16
WINDSHIELD WIPERS AND WASHERS 6-19
INSTRUMENTS AND SWITCHES 6-21
LIGHTING 6-23
WIRING DIAGRAMS 6-41

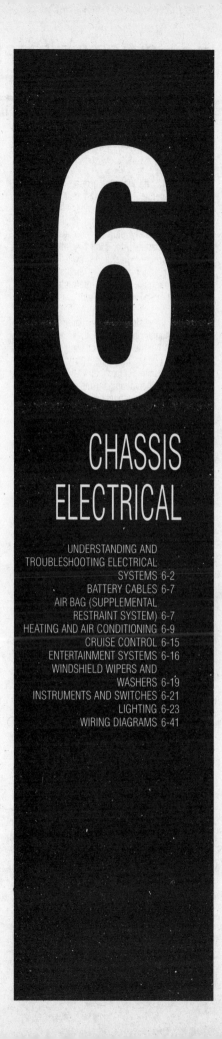

# UNDERSTANDING AND TROUBLESHOOTING ELECTRICAL SYSTEMS

## Basic Electrical Theory

**See Figure 1**

For any 12 volt, negative ground, electrical system to operate, the electricity must travel in a complete circuit. This simply means that current (power) from the positive (+) terminal of the battery must eventually return to the negative (-) terminal of the battery. Along the way, this current will travel through wires, fuses, switches and components. If, for any reason, the flow of current through the circuit is interrupted, the component fed by that circuit will cease to function properly.

Perhaps the easiest way to visualize a circuit is to think of connecting a light bulb (with two wires attached to it) to the battery—one wire attached to the negative (-) terminal of the battery and the other wire to the positive (+) terminal. With the two wires touching the battery terminals, the circuit would be complete and the light bulb would illuminate. Electricity would follow a path from the battery to the bulb and back to the battery. It's easy to see that with longer wires on our light bulb, it could be mounted anywhere. Further, one wire could be fitted with a switch so that the light could be turned on and off.

The normal automotive circuit differs from this simple example in two ways. First, instead of having a return wire from the bulb to the battery, the current travels through the frame of the vehicle. Since the negative (-) battery cable is attached to the frame (made of electrically conductive metal), the frame of the vehicle can serve as a ground wire to complete the circuit. Secondly, most automotive circuits contain multiple components which receive power from a single circuit. This lessens the amount of wire needed to power components on the vehicle.

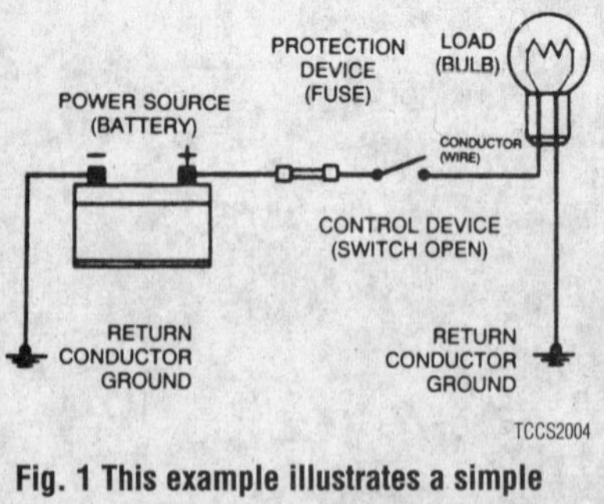


**Fig. 1 This example illustrates a simple circuit. When the switch is closed, power from the positive (+) battery terminal flows through the fuse and the switch, and then to the light bulb. The light illuminates and the circuit is completed through the ground wire back to the negative (-) battery terminal. In reality, the two ground points shown in the illustration are attached to the metal frame of the vehicle, which completes the circuit back to the battery**

### HOW DOES ELECTRICITY WORK: THE WATER ANALOGY

Electricity is the flow of electrons—the subatomic particles that constitute the outer shell of an atom. Electrons spin in an orbit around the center core of an atom. The center core is comprised of protons (positive charge) and neutrons (neutral charge). Electrons have a negative charge and balance out the positive charge of the protons. When an outside force causes the number of electrons to unbalance the charge of the protons, the electrons will split off the atom and look for another atom to balance out. If this imbalance is kept up, electrons will continue to move and an electrical flow will exist.

Many people have been taught electrical theory using an analogy with water. In a comparison with water flowing through a pipe, the electrons would be the water and the wire is the pipe.

The flow of electricity can be measured much like the flow of water through a pipe. The unit of measurement used is amperes, frequently abbreviated as amps (a). You can compare amperage to the volume of water flowing through a pipe. When connected to a circuit, an ammeter will measure the actual amount of current flowing through the circuit. When relatively few electrons flow through a circuit, the amperage is low. When many electrons flow, the amperage is high.

Water pressure is measured in units such as pounds per square inch (psi); The electrical pressure is measured in units called volts (v). When a voltmeter is connected to a circuit, it is measuring the electrical pressure.

The actual flow of electricity depends not only on voltage and amperage, but also on the resistance of the circuit. The higher the resistance, the higher the force necessary to push the current through the circuit. The standard unit for measuring resistance is an ohm. Resistance in a circuit varies depending on the amount and type of components used in the circuit. The main factors which determine resistance are:

- Material—some materials have more resistance than others. Those with high resistance are said to be insulators. Rubber materials (or rubber-like plastics) are some of the most common insulators used in vehicles as they have a very high resistance to electricity. Very low resistance materials are said to be conductors. Copper wire is among the best conductors. Silver is actually a superior conductor to copper and is used in some relay contacts, but its high cost prohibits its use as common wiring. Most automotive wiring is made of copper.
- Size—the larger the wire size being used, the less resistance the wire will have. This is why components which use large amounts of electricity usually have large wires supplying current to them.
- Length—for a given thickness of wire, the longer the wire, the greater the resistance. The shorter the wire, the less the resistance. When determining the proper wire for a circuit, both size and length must be considered to design a circuit that can handle the current needs of the component.
- Temperature—with many materials, the higher the temperature, the greater the resistance (positive temperature coefficient). Some materials exhibit the opposite trait of lower resistance with higher temperatures (negative temperature coefficient). These principles are used in many of the sensors on the engine.

### OHM'S LAW

There is a direct relationship between current, voltage and resistance. The relationship between current, voltage and resistance can be summed up by a statement known as Ohm's law.

Voltage (E) is equal to amperage (I) times resistance ®: E=I x R

Other forms of the formula are R=E/I and I=E/R

In each of these formulas, E is the voltage in volts, I is the current in amps and R is the resistance in ohms. The basic point to remember is that as the resistance of a circuit goes up, the amount of current that flows in the circuit will go down, if voltage remains the same.

The amount of work that the electricity can perform is expressed as power. The unit of power is the watt (w). The relationship between power, voltage and current is expressed as:

Power (w) is equal to amperage (I) times voltage (E): W=I x E

This is only true for direct current (DC) circuits; The alternating current formula is a tad different, but since the electrical circuits in most vehicles are DC type, we need not get into AC circuit theory.

## Electrical Components

### POWER SOURCE

Power is supplied to the vehicle by two devices: The battery and the alternator. The battery supplies electrical power during starting or during periods when the current demand of the vehicle's electrical system exceeds the output capacity of the alternator. The alternator supplies electrical current when the engine is running. Just not does the alternator supply the current needs of the vehicle, but it recharges the battery.

#### The Battery

In most modern vehicles, the battery is a lead/acid electrochemical device consisting of six 2 volt subsections (cells) connected in series, so that the unit is capable of producing approximately 12 volts of electrical pressure. Each subsection consists of a series of positive and negative plates held a short distance apart in a solution of sulfuric acid and water.

The two types of plates are of dissimilar metals. This sets up a chemical reaction, and it is this reaction which produces current flow from the battery when its positive and negative terminals are connected to an electrical load. The power removed from the battery is replaced by the alternator, restoring the battery to its original chemical state.

### The Alternator

On some vehicles there isn't an alternator, but a generator. The difference is that an alternator supplies alternating current which is then changed to direct current for use on the vehicle, while a generator produces direct current. Alternators tend to be more efficient and that is why they are used.

Alternators and generators are devices that consist of coils of wires wound together making big electromagnets. One group of coils spins within another set and the interaction of the magnetic fields causes a current to flow. This current is then drawn off the coils and fed into the vehicles electrical system.

## GROUND

Two types of grounds are used in automotive electric circuits. Direct ground components are grounded to the frame through their mounting points. All other components use some sort of ground wire which is attached to the frame or chassis of the vehicle. The electrical current runs through the chassis of the vehicle and returns to the battery through the ground (-) cable; if you look, you'll see that the battery ground cable connects between the battery and the frame or chassis of the vehicle.

**➡It should be noted that a good percentage of electrical problems can be traced to bad grounds.**

## PROTECTIVE DEVICES

**➧ See Figure 2**

It is possible for large surges of current to pass through the electrical system of your vehicle. If this surge of current were to reach the load in the circuit, the surge could burn it out or severely damage it. It can also overload the wiring, causing the harness to get hot and melt the insulation. To prevent this, fuses, circuit breakers and/or fusible links are connected into the supply wires of the electrical system. These items are nothing more than a built-in weak spot in the system. When an abnormal amount of current flows through the system, these protective devices work as follows to protect the circuit:

- Fuse—when an excessive electrical current passes through a fuse, the fuse "blows" (the conductor melts) and opens the circuit, preventing the passage of current.
- Circuit Breaker—a circuit breaker is basically a self-repairing fuse. It will open the circuit in the same fashion as a fuse, but when the surge subsides, the circuit breaker can be reset and does not need replacement.
- Fusible Link—a fusible link (fuse link or main link) is a short length of special, high temperature insulated wire that acts as a fuse. When an excessive electrical current passes through a fusible link, the thin gauge wire inside the link melts, creating an intentional open to protect the circuit. To repair the circuit, the link must be replaced. Some newer type fusible links are housed in plug-in modules, which are simply replaced like a fuse, while older type fusible links must be cut and spliced if they melt. Since this link is very early in the electrical path, it's the first place to look if nothing on the vehicle works, yet the battery seems to be charged and is properly connected.

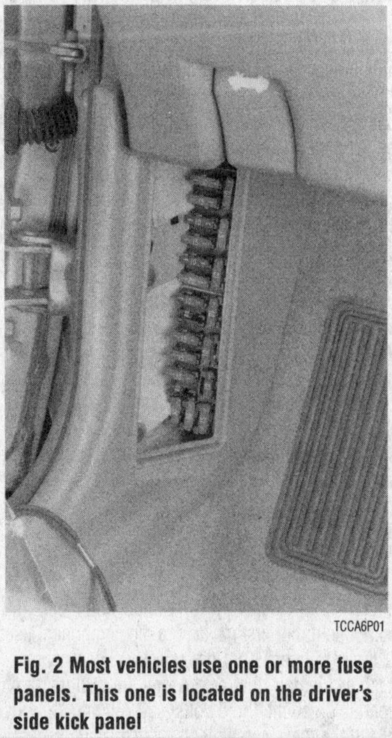

TCCA6P01

**Fig. 2 Most vehicles use one or more fuse panels. This one is located on the driver's side kick panel**

**⁂ CAUTION**

**Always replace fuses, circuit breakers and fusible links with identically rated components. Under no circumstances should a component of higher or lower amperage rating be substituted.**

## SWITCHES & RELAYS

**➧ See Figures 3 and 4**

Switches are used in electrical circuits to control the passage of current. The most common use is to open and close circuits between the battery and the various electric devices in the system. Switches are rated according to the amount of amperage they can handle. If a sufficient amperage rated switch is not used in a circuit, the switch could overload and cause damage.

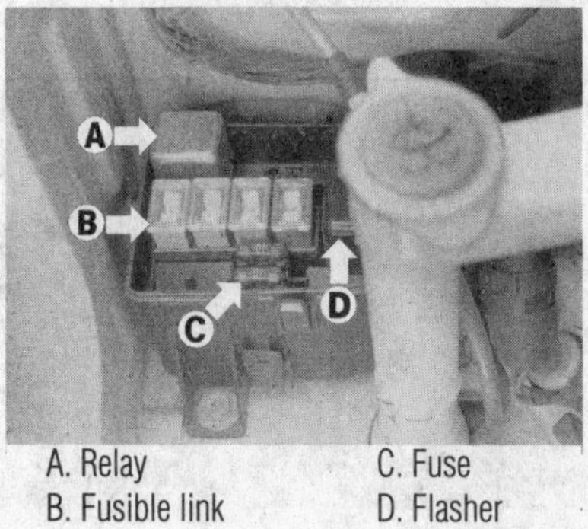


A. Relay C. Fuse
B. Fusible link D. Flasher

TCCA6P02

**Fig. 3 The underhood fuse and relay panel usually contains fuses, relays, flashers and fusible links**

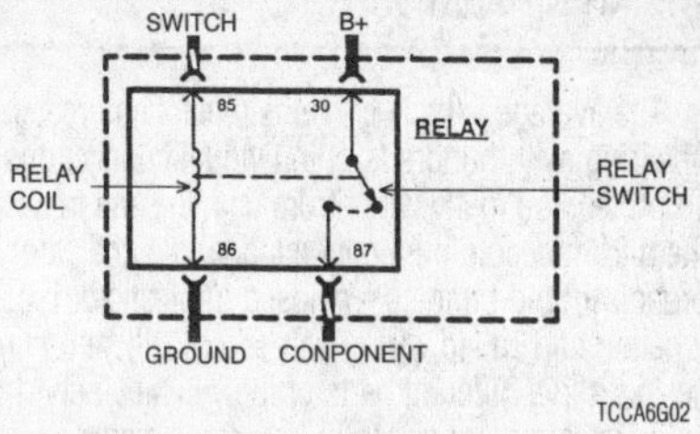


TCCA6G02

**Fig. 4 Relays are composed of a coil and a switch. These two components are linked together so that when one operates, the other operates at the same time. The large wires in the circuit are connected from the battery to one side of the relay switch (B+) and from the opposite side of the relay switch to the load (component). Smaller wires are connected from the relay coil to the control switch for the circuit and from the opposite side of the relay coil to ground**

Some electrical components which require a large amount of current to operate use a special switch called a relay. Since these circuits carry a large amount of current, the thickness of the wire in the circuit is also greater. If this large wire were connected from the load to the control switch, the switch would have to carry the high amperage load and the fairing or dash would be twice as large to accommodate the increased size of the wiring harness. To prevent these problems, a relay is used.

Relays are composed of a coil and a set of contacts. When the coil has a current passed though it, a magnetic field is formed and this field causes the contacts to move together, completing the circuit. Most relays are normally open, preventing current from passing through the circuit, but they can take any electrical form depending on the job they are intended to do. Relays can be considered "remote control switches." They allow a smaller current to operate devices that require higher amperages. When a small current operates the coil, a larger current is allowed to pass by the contacts. Some common circuits which may use relays are the horn, headlights, starter, electric fuel pump and other high draw ciruits.

## LOAD

Every electrical circuit must include a "load" (something to use the electricity coming from the source). Without this load, the battery would attempt to deliver its entire power supply from one pole to another. This is called a "short circuit." All this electricity would take a short cut to ground and cause a great amount of damage to other components in the circuit by developing a tremendous amount of heat. This condition could develop sufficient heat to melt the insulation on all the surrounding wires and reduce a multiple wire cable to a lump of plastic and copper.

## WIRING & HARNESSES

The average vehicle contains meters and meters of wiring, with hundreds of individual connections. To protect the many wires from damage and to keep them from becoming a confusing tangle, they are organized into bundles, enclosed in plastic or taped together and called wiring harnesses. Different harnesses serve different parts of the vehicle. Individual wires are color coded to help trace them through a harness where sections are hidden from view.

Automotive wiring or circuit conductors can be either single strand wire, multi-strand wire or printed circuitry. Single strand wire has a solid metal core and is usually used inside such components as alternators, motors, relays and other devices. Multi-strand wire has a core made of many small strands of wire twisted together into a single conductor. Most of the wiring in an automotive electrical system is made up of multi-strand wire, either as a single conductor or grouped together in a harness. All wiring is color coded on the insulator, either as a solid color or as a colored wire with an identification stripe. A printed circuit is a thin film of copper or other conductor that is printed on an insulator backing. Occasionally, a printed circuit is sandwiched between two sheets of plastic for more protection and flexibility. A complete printed circuit, consisting of conductors, insulating material and connectors for lamps or other components is called a printed circuit board. Printed circuitry is used in place of individual wires or harnesses in places where space is limited, such as behind instrument panels.

Since automotive electrical systems are very sensitive to changes in resistance, the selection of properly sized wires is critical when systems are repaired. A loose or corroded connection or a replacement wire that is too small for the circuit will add extra resistance and an additional voltage drop to the circuit.

The wire gauge number is an expression of the cross-section area of the conductor. Vehicles from countries that use the metric system will typically describe the wire size as its cross-sectional area in square millimeters. In this method, the larger the wire, the greater the number. Another common system for expressing wire size is the American Wire Gauge (AWG) system. As gauge number increases, area decreases and the wire becomes smaller. An 18 gauge wire is smaller than a 4 gauge wire. A wire with a higher gauge number will carry less current than a wire with a lower gauge number. Gauge wire size refers to the size of the strands of the conductor, not the size of the complete wire with insulator. It is possible, therefore, to have two wires of the same gauge with different diameters because one may have thicker insulation than the other.

It is essential to understand how a circuit works before trying to figure out why it doesn't. An electrical schematic shows the electrical current paths when a circuit is operating properly. Schematics break the entire electrical system down into individual circuits. In a schematic, usually no attempt is made to represent wiring and components as they physically appear on the vehicle; switches and other components are shown as simply as possible. Face views of harness connectors show the cavity or terminal locations in all multi-pin connectors to help locate test points.

## CONNECTORS

**See Figures 5 and 6**

Three types of connectors are commonly used in automotive applications—weatherproof, molded and hard shell.

- Weatherproof—these connectors are most commonly used where the connector is exposed to the elements. Terminals are protected against moisture and dirt by sealing rings which provide a weathertight seal. All repairs require the use of a special terminal and the tool required to service it. Unlike standard blade type terminals, these weatherproof terminals cannot be straightened once they are bent. Make certain that the connectors are properly seated and all of the sealing rings are in place when connecting leads.
- Molded—these connectors require complete replacement of the connector if found to be defective. This means splicing a new connector assembly into the harness. All splices should be soldered to insure proper contact. Use care when probing the connections or replacing terminals in them, as it is possible to create a short circuit between opposite terminals. If this happens to the wrong terminal pair, it is possible to damage certain components. Always use jumper wires between connectors for circuit checking and NEVER probe through weatherproof seals.
- Hard Shell—unlike molded connectors, the terminal contacts in hard-shell connectors can be replaced. Replacement usually involves the use of a special terminal removal tool that depresses the locking tangs (barbs) on the connector terminal and allows the connector to be removed from the rear of the shell. The connector shell should be replaced if it shows any evidence of burning, melting, cracks, or breaks. Replace individual terminals that are burnt, corroded, distorted or loose.

TCCA6P03

**Fig. 5 Hard shell (left) and weatherproof (right) connectors have replaceable terminals**

TCCA6P04

**Fig. 6 Weatherproof connectors are most commonly used in the engine compartment or where the connector is exposed to the elements**

## Test Equipment

Pinpointing the exact cause of trouble in an electrical circuit is most times accomplished by the use of special test equipment. The following describes different types of commonly used test equipment and briefly explains how to use them in diagnosis. In addition to the information covered below, the tool manufacturer's instructions booklet (provided with the tester) should be read and clearly understood before attempting any test procedures.

### JUMPER WIRES

**** CAUTION**

**Never use jumper wires made from a thinner gauge wire than the circuit being tested. If the jumper wire is of too small a gauge, it may overheat and possibly melt. Never use jumpers to bypass high resistance loads in a circuit. Bypassing resistances, in effect, creates a short circuit. This may, in turn, cause damage and fire. Jumper wires should only be used to bypass lengths of wire or to simulate switches.**

Jumper wires are simple, yet extremely valuable, pieces of test equipment. They are basically test wires which are used to bypass sections of a circuit. Although jumper wires can be purchased, they are usually fabricated from lengths of standard automotive wire and whatever type of connector (alligator clip, spade connector or pin connector) that is required for the particular application being tested. In cramped, hard-to-reach areas, it is advisable to have insulated boots over the jumper wire terminals in order to prevent accidental grounding. It is also advisable to include a standard automotive fuse in any jumper wire. This is commonly referred to as a "fused jumper". By inserting an in-line fuse holder between a set of test leads, a fused jumper wire can be used for bypassing open circuits. Use a 5 amp fuse to provide protection against voltage spikes.

Jumper wires are used primarily to locate open electrical circuits, on either the ground (-) side of the circuit or on the power (+) side. If an electrical component fails to operate, connect the jumper wire between the component and a good ground. If the component operates only with the jumper installed, the ground circuit is open. If the ground circuit is good, but the component does not operate, the circuit between the power feed and component may be open. By moving the jumper wire successively back from the component toward the power source, you can isolate the area of the circuit where the open is located. When the component stops functioning, or the power is cut off, the open is in the segment of wire between the jumper and the point previously tested.

You can sometimes connect the jumper wire directly from the battery to the "hot" terminal of the component, but first make sure the component uses 12 volts in operation. Some electrical components, such as fuel injectors or sensors, are designed to operate on about 4 to 5 volts, and running 12 volts directly to these components will cause damage.

## TEST LIGHTS

**See Figure 7**

The test light is used to check circuits and components while electrical current is flowing through them. It is used for voltage and ground tests. To use a 12 volt test light, connect the ground clip to a good ground and probe wherever necessary with the pick. The test light will illuminate when voltage is detected. This does not necessarily mean that 12 volts (or any particular amount of voltage) is present; it only means that some voltage is present. It is advisable before using the test light to touch its ground clip and probe across the battery posts or terminals to make sure the light is operating properly.

**WARNING**

**Do not use a test light to probe electronic ignition, spark plug or coil wires. Never use a pick-type test light to probe wiring on computer controlled systems unless specifically instructed to do so. Any wire insulation that is pierced by the test light probe should be taped and sealed with silicone after testing.**

Like the jumper wire, the 12 volt test light is used to isolate opens in circuits. But, whereas the jumper wire is used to bypass the open to operate the load, the 12 volt test light is used to locate the presence of voltage in a circuit. If the test light illuminates, there is power up to that point in the circuit; if the test light does not illuminate, there is an open circuit (no power). Move the test light in successive steps back toward the power source until the light in the handle illuminates. The open is between the probe and a point which was previously probed.

The self-powered test light is similar in design to the 12 volt test light, but contains a 1.5 volt penlight battery in the handle. It is most often used in place of a multimeter to check for open or short circuits when power is isolated from the circuit (continuity test).

The battery in a self-powered test light does not provide much current. A weak battery may not provide enough power to illuminate the test light even when a complete circuit is made (especially if there is high resistance in the circuit). Always make sure that the test battery is strong. To check the battery, briefly touch the ground clip to the probe; if the light glows brightly, the battery is strong enough for testing.

TCCS2006

**Fig. 7 A 12 volt test light is used to detect the presence of voltage in a circuit**

**➡A self-powered test light should not be used on any computer controlled system or component. The small amount of electricity transmitted by the test light is enough to damage many electronic automotive components.**

## MULTIMETERS

Multimeters are an extremely useful tool for troubleshooting electrical problems. They can be purchased in either analog or digital form and have a price range to suit any budget. A multimeter is a voltmeter, ammeter and ohmmeter (along with other features) combined into one instrument. It is often used when testing solid state circuits because of its high input impedance (usually 10 megaohms or more). A brief description of the multimeter main test functions follows:

- Voltmeter—the voltmeter is used to measure voltage at any point in a circuit, or to measure the voltage drop across any part of a circuit. Voltmeters usually have various scales and a selector switch to allow the reading of different voltage ranges. The voltmeter has a positive and a negative lead. To avoid damage to the meter, always connect the negative lead to the negative (-) side of the circuit (to ground or nearest the ground side of the circuit) and connect the positive lead to the positive (+) side of the circuit (to the power source or the nearest power source). Note that the negative voltmeter lead will always be black and that the positive voltmeter will always be some color other than black (usually red).
- Ohmmeter—the ohmmeter is designed to read resistance (measured in ohms) in a circuit or component. Most ohmmeters will have a selector switch which permits the measurement of different ranges of resistance (usually the selector switch allows the multiplication of the meter reading by 10, 100, 1,000 and 10,000). Some ohmmeters are "auto-ranging" which means the meter itself will determine which scale to use. Since the meters are powered by an internal battery, the ohmmeter can be used like a self-powered test light. When the ohmmeter is connected, current from the ohmmeter flows through the circuit or component being tested. Since the ohmmeter's internal resistance and voltage are known values, the amount of current flow through the meter depends on the resistance of the circuit or component being tested. The ohmmeter can also be used to perform a continuity test for suspected open circuits. In using the meter for making continuity checks, do not be concerned with the actual resistance readings. Zero resistance, or any ohm reading, indicates continuity in the circuit. Infinite resistance indicates an opening in the circuit. A high resistance reading where there should be none indicates a problem in the circuit. Checks for short circuits are made in the same manner as checks for open circuits, except that the circuit must be isolated from both power and normal ground. Infinite resistance indicates no continuity, while zero resistance indicates a dead short.

**WARNING**

**Never use an ohmmeter to check the resistance of a component or wire while there is voltage applied to the circuit.**

- Ammeter—an ammeter measures the amount of current flowing through a circuit in units called amperes or amps. At normal operating voltage, most circuits have a characteristic amount of amperes, called "current draw" which can be measured using an ammeter. By referring to a specified current draw rating, then measuring the amperes and comparing the two values, one can determine what is happening within the circuit to aid in diagnosis. An open circuit, for example, will not allow any current to flow, so the ammeter reading will be zero. A damaged component or circuit will have an increased current draw, so the reading will be high. The ammeter is always connected in series with the circuit being tested. All of the current that normally flows through the circuit must also flow through the ammeter; if there is any other path for the current to follow, the ammeter reading will not be accurate. The ammeter itself has very little resistance to current flow and, therefore, will not affect the circuit, but it will measure current draw only when the circuit is closed and electricity is flowing. Excessive current draw can blow fuses and drain the battery, while a reduced current draw can cause motors to run slowly, lights to dim and other components to not operate properly.

# Troubleshooting Electrical Systems

When diagnosing a specific problem, organized troubleshooting is a must. The complexity of a modern automotive vehicle demands that you approach any problem in a logical, organized manner. There are certain troubleshooting techniques, however, which are standard:

- Establish when the problem occurs. Does the problem appear only under certain conditions? Were there any noises, odors or other unusual symptoms? Isolate the problem area. To do this, make some simple tests and observations, then eliminate the systems that are working properly. Check for obvious problems, such as broken wires and loose or dirty connections. Always check the obvious before assuming something complicated is the cause.
- Test for problems systematically to determine the cause once the problem area is isolated. Are all the components functioning properly? Is there power going to electrical switches and motors. Performing careful, systematic checks will often turn up most causes on the first inspection, without wasting time checking components that have little or no relationship to the problem.
- Test all repairs after the work is done to make sure that the problem is fixed. Some causes can be traced to more than one component, so a careful verification of repair work is important in order to pick up additional malfunctions that may cause a problem to reappear or a different problem to arise. A blown fuse, for example, is a simple problem that may require more than another fuse to repair. If you don't look for a problem that caused a fuse to blow, a shorted wire (for example) may go undetected.

Experience has shown that most problems tend to be the result of a fairly simple and obvious cause, such as loose or corroded connectors, bad grounds or damaged wire insulation which causes a short. This makes careful visual inspection of components during testing essential to quick and accurate troubleshooting.

## Testing

### OPEN CIRCUITS

➧ **See Figure 8**

This test already assumes the existence of an open in the circuit and it is used to help locate the open portion.

1. Isolate the circuit from power and ground.
2. Connect the self-powered test light or ohmmeter ground clip to the ground side of the circuit and probe sections of the circuit sequentially.
3. If the light is out or there is infinite resistance, the open is between the probe and the circuit ground.
4. If the light is on or the meter shows continuity, the open is between the probe and the end of the circuit toward the power source.

### SHORT CIRCUITS

➡**Never use a self-powered test light to perform checks for opens or shorts when power is applied to the circuit under test. The test light can be damaged by outside power.**

1. Isolate the circuit from power and ground.
2. Connect the self-powered test light or ohmmeter ground clip to a good ground and probe any easy-to-reach point in the circuit.
3. If the light comes on or there is continuity, there is a short somewhere in the circuit.
4. To isolate the short, probe a test point at either end of the isolated circuit (the light should be on or the meter should indicate continuity).
5. Leave the test light probe engaged and sequentially open connectors or switches, remove parts, etc. until the light goes out or continuity is broken.
6. When the light goes out, the short is between the last two circuit components which were opened.

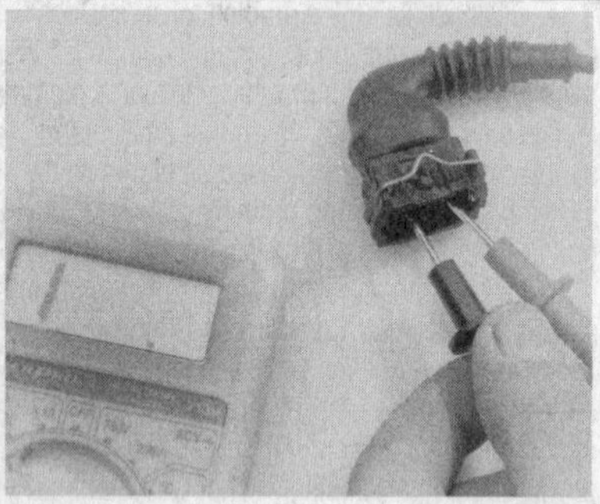

TCCA6P10

**Fig. 8 The infinite reading on this multimeter indicates that the circuit is open**

### VOLTAGE

This test determines voltage available from the battery and should be the first step in any electrical troubleshooting procedure after visual inspection. Many electrical problems, especially on computer controlled systems, can be caused by a low state of charge in the battery. Excessive corrosion at the battery cable terminals can cause poor contact that will prevent proper charging and full battery current flow.

1. Set the voltmeter selector switch to the 20V position.
2. Connect the multimeter negative lead to the battery's negative (-) post or terminal and the positive lead to the battery's positive (+) post or terminal.
3. Turn the ignition switch **ON** to provide a load.
4. A well charged battery should register over 12 volts. If the meter reads below 11.5 volts, the battery power may be insufficient to operate the electrical system properly.

### VOLTAGE DROP

➧ **See Figure 9**

When current flows through a load, the voltage beyond the load drops. This voltage drop is due to the resistance created by the load and also by small resistances created by corrosion at the connectors and damaged insulation on the wires. The maximum allowable voltage drop under load is critical, especially if there is more than one load in the circuit, since all voltage drops are cumulative.

1. Set the voltmeter selector switch to the 20 volt position.
2. Connect the multimeter negative lead to a good ground.
3. Operate the circuit and check the voltage prior to the first component (load).
4. There should be little or no voltage drop in the circuit prior to the first component. If a voltage drop exists, the wire or connectors in the circuit are suspect.
5. While operating the first component in the circuit, probe the ground side of the component with the positive meter lead and observe the voltage readings. A small voltage drop should be noticed. This voltage drop is caused by the resistance of the component.
6. Repeat the test for each component (load) down the circuit.
7. If a large voltage drop is noticed, the preceding component, wire or connector is suspect.

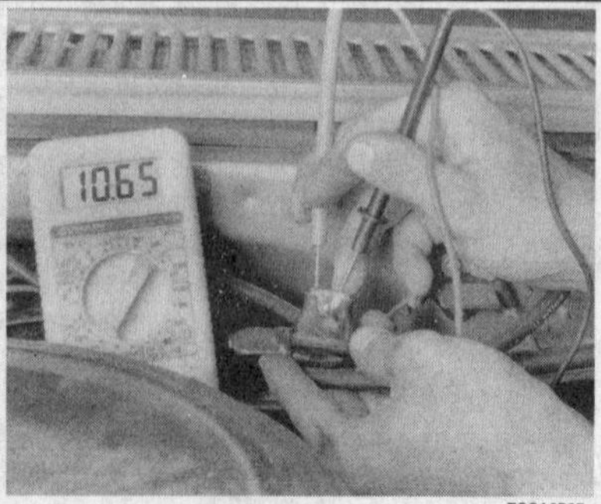


TCCA6P07

**Fig. 9 This voltage drop test revealed high resistance (low voltage) in the circuit**

### RESISTANCE

➧ **See Figures 10 and 11**

**⁂ WARNING**

**Never use an ohmmeter with power applied to the circuit. The ohmmeter is designed to operate on its own power supply. The normal 12 volt electrical system voltage could damage the meter!**

1. Isolate the circuit from the vehicle's power source.
2. Ensure that the ignition key is **OFF** when disconnecting any components or the battery.
3. Where necessary, also isolate at least one side of the circuit to be checked, in order to avoid reading parallel resistances. Parallel circuit resistances will always give a lower reading than the actual resistance of either of the branches.
4. Connect the meter leads to both sides of the circuit (wire or component) and read the actual measured ohms on the meter scale. Make sure the selector switch is set to the proper ohm scale for the circuit being tested, to avoid misreading the ohmmeter test value.

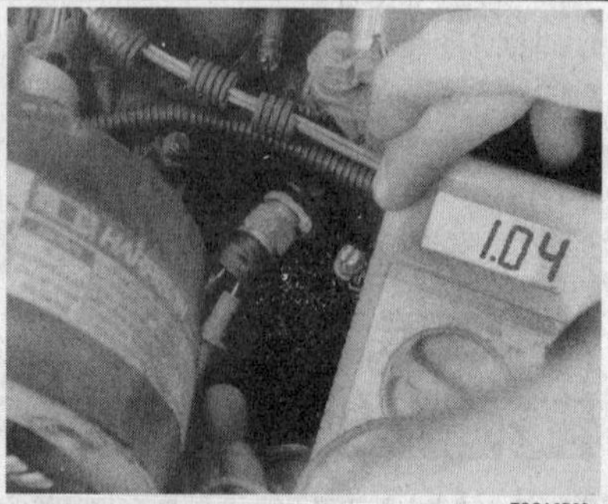


TCCA6P08

**Fig. 10 Checking the resistance of a coolant temperature sensor with an ohmmeter. Reading is 1.04 kilohms**

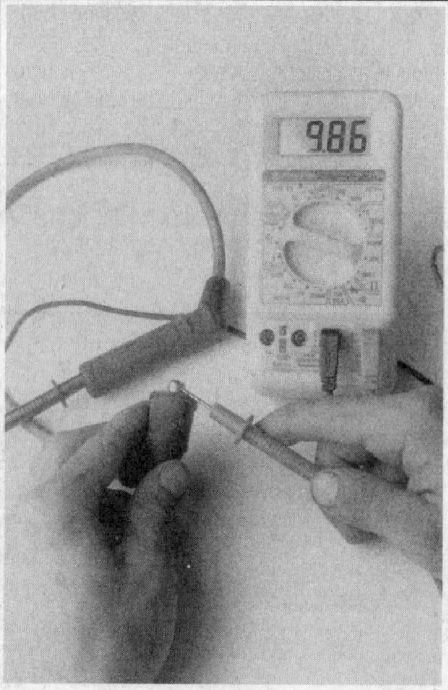


TCCA6P09

**Fig. 11 Spark plug wires can be checked for excessive resistance using an ohmmeter**

## Wire and Connector Repair

Almost anyone can replace damaged wires, as long as the proper tools and parts are available. Wire and terminals are available to fit almost any need. Even the specialized weatherproof, molded and hard shell connectors are now available from aftermarket suppliers.

Be sure the ends of all the wires are fitted with the proper terminal hardware and connectors. Wrapping a wire around a stud is never a permanent solution and will only cause trouble later. Replace wires one at a time to avoid confusion. Always route wires exactly the same as the factory.

**➡If connector repair is necessary, only attempt it if you have the proper tools. Weatherproof and hard shell connectors require special tools to release the pins inside the connector. Attempting to repair these connectors with conventional hand tools will damage them.**

# BATTERY CABLES

## Disconnecting the Cables

When working on any electrical component on the vehicle, it is always a good idea to disconnect the negative (-) battery cable. This will prevent potential damage to many sensitive electrical components such as the Powertrain Control Module (PCM), radio, alternator, etc.

**➡Any time you disengage the battery cables, it is recommended that you disconnect the negative (-) battery cable first. This will prevent your accidentally grounding the positive (+) terminal to the body of the vehicle when disconnecting it, thereby preventing damage to the above mentioned components.**

Before you disconnect the cable(s), first turn the ignition to the **OFF** position. This will prevent a draw on the battery that could cause arcing (electricity trying to ground itself to the body of a vehicle). It will also help prevent a spike (like a spark plug jumping the gap) when the cables are reconnected; and, of course, damaging some components such as the alternator diodes.

When the battery cable(s) are reconnected (negative cable last), be sure to check that your lights, windshield wipers and other electrically operated safety components are all working correctly. If your vehicle contains an Electronically Tuned Radio (ETR), don't forget to also reset your radio stations. Ditto for the clock.

# AIR BAG (SUPPLEMENTAL RESTRAINT SYSTEM)

The Supplemental Air Bag Restraint System is designed to provide increased collision protection for front seat occupants in addition to that provided by the three point safety belt system. In the event of an accident, the air bag(s) will be the most effective if the vehicle occupant(s) is held in position by the seat belts.

A driver's side air bag first became standard equipment on 1990 vehicles.

## General Information

➧ See Figures 12 and 13

The supplemental restraint system was designed to provide increased protection in case of an accident for those in the front seat of the car, when used along with the safety belt system. The system **MUST** be disarmed before any work is performed on or around the supplemental air bag system.

The system is an electronically controlled, mechanically operated system. The system contains two basic subsystems: the driver's side air bag module assembly and the passenger side air bag assembly, and the electrical system that connects them. The system consists of:

- The crash sensors
- The safing sensor
- The air bag module(s)
- The diagnostic monitor
- The back-up power supply
- The instrument cluster indicator
- The sliding contacts (clock spring assembly)

The system is operates as follows: The system remains out of sight until activated in an accident that is determined to be the equivalent of hitting a parked car of the same size and weight at 28 mph (40 km/h) with the vehicle receiving severe front end damage. This determination is made by crash and safing sensors mounted on the vehicle which when a sufficient impact occurs, close their contacts completing the electrical circuit and inflating the air bags. When not activated the system is monitored by the air bag diagnostic monitor and system readiness is indicated by the lamp located on the instrument cluster. Any fault detected by the diagnostic monitor will illuminate the lamp and store a Diagnostic Trouble Code (DTC).

### SERVICE PRECAUTIONS

Whenever working around, or on, the air bag supplemental restraint system, ALWAYS adhere to the following warnings and cautions.

**➡Please refer to the appropriate vehicle shop manual to determine location of the front air bag sensors.**

**➡The side air bag sensors are located at or near the base of the B-pillar.**

**➡To deplete the backup power supply energy, disconnect the battery ground cable and wait at least one minute. Be sure to disconnect auxiliary batteries and power supplies (if equipped).**

- Always wear safety glasses when servicing an air bag vehicle and when handling an air bag module.
- Carry a live air bag module with the bag and trim cover facing away from your body, so that an accidental deployment of the air bag will have a small chance of personal injury.
- Place an air bag module on a table or other flat surface with the bag and trim cover pointing up.
- Wear gloves, a dust mask and safety glasses whenever handling a deployed air bag module. The air bag surface may contain traces of sodium hydroxide, a by-product of the gas that inflates the air bag and which can cause skin irritation.
- After deployment, the air bag surface can contain deposits of sodium hydroxide, a product of the

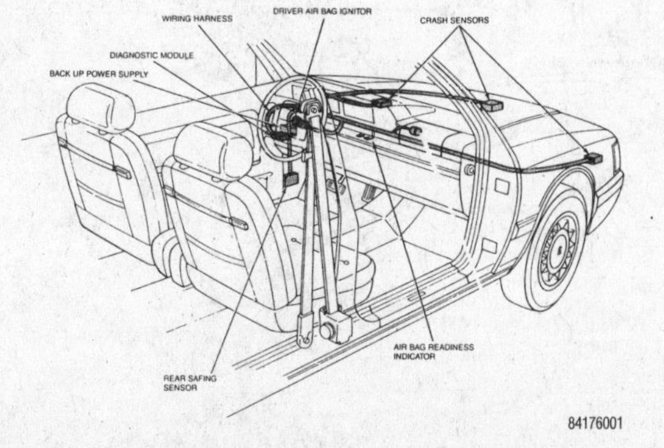


Fig. 12 Air bag system component locations—1990–91 vehicles

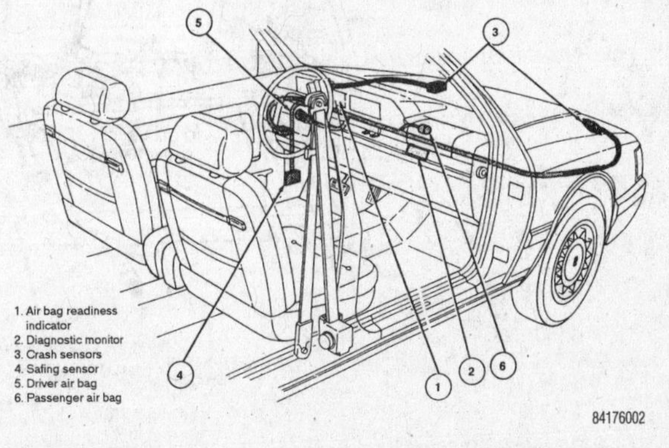


Fig. 13 Air bag system component locations—1992–00 vehicles

gas generant combustion that is irritating to the skin. Wash your hands with soap and water afterwards.

- All air bag modules with discolored or damaged cover trim must be replaced, not repainted.
- All component replacement and wiring service must be made with the negative and positive battery cables disconnected from the battery for a minimum of one minute prior to attempting service or replacement.
- NEVER probe the air bag electrical terminals. Doing so could result in air bag deployment, which can cause serious physical injury.
- If the vehicle is involved in a fender-bender that results in a damaged front bumper or grille, have the air bag sensors inspected by a qualified automotive technician to ensure that they were not damaged.
- If at any time, the air bag light indicates that the computer has noted a problem, have your vehicle's SRS serviced immediately by a qualified automotive technician. A faulty SRS can cause severe physical injury or death.

## DISARMING THE SYSTEM

**See Figures 14 and 15**

1. Disconnect the negative battery cable.
2. Disconnect the electrical connector from the backup power supply.

**➥The backup power supply allows air bag deployment if the battery or battery cables are damaged in an accident before the crash sensors close. The power supply is a capacitor that will leak down in approximately 15 minutes after the battery is disconnected or in 1 minute if the battery positive cable is grounded. It is located in the instrument panel and is combined with the diagnostic monitor. The backup power supply must be disconnected before any air bag related service is performed.**

3. Remove the four nut and washer assemblies retaining the driver air module to the steering wheel.
4. Disengage the driver air bag module and attach a jumper wire to the air bag terminals on the clockspring.

### 1992–00 Vehicles

**See Figures 16 thru 19**

**➥For this procedure, you will need the Rotunda Air Bag Simulator 105-00008 or equivalent, for early models, or 105-00010 or equivalent for later model vehicles. Since dif-**

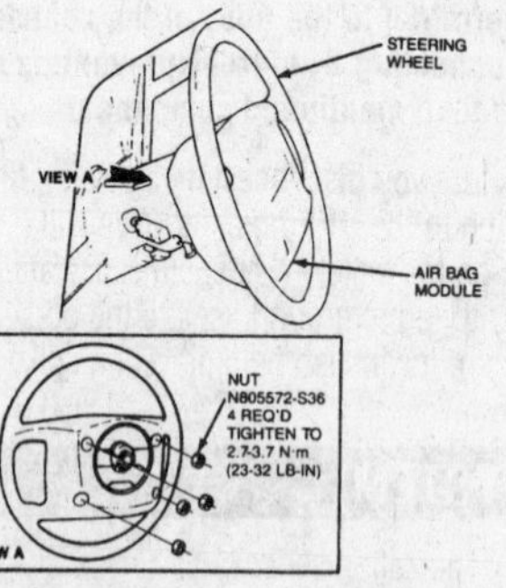


**Fig. 14 Air bag module mounting—1990–91 vehicles**

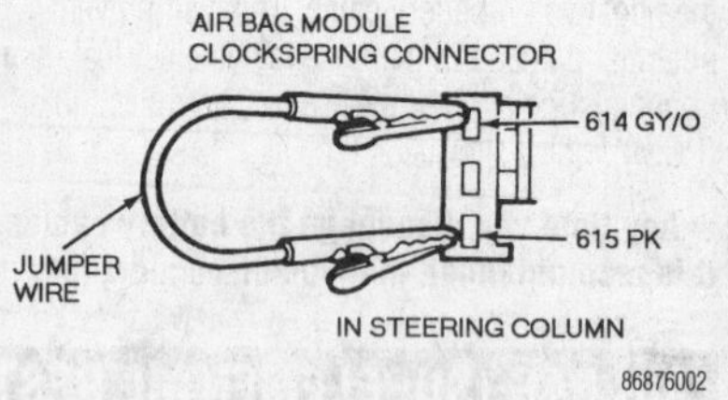


**Fig. 15 Connecting a jumper wire to the air bag terminals on the clockspring—1990–91 vehicles**

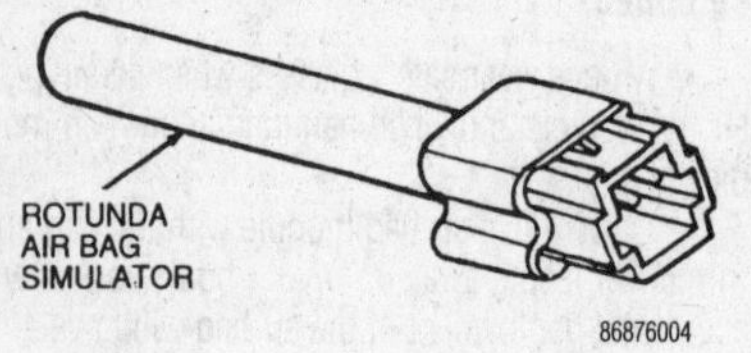

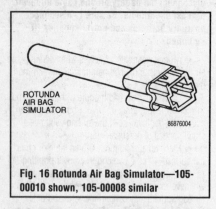

**Fig. 16 Rotunda Air Bag Simulator—105-00010 shown, 105-00008 similar**

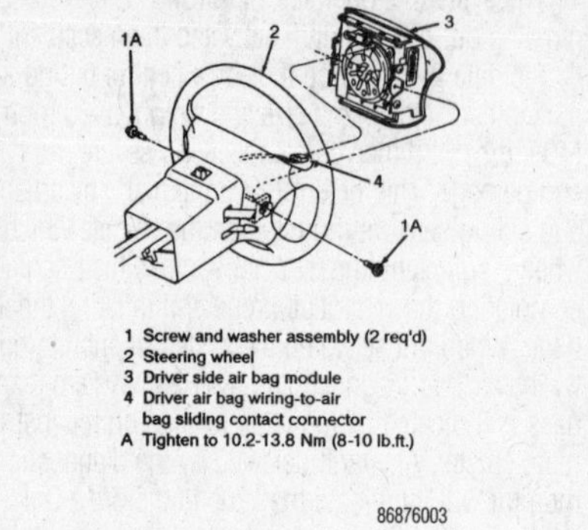


**Fig. 17 Driver air bag module mounting—1995 vehicle shown**

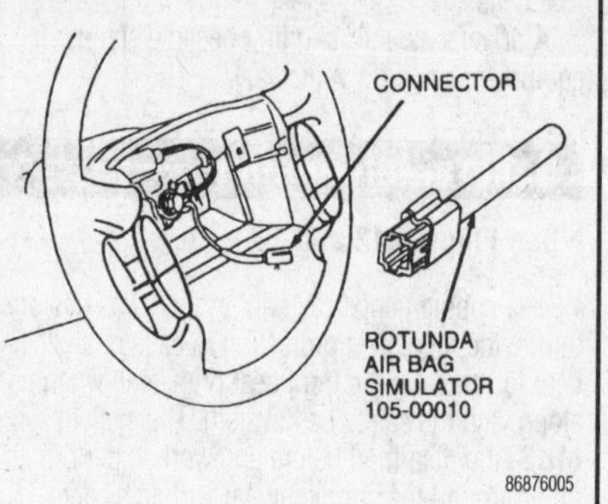


**Fig. 18 Connecting the air bag simulator tool**

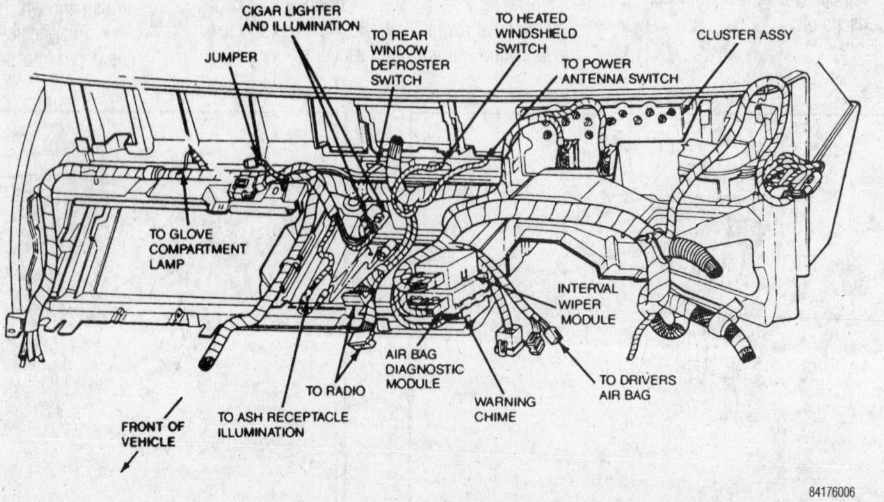


**Fig. 19 Rear view of instrumental panel showing diagnostic monitor location—1990–91 vehicles**

**ferent models use different simulators in the same year, always check and be sure the right tool is being used.**

1. Disconnect the negative, then the positive battery cables.
2. Wait one minute for the backup power supply in the diagnostic monitor to deplete its stored energy.
3. Remove the fasteners attaching the air bag module to the steering wheel.
4. Disengage the driver air bag electrical connector, then attach Air Bag Simulator Tool, or equivalent to the vehicle harness connector.

**➡If your vehicle is equipped with a passenger side air bag, both the driver and the passenger air bag modules must be disconnected.**

5. If equipped with a passenger air bag, proceed as follows:
   a. Remove the right-hand and passenger side finish panels.
   b. Remove the instrument panel finish panel retaining spear clips.
   c. Open the glove compartment, press the sides inward, and then lower the glove compartment to the floor.
   d. Working through the glove compartment opening, remove the two lower air bag module retaining bolts.
   e. Remove the four remaining air bag module retaining screws from the side of the air bag cover.
   f. Disengage the electrical connector from the left side of the air bag, then remove the air bag module.

**⁂ CAUTION**

**When carrying a live air bag, make sure the bag and trim cover are pointed away from the body. In the unlikely event of an accidental deployment, the bag will then deploy with the minimal chance of injury. In addition, when placing a live air bag on a bench or other surface, always face the bag and trim cover up, away from the surface. This will reduce the motion of the unit if it is accidentally deployed.**

   g. Attach the Air Bag Simulator Tool, or equivalent to the vehicle harness connector.
6. Connect the positive battery cable, then the negative battery cable.

### ARMING THE SYSTEM

#### 1990–91

1. Disconnect the negative battery cable and the backup power supply.
2. Remove the jumper wire from the air bag terminals on the clockspring assembly and reattach the air bag connector.
3. Position the driver air bag on the steering wheel with the 4 nut and washer assemblies. Tighten the nuts to 24–32 inch lbs. (2.7–3.7 Nm).
4. Connect the backup power supply and negative battery cable. Verify the air bag light

#### 1992–00

1. Disconnect the negative, then the positive battery cables. Wait 1 minute for the backup power supply in the diagnostic monitor to deplete its stored energy.
2. Remove the air bag simulator from the vehicle harness connector at the top of the steering column. Reconnect the driver air bag connector.
3. Position the driver air bag on the steering wheel with the 4 nut and washer assemblies. Tighten the nuts to 24–32 inch lbs. (3–4 Nm).
4. If equipped with a passenger air bag, remove the air bag simulator from the vehicle harness connector and reconnect the passenger air bag. Proceed as follows:
   a. Position the air bag module in the instrument panel.
   b. Install the 2 rear screws and tighten to 24–32 inch lbs. (3–4 Nm). Install the 2 front screws and tighten to 68–92 inch lbs. (8–10 Nm).
   c. Return the glove compartment to its proper position.
   d. Install the instrument cluster finish panel and tighten the screws to 17–27 inch lbs. (2–3 Nm).
   e. If removed, install the right-hand register applique and tighten the screws to 17–27 inch lbs. (2–3 Nm).
   f. Install the instrument panel lower moulding.
5. Connect the positive, then the negative battery cables and verify the air bag light.
6. Ensure the air bag indicator light turns off after approximately 6 seconds. If the light does not illuminate at all, does not turn off, or starts to flash, have the system tested by a qualified automotive technician. If the light does turn off after 6 seconds and does not flash, the SRS is working properly.

## HEATING AND AIR CONDITIONING

Vehicle air conditioning is the cooling r refrigeration of the air in the passenger compartment. Refrigeration I accomplished by making practical use of the laws of nature. HEAT GOES TO LESS HEAT. All this means is that heat transfers. If two substances of different temperature are placed near each other, the heat in the warmer substance will always travel to the colder substance until both are of equal temperature.

As a fail-safe, the air handling system is designed to provide defrost when no vacuum is applied to any of the vacuum control motors. This is done to prevent a situation where defrost cannot be obtained due to a system vacuum leak. Instead, a leak in the vacuum control circuit will send all airflow to the defroster outlets. This condition may occur during acceleration (slow vacuum leak), may exist at all times (large vacuum leak), and may happen only when certain specific functions are selected, indicating a leak in that portion of the circuit.

## Blower Motor

### REMOVAL & INSTALLATION

#### Continental 1988–94

➧ See Figures 20 thru 27

1. Disconnect the negative battery cable.
2. Open the glove compartment door, release the door retainers and lower the door.
3. Remove the screw attaching the recirculation duct support bracket to the instrument panel cowl.
4. Remove the vacuum connection to the recirculation door vacuum motor.Remove the aspirator hoses to the muffler. Remove the screws attaching the recirculation duct to the heater assembly.
5. Remove the recirculation duct from the heater assembly, lowering the duct from between the instrument panel and the heater case.
6. Disconnect the blower motor electrical lead. Remove the blower motor wheel clip and remove the blower motor wheel.
7. Remove the blower motor mounting plate screws and remove the blower motor from the evaporator case.

**To install:**

8. Feed the blower motor electrical connector through the evaporator housing.
9. Position the blower motor into the evaporator housing. Install the retaining screws, making sure the mounting seal is in place.
10. Assembly to blower motor to the shaft aligning the flat on the shaft with the flat on the inside diameter of the blower wheel hub. Slide the blower motor wheel onto the blower motor shaft until the wheel is fully seated.

86876007

**Fig. 20 Release the glove compartment door retainers, then lower the door**

86876008

**Fig. 21 Remove the screws attaching the recirculation duct to the heater assembly, then remove the duct**

86876009

Fig. 22 Remove the blower motor wheel clip

86876010

Fig. 23 Remove the blower motor wheel

86876011

Fig. 24 Disengage the electrical connector

86876012

Fig. 25 Remove the blower motor retaining screws

86876013

Fig. 26 Remove the blower motor assembly from the vehicle

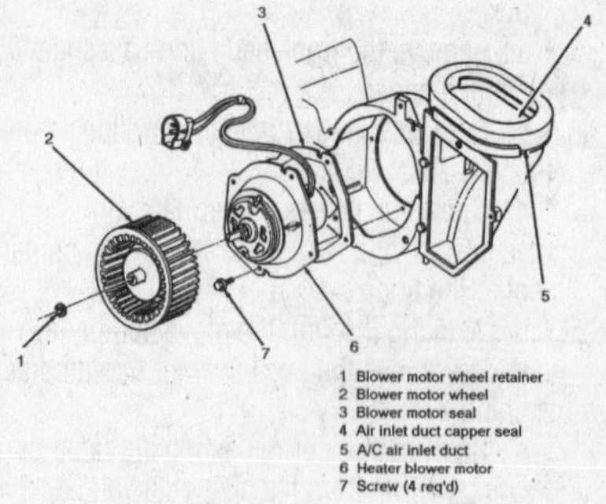

86876014

Fig. 27 Exploded view of a blower motor and wheel assembly—typical

11. Install a new blower motor retainer on the blower shaft to retain the blower motor wheel.

12. Connect the blower motor electrical lead to the wiring harness.

13. Install the recirculation duct using the retaining screws.

14. Install the glove compartment door to its original closed position, then connect the negative battery cable.

### Continental 1995–00

1. Disengage the two pushpins retaining the instrument panel insulator to the instrument panel. Disconnect the courtesy lamp from the instrument panel insulator.

2. Remove the passenger side scuff plate.

3. Remove the instrument panel upper finish panel (044A90) and disconnect the A/C sunload sensor wire harness connector.

4. Remove the screws retaining the passenger side and center instrument panel (04320) to the dash panel (01610).

5. Remove the passenger door trim panel, pull back the carpet and reposition the main wire harness connector and bracket to improve access to the blower motor.

6. Working from under the instrument panel, disconnect the electrical harness connector from the blower motor

7. Remove the passenger side instrument panel-to-cowl retaining nut.

8. Remove the three heater blower motor mounting plate screws. Remove the blower motor from the A/C evaporator housing.

9. Installation is the reverse of removal

### Town Car 1988–94

➧ See Figure 28

1. Disconnect the negative battery cable.

2. Disconnect the blower motor lead connector from the wiring harness connector.

3. Remove the blower motor cooling tube from the blower motor.

4. Remove the 4 retaining screws.

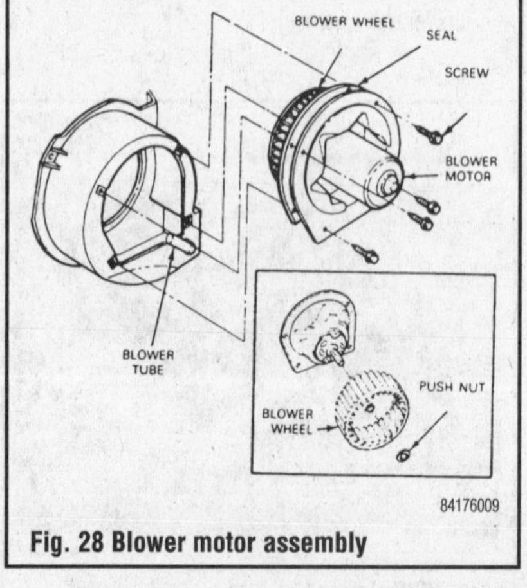

84176009

Fig. 28 Blower motor assembly

5. Turn the blower motor and wheel assembly slightly to the right so the bottom edge of the mounting plate follows the contour of the wheel well splash panel. While still in the blower housing, lift the motor and wheel assembly up and maneuver it out of the blower housing.

6. If necessary, remove the pushnut from the motor shaft and slide the wheel from the shaft.

7. Installation is the reverse of removal. If the wheel was removed from the motor shaft, make sure it is reinstalled so the outside of the wheel is 3.62–3.70 in. (92–94mm) from the blower motor mounting plate.

8. Connect the negative battery cable and check for proper blower motor operation.

### Town Car 1995–00

1. Disconnect the negative battery cable.

2. Remove the radiator coolant recovery tank.

3. Slide the connector from the top of the blower motor.

4. Detach the blower motor lead connector from the wiring harness connector.

5. Remove the blower motor cooling tube from the blower motor.

6. Remove the 4 retaining screws.

7. Turn the blower motor and wheel assembly slightly to the right so the bottom edge of the mounting plate follows the contour of the wheel well splash panel. While still in the blower housing, lift the motor and wheel assembly up and maneuver it out of the blower housing.

8. If necessary, remove the pushnut from the motor shaft and slide the wheel from the shaft.

9. Installation is the reverse of removal. If the wheel was removed from the motor shaft, make sure it is reinstalled so the outside of the wheel is 3.62–3.70 in. (92–94mm) from the blower motor mounting plate.

10. Connect the negative battery cable and check for proper blower motor operation.

**Mark VII**

1. Disconnect the negative battery cable.
2. Remove the glove box liner.
3. Use a small flat bladed tool to remove the clip retaining the hydraulic damper strut, if equipped.
4. Disconnect the wires at the blower motor.
5. Remove the four retaining screws and pull the blower motor from the heater case.
6. Remove the pushnut and slide the blower wheel from the shaft.

**To install:**

7. Using a new seal, position the blower motor and motor wheel assembly to the motor housing with the flat side of the flange near motor switch resistor.
8. Install the four retaining screws.
9. Tape the blower motor power lead to the air inlet duct to keep the wire away from the blower outlet during installation.
10. Install the blower motor and motor wheel assembly into the vehicle.
11. Attach the blower motor wiring.
12. Connect the negative battery cable.
13. Check the blower motor operation in all speeds.
14. Install the glove compartment liner.
15. Check the operation of the system.

**Mark VIII**

1. Lower the glove compartment door to gain access to the rear of the evaporator case.
2. Disconnect the blower motor electrical connector.
3. Remove the two screws and remove the A/C evaporator air control venturi and automatic temperature control sensor hose and elbow.
4. Remove the two screws and remove the A/C blower motor speed control.
5. Remove the attaching screws and pull the A/C blower motor out of the A/C evaporator housing.
6. Pull the blower motor wheel retainer off of the A/C blower motor shaft and remove the A.C blower wheel from the shaft.

**To install:**

7. Install the A/C blower wheel on the A/C blower motor shaft.
8. Install the A/C blower motor assembly in the AC evaporator housing and install the last screw removed.
9. Install the A.C blower motor speed control module.
10. Install the A.C evaporator air control venturi and connect the automatic temperature control sensor hose and elbow.
11. Connect the A/C blower motor electrical connector.

## Heater Core

**⁂ CAUTION**

**Never open, service or drain the radiator or cooling system when hot; serious burns can occur from the steam and hot coolant. Also, when draining engine coolant, keep in mind that cats and dogs are attracted to ethylene glycol antifreeze and could drink any that is left in an uncovered container or in puddles on the ground. This will prove fatal in sufficient quantities. Always drain coolant into a sealable container. Coolant should be reused unless it is contaminated or is several years old**

### REMOVAL & INSTALLATION

**Town Car**

1. Disconnect the negative battery cable.
2. Drain the cooling system and disconnect the heater hoses from the heater core tubes. Plug the hoses and the heater core tubes to prevent coolant leakage.
3. Remove the 3 nuts located below the windshield wiper motor attaching the left end of the plenum to the dash panel. Remove the 1 nut retaining the upper left corner of the evaporator case to the dash panel.
4. Disconnect the vacuum supply hose(s) from the vacuum source. Push the grommet and vacuum supply hose(s) into the passenger compartment.
5. Remove the right and left lower instrument panel insulators.
6. On 1988–93 vehicles:
   a. Remove the 3 glove compartment hinge screws, disconnect the check arms and remove the glove compartment. Loosen the right door sill plate and remove the right side cowl trim panel. Remove the bolt attaching the lower right end of the instrument panel to the side cowl. Remove the instrument panel pad as follows:
   b. Remove the 2 screws attaching the pad to the instrument panel at each defroster opening. Be careful not to drop the screws into the defroster openings.
   c. Remove the one (shouldered) screw attaching each outboard end of the pad to the instrument panel.
   d. Remove the line of screws attaching the lower edge of the pad to the instrument panel. Pull the instrument panel pad rearward and remove it from the vehicle.
7. On 1988–89 vehicles:
   a. Remove all instrument panel mounting screws and pull the instrument panel back as far as it will go without disconnecting any wiring harnesses.
   b. Make sure the nuts attaching the instrument panel braces to the dash panel are removed.
   c. Loosen the right door sill plate and remove the right side cowl trim panel.
   d. Disconnect the temperature control cable from the ATC sensor. Disconnect the vacuum harness line connector from the ATC sensor harness and disconnect the electrical connector from the ATC servo connector.
8. On 1990–00 vehicles:
   a. Remove the cross body brace and disconnect the wiring harness from the temperature blend door actuator.
   b. Disconnect the ATC sensor tube from the evaporator case connector.
9. Disconnect the vacuum jumper harness at the multiple vacuum connector near the floor air distribution duct. Disconnect the white vacuum hose from the outside-recirculating door vacuum motor.
10. Remove the 2 hush panels.
11. Remove 1 plastic push fastener retaining the floor air distribution duct to the left end of the plenum. Remove the left screw and loosen the right screw on the rear face of the plenum and remove the floor air distribution duct.
12. Remove the 2 nuts from the 2 studs along the lower flange of the plenum.
13. Carefully move the plenum rearward to allow the heater core tubes and the stud at the top of the plenum to clear the holes in the dash panel. Remove the plenum from the vehicle by rotating the top of the plenum forward, down and out from under the instrument panel. Carefully pull the lower edge of the instrument panel rearward, as necessary, while rolling the plenum from behind the instrument panel.
14. On 1988–1989 vehicles, remove the ATC servo from the plenum.
15. Remove the 4 retaining screws from the heater core cover and remove the cover from the plenum assembly. Pull the heater core and seal assembly from the plenum assembly.

**To install:**

16. Carefully install the heater core and seal assembly into the plenum assembly. Visually check to ensure that the core seal is properly positioned. Position the heater core cover and install the 4 retaining screws.
17. On 1988–1989 vehicles, install the ATC servo on the plenum.
18. Route the vacuum supply hose through the dash panel and seat the grommet in the opening.
19. Position the plenum under the instrument panel with the register duct opening up and the heater core tubes down. Rotate the plenum up behind the instrument panel and position the plenum to the dash panel. Insert the heater core tubes and mounting studs through their respective holes in the dash panel and the evaporator case.
20. Install the 3 nuts on the studs along the lower flange and one on the upper flange of the plenum. Install the 3 nuts below the windshield wiper motor to attach the left end of the plenum to the dash panel and the one nut to retain the upper left corner of the evaporator case to the dash panel.
21. Position the floor air distribution duct on the plenum. Install the 2 screws and plastic push fastener. If removed, position the panel door vacuum motor to the mounting bracket and install the 2 attaching screws.
22. Connect the white vacuum hose to the outside-recirculating door vacuum motor. Connect the vacuum jumper harness to the plenum harness at the multiple vacuum connector near the floor air distribution duct. Install the floor duct.
23. If equipped with manual air conditioning,

connect the temperature control cable housing to the bracket on top of the plenum and connect the temperature control cable to the temperature blend door crank arm. Adjust the temperature cable.

24. If equipped with ATC, proceed as follows:
25. Connect the temperature control cable to the ATC sensor and adjust the cable. Route and connect the vacuum harness connector to the ATC sensor and connect the electrical connector to the ATC servo connector. Do not block the sensor aspirator exhaust port with the excess vacuum harness. Install the ATC sensor tube between the sensor and the evaporator connector.
26. On 1990–00vehicles:
    a. Connect the ATC sensor tube to the evaporator case connector.
    b. Install the cross body brace and connect the wiring harness to the blend door actuator.
    c. Install the bolt to attach the lower right end of the instrument panel to the side cowl. Install the right side cowl trim panel and tighten the right door sill plate attaching screws.
27. On 1988–1989 vehicles install the instrument panel pad and the glove compartment door.
28. On 1990–99 vehicles, push the instrument panel back into position and install all instrument panel mounting screws. Install the right and left lower instrument panel insulators.
29. Connect the vacuum supply hose(s) to the vacuum source.
30. Install the right and left lower instrument panel insulators and install the 2 hush panels.
31. Unplug the heater core tubes and the heater hoses and connect the heater hoses to the heater core tubes. Fill the cooling system.
32. Connect the negative battery cable and check the system for proper operation.

#### Continental 1988–94

**➡It is necessary to remove the evaporator case in order to remove the heater core. Due to this fact the A/C system refrigerant must be recovered. If necessary, take the vehicle to an MVAC certified tech to recover the A/C system refrigerant before beginning work.**

**Whenever an evaporator case is removed, it will be necessary to replace the suction accumulator/drier.**

1. Disconnect the negative battery cable.
2. Remove the instrument panel on 1988–94 vehicles as follows:
    a. Remove the four screws retaining the steering column opening cover and remove the cover.
    b. Remove the sound insulator under the glove compartment by removing the two push nuts securing the insulator to the studs on the climate control case.
    c. Remove the steering column trim shrouds and disconnect all electrical connections from the steering column switches.
    d. Remove the four screws at the steering column bracket to remove the steering column.
    e. Remove the screws retaining the lower left and radio finish panels and remove the panels by snapping out.
    f. Remove the cluster opening finish panel retaining screws.
    g. Disconnect the speedometer cable by reaching up under the instrument panel and pressing on the flat surface of the plastic connector, where applicable. The panel can be removed with the cluster installed.
    h. Release the glove compartment assembly by depressing the side of the glove compartment bin and swinging the door/bin down.
    i. Using the steering column, cluster and glove compartment openings and by reaching under the instrument panel, tag and disconnect all electrical connections, vacuum hoses, heater/air conditioner control cables and the radio antenna cable.
    j. Disconnect all under hood electrical connectors of the main wire loom. Disengage the rubber grommet from the dash panel and push the wire and connectors into the instrument panel area.
    k. Remove the right and left speaker opening covers by snapping out.
    l. Remove the two lower instrument panel-to-cowl side retaining screws from the right and left side. Remove the instrument panel brace retaining screw from under the radio area..
    m. Remove the three instrument panel upper retaining screws and remove the instrument panel.
3. Remove the instrument panel on 1988–94vehicles as follows:
    a. Position the front wheels in the straight-ahead position.
    b. Remove the ignition lock cylinder and, remove the tilt lever stalk.
    c. Remove the steering column trim shrouds. Disconnect all electrical connections from the steering column switches.
    d. Remove the four bolts and opening cover and the two bolts and reinforcement from under the steering column.
    e. Disengage the insulator retainer and remove the insulator. Remove the four nuts and reinforcement from under the steering column.

**➡Do not rotate the steering column shaft.**

    f. Remove the four nuts retaining the steering column to the instrument panel, disconnect the shift indicator cable and lower the column on the front seat. Install the lock cylinder to make sure the steering column shaft does not turn.
    g. Remove the bolt at the steering column opening attaching the instrument panel to the brace. Remove instrument panel brace retaining bolt from under the radio area.
    h. Remove the sound insulator under the glove compartment by removing the two push nuts that secure the insulator to the studs on the climate control case.
    i. Disconnect the wires of the main wire loom in the engine compartment. Disengage the rubber grommet from the dash panel, then feed the wiring through the hole in the dash panel into the passenger compartment.
    j. Remove the right and left cowl sides trim panels. Disconnect the wires from the instrument panel at the right and left cowl sides.
    k. Remove one screw from each the left and right side retaining the instrument panel. Pull up to unsnap the right and left speaker opening covers and remove.
    l. Release the glove compartment assembly by depressing the side of the glove compartment bin and swinging the door/bin down.
    m. Using the steering column and glove compartment openings and by reaching under the instrument panel, tag and disconnect all electrical connections, vacuum hoses, heater/air conditioner control cables, speedometer cable and radio antenna cable.
    n. Close the glove compartment door, support the panel and remove the three screws attaching the top of the instrument panel to the cowl top and disconnect any remaining wires. Remove the panel from the vehicle.
4. Drain the coolant from the radiator.
5. Have a MVAC certified tech recover the A/C system refrigerant.
6. Disconnect and plug the heater hoses at the heater core. Plug the heater core tubes.
7. Disconnect the vacuum supply hose from the inline vacuum check valve in the engine compartment.
8. Disconnect the air conditioning lines from the evaporator core at the dash panel. Cap the lines and the core to prevent entrance of dirt and moisture.
9. Remove the screw holding the instrument panel shake brace to the evaporator case and remove the shake brace.
10. Remove the two screws attaching the floor register and rear seat duct to the bottom of the evaporator case. Remove the three nuts attaching the evaporator case to the dash panel in the engine compartment.
11. Remove the two screws attaching the support brackets to the cowl top panel. Carefully pull the evaporator assembly away from the dash panel and remove the evaporator case from the vehicle.
12. Remove the vacuum source line from the heater core tube seal and remove the seal from the heater core tubes.
13. Remove the three screws attaching the blend door actuator to the evaporator case and remove the actuator.
14. Remove the four heater-core access cover attaching screws and remove the access cover and seal from the evaporator case. Lift the heater core and seals from the evaporator case.

**To install:**

15. Transfer the seal to the new heater core, then install the heater core into the evaporator case.
16. Position the heater core access cover on the evaporator case and install the four attaching screws. If equipped with automatic temperature control, position the blend door actuator to the blend door shaft and install the three attaching screws.
17. Install the seal on the heater core tubes and install the vacuum source line through the seal.
18. Position the evaporator case assembly to the dash panel and cowl top panel at the air inlet opening. Install the two screws attaching the support brackets to the cowl top panel.
19. Install the three nuts in the engine compartment attaching the evaporator case to the dash panel. Install the floor register and rear seats duct to the evaporator case and tighten the two attaching screws.
20. Install the instrument panel shake brace and screw to the evaporator case. Install the instrument panel in the reverse order of removal.
21. Connect the air conditioning lines to the evaporator core and the heater hoses to the heater core.

22. Connect the black vacuum supply hose to the vacuum check valve in the engine compartment.
23. Fill and bleed the cooling system. Connect the negative battery cable.
24. Have a MVAC certified tech leak test, evacuate, and charge the air conditioning system.
25. Check the system for proper operation.

**Continental 1995–00**

1. Disconnect the battery ground cable
2. Remove the console glove compartment. Disconnect the power point electrical connector. If equipped, disconnect the cellular phone antenna cable and coaxial cable from the console glove compartment. If equipped, disconnect the cellular phone antenna cable and coaxial cable.
3. If equipped, remove the compact disc changer. Remove the screws. Disconnect the electrical connector. Remove the digital audio compact disc player.
4. Place the gearshift lever in the 1 position.
5. Remove the console top panel. Disconnect the cigar lighter electrical connector.
6. Remove the floor console to floor bracket screws.
7. Remove the floor console to gearshift bracket screws.
8. Remove the floor console. Slide the floor console rearward. Remove the floor console. Disconnect the three electrical connectors.

**CAUTION**

**Electronic modules are sensitive to static electrical charges. If exposed to these charges, damage may result.**

9. Remove the passenger side air bag module.

**WARNING**

**Always wear safety glasses when repairing an air bag supplemental restraint system (SRS) vehicle and when handling an air bag module. This will reduce the risk of injury in the event of an accidental deployment.**

**WARNING**

**Carry a live air bag module with the air bag and deployment door pointed away from your body. This will reduce the risk of injury in the event of an accidental deployment.**

**WARNING**

**Do not set a live air bag module down with the deployment door face down. This will reduce the risk of injury in the event of an accidental deployment.**

10. Disconnect the battery ground cable and wait at least one minute.
11. Push in on the two glove compartment door tabs and position downward.
12. Disconnect the passenger air bag module electrical connector. Remove the passenger air bag module retaining bolts.
13. Remove the passenger air bag module.

Note: When the battery is disconnected and reconnected, some abnormal drive symptoms may occur while the vehicle relearns its adaptive strategy. The vehicle may need to be driven 16 km (10 mi) or more to relearn the strategy.

14. If equipped, remove the rear seat climate control air duct sleeve.
15. Remove the steering column.

**CAUTION**

**Do not remove the steering column, steering wheel and air bag module as an assembly from the vehicle. Unless the steering column is locked to prevent rotation; or the lower end of the steering shaft is wired to prevent the steering wheel from being rotated, damage to the air bag sliding contact will occur.**

➡**All steering column components are assembled with specific fasteners. They are designed with a thread locking system to prevent loosening due to vibrations associated with normal vehicle operation. Make sure vehicle front wheels are in the straight-ahead position**

16. Remove the ignition switch lock
17. Remove the steering wheel.
18. Remove the air bag sliding contact.
19. Remove the tilt wheel handle and shank by unscrewing it from the steering column.
20. Remove the four upper and lower steering column shroud retaining screws. Remove the upper steering column shroud and lower steering column shroud.
21. Remove the lower instrument panel trim cover.
22. Unsnap the steering column lower trim panel.
23. Remove the release lever hood retaining screws.
24. Remove the brake release retaining screws.
25. Remove the instrument panel steering column opening cover reinforcement
26. Remove the instrument panel reinforcement brace.
27. Disconnect the shift cable and bracket from the steering column by removing two screws.
28. Disconnect the transmission shift cable loop from the shift tube hook (column shift).
29. Remove the two multi-function switch retaining screws and set the multi-function switch aside.
30. Remove the retaining screw and remove the wiring connector from the ignition switch.
31. Remove two front steering column nuts and the steering column impact absorber
32. Remove the pinch bolt from the steering column lower yoke.
33. While supporting the column assembly, remove two rear column assembly retaining nuts.
34. Disconnect the shift cable and bracket from the selector lever pivot. Disconnect the shift cable from the steering column shift tube lever. Disconnect the shift cable from the steering column bracket.
35. Remove the shift cable and bracket from the lower column mounting.
36. Remove two shift lock actuator-retaining screws and remove the shift lock actuator (console shift only).
37. Remove the steering column from the vehicle.
38. Release the cable from the parking brake actuator.
39. Release the cable conduit from the parking brake actuator.
40. To disconnect the driver's side outboard bulkhead electrical connector. Loosen the bolt. Disconnect the driver's side bulkhead electrical connector.
41. To disconnect the driver's side inboard bulkhead electrical connector. Loosen the bolt. Disconnect the driver's side bulkhead electrical connector.
42. If equipped, disconnect the heated seat switch electrical connectors.
43. Remove the steering column mounting support to instrument cowl brace bolts.
44. Remove the instrument panel dash brace to instrument panel bolt.
45. Loosen the nut that secures the instrument panel dash brace. Position the instrument panel dash brace aside.
46. Remove the pin-type retainers. Remove the passenger side instrument panel insulator. Remove the courtesy lamp.
47. Disconnect the vacuum harness connector.
48. Disconnect the in-line electrical harness connector.
49. Position the passenger side scuff plate aside.
50. Remove the passenger side cowl trim panel.
51. Disconnect the antenna in-line connector.
52. Remove the ignition/shifter interlock cable from the bracket and the shifter interlock cam.
53. Remove the instrument panel defroster opening grille assembly.
54. Lift upward to release the instrument panel defroster opening grille assembly from the instrument panel.
55. Disconnect the two electrical connectors (one each side).
56. Remove the instrument panel defroster opening grille assembly.
57. Remove the instrument panel cowl top screws.
58. Remove the passenger side instrument panel support to cowl side nut.
59. Remove the driver's side instrument panel support to cowl side bolts.
60. Loosen the driver's side instrument panel support to cowl side captive bolt.
61. Position the instrument panel away from the cowl.
62. Disconnect the electronic air temperature control (EATC) hose from the heater plenum.

➡**Two technicians are required to carry out this step.**

63. Remove the instrument panel.

➡**Check the cowl top clips for damage, looseness, or stripped fasteners.**

64. Drain the coolant from the radiator so that the coolant level is below the heater core
65. Loosen the screw and disconnect the electrical connector from the powertrain control module (PCM).
66. Disconnect the heater water hoses from the heater core.
67. Remove the screws and the metal cover.
68. Remove the A/C electronic blend door actuator.
69. Disconnect the wire harness connector.

70. Remove the screws and remove the A/C electronic blend door actuator.
71. Remove the A/C air intake flue damper assist spring.

**CAUTION**

**Do not attempt to bend any part of the A/C damper door shaft. It is brittle and will break.**

72. Depress the locking ramp and remove the A/C damper door shaft from the air temperature control door shaft.

**CAUTION**

**Do not attempt to bend any part of the lever. It is brittle and will break.**

73. Remove the A/C evaporator case outlet door shaft.
74. Remove the screws and the heater core cover.
75. Remove the heater core cover seal.
76. Remove the heater core.
77. Installation is the reversal of the removal process.
78. To exchange a loose or damaged cowl top clip with a new clip, remove the metal insert and then carefully release the clip from the cowl. Do not pry on the clip or damage to the cowl sheet metal may occur.

**➡To install a new fastener, remove the metal insert from the cowl top clip and exchange it with the new fastener. If any portion of the cowl top clip falls into the cowl, use Clear Silicone Rubber D6AZ-19562-AA or equivalent meeting Ford specification ESB-M4G92-A to prevent the broken portion from rattling within the cowl.**

**➡Two technicians are required to carry out this step.**

79. Position the instrument panel. Connect the EATC hose to the heater plenum.
80. Install the instrument panel cowl top screws.
81. Install the instrument panel defroster opening grille assembly.
82. Connect the electrical connectors (one each side).
83. Install the instrument panel defroster opening grille assembly.
84. Install the driver's side instrument panel support to cowl side bolts.
85. Tighten the driver's side instrument panel support to cowl side captive bolt.
86. Install the passenger side instrument panel support to cowl side nut.
87. Install the ignition/shifter interlock cable into the bracket and the shifter interlock cam.
88. Connect the antenna in-line connector.
89. Install the passenger side cowl trim panel.
90. Install the passenger side scuff plate.
91. Connect the in-line electrical harness connector.
92. Connect the vacuum harness connector.
93. Position the passenger side instrument panel insulator. Install the pin-type retainers. Install the courtesy lamp.
94. Position the instrument panel dash brace.
95. Install the instrument panel dash brace to instrument panel bolt.
96. Install the steering column mounting support to instrument panel cowl brace bolts.
97. Tighten the instrument panel dash brace nut.
98. Installation from this point is the reversal of the removal process.

### Mark VII

**➡If your vehicle is equipped with air conditioning, refer to Section 1 for information regarding the implications of servicing your A/C system yourself. Only an MVAC-trained, EPA-certified, automotive technician should service the A/C system or its components.**

1. Reclaim the refrigerant.
2. Drain the cooling system.

**➡The next set of instructions applies for removing the center console, where necessary.**

3. Remove the console top panel. Disconnect the electrical connector.
4. Place the gearshift lever in the 1 position.
5. Remove the floor console to floor bracket screws.
6. Remove the floor console to gearshift bracket screws.
7. Slide the floor console rearward. Remove the floor console. Disconnect the electrical connectors.
8. Remove the lower instrument panel trim cover.
9. Remove the steering column trim shrouds and disconnect all electrical connections from the steering column switches.
10. Disconnect the shift cable and bracket from the selector lever pivot.
    a. Remove the four screws at the steering column bracket to lower the steering column.

**CAUTION**

**Do not remove the steering column, steering wheel and air bag module (if equipped) as an assembly from the vehicle. Unless the steering column is locked to prevent rotation; or the lower end of the steering shaft is wired to prevent the steering wheel from being rotated, damage to the air bag sliding contact will occur.**

**➡All steering column components are assembled with specific fasteners. They are designed with a thread locking system to prevent loosening due to vibrations associated with normal vehicle operation. Make sure vehicle front wheels are in the straight-ahead position**

11. Remove the instrument panel and lay it on the front seat.
12. Remove the high and low pressure hoses and cap the openings to prevent dirt and moisture from entering.
13. Disconnect the liquid line and the accumulator/drier inlet tube from the evaporator core at the dash panel and cap the lines.
14. Remove the suction accumulator/drier and bracket. If necessary, remove the throttle cable bracket and position it out of the way.
15. Disconnect the heater hoses from the heater core. Plug the hoses and cap the heater core tubes to prevent coolant loss during removal of the evaporator case.
16. Disconnect the vacuum supply hose (black) from the inline vacuum check valve in the engine compartment.
17. Working under the hood, remove the three nuts retaining the evaporator case to the dash panel.
18. In the passenger compartment, remove the screw attaching the evaporator case support bracket to the cowl top panel.
19. Remove one nut retaining the bracket below the evaporator case to the dash panel.
20. Carefully pull the evaporator case away from the dash panel and remove assembly from vehicle.
21. Remove the screws and pull air inlet duct away from evaporator case.
22. Remove the heater core from the case.

**To install:**

23. Install a new heater core into the case.
24. Run a bead of caulk/sealer between evaporator case and service cover.
25. Install the service cover and retaining screws onto the evaporator case.
26. Position air inlet duct on case and install the screws.
27. Install evaporator case into dash panel, reverse of the removal procedures.
    a. Make sure that the drain hose is not kinked.
    b. Always use new O-rings coated with clean refrigerant oil.
    c. When connecting the refrigerant lines, make ALL connections loosely BEFORE tightening any of them.
    d. Make sure that the core seal fits over the case lower half edge.
    e. Always use new sealer between the case halves.
    f. When everything is back together, turn on the blower and check for air leaks around the case.

### Mark VIII

**➡If your vehicle is equipped with air conditioning, refer to Section 1 for information regarding the implications of servicing your A/C system yourself. Only an MVAC-trained, EPA-certified, automotive technician should service the A/C system or its components.**

1. Reclaim the refrigerant.
2. Drain the cooling system.
3. Place the gearshift lever in the 1 position.

**➡The next set of instructions applies for removing the center console, where necessary.**

4. Remove the console top panel. Disconnect the electrical connector.
5. Remove the floor console to floor bracket screws.
6. Remove the floor console to gearshift bracket screws.
7. Slide the floor console rearward. Remove the floor console. Disconnect the electrical connectors
8. Remove the lower instrument panel trim cover.

9. Remove the steering column trim shrouds and disconnect all electrical connections from the steering column switches.

10. Disconnect the shift cable and bracket from the selector lever pivot.

a. Remove the four screws at the steering column bracket to lower the steering column.

11. Remove the instrument panel, and lay it on the front seat.

12. Remove the seal from around the heater core tubes. Disconnect the heater hoses from the heater core tubes.

13. Remove the three screws retaining the A/C electronic door actuator motor to the evaporator housing, and remove the actuator.

14. Remove the four heater core cover retaining screws and remove the heater core cover and seal.

15. Remove the heater core from the housing.

**To install:**

16. Transfer the foam heater core cover seals to the new heater core.

17. Install the heater core cover and secure it into the A/C evaporator housing.

18. Position the heater core cover on the A/C evaporator housing and install the four retaining screws.

19. Position the A/C electronic door actuator motor to the blend door shaft. Install the three screws retaining the A/C electronic door actuator motor to the A/C evaporator housing.

20. Install the seals onto ht heater core tubes .

21. Connect the heater hoses, fill the radiator with the specified coolant and check the operation of the system.

## Air Conditioning Components

### REMOVAL & INSTALLATION

Repair or service of air conditioning components is not covered by this manual, because of the risk of personal injury or death, and because of the legal ramifications of servicing these components without the proper EPA certification and experience. Cost, personal injury or death, environmental damage, and legal considerations (such as the fact that it is a federal crime to vent refrigerant into the atmosphere), dictate that the A/C components on your vehicle should be serviced only by a Motor Vehicle Air Conditioning (MVAC) trained, and EPA certified automotive technician.

**➡If your vehicle's A/C system uses R-12 refrigerant and is in need of recharging, the A/C system can be converted over to R-134a refrigerant (less environmentally harmful and expensive). Refer to Section 1 for additional information on R-12 to R-134a conversions, and for additional considerations dealing with your vehicle's A/C system.**

## CRUISE CONTROL

All models covered by this manual were available with an optional speed control system. This system automatically controls the speed of the vehicle when cruising at a stable highway speed.

The speed control system consists of the following:

- Speed control amplifier/servo assembly
- Speed control cable
- Vehicle Speed Sensor (VSS)
- Speed control actuator switch
- Stop light switch
- Deactivator switch

The speed control system operates independently of engine vacuum and, therefore, does not utilize any vacuum lines.

The speed control amplifier integrates the system electronics, thereby eliminating any other electronic control modules in the vehicle. The amplifier controls the vehicle's speed via a cable attached to the throttle body lever.

The speed control actuator switch assembly is mounted on the steering wheel and allows the driver to control the system's operation. The switch assembly contains five control buttons for system functioning, namely: ON, OFF, RESUME, SET ACCEL, COAST.

The system will continue to control the vehicle's speed until the OFF button is used, or the brake pedal or clutch pedal (manual transmissions only) is depressed.

## CRUISE CONTROL TROUBLESHOOTING

| Problem | Possible Cause |
|---|---|
| Will not hold proper speed | Incorrect cable adjustment<br>Binding throttle linkage<br>Leaking vacuum servo diaphragm<br>Leaking vacuum tank<br>Faulty vacuum or vent valve<br>Faulty stepper motor<br>Faulty transducer<br>Faulty speed sensor<br>Faulty cruise control module |
| Cruise intermittently cuts out | Clutch or brake switch adjustment too tight<br>Short or open in the cruise control circuit<br>Faulty transducer<br>Faulty cruise control module |
| Vehicle surges | Kinked speedometer cable or casing<br>Binding throttle linkage<br>Faulty speed sensor<br>Faulty cruise control module |
| Cruise control inoperative | Blown fuse<br>Short or open in the cruise control circuit<br>Faulty brake or clutch switch<br>Leaking vacuum circuit<br>Faulty cruise control switch<br>Faulty stepper motor<br>Faulty transducer<br>Faulty speed sensor<br>Faulty cruise control module |

Note: Use this chart as a guide. Not all systems will use the components listed.

TCCA6C01

## ENTERTAINMENT SYSTEMS

**➡The premium sound system is available with all electronic radios. It consists of a maximum of six speakers (two high frequency instrument panel speakers, two premium front door speakers, and two premium rear speakers). The door and instrument panel speakers are wired in parallel. Separate signal return wiring to each speaker is used. The amplifier is in operation and is part of the circuit at all times.**

## Radio Receiver/Amplifier/Tape Player/CD Player

### REMOVAL & INSTALLATION

#### Continental 1988–1994

1. Disconnect the negative battery cable.
2. Remove the center instrument trim panel.
3. Use the radio removal tools to pull the radio from the instrument panel.
4. Pull the radio to the front and raise the back end of the radio slightly so that the rear support bracket clears the track in the instrument panel. Pull the radio out of the instrument panel slowly.
5. Disconnect the wiring connectors and antenna cable and remove the rear support bracket.

**To install:**

6. Connect the wiring connectors and antenna cable to radio. Install the rear support bracket.
7. Slide the radio into the instrument panel until the spring clips on both sides of the radio are fully seated.
8. Install the center instrument trim panel.
9. Connect the negative battery cable.

#### Continental 1995–00

Two sound systems are available in the Continental.

- The base sound system is the luxury analog cassette radio chassis.
- The optional sound system is the JBL ® audio system which features two radio speakers mounted in the package tray, a sub-woofer and can be equipped with a digital audio compact disc player.

Both systems utilize a two-chassis design (distributed radio system).

- The luxury analog cassette radio chassis consists of: a housing, a cassette player, a bezel assembly, a large graphic digital display window and electronic control switches and circuitry.
- The rear chassis unit is mounted below the rear package tray and consists of AM and FM tuners; signal processing hardware, and a four-channel power amplifier.
- The luxury analog cassette radio chassis and the rear chassis unit communicate via a Society of Automotive Engineers (SAE) J1708-based audio control protocol. Audio control protocol will also be used to control the digital audio compact disc player and handle commands from the mobile phone.
- Audio signal inputs to the rear chassis units are analog. The analog signal from the cassette is two channels (left and right) of differential signal with twisted and shielded wiring. Inputs for cellular telephone and CD player functions use twisted and shielded wiring.
- Outpputs from the rear chassis unit are bridge outputs. The power amplifiers are distortion-limited to prevent severe clipping. The four-channel amplifier is fed with full-range signals.
- The rear chassis unit will process analog signals from the tuner, tape audio, CD player audio and mobile phone audio.

#### *LUXURY*

The luxury audio system consists of:

- Two premium front door radio speakers.
- Two rear door radio speakers.
- Separate signal and return wiring to each radio speaker. The rear chassis unit is in operation and is part of the circuit at all times.

#### *JBL*

The JBL® sound system consists of:

- Two JBL® two-way radio speakers mounted in the front doors.
- Two JBL® two-way radio speakers mounted in the rear doors.
- Two sub-woofer radio speakers mounted on the package tray and a sub-woofer amplifier mounted under the package tray.
- A rear chassis unit mounted in the luggage compartment.

A console mounted digital audio compact disc player is available as an option with the JBL® sound systems.

**⁂ WARNING**

**Use of controls and adjustments of performance of procedures other than those specified may result in hazardous radiation exposure.**

### REMOVAL & INSTALLATION

#### Radio Chassis—Front Control Unit

1. Disconnect the negative battery cable.
2. Install the radio removing tool into the radio face plate far enough to engage the retaining clips.
3. Apply a slight spreading force on the tools and pull the radio chassis out of the instrument panel.
4. Disconnect the wiring connectors and remove the radio chassis.

**To install:**

5. Connect the wiring connectors to the radio chassis.
6. Slide the radio chassis into the instrument panel. Making sure it is squarely inserted.
7. Push the radio chassis inward until the retaining clips are fully engaged.
8. Connect the negative battery cable.

#### Radio Chassis—Rear Chassis Unit

1. Disconnect the negative battery cable.
2. Remove the luggage compartment front cover from the luggage compartment.
3. Pull down the rear of the module tray.
4. Disconnect
5. Remove the ground screw and ground strap from the rear chassis unit.
6. Remove the rear chassis unit from the module tray.

**To install:**

7. Install the rear chassis unit into the module tray.
8. Install the ground strap to the rear chassis unit with the ground screw.
9. Connect the radio antenna isolator to the rear chassis unit cable and the wiring connectors to the rear chassis unit.
10. Secure the module tray with pushpins and install the luggage compartment front cover.
11. Connect the negative battery cable.

#### Town Car 1988–94

**➧ See Figure 29**

1. The premium sound system is standard on Lincoln Town Car. It consists of Electronic Premium Cassette radio, four speakers (two premium front door speakers and two premium rear speakers). Separate signal return wiring to each speaker is used. The amplifier is in operation and is part of the circuit at all times.
2. The JBL ® sound system consists of the Electronic Premium Cassette radio, four JBL ® two-way speakers mounted in the doors and rear package tray, one sub-woofer assembly with built-in amplifier mounted under the rear package tray, and an amplifier mounted in the luggage compartment.

**➡A compact disc radio (CDR) is available with the JBL ® sound system.**

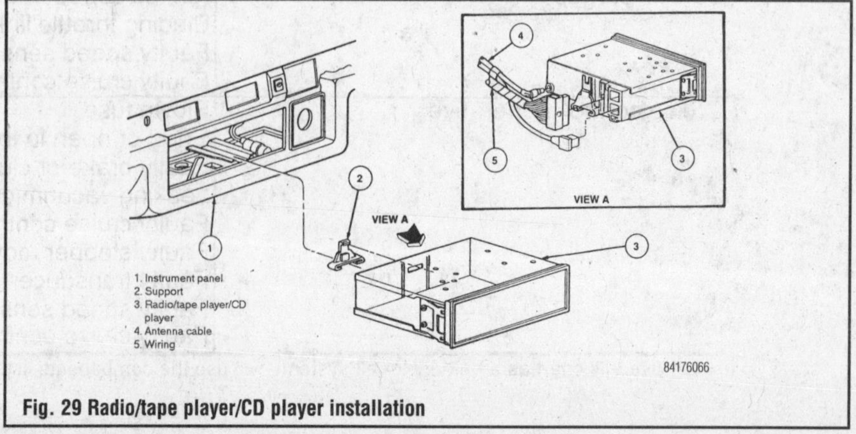


**Fig. 29 Radio/tape player/CD player installation**

3. Disconnect the negative battery cable.
4. Remove the radio trim panel (1988–90).
5. Remove the four trim screws securing the radio to the instrument panel. (as necessary).
6. Install the radio removing tools (1990–95)
7. Apply a slight spreading force on the tools and pull the radio from the dash.
8. Disconnect the power, antenna and speaker leads and remove the radio.

**To install:**

9. Connect the power lead, antenna, and speaker leads.
10. Slide the radio into the dash ensuring that the rear bracket is engaged on the lower support rail.
11. Push the radio inward until the retaining clips are fully engaged (1990–95).
12. Secure the radio by installing the trim screws to the instrument panel (1988–90).
13. Install the radio trim panel (1988–90).

#### Town Car 1995–00

The luxury sound system is standard on Town Car. This audio system uses a two-chassis design (distributed radio system).

- The luxury analog cassette radio chassis consists of a housing, a cassette player, a bezel assembly, a large graphic vacuum fluorescent display and electronic control switches and circuitry. The front chassis has selective lighting.
- The remote chassis unit is mounted below the rear package tray and consists of AM and FM tuners, signal processing hardware, and a four-channel power amplifier.
- The front control unit and the remote chassis unit communicate via a Society of Automotive Engineers (SAE) J1708-based audio control protocol. Audio control protocol will also be used to control the digital audio compact disc player and handle commands from the mobile phone.
- Audio signal inputs to the remote chassis unit are analog. The analog signal from the cassette is two channels (left and right) of differential signal with twisted and shielded wiring. Inputs for cellular telephone and CD player functions use twisted and shielded wiring.
- Outputs from the rear chassis unit are bridge outputs. The power amplifiers are distortion-limited to prevent severe clipping. The four-channel amplifier is fed with full-range signals.
- The remote chassis unit will process analog signals from the tuner, tape audio, CD player audio and mobile phone audio.

The front control unit contains the input bezel assembly, the output display and the cassette player. The bezel is backlit with a single electroluminescent lamp for selective back-lighting.

- A five-digit vacuum fluorescent display will be used. The display will indicate the station frequency, band (AM and FM), volume setting, cassette player, CD changer and cellular telephone information.
- The ACP and cassette player signals use shielded wire. Pins are reserved in the front control unit to terminate the drain wire of the shields.
- The front control unit holds a switching power supply which generates sufficient voltage to illuminate the EL panel.
- The microcontroller in the front control unit monitors the switch settings, handles commands to ht display and performs ACP network tasks.

The remote chassis unit consists of three major sections.

- The AM/FM tuner processes the radio frequency signal and produces the left and right analog audio signals.
- The microprocessor control and audio processor board controls the remote chassis unit and processes all of the audio input signals from the front control unit, tuner and cellular phone.
- The 4 channel 20-Watt audio power amplifier and RCU power supply board.

All sections are contained in a single aluminum heat sink casting.

Antenna—Town Car

- Antennas are concealed on all vehicles.
- The diversity antenna system uses two concealed antennas
- The AM antenna consists of the rear window defroster grid on the interior of the rear window.
- The FM antenna consists of conductive tracing on the rear window above the rear window defroster grid.
- Active and wide-band antenna elements are used.
- A multipath circuit and the microprocessor monitor FM signal level.
- The antenna-switching scheme is controlled by the microprocessor.

#### Mark VII 1988–90

1. Disconnect the negative battery cable.

**➡If the gear shift on console interferes with removal and installation, set parking brake and place in 1 or 2 for automatic transmission.**

2. Remove the center instrument trim panel..
3. Remove the 4 screws retaining the radio and mounting bracket to the instrument panel.
4. Pull the radio towards the front seat to disengage it from the lower bracket.
5. Pull the radio out slowly Disconnect the radio and antenna connections
6. Remove the radio.
7. Installation is the reverse of removal..

**To install:**

8. Attach the antenna and wiring to back of the unit.
9. Insert the radio into the dash, tighten the mounting screws to the bracket to retain the unit.
10. Connect the negative battery cable
11. Test the unit for proper operation
12. If the system works well, install the center trim panel.

#### Mark VII 1991–92

**➡A special radio removal tool, must be used in order to remove radio components with out damage to unit.**

1. Disconnect negative battery cable.
2. Insert two radio removal tools into the radio face plates holes, until tension of spring clips is felt.
3. Flex outward on both sides simultaneously and pull the radio out.
4. Disconnect wiring connectors and antenna cable.

**To install:**

5. Attach the antenna and wiring to back of the unit.
6. Insert the radio into the dash, then push on the radio until the clips "click".
7. Connect the negative battery cable. Test the unit for proper operation.

#### Mark VIII 1993–98

The Mark VIII has two systems available, the premium sound system and the JBL®.

The premium sound system, which is standard on Mark VIII, consists of the following features.

- Premium analog cassette radio chassis.
- Four radio speakers (two premium front door radio speakers and two premium quarter trim panel mounted radio speakers.
- Separate signal return wiring to each radio speaker.
- A premium radio amplifier that is in operation and is part of the circuit at all times.

The JBL® sound system consists of the following features.

- Premium analog cassette radio chassis.
- Four premium radio speakers in the doors and quarter trim panels.
- Four additional JBL® radio speakers mounted in the doors and quarter trim panels.
- JBL®audiophile radio amplifier.
- An optional radio chassis is available.
- An optional luggage compartment-mounted digital audio compact disc player is available with the standard premium or JBL®sound systems.

1. Disconnect the negative battery cable.
2. Install the radio-removing tool into the radio faceplate far enough to engage the retaining clips.
3. Apply a slight spreading force on the tools and pull the radio chassis out of the instrument panel.
4. Dilsconnect the wiring connectors and remove the radio chassis.

**To install:**

5. Connect the wiring connectors to the radio chassis.
6. Slide the radio chassis into the instrument panel. Making sure it is squarely inserted.
7. Push the radio chassis inward until the retaining clips are fully engaged.
8. Connect the negative battery cable.

## Speakers

### REMOVAL & INSTALLATION

#### Front—Town Car

##### *1988–94*

**➧ See Figure 30**

1. Disconnect the negative battery cable.
2. Remove the instrument panel pad as follows:
   a. Remove the 2 screws attaching the pad to the instrument panel at each defroster opening. Be careful not to drop the screws into the defroster openings.
   b. Remove the one screw attaching each outboard end of the pad to the instrument panel.
   c. Remove the row of screws attaching the lower edge of the pad to the instrument panel. Pull

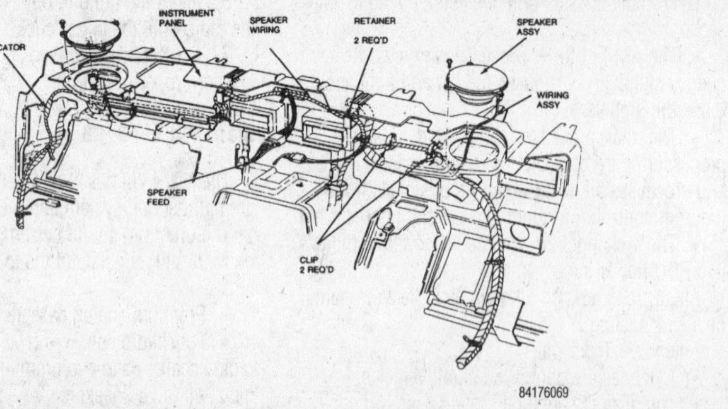


Fig. 30 Front speaker removal

the instrument panel pad rearward and remove it from the vehicle.

3. Remove the 3 retaining screws for each of the front speakers.

4. Raise the speakers and disconnect the leads at the connectors.

5. Installation is the reverse of the removal procedure.

### Door Mounted —Town Car

#### *1988 -94*

➧ See Figure 31

1. Disconnect the negative battery cable.

2. Remove the door panel as explained in Section 10.

3. Remove the retaining screws and pull the speaker from the opening.

4. Disconnect the speaker lead at the connector and remove the speaker.

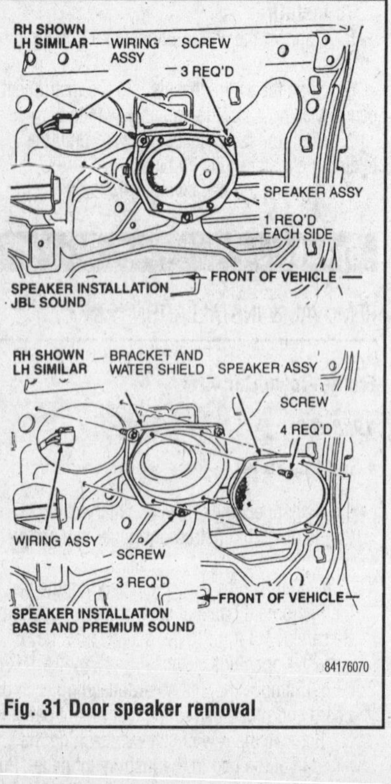


Fig. 31 Door speaker removal

5. Installation is the reverse of the removal procedure.

### Rear—Town Car

#### *1988–94*

➧ See Figure 32

1. Disconnect the negative battery cable.

2. Remove the spare tire and jack assembly from the luggage compartment, if necessary.

3. Working inside the luggage compartment, disconnect the speaker lead from the wire harness.

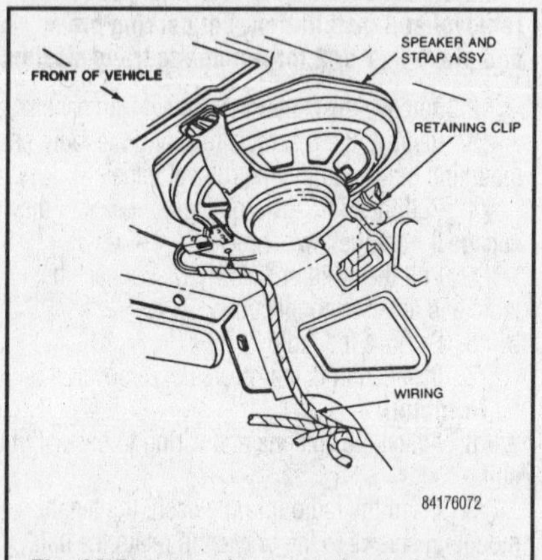


Fig. 32 Rear speaker mounting in luggage compartment

4. Disengage the strap from the retaining clips and remove the speaker.

5. Installation is the reverse of the removal procedure.

#### *1995–00*

➧ See Figure 33

1. Disconnect the negative battery cable.

2. Remove the package tray trim.

3. Remove the 4 speaker retaining screws.

4. Disconnect the connector and lift out the speaker.

5. If equipped with standard speakers, remove the NVH cover if necessary.

6. Installation is the reverse of the removal procedure.

### Subwoofer

1. Disconnect the negative battery cable.

2. Remove the spare tire.

3. Remove the 4 nut and washer assemblies from the bottom of the subwoofer. Remove the subwoofer by lowering straight down.

4. Disconnect the power connector and amplifier input connector located on the forward face of the subwoofer enclosure.

5. The subwoofer and amplifier assembly is now free of the vehicle.

6. To remove the subwoofer amplifier from the enclosure, disconnect the power and input connectors.

7. Remove the 4 retaining screws from the amplifier and remove the amplifier from the subwoofer enclosure.

8. Installation is the reverse of the removal procedure.

### Front Door Mounted Continental

#### *1988–94*

➧ See Figure 34

1. Disconnect the negative battery cable.

2. Remove the front door trim panel.

3. Remove the screws retaining the speaker to its mounting bracket.

4. Pull the speaker away from the mounting bracket far enough to disconnect the speaker electrical wires.

5. Remove the speaker from the vehicle.

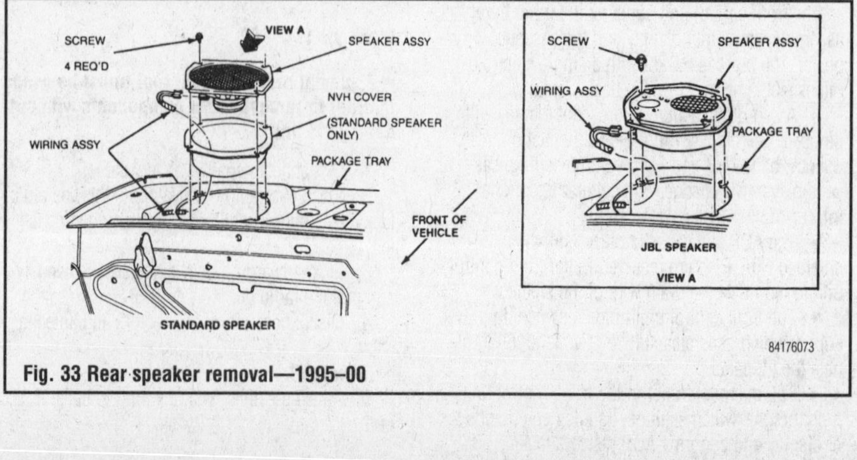


Fig. 33 Rear speaker removal—1995–00

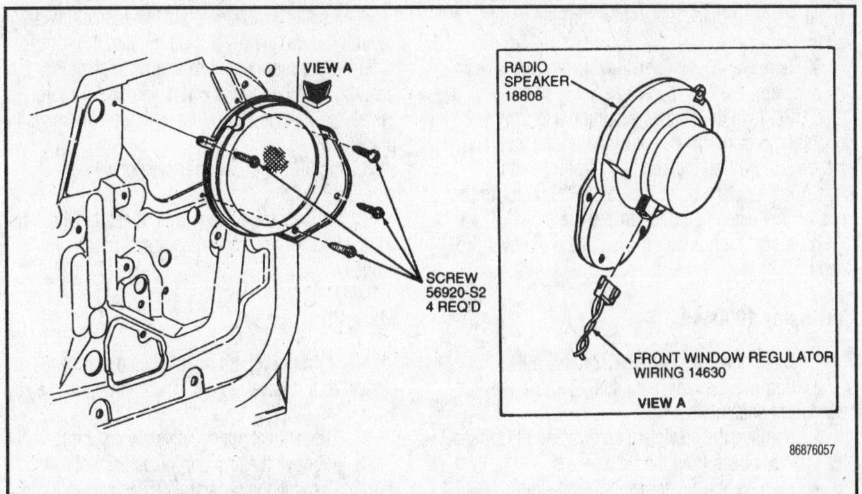


**Fig. 34 Common front door mounted speaker assembly**

**To install:**

6. Connect the speaker electrical wires, then install the speaker to the mounting bracket using the retaining screws.
7. Install the front door trim panel.
8. Connect the negative battery cable.

***1995–00***

1. Remove the lower door panel.
2. Remove the four screws retaining the speaker to the door
3. Pull the speaker away from the door and disconnect the speaker lead. Remove the speaker from the vehicle.

**To install:**

4. Firmly push the radio speaker lead into the radio speaker connector.
5. Position the speaker to the door and install the retaining screws.
6. Install the lower door panel.

**Package Tray Speaker**

***1988–94 CONTINENTAL***

**➧ See Figure 35**

1. Disconnect the negative battery cable.
2. Remove the speaker cover.

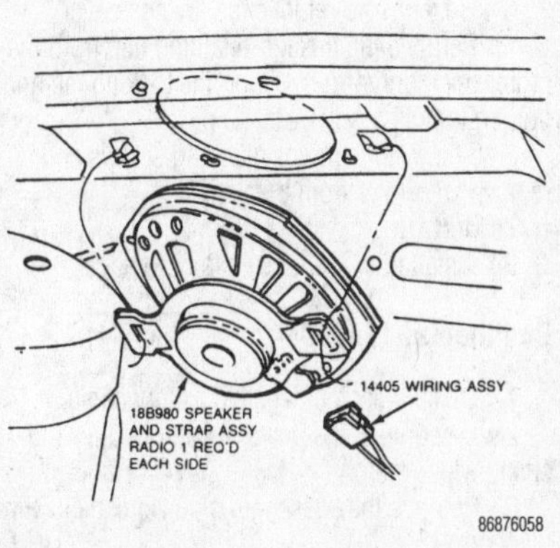


**Fig. 35 Standard rear speaker mounting**

3. From the inside of the trunk, disconnect the speaker wiring harness from the speaker.
4. Pull one end of the speaker rubber retaining strap to disengage it from the tab on the package tray, then remove the speaker from the vehicle.

**To install:**

5. Position the speaker and strap assembly in place with one end of the strap over the tab on the package tray. Pull the opposite end of the strap to index over the other tab, securing the assembly.
6. Connect the speaker harness wiring, then connect the negative battery cable and check speaker operation.
7. Connect the negative battery cable.

***1995–00 CONTINENTAL***

1. Remove the package tray panel.
2. Remove the four screws retaining the speaker to the package tray.
3. Pull the speaker away from the package tray and disconnect the speaker lead. Remove the speaker from the vehicle.

**To install:**

4. Firmly push the radio speaker lead into the radio speaker connector.
5. Position the speaker to the package tray and install the retaining screws.
6. Install the package tray panel.

**Mark VII 1988–1992**

***DOOR SPEAKERS***

1. Remove the front door trim panel. Remove the radio speaker retaining screws.
2. Disconnect the radio speaker connector and remove the radio speaker.

**To install:**

3. Connect the radio speaker connector.
4. Installation is the reversal of the removal process.

***QUARTER TRIM SPEAKERS***

1. Remove the quarter trim panel.
2. Remove the radio speaker retaining screws.
3. Remove the radio speaker and disconnect the radio speaker connector.

**To install:**

4. Connect the radio speaker connector .
5. Installation is the reversal of the removal process.

# WINDSHIELD WIPERS AND WASHERS

## Windshield Wiper Blade and Arm

### REMOVAL & INSTALLATION

**➧ See Figures 36, 37 and 38**

**➡To prevent damage, do not pry arm from pivot with metal or sharp tool.**

Raise the blade end of the arm off the windshield and move the slide latch away from the pivot shaft. This will unlock the wiper arm from the pivot shaft and hold the blade end of the arm off the glass at the same time. The wiper arm can now be pulled off the pivot shaft without the aid of any tools.

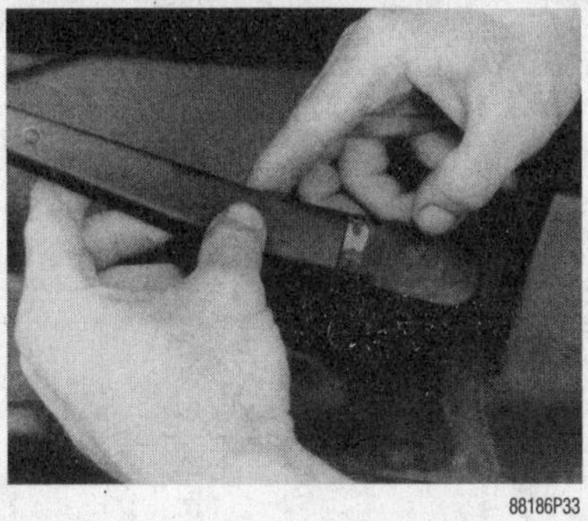


**Fig. 36 Raise the wiper arm off the windshield**

**Fig. 37 Move the slide latch away from the pivot shaft. This will unlock the wiper arm from the pivot shaft**

To install, position the auxiliary arm over the pivot pin, (on 1989 and later models align the keyway on the pivot shaft) hold it down and push the main arm head over the pivot shaft. Ensure pivot shaft is in position, and that the blade assembly is positioned to the correct dimension. Hold the main arm head onto the pivot shaft while raising the blade end of the wiper arm and push the slide latch into the lock under the pivot shaft. Then, lower the blade to the windshield. If the blade does not touch the windshield, the slide latch is not completely in place.

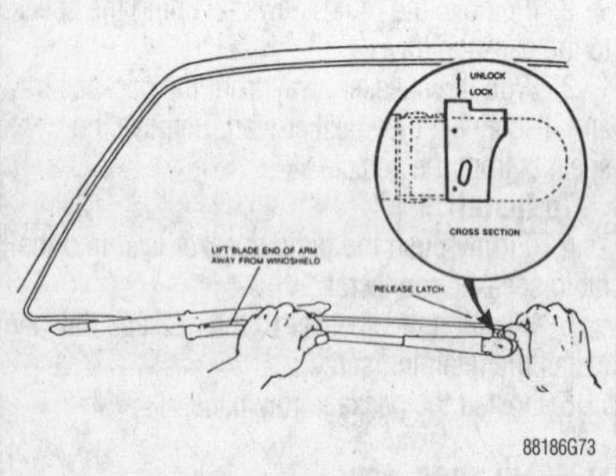


**Fig. 38 Removing the wiper arm and blade from the pivot shaft with the release latch**

## Windshield Wiper Motor

### REMOVAL & INSTALLATION

➡**The internal permanent magnets used in the wiper motor are a ceramic (glass-like) material. Be careful when handling the motor to avoid damaging the magnets. The motor must not be struck or tapped with a hammer or other object.**

#### Town Car 1988–89

▶ **See Figure 39**

1. Disconnect the negative battery cable.
2. Disconnect the push-on wire connectors from the motor.
3. Remove the hood seal. Remove the right wiper arm and blade assembly from the pivot shaft.
4. Remove the windshield wiper linkage cover by removing the two attaching screws and hose clip.
5. Remove the linkage-retaining clip from the operating arm on the motor by lifting the locking tab up and pulling the clip away from the pin.
6. Remove the bolts that retain the motor to the dash panel extension and remove the motor.
7. Installation is the reverse of the removal procedure.

#### Town Car 1990–00

1. Disconnect the negative battery cable.
2. Remove the rear hood seal. Remove the wiper arm assemblies.
3. Remove the cowl vent screws and disconnect the washer hoses from the washer jets.
4. Remove the wiper assembly attaching screws, lift the assembly out, and disconnect the washer hose.
5. Disconnect the electrical connectors from the wiper motor.
6. Unsnap and remove the linkage cover.
7. Remove the linkage-retaining clip from the motor operating arm by lifting the locking tab and pulling the clip away from the pin.
8. Remove the motor retaining screws and remove the motor from the vehicle.

**To install:**

9. Installation is the reverse of removal.

#### Continental 1988–94

1. Disconnect the negative battery cable.
2. Disconnect the power lead from the windshield wiper motor.
3. Remove the passenger side windshield wiper pivot arm.
4. Remove linkage-retaining clip from the windshield wiper mounting arm and pivot shaft to the windshield wiper motor by lifting the locking tab up and pulling clip away from the pin.

**To install:**

5. Position the windshield wiper motor assembly and install the retaining bolts.
6. Install the retaining clip on the windshield wiper mounting arm and pivot shaft.

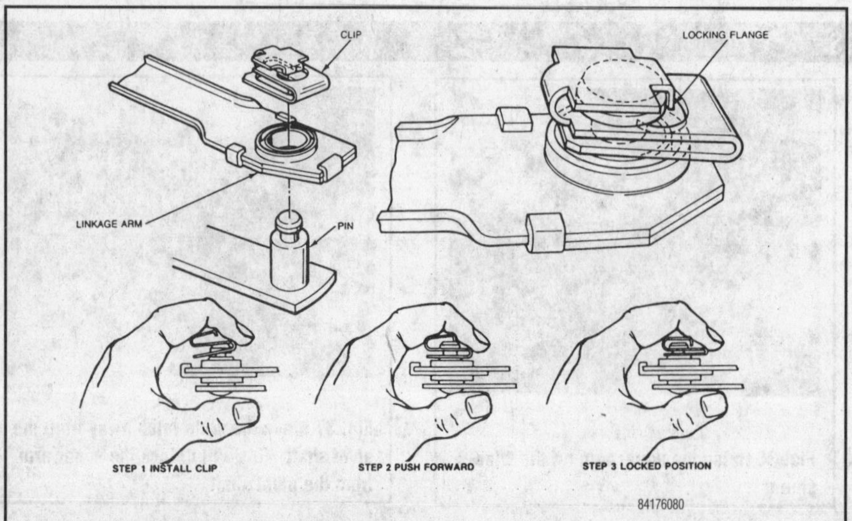


**Fig. 39 Linkage retaining clip installation**

7. Install the linkage on the windshield wiper mounting arm and pivot shaft. Ensure the windshield wiper mounting arm and pivot shaft is securely attached to the windshield wiper motor. Install the linkage by pulling until the clip snaps in place.
8. Install the passenger side cowl vent screen.
9. Connect the battery ground cable. Check the windshield wiper motor operation through all modes.

#### Mark VII

1. Turn the wipers on and when the blades are closest to full travel on the windshield, turn the key off.
2. Disconnect the negative battery cable.
3. Remove the arm and blade assemblies.
4. Remove the passenger side cowl vent screen.
5. Disconnect the linkage drive arm from the motor crankpin after removing the clip.
6. Disconnect the electrical connector of the wiper motor and remove the three retaining bolts of the wiper motor.
7. Pull the motor from the opening.

**To install:**

8. Reverse the removal procedure. Tighten all motor retaining bolts to 60–80 inch lbs. (7–9Nm)
9. Install the clip to wiper linkage.
10. Connect the linkage to motor by pushing linkage onto motor crankpin. Ensure the linkage is securely attached.

#### Mark VIII and 1995–00 Continental

➡**When installing the drive arm to a new motor, follow the instructions included in the new motor kit.**

1. Turn the ignition to the **RUN**position. Turn on the wipers and cycle to the mid-wipe position (straight up) and turn the ignition **OFF**.
2. Disconnect the negative battery cable.
3. Remove the passenger side and right-hand wiper arms.
4. Remove cowl top to hood seal.
5. Remove the driver's side and passenger side cowl vent screens.
6. Remove the four retaining screws and washers, and remove the cowl top extension.
7. Disconnect the two wiring connectors from the motor.
8. Remove the five retaining bolt and washer assemblies and one nut from the wiper module.
9. Lift the module slightly to disengage the support bracket from the dash panel mounting stud, move the module sideways about 2 inches (50.8mm) toward the passenger side and remove the module form the vehicle.
10. Disconnect the linkage drive arm from the motor crankpin after removing the clip.

➡**Check the location of the support bracket on the module.**

11. Remove the three retaining screws of the wiper motor and remove the motor from the module.

**To install:**

12. Installation is the reversal of the removal procedure.

# INSTRUMENTS AND SWITCHES

## Instrument Cluster

**➡Fedreral law requires that the odometer in any replacement speedometer must register the same mileage as that registered on the removed speedometer/odometer. Service replacement speedometer/odometer and odometer modules with the mileage preset to actual vehicle mileage are available through Ford Electronic service centers. In nearly all instances, the mileage continues to accumulate in the odometer memory even if the odometer does not display mileage. This mileage can usually be verified by the electronic service centers. Contact the service center for instructions to receive a replacement speed meter/odometer or odometer module with the mileage preset to actual mileage.**

If the actual vehicle mileage cannot be certified, the service center will supply a speedometer/odometer module with the odometer/display preset to zero miles ("0") miles and the service odometer segment ("s") illuminated in the vicinity of the odometer display. In addition, an odometer mileage sticker is supplied with the replacement odometer. This sticker must display the estimated vehicle mileage and is to be affixed to the driver's door.

### REMOVAL & INSTALLATION

#### Town Car

##### *CONVENTIONAL CLUSTER*

1. Disconnect the negative battery cable.
2. On 1988–89 vehicles, disconnect the speedometer cable.
3. Remove the instrument cluster trim cover attaching screws and remove the trim cover.
4. Remove the lower steering column cover retaining screws and remove the lower cover.
5. Remove the lower half of the steering column shroud.
6. Remove the screw holding the transmission range indicator column bracket to the steering column. Detach the cable loop from the pin and cane shift lever. Remove the column bracket from the column.
7. Remove the 4 cluster retaining screws. Disconnect the cluster feed plugs from the receptacle and remove the cluster assembly.
8. Installation is the reverse of the removal procedure.

##### *ELECTRONIC CLUSTER*

**➡The electronics within the electronic instrument cluster are not serviceable. In case of an electronic failure, the entire instrument cluster must be replaced or returned to the manufacturer for repair.**

1. Disconnect the negative battery cable and set the parking brake.
2. Unsnap the center moulding on the left and right sides of the instrument panel. Remove the steering column cover and column shroud.
3. Remove the knobs from the auto dim and auto lamp switches, if equipped. Remove the 13 screws retaining the instrument panel and pull the panel out.
4. Move the shift lever to the **1** position, if required, for easier access.
5. Detach the electrical connectors from the warning lamp module, switch module and center panel switches, if equipped.
6. Remove the instrument cluster carefully so as not to scratch the cluster lens. Detach the electrical connector from the front of the cluster.
7. Disconnect the transmission range indicator assembly from the cluster by carefully bending the bottom tab down and pulling the indicator assembly forward.
8. Pull the cluster out and detach the electrical connectors on the rear of the cluster. Remove the instrument cluster.
9. Installation is the reverse of the removal procedure.

#### Continental 1988–94

➧ See Figures 40 thru 56

1. Disconnect the negative battery cable.
2. Positon vehicle on a flat surface to prevent movement when shift control selector lever is out of position
3. Apply the parking brake, block the wheels.
4. Turn the ignition switch to unlock the shift control selector lever and move the lever down from the front of the Electronic Instrument Cluster (EIC).
5. Tilt the steering column down as far as possible.
6. Remove the passenger side and driver's side instrument panel moulding by pulling upward to unsnap the two clips. Disconnect the electrical connectors. Set the instrument panel moldings aside.
7. Remove the Torx® screws below the instrument cluster that retain the instrument panel finish panel applique.
8. Unsnap the instrument panel finish panel applique along the top and pull the instrument panel finish panel applique away from the instrument panel.
9. Disconnect the switch assembly electrical connectors. Set the instrument panel finish panel applique aside.
10. Remove the three screws from the bottom of the instrument panel steering column cover.
11. Lift up the top section f the instrument panel steering column cover to undo a clip located on the driver's side side near the steering wheel. Separate the upper section of the steering wheel from the side section near the ignition switch. Slip the upper section off the shift control selection lever and housing.
12. Remove the four Torx® screws retaining the instrument cluster to the instrument panel.
13. Place a clean, soft cloth on the steering column shroud to prevent scratching the front surface of the instrument cluster as it is removed.
14. Tilt the top of the instrument cluster slightly toward the rear of the vehicle. Undo the two snaps beneath the instrument cluster retaining the transmission control selector indicator (PRNDL) in the instrument cluster.
15. Reach around to the back of the instrument cluster to unplug the three connectors.

**➡The connectors have locking tabs that must be pressed in to unplug the connection.**

16. Loosen the two clips retaining the transmission control selector indicator to the instrument cluster.
17. Pull the transmission control selector indicator down and to the right to position it out of the way.
18. Push the bottom to the instrument cluster into the instrument panel cavity. Tilt the top of the instrument cluster toward the rear of the vehicle. Pull the instrument cluster up and out of the cavity.

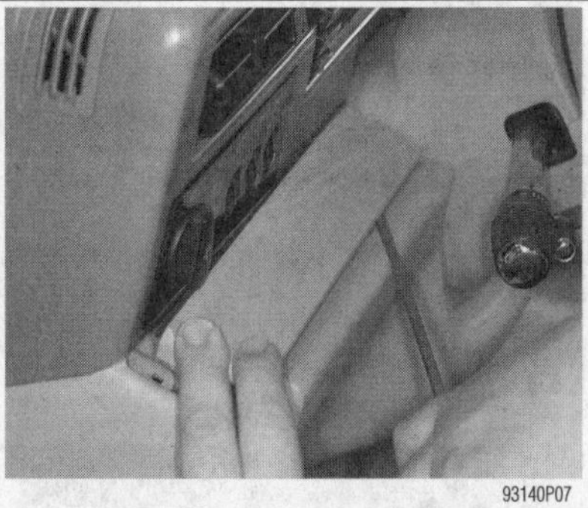

93140P07

**Fig. 40 Use a small pry tool to remove the cover panel on the left side of the steering column**

93140P06

**Fig. 41 Then use a prytool to remove the right side**

93140P05

**Fig. 42 Start from one side and disengage the clips**

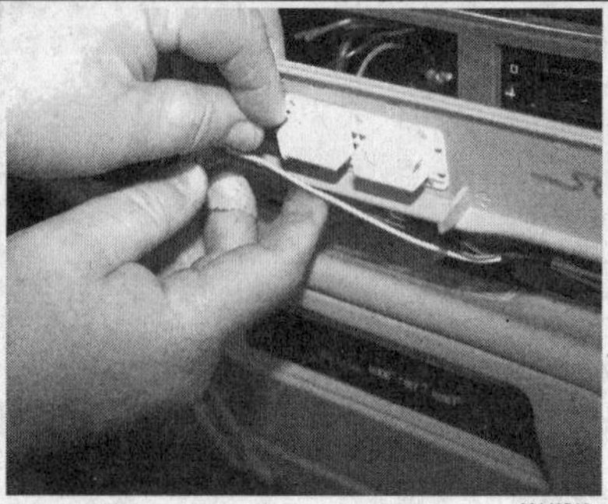
93140P03

Fig. 43 Unplug the sockets from the housings

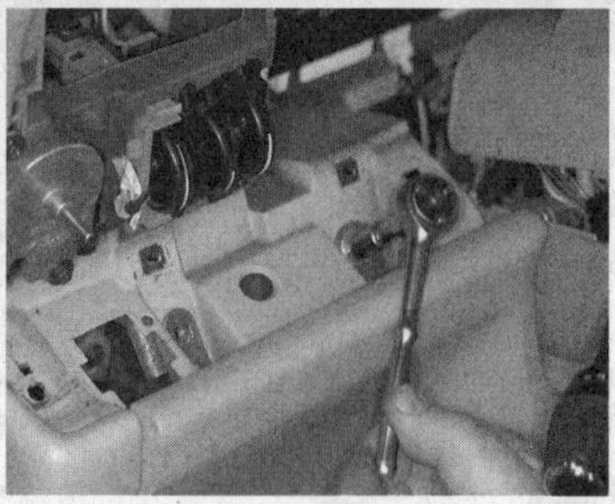
93146P09

Fig. 44 Unbolt the lower dash panel (knee brace) . . .

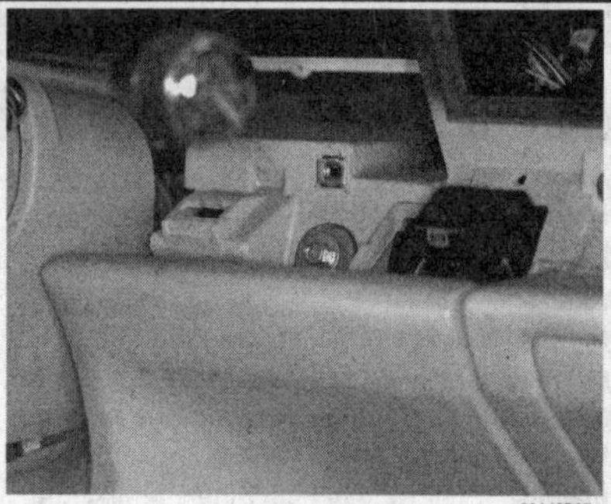
93146P07

Fig. 45 . . . on the left and right side of the steering column . . .

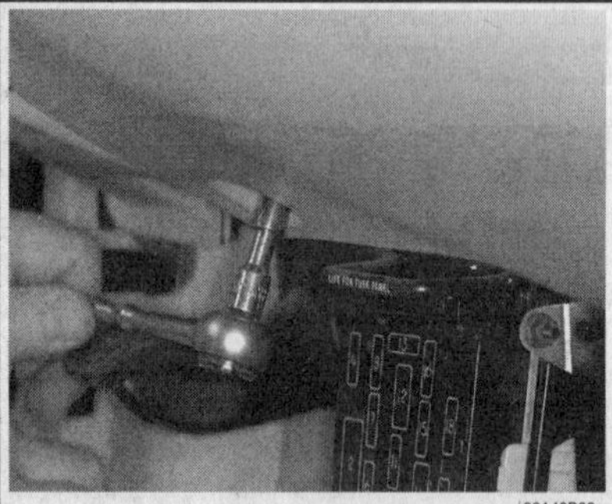
93146P06

Fig. 46 . . . and at the bottom of the panel . . .

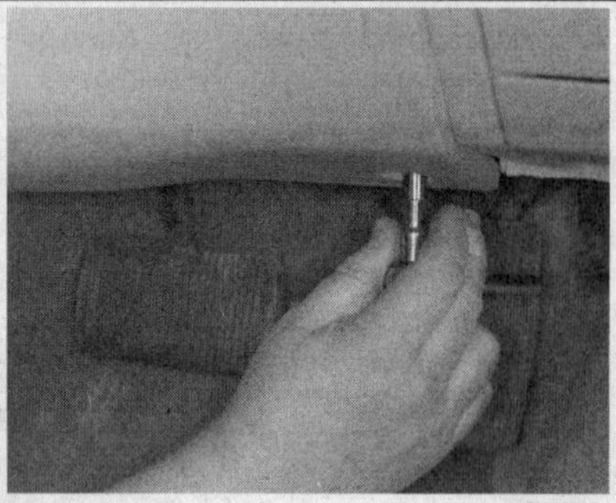
93146P20

Fig. 47 . . . on both sides of the column

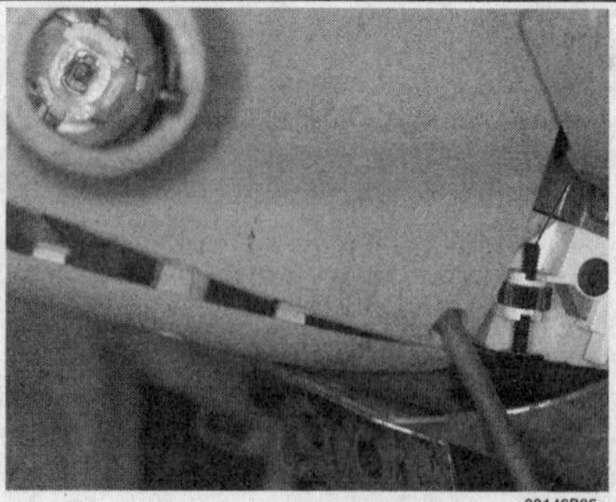
93146P05

Fig. 48 Remove the steering column shroud retaining screws and remove the shrouds

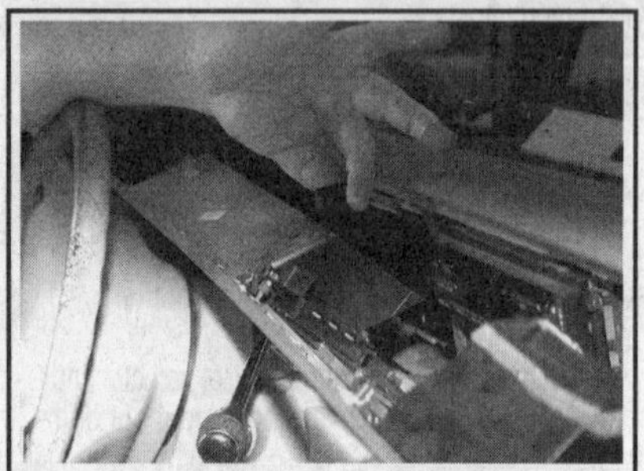
93140P59

Fig. 49 Remove the trim screws from the dash trim, unsnap the top and flip it down and away from the instrument cluster. Slide it out from behind the steering wheel

93146P22

Fig. 50 With the lower panel removed, you can disengage the PRNDL cable . . .

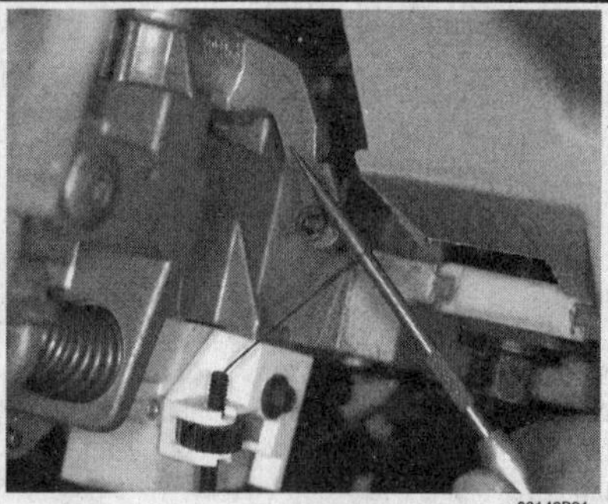
93146P21

Fig. 51 . . . using a seal pick or another thin tool, pick the cable off the stud

93146P23

Fig. 52 With the cable removed, the adjuster is now easy to access

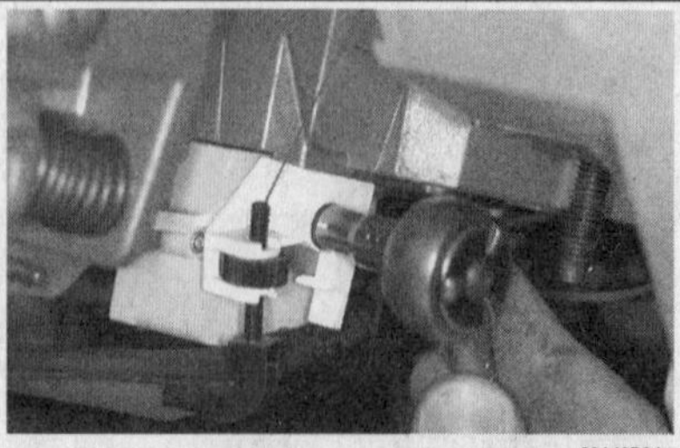
93146P24

Fig. 53 Remove the mounting screw, and release the adjuster from the column stand. Let it hang. Do not turn the adjusting star, and you won't have to adjust it when it is installed

93146P12

Fig. 54 Remove these two screws on the right side of the cluster . . .

93146P13

**Fig. 55 . . . and these two on the left side of the cluster**

93146P11

**Fig. 56 Pull the cluster forward and release the PRNDL display, unplug the connections from the rear of the cluster and remove the cluster**

**To install:**

19. Installation is the reversal of the removal procedure.
20. Connect the negative battery cable.

**➡The fuel computer internal fuel economy values will be re-initialized after the battery has been disconnected. There may be a noticeable change in AVE ECON (average economy) and DTE (distance to empty) calculations from this. Accuracy will improve gradually as the new fuel economy history is developed. This may take about 525 miles.**

#### Continental 1995–00

1. Disconnect the negative battery cable.
2. Turn the ignition switch to **RUN** and move the transmission range selector lever to low position. Turn the ignition OFF.
3. Remove the radio front control unit using the special radio tools.
4. Remove the two lower screws, then unsnap, and remove the instrument panel lower cover.
5. Unsnap and remove the driver's side and passenger side instrument panel center wood grain trim moulding.
6. Remove the plush pins, disconnect the courtesy lamp socket an remove the instrument panel insulator.
7. Remove the three screws, then unsnap, and remove he instrument panel steering column cover.
8. Remove the five screws and remove the instrument panel brace.
9. Loosen the steering column retaining nuts and lower the steering column.
10. Protect the upper bowl of the steering column trim with cloth or tape to avoid scratches during the instrument cluster removal.
11. Remove he five screws retaining the instrument panel finish panel, then remove the instrument panel finish panel.
12. Remove the six screws retaining the instrument cluster to the instrument panel.
13. Pull the driver's side side of the instrument cluster forward and disconnect the two electrical connectors at the rear of the instrument cluster.
14. On column shift models, disconnect the transmission range indicator assembly. Remove the instrument cluster.

**To install:**

15. Installlation is the reversal of the removal procedure.

#### Mark VII

1. Disconnect the negative battery cable.
2. Remove the instrument cluster finish panel, disconnecting the warning lamp module connectors.
3. Remove the instrument panel binnacle moulding.
4. Remove the five screws holding the mask to the back plate mounting. Do not remove the two top screws fastening the lens to the mask. Remove the lens and mask as an assembly.
5. Lift the main assembly from the backplate. The speedometer is permanently mounted to the main dial and the other gauges are mounted to the dial. Some effort may be required to pull quick connect terminals from the clips.

**To install:**

6. Install the quick connect terminals to the clips and position the main dial assembly onto the backplate. Ensure that the foam gasket under the indicator lamp baffle is correctly positioned in the backplate.
7. Install the lens and mask assembly and tighten the five mask to backplate mounting screws.
8. Install the instrument panel binnacle moulding.
9. Install the warning lamp module connectors and instrument cluster finish panel.
10. Connect the negative battery cable.

#### Mark VIII

**➡There is no speedometer cable required for this instrument cluster.**

1. Disconnect the negative battery cable.
2. Remove the instrument panel finish panel.
3. Remove the four cluster to panel retaining screws. Do not remove the screws securing the instrument cluster main lens and the instrument cluster mask to the instrument cluster back plate.
4. Rotate the instrument cluster face down and disconnect the instrument cluster connector.
5. Slide the instrument cluster to the right of the instrument panel opening and unhook on the back of he instrument cluster.
6. Remove the instrument cluster form the instrument panel,

**To install:**

7. Installation is the reversal of the removal process.

## Gauges

### REMOVAL & INSTALLATION

1. Disconnect the negative battery cable.
2. Remove the instrument cluster.
3. Remove the retaining screws for the instrument cluster lens and cover assembly. Remove the cover and lens.
4. Remove the retaining screws for the gauge or warning lamp to be replaced and remove the gauge or warning lamp.

**To install:**

5. Place the gauge or warning lamp into place and tighten the retaining screws.
6. Install the instrument cluster lens and cover assembly.
7. Install the instrument cluster.
8. Connect the negative battery cable.

# LIGHTING

## Headlights

All 1988–89Town Cars are equipped with sealed-beam halogen headlights. All 1990–99 vehicles are equipped with aerodynamically styled headlight bodies using replaceable halogen bulbs.

**⁂ CAUTION**

**The halogen headlight bulb contains gas under pressure. The bulb may shatter if the glass envelope is scratched or the bulb is dropped. Handle the bulb carefully. Grasp the bulb only by its plastic base. Avoid touching the glass envelope. Keep the bulb out of the reach of children.**

### REMOVAL & INSTALLATION

#### 1988–89 Town Car

1. Open the hood and from inside the engine compartment remove the three retainers attaching the headlight assembly to the grille opening panel.
2. Remove the headlight door mounting screws and remove the headlight door.
3. Remove the 4 retainer ring screws and remove the retainer ring from the headlight.
4. Pull the headlight bulb forward and detach the wiring connector.

**To install:**

5. Attach the wiring connector to the headlight bulb and place the bulb in position, locating the bulb glass tabs in the positioning slots.
6. Attach the bulb retainer ring to the assembly with the retainer ring screws.

7. Install the headlight door and secure with the screws.
8. Check the headlight bulb aim and adjust as necessary.

### All Vehicles With Halogen Bulbs

➧ **See Figures 57 thru 65**

1. Make sure the headlight switch is in the OFF position.
2. Lift the hood and remove the trim panel located above the headlight bulb, where necessary.
3. Rotate the bulb retainer counterclockwise (when viewed from the rear) about an ⅛–¼ turn.
4. Carefully remove the bulb from the socket in the reflector by gently pulling straight out of the socket. Do not rotate the bulb during removal.
5. Detach the electrical connector from the bulb.

**To install:**

6. Attach the electrical connector to the bulb.
7. Insert the glass envelope of the bulb into the socket while aligning the locking tabs.
8. Rotate the bulb retainer ¼ turn to lock it in.
9. Turn the headlights on and check for proper operation.

**➡A properly aimed headlight normally does not need to be re-aimed after bulb installation. A burned out bulb should not be removed from the headlight reflector until just before a replacement bulb is to be installed. Removal of a bulb for an extended period of time may allow contaminants to enter the headlight body and affect the performance of the headlight. The headlight bulb should be energized only while it is contained within the headlight body.**

## AIMING THE HEADLIGHTS

➧ **See Figures 66, 67 and 68**

On 1989–91 vehicles, the headlights can be aimed using the adjusting screws located above and to the side of the headlight bulbs. A rough adjustment can be made while shining the headlights on a wall or on the rear of another vehicle, but headlight adjustment should really be made using proper headlight aiming equipment.

On 1992–98 vehicles, the aerodynamically styled

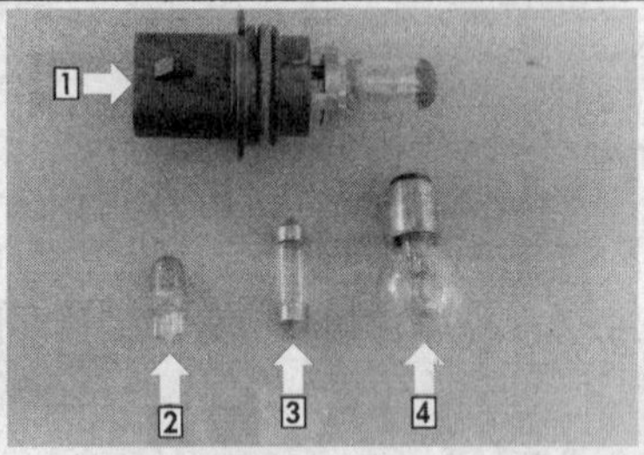


1. Halogen headlight bulb
2. Side marker light bulb
3. Dome light bulb
4. Turn signal/brake light bulb

TCCA6P11

**Fig. 57 Examples of various types of automotive light bulbs**

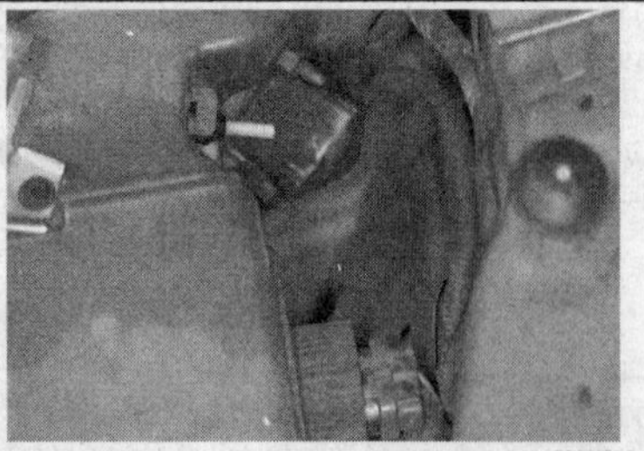

93146P59

**Fig. 58 This is the view of the headlamp assembly looking straight down in front of the radiator support. There is not a great deal of clearance to work in this vicinity, but it is manageable**

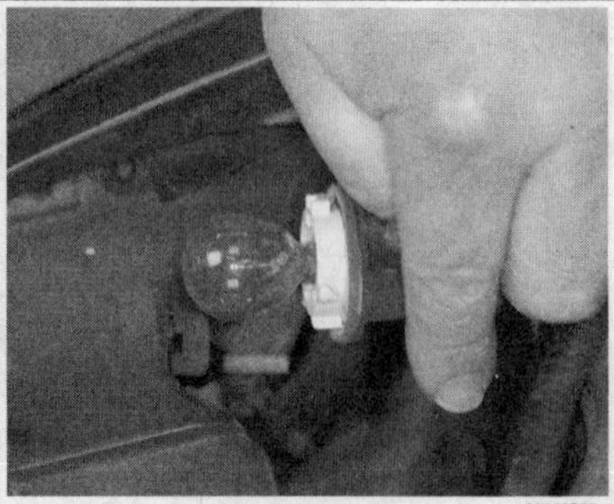

93146P58

**Fig. 59 You can get the front turn signal bulb out by giving it a half-twist**

93146P56

**Fig. 60 Removing the locking ring on the headlamp halogen bulb . . .**

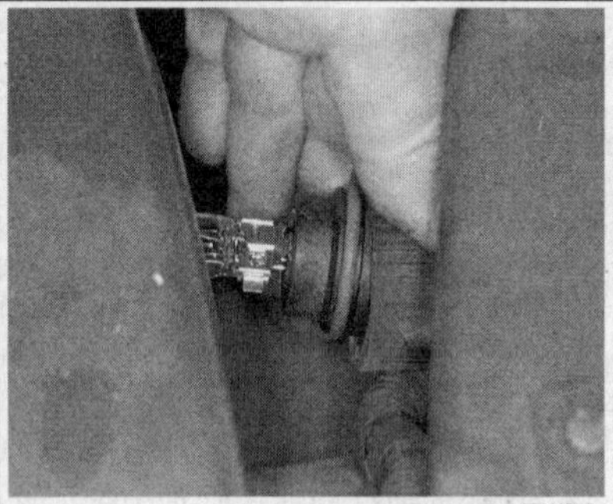

93146P57

**Fig. 61 . . . allows you to unplug the bulb**

93146P55

**Fig. 62 This is the view of the headlamp housing from the back. Notice the locking clip**

93146P54

**Fig. 63 The locking clip can be removed to facilitate easy removal of the headlamp assembly**

93146P53

**Fig. 64 The headlamp assemblies are marked for left or passenger side installation. This one is passenger side**

93146P52

**Fig. 65 The retaining clip removal and installation is accomplished with a special tool. If the clips are in good shape, they can be removed with an inside snap ring pliers. But be ready to replace them if they distort**

headlights necessitate the use of headlight aiming kit 107–00003 or equivalent. The adjustable aimer adapters provided in the kit must be used to aim the headlights. Adjustment aimer adapter positions are molded into the bottom edge of the headlight lens. Set and lock the adjustable adapters, attach each adapter to its mechanical aimer and aim the headlights according to the instructions in the kit.

Headlight aim adjustment should be made with the fuel tank approximately half full, the vehicle unloaded and the trunk empty, except for the spare tire and jacking equipment. Make sure all tires are inflated to the proper pressure.

The headlights must be properly aimed to provide the best, safest road illumination. The lights should be checked for proper aim and adjusted as necessary. Certain state and local authorities have requirements for headlight aiming; these should be checked before adjustment is made.

**CAUTION**

**About once a year, when the headlights are replaced or any time front end work is performed on your vehicle, the headlight should be accurately aimed by a reputable repair shop using the proper equipment. Headlights not properly aimed can make it virtually impossible to see and may blind other drivers on the road, possibly causing an accident. Note that the following procedure is a temporary fix, until you can take your vehicle to a repair shop for a proper adjustment.**

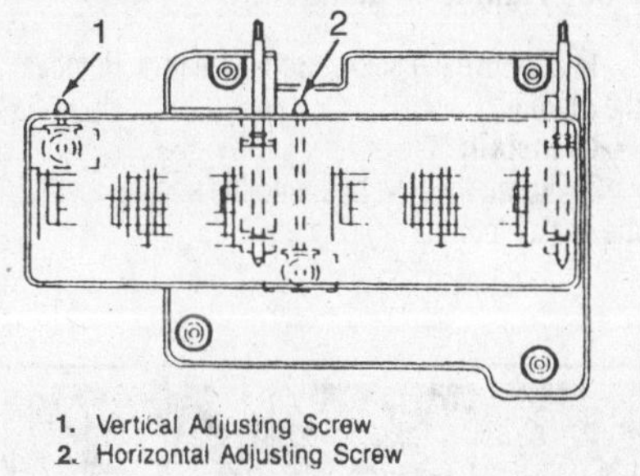


**Fig. 66 Example of headlight adjustment screw location for composite headlamps**

Headlight adjustment may be temporarily made using a wall, as described below, or on the rear of another vehicle. When adjusted, the lights should not glare in oncoming car or truck windshields, nor should they illuminate the passenger compartment of vehicles driving in front of you. These adjustments are rough and should always be fine-tuned by a repair shop which is equipped with headlight aiming tools. Improper adjustments may be both dangerous and illegal.

For most of the vehicles covered by this manual, horizontal and vertical aiming of each sealed beam unit is provided by two adjusting screws which move the retaining ring and adjusting plate against the tension of a coil spring. There is no adjustment for focus; this is done during headlight manufacturing.

**➡Because the composite headlight assembly is bolted into position, no adjustment should be necessary or possible. Some applications, however, may be bolted to an adjuster plate or may be retained by adjusting screws. If so, follow this procedure when adjusting the lights, BUT always have the adjustment checked by a reputable shop.**

Before removing the headlight bulb or disturbing the headlamp in any way, note the current settings in order to ease headlight adjustment upon reassembly. If the high or low beam setting of the old lamp still works, this can be done using the wall of a garage or a building:

1. Park the vehicle on a level surface, with the fuel tank about ½ full and with the vehicle empty of all extra cargo (unless normally carried). The vehicle should be facing a wall which is no less than 6 feet (1.8m) high and 12 feet (3.7m) wide. The front of the vehicle should be about 25 feet from the wall.
2. If aiming is to be performed outdoors, it is advisable to wait until dusk in order to properly see the headlight beams on the wall. If done in a garage, darken the area around the wall as much as possible by closing shades or hanging cloth over the windows.
3. Turn the headlights **ON** and mark the wall at the center of each light's low beam, then switch on the bright lights and mark the center of each light's high beam. A short length of masking tape that is visible from the front of the vehicle may be used. Although marking all four positions is advisable, marking one position from each light should be sufficient.
4. If neither beam on one side is working, and if another like-sized vehicle is available, park the second one in the exact spot where the vehicle was and mark the beams using the same-side light. Then switch the vehicles so the one to be aimed is back in the original spot. It must be parked no closer to or farther away from the wall than the second vehicle.
5. Perform any necessary repairs, but make sure the vehicle is not moved, or is returned to the exact spot from which the lights were marked. Turn the headlights **ON** and adjust the beams to match the marks on the wall.
6. Have the headlight adjustment checked as soon as possible by a reputable repair shop.

## Signal and Marker Lights

### REMOVAL & INSTALLATION

#### Turn Signal and Brake Lights

See Figure 69

1. Depending on the vehicle and bulb application, either unscrew and remove the lens or disengage the bulb and socket assembly from the rear of the lens housing.
2. To remove a light bulb with retaining pins from its socket, grasp the bulb, then gently depress and twist it 1/8 turn counterclockwise, and pull it from the socket.

**To install:**

3. Before installing a light bulb into the socket, ensure that all electrical contact surfaces are free of corrosion or dirt.

**➡Before installing the light bulb, note the positions of the two retaining pins on the bulb. They will likely be at different heights on the bulb, to ensure that the bulb is installed correctly. If, when installing the bulb, it does not turn easily, do not force it. Remove the bulb and rotate it 180 degrees from its former position, then reinsert it into the bulb socket.**

4. Insert the light bulb into the socket and, while depressing the bulb, twist it 1/8 turn clockwise until the two pins on the light bulb are properly engaged in the socket.
5. To ensure that the replacement bulb functions properly, activate the applicable switch to illuminate the bulb which was just replaced. If the replacement light bulb does not illuminate, either it

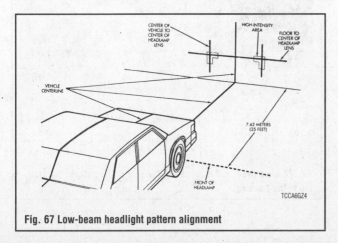

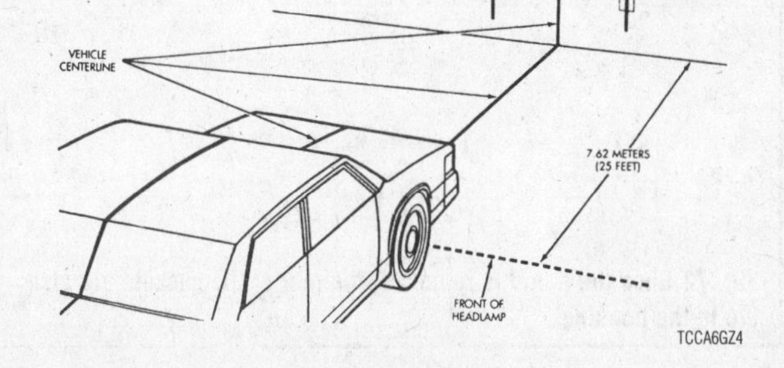


**Fig. 67 Low-beam headlight pattern alignment**

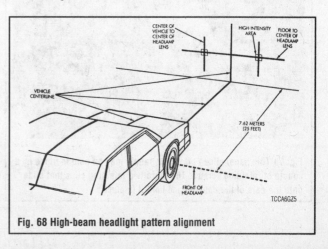

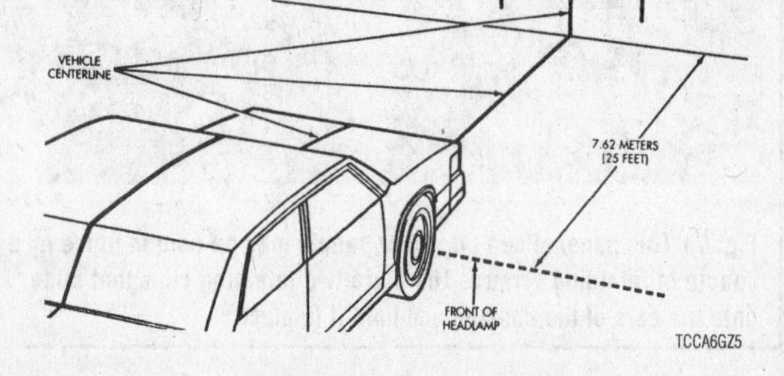


**Fig. 68 High-beam headlight pattern alignment**

too is faulty or there is a problem in the bulb circuit or switch. Correct if necessary.

6. If applicable, install the socket and bulb assembly into the rear of the lens housing; otherwise, install the lens over the bulb.

### High-mount Brake Light and Side Marker Light

**See Figures 70 thru 75**

1. Disengage the bulb and socket assembly from the lens housing.
2. Gently grasp the light bulb and pull it straight out of the socket.

**To install:**

3. Before installing the light bulb into the socket, ensure that all electrical contact surfaces are free of corrosion or dirt.
4. Line up the base of the light bulb with the socket, then insert the light bulb into the socket until it is fully seated.
5. To ensure that the replacement bulb functions properly, activate the applicable switch to illuminate the bulb which was just replaced. If the replacement light bulb does not illuminate, either it too is faulty or there is a problem in the bulb circuit or switch. Correct as necessary.
6. Install the socket and bulb assembly into the lens housing.

### Rear Turn Signal, Brake and Parking Lights

**See Figures 76 and 77**

1. Open the trunk and remove the luggage compartment trim.
2. Remove the eight nuts retaining the reflector to lower back of luggage compartment
3. Remove the rear panel reflector assembly from the vehicle.

**To install:**

4. Installation is the reversal of the removal procedure.

### Dome Light

**See Figures 78, 79, 80, 81 and 82**

1. Using a small prytool, carefully remove the cover lens from the lamp assembly.
2. Remove the bulb from its retaining clip contacts. If the bulb has tapered ends, gently depress the spring clip/metal contact and disengage the light bulb, then pull it free of the two metal contacts.

**To install:**

3. Before installing the light bulb into the metal contacts, ensure that all electrical conducting surfaces are free of corrosion or dirt.
4. Position the bulb between the two metal contacts. If the contacts have small holes, be sure that the tapered ends of the bulb are situated in them.
5. To ensure that the replacement bulb functions properly, activate the applicable switch to illuminate the bulb which was just replaced. If the replacement light bulb does not illuminate, either it is faulty or there is a problem in the bulb circuit or switch. Correct as necessary.
6. Install the cover lens until its retaining tabs are properly engaged.

### License Plate Lights

#### TOWN CAR

1. Remove the two screws retaining the lamp assembly to the rear bumper/ bumper cover.
2. Pull the lamp assembly from the bumper/bumper cover.
3. Grasp and twist the socket ⅛turn counterclockwise and remove the socket from the lamp housing.

#### CONTINENTAL AND MARK

**See Figures 83 and 84**

1. Remove the socket from the lamp. Remove the old bulb.

**To install:**

2. Install the new bulb into the socket. Install the socket into the lamp.

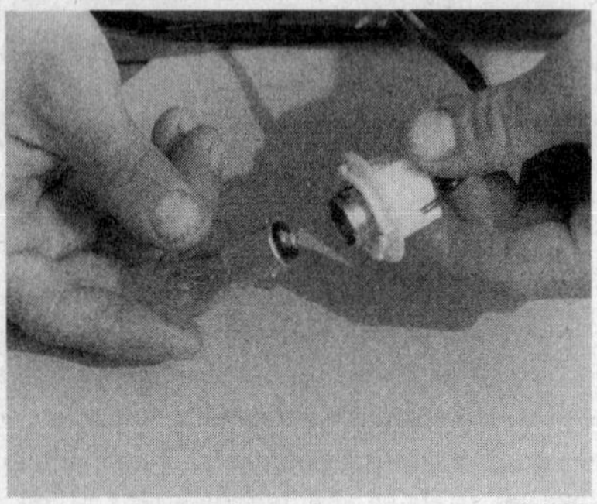

TCCA6P13

**Fig. 69 Depress and twist this type of bulb counterclockwise, then pull the bulb straight from its socket**

93146P65

**Fig. 70 This is the finish panel that covers the high-mount brake light assembly. It is a removable housing**

93146P64

**Fig. 71 This panel slides off. Other panels may be held in place by a couple of retaining screws. There are two retaining clips that slide onto the ears of the housing and hold it in place**

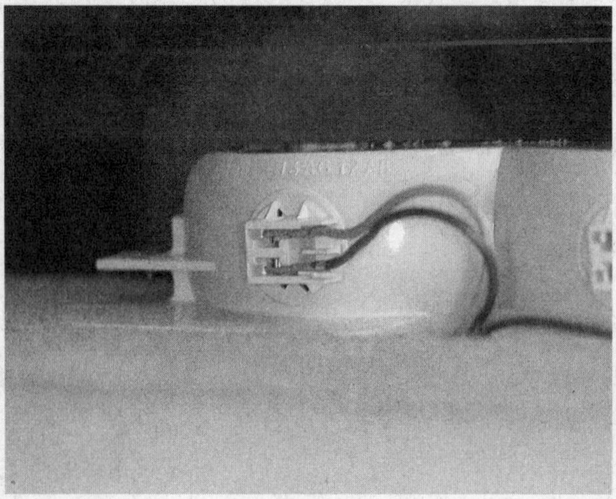

93146P61

**Fig. 72 Once the panel is removed, the rear of the sockets are visible in the housing**

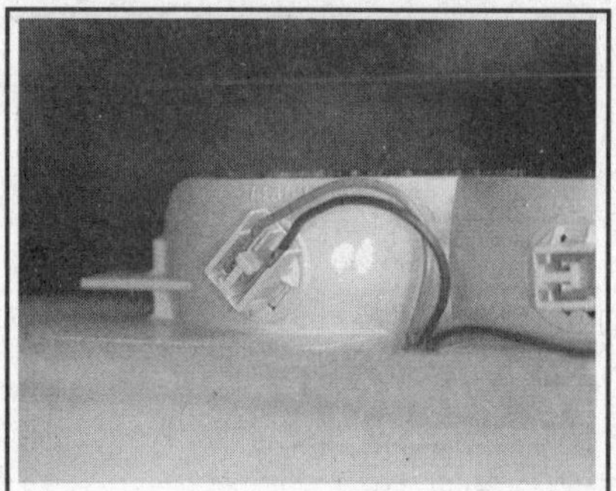

93146P62

Fig. 73 Give the sockets a quarter twist . . .

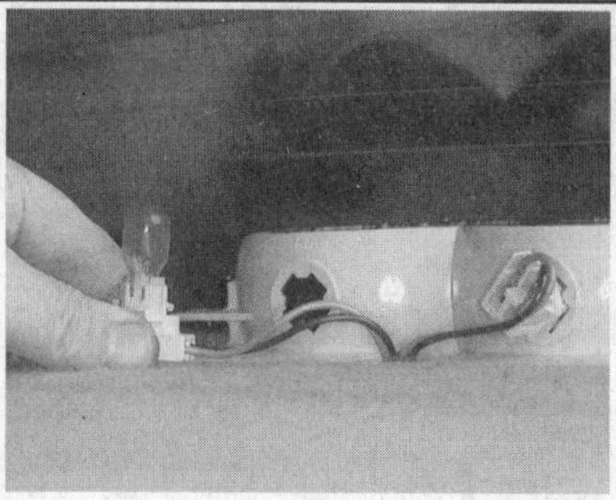

93146P63

Fig. 74 . . . to extract them from the housing. The bulbs pull straight out

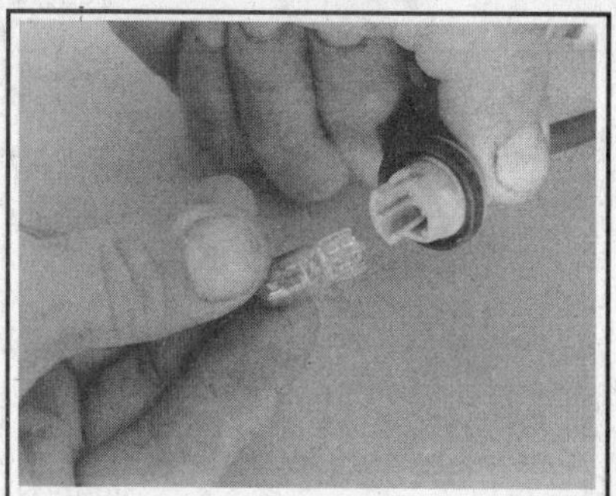

TCCA6P14

Fig. 75 Simply pull this side marker light bulb straight from its socket

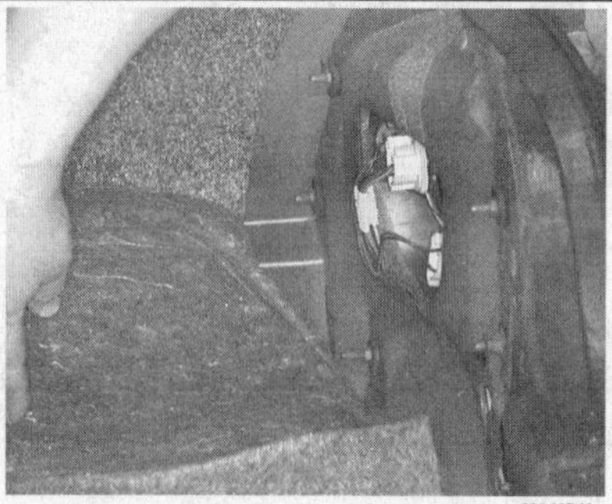

93146P43

Fig. 76 Pull the trunk trim away from the lamp housing assembly

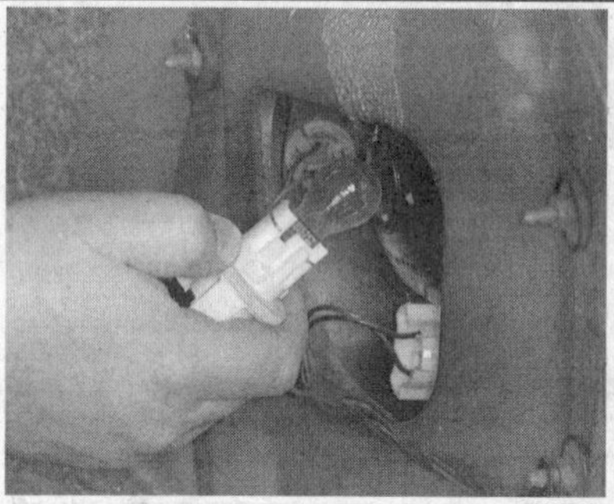

93146P44

Fig. 77 Twist the socket assembly and remove it from the housing

TCCA6P15

Fig. 78 Disengage the spring clip that retains one tapered end of this dome light bulb, then withdraw the bulb

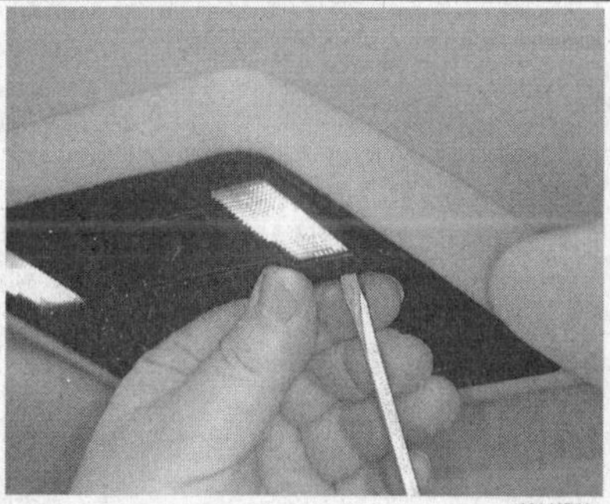

93146P80

Fig. 79 Use a small pry tool to "pop" out the lens assembly

93146P81

Fig. 80 The lens assembly comes free from the housing and reveals the dome light bulb

93146P82

Fig. 81 The dome light sits in its own special socket and housing. Easier to remove if you use a long nose pliers

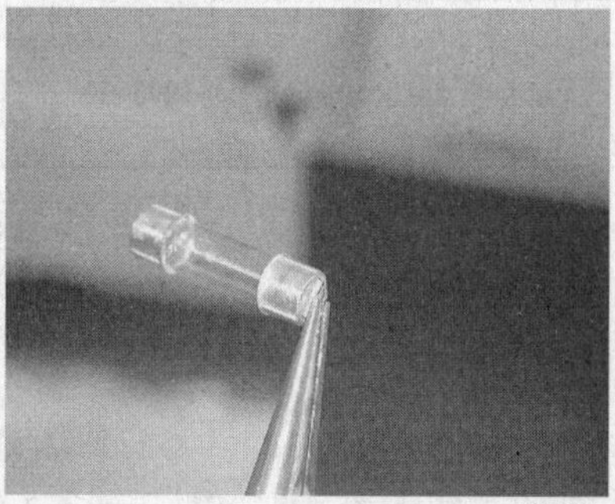

93146P83

Fig. 82 Be careful in handling the bulb, they get very hot very quickly!

93146P45

Fig. 83 This is the location of the license plate lamps

93146P46

Fig. 84 Remove the three screws to gain access to the bulbs. The bulbs pull straight out

| Function | Trade number |
|---|---|
| **Exterior lights** | |
| Tail lamp, brakelamp, turn lamp | 3157 |
| Backup lamp | 3156 |
| Side marker lamp | 194 |
| Front park, turn lamp | 3157NA** |
| Headlamp—Aero | 9004* |
| Cornering lamp | 3156 |
| Fog lamp | H-2 |
| License plate lamp | 168 |
| High mounted brakelamp | 912 |
| **Interior lights** | |
| Luggage compartment lamp | 912 |
| Visor vanity lamp | 168 |
| Door courtesy lamp | 904 |
| Engine compartment lamp | 912 |
| Front overhead map/courtesy lamp | 912 |
| Reading lamp — rear | 912 |
| Dual floorwell lamp | 906 |
| Ashtray lamp (Armrest) | 1893 |
| **Instrument panel lights** | |
| Glove box | 194 |
| Instrument courtesy lamps | 89 |
| Warning lights (all) | 37 |
| Radio illumination | • |
| Speedometer illumination | 168 |
| "PRN(D)D1" bulb | 168 |
| Tripminder® illumination | 194 |
| High beam indicator | 37 |
| Turn signal indicator | 194 |
| Climate control panel lights | 37 |
| Instrument panel lights | 194 |
| Headlamp nomenclature | 37 |
| Autolamp nomenclature | 1816 |
| Ashtray lamp (console) | 1815 |
| Cigarette lighter lamp | 1445 |

*Use only original equipment bulbs or equivalent, if you do not, it may result in false warning or no headlamp burnout warning from the message center.

**NA means Natural Amber

• Refer bulb replacement to a Ford authorized radio service center.

93146G01

**Light bulb application chart—1988-92 Mark VII.**

| Function | Trade number |
|---|---|
| **Exterior lights** | |
| Tail lamp, brakelamp, turn lamp | 3157 |
| Backup lamp | 3156 |
| Side marker lamp - front | 194 NA** |
| Front park, turn lamp | 3157NA** |
| Headlamp (hi & lo) | 9004* |
| Cornering lamp | 2456 |
| License plate lamp | 194 |
| High-mounted brakelamp | 912 |
| **Interior lights** | |
| Luggage compartment lamp | 906 |
| Map lamp | 211-2 |
| Visor vanity lamp | 168 |
| Door courtesy lamp | 168 |
| Engine compartment lamp | 906 |
| Dual floorwell lamps | 906 |
| Armrest ashtray lamp | 161 |
| **Instrument panel lights** | |
| Glove compartment | 194 |
| Warning lights (all) | 37 |
| Radio illumination | • |
| Compact disk illumination (opt.) | •• |
| High beam indicator | 194 |
| Turn signal indicator | 194 |
| Low fuel warning light | 194 |
| I/P ashtray lamp | 161 |
| Cigarette lighter lamp | 1445 |
| Instrument panel lights | 194 |
| Headlamp nomenclature | 1816 |
| Autolamp nomenclature | 1816 |
| Automatic climate control | 161 |
| "PRNDL" | 37 |

*Use only original equipment bulbs or equivalent, if you do not, it may result in false warning or no headlamp burnout warning from the message center.

**NA means Natural Amber

• Refer bulb replacement to Ford authorized radio service center

•• Refer bulb replacement to manufacturer (Sony)

93146G02

**Light bulb application chart—1988-90 Town Car**

| Function | Trade number |
|---|---|
| **Exterior illumination** | |
| Backup lamp | 3156 |
| Cornering lamp | 3156 |
| Headlamp | 9004 |
| High-mount brakelamp | 921 |
| License plate lamp | 168 |
| Luggage compartment lamp | 912 |
| Side marker—front lamp | 194 |
| Side marker—rear lamp | 168 |
| Turn signal and park lamp—front | 3157NA*** |
| Turn signal, stoplamp and taillamp—rear | 3157NA*** |
| Under hood lamp | 912 |
| **Instrument panel** | |
| EATC | * |
| Air bag readiness light | 37 |
| Anti-lock warning lamp | 37 |
| Anti-theft warning lamp | 37 |
| Ash receptacle | 1445 |
| Clock | (*) |
| Cluster illumination | * |
| Cluster control button | 37 |
| Compact disc player | ** |
| Glove compartment | 194 |
| Headlamp switch nomenclature | 37 |
| Heated windshield switch nomenclature | 37 |
| Message center control buttons | * |
| Rear window defrost switch nomenclature | 37 |
| Radio | ** |
| Warning lights (cluster) | 37 |

*Refer bulb replacement to dealer.

**Refer bulb replacement to a Ford authorized radio service center.

***NA means natural amber.

93146G08

**Light bulb application chart—1988-92 Continental**

| Function | Trade number |
|---|---|
| **Exterior lights** | |
| Tail lamp, brakelamp, turn lamp | 3157 |
| Backup lamp | 3156 |
| Side marker lamp - front | 194 NA** |
| Front park, turn lamp | 3157NA** |
| Headlamp (hi & lo) | 9004 |
| Cornering lamp | 3156 |
| License plate lamp | 194 |
| High-mounted brakelamp | 912 |
| **Interior lights** | |
| Luggage compartment lamp | 906 |
| Map lamp | 211-2 |
| Visor vanity lamp | 168 |
| Door courtesy lamp | 904 |
| Engine compartment lamp | 906 |
| Dual floorwell lamps | 906 |
| **Instrument panel lights** | |
| Glove compartment | 194 |
| Rear window defroster switch*** | |
| Heated windshield switch*** | |
| Fuel door release switch*** | |
| Warning lights (all) (std.) | 194 |
| Radio illumination | • |
| Compact disc illumination (opt.) | •• |
| High beam indicator (std.) | 194 |
| Turn signal indicator (std.) | 194 |
| Low fuel warning light (std.) | 194 |
| I/P ashtray lamp | 161 |
| Cigarette lighter lamp | 1445 |
| Instrument panel lights | 194 |
| Headlamp nomenclature | 1816 |
| Autolamp nomenclature | 1816 |
| Automatic climate control | 161 |
| "PRNDL" (std./elect.) | 194/37 |

**NA means Natural Amber

***Refer bulb replacement to a Ford or Lincoln-Mercury dealer.

• Refer bulb replacement to Ford authorized radio service center

•• Refer bulb replacement to manufacturer (Sony)

93146G06

**Light bulb application chart—1991-92 Town Car**

| Function | Trade number |
|---|---|
| **Exterior illumination** | |
| Backup lamp | 3156 |
| Cornering lamp | 3156 |
| Headlamp | 9004 |
| High-mount brakelamp | 921 |
| License plate lamp | 168 |
| Luggage compartment lamp | 912 |
| Side marker—front lamp | 194 |
| Side marker—rear lamp | 168 |
| Turn signal and park lamp—front | 3157NA*** |
| Turn signal, stoplamp and taillamp—rear | 3157NA*** |
| Under hood lamp | 912 |
| **Instrument panel** | |
| Electronic automatic temperature control | * |
| Air bag readiness light | 37 |
| Anti-lock warning lamp | 37 |
| Anti-theft warning lamp | 37 |
| Ash receptacle | 1445 |
| Clock | (*) |
| Cluster illumination | * |
| Cluster control button | 37 |
| Compact disc player | ** |
| Glove compartment | 194 |
| Headlamp switch nomenclature | 37 |
| Message center control buttons | * |
| "PRNDL" bulb (floor console) | 194 |
| Rear window defrost switch nomenclature | 37 |
| Radio | ** |
| Warning lights (cluster) | 37 |

*Refer bulb replacement to dealer.

**Refer bulb replacement to a Ford authorized radio service center.

***NA means natural amber.

93146G03

**Light bulb application chart—1993-00 Continental**

| Function | Trade number |
|---|---|
| **Exterior lights** | |
| Tail lamp, brakelamp, turn lamp | 3157 |
| Backup lamp | 3156 |
| Side marker lamp - front | 194 NA** |
| Front park, turn lamp | 3157NA** |
| Headlamp (hi & lo) | 9004 |
| Cornering lamp | 3156 |
| License plate lamp | 194 |
| High-mounted brakelamp | 912 |
| **Interior lights** | |
| Luggage compartment lamp | 906 |
| Map lamp | 211-2 |
| Visor vanity lamp | 168 |
| Door courtesy lamp | 904 |
| Engine compartment lamp | 906 |
| **Instrument panel lights** | |
| Glove compartment | 194 |
| Rear window defroster switch*** | |
| Heated windshield switch*** | |
| Fuel door release switch*** | |
| Warning lights (all) (std.) | 194 |
| Radio illumination | • |
| Compact disc illumination (opt.) | •• |
| High beam indicator (std.) | 194 |
| Turn signal indicator (std.) | 194 |
| Low fuel warning light (std.) | 194 |
| I/P ashtray lamp | 161 |
| Cigarette lighter lamp | 1445 |
| Instrument panel lights | 194 |
| Headlamp nomenclature | 1816 |
| Autolamp nomenclature | 1816 |
| Automatic climate control | 161 |
| "PRNDL" (std./elect.) | 194/37 |

**NA means Natural Amber

***Refer bulb replacement to a Ford or Lincoln-Mercury dealer.

• Refer bulb replacement to Ford authorized radio service center

•• Refer bulb replacement to manufacturer (Sony)

93146G04

**Light bulb application chart—1993-00 Town Car**

| Function | Trade number |
|---|---|
| **Exterior lights front** | |
| Headlamps low beam | 9005 |
| Headlamps high beam | 9005 |
| Park and turn lamp | 3457NA* |
| Side marker lamp | 194 |
| Cornering lamp | 3156 |
| **Exterior lights rear** | |
| Tail lamp, brakelamp, turn lamp | 3357 |
| Side marker | 916 |
| Backup lamp | 3156 |
| License plate lamp | 168 |
| High-mounted brakelamp | 3156 |
| Decklid reflector | 168 |
| **Interior lights** | |
| Luggage compartment lamp | 912 |
| Engine compartment lamp | 912 |
| Dome/map (with moon roof) | 906 |
| Dome/map lamp | |
| Dome | 906 |
| Map | 168 |
| Sun visor lighted mirror | ••• |
| Front door courtesy lamp | 168 |

| Function | Trade number |
|---|---|
| Dual floorwell lamps | 168 |
| Rear reading/courtesy | 912 |
| **Instrument panel lights** | |
| Glove compartment | 194 |
| Ashtray lamp (console) | 161 |
| Headlamp switch illumination | 37 |
| Instrument courtesy lamps | 89 |
| Rear window defroster switch | •• |
| Warning lights (all) | 37 |
| Radio illumination | • |
| Speedometer illumination | 194 |
| "PRND21" bulb | 168 |
| High beam indicator | 37 |
| Turn signal indicator | 37 |
| Climate Control panel lights | 37 |
| Instrument panel lights | 194 |
| Headlamp nomenclature | 37 |

*NA means Natural Amber.
• Refer bulb replacement to a Ford-authorized radio service center.
•• Refer replacement to a Ford or Lincoln-Mercury dealer.
••• E9SZ-13466-B (Part No.)

93146G05

**Light bulb application chart—1993–98 Mark VIII**

# CIRCUIT PROTECTION

## Fuses

**See Figures 85, 86, 87 and 88**

All vehicles are equipped with a fuse panel located on the left side of the lower instrument panel. In addition, 1992–98 vehicles are equipped with a combination fuse/relay panel called the "engine compartment fuse box" which is located in the vicinity of the battery in the engine compartment.

### REPLACEMENT

1. Locate the fuse panel and remove the cover, if necessary.
2. Look through the clear side of the fuse in question, to see if the metal wire inside is separated. If the wire is separated, the fuse is blown and must be replaced.
3. Remove the fuse by pulling it from its cavity; no special tools are required.
4. Replace the blown fuse only with one having the same amp rating for that particular circuit. Push the fuse straight in until the fuse seats fully in the cavity.

## Fusible Links

Fuse links are used to protect the main wiring harness and selected branches from complete burn-out, should a short circuit or electrical overload occur. A fuse link is a short length of insulated wire, integral with the engine compartment wiring harness. It is several wire gauges smaller than the circuit it protects and generally located in-line directly from the positive terminal of the battery.

Production fuse links are color coded as follows:

- Gray: 12 gauge
- Dark Green: 14 gauge
- Black: 16 gauge
- Brown: 18 gauge
- Dark Blue: 20 gauge

When a heavy current flows, such as when a booster battery is connected incorrectly or when a short to ground occurs in the wiring harness, the fuse link burns out and protects the alternator or wiring.

A burned out fuse link may have bare wire ends protruding from the insulation, or it may have only expanded or bubbled insulation with illegible identification. When it is hard to determine if the fuse link is burned out, perform the continuity test:

1. Make sure the battery is okay, then turn on the headlights or an accessory. If the headlights or accessory do not work, the fuse link is probably burned out.
2. If equipped with more than one fuse link, use the same procedure as in Step 1 to test each link separately.

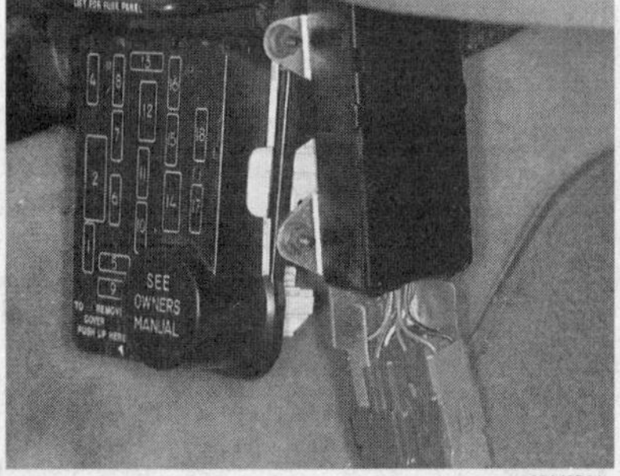


93146P01

**Fig. 85 This fuse panel will actually fold down to give you easier access to the fuses and flashers**

93146P48

**Fig. 86 The cover for the engine compartment fuse box is easily removable. The engine compartment fuse box, with its fuses and relays, takes the place of the bundle of fusible links**

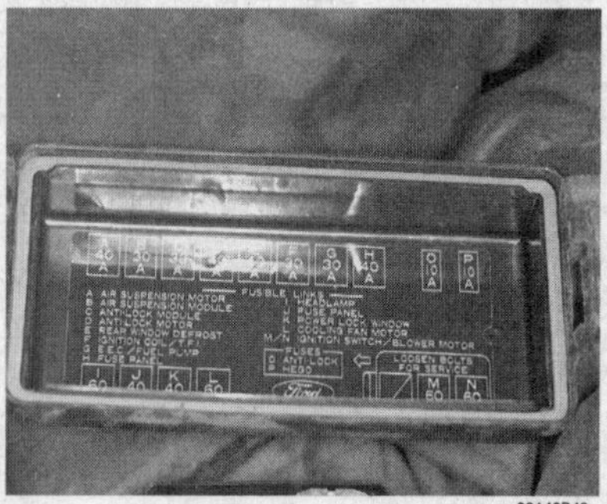

93146P49

**Fig. 87 The inside of the lid gives you the explanation of the fuse locations**

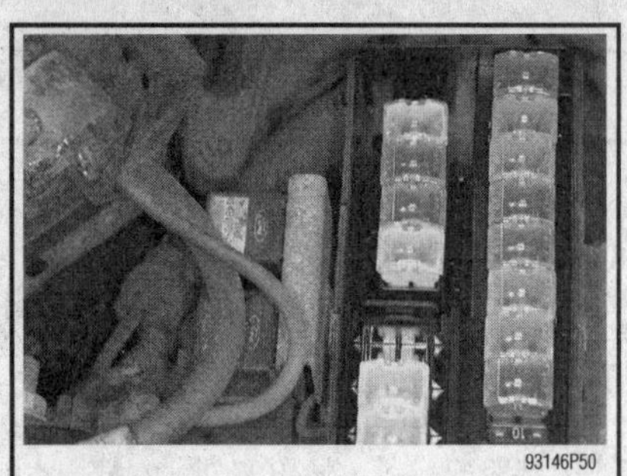


**Fig. 88 This gives you the view of all the Maxi Fuse® locations in the box. It is easy to see if any fuses are "blown" with a bright light**

3. To test the fuse link that protects the alternator, make sure the battery is okay, then check with a voltmeter for voltage at the BAT terminal of the alternator. No voltage indicates that the fuse link is probably burned out.

## REPLACEMENT

**See Figures 89, 90, 91, 92 and 93**

When replacing a fuse link, always make sure the replacement fuse link is a duplicate of the one removed with respect to gauge, length and insulation. Original equipment and original equipment specification replacement fuse links have insulation that is flame proof. Do not fabricate a fuse link from ordinary wire because the insulation may not be flame proof.

If a circuit protected by a fuse link becomes inoperative, inspect for a blown fuse link. If the fuse link wire insulation is burned or opened, disconnect the feed as close as possible behind the splice in the harness. If the damaged fuse link is between 2 splices (weld points in the harness), cut out the damaged portion as close as possible to the weld points.

Replace the fuse link as follows:

1. To service a 2-link group when only one link has blown and the other link is not damaged, proceed as follows:
   a. Disconnect the negative battery cable.
   b. Cut out the blown fusible link (2 places).
   c. Position the correct eyelet type service fusible link with the bare end to the correct size wire connector and crimp to the wire ends.
   d. Heat the splice insulation until the tubing shrinks and adhesive flows from each end of the connector.
   e. Connect the negative battery cable.
2. To service a fuse link in a multi-feed or single circuit, proceed as follows:
   a. Disconnect the negative battery cable.
   b. Determine which circuit is damaged, its location and the cause of the open fuse link. If the damaged fuse link is one of 3 fed by a common number 10 or 12 gauge feed wire, determine the specific affected circuit.
   c. Cut the damaged fuse link from the wiring harness and discard. If the fuse link is one of 3 circuits fed by a single feed wire, cut it out of the harness at each splice end and discard.
   d. Obtain the proper fuse link and butt connectors for attaching the fuse link to the harness.
   e. Strip 5/16in. (7.6mm) of insulation from the wire ends and insert into the proper size wire connector. Crimp and heat the splice insulation until the tubing shrinks and adhesive flows from each end of the connector.
   f. To replace a fuse link on a single circuit in a harness, cut out the damaged portion. Strip approximately ½ in. (12.7mm) of insulation from the 2 wire ends and attach the correct size fuse link to each wire end with the proper gauge

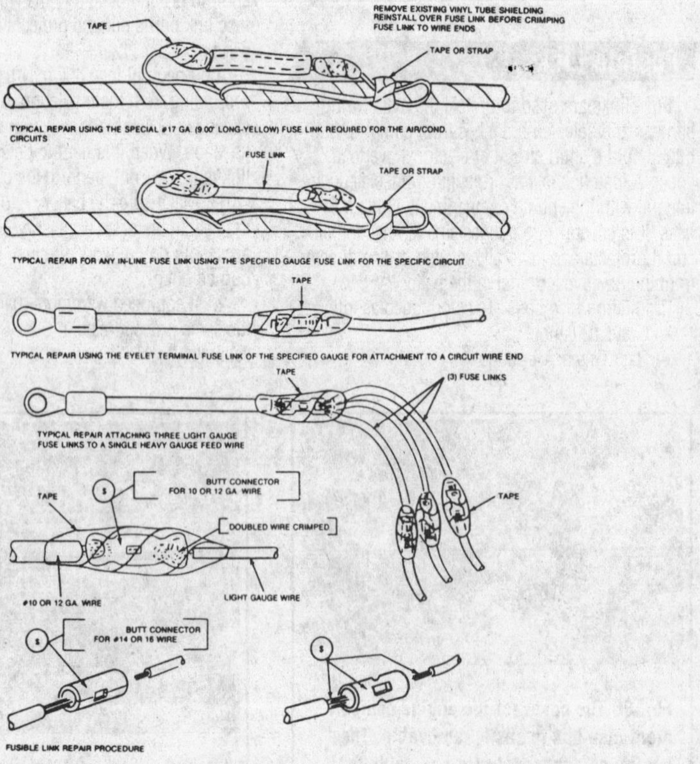


**Fig. 89 General fusible link repair procedures**

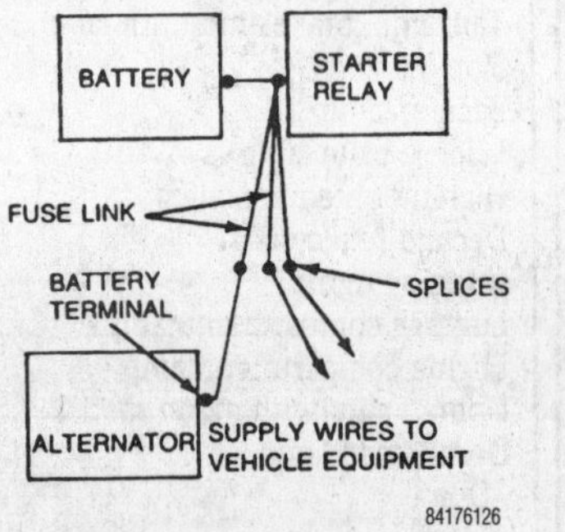


**Fig. 90 Functional schematic showing fuse link locations**

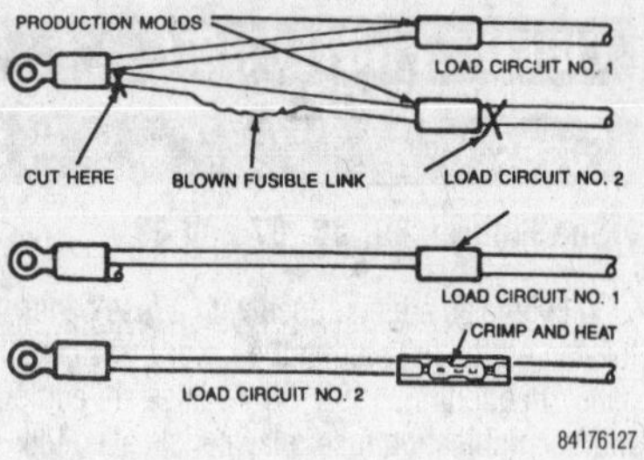


**Fig. 91 Fusible link replacement in a 2-link group when only one link has blown**

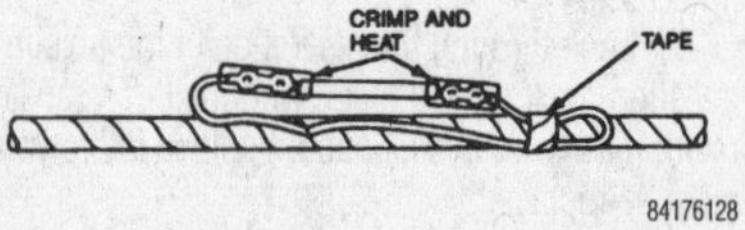


**Fig. 92 Fusible link replacement in a single circuit**

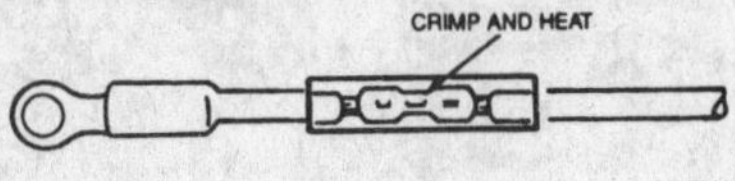

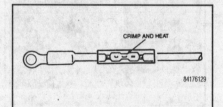

**Fig. 93 Fusible link repair using the eyelet terminal fuse link of the specified gauge for attachment to a circuit wire end**

wire connectors. Crimp and heat the splice insulation until the tubing shrinks and adhesive flows from each end of the connector.

g. Connect the negative battery cable.

3. To service a fuse link with an eyelet terminal on one end, such as the charging circuit, proceed as follows:

a. Disconnect the negative battery cable.

b. Cut off the fuse link behind the weld, strip approximately ½ in. (12.7mm) of insulation from the cut end, and attach the appropriate new eyelet fuse link to the cut stripped wire with the proper size connector.

c. Crimp and heat the splice insulation until the tubing shrinks and adhesive flows from each end of the connector.

d. Connect the negative battery cable.

**➡Do not mistake a resistor wire for a fuse link. The resistor wire is generally longer and has print stating "Resistor—do not cut or splice. "When attaching a No. 16, 18 or 20 gauge fuse link to a heavy gauge wire, always double the stripped wire end of the fuse link before inserting and crimping it into the wire connector for positive wire retention.**

## Circuit Breakers

Circuit breakers are located inside the fuse panel. They are automatically reset when the problem corrects itself, is repaired, or the circuit cools down to allow operation again.

## Flashers

The turn signal and emergency flashers are attached to the interior fuse panel. They are replaced in the same manner as the fuses and circuit breakers.

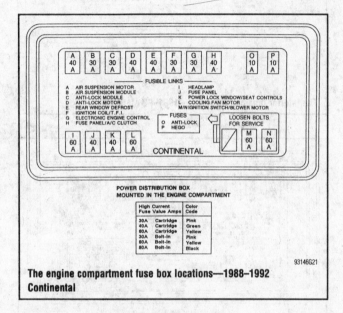

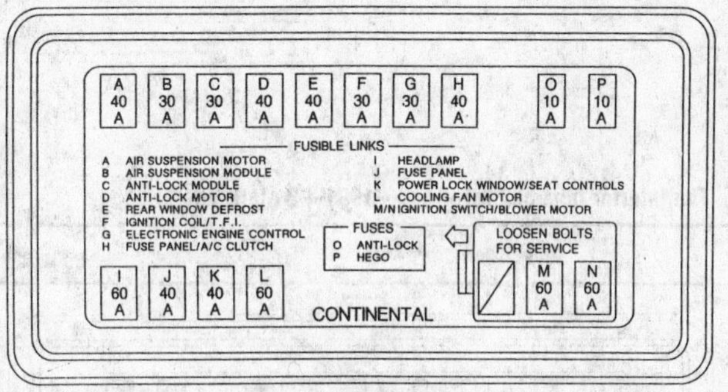


POWER DISTRIBUTION BOX
MOUNTED IN THE ENGINE COMPARTMENT

| High Current Fuse Value Amps | | Color Code |
|---|---|---|
| 30A | Cartridge | Pink |
| 40A | Cartridge | Green |
| 60A | Cartridge | Yellow |
| 30A | Bolt-In | Pink |
| 60A | Bolt-In | Yellow |
| 80A | Bolt-In | Black |

93146G21

**The engine compartment fuse box locations—1988–1992 Continental**

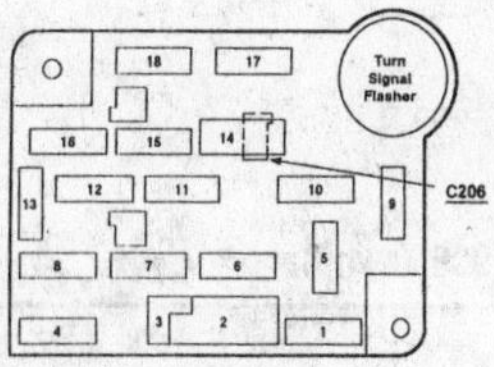


| Fuse Value Amps | Color Code |
|---|---|
| 4 | Pink |
| 5 | Tan |
| 10 | Red |
| 15 | Light Blue |
| 20 | Yellow |
| 25 | Natural |
| 30 | Light Green |

| Fuse Position | Amps | Circuits Protected |
|---|---|---|
| 1 | 15 | Cornering Lamp Relays, Stop/Hazard Lamps, Speed Control Servo, Electronic Engine Control (EEC) Module |
| 2 | 6 c.b. | Windshield Wiper Washer and Governor, Washer Fluid Level Warning |
| 3 | — | (Not Used) |
| 4 | 15 | Exterior Lamps, Ashtray, Climate Control and Load on Fuses 13 and 15, Instrument Cluster, Radio Illumination, Headlamp Switch |
| 5 | 15 | Turn Signals, Backup Lamps, Keyless Entry, Electronic Rear View Mirror, Electronic Engine Control, Rear Window Defrost, Daytime Running Lamps |
| 6 | 15 | Electronic Compass, Lamp Out Warning, Cornering Lamps, Reading Lamps, Anti-theft, Keyless Entry Module, Blower Motor, ATC Control, Warning Chime, Deck Lid Release, Speed Control, Outside Temp. Display |
| 7 | 15 | Heated Mirrors |
| 8 | 15 | Courtesy Lamps, Radio, Reading Lamp, Instrument Panel Illumination Dimming Control, Keyless Entry, Key Warning Buzzer, Illuminated Entry Module, Power Mirror |
| 9 | 30 | ATC Control |
| 10 | 15 | Air Bags |
| 11 | 20 | Radio, Power Antenna |
| 12 | 20 c.b. | Cigar Lighters, Horn |
| 13 | 5 | Instrument Illumination, Warning Indicators, Outside Temp. Display |
| 14 | 20 c.b. | Power Windows, Moonroof, Automatic Headlamps Dimmer, Headlamps |
| 15 | 10 | Exterior Lamps, Anti-theft, ATC, Lamp Out Warning |
| 16 | 4 | Trip Minder, Instrument Cluster |
| 17 | 4 | Interior Lamp Relay, Instrument Cluster Illumination Module |
| 18 | 10 | Roof Console, Autolamp Sensor, Flash-To-Pass Relay, Voice Alert/Chime, Low Oil Level Relay, Upper, Lower Warning Indicators, Air Bags |

93146G23

**The interior fuse box locations—1988–1990 Mark VII**

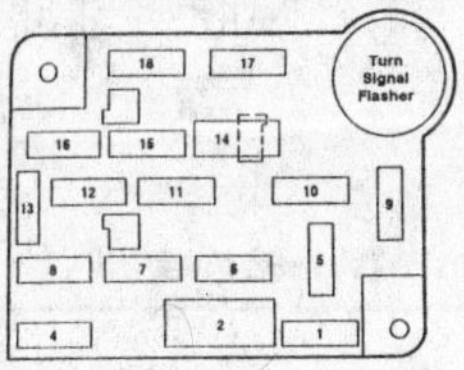


| Fuse Value Amps | Color Code |
|---|---|
| 4 | Pink |
| 5 | Tan |
| 10 | Red |
| 15 | Light Blue |
| 20 | Yellow |
| 25 | Natural |
| 30 | Light Green |

| Fuse Position | Amps | Circuits Protected |
|---|---|---|
| 1 | 15 | Stop/Hazard Lamps; Electronic Control Assembly |
| 2 | 8.25 c.b. | Interval Wiper/Washer Module; Wiper Motor and Switch |
| 4 | 15 | Exterior Lamps; Main Light Switch; Automatic Headlamps; Lamp Out Warning; and load on Fuse 13 and 15; Instrument Panel Illumination |
| 5 | 15 | Turn Lamps; Backup Lamps; Keyless Entry; Variable Assist Stepper Motor; EATC; Backup/Neutral Switch; Steering Rate Sensor; Air Suspension Electronic Control Module; Rear Window Defrost; Day/Night Mirror; D.R.L.; Heated Windshield; Digital Cluster; Air Bag Module; Air Suspension |
| 6 | 15 | Trunk Release; LCD Dimming Relay; Moonroof; Anti-Theft Module; Reading Lamps; Main Light Switch; Compass; Warning Chime Module; Digital Cluster; Daytime Cluster Illumination |
| 7 | 10 | Mirror Heater |
| 8 | 15 | Courtesy Lamps; Clock; Radio; Power Mirrors; Hood and Trunk Lamps; Memory Seats; Keyless Entry; Anti-Theft Control Module; C.D. Player; Power Antenna Module; Overhead Console; Illumination Dimming Control; Glove Box Lamp; Dimming Module |
| 9 | 30 | Blower Motor |
| 10 | 20 | Horn; Fuel Filler Door; Cigar Lighters |
| 11 | 15 | Radio; Power Antenna; Premium Sound & JBL Amplifiers |
| 12 | 15 | Air Bag Diagnostic Module; Air Bag Power Supply |
| 13 | 5 | Dimming Module; Radio; Compass; Clock; Shift Indicator; Climate Control |
| 14 | 15 | EATC; Window Safety Relay; Cluster Illumination |
| 15 | 10 | License Lamp, Side Marker Lamps, Tail Lamps, Rear Side Marker Lamp |
| 16 | 5 | Message Center; Digital Cluster; EATC |
| 17 | 20 | Flash To Pass; Daytime Running Lamps; Auto Dimmer Relay |
| 18 | 15 | Warning Chime Module; Automatic Headlamps; Brake Warning Lamp; Anti-Lock Warning Lamp; Digital Cluster; Air Bag Lamp |

93146G22

**The interior fuse box locations—1988–1992 Continental**

| Position | Description | Color | Circuit Protected |
|---|---|---|---|
| A | 60 Amp Maxi Fuse | Light Blue | Lamps |
| B | 50 Amp Maxi Fuse | Red | Antilock Brakes |
| C | 50 Amp Maxi Fuse | Red | Ignition Switch |
| D | 40 Amp Maxi Fuse | Amber | Heated Backlight |
| E | 50 Amp Maxi Fuse | Light Red | Ignition Switch |
| F | 30 Amp C.B. | | Power Windows |
| G | Spare | | |
| H | 30 Amp C.B. | | Power Seats, Power Door Locks |
| J | 10 Amp Std. Fuse | Red | Alternator |
| K | 10 Amp Std. Fuse | Red | Air Bag |
| L | 15 Amp Std. Fuse | Light Blue | Horn |
| M | 20 Amp Std. Fuse | Yellow | Hazard |
| N | 20 Amp Std. Fuse | Yellow | Fuel Pump |
| P | 25 Amp Std. Fuse | White | Ignition Switch |
| R | 25 Amp Std. Fuse | White | Radio |
| S | 30 Amp Std. Fuse | Light Green | Antilock Brakes |
| T | 30 Amp Std. Fuse | Light Green | Electronic Engine Control |
| U | 30 Amp Std. Fuse | Light Green | Air Suspension |
| V | 30 Amp Std. Fuse | Light Green | Trailer Tow |
| W | 30 Amp Std. Fuse | Light Green | Trailer Tow |
| X | 30 Amp Std. Fuse | Light Green | Trailer Tow |
| Y | 40 Amp Maxi Fuse | Amber | Heated Windshield |

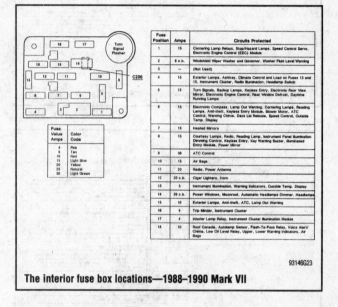

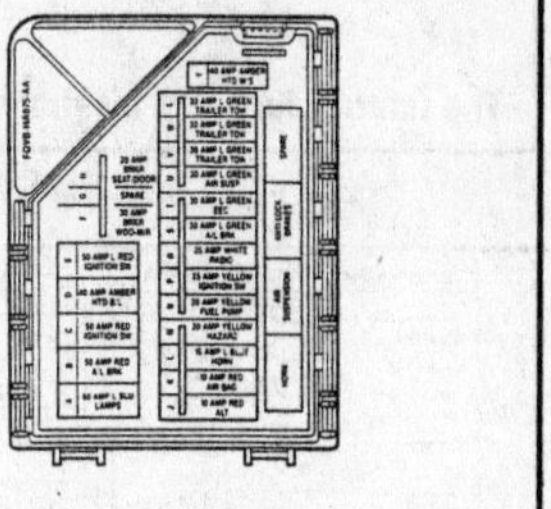

93146G07

**The engine compartment fuse box locations—1988–1990 Town Car**

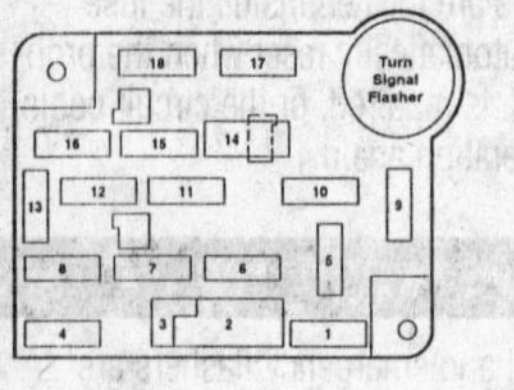

| Fuse Position | Amps | Circuits Protected |
|---|---|---|
| 1 | 15 | Memory Seats, Clock, Radio, Instrument Panel, Heated Windshield, Air Suspension, Antenna Module, Daytime Running Lamps |
| 2 | 8.25 c.b. | Wiper/Washer, Windshield Wiper Module |
| 3 | — | Not Used |
| 4 | 10 | Instrument Panel, Air Suspension, Heated Windshield, Warning Chime, Air Bag |
| 5 | 10. | Power Mirrors |
| 6 | 10 | Radio, Warning Chime, Dome/Reading/Map Lamps, Window Regulator Safety Relay, Antenna Module, Clock |
| 7 | 5 | Illumination Lamps |
| 8 | 15 | Neutral Safety Switch, Keyless Entry, Daytime Running Lamps, ATC Mode Switch, Day/Nite Sensor, Electronic Day/night Mirror |
| 9 | 30 | ATC Blower Motor |
| 10 | 30 | Cigar Lighters |
| 11 | 20. | Exterior Lamps, Delay Exit Relay, Anti-theft, Keyless Entry |
| 12 | 20 c.b. | Trunk Lid Release Switch |
| 13 | 15 | Ignition Coil, TFI Ignition Module |
| 14 | — | Not Used |
| 15 | 5 | Rear Window Defrost, Trailer Adapter, Anti-theft |
| 16 | 20 | Stop/Hazard Lamps, HEGO Sensors, Multi-function Switch |
| 17 | 10 | Courtesy Lamps, Automatic Temperature Control Blower Switch, Power Door Locks, Instrument Panel, Power Mirrors, Keyless Entry |
| 18 | 5 | Anti-lock Brakes |

93146G09

**The interior fuse box locations—1988–1990 Town Car**

| Fuse Position | Amps | Circuits Protected |
|---|---|---|
| 1 | 15 | Stop/Hazard Lamps |
| 2 | 6 c.b. | Windshield Wiper/Washer and Governor, Washer Fluid Level Warning |
| 3 | — | Not Used |
| 4 | 15 | Exterior Lamps, Headlamps, Load on Fuses 13 and 15, Autolamps |
| 5 | 15 | Turn Signals, Backup Lamps, Keyless Entry, Rear Window Defrost, Daytime Running Lamps, Air Bags |
| 6 | 15 | Electronic Compass, Lamp Out Warning, Reading Lamps, Anti-theft, Warning Chime, Trunk Lid Release, Outside Temp., Display, Automatic Temperature Control |
| 7 | 10 | Heated Mirrors |
| 8 | 15 | Courtesy Lamps, Radio, Reading Lamps, Instrument Panel Illumination Dimming Control, Warning Indicators, Keyless Entry, Power Mirrors, Power Antenna |
| 9 | 30 | Blower Motor, Automatic Temperature Control |
| 10 | 15 | Air Bags |
| 11 | 15 | Radio, Power Antenna, Mobile Telephone |
| 12 | 20 c.b. | Cigar Lighters, Horn |
| 13 | 5 | Instrument Illumination |
| 14 | 20 c.b. | Power Windows, Moonroof |
| 15 | 10 | Exterior Lamps |
| 16 | 4 | Trip Minder, Digital Instrument Cluster |
| 17 | 4 | Trip Minder Module, Instrument Cluster |
| 18 | 10 | Roof Console, Autolamp Sensor, Warning Chime, Low Oil Level Relay, Analog Instrument Cluster, Warning Indicators, Electronic Day/Night Mirror, Outside Temperature/Compass Module |

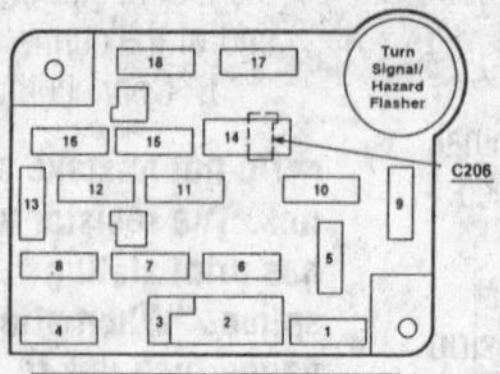

**BLADE FUSE COLOR CODING**

| AMPERE RATING | HOUSING COLOR |
|---|---|
| 4 | Pink |
| 5 | Tan |
| 10 | Red |
| 15 | Light Blue |
| 20 | Yellow |
| 25 | Natural |
| 30 | Light Green |

93146G28

**The interior fuse box locations—1991–92 Mark VII**

**INSTRUMENT PANEL FUSE PANEL**

| FUSE POSITION | AMPS | CIRCUITS PROTECTED |
|---|---|---|
| 1 | 15 | Memory Seats, Clock Memory, Radio Memory, Instrument Cluster Warning Indicators (Door Ajar, Anti-theft, Air Suspension), Heated Windshield, Air Suspension, Power Antenna, Daytime Running Lamps |
| 2 | 8.25 c.b. | Interval Wiper/Washer System |
| 3 | — | Not Used |
| 4 | 10 | Instrument Cluster, Air Suspension, Heated Windshield, Warning Chime, Air Bag, EVO Steering |
| 5 | 10 | Heated Mirrors |
| 6 | 10 | Radio, Warning Chime, Dome/Reading/Map Lamps, Power Antenna, Clock, Speed Control, Power Windows |
| 7 | 5 | Instrument Panel Illumination Lamps |
| 8 | 15 | Backup/Neutral Safety Switch, Keyless Entry, Daytime Running Lamps, ATC Module, Electronic Day/Night Mirror, Autolamps |
| 9 | 30 | Blower Motor |
| 10 | 30 | Cigar Lighters |
| 11 | 20 | Exterior Lamps, Courtesy Lamps, Anti-theft, Autolamps |
| 12 | 20 c.b. | Trunk Lid Release |
| 13 | 15 | Ignition Coils, EEC System |
| 14 | — | Not Used |
| 15 | 15 | Rear Window Defrost, Trailer Adapter, Anti-theft, Headlamp Flash-to-Pass, Turn Signals, A/C Compressor Clutch |
| 16 | 15 | HEGO Sensors |
| 17 | 10 | Courtesy Lamps, ATC Control, Module, Power Door Locks, Instrument Panel, Power Mirrors, Keyless Entry |
| 18 | 5 | Anti-lock Brake System |

93146G25

**The interior fuse box locations—1991 Town Car**

| | | |
|---|---|---|
| A | 40 A | |
| B | 30 A | |
| C | 30 A | |
| D | 40 A | |
| E | 40 A | |
| F | 30 A | |
| G | 30 A | |
| H | 40 A | |
| O | 10 A | |
| P | 10 A | |

FUSIBLE LINKS

| A | AIR SUSPENSION MOTOR | I | MAIN LIGHT SWITCH |
|---|---|---|---|
| B | SHOCK ACTUATORS | J | FUSE PANEL |
| C | ANTI-LOCK BRAKE CONTROL MODULE | K | POWER LOCK WINDOW/SEAT CONTROLS |
| D | ANTI-LOCK BRAKE MOTOR | L | INTEGRATED CONTROL MODULE |
| E | REAR WINDOW DEFROST CONTROL | M/N | IGNITION SWITCH |
| F | IGNITION COIL/T.F.I. DISTRIBUTOR | | |
| G | ELECTRONIC ENGINE CONTROL | | FUSES |
| H | FUSE PANEL | O | ANTI-LOCK |
| | | P | HEGO |

LOOSEN BOLTS FOR SERVICE

| I | 60 A | J | 40 A | K | 40 A | L | 60 A |
|---|---|---|---|---|---|---|---|

| M | 60 A | N | 60 A |
|---|---|---|---|

CONTINENTAL

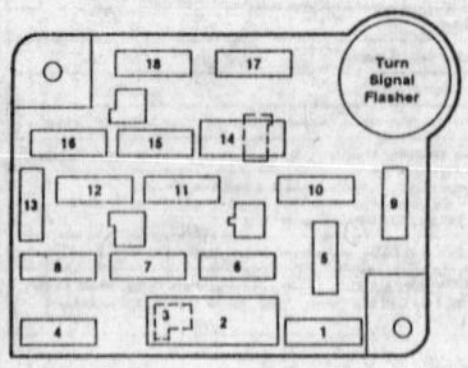

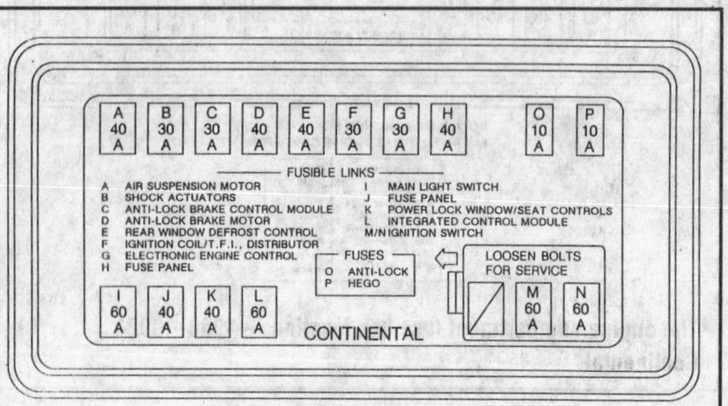

**POWER DISTRIBUTION BOX MOUNTED IN THE ENGINE COMPARTMENT**

| High Current Fuse Value Amps | Color Code |
|---|---|
| 30A Cartridge | Pink |
| 40A Cartridge | Green |
| 60A Cartridge | Yellow |
| 30A Bolt-In | Pink |
| 60A Bolt-In | Yellow |
| 80A Bolt-In | Black |

**MAXI-FUSE CARTRIDGE TOP VIEW**

30A GOOD / 30A BLOWN

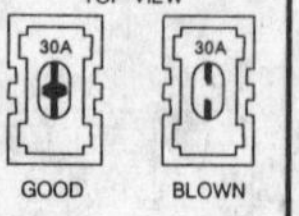

93146G29

**The engine compartment fuse box locations—1991–92 Mark VII**

**ENGINE COMPARTMENT FUSE BOX**

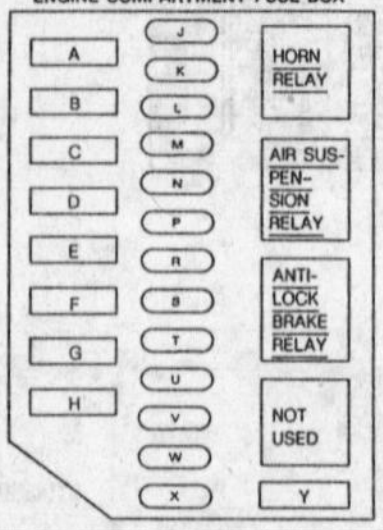

HORN RELAY / AIR SUSPENSION RELAY / ANTI-LOCK BRAKE RELAY / NOT USED

| FUSE LINK CARTRIDGE | AMPS | CIRCUITS PROTECTED |
|---|---|---|
| A | 60 | Lamps |
| B | 50 | Anti-lock Brakes |
| C | 50 | Ignition Switch |
| D | 40 | Rear Window Defrost/Heated Mirrors |
| E | 50 | Ignition Switch |
| Y | 40 | Heated Windshield |

| FUSE | AMPS | CIRCUITS PROTECTED |
|---|---|---|
| F | 30 c.b. | Power Windows/Moonroof |
| G | — | NOT USED |
| H | 30 c.b. | Power Seats/Door Locks/Fuel Filler Door Release/Trunk Lid Pull-Down |
| J | 10 | Alternator |
| K | 10 | Air Bag Restraints |
| L | 15 | Horn |
| M | 20 | Turn/Stop/Hazard Lamps |
| N | 20 | Fuel Pump/Fuel Gauge Sender |
| P | 25 | Ignition Switch |
| R | 25 | Radio Amplifier |
| S | 30 | Anti-lock Brakes |
| T | 30 | Electronic Engine Control |
| U | 30 | Air Suspension |
| V | 30 | Trailer Tow Battery Charging |
| W | 30 | Trailer Tow Brakes |
| X | 30 | Trailer Tow Lamps |

| AMPERE RATING | HOUSING COLOR |
|---|---|
| **BLADE TYPE FUSE** | |
| 10 | Red |
| 15 | Blue |
| 20 | Yellow |
| 30 | Green |
| **FUSE LINK CARTRIDGE** | |
| 20 | Light Blue |
| 30 | Pink |
| 40 | Green |
| 50 | Red |
| 60 | Yellow |
| 80 | Black |
| 100 | Dark Blue |

93146G24

**The engine compartment fuse box locations—1991 Town Car**

**INSTRUMENT PANEL FUSE PANEL**

| FUSE POSITION | AMPS | CIRCUITS PROTECTED |
|---|---|---|
| 1 | 15 | CD Changer, Clock Memory, Radio Memory, Instrument Cluster, Trunk Lid Pull-down, Cellular Telephone Connector, Heated Windshield, Air Suspension, Power Antenna, Daytime Running Lamps |
| 2 | 8.25 c.b. | Interval Wiper/Washer System |
| 3 | — | Not Used |
| 4 | 10 | Instrument Cluster, Warning Lamps, Heated Windshield, Warning Chime, Air Bag, EVO Steering |
| 5 | 10 | Heated Mirrors |
| 6 | 10 | Radio, Warning Chime, Dome/Reading/Map Lamps, Power Antenna, Clock, Speed Control, Power Windows, Shift Lock |
| 7 | 5 | Instrument Panel Illumination Lamps |
| 8 | 15 | Manual Lever Position Sensor, Keyless Entry, Daytime Running Lamps, ATC Module, Electronic Day/Night Mirror, Autolamps, Air Suspension/EVO Steering, Anti-theft |
| 9 | 30 | Blower Motor |
| 10 | 30 | Cigar Lighters |
| 11 | 20 | Exterior Lamps, Courtesy Lamps, Anti-theft, Autolamps |
| 12 | 15 | Speed Control, Stop Lamps, Hazard Flashers, Warning Lamps |
| 13 | 15 | Ignition Coils, EEC System |
| 14 | — | Not Used |
| 15 | 15 | Rear Window Defrost, Trailer Adapter, Headlamp Flash-to-Pass, Turn Signals, A/C Compressor Clutch |
| 16 | 15 | HEGO Sensors |
| 17 | 10 | Courtesy Lamps, ATC Control, Module, Power Door Locks, Warning Lamps, Power Mirrors, Keyless Entry, Memory Seats |
| 18 | 5 | Anti-lock Brake System |

93146G26

**The interior fuse box locations—1992 Town Car**

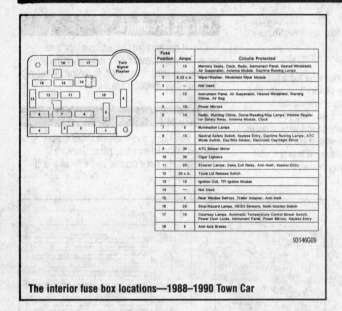

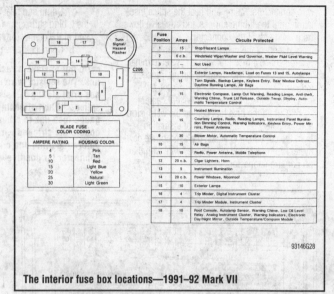

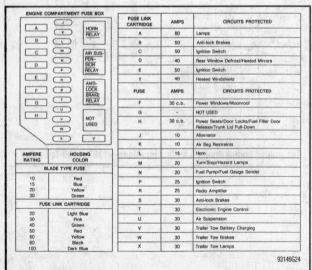

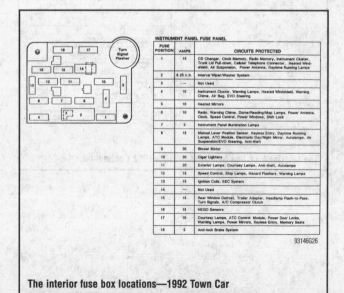

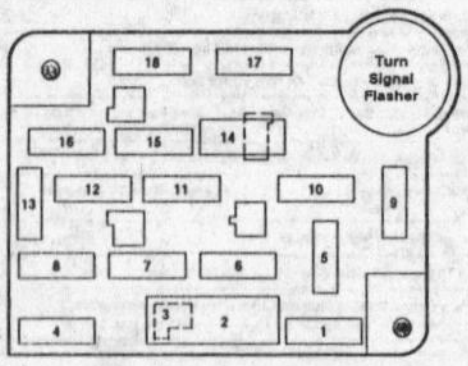

ENGINE COMPARTMENT FUSE BOX

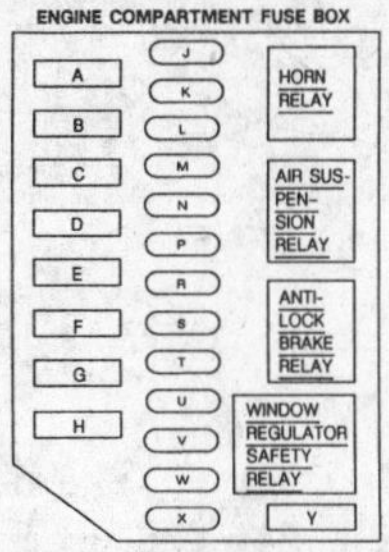


| AMPERE RATING | HOUSING COLOR |
|---|---|
| BLADE TYPE FUSE | |
| 10 | Red |
| 15 | Blue |
| 20 | Yellow |
| 30 | Green |
| MAXI-FUSE | |
| 20 | Light Blue |
| 30 | Pink |
| 40 | Green |
| 50 | Red |
| 60 | Yellow |
| 80 | Black |
| 100 | Dark Blue |

| FUSE LINK CARTRIDGE | AMPS | CIRCUITS PROTECTED |
|---|---|---|
| A | 50 | Lamps |
| B | 40 | Anti-lock Brakes |
| C | 50 | Ignition Switch |
| D | 40 | Rear Window Defrost/Heated Mirrors |
| E | 40 | Ignition Switch |
| Y | 40 | Heated Windshield |
| **FUSE** | **AMPS** | **CIRCUITS PROTECTED** |
| F | 30 c.b. | Power Windows/Moonroof |
| G | - | NOT USED |
| H | 30 c.b. | Power Seats/Door Locks/Fuel Filler Door Release/ Trunk Lid Pull-down/ Trunk Lid Release Switch |
| J | 10 | Alternator |
| K | 10 | Air Bag Restraints |
| L | 15 | Horn |
| M | - | |
| N | 20 | Fuel Pump |
| P | 25 | Ignition Switch |
| R | 25 | Radio Amplifier |
| S | 30 | Anti-lock Brakes |
| T | 30 | Electronic Engine Control |
| U | 30 | Air Suspension |
| V | 30 | Trailer Tow Battery Charging |
| W | 30 | Trailer Tow Brakes |
| X | 30 | Trailer Tow Lamps |

93146G27

**The engine compartment fuse box locations—1992 Town Car**

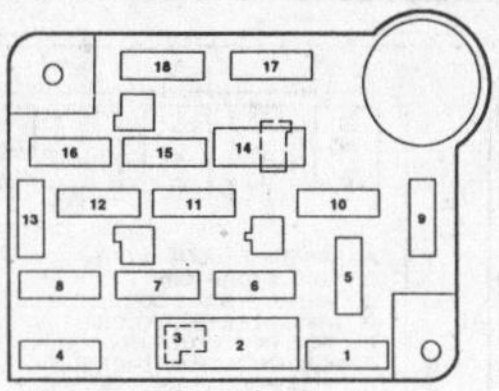


INSTRUMENT PANEL FUSE PANEL

| FUSE | AMPS | CIRCUITS PROTECTED |
|---|---|---|
| 1 | 30 | Blower Motor Speed Controller |
| 2 | — | Not Used |
| 3 | 30 | Interval Wiper/Washer System |
| 4 | 25 | Park Lamp Relay, Main Light Switch |
| 5 | 10 | EATC Module, Shift Lock Actuator, Temperature Blend Actuator, Rear Window Defrost, Traction Assist |
| 6 | 15 | Autolamp Switch/Pulse Width Dimming Module, Anti-Theft System, Keyless Entry System, Power Seats, Power Mirrors, Memory Mirror System |
| 7 | 10 | Start Interrupt Relay, Power Antenna Switch, Left Memory Seat Module, Memory Mirror Module |
| 8 | 20 | Cigar Lighters |
| 9 | 10 | Electronic Day/Night Mirror, Shock Damping Control, Transmission Control Switch, Day/Night Sensor/Amplifier |
| 10 | 15 | Multi-Fuction Switch, Air Bag System, Anti Lock Brakes, Air Suspension, Manual Lever Position Switch, Daytime Running Lamps, Electronic Flasher, Back-up Lamps |
| 11 | 10 | Multi-Function Switch, Brake ON/OFF (BOO) Switch, Brake Pressure Switch, Hazard Flasher |
| 12 | 20 c.b. | Power Seats, Shock Damping Control Relays, Remote/Keyless Entry, Fuel Filler Door and Trunk Lid Release Switches |
| 13 | 10 | Rear Window Defrost/Heated Mirrors |
| 14 | 20 c.b. | Master Window Control Switch, Moonroof Control Switch, Right Front Window Switch, One Touch Window Down Module |
| 15 | 10 | Instrument Cluster, Warning Chime Module, I/P Warning Indicator Display, Delayed Accessory Module |
| 16 | 10 | Radio, Power Antenna, Message Center, Air Bag System, EATC Module, I/P Warning Indicator |
| 17 | 10A | Power Antenna Switch, Warning Chime Module, Message Center, Anti-Theft Controller Module, Mobile Telephone Transceiver Radio, Memory Seat Modules, Keyless Entry Module, Compass Module |
| 18 | 10 | Exterior Lamps, Warning Chime Module |

93146G12

**The interior fuse box locations—1993–98 Mark VIII**

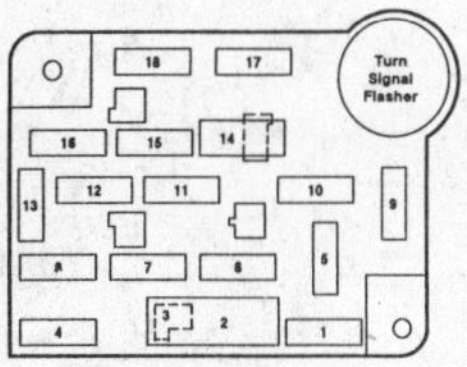


INSTRUMENT PANEL FUSE PANEL

| FUSE POSITION | AMPS | CIRCUITS PROTECTED |
|---|---|---|
| 1 | 15 | CD Changer, Clock Memory, Radio Memory, Instrument Cluster, Trunk Lid Pull-down, Cellular Telephone Connector, Air Suspension, Power Antenna, Daytime Running Lamps |
| 2 | 8.25 c.b. | Interval Wiper/Washer System |
| 3 | — | Not Used |
| 4 | 10 | Instrument Cluster, Warning Lamps, Warning Chime, Air Bag, EVO Steering |
| 5 | 10 | Heated Mirrors |
| 6 | 10 | Radio, Warning Chime, Dome/Reading/Map Lamps, Power Antenna, Clock, Power Windows, Shift Lock, Remote Keyless Entry, Anti-theft |
| 7 | 5 | Instrument Panel Illumination Lamps |
| 8 | 15 | Manual Lever Position Sensor, Remote Keyless Entry, Daytime Running Lamps, EATC Controller Module, Electronic Day/Night Mirror, Autolamps, Air Suspension/EVO Steering, Anti-theft |
| 9 | 30 | Blower Motor |
| 10 | 30 | Cigar Lighters |
| 11 | 20 | Exterior Lamps, Courtesy Lamps, Anti-theft, Autolamps |
| 12 | 15 | Speed Control, Stop Lamps, Hazard Flashers, Warning Lamps |
| 13 | 15 | Ignition Coils, EEC System |
| 14 | — | Not Used |
| 15 | 15 | Rear Window Defrost, Trailer Adapter, Headlamp Flash-to-Pass, Turn Signals, A/C Compressor Clutch |
| 16 | 15 | HO2S Sensors |
| 17 | 10 | Courtesy Lamps, EATC Controller Module, Warning Lamps, Power Mirrors, Remote Keyless Entry, Memory Seats |
| 18 | 5 | Anti-lock Brake System |

93146G10

**The interior fuse box locations—1993–94 Town Car**

ENGINE COMPARTMENT FUSE BOX

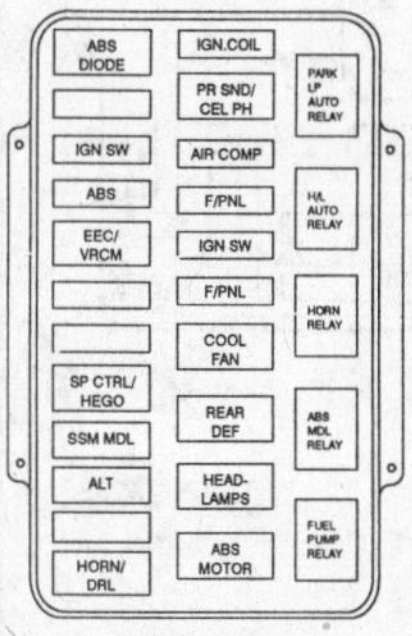


| MAXI-FUSE | AMPS | CIRCUITS PROTECTED |
|---|---|---|
| IGN. COIL | 20 | Fuel Pump Relay, Ignition Coils, Radio Noise Capacitors, Variable Control Relay Module (VCRM) |
| PR SND/CELL PH | 20 | Radio Amplifier, Cellular Phone |
| AIR COMP | 50 | Air Compressor Relay |
| F/PNL | 40 | See Fuses 6 and 11 |
| IGN SW | 40 | Ignition, Delayed Accessory Module |
| F/PNL | 50 | See Fuses 4, 8, 16 and Circuit Breaker 12 |
| COOL FAN | 40 | Variable Control Relay Module (VCRM) |
| REAR DEF | 40 | Rear Window Defrost Control |
| HEADLAMPS | 40 | Main Light Switch |
| ABS MOTOR | 40 | Anti-Lock Pump Motor Relay |
| IGN SW | 50 | Ignition Switch |
| ABS | 30 | Anti-Lock Brake Relay, Anti-Lock Brake Control Module |
| EEC/VRCM | 20 | High Speed Fuel Pump Relay, Variable Control Relay Module (VCRM), Powertrain Control Module (PCM) |
| **FUSE** | **AMPS** | **CIRCUITS PROTECTED** |
| SP CTRL/HEGO | 10 | Speed Control Amplifier, Heated Oxygen Sensors |
| SSM MDL | 15 | Air Suspension/EVO Steering Module |
| ALT | 20 | Integral Alternator Regulator |
| HORN/DRL | 25 | Horn Relay, Daytime Running Lamps (DRL) Resistor (If equipped) |

93146G14

**The engine compartment fuse box locations—1993–98 Mark VIII**

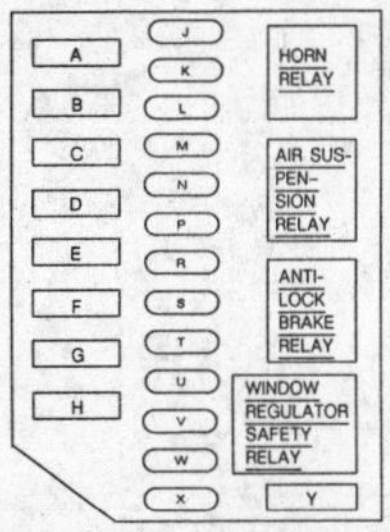


| AMPERE RATING | HOUSING COLOR |
|---|---|
| BLADE TYPE FUSE | |
| 10 | Red |
| 15 | Blue |
| 20 | Yellow |
| 30 | Green |
| MAXI-FUSE | |
| 20 | Light Blue |
| 30 | Pink |
| 40 | Green |
| 50 | Red |
| 60 | Yellow |
| 80 | Black |
| 100 | Dark Blue |

| FUSE LINK CARTRIDGE | AMPS | CIRCUITS PROTECTED |
|---|---|---|
| A | 50 | Lamps |
| B | 40 | Anti-lock Brakes |
| C | 50 | Ignition Switch |
| D | 40 | Rear Window Defrost/Heated Mirrors |
| E | 40 | Ignition Switch |
| **FUSE** | **AMPS** | **CIRCUITS PROTECTED** |
| F | 30 c.b. | Power Windows/Moonroof |
| G | - | NOT USED |
| H | 30 c.b. | Power Seats/Door Locks/Fuel Filler Door Release/ Trunk Lid Pull-down/ Trunk Lid Release Switch |
| J | 10 | Alternator |
| K | 10 | Air Bag Restraints |
| L | 15 | Horn |
| N | 20 | Fuel Pump |
| M | 15 | Daytime Running Lamp |
| P | 25 | Ignition Switch |
| R | 25 | Radio Amplifier |
| S | 30 | Anti-lock Brakes |
| T | 30 | Powertrain Control Module (PCM) |
| U | 30 | Air Suspension |
| V | 30 | Trailer Tow Battery Charging |
| W | 30 | Trailer Tow Brakes |
| X | 30 | Trailer Tow Lamps |

93146G11

**The engine compartment fuse box locations—1993–94 Town Car**

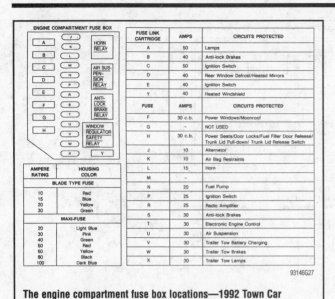

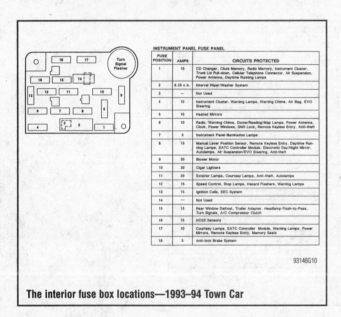

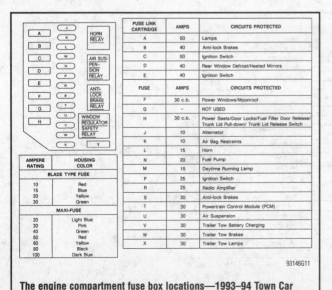

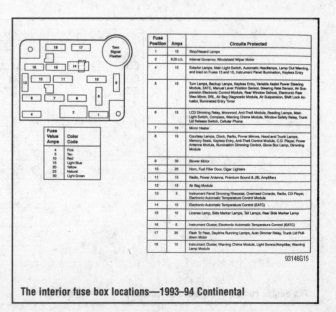

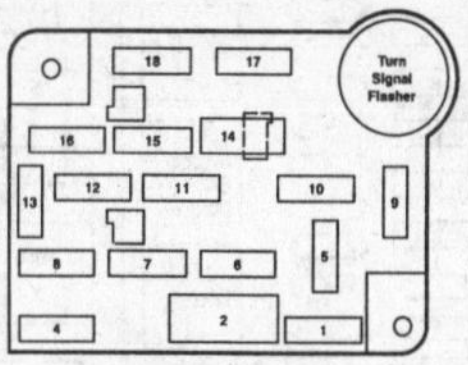


| Fuse Value Amps | Color Code |
|---|---|
| 4 | Pink |
| 5 | Tan |
| 10 | Red |
| 15 | Light Blue |
| 20 | Yellow |
| 25 | Natural |
| 30 | Light Green |

| Fuse Position | Amps | Circuits Protected |
|---|---|---|
| 1 | 15 | Stop/Hazard Lamps |
| 2 | 8.25 c.b. | Interval Governor, Windshield Wiper Motor |
| 4 | 15 | Exterior Lamps, Main Light Switch, Automatic Headlamps, Lamp Out Warning, and load on Fuses 13 and 15, Instrument Panel Illumination, Keyless Entry |
| 5 | 15 | Turn Lamps, Backup Lamps, Keyless Entry, Variable Assist Power Steering Module, EATC, Manual Lever Position Sensor, Steering Rate Sensor, Air Suspension Electronic Control Module, Rear Window Defrost, Electronic Rear View Mirror, DRL, Air Bag Diagnostic Module, Air Suspension, Shift Lock Actuator, Illuminated Entry Timer |
| 6 | 15 | LCD Dimming Relay, Moonroof, Anti-Theft Module, Reading Lamps, Main Light Switch, Compass, Warning Chime Module, Window Safety Relay, Trunk Lid Release Switch, Cellular Phone |
| 7 | 10 | Mirror Heater |
| 8 | 15 | Courtesy Lamps, Clock, Radio, Power Mirrors, Hood and Trunk Lamps, Memory Seats, Keyless Entry, Anti-Theft Control Module, C.D. Player, Power Antenna Module, Illumination Dimming Control, Glove Box Lamp, Dimming Module |
| 9 | 30 | Blower Motor |
| 10 | 20 | Horn, Fuel Filler Door, Cigar Lighters |
| 11 | 15 | Radio, Power Antenna, Premium Sound & JBL Amplifiers |
| 12 | 15 | Air Bag Module |
| 13 | 5 | Instrument Panel Dimming Rheostat, Overhead Console, Radio, CD Player, Electronic Automatic Temperature Control Module |
| 14 | 15 | Electronic Automatic Temperature Control (EATC) |
| 15 | 10 | License Lamp, Side Marker Lamps, Tail Lamps, Rear Side Marker Lamp |
| 16 | 5 | Instrument Cluster, Electronic Automatic Temperature Control (EATC) |
| 17 | 20 | Flash To Pass, Daytime Running Lamps, Auto Dimmer Relay, Trunk Lid Pull-down Motor |
| 18 | 15 | Instrument Cluster, Warning Chime Module, Light Sensor/Amplifier, Warning Lamp Module |

93146G15

**The interior fuse box locations—1993–94 Continental**

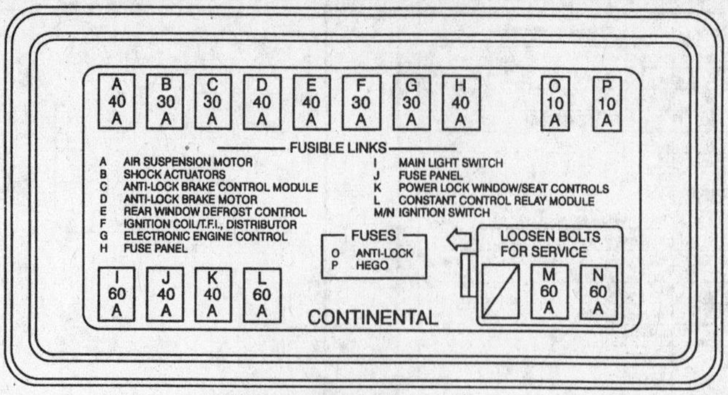


POWER DISTRIBUTION BOX
MOUNTED IN THE ENGINE COMPARTMENT

| High Current Fuse Value Amps | | Color Code |
|---|---|---|
| 30A | Cartridge | Pink |
| 40A | Cartridge | Green |
| 60A | Cartridge | Yellow |
| 30A | Bolt-In | Pink |
| 60A | Bolt-In | Yellow |
| 80A | Bolt-In | Black |

MAXI-FUSE CARTRIDGE
TOP VIEW

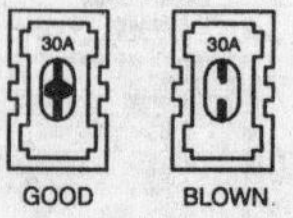


93146G16

**The engine compartment fuse box locations—1993–94 Continental**

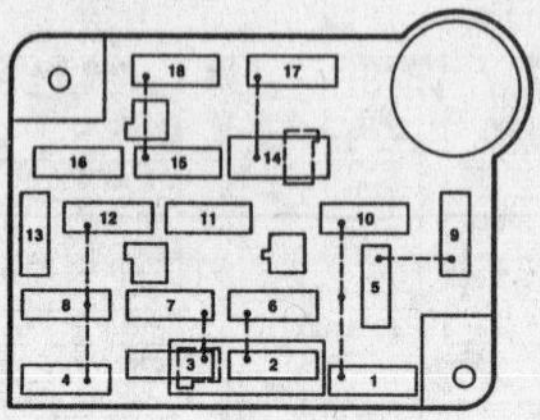


INSTRUMENT PANEL FUSE PANEL

| FUSE POSITION | AMPS | CIRCUITS PROTECTED |
|---|---|---|
| 1 | 15 | Electronic Automatic Temperature Control (EATC) Module, Backup Lamps, Turn Signal Indicators, Trailer Battery Charging Relay, Heated Seats, Shift Lock |
| 2 | 30 | Wiper/Washer Controller Module, Windshield Wiper Motor |
| 3 | 5 | Instrument Cluster |
| 4 | 10 | Lighting Control Module (LCM) |
| 5 | 15 | Ignition Coils, PCM Power Relay |
| 6 | 10 | Lighting Control Module (LCM), Front Radio Control Unit, Clock, Cellular Phone, Electronic Day/Night Mirror, Compass Module |
| 7 | 15 | Air Bag Diagnostic Module, Air Suspension/EVO Steering Module, Steering Wheel Rotation Sensor, EATC Module, Anti-Lock Brake Module, Instrument Cluster, Daytime Running Lamps, Speed Control Amplifier, Warning Indicators, Transmission Control Switch |
| 8 | 15 | Keyless Entry, Power Mirrors, Trunk Lid Pull-Down, Memory Seats, Redundant Steering Control Module, CD Changer, Cellular Phone |
| 9 | 5 | Air Bag Diagnostic Module, Day/Night Sensor Amplifier, Lighting Control Module (LCM), Warning Indicators, Front Radio Control Unit |
| 10 | 30 | EATC Module |
| 11 | 5 | LF Seat Module, LF Door Module |
| 12 | 18 c.b. | Headlamps, Lighting Control Module (LCM) |
| 13 | 10 | Rear Window Defrost/Heated Mirror |
| 14 | 20 c.b. | Keyless Entry, Fuel Fill Door Release, LF Seat Module, Power Seats, LF Door Module |
| 15 | 15 | I/P Illumination, Courtesy Lamps, Daytime Running Lamps, Lighting Control Module (LCM) |
| 16 | 15 | Brake ON–OFF Switch, Brake Pressure Switch, Hazard Flasher, Trailer Adapter |
| 17 | 30 | Cigar Lighters |
| 18 | 10 | EATC Module, Instrument Cluster, On Board Diagnostic (OBD) Data Link Connector, Clock, Front Radio Control Unit |

93146G31

**The interior fuse box locations—1995–97 Town Car**

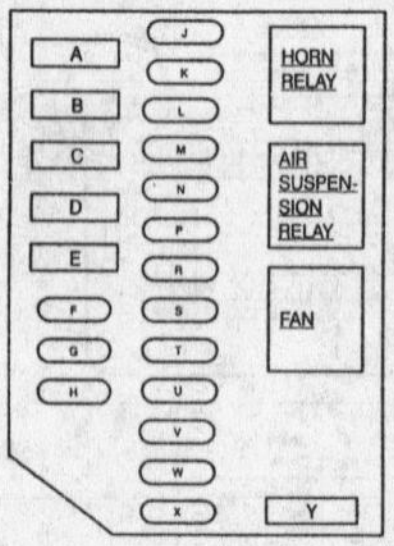


| MAXI–FUSE | AMPS | CIRCUITS PROTECTED |
|---|---|---|
| A | 50 | Lamps |
| B | 50 | Anti-lock Brakes |
| C | 50 | Ignition Switch |
| D | 40 | Rear Window Defrost/Heated Mirrors |
| E | 40 | Ignition Switch |
| **MINI–FUSE** | **AMPS** | **CIRCUITS PROTECTED** |
| F | 30 c.b. | Power Windows/Moonroof |
| G | – | NOT USED |
| H | – | NOT USED |
| J | 10 | Generator/Voltage Regulator |
| K | 10 | Air Bag Restraints |
| L | 20 | Horn |
| M | – | NOT USED |
| N | 20 | Fuel Pump |
| P | 30 | Cooling Fan |
| R | 25 | Radio Amplifier |
| S | 30 | Heated Seat |
| T | 30 | Powertrain Control Module (PCM) |
| U | 30 | Air Suspension |
| V | 30 | Trailer Battery Charging |
| W | 30 | Trailer Brakes |
| X | 30 | Trailer Exterior Lamps |
| Y | – | NOT USED |

93146G30

**The engine compartment fuse box locations—1995–97 Town Car**

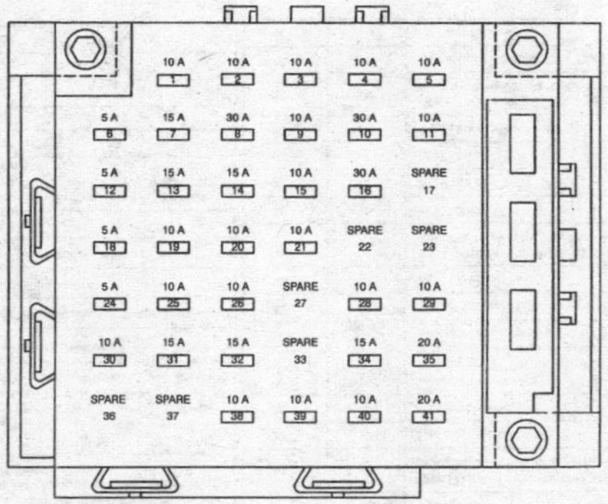


| FUSE | AMPS | CIRCUITS PROTECTED |
|---|---|---|
| 1 | 10 | Lighting Control Module: Anti–Theft Indicator Lamp, PWM Dimming Output Illumination Lamps for Microphone, RR and LR Door Ashtrays, Heated Seat Switches, Rear Defrost Control Switch, EATC Control Panel, Message Center Switches, Speed Control Switches, Cigar Lighter, Console and Ashtray, Navigation Display Module and Navigation Switches |
| 2 | 10 | Front Control Unit, Mobile Telephone Transceiver, Clock |
| 3 | 10 | Multi–Function Switch, Cornering Lamps |
| 4 | 10 | Power Door Locks and Power Windows Switch Backlights, Front Radio Control Unit, Mobile Telephone Transceiver, Lighting Control Module, Electronic Day/Night Mirror, Compass Module, Clock |
| 5 | 10 | Front Control Unit, Virtual Image Instrument Cluster, Air Bag Diagnostic Monitor, Traction Control Switch, Lighting Control Module (LCM), Light Sensor Amplifier |
| 6 | 5 | SCP Bus + |
| 7 | 15 | Lighting Control Module (LCM): LF Turn Lamp, Left Turn Indicator (VIC), Multi–Function Switch, LF and RF Side Marker Lamps, RF and LF Park Lamps, RR and LR Tail Lamps, RR Stop/Turn Lamps |
| 8 | 30 | Fuel Filler Door Release Switch, Trunk Lid Relay, Navigation Module |
| 9 | 10 | Air Bag Diagnostic Monitor, EATC Module, Blower Motor Relay |
| 10 | 30 | Windshield Wiper Motor, Wiper Control Module |
| 11 | 10 | Ignition Coils, Radio Interference Capacitor, PCM Power Relay |
| 12 | 5 | SCP Bus + |
| 13 | 15 | Lighting Control Module (LCM): RF Turn Lamp, Right Turn Indicator (VIC), RR Side Marker Lamps, Tail Lamps, License Lamps, LR Stop/Turn Lamps, Clock Illumination. |
| 14 | 15 | Cigar Lighter |
| 15 | 10 | Heated Seat Switch Assembly, Navigation Module, Navigation Display Module |
| 16 | 30 | Moonroof Switch |
| 17 | – | NOT USED |
| 18 | 5 | SCP Bus – |

| FUSE | AMPS | CIRCUITS PROTECTED |
|---|---|---|
| 19 | 10 | Lighting Control Module (LCM): Left Headlamp, DHL |
| 20 | 10 | Multi–Function Switch: Flash to Pass, Cornering Lamps |
| 21 | 10 | ABS EVAC and Fill Connector, ABS Control Module |
| 22 | – | NOT USED |
| 23 | – | NOT USED |
| 24 | 5 | SCP Bus – |
| 25 | 10 | Lighting Control Module (LCM): Right Headlamp |
| 26 | 10 | Virtual Image Instrument Cluster, EATC Module |
| 27 | – | NOT USED |
| 28 | 10 | Shift Lock Actuator, Vehicle Dynamic Module, Virtual Image Instrument Cluster, Rear Window Defrost Control |
| 29 | 10 | Remote Chassis Unit, Navigation Module |
| 30 | 10 | Heated Mirrors |
| 31 | 15 | Lighting Control Module (LCM): FCU, Navigation Display Module, Electronic Day/Night Mirror, RH and LH I/P Courtesy Lamp, Door Courtesy Lamps, RH and LH Map Lamps, RR and LR Reading Lamps, Engine Compartment Lamp, RH and LH Visor Lamps, Storage Bin Lamp, Trunk Lid Lamp, Glove Box Lamp. |
| 32 | 15 | Speed Control DEAC. Switch, Brake ON/OFF (BOO) Switch |
| 33 | – | NOT USED |
| 34 | 15 | EATC Module, Transmission Range Sensor, Speed Control Servo/Amplifier Assembly, DRL Module, Intake Manifold Runner Control |
| 35 | 20 | Heated Seat Modules |
| 36 | – | NOT USED |
| 37 | – | NOT USED |
| 38 | 10 | Data Link Connector (DLC) |
| 39 | 10 | Power Door Locks, Power Seats, Power Mirrors, Keyless Entry, Memory Seat/Mirrors, LF Seat Module, LF Door Module |
| 40 | 10 | Blend Door Actuator, Low Tire Pressure Sensor (LTPS) |
| 41 | 20 | LF Door Module |

93146G34

**The interior fuse box locations—1995–96 Continental**

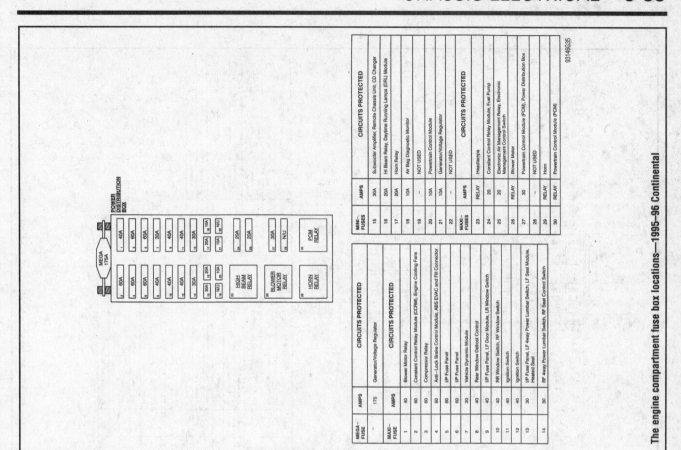

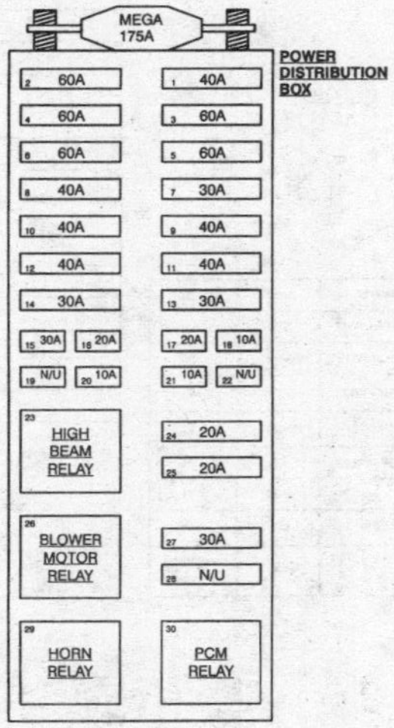


| MEGA–FUSE | AMPS | CIRCUITS PROTECTED |
|---|---|---|
| – | 175 | Generator/Voltage Regulator |
| **MAXI–FUSE** | **AMPS** | **CIRCUITS PROTECTED** |
| 1 | 40 | Blower Motor Relay |
| 2 | 60 | Constant Control Relay Module (CCRM), Engine Cooling Fans |
| 3 | 60 | Compressor Relay |
| 4 | 60 | Anti–Lock Brake Control Module, ABS EVAC and Fill Connector |
| 5 | 60 | I/P Fuse Panel |
| 6 | 60 | I/P Fuse Panel |
| 7 | 30 | Vehicle Dynamic Module |
| 8 | 40 | Rear Window Defrost Control |
| 9 | 40 | I/P Fuse Panel, LF Door Module, LR Window Switch |
| 10 | 40 | RR Window Switch, RF Window Switch |
| 11 | 40 | Ignition Switch |
| 12 | 40 | Ignition Switch |
| 13 | 30 | I/P Fuse Panel, LF 4way Power Lumbar Switch, LF Seat Module, Heated Seat |
| 14 | 30 | RF 4way Power Lumbar Switch, RF Seat Control Switch |

| MINI–FUSES | AMPS | CIRCUITS PROTECTED |
|---|---|---|
| 15 | 30A | Subwoofer Amplifier, Remote Chassis Unit, CD Changer |
| 16 | 20A | HI Beam Relay, Daytime Running Lamps (DRL) Module |
| 17 | 20A | Horn Relay |
| 18 | 10A | Air Bag Diagnostic Monitor |
| 19 | – | NOT USED |
| 20 | 10A | Powertrain Control Module |
| 21 | 10A | Generator/Voltage Regulator |
| 22 | – | NOT USED |
| **MAXI–FUSES** | **AMPS** | **CIRCUITS PROTECTED** |
| 23 | RELAY | Headlamps |
| 24 | 20 | Constant Control Relay Module, Fuel Pump |
| 25 | 20 | Electronic Air Management Relay, Electronic Management Control Switch |
| 26 | RELAY | Blower Motor |
| 27 | 30 | Powertrain Control Module (PCM), Power Distribution Box |
| 28 | – | NOT USED |
| 29 | RELAY | Horn |
| 30 | RELAY | Powertrain Control Module (PCM) |

93146G35

**The engine compartment fuse box locations—1995–96 Continental**

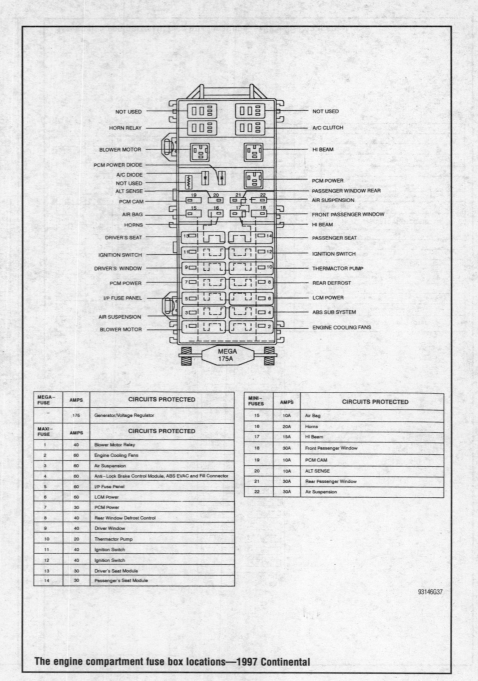

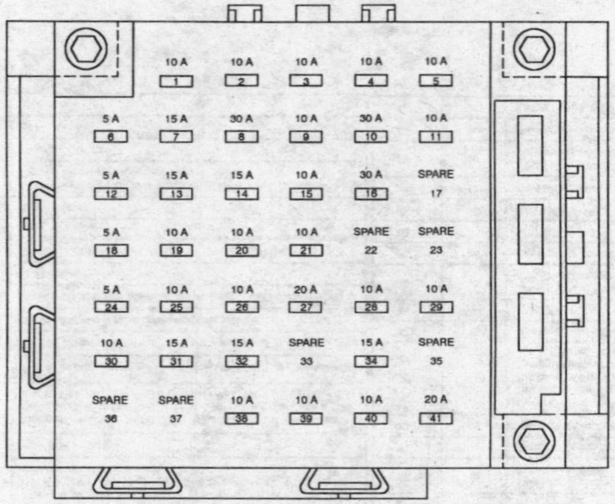


| FUSE | AMPS | CIRCUITS PROTECTED |
|---|---|---|
| 1 | 10 | Lighting Control Module: Anti–Theft Indicator Lamp, PWM Dimming Output Illumination Lamps for Microphone, RR and LR Door Ashtrays, Heated Seat Switches, Rear Defrost Control Switch, EATC Control Panel, Message Center Switches, Speed Control Switches, Cigar Lighter, Console and Ashtray |
| 2 | 10 | Front Control Unit, Mobile Telephone Transceiver, Clock, RESCU Module, Compact Disc Changer |
| 3 | 10 | Multi–Function Switch, Cornering Lamps, High Beam and Turn Signal Input to LCM |
| 4 | 10 | Power Door Locks and Power Windows Switch Backlights, Front Radio Control Unit, Mobile Telephone Transceiver, Lighting Control Module, (RUN/ACC Sense), Digital Clock |
| 5 | 10 | Front Control Unit, Virtual Image Instrument Cluster, Air Bag Diagnostic Monitor, Traction Control Switch, Lighting Control Module (LCM RUN/START Sense), Light Sensor Amplifier |
| 6 | 5 | SCP Bus + To PCM, VIC, OBDII, FCU, EATC, DSM |
| 7 | 15 | Lighting Control Module (LCM): LF Turn Lamp, Left Turn Indicator (VIC), Multi–Function Switch, LF and RF Side Marker Lamps, RF and LF Park Lamps, RR and LR Tail Lamps, RR Stop/Turn Lamps |
| 8 | 30 | Fuel Filler Door Release Switch, Trunk Lid Relay |
| 9 | 10 | Air Bag Diagnostic Monitor, EATC Module, Blower Motor Relay |
| 10 | 30 | Windshield Wiper Motor, Wiper Control Module |
| 11 | 10 | Ignition Coils, Radio Interference Capacitor, PCM Power Relay |
| 12 | 5 | SCP Bus + To Phone, VDM, DDM, LCM, ABS/TA, EVAC & Fill |
| 13 | 15 | Lighting Control Module (LCM): RF Turn Lamp, Right Turn Indicator (VIC), RR Side Marker Lamps, Tail Lamps, License Lamps, LR Stop/Turn Lamps, Clock Illumination |
| 14 | 15 | Cigar Lighter |
| 15 | 10 | Heated Seat Switch Assembly |
| 16 | 30 | Moonroof Switch |
| 17 | – | NOT USED |
| 18 | 5 | SCP Bus – To PCM, VIC, OBDII, FCU, EATC, DSM |

| FUSE | AMPS | CIRCUITS PROTECTED |
|---|---|---|
| 19 | 10 | Lighting Control Module (LCM): Left Headlamp, DRL |
| 20 | 10 | Multi–Function Switch: Flash to Pass, and Hazard Warning Input to LCM |
| 21 | 10 | ABS EVAC and Fill Connector, ABS Control Module |
| 22 | – | NOT USED |
| 23 | – | NOT USED |
| 24 | 5 | SCP Bus – To Phone, VDM, DDM, LCM, ABS/TA |
| 25 | 10 | Lighting Control Module (LCM): Right Headlamp |
| 26 | 10 | Virtual Image Instrument Cluster, EATC Module |
| 27 | 20 | Power Point |
| 28 | 10 | Shift Lock Actuator, Vehicle Dynamic Module, Virtual Image Instrument Cluster, Rear Window Defrost Control |
| 29 | 10 | Remote Chassis Unit |
| 30 | 10 | Heated Mirrors |
| 31 | 15 | Lighting Control Module (LCM): FCU, Electronic Day/Night Mirror, RH and LH I/P Courtesy Lamp, Door Courtesy Lamps, RH and LH Map Lamps, RR and LR Reading Lamps, RH and LH Visor Lamps, Storage Bin Lamp, Trunk Lid Lamp, Glove Box Lamp |
| 32 | 15 | Speed Control DEAC. Switch, Brake ON/OFF (BOO) Switch |
| 33 | – | NOT USED |
| 34 | 15 | EATC Module, Transmission Range Sensor, Speed Control Servo/Amplifier Assembly, DRL Module, Intake Manifold Runner Control |
| 35 | – | NOT USED |
| 36 | – | NOT USED |
| 37 | – | NOT USED |
| 38 | 10 | Data Link Connector (DLC) |
| 39 | 10 | Power Door Locks, Power Seats, Power Mirrors, Keyless Entry, Memory Seat/Mirrors, LF Seat Module, LF Door Module |
| 40 | 10 | Blend Door Actuator, Low Tire Pressure Sensor (LTPS) |
| 41 | 20 | LF Door Module |

93146G36

**The interior fuse box locations—1997 Continental**

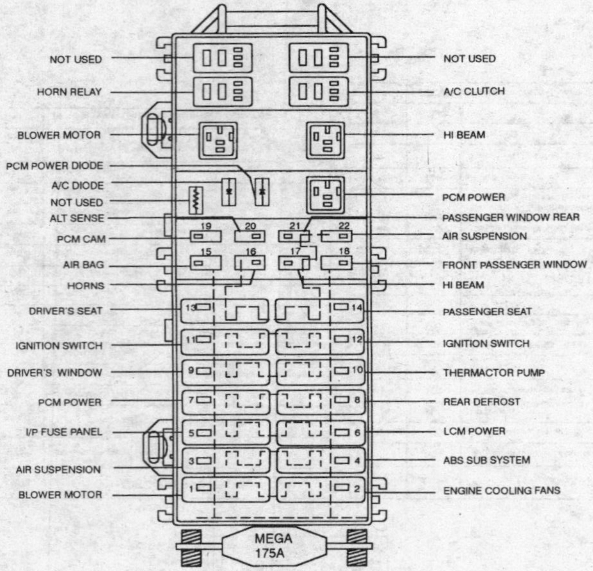


| MEGA–FUSE | AMPS | CIRCUITS PROTECTED |
|---|---|---|
| – | 175 | Generator/Voltage Regulator |
| **MAXI–FUSE** | **AMPS** | **CIRCUITS PROTECTED** |
| 1 | 40 | Blower Motor Relay |
| 2 | 60 | Engine Cooling Fans |
| 3 | 60 | Air Suspension |
| 4 | 60 | Anti–Lock Brake Control Module, ABS EVAC and Fill Connector |
| 5 | 60 | I/P Fuse Panel |
| 6 | 60 | LCM Power |
| 7 | 30 | PCM Power |
| 8 | 40 | Rear Window Defrost Control |
| 9 | 40 | Driver Window |
| 10 | 20 | Thermactor Pump |
| 11 | 40 | Ignition Switch |
| 12 | 40 | Ignition Switch |
| 13 | 30 | Driver's Seat Module |
| 14 | 30 | Passenger's Seat Module |

| MINI–FUSES | AMPS | CIRCUITS PROTECTED |
|---|---|---|
| 15 | 10A | Air Bag |
| 16 | 20A | Horns |
| 17 | 15A | Hi Beam |
| 18 | 30A | Front Passenger Window |
| 19 | 10A | PCM CAM |
| 20 | 10A | ALT SENSE |
| 21 | 30A | Rear Passenger Window |
| 22 | 30A | Air Suspension |

93146G37

**The engine compartment fuse box locations—1997 Continental**

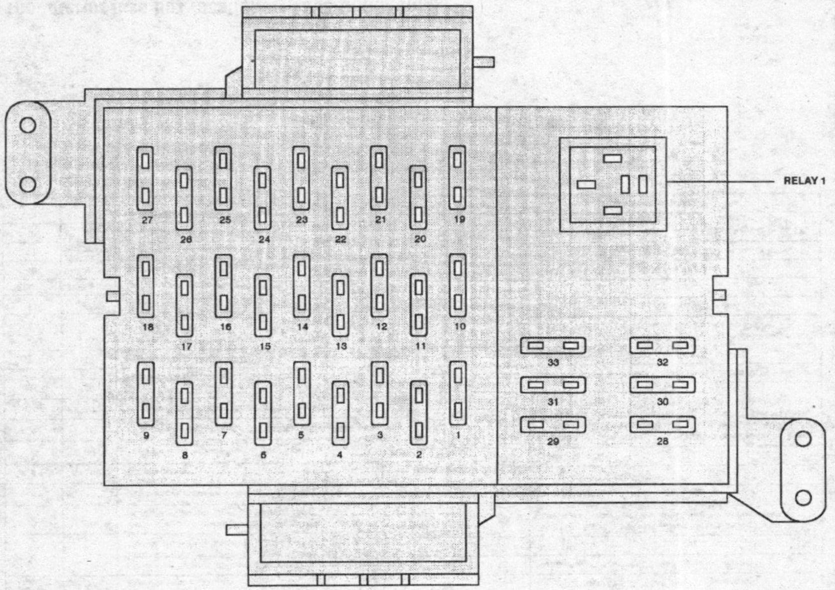


| FUSE | Amps | Circuits Protected |
|---|---|---|
| 1 | 10 | Lighting Control Module (LCM) |
| 2 | 30 | EATC Blower Motor |
| 3 | 10 | Lighting Control Module (LCM) |
| 4 | 7.5 | Instrument Cluster |
| 5 | 7.5 | Lighting Control Module (LCM) |
| 6 | 15 | EATC, Heated Seats |
| 7 | 15 | Lighting Control Module (LCM), Day/Night Sensor/Amplifier |
| 8 | 10 | Shift Lock, Speed Control, Air Suspension, Steering Wheel Rotation Sensor |
| 9 | 20 | Lighting Control Module (LCM), Multi–Function Switch |
| 10 | 20 | Brake Pedal Position (BPP) Switch, Brake Pressure Switch |
| 11 | 10 | Electronic Crash Sensor |
| 12 | 15 | Instrument Cluster, Anti–Theft, Ignition Switch, Ignition Coils |
| 13 | 10 | Anti–Lock Brake Module, Traction Control Switch |
| 14 | 7.5 | Transmission Control Switch, Lighting Control Module |
| 15 | 20 | Multi–Function Switch |
| 16 | 30 | Wiper Control Module (WCM), Windshield Wiper Motor |
| 17 | 10 | Digital Transmission Range (DTR) Sensor |
| 18 | 7.5 | Lighting Control Module, Front Radio Control Unit, Cellular Telephone Transceiver, Electronic Day/Night Mirror, Compass Module |
| 19 | 10 | EATC, Clock, Instrument Cluster, PCM |
| 20 | 7.5 | Lighting Control Module, ABS, Shift Lock |
| 21 | 20 | Multi–Function Switch |
| 22 | 20 | Multi–Function Switch, High Mount Stop Lamps |
| 23 | 20 | Data Link Connector, I/P Cigar Lighter |
| 24 | 5 | Front Radio Control Unit |
| 25 | 15 | Lighting Control Module (LCM) |
| 26 | 5 | Digital Transmission Range (DTR) Sensor |
| 27 | 20 | Fuel Filler Door Release Switch |
| 28 | 10 | Heated Mirrors |
| 29 | 20 | LF Door Module |
| 30 | 7.5 | LF Seat Module, Trunk Lid Release Switch, Door Lock Switches, LF Seat Control Switch, LF Door Module, Power Mirror Switch |
| 31 | 7.5 | Main Light Switch, Lighting Control Module (LCM) |
| 33 | 15 | Front Radio Control Unit, Digital Compact Disc Changer, Cellular Telephone Transceiver |
| RELAY POSITION | | RELAY |
| 1 | | ACCY Delay Relay (Signature/Cartier), Power Window Relay (Executive) |

93146G32

**The interior fuse box locations—1998 Town Car**

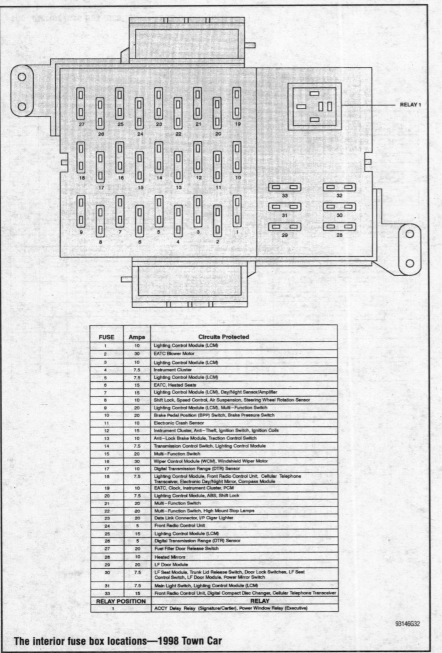

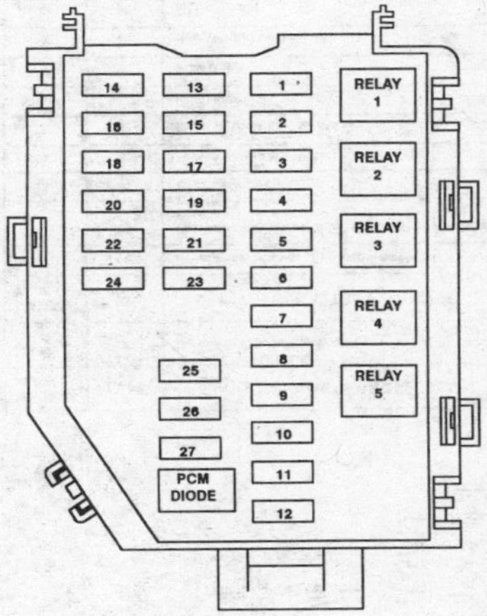


POWER DISTRIBUTION BOX

| MAXI FUSE | Amps | Circuits Protected |
|---|---|---|
| 1 | 50 | Ignition Switch |
| 2 | 40 | Ignition Switch |
| 3 | 50 | Cooling Fan (Hi Speed) |
| 4 | 30 | PCM Power Relay |
| 5 | 40 | I/P fuse Panel, Fuses 10, 19, 21, 23, 25, 27 |
| 6 | 30 | Starting System |
| 7 | 50 | I/P Fuse Panel, Fuses 1, 3, 5, 7, 9, 31 |
| 8 | 30 | Driver's Power Seat, I/P Fuse Panel, Fuse 30 |
| 9 | 50 | Anti–Lock Brakes |
| 10 | 40 | Rear Defrost |
| 11 | 40 | ACCY Delay Relay (LTS/Signature/Cartier), Power Window Relay (Executive), I/P Fuse Panel, Fuse 29 |
| 12 | 30 | Air Suspension |
| 25 | 30 | Power Lumbar, Passenger Power Seat |
| 26 | 30 c.b. | Cooling Fan (Lo Speed) |
| 27 | — | NOT USED |
| **MINI FUSE** | **Amps** | **Circuits Protected** |
| 13 | 15 | Charging System |
| 14 | 20 | Fuel Pump |
| 15 | 10 | Air Bags |
| 16 | 30 | Heated Seats |
| 17 | 10 | Air Suspension |
| 18 | 15 | Horn |
| 19 | 30 | Subwoofer, I/P Fuse Panel, Fuse 23 |
| 20 | 15 | Fuel Injectors, PCM |
| 21 | 15 | Heated Oxygen Sensor, Trans Solenoids |
| 22 | – | NOT USED |
| 23 | – | NOT USED |
| 24 | 20 | Auxiliary Power Outlet |
| **RELAY POSITION** | | **RELAY** |
| 1 | | Fuel Pump Relay |
| 2 | | AC Clutch Relay |
| 3 | | PCM Power Relay |
| 4 | | Air Suspension Relay |
| 5 | | Rear Defrost Relay |

93146G33

**The engine compartment fuse box locations—1998 Town Car**

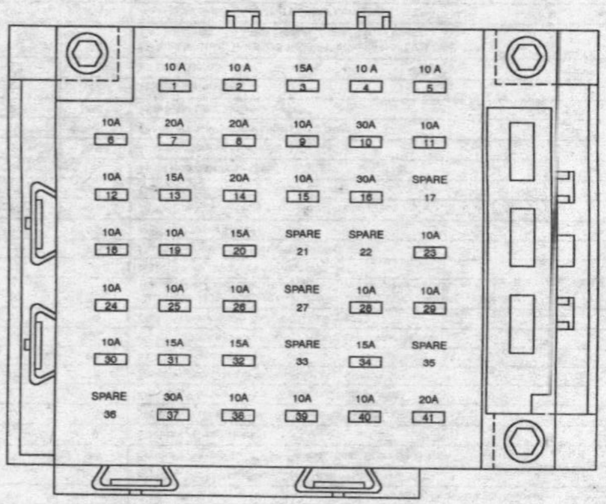


| FUSE | AMPS | CIRCUITS PROTECTED |
|---|---|---|
| 1 | 10 | Lighting Control Module: Anti-Theft Indicator Lamp, PWM Dimming Output Illumination Lamps for Microphone, Heated Seat Switches, Rear Defrost Control Switch, EATC Control Panel, Message Center Switches, Speed Control Switches, Cigar Lighter, Console and Ashtray |
| 2 | 10 | Data Link Connector (DLC), Powertrain Control Module (PCM) |
| 3 | 15 | Multi-Function Switch, Cornering Lamps, High Beam and Turn Signal input to LCM |
| 4 | 10 | Power Door Locks and Power Windows Switch Backlights, Front Radio Control Unit, Mobile Telephone Transceiver, Lighting Control Module, (RUN/ACC Sense), RESCU, Electronic Day/Night Mirror |
| 5 | 10 | Virtual Image Instrument Cluster, Lighting Control Module (LCM RUN/START Sense), Light Sensor/Amplifier |
| 6 | 10 | Virtual Image Instrument Cluster, RF Park/Turn Lamp |
| 7 | 20 | Power Point |
| 8 | 20 | Fuel Filler Door Release Switch, Trunk Lid Relay |
| 9 | 10 | Air Bag Diagnostic Monitor, EATC Module, Blower Motor Relay |
| 10 | 30 | Windshield Wiper Motor, Windshield Wiper Module |
| 11 | 10 | Ignition Coils, Radio Interference Capacitor, PCM Power Relay, Passive Anti-Theft System (PATS) Module |
| 12 | 10 | Lighting Control Module (LCM) |
| 13 | 15 | Lighting Control Module (LCM): RF Turn Lamp, Right Turn Indicator (VIC), RR Side Marker Lamps, Tail Lamps, License Lamps, LR Stop/Turn Lamps, Clock Illumination |
| 14 | 20 | Cigar Lighter |
| 15 | 10 | ABS Evac and Fill Connector |
| 16 | 30 | Moonroof Switch |
| 17 | — | NOT USED |
| 18 | 10 | Lighting Control Module (LCM) |
| 19 | 10 | Lighting Control Module (LCM): Left Headlamp, DRL |
| 20 | 15 | Multi-Function Switch: Flash to Pass, and Hazard Warning Input to LCM |
| 21 | — | NOT USED |
| 22 | — | NOT USED |
| 23 | 10 | Digital Transmission Range (DTR) Sensor |
| 24 | 10 | Virtual Image Instrument Cluster (VIC), LF Park/Turn Lamp |
| 25 | 10 | Lighting Control Module (LCM): Right Headlamp |
| 26 | 10 | Virtual Image Instrument Cluster (VIC), EATC Module |
| 27 | — | NOT USED |
| 28 | 10 | Shift Lock Actuator, Vehicle Dynamic Module, Virtual Image Instrument Cluster, Rear Window Defrost, Heated Seat Switch Assembly, Low Tire Pressure Module, Speed Control Servo / Amplifier Assembly |
| 29 | 10 | Front Control Unit (Radio) |
| 30 | 10 | Heated Mirrors |
| 31 | 15 | Lighting Control Module (LCM): FCU, Electronic Day/Night Mirror, RH and LH I/P Courtesy Lamp, Door Courtesy Lamps, RH and LH Map Lamps, RR and LR Reading Lamps, RH and LH Visor Lamps, Storage Bin Lamp, Trunk Lid Lamp, Glove Box Lamp, Light Sensor Amplifier |
| 32 | 15 | Speed Control DEAC Switch, Brake Pedal Position (BPP) Switch |
| 33 | — | NOT USED |
| 34 | 15 | Console Shift Illumination, A/C Clutch Cycling Pressure Switch, A/C Clutch Relay, DTR Sensor, Intake Manifold Runner Control |
| 35 | — | NOT USED |
| 36 | — | NOT USED |
| 37 | 30 | Subwoofer Amplifier, Front Control Unit (Radio) |
| 38 | 10 | Digital Clock, CD Player, Mobile Telephone Transceiver, RESCU |
| 39 | 10 | Power Door Locks, Power Seats, Power Mirrors, Keyless Entry, LF Seat Module, LF Door Module |
| 40 | 10 | Multi-Function Switch, Cornering Lamps |
| 41 | 20 | LF Door Module |

93146G38

**The interior fuse box locations—1998 Continental**

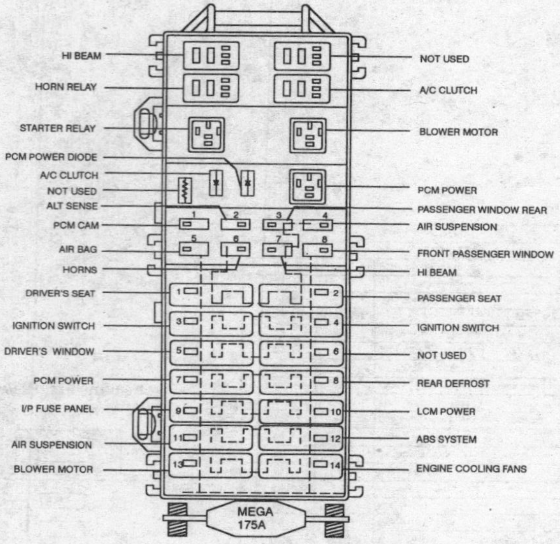


| MEGA-FUSE | AMPS | CIRCUITS PROTECTED |
|---|---|---|
| — | 175 | Generator/Voltage Regulator |
| **MAXI-FUSE** | **AMPS** | **CIRCUITS PROTECTED** |
| 1 | 30 | Driver's Seat Module, LF Heated Seat Module, LF Power Lumbar |
| 2 | 30 | Passenger's Seat Module, RF Heated Seat Module, RF Power Lumbar |
| 3 | 40 | Ignition Switch |
| 4 | 40 | Ignition Switch, Starter Relay |
| 5 | 40 | Driver Window, LF Door Module |
| 6 | — | NOT USED |
| 7 | 30 | PCM Power |
| 8 | 40 | Rear Window Defrost Control |
| 9 | 60 | I/P Fuse Panel |
| 10 | 60 | LCM Power, Power Point |
| 11 | 60 | Compressor Relay |
| 12 | 60 | Anti-Lock Brake Control Module, ABS EVAC and Fill Connector |
| 13 | 40 | Blower Motor Relay |
| 14 | 60 | Dual Auxiliary Relay Box |

| MINI-FUSES | AMPS | CIRCUITS PROTECTED |
|---|---|---|
| 1 | 30 | PCM Components, AX4N Transaxle, A/C Clutch Relay |
| 2 | 10 | Generator/Voltage Regulator |
| 3 | 30 | Rear Passenger Window |
| 4 | 30 | Air Suspension |
| 5 | 10 | Air Bag Diagnostic Monitor |
| 6 | 20 | Horn Relay |
| 7 | 15 | Hi Beam Relay |
| 8 | 30 | Front Passenger Window |

93146G39

**The engine compartment fuse box locations—1998 Continental**

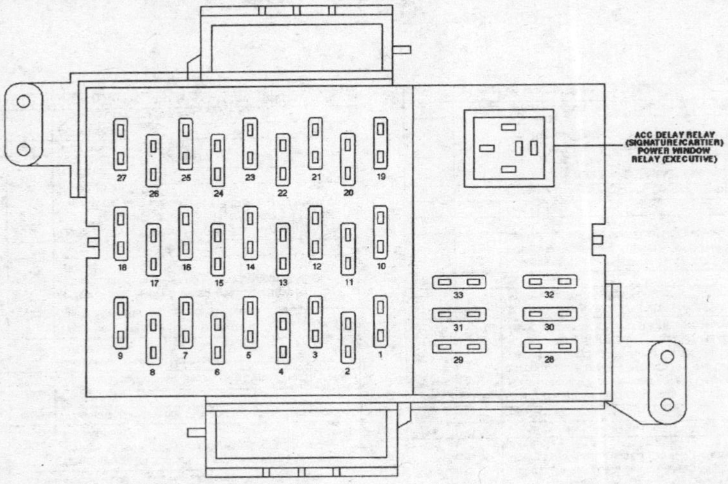


| FUSE | Amps | Circuits Protected |
|---|---|---|
| 1 | 10 | Lighting Control Module (LCM) |
| 2 | 30 | EATC Blower Motor |
| 3 | 10 | Lighting Control Module (LCM) |
| 4 | 7.5 | Instrument Cluster |
| 5 | 7.5 | Lighting Control Module (LCM) |
| 6 | 15 | EATC, Heated Seats |
| 7 | 15 | Lighting Control Module (LCM), Day/Night Sensor/Amplifier |
| 8 | 10 | Shift Lock, Speed Control, Air Suspension, Steering Wheel Rotation Sensor |
| 9 | 20 | Lighting Control Module (LCM), Multifunction Switch |
| 10 | 20 | Brake Pedal Position (BPP) Switch, Brake Pressure Switch |
| 11 | 10 | Restraint Control Module (RCM) |
| 12 | 15 | Instrument Cluster, Anti-Theft, Ignition Coils |
| 13 | 10 | Anti-Lock Brake Module, Traction Control Switch |
| 14 | 7.5 | Transmission Control Switch (TCS), Lighting Control Module (LCM) |
| 15 | 20 | Multifunction Switch |
| 16 | 30 | Wiper Control Module (WCM), Windshield Wiper Motor |
| 17 | 10 | Digital Transmission Range (DTR) Sensor |
| 18 | 7.5 | Lighting Control Module (LCM), Front Radio Control Unit, Cellular Telephone Transceiver, Electronic Day/Night Mirror, Compass Module |
| 19 | 10 | EATC, Clock, Instrument Cluster, PCM |
| 20 | 7.5 | Lighting Control Module (LCM), ABS, Shift Lock |
| 21 | 20 | Multifunction Switch |
| 22 | 20 | Multifunction Switch, High Mounted Stoplamps |
| 23 | 20 | Data Link Connector (DLC), I/P Cigar Lighter |
| 24 | 5 | Front Radio Control Unit |
| 25 | 15 | Lighting Control Module (LCM) |
| 26 | 5 | Digital Transmission Range (DTR) Sensor |
| 27 | 20 | Fuel Filler Door Release Switch |
| 28 | 10 | Heated Mirrors |
| 29 | 20 | LF Door Module |
| 30 | 7.5 | LF Seat Module, Luggage Compartment Lid Release Switch, Door Lock Switches, LF Seat Control Switch, LF Door Module, Exterior Rear View Mirror Switch |
| 31 | 7.5 | Main Light Switch, Lighting Control Module (LCM) |
| 33 | 16 | Front Radio Control Unit, Digital Compact Disc (CD) Changer, Cellular Telephone Transceiver |

93146G17

**The interior fuse box locations—1999–00 Town Car**

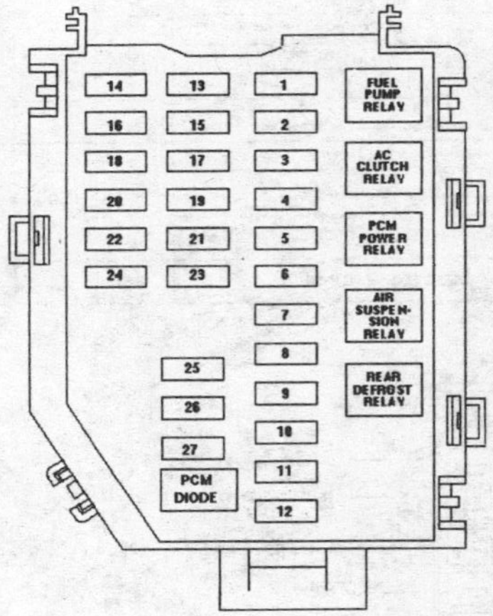


| MAXI FUSE | Amps | Circuits Protected |
|---|---|---|
| 1 | 50 | Ignition Switch |
| 2 | 40 | Ignition Switch |
| 3 | 50 | Cooling Fan (High Speed) |
| 4 | 30 | PCM Power Relay |
| 5 | 40 | Fuse Junction Panel, Fuses 10, 19, 21, 23, 25, 27 |
| 6 | 30 | Starting System |
| 7 | 50 | Fuse Junction Panel, Fuses 1, 3, 5, 7, 9, 31 |
| 8 | 30 | Driver Power Seat, Fuse Junction Panel, Fuse 30 |
| 9 | 50 | Anti-Lock Brakes |
| 10 | 40 | Rear Defrost |
| 11 | 40 | Accessory Delay Relay (Signature/Cartier), Power Window Relay (Executive), Fuse Junction Panel, Fuse 29 |
| 12 | 30 | Air Suspension |
| 25 | 30 | Power Lumbar, Passenger Power Seat |
| 26 | 30 c.b. | Cooling Fan (Low Speed) |
| 27 | — | NOT USED |
| **MINI FUSE** | **Amps** | **Circuits Protected** |
| 13 | 15 | Charging System |
| 14 | 20 | Fuel Pump |
| 15 | - | NOT USED |
| 16 | 30 | Heated Seats |
| 17 | 10 | Air Suspension |
| 18 | 15 | Horn |
| 19 | 30 | Subwoofer, Fuse Junction Panel, Fuse 33 |
| 20 | 15 | Fuel Injectors, PCM |
| 21 | 15 | Heated Oxygen Sensor, Trans Solenoids, EVAP Canister Vent Solenoid Valve, EGR Vacuum Regulator, EVAP Canister Purge Solenoid |
| 22 | - | NOT USED |
| 23 | - | NOT USED |
| 24 | 20 | Auxiliary Power Outlet |

93146G18

**The engine compartment fuse box locations—1999–00 Town Car**

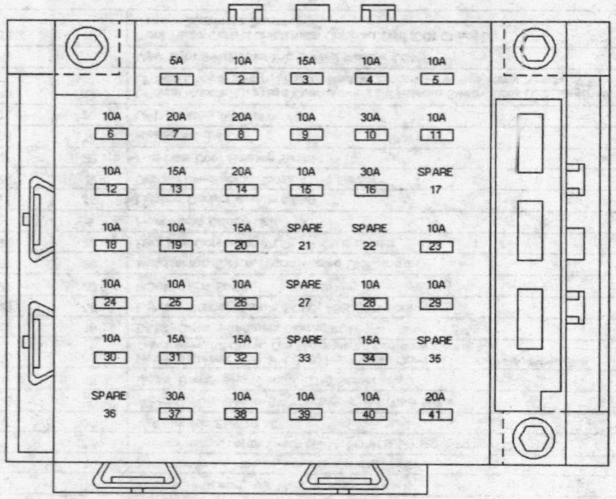


| FUSE | AMPS | CIRCUITS PROTECTED |
|---|---|---|
| 1 | 5 | Lighting Control Module: Anti–Theft Indicator Lamp, PWM Dimming Output Illumination Lamps for Microphone, Heated Seat Switches, Rear Defrost Control Switch, EATC Control Panel, Message Center Switches, Speed Control Switches, Cigar Lighter, Console and Ashtray |
| 2 | 10 | Data Link Connector (DLC), Powertrain Control Module (PCM) |
| 3 | 15 | Multifunction Switch, Cornering Lamps, High Beam and Turn Signal Input to LCM |
| 4 | 10 | Power Door Locks and Power Windows Switch Backlights, Front Radio Control Unit, Cellular Telephone Transceiver, Lighting Control Module, (RUN/ACC Sense), RESCU, Electronic Day/Night Mirror |
| 5 | 10 | Virtual Image Instrument Cluster, Lighting Control Module (LCM RUN/START Sense), Light Sensor/Amplifier |
| 6 | 10 | Virtual Image Instrument Cluster, RF Park/Turn Lamp |
| 7 | 20 | Power Point |
| 8 | 20 | Fuel Filler DoorRelease Switch,Luggage Comp Lid Relay |
| 9 | 10 | Restraints Control Module, EATC Module, Blower Motor Relay |
| 10 | 30 | Windshield Wiper Motor, Windshield Wiper Module |
| 11 | 10 | Ignition Coils, Radio Interference Capacitor, PCM Power Relay, Passive Anti–Theft System (PATS) Module |
| 12 | 10 | Lighting Control Module (LCM) |
| 13 | 15 | Lighting Control Module (LCM): RF Turn Lamp, Right Turn Indicator (VIC), RR Side Marker Lamps, Tail Lamps, License Lamps, LR Stop/Turn Lamps, Clock Illumination |
| 14 | 20 | Cigar Lighter |
| 15 | 10 | ABS Evac and Fill Connector |
| 16 | 30 | Roof opening Panel Switch |
| 17 | — | NOT USED |
| 18 | 10 | Lighting Control Module (LCM) |
| 19 | 10 | Lighting Control Module (LCM): Left Headlamp, DRL |

| FUSE | AMPS | CIRCUITS PROTECTED |
|---|---|---|
| 20 | 15 | Multifunction Switch: Flash to Pass, and Hazard Warning Input to LCM |
| 21 | — | NOT USED |
| 22 | — | NOT USED |
| 23 | 10 | Digital Transmission Range (DTR) Sensor |
| 24 | 10 | Virtual Image Instrument Cluster (VIC), LF Park/Turn Lamp |
| 25 | 10 | Lighting Control Module (LCM): Right Headlamp |
| 26 | 10 | Virtual Image Instrument Cluster (VIC), EATC Module |
| 27 | — | NOT USED |
| 28 | 10 | Shift Lock Actuator, Vehicle Dynamic Module, Virtual Image Instrument Cluster, Rear Window Defrost, Heated Seat Switch Assembly, Low Tire Pressure Module, Speed Control Servo/Amplifier Assembly |
| 29 | 10 | Front Control Unit (Radio) |
| 30 | 10 | Heated Mirrors |
| 31 | 15 | Lighting Control Module (LCM): FCU, Electronic Day/Night Mirror, RH and LH I/P Courtesy Lamp, Door Courtesy Lamps, RH and LH Map Lamps, RR and LR Reading Lamps, RH and LH Visor Lamps, Storage Bin Lamp, Trunk Lid Lamp, Glove Box Lamp, Light Sensor Amplifier |
| 32 | 15 | Speed Control DEAC Switch, Brake Pedal Position (BPP) Switch |
| 33 | — | NOT USED |
| 34 | 15 | Console Shift Illumination, A/C Clutch Cycling Pressure Switch, A/C Clutch Relay, DTR Sensor, Intake Manifold Runner Control |
| 35 | — | NOT USED |
| 36 | — | NOT USED |
| 37 | 30 | Subwoofer Amplifier, Front Control Unit (Radio) |
| 38 | 10 | Digital Clock, CD Player, Mobile Telephone Transceiver, RESCU |
| 39 | 10 | Power Door Locks, Power Seats, Power Mirrors, Keyless Entry, LF Seat Module, LF Door Module |
| 40 | 10 | Multifunction Switch, Cornering Lamps |
| 41 | 20 | LF Door Module |

93146G19

**The interior fuse box locations—1999–00 Continental**

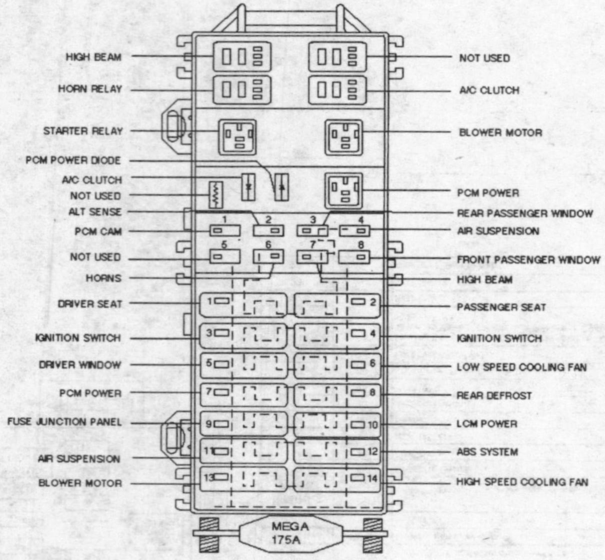


| MEGA-FUSE | AMPS | CIRCUITS PROTECTED |
|---|---|---|
| - | 175 | Generator |

| MAXI-FUSE | AMPS | CIRCUITS PROTECTED |
|---|---|---|
| 1 | 30 | Driver Seat Module, LF Heated Seat Module, LF Power Lumbar |
| 2 | 30 | Passenger Seat Module, RF Heated Seat Module, RF Power Lumbar |
| 3 | 40 | Ignition Switch |
| 4 | 40 | Ignition Switch, Starter Relay |
| 5 | 40 | Rear Driver Window, LF Door Module |
| 6 | 30 | Low Speed Cooling Fan Relay |
| 7 | 30 | PCM Power |
| 8 | 40 | Rear Window Defrost Control |
| 9 | 60 | Fuse Junction Panel |
| 10 | 60 | LCM Power, Power Point |
| 11 | 60 | Compressor Relay |
| 12 | 60 | Anti-Lock Brake Control Module, ABS EVAC and Fill Connector |
| 13 | 40 | Blower Motor Relay |
| 14 | 60 | High Speed Cooling Fan Relay |

| MINI-FUSES | AMPS | CIRCUITS PROTECTED |
|---|---|---|
| 1 | 30 | PCM Components, AX4N Transaxle |
| 2 | 20 | Generator |
| 3 | 30 | Rear Passenger Window |
| 4 | 30 | Air Suspension |
| 5 | - | NOT USED |
| 6 | 20 | Horn Relay |
| 7 | 15 | High Beam Relay |
| 8 | 30 | Front Passenger Window |

93146G20

**The engine compartment fuse box locations—1999–00 Continental**

## WIRING DIAGRAMS

### INDEX OF WIRING DIAGRAMS


| | |
|---|---|
| DIAGRAM 1 | Sample Diagram: How To Read & Interpret Wiring Diagrams |
| DIAGRAM 2 | Sample Diagram: Wiring Diagram Symbols |
| DIAGRAM 3 | 1989-92 Continental 3.8L Engine Schematic |
| DIAGRAM 4 | 1993-94 Continental 3.8L Engine Schematic |
| DIAGRAM 5 | 1995-97 Continental 4.6L Engine Schematic |
| DIAGRAM 6 | 1998-00 Continental 4.6L Engine Schematic |
| DIAGRAM 7 | 1989-92 Mark VII (EEC IV) 5.0L Engine Schematic |
| DIAGRAM 8 | 1993-95 Mark VIII 4.6L Engine Schematic |
| DIAGRAM 9 | 1996-97 Mark VIII 4.6L Engine Schematic |
| DIAGRAM 10 | 1998-00 Mark VIII 4.6L Engine Schematic |
| DIAGRAM 11 | 1989-90 Town Car (EEC IV) 5.0L Engine Schematic |
| DIAGRAM 12 | 1991-94 Town Car 4.6L Engine Schematic |
| DIAGRAM 13 | 1995 Town Car 4.6L Engine Schematic |
| DIAGRAM 14 | 1996-97 Town Car 4.6L Engine Schematic |
| DIAGRAM 15 | 1998-00 Town Car 4.6L Engine Schematic |
| DIAGRAM 16 | 1989-94 Continental Starting Chassis Schematics |
| DIAGRAM 17 | 1995-00 Continental Starting Chassis Schematics |
| DIAGRAM 18 | 1989-92 Continental Charging Chassis Schematics |
| DIAGRAM 19 | 1993-00 Continental Charging Chassis Schematics |
| DIAGRAM 20 | 1989-94 Continental Headlights w/o DRL Chassis Schematic |
| DIAGRAM 21 | 1989-94 Continental Headlights w/ DRL Chassis Schematic |
| DIAGRAM 22 | 1995-00 Continental Headlights w/o DRL Chassis Schematic |
| DIAGRAM 23 | 1989-94 Continental Parking/Marker Lights Chassis Schematic |
| DIAGRAM 24 | 1995-00 Continental Parking/Marker Lights Chassis Schematic |
| DIAGRAM 25 | 1995-97 Continental Headlights w/ DRL Chassis Schematic |
| DIAGRAM 26 | 1989-94 Continental Turn/Hazard/Stop Lights Chassis Schematic |
| DIAGRAM 27 | 1995-00 Continental Turn/Hazard/Stop Lights Chassis Schematic |
| DIAGRAM 28 | 1989-92 Mark VII Starting Chassis Schematics |
| DIAGRAM 29 | 1993-00 Mark VIII Starting Chassis Schematics |
| DIAGRAM 30 | 1989-00 Mark VIII Charging Chassis Schematics |
| DIAGRAM 31 | 1989-92 Mark VII Headlights w/o DRL Chassis Schematic |
| DIAGRAM 32 | 1989-92 Mark VII Headlights w/ DRL Chassis Schematic |
| DIAGRAM 33 | 1993-96 Mark VIII Headlights w/o DRL Chassis Schematic |
| DIAGRAM 34 | 1993-96 Mark VIII Headlights w/ DRL Chassis Schematic |
| DIAGRAM 35 | 1997-00 Mark VIII Headlights w/ DRL Chassis Schematic |
| DIAGRAM 36 | 1989-96 Mark VII/VIII Turn/Hazard/Stop Lights Chassis Schematic |
| DIAGRAM 37 | 1997-00 Mark VIII Turn/Hazard/ Stop Lights Chassis Schematic |
| DIAGRAM 38 | 1989-92 Mark VII Parking/Marker Lights Chassis Schematic |
| DIAGRAM 39 | 1993-96 Mark VIII Parking/Marker Lights Chassis Schematic |
| DIAGRAM 40 | 1997-00 Mark VIII Parking/Marker Lights Chassis Schematic |
| DIAGRAM 41 | 1989-00 Town Car Starting Chassis Schematics |
| DIAGRAM 42 | 1989-90 Town Car Charging Chassis Schematics |
| DIAGRAM 43 | 1991-95 Town Car Charging Chassis Schematics |
| DIAGRAM 44 | 1992-00Town Car Charging Chassis Schematics |
| DIAGRAM 45 | 1989-94 Town Car Turn/Hazard/Stop Lights Chassis Schematic |
| DIAGRAM 46 | 1995-97 Town Car Turn/Hazard/Stop Lights Chassis Schematic |
| DIAGRAM 47 | 1998-00 Town Car Turn/Hazard/Stop Lights Chassis Schematic |
| DIAGRAM 48 | 1989-97 TownCar Parking/Marker Lights Chassis Schematics |
| DIAGRAM 49 | 1998-00 Town Car Parking/Marker Lights Chassis Schematic |
| DIAGRAM 50 | 1989-00 Continental/Mark VII/VII/Town Car Back-up Lights Chassis Schematic |
| DIAGRAM 51 | 1989-00 Continental/Mark VII/VII/Town Car Fuel Pump Chassis Schematics |
| DIAGRAM 52 | 1989-00 Continental Horns Chassis Schematics |
| DIAGRAM 53 | 1989-00 Mark VIII/Town Car Horns Chassis Schematics |
| DIAGRAM 54 | 1989-00 Continental/Mark VII/VII/Town Car Windshield Wiper/Washer Chassis Schematics |


93146W01

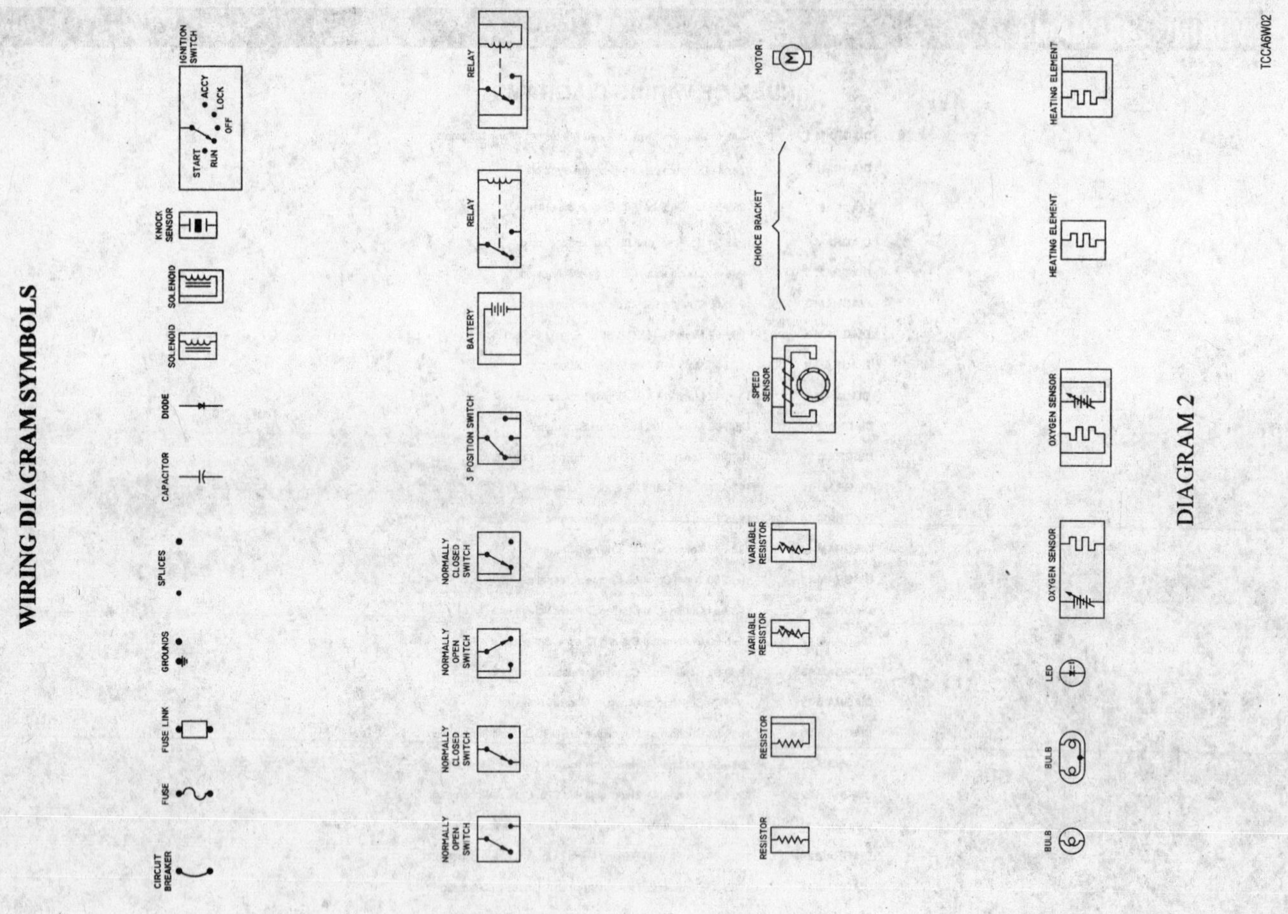

DIAGRAM 2

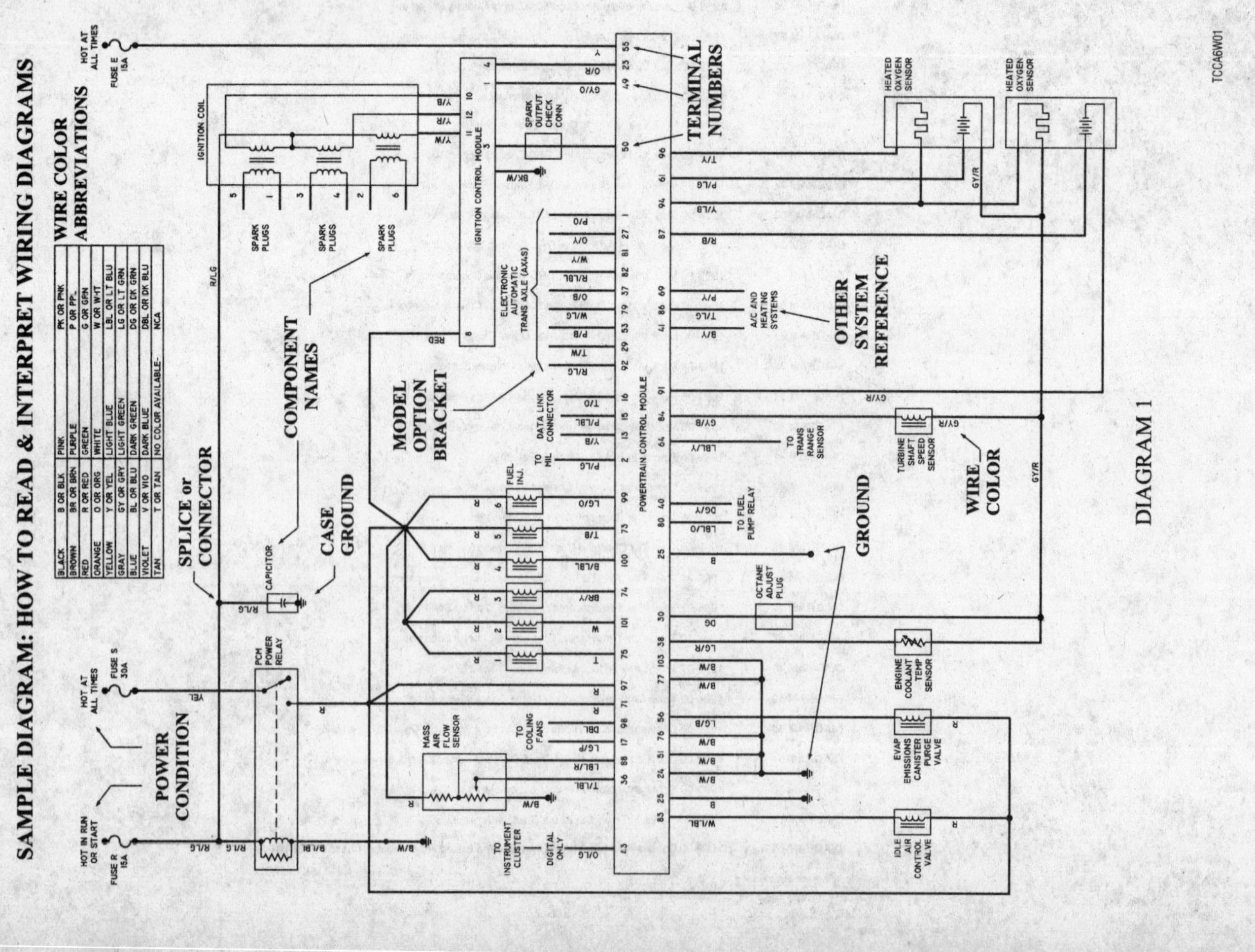

DIAGRAM 1

1993-94 CONTINENTAL 3.8L ENGINE SCHEMATIC

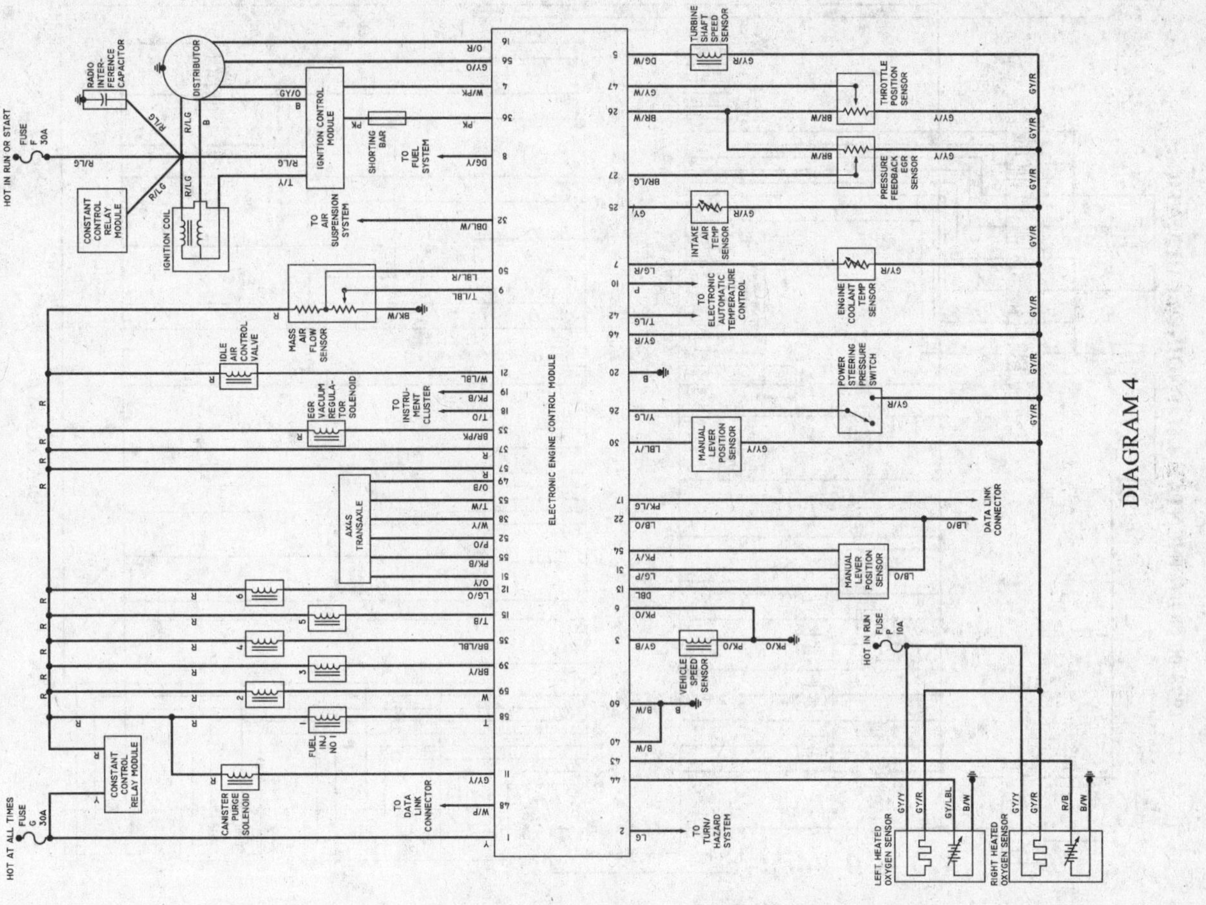

DIAGRAM 4

93146E02

1989-92 CONTINENTAL 3.8L ENGINE SCHEMATIC

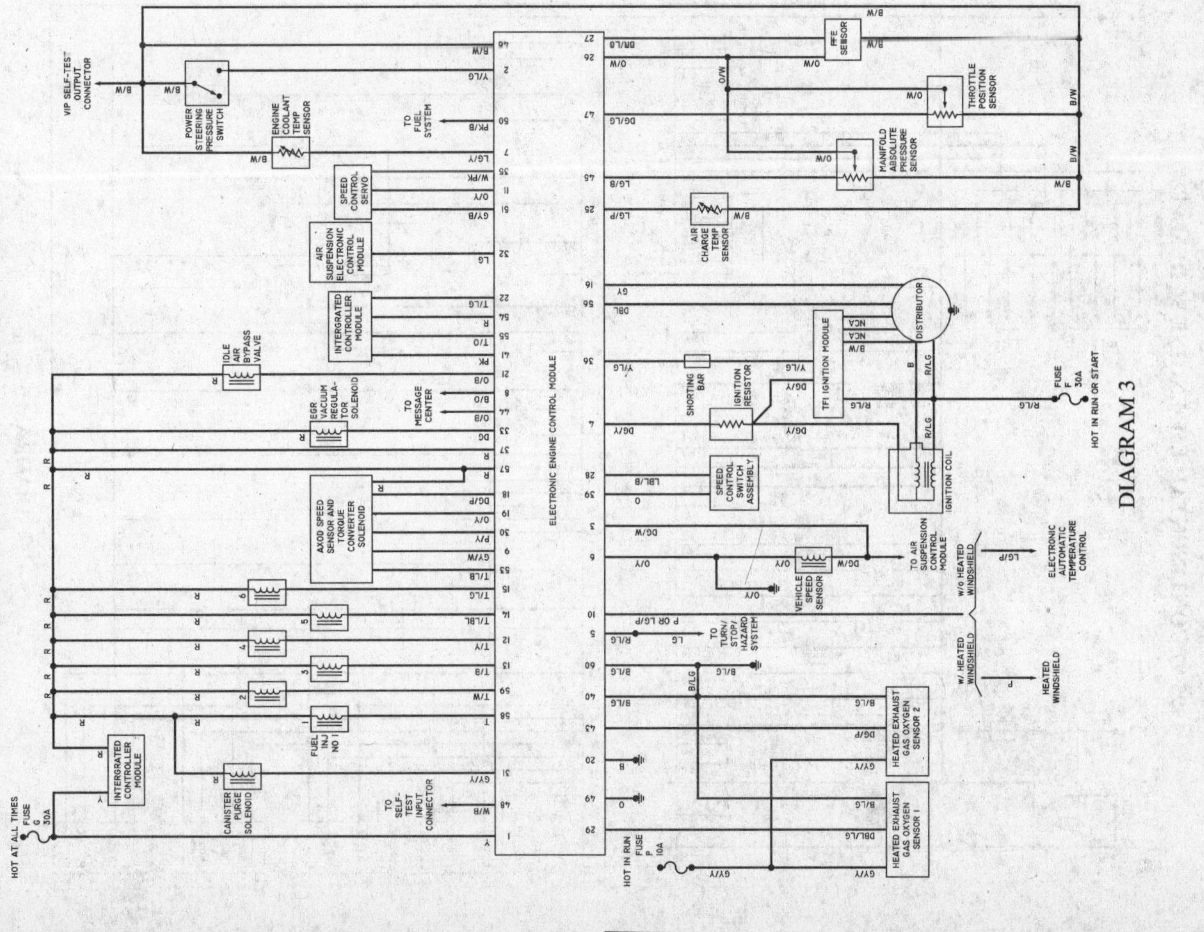

DIAGRAM 3

93146E01

## 1998-00 CONTINENTAL 4.6L ENGINE SCHEMATIC

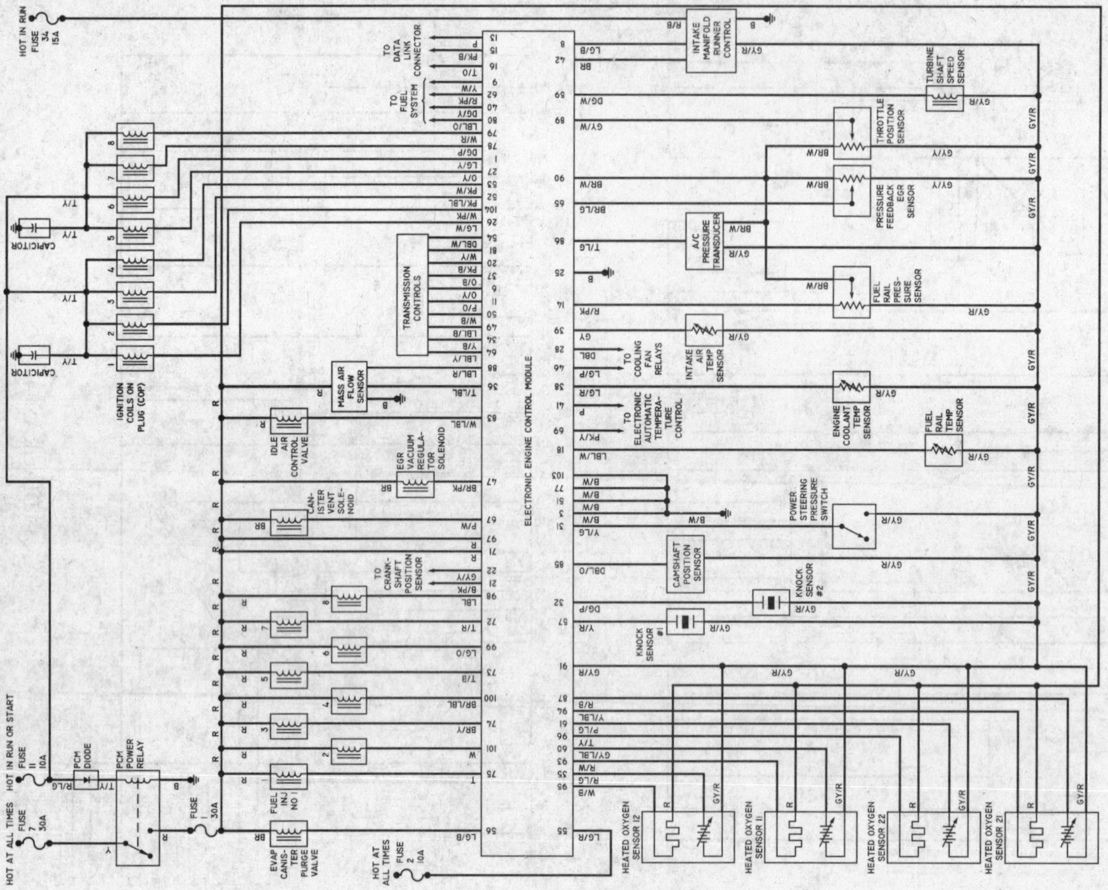

93146E04

DIAGRAM 6

## 1995-97 CONTINENTAL 4.6L ENGINE SCHEMATIC

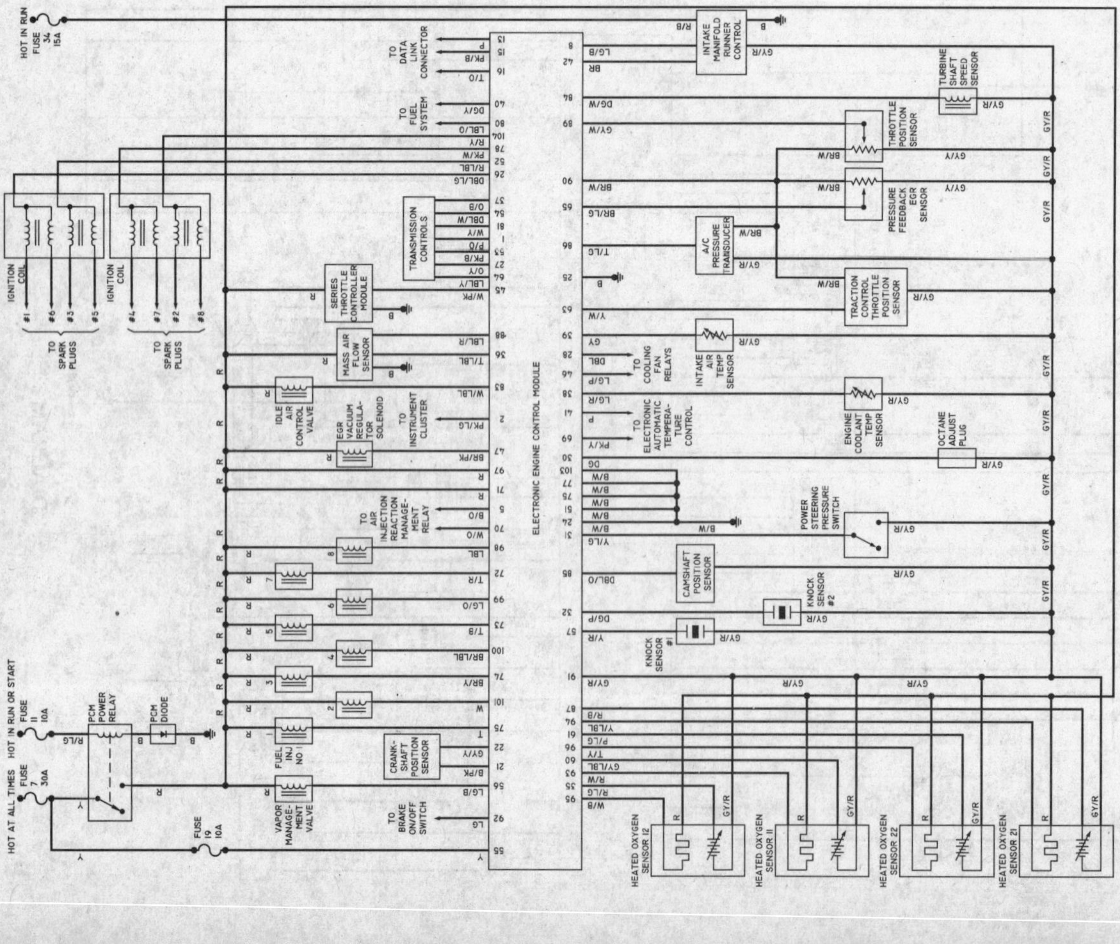

93146E03

DIAGRAM 5

## 1993-95 MARK VIII 4.6L ENGINE SCHEMATIC

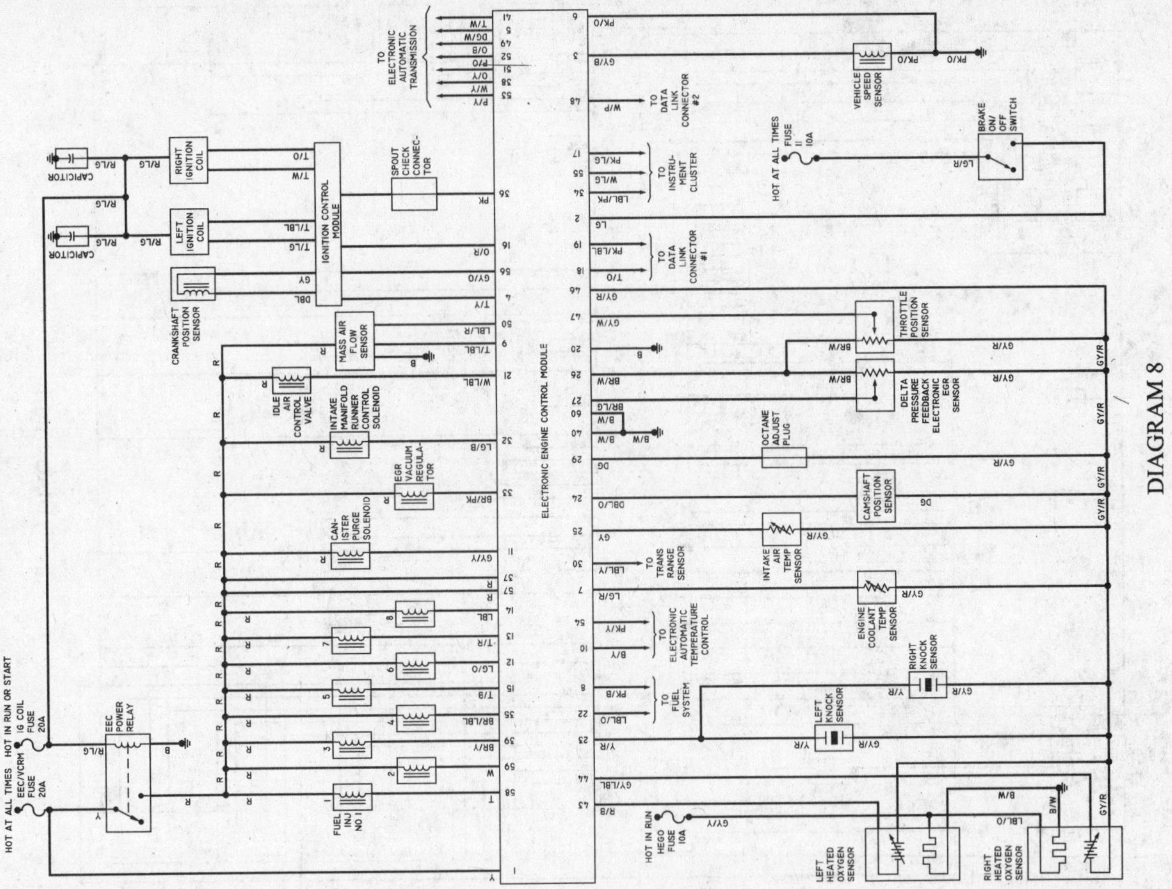


DIAGRAM 8

93146E11

## 1989-92 MARK VII (EEC IV) 5.0L ENGINE SCHEMATIC

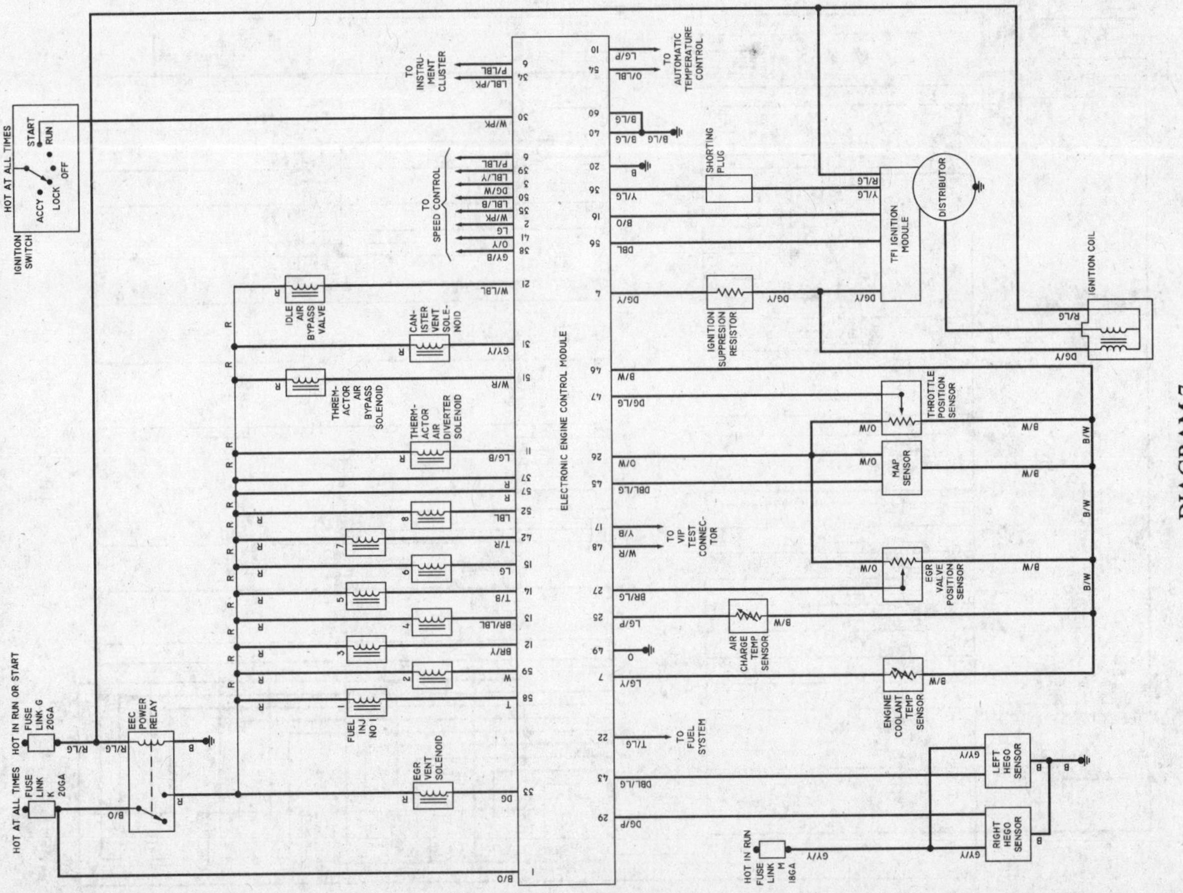


DIAGRAM 7

93146E10

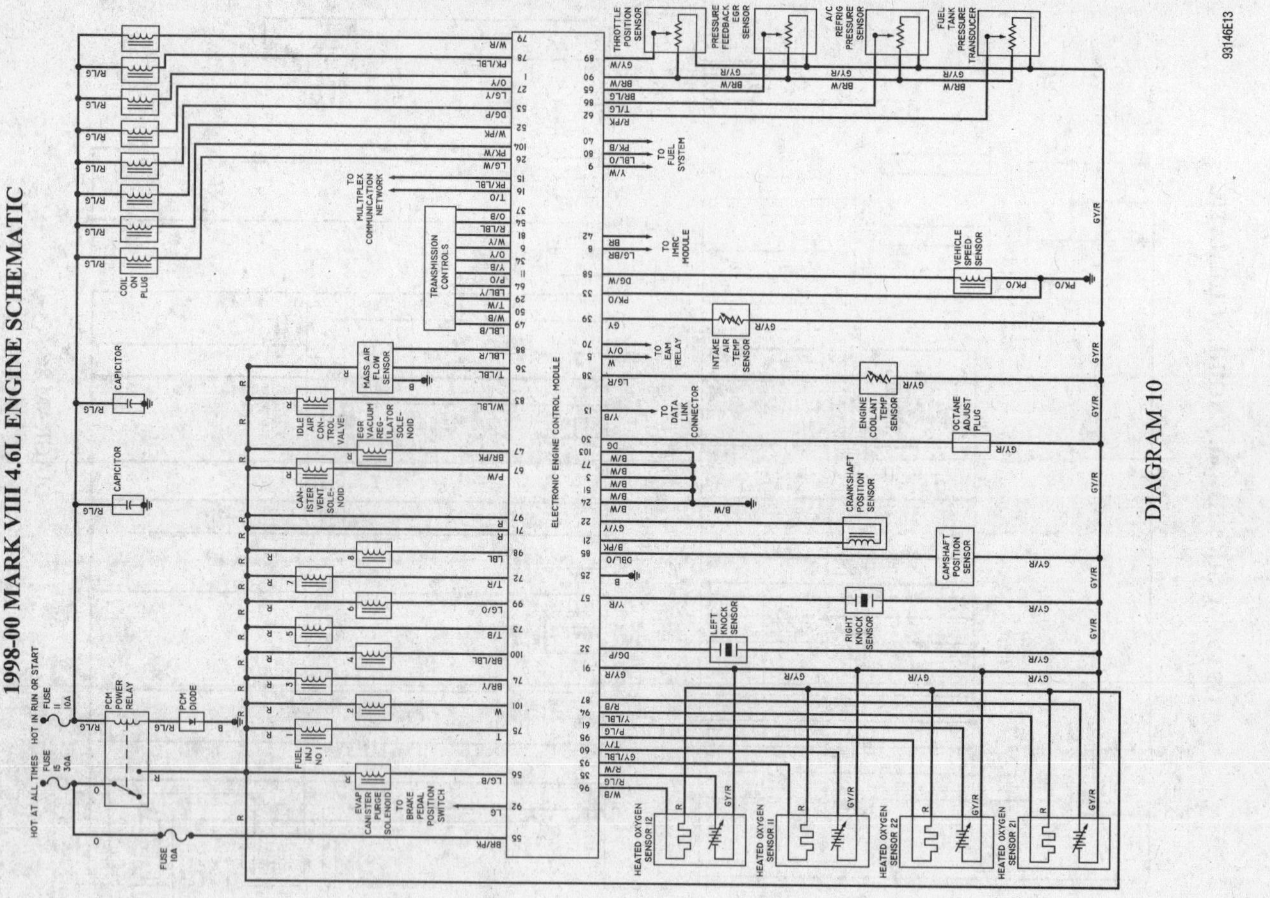


DIAGRAM 10

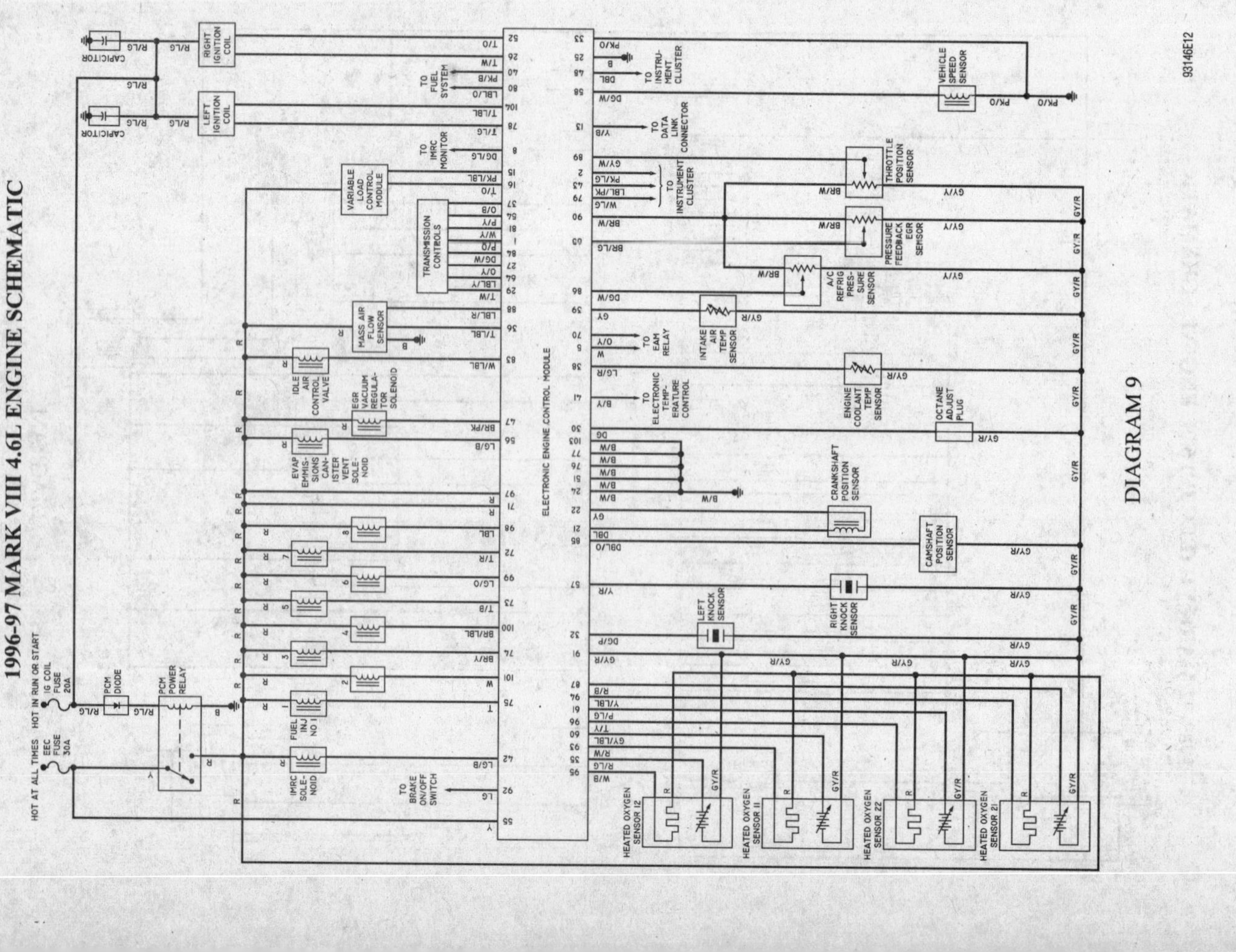


DIAGRAM 9

1991-94 TOWN CAR 4.6L ENGINE SCHEMATIC

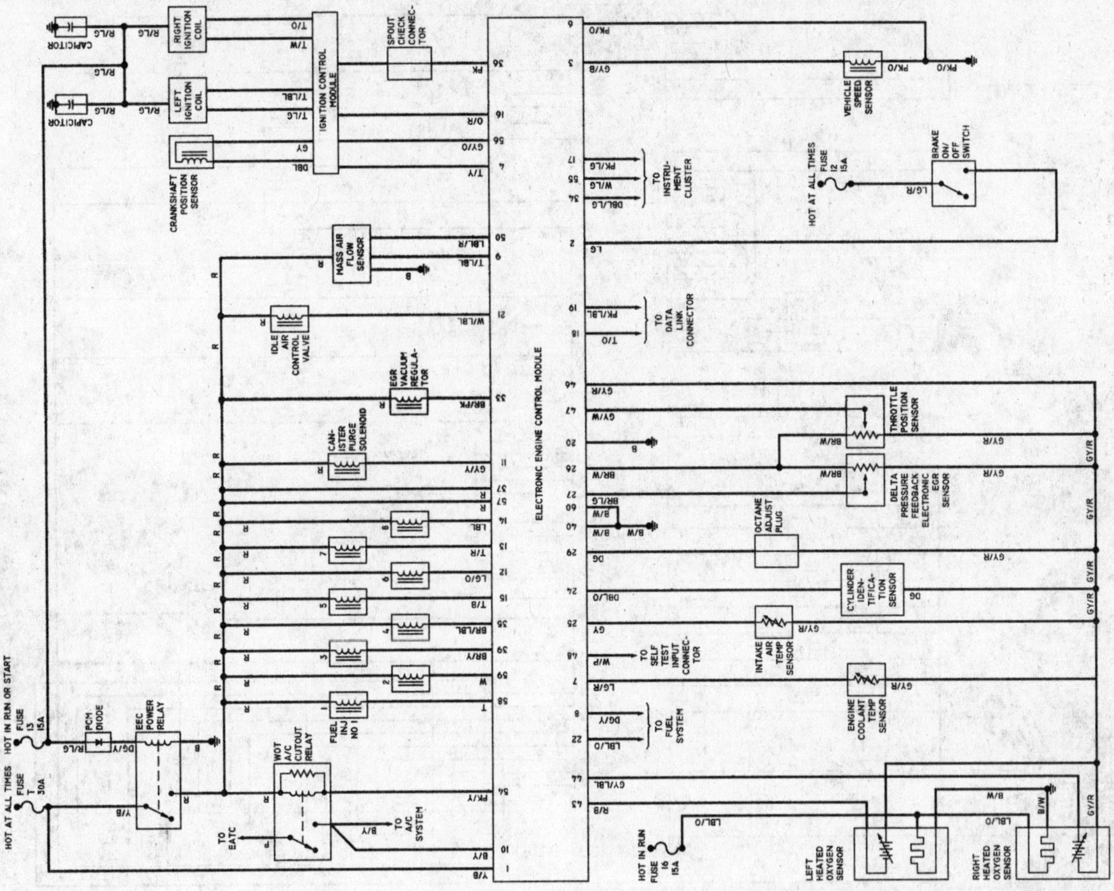

DIAGRAM 12

93146E06

1989-90 TOWN CAR (EEC IV) 5.0L ENGINE SCHEMATIC

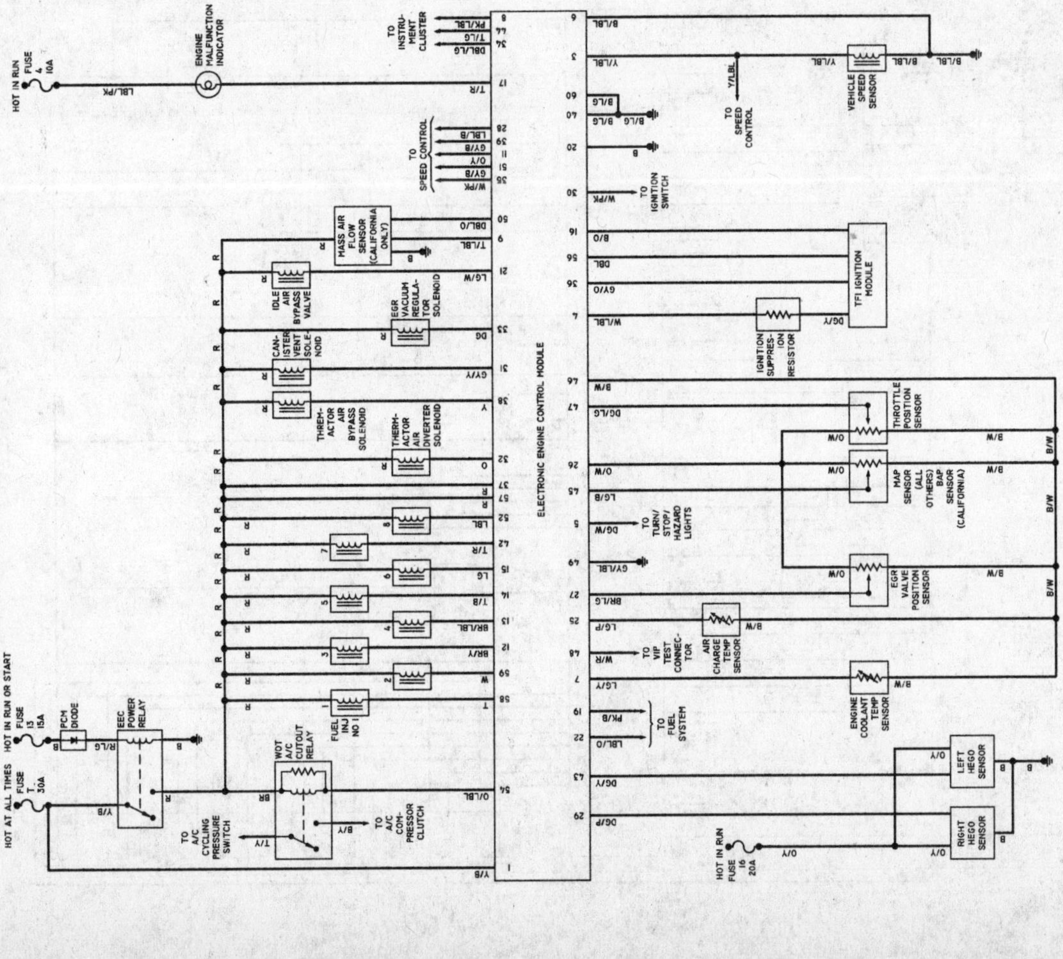

DIAGRAM 11

93146E05

## 1996-97 TOWN CAR 4.6L ENGINE SCHEMATIC

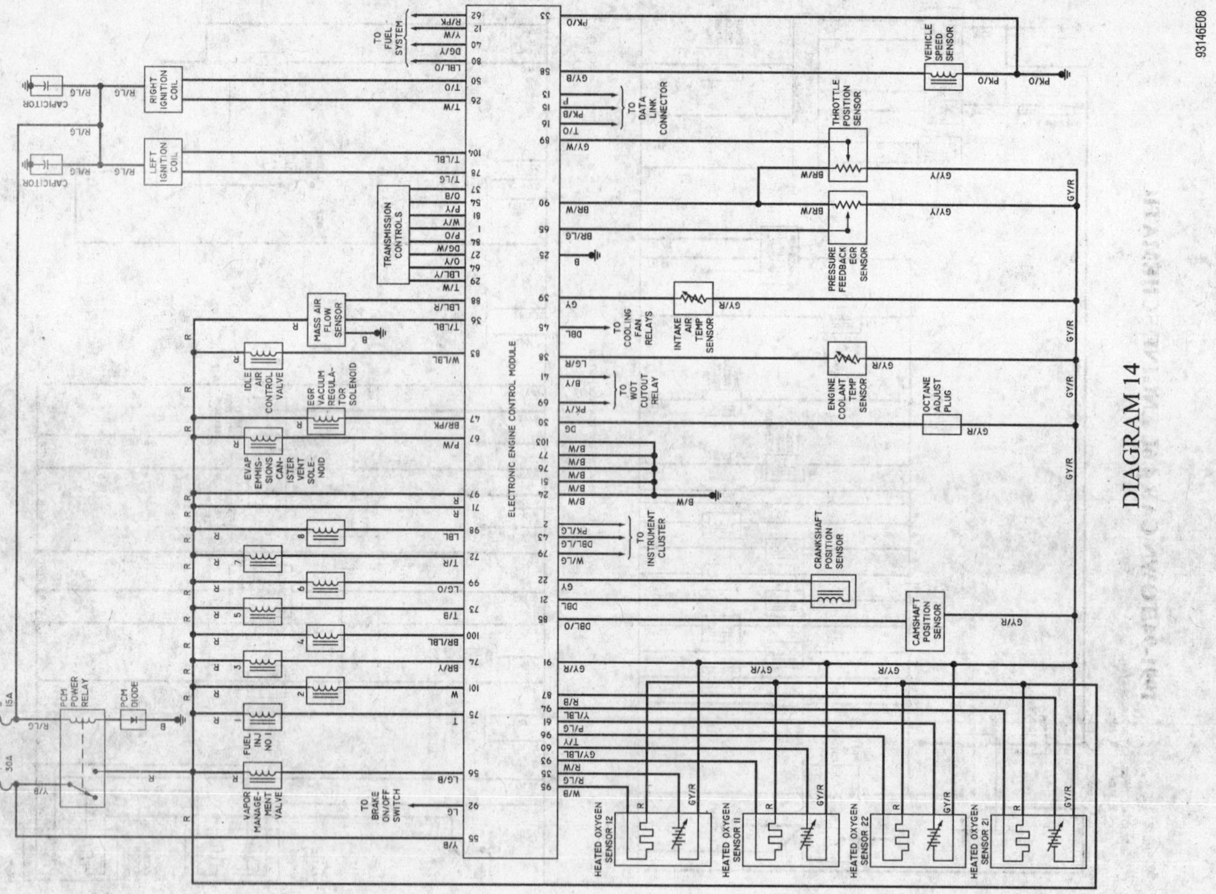


DIAGRAM 14

## 1995 TOWN CAR 4.6L ENGINE SCHEMATIC

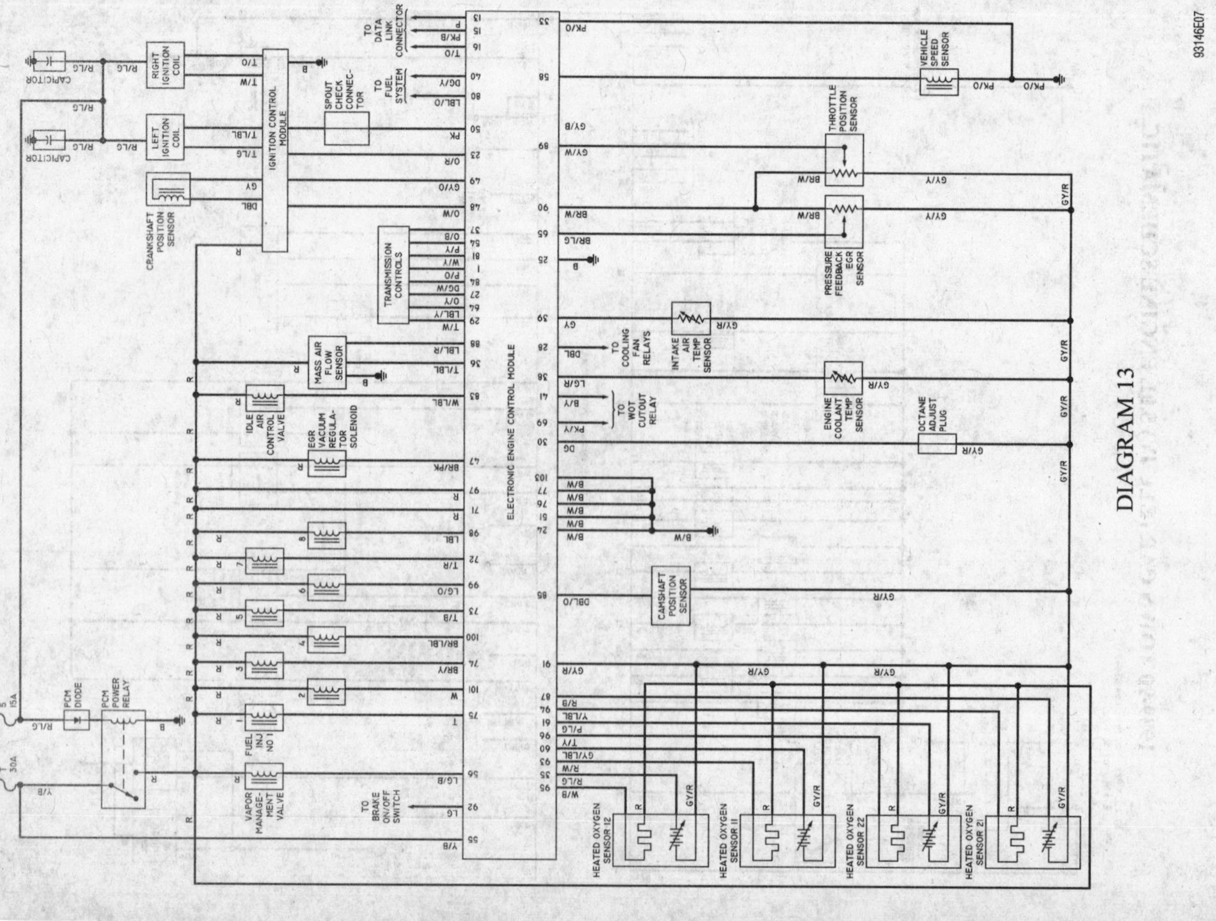


DIAGRAM 13

## 1989-94 CONTINENTAL CHASSIS SCHEMATICS

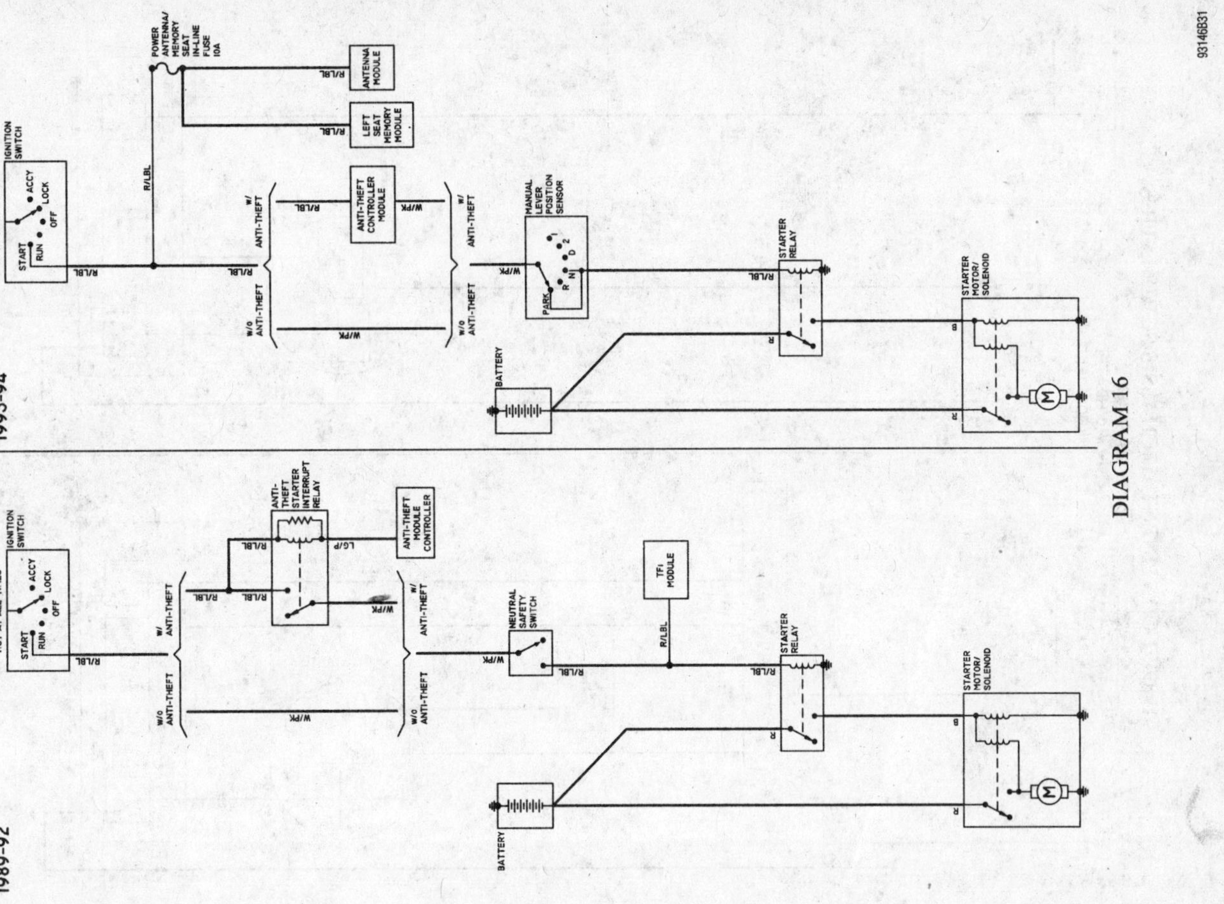

DIAGRAM 16

## 1998-00 TOWN CAR 4.6L ENGINE SCHEMATIC

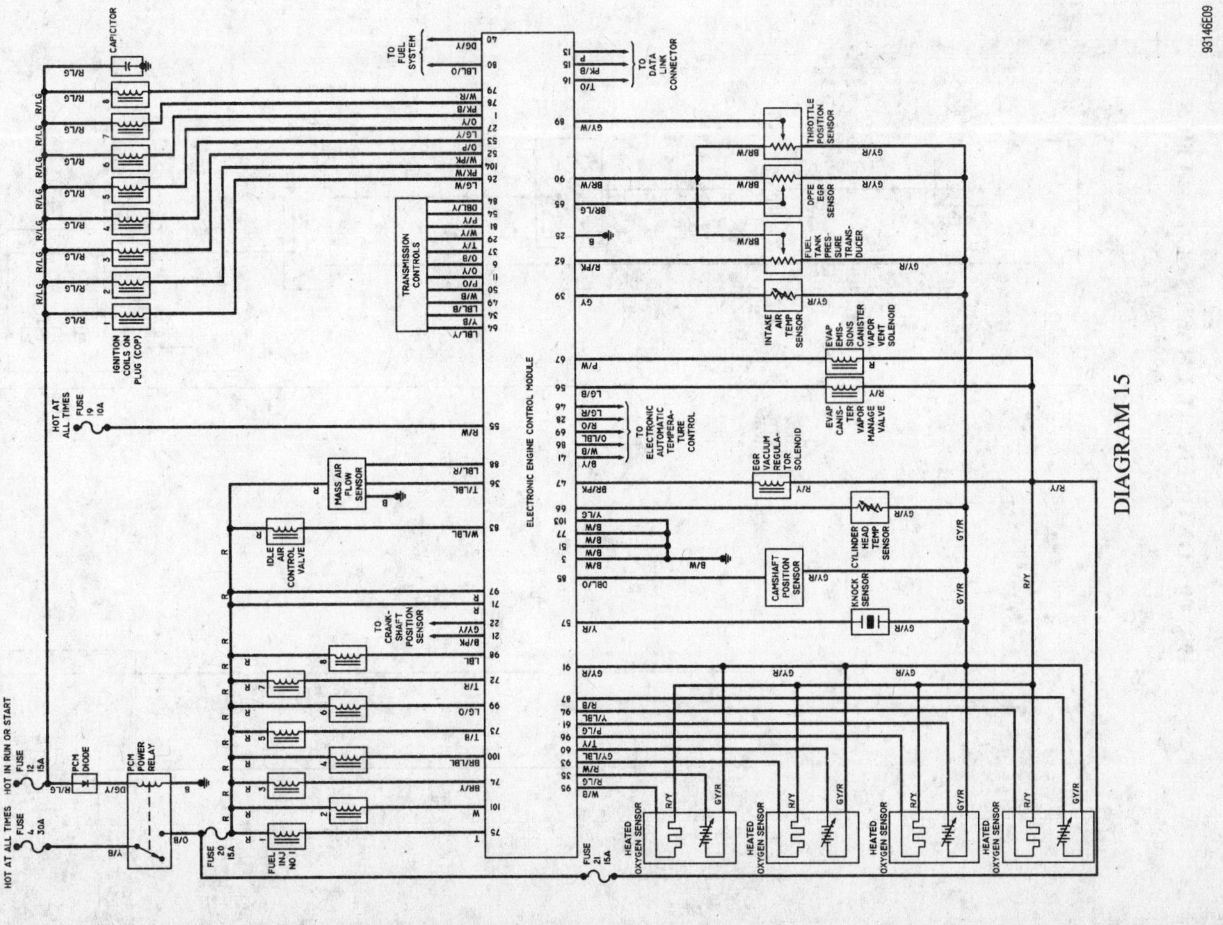

DIAGRAM 15

## 1989-92 CONTINENTAL CHASSIS SCHEMATICS

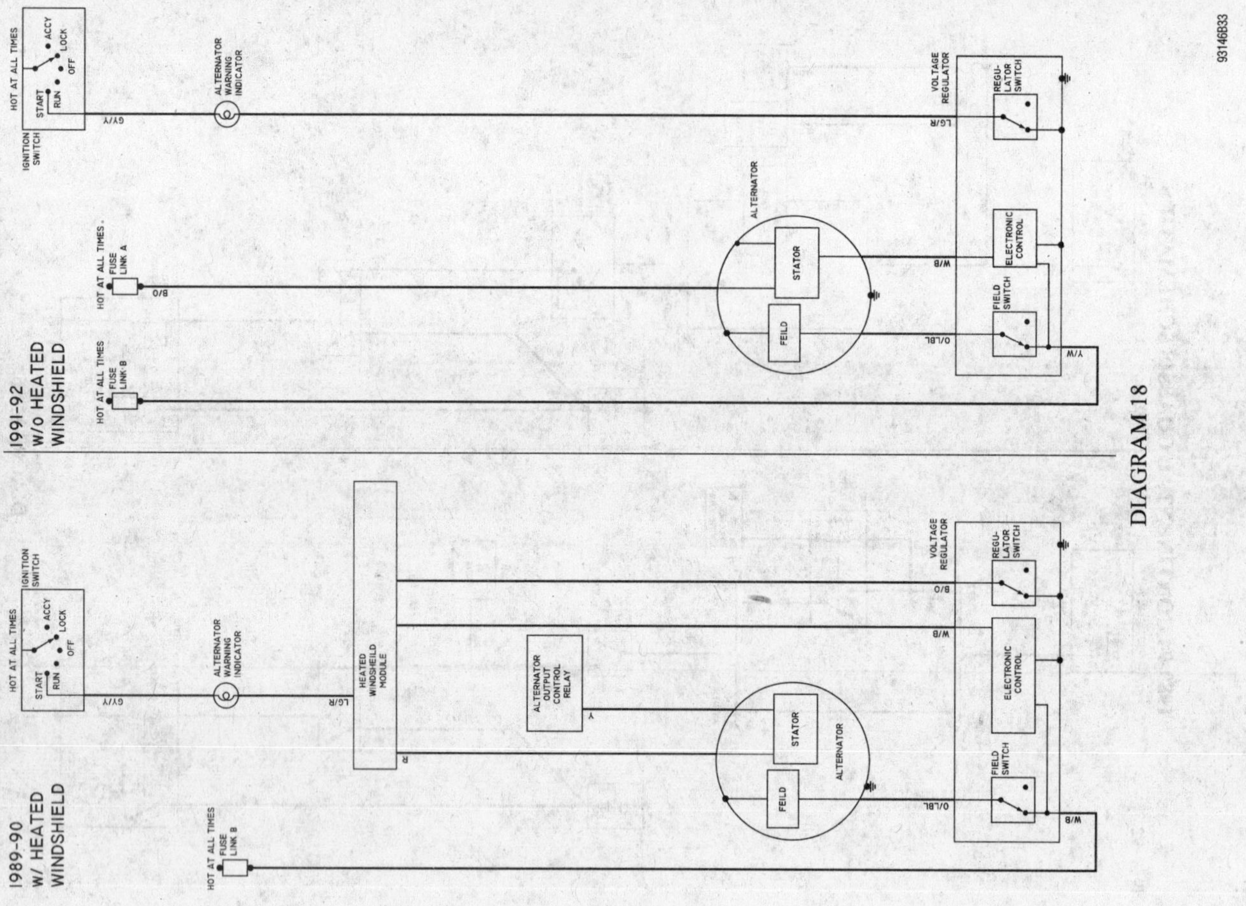


DIAGRAM 18

## 1995-00 CONTINENTAL CHASSIS SCHEMATICS

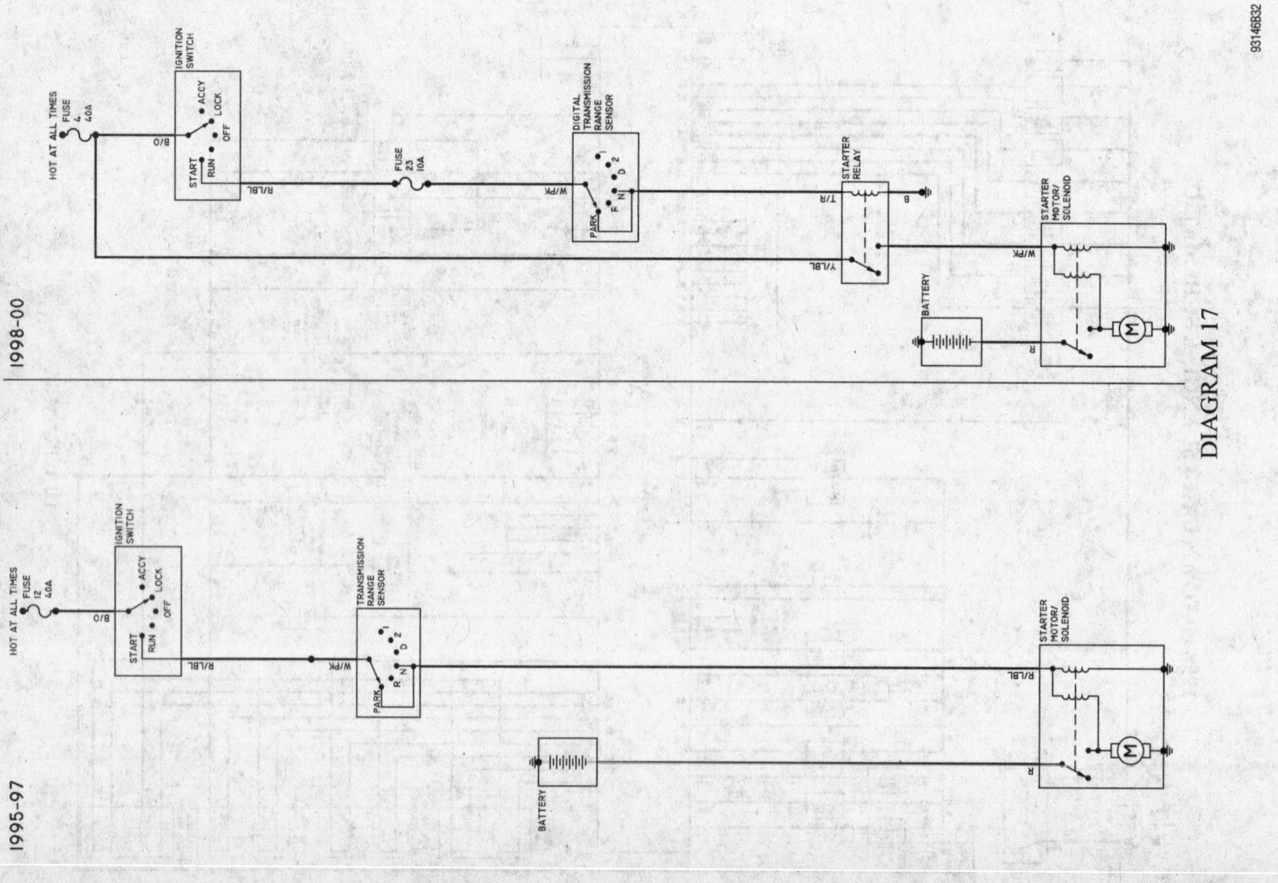


DIAGRAM 17

## 1993-00 CONTINENTAL CHASSIS SCHEMATICS

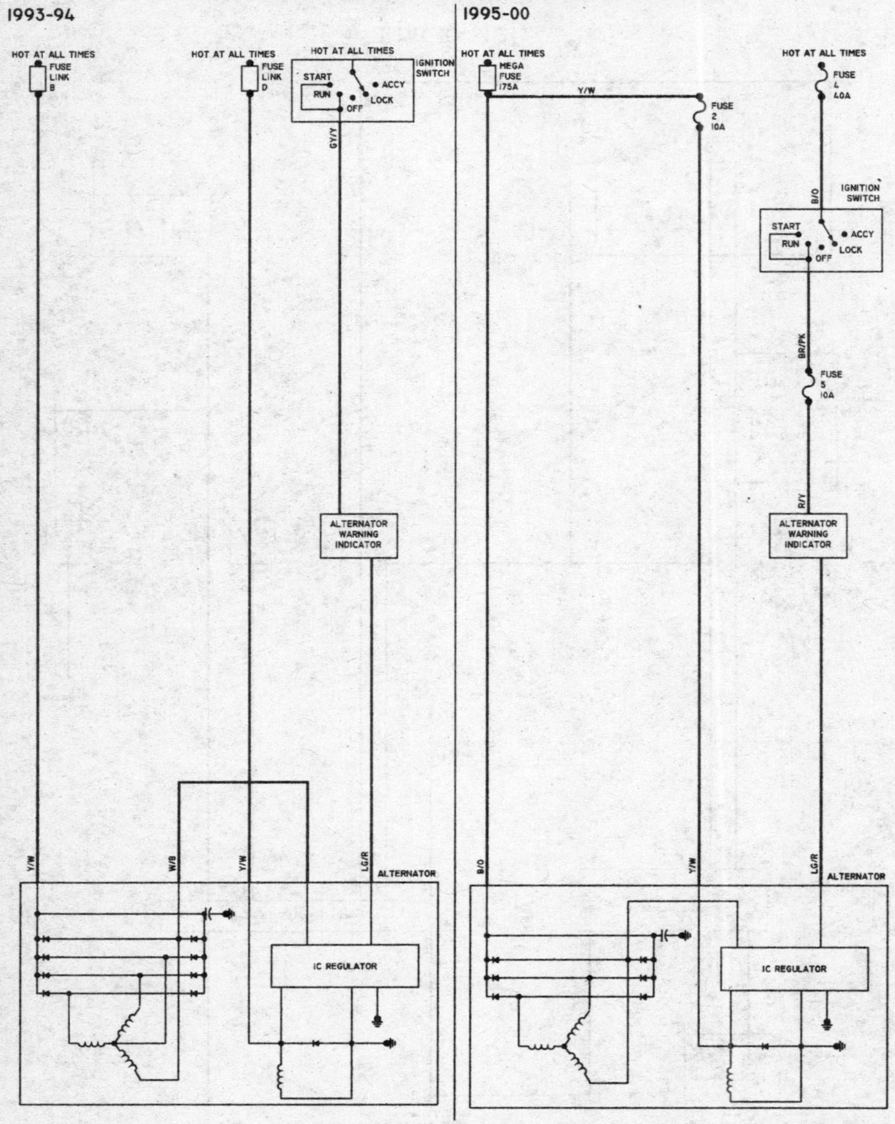


DIAGRAM 19

93146B34

## 1989-94 CONTINENTAL CHASSIS SCHEMATIC

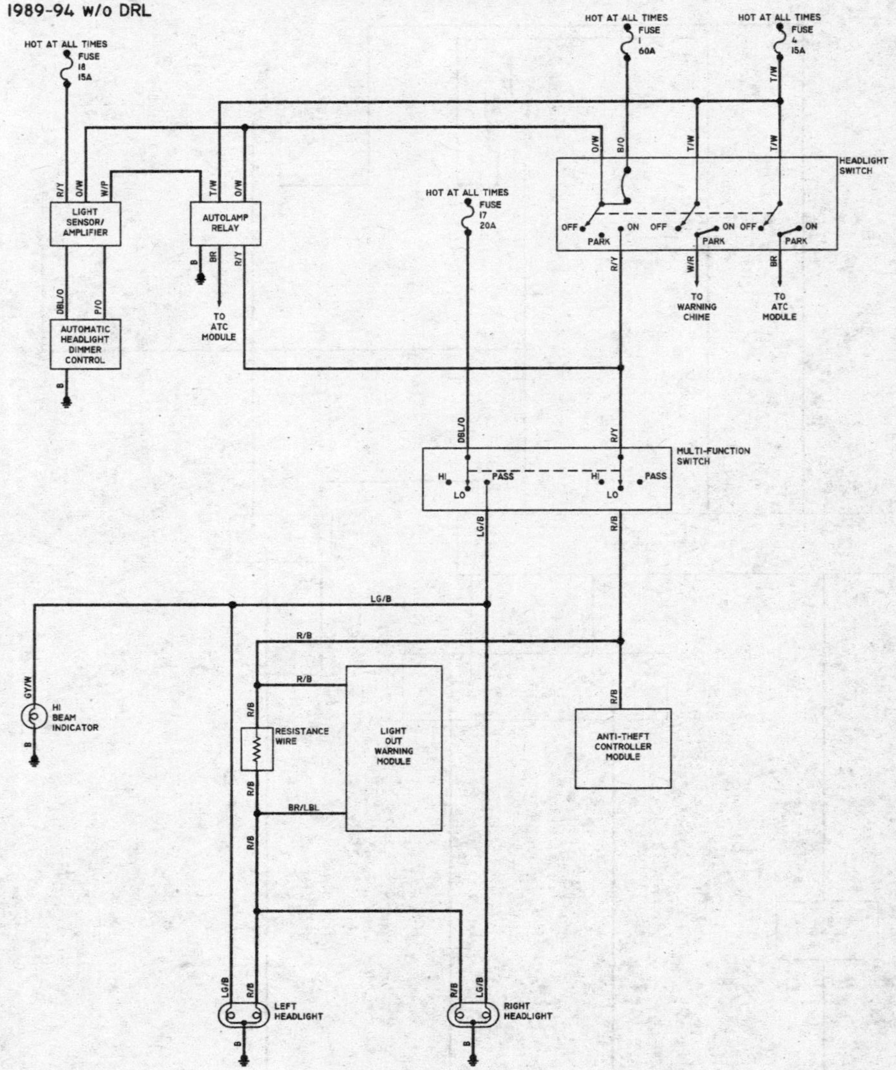


DIAGRAM 20

93146B35

## 1995-00 CONTINENTAL CHASSIS SCHEMATIC

1995-00 W/o DRL

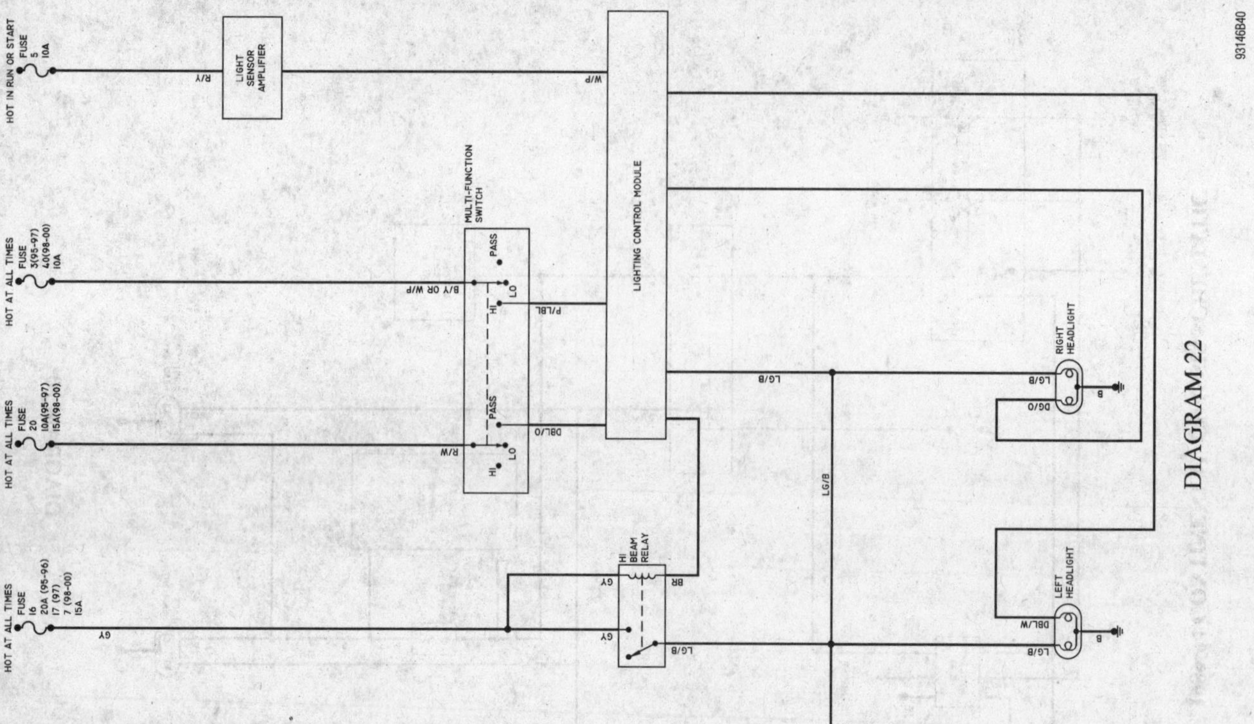


DIAGRAM 22

## 1989-94 CONTINENTAL CHASSIS SCHEMATIC

1989-94 W/ DRL

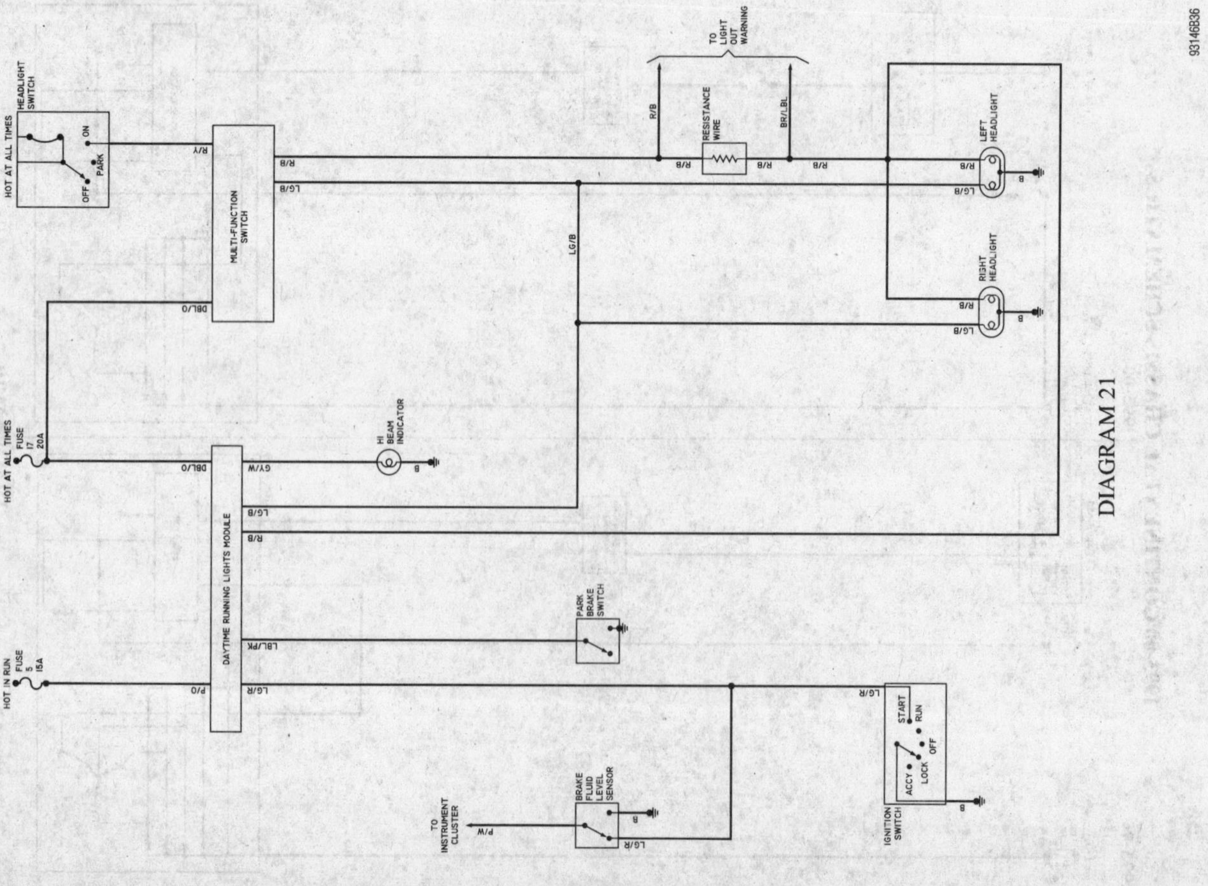


DIAGRAM 21

## 1995-00 CONTINENTAL CHASSIS SCHEMATIC

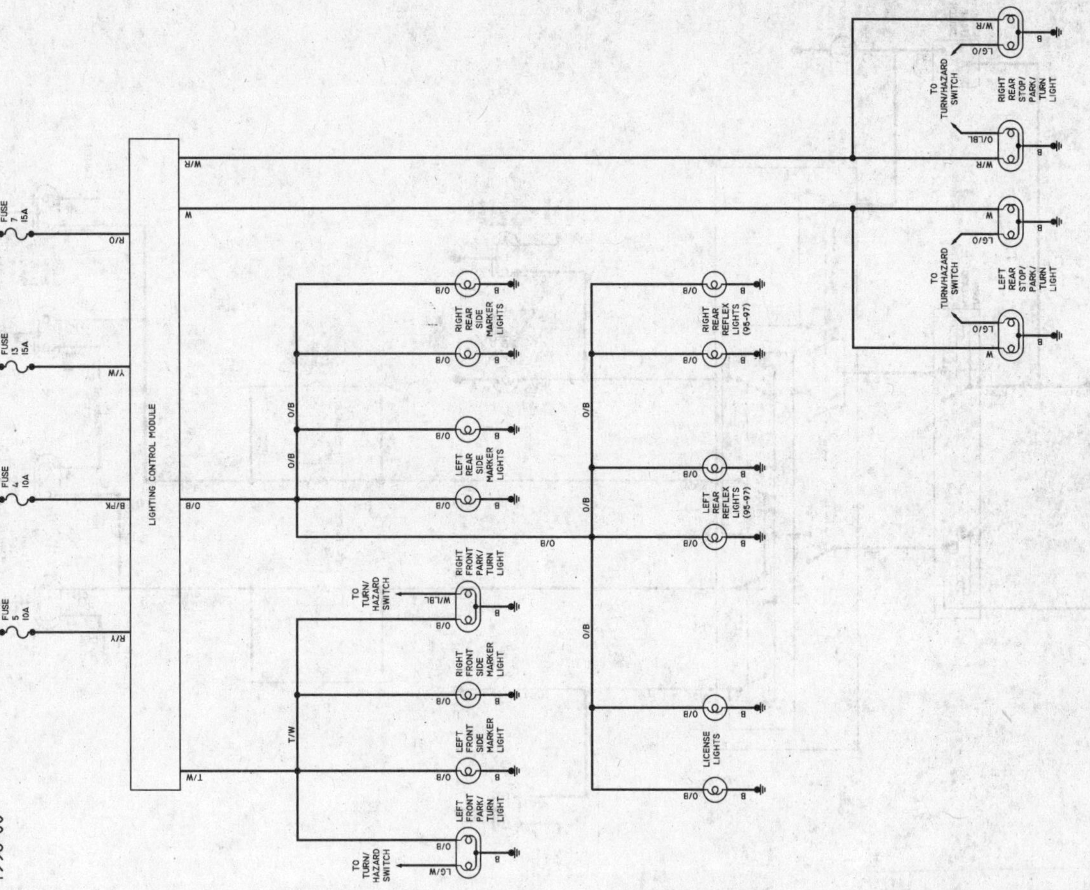


DIAGRAM 24

93146B39

## 1989-94 CONTINENTAL CHASSIS SCHEMATIC

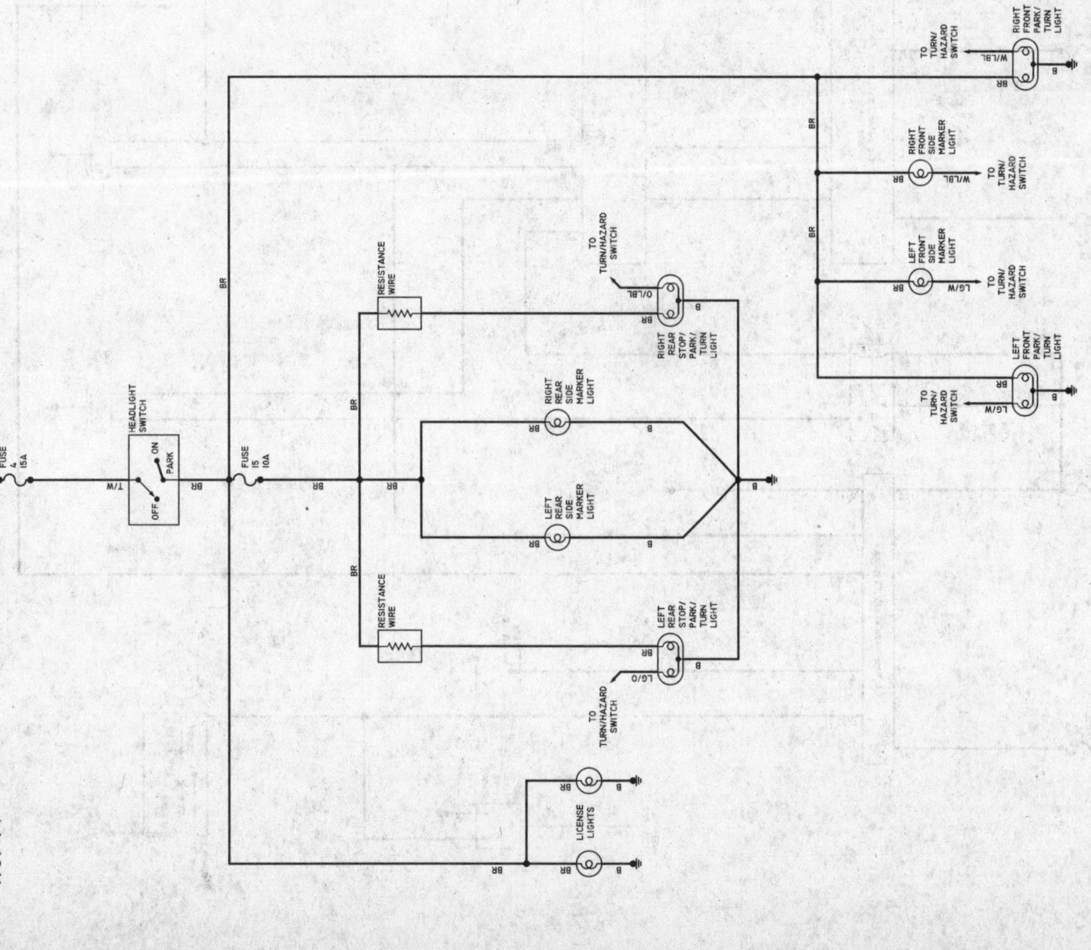


DIAGRAM 23

93146B38

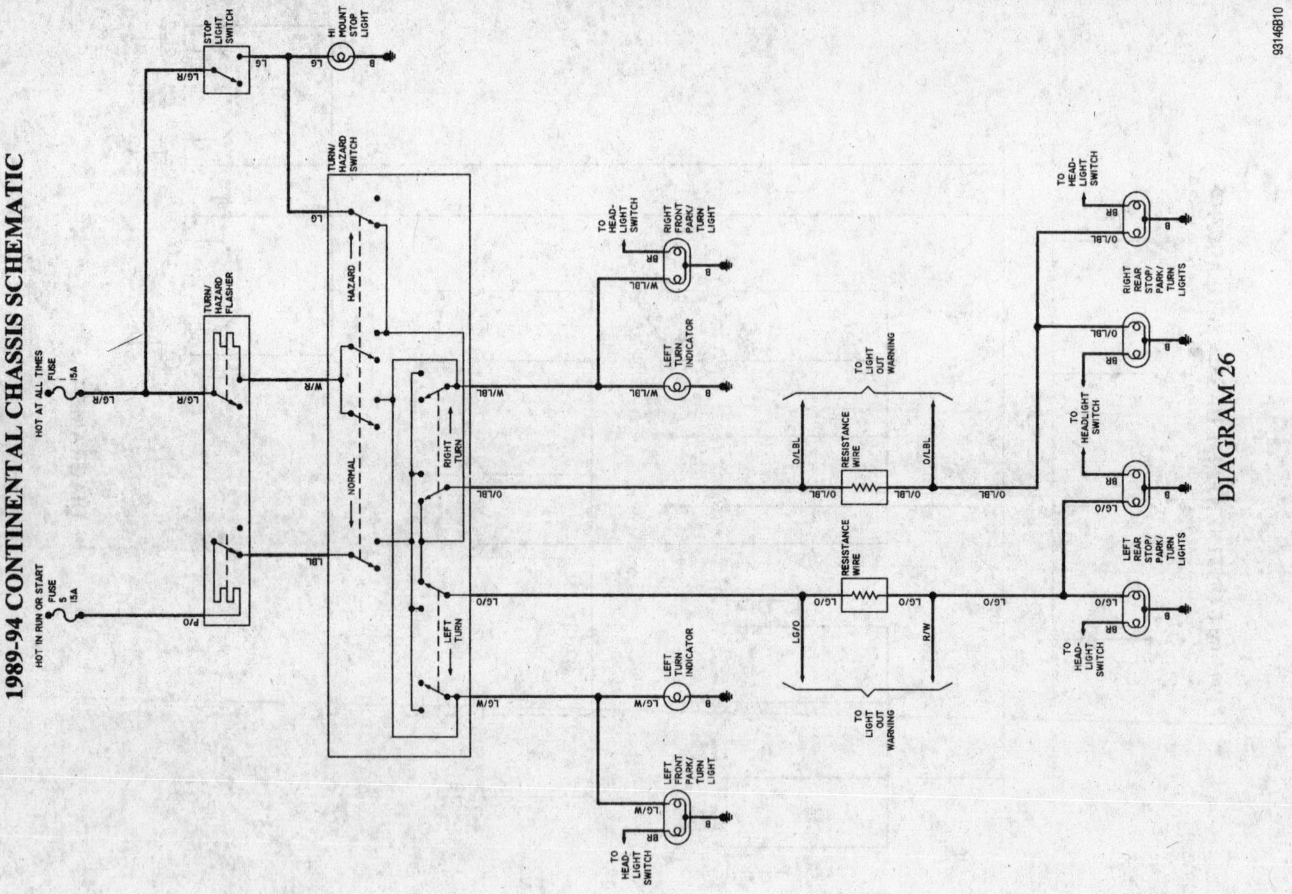
1989-94 CONTINENTAL CHASSIS SCHEMATIC
HOT AT ALL TIMES FUSE 1 15A
HOT IN RUN OR START FUSE 5 15A
TURN/ HAZARD FLASHER
STOP LIGHT SWITCH
HI MOUNT STOP LIGHT
TURN/ HAZARD SWITCH
HAZARD
NORMAL
RIGHT TURN
LEFT TURN
RIGHT FRONT PARK/ TURN LIGHT
LEFT TURN INDICATOR
LEFT FRONT PARK/ TURN LIGHT
TO HEAD- LIGHT SWITCH
RESISTANCE WIRE
TO LIGHT OUT WARNING
RIGHT REAR STOP/ PARK/ TURN LIGHTS
LEFT REAR STOP/ PARK/ TURN LIGHTS
TO HEADLIGHT SWITCH
DIAGRAM 26
93146810

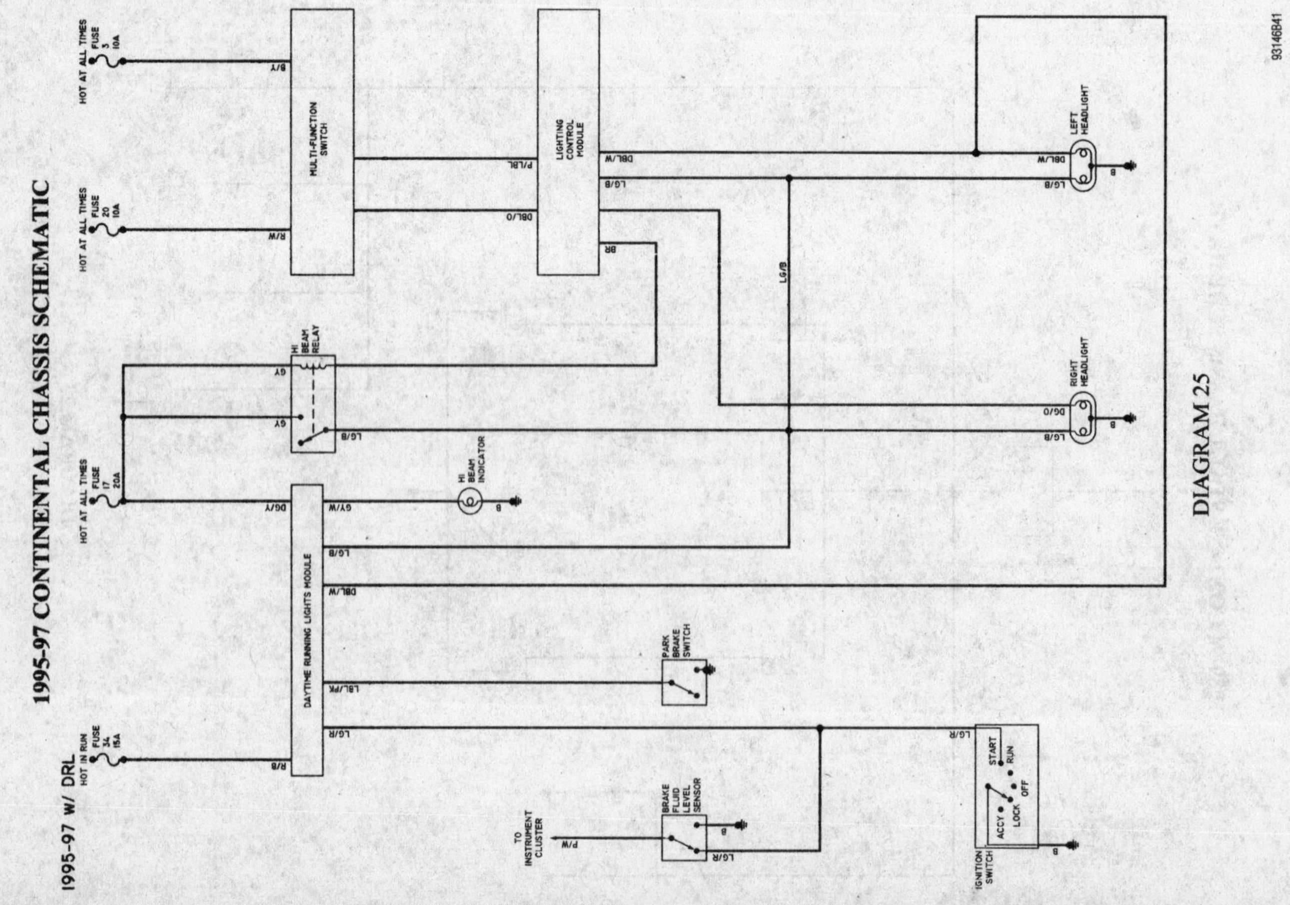
1995-97 CONTINENTAL CHASSIS SCHEMATIC
1995-97 W/ DRL
HOT AT ALL TIMES FUSE 3 10A
HOT AT ALL TIMES FUSE 20 10A
HOT AT ALL TIMES FUSE 17 20A
HOT IN RUN FUSE 34 15A
MULTI-FUNCTION SWITCH
LIGHTING CONTROL MODULE
HI BEAM RELAY
HI BEAM INDICATOR
DAYTIME RUNNING LIGHTS MODULE
PARK BRAKE SWITCH
BRAKE FLUID LEVEL SENSOR
TO INSTRUMENT CLUSTER
IGNITION SWITCH
ACCY LOCK OFF RUN START
LEFT HEADLIGHT
RIGHT HEADLIGHT
DIAGRAM 25
93146841

## 1989-92 MARK VII CHASSIS SCHEMATICS

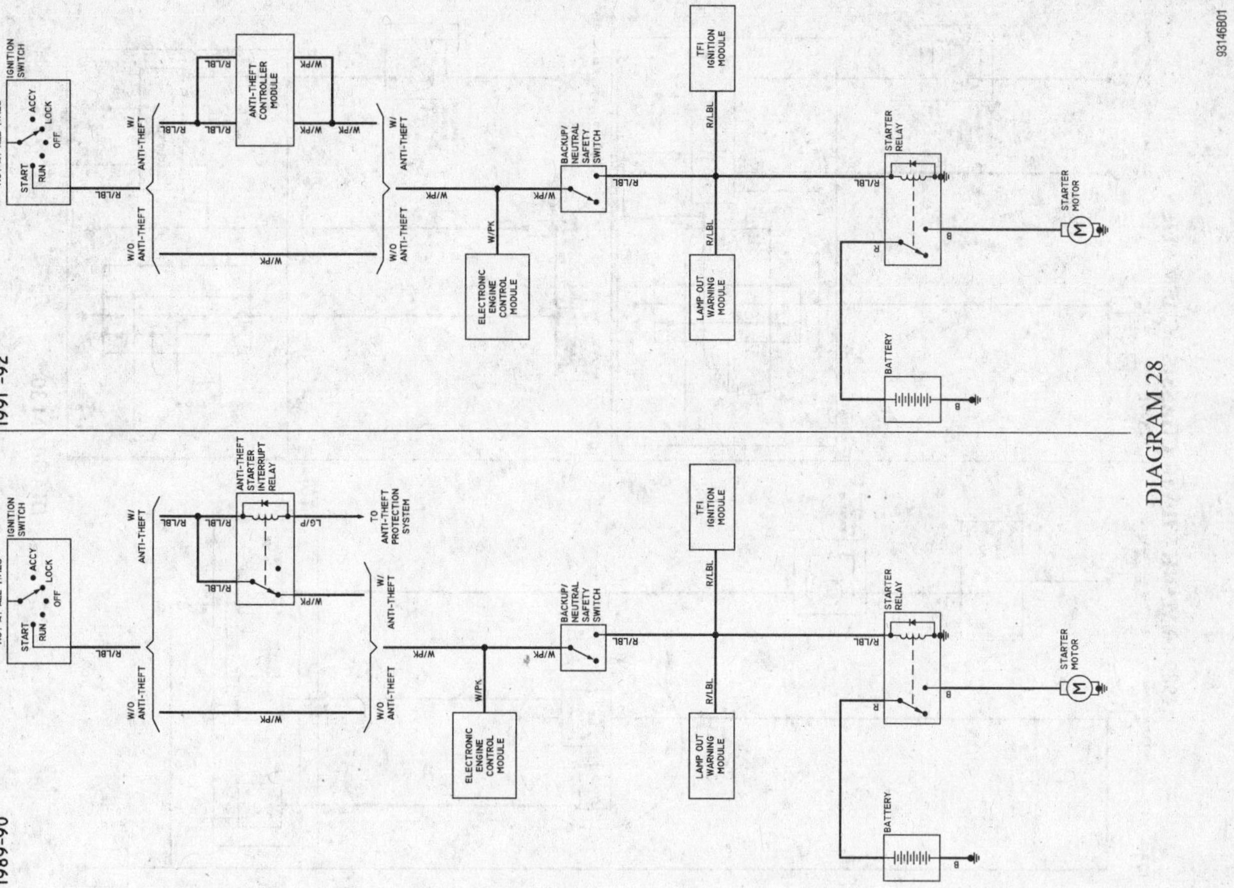


DIAGRAM 28

## 1995-00 CONTINENTAL CHASSIS SCHEMATIC

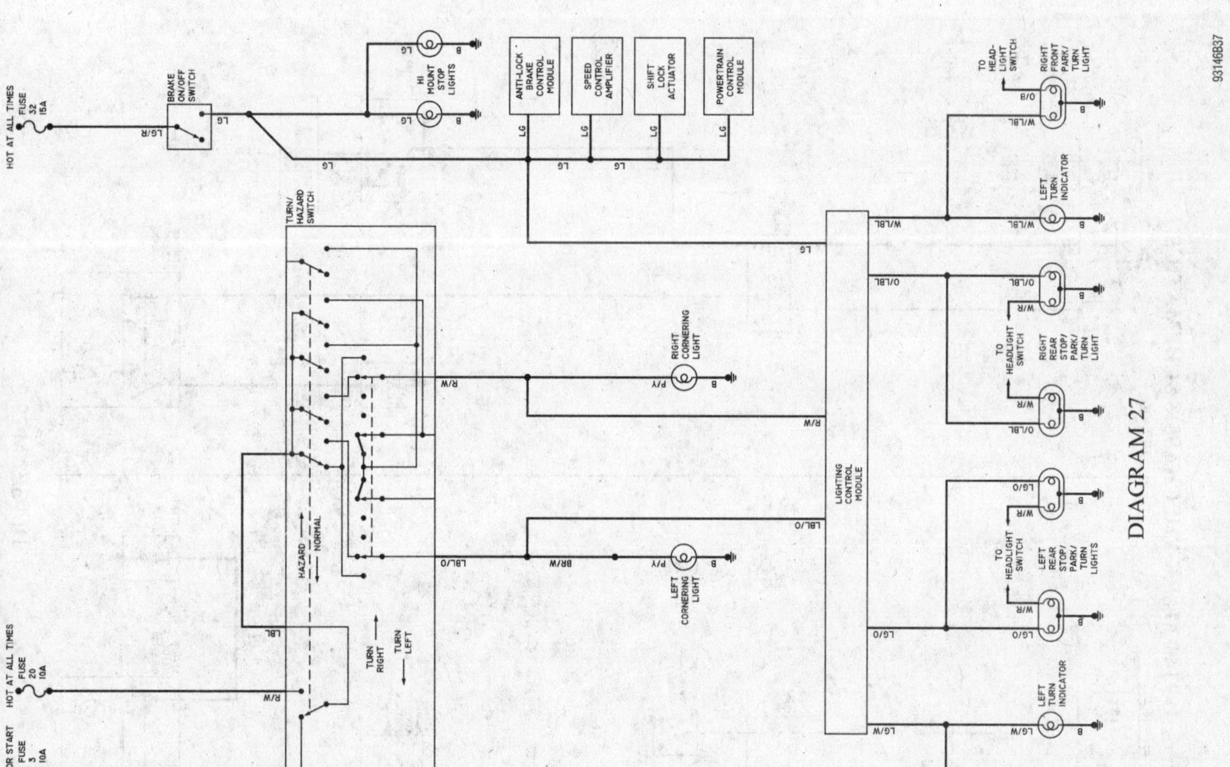


DIAGRAM 27

1989-00 MARK VII/VIII CHASSIS SCHEMATICS

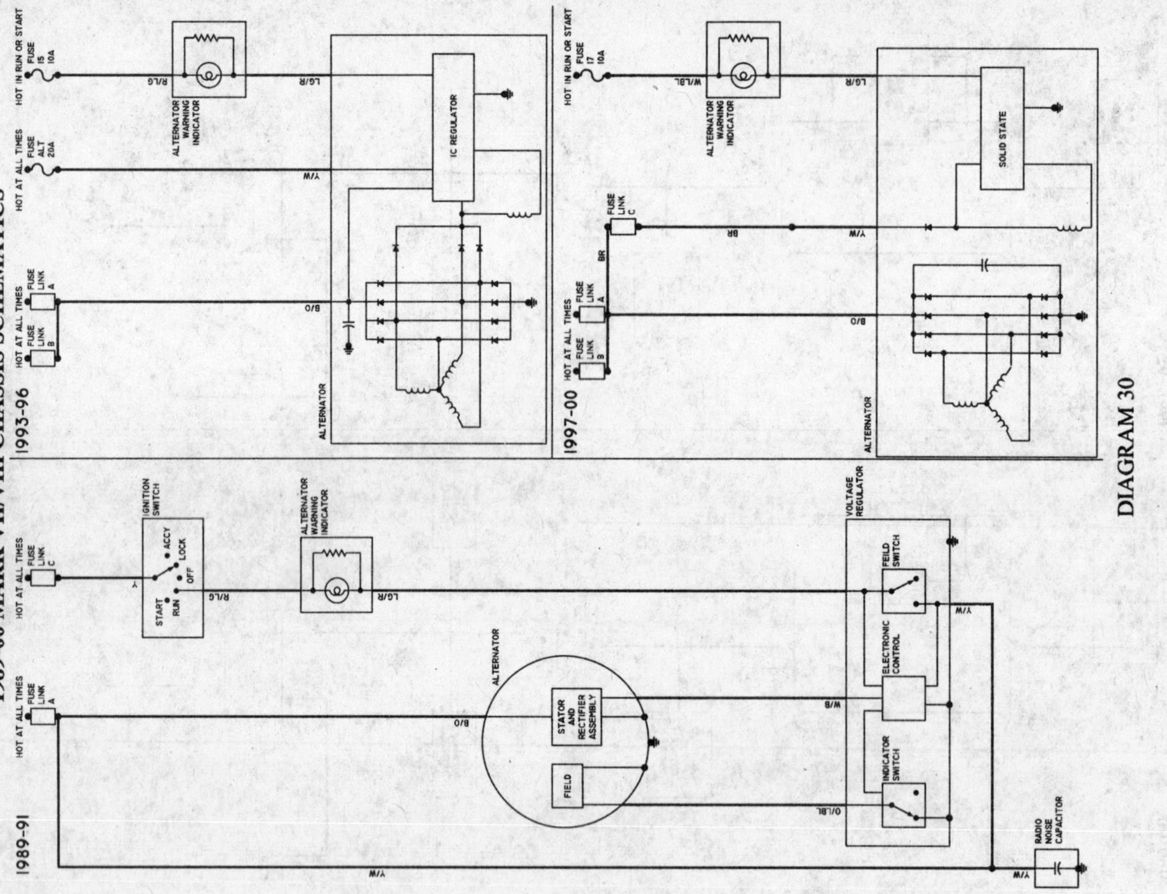


DIAGRAM 30

1993-00 MARK VIII CHASSIS SCHEMATICS

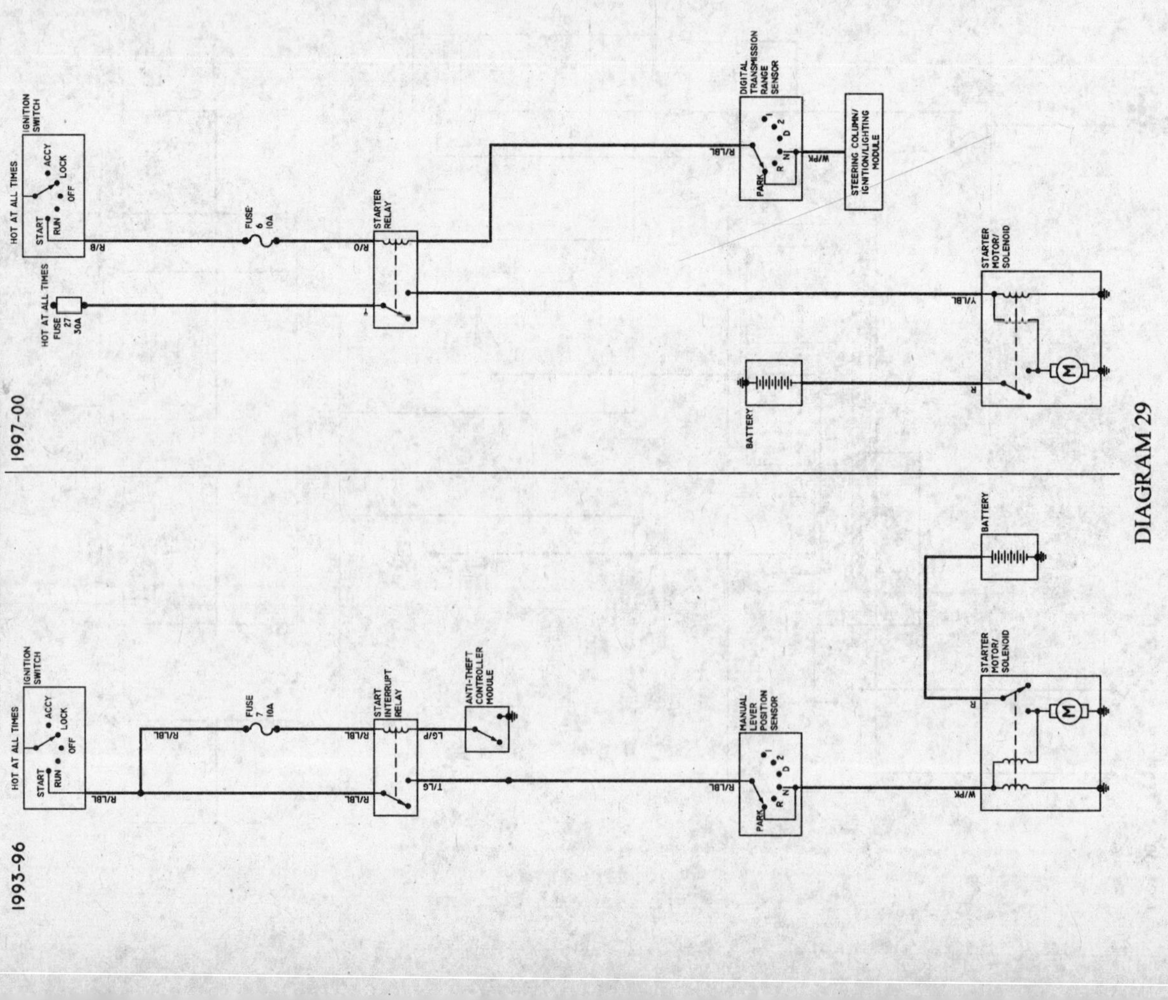


DIAGRAM 29

## 1989-92 MARK VII CHASSIS SCHEMATIC

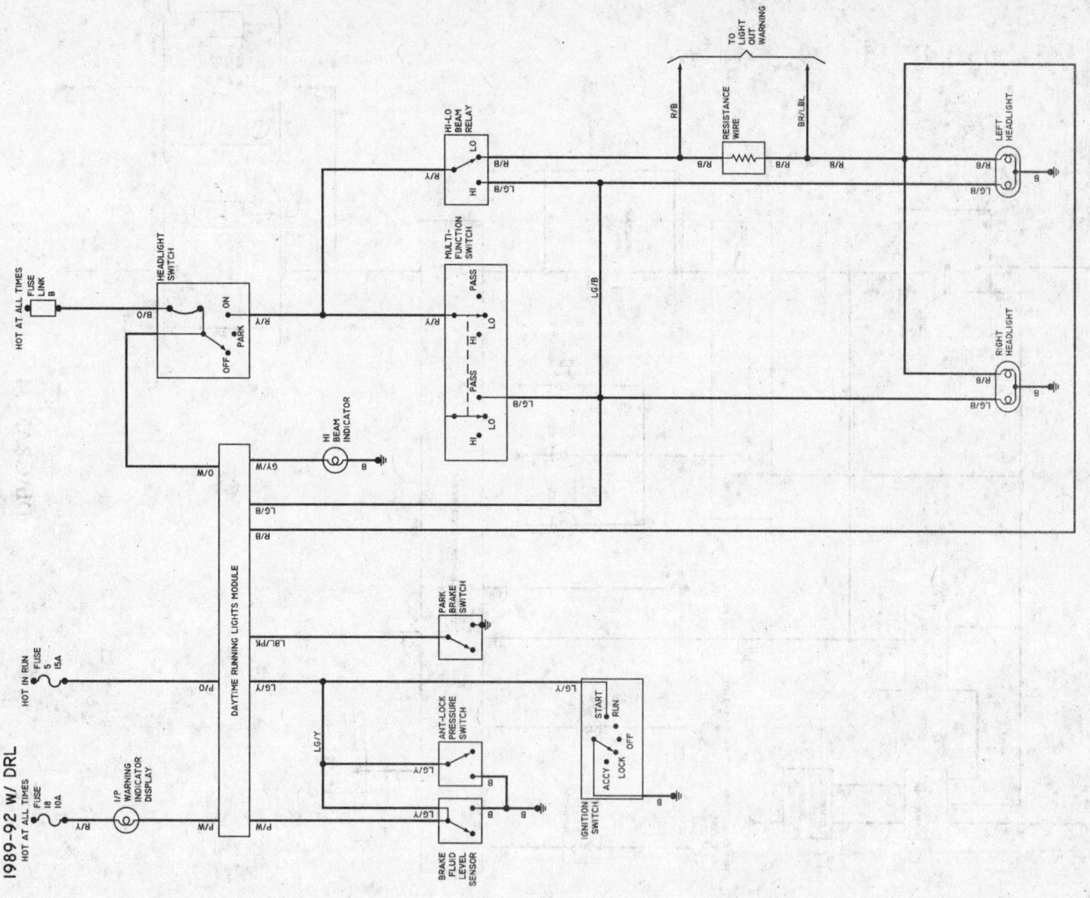


DIAGRAM 32

93146B09

## 1989-92 MARK VII CHASSIS SCHEMATIC

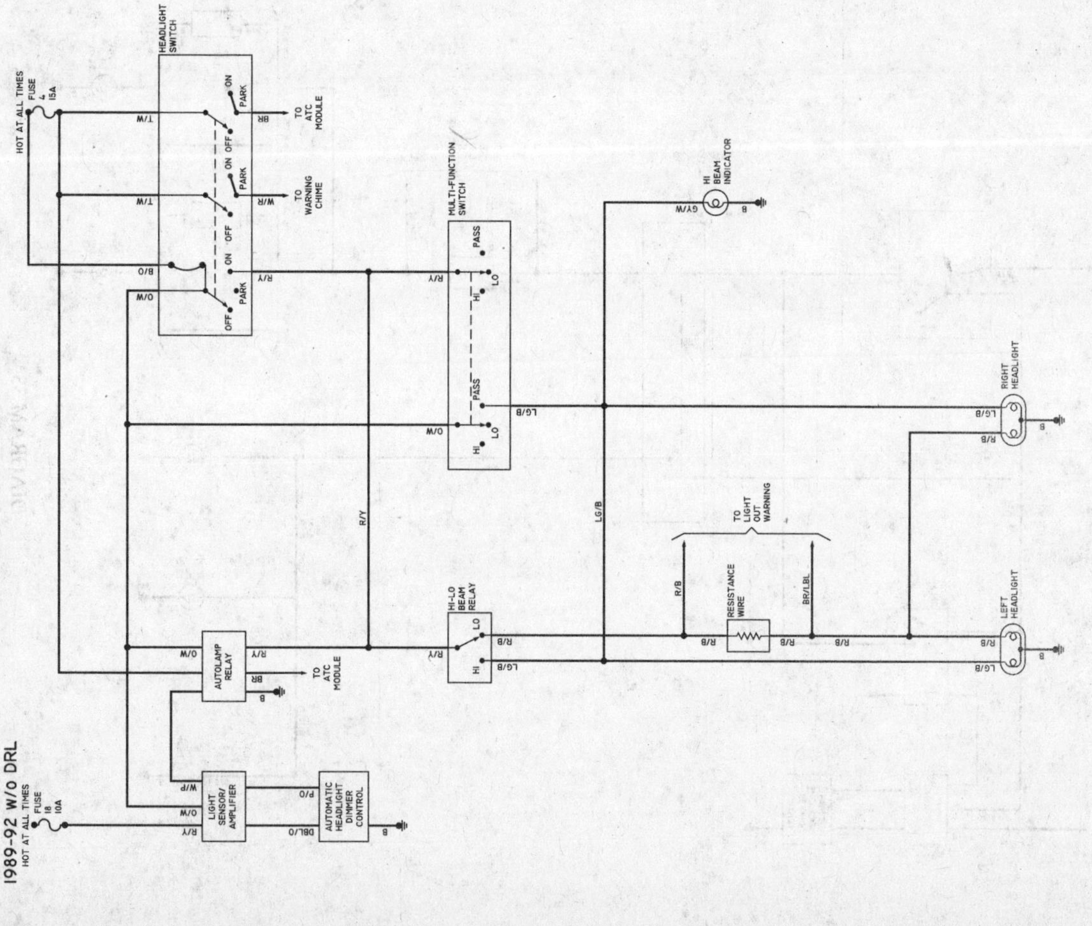


DIAGRAM 31

93146B08

## 1993-96 MARKVIII CHASSIS SCHEMATIC

1993-96 W/ DRL

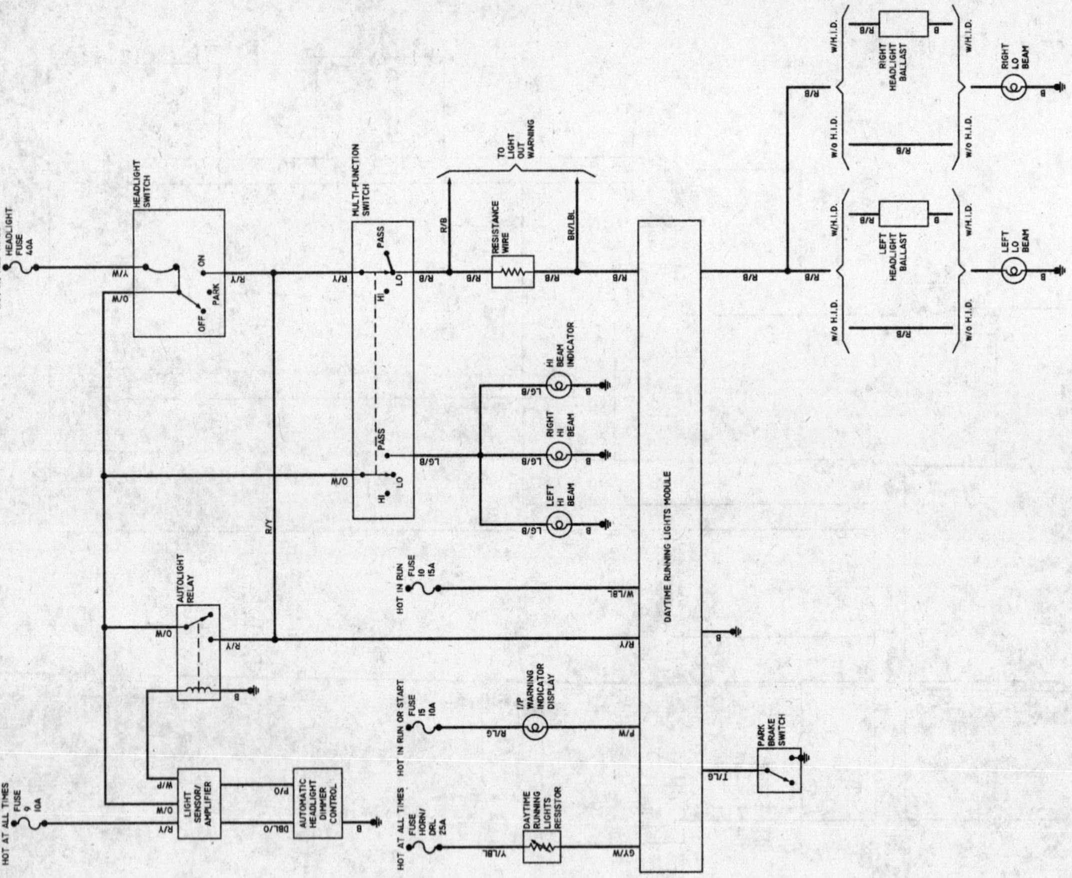

DIAGRAM 34

93146B14

## 1993-96 MARK VIII CHASSIS SCHEMATIC

1993-96 W/O DRL

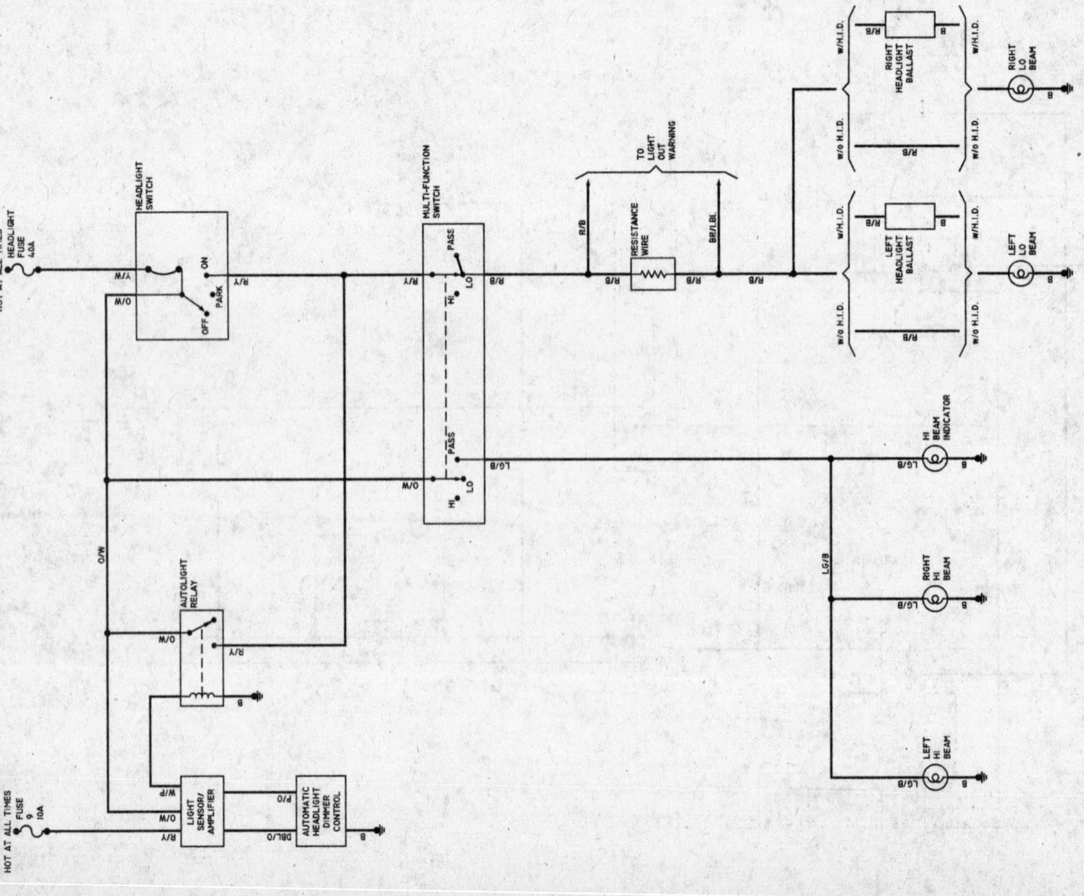

DIAGRAM 33

93146B13

1989-96 MARK VII/VIII CHASSIS SCHEMATIC

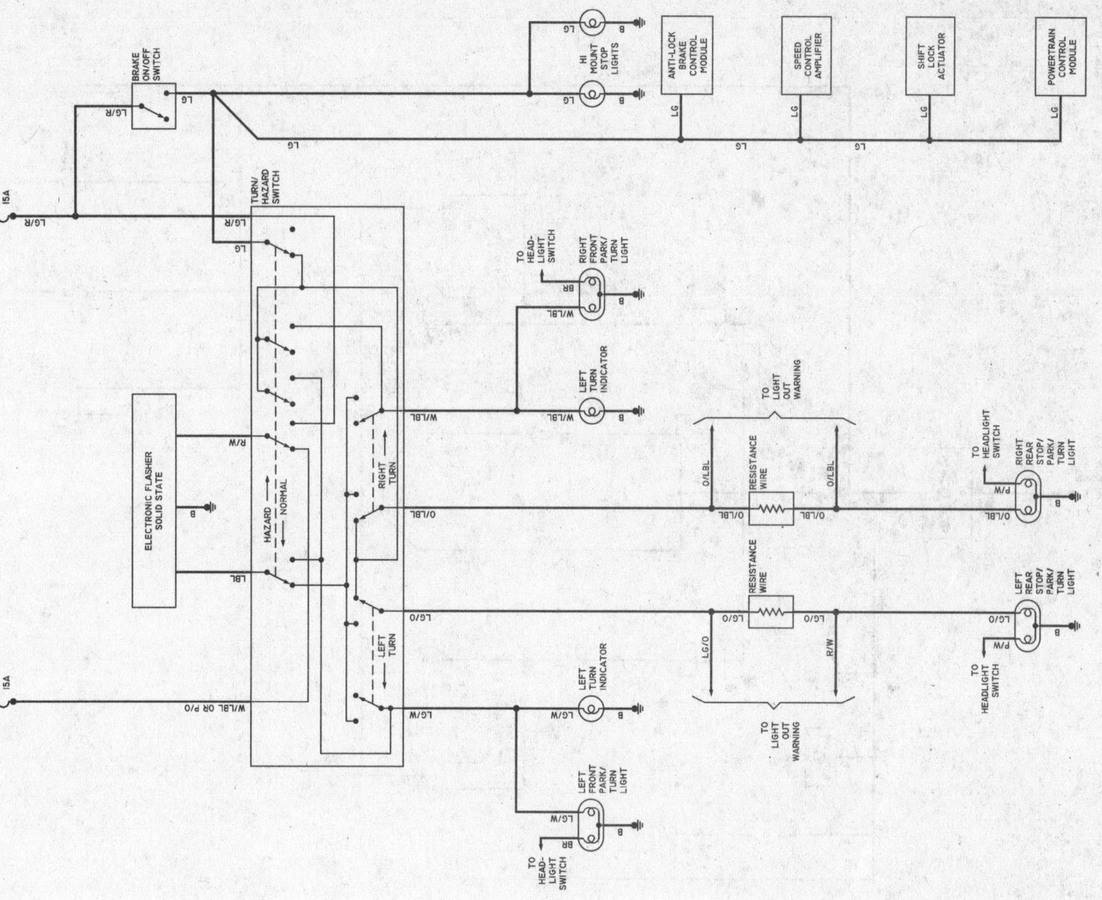


93146B16

DIAGRAM 36

1997-00 MARK VIII CHASSIS SCHEMATIC

1997-00 W/ DRL

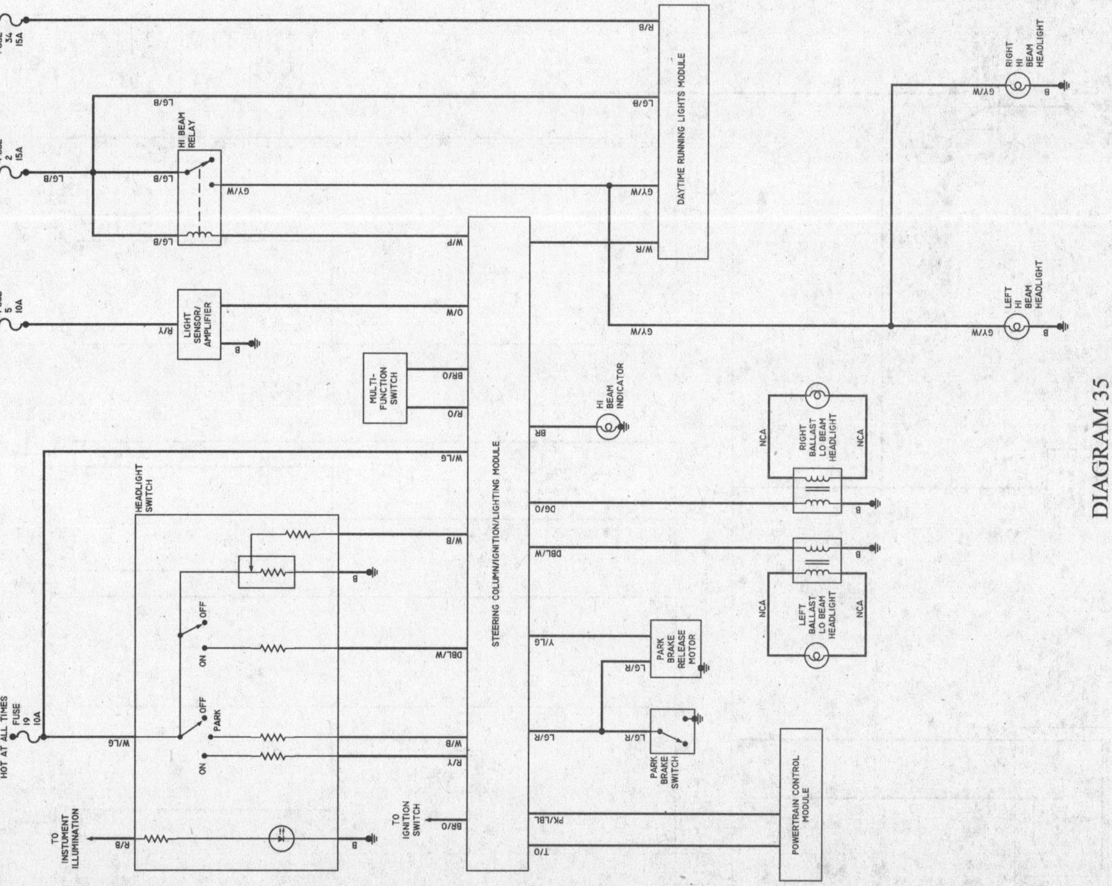


93146B15

DIAGRAM 35

## 1989-92 MARK VII CHASSIS SCHEMATIC

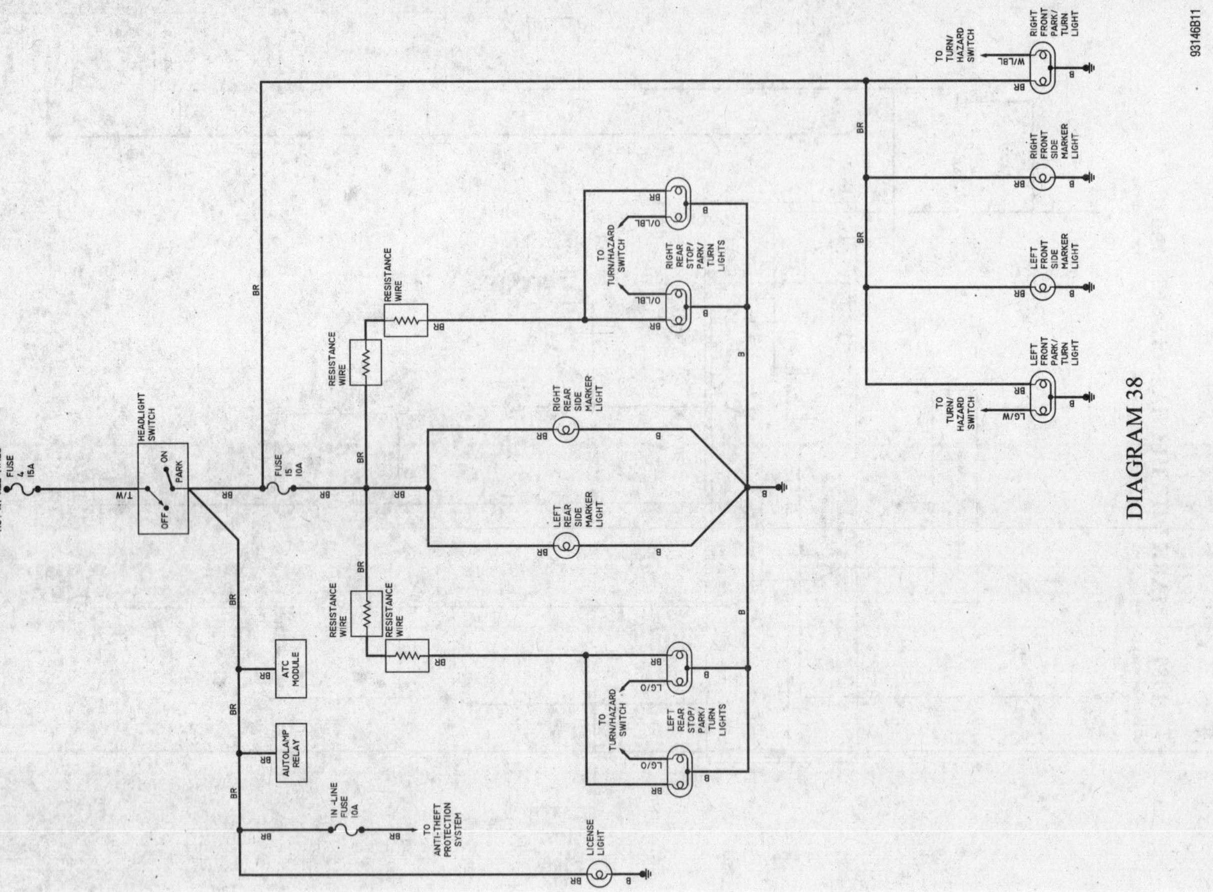


DIAGRAM 38

## 1997-00 MARK VIII CHASSIS SCHEMATIC

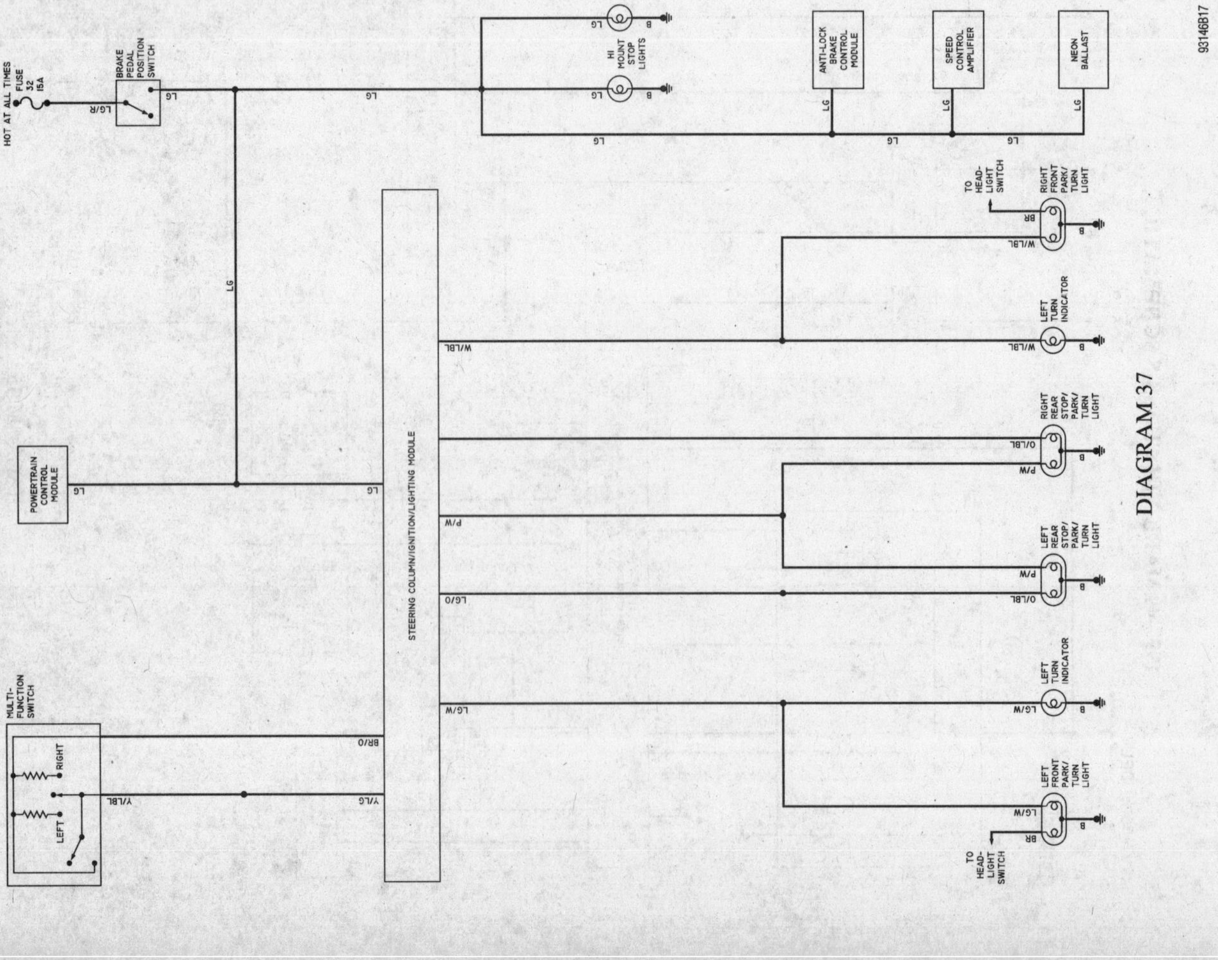


DIAGRAM 37

## 1997-00 MARK VIII CHASSIS SCHEMATIC

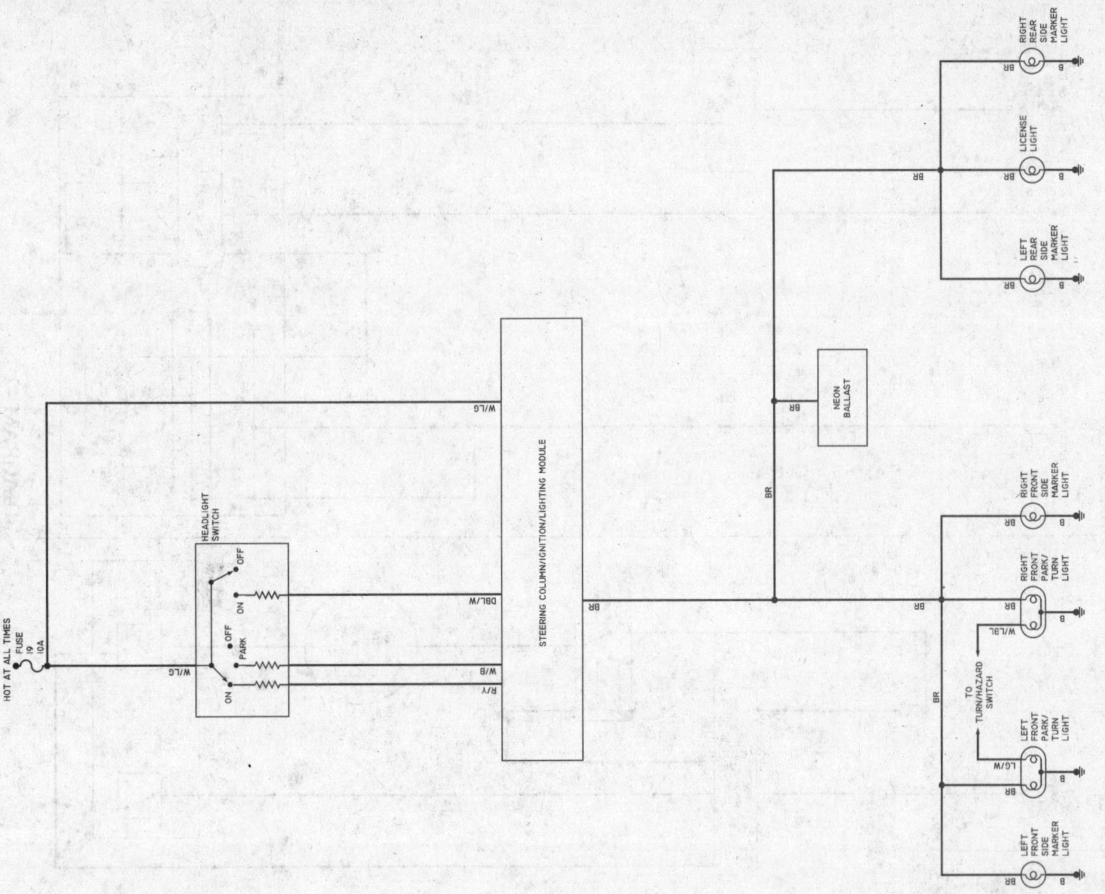


DIAGRAM 40

93146B19

## 1993-96 MARK VIII CHASSIS SCHEMATIC

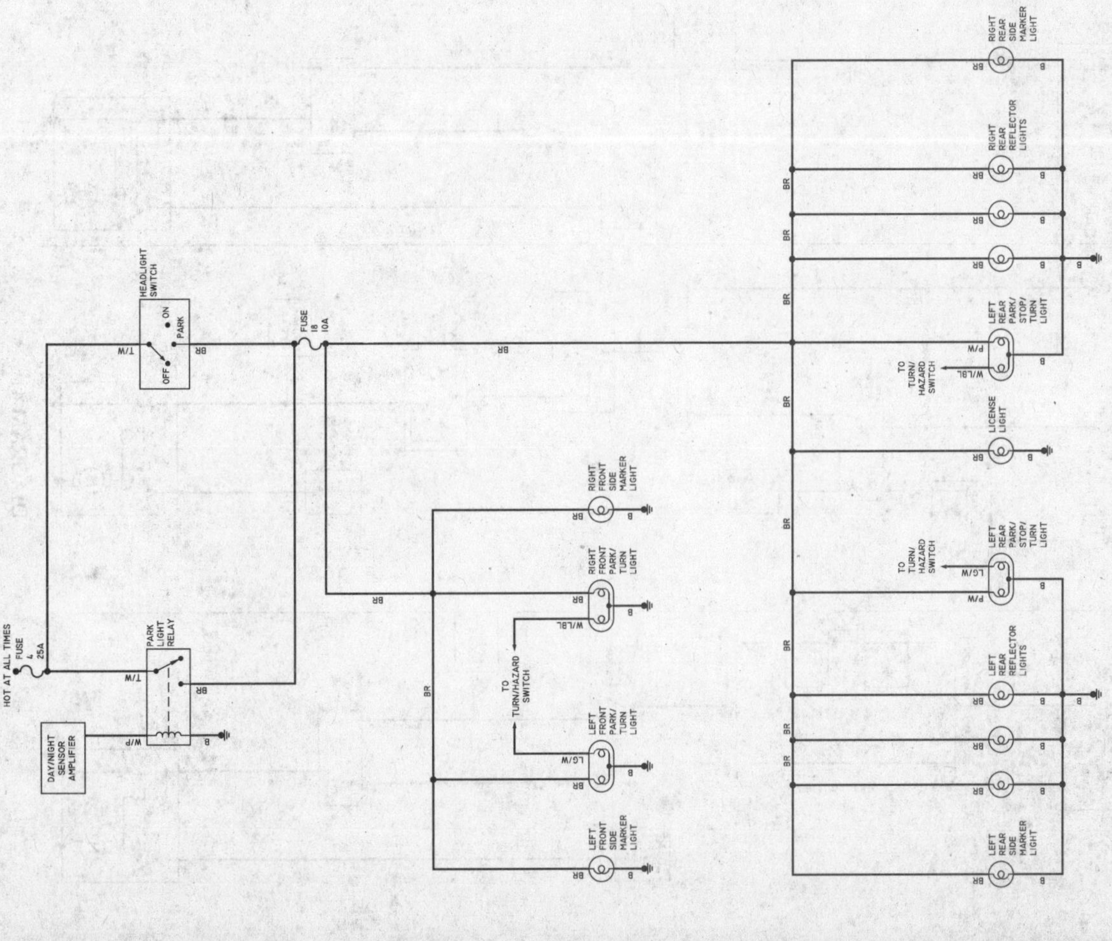


DIAGRAM 39

93146B18

## 1989-90 TOWN CAR CHASSIS SCHEMATICS

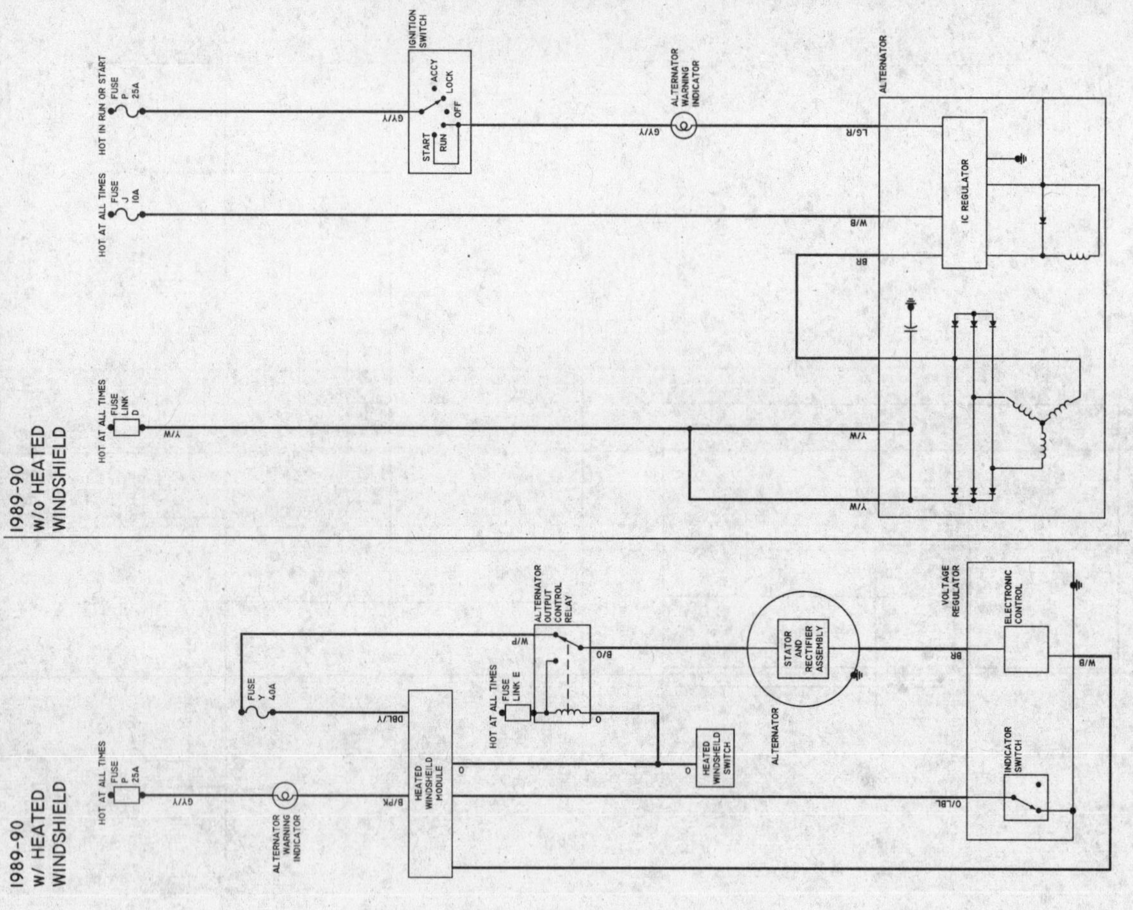


DIAGRAM 42

93146822

## 1989-00 TOWN CAR CHASSIS SCHEMATICS

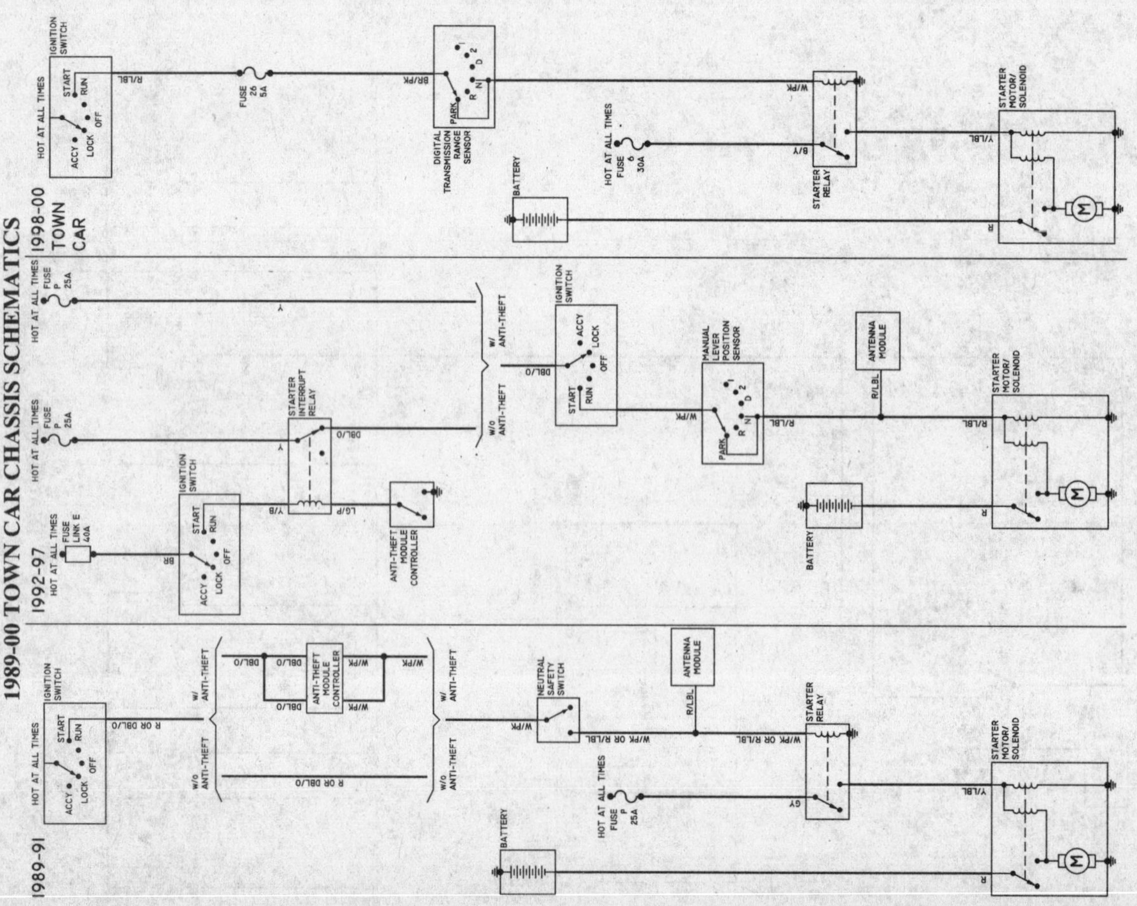


DIAGRAM 41

93146820

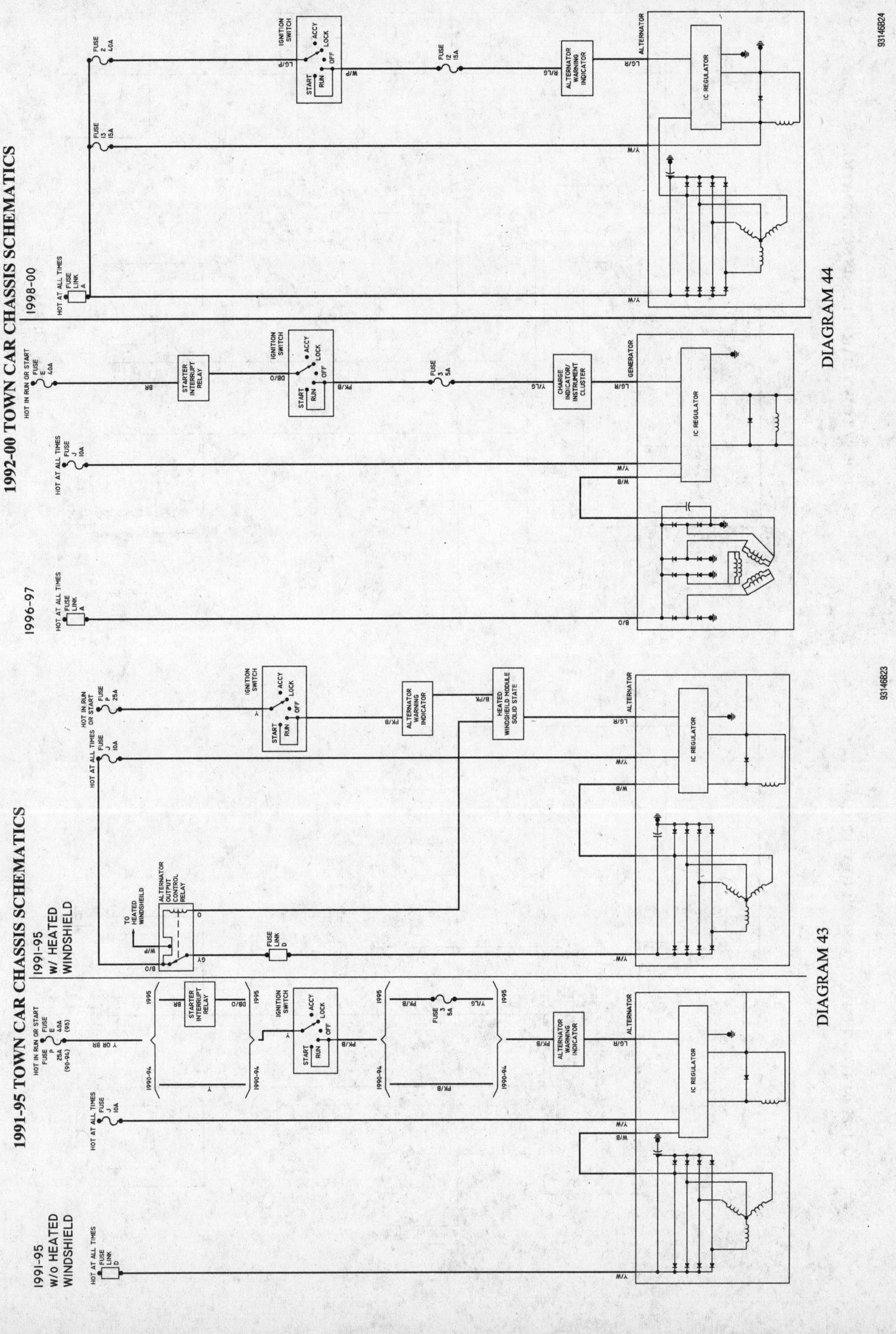
1992-00 TOWN CAR CHASSIS SCHEMATICS
1998-00
1996-97
DIAGRAM 44
93146B24
1991-95 TOWN CAR CHASSIS SCHEMATICS
1991-95 W/ HEATED WINDSHIELD
1991-95 W/o HEATED WINDSHIELD
DIAGRAM 43
93146B23
HOT AT ALL TIMES
HOT IN RUN OR START
FUSE LINK A
FUSE LINK D
IGNITION SWITCH
START
RUN
OFF
LOCK
ACCY
STARTER INTERRUPT RELAY
ALTERNATOR WARNING INDICATOR
CHARGE INDICATOR INSTRUMENT CLUSTER
HEATED WINDSHEILD MODULE SOLID STATE
ALTERNATOR OUTPUT CONTROL RELAY
TO HEATED WINDSHIELD
IC REGULATOR
ALTERNATOR
GENERATOR

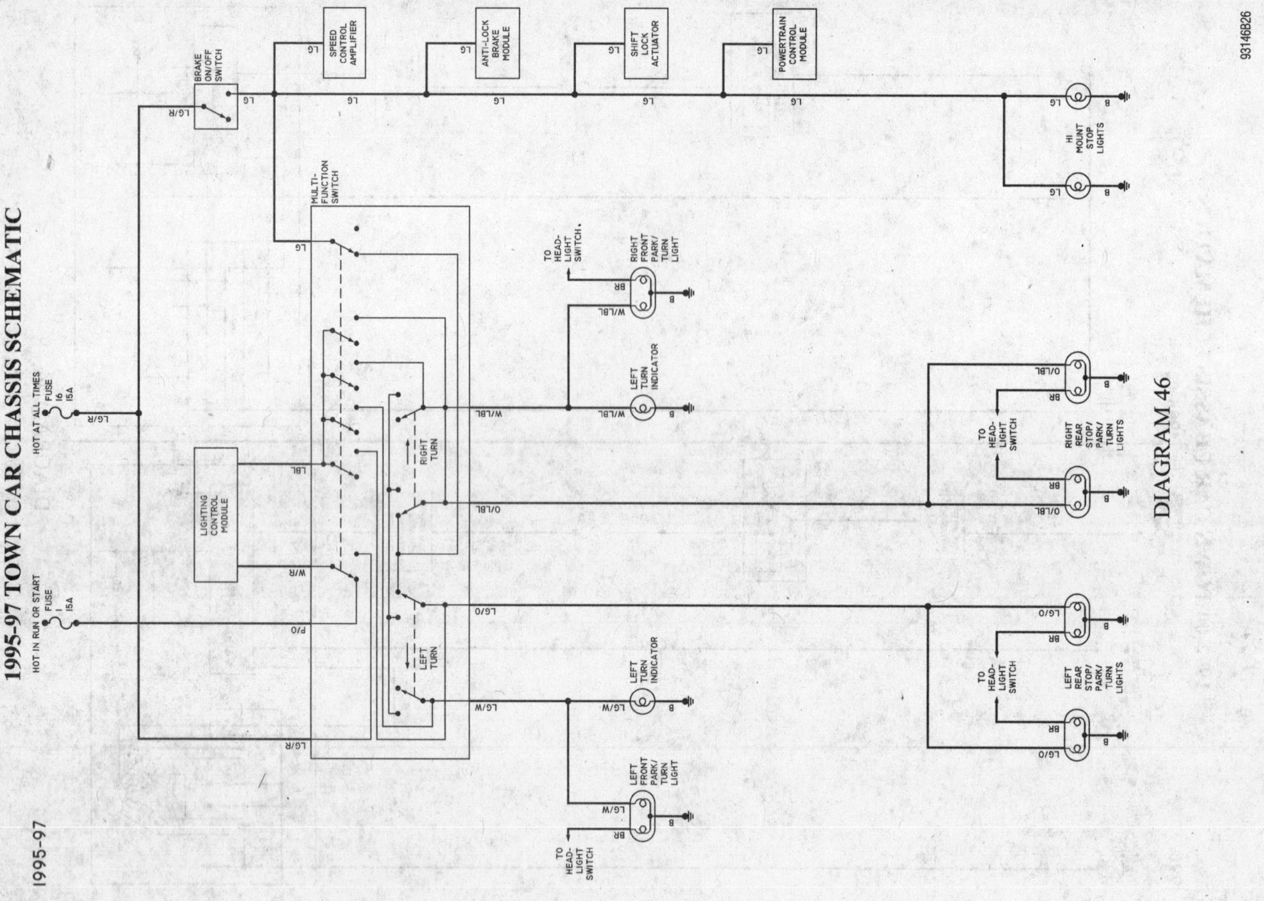

DIAGRAM 46

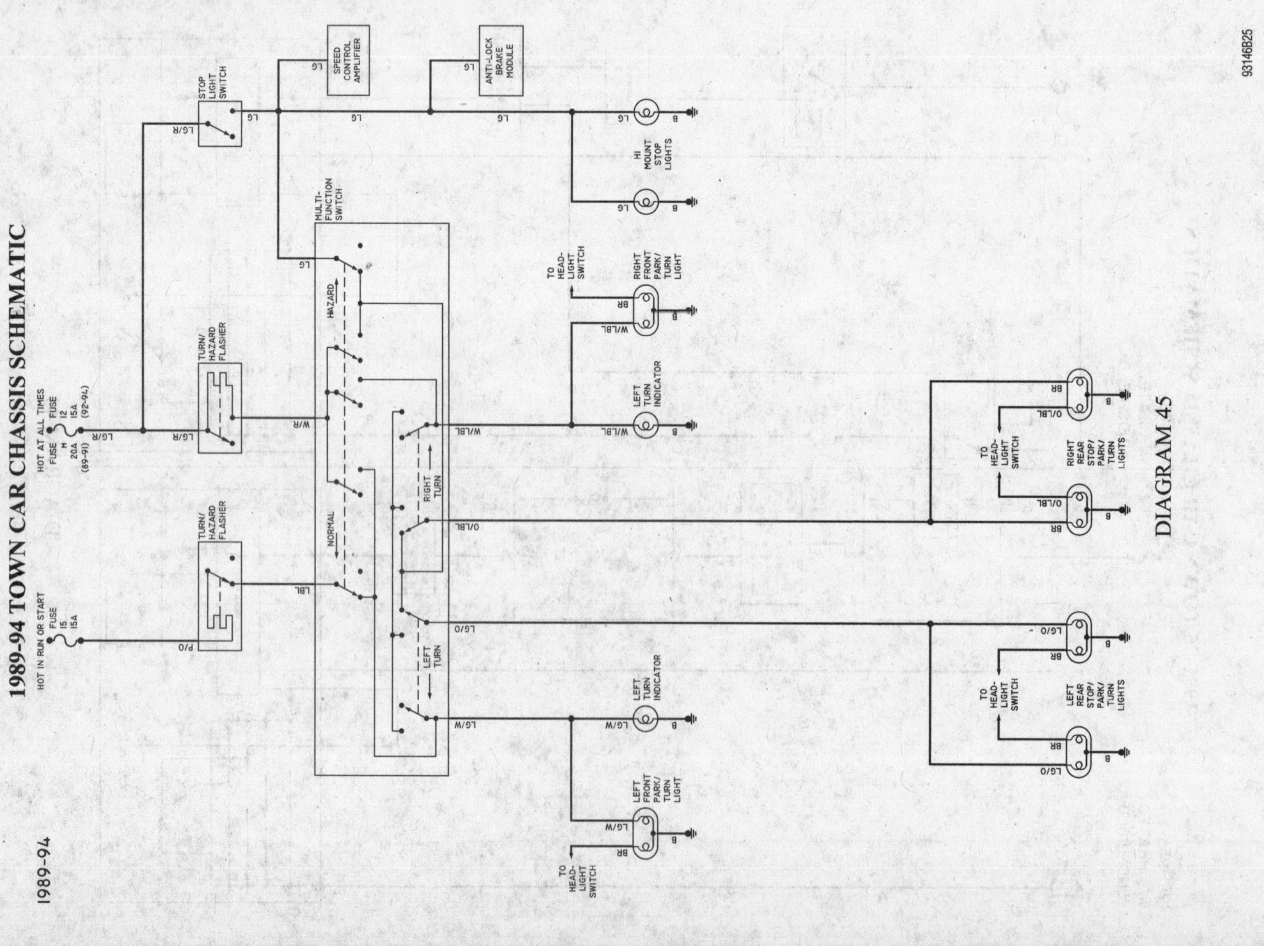

DIAGRAM 45

## 1989-97 TOWN CAR CHASSIS SCHEMATICS

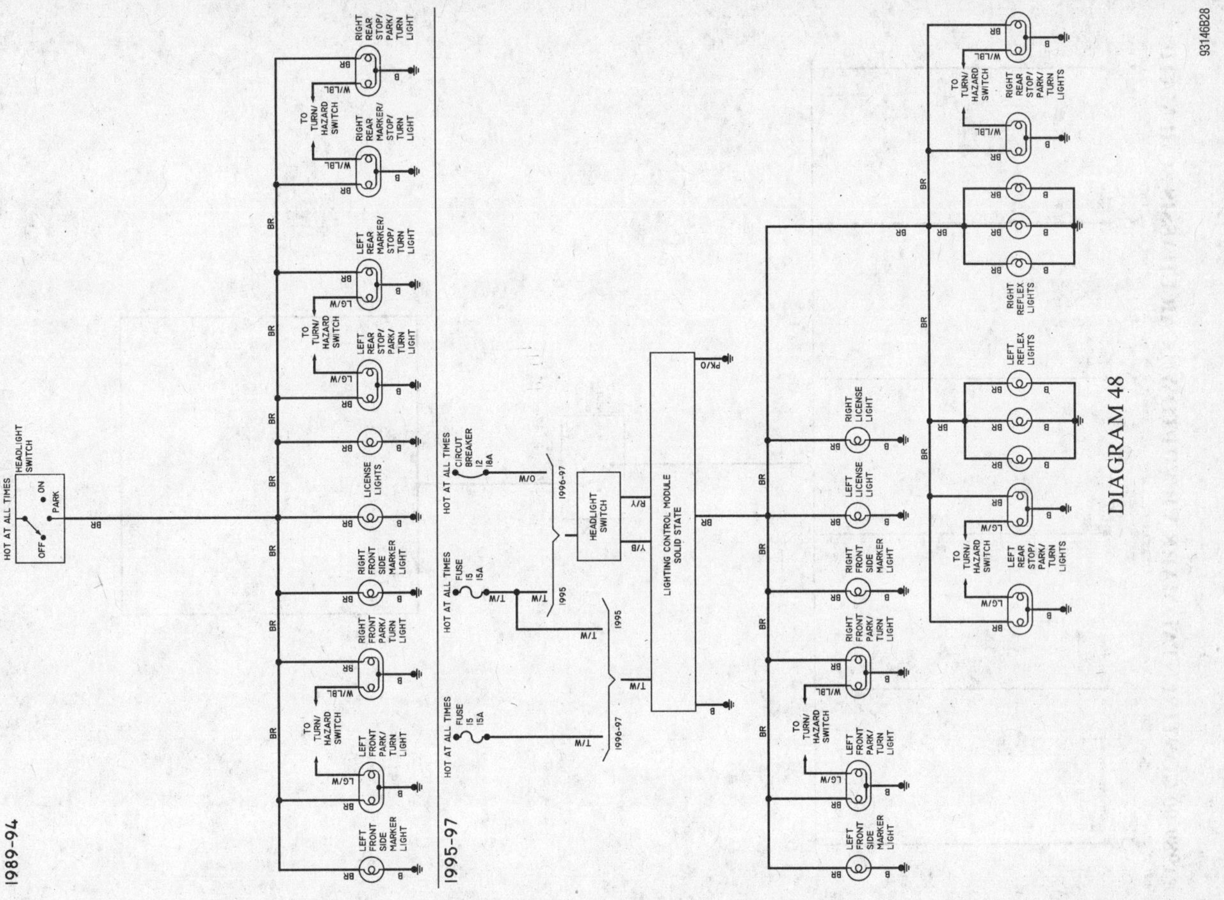


## 1998-00 TOWN CAR CHASSIS SCHEMATIC

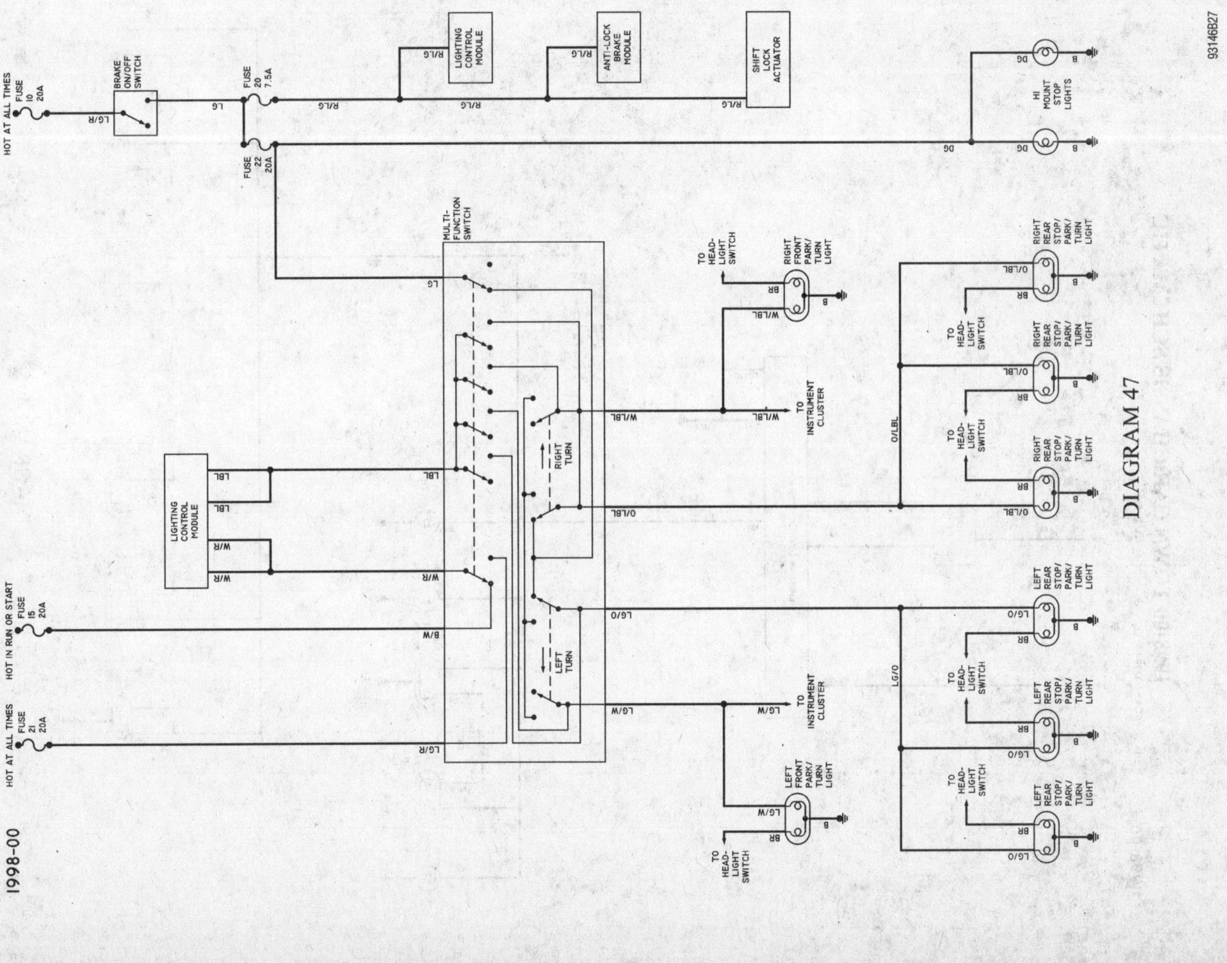

## 1989-00 CONTINENTAL/MARK VII/VIII/TOWN CAR CHASSIS SCHEMATIC

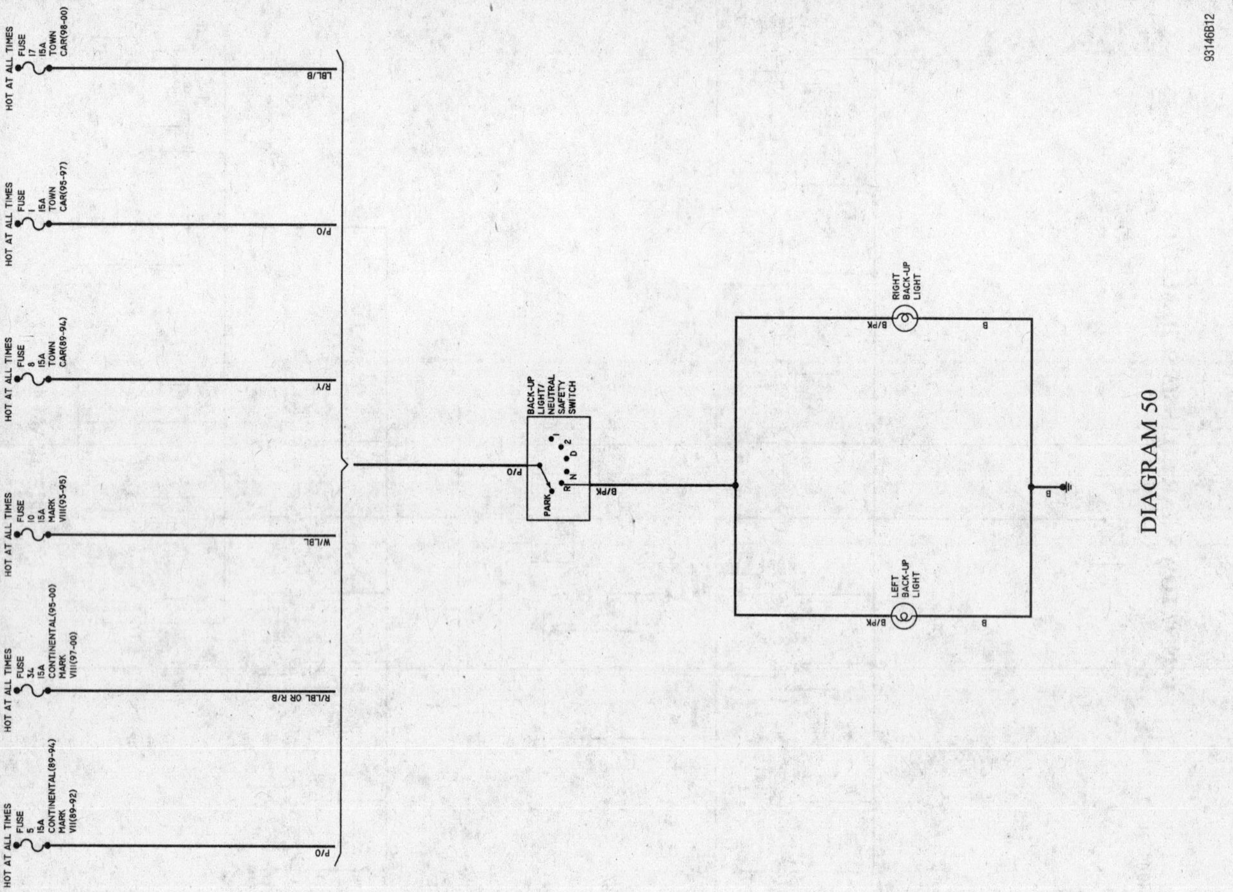


DIAGRAM 50

## 1998-00 TOWN CAR CHASSIS SCHEMATIC

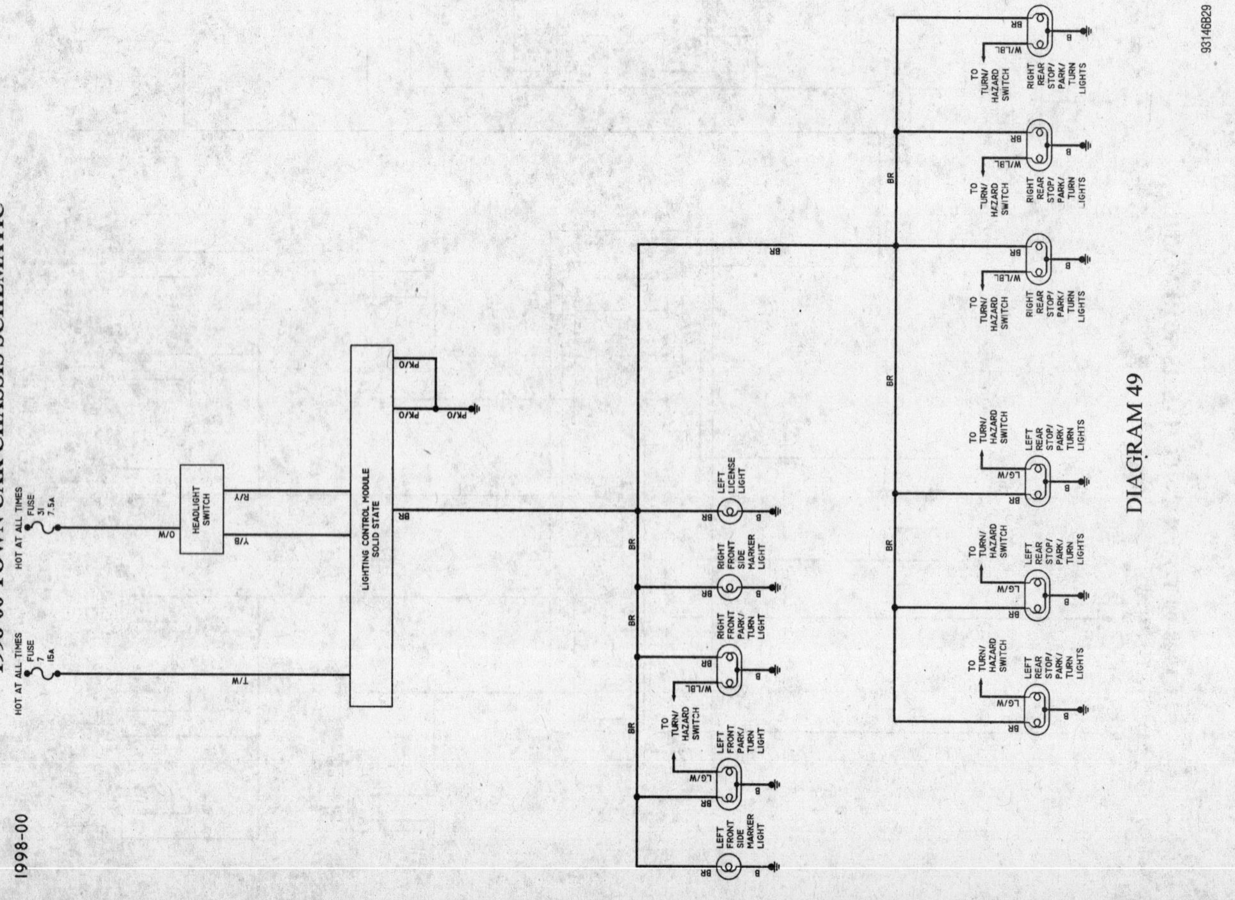


DIAGRAM 49

1998-00

## 1989-00 CONTINENTAL/MARK VII/VIII/TOWN CAR CHASSIS SCHEMATICS

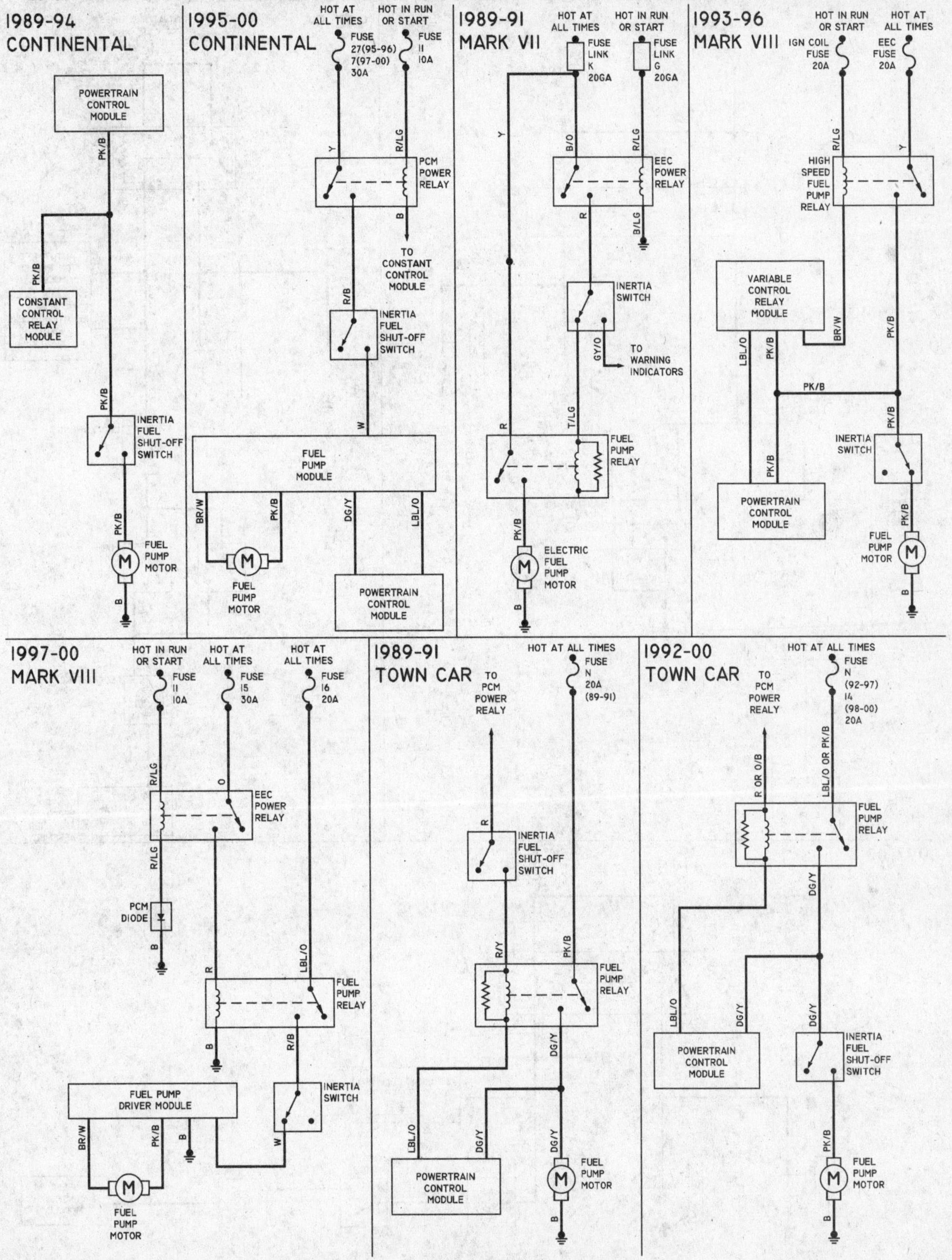


DIAGRAM 51

93146B42

# 1989-00 CONTINENTAL CHASSIS SCHEMATICS

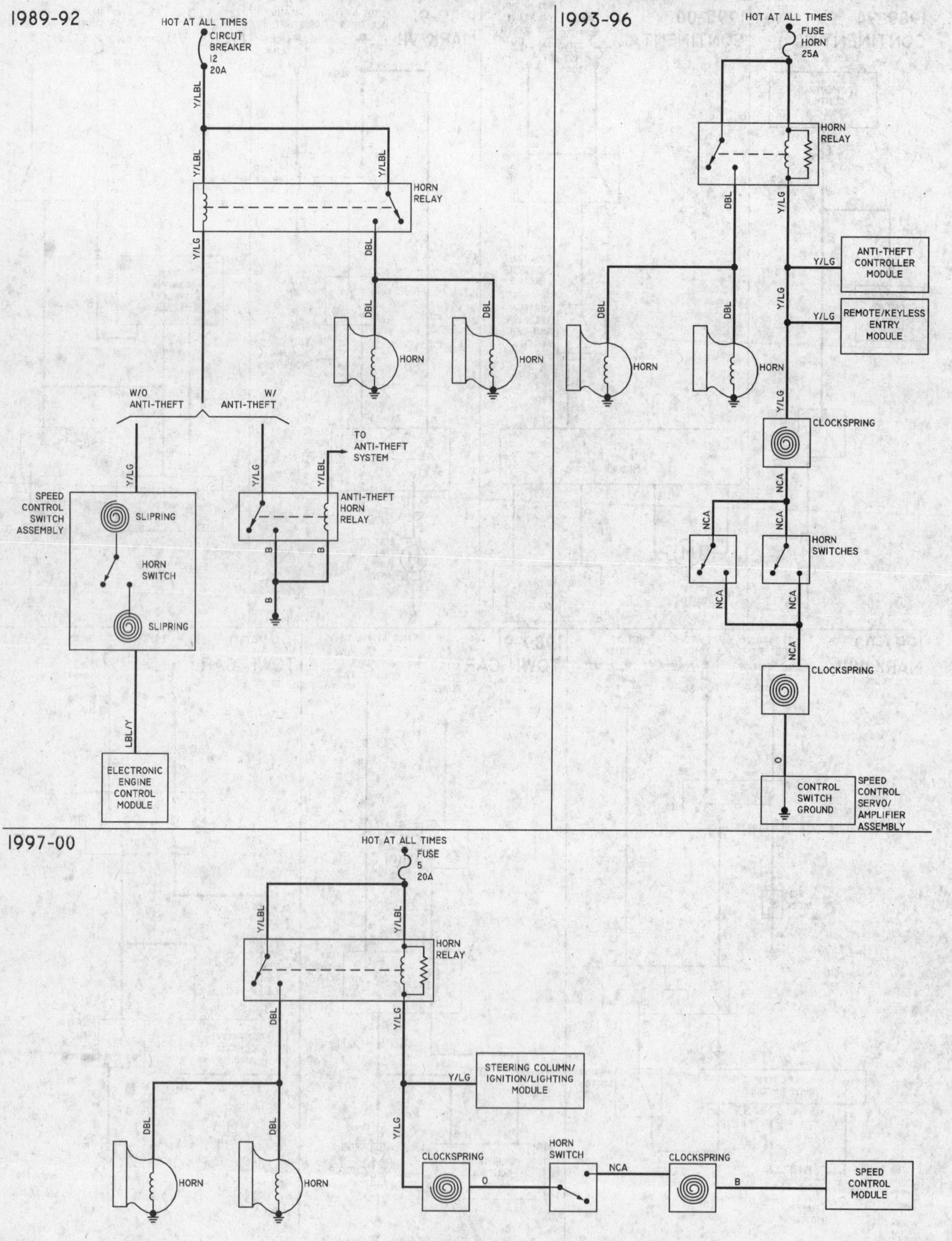


DIAGRAM 52

93146B05

# 1989-00 MARK VIII/TOWN CAR CHASSIS SCHEMATICS

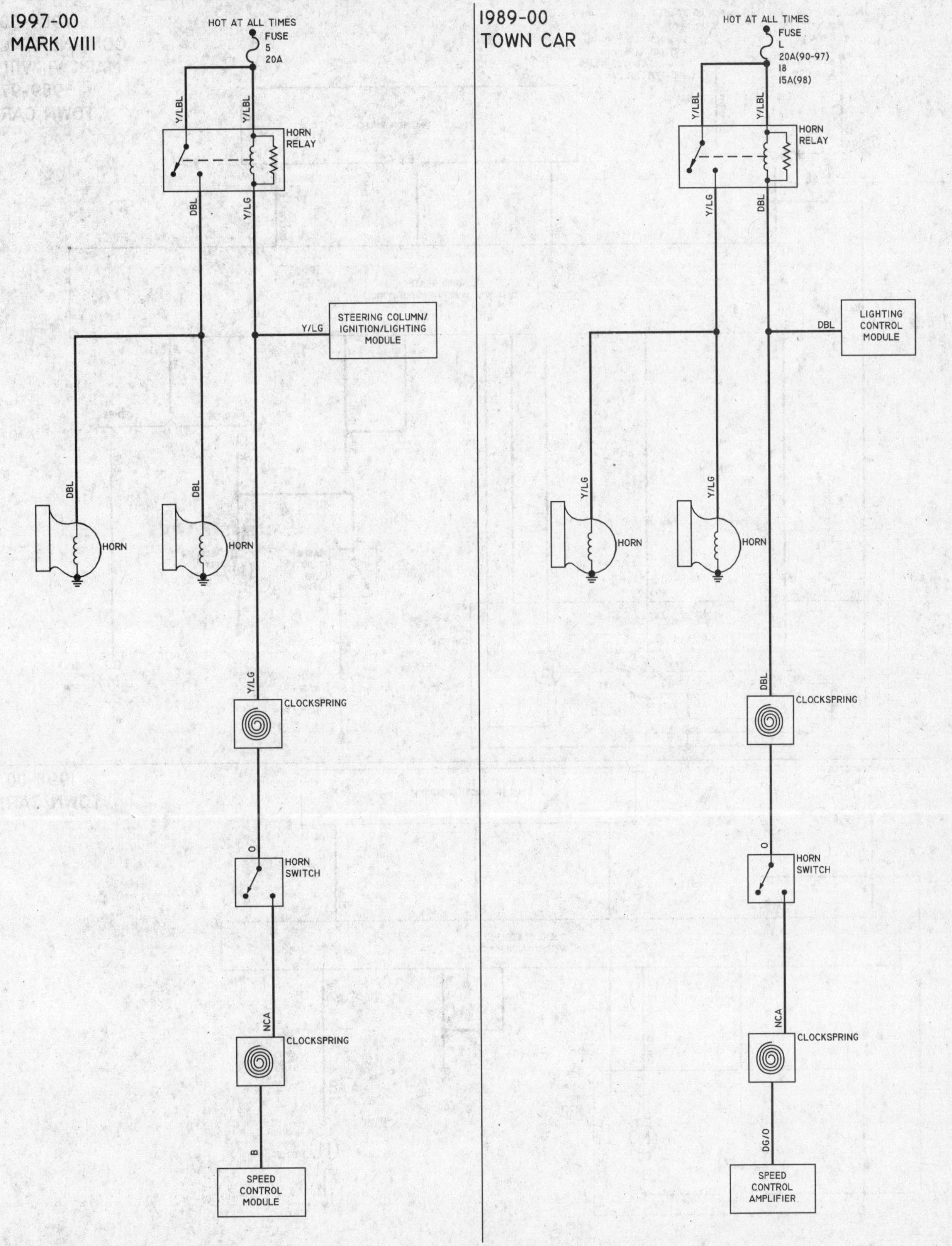


DIAGRAM 53

93146B06

# 1989-00 CONTINENTAL/MARK VII/VIII/TOWN CAR CHASSIS SCHEMATICS

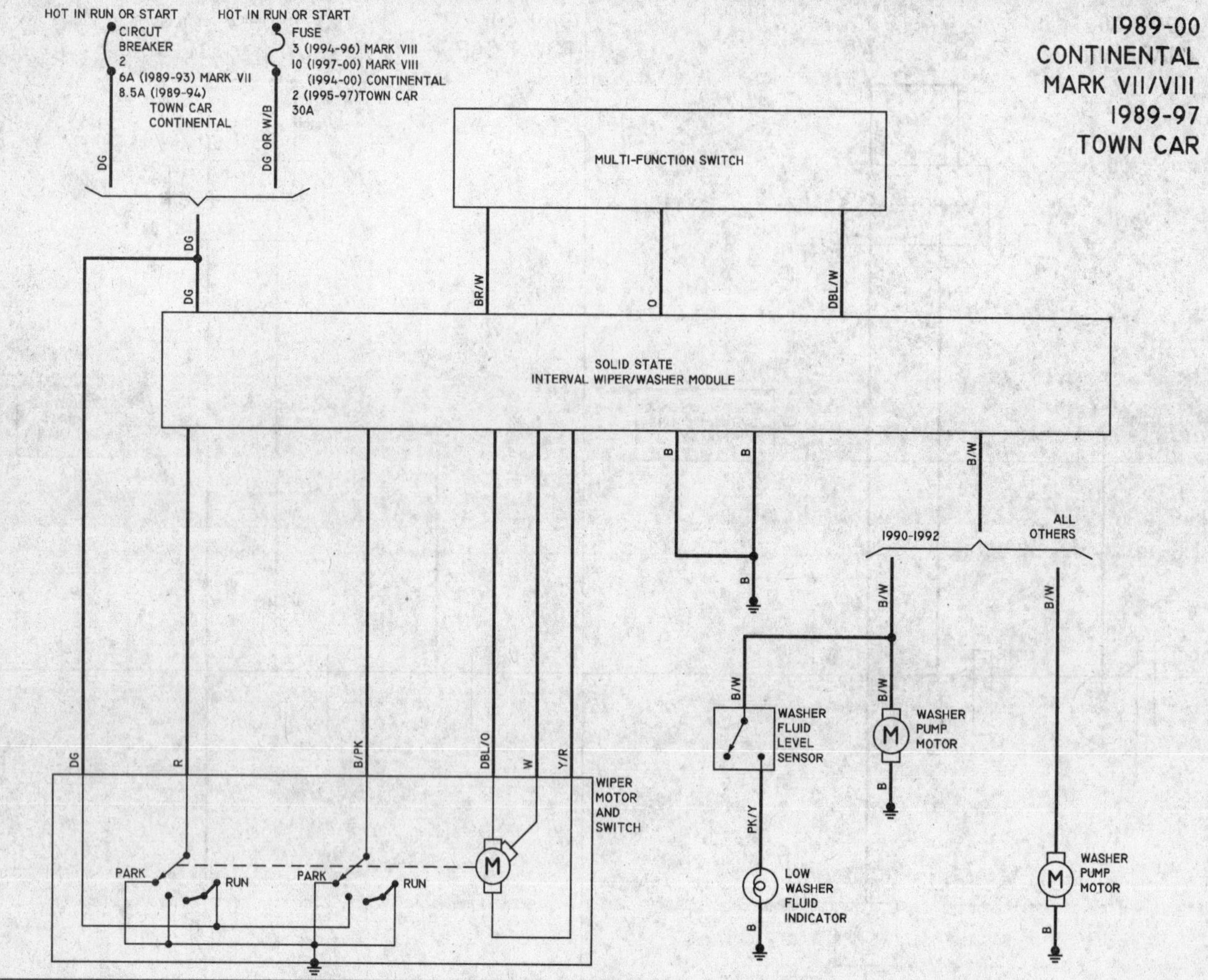


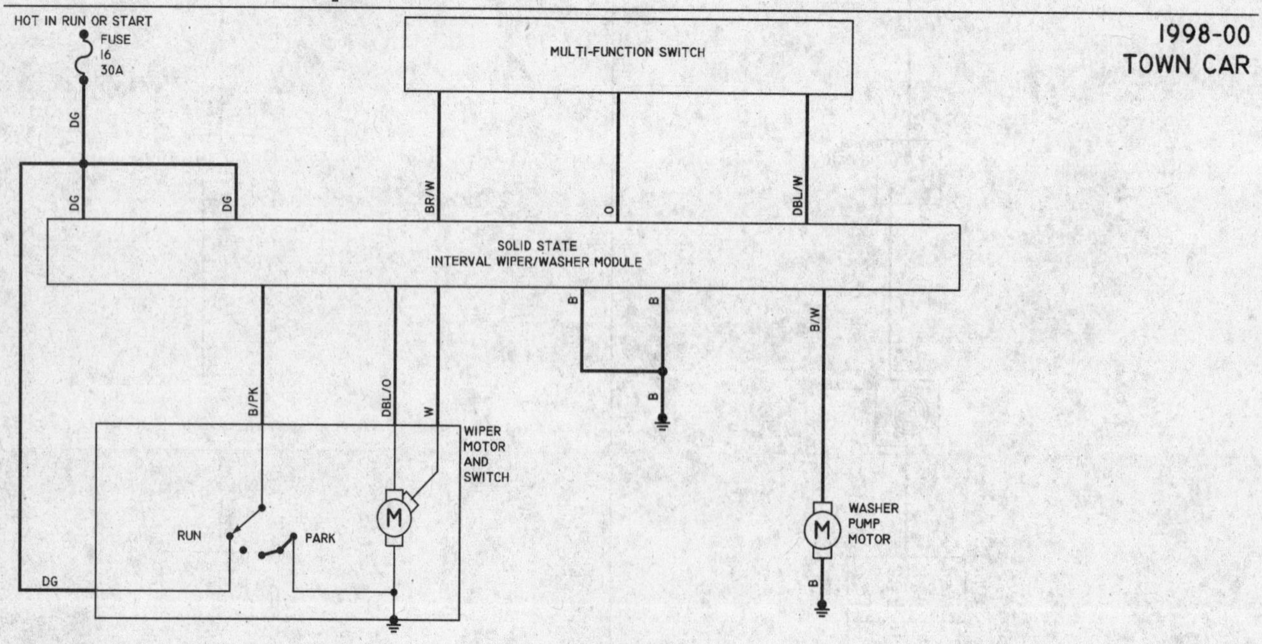


DIAGRAM 54

93146B07

# 7

# DRIVE TRAIN

AUTOMATIC TRANSMISSION 7-2
AUTOMATIC TRANSAXLE 7-4
DRIVELINE 7-9

**AUTOMATIC TRANSMISSION 7-2**
FLUID PAN AND FILTER SERVICE 7-2
REMOVAL & INSTALLATION 7-2
NEUTRAL SAFETY SWITCH 7-2
REMOVAL & INSTALLATION 7-2
ADJUSTMENT 7-2
MANUAL LEVER POSITION (MLP) SENSOR/TRANSMISSION RANGE (TR) SENSOR 7-2
REMOVAL & INSTALLATION 7-2
ADJUSTMENT 7-2
EXTENSION HOUSING SEAL 7-3
REMOVAL & INSTALLATION 7-3
AUTOMATIC TRANSMISSION ASSEMBLY 7-3
REMOVAL & INSTALLATION 7-3
**AUTOMATIC TRANSAXLE 7-4**
FLUID PAN 7-4
REMOVAL & INSTALLATION 7-4
ADJUSTMENTS 7-4
SHIFT LINKAGE 7-4
THROTTLE CABLE 7-4
THROTTLE VALVE CONTROL LINKAGE 7-4
NEUTRAL SAFETY SWITCH 7-4
REMOVAL & INSTALLATION 7-4
TRANSAXLE 7-5
REMOVAL & INSTALLATION 7-5
HALFSHAFTS 7-6
REMOVAL & INSTALLATION 7-7
**DRIVELINE 7-9**
DRIVESHAFT AND U-JOINTS 7-9
REMOVAL & INSTALLATION 7-9
U-JOINT REPLACEMENT 7-10
AXLE SHAFT, BEARING AND SEAL 7-10
REMOVAL & INSTALLATION 7-10
PINION SEAL 7-12
REMOVAL & INSTALLATION 7-12
AXLE HOUSING 7-12
REMOVAL & INSTALLATION 7-12
**SPECIFICATION CHARTS**
AXODE (AX4S) TORQUE SPECIFICATIONS 7-13
AX4N TORQUE SPECIFICATIONS 7-14
AODE TORQUE SPECIFICATIONS 7-14

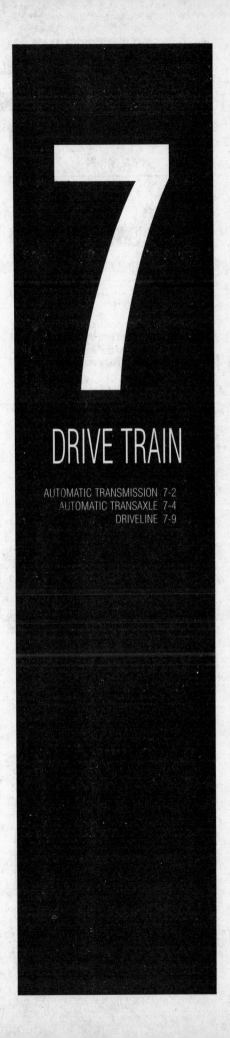

# AUTOMATIC TRANSMISSION

## Fluid Pan and Filter Service

### REMOVAL & INSTALLATION

Refer to Section 1 for transmission pan removal and filter service.

## Neutral Safety Switch

### REMOVAL & INSTALLATION

**1988–91 Models Only**

**➡On 1992 and later models, the neutral safety switch is incorporated into the Manual Lever Position or Transmission Range MLP/TR sensor. Refer to the MLP/TR sensor procedure in this section.**

The neutral safety switch is located on the transmission case above the manual lever.

1. Set the parking brake.
2. Place the selector lever in the manual **L** position.
3. Remove the air cleaner assembly.
4. Disconnect the negative battery cable.
5. Disconnect the neutral safety switch electrical harness from the switch by lifting the harness straight up off the switch without side-to-side motion.
6. Reach in the area of the left hand dash panel, using a 24 inch extension, universal adapter and socket tool T74P–77247–A or equivalent, and remove the neutral safety switch and O-ring.

**➡Use of different tools could crush or puncture the walls of the switch.**

**To install:**

7. Install the neutral safety switch and new O-ring using socket tool T74P–77247–A or equivalent.
8. Tighten the switch to 8–11 ft. lbs. (11–15 Nm).
9. Connect the neutral safety switch to the wiring harness.
10. Connect the negative battery cable.
11. Check that the vehicle starts in the **N** or **P** position.

### ADJUSTMENT

No adjustment is possible on the neutral safety switch.

## Manual Lever Position (MLP) Sensor/Transmission Range (TR) Sensor

### REMOVAL & INSTALLATION

**➧ See Figures 1, 2, 3, 4 and 5**

1. Disconnect the negative battery cable.
2. Raise and support the vehicle safely on jackstands.

91197P03

**Fig. 1 Unfasten the nut for the manual control lever and . . .**

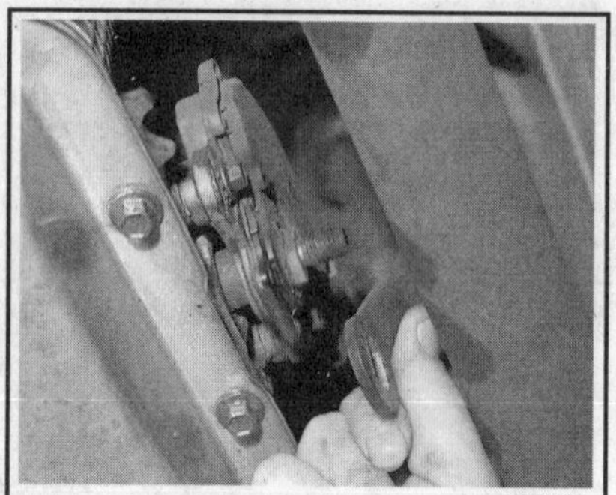

91197P02

**Fig. 2 . . . remove the lever from the sensor**

91197P01

**Fig. 3 Detach the connector from the TR sensor**

3. Place the transmission in Neutral.
4. Remove and discard the manual control lever nut, then remove the lever from the transmission.
5. Detach the TR sensor electrical harness connector, remove the TR sensor retaining bolts, and then pull the TR sensor off the transmission case.

**To install:**

6. Position the TR sensor against the transmission case and loosely install the 2 retaining screws.

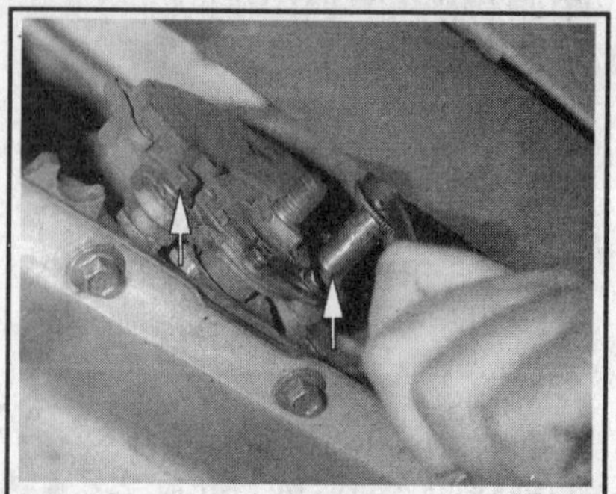

91197P05

**Fig. 4 Unfasten the retaining bolts and . . .**

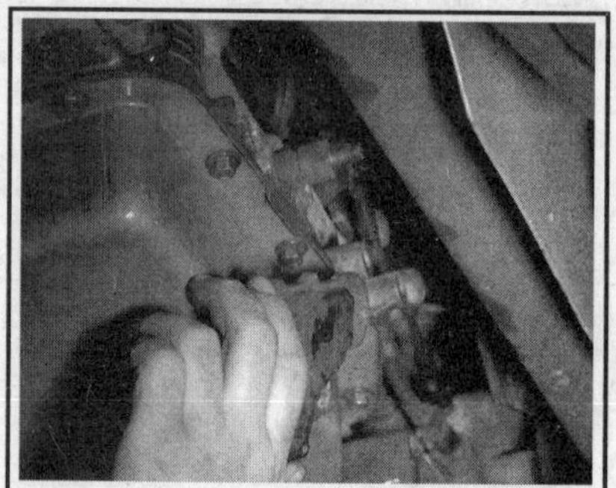

91197P04

**Fig. 5 . . . remove the sensor from the transmission**

7. Attach the TR sensor electrical harness connector.
8. Use an alignment tool, such as the TR Sensor Alignment Tool T93P-70010-A, to align the TR sensor slots.
9. Tighten the TR sensor bolts to 80–100 inch lbs. (9–11 Nm).
10. Position the manual control lever onto the TR sensor, then install the new lever nut to 22–26 ft. lbs. (30–35 Nm).
11. Lower the vehicle.
12. Connect the negative battery cable.

### ADJUSTMENT

**➧ See Figure 6**

**➡Park is the last detent when the manual control lever is full forward. Return 2 detents toward the output shaft for Neutral.**

1. Position the manual control lever in **Neutral**.
2. Raise and safely support the vehicle.
3. Loosen the sensor retaining bolts.
4. Insert Gear Position Sensor Adjuster tool T93P-700 10-A or equivalent, into the slots.
5. Align all 3 slots on the MLP sensor with 3 tabs on the tool.
6. Tighten the attaching screws to 80–100 inch lbs. (9–11 Nm).
7. Lower the vehicle.

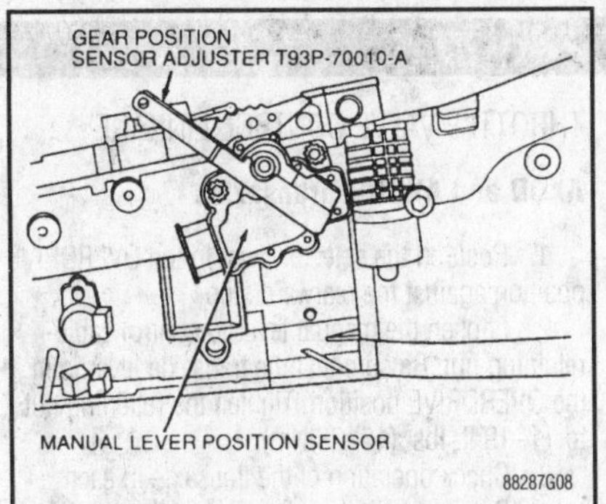


**Fig. 6 Adjusting the MLP sensor**

## Extension Housing Seal

### REMOVAL & INSTALLATION

1. Raise and safely support the vehicle.
2. Remove the driveshaft according to the procedure in this section.
3. Carefully remove the seal, using a suitable seal removal tool.
4. Inspect the sealing surface of the driveshaft yoke for scoring or damage. If scored or damaged, the yoke must be replaced.
5. Inspect the seal bore in the extension housing for burrs or damage. Burrs can be removed with crocus cloth.

**To install:**

6. Install the seal in the housing using a suitable seal installer; the seal should be firmly seated in the bore.
7. Coat the inside diameter of the rubber portion of the seal with grease.
8. Install the driveshaft as described in this Section.
9. Lower the vehicle. Operate the vehicle and check for leaks.

## Automatic Transmission Assembly

### REMOVAL & INSTALLATION

1. Disconnect the negative battery cable.
2. Raise the vehicle and support safely.
3. Drain the fluid from the transmission by removing all the transmission pan bolts except for one on each corner. Loosen the 4 bolts on the corner and drop the oil pan to allow the fluid to drain into a container. When drained, reinstall a few of the bolts to hold the pan in place.
4. Remove the converter bottom cover and remove the converter drain plug, to allow the converter to drain. After the converter has drained, reinstall the drain plug and tighten.
5. Remove the converter to flywheel nuts by turning the converter to expose the nuts.

**➡Crank the engine over with a wrench on the crankshaft pulley-attaching bolt.**

6. Mark the position of the driveshaft on the rear axle flange and remove the driveshaft. Install a suitable plug in the transmission extension housing to prevent fluid leakage.
7. Disconnect the starter cable and remove the starter.
8. Disconnect the wiring from the neutral safety switch.
9. Remove the mount-to-crossmember and crossmember-to-frame bolts.
10. Remove the mount-to-transmission bolts.
11. On 1988–89 vehicles, disconnect the manual rod from the transmission manual lever using grommet removal tool T84P–7341–A or equivalent. On 1990–92 vehicles, disconnect the shift cable from the transmission. If equipped, disconnect the throttle valve cable from the transmission throttle valve lever.
12. On 1993–00vehicles, detach the wiring connectors.
13. Remove the bellcrank bracket from the converter housing.
14. Position a suitable jack and raise the transmission.
15. Remove the transmission mount and crossmember.

**➡It may be necessary to disconnect or remove interfering exhaust system components.**

16. Lower the transmission to gain access to the oil cooler lines.
17. Disconnect the oil cooler lines from the transmission.
18. If equipped, disconnect the speedometer cable from the extension housing.
19. Remove the transmission dipstick tube-to-engine-block retaining bolt and remove the tube and dipstick from the transmission.
20. Secure the transmission to the jack with a chain and remove the transmission-to-engine bolts.
21. Carefully pull the transmission and converter assembly rearward and lower them from the vehicle.

**To install:**

22. Tighten the converter drain plug to 21–23 ft. lbs. (28–30 Nm).
23. If removed, position the converter on the transmission and rotate into position to make sure the drive flats are fully engaged in the pump gear.

**➡Lubricate the pilot with chassis grease.**

24. Raise the converter and transmission assembly.
25. Rotate the converter until the studs and drain plug are in alignment with the holes in the flywheel. Align the orange balancing marks on the converter stud and flywheel boltholes if balancing marks are present.
26. Move the converter and transmission assembly forward into position, being careful not to damage the flywheel and converter pilot.

**➡The converter face must rest squarely against the flywheel. This indicates that the converter pilot is not binding in the engine crankshaft. To ensure the converter is properly seated, grasp a converter stud. It should move freely back and forth in the flywheel hole. If the converter will not move, the transmission must be removed and the converter repositioned so the impeller hub is properly engaged in the pump gear.**

27. Install the transmission-to-engine attaching bolts. Tighten the bolts to 40–50 ft. lbs. (55–68 Nm).
28. Remove the safety chain from around the transmission.
29. Install a new O-ring on the lower end of the transmission dipstick tube and install the tube to the transmission case.
30. If equipped, connect the speedometer cable to the transmission case.
31. Connect the oil cooler lines to the right side of the transmission case.
32. Position the crossmember on the side supports.
33. Position the rear mount on the crossmember and install the attaching bolt/nut.
34. Secure the engine rear support to the transmission extension housing.
35. Install any exhaust system components, if removed.
36. Lower the transmission and remove the jack.
37. Secure the crossmember to the side supports with the attaching bolts.
38. If equipped, connect the throttle valve linkage to the throttle valve lever. On 1993–00 vehicles, attach the wiring harness connectors.
39. On 1988–89 vehicles, connect the manual linkage rod to the transmission manual lever using grommet installation tool T84P–7341–B or equivalent. On 1990–92 vehicles, connect the shift cable.
40. Install the converter to flywheel attaching nuts and tighten to 20–34 ft. lbs. (27–46 Nm).
41. Install the converter housing cover.
42. Secure the starter motor in place and attach all electrical connections.
43. Install the driveshaft, aligning the marks that were made during removal.
44. Install the transmission fluid pan bolts and tighten, evenly, to 107–119 inch lbs. (12–13.5 Nm).
45. Lower the vehicle.
46. Fill the transmission with the proper type and quantity of fluid, start the engine, and check the transmission for leakage.
47. Adjust the linkage as required.

# AUTOMATIC TRANSAXLE

## Fluid Pan

### REMOVAL & INSTALLATION

Refer to Section 1 for transaxle pan removal and filter service.

## Adjustments

### SHIFT LINKAGE

#### AXOD And AXOD-E Transaxle

1. Position the selector lever in the **OD** position against the rearward stop. The shift lever must be held in the rearward position using a constant force of 3 lbs. (1.4 Kg) while the linkage is being adjusted.
2. Loosen the manual lever-to-control cable-retaining nut.
3. Move the transaxle manual lever to the **OD** position, second detent from the most rearward position.
4. Tighten the retaining nut to 11–19 ft. lbs. (15–26 Nm).
5. Check the operation of the transaxle in each selector lever position. Make sure the park and neutral start switch are functioning properly.

### THROTTLE CABLE

**➡Transaxle downshift control is controlled through the throttle position switch on 1991–95 vehicles equipped with the electronic automatic overdrive transaxle.**

#### 1988–90 Continental

**➧ See Figures 7 and 8**

The Throttle Valve (TV) cable normally does not need adjustment. The cable should be adjusted only

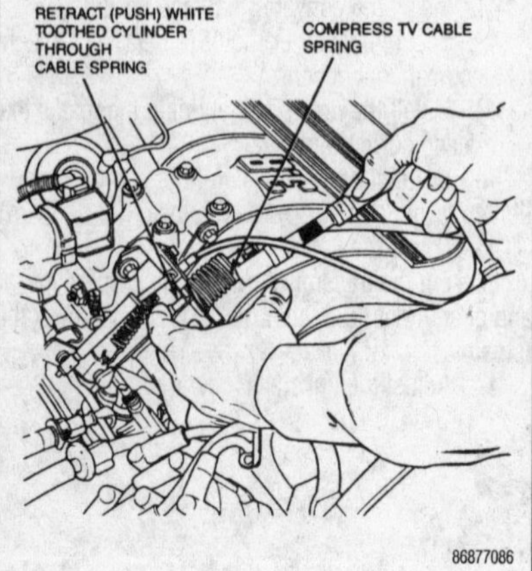


**Fig. 7 While the spring is compressed, push the threaded shank toward the spring with the index and middle fingers of the left hand. Do not pull on the cable sheath**

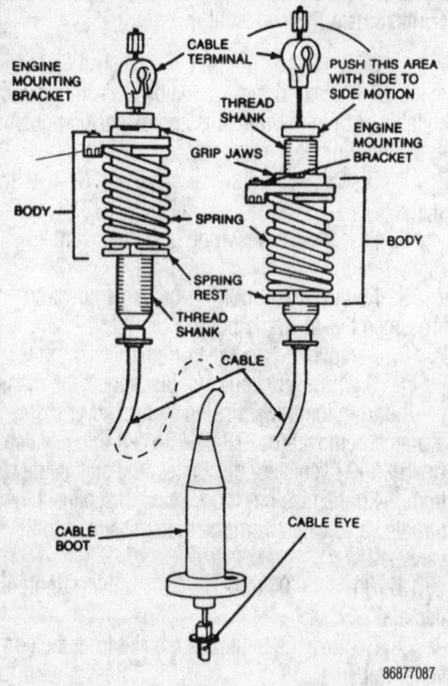


**Fig. 8 The threaded shank must show movement or "ratchet" out of the grip jaws. If there is no movement, inspect the TV cable system for broken or disconnected components then repeat the procedure**

if one of the following components is removed for service or replacement:

- Main control assembly
- Throttle valve cable
- Throttle valve cable engine mounting bracket
- Throttle control lever link or lever assembly
- Engine throttle body
- Transaxle assembly

1. Connect the TV cable eye to the transaxle throttle control lever link, then attach the cable boot to the chain cover.
2. The TV cable must be unclipped from the right intake manifold clip. To retract the shank, span the crack between the two 180 degree segments of the adjuster spring rest with a suitable tool. Compress the spring by pushing the rod toward the throttle body with the right hand. While the spring is compressed, push the threaded shank toward the spring with the index and middle fingers of the left hand. Do not pull on the cable sheath.
3. Attach the end of the TV cable to the throttle body.
4. Rotate the throttle body primary lever by hand, the lever to which the TV-driving nailhead is attached, to the wide-open-throttle position. The white adjuster shank must be seen to advance. If not, look for cable sheath/foam hang-up on engine/body components. Attach the TV cable into the top position of the right intake manifold clip.

**➡The threaded shank must show movement or "ratchet" out of the grip jaws. If there is no movement, inspect the TV cable system for broken or disconnected components then repeat the procedure.**

### THROTTLE VALVE CONTROL LINKAGE

#### AXOD and AXOD-E Transaxles

1. Position the selector lever in the OVERDRIVE position against the rearward stop.
2. Loosen the manual lever to control cable-retaining nut. Be sure that the transaxle lever is in the OVERDRIVE position. Tighten the retaining nut to 11–19 ft. lbs. (15–26 Nm).
3. Check operation of the transaxle in each range. Be sure that the park switch and neutral safety switch are working properly.

## Neutral Safety Switch

### REMOVAL & INSTALLATION

**➧ See Figures 9 and 10**

1. Make sure the shift selector in the **Park** position, then apply the emergency brake.
2. Disconnect the negative battery cable.
3. Disengage the neutral start switch electrical connector, then remove the shift control lever on top of the switch.
4. Remove the two neutral switch-attaching bolts, then remove the switch.

**To install:**

5. Install the switch on the manual shaft.
6. Loosely install the two attaching bolts and washers.

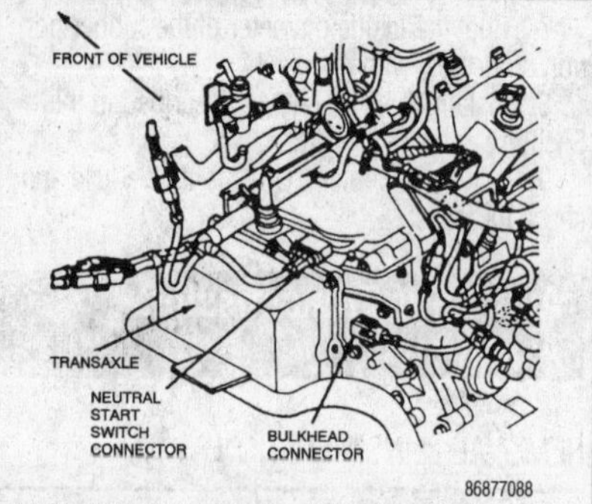


**Fig. 9 Neutral safety switch location—vehicles equipped with automatic transaxle**

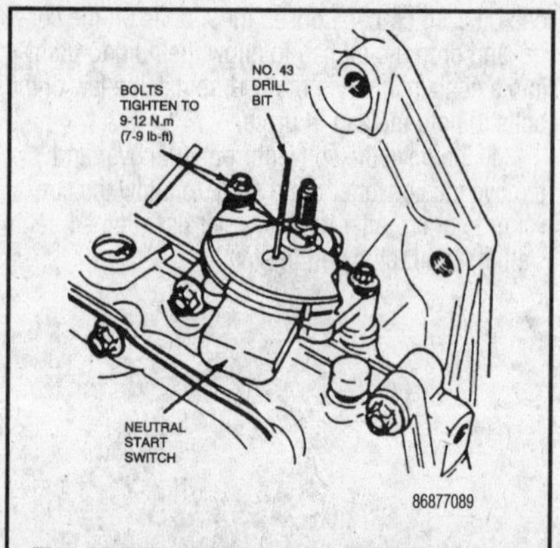


**Fig. 10 Adjusting the neutral safety switch**

7. Insert a No. 43 drill (0.089 in.) through the hole.

8. Tighten the attaching bolts to 7–9 ft. lbs. (9–12 Nm), then remove the drill.

9. Engage the switch electrical connector, then connect the negative battery cable.

## Transaxle

### REMOVAL & INSTALLATION

#### 1988–94 Vehicles

➧ **See Figures 11 thru 20**

1. Disconnect the negative battery cable.
2. Remove the air cleaner assembly.
3. Remove the bolt retaining the shift cable and bracket assembly to the transaxle.

**➡Hold the bracket with a prybar in the slot to prevent the bracket from moving.**

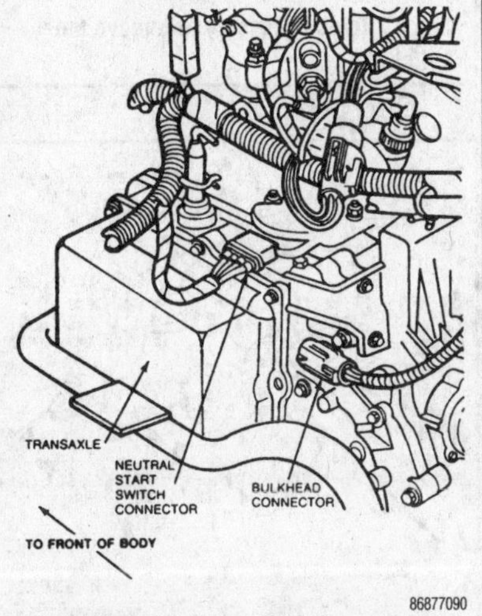


**Fig. 11 Detach the connectors from the neutral safety switch and the bulkhead connector**

4. Remove the shift cable bracket bolts and bracket from the transaxle.
5. Disengage the electrical connector from the neutral safety switch.
6. Detach the electrical bulkhead connector from the rear of the transaxle.
7. Remove the oil dipstick.
8. Remove the throttle valve cable cover. Unsnap the throttle valve cable from the throttle body lever. Remove the throttle valve cable from the transaxle case
9. Carefully pull up on the throttle valve cable and disconnect the throttle valve cable from the TV link.

**➡Pulling too hard on the throttle valve may bend the internal TV bracket.**

10. Install engine-lifting brackets.
11. Disconnect the power steering pump pressure and return line bracket.
12. Remove the converter housing bolts from the top of the transaxle.
13. Install a suitable engine support fixture.
14. Raise the and safely support the vehicle.
15. Remove both front wheels. Remove the left-side outer tie rod end.
16. Remove the lower ball joint attaching nuts and bolts. Remove the lower ball joints and remove the lower control arms from each spindle. Remove stabilizer bar bolts.
17. Remove the nuts securing the steering rack to the subframe.
18. Disengage the oxygen sensor electrical connection, then remove the exhaust pipe, converter assembly and mounting bracket.
19. Remove the two 15mm bolts from the transaxle mount. Remove the four 15mm bolts from the left engine support, then remove the bracket.
20. Position a suitable subframe removal tool.
21. Remove the steering gear from the subframe and secure to the rear of the engine compartment. Remove the subframe-to-body retaining bolts, then remove the subframe.
22. Remove the dust cover retaining bolt and the starter retaining bolts then position the starter out of the way. Remove the dust cover.
23. Rotate the engine by the crankshaft pulley bolt to align the torque converter bolts with the starter drive hole. Remove the torque converter-to-flywheel retaining nuts.

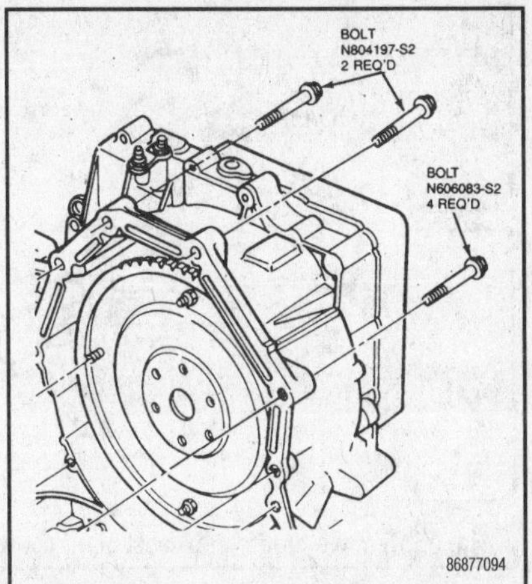


**Fig. 13 Remove the four torque converter housing bolts from the top of the transaxle**

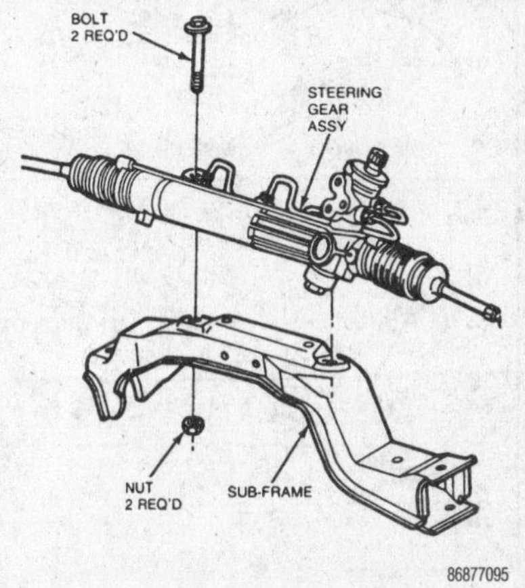


**Fig. 14 Remove the nut securing the steering rack to the subframe**

24. Remove the transaxle cooler line fitting retaining clips. Using Cooler Line Disconnect Tool T86P-77265-AH or equivalent, disconnect the transaxle cooler lines.
25. Remove the engine-to-transaxle retaining bolts.
26. Remove the speedometer sensor heat shield.
27. Remove the vehicle speed sensor from the transaxle.

**➡Vehicles with electronic instrument clusters do not use a speedometer cable.**

28. Position a suitable transaxle jack.
29. Remove the halfshafts as follows:
    a. Screw Extension T86P-3514-A2 into CV Joint Puller T86P-3514-A1, and insert Slide Hammer D79P-100-A or equivalent into the extension.
    b. Position the puller behind the CV joint, then remove the joint.
    c. Install shipping plugs.
30. Remove the two remaining torque converter housing bolts.

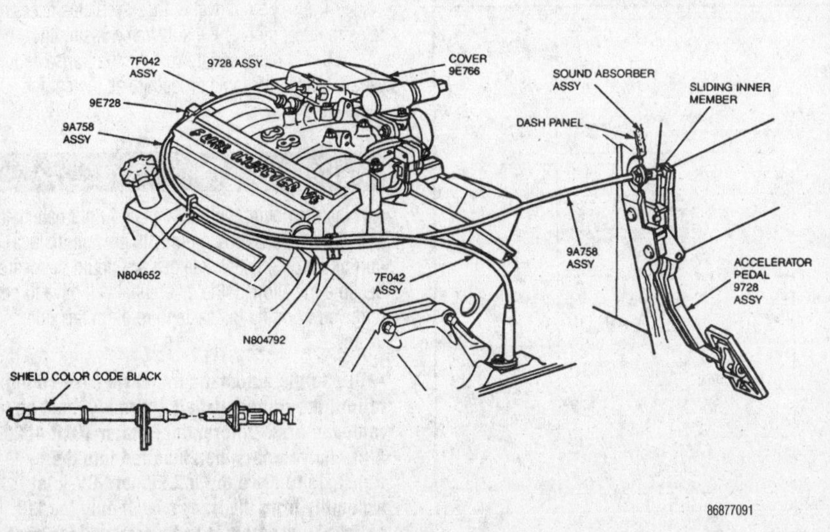


**Fig. 12 Location of the throttle valve cable cover**

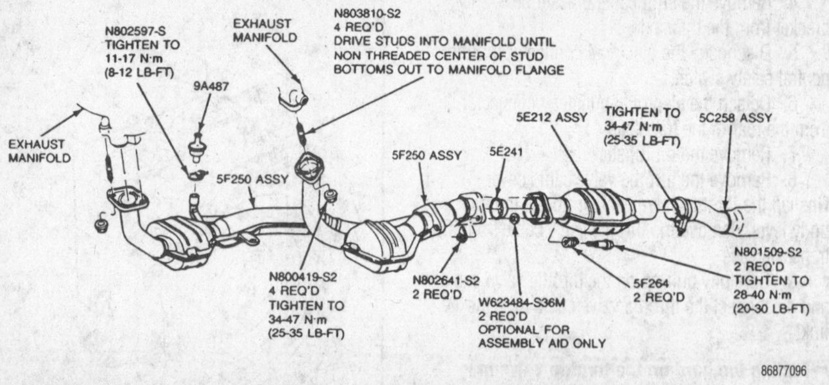


**Fig. 15 Remove the front exhaust pipe, converter assembly, and mounting bracket**

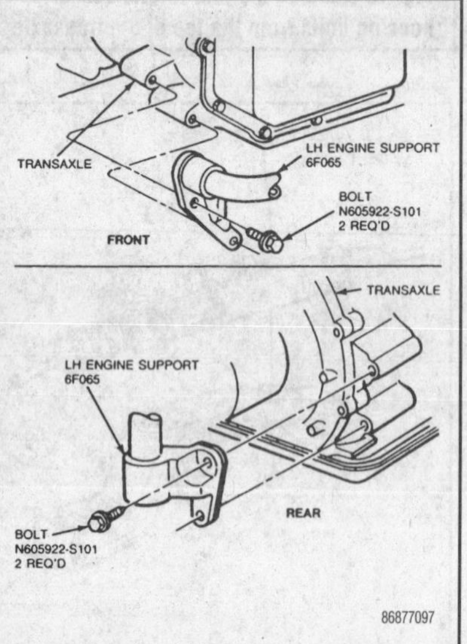


**Fig. 16 Remove the bolts from the left engine support, then remove the support**

31. Separate the transaxle from the engine, then carefully lower the transaxle from the vehicle.

**To install:**

a. Clean the transaxle oil cooler lines.

b. Install new circlips on the CV-joint seals.

c. Carefully install the halfshafts in the transaxle by aligning the splines of the CV-joint with the splines of the differential.

d. Attach the lower ball joint to the steering knuckle with a new nut and bolt. Tighten the nut to 37–44 ft. lbs.

e. When installing the transaxle to the engine, verify that the converter-to-transaxle engagement is maintained. Prevent the converter from moving forward and disengaging during installation.

f. Adjust the TV and manual linkages. Check the transaxle fluid level.

g. Tighten the following bolts to the torque specifications listed:

- Transaxle-to-engine bolts: 41–50 ft. lbs. (55–68 Nm)
- Control arm-to-knuckle bolts: 36–44 ft. lbs. (49–60 Nm)
- Stabilizer U-clamp-to-bracket bolts: 60–70 ft. lbs. (81–95 Nm)
- Tie rod-to-knuckle nut: 23–35 ft. lbs. (31–47 Nm)
- Starter-to-transaxle bolts: 30–40 ft. lbs. (41–54 Nm)
- Converter-to-flywheel bolts: 23–39 ft. lbs. (31–53 Nm)
- Insulator-to-bracket bolts: 55–70 ft. lbs. (75–95 Nm)

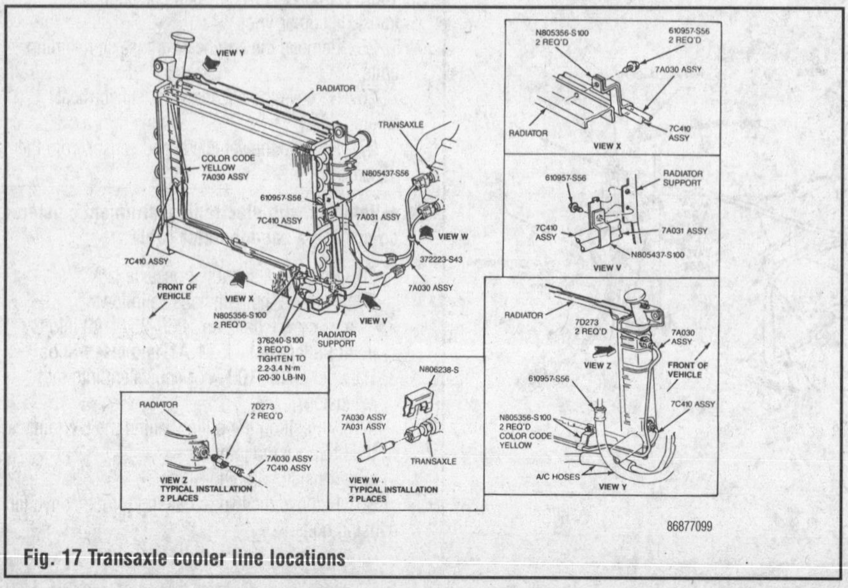


**Fig. 17 Transaxle cooler line locations**

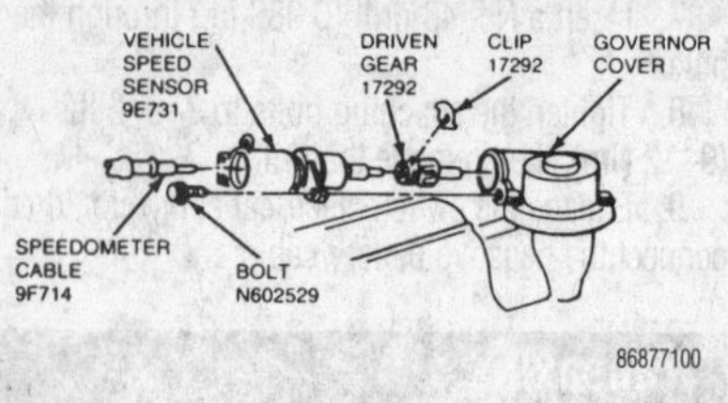


**Fig. 18 Remove the vehicle speed sensor from the transaxle**

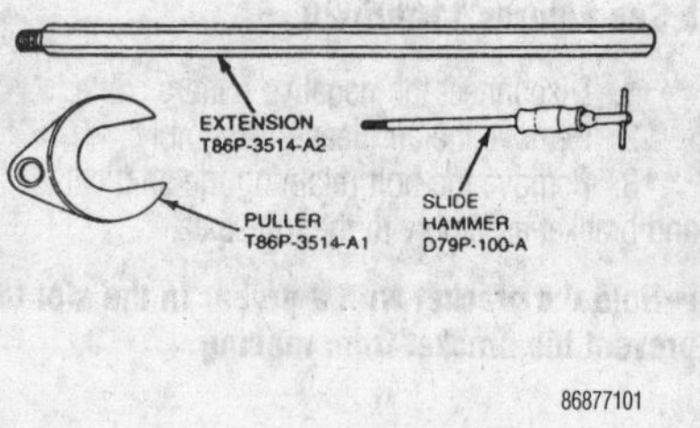


**Fig. 19 Tools necessary to remove the halfshafts**

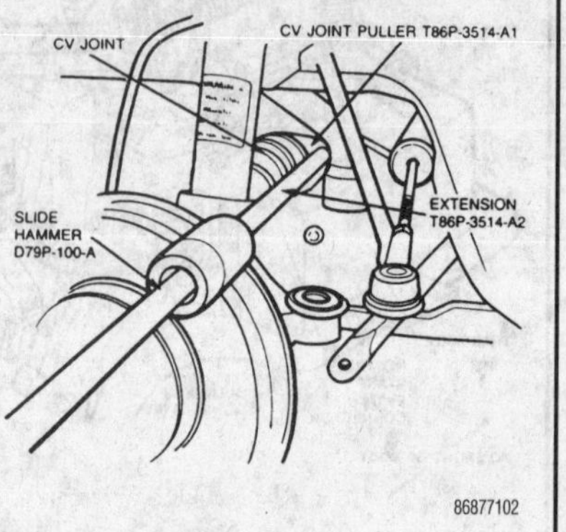


**Fig. 20 Position the puller behind the CV-joint, then remove the joint**

**Continental 1995–00**

1. Transaxle removal in these vehicles necessitates the dropping of the sub-frame assembly.

2. If it is necessary to remove the transaxle for repair, follow the same procedure as the engine removal.

## Halfshafts

When removing both the left and right halfshafts, install suitable shipping plugs to prevent dislocation of the differential side gears. Should the gears become misaligned, the differential will have to be removed from the transaxle to re-align the side gears.

**➡Due to the automatic transaxle case configuration, the right halfshaft assembly must be removed first. Differential Rotator T81P-4026-A or equivalent is then inserted into the transaxle to drive the left inboard CV-joint assembly from the transaxle. If only the left halfshaft assembly is to be removed for ser-**

**vice, remove only the right halfshaft assembly from the transaxle. After removal, support it with a length of wire. Then, drive the left halfshaft assembly from the transaxle.**

## REMOVAL & INSTALLATION

**See Figures 21 thru 39**

1. Disconnect the negative battery cable.
2. Remove the wheel cover/hub cover from the wheel and tire assembly, then loosen the lug nuts.
3. Raise and safely support the vehicle, then remove the wheel and tire assembly. Insert a steel rod in the rotor to prevent it from turning, then remove the hub nut and washer. Discard the old hub nut.

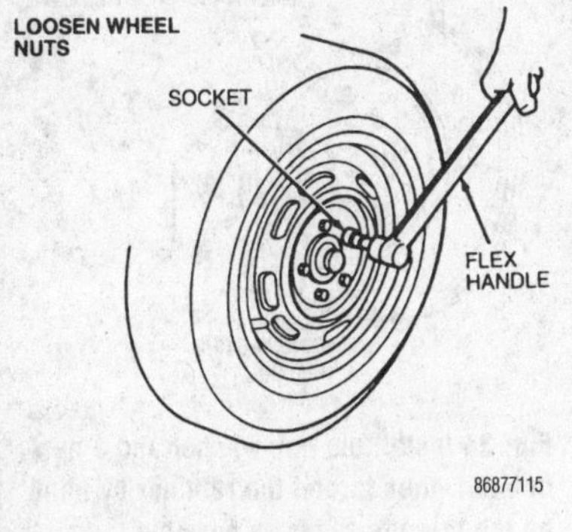


**Fig. 21 After removing the wheel/hub cover, loosen the lug nuts**

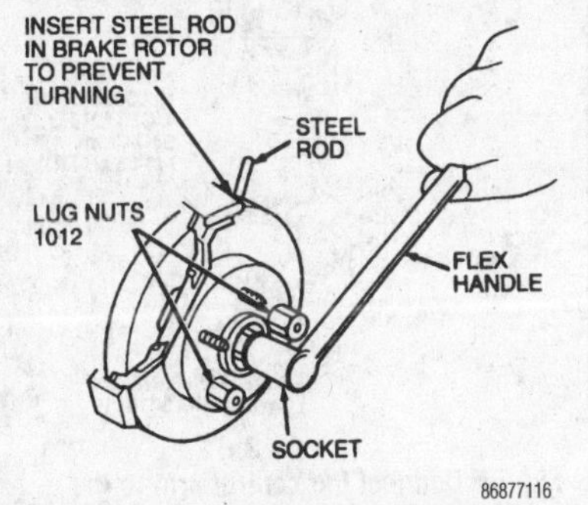


**Fig. 22 Before removing the hub nut and washer, insert a steel rod in the rotor to prevent it from turning**

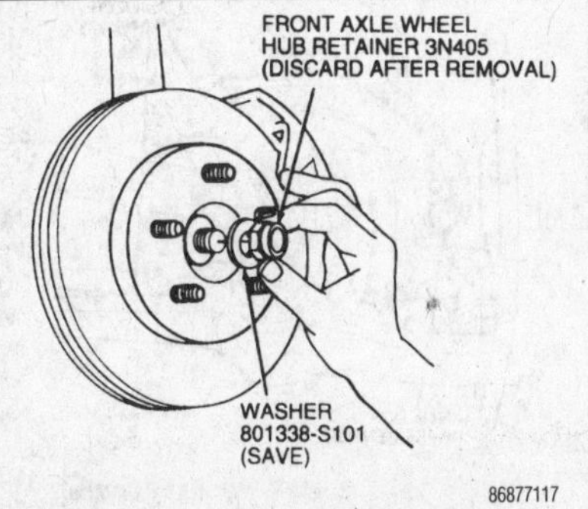


**Fig. 23 Remove the hub nut and washer, then discard the nut, and replace with a new one during installation**

4. Remove the nut from the ball joint to steering knuckle attaching bolts.
5. Drive the bolt out of the steering knuckle using a punch and hammer. Discard this bolt and nut after removal.
6. If equipped with anti-lock brakes, remove the anti-lock brake sensor and position it aside. If equipped with air suspension, remove the height sensor bracket retaining bolt and wire sensor bracket to inner fender. Position the sensor link aside.
7. Separate the ball joint from the steering knuckle using a suitable prybar. Position the end of the prybar outside of the bushing pocket to avoid damage to the bushing. Use care to prevent damage to the ball joint boot. Remove the stabilizer bar link at the stabilizer bar.
   a. Slide the link shaft out of the transaxle. Support the end of the shaft by suspending it from a convenient underbody component with a piece of wire. Do not allow the shaft to hang unsupported, damage to the outboard CV-joint may occur.
   b. Separate the outboard CV-joint from the hub using front hub remover tool T81P-1104-C or equivalent and metric adapter tools T83P-1104-BH, T86P-1104-AI and T81P-1104-A or equivalent.

**➡Never use a hammer to separate the outboard CV-joint stub shaft from the hub. Damage to the CV-joint threads and internal components may result. The halfshaft assembly is removed as a complete unit.**

   c. Install the CV-joint puller tool T86P-3514-A1 or equivalent, between CV-joint and transaxle case. Turn the steering hub and/or wire strut assembly aside.
   d. Screw extension tool T86P-3514-A2 or equivalent, into the CV-joint puller and hand tighten. Screw an impact slide hammer onto the extension and remove the CV-joint.
   e. Support the end of the shaft by suspending it from a convenient underbody component with a piece of wire. Do not allow the shaft to hang unsupported, damage to the outboard CV-joint may occur.
   f. Separate the outboard CV-joint from the hub using front hub remover tool T81P-1104-C

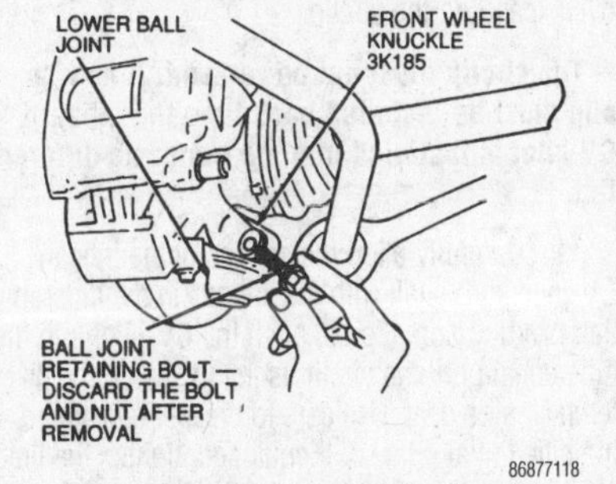


**Fig. 24 Drive the bolt out of the front wheel knuckle using a punch and hammer, then discard the nut and bolt and replace with new ones during installation**

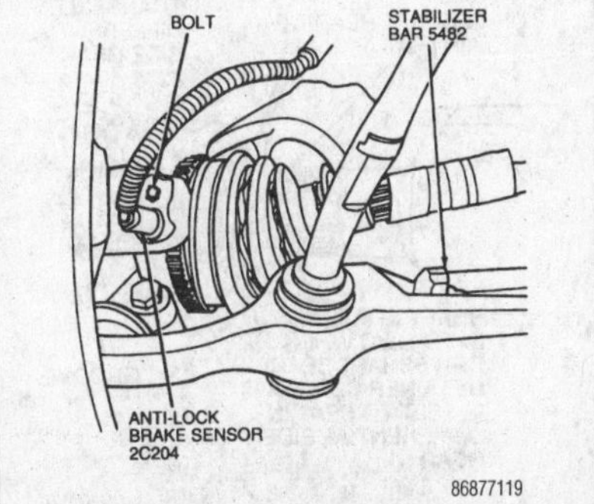


**Fig. 25 If so equipped, remove the anti-lock brake sensor and position it aside**

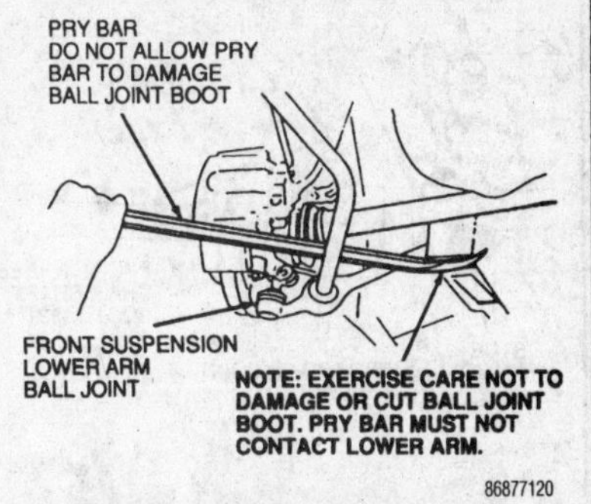


**Fig. 26 When separating the ball joint from the steering knuckle, be careful not to damage to ball joint boot**

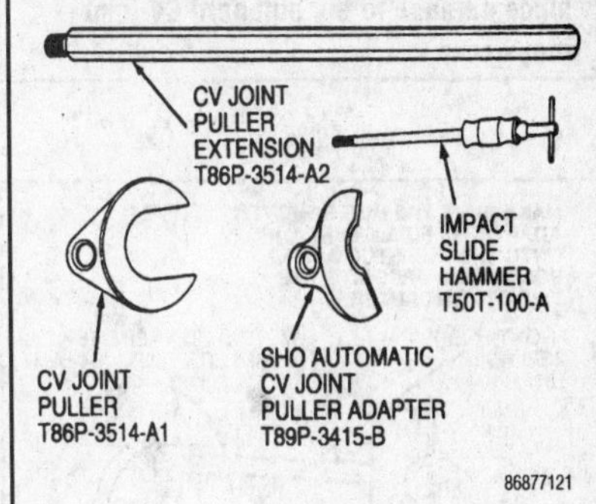


**Fig. 27 These tools are necessary for halfshaft removal**

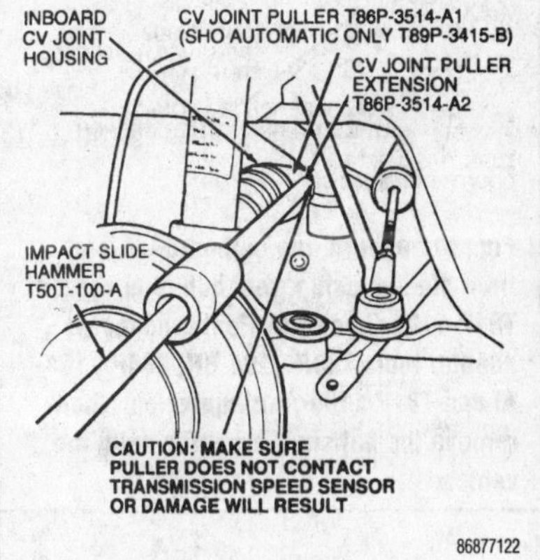


**Fig. 28 Installing the specified tools to remove the halfshaft assembly from the vehicle**

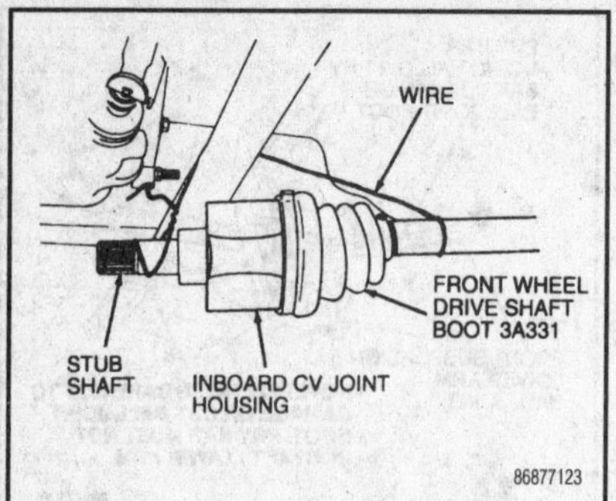


**Fig. 29 Support the end of the shaft by suspending it from a convenient underbody component with a piece of wire. Do not allow the shaft to hang unsupported, since damage to the outboard CV-joint may occur**

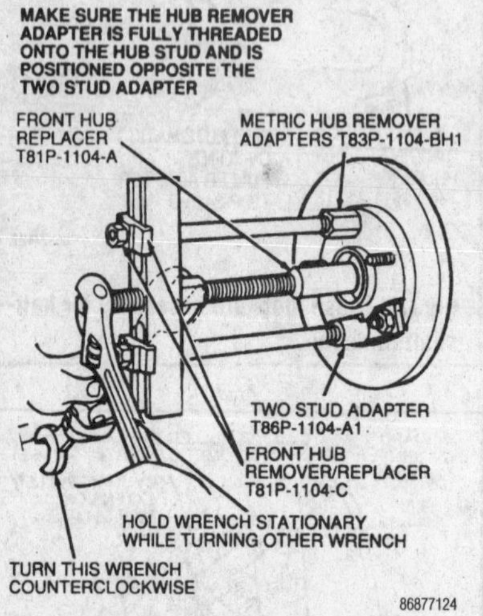


**Fig. 30 Separate the outboard CV-joint from the hub using front hub remover tool T81P-1104-C or equivalent, and metric adapter tools T83P-1104-BH, T86P-1104-AI and T81P-1104-A or equivalent, then remove the halfshaft assembly from the vehicle**

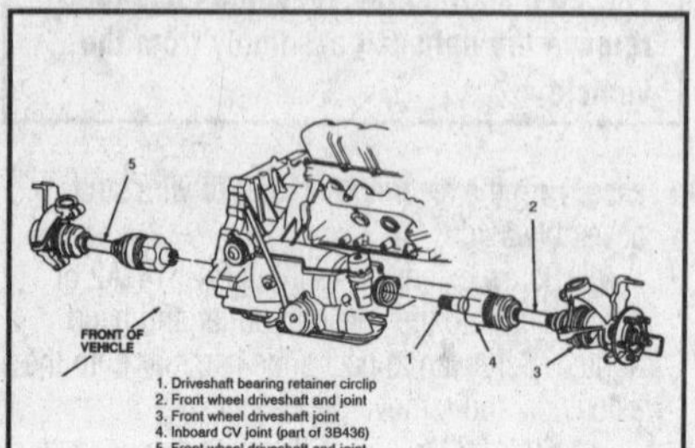


**Fig. 31 Exploded view of the halfshaft assemblies and related components—automatic transaxle**

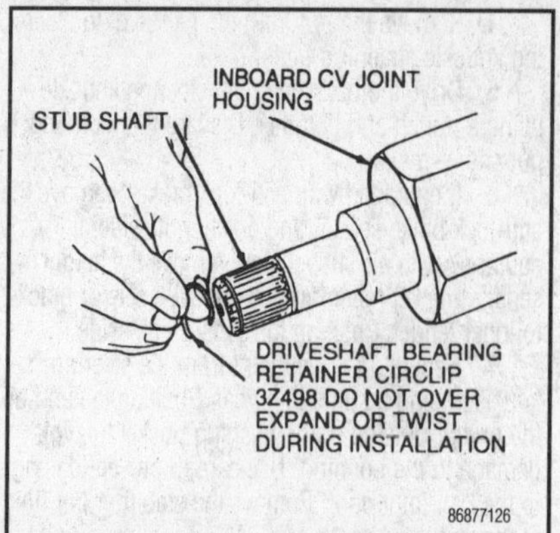


**Fig. 32 Always use a new circlip on the inboard CV-joint stub shaft and/or link shaft. When installing the new circlip, start one end in the groove and work the circlip over the stub shaft end into the groove. This will avoid overexpanding the circlip**

or equivalent and metric adapter tools T83P-1104-BH, T86P-1104-AI and T81P-1104-A or equivalent.

g. Remove the halfshaft assembly from the vehicle.

**To install:**

8. Install a new circlip on the inboard CV-joint stub shaft and/or link shaft. The outboard CV-joint does not have a circlip. When installing the circlip, start one end in the groove and work the circlip over the stub shaft end into the groove. This will avoid overexpanding the circlip.

**➡The circlip must not be re-used. A new circlip must be installed each time the inboard CV-joint is installed into the transaxle differential.**

9. Carefully align the splines of the inboard CV-joint stub shaft with the splines in the differential. Exerting some force, push the CV-joint into the differential until the circlip is felt to seat in the differential side gear. Use care to prevent damage to the differential oil seal. If equipped, tighten the link shaft bearing to 16–23 ft. lbs. (22–31 Nm).

**➡A non-metallic mallet may be used to aid in seating the circlip into the differential side gear groove. If a mallet is necessary, tap only on the outboard CV-joint stub shaft.**

10. Carefully align the splines of the outboard CV-joint stub shaft with the splines in the hub and push the shaft into the hub as far as possible.

11. Temporarily fasten the rotor to the hub with washers and two wheel lug nuts. Insert a steel rod into the rotor and rotate clockwise to contact the knuckle to prevent the rotor from turning during the CV-joint installation.

12. Install the hub nut washer and a new hub nut. Manually thread the retainer onto the CV-joint as far as possible.

13. Connect the control arm to the steering

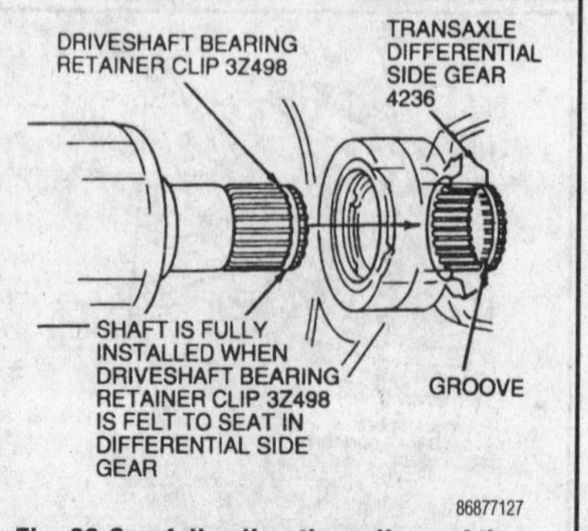


**Fig. 33 Carefully align the splines of the inboard CV-joint stub shaft with the splines in the differential**

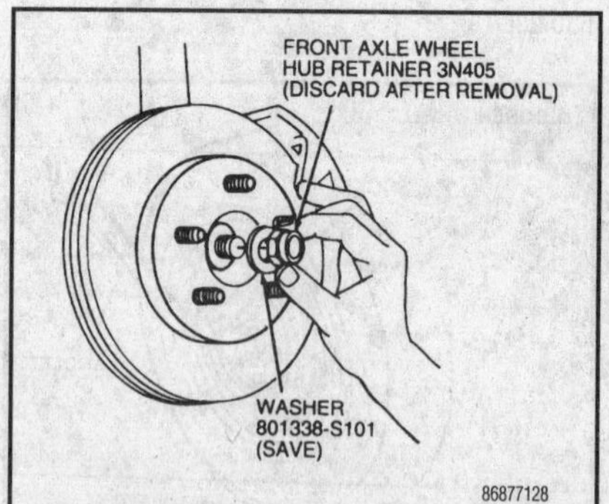


**Fig. 34 Install the hub washer and a new hub nut, then thread the retainer by hand on the threads as far as possible**

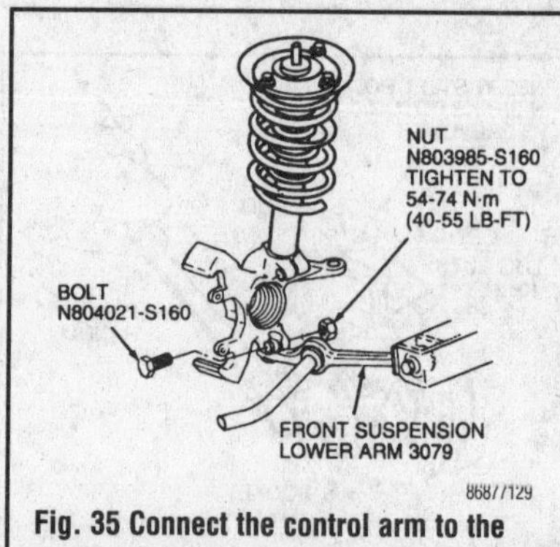


**Fig. 35 Connect the control arm to the steering knuckle and install a new nut and bolt. Tighten to 40–55 ft. lbs. (54–74 Nm)**

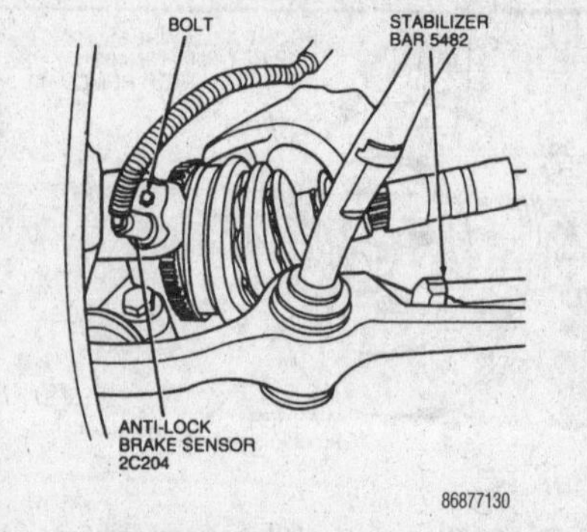


**Fig. 36 If equipped, install the anti-lock brake sensor**

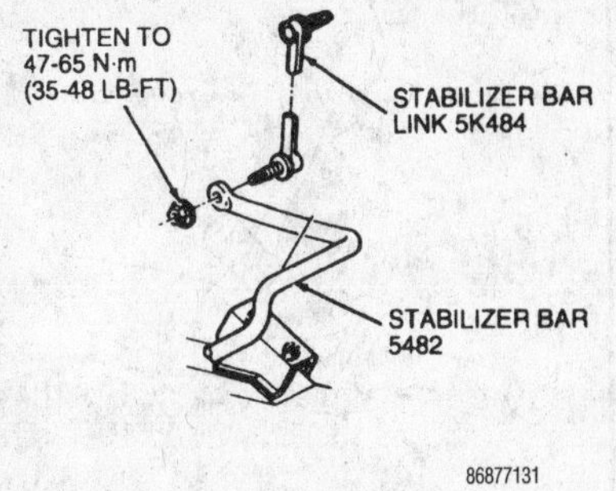

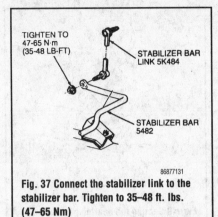

**Fig. 37 Connect the stabilizer link to the stabilizer bar. Tighten to 35–48 ft. lbs. (47–65 Nm)**

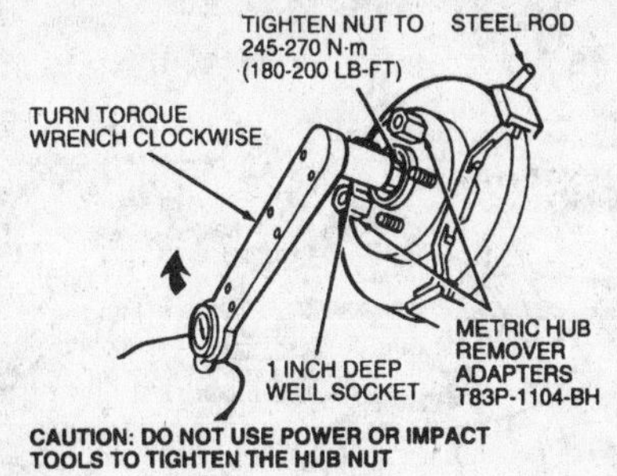

**Fig. 38 Install a new hub retainer nut, then tighten to specification using a torque wrench. Do NOT use an air gun or impact tool to tighten the nut**

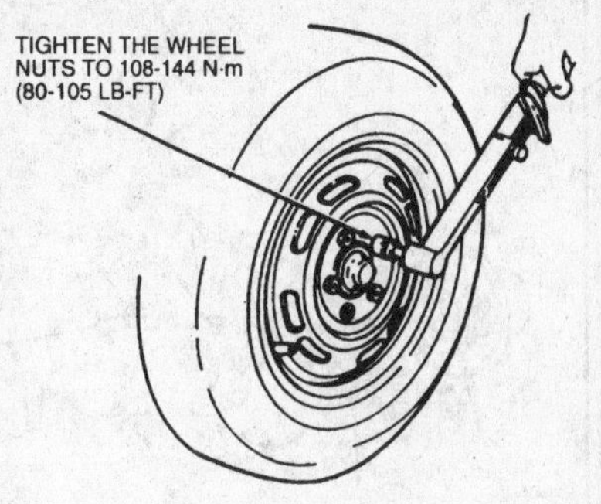

**Fig. 39 After the vehicle is lowered, tighten the lug nuts to 80–105 ft. lbs. (108–142 Nm)**

knuckle, then install a new nut and bolt. Tighten the nut to 40–55 ft. lbs. (54–74 Nm).

14. If equipped, install the anti-lock brake sensor and/or the ride height sensor bracket.

15. Connect the stabilizer link to the stabilizer bar. Tighten to 35–48 ft. lbs. (47–65 Nm).

16. Install a new hub retainer nut, then tighten the nut to 180–200 ft. lbs. (245–270 Nm). Remove the steel rod.

17. Install the wheel and tire assembly, snugging the lug nuts by hand, then lower the vehicle. Tighten the wheel lug nuts to 80–105 ft. lbs. (108–142 Nm). Fill the transaxle to the proper level with the specified fluid.

# DRIVELINE

## Driveshaft and U-Joints

### REMOVAL & INSTALLATION

**Town Car and Mark VII-VIII**

**See Figures 40, 41, 42, 43 and 44**

1. Raise and safely support the vehicle.
2. Mark the position of the driveshaft yoke on the axle companion flange so they can be reassembled in the same way to maintain balance.
3. Remove the flange bolts and disconnect the driveshaft from the axle companion flange.
4. Allow the rear of the driveshaft to drop down slightly.
5. Pull the driveshaft and slip yoke rearward until the yoke just clears the transmission extension housing seal. Mark the position of the slip yoke in relation to the transmission output shaft, then remove the driveshaft.

91197P12

**Fig. 40 The bolts retaining the rear driveshaft yoke-to-differential flange require a 12mm, 12 point wrench or socket to loosen them**

6. Plug the transmission to prevent fluid leakage.

**To install:**

7. Lubricate the yoke splines with suitable grease.
8. Remove the plug from the transmission and inspect the extension housing seal; replace if necessary.
9. Align the slip yoke and output shaft with the marks made at removal and install the yoke into the transmission extension housing. Be careful not to bottom the slip yoke hard against the transmission seal.

91197P11

**Fig. 41 Remove the bolts retaining the rear driveshaft yoke-to-differential flange**

91197P13

**Fig. 42 Separate the driveshaft from the axle flange and . . .**

91197P14

**Fig. 43 . . . disengage the driveshaft from the transmission output shaft**

91197P15

**Fig. 44 Insert a plug onto the splines of the transmission output shaft to prevent fluid from leaking out**

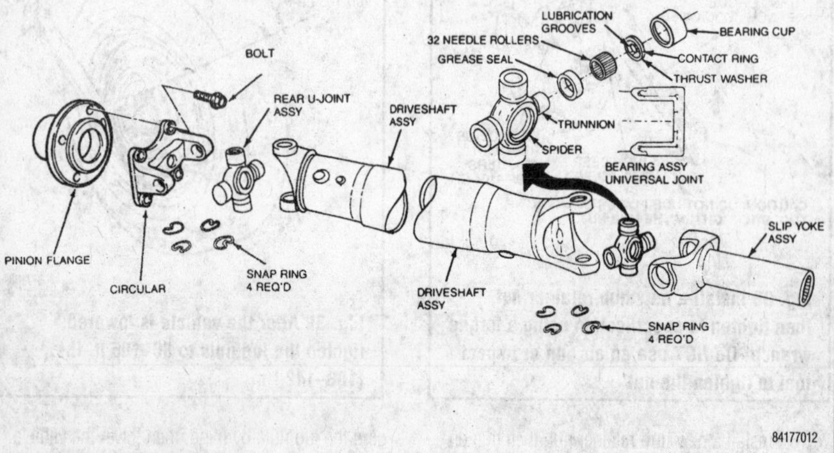


**Fig. 45 Driveshaft assembly**

10. Rotate the axle flange, as necessary, to align the marks made during removal.
11. Install the driveshaft yoke to the axle flange. Install the bolts and tighten to 71–95 ft. lbs. (95–130 Nm).
12. Lower the vehicle.

## U-JOINT REPLACEMENT

**➧ See Figures 45, 46, 47, 48 and 49**

1. Remove the driveshaft from the vehicle and place it in a vise, being careful not to damage it.
2. Mark the position of the yokes in relation to the driveshaft tube, so they can be reinstalled the same way.
3. Remove the snap-rings that retain the bearing cups in the yokes and in both ends of the driveshaft.
4. Remove the driveshaft tube from the vise and position the U-joint in the vise with a socket smaller than the bearing cup on one side and a socket larger than the bearing cup on the other side.
5. Slowly tighten the jaws of the vise so that the smaller socket forces the U-joint spider and the opposite bearing cup out of the driveshaft and into the larger socket.
6. Remove the U-joint from the vise and remove the socket from over the bearing cup. The bearing cup should be forced out of the driveshaft enough to grip and remove with pliers.
7. Drive the spider in the opposite direction in the same manner as in Step 4 in order to make the opposite bearing cup accessible, and pull it free with pliers. Use this procedure to remove all bearing cups from both U-joints.
8. After removing the bearing cups, remove the spiders from the driveshaft and yokes.
9. Thoroughly clean all dirt and foreign material from the yoke areas of the driveshaft and yokes.
10. Start a new bearing cup into the yoke of the driveshaft. Install the new spider in the driveshaft yoke and bearing. Position the yoke in the vise. Slowly close the vise, pressing the bearing cup into the yoke. Use the smaller socket to press the cup in far enough so that the retaining snapring can be installed.
11. Open the vise and start a new bearing cup in the opposite hole. Press the bearing cup into the yoke in the same manner as in Step 9. Make sure the spider assembly is in line with the bearing cup as it is pressed in.

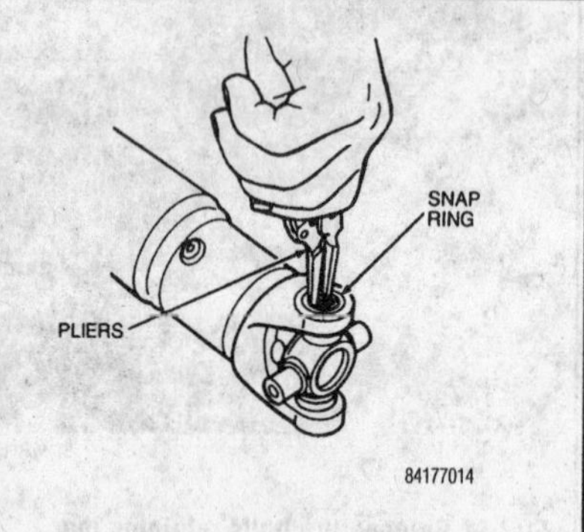


**Fig. 47 Installing a new snapring**

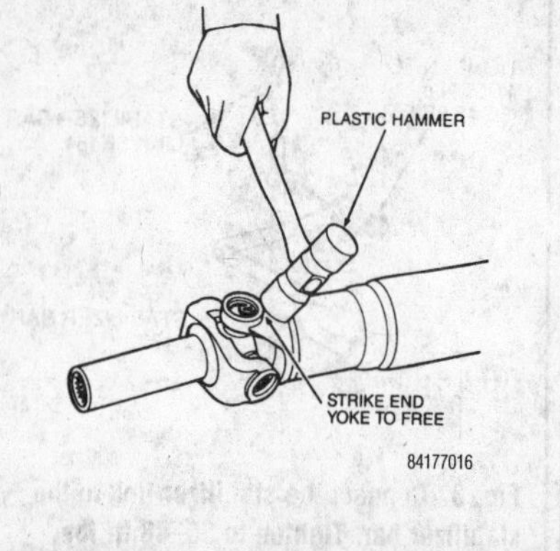


**Fig. 49 Seating the bearing needles**

**✲✲ WARNING**

**It is very easy to damage or misalign the needle rollers in the bearing cup if the spider assembly is not kept in line with the bearing cup during assembly. If the U-joint binds easily and/or the bearing cup cannot be pressed in far enough to install the snapring, one or more needle rollers has probably been knocked to the bottom of the cup. Remove the bearing cup, reposition the needle rollers and reinstall.**

12. Install all remaining U-joint cups in the same manner. When installing the slip yoke and rear yoke, make sure the marks align that were made during removal. Make sure all snap-rings are properly installed.
13. Check the U-joints for freedom of movement. If binding has resulted from misalignment during assembly, a sharp rap on the yoked with a brass or plastic hammer will seat the bearing cups. Take care to support the shaft end and do not strike the bearing cups during this procedure. Make sure the U-joints are free to rotate easily without binding before installing the driveshaft.
14. If supplied, install the grease fittings in the U-joints.
15. Install the driveshaft.
16. Grease the new U-joints if they are equipped with grease fittings.

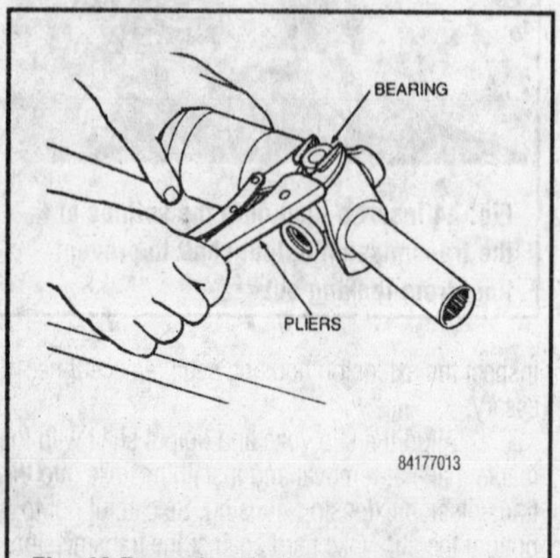


**Fig. 46 Removing the bearing cup**

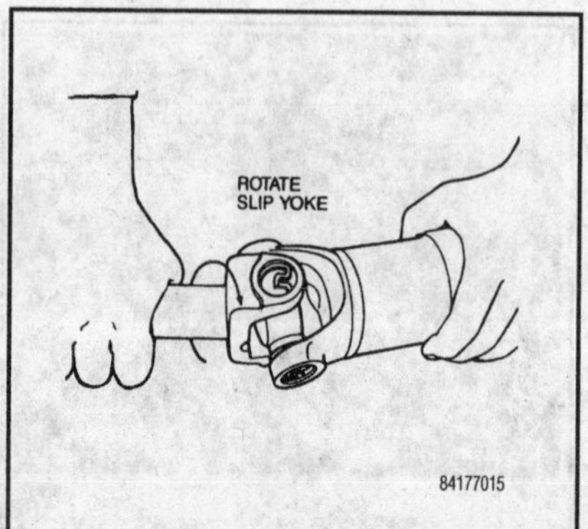


**Fig. 48 Checking U-joint for freedom of movement**

# Axle Shaft, Bearing and Seal

## REMOVAL & INSTALLATION

**➧ See Figures 50 thru 56**

1. Raise and safely support the vehicle. Remove the wheel and tire assembly and remove the brake drum or brake rotor.

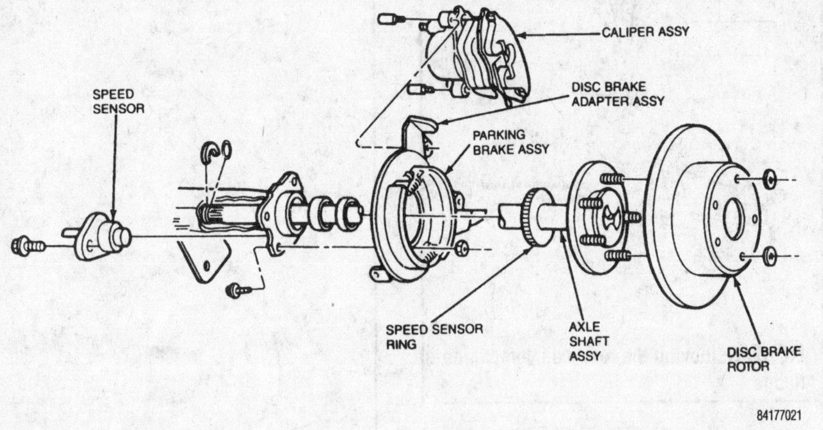


**Fig. 50 Axle shaft, bearing, seal and related components—1992–93 vehicles with anti-lock brakes**

2. If equipped, remove the anti-lock brake speed sensor.
3. Clean all dirt from the area of the carrier cover. Drain the axle lubricant by removing the housing cover.
4. Remove the differential pinion shaft lock bolt and differential pinion shaft.
5. Push the flanged end of axle shafts toward the center of the vehicle and remove the C-lock from the button end of the axle shaft. Remove the axle shaft from the housing, being careful not to damage the anti-lock brake sensor ring, if equipped.
6. Insert wheel bearing and seal replacer tool T85L–1225–AH or equivalent, in the bore and position it behind the bearing so the tangs on the tool engage the bearing outer race. Remove the bearing and seal as a unit using an impact slide hammer.

**To install:**

7. Lubricate the new bearing with rear axle lubricant. Install the bearing into the housing bore using a suitable bearing installer.
8. Install a new axle seal using a seal installer.

**➡Check for the presence of an axle shaft O-ring on the splined end of the shaft and install, if not present.**

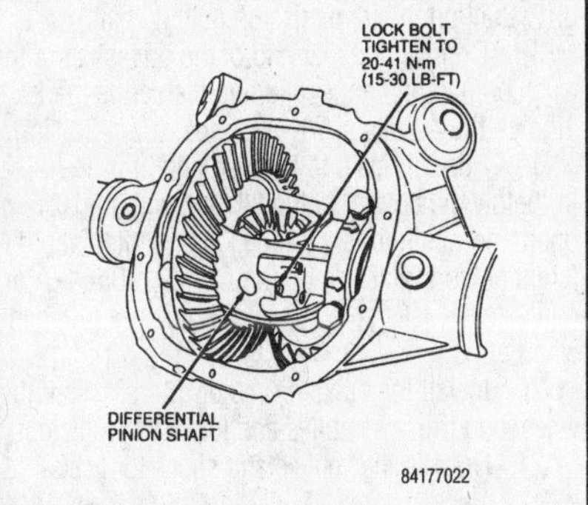


**Fig. 51 Differential pinion shaft and lock bolt**

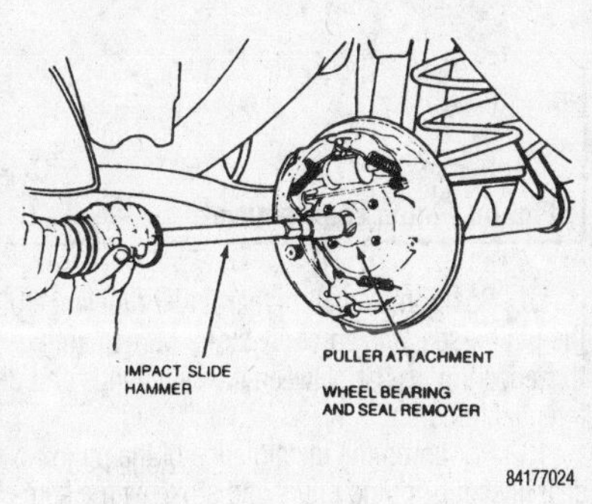


**Fig. 53 Wheel bearing and seal removal—1989–91 vehicles shown**

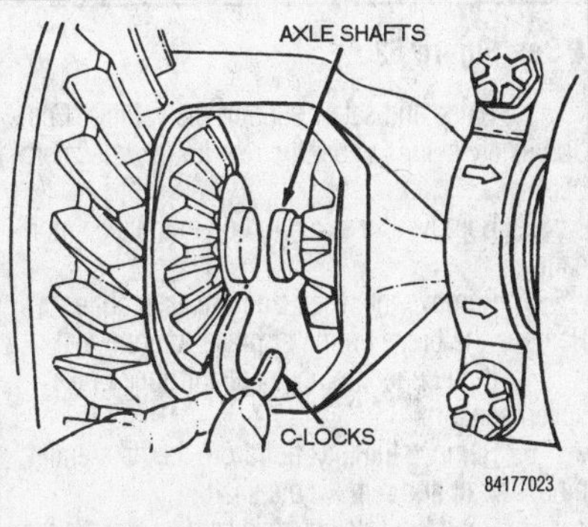


**Fig. 52 C-lock removal**

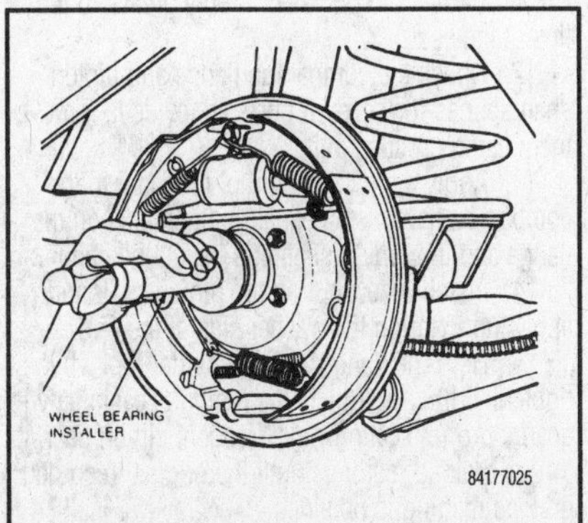


**Fig. 54 Wheel bearing installation—1989–91 vehicles shown**

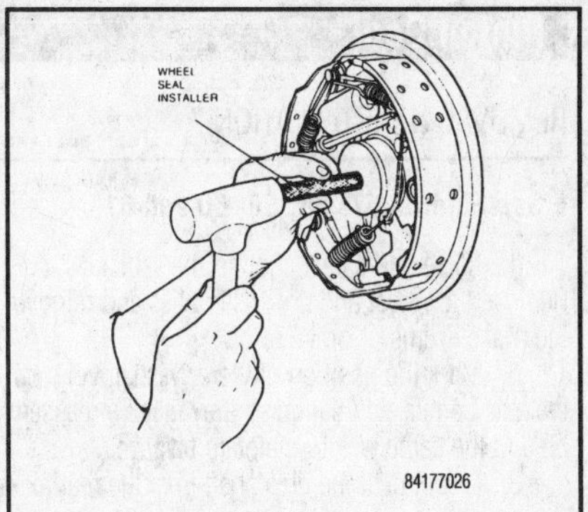


**Fig. 55 Axle seal installation—1989–91 vehicles shown**

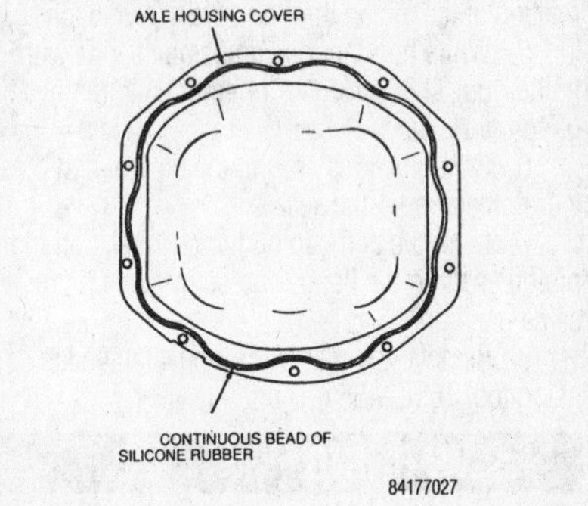


**Fig. 56 Apply sealer to the axle housing cover before installation**

9. Carefully slide the axle shaft into the axle housing, without damaging the bearing/seal assembly or anti-lock brake sensor ring, if equipped. Start the splines into the side gear and push firmly until the button end of the axle shaft can be seen in the differential case.
10. Install the C-lock on the button end of the axle shaft splines, then push the shaft outboard until the shaft splines engage and the C-lock seats in the counterbore of the differential side gear.
11. Insert the differential pinion shaft through the case and pinion gears, aligning the hole in the shaft with the lock bolt hole. Apply locking compound to the lock bolt and install in the case and pinion shaft. Tighten to 15–30 ft. lbs. (20–41 Nm).
12. Cover the inside of the differential case with a shop rag and clean the machined surface of the carrier and cover. Remove the shop rag.
13. Apply a 1/8–3/16 in. wide bead of silicone sealer to the cover and install on the carrier. Tighten the bolts in a crisscross pattern. Final torque the cover retaining bolts to 28–35 ft. lbs. (38–47 Nm).
14. Add rear axle lubricant to the carrier to a level 1/4–9/16 in. below the bottom of the fill hole. If equipped with limited slip differential, add friction modifier C8AZ–19B564–A or equivalent. Install the filler plug and tighten to 15–30 ft. lbs. (20–41 Nm).
15. Install the anti-lock brake speed sensor, if equipped. Tighten the retaining bolt to 40–60 inch lbs. (4.5–6.8 Nm).
16. Install the brake calipers and rotors or the brake drums, as required. Install the wheel and tire assembly and lower the vehicle.

## Pinion Seal

### REMOVAL & INSTALLATION

**➧ See Figures 57, 58, 59, 60 and 61**

1. Raise and safely support the vehicle. Remove the wheel and tire assemblies and remove the brake drums or brake rotors.
2. Mark the position of the driveshaft yoke on the axle companion flange so they may be reassembled in the same way to maintain balance.
3. Disconnect the driveshaft from the rear axle companion flange, remove the driveshaft and remove the driveshaft from the extension housing. Plug the extension housing to prevent leakage.
4. Install an inch pound torque wrench on the pinion nut and record the torque required to maintain rotation of the pinion through several revolutions.
5. While holding the companion flange with holder tool T78P–4851–A or equivalent, remove the pinion nut.
6. Clean the area around the oil seal and place a drain pan under the seal.
7. Mark the companion flange in relation to the pinion shaft so the flange can be installed in the same position.
8. Remove the rear axle companion flange using tool T65L–4851–B or equivalent.

**⁂ WARNING**

**Never strike the companion flange with a hammer.**

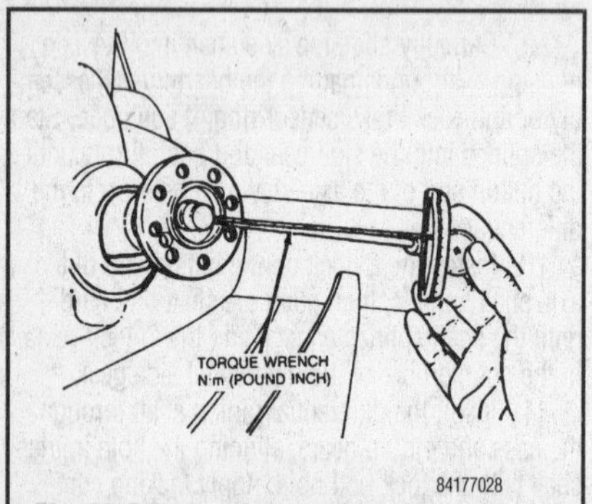


**Fig. 57 Prior to disassembly, record the torque required to maintain pinion rotation through several revolutions**

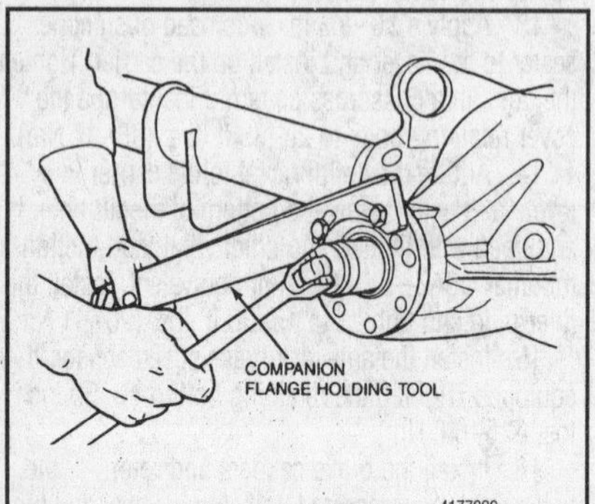


**Fig. 58 Removing the pinion nut**

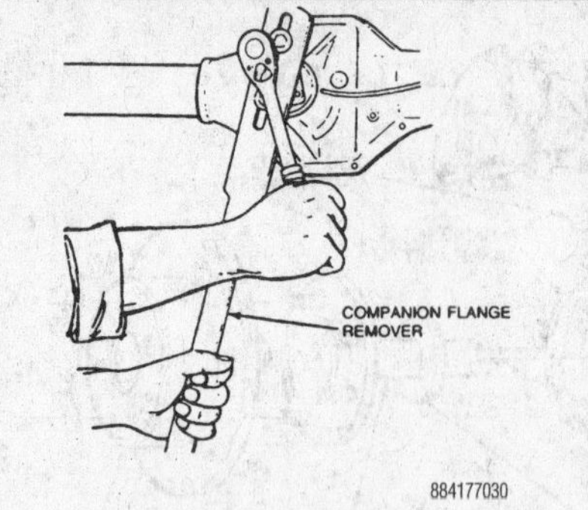


**Fig. 59 Removing the rear axle companion flange**

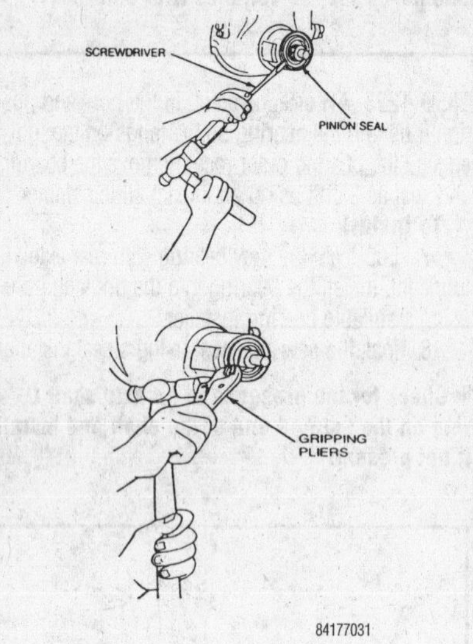


**Fig. 60 Pinion seal removal**

9. Position a small prybar under the flange of the pinion seal and carefully strike with a hammer to wedge the prybar between the seal flange and differential housing.
10. Pry up on the metal flange of the pinion seal. Install gripping pliers and strike with a hammer until the pinion seal is removed.

**To install:**

11. Clean the oil seal seat surface and install the seal in the carrier using seal replacer tool T79P–4676–A or equivalent. Apply grease to the lips of the seal.
12. Check the companion flange and pinion shaft splines for burrs. If burrs are evident, remove them using crocus cloth.
13. Apply a small amount of lubricant to the companion flange splines, align the marks on the flange and the pinion shaft and install the flange.
14. Install a new nut on the pinion shaft and apply lubricant on the washer side of the nut.
15. Hold the flange with the holder tool while tightening the nut. Rotate the pinion occasionally to ensure proper seating. Take frequent pinion bearing torque preload readings until the original recorded preload reading is obtained.
16. If the original recorded preload is less than 8–14 inch lbs. (0.9–1.6 Nm), then tighten the nut

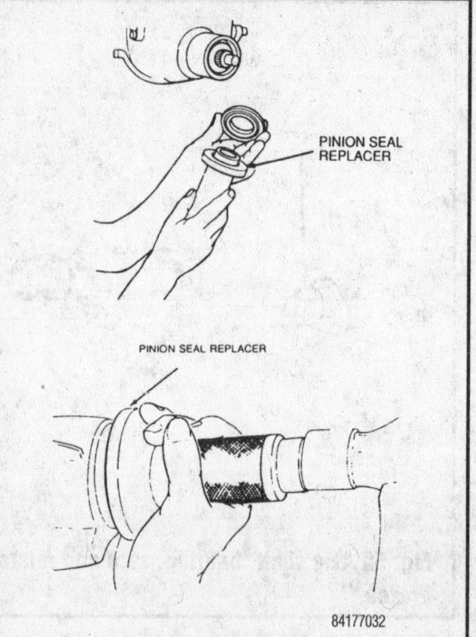


**Fig. 61 Pinion seal installation**

until the rotational torque of to 8–14 inch lbs. (0.9–1.6 Nm) is obtained. If the original preload is higher than 8–14 inch lbs. (0.9–1.6 Nm), tighten to the original recorded preload.

**➡Under no circumstances should the pinion nut be backed off to reduce preload. If reduced preload is required, a new collapsible pinion spacer and pinion nut must be installed.**

17. Remove the plug from the transmission extension housing and install the front end of the driveshaft on the transmission output shaft.
18. Connect the rear end of the driveshaft to the axle companion flange, aligning the scribe marks. Tighten the 4 bolts to 71–95 ft. lbs. (95–130 Nm).
19. Add lubricant to the axle until it is 1/4–5/16 in. below the bottom of the fill hole with the axle in operating position. If equipped with limited slip differential, add friction modifier C8AZ–19B564–A or equivalent. Make sure the axle vent is not plugged with debris.
20. Install the brake drums or rotors. Install the wheel and tire assemblies and lower the vehicle.
21. Operate the vehicle and check for leaks.

## Axle Housing

### REMOVAL & INSTALLATION

**➧ See Figure 62**

1. Raise and safely support the vehicle. Position safety stands under the rear frame crossmember.
2. Remove the cover and drain the axle lubricant.
3. Remove the wheel and tire assemblies. Remove the brake drums or brake rotors.
4. If equipped, remove the anti-lock brake speed sensors.
5. Remove the lock bolt from the differential pinion shaft and remove the shaft.
6. Push the axle shafts inward to remove the C-locks and remove the axle shafts.
7. If equipped with drum brakes, remove the 4

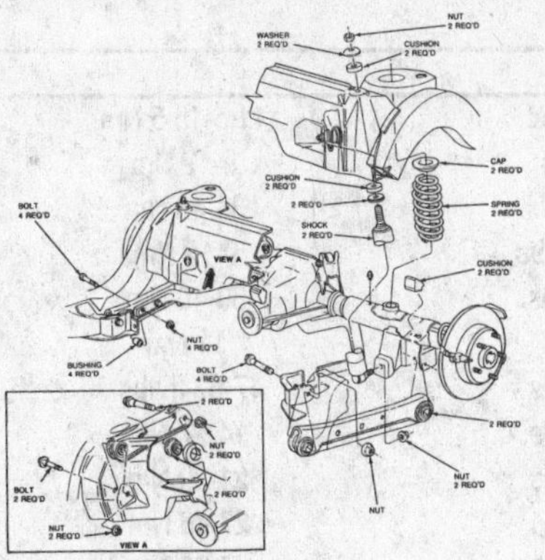


84177033

**Fig. 62 Rear axle housing assembly—typical**

retaining nuts from each backing plate and wire the backing plate to the underbody.

8. If equipped with disc brakes, remove the disc brake adapter bracket, bolts and J-nuts. Remove the 4 retaining nuts from each adapter and wire the adapters to the underbody.

9. Mark the position of the driveshaft yoke on the axle companion flange. Disconnect the driveshaft at the companion flange and wire it to the underbody.

10. Support the axle housing with jackstands. Disengage the brake line from the clips that retain the line to the axle housing.

11. Disconnect the vent from the rear axle housing.

12. If equipped with air springs, remove them according to the procedure in Section 8.

13. Disconnect the lower shock absorber studs from the mounting brackets on the axle housing.

14. Remove the nuts and bolts and disconnect the upper arms from the mountings on the axle housing ear brackets.

15. Lower the axle housing assembly until the springs are released and lift out the springs.

16. Remove the nuts and bolts and disconnect the suspension lower arms at the axle housing.

17. Lower the axle housing and remove it from the vehicle.

**To install:**

18. Position the axle housing under the vehicle and raise the axle with a hoist or jack. Connect the lower suspension arms to their mounting brackets on the axle housing. Do not tighten the bolts and nuts at this time.

19. Reposition the rear springs.

20. Raise the housing into position.

21. Connect the upper arms to the mounting ears on the housing. Tighten the nuts and bolts to 103–133 ft. lbs. (140–180 Nm). Tighten the lower arm bolts and nuts to 103–133 ft. lbs. (140–180 Nm).

22. Install the axle vent and install the brake line to the clips that retain the line to the axle housing. Secure the brake junction block to the housing cast boss.

23. Connect the air spring lines as described in Section 8.

24. If equipped with drum brakes, install the brake backing plates on the axle housing flanges. If equipped with disc brakes, install the disc brake adapters and tighten the nuts to 20–29 ft. lbs. (27–40 Nm). Install the disc brake adapter brackets, bolts and J-nuts. Tighten to 20–39 ft. lbs. (27–54 Nm).

25. Connect the lower shock absorber studs to the mounting bracket on the axle housing.

26. Connect the driveshaft to the companion flange and tighten the bolts and nuts to 70–95 ft. lbs. (95–130 Nm).

27. Slide the rear axle shafts into the housing until the splines enter the side gear. Push the axle shafts inward and install the C-lock at the end of each shaft splined. Pull the shafts outboard until the C-lock enters the recess in the side gears.

28. Install the pinion shaft. Apply locking compound to the pinion shaft lock bolt. Install and tighten to 15–30 ft. lbs. (20–41 Nm).

29. Install the rear brake drums or disc brake rotors and calipers.

30. Install the anti-lock brake speed sensor, if equipped.

31. Install the rear carrier cover using new silicone sealer. Tighten to 28–35 ft. lbs. (38–47 Nm).

32. Add rear axle lubricant to the carrier to a level ¼–⁹⁄₁₆ in. below the bottom of the fill hole. If equipped with limited slip, add friction modifier C8AZ–19B564–A or equivalent. Install the filler plug and tighten to 15–30 ft. lbs. (20–41 Nm).

33. Install the wheel and tire assemblies and lower the vehicle. Road test.

## AXODE (AX4S) TORQUE SPECIFICATIONS

| Components | English | Metric |
|---|---|---|
| Pump cover-to-pump body bolts | 7-9 ft. lbs. | 9-12 Nm |
| Filler tube-to-case retaining nut | 7-9 ft. lbs. | 9-12 Nm |
| Governor cover-to-case bolts | 7-9 ft. lbs. | 9-12 Nm |
| Park/Neutral position switch-to-case retaining bolts | 7-9 ft. lbs. | 9-12 Nm |
| Manual lever-to-manual shaft nut | 12-16 ft. lbs. | 16-22 Nm |
| Differential brace-to-case retaining bolts | 25-35 ft. lbs. | 55-68 Nm |
| Oil pan-to-case retaining bolts | 8-11 ft. lbs. | 13-15 Nm |
| Speedometer cover-to-case bolts | 7-9 ft. lbs. | 9-12 Nm |
| Transaxle-to-engine bolts | 55-68 ft. lbs. | 41-50 Nm |
| Stabilizer U-Clamp-to-bracket bolt | 23-29 ft. lbs. | 30-40 Nm |
| Brake hose routing clip bolt | 8 ft. lbs. | 11 Nm |
| Tie rod-to-knuckle bolt | 23-35 ft. lbs. | 31-47 Nm |
| Manual cable bracket bolt | 10-20 ft. lbs. | 14-27 Nm |
| Starter bolt | 30-40 ft. lbs. | 41-54 Nm |
| Dust cover bolt | 7-9 ft. lbs. | 9-12 Nm |
| Torque converter-to-flywheel bolt | 23-29 ft. lbs. | 31-53 Nm |
| Vehicle speed sensor bolt | 31-39 inch. lbs. | 3.4-4.5 Nm |
| Subframe bolts | 55-75 ft. lbs. | 75-102 Nm |
| Lower control arm pinch bolt | 40-53 ft. lbs. | 53-72 Nm |
| Power steering line bracket bolts | 40-50 inch lbs. | 4.5-5.7 Nm |
| Steering gear bolts | 85-100 ft. lbs. | 115-135 Nm |
| Engine mount bolts | 60-85 ft. lbs. | 81-116 Nm |
| LH engine support bolts | 40-55 ft. lbs. | 54-75 Nm |
| Lug nuts | 80-105 ft. lbs. | 108-144 Nm |
| Front hub retaining nut | 180-200 ft. lbs. | 245 – 270 Nm |
| Control arm-to-steering knuckle nut | 40-55 ft. lbs. | 54-75 Nm |
| Stabilizer link-to-stabilizer bar nuts | 35-48 ft. lbs. | 47-65 Nm |
| Ride height sensor bracket retaining bolts | 8-12 ft. lbs. | 11-16 Nm |

93147C01

## AX4N TORQUE SPECIFICATIONS

| Components | | |
|---|---|---|
| Manual lever-to-manual shaft | 9-11 ft. lbs. | 11.5-15.5 Nm |
| Fluid pan-to-case retaining bolts | 7-9 ft. lbs. | 9-12 Nm |
| Upper transaxle-to-engine bolts | 25-34 ft. lbs. | 34-46 Nm |
| Lower engine-to-transaxle bolts | 80-106 in. lbs. | 9-12 Nm |
| Stabilizer U-clamp-to-bracket bolts | 23-29 ft. lbs. | 30-40 Nm |
| Brake hose routing clip bolt | 8 ft. lbs. | 11 Nm |
| Tie rod-to-knuckle nuts | 35-46 ft. lbs. | 47-63 ft. lbs. |
| Manual cable bracket bolt | 10-20 ft. lbs. | 14-27 Nm |
| Starter bolt and stud | 15-21 ft. lbs. | 21-29 Nm |
| Torque converter-to-flywheel nuts | 20-34 ft. lbs. | 27-46 Nm |
| Shaft cable stud | 20-26 ft. lbs. | 27-35 Nm |
| Over-drive servo retaining bolts | 7-9 ft. lbs. | 9-12 Nm |
| Turbine Shaft speed sensor (TSS) retaining bolt | 7-10 ft. lbs. | 10-14 Nm |
| Fluid Filler tube retaining bolt | 7-9 ft. lbs. | 9-12 Nm |
| Rear Engine support-to-transaxle bolts | 44-60 ft. lbs. | 60-80 Nm |
| Ground strap nut | 13-17 ft. lbs. | 17-23Nm |
| Control arm-to-steering knuckle nuts | 50-68 ft. lbs. | 68-92 Nm |
| Stabilizer bar link nuts | 35-46 ft. lbs. | 47-63 Nm |
| Transaxle shift cable retaining nut | 14-19 ft. lbs. | 19-26 Nm |
| Subframe bolts | 55-75 ft. lbs. | 75-102 Nm |
| Lower control arm pinch bolt | 40-53 ft. lbs. | 53-72 Nm |
| Lug nuts | 80-105 ft. lbs. | 108-144 Nm |
| Steering gear bolts | 85-100 ft. lbs. | 115-135 Nm |
| Engine mount bolts | 60-85 ft. lbs. | 81-116 Nm |
| Rear engine support bolts | 44-60 ft. lbs. | 60-80 Nm |
| Engine mount-to-support retaining bolts | 55-75 ft. lbs. | 75-102 Nm |
| Y-Pipe assembly nuts and bolts | 25-34 ft. lbs. | 34-46 Nm |

93147C01

## AODE TORQUE SPECIFICATIONS

| Components | English | Metric |
|---|---|---|
| Converter end play | | |
| New or rebuilt | 0.023 inches | 0.58 mm |
| Used | 0.050 inches | 1.27 mm |
| Manual lever position sensor retaining bolts | 62-88 in. lbs. | 7-10 Nm |
| Extension housing bolts | 18-22 ft. lbs. | 25-30 Nm |
| Oil pan retaining bolts | 107-132 in. lbs. | 12-15 Nm |
| Crossmember-to-side support bolts | 70-100 ft. lbs. | 95-136 Nm |
| Crossmember-to-transmission mount nuts | 64-81 ft. lbs. | 87-110 Nm |
| Converter-to-flywheel nuts | 20-34 ft. lbs. | 27-46 Nm |
| Converter housing access cover retaining bolts | 12 -16 ft. lbs. | 16-22 Nm |
| Converter drain plug | 21-23 ft. lbs. | 28-30 Nm |
| Converter housing-to-engine bolts | 40-50 ft. lbs. | 55-68 Nm |
| Pressure tap plugs | 6-12 ft. lbs. | 8-16 Nm |
| Transmission speed sensor retaining bolt | 5-7 ft. lbs. | 7-10 Nm |
| Manual shift lever-to-case retaining nut | 20-27 ft. lbs. | 26-37 Nm |

93147C02

# 8

# SUSPENSION AND STEERING


**WHEELS 8-2**
WHEELS 8-2
REMOVAL & INSTALLATION 8-2
INSPECTION 8-2
WHEEL LUG STUDS 8-2
REMOVAL & INSTALLATION 8-2
**FRONT SUSPENSION 8-4**
COIL SPRINGS 8-4
REMOVAL & INSTALLATION 8-4
SHOCK ABSORBERS 8-5
REMOVAL & INSTALLATION 8-5
TESTING 8-5
MACPHERSON STRUTS 8-5
REMOVAL & INSTALLATION 8-5
UPPER BALL JOINT 8-8
INSPECTION 8-8
REMOVAL & INSTALLATION 8-8
LOWER BALL JOINT 8-9
INSPECTION 8-9
REMOVAL & INSTALLATION 8-9
STABILIZER BAR 8-9
REMOVAL & INSTALLATION 8-9
UPPER CONTROL ARM 8-9
REMOVAL & INSTALLATION 8-9
CONTROL ARM BUSHING REPLACEMENT 8-10
LOWER CONTROL ARM 8-10
REMOVAL & INSTALLATION 8-10
CONTROL ARM BUSHING REPLACEMENT 8-11
SPINDLE 8-11
REMOVAL & INSTALLATION 8-11
FRONT WHEEL BEARINGS 8-11
REPLACEMENT 8-11
WHEEL ALIGNMENT 8-12
CASTER 8-12
CAMBER 8-12
TOE 8-12
**REAR SUSPENSION 8-12**
COIL SPRINGS 8-12
REMOVAL & INSTALLATION 8-12
AIR SPRINGS 8-14
REMOVAL & INSTALLATION 8-14
SHOCK ABSORBERS 8-17
REMOVAL & INSTALLATION 8-17
TESTING 8-18
CONTROL ARMS 8-18
REMOVAL & INSTALLATION 8-18
STABILIZER BAR 8-18
REMOVAL & INSTALLATION 8-18
**STEERING 8-18**
STEERING WHEEL 8-18
REMOVAL & INSTALLATION 8-18
MULTI-FUNCTION/COMBINATION SWITCH 8-19
REMOVAL & INSTALLATION 8-19
WINDSHIELD WIPER SWITCH 8-20
REMOVAL & INSTALLATION 8-20
IGNITION SWITCH 8-20
REMOVAL & INSTALLATION 8-20
IGNITION LOCK CYLINDER 8-21
REMOVAL & INSTALLATION 8-21
STEERING LINKAGE 8-22
REMOVAL & INSTALLATION 8-22
POWER STEERING GEAR 8-24
REMOVAL & INSTALLATION 8-24
POWER STEERING PUMP 8-25
REMOVAL & INSTALLATION 8-25
BLEEDING 8-25
POWER RACK AND PINION STEERING GEAR 8-26
REMOVAL & INSTALLATION 8-26
**SPECIFICATIONS CHART**
TORQUE SPECIFICATIONS 8-28

WHEELS 8-2
FRONT SUSPENSION 8-4
REAR SUSPENSION 8-12
STEERING 8-18

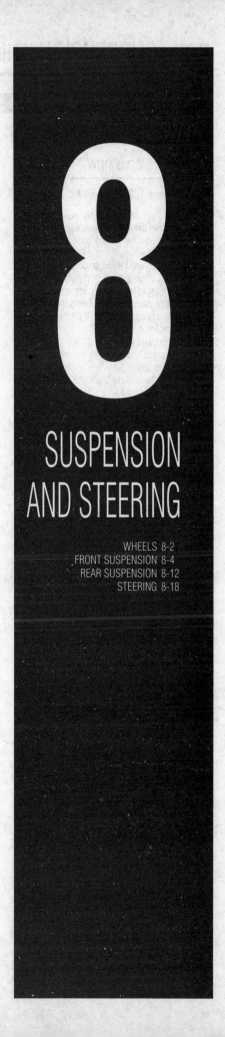

# WHEELS

## Wheels

### REMOVAL & INSTALLATION

➧ **See Figures 1, 2, 3, 4 and 5**

1. Park the vehicle on a level surface.
2. Remove the jack, tire iron and, if necessary, the spare tire from the storage compartment.
3. Check the owner's manual or refer to Section 1 of this manual for the jacking points on your vehicle. Then, place the jack in the proper position.
4. If equipped with lug nut trim caps, remove them by either unscrewing or pulling them off the lug nuts, as appropriate. Consult the owner's manual, if necessary.
5. If equipped with a wheel cover or hubcap, insert the tapered end of the tire iron in the groove and pry off the cover.
6. Apply the parking brake and block the diagonally opposite wheel with a wheel chock or two.

**➡Wheel chocks may be purchased at your local auto parts store, or a block of wood cut into wedges may be used. If possible, keep one or two of the chocks in your tire storage compartment, in case any of the tires has to be removed on the side of the road.**

7. If equipped with an automatic transmission/transaxle, place the selector lever in **P** or Park; with a manual transmission/transaxle, place the shifter in Reverse.
8. With the tires still on the ground, use the tire iron/wrench to break the lug nuts loose.

**➡If a nut is stuck, never use heat to loosen it or damage to the wheel and bearings may occur. If the nuts are seized, one or two heavy hammer blows directly on the end of the bolt usually loosens the rust. Be careful, as continued pounding will likely damage the brake drum or rotor.**

9. Using the jack, raise the vehicle until the tire is clear of the ground. Support the vehicle safely using jackstands.
10. Remove the lug nuts, then remove the tire and wheel assembly.

93149P18

**Fig. 1 Most styled wheels from Lincoln have a special lug nut that requires a special key. Be careful not to lose the key when changing the lugs**

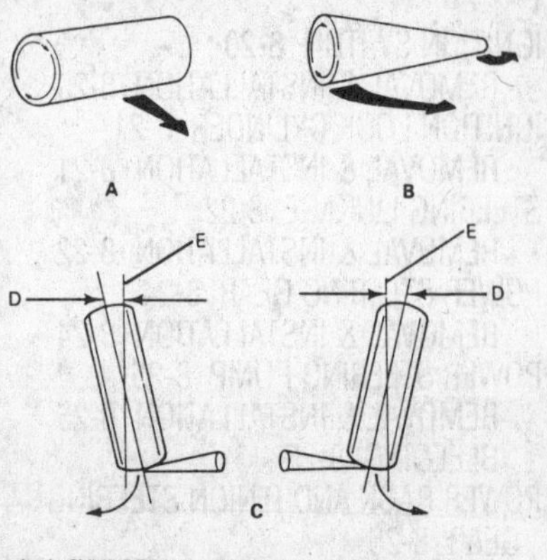


A A CYLINDER WILL ROLL STRAIGHT AHEAD
B A CONE WILL ROLL IN A CIRCLE TOWARD THE SMALL END
C TIRE CONTACTS THE ROAD SURFACE
D POSITIVE CAMBER ANGLE
E VERTICAL

TCCA8P02

**Fig. 2 With the vehicle still on the ground, break the lug nuts loose using the wrench end of the tire iron**

**To install:**

11. Make sure the wheel and hub mating surfaces, as well as the wheel lug studs, are clean and free of all foreign material. Always remove rust from the wheel mounting surface and the brake rotor or drum. Failure to do so may cause the lug nuts to loosen in service.
12. Install the tire and wheel assembly and hand-tighten the lug nuts.
13. Using the tire wrench, tighten all the lug nuts, in a crisscross pattern, until they are snug.
14. Raise the vehicle and withdraw the jackstand, then lower the vehicle.
15. Using a torque wrench, tighten the lug nuts in a crisscross pattern to 85–105 ft. lbs. ( 115–142 Nm). Check your owner's manual or refer to Section 1 of this manual for the proper tightening sequence.

**⁂ WARNING**

**Do not overtighten the lug nuts, as this may cause the wheel studs to stretch or the brake disc (rotor) to warp.**

16. If so equipped, install the wheel cover or hubcap. Make sure the valve stem protrudes through the proper opening before tapping the wheel cover into position.
17. If equipped, install the lug nut trim caps by pushing them or screwing them on, as applicable.
18. Remove the jack from under the vehicle, and place the jack and tire iron/wrench in their storage compartments. Remove the wheel chock(s).
19. If you have removed a flat or damaged tire, place it in the storage compartment of the vehicle and take it to your local repair station to have it fixed or replaced as soon as possible.

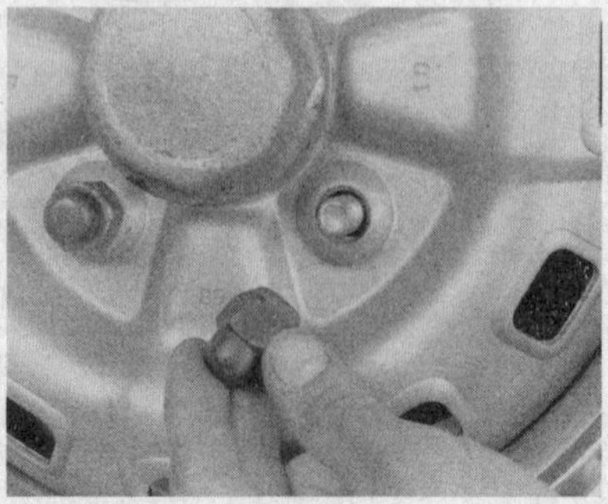

TCCA8P04

**Fig. 3 Remove the lug nuts from the studs**

TCCA8P05

**Fig. 4 Remove the wheel and tire assembly from the vehicle**

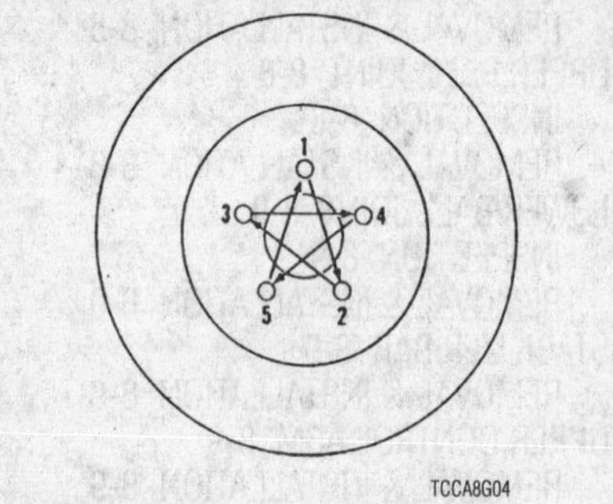


TCCA8G04

**Fig. 5 Typical wheel lug tightening sequence**

### INSPECTION

Inspect the tires for lacerations, puncture marks, nails and other sharp objects. Repair or replace as necessary. Also, check the tires for treadwear and air pressure as outlined in Check the wheel assemblies for dents, cracks, rust, and metal fatigue. Repair or replace as necessary.

## Wheel Lug Studs

### REMOVAL & INSTALLATION

**With Disc Brakes**

➧ **See Figures 6, 7 and 8**

1. Raise and support the appropriate end of the vehicle safely using jackstands, then remove the wheel.

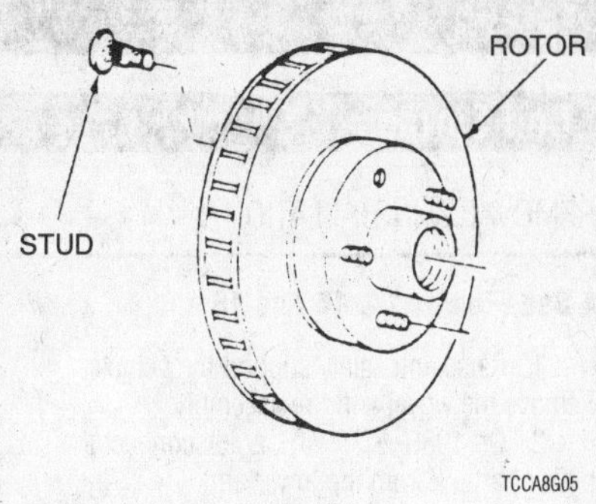


Fig. 6 View of the rotor and stud assembly

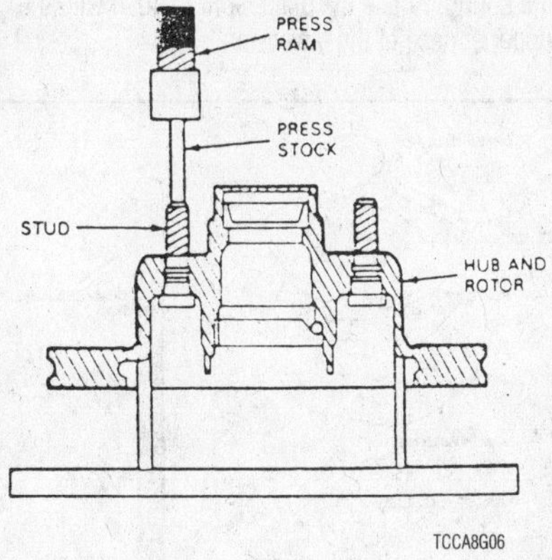


Fig. 7 Pressing the stud from the rotor

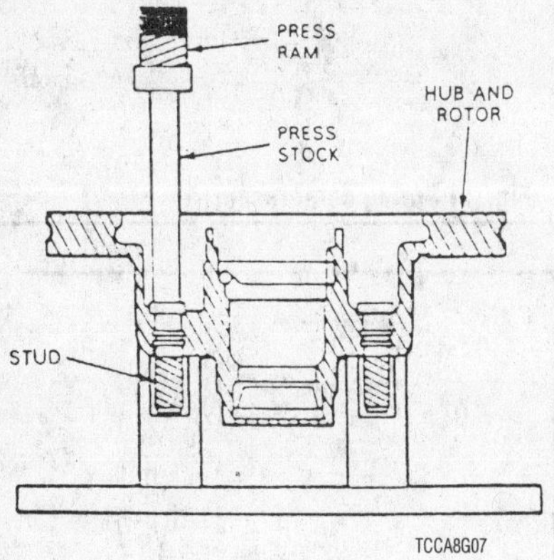


Fig. 8 Use a press to install the stud into the rotor

2. Remove the brake pads and caliper. Support the caliper aside using wire or a coat hanger. For details, please refer to Section 9 of this manual.
3. Remove the outer wheel bearing and lift off the rotor. For details on wheel bearing removal, installation, and adjustment, please refer to Section 1 of this manual.
4. Properly support the rotor using press bars, then drive the stud out using an arbor press.

**➡If a press is not available, CAREFULLY drive the old stud out using a blunt drift. MAKE SURE the rotor is properly supported or it may be damaged.**

**To install:**

5. Clean the stud hole with a wire brush and start the new stud with a hammer and drift pin. Do not use any lubricant or thread sealer.
6. Finish installing the stud with the press

**➡If a press is not available, start the lug stud through the bore in the hub, then position about four flat washers over the stud, and thread the lug nut. Hold the hub/rotor while tightening the lug nut, and the stud should be drawn into position. MAKE SURE THE STUD IS FULLY SEATED, then remove the lug nut and washers.**

7. Install the rotor and adjust the wheel bearings.
8. Install the brake caliper and pads.
9. Install the wheel, then remove the jackstands, and carefully lower the vehicle.
10. Tighten the lug nuts to the proper torque.

### With Drum Brakes

**➧ See Figures 9, 10 and 11**

1. Raise the vehicle and safely support it with jackstands, then remove the wheel.
2. Remove the brake drum.
3. If necessary to provide clearance, remove the brake shoes, as outlined in Section 9 of this manual.
4. Using a large C-clamp and socket, press the stud from the axle flange.
5. Coat the serrated part of the stud with liquid soap and place it into the hole.

**To install:**

6. Position about four flat washers over the stud and thread the lug nut. Hold the flange while tightening the lug nut, and the stud should be drawn into position. MAKE SURE THE STUD IS FULLY SEATED, then remove the lug nut and washers.
7. If applicable, install the brake shoes.
8. Install the brake drum.
9. Install the wheel, then remove the jackstands, and carefully lower the vehicle.
10. Tighten the lug nuts to the proper torque.

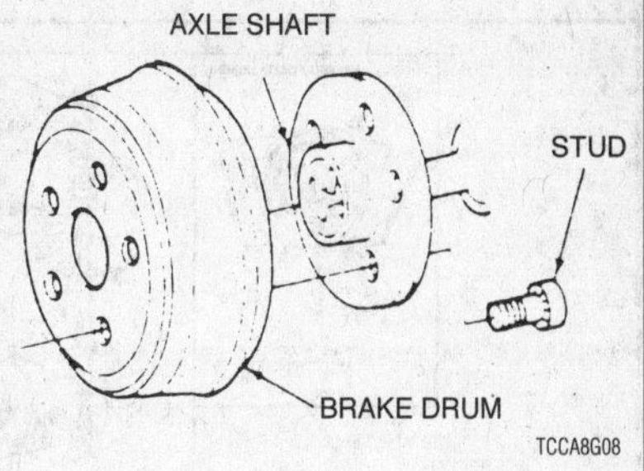


Fig. 9 Exploded view of the drum, axle flange and stud

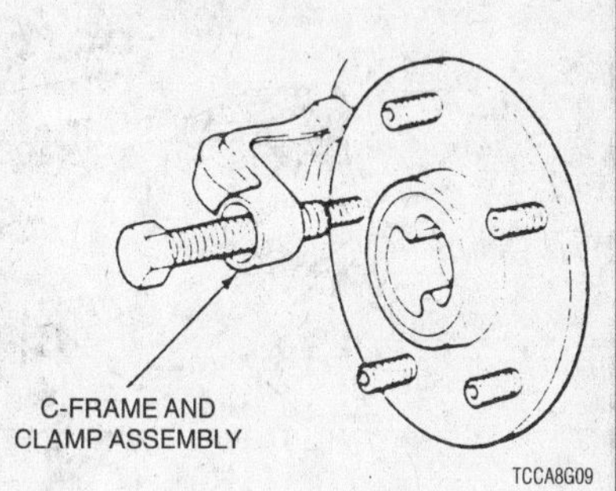


Fig. 10 Use a C-clamp and socket to press out the stud

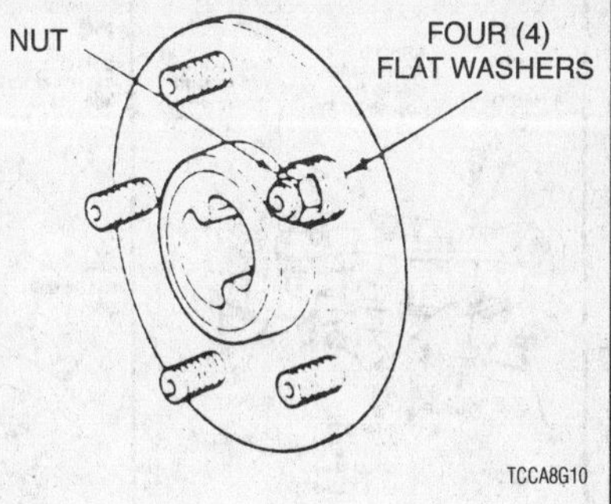


Fig. 11 Force the stud onto the axle flange using washers and a lug nut

## FRONT SUSPENSION

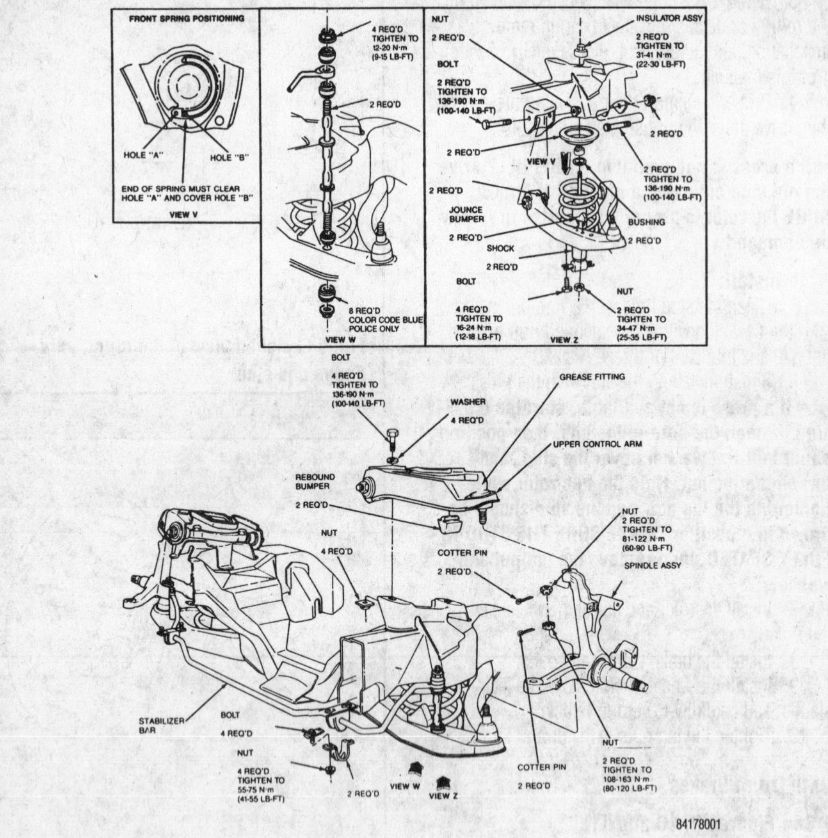


Fig. 12 Typical front suspension—1988-91

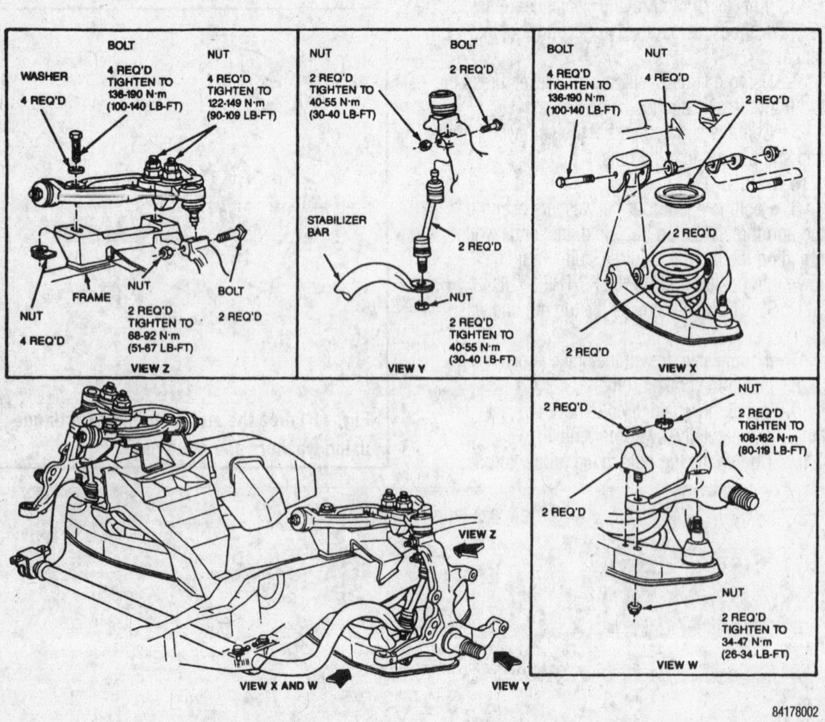


Fig.13 Typical front suspension—1992-00

## Coil Springs

### REMOVAL & INSTALLATION

**▶ See Figures 14, 15 and 16**

1. Raise and safely support the vehicle. Remove the wheel and tire assembly.
2. On 1988–91 Town Car, disconnect the stabilizer bar link from the lower arm.
3. Remove the shock absorber. Remove the steering link from the pitman arm.
4. Using spring compressor tool D78P–5310–A or equivalent, install one plate with the pivot ball seat facing downward into the coils of the spring. Rotate the plate, so it is flush with the upper surface of the lower arm.

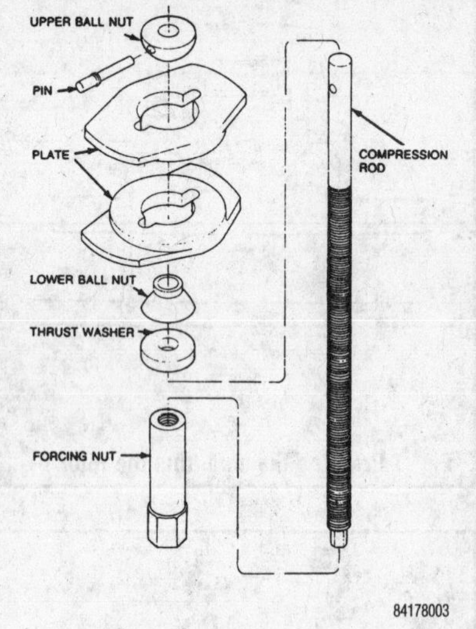


Fig. 14 Spring compressor

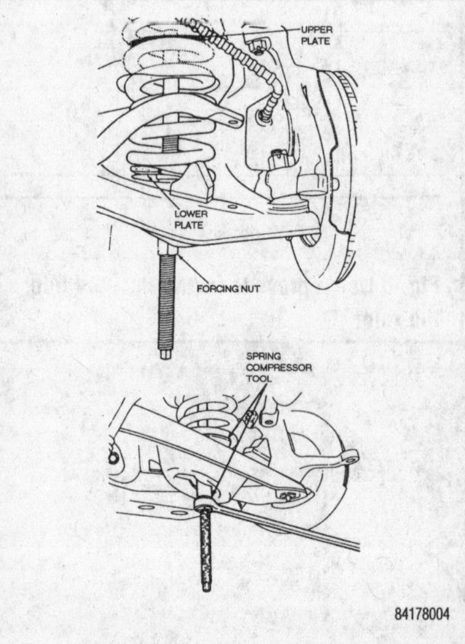


Fig. 15 Compressing the coil spring

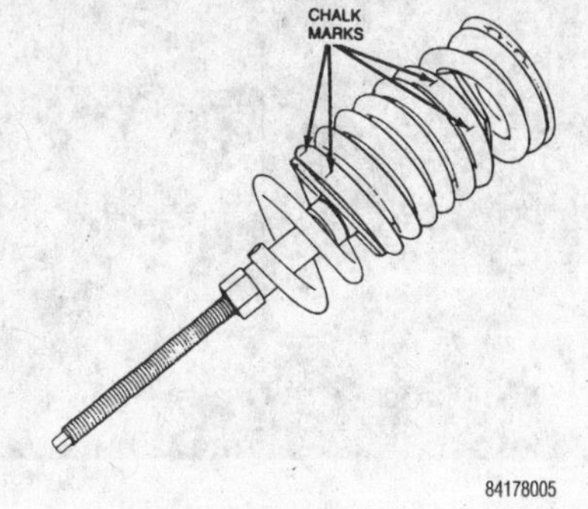


**Fig. 16 Positioning the coil spring in the compressor**

5. Install the other plate with the pivot ball seat facing upward into the coils of the spring. Insert the upper ball nut through the coils of the spring, so the nut rests in the upper plate.

6. Insert the compression rod into the opening in the lower arm, through the upper and lower plate and upper ball nut. Insert the securing pin through the upper ball nut and compression rod.

**➡This pin can only be inserted one way into the upper ball nut because of a stepped hole design.**

7. With the upper ball nut secured, turn the upper plate so it walks up the coil until it contacts the upper spring seat. Then back off ½ turn.

8. Install the lower ball nut and thrust washer on the compression rod and screw on the forcing nut. Tighten the forcing nut until the spring is compressed enough so it is free in its seat.

9. Remove the two lower arm pivot bolts, disengage the lower arm from the frame crossmember, and remove the spring.

10. If a new spring is to be installed, perform the following:

a. Mark the position of the upper and lower plates on the spring with chalk.

b. With an assistant, compress a new spring for installation and measure the compressed length and the amount of curvature of the old spring.

11. Loosen the forcing nut to relieve the spring tension and remove the tools from the spring.

**To install:**

12. Assemble the spring compressor and locate in the same position as indicated in Step 10a.

13. Before compressing the coil spring, make sure the upper ball nut securing the pin is inserted properly.

14. Compress the coil spring until the spring height reaches the dimension obtained in Step 10b.

15. Position the coil spring assembly into the lower arm and reverse the removal procedure.

## Shock Absorbers

### REMOVAL & INSTALLATION

**⁂ CAUTION**

**All vehicle applications are equipped with gas-pressurized shock absorbers that will extend unassisted. Do not apply heat or flame to the shock absorber tube.**

1. Remove the nut, washer and bushing from the upper end of the shock absorber.

2. Raise and safely support the vehicle by the frame rails allowing the front wheels to hang.

3. Remove the 2 bolts securing the shock absorber to the lower control arm and remove the shock absorber.

**To install:**

4. Before installation, purge a new shock of air by repeatedly extending it in its normal position and compressing it while inverted.

5. Install a new bushing and washer on the top of the shock absorber and position the unit inside the front spring. Install the two lower attaching bolts and torque them to 13–16 ft. lbs. (17–23 Nm).

6. Lower the vehicle.

7. Place a new bushing and washer on the shock absorber top stud and install a new attaching nut. Tighten to 26 ft. lbs. (41 Nm).

### TESTING

1. Remove the shock absorber from the vehicle.

2. Extend the shock absorber fully while it is right side up, as installed in the vehicle. Then turn it upside down and fully compress it. Repeat this procedure at least 3 times to make sure any trapped air has been expelled.

3. Place the shock absorber right side up in a vise and hand stroke the shock absorber. Check the shock absorber insulators for damage and wear.

4. If the shock absorber is properly primed, in its installed position, and there is a lag or a skip occurring near mid-stroke of the shaft reverse travel direction, the shock absorber must be replaced.

5. Replace the shock absorber if there is any seizing during the shaft full travel, except at either end of the travel.

6. Replace the shock absorber if upon the shaft fast, reverse stroke, there is any noise encountered other than a faint swish, such as a clicking sound.

7. If there are excessive fluid leaks, and the shock absorber action remains erratic after purging air, replace the shock absorber.

## MacPherson Struts

### REMOVAL & INSTALLATION

**➧ See Figures 17 thru 47**

1. Place the ignition switch in the **OFF** position and the steering column in the **UNLOCKED** position.

2. Remove the plastic cover from the shock tower to gain access to the upper mounting nuts and dual damping actuator.

3. Remove the two actuator screws and move the actuator aside.

4. Loosen the 3 top mount-to-airspring tower nuts; but do not remove all the nuts at this time.

5. Remove the hub nut.

6. Raise and safely support the vehicle.

**➡When raising the vehicle, do not lift by using the lower control arms.**

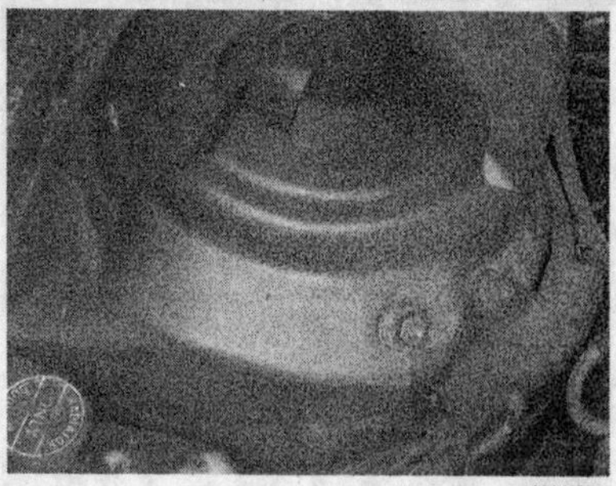


**Fig. 17 This shield covers the strut housing. You will use a 13mm wrench to remove the nut**

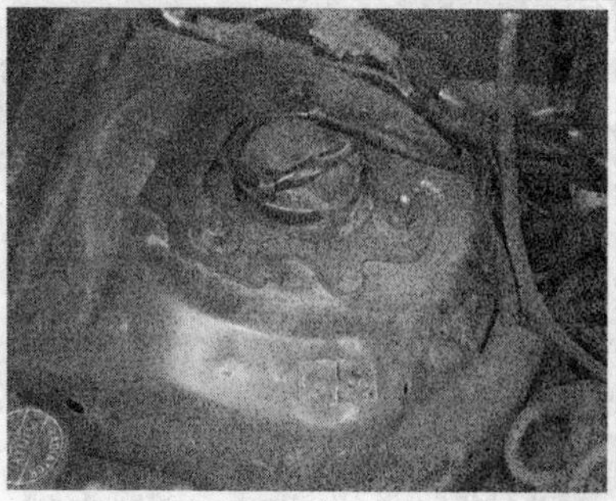


**Fig. 18 After removing the shield, you will see the suspension actuator**

**Fig. 19 You can unplug the actuator, although it is not necessary to replace the air spring**

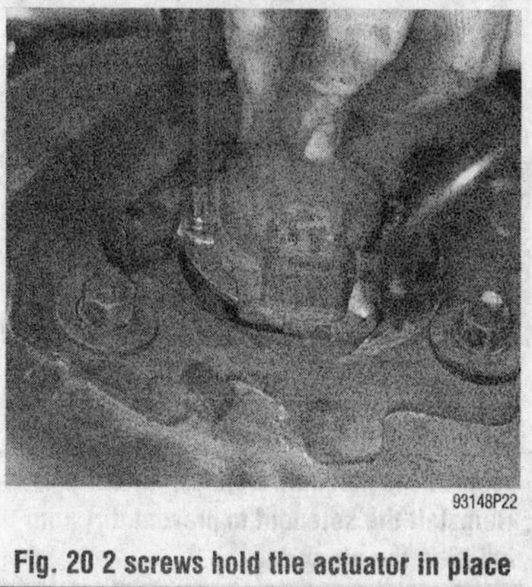


**Fig. 20 2 screws hold the actuator in place**

93148P21

**Fig. 21 The actuator just lifts off once the screws have been removed**

93148P20

**Fig. 22 Loosen but do not remove all the top mounted screws**

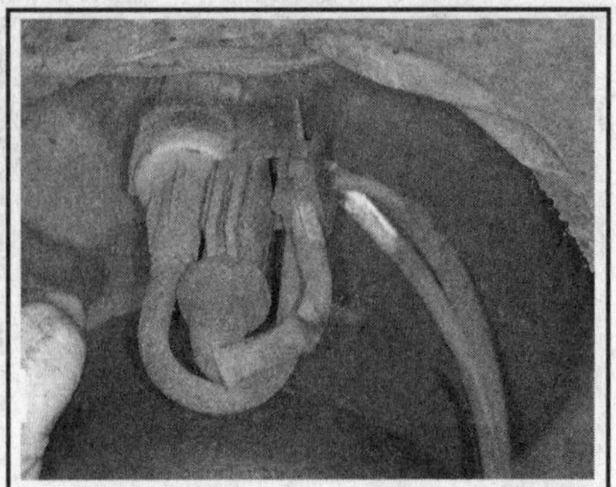

93148P30

**Fig. 23 The air spring solenoid must be removed to remove the air spring**

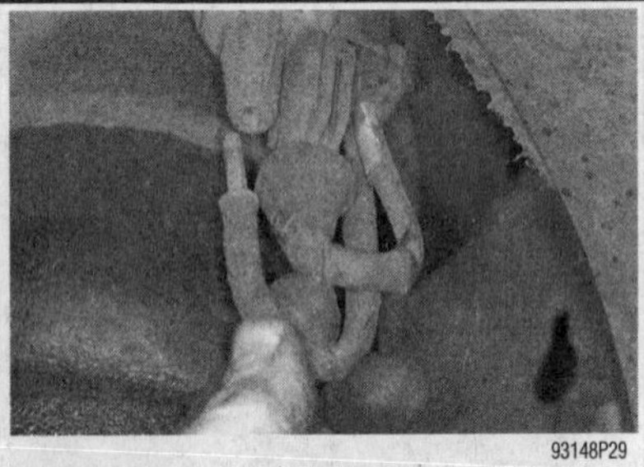

93148P29

**Fig. 24 Unplug the air line by pushing in on the air line and colored ring.The ring will seat against the base. Hold the ring against the base and pull the line out of the ring**

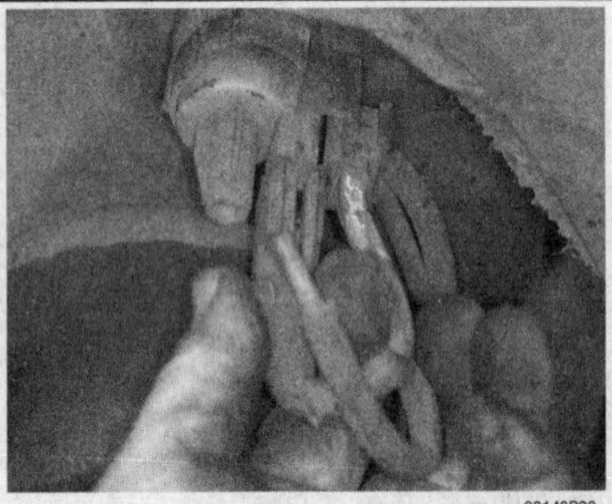

93148P28

**Fig. 25 Unplug the electrical connection to the solenoid**

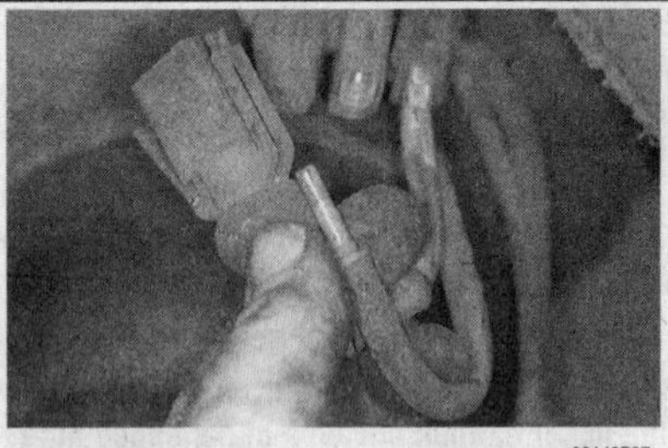

93148P27

**Fig. 26 There may be a slight hiss of air when the airline is first disconnected, but even with both connectors in your hand, there should be no air loss from the air spring**

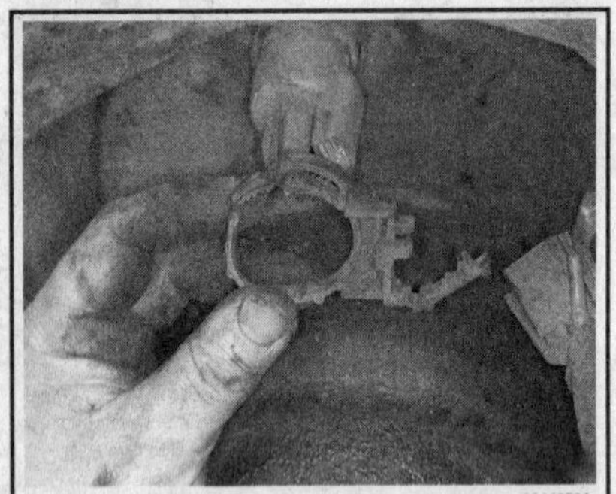

93148P26

**Fig. 27 Slid the connector retaining clip off the solenoid**

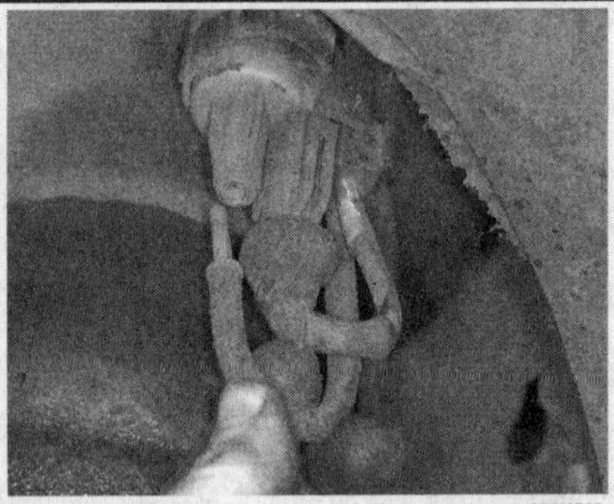

93148P25

**Fig. 28 The locking clip has to be removed to release the air pressure from the spring**

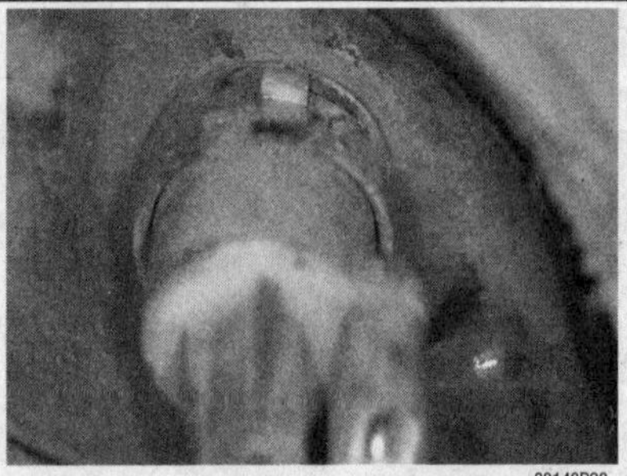

93148P23

**Fig. 29 Rotate the air spring solenoid by giving it a twist counterclockwise until it comes to the first stop. Allow the air pressure to release slowly at this position**

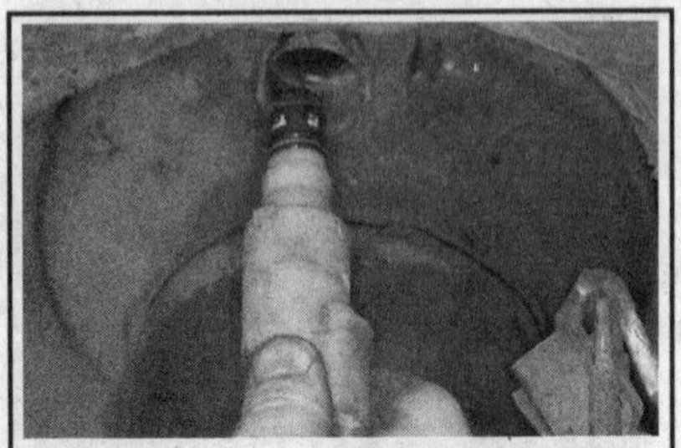

93148P24

**Fig. 30 Twist counterclockwise again to the second stop and pull straight down to remove the solenoid from the air spring. Reinstall the solenoid to prevent dirt from entering the air spring**

93148P34

**Fig. 31 You will have to disassemble the components shown here to remove the air spring assembly**

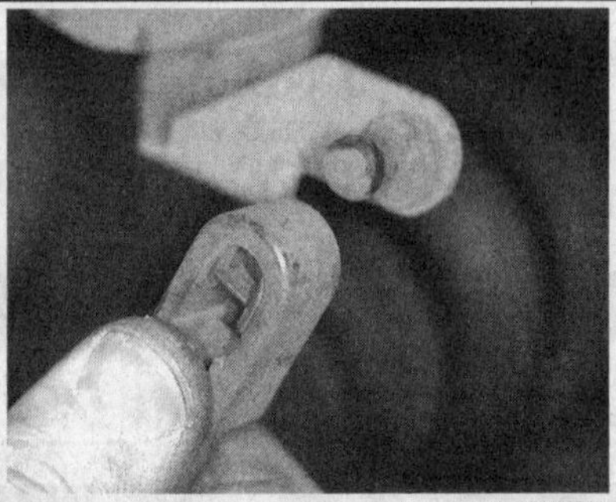

93149P15

**Fig. 32 Push on the clip to relieve the tension and pull the height adjusting sensor off the stud**

93149P17

**Fig. 33 It is safer to remove the brake sensor, but not always possible without destroying it. You can work around it, but do it carefully!!**

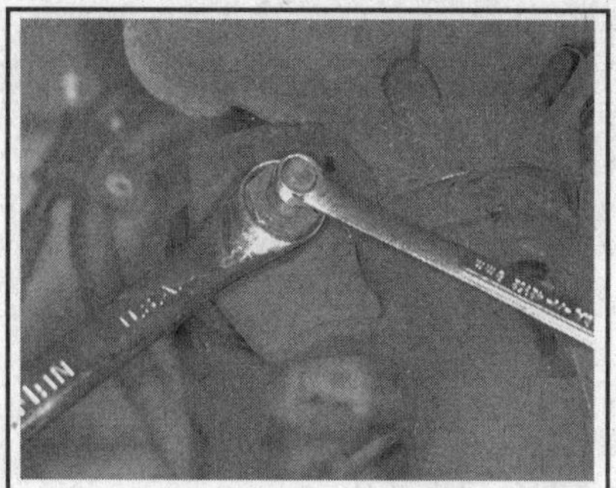
93148P33

**Fig. 34 To remove the stabilizer link from the air spring housing, use two wrenches**

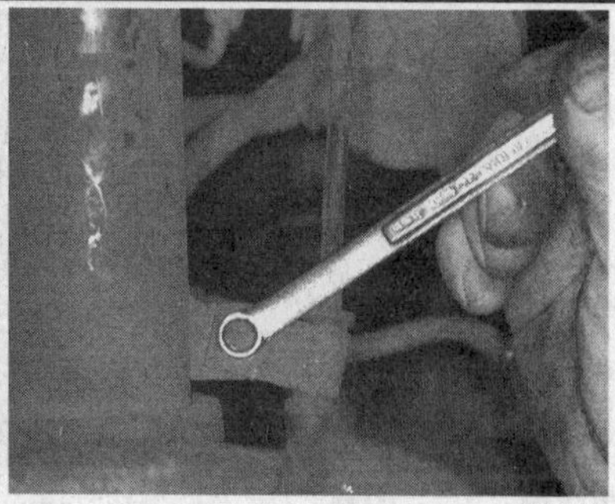
93148P32

**Fig. 35 Unbolt the anti-lock brake sensor line from the air spring housing**

93149P19

**Fig. 36 Match mark the rotor and a stud the way you see here**

93149P20

**Fig. 37 Using a Torx®driver, remove the caliper bolts**

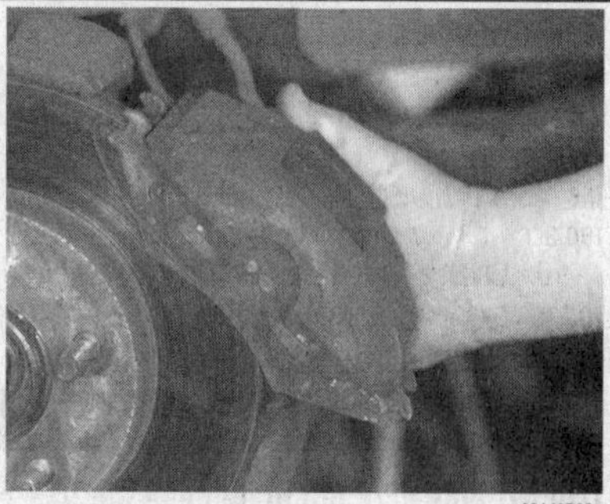
93149P06

**Fig. 38 Remove the caliper by sliding it off the spindle**

93149P07

**Fig. 39 Now slide the rotor off the studs, after making sure you have them match-marked**

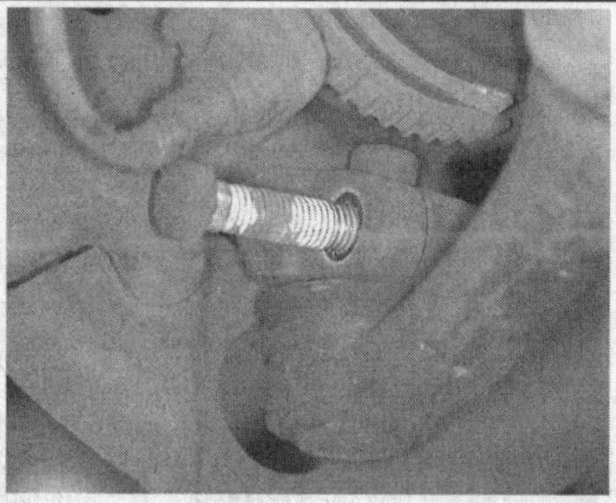
93149P11

**Fig. 40 Remove the pinch bolt from the lower arm assembly**

93148P31

**Fig. 41 Remove the airspring mounting bolt**

93148P38

**Fig. 42 Remove the tie rod from the spindle, using the special tool . . .**

93148P12

**Fig. 43 . . . or you can use the peen end of a ball-peen hammer to jar and separate the taper of the tie rod as it sits in the spindle**

93149P14

**Fig. 44 We broke this nut loose with the car on the ground. Now it's just a matter of unscrewing the nut and removing the washer**

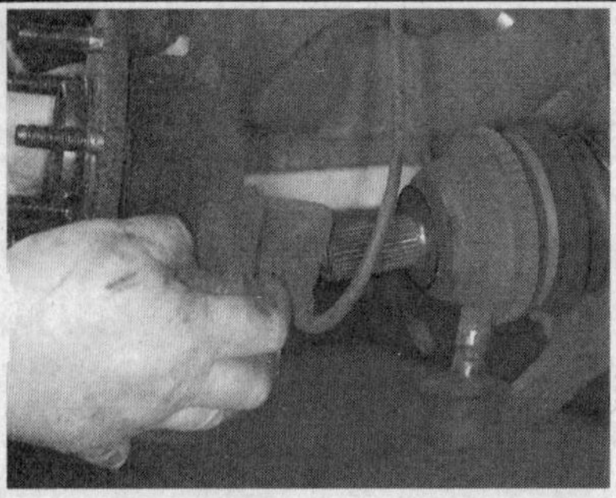
93149P13

Fig. 45 Slide the axle shaft out of the spindle/hub assembly. Be sure to support the axle. Don't let it hang!

93148P19

Fig. 46 The airspring removed from the car

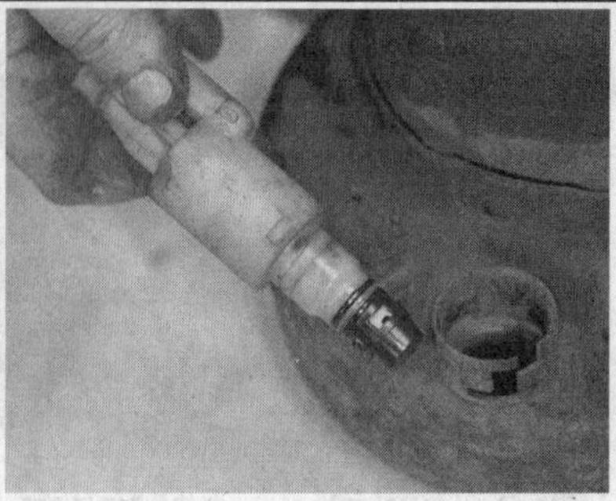
93148P18

Fig. 47 Check the solenoid and airspring to make sure you haven't lost the sealing O-rings

7. Remove the tire and wheel assembly.
8. Remove the brake caliper, then support it on a wire, out of the way. Remove the rotor.
9. At the tie rod end, remove the cotter pin and the castle nut. Discard the cotter pin and nut, and replace with new ones during installation.
10. Using a tie rod end remover tool and the tie rod remover adapter tool, separate the tie rod from the steering knuckle.

**WARNING**

**Use extreme care not to damage the link ball joint boot seal.**

11. Unfasten the stabilizer bar link nut, then remove the stabilizer bar link from the strut.
12. Remove the lower arm-to-steering knuckle pinch bolt and nut; it may be necessary to use a drift punch to remove the bolt. Using a suitable tool, spread the knuckle-to-lower arm pinch joint, then remove the lower arm from the steering knuckle. Discard the pinch nut/bolt and replace with a new one during installation.
13. Remove the halfshaft from the hub and support it with a wire to maintain a level position.

**➡When removing the halfshaft, do not allow it to move outward as the internal parts of the tripod CV-joint could separate, causing failure of the joint.**

14. Remove the strut-to-steering knuckle pinch bolt. Using a small prybar, spread the pinch bolt joint and separate the strut from the steering knuckle. Remove the steering knuckle/hub assembly from the strut.
15. Remove the 3 top mount-to-airspring tower nuts, then remove the air spring from the vehicle.

**To install:**

16. Install the air spring assembly and the three top mount-to-airspring tower nuts.
17. Install the steering knuckle and hub assembly to the strut.
18. Install a new strut-to-steering knuckle pinch bolt. Tighten the bolt to 73–97 ft. lbs. (98–132 Nm).
19. Install the halfshaft into the hub.
20. Install the lower arm to the steering knuckle, making sure the ball stud groove is properly positioned. Be very careful not to damage the ball joint seal. Fasten using a new pinch bolt and nut. Tighten to 40–53 ft. lbs. (54–72 Nm).

**➡The letters "Top LH" and "Top RH" are molded into the stabilizer bar link for correct assembly to the strut.**

21. Install the stabilizer link to the strut, making sure the link is positioned properly, then install a new stabilizer bar link nut. Tighten to 57–75 ft. lbs. (77–102 Nm).
22. Using a new castle/slotted nut, install the tie rod end onto the knuckle. Tighten the nut to 23–35 ft. lbs. (31–47 Nm).
23. Install the disc brake rotor, caliper, and tire/wheel assembly. Tighten the wheel lug nuts to 85–105 ft. lbs. (115–142 Nm).
24. Tighten the three top mount-to-air spring tower nuts to 23–29 ft. lbs. (31–40 Nm).
25. Lower the vehicle partially.
26. Turn on the air suspension switch and fill the air spring as follows:

- Place the air suspension service switch in the **ON**position.
- Turn the ignition switch **OFF**.
- Connect a battery charger to reduce the battery drain.
- Open the access door in the left-hand luggage compartment trim panel to plug the Super Star II tester or an equivalent scan tool, into the air suspension diagnostics wiring harness connector.
- Set the tester to EEC-IV/MCU mode. Also set the tester to FAST mode. Release the tester button to the HOLD (up) position and turn the tester **ON**.
- Depress the tester button to TEST (down) position. A Code 10 will be displayed. Within 2 minutes, a Code 13 will be displayed. After Code 13 is displayed, release the tester button to HOLD (up) position, wait 5 seconds, and depress the tester button to TEST (down) position. Ignore any codes displayed.
- Release the tester button to the HOLD (up) position. Wait at least 20 seconds, then depress the tester button to TEST (down) position. Within 10 seconds, the codes will be displayed in the order shown.
- Within 4 seconds after Code 24/25 is displayed, release the tester button to the HOLD (up) position. Waiting longer than 4 seconds may result in Functional Test 31 being entered. The compressor will fill the air springs with air as long as the tester button is in the HOLD (up) position. To stop filling the air springs, depress the tester button to the TEST (down) position.

**➡It is possible to overheat the compressor during this operation. If the compressor overheats, the self-resetting circuit breaker in the compressor will open and remain open for about 15 minutes. This allows the compressor to cool down.**

- To exit Functional Test 24/25, disconnect the tester and turn the ignition switch OFF.

27. Lower the vehicle.
28. Then tighten the hub nut to 170–203 ft. lbs. (230–275 Nm).
29. Depress the brake pedal a few times before moving the vehicle.

## Upper Ball Joint

### INSPECTION

➧ **See Figure 48**

1. Raise the vehicle and place floor jacks beneath the lower control arms.
2. Make sure the front wheel bearings are properly adjusted.
3. Inspect the lower ball joint and replace the lower control arm assembly, if required.
4. Have an assistant grasp the bottom of the tire and move the wheel in and out.
5. As the wheel is being moved, observe the upper control arm where the spindle attaches to it. Any movement between the upper part of the spindle and the upper control arm indicates a bad ball joint, which must be replaced.

### REMOVAL & INSTALLATION

#### 1988–91 Vehicles

**➡Ford Motor Company recommends replacement of the upper control arm and ball joint as an assembly. However, aftermarket replacement parts are available, which can be installed using the following procedure.**

1. Raise the vehicle and support it on the frame points so the front wheels fall to their full down position. Remove the wheel and tire assembly.
2. Drill a ⅛ in. hole completely through each ball joint attaching rivet.

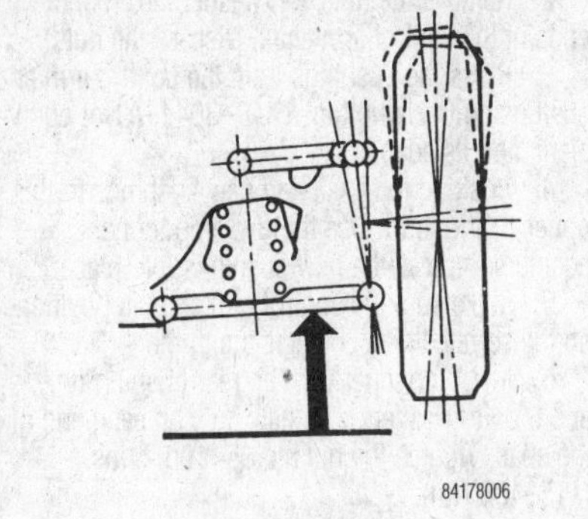


Fig. 48 Checking the upper ball joint

3. Using a large chisel, cut off the head of each rivet and drive them from the arm.

4. Place a jack under the lower arm and raise the arm to compress the coil spring.

5. Remove the cotter pin and attaching nut from the ball joint stud.

6. Using a ball joint removal tool, loosen the ball joint stud from the spindle and remove the ball joint from the arm.

**To install:**

7. Clean all metal burrs from the arm and install the new ball joint, using the service part nuts and bolts to attach the ball joint. Do not attempt to rivet the ball joint once it has been removed.

8. Install the ball joint stud into the spindle. Tighten the ball joint-to-upper spindle nut to 60–90 ft. lbs. (81–122 Nm). Continue to tighten until the slot for the cotter pin is aligned. Install a new cotter pin.

9. Install the wheel and tire assembly and lower the vehicle. Check front end alignment.

#### 1992–00 Vehicles

**➧ See Figure 49**

1. Raise and safely support the vehicle with safety stands under the frame behind the lower arm. Remove the wheel and tire assembly.

2. Position a floor jack under the lower arm at the lower ball joint area. The floor jack will support the spring load on the lower arm.

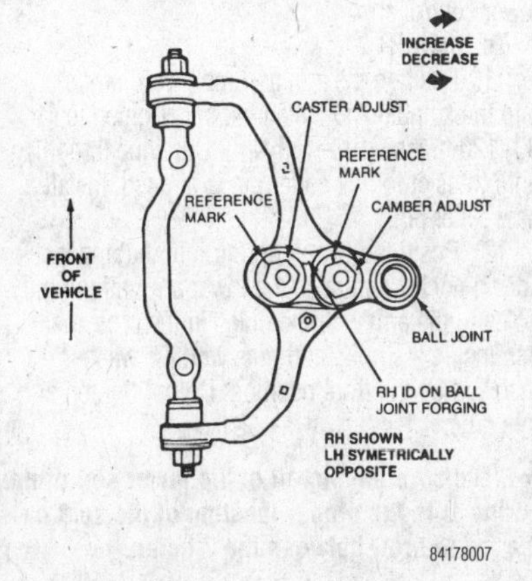


Fig. 49 Upper control arm assembly—1992–99 Town Cars

3. Remove the retaining nut and pinch bolt from the upper ball joint stud.

4. Mark the position of the alignment cams. When replacing the ball joint this will approximate the current alignment.

5. Remove the 2 nuts retaining the ball joint to the upper arm. Remove the ball joint and spread the slot with a suitable prybar to separate the ball joint stud from the spindle.

**To install:**

**➡The upper ball joints differ from side to side. Be sure to use the proper ball joint on each side.**

6. Position the ball joint on the upper arm and insert the ball stud into the spindle.

7. Install the pinch bolt and retaining nut. Tighten to 67 ft. lbs. (92 Nm).

8. Install the alignment cams to the approximate position at removal. If not marked, install in neutral position.

9. Install the 2 nuts attaching the ball joint to the arm. Hold the cams and tighten the nuts to 90–109 ft. lbs. (122–149 Nm) on 1992 vehicles or 107–129 ft. lbs. (145–175 Nm) on 1999–99 Town Cars.

10. Remove the floor jack from the lower arm and install the wheel and tire assembly. Remove the safety stands and lower the vehicle.

11. Check and adjust the front end alignment.

## Lower Ball Joint

### INSPECTION

**➧ See Figure 50**

1. Support the vehicle in normal driving position with ball joints loaded.

2. Wipe the grease fitting and ball joint cover checking surface clean. The checking surface is the round boss into which the grease fitting is threaded.

3. The checking surface should project outside the cover. If the checking surface is inside the cover, replace the lower control arm assembly.

### REMOVAL & INSTALLATION

The ball joint is an integral part of the lower control arm. If the ball joint is defective, the entire lower control arm must be replaced.

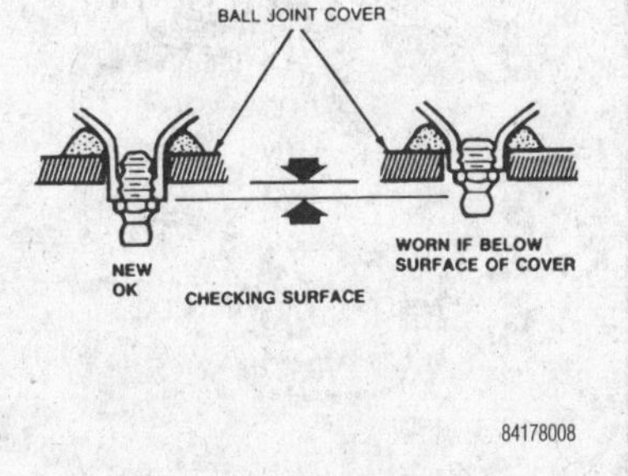


Fig. 50 Checking the lower ball joint

## Stabilizer Bar

### REMOVAL & INSTALLATION

1. Raise the front of the vehicle and place jackstands under the lower control arms.

2. On 1988–91 vehicles, remove the link nuts and disconnect the stabilizer bar from the links.

3. On 1992–00 vehicles, remove the retaining nuts from the pinch bolts at the spindles. Spread the slots in the spindles with a prybar to free the ball studs. Be careful not to damage the ball joint stud seal.

4. Remove the stabilizer bar brackets from the frame and remove the stabilizer bar. If worn, cut the insulators from the stabilizer bar.

5. On 1992–00 vehicles, remove the retaining nuts from the ball joint studs at the end of the bar. Use removal tool 3290–D or equivalent to separate the links from the ends of the stabilizer bar.

**To install:**

6. Coat the necessary parts of the stabilizer bar with rubber lubricant. Slide new insulators onto the stabilizer bar.

7. On 1992–00 vehicles, install the ball joint links into the ends of the bar with the retaining nuts. Tighten to 30–40 ft. lbs. (40–55 Nm).

8. On 1988–91 vehicles, attach the ends of the stabilizer bar to the lower control arm with new nuts and links. Tighten the nuts to 9–15 ft. lbs. (12–20 Nm). Install the insulator brackets and tighten the bolts to 14–26 ft. lbs. (19–35 Nm).

9. On 1992–00 vehicles, position the bar under the vehicle and engage the upper ball joint links to the spindles. Install the insulator brackets with the retaining nuts. Tighten the pinch bolts and nuts at the spindles to 30–40 ft. lbs. (40–55 Nm) Tighten the bracket-to-frame nuts to 44–59 ft. lbs. (59–81 Nm).

## Upper Control Arm

### REMOVAL & INSTALLATION

#### 1988–91 Town Car

1. Raise and safely support the vehicle on safety stands positioned on the frame just behind the lower arm. Remove the wheel and tire assembly.

2. Remove the cotter pin from the upper ball joint stud nut. Loosen the nut a few turns but do not remove.

3. Install ball joint press T57P–3006–B or equivalent, between the upper and lower ball joint studs with the adapter screw on top.

**➡This tool should be seated firmly against the ends of both studs, not against the nuts or lower stud cotter pin.**

4. With a wrench, turn the adapter screw until the tool places the stud under compression. Tap the spindle near the upper stud with a hammer to loosen the stud in the spindle.

**➡Do not loosen the stud from the spindle with tool pressure only. Do not contact the boot seal with the hammer.**

5. Remove the tool from between the ball joint studs and place a floor jack under the lower arm.

6. Remove the upper arm attaching bolts and the upper arm.

**To install:**

7. Transfer the rebound bumper from the old arm to the new arm, or replace the bumper if worn or damaged.

8. Position the upper arm shaft to the frame bracket. Install the 2 attaching bolts and washers. Tighten to 100–140 ft. lbs. (136–190 Nm).

9. Connect the upper ball joint stud to the spindle and install the attaching nut. Tighten the nut to 60–90 ft. lbs. (81–122 Nm). Continue to tighten the nut until the slot for the cotter pin is aligned. Install a new cotter pin.

10. Install the wheel and tire assembly and lower the vehicle. Check the front end alignment.

**1992–00 Town Cars**

1. Raise and safely support the vehicle on safety stands positioned on the frame just behind the lower arm.

2. Remove the wheel and tire assembly and position a floor jack under the lower arm.

3. Remove the retaining nut from the upper ball joint stud to spindle pinch bolt. Tap the pinch bolt to remove from the spindle.

4. Using a suitable prybar, spread the slot to allow the ball joint stud to release out of the spindle.

5. Remove the upper arm retaining bolts and the upper arm.

**To install:**

6. Transfer the rebound bumper from the old arm to the new arm, or replace the bumper if worn or damaged.

7. Use reference marks from the camber and caster cams as initial settings.

8. Position the upper arm shaft to the frame bracket. Install the 2 retaining bolts and washers. Position the arm in the center of the slot adjustment range and tighten to 100–140 ft. lbs.

9. Connect the upper ball joint stud to the spindle and install the retaining pinch bolt and nut. Tighten the nut to 67 ft. lbs. (92 Nm).

10. Install the wheel and tire assembly and lower the vehicle. Check the front end alignment.

## CONTROL ARM BUSHING REPLACEMENT

**See Figures 51, 52, 53, 54 and 55**

1. Remove the upper control arm from the vehicle.

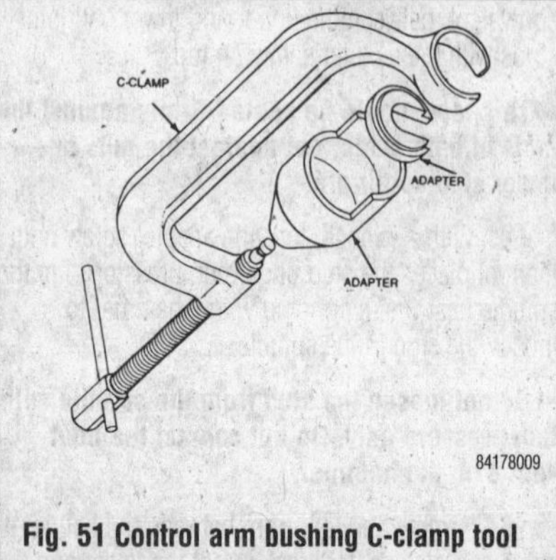


**Fig. 51 Control arm bushing C-clamp tool and adapters**

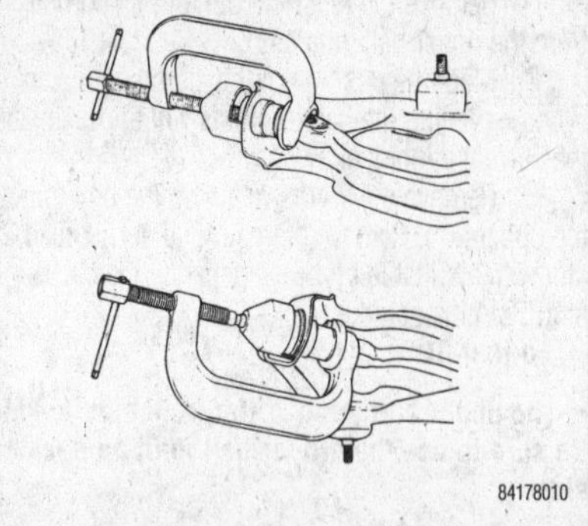


**Fig. 52 Control arm bushing removal—1988–91 vehicles**

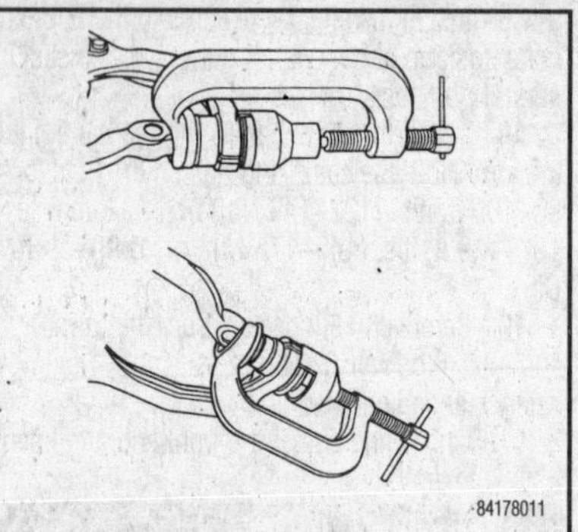


**Fig. 53 Control arm bushing removal—1992–99 vehicles**

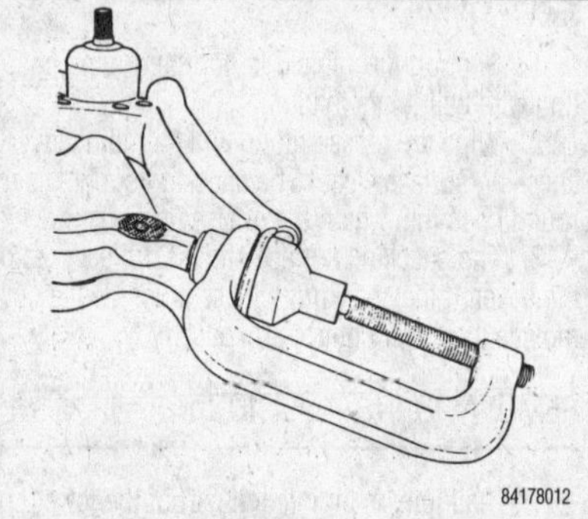


**Fig. 54 Control arm bushing installation—1988–91 vehicles**

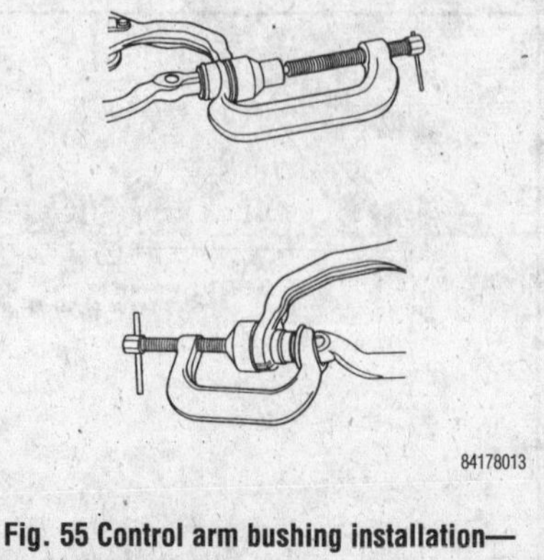


**Fig. 55 Control arm bushing installation—1992–99 vehicles**

2. Remove the nuts and washers from both ends of the control arm shaft. Discard the nuts.

3. Press the bushings from the control arm and shaft using C-clamp tool T74P–3044–A1 or equivalent, and its adapters.

4. Position the shaft and new bushings to the upper control arm. Use the C-clamp tool and adapters to press the new bushings into place.

5. Make sure the control arm shaft is positioned so the serrated side contacts the frame.

6. Install an inner washer, rear bushing only, and 2 outer washers with new nuts on each end of the shaft. Tighten the nuts to 85–100 ft. lbs. (115–136 Nm).

# Lower Control Arm

## REMOVAL & INSTALLATION

1. Raise the front of the vehicle and position safety stands on the frame behind the lower control arms. Remove the wheel and tire assembly.

2. Remove the brake caliper and suspend with a length of wire; do not let the caliper hang by the brake hose. Remove the brake rotor and dust shield. Remove the anti-lock brake sensor, if equipped.

3. Remove the jounce bumper; inspect and save for installation if in good condition. Remove the shock absorber.

4. On 1988–91 vehicles, disconnect the stabilizer link from the lower arm.

5. Disconnect the steering center link from the pitman arm.

6. Remove the cotter pin and loosen the lower ball joint stud nut 1–2 turns.

**➡Do not remove the nut at this time.**

7. On 1988–91 vehicles, install a suitable ball joint press tool to place the ball joint stud under compression. With the stud under compression, tap the spindle sharply with a hammer to loosen the stud in the spindle. Remove the ball joint press tool.

8. On 1992–99 vehicles, tap the spindle boss sharply to relieve the stud pressure. Tap the spindle sharply, near the lower stud, with a hammer to loosen the stud in the spindle.

9. Place a floor jack under the lower arm. Remove the coil spring as described in this Section.

10. Remove the ball joint nut and remove the lower control arm.

**To install:**

11. Position the arm assembly ball joint stud into the spindle and install the nut. Tighten to 80–120 ft. lbs. (108–163 Nm). Continue to tighten until the slot for the cotter pin is aligned. Install a new cotter pin.

12. Position the coil spring into the upper spring pocket and raise the lower arm, aligning the holes in the arm with the holes in the crossmember. Install the bolts and nuts with the washer installed on the front bushing. Do not tighten at this time.

**➡Make sure the pigtail of the lower coil of the spring is in the proper location of the seat on the lower arm, between the 2 holes.**

13. Remove the spring compressor tool.

14. Connect the steering center link at the pitman arm and install the nut. Tighten to 44–46 ft.

lbs. (59–63 Nm). Continue to tighten until the slot for the cotter pin is aligned. Install a new cotter pin.

15. Install the shock absorber and the jounce bumper.

16. Install the dust shield, rotor and caliper. Install the anti-lock brake sensor, if equipped.

17. On 1988–91 vehicles, position the stabilizer link to the lower control arm and install the link, bushing and retaining nut. Tighten to 9–15 ft. lbs. (12–20 Nm).

18. Install the wheel and tire assembly and lower the vehicle. With the vehicle supported on the wheels and tires at normal curb height, tighten the lower control arm-to-crossmember bolts to 109–140 ft. lbs. (148–190 Nm).

19. Check the front end alignment.

### CONTROL ARM BUSHING REPLACEMENT

The control arm bushings are integral with the lower control arm. If the bushings are defective, the entire lower control arm must be replaced.

## Spindle

### REMOVAL & INSTALLATION

1. Raise and safely support the front of the vehicle securely on jackstands.

2. Position safety stands on the frame behind the lower control arms. Remove the wheel and tire assembly.

3. Remove the brake caliper and suspend with a length of wire; do not let the caliper hang by the brake hose. Remove the brake rotor and dust shield. Remove the anti-lock brake sensor, if equipped.

4. Disconnect the tie rod end from the spindle using removal tool 3290–D or equivalent.

5. On 1988–91 vehicles, proceed as follows:

   a. Remove and discard the cotter pins from both ball joint studs and loosen the stud nuts 1–two turns. Do not remove the nuts at this time.

   b. Position a suitable ball joint press tool between the upper and lower ball joint studs. Turn the tool with a wrench until the tool places the studs under compression.

   c. Using a hammer sharply hit the spindle near the studs to loosen the studs from the spindle.

6. On 1992–00 vehicles, proceed as follows:

   a. Remove and discard the cotter pin from the lower ball joint stud and loosen the stud nut 1–two turns. Do not remove the nut at this time.

   b. Using a hammer sharply hit the spindle near the stud to loosen the stud from the spindle.

   c. Remove the pinch bolts from the upper ball joint and stabilizer link ball joint at the spindle.

7. Position a floor jack under the lower control arm at the lower ball joint area, and raise the jack to support the lower arm.

**➡The jack will support the spring load on the lower control arm.**

8. On 1988–91 vehicles, remove the upper and lower ball joint stud nuts and remove the spindle.

9. On 1992–00 vehicles, remove the lower ball joint stud nut. Pry the slots with a suitable prybar at the upper ball joint and link ball joint to separate from the spindle. Remove the spindle.

**To install:**

10. On 1992–00 vehicles, position the spindle on the stabilizer bar upper ball joint stud. Install the pinch bolt and loosely install the nut.

11. Position the spindle on the lower ball joint stud and install the stud nut. Tighten the nut to 80–119 ft. lbs. (108–162 Nm). Continue to tighten the nut until a slot for the cotter pin is aligned. Install a new cotter pin.

12. Raise the lower arm and guide the upper ball joint stud into the spindle.

13. On 1988–91 vehicles, install the upper ball joint stud nut and tighten to 60–90 ft. lbs. (81–122 Nm). Continue to tighten the nut until a slot for the cotter pin is aligned. Install a new cotter pin.

14. On 1992–00 vehicles, install the upper ball joint stud pinch bolt and nut. Tighten the nut to 67 ft. lbs. (92 Nm). Tighten the stabilizer link to spindle pinch bolt nut to 30–50 ft. lbs. (40–55 Nm).

15. Connect the tie rod end to the spindle. Install the nut and tighten to 43–46 ft. lbs. (59–63 Nm). Continue to tighten the nut until the slot for the cotter pin is aligned with the cut in the bolt and install a new cotter pin.

16. Install the brake dust shield, caliper, rotor, and anti-lock brake sensor, if equipped.

17. Install the wheel and tire assembly and lower the vehicle.

18. Check the front end alignment.

## Front Wheel Bearings

### REPLACEMENT

#### 1988–91 Vehicles

1. Raise and support the vehicle safely.

2. Remove the wheel and tire assembly and the disc brake caliper. Suspend the caliper with a length of wire; do not let it hang from the brake hose.

3. Pry off the dust cap. Tap out and discard the cotter pin. Remove the nut retainer.

4. Being careful not to drop the outer bearing, pull off the brake disc and wheel hub assembly.

5. Remove the inner grease seal using a prybar. Remove the inner wheel bearing.

6. Clean the wheel bearings with solvent and inspect them for pits, scratches, and excessive wear. Wipe all the old grease from the hub and inspect the bearing races (cups). If either bearings or races are damaged, the bearing races must be removed and the bearings and races replaced as an assembly.

7. If the bearings are to be replaced, drive out the races (cups) from the hub using a brass drift, or pull them from the hub using a puller.

8. Make sure the spindle, hub and bearing assemblies are clean before installation.

**To install:**

9. If the bearing races (cups) were removed, install new ones using a suitable bearing race installer. Pack the bearings with high-temperature wheel bearing grease using a bearing packer. If a packer is not available, work as much grease as possible between the rollers and cages using your hands.

10. Coat the inner surface of the hub and bearing races (cups) with grease.

11. Install the inner bearing in the hub. Using a seal installer, install a new grease seal into the hub. Lubricate the lip of the seal with grease.

12. Install the hub/disc assembly on the spindle, being careful not to damage the oil seal.

13. Install the outer bearing, washer, and spindle nut. Install the caliper and the wheel and tire assembly. Adjust the bearings as follows:

   a. Loosen the adjusting nut three turns and rock the wheel in and out a few times to release the brake pads from the rotor.

   b. While rotating the wheel and hub assembly in a counterclockwise direction, tighten the adjusting nut to 17–25 ft. lbs. (23–34 Nm).

   c. Back off the adjusting nut ½ turn, then retighten to 10–28 inch lbs. (1.1–3.2 Nm).

   d. Install the nut retainer and a new cotter pin. Replace the grease cap.

14. Lower the vehicle. Before driving the vehicle, pump the brake pedal several times to restore normal brake pedal travel.

#### 1992–00 Vehicles

➧ See Figures 56, 57 and 58

1. Raise and safely support the vehicle. Remove the wheel and tire assembly.

2. Remove and discard the grease cap from the hub.

3. Remove the brake caliper. Suspend the caliper with a length of wire; do not let it hang from the brake hose.

4. Remove the rotor. If the factory installed push on nuts are installed, remove them first.

5. Remove and discard the wheel hub nut.

6. Remove the hub and bearing assembly.

**To install:**

7. Install the hub and bearing assembly. Install a new wheel hub nut and tighten to 189–254 ft. lbs. (255–345 Nm).

8. Install the rotor and push on nuts, if equipped. Install a new grease cap.

9. Install the brake caliper.

10. Install the wheel and tire assembly and lower the vehicle.

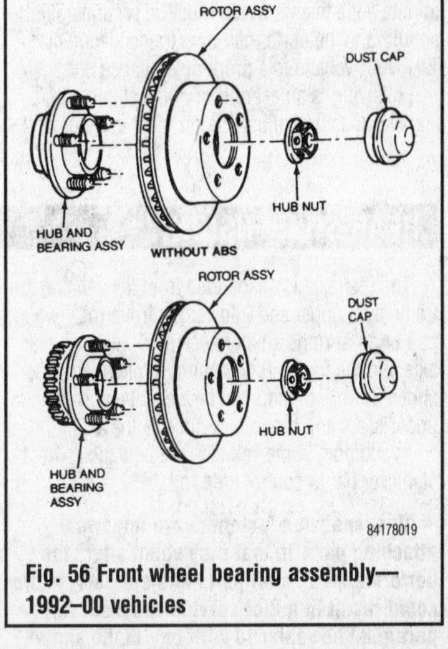


**Fig. 56 Front wheel bearing assembly—1992–00 vehicles**

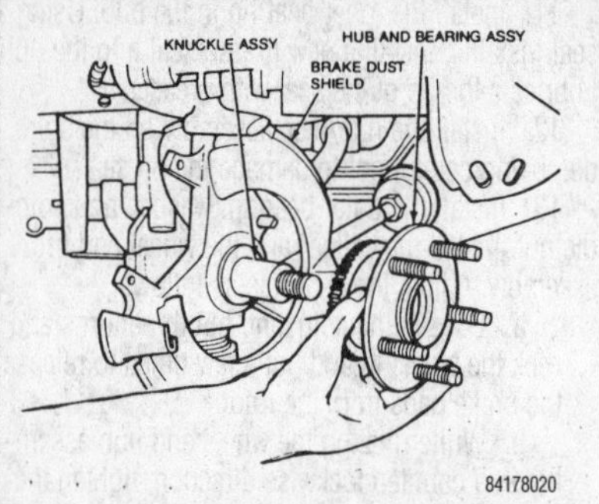


**Fig. 57 Front wheel hub and bearing assembly removal—1992–00 vehicles**

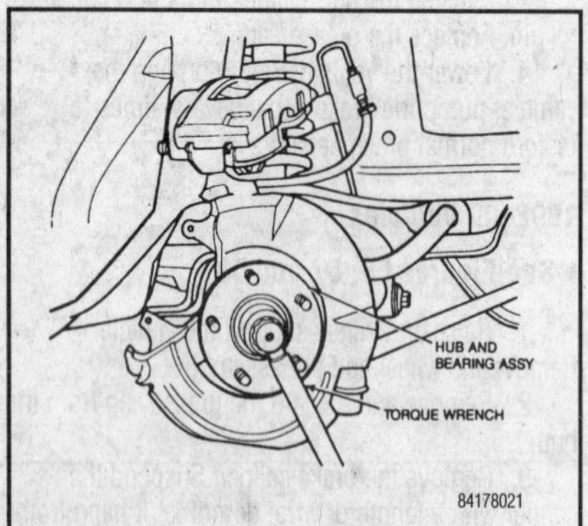


**Fig. 58 Front wheel hub and bearing assembly installation—1992–00 vehicles**

## Wheel Alignment

If the tires are worn unevenly, if the vehicle is not stable on the highway or if the handling seems uneven in spirited driving, the wheel alignment should be checked. If an alignment problem is suspected, first check for improper tire inflation and other possible causes. These can be worn suspension or steering components, accident damage or even unmatched tires. If any worn or damaged components are found, they must be replaced before the wheels can be properly aligned. Wheel alignment requires very expensive equipment and involves minute adjustments which must be accurate; it should only be performed by a trained technician. Take your vehicle to a properly equipped shop.

Following is a description of the alignment angles which are adjustable on most vehicles and

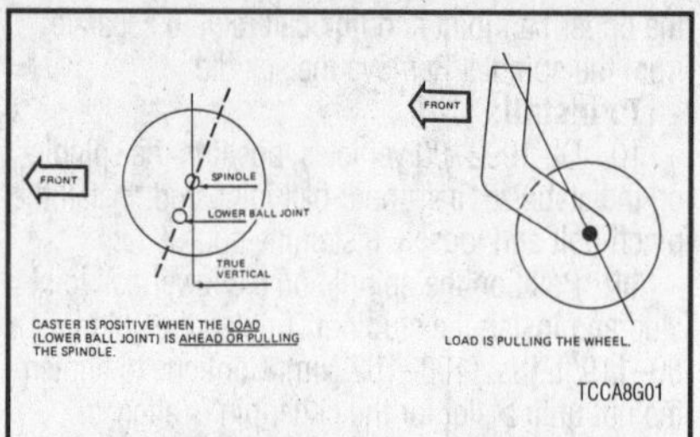


**Fig. 59 Caster affects straight-line stability. Caster wheels used on shopping carts, for example, employ positive caster**

how they affect vehicle handling. Although these angles can apply to both the front and rear wheels, usually only the front suspension is adjustable.

### CASTER

➧ **See Figure 59**

Looking at a vehicle from the side, caster angle describes the steering axis rather than a wheel angle. The steering knuckle is attached to a control arm or strut at the top and a control arm at the bottom. The wheel pivots around the line between these points to steer the vehicle. When the upper point is tilted back, this is described as positive caster. Having a positive caster tends to make the wheels self-centering, increasing directional stability. Excessive positive caster makes the wheels hard to steer, while an uneven caster will cause a pull to one side. Overloading the vehicle or sagging rear springs will affect caster, as will raising the rear of the vehicle. If the rear of the vehicle is lower than normal, the caster becomes more positive.

### CAMBER

➧ **See Figure 60**

Looking from the front of the vehicle, camber is the inward or outward tilt of the top of wheels. When the tops of the wheels are tilted in, this is negative camber; if they are tilted out, it is positive. In a turn, a slight amount of negative camber helps maximize contact of the tire with the road. However, too much negative camber compromises straight-line stability, increases bump steer and torque steer.

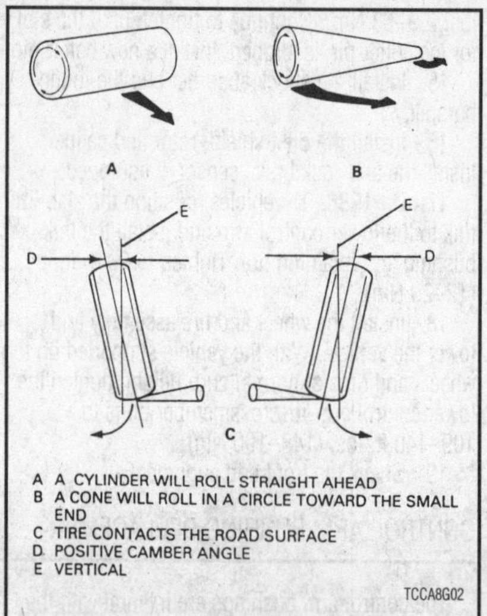


**Fig. 60 Camber influences tire contact with the road**

### TOE

➧ **See Figure 61**

Looking down at the wheels from above the vehicle, toe angle is the distance between the front of the wheels, relative to the distance between the back of the wheels. If the wheels are closer at the front, they are said to be toed-in or to have negative toe. A small amount of negative toe enhances directional stability and provides a smoother ride on the highway.

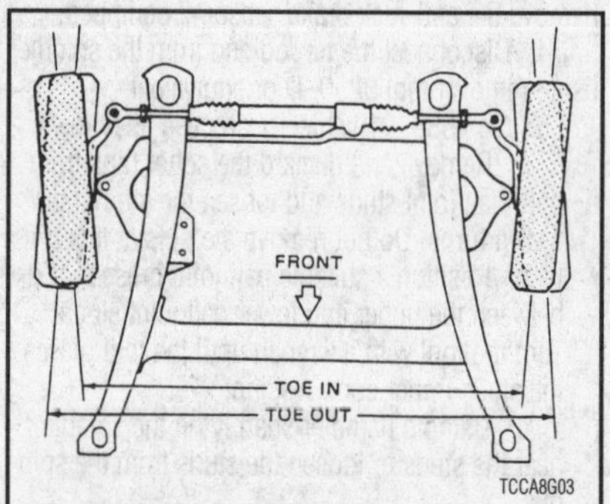


**Fig. 61 With toe-in, the distance between the wheels is closer at the front than at the rear**

# REAR SUSPENSION

The rear axle is suspended from the vehicle frame by 2 upper and 2 lower control arms. Two coil or air springs are connected between the rear axle and the frame. Ride control is provided by 2 shock absorbers mounted between the coil springs upper seats and brackets welded to the axle tube.

In addition, some vehicles are equipped with a stabilizer bar to control side roll.

**➡All suspension fasteners are important attaching parts in that they could affect the performance of vital parts and systems, and/or could result in major service expense. Any part must be replaced with one of the same part number or with an exact equivalent part if replacement becomes necessary. Do not use a replacement part of lesser quality or substitute design. Torque values must be used as specified during assembly to ensure proper part retention.**

**⁂ CAUTION**

**If equipped with air suspension, the air suspension switch, located in the trunk on the right-hand trim panel, must be turned OFF before raising the vehicle. Failure to turn the air suspension switch off may result in unexpected inflation or deflation of the air springs, which may result in the vehicle shifting, possibly causing personal injury.**

## Coil Springs

### REMOVAL & INSTALLATION

➧ **See Figures 64, 65, 66, 67 and 68**

1. Raise and safely support the vehicle. Place jack stands under the frame side rails.
2. Support the rear axle housing.

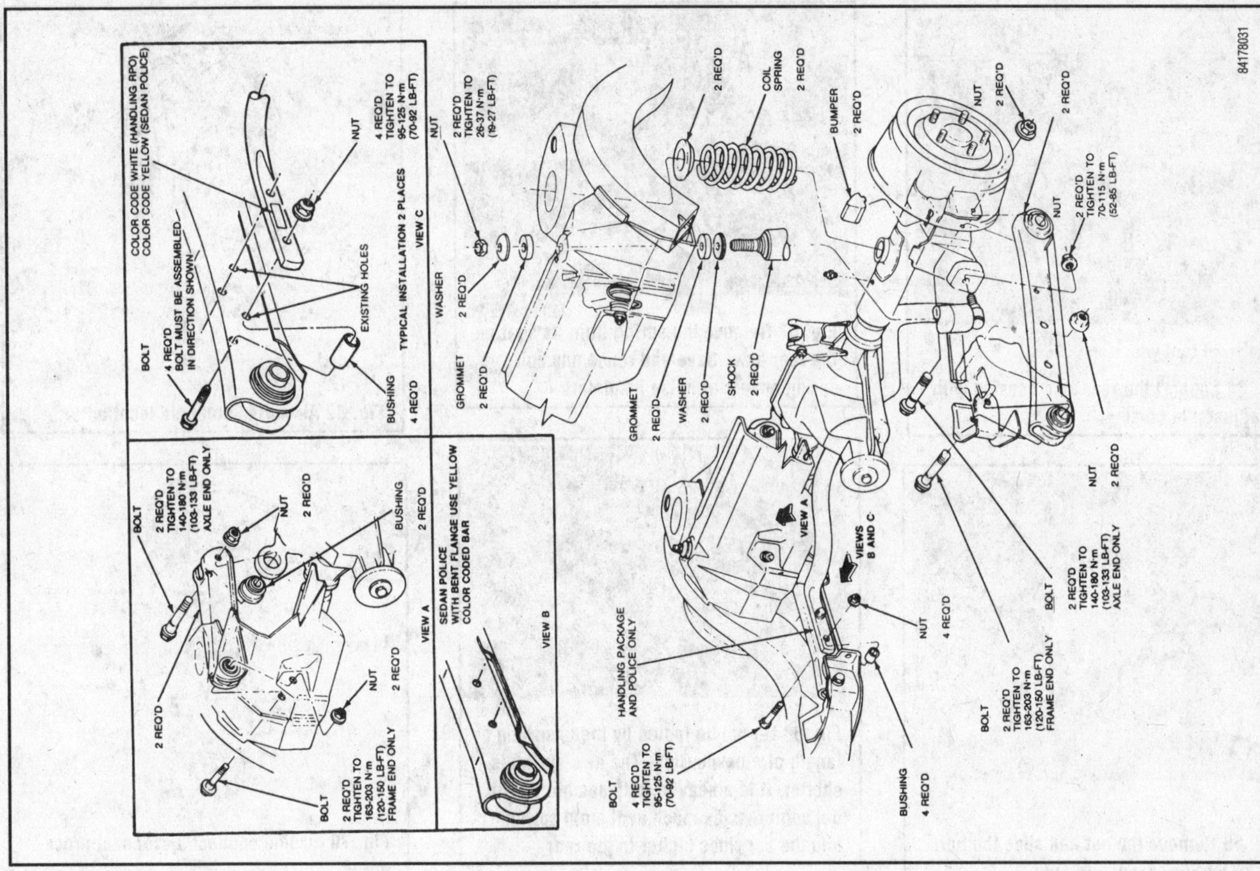


Fig. 63 Rear suspension—1992–93 vehicles, except air suspension

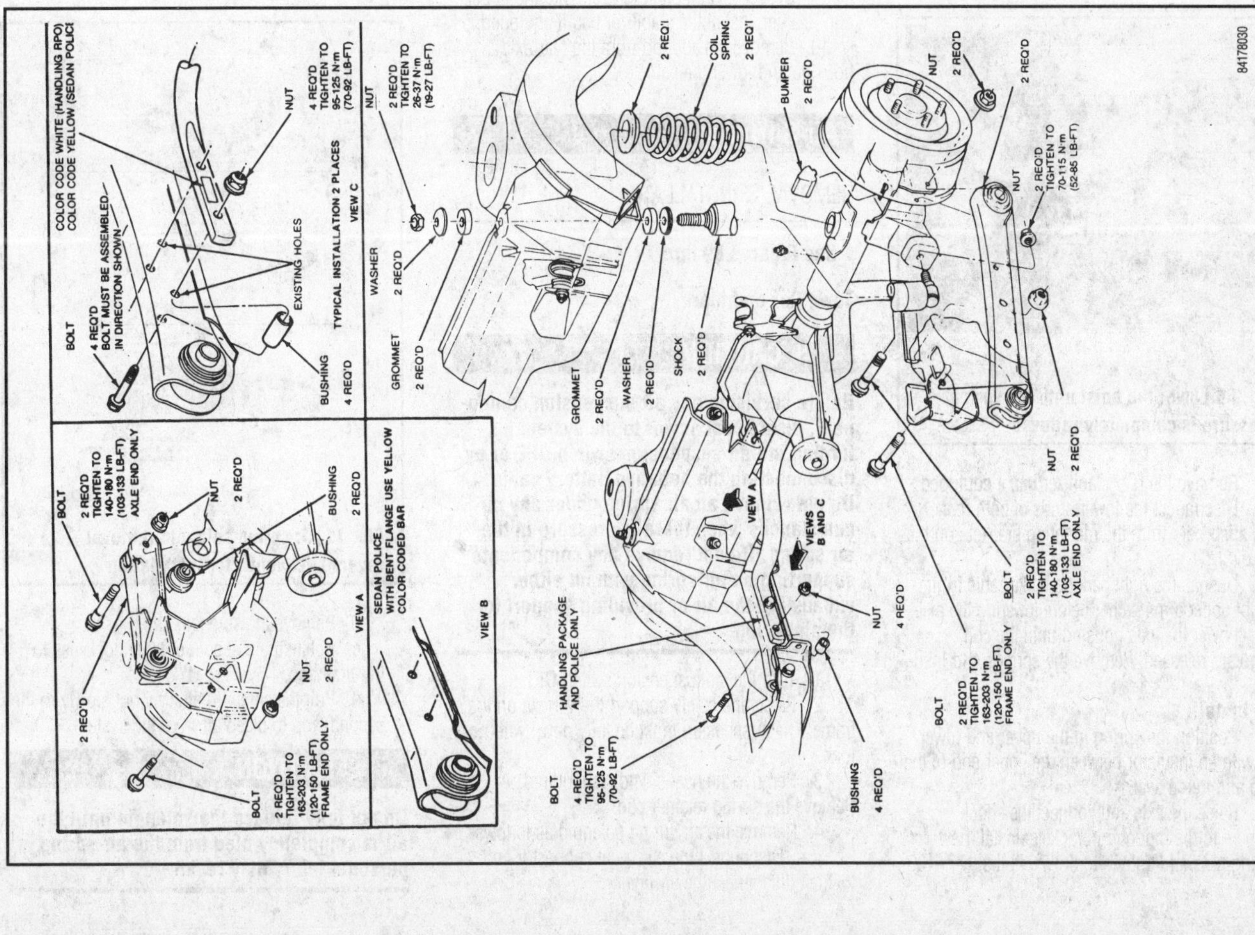


Fig. 62 Rear suspension—1988–91 vehicles

Fig. 64 Support the rear axle housing with an adjustable hoist

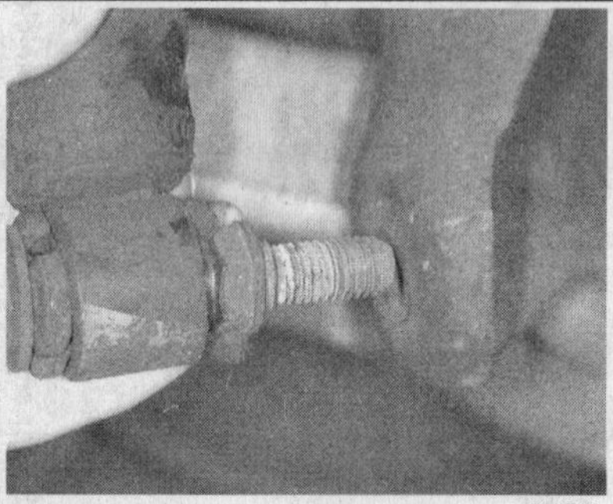


Fig. 65 Remove the nut and slide the bolt out of the lower mounting ear

Fig. 66 Lower the hoist until the spring pressure is completely relieved

3. Remove the rear stabilizer bar, if equipped.

4. Disconnect the lower studs of both rear shock absorbers from the mounting brackets on the axle tube.

5. Unsnap the right parking brake cable from the right upper arm retainer before lowering the axle.

6. Lower the axle housing until the coil springs are released. Remove the springs and insulators.

**To install:**

7. Position the spring in the upper and lower seats with an insulator between the upper end of the spring and frame seat.

8. Raise the axle and connect the shock absorbers to the mounting brackets. Install new retaining nuts and tighten to 56–76 ft. lbs. (77–103 Nm).

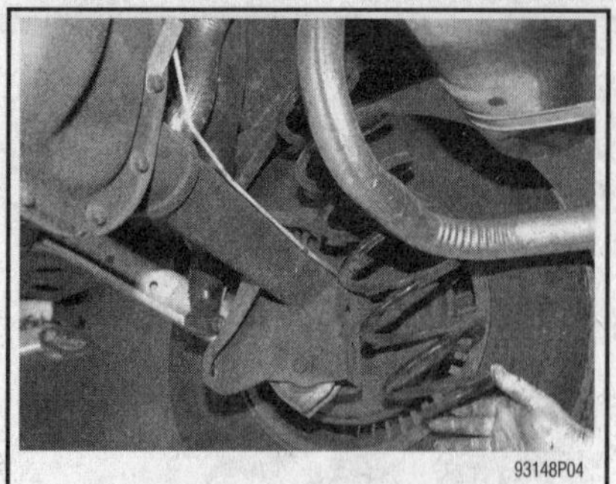


Fig. 67 Remove the spring from its seat on the rear axle. Save and reuse any coil spring covers or noise insulators

Fig. 68 Do not be fooled by the unsprung length of a new spring. The new spring is shorter, it is a heavier duty design. It will not compress as much as the old spring and the car rides higher in the rear

9. Snap the right parking cable into the upper arm retainer. Install the stabilizer bar, if equipped.

10. Remove the support from the rear axle housing and lower the vehicle.

## Air Springs

### REMOVAL & INSTALLATION

➧ See Figures 69 thru 79

**Town Car and Mark**

**⁂ CAUTION**

**Before servicing any air suspension component, disconnect power to the system by turning the air suspension switch OFF or by disconnecting the negative battery cable. Do not remove an air spring under any circumstances when there is pressure in the air spring. Do not remove any components supporting an air spring without either exhausting the air or providing support for the air spring.**

1. Turn the air suspension switch **OFF**.

2. Raise and safely support the vehicle on the frame. The suspension must be fully down with no load.

3. Remove the heat shield, as required. Remove the spring retainer clip.

4. Remove the air spring solenoid as follows:

a. Disconnect the electrical connector and then disconnect the air line.

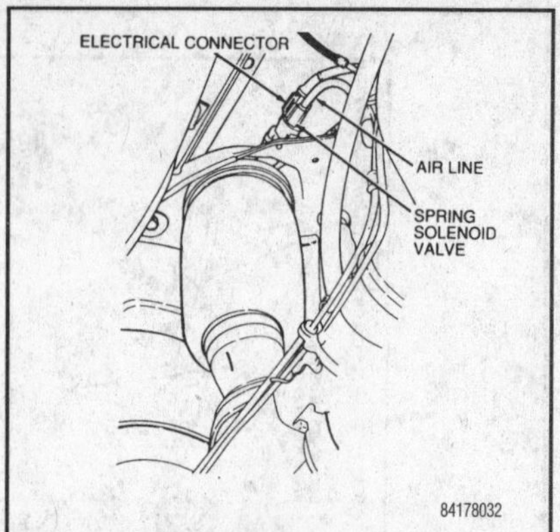


Fig. 69 Air spring solenoid location

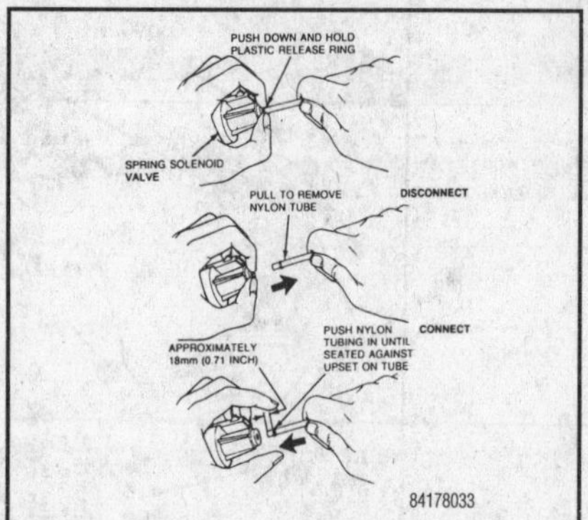


Fig. 70 Air line connect/disconnect procedure

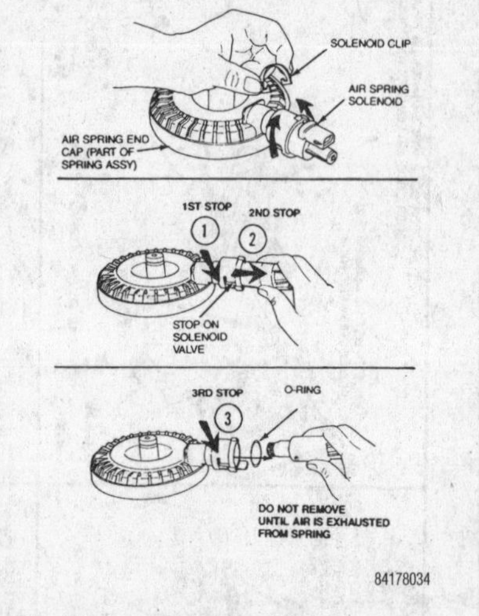


Fig. 71 Air spring solenoid removal—reverse sequence for installation

b. Remove the solenoid clip.

c. Rotate the solenoid counterclockwise to the first stop.

d. Pull the solenoid straight out slowly to the second stop to bleed air from the system.

**⁂ CAUTION**

**Do not fully release the solenoid until the air is completely bled from the air spring or personal injury may result.**

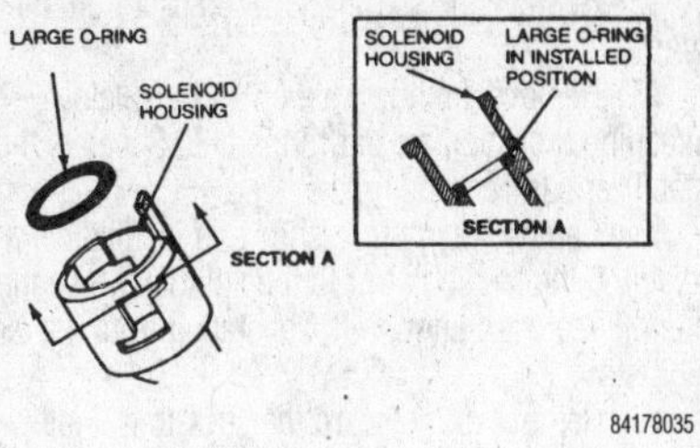


**Fig. 72 Large solenoid housing O-ring**

e. After the air is fully bled from the system, rotate counterclockwise to the third stop and remove the solenoid from the solenoid housing. Remove the large O-ring from the solenoid housing.

5. Remove the spring piston-to-axle spring seat as follows:

a. Insert air spring removal tool T90P–5310–A or equivalent, between the axle tube and the spring seat on the forward side of the axle.

b. Position the tool so its flat end rests on the piston knob. Push downward, forcing the piston and retainer clip off the axle spring seat.

6. Remove the air spring.

**To install:**

7. Install the air spring solenoid as follows:

a. Check the solenoid O-rings for cuts or abrasion. Replace the O-rings as required. Lightly grease the O-ring area of the solenoid and the larger solenoid housing O-ring with silicone dielectric compound.

b. Insert the solenoid into the air spring end cap and rotate clockwise to the third stop, push in to the second stop, then rotate clockwise to the first stop.

c. Install the solenoid clip. Inspect the wire harness connector and ensure the rubber gasket is in place at the bottom of the connector cavity.

8. Install the air spring into the frame spring seat, taking care to keep the solenoid air and electrical connections clean and free of damage.

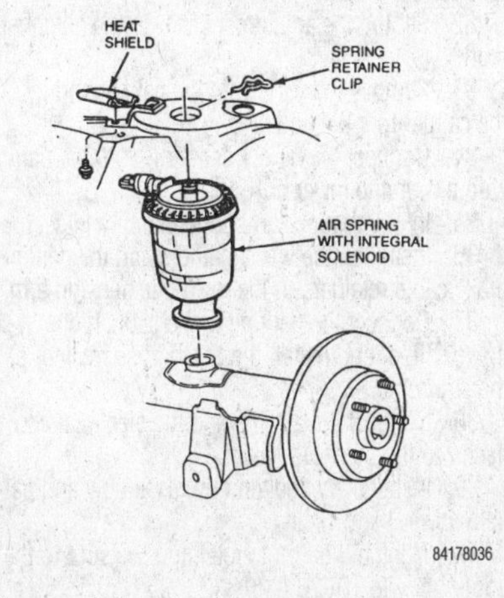


**Fig. 73 Air spring removal**

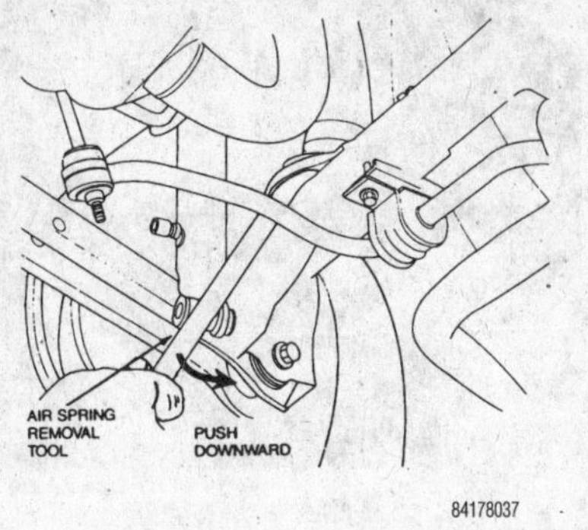


**Fig. 74 Removing the spring piston-to-axle spring seat**

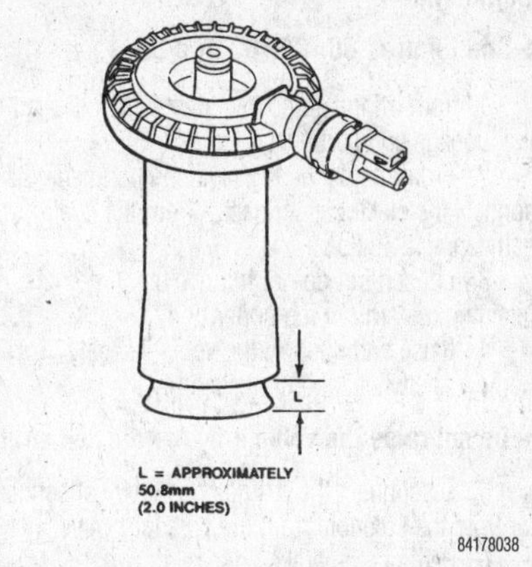


**Fig. 75 New air spring appearance prior to installation**

9. Connect the push on spring retainer clip to the knob of the spring cap from the top side of the frame spring seat.

10. Connect the air line and electrical connector to the solenoid. Install the heat shield to frame spring seat, if required.

11. Align the air spring piston to axle seats. Squeeze to increase pressure and push downward on the piston, snapping the piston to axle seat at rebound and supported by the shock absorber.

**➡The air springs may be damaged if the suspension is allowed to compress before the spring is inflated.**

12. Refill the air spring as follows:

a. Turn the air suspension switch **ON**. The ignition switch must be **ON** and the engine running or a battery charger must be connected to the battery to reduce battery drain.

b. Fold back or remove the right luggage compartment trim panel and connect SUPER STAR II tester 007–0041–A or equivalent to the air suspension diagnostic connector, which is located near the air suspension switch.

c. Set the tester to EEC-IV/MCU mode. Also set the tester to FAST mode. Release the tester button to the HOLD (up) position and turn the tester **ON**.

d. Depress the tester button to TEST (down) position. A Code 10 will be displayed. Within 2 minutes, a Code 13 will be displayed. After Code 13 is displayed, release the tester button to

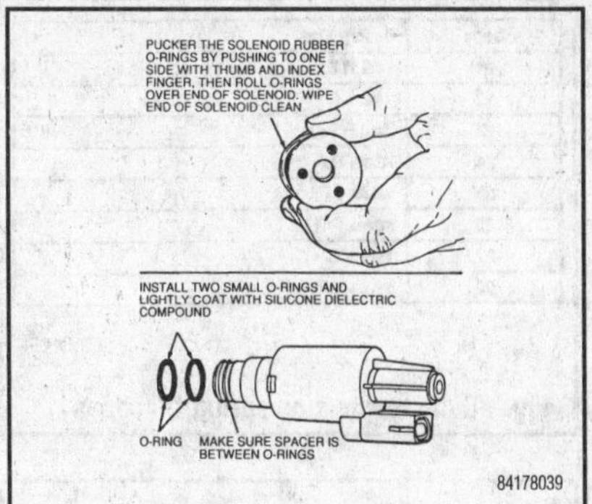


**Fig. 76 Installing new O-rings on the air spring solenoid**

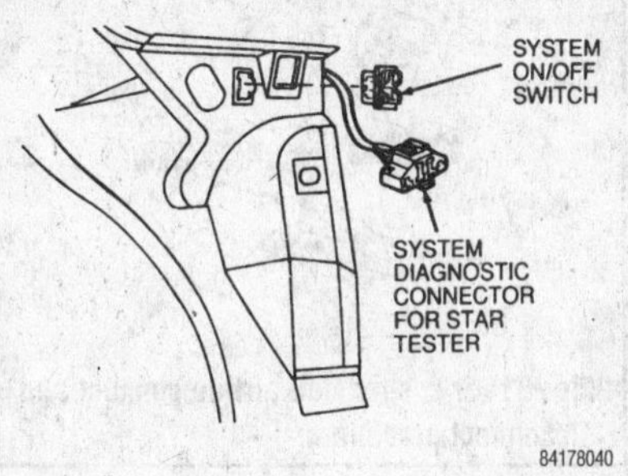


**Fig. 77 Air suspension diagnostic connector location**

| Code | Description |
|---|---|
| 23 | Vent Rear |
| 26 | Compress Rear |
| 31 | Cycle Compressor On and Off Repeatedly |
| 32 | Cycle Vent Solenoid Valve Open and Closed Repeatedly |
| 33 | Cycle Spring Solenoid Valves Open and Closed Repeatedly |

84178041

**Fig. 78 Air suspension codes**

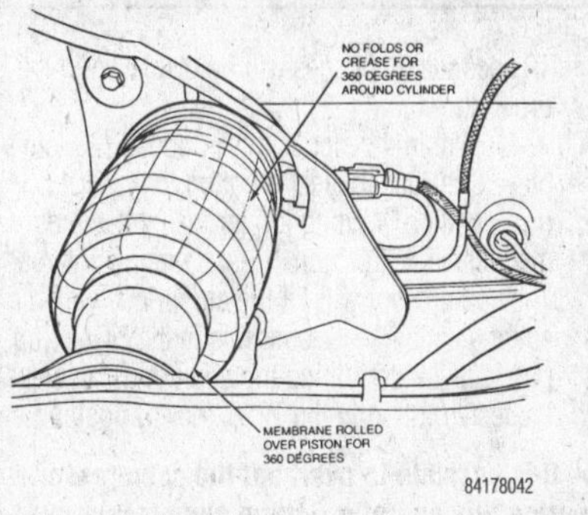


**Fig. 79 Correct air spring appearance after installation**

HOLD (up) position, wait 5 seconds, and depress the tester button to TEST (down) position. Ignore any codes displayed.

e. Release the tester button to the HOLD (up) position. Wait at least 20 seconds, then depress the tester button to TEST (down) position. Within

| Code | Description |
|---|---|
| 21 | Vent R.F. |
| 22 | Vent L.F. |
| 23 | Vent R.R. |
| 24 | Inflate R.F. |
| 25 | Inflate L.F. |
| 26 | Inflate R.R. |
| 27 | Vent L.R. |
| 28 | Inflate L.R. |

93148G01

**Fig. 80 Air suspension spring fill codes**

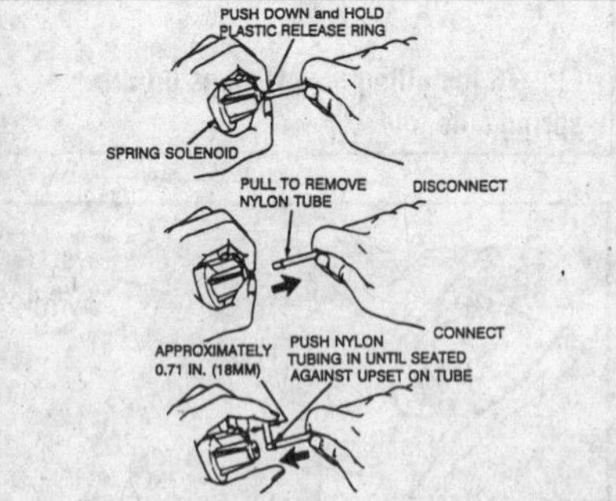


93148G02

**Fig. 81 Air suspension airline connect and disconnect procedure**

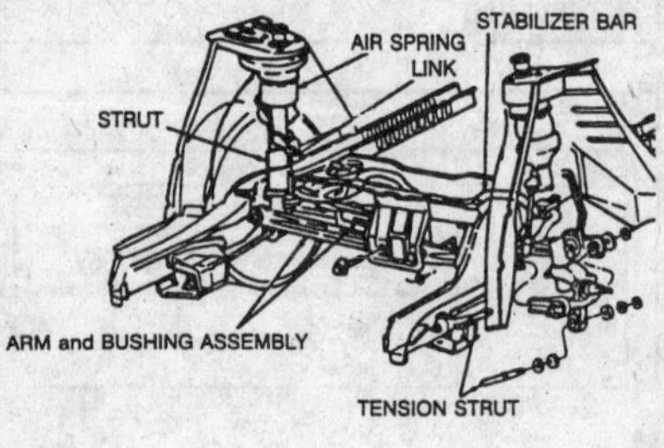


93148G03

**Fig. 82 Rear suspension schematic for Continental**

10 seconds, the codes will be displayed in the order shown.

f. Within 4 seconds after Code 26/28 is displayed, release the tester button to the HOLD (up) position. Waiting longer than 4 seconds may result in Functional Test 31 being entered. The compressor will fill the air springs with air as long as the tester button is in the HOLD (up) position. To stop filling the air springs, depress the tester button to the TEST (down) position.

**➡It is possible to overheat the compressor during this operation. If the compressor overheats, the self-resetting circuit breaker in the compressor will open and remain open for about 15 minutes. This allows the compressor to cool down.**

g. To exit Functional Test 26/28, disconnect the tester and turn the ignition switch OFF.

13. Lower the vehicle.

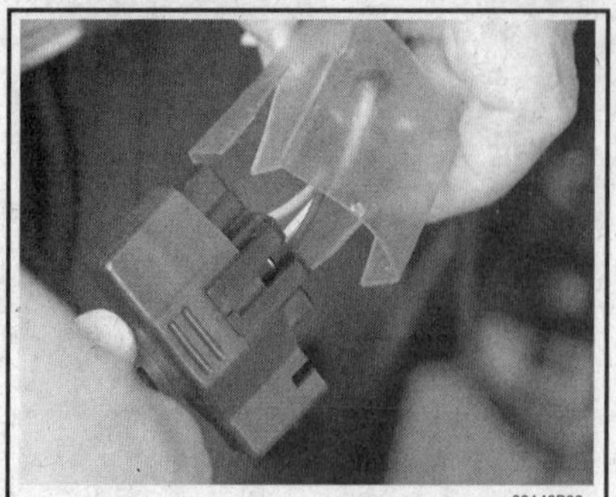

93148P08

**Fig. 83 Plugging in to the diagnostic connector in the luggage compartment**

### Continental

**▶ See Figures 80, 81, 82 and 83**

1. Turn off the air suspension switch located in the luggage compartment.
2. From inside the luggage compartment, disconnect the electrical connector from the dual dampening actuator.
3. Loosen but do not remove the three nuts retaining the strut to the upper body.
4. Raise and support the vehicle sagely. Remove the wheel and tire assembly.

**➡Do not raise the vehicle by the tension strut.**

5. Disconnect the airline and electrical connector from the solenoid from the solenoid valve.
6. Remove the brake hose retainer at the strut bracket.
7. Disconnect the parking brake cable from the brake caliper. Remove all the wire retainer and parking brake cable retainers from the lower suspension arm.
8. Disconnect the height sensor link from the ball stud pin on the lower arm.
9. Remove the caliper assembly from the spindle and position it off to the side with a piece of wire. Do not kink or place a load on the brake hose.
10. Blccd the air spring by performing the following:
   - Remove the solenoid clip.
   - Rotate the solenoid counterclockwise to the first stop.
   - Slowly pull the solenoid straight out to the second stop and bleed the air from the system.
   - After the air is fully bled from the system, rotate the solenoid to the third stop and remove the solenoid from the housing.
11. Mark the position of the notch on the toe adjustment cam.
12. Remove the torsion spring clamp from the spindle-to-strut bolt.
13. Remove the nut from the inboard bushing on the suspension arm.
14. Install the torsion spring remover tool T88p-5310-a or the equivalent, on the suspension arm. Pry up on the tool and arm using a ¾ inch drive ratchet to relieve the pressure on the pivot bolt. An assistant may be required to pull outboard on the spindle simultaneously to fully relieve the tension on the bolt. Remove the bolt and lower arm. Repeat this procedure for the opposite arm.
15. Remove the torsion spring from the arms.
16. Remove the stabilizer `U' bracket from the body.
17. Remove the nut, washer, and insulator attaching the stabilizer bar to the link. Separate the stabilizer bar from the link.
18. Remove the nut, washer, and insulator retaining the tension strut to the spindle. Move the spindle rearward enough to separate it from the tension strut.
19. Remove and discard the strut-to-spindle pinch joint as required to assist in removing the bolt.
20. Separate the spindle from the strut. Remove the spindle as an assembly with the arms attached.
21. From inside the luggage compartment area, support the shock strut by hand and remove and discard the 3 upper mount-to-body nuts. Do not drop the strut when removing the upper nuts. Guide the electric actuator wire through the opening to prevent snagging and damage while removing the strut assembly.

**To install:**

22. Install the solenoid valve on the air spring.
23. Guide the electric actuator wire through the opening and install the strut assembly. Install the 3 new upper mount nuts.
24. Install the spindle and arms to the strut. Install a new strut-too-spindle pinch bolt. Do not tighten the bolt until the control arms are attached to the body and the cams are centered.
25. Position the tension strut to the spindle. Install the insulator, washer and nut retaining the tension strut to the spindle. Tighten the nut to 35–50 ft. lbs. (48–68Nm).
26. Install the stabilizer to the link. Install the insulator, washer, and retaining nut. Tighten the nut to 5–7 ft. lbs. (7–9.5 Nm).
27. Install the stabilizer `U' bracket to the body. Tighten the bolt to 25–37 ft. lbs. (34–50 Nm).
28. Install the torsion spring to the arms.
29. Position the inboard bushing using the torsion spring remover tool, and install the bolt. An assistant may be required to pull out board on the spindle to align the bushing so the bolt can be inserted. Repeat the procedure for the opposite lower arm.
30. Install the nut to the inboard bushing on the suspension arm but do not tighten at this time.
31. Tighten the spindle to strut bolt to 51–70 ft. lbs. 68–95 Nm).
32. Set the toe adjustment cam to the alignment mark.
33. Remove the wire from the caliper and install the caliper to the spindle.
34. Connect the height sensor link to the ball stud pin on the lower arm.
35. Install the torsion spring clamp and secure.
36. Install all the wire retainers and the parking brake cable retainers to the lower suspension arm.
37. Connect the parking brake cable to the brake caliper and install the brake hose retainer at the strut bracket.
38. Connect the air line and the electrical connector to the solenoid valve.
39. Install the wheel and tire assembly and partially lower the vehicle.
40. Tighten the 3 nuts retaining the strut to the upper body to 19–26 ft. lbs. (26–35 Nm).
41. From inside the luggage compartment, con-

nect the electrical connector for the dual dampening actuator.

42. Turn on the air suspension switch and fill the air spring as follows:

- Place the air suspension service switch in the **ON**position.
- Turn the ignition switch **OFF**.
- Connect a battery charger to reduce the battery drain.
- Open the access door in the left-hand luggage compartment trim panel to plug the Super Star II tester or an equivalent scan tool, into the air suspension diagnostics wiring harness connector.
- Set the tester to EEC-IV/MCU mode. Also set the tester to FAST mode. Release the tester button to the HOLD (up) position and turn the tester **ON**.
- Depress the tester button to TEST (down) position. A Code 10 will be displayed. Within 2 minutes, a Code 13 will be displayed. After Code 13 is displayed, release the tester button to HOLD (up) position, wait 5 seconds, and depress the tester button to TEST (down) position. Ignore any codes displayed.
- Release the tester button to the HOLD (up) position. Wait at least 20 seconds, then depress the tester button to TEST (down) position. Within 10 seconds, the codes will be displayed in the order shown.
- Within 4 seconds after Code 26/28 is displayed, release the tester button to the HOLD (up) position. Waiting longer than 4 seconds may result in Functional Test 31 being entered. The compressor will fill the air springs with air as long as the tester button is in the HOLD (up) position. To stop filling the air springs, depress the tester button to the TEST (down) position.

**➡It is possible to overheat the compressor during this operation. If the compressor overheats, the self-resetting circuit breaker in the compressor will open and remain open for about 15 minutes. This allows the compressor to cool down.**

- To exit Functional Test 26/28, disconnect the tester and turn the ignition switch OFF.

43. Lower the vehicle.

## Shock Absorbers

### REMOVAL & INSTALLATION

#### Without Automatic Leveling

➧ See Figure 84

**CAUTION**

**All vehicle applications are equipped with gas-pressurized shock absorbers that will extend unassisted. Do not apply heat or flame to the shock absorber tube.**

1. If equipped with air suspension, turn the air suspension switch **OFF**.
2. Raise and safely support the vehicle. Make sure the rear axle is supported.

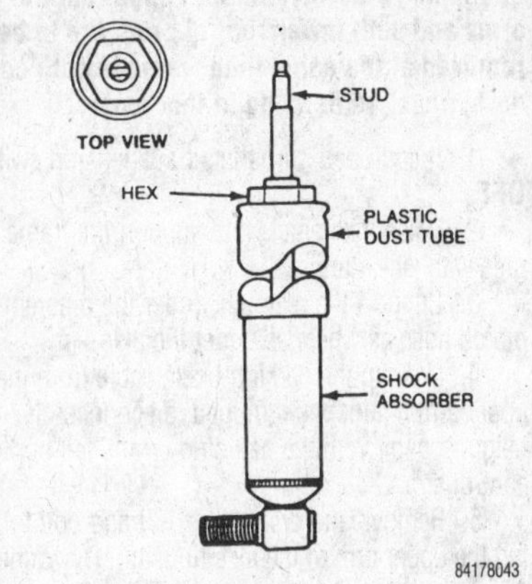


84178043

**Fig. 84 Rear shock absorber—except with automatic leveling suspension**

3. To assist in removing the upper attachment on shock absorbers using a plastic dust tube, place and open end wrench onto the hex stamped into the metal cap of the dust tube. For shock absorbers with a steel dust tube, simply grasp the tube to prevent stud rotation when loosening the retaining nut.
4. Remove the shock absorber retaining nut, washer, and insulator from the stud on the upper side of the frame. Discard the nut. Compress the shock to clear the hole in the frame and remove the inner insulator and washer from the upper retaining stud.
5. Remove the self-locking retaining nut and disconnect the shock absorber lower stud from the mounting bracket on the rear axle.

**To install:**

6. Prime the new shock absorber as follows:
   a. With the shock absorber right side up (as installed in the vehicle), extend it fully.
   b. Turn the shock upside down and fully compress it.
   c. Repeat the previous 2 steps at least 3 times to make sure any trapped air has been expelled.
7. Place the inner washer and insulator on the upper retaining stud and position the shock absorber with the stud through the hole in the frame.
8. While holding the shock absorber in position, install the outer insulator, washer, and a new stud nut on the upper side of the frame. Tighten the nut to 25 ft. lbs. (34 Nm).
9. Extend the shock absorber and place the lower stud in the mounting bracket hole on the rear axle housing. Install a new self-locking nut and tighten to 56–76 ft. lbs. (77–103 Nm).
10. Lower the vehicle and, if equipped, turn the air suspension switch **ON**.

#### With Automatic Leveling

➧ See Figures 85, 86 and 87

**WARNING**

**When removing and installing rear air shock absorbers, it is very important that this procedure be followed exactly. Failure to do so may result in damaged shock absorbers.**

1. Make sure the ignition switch is in the **OFF** position.
2. Disconnect the height sensor connector link before allowing the rear axle to hang free.
3. Raise and safely support the vehicle so the suspension arms hang free. The rear shock absorbers will vent air through the compressor and a hissing noise will be heard. When the noise stops, the air lines can be disconnected. A residual pressure of 8–24 psi will remain in the air lines.
4. Disconnect the air line by pushing in on the retainer ring(s) and pulling the line(s) out.
5. Remove the top retaining nut, washer, and bushing.
6. Remove the bottom retaining nut and washer. Remove the shock absorber.

**To install:**

7. Position the shock absorber and install the bottom retaining washer and nut. Tighten to 52–85 ft. lbs. (70–115 Nm).

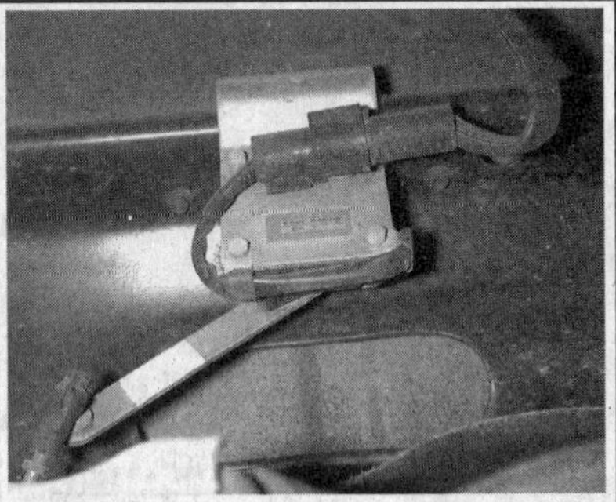

93148P01

**Fig. 85 This is the height sensor for air adjustable rear shocks**

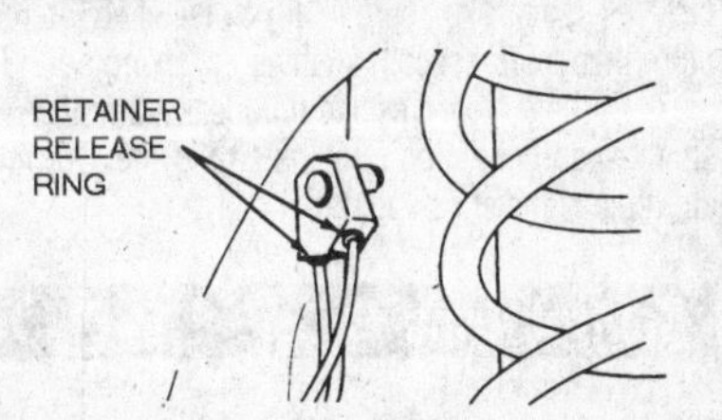


84178044

**Fig. 86 Disconnect/connect the air lines here**

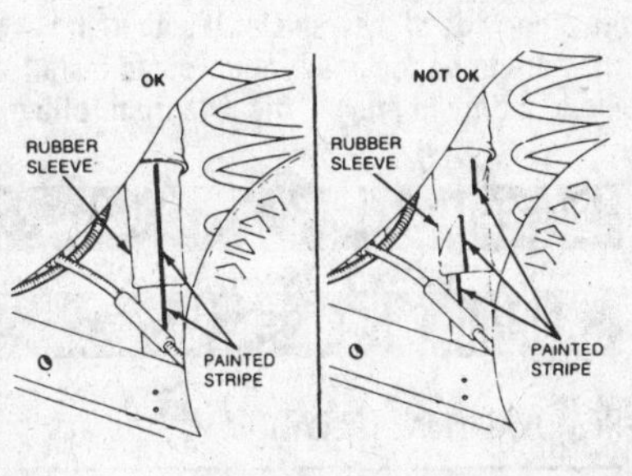


84178045

**Fig. 87 Make sure the rubber sleeve on the air shock absorber is not wrapped up**

8. Install the top bushing, washer, and retaining nut. Tighten to 14–26 ft. lbs. (19–35 Nm).

**➡Check the rubber sleeve on the shock absorber to be sure it is not wrapped up. To assist in identifying wrap-up during installation, a white stripe is on the rubber sleeve and on the shock absorber body. The stripes should align. To correct a wrap-up condition, loosen the upper shock retaining nut and turn the shock to align the stripes. Retighten the retaining nut.**

9. Connect the air line to the shock absorber by pushing in on the retainer ring and installing the air line.
10. Connect the height sensor connecting link and lower the vehicle.

### TESTING

#### Except Air Shock Absorbers

1. Remove the shock absorber from the vehicle.
2. Extend the shock absorber fully while it is right side up, as installed in the vehicle. Then turn it upside down and fully compress it. Repeat this procedure at least 3 times to make sure any trapped air has been expelled.
3. Place the shock absorber right side up in a vise and hand stroke the shock absorber. Check the shock absorber insulators for damage and wear.
4. If the shock absorber is properly primed, in its installed position, and there is a lag or a skip occurring near mid-stroke of the shaft reverse travel direction, the shock absorber must be replaced.
5. Replace the shock absorber if there is any seizing during the shaft full travel, except at either end of the travel.
6. Replace the shock absorber if upon the shaft fast, reverse stroke, there is any noise encountered other than a faint swish, such as a clicking sound.
7. If there are excessive fluid leaks, and the shock absorber action remains erratic after purging air, replace the shock absorber.

## Control Arms

### REMOVAL & INSTALLATION

#### Upper Control Arm

**➡If one upper control arm requires replacement, also replace the upper control arm on the other side of the vehicle. If both upper arms are to be replaced, remove and install one at a time to prevent the axle from rolling or slipping sideways. If both upper control arms and both lower control arms are to be removed at the same time, remove both coil or air springs, as detailed in this Section.**

1. If equipped, turn the air suspension switch **OFF**.
2. Raise the vehicle and support the frame side rails with jack stands.
3. Support the rear axle under the differential pinion nose as wheel as under the axle.
4. Unsnap the parking brake cable from the upper arm retainer. If equipped, disconnect the height sensor from the ball stud on the left upper control arm.
5. Remove and discard the nut and bolt retaining the upper arm to the axle housing. Disconnect the arm from the housing.
6. Remove and discard the nut and bolt retaining the upper arm to the frame bracket and remove the arm.

**To install:**

7. Hold the upper arm in place on the front arm bracket and install a new retaining bolt and self-locking nut. Do not tighten at this time.
8. Secure the upper arm to the axle housing with new retaining bolts and nuts. The bolts must be pointed toward the front of the vehicle.
9. Raise the suspension with a jack until the upper arm rear pivot hole is in position with the hole in the axle bushing. Install a new pivot bolt and nut with the nut facing inboard.
10. Tighten the upper arm-to-axle pivot bolts to 103–132 ft. lbs. (140–180 Nm) and upper arm-to-frame pivot bolts to 119–149 ft. lbs. (162–203 Nm).
11. Snap the parking brake cable into the upper arm retainer. Connect the height sensor to the ball stud on the left upper arm, if equipped.
12. Remove the supports from the frame and axle and lower the vehicle. If equipped, turn the air suspension switch **ON**.

#### Lower Control Arm

**➡If one lower control arm requires replacement, also replace the lower control arm on the other side of the vehicle. If both upper control arms and both lower control arms are to be removed at the same time, remove both coil or air springs, as detailed in this Section.**

1. If equipped, turn the air suspension switch **OFF**.
2. Mark the rear shock absorber tube relative to the protective sleeve with the vehicle in the normal ride height position.
3. Raise the vehicle and support the frame side rails with jack stands. Allow the axle housing to hang with the shock absorbers fully extended to relieve spring pressure.
4. Remove the stabilizer bar, if equipped.
5. Support the axle with jack stands under the differential pinion nose as well as under the axle.
6. Remove and discard the lower arm pivot bolts and nuts and remove the lower arm.

**To install:**

7. Position the lower arm to the frame bracket and axle. Install new bolts and nuts with the nuts facing outboard.
8. Raise the axle to the normal ride height position, compressing the shock absorbers to the marks made during the removal procedure. Tighten the lower arm-to-axle pivot bolt to 103–132 ft. lbs. (140–180 Nm) and lower arm-to-frame pivot bolt to 119–149 ft. lbs. (162–203 Nm).
9. Install the stabilizer bar, if equipped.
10. Remove the jack stands and lower the vehicle. If equipped, turn the air suspension switch **ON**.

## Stabilizer Bar

### REMOVAL & INSTALLATION

1. If equipped, turn the air suspension switch **OFF**.
2. Raise the vehicle and support the frame side rails with jack stands. Allow the axle housing to hang with the shock absorbers fully extended.
3. On 1988–91 vehicles, remove the bolts, nuts and spacers retaining the stabilizer bar to the lower control arms and remove the stabilizer bar. Discard the bolts and nuts.
4. On 1992–99 vehicles, disconnect the stabilizer bar arms from the links. Remove the bolts and brackets retaining the stabilizer bar to the rear axle and remove the stabilizer bar.

**To install:**

5. On 1988–91 vehicles, align the 4 holes in the stabilizer bar with the holes in the lower control arms. Install the color coded end of the bar on the right side of the vehicle. Install 4 new bolts and nuts and the existing spacers. Tighten to 70–92 ft. lbs. (95–125 Nm).
6. On 1992–99 vehicles, install 2 brackets onto the stabilizer bar insulators and hook both brackets into the T-slot of the rear axle bracket. Install the retaining bolts and tighten to 16–21 ft. lbs. (21–29 Nm). Connect the stabilizer bar eyes to the links using insulators, nuts and washers. Tighten to 13–17 ft. lbs. (17–23 Nm).
7. Remove the jack stands and lower the vehicle. If equipped, turn the air suspension switch **ON**.

# STEERING

## Steering Wheel

### REMOVAL & INSTALLATION

#### 1988 –89 Vehicles

1. Disconnect the negative battery cable.
2. Remove the horn pad and cover assembly. Disconnect the horn electrical connector.
3. Disconnect the cruise control switch electrical connector, if equipped.
4. Remove and discard the steering wheel bolt. Remove the steering wheel using a suitable puller.

**➡Do not use a knock-off type steering wheel puller or strike the retaining bolt with a hammer. This could cause damage to the steering shaft bearing.**

**To install:**

5. Align the index marks on the steering wheel and shaft and install the steering wheel.
6. Install a new steering wheel retaining bolt and tighten to 30–35 ft. lbs. (41–47 Nm).
7. Connect the cruise control electrical connector, if equipped.
8. Connect the horn electrical connector and install the horn pad and cover.
9. Connect the negative battery cable.

#### 1990–00 Vehicles

➧ See Figures 88 and 89

**✲✲ CAUTION**

**The air bag system must be disarmed, before working on the system. Failure to do so may result in deployment of the air bag and possible personal injury.**

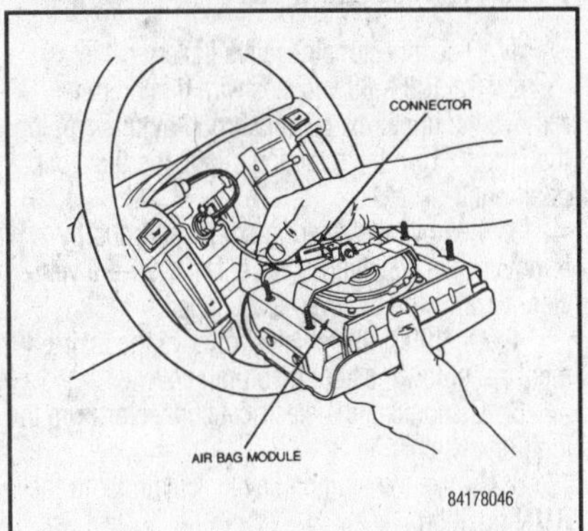


**Fig. 88 Removing the air bag module from the steering wheel**

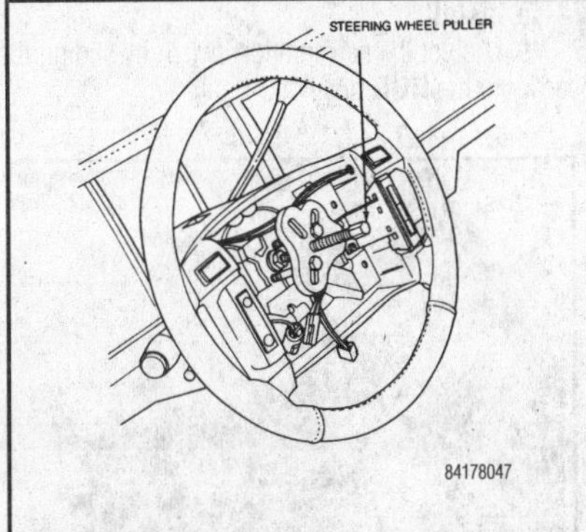


**Fig. 89 Removing the steering wheel using a puller**

1. Center the front wheels in the straight-ahead position.
2. Properly disarm the air bag system; see the procedure in Section 6.
3. Remove the 4 air bag module retaining nuts and lift the module off the steering wheel. Disconnect the air bag wire harness from the air bag module and remove the module from the steering wheel.

**✲✲ CAUTION**

**When carrying a live air bag, make sure the bag and trim cover are pointed away from the body. In the unlikely event of an accidental deployment, the bag will then deploy with minimal chance of injury. When placing a live air bag on a bench or other surface, always face the bag and trim cover up, away from the surface. This will reduce the motion of the module if it is accidentally deployed.**

4. Disconnect the cruise control wire harness from the steering wheel, if equipped.
5. Remove and discard the steering wheel bolt. Remove the steering wheel using a suitable puller. Route the contact assembly wire harness through the steering wheel as the wheel is lifted off the shaft.

**➡Do not use a knock-off type steering wheel puller or strike the retaining bolt with a hammer. This could cause damage to the steering shaft bearing.**

**To install:**

6. Make sure the front wheels are in the straight-ahead position.
7. Route the contact assembly wire harness through the steering wheel opening at the 3 o'clock position and install the steering wheel on the steering shaft. The steering wheel and shaft alignment marks should be aligned. Make sure the air bag contact wire is not pinched.
8. Install a new steering wheel retaining bolt and tighten to 23–33 ft. lbs. (31–45 Nm).
9. Connect the cruise control wire harness to the wheel and snap the connector assembly into the steering wheel clip. Make sure the wiring is not trapped between the steering wheel and contact assembly.
10. Connect the air bag wire harness to the air bag module and install the module to the steering wheel. Tighten the module retaining nuts to 24–32 inch lbs. (2.7–3.7 Nm).
11. Enable the air bag system according to the procedure in Section 6.

## Multi-Function/Combination Switch

The combination switch incorporates the turn signal, dimmer and windshield wiper switch functions on 1990–99 vehicles. The combination switch incorporates only the turn signal and dimmer function on 1988–89 vehicles. For windshield wiper switch removal and installation on 1988–89 vehicles, refer to the procedure in this Section.

### REMOVAL & INSTALLATION

#### 1988–89 Vehicles

➧ See Figure 90

1. Disconnect the negative battery cable.
2. Remove the switch lever by grasping and pulling straight out.
3. Remove the steering column cover retaining screws and remove the cover.
4. Remove the shroud retaining screws and remove the shroud.
5. With the wiring connectors exposed, carefully lift the connector retainer tabs and disconnect the connectors.
6. Remove the switch retaining screws and lift up the switch assembly.
7. Installation is the reverse of the removal procedure.

#### 1990–00 Vehicles

➧ See Figures 91, 92, 93 and 94

1. Disconnect the negative battery cable.
2. If equipped with tilt column, move to the lowest position and remove the tilt lever.

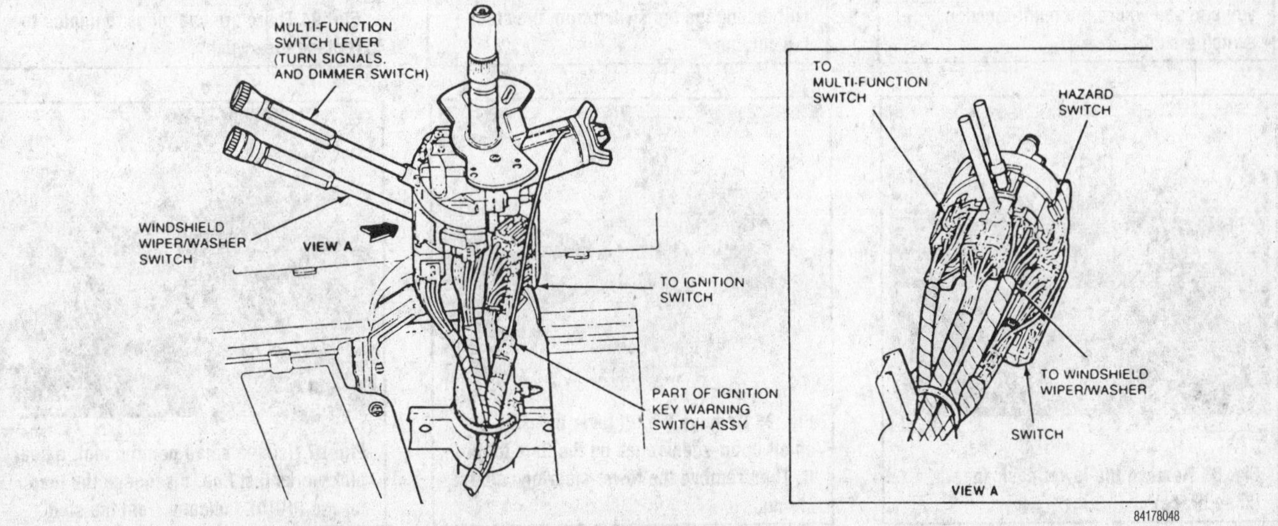


**Fig. 90 Combination switch and windshield wiper switch locations—1988 vehicles**

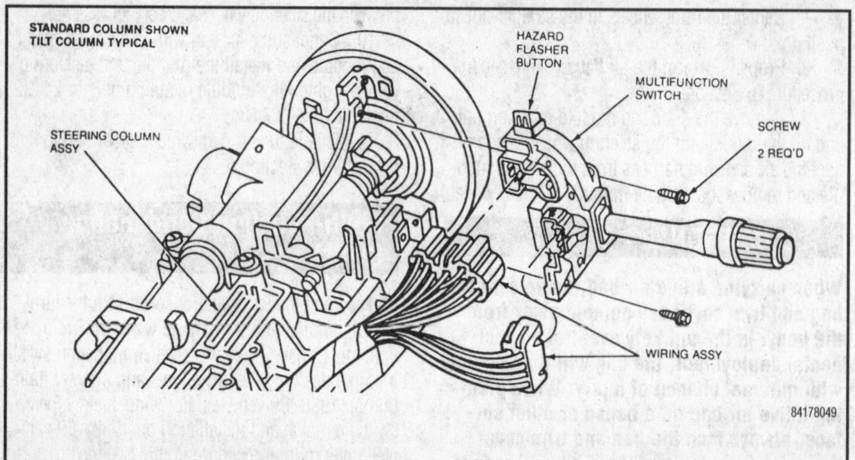

**Fig. 91 Combination switch—1990–93 vehicles**

3. Remove the ignition lock cylinder; refer to the procedure in this Section.
4. Remove the shroud screws and remove the upper and lower shrouds.
5. Remove the 2 self-tapping screws attaching the combination switch to the steering column casting and remove the switch.
6. Remove the wiring harness retainer and disconnect the 2 electrical connectors.

**To install:**

7. Installation is the reverse of the removal procedure.

## Windshield Wiper Switch

### REMOVAL & INSTALLATION

#### 1988–89 Vehicles

1. Disconnect the negative battery cable.
2. Remove the split steering column cover retaining screws.
3. Separate the halves and remove the wiper switch retaining screws.
4. Disconnect the electrical connector and remove the wiper switch.
5. The installation of the wiper switch is the reverse of the removal procedure.

## Ignition Switch

### REMOVAL & INSTALLATION

**See Figures 95 thru 105**

1. Disconnect the negative battery cable.
2. On 1988–89 vehicles with tilt column, remove the upper extension shroud by unsnapping the shroud from the retaining clip at the 9 o'clock position.
3. Remove the steering column shroud by removing the attaching screws. On 1990–99 vehicles, remove the tilt lever, if equipped.
4. On 1990–99 vehicles, remove the instrument panel lower steering column cover.
5. Disconnect the electrical connector from the ignition switch.
6. Rotate the ignition key lock cylinder to the **RUN** position.
7. Remove the 2 screws attaching the ignition switch.
8. Disengage the ignition switch from the actuator pin and remove the switch.

**To install:**

9. Adjust the new ignition switch by sliding the carrier to the **RUN** position.

93146P04

**Fig. 92 After removing the upper shroud, you can see where the multi-function switch mounts**

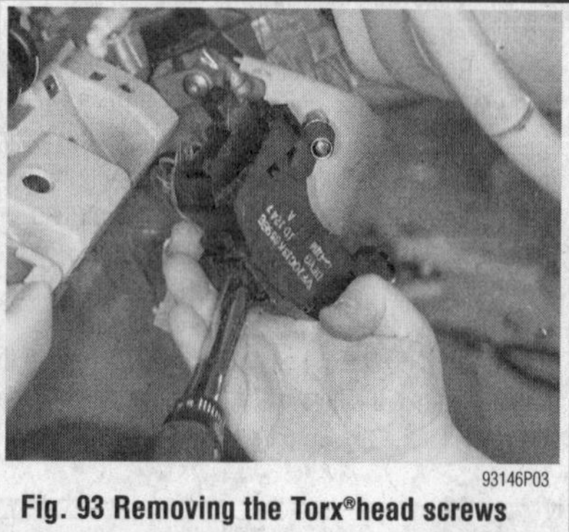
93146P03

**Fig. 93 Removing the Torx®head screws will disengage the switch from the steering column**

93146P02

**Fig. 94 There are two plugs to unplug to replace the switch**

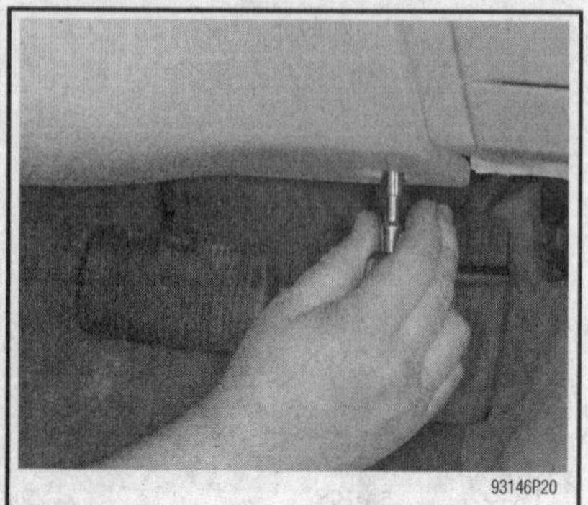
93146P20

**Fig. 95 Remove the lower dash panel (knee brace)**

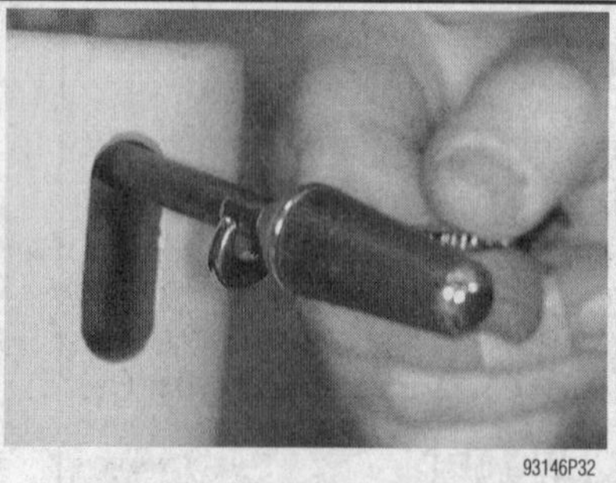
93146P32

**Fig. 96 Remove the tilt lever by using a small open-end wrench on the flats to turn it. Then remove the lower steering column shroud**

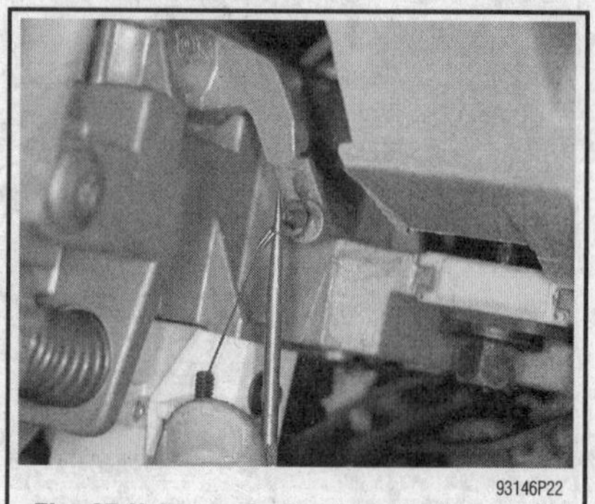
93146P22

**Fig. 97 Using a small pointed tool, a seal pick works just fine, disengage the loop for the PRNDL indicator from the stud**

**Fig. 98 Just insert the pick into the loop and allow the wire to slid down the pick**

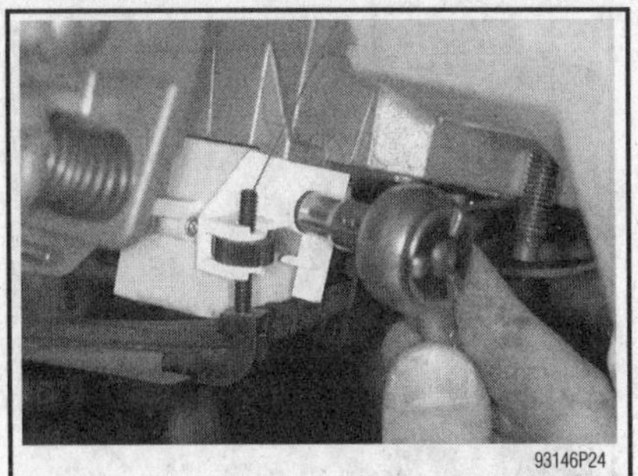


**Fig. 99 Unscrew the one retaining screw from the adjuster, although there is no reason to completely remove it from the adjusting block**

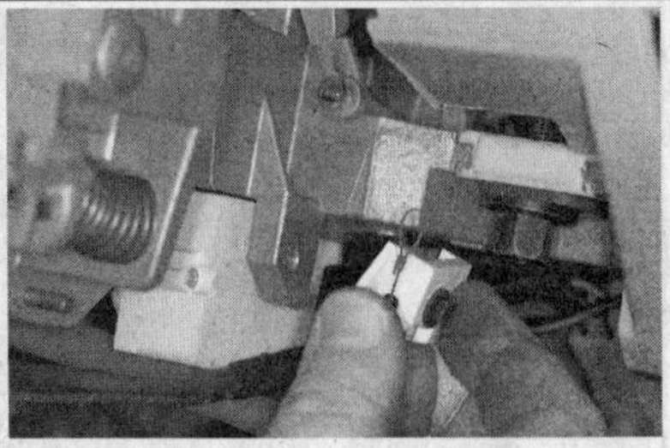


**Fig. 100 Pull it away from the column and allow it to hang out of the way. Do not allow the thumbscrew to turn and no adjustments to the PRNDL indicator should be needed on installation**

**Fig. 101 Unscrew the four nuts holding the steering column up in place. It is not necessary to totally remove all of them from the mounting studs. Just drop the column enough for working clearance**

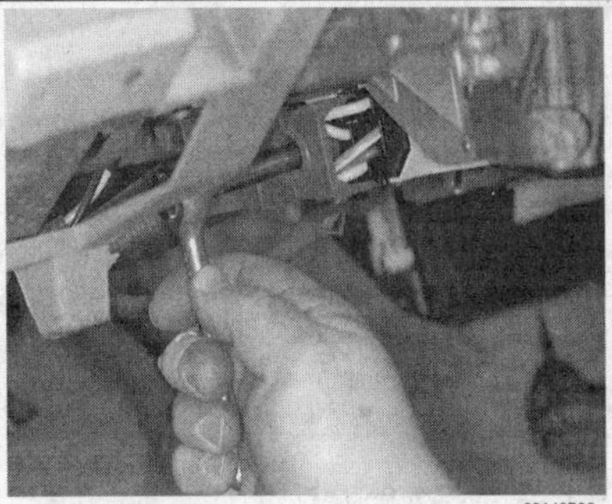


**Fig. 102 Using a small ratchet set, unbolt the electrical connector from the left side of the steering column**

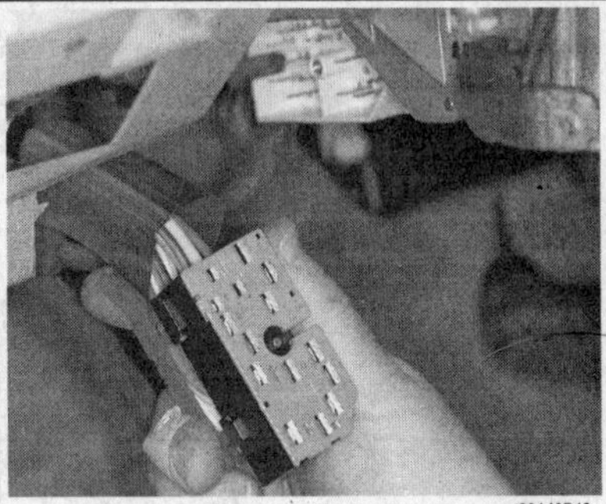


**Fig. 103 Pull gently on the connector to disengage all the terminals from the harness connector**

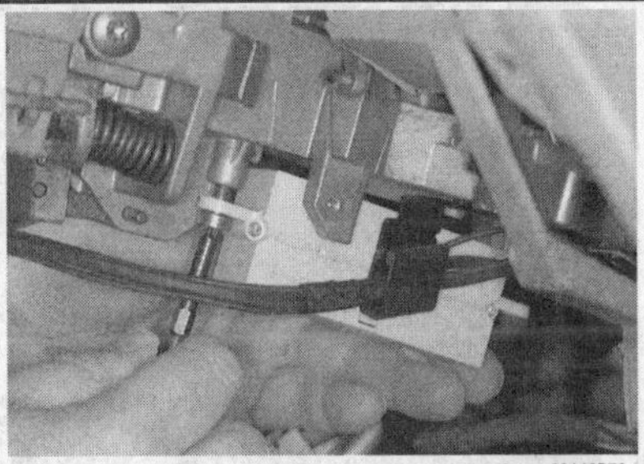


**Fig. 104 This is the right side of the steering column. It houses the ignition switch. You will need a Torx ®driver to remove the screws holding the ignition switch in place**

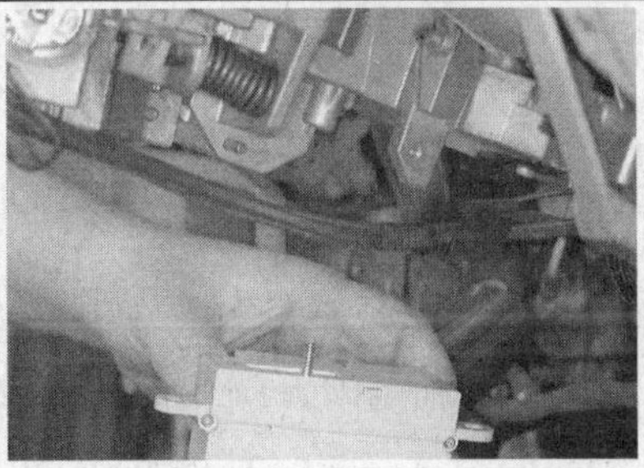


**Fig. 105 When removing the ignition switch, remember that the locator pin is in the RUNposition. Be sure to install the new one in the same position**

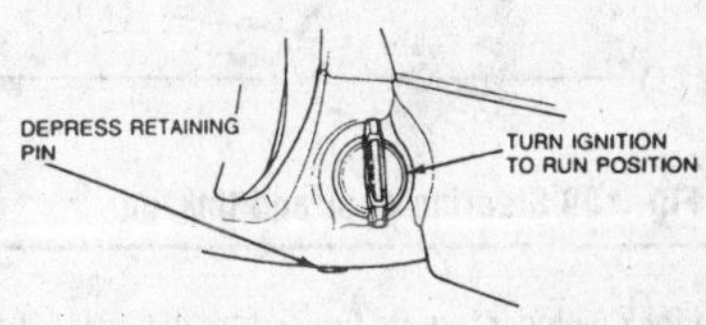


**Fig. 106 Lock cylinder removal—vehicles with functional locks**

10. Check to ensure that the ignition key lock cylinder is in the **RUN** position. The **RUN** position is achieved by rotating the key lock cylinder approximately 90 degrees from the **LOCK** position.

11. Install the ignition switch onto the actuator pin.

12. Align the switch mounting holes and install the attaching screws. Tighten the screws to 50–69 inch lbs. (5.6–7.9 Nm).

13. Connect the electrical connector to the ignition switch.

14. Connect the negative battery cable. Check the ignition switch for proper function in **START** and **ACC** positions. Make sure the column is locked in the **LOCK** position.

15. Install the remaining components in the reverse order of removal.

## Ignition Lock Cylinder

### REMOVAL & INSTALLATION

#### Functional Lock

**➧ See Figures 106, 107 and 108**

The following procedure is for vehicles with functioning lock cylinders. Ignition keys are available for these vehicles or the ignition key numbers are known and the proper key can be made.

1. Disconnect the negative battery cable. If equipped, properly disarm the air bag system; refer to Section 6.

2. On 1988 vehicles, remove the trim shroud halves by removing the attaching screws. Remove the electrical connector from the key warning switch.

3. Turn the ignition to the **RUN** position.

4. Place a ⅛ in. diameter wire pin or small drift punch in the hole in the casting surrounding the lock cylinder and depress the retaining pin while pulling out on the lock cylinder to remove it from the column housing.

**To install:**

5. To install the lock cylinder, turn it to the **RUN** position and depress the retaining pin. Insert

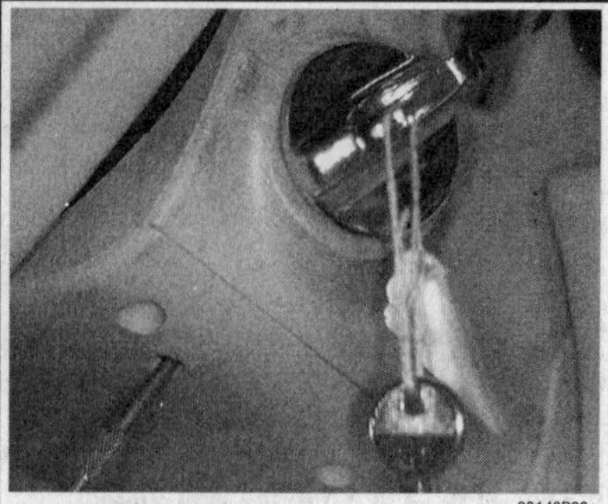

93148P39

**Fig. 107 Move the key to the RUN position, insert a probe or small diameter tool into the access hole to depress the button**

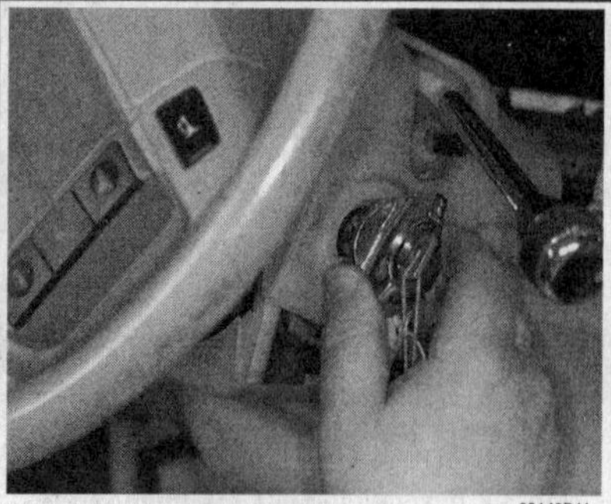

93148P41

**Fig. 108 Once the button is depressed, you can pull the lock switch out of the steering column housing**

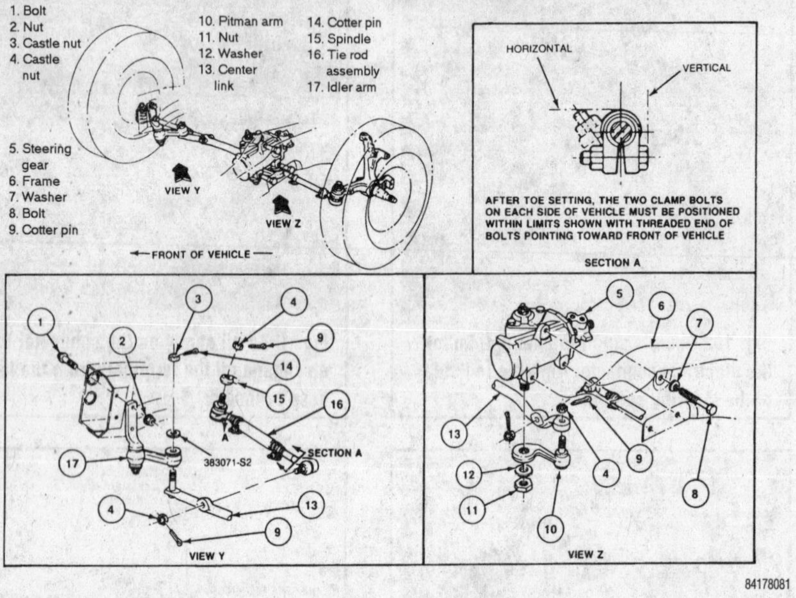


**Fig. 109 Steering gear and linkage**

the lock cylinder into its housing in the lock cylinder casting.

6. Make sure the cylinder is fully seated and aligned in the interlocking washer before turning the key to the **OFF** position. This action will permit the cylinder retaining pin to extend into the hole in the lock cylinder housing.

7. Using the ignition key, rotate the cylinder to ensure the correct mechanical operation in all positions.

8. Check for proper start in **P** or **N**. Also make sure the start circuit cannot be actuated in **D** or **R** positions and that the column is locked in the **LOCK** position.

9. Connect the key warning buzzer electrical connector and install the trim shrouds, if required.

#### Non-Functional Lock

The following procedure is for vehicles with non-functioning locks. On these vehicles, the lock cylinder cannot be rotated due to a lost or broken key, the key number is not known, or the lock cylinder cap is damaged and/or broken, preventing the lock cylinder from rotating.

1. Disconnect the negative battery cable. If equipped, properly disarm the air bag system; refer to Section 6.

2. Remove the steering wheel; refer to the procedure in this Section.

3. On 1988–89 vehicles, remove the trim shroud halves by removing the attaching screws. Remove the electrical connector from the key warning switch.

4. On 1988–90 vehicles, drill out the retaining pin using a ⅛ in. diameter drill, being careful not to drill deeper than ½ in. Position a chisel at the base of the ignition lock cylinder. Strike the chisel with sharp blows, using a hammer, to break the cap away from the lock cylinder.

5. On 1991–99 vehicles, use channel lock or vise grip type pliers to twist the lock cylinder cap until it separates from the lock cylinder.

6. Drill approximately 1¾ in. into the middle of the ignition key slot, using a ⅜ in. diameter drill bit. Drill until the lock cylinder breaks loose from the breakaway base of the lock cylinder. Remove the lock cylinder and drill shavings from the lock cylinder housing.

7. Remove the snapring or retainer, washer, and steering column lock gear. Thoroughly clean all drill shavings and other foreign materials from the casting.

8. Inspect the lock cylinder housing for damage and replace, as necessary.

**To install:**

9. Install the ignition lock cylinder and check for smooth operation.

10. Connect the electrical connector to the key warning switch and install the trim shrouds, if necessary.

11. Install the steering wheel and connect the negative battery cable.

## Steering Linkage

**➧ See Figure 109**

### REMOVAL & INSTALLATION

#### Pitman Arm

**➧ See Figures 110 thru 116**

1. Position the front wheels in the straight-ahead position.

2. Raise and safely support the vehicle.

3. Remove and discard the cotter pin from the castellated nut that attaches the center link to the pitman arm. Remove the castellated nut.

4. Disconnect the center link from the pitman arm using removal tool 3290–D or equivalent.

5. Remove the pitman arm retaining nut and lockwasher

6. Make sure the front wheel are in the straight-ahead position. Remove the pitman arm from the steering gear sector shaft using pitman arm puller T64P–3590–F or equivalent.

89608P35

**Fig. 110 Remove and discard the cotter pin from the castellated nut that attaches the center link to the pitman arm**

89608P36

**Fig. 111 Remove the castellated nut**

89608P30

Fig. 112 A large deepwell socket, typically 1 5/16 in., is needed to remove the pitman arm retaining nut

89608P31

Fig. 113 Remove the pitman arm retaining nut and lockwasher

89608P32

Fig. 114 Install a suitable pitman arm puller onto the pitman arm

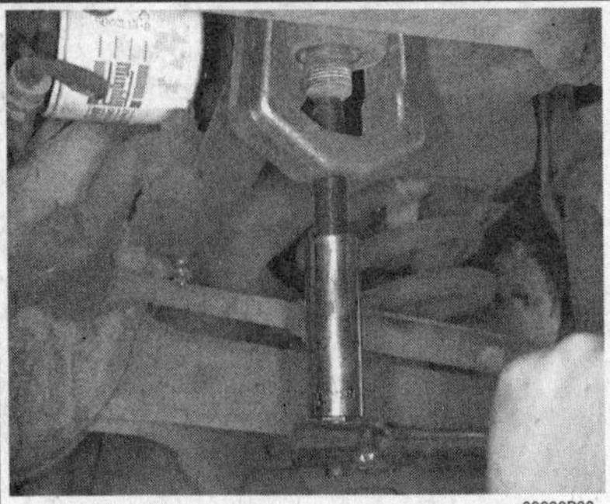

89608P33

Fig. 115 Carefully tighten the puller's forcing screw until the pitman arm breaks loose

89608P34

Fig. 116 Remove the pitman arm from the steering gear sector shaft

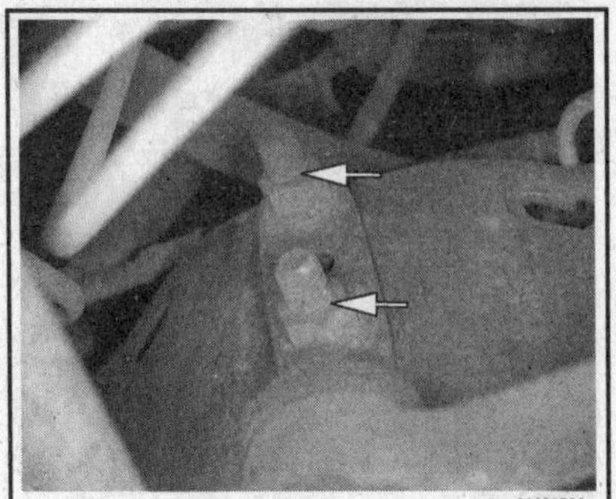

89608P26

Fig. 117 Remove the bolts and nuts holding the idler arm to the frame

**To install:**

7. With the front wheels in the straight-ahead position, place the pitman arm, pointing it rearward, on the sector shaft. Align the blind tooth on the pitman arm with the blind tooth on the steering gear sector shaft.

8. Install the nut and lockwasher and tighten to 233–250 ft. lbs. (316–338 Nm).

9. Install the center link on the pitman arm and install the castellated nut. Tighten the nut to 43–47 ft. lbs. (59–63 Nm) and install a new cotter pin.

**➡If, after the nut has been torqued, the nut castellations and stud hole do not align for cotter pin installation, tighten the nut further until the cotter pin can be installed. Never back off the nut.**

10. Lower the vehicle.

### Idler Arm

**➧ See Figure 117**

1. Raise and safely support the vehicle.

2. Remove the cotter pin, nut, and washer retaining the center link to the idler arm. Discard the cotter pin.

3. Remove the center link from the idler arm.

4. Remove the bolts and nuts holding the idler arm to the frame and remove the idler arm.

**To install:**

5. Install the idler arm to the frame with the bolts and nuts. Tighten to 85–97 ft. lbs. (115–132 Nm).

6. Place the idler arm and front wheels in the straight-ahead position to maintain steering wheel alignment and prevent bushing damage.

7. Install the center link nut and washer and tighten to 43–47 ft. lbs. (59–63 Nm). Install a new cotter pin.

**➡If, after the nut has been torqued, the nut castellations and stud hole do not align for cotter pin installation, tighten the nut further until the cotter pin can be installed. Never back off the nut.**

8. Lower the vehicle.

### Center Link

**➧ See Figure 118**

1. Raise and safely support the vehicle.

2. Remove the cotter pins and nuts that attach the inner tie rod ends to the center link. Discard the cotter pins.

3. Disconnect the inner tie rod ends from the center link using removal tool 3290–D or equivalent.

4. Remove the cotter pin and nut that retains the pitman arm to the center link. Disconnect the pitman arm from the center link using removal tool 3290–D or equivalent.

5. Remove the cotter pin and nut retaining the idler arm to the center link and remove the center link. Discard the cotter pin.

**To install:**

6. Position the center link to the pitman arm and idler arm and loosely install the nuts. Place the idler arm and front wheels in the straight-ahead position to maintain steering wheel alignment and prevent bushing damage. Tighten the nuts to 43–47 ft. lbs. (59–63 Nm) and install new cotter pins.

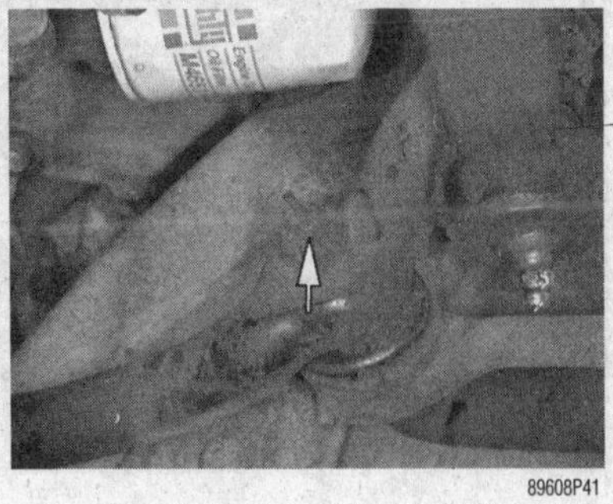

89608P41

Fig. 118 Remove the cotter pins and nuts that attach the inner tie rod ends to the center link

**➡If, after the nut has been torqued, the nut castellations and stud hole do not align for cotter pin installation, tighten the nut further until the cotter pin can be installed. Never back off the nut.**

7. Install the tie rode ends on the center link and tighten the nuts to 43–47 ft. lbs. (59–63 Nm). Install new cotter pins.

8. Lower the vehicle.

9. Check the toe and adjust, if necessary.

### Tie Rod Ends

➧ See Figures 119 thru 125

1. Raise and support the vehicle safely.
2. Remove the cotter pin and nut from the tie rod end ball stud.
3. Loosen the tie rod adjusting sleeve clamp bolts and remove the rod end from the spindle arm or center link, using removal tool 3290–D or equivalent.
4. Remove the tie rod end from the sleeve, counting the exact number of turns required doing so. Discard all parts removed from the sleeve.

**To install:**

5. Install the new tie rod end into the sleeve, using the exact number of turns it took to remove the old one. Install the tie rod end ball stud into the spindle arm or center link.
6. Install the stud nut. Tighten to 43–47 ft. lbs. (59–63 Nm) and install a new cotter pin.

**➡If, after the nut has been torqued, the nut castellations and stud hole do not align for cotter pin installation, tighten the nut further until the cotter pin can be installed. Never back off the nut.**

7. Check the toe and adjust if necessary. Loosen the clamps from the sleeve and oil the sleeve, clamps, bolts, and nuts. Position the adjusting sleeve clamps as shown in the figure, then tighten the clamp nuts to 20–22 ft. lbs. (27–29 Nm).

## Power Steering Gear

### REMOVAL & INSTALLATION

➧ See Figure 126

1. Disconnect the negative battery cable.
2. Remove the stone shield.
3. Tag the pressure and return lines so they may be reassembled in their original positions.
4. Disconnect the pressure and return lines from the steering gear. Plug the lines and ports in the gear to prevent the entry of dirt.
5. Remove the clamp bolts retaining the flexible coupling to the steering gear.
6. Raise and safely support the vehicle.

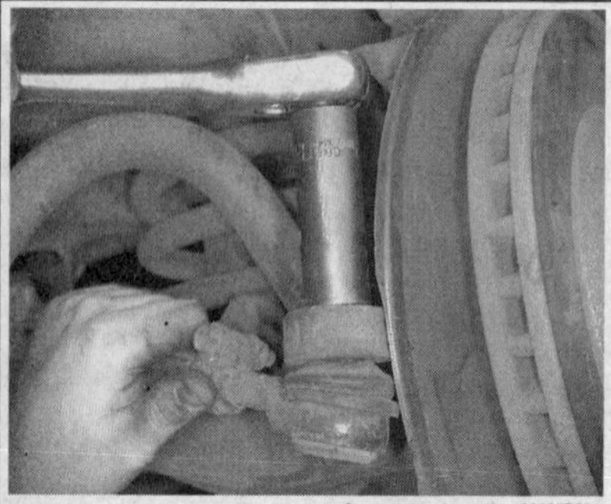

89608P37

**Fig. 119 Remove the tie rod end-to-steering knuckle retaining nut**

89608P38

**Fig. 120 A special removal tool like this one from Lisle® can be used to remove the tie rod end from the knuckle. Just install the tool on the tie rod end and tighten the forcing screw to . . .**

89608P39

**Fig. 121 . . . remove the tie rod end from the knuckle**

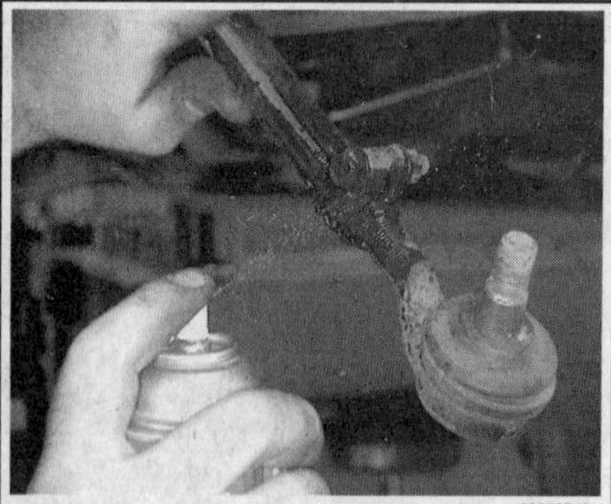

89608P40

**Fig. 122 Spraying a quality rust penetrant onto the tie rod adjusting sleeve is a good idea before attempting to remove it**

89608P42

**Fig. 123 Loosen the adjusting sleeve bolt**

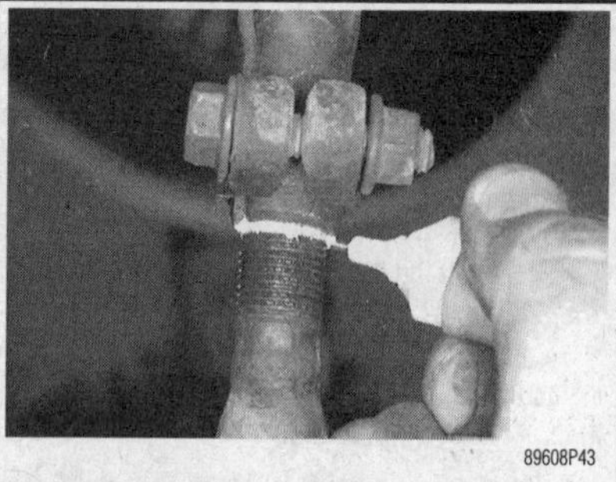

89608P43

**Fig. 124 Mark the tie rod end before removal to ensure reinstallation as close as possible to the previous alignment position**

89608P44

**Fig. 125 Grasp the tie rod end with a pair of pliers or other suitable tool and slowly turn it out of the adjusting sleeve to remove it**

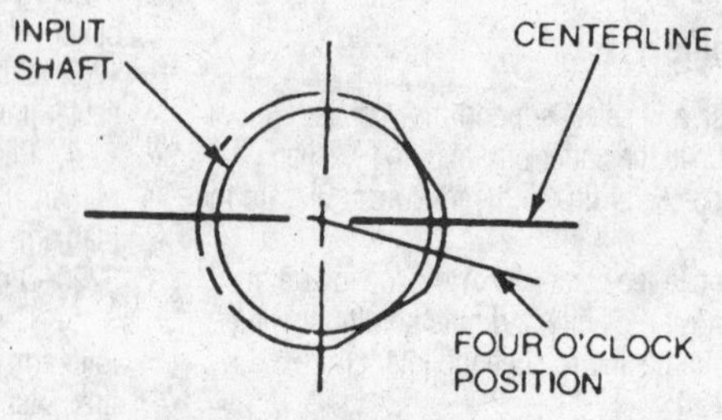


84178085

**Fig. 126 During installation, position the steering gear input shaft as shown on 1992–00 vehicles**

7. Remove the nut from the sector shaft.
8. Remove the pitman arm from the sector shaft with pitman arm removal tool T64P–3590–F or equivalent. Remove the tool from the pitman arm.

**⁂ WARNING**

**Do not damage the seals and/or gear housing. Do not use a non-approved tool such as a pickle fork.**

9. Support the steering gear and remove the steering gear retaining bolts.
10. Work the gear free of the flex coupling and remove the gear.
11. If the flex coupling did not come off with the gear, lift it off the shaft.

**To install:**

12. Turn the steering wheel to the straight-ahead position.
13. Center the steering gear input shaft with the indexing flat facing downward on 1989–91 vehicles. On 1992–98 vehicles, center the steering gear input shaft with the centerline of the 2 indexing flats at 4 o'clock.
14. Slide the steering gear input shaft into the flex coupling and into place on the frame side rail. Install the retaining bolts and tighten to 50–65 ft. lbs. (68–88 Nm).
15. Make sure the wheels are in the straight-ahead position. Install the pitman arm on the sector shaft and install the lockwasher and nut. Tighten the nut to 233–250 ft. lbs. (316–338 Nm).
16. Move the flex coupling into place on the steering gear input shaft. Install the retaining bolt and tighten to 20–30 ft. lbs. (27–41 Nm).
17. Connect the pressure and return lines to the steering gear and tighten the lines. Fill the reservoir and turn the steering wheel from stop-to-stop to distribute the fluid. Check the fluid level and add fluid, if necessary.
18. Start the engine and turn the steering wheel from left to right.
19. Check for leaks.
20. Install the stone shield.

## Power Steering Pump

### REMOVAL & INSTALLATION

**➧ See Figures 127 and 128**

1. Disconnect the negative battery cable.
2. Disconnect the fluid return hose at the pump and drain the fluid into a container.
3. Remove the pressure hose from the pump and, if necessary, drain the fluid into a container. Do not remove the fitting from the pump.
4. Disconnect the belt from the pulley. On 5.0L engines, use pulley removal tool T69L–10300–B or equivalent, to remove the pulley.
5. Remove the mounting bolts and remove the pump.

**To install:**

6. On 5.0L engines, place the pump on the mounting bracket and install the bolts at the front of the pump. Tighten to 30–45 ft. lbs. (40–62 Nm).
7. On 4.6L engines, place the pump on the mounting bosses of the engine block and install the bolts at the side of the pump. Tighten to 15–22 ft. lbs. (20–30 Nm).

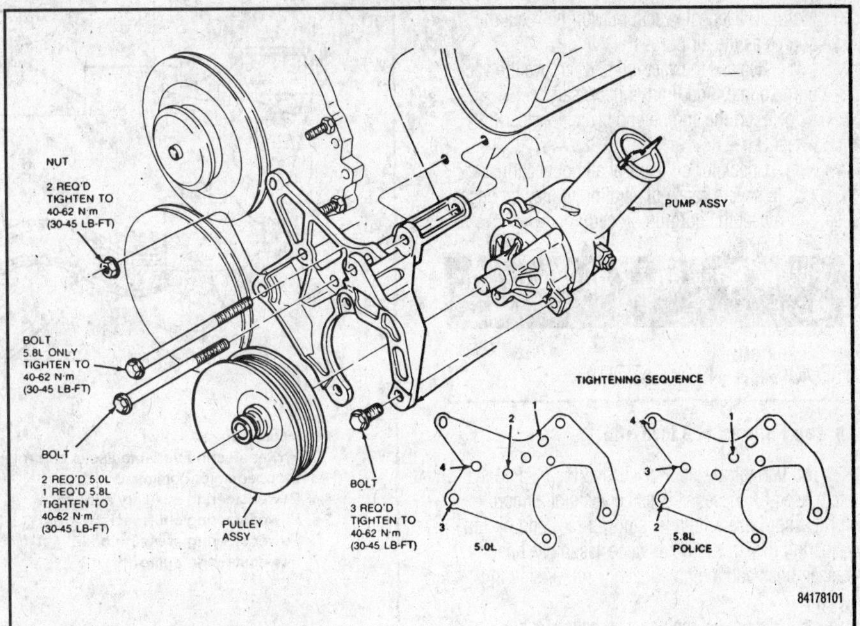


**Fig. 127 Power steering pump—5.0L**

8. On 5.0L engines, install the pump pulley using pulley replacer tool T65P–3A733–C or equivalent.
9. Place the belt on the pump pulley and adjust the tension, if necessary.
10. Install the pressure hose to the pump fitting. Tighten the tube nut with a tube nut wrench rather than with an open-end wrench. Tighten to 20–25 ft. lbs. (27–34 Nm) on 1989–91 vehicles or 35–45 ft. lbs. (47–60 Nm) on 1992–98 vehicles.

**➡Do not overtighten this fitting. Swivel and/or end play of the fitting is normal and does not indicate a loose fitting. Over-tightening the tube nut can collapse the tube nut wall, resulting in a leak and requiring replacement of the entire pressure hose assembly. Use of an open-end wrench to tighten the nut can deform the tube nut hex, which may result in improper torque and may make further servicing of the system difficult.**

11. Connect the return hose to the pump and tighten the clamp.
12. Fill the reservoir with the proper type and quantity of fluid.
13. Bleed the air from the system.

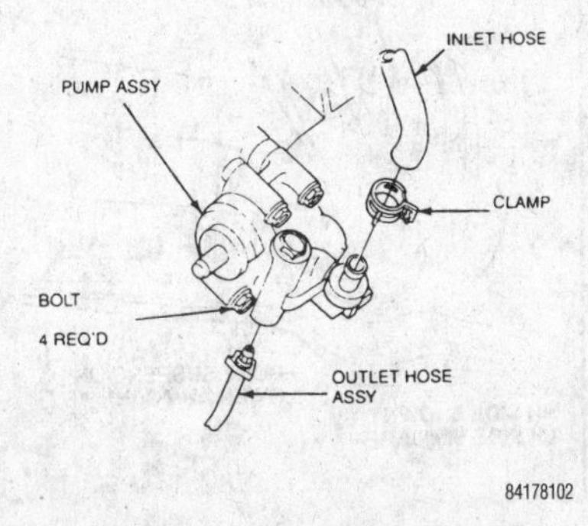


**Fig. 128 Power steering pump—4.6L engine**

### BLEEDING

1. Disconnect the ignition coil.
2. Raise and safely support the vehicle so the front wheels are off the floor.
3. Fill the power steering fluid reservoir.
4. Crank the engine with the starter and add fluid until the level remains constant.
5. While cranking the engine, rotate the steering wheel from lock-to-lock.

**➡The front wheels must be off the floor during lock-to-lock rotation of the steering wheel.**

6. Check the fluid level and add fluid, if necessary.
7. Connect the ignition coil wire. Start the engine and allow it to run for several minutes.
8. Rotate the steering wheel from lock-to-lock.
9. Shut off the engine and check the fluid level. Add fluid, if necessary.
10. If air is still present in the system, purge the system of air using power steering pump air evacuator tool 021–00014 or equivalent, as follows:
    a. Make sure the power steering pump reservoir is full to the COLD FULL mark on the dipstick or to just above the minimum indication on the reservoir.
    b. Tightly insert the rubber stopper of the air evacuator assembly into the pump reservoir fill neck.
    c. Apply 15 in. Hg maximum vacuum on the pump reservoir for a minimum of 3 minutes with the engine idling. As air purges from the system, vacuum will fall off. Maintain adequate vacuum with the vacuum source.
    d. Release the vacuum and remove the vacuum source. Fill the reservoir to the COLD FULL mark or to just above the minimum indication on the reservoir.
    e. With the engine idling, apply 15 in. Hg vacuum to the pump reservoir. Slowly cycle the steering wheel from lock-to-lock every 30 seconds for approximately 5 minutes. Do not hold the steering wheel on the stops while cycling.

Maintain adequate vacuum with the vacuum source as the air purges.

f. Release the vacuum and remove the vacuum source. Add fluid, if necessary.

g. Start the engine and cycle the steering wheel.

h. Check for oil leaks at all connections.

11. In severe cases of aeration, it may be necessary to repeat the purging procedure.

## Power Rack and Pinion Steering Gear

### REMOVAL & INSTALLATION

**➧ See Figures 129 thru 135**

The Variable Assist Power Steering (VAPS) system used on these vehicles consists of a microprocessor based module, a power rack and pinion steering gear, an actuator valve assembly, hose assemblies and a high efficiency power steering pump.

1. Disconnect the negative battery cable.
2. From inside the vehicle, remove the nuts securing the steering column tube boot to the cowl panel.
3. Remove the two bolts retaining the steering column gear input shaft coupling to the power steering gear shaft and yoke assembly.
4. Set the steering column tube boot aside. Remove the pinch bolt at the power steering gear shaft and yoke assembly, then remove the steering column gear input shaft coupling.
5. Raise the vehicle and support safely. Remove the front wheel and tire assemblies. Support the vehicle under the rear edge of the subframe with jack stands.
6. Remove the tie rod cotter pins and nuts. Remove the left and right-side tie rod ends from the steering knuckle.
7. Mark the position of the jam nut (to maintain the alignment), then remove the tie rod ends from the spindle tie rod.
8. Remove the nuts from the gear-to-subframe attaching bolts.
9. Remove the rear subframe-to-body attaching bolts.
10. Remove the exhaust pipe-to-catalytic converter attachment.
11. Lower the vehicle carefully until the sub-

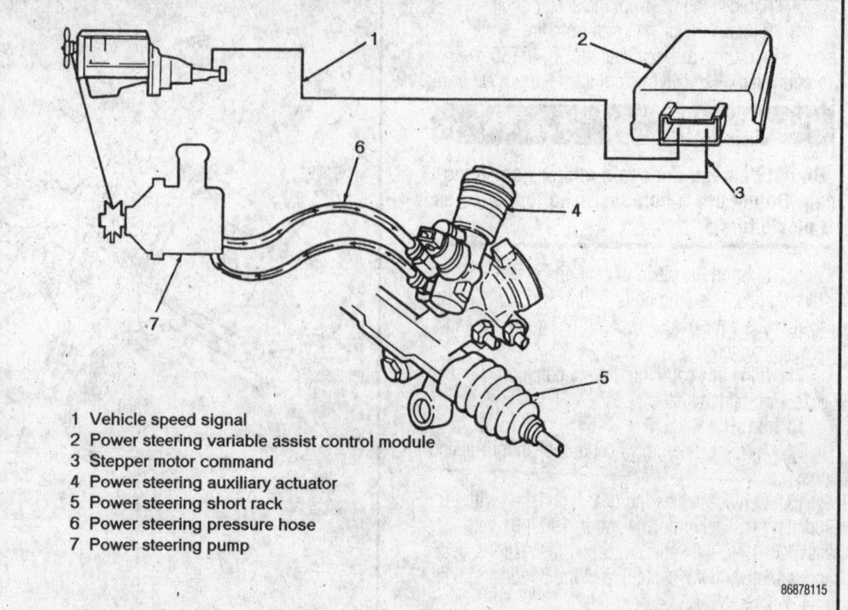


**Fig. 129 View of the Variable Assist Power Steering (VAPS) system components**

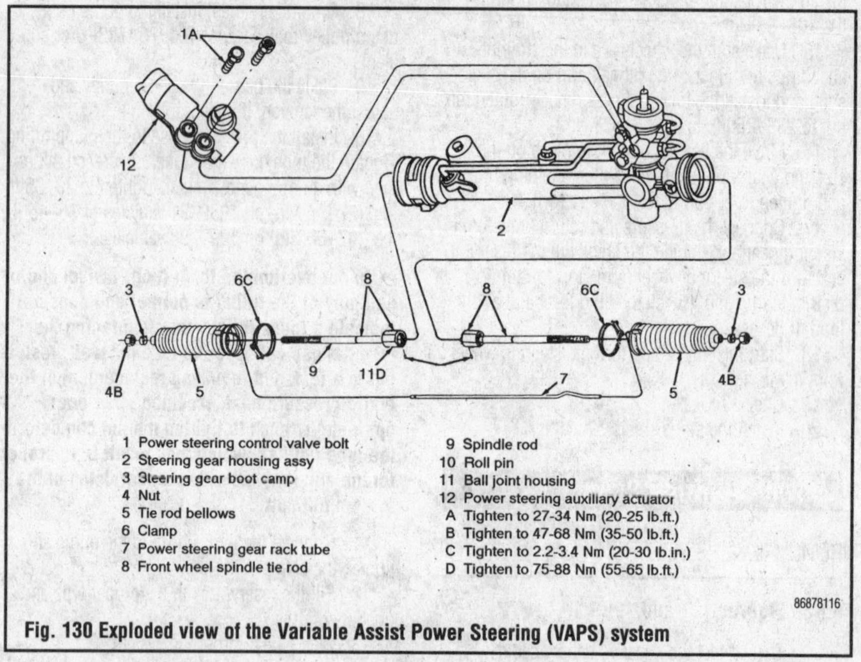


**Fig. 130 Exploded view of the Variable Assist Power Steering (VAPS) system**

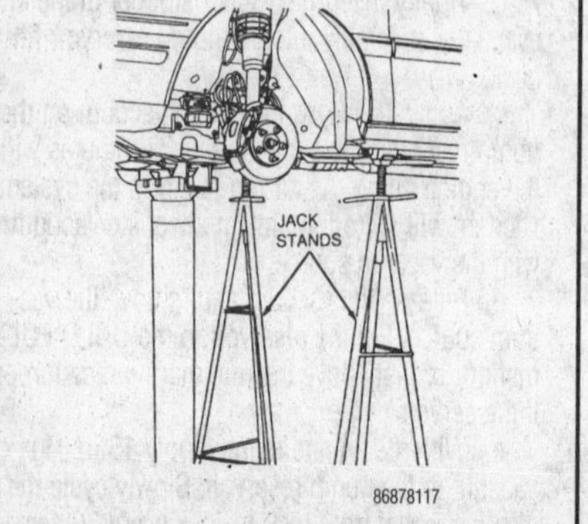


**Fig. 131 Support the vehicle under the rear edge of the subframe with jack stands**

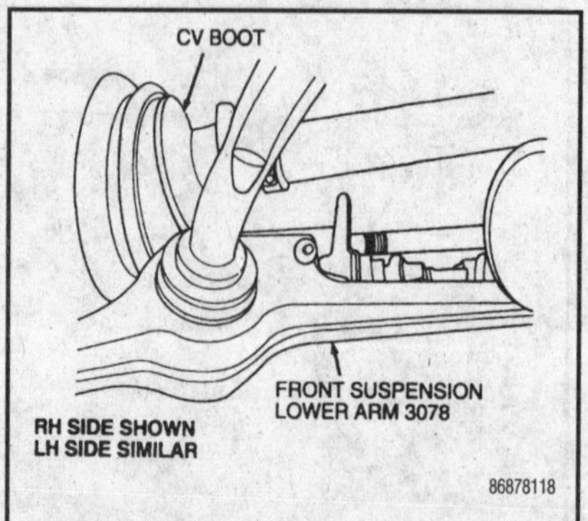


**Fig. 132 Remove the nuts from the gear-to-subframe attaching bolts**

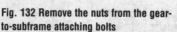

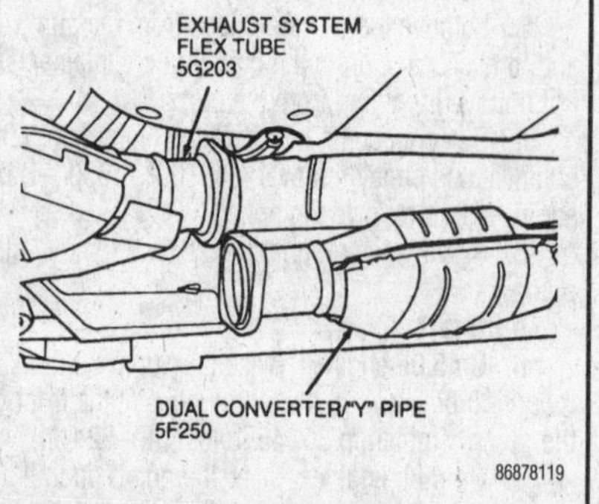


**Fig. 133 Remove the exhaust pipe-to-catalytic converter attachment**

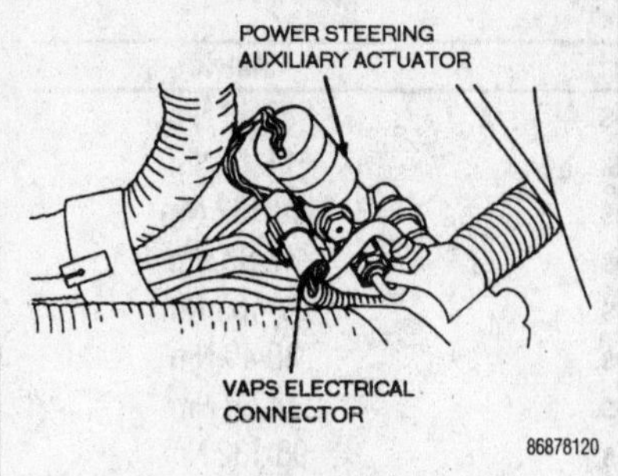


**Fig. 134 Disengage the VAPS electrical connectors from the actuator assembly**

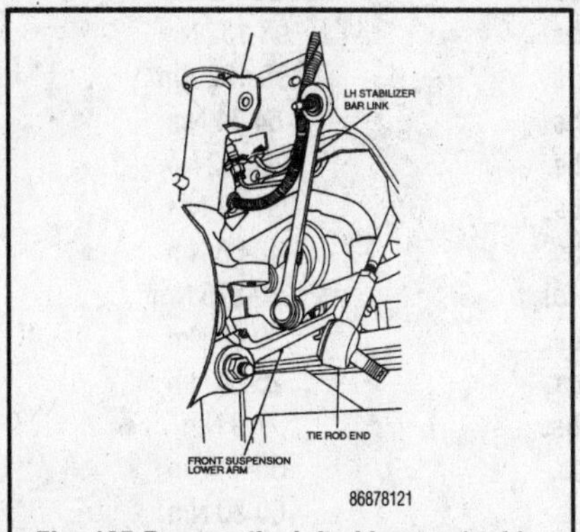


**Fig. 135 Remove the left-side sway/stabilizer bar link**

frame separates from the body approximately 4 in. (102 mm).

12. Remove the heat shield band, then fold the shield down.

13. Disengage the VAPS electrical connectors from the actuator assembly.

14. Rotate the gear to clear the bolts from the subframe and pull to the left to facilitate line fitting removal.

15. Position a suitable drain pan under the vehicle, then remove the line fittings. Remove the O-rings from the fitting connections, then replace with new ones during installation.

16. Remove the left-hand side sway/stabilizer bar link.

17. Remove the steering gear assembly through the left wheel well.

**To install:**

18. Install new Teflon® O-rings into the line fittings.

19. Place the gear attachment bolts in the gear housing.

20. Install the steering gear assembly through the left wheel well.

21. Connect and tighten the line fittings to the steering gear assembly.

22. Engage the VAPS electrical connectors.

23. Position the steering gear into the subframe.

24. Install the tie rod ends onto the front wheel spindle tie rod.

25. Install the heat shield band.

26. Attach the tie rod ends onto the knuckle. Install the nuts and secure with new cotter pins.

27. Attach the sway/stabilizer bar link.

28. Raise the vehicle until the subframe contacts the body. Install the rear subframe attaching bolts.

29. Install the gear-to-front subframe nuts, then tighten to 85–100 ft. lbs. (115–135 Nm).

30. Attach the exhaust pipe to the catalytic converter.

31. Install the wheels, then remove the jackstands, and carefully lower the vehicle. Tighten the lug nuts to 85–105 ft. lbs. (115–142 Nm).

32. From inside the vehicle, push the steering column tube boot end out of the vehicle, then install over the steering gear housing.

33. Install the steering column gear input shaft coupling to the power steering gear shaft and yoke assembly. Tighten the bolt to 30–38 ft. lbs. (41–51 Nm).

34. Install the inner steering column tube boot to the cowl panel.

35. Install the input shaft coupling to the steering gear shaft and yoke assembly.

36. Fill the power steering system with Premium Power Steering Fluid E6AZ-19582-AA or equivalent.

37. Bleed the power steering system. For details, please refer to the procedure located later in this section.

38. Connect the negative battery cable, then check the system for leaks and proper operation.

39. If necessary, have the alignment checked by a reputable repair shop.

## TORQUE SPECIFICATIONS

| Components | English | Metric |
|---|---|---|
| Front strut top mount-to-body nut | 23-29 ft. lbs. | 30-40 Nm |
| Air bag retaining screws | 8-10 ft. lbs. | 11-13 Nm |
| Front tension strut-to-body nut | 73-97 ft. lbs. | 98-132 Nm |
| Front stabilizer link-to-bar nuts | 35-46 ft. lbs. | 47-63 Nm |
| Front stabilizer link-to-strut nuts | 57-75 ft. lbs. | 77-103 Nm |
| Front stabilizer U-bracket | 23-29 ft. lbs. | 30-40 Nm |
| Front height sensor service stud | 11-14 ft. lbs. | 14-20 Nm |
| Strut-to-knuckle retaining nuts | 73-97 ft. lbs. | 98-132 Nm |
| Tension strut-to-subframe | 73-97 ft. lbs. | 98-132 Nm |
| Tension strut-to-control arm | 73-97 ft. lbs. | 98-132 Nm |
| Control arm-to-knuckle retaining nut | 39-53 ft. lbs. | 53-72 Nm |
| Control arm-to-subframe bolts | 73-97 ft. lbs. | 98-132 Nm |
| Front strut-to-spindle bolt | 73-97 ft. lbs. | 98-132 Nm |
| Front control arm-to-spindle nut | 40-52 ft. lbs. | 54-71 Nm |
| Front tension strut-to-spindle nut | 73-97 ft. lbs. | 98-132 Nm |
| Tie rod end-to-steering knuckle nut | 23-25 ft. lbs. | 31-47 Nm |
| Tie rod end jam nuts | 35-50 ft. lbs. | 48-68 Nm |
| Hub nut | 170-202 ft. lbs. | 230-275 Nm |
| Rear control arm-to-spindle nuts | 45-59 ft. lbs. | 60-80 Nm |
| Rear strut top mount-to-body nut | 20-25 ft. lbs. | 26-34 Nm |
| Rear stabilizer link-to-strut nut | 62-79 in. lbs. | 7-9 Nm |
| Rear stabilizer U-bracket bolt | 27-32 ft. lbs. | 36-44 Nm |
| Rear strut-to-spindle bolt | 45-59 ft. lbs. | 60-80 Nm |
| Rear tension strut-to-spindle nut | 35-46 ft. lbs. | 47-63 Nm |
| Rear control arm-to-body nut | 51-67 ft. lbs. | 68-92 Nm |
| Wheel lug nuts | 80-105 ft. lbs. | 115-142 Nm |
| Power rack and pinion | | |
| Rack-to-subframe retaining bolts | 85-105 ft. lbs. | 115-142 Nm |
| Power steering hose unions | 23 ft. lbs. | 31 Nm |
| Power steering pump | | |
| Pressure hose fitting | 25-34 ft. lbs. | 34-47 Nm |
| Pump retaining bolts | 30-45 ft. lbs. | 40-62 Nm |
| Intermediate shaft-to-steering gear retaining bolt | 30-38 ft. lbs. | 41-51 Nm |
| VAPS actuator-to-rack | 20-25 ft. lbs. | 27-34 Nm |
| Steering wheel retaining bolt | 37 ft. lbs. | 50 Nm |
| Steering yoke-to-steering gear shaft retaining bolt | 15-20 ft. lbs. | 20-27 Nm |
| Subframe bolts | 81-110 ft. lbs. | 110-150 Nm |
| Wheel lug nuts | 62 ft. lbs. | 85 Nm |
| Inner tie rod-to-rack | 55-65 ft. lbs. | 75-88 Nm |

93148C01

**BRAKE OPERATING SYSTEM 9-2**
BASIC OPERATING PRINCIPLES 9-2
DISC BRAKES 9-2
DRUM BRAKES 9-2
POWER BOOSTERS 9-3
BRAKE LIGHT SWITCH 9-3
REMOVAL & INSTALLATION 9-3
MASTER CYLINDER 9-3
REMOVAL & INSTALLATION 9-3
BRAKE PRESSURE CONTROL VALVE 9-4
REMOVAL & INSTALLATION 9-4
METERING VALVE 9-4
REMOVAL & INSTALLATION 9-4
BLEEDING THE BRAKE SYSTEM 9-4
**DISC BRAKES 9-5**
BRAKE PADS 9-5
REMOVAL & INSTALLATION 9-5
INSPECTION 9-7
BRAKE CALIPER 9-7
REMOVAL & INSTALLATION 9-7
BRAKE DISC (ROTOR) 9-8
REMOVAL & INSTALLATION 9-8
INSPECTION 9-9
**DRUM BRAKES 9-10**
BRAKE DRUMS 9-11
REMOVAL & INSTALLATION 9-11
INSPECTION 9-11
BRAKE SHOES 9-11
INSPECTION 9-11
REMOVAL & INSTALLATION 9-11
ADJUSTMENTS 9-14
WHEEL CYLINDERS 9-14
INSPECTION 9-14
REMOVAL & INSTALLATION 9-14
**PARKING BRAKE 9-15**
BRAKE SHOES (PARKING) 9-15
REMOVAL & INSTALLATION 9-15
**ANTI-LOCK BRAKE SYSTEM 9-16**
GENERAL INFORMATION 9-16
SYSTEM COMPONENTS 9-16
ABS MODULE 9-16
REMOVAL & INSTALLATION 9-16
HYDRAULIC CONTROL UNIT 9-17
REMOVAL & INSTALLATION 9-17
SPEED SENSORS 9-17
REMOVAL & INSTALLATION 9-17
BLEEDING THE ABS SYSTEM 9-19
**COMPONENT LOCATIONS**
REAR DRUM BRAKE COMPONENTS 9-10
**SPECIFICATIONS CHART**
BRAKE SPECIFICATIONS 9-20

# 9

# BRAKES

BRAKE OPERATING SYSTEM 9-2
DISC BRAKES 9-5
DRUM BRAKES 9-10
PARKING BRAKE 9-15
ANTI-LOCK BRAKE SYSTEM 9-16

# BRAKE OPERATING SYSTEM

## Basic Operating Principles

Hydraulic systems are used to actuate the brakes of all modern automobiles. The system transports the power required to force the frictional surfaces of the braking system together from the pedal to the individual brake units at each wheel. A hydraulic system is used for two reasons.

First, fluid under pressure can be carried to all parts of an automobile by small pipes and flexible hoses without taking up a significant amount of room or posing routing problems.

Second, a great mechanical advantage can be given to the brake pedal end of the system, and the foot pressure required to actuate the brakes can be reduced by making the surface area of the master cylinder pistons smaller than that of any of the pistons in the wheel cylinders or calipers.

The master cylinder consists of a fluid reservoir along with a double cylinder and piston assembly. Double type master cylinders are designed to separate the front and rear braking systems hydraulically in case of a leak. The master cylinder coverts mechanical motion from the pedal into hydraulic pressure within the lines. This pressure is translated back into mechanical motion at the wheels by either the wheel cylinder (drum brakes) or the caliper (disc brakes).

Steel lines carry the brake fluid to a point on the vehicle's frame near each of the vehicle's wheels. The fluid is then carried to the calipers and wheel cylinders by flexible tubes in order to allow for suspension and steering movements.

In drum brake systems, each wheel cylinder contains two pistons, one at either end, which push outward in opposite directions and force the brake shoe into contact with the drum.

In disc brake systems, the cylinders are part of the calipers. At least one cylinder in each caliper is used to force the brake pads against the disc.

All pistons employ some type of seal, usually made of rubber, to minimize fluid leakage. A rubber dust boot seals the outer end of the cylinder against dust and dirt. The boot fits around the outer end of the piston on disc brake calipers, and around the brake actuating rod on wheel cylinders.

The hydraulic system operates as follows: When at rest, the entire system, from the piston(s) in the master cylinder to those in the wheel cylinders or calipers, is full of brake fluid. Upon application of the brake pedal, fluid trapped in front of the master cylinder piston(s) is forced through the lines to the wheel cylinders. Here, it forces the pistons outward, in the case of drum brakes, and inward toward the disc, in the case of disc brakes. The motion of the pistons is opposed by return springs mounted outside the cylinders in drum brakes, and by spring seals, in disc brakes.

Upon release of the brake pedal, a spring located inside the master cylinder immediately returns the master cylinder pistons to the normal position. The pistons contain check valves and the master cylinder has compensating ports drilled in it. These are uncovered as the pistons reach their normal position. The piston check valves allow fluid to flow toward the wheel cylinders or calipers as the pistons withdraw. Then, as the return springs force the brake pads or shoes into the released position, the excess fluid reservoir through the compensating ports. It is during the time the pedal is in the released position that any fluid that has leaked out of the system will be replaced through the compensating ports.

Dual circuit master cylinders employ two pistons, located one behind the other, in the same cylinder. The primary piston is actuated directly by mechanical linkage from the brake pedal through the power booster. The secondary piston is actuated by fluid trapped between the two pistons. If a leak develops in front of the secondary piston, it moves forward until it bottoms against the front of the master cylinder, and the fluid trapped between the pistons will operate the rear brakes. If the rear brakes develop a leak, the primary piston will move forward until direct contact with the secondary piston takes place, and it will force the secondary piston to actuate the front brakes. In either case, the brake pedal moves farther when the brakes are applied, and less braking power is available.

All dual circuit systems use a switch to warn the driver when only half of the brake system is operational. This switch is usually located in a valve body which is mounted on the firewall or the frame below the master cylinder. A hydraulic piston receives pressure from both circuits, each circuit's pressure being applied to one end of the piston. When the pressures are in balance, the piston remains stationary. When one circuit has a leak, however, the greater pressure in that circuit during application of the brakes will push the piston to one side, closing the switch and activating the brake warning light.

In disc brake systems, this valve body also contains a metering valve and, in some cases, a proportioning valve. The metering valve keeps pressure from traveling to the disc brakes on the front wheels until the brake shoes on the rear wheels have contacted the drums, ensuring that the front brakes will never be used alone. The proportioning valve controls the pressure to the rear brakes to lessen the chance of rear wheel lock-up during very hard braking.

Warning lights may be tested by depressing the brake pedal and holding it while opening one of the wheel cylinder bleeder screws. If this does not cause the light to go on, substitute a new lamp, make continuity checks, and, finally, replace the switch as necessary.

The hydraulic system may be checked for leaks by applying pressure to the pedal gradually and steadily. If the pedal sinks very slowly to the floor, the system has a leak. This is not to be confused with a springy or spongy feel due to the compression of air within the lines. If the system leaks, there will be a gradual change in the position of the pedal with a constant pressure.

Check for leaks along all lines and at wheel cylinders. If no external leaks are apparent, the problem is inside the master cylinder.

### DISC BRAKES

Instead of the traditional expanding brakes that press outward against a circular drum, disc brake systems utilize a disc (rotor) with brake pads positioned on either side of it. An easily-seen analogy is the hand brake arrangement on a bicycle. The pads squeeze onto the rim of the bike wheel, slowing its motion. Automobile disc brakes use the identical principle but apply the braking effort to a separate disc instead of the wheel.

The disc (rotor) is a casting, usually equipped with cooling fins between the two braking surfaces. This enables air to circulate between the braking surfaces making them less sensitive to heat buildup and more resistant to fade. Dirt and water do not drastically affect braking action since contaminants are thrown off by the centrifugal action of the rotor or scraped off the by the pads. Also, the equal clamping action of the two brake pads tends to ensure uniform, straight line stops. Disc brakes are inherently self-adjusting. There are three general types of disc brake:

- A fixed caliper.
- A floating caliper.
- A sliding caliper.

The fixed caliper design uses two pistons mounted on either side of the rotor (in each side of the caliper). The caliper is mounted rigidly and does not move.

The sliding and floating designs are quite similar. In fact, these two types are often lumped together. In both designs, the pad on the inside of the rotor is moved into contact with the rotor by hydraulic force. The caliper, which is not held in a fixed position, moves slightly, bringing the outside pad into contact with the rotor. There are various methods of attaching floating calipers. Some pivot at the bottom or top, and some slide on mounting bolts. In any event, the end result is the same.

### DRUM BRAKES

Drum brakes employ two brake shoes mounted on a stationary backing plate. These shoes are positioned inside a circular drum which rotates with the wheel assembly. The shoes are held in place by springs. This allows them to slide toward the drums (when they are applied) while keeping the linings and drums in alignment. The shoes are actuated by a wheel cylinder which is mounted at the top of the backing plate. When the brakes are applied, hydraulic pressure forces the wheel cylinder's actuating links outward. Since these links bear directly against the top of the brake shoes, the tops of the shoes are then forced against the inner side of the drum. This action forces the bottoms of the two shoes to contact the brake drum by rotating the entire assembly slightly (known as servo action). When pressure within the wheel cylinder is relaxed, return springs pull the shoes back away from the drum.

Most modern drum brakes are designed to self-adjust themselves during application when the vehicle is moving in reverse. This motion causes both shoes to rotate very slightly with the drum, rocking an adjusting lever, thereby causing rotation of the adjusting screw. Some drum brake systems are designed to self-adjust during application whenever the brakes are applied. This on-board adjustment system reduces the need for maintenance adjustments and keeps both the brake function and pedal feel satisfactory.

## POWER BOOSTERS

Virtually all modern vehicles use a vacuum assisted power brake system to multiply the braking force and reduce pedal effort. Since vacuum is always available when the engine is operating, the system is simple and efficient. A vacuum diaphragm is located on the front of the master cylinder and assists the driver in applying the brakes, reducing both the effort and travel he must put into moving the brake pedal.The vacuum diaphragm housing is normally connected to the intake manifold by a vacuum hose. A check valve is placed at the point where the hose enters the diaphragm housing, so that during periods of low manifold vacuum brakes assist will not be lost.Depressing the brake pedal closes off the vacuum source and allows atmospheric pressure to enter on one side of the diaphragm. This causes the master cylinder pistons to move and apply the brakes. When the brake pedal is released, vacuum is applied to both sides of the diaphragm and springs return the diaphragm and master cylinder pistons to the released position.If the vacuum supply fails, the brake pedal rod will contact the end of the master cylinder actuator rod and the system will apply the brakes without any power assistance. The driver will notice that much higher pedal effort is needed to stop the car and that the pedal feels harder than usual.

### Vacuum Leak Test

1. Operate the engine at idle without touching the brake pedal for at least one minute.
2. Turn off the engine and wait one minute.
3. Test for the presence of assist vacuum by depressing the brake pedal and releasing it several times. If vacuum is present in the system, light application will produce less and less pedal travel. If there is no vacuum, air is leaking into the system.

### System Operation Test

1. With the engine **OFF**, pump the brake pedal until the supply vacuum is entirely gone.
2. Put light, steady pressure on the brake pedal.
3. Start the engine and let it idle. If the system is operating correctly, the brake pedal should fall toward the floor if the constant pressure is maintained.

Power brake systems may be tested for hydraulic leaks just as ordinary systems are tested.

**✱✱ WARNING**

**Clean, high quality brake fluid is essential to the safe and proper operation of the brake system. You should always buy the highest quality brake fluid that is available. If the brake fluid becomes contaminated, drain and flush the system, then refill the master cylinder with new fluid. Never reuse any brake fluid. Any brake fluid that is removed from the system should be discarded.**

# Brake Light Switch

## REMOVAL & INSTALLATION

1. Disconnect the negative battery cable.
2. Disconnect the electrical connector at the switch. The locking tab on the connector must be lifted before the connector can be removed.
3. Remove the hairpin retainer, slide the brake light switch, the pushrod and the nylon washers and bushings away from the pedal and remove the switch.

**➡Since the switch side plate nearest the brake pedal is slotted, it is not necessary to remove the brake master cylinder pushrod and 1 washer from the brake pedal pin.**

**To install:**

4. Position the switch so the U-shaped side is nearest the pedal and directly over/under the pin. Then slide the switch down/up trapping the master cylinder pushrod and black bushing between the switch side plates. Push the switch and pushrod assembly firmly toward the brake pedal arm. Assemble the outside white plastic washer to the pin and install the hairpin retainer to trap the whole assembly.
5. Assemble the wire harness connector to the switch. Check the switch for proper operation.

**➡The brake light switch wire harness must be long enough to travel with the switch during full pedal stroke. If wire length is insufficient, reroute the harness or service, as required.**

# Master Cylinder

## REMOVAL & INSTALLATION

### 1988–94 Vehicles

**➧ See Figures 1, 2, 3 and 4**

1. Disconnect the negative battery cable.
2. For vehicles equipped with ABS, apply the brake pedal a few times to exhaust all the vacuum in the system.
3. Disengage the brake warning indicator electrical connector.
4. Disconnect the brake lines from the primary and secondary outlet ports of the master cylinder and the brake pressure control valve.

**➡The master cylinder on the 1988–89 Lincoln Continental is part of the anti-lock brake hydraulic actuation unit and cannot be removed separately.**

5. For vehicles equipped with ABS, disconnect the Hydraulic Control Unit (HCU) supply hose at the master cylinder, then secure in a position to prevent the loss of brake fluid.
6. Remove the nuts attaching the master cylinder to the brake booster assembly.
7. Slide the master cylinder forward and upward from the vehicle.

**To install:**

8. In order to ease installation, bench bleed the master cylinder before installation:
   a. Mount the master cylinder in a holding fixture, such as a soft jawed vise. Be careful not to damage the master cylinder housing.
   b. Fill the master cylinder with brake fluid.
   c. Place a suitable container under the master cylinder to catch the fluid being expelled from the outlet ports. Using a suitable tool inserted into the booster pushrod cavity, push the master cylinder piston in slowly.
   d. Place a finger tightly over each outlet port, then allow the master cylinder piston to return.
   e. Repeat the procedure until only clear fluid is expelled from the master cylinder. Plug the outlet ports, then remove the master cylinder from the holding fixture.
9. For vehicles equipped with ABS, install a new seal in the groove in the master cylinder mounting face.

86879004

**Fig. 1 Disengage the electrical connector from the brake warning indicator**

86879005

**Fig. 2 Disconnect the brake lines from the primary and secondary outlet ports of the master cylinder**

86879006

**Fig. 3 Remove the retaining nuts attaching the master cylinder to the brake booster assembly, then . . .**

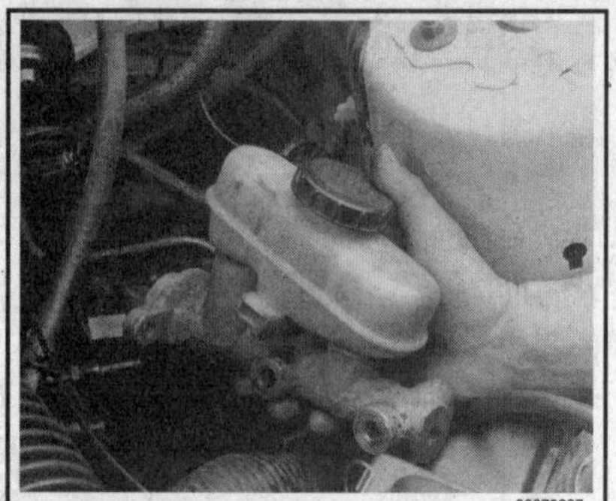

86879007

**Fig. 4 . . . slide the master cylinder assembly forward and upward from the vehicle**

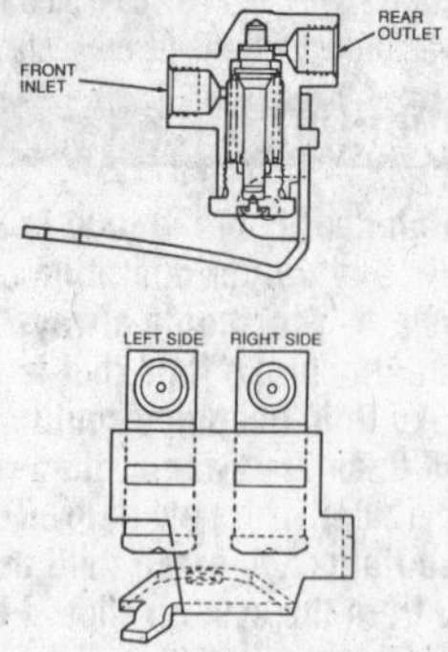


84179011

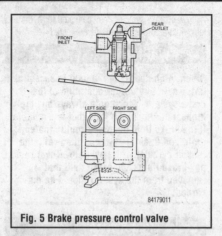

**Fig. 5 Brake pressure control valve**

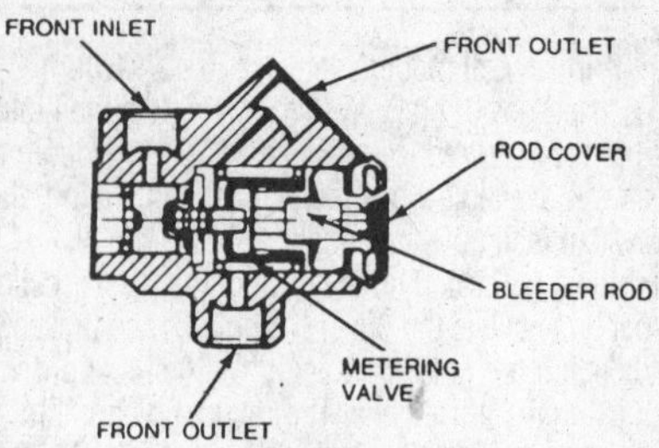


84179012

**Fig. 6 Metering valve—1989 vehicles and 1990–91 vehicles with 5.8L engine**

10. Mount the master cylinder over the booster pushrod and onto the two studs on the power brake booster assembly.
11. Install the retaining nuts, then tighten them to 16–21 ft. lbs. (21–29 Nm).
12. Attach the brake fluid lines to the master cylinder and the brake pressure control valve ports.
13. For vehicles equipped with ABS, install the HCU supply hose to the master cylinder fitting, then secure it with the hose clamp.
14. Connect the brake warning light wire.
15. Fill the brake master cylinder with DOT 3 brake fluid to 0.16 in. (4.0mm) below the MAX lines on the side of the reservoir.
16. Connect the negative battery cable, then bleed the brake system. For details, please refer to the procedure located later in this section.
17. Operate the brakes several times, then check for external hydraulic leaks.

#### 1995–00 Vehicles

1. Disconnect the negative battery cable.
2. Depress the brake pedal several times to exhaust all vacuum in the power brake booster.
3. Remove and plug the brake lines from the primary and secondary outlet ports of the master cylinder.
4. Detach the brake warning indicator switch connector.
5. If equipped with ABS and traction assist, remove 2 bolts retaining the proportioning valve bracket to the master cylinder. Secure the proportioning valve and brake lines in a position to prevent damage or loss of brake fluid.
6. Remove 2 nuts retaining the brake master cylinder to the power brake booster assembly.
7. Slide the master cylinder forward and upward from the vehicle and remove.

**To install:**

8. If replacing the brake master cylinder, bench bleed the master cylinder before installation.
9. Install the brake master cylinder to the power brake booster mounting studs and install 2 retaining nuts. Torque the nuts to 16–21 ft. lbs. (21–29 Nm).
10. If equipped with ABS and traction assist, place the proportioning valve bracket in position and install 2 retaining bolts. Torque the bolts to 14–19 ft. lbs. (19–26 Nm).
11. Unplug and install the primary and secondary brake lines to the brake master cylinder outlet ports. Torque the brake line fittings to 10–15 ft. lbs. (14–20 Nm).
12. Reconnect the brake warning indicator switch connector.
13. Properly bleed the brake system using clean DOT 3 or equivalent, brake fluid from a closed container.

**CAUTION**

**If raising the vehicle for brake bleeding and the vehicle is equipped with air suspension, the air suspension switch, located on the right-hand side of the luggage compartment, must be turned to the OFF position before raising the vehicle.**

14. Fill the master cylinder reservoir to the proper level.
15. Operate the brakes several times, then check for external hydraulic leaks.
16. Reconnect the negative battery cable.
17. If equipped with air suspension, turn the air suspension switch to the **ON** position, if disabled.
18. Road test the vehicle and check the brake system for proper operation.

## Brake Pressure Control Valve

### REMOVAL & INSTALLATION

**See Figure 5**

1. Disconnect the brake inlet lines and the rear lines from the brake control valve assembly.
2. Remove the screw retaining the control valve assembly to the frame and remove the brake control valve.

**To install:**

3. Position the control valve on the frame and secure with the retaining screw.
4. Connect the rear brake outlet lines to the control valve assembly and tighten the line nuts to 10–18 ft. lbs. (14–24 Nm).
5. Connect the inlet lines to the control valve assembly and tighten the line nuts to 10–18 ft. lbs. (14–24 Nm).
6. Bleed the brake system.

## Metering Valve

### REMOVAL & INSTALLATION

**See Figure 6**

1. Disconnect the front brake system inlet line and the left and right front brake outlet lines from the metering valve.
2. Remove the screw retaining the metering valve to the frame and remove the metering valve from the vehicle.

**To install:**

3. Position the metering valve on the frame and secure with the retaining screw. Tighten the screw to 7–11 ft. lbs. (10–14 Nm).
4. Connect the front brake outlet lines to the metering valve assembly and tighten the line nuts to 10–18 ft. lbs. (14–24 Nm).
5. Connect the front brake inlet line to the metering valve assembly and tighten the line nut to 10–18 ft. lbs. (14–24 Nm).
6. Bleed the brake system.

**➡If the brake system is pressure bled, the metering valve bleeder rod must be pushed in.**

## Bleeding the Brake System

**See Figures 7, 8, 9 and 10**

When any part of the hydraulic system has been disconnected for repair or replacement, air may get into the lines and cause spongy pedal action (because air can be compressed and brake fluid cannot). To correct this condition, it is necessary to bleed the hydraulic system so to be sure all air is purged.

When bleeding the brake system, bleed one brake cylinder at a time, beginning at the cylinder with the longest hydraulic line (farthest from the master cylinder) first. ALWAYS keep the master cylinder reservoir filled with brake fluid during the bleeding operation. Never use brake fluid that has been drained from the hydraulic system, no matter how clean it is.

The primary and secondary hydraulic brake systems are separate and are bled independently. During the bleeding operation, do not allow the

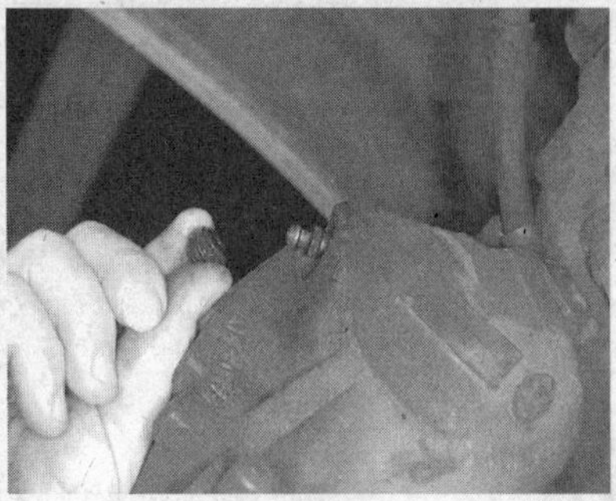

89609P01

Fig. 7 Remove the bleeder screw rubber dust cover—front caliper

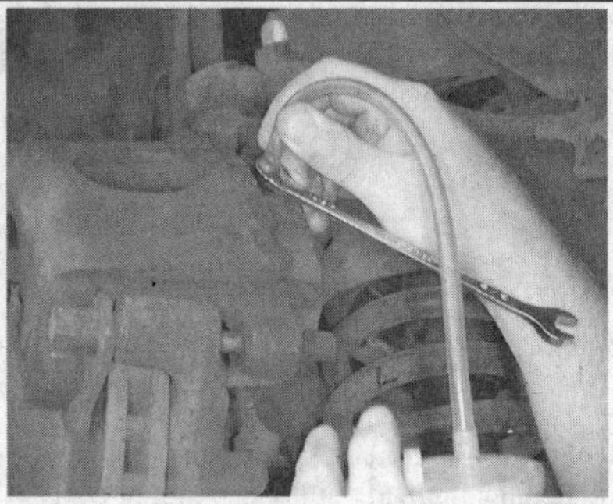

89609P02

Fig. 8 Attach a length of rubber hose over the bleeder screw and place the other end of the hose in a glass jar

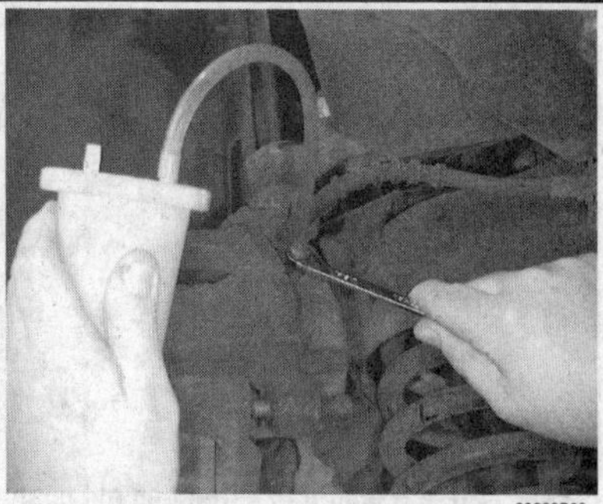

89609P03

Fig. 9 Open the bleeder valve using a suitable size wrench while an assistant depresses the brake pedal

89609P38

Fig. 10 Bleeder screw location—rear caliper

reservoir to run dry. Keep the master cylinder reservoir filled with brake fluid.

1. Clean all dirt from around the master cylinder fill cap, remove the cap and fill the master cylinder with brake fluid until the level is within ¼ in. (6mm) of the top edge of the reservoir.
2. Clean the bleeder screws at all 4 wheels. The bleeder screws are located on the back of the brake backing plate (drum brakes) and on the top of the brake calipers (disc brakes).
3. Attach a length of rubber hose over the bleeder screw and place the other end of the hose in a glass jar, submerged in brake fluid.
4. Open the bleeder screw ½–¾ turn. Have an assistant slowly depress the brake pedal.
5. Close the bleeder screw and tell your assistant to allow the brake pedal to return slowly. Continue this process to purge all air from the system.
6. When bubbles cease to appear at the end of the bleeder hose, close the bleeder screw and remove the hose. Tighten the bleeder screw to the proper torque.
7. Check the master cylinder fluid level and add fluid accordingly. Do this after bleeding each wheel.
8. Repeat the bleeding operation at the remaining 3 wheels, ending with the one closet to the master cylinder.
9. Fill the master cylinder reservoir to the proper level.

## DISC BRAKES

### ** CAUTION

**Older brake pads or shoes may contain asbestos, which has been determined to be cancer-causing agent. Never clean the brake surfaces with compressed air! Avoid inhaling any dust from any brake surface! When cleaning brake surfaces, use a commercially available brake cleaning fluid. Also use this caution:**

### Brake Pads

#### REMOVAL & INSTALLATION

**Front**

**➧ See Figures 11 thru 16**

1. Remove and discard half the brake fluid from the master cylinder. Properly dispose of the used brake fluid.
2. Raise and safely support vehicle. Remove the front wheel and tire assemblies.
3. Remove the caliper locating pins and remove the caliper from the anchor plate and rotor, but do not disconnect the brake hose.
4. Remove the outer brake pad from the caliper assembly and remove the inner brake pad from the caliper piston.
5. Inspect the disc brake rotor for scoring and wear. Replace or machine, as necessary.
6. Suspend the caliper inside the fender hous-

84179016

Fig. 11 Front disc brake caliper

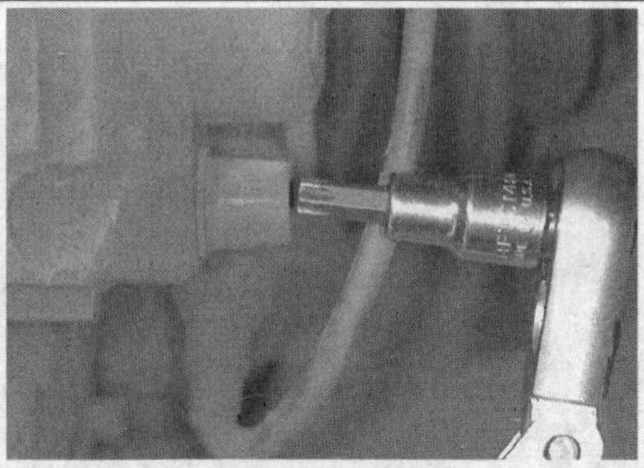

93149P20

Fig. 12 This Continental uses a Torx ® driver to remove the caliper pins. Make sure the proper size is used and the driver is seated in the pin tightly

93149P06

Fig. 13 When the pins have been removed, the caliper slides off the rotor. If the rotor has been scored, the caliper may be a little tough to remove. Use a small pry tool if necessary

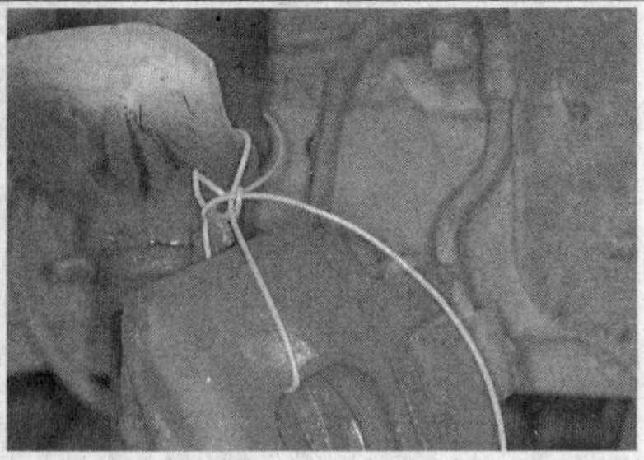
93149P10

**Fig. 14 Use a length of wire or an old coat hanger to suspend the caliper. Do not allow the weight of the caliper to hang on the brake hose**

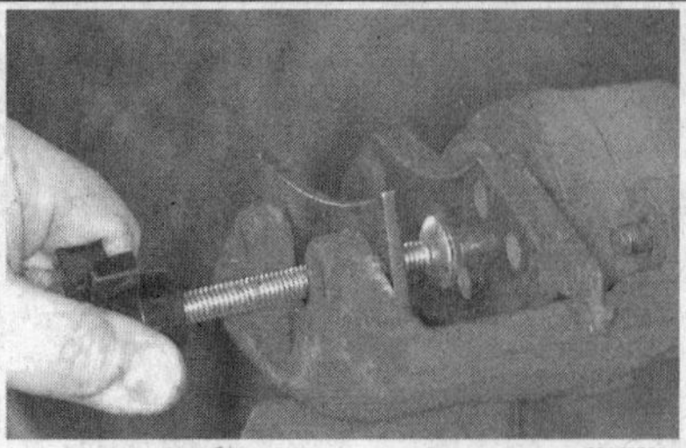
93149P08

**Fig. 15 This special collapsing tool is readily available at the local parts store. It will fit many different vehicles. Leave the old shoe in place when collapsing the piston into the caliper**

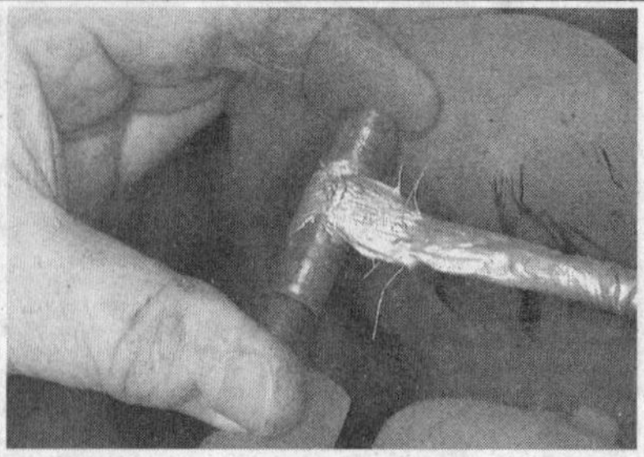
93149P09

**Fig. 16 When replacing brakes, make sure to service the caliper pins. Lube the pins with special "brake" grease that has a silicone compound base**

ing with a length of wire. Do not let the caliper hang by the brake hose.

**To install:**

7. Use a large C-clamp and wood block to push the caliper piston back into its bore.

**WARNING**

**Never apply the C-clamp directly to the phenolic caliper piston; damage to the piston may result.**

8. Install new locating pin insulators in the caliper housing, Check to see if both insulator flanges straddle the housing holes.

**➡Do not attempt to install the rubber insulators with a sharp edged tool.**

9. Install the inner brake pad in the caliper piston. Be careful not to bend the pad clips in the piston, or distortion and rattles can result.

10. Install the outer brake pad, making sure the clips are properly seated. The outer pads are marked left-hand (LH) and right-hand (RH) and must be installed in the proper caliper.

**➡Make sure that the large diameter of the pins is through the outer pad hole to prevent possible binding or bending.**

11. Install the caliper over the rotor with the outer brake pad against the rotor's braking surface. This prevents pinching the piston boot between the inner brake pad and the piston.

12. Lubricate the caliper locating pins and the inside of the locating pin insulators with silicone dielectric grease. Install the caliper locating pins and thread them into the spindle/anchor plate assembly by hand.

13. Tighten the caliper locating pins to 45–65 ft. lbs. (61–88 Nm).

14. Install the wheel and tire assembly. Lower the vehicle.

15. Pump the brake pedal prior to moving the vehicle to seat the brake pads. Refill the master cylinder.

16. Road test the vehicle.

## Rear

**➧ See Figures 17 thru 25**

1. Turn the air suspension service off.
2. Raise and safely support the rear of the vehicle securely on jackstands.
3. Remove the wheel and tire assembly.
4. Remove the bolt retaining rear brake hose support bracket, where necessary.
5. Remove the retaining clip from the parking brake rear cable an conduit at the rear disc brake caliper.
6. Remove the cable end from the parking brake lever.
7. Remove the upper disc brake caliper-locating pin.
8. Remove the lower disc brake caliper-locating pin.
9. Rotate the rear disc brake caliper away from the rear disc brake rotor.
10. Remove the inner and outer rear brake shoe and lining assemblies from the rear disc support bracket.

**➡Unless the tabs on the back of the brake pads are seated in the slots of the piston, and the piston seated in the caliper, the brake pads and the caliper will not fit into the disc support bracket.**

**To install:**

11. Make sure that one of the two slots in the piston face is positioned so it will engage the nib on the brake shoe.
12. Using the rear caliper piston adjuster rotate the piston clockwise while applying pressure inward, until it is fully seated.
13. Install the inner and outer rear brake shoe and lining assemblies in the rear disc support bracket.
14. Rotate the rear disc brake caliper over the rear disc brake rotor into position on the rear disc support bracket. Make sure that the rear brake shoe and lining assemblies are installed correctly.
15. Remove any residue from the rear brake pin retainer bolt threads and apply one drop of a thread sealer. Install the disc brake caliper locating pin and tighten .
16. Attach the cable end to the parking brake lever. Install the cable retaining clip on the rear disc brake caliper.
17. Position the rear wheel brake hose to the side rail and install the retaining bolt.
18. Install the wheel and tire assembly.

93149P36

**Fig. 17 Pull the caliper out of the support bracket and support it. Notice the brake pads stay in the support bracket, they are not attached to the caliper**

93149P22

**Fig. 18 This is the rear caliper with the parking brake cable ready to be unhooked**

93149P39

**Fig. 19 Removing the upper disc caliper locating pin, using an open end and a box end wrench**

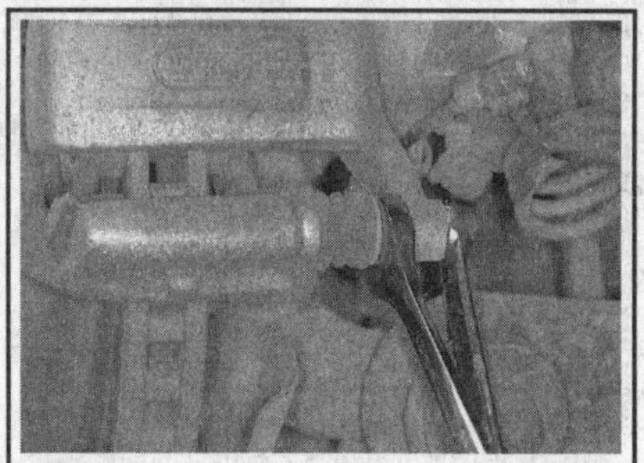

93149P37

Fig. 20 Removing the lower disc caliper locating pin, This application used a 10 mm box wrench and a 15 mm open end wrench

93149P32

Fig. 21 With the brake caliper removed, you can see the way the brake pads are mounted in the support bracket

93149P28

Fig. 22 Replacing the brake pads, is a good time to service the caliper pins. Use a brake grease compound with a silicone base to lube the pins

93149P35

Fig. 23 The parking brake is built into the rear caliper requiring a special tool for brake installation, the piston has to be twisted into the boot

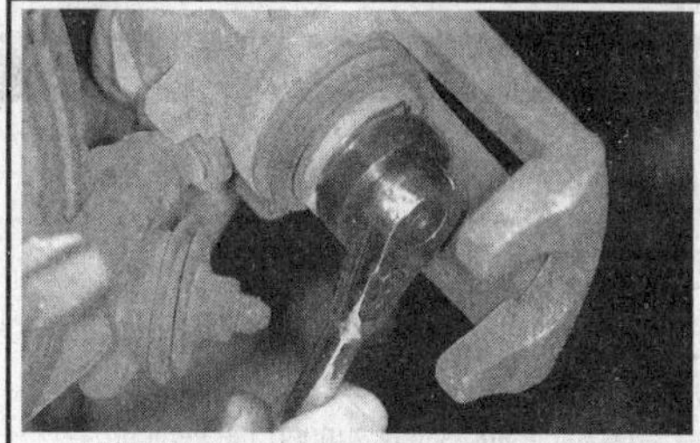

93149P34

Fig. 24 To collapse the piston back into the caliper, align the two pins in the special tool to the piston's two slots and screw it back in slowly, while applying an inward pressure to the piston

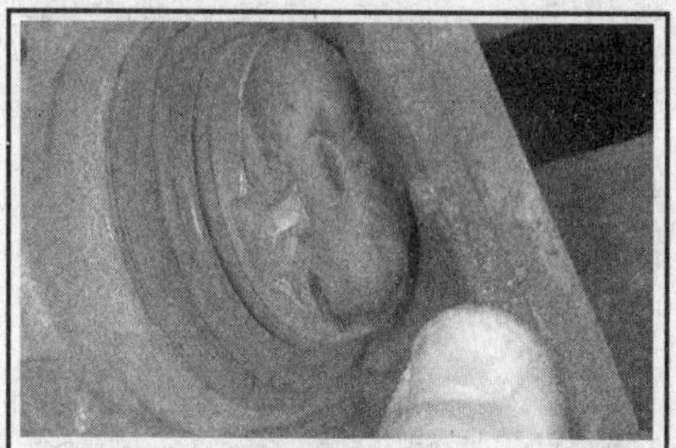

93149P41

Fig. 25 When the piston is pushed into the piston and seated, be sure the piston's slots are at 6 and 12 o'clock. There are two tabs on the back of the pad that seat in the slots

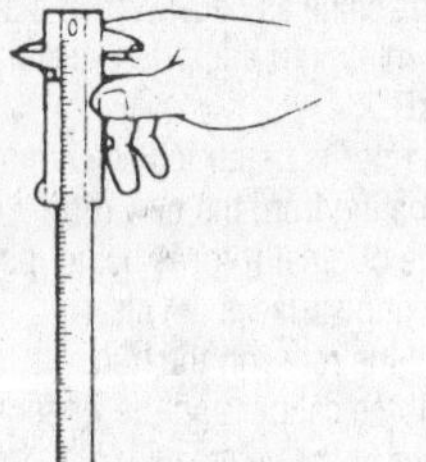

84179023

Fig. 26 Checking disc brake pad thickness

19. Lower the vehicle and turn the air suspension on.

## INSPECTION

➧ **See Figure 26**

Inspect the disc brake pads for oil or grease contamination, abnormal wear or cracking, and for deterioration or damage due to heat. Check the thickness of the pads; the minimum allowable thickness is ⅛ in. Always replace the brake pads in axle sets; never replace just one pad of a brake assembly.

# Brake Caliper

## REMOVAL & INSTALLATION

### Front

➧ **See Figure 27**

1. Raise and safely support the vehicle. Remove the front wheel and tire assembly.
2. Loosen the brake line fitting that connects the brake hose to the brake line at the frame bracket. Plug the brake line. Remove the retaining clip from the hose and bracket and disengage the hose from the bracket.
3. Remove the hollow bolt attaching the brake hose to the caliper and remove the brake hose. Discard the sealing washers.
4. Remove the caliper locating pins and remove the caliper. If removing both calipers, mark the right and left sides so they may be reinstalled correctly.

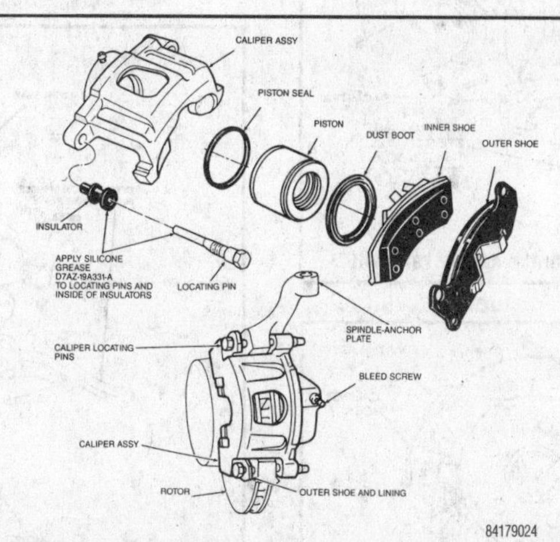


84179024

Fig. 27 Front disc brake caliper assembly

**To install:**

5. Install the caliper over the rotor with the outer brake pad against the rotor's braking surface. This prevents pinching the piston boot between the inner brake pad and the piston.

6. Lubricate the locating pins and the inside of the locating pin insulators with silicone dielectric grease. Install the caliper locating pins and thread them into the spindle/anchor plate assembly by hand.

7. Tighten the caliper locating pins to 45–65 ft. lbs. (61–88 Nm).

8. Install new sealing washers on each side of the brake hose fitting outlet and install the hollow bolt, through the hose fitting and into the caliper. Tighten the bolt to 30 ft. lbs. (41 Nm).

9. Position the other end of the brake hose in the bracket and install the retaining clip. Make sure the hose is not twisted.

10. Remove the plug from the brake line, connect the brake line to the brake hose and tighten the fitting nut to 10–18 ft. lbs. (13–24 Nm).

11. Bleed the brake system, install the wheel and tire assembly and lower the vehicle.

12. Apply the brake pedal several times before moving the vehicle, to position the brake pads.

13. Road test the vehicle.

### Rear

➧ See Figures 28 and 29

1. Raise and safely support the vehicle.
2. Remove the rear wheel and tire assembly.
3. Remove the brake fitting retaining bolt from the caliper and disconnect the flexible brake hose from the caliper. Plug the hose and the caliper fitting.
4. Remove the caliper locating pins. Lift the caliper off the rotor and anchor plate using a rotating motion.

**✱✱ WARNING**

**Do not pry directly against the plastic piston or damage to the piston may occur.**

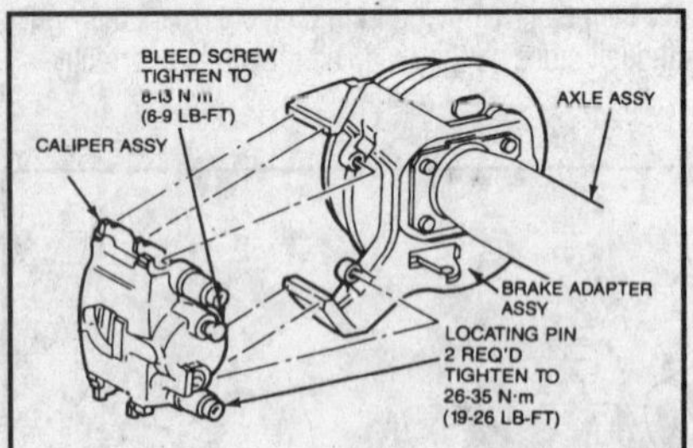


**Fig. 28 Rear disc brake caliper removal**

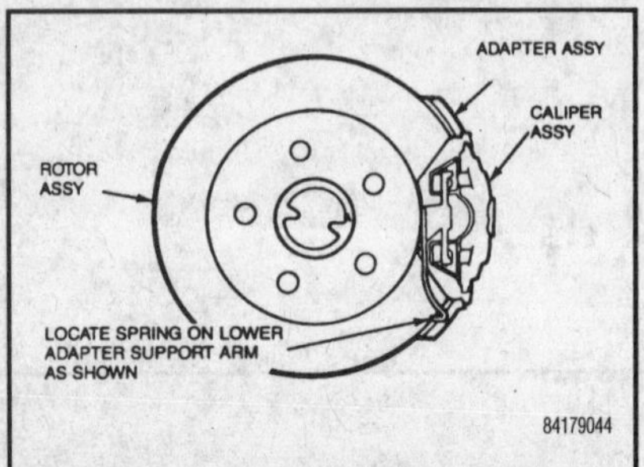


**Fig. 29 Rear disc brake caliper installation**

**To install:**

5. Position the caliper assembly above the rotor with the anti-rattle spring located on the lower adapter support arm. Install the caliper over the rotor with a rotating motion. Make sure the inner pad is properly positioned.

6. Install the caliper locating pins and start them in the threads by hand. Tighten them to 19–26 ft. lbs. (26–35 Nm).

7. Install the brake hose on the caliper with a new gasket on each side of the fitting outlet. Insert the retaining bolt and tighten to 30–40 ft. lbs. (40–54 Nm).

8. Bleed the brake system, install the wheel and tire assembly and lower the vehicle.

9. Pump the brake pedal prior to moving the vehicle to position the linings.

10. Road test the vehicle.

## Brake Disc (Rotor)

### REMOVAL & INSTALLATION

#### 1988–91 Vehicles

➧ See Figure 30

1. Raise and safely support the vehicle.
2. Remove the wheel and tire assembly.
3. Remove the caliper from the spindle and rotor, but do not disconnect the brake hose. Suspend the caliper inside the fender housing with a length of wire. Do not let the caliper hang by the brake hose.
4. Remove the grease cap from the hub and remove the cotter pin, nut retainer and adjusting nut.
5. Grasp the hub/rotor assembly and pull it out far enough to loosen the washer and outer wheel bearing. Push the hub/rotor assembly back onto the spindle and remove the washer and outer wheel bearing.
6. Remove the hub/rotor assembly from the spindle.
7. Inspect the rotor for scoring and wear. Replace or machine as necessary. If machining, observe the minimum thickness specification.

**To install:**

8. If the rotor is being replaced, remove the protective coating from the new rotor with brake cleaner. Pack a new set of bearings with high-temperature wheel bearing grease and install the inner roller bearing in the inner cup. Pack grease lightly between the lips of a new seal and install the seal, using a seal installer.

9. If the original rotor is being installed, make sure the grease in the hub is clean and adequate, the inner bearing and grease seal are lubricated and in good condition, and the rotor braking surfaces are clean.

10. Install the hub/rotor assembly on the spindle. Keep the assembly centered on the spindle to prevent damage to the grease seal or spindle threads.

11. Install the outer wheel bearing, washer and adjusting nut. Adjust the wheel bearings according to the procedure in Section 8, then install the nut retainer, cotter pin and grease cap.

12. Install the caliper and the wheel and tire assembly. Lower the vehicle.

13. Apply the brake pedal several times before moving the vehicle, to position the brake pads.

#### 1992–99 Vehicles

➧ See Figures 31 thru 36

1. Raise and safely support the vehicle.
2. Remove the wheel and tire assembly.
3. Remove the caliper from the spindle and rotor, but do not disconnect the brake hose. Suspend the caliper inside the fender housing with a length of wire. Do not let the caliper hang by the brake hose.
4. Remove the rotor retaining push nuts, if equipped, and remove the rotor from the hub.
5. Inspect the rotor for scoring and wear. Replace or machine as necessary. If machining, observe the minimum thickness specification.

**To install:**

6. If the rotor is being replaced, remove the protective coating from the new rotor with brake cleaner. If the original rotor is being installed, make sure the braking surfaces are clean.
7. Install the rotor on the hub.
8. Install the caliper and the wheel and tire assembly. Lower the vehicle.

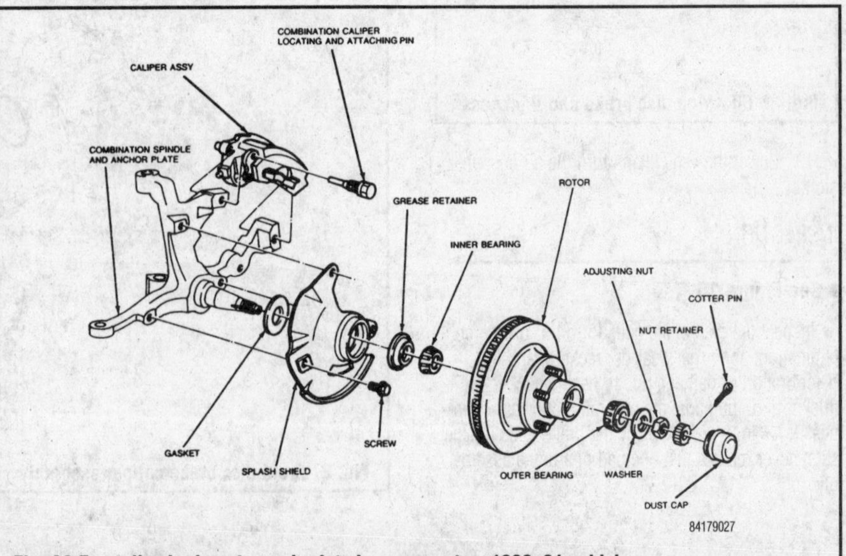


**Fig. 30 Front disc brake rotor and related components—1988–91 vehicles**

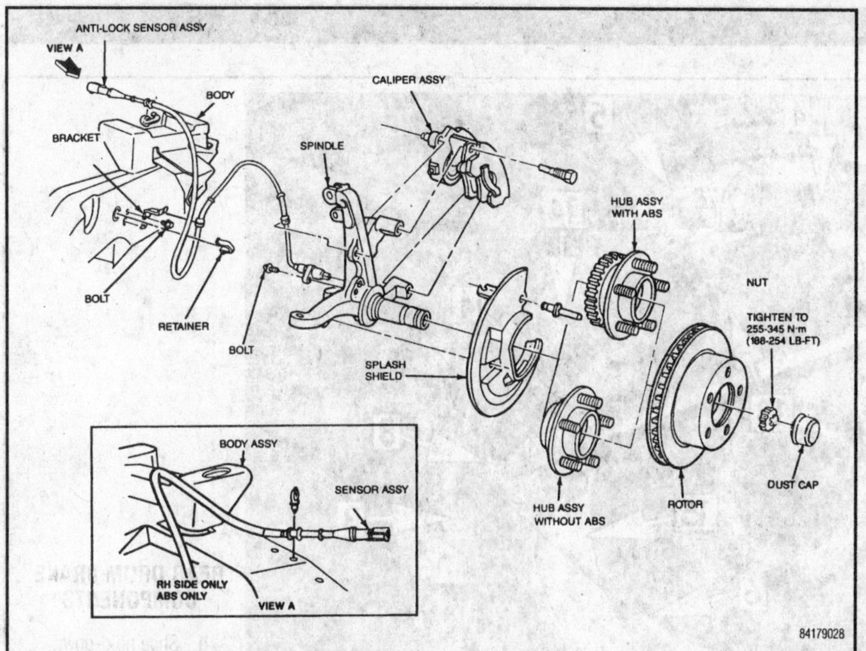


**Fig. 31 Front disc brake rotor and related components—typical**

**Fig. 32 After removing the disc pads you can inspect the brake rotor thoroughly for scoring**

**Fig. 33 If the rotor has to come off, the disc support bracket has to be removed. This bracket has two bolts that hold it in place**

9. Apply the brake pedal several times before moving the vehicle, to position the brake pads.

## INSPECTION

Check the disc brake rotor for scoring, cracks or other damage. Check the minimum thickness and rotor runout.

Either foreign material build-up or contamination on the rotor braking surface or uneven rotor thickness causes a brake pulsation that is present during brake application. If there is a foreign material build-up or contamination found on the rotor or lining surfaces, hand sand the linings and rotors. Uneven rotor thickness (thickness variation) may be caused by excessive runout, caliper drag or the abrasive action of the brake lining. If brake pulsation is present, attempt stopping the vehicle with the transmission in the NEUTRAL position. If the pulsation is gone, the drivetrain should be inspected. If the pulsation remains, inspect the brakes.

Check the rotor thickness using a micrometer or calipers. The brake rotor minimum thickness must not be less than 0.972 in. on 1988–91 vehicles or 0.974 in. on 1992–99 vehicles.

Rotor runout can be checked using a dial indicator. Mount the indicator to the spindle or upper control arm and position the indicator foot on the center of the braking surface. Rotate the rotor to check the runout. On 1992–99 vehicles, make sure there is no rust or foreign material between the rotor and hub face. Hold the rotor to the hub by inverting the lugnuts and tightening them to 85–105 ft. lbs. (115–142 Nm). Rotor runout must not exceed 0.003 in.

If rotor runout exceeds specification on 1988–91 vehicles, machine the rotor if it will not be below the minimum thickness specification after machining. On 1992–00 vehicles, the rotor can be repositioned on the hub to obtain the lowest possible runout. If runout remains excessive, remove the rotor and check the hub runout. Replace the hub if hub runout exceeds 0.002 in. If after replacing the hub, rotor runout remains excessive, machine the rotor if it will not be below the minimum thickness specification after machining.

**Fig. 34 Before removing the caliper, matchmark the rotor and the stud (lug) to help prevent vibration from a rotor that is out of round**

**Fig. 35 To remove the rotor, just slide it off the hub. Make sure it is marked on a stud and on the rotor "hat" for proper installation**

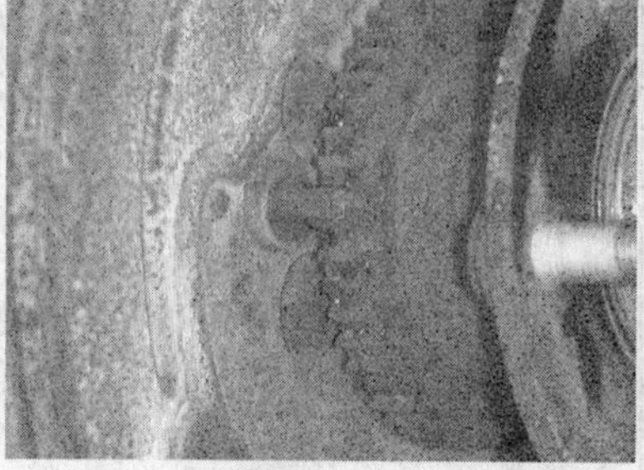


**Fig. 36 When the rotor has been removed, the anti-lock hub and sensor can be cleaned and inspected**

## DRUM BRAKES

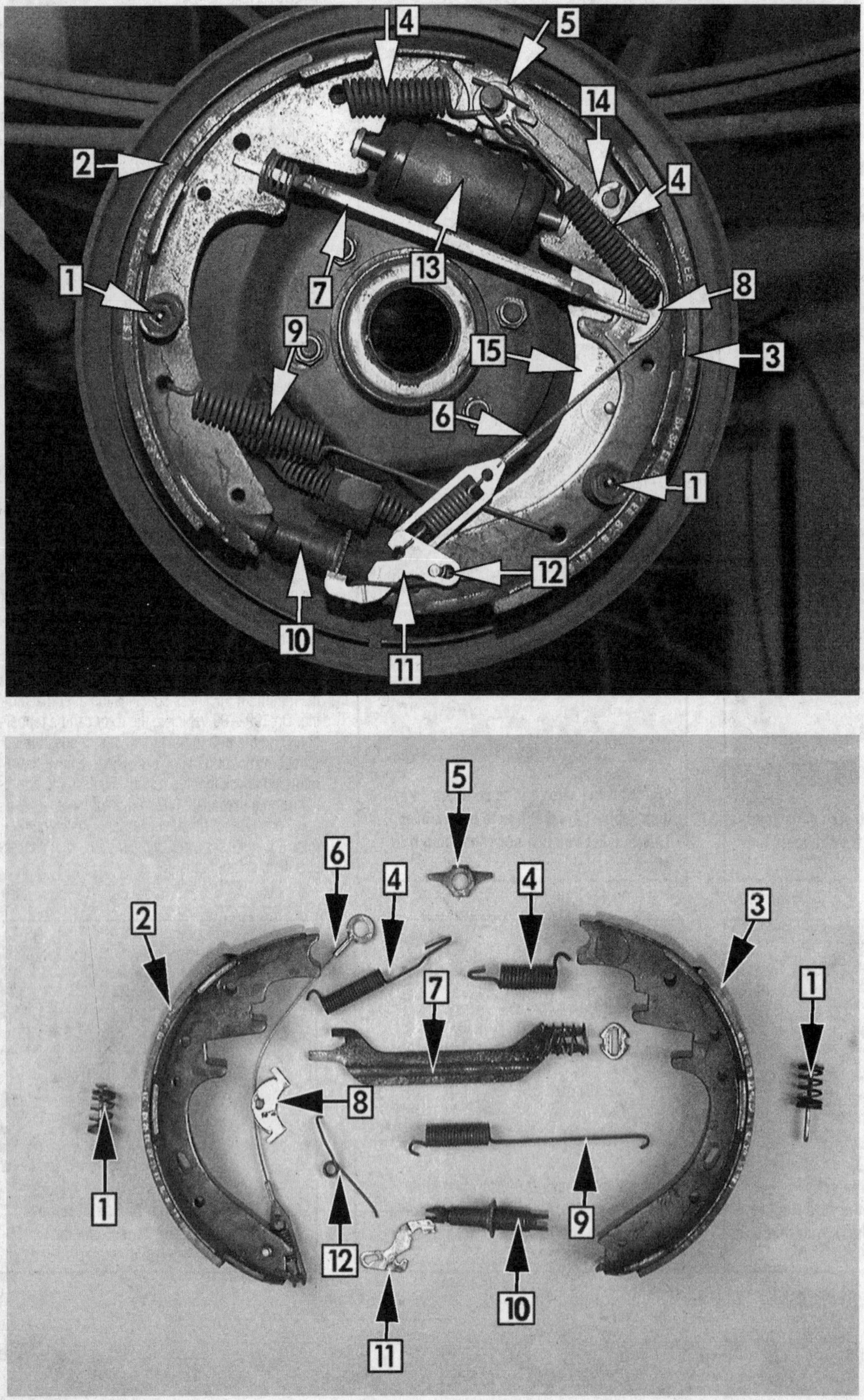


**REAR DRUM BRAKE COMPONENTS**

1. Shoe hold-down spring and retainer
2. Primary brake shoe
3. Secondary brake shoe
4. Brake shoe retracting springs
5. Anchor pin guide plate
6. Shoe adjusting lever cable
7. Parking brake strut
8. Shoe adjusting lever cable guide
9. Brake shoe adjusting screw spring
10. Brake adjuster screw
11. Brake shoe adjusting lever
12. Adjusting lever return spring
13. Wheel cylinder
14. Parking brake lever retaining clip
15. Parking brake lever

91199P75

**CAUTION**

**Older brake pads or shoes may contain asbestos, which has been determined to be cancer causing agent. Never clean the brake surfaces with compressed air! Avoid inhaling any dust from any brake surface! When cleaning brake surfaces, use a commercially available brake cleaning fluid.**

## Brake Drums

### REMOVAL & INSTALLATION

**See Figure 37**

**CAUTION**

**Older brake pads or shoes may contain asbestos, which has been determined to be cancer causing agent. Never clean the brake surfaces with compressed air! Avoid inhaling any dust from any brake surface! When cleaning brake surfaces, use a commercially available brake cleaning fluid.**

1. Raise and safely support the vehicle securely on jackstands.
2. Remove the tire and wheel assembly.
3. Remove the three retaining clips (if equipped), then remove the brake drum.

**It may be necessary to back off the brake shoe adjustment in order to remove the brake drum. This is because the drum might be grooved or worn from being in service for an extended period of time.**

**Before installing a new brake drum, be sure to remove any protective coating with brake cleaner or a suitable fast-drying degreaser.**

4. Install the brake drum in the reverse order of removal, then adjust the brakes as outlined later in this section.

### INSPECTION

**See Figures 38 and 39**

Check that there are no cracks or chips in the braking surface. Excessive bluing indicates overheating and a replacement drum is needed. The drum can be machined to remove minor damage and to establish a rounded braking surface on a warped drum. Never exceed the maximum oversize of the drum when machining the braking surface.

**CAUTION**

**Older brake pads or shoes may contain asbestos, which has been determined to be cancer causing agent. Never clean the brake surfaces with compressed air! Avoid inhaling any dust from any brake surface! When cleaning brake surfaces, use a commercially available brake cleaning fluid.**

The brake drum inside diameter and run-out can be measured using a brake drum micrometer. The drum should be measured every time a brake inspection is performed. Take the inside diameter readings at points 90° apart from each other on the drum to measure the run-out. The maximum inside diameter is stamped on the rim of the drum or on the inside above the lug nut stud holes and is also contained in the brake specifications chart at the end of this section.

## Brake Shoes

### INSPECTION

**See Figure 40**

**CAUTION**

**Older brake pads or shoes may contain asbestos, which has been determined to be cancer causing agent. Never clean the brake surfaces with compressed air! Avoid inhaling any dust from any brake surface! When cleaning brake surfaces, use a commercially available brake cleaning fluid.**

Inspect the brake shoes for wear using a ruler or Vernier caliper. Compare measurements to the brake specifications chart. If the lining is thinner than specification or there is evidence of the lining being contaminated by brake fluid or oil, repair the leak and replace all brake shoe assemblies (a complete axle set). In addition to the shoes inspect all springs and brake shoe hardware for wear and replace as necessary.

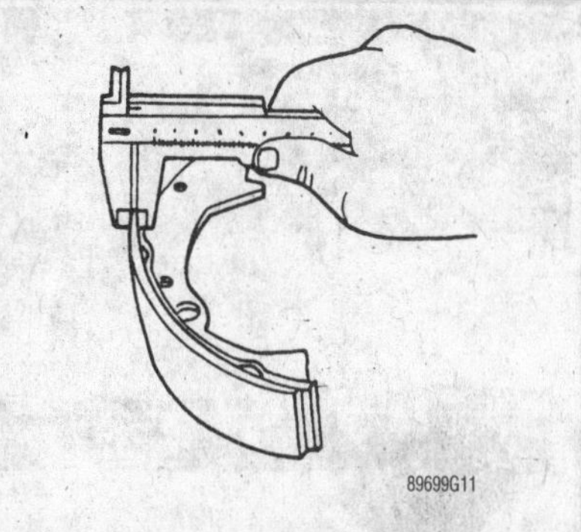


**Fig. 40 Measure brake shoe thickness in several places around the shoe**

### REMOVAL & INSTALLATION

**See Figures 41 thru 59**

1. Raise and safely support the vehicle securely on jackstands.
2. Remove the wheel and tire assembly, then remove the brake drum.

**When servicing drum brakes, only dissemble and assemble one side at a time, leaving the remaining side intact for reference.**

**CAUTION**

**Older brake pads or shoes may contain asbestos, which has been determined to be cancer causing agent. Never clean the brake surfaces with compressed air! Avoid inhaling any dust from any brake surface! When cleaning brake surfaces, use a commercially available brake cleaning fluid.**

3. Contract the brake shoes by pulling the self-adjusting lever away from the starwheel adjustment screw and turn the starwheel up and back until the pivot nut is drawn onto the starwheel as far as it will come.
4. Pull the adjusting lever, cable and automatic adjuster spring down and toward the rear to unhook the pivot hook from the large hole in the secondary shoe web. Do not attempt to pry the pivot hook from the hole.
5. Remove the automatic adjuster spring and the adjusting lever.
6. Remove the secondary shoe-to-anchor

**Fig. 37 Lift the brake drum from the shoes and backing plate**

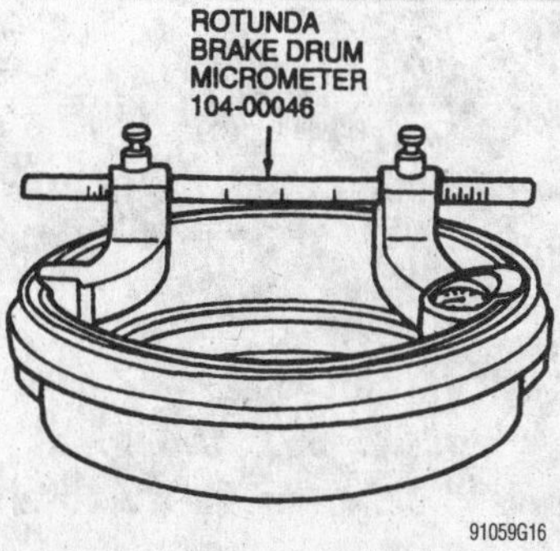


**Fig. 38 Measure the drum using a micrometer made especially for brake drums**

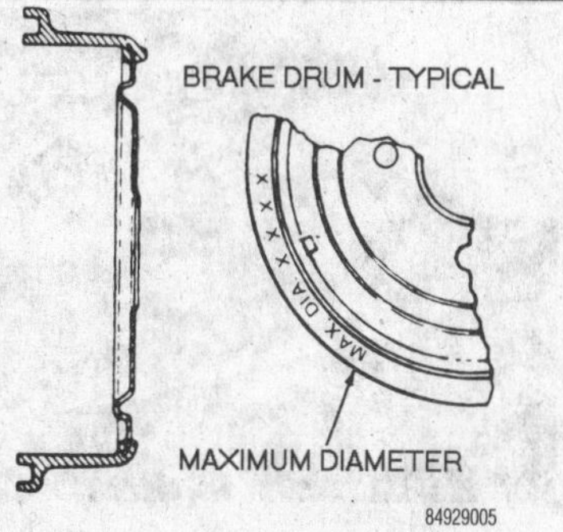


**Fig. 39 Brake drum maximum diameter location**

91199P04

**Fig. 41 Remove the brake shoe retracting springs . . .**

91199P05

**Fig. 42 . . . from both sides**

91199P06

**Fig. 43 Rotate the hold down spring retainer and . . .**

91199P07

**Fig. 44 . . . remove the hold down spring from the primary brake shoe**

91199P08

**Fig. 45 Remove the primary shoe and unhook the adjusting spring from the shoe**

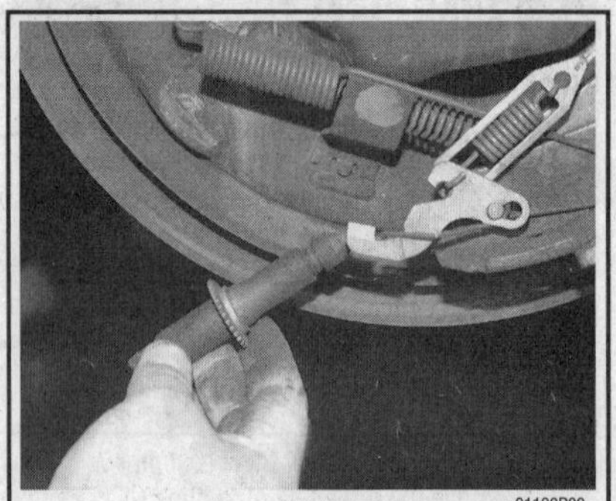

91199P09

**Fig. 46 Remove the adjusting screw**

91199P10

**Fig. 47 Remove the brake shoe adjusting lever cable**

91199P11

**Fig. 48 Remove the adjusting spring**

91199P12

**Fig. 49 Remove the adjusting lever return spring**

91199P13

**Fig. 50 Remove the anchor pin guide plate**

91199P15

**Fig. 51 Remove the parking brake strut**

91199P14

**Fig. 52 Remove the secondary shoe hold down spring and . . .**

91199P16

**Fig. 53 . . . lift the secondary shoe from the backing plate**

91199P17

**Fig. 54 Remove the parking brake lever horseshoe clip and . . .**

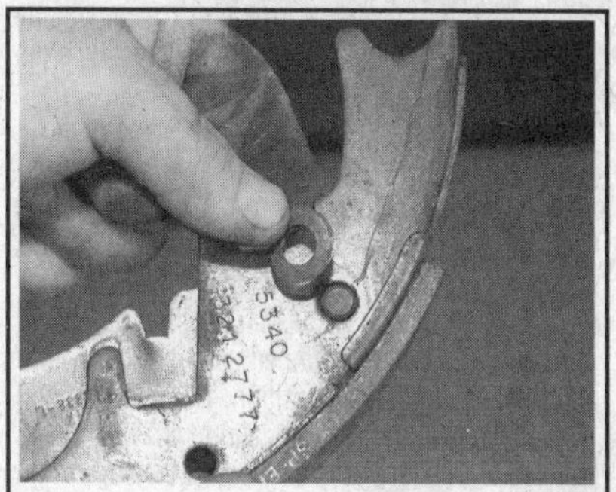
91199P18

**Fig. 55 . . . remove the washer from under the horseshoe clip**

91199P19

**Fig. 56 Remove the secondary brake shoe from the parking brake lever**

91199P20

**Fig. 57 Thoroughly clean and . . .**

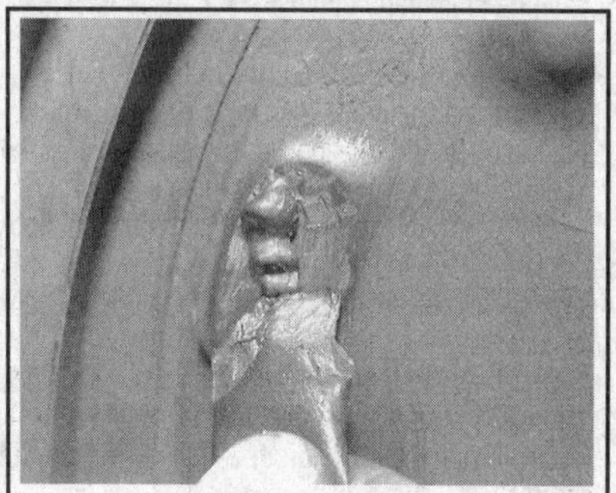
91199P21

**Fig. 58 . . . lubricate the . . .**

91199P22

**Fig. 59 . . . shoe contact points on the backing plate**

spring. Remove the primary shoe-to-anchor spring and unhook the cable anchor. Remove the anchor pin plate.

7. Remove the cable guide from the secondary shoe.

8. Remove the shoe hold-down springs, shoes, adjusting screw, pivot nut, and socket. Note the color of each hold-down spring for assembly. To remove the hold-down springs, reach behind the brake backing plate and place one finger on the end of one of the brake hold-down spring mounting pins. Using a pair of pliers, grasp the washer type retainer on top of the hold-down spring that corresponds to the pin which you are holding. Push down on the pliers and turn them 90° to align the slot in the washer with the head on the spring mounting pin. Remove the spring and washer retainer and repeat this operation on the hold down spring on the other shoe.

9. Remove the parking brake link and spring. Disconnect the parking brake cable from the parking brake lever.

10. After removing the rear brake secondary shoe, disassemble the parking brake lever from the shoe by removing the retaining clip and spring washer.

**To install:**

11. Assemble the parking brake lever to the secondary shoe and secure it with the spring washer and retaining clip.

12. Apply a light coating of Lubriplate®, or equivalent, at the points where the brake shoes contact the backing plate.

13. Position the brake shoes on the backing plate, and install the hold-down spring pins, springs, and spring washer type retainers. On the rear brake, install the parking brake link, spring and washer. Connect the parking brake cable to the parking brake lever.

14. Install the anchor pin plate, and place the cable anchor over the anchor pin with the crimped side toward the backing plate.

15. Install the primary shoe-to-anchor spring with the brake tool.

16. Install the cable guide on the secondary shoe web with the flanged holes fitted into the hole in the secondary shoe web. Thread the cable around the cable guide groove.

17. Install the secondary shoe-to-anchor (long) spring. Be sure that the cable end is not cocked or binding on the anchor pin when installed. All of the parts should be flat on the anchor pin. Remove the wheel cylinder piston clamp.

18. Apply Lubriplate®, or equivalent, to the threads and the socket end of the adjusting starwheel screw. Turn the adjusting screw into the adjusting pivot nut to the limit of the threads and then back off ½ turn.

**➡Interchanging the brake shoe adjusting screw assemblies from one side of the vehicle to the other would cause the brake shoes to retract rather than expand each time the automatic adjusting mechanism is operated. To prevent this, the socket end of the adjusting screw is stamped with an "R" or an "L" for "RIGHT" or "LEFT". The adjusting pivot nuts can be distinguished by the number of lines machined around the body of the nut; one line indicates left hand nut and two lines indicate a right hand nut.**

19. Place the adjusting socket on the screw and install this assembly between the shoe ends with the adjusting screw nearest to the secondary shoe.

20. Place the cable hook into the hole in the adjusting lever from the backing plate side. The adjusting levers are stamped with an **R** (right) or a **L** (left) to indicate their installation on the right or left hand brake assembly.

21. Position the hooked end of the adjuster spring in the primary shoe web and connect the loop end of the spring to the adjuster lever hole.

22. Pull the adjuster lever, cable and automatic

adjuster spring down toward the rear to engage the pivot hook in the large hole in the secondary shoe web.

23. After installation, check the action of the adjuster by pulling the section of the cable guide and the adjusting lever toward the secondary shoe web far enough to lift the lever past a tooth on the adjusting screw starwheel. The lever should snap into position behind the next tooth, and release of the cable should cause the adjuster spring to return the lever to its original position. This return action of the lever will turn the adjusting screw starwheel one tooth. The lever should contact the adjusting screw starwheel one tooth above the centerline of the adjusting screw.

If the automatic adjusting mechanism does not perform properly, check the following:

24. Check the cable and fittings. The cable ends should fill or extend slightly beyond the crimped section of the fittings. If this is not the case, replace the cable.

25. Check the cable guide for damage. The cable groove should be parallel to the shoe web, and the body of the guide should lie flat against the web. Replace the cable guide if this is not so.

26. Check the pivot hook on the lever. The hook surfaces should be square with the body on the lever for proper pivoting. Repair or replace the hook as necessary.

27. Make sure that the adjusting screw starwheel is properly seated in the notch in the shoe web.

28. Install the brake drum and the wheel and tire assembly

29. Carefully lower the vehicle.

### ADJUSTMENTS

The drum brakes are self-adjusting and require a manual adjustment only after the brake shoes have been replaced, or when the length of the adjusting screw has been changed while performing some other service operation, as, for example, when taking off brake drums.

To adjust the brakes, perform the procedures that follow:

#### Drum Installed

➧ See Figure 60

1. Raise and support the rear of the vehicle on jackstands.

2. Remove the rubber plug from the adjusting slot on the backing plate.

**⁂ CAUTION**

**Brake shoes may contain asbestos, which has been determined to be a cancer causing agent. Never clean the brake surfaces with compressed air! Avoid inhaling any dust from any brake surface! When cleaning brake surfaces, use a commercially available brake cleaning fluid.**

3. Insert a brake adjusting spoon into the slot and engage the lowest possible tooth on the starwheel. Move the end of the brake spoon downward to move the starwheel upward and expand the adjusting screw. Repeat this operation until the brakes lock the wheels.

4. Insert a small screwdriver or piece of firm wire (coat hanger wire) into the adjusting slot and push the automatic adjusting lever out and free of the starwheel on the adjusting screw and hold it there.

5. Engage the topmost tooth possible on the starwheel with the brake adjusting spoon. Move the end of the adjusting spoon upward to move the adjusting screw starwheel downward and contact the adjusting screw. Back off the adjusting screw starwheel until the wheel spins freely with a minimum of drag. Keep track of the number of turns that the starwheel is backed off, or the number of strokes taken with the brake adjusting spoon.

6. Repeat this operation for the other side. When backing off the brakes on the other side, the starwheel adjuster must be backed off the same number of turns to prevent side-to-side brake pull.

7. Remove the jackstands and lower the vehicle.

8. After the brakes are adjusted make several stops while backing the vehicle up, to equalize the brakes at both of the wheels. Road test the vehicle.

#### Drum Removed

➧ See Figures 61 and 62

**⁂ CAUTION**

**Brake shoes may contain asbestos, which has been determined to be a cancer causing agent. Never clean the brake surfaces with compressed air! Avoid inhaling any dust from any brake surface! When cleaning brake surfaces, use a commercially available brake cleaning fluid.**

1. Make sure that the shoe-to-contact pad areas are clean and properly lubricated.

2. Using an inside caliper check the inside diameter of the drum. Measure across the diameter of the assembled brake shoes, at their widest point.

3. Turn the adjusting screw so that the diameter of the shoes is 0.030 in. (0.76mm) less than the brake drum inner diameter.

4. Install the drum.

## Wheel Cylinders

### INSPECTION

Carefully pull the lower edges of the wheel cylinder boots away from the cylinders to see if the interior of the cylinder is wet with brake fluid. Excessive fluid at this point indicates leakage past the piston cups and a need for wheel cylinder replacement.

**➥A slight amount of fluid is nearly always present and acts as a lubricant for the piston.**

### REMOVAL & INSTALLATION

➧ See Figures 63, 64, 65 and 66

1. Raise and safely support the vehicle.
2. Remove the rear wheel and tire assembly.
3. Remove the brake drum retainers, if equipped.
4. Grasp the brake drum and remove.
5. If the drum will not slide off with light force, then the brake shoes need to be backed off.

**⁂ CAUTION**

**Brake shoes may contain asbestos, which has been determined to be a cancer causing agent. Never clean the brake surfaces with compressed air! Avoid inhaling any dust from any brake surface! When cleaning brake surfaces, use a commercially available brake cleaning fluid.**

6. Remove the brake drum.
7. Remove the brake shoes.

**⁂ CAUTION**

**Brake fluid contains polyglycol ethers and polyglycols. Avoid contact with the eyes and wash your hands thoroughly after handling brake fluid. If you do get brake fluid in your**

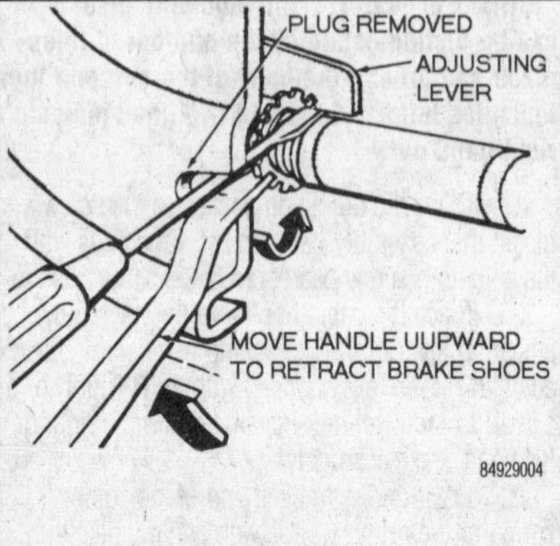

**Fig. 60 Rear brake shoe adjustment**

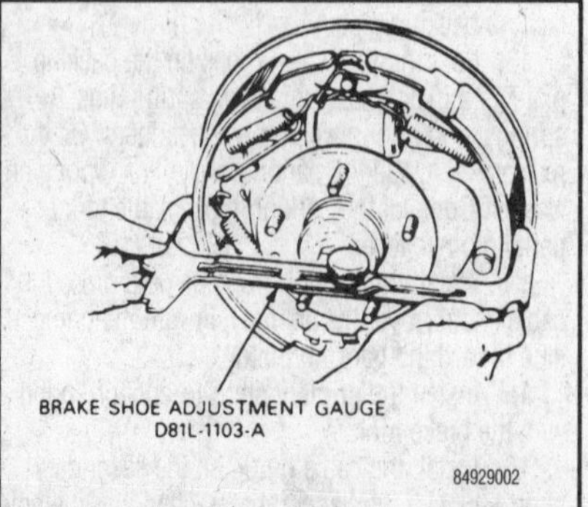

**Fig. 61 Use a gauge as shown to measure the brake shoes**

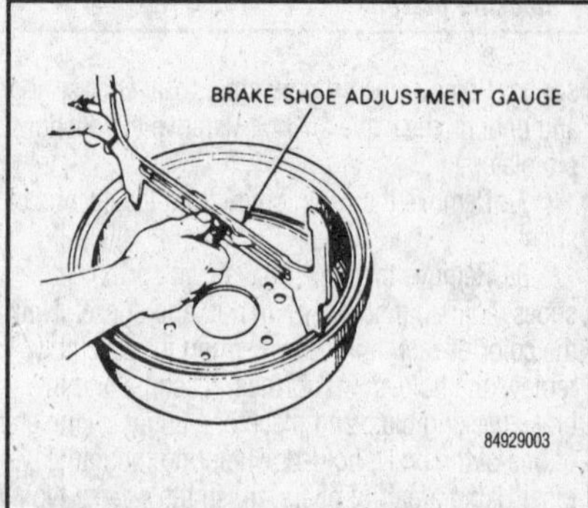

**Fig. 62 Use a gauge as shown to measure the drum**

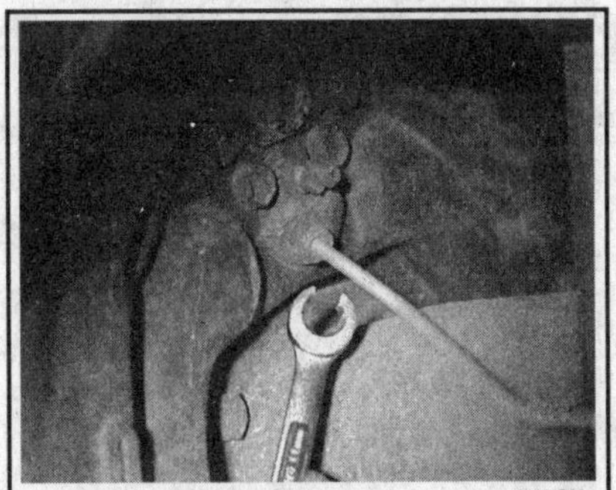
91199P23

Fig. 63 Use a suitable size flare nut wrench to . . .

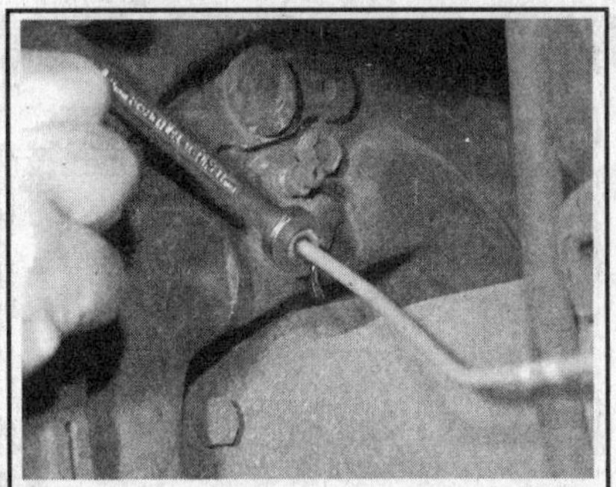
91199P24

Fig. 64 . . . loosen the brake line fitting on the wheel cylinder

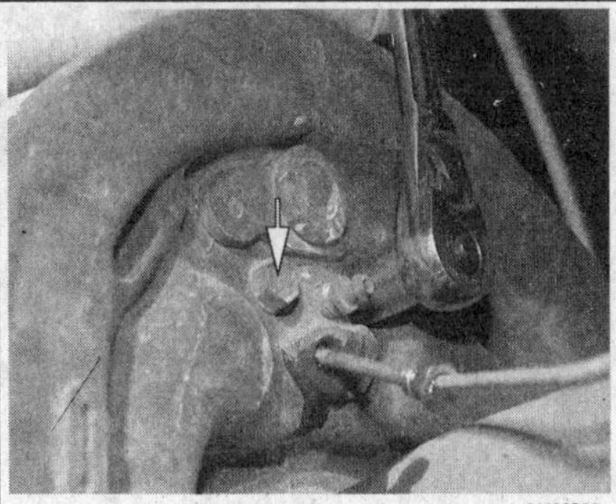
91199P25

Fig. 65 Remove the wheel cylinder retaining bolts and . . .

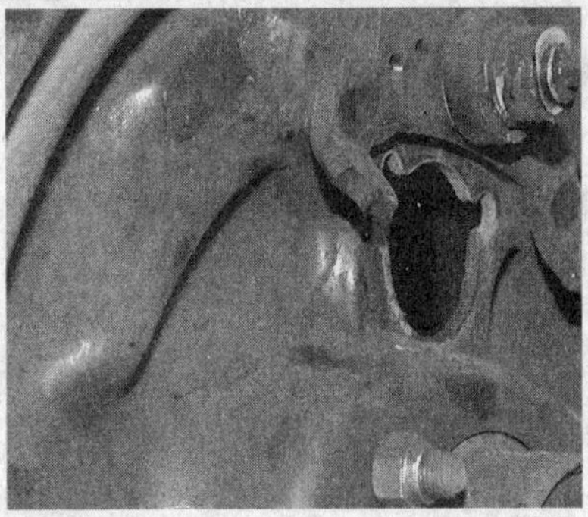
91199P26

Fig. 66 . . . remove the wheel cylinder from the backing plate

**eyes, flush your eyes with clean, running water for 15 minutes. If eye irritation persists, or if you have taken brake fluid internally, IMMEDIATELY seek medical assistance.**

8. Disconnect the brake line at the wheel cylinder.
9. Remove the 2 bolts securing the wheel cylinder to the backing plate and remove the wheel cylinder.

**To install:**

10. Reinstall the wheel cylinder to the brake backing plate and install the 2 retaining bolts. Torque the retaining bolts to 84–108 inch. lbs. (10–13 Nm).
11. Reconnect the brake line to the wheel cylinder and torque the fitting to 10–18 ft. lbs. (14–24 Nm).
12. Lubricate the rear brake shoe contact points on the backing plate with an appropriate grease.
13. Install the brake shoes.
14. Make sure that the brake drum and brake shoes are clean of any oils or protective coatings.
15. Reinstall the brake drum.
16. Bleed the brake system of air until a firm pedal is achieved. Top off the brake fluid in the master cylinder.

**WARNING**

**Clean, high quality brake fluid is essential to the safe and proper operation of the brake system. You should always buy the highest quality brake fluid that is available. If the brake fluid becomes contaminated, drain and flush the system, then refill the master cylinder with new fluid. Never reuse any brake fluid. Any brake fluid that is removed from the system should be discarded. Also, do not allow any brake fluid to come in contact with a painted surface; it will damage the paint.**

17. Reinstall the wheel and tire assembly.
18. Lower the vehicle.
19. Pump the brake pedal several times to assure a good pedal.
20. Road test the vehicle and check the brake system for proper operation.

# PARKING BRAKE

## Brake Shoes (Parking)

### REMOVAL & INSTALLATION

**See Figures 67 and 68**

1. Raise and safely support the vehicle.
2. Remove the rear axle shaft; refer to Section 7.
3. Disconnect the brake cable from the lever.
4. Remove the brake shoe retaining springs and pins.
5. Set the adjuster assembly to the shortest length. Pull the shoes away from the backing plate slightly and spread them enough to remove the adjuster assembly.
6. Remove the upper return (adjuster) spring.
7. Lift the shoes over the support and remove the shoes and actuating lever as an assembly. Make sure the lever does not damage the boot or pull the boot out of position.
8. Disassemble the shoes, lever and springs.

**To install:**

9. Install the lower return springs and actuating lever to the brake shoes.
10. Make sure the boot is properly positioned in the backing plate. Install the shoes by first inserting the lever through the boot, then lowering the shoes into position.
11. Install the upper return (adjuster) spring and install the adjuster assembly.
12. Install the brake shoe retaining springs and pins.
13. Connect the brake cable to the lever.
14. Install the rear axle shaft.
15. Center the brake shoes on the backing plate. Using an 8-in. micrometer or calipers, gauge the brake shoes.

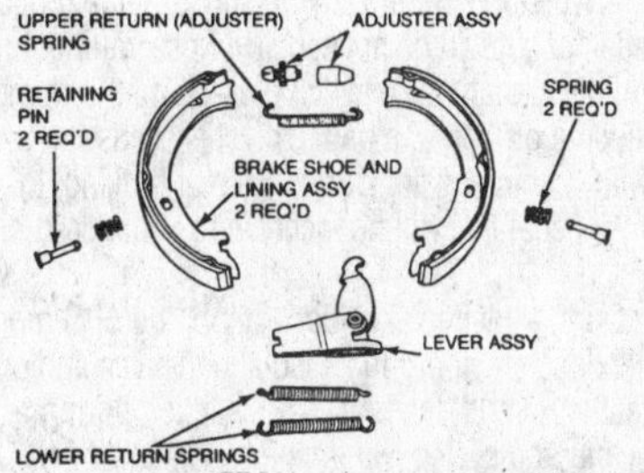


Fig. 67 Parking brake shoe assembly

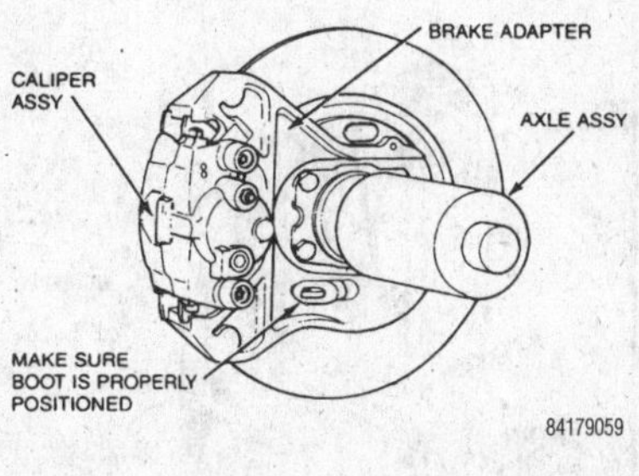


Fig. 68 Rear view of the brake backing plate

# ANTI-LOCK BRAKE SYSTEM

## General Information

The 4-Wheel Anti-lock Brake System (ABS) is an electronically operated, all wheel brake control system. Major components include the power brake booster, master cylinder, the wheel speed sensors, and the Hydraulic Control Unit (HCU) which contains the control module, a relay, and the pressure control valves.

The system is designed to retard wheel lockup during periods of high wheel slip when braking. Retarding wheel lockup is accomplished by modulating fluid pressure to the wheel brake units. When the control module detects a variation in voltage across the wheel speed sensors, the ABS is activated. The control module opens and closes various valves located inside the HCU. These valves, called dump and isolation valves, modulate the hydraulic pressure to the wheels by applying and venting the pressure to the brake fluid circuits.

Some models are equipped with a Traction Assist (TA) system. The TA system senses wheel spin upon acceleration, turns on the Hydraulic Control Unit (HCU) pump and applies fluid pressure to the appropriate rear wheel. Two additional isolation valves in the HCU will also close to permit fluid to flow only to the rear wheels.

The TA system monitors TA usage to avoid overheating the rear brakes. If the system does sense brake overheating, the ABS module will inhibit TA operation until the rear brakes are permitted to cool down.

### SYSTEM COMPONENTS

The anti-lock brake system consists of the following components:

- Vacuum booster and master cylinder assembly
- Hydraulic Control Unit (HCU)
- ABS module
- Wheel sensors
- Pedal travel switch

## ABS Module

➧ See Figures 69, 70 and 71

The ABS module is an on-board, self-test, nonrepairable unit consisting of 2 microprocessors and

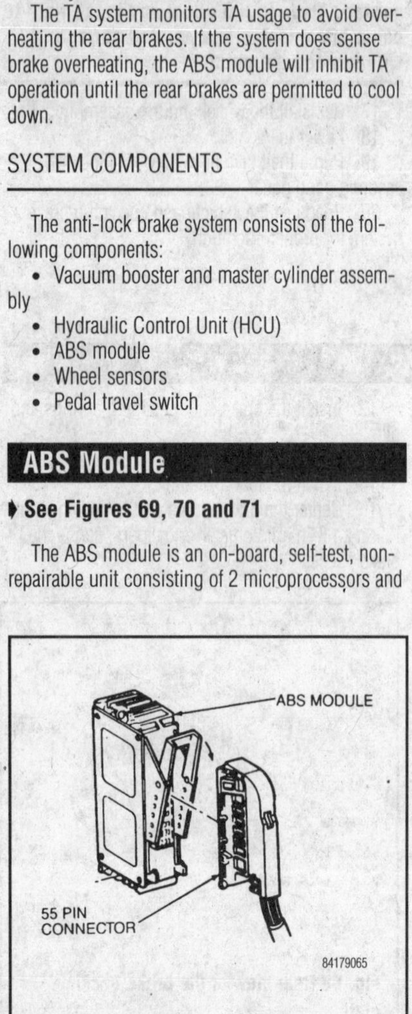


**Fig. 69 ABS module**

| SERVICE CODE (COMPONENT) |
|---|
| 11 (Electronic Controller) |
| 12 (Electronic Controller-Replacer) |
| [1]21 (Main Valve) |
| [1]22 (LH Front Inlet Valve) |
| [1]23 (LH Front Outlet Valve) |
| [1]24 (RH Front Inlet Valve) |
| [1]25 (RH Front Outlet Valve) |
| [1]26 (Rear Inlet Valve) |
| [1]27 (Rear Outlet Valve and Ground) |
| 31 (LH Front Sensor) |
| 32 (RH Front Sensor) |
| 33 (RH Rear Sensor) |
| 34 (LH Rear Sensor) |
| 35 (LH Front Sensor) |
| 36 (RH Front Sensor) |
| 37 (RH Rear Sensor) |
| 38 (LH Rear Sensor) |
| 41 (LH Front Sensor) |
| 42 (RH Front Sensor) |
| 43 (RH Rear Sensor) |

93149G01

**Fig. 70 The on-board self test service codes (1 of 2)**

| SERVICE CODE (COMPONENT) |
|---|
| 44 (LH Rear Sensor) |
| 45 (LH Front Sensor) |
| 46 (RH Front Sensor) |
| 47 (RH and LH Rear Sensors) |
| 48 (Any 3 Sensors missing) |
| 51 (LH Front Outlet Valve) |
| 52 (RH Front Outlet Valve) |
| 53 (Rear Outlet Valve) |
| 54 (Rear Outlet Valve) |
| 55 (LH Front Sensor) |
| 56 (RH Front Sensor) |
| 57 (RH Rear Sensor) |
| 58 (LH Rear Sensor) |
| 61 (FLI and PWS Circuit) |
| 71 (LH Front Sensor) |
| 72 (RH Front Sensor) |
| 73 (RH Rear Sensor) |
| 74 (LH Rear Sensor) |
| 75 (LH Front Sensor) |
| 76 (RH Front Sensor) |
| 77 (RH Rear Sensor) |
| 78 (LH Rear Sensor) |
| 88 (Electronic Controller) |
| 99 (Electronic Controller) |

93149G02

**Fig. 71 The on-board self test service codes (2 of 2)**

the necessary circuitry for their operation. These microprocessors are programmed identically. The ABS module monitors system operation during normal driving as well as during anti-lock braking and traction assist cycling.

Under normal driving conditions, the microprocessors produce short test pulses to the solenoid valves that check the electrical system without any mechanical reaction. Impending wheel lock conditions trigger signals from the ABS module that open and close the appropriate solenoid valves. This results in moderate pulsation in the brake pedal. If brake pedal travel exceeds a preset dimension determined by the pedal travel switch setting, the ABS module will send a signal to the pump to turn on and provide high pressure to the brake system. When the pump starts to run, a gradual rise in pedal height will be noticed. This rise will continue until the pedal travel switch closes and the pump will shut off until the pedal travel exceeds the travel switch setting again. During normal braking, the brake pedal feel will be identical to a standard brake system.

During traction assist operation, the ABS module will close the appropriate isolation valves and operate the pump. If the brakes are applied during cycling, the system will automatically shut off. The ABS module monitors traction assist usage and will shut off the traction assist features to prevent overheating of the rear brakes. If the system shuts off, there is a cool down period required before it becomes functional again. This cool down period varies depending on brake usage during the cool down period. Anti-lock braking is still fully functional during the cool down period.

Most malfunctions, which occur to the anti-lock brake system and the traction assist, will be stored as a coded number in the keep-alive memory of the ABS module. The codes can be retrieved from memory by following the on-board self-test procedures.

**➡Any brake code between 20–29 must be serviced before the processor will output any other codes**

### REMOVAL & INSTALLATION

#### 1988–94 Continental and Mark VII

➧ See Figures 72, 73 and 74

#### 1990–94 Town Car and 1993–94 Mark VIII

➧ See Figure 75

1. Disconnect the negative battery cable.
2. Locate the ABS module at the left front side of the radiator support.
3. Detach the 55-pin connector from the ABS module. Unlock the connector by pulling up the lever completely. Move the end of the connector away from the ABS module until all terminals are clear, then pull the connector up and out of the slots in the ABS module.
4. Remove the 3 screws attaching the ABS

93149P05

**Fig. 72 This is the ABS module. It is located in the luggage compartment, mounted against the rear seat supports**

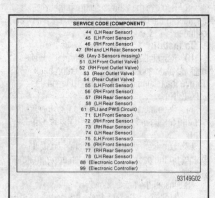

93149P04

**Fig. 73 You will find the ABS module mounted next to the door lock module**

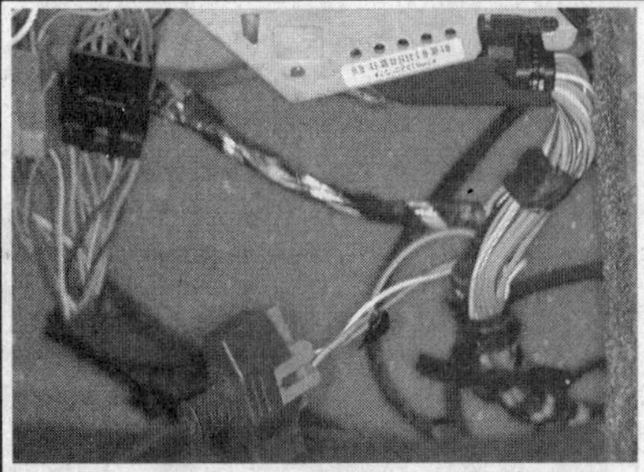


**Fig. 74 This is the test connector for the ABS system. Use the Ford Super Star II tester or an equivalent scan tool to access the ABS system**

module to the mounting bracket and remove the ABS module.

**To install:**

5. Align the ABS module with the bracket so that the lever is facing the drivers side of the vehicle. If all 3 mounting holes in the ABS module do not line up with the holes in the mounting bracket, the ABS module is incorrectly aligned with the bracket. Install the 3 attaching screws and tighten to 40–60 inch lbs. (4.5–6.8 Nm).
6. Attach the 55-pin connector by installing the bottom part of the connector into the slots in the ABS module and pushing the top portion of the connector into the ABS module. Then, pull the locking lever completely down to ensure proper installation.
7. Connect the negative battery cable.

### 1995–00 Vehicles

**➡The control module is located on the HCU. To facilitate the removal of the module, the HCU must be removed. If the proper tools for bleeding the ABS system are not available, you will need to have a professional technician perform this repair.**

**WARNING**

**Electronic modules are sensitive to static electrical charges. If exposed to these charges, damage may result.**

1. Disconnect the negative battery cable.
2. Remove the HCU as describe din this section.
3. Remove the module retaining screws and remove the anti-lock brake control module.
4. The installation is the reverse of the removal.

## Hydraulic Control Unit

### REMOVAL & INSTALLATION

### 1992–94

**➧ See Figure 76**

1. Disconnect the negative battery cable and remove the air cleaner and air outlet tube.
2. Detach the 19-pin connector from the HCU

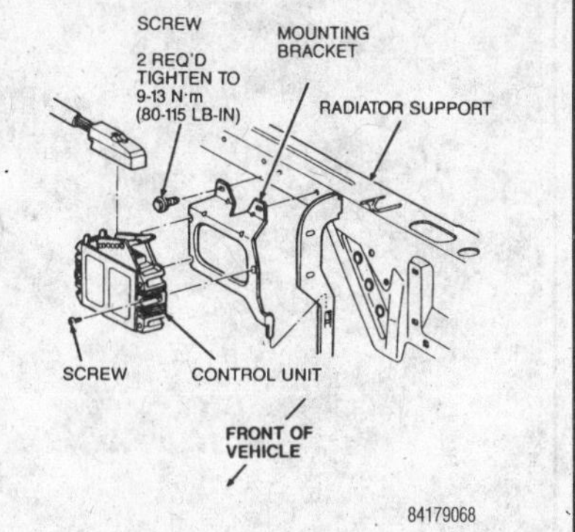


**Fig. 75 ABS module installation**

to the wire harness and detach the 4-pin connector from the HCU to the pump motor relay.

3. Remove the 2 lines from the inlet ports and the 4 lines from the outlet ports of the HCU. Plug each port to prevent brake fluid from spilling onto the paint and wiring.
4. Remove the 3 nuts retaining the HCU assembly to the mounting bracket and remove the assembly from the vehicle.

**➡The nut on the front of the HCU also retains the relay-mounting bracket.**

**To install:**

5. Position the HCU assembly into the mounting bracket. Install the 3 retaining nuts and tighten to 12–18 ft. lbs. (16–24 Nm). Make sure the ABS pump motor relay bracket is retained by the front bracket nut.
6. Connect 4 lines to the outlet ports on the side of the HCU and 2 lines to the inlet ports on the rear of the HCU and tighten the fittings to 10–18 ft. lbs. (14–24 Nm).
7. Attach the 19-pin connector to the harness and the 4-pin connector to the pump motor relay.
8. Install the air cleaner and air outlet tube.
9. Connect the battery cables, properly bleed the brake system and check for fluid leaks.

### 1995–00

1. Disconnect the negative battery cable.
2. Detach the anti-lock brake control module electrical connectors.

**CAUTION**

**Brake fluid contains polyglycol ethers and polyglycols. Avoid contact with the eyes and wash your hands thoroughly after handling brake fluid. If you do get brake fluid in your eyes, flush your eyes with clean, running water for 15 minutes. If eye irritation persists, or if you have taken brake fluid internally, IMMEDIATELY seek medical assistance.**

3. Disconnect and plug the hydraulic brake lines.
4. Remove the HCU retaining bolts and remove the HCU.
5. If necessary, remove the HCU bracket.

**To install:**

6. If removed, install the HCU bracket.
7. Position the HCU.
8. Install and tighten the retaining bolts.
9. Connect the hydraulic brake lines.
10. Connect the anti-lock brake control module electrical connectors.
11. Connect the negative battery cable.
12. Bleed the 4-wheel ABS.

## Speed Sensors

### REMOVAL & INSTALLATION

### Front

**➧ See Figures 77, 78, 79, 80 and 81**

1. Disconnect the negative battery cable.
2. From inside engine compartment, detach sensor assembly 2-pin connector from the wiring harness.
3. Remove the steel routing clip attaching the sensor wire to the tube bundle on the left sensor or remove the plastic routing clip attaching the sensor wire to the frame on the right sensor.
4. Remove the rubber coated spring steel clip holding the sensor wire to the frame.
5. Remove the sensor wire from the steel routing clip on the frame and from the dust shield.
6. Remove the sensor attaching bolt from the front spindle and slide the sensor out of the mounting hole.

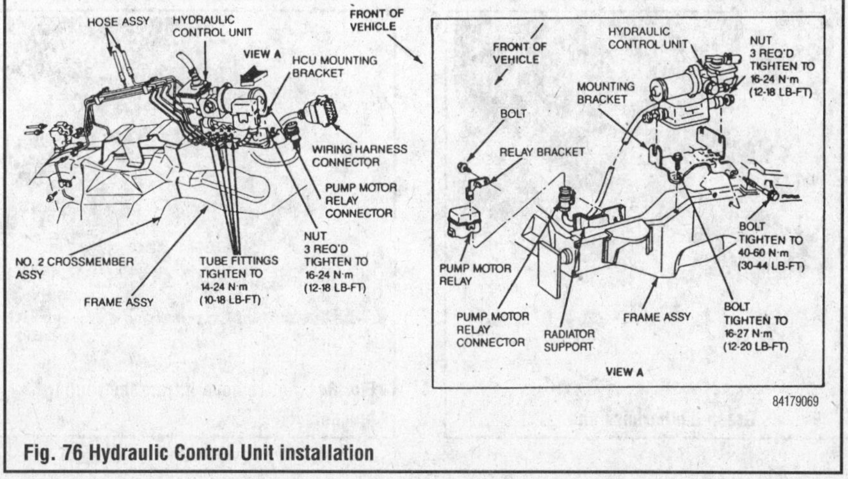


**Fig. 76 Hydraulic Control Unit installation**

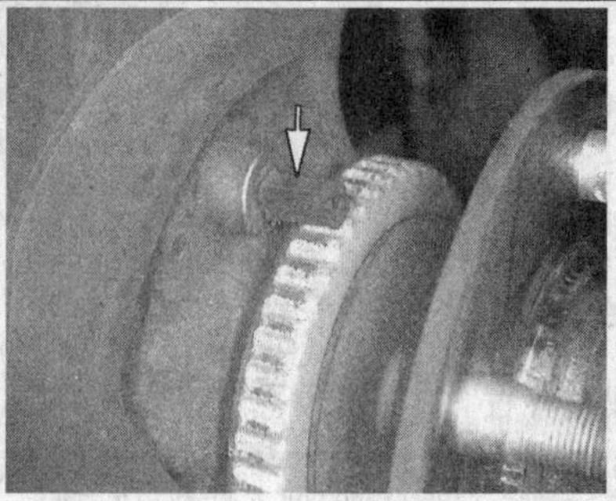
89609P51

**Fig. 77 The speed sensor sits directly over the exciter ring in the front knuckle**

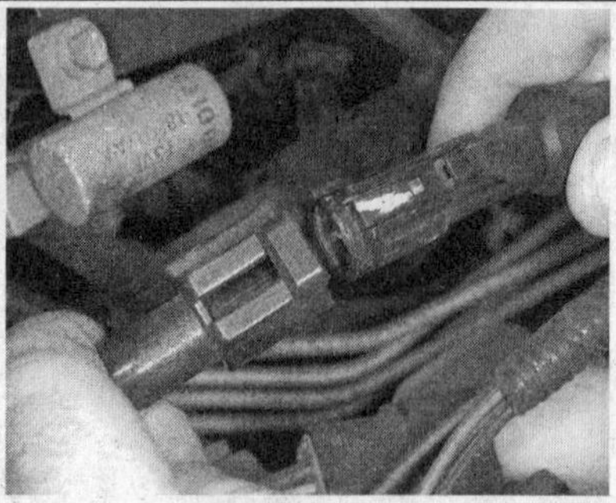
89609P55

**Fig. 78 Detach the speed sensor connector in the engine compartment**

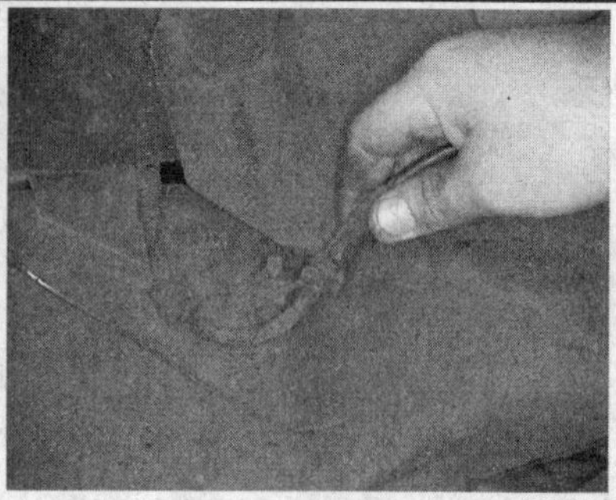
89609P53

**Fig. 79 Remove the speed sensor harness from the routing clips**

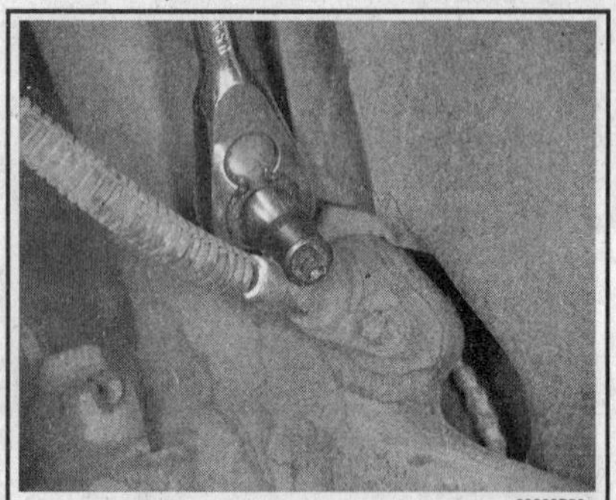
89609P52

**Fig. 80 A special E6 Torx® socket is required to remove the speed sensor-retaining bolt**

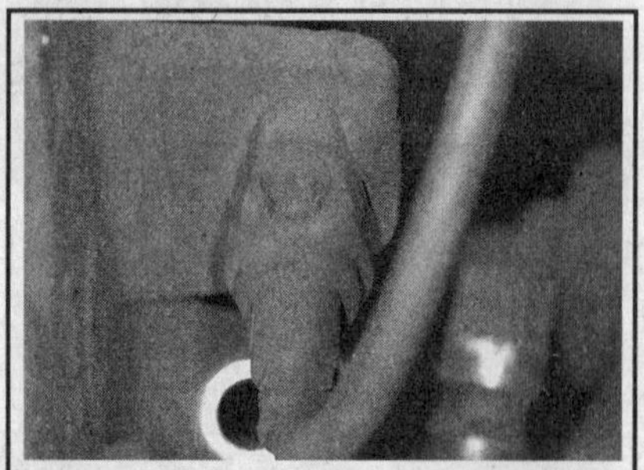
93149P17

**Fig. 81 The sensor sits in a special mounting boss that does not allow an adjustable air gap between the sensor and exciter ring**

89609P04

**Fig. 82 Detach the speed sensor connector in the luggage compartment**

**To install:**

7. Install the sensor into the mounting hole in the front spindle and attach with the mounting bolt. Torque to 40–60 inch lbs. (4.5–6.8 Nm).

8. Insert the sensor routing grommets into the dust shield and steel bracket on the frame. Route the wire into the engine compartment.

9. Install the rubber coated steel clip that holds the sensor wire to the frame into the hole in the frame.

10. Install the steel clip that holds sensor wire to tube bundle on left side or plastic clip that holds sensor to frame on right side.

11. Reconnect the 2-pin connector to wire harness. Reconnect the negative battery cable.

### Rear

➧ **See Figures 82 thru 88**

1. Disconnect the negative battery cable.

2. From inside luggage compartment, detach 2-pin sensor connector from wiring harness and push sensor wire through hole in floor.

3. From below vehicle, remove sensor wire from routing bracket located on top of rear axle carrier housing and remove steel clip holding sensor wire and brake tube against axle housing.

4. Remove screw from clip holding sensor wire and brake tube to bracket on axle.

5. Remove sensor to rear adapter retaining bolt and remove sensor.

**To install:**

6. Insert sensor adapter and install retaining bolt. Torque to 40–60 inch lbs. (4.5–6.8 Nm).

7. Attach clip holding sensor and brake tube to bracket on axle housing and secure with screw. Torque to 40–60 inch lbs. (4.5–6.8 Nm).

8. Install steel clip around axle tube that holds sensor wire and brake tube against axle tube and push spool-shaped grommet into clip located on top of axle carrier housing.

9. Push sensor wire connector up through hole in floor and seat large round grommet into hole.

10. Push sensor wire connector up through hole in floor and seat large round grommet into hole.

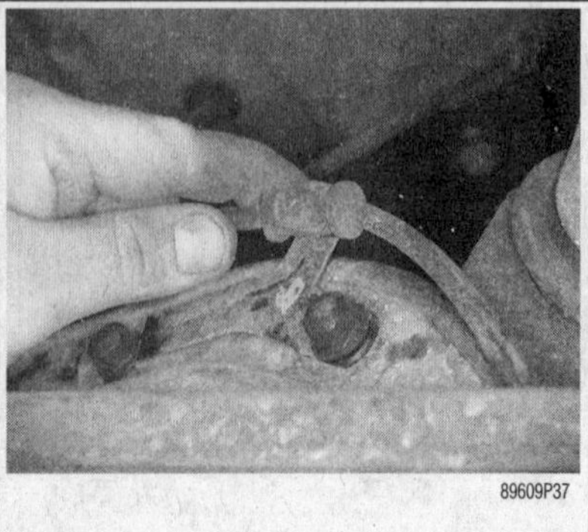
89609P37

**Fig. 83 Grasp the harness and . . .**

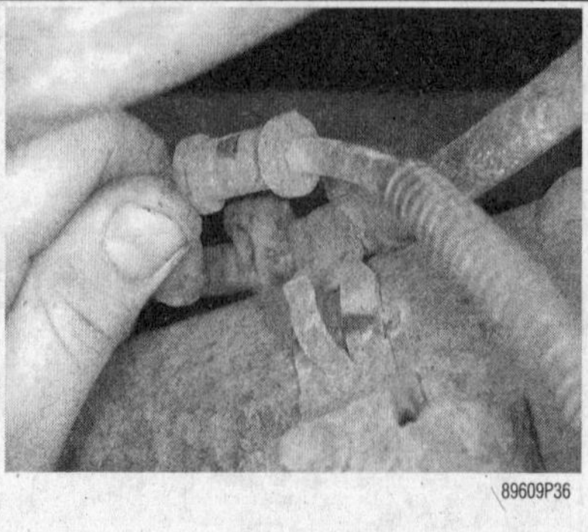
89609P36

**Fig. 84 . . . remove it from the routing brackets**

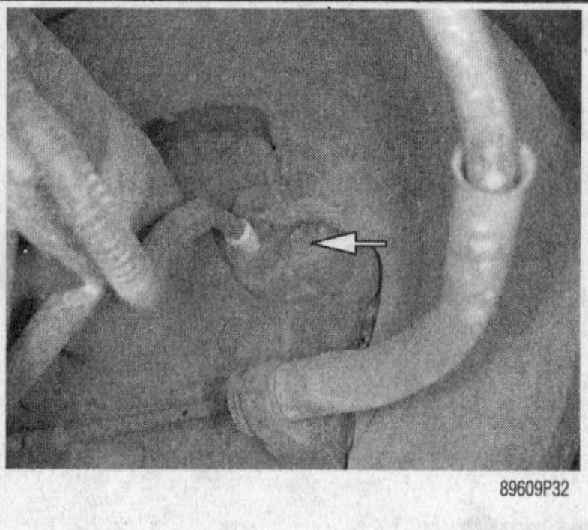
89609P32

**Fig. 85 The rear speed sensor is mounted on the back of the hub assembly**

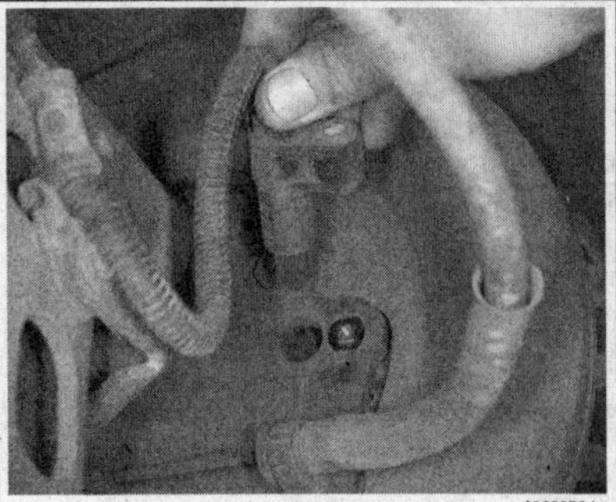


**Fig. 86 Remove the sensor retaining bolt and remove the sensor from the hub**

**Fig. 87 The sensor is bolted through the back of the plate on the rear wheels, and is held in place by an external Torx®head bolt. The same as the front**

**Fig. 88 When the head comes through the backing plate it mounts next to the exciter ring**

11. Reconnect sensor 2-pin connector to wiring harness inside luggage compartment.

## Bleeding the ABS System

### 1992–1994

**➡The ABS brake system must be bled using Anti-lock Test Adapter T90P-50-ALA, or equivalent. If the procedure is not followed correctly, air will stay trapped in the Hydraulic Control Unit (HCU) which will lead to a spongy brake pedal.**

1. To bleed the master cylinder and the HCU, connect the anti-lock tester wiring harness to the 55-pin harness connector of the ABS module.
2. Place the bleed/harness switch in the bleed position.
3. Turn the ignition switch to the ON position.
4. Push the motor button on the tester down, starting the pump motor. The pump motor will run for 60 seconds.
5. After 20 seconds of pump motor operation, push and hold the valve button down. Hold the valve button down for 20 seconds.
6. The pump motor will continue to run for an additional 20 seconds.
7. The master cylinder and HCU should be free of air and the brake lines must now be bleed using the conventional method for non-ABS brake systems by bleeding the wheels in the following sequence: right-hand rear, left-hand front, left-hand rear and right-hand front.
8. Road test the vehicle and check for proper brake system operation.

### 1995–00

Whenever service is performed on the ABS valve block or pump and motor assembly, the following procedure must be performed to make sure no air is trapped in the ABS control and modulator assembly. If this procedure is not done, the vehicle operator could experience a spongy pedal after the ABS is actuated. This procedure requires the use of the Ford New Generation STAR (NGS) Tester, or equivalent.

1. First bleed the entire brake system conventionally as described above.
2. Reattach the NGS Tester to the data link connector as though retrieving codes.
3. Make sure the ignition is in the **RUN** position.
4. Follow the instructions on the NGS screen. Choose the correct vehicle and model year, go to DIAGNOSTIC DATA LINK menu item, choose ABS MODULE, choose FUNCTION TESTS and choose SERVICE BLEED.
5. The NGS will prompt you to depress the brake pedal. Make sure you press hard on the brake pedal, and hold it down for approximately 5 seconds while the NGS opens the outlet valves in the brake pressure control valve block. When the outlet valves are opened, you should immediately feel the pedal drop. It is very important that you continue pushing the pedal all the way to the floor. The NGS will then instruct you to release the brake pedal. After you release the brake pedal, the NGS will run the ABS hydraulic pump motor for approximately 15 seconds.
6. Repeat the previous step to ensure that all air is bleed from the ABS unit. Upon completion, the NGS will display SERVICE BLEED PROCEDURE COMPLETED.
7. Repeat the conventional bleeding procedure.
8. Once complete, road test the vehicle and check for proper brake system operation.

## BRAKE SPECIFICATIONS

All measurements in inches unless noted

| Year | Model | Master Cylinder Bore | Front Brake Disc Original Thickness | Front Brake Disc Minimum Thickness | Front Brake Disc Maximum Run-out | Rear Brake Disc Original Thicknes | Rear Brake Disc Minimum Thickness | Rear Brake Disc Maximum Run-out | Minimum Lining Thickness | Brake Caliper Bracket Bolts (ft. lbs.) | Brake Caliper Mounting Bolts (ft. lbs.) |
|---|---|---|---|---|---|---|---|---|---|---|---|
| 1988 | Mark VII | N/A | 1.024 | 0.972 | 0.003 | N/A | 0.895 | 0.004 | 0.123 | 125-169 | 21-26 |
| | Contintental | N/A | 1.024 | 0.970 | 0.002 | N/A | 0.974 A | 0.002 | 0.123 | 125-169 | 21-26 |
| | Town Car E | 1.000 | 1.024 | 0.972 | 0.003 | 10.00 B | 10.90 C | 0.005 | 0.030 D | 125-169 | 21-26 |
| 1989 | Mark VII | N/A | 1.024 | 0.972 | 0.003 | N/A | 0.895 | 0.004 | 0.123 | 125-169 | 21-26 |
| | Contintental | N/A | 1.024 | 0.970 | 0.002 | N/A | 0.974 A | 0.035 | 0.123 | 125-169 | 21-26 |
| | Town Car E | 1.000 | 1.024 | 0.972 | 0.003 | 10.00 B | 10.90 C | 0.005 | 0.030 D | 125-169 | 21-26 |
| 1990 | Mark VII | N/A | 1.024 | 0.972 | 0.003 | N/A | 0.895 | 0.004 | 0.123 | 125-169 | 21-26 |
| | Contintental | N/A | 1.024 | 0.970 | 0.002 | N/A | 0.974 A | 0.035 | 0.123 | 125-169 | 21-26 |
| | Town Car E | 1.000 | 1.024 | 0.972 | 0.003 | 10.00 B | 10.90 C | 0.005 | 0.030 D | 125-169 | 21-26 |
| 1991 | Mark VII | 1.000 | 1.024 | 0.974 | 0.002 | 0.550 | 0.510 | 0.002 | 0.123 | 125-169 | 21-26 |
| | Contintental | 1.000 | 1.024 | 0.974 | 0.002 | 9.400 | 0.510 | 0.035 | 0.123 | 125-169 | 21-26 |
| | Town Car | 1.000 | 1.024 | 0.974 | 0.002 | 0.550 | 0.510 | 0.002 | 0.125 | 125-169 | 21-26 |
| 1992 | Mark VII | 1.000 | 1.024 | 0.974 | 0.002 | 0.550 | 0.510 | 0.002 | 0.123 | 125-169 | 21-26 |
| | Contintental | 1.000 | 1.024 | 0.974 | 0.002 | 0.550 | 0.510 | 0.035 | 0.123 | 125-169 | 21-26 |
| | Town Car | 1.000 | 1.024 | 0.974 | 0.002 | 0.550 | 0.510 | 0.002 | 0.125 | 125-169 | 21-26 |
| 1993 | Mark VIII | 1.000 | 1.024 | 0.974 | 0.002 | 0.550 | 0.510 | 0.002 | 0.123 | 125-169 | 21-26 |
| | Contintental | 1.000 | 1.024 | 0.974 | 0.002 | 0.550 | 0.510 | 0.035 | 0.123 | 125-169 | 21-26 |
| | Town Car | 1.000 | 1.024 | 0.974 | 0.002 | 0.550 | 0.510 | 0.002 | 0.125 | 125-169 | 21-26 |
| 1994 | Mark VIII | 1.000 | 1.024 | 0.974 | 0.002 | 0.550 | 0.510 | 0.002 | 0.123 | 125-169 | 21-26 |
| | Contintental | 1.000 | 1.024 | 0.974 | 0.002 | 0.550 | 0.502 | 0.035 | 0.123 | 125-169 | 21-26 |
| | Town Car | 1.000 | 1.024 | 0.974 | 0.002 | 0.550 | 0.510 | 0.002 | 0.125 | 125-169 | 21-26 |
| 1995 | Mark VIII | 1.000 | 1.024 | 0.974 | 0.002 | 0.550 | 0.510 | 0.002 | 0.123 | 125-169 | 21-26 |
| | Contintental | 1.000 | 1.024 | 0.974 | 0.002 | 0.550 | 0.502 | 0.035 | 0.123 | 125-169 | 21-26 |
| | Town Car | 1.000 | 1.024 | 0.974 | 0.002 | 0.550 | 0.510 | 0.002 | 0.125 | 125-169 | 21-26 |
| 1996 | Mark VIII | 1.000 | 1.024 | 0.974 | 0.002 | 0.550 | 0.510 | 0.002 | 0.123 | 125-169 | 21-26 |
| | Contintental | 1.000 | 1.024 | 0.974 | 0.002 | 0.550 | 0.502 | 0.035 | 0.123 | 125-169 | 21-26 |
| | Town Car | 1.000 | 1.024 | 0.974 | 0.002 | 0.550 | 0.510 | 0.002 | 0.125 | 125-169 | 21-26 |
| 1997 | Mark VIII | 1.000 | 1.024 | 0.974 | 0.002 | 0.550 | 0.510 | 0.002 | 0.123 | 125-169 | 21-26 |
| | Contintental | 1.000 | 1.024 | 0.974 | 0.002 | 0.550 | 0.502 | 0.035 | 0.123 | 125-169 | 21-26 |
| | Town Car | 1.000 | 1.024 | 0.974 | 0.002 | 0.550 | 0.510 | 0.002 | 0.125 | 125-169 | 21-26 |
| 1998 | Mark VIII | 1.000 | 1.024 | 0.974 | 0.002 | 0.550 | 0.510 | 0.002 | 0.123 | 125-169 | 21-26 |
| | Contintental | 1.000 | 1.024 | 0.974 | 0.002 | 0.550 | 0.502 | 0.035 | 0.123 | 125-169 | 21-26 |
| | Town Car | 1.000 | 1.024 | 0.974 | 0.002 | 0.550 | 0.510 | 0.002 | 0.125 | 125-169 | 21-26 |
| 1999 | Contintental | 1.000 | 1.024 | 0.974 | 0.002 | 0.550 | 0.502 | 0.035 | 0.123 | 125-169 | 21-26 |
| | Town Car | 1.000 | 1.024 | 0.974 | 0.002 | 0.550 | 0.510 | 0.002 | 0.125 | 125-169 | 21-26 |
| 2000 | Contintental | 1.000 | 1.024 | 0.974 | 0.002 | 0.550 | 0.502 | 0.035 | 0.123 | 125-169 | 21-26 |
| | Town Car | 1.000 | 1.024 | 0.974 | 0.002 | 0.550 | 0.510 | 0.002 | 0.125 | 125-169 | 21-26 |

NOTE: Follow specifications stamped on rotor or drum if figures differ from those in this chart.

A - Minimum safe thickness is shown on each rotor.

B - Original diameter for standard drum brake.

C - Maximum allowable diameter.

D - Rear Drum shoe measurement.

E - Rear drum brakes were standard on these vehicles.

93149C01

**EXTERIOR 10-2**
DOORS 10-2
ADJUSTMENT 10-2
HOOD 10-2
REMOVAL & INSTALLATION 10-2
TRUNK LID 10-3
ALIGNMENT 10-3
OUTSIDE MIRRORS 10-3
REMOVAL & INSTALLATION 10-3
ANTENNA 10-4
REPLACEMENT 10-4
**INTERIOR 10-6**
INSTRUMENT PANEL AND PAD 10-6
REMOVAL & INSTALLATION 10-6
CENTER CONSOLE 10-9
REMOVAL & INSTALLATION 10-9
OVERHEAD CONSOLE 10-10
REMOVAL & INSTALLATION 10-10
DOOR PANELS 10-10
REMOVAL & INSTALLATION 10-10
DOOR LOCKS 10-13
REMOVAL & INSTALLATION 10-13
DOOR GLASS AND REGULATOR 10-15
REMOVAL & INSTALLATION 10-15
DOOR WINDOW REGULATOR 10-17
REMOVAL & INSTALLATION 10-17
POWER WINDOW MOTOR 10-18
REMOVAL & INSTALLATION 10-18
INSIDE REAR VIEW MIRROR 10-18
REMOVAL & INSTALLATION 10-18
SEATS 10-19
REMOVAL & INSTALLATION 10-19
**SPECIFICATIONS CHART**
TORQUE SPECIFICATIONS 10-20

# 10

# BODY AND TRIM

EXTERIOR 10-2
INTERIOR 10-6

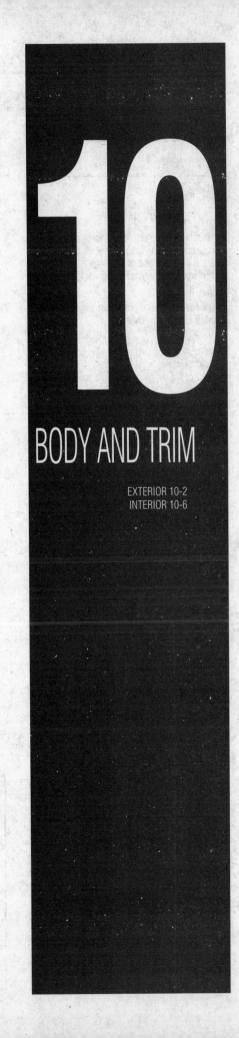

# EXTERIOR

## Doors

### ADJUSTMENT

#### Door Hinges

**➧ See Figures 1, 2 and 3**

The door hinges provide sufficient adjustment to correct most door misalignment conditions. The holes of the hinge and/or the hinge attaching points are enlarged or elongated to provide for hinge and door alignment.

**➡Do not cover up a poor door alignment with a latch striker adjustment.**

1. Refer to the figures to determine which hinge bolts must be loosened to move the door in the desired direction.
2. Loosen the hinge bolts just enough to permit movement of the door with a padded prybar.
3. Move the door the estimated necessary distance, then tighten the hinge bolts to 19–25 ft. lbs. (25–35 Nm).
4. Check the door fit to make sure there is no bind or interference with the adjacent panel.
5. Repeat the operation until the desired fit is obtained.
6. Check the striker plate alignment for proper door closing.

#### Door Latch Striker

**➧ See Figures 4 and 5**

The latch striker should be shimmed to get the clearance between the striker and the latch. To check this clearance, clean the latch jaws and the striker area. Apply a thin layer of dark grease to the striker. As the door is opened and closed, a measurable pattern will result on the latch striker. Use a maximum of 2 shims on 1988–90 vehicles or one shim on 1991–00 vehicles, under the striker. Use Torx® drive bit set D79P–2100–T or equivalent, to loosen and tighten the latch striker to 25–32 ft. lbs. (35–45 Nm).

## Hood

### REMOVAL & INSTALLATION

1. Open and support the hood. Mark the position of the hood hinges on the hood.
2. Protect the body with covers to prevent damage to the paint.
3. Disconnect the gas charged cylinders (where applicable).
4. With the help of an assistant, remove the 2 bolts attaching each hinge to the hood, being careful not to let the hood slip when the bolts are removed.
5. Remove the hood from the vehicle.

**To install:**

6. With the help of an assistant, position the hood on its hinges and install the attaching bolts.
7. Reconnect the gas charged cylinders. Remove the body covers..
8. Adjust the hood for an even fit between the fenders and a flush fit with the front of the fenders.
9. Adjust the hood latch, if necessary.

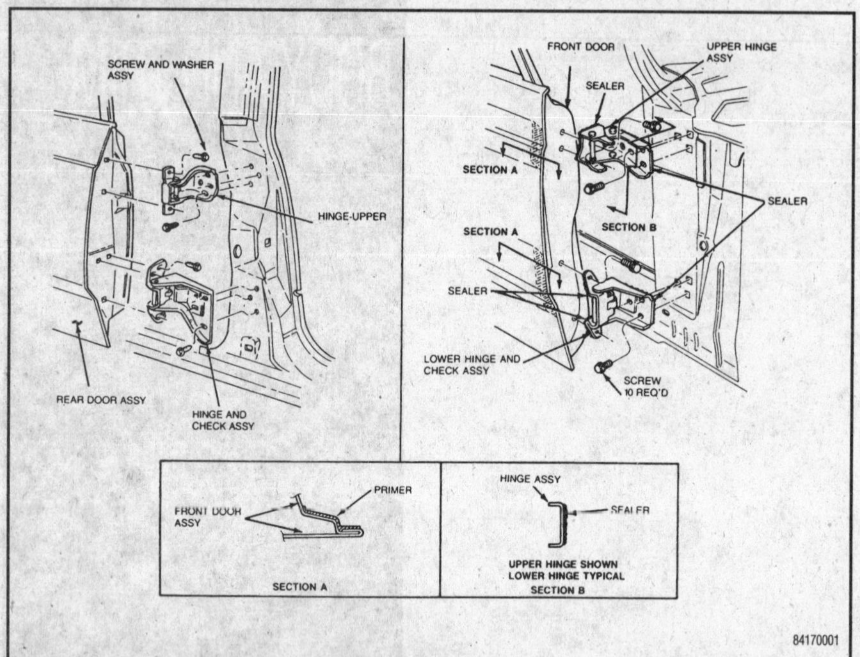


Fig. 1 Front and rear door hinges—1988–91 vehicles

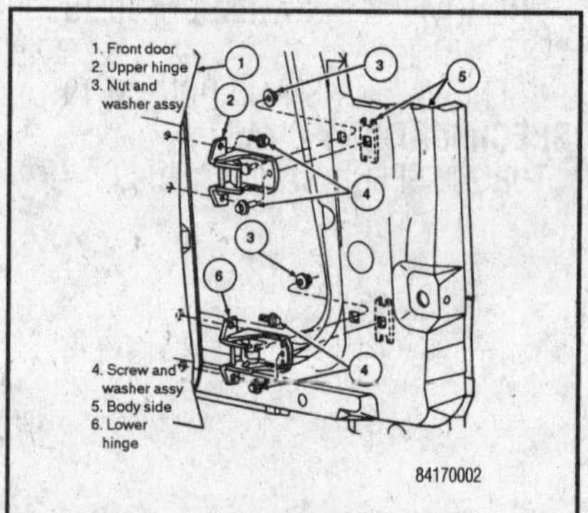


Fig. 2 Front door hinges—1992–00 vehicles

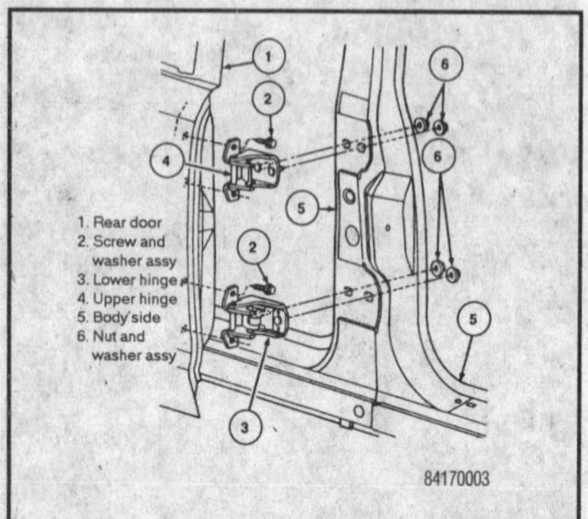


Fig. 3 Rear door hinges—1992–00 vehicles

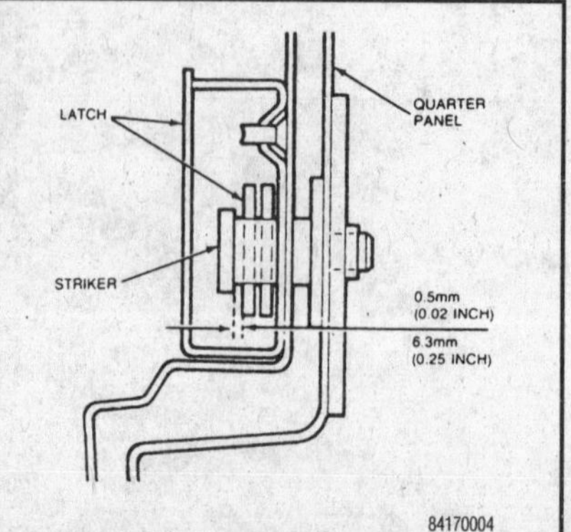


Fig. 4 Latch and striker clearance

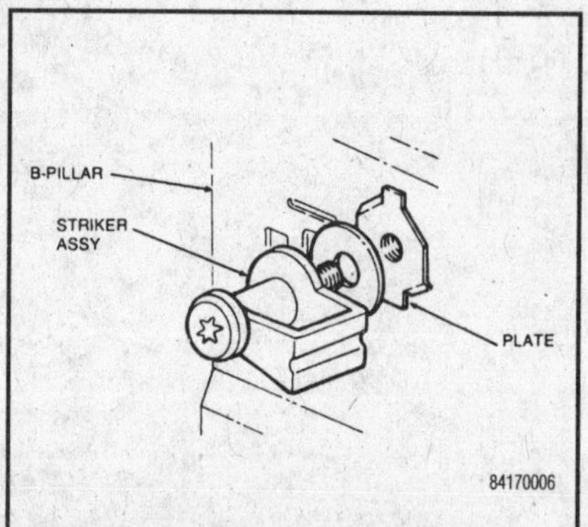


Fig. 5 Door latch striker—1990–00 vehicles

## ALIGNMENT

### Hood Alignment

**➧ See Figures 6 and 7**

The hood can be adjusted fore-and-aft and side-to-side by loosening the hood-to-hinge retaining bolts and repositioning the hood. To raise or lower the hood, loosen the hinge-to-fender reinforcement retaining bolts and raise or lower the hinge as necessary.

# Trunk Lid

## ALIGNMENT

### Trunk Lid Alignment

The trunk lid can be shifted fore-and-aft by loosening the hinge-to-trunk lid retaining screws.

The trunk lid should be adjusted for an even and parallel fit with the trunk lid opening. The trunk lid should also be adjusted up and down for a flush fit with the surrounding panels. Be careful not to damage the trunk lid or surrounding body panels.

### Trunk Lid Latch/Striker

**➡The latch assembly is fixed and not adjustable on all vehicles. Any latch adjustment must be made at the striker.**

**➡Before adjusting the striker, open and close the trunk lid to double-check the striker alignment.**

1. Remove the scuff plate striker covering before attempting any striker adjustment.
2. Loosen the 2 screw and washer assemblies and adjust the striker by moving up and down or from side-to-side as necessary.
3. Tighten the screw and washer assemblies to 7–10 ft. lbs. (9–14 Nm).

**➡Do not try to correct a poor trunk lid alignment with a latch striker adjustment.**

# Outside Mirrors

## REMOVAL & INSTALLATION

### 1988–91 Town Car

**➧ See Figure 8**

1. Disconnect the negative battery cable.
2. Remove the interior door handle.
3. On the left door, remove the bezel from the power mirror control switch.
4. Remove the switch housing from the armrest and detach all electrical connectors.
5. Using a putty knife or similar tool, pry the trim panel retaining clips from the door inner panel and remove the panel.
6. Detach the mirror wiring connectors and remove the necessary wiring guides.
7. Remove the 2 mirror retaining screws and remove the mirror, guiding the wiring and connectors through the hole in the door.

**To install:**

8. Guide the wiring and connectors through the hole in the door.
9. Install the mirror on the door and secure with the retaining screws.
10. Position and install the wiring guides.
11. Attach the mirror wiring connectors.
12. Install the door trim panel.
13. Attach all electrical connectors to the switch housing and install the switch housing on the armrest.
14. On the left door, install the bezel nut to the power mirror control switch.
15. Install the interior door handle.
16. Connect the negative battery cable and check mirror operation.

### 1992–00 Town Car

1. Disconnect the negative battery cable.
2. Remove the door trim panel.
3. Remove the push pin from the mirror access hole cover and remove the access hole cover.
4. Detach the mirror wiring connectors and remove the necessary wiring guides.
5. Remove the 3 mirror retaining nuts and remove the mirror, guiding the wiring and connectors through the hole in the door.

**To install:**

6. Guide the wiring and connectors through the hole in the door.
7. Install the mirror on the door and secure with the retaining nuts.
8. Position and install the wiring guides.
9. Attach the mirror wiring connectors.
10. Install the mirror access hole cover. Install the push pin.
11. Install the door trim panel.
12. Attach all electrical connectors to the switch housing and install the switch housing on the armrest.
13. On the left door, install the bezel nut to the power mirror control switch.
14. Connect the negative battery cable and check mirror operation.

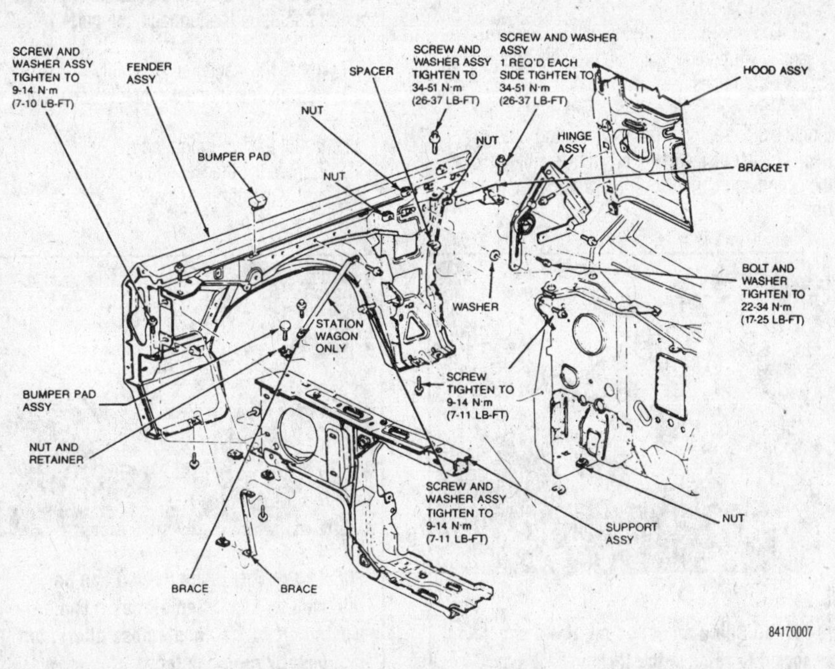


**Fig. 6 Hood hinge and related components—1988–91 vehicles**

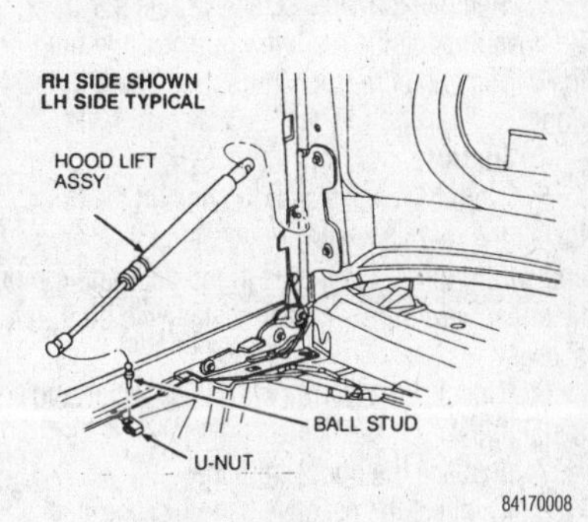


**Fig. 7 Hood hinge (shown with gas cylinder removed)—1992–00 vehicles**

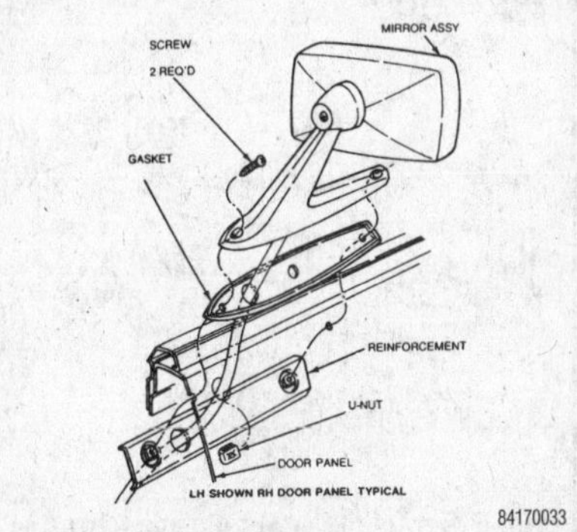


**Fig. 8 Power mirror installation—1988–91 vehicles**

#### Continental 1988–94

➧ See Figure 9

**➡Outside mirrors that are frozen must be thawed prior to adjustment. Do not attempt to free up the mirror by pressing on the glass.**

1. Disconnect the negative battery cable.
2. Remove the retaining cover.
3. Remove the front door trim panel.
4. Disengage the mirror assembly wiring connector. Remove the necessary-wiring guides.
5. Remove the mirror retaining nuts on the mirror. Remove the mirror while guiding the wiring and connector through the hole in the door.

**To install:**

6. Install the mirror assembly by routing the connector and wiring through the hole in the door. Attach the retaining nuts to the mirror. Tighten the retaining nuts to 53–71 inch lbs. (6–8 Nm).
7. Engage the mirror electrical wiring connector, then install the wiring guides.
8. Position the mirror mounting hole cover, then install the retaining screw.
9. Install the door trim panel.
10. Connect the negative battery cable.
11. If a new mirror has been installed, snap on the new trim, the top finish panel.

#### Continental 1995–00

1. Disconnect the negative battery cable.
2. Remove the door trim panel.
3. Disconnect the mirror assembly wiring connectors. Remove the necessary wiring pushpins.
4. Remove the three screws on the mirror. Remove the outside rear view mirror while guiding the wiring and connector through the hole in the door.

**To install:**

5. Hold the gasket over the hole in the door. Install the rear view mirror by routing the connector and wiring through the hole in the door and the outside rear view mirror gasket. Install with the three screws.
6. Connect the mirror wiring connector and install the wiring pushpins.
7. Replace the door trim panel.
8. Connect the negative battery cable.
9. Snap on a new trim (top finish panel) if a new mirror assembly has been installed.

#### Mark VII

**➡The following instructions are given as the general repair procedure for the vehicle and years given.**

**➡If the wire assembly to the motor is not damaged, the mirror assembly can be replaced without removing the door trim panel. Disconnect the wiring assembly at the motor.**

1. Disconnect the negative battery cable.
2. Remove the retaining cover.
3. Remove the door trim panel, if necessary.
4. Disconnect the mirror assembly wiring connector and remove the wiring guides, as necessary.
5. Remove the plug button and remove the three outside rear view mirror retaining nuts. Remove the outside rear view mirror while guiding the wiring and connector through the hole in the front door.

**To install:**

6. Hold the gasket over the hole in the door. Install the rear view mirror by routing the connector and wiring through the hole in the door and the outside rear view mirror gasket. Install with the three screws.
7. Engage the mirror electrical wiring connector, then install the wiring guides.
8. Install the rear view mirror mounting hole cover.
9. Install the front door trim panel.
10. Connect the negative battery cable.

#### Mark VIII

1. Disconnect the negative battery cable.
2. Remove the front door trim panel. Remove the rear view mirror mounting hole cover from the front door trim panel.
3. Disconnect the outside rear view mirror assembly wiring connector and remove the necessary wiring guides.
4. Remove the plug button and remove the three outside rear view mirror retaining nuts. Remove the outside rear view mirror while guiding the wiring and connector through the hole in the front door.

**To install:**

5. Install the outside rear view mirror assembly by routing the connector and wiring through the hole in the front door and attach with the three retaining nuts. Install the plug button.
6. Connect the outside rear view mirror wiring connector and install the wiring guides.
7. Install the rear view mirror mounting hole cover.
8. Install the front door trim panel.
9. Connect the negative battery cable.

## Antenna

### REPLACEMENT

➧ See Figures 10 thru 23

1. Lower the antenna and remove the luggage compartment trim panel.
2. Disconnect the lead-in cable from the antenna and ground strap.
3. Disconnect the antenna motor wires at the connectors and disconnect the control box connectors.
4. Remove the top mounting nut and stanchion assembly.
5. Remove the two nuts retaining the antenna bracket assembly to the quarter panel.
6. Remove the antenna assembly from the vehicle.

**To install:**

**➡Correct sequencing for installation is important to prevent water leakage or dimpling of the quarter panel**

7. Connect the antenna cable, power connector and control box connector.
8. Insert the antenna mast through the quarter panel hole and position bracket on mounting studs in the luggage compartment.
9. Install the stanchion assembly.
10. Loosely install the two bracket retaining nuts.
11. Install the top-mounting nut.
12. Tighten the bracket retaining nuts.
13. Install the ground strap.

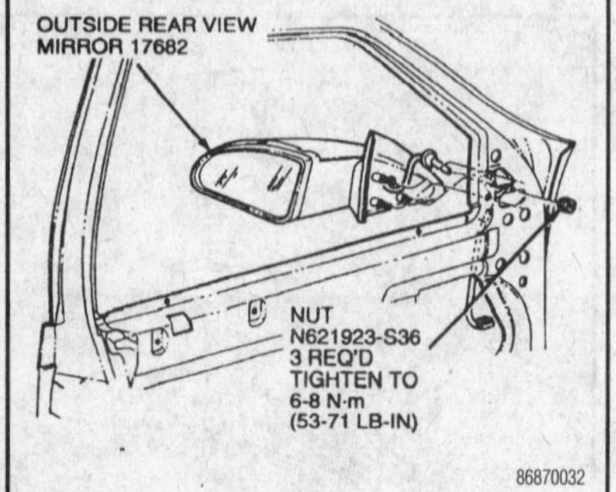


**Fig. 9 View of the power outside mirror mounting**

**Fig. 10 Some antennas require a special socket to remove the locknut**

**Fig. 11 Once its loose the nut can be removed by hand. Sometimes it can be twisted off with a needle nose pliers, but that usually ruins the tool**

93140P33

Fig. 12 The antenna mounts in the luggage compartment against the support member

93140P11

Fig. 13 The motor and housing sit on a stand that is bolted to the support member

93140P12

Fig. 14 Unplug the antenna lead from the staff tube

93140P58

Fig. 15 Unplug the connector to the motor

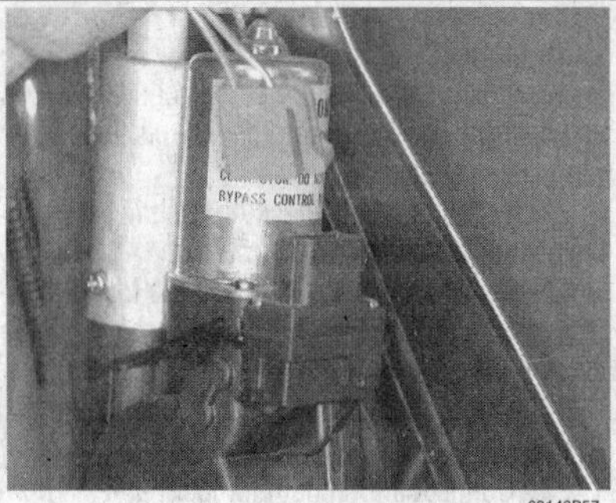
93140P57

Fig. 16 Unplug the connector to the relay

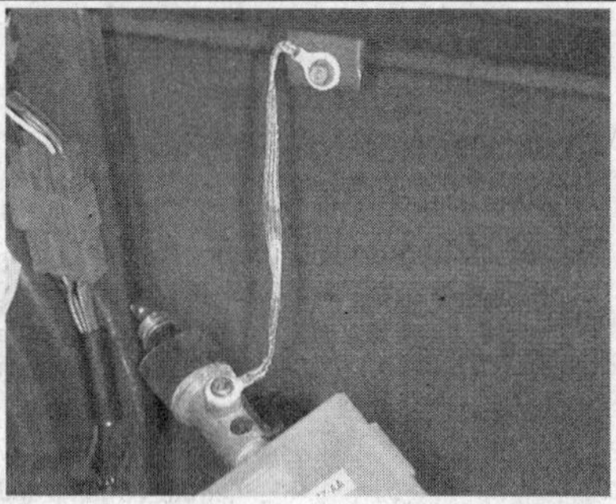
93140P56

Fig. 17 Its easier to remove the antenna from the support to gain access to the ground strap screws

93140P42

Fig. 18 If the antenna motor still operates, but the staff does not move, or the staff is bent, or does not extend to its full height, a replacement staff kit is available that can be used without replacing the motor

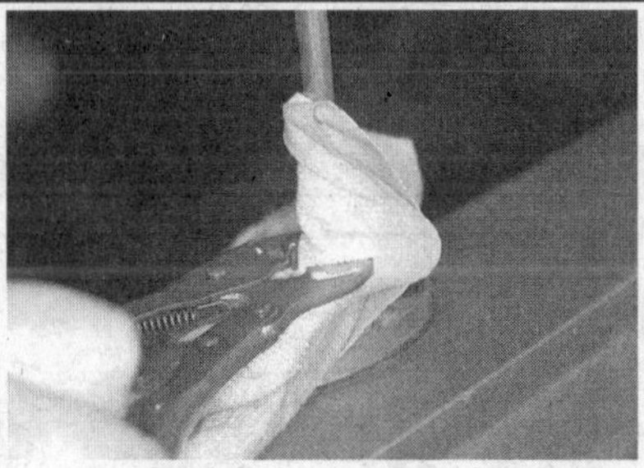
93140P41

Fig. 19 This locknut was removable using a locking pliers and a shop cloth (to protect the chrome nut). Unscrew the locknut to remove it

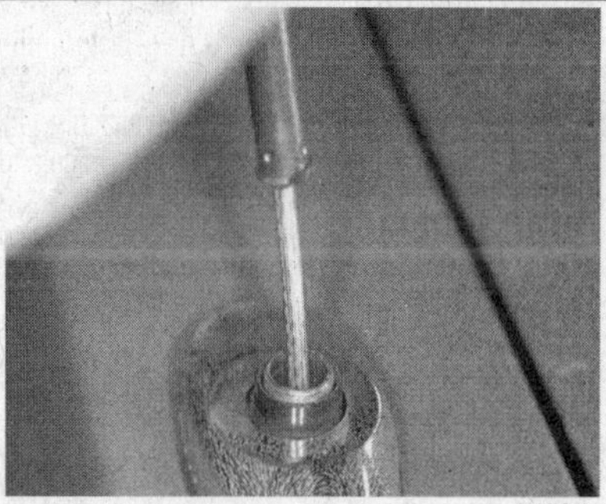
93140P43

Fig. 20 With the help of an assistant to raise the antenna, gently pull up on the staff to extricate it from the fender

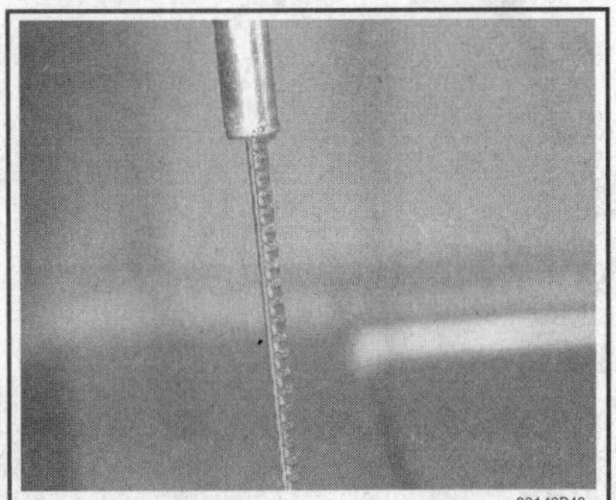
93140P40

Fig. 21 Continue pulling while raising the antenna until the entire drive comes out of the base

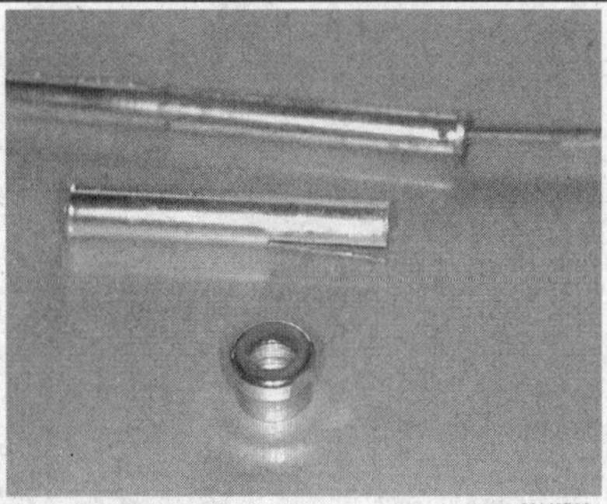
93140P38

Fig. 22 When the antenna is out, slide the bushing off and install it on the new staff, if not supplied

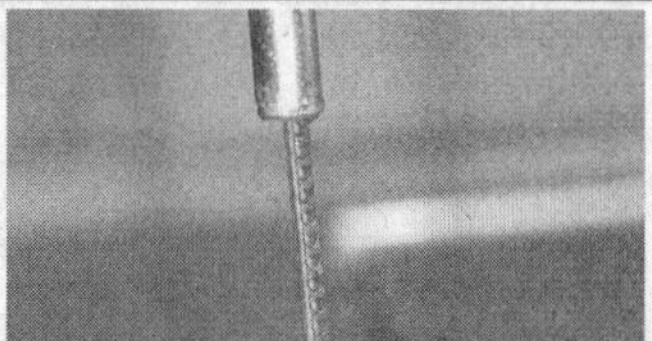
93140P39

Fig. 23 Feed the new nylon drive into the antenna hole, while an assistant is lowering the antenna by turning the radio off or pushing the antenna switch down. Feed about half of the drive, then install the staff and lock nut. Cycle the antenna up and down

## INTERIOR

### Instrument Panel and Pad

The instrument panel houses the controls for most of the electrical systems of the vehicle. The glove compartment is located in the lower RH side of the instrument panel. The LH side of the instrument panel frames the steering column and houses the instrument cluster.

#### REMOVAL & INSTALLATION

**1988 –94 Town Car**

**See Figures 24 and 25**

1. Disconnect the negative battery cable.
2. Remove the 2 screws attaching the instrument panel pad to the instrument panel at each defroster opening. Be careful not to drop the screws into the defroster openings.
3. Remove the one screw attaching each outboard end of the instrument panel pad to the instrument panel.
4. Remove the screws attaching the lower edge of the instrument panel pad to the instrument panel. Pull the instrument panel pad rearward and remove it from the vehicle.
5. Remove the screws attaching the steering column opening cover to the instrument panel and remove the cover.
6. Loosen the right and left front door sill plate screws then remove the right and left cowl sides trim panels.
7. Disconnect the wiring harnesses from the steering column at the multiple connectors.
8. Disconnect the transmission selector indicator from the steering column.
9. Remove the nuts and washers attaching the steering column to the instrument panel brace and lay the steering column down on the seat.
10. Remove the one screw attaching the lower flange brace to the lower flange of the instrument panel just to the right of the steering column opening.
11. Remove the one screw attaching the instrument panel support to the lower edge of the instrument panel below the A/C-heater control assembly.
12. Disconnect the speedometer cable from the speedometer by pushing the cable retainer sideways and pulling the cable from the speedometer (where applicable).
13. Remove the glove compartment from the instrument panel.
14. Disconnect the vacuum jumper harness at the vacuum multiple connector located above the floor air distribution duct.
15. Disconnect the antenna cable from the radio, if equipped.
16. Remove the screws attaching the top of the instrument panel to the cowl at the windshield opening.
17. Remove the one bolt attaching each lower end of the instrument panel to the cowl side (A-pillar).
18. Cover the steering column and seat with a protective cover and lay the instrument panel on the seat, disconnecting any wiring or other connections as necessary to allow the instrument panel to lay on the seat.

**To install:**

19. Position the instrument panel near the cowl and connect any wiring or other connections that were disconnected.
20. Install one bolt attaching each lower end of the instrument panel to the cowl side (A-pillar).
21. Install the screws to attach the top of the instrument panel to the cowl panel at the windshield opening.
22. Connect the antenna cable to the radio, if equipped.
23. Connect the vacuum jumper harness (from the control assembly) to the plenum vacuum harness at the vacuum multiple connector located above the floor air distribution duct.
24. Connect the speedometer cable to the speedometer (where applicable).
25. Install one screw to attach the instrument panel support to the lower edge of the instrument panel below the A/C-heater control assembly.
26. Install one screw to attach the lower flange brace to the lower flange of the instrument panel just to the right of the steering column opening.
27. Install the glove compartment and check the arms.
28. Install the right and left cowl side trim panels and tighten the door sill plate attaching screws.
29. Position the steering column to the instrument panel brace and install the retaining nuts and washers.
30. Connect the transmission indicator to the steering column.
31. Connect the wire harnesses to the steering column at the multiple connectors. Install the steering column opening cover.
32. Position the instrument panel pad to the instrument panel and install the screws along the lower edge of the pad.
33. Install one screw to attach each outboard end of the pad to the instrument panel.
34. Install 2 instrument panel pad attaching screws at each defroster opening. Be careful not to drop the screws into the defroster opening.
35. Connect the negative battery cable. Check operation of all instruments, lights, controls and the A/C-heater system.

**Town Car 1995–00**

1. Position the wheels straight ahead.
2. Disconnect the negative battery cable.
3. Loosen the lug nuts on the front wheels.
4. Apply the parking brake, block the rear wheels, then raise and safely support the front of the vehicle securely on jackstands.
5. Remove the front wheels.
6. Remove the retaining nut in the radiator coolant recovery reservoir assembly.

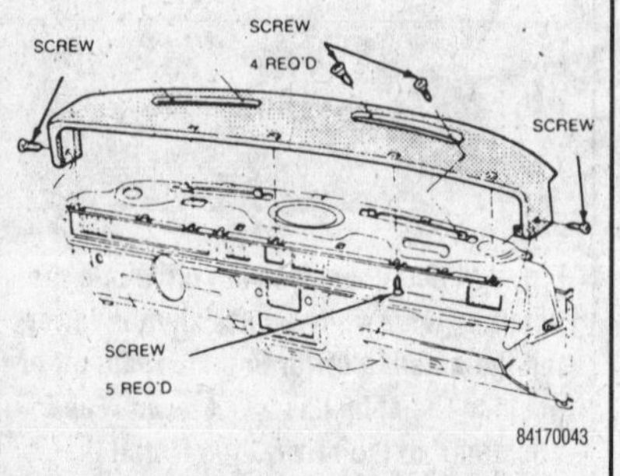


**Fig. 24 Instrument panel pad removal — typical**

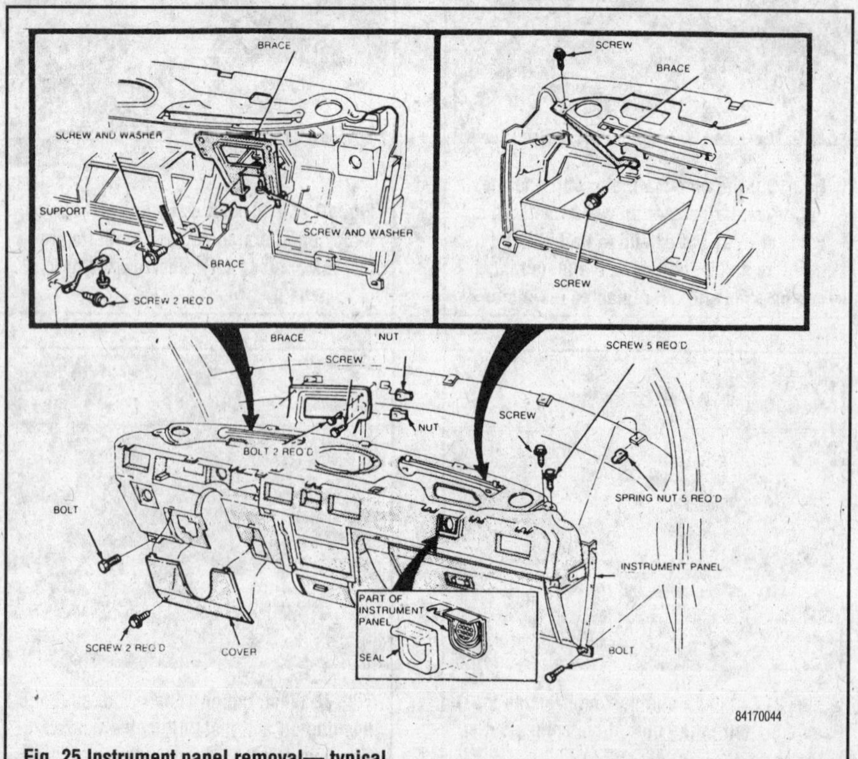


**Fig. 25 Instrument panel removal— typical**

7. Remove the retaining bolt in the front fender splash shield.
8. Position the front fender splash shield out of the way.
9. Lower the vehicle.
10. Tag and remove the wiring connectors.
11. Remove the retaining screw in the parking brake control.
12. Remove the parking brake control.
13. Remove the retaining screw in the instrument panel finish panel in the lower instrument panel.
14. Remove the retaining screw in the steering column opening reinforcement.
15. Remove the retaining screw in the steering gear housing.
16. Remove the tilt wheel handle and shank.
17. Remove the ignition switch.
18. Disconnect the upper steering column shroud and remove the retaining bolts.
19. Disconnect the ignition switch assembly.
20. Tag and remove the electrical connector.
21. Disconnect the vacuum hose.
22. Remove the retaining nut in the steering column assembly.
23. Lower the steering column tube assembly.
24. Disconnect the shift cable assembly.
25. Remove the steering column shroud retaining screw.
26. Remove the retaining screws from the multi-function switch.
27. Position the multi-function switch out of the way.
28. Remove the retaining screw from the cowl side trim panel.
29. Remove the lower panel door trim, remove the retaining screw, and position the panel out of the way.
30. Tag and disconnect the wiring connectors, and remove the ground wire assembly.
31. Remove the retaining screw on the cowl side (RH) panel.
32. Remove the lower panel door trim, remove the retaining screw, and position the panel out of the way.
33. Tag and disconnect the wiring connectors, and remove the ground wire assembly.
34. Remove the retaining rivet in the passenger side of the instrument panel.
35. Disconnect the generator.
36. Disconnect the radio feed of the wire assembly.
37. Unsnap the I/P finish center (LH) on the panel assembly.
38. Remove the radio chassis.
39. Remove the retaining screw in the instrument panel, and position the panel out of the way.
40. Tag and disconnect the wiring connectors.
41. Remove the retaining screw in the air bag restraining module assembly, and disconnect it.
42. Remove and disconnect the instrument panel defroster-opening grille.
43. Remove the instrument panel to cowl brace retaining screw.
44. Remove the instrument panel finish panel retaining screw.
45. Remove the retaining nut on the instrument LH lower finish panel.
46. Remove the retaining brace.
47. Disconnect the vacuum hose on the harness assembly.
48. If the instrument panel is being replaced, transfer all parts to the new instrument panel.

**To install:**

49. Installation is the reversal of the removal procedure. Check air bag indicator operation.

### Continental 1988–94

➧ **See Figure 26**

**➡Some vehicles are equipped with air bags. Before attempting to service air bag equipped vehicles, be sure that the system is properly disarmed and all safety precautions are taken. Serious personal injury and vehicle damage could result if this note is disregarded.**

1. Position the wheels in the straight-ahead position. Disable the air bag system. For details, please refer to the procedure in Section 6 of this manual. Disconnect the negative battery cable.
2. Remove the ignition lock cylinder. Remove the tilt lever. Remove the steering column trim shrouds. Disengage all electrical connectors from the steering column switches.
3. Remove the two bolts and reinforcement from under the steering column. Disengage the insulator, then remove the insulator.
4. Remove the four nuts and the reinforcement from under the steering column. Do NOT rotate the steering column shaft.
5. Remove the four nuts retaining the steering column to the instrument panel, disconnect the PRNDL cable, and lower the steering column on the front seat. Cover the front seat to protect it from damage.
6. Install the ignition lock cylinder to ensure that the steering column shaft does not turn. Remove the one bolt at the steering column opening attaching the instrument panel brace retaining bolt under the radio.
7. Remove the sound insulator from under the glove compartment by removing the two push nuts that secure the insulator to the studs on the climate control case assembly.
8. Disconnect the wires of the main wire loom inside the engine compartment. Disengage the rubber grommet from the dash panel, then feed the wiring through the hole in the dash panel into the passenger compartment.
9. Remove the right and left-hand cowl sides trim panels. Remove the two screws (one on each side) retaining the instrument panel to the left and right side.
10. Remove both speaker covers by pulling upward on them. Open the glove compartment door and allow it to hang open.
11. Using all openings, tag and remove all instrument panel electrical connections, air conditioning outlets, air conditioning controls, antenna wires, and anything else that may interfere with panel removal.
12. Close the glove compartment lid. Remove the three instrument panel screws at the top of the assembly. Disconnect any remaining electrical wires. Remove the instrument panel assembly from the vehicle.
13. If the panel is being replaced, transfer all components, wiring, and hardware to the new instrument panel.

**To install:**

14. Position the instrument panel in place. Engage the underhood electrical connections. Install the instrument panel upper and lower retaining screws.
15. Install the lower brace and tighten the bolt to 5–8 ft. lbs. (6.8–10.8 Nm) Install the radio speaker grilles.
16. Using all necessary openings, engage all instrument panel electrical connections, air conditioning outlets, air conditioning controls, antenna wires, and anything else that may have been removed.
17. Continue the installation in the reverse order of the removal procedure.
18. Connect the negative battery cable. Enable the air bag system following the procedure in Section 6 of this manual. Check for proper operation of the air bag indicator. Check for proper operation of all components.

### Continental 1995–00

1. Disconnect the negative battery cable.
2. Remove the defroster grille by pulling

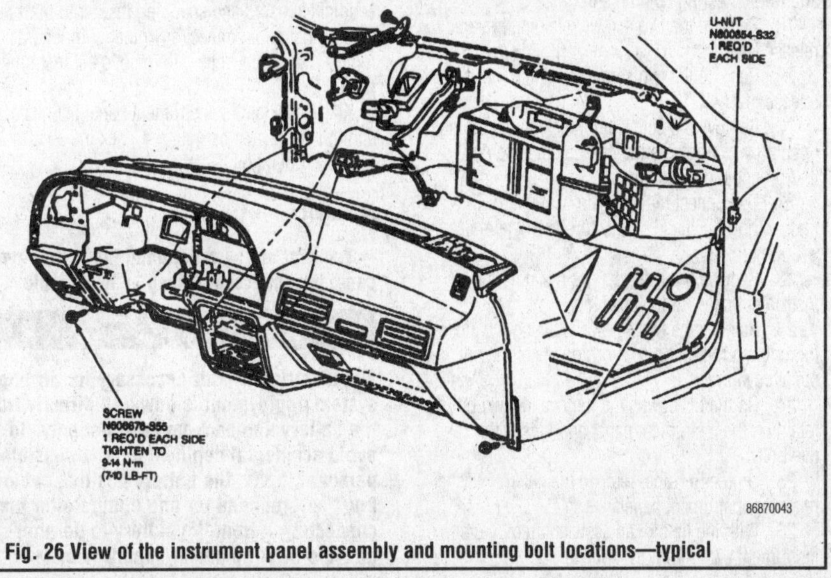


**Fig. 26 View of the instrument panel assembly and mounting bolt locations—typical**

upward to unsnap the six clips and disconnect the wiring.

3. Open the glove compartment door and unsnap the glove box damper wire.

4. Press the sides inward and lower the glove compartment assembly toward the floor.

5. Through the glove box opening, remove the automatic temperature sensor hose from the blower assembly, and disconnect the electronic automatic temperature control vacuum lines.

6. Remove the five pushpins from the RH and LH lower instrument panel insulators. Remove the instrument panel insulators.

7. For traction assist equipped vehicles, disconnect the traction assist switch connector.

8. Remove the three screws retaining lower instrument panel steering column cover and remove the cover.

9. Remove the five screws retaining the lower instrument panel steering column reinforcement. Remove the reinforcement.

10. Remove the steering column.

**CAUTION**

**Do not remove the steering column, steering wheel, and air bag module as an assembly from the vehicle. Unless the steering column is locked to prevent rotation, or the lower end of steering shaft is wired in such a way to prevent the steering wheel from being rotated; as this will damage the air bag sliding contact.**

11. Make sure that the vehicle front wheels are in the straight ahead position.

12. Remove the steering wheel.

13. Remove the instrument panel lower trim cover.

14. Remove the air bag sliding contact.

15. Remove the tilt wheel handle and shank by unscrewing it from the column and removing the four screws.

16. Rotate the ignition switch lock cylinder to the **RUN** position. Using a 1/8inch drift, press the lock cylinder retaining pin through the access hole and remove the ignition switch lock cylinder.

17. Remove the four upper and lower steering column shroud retaining screws. Remove the upper and lower steering column shrouds.

18. Remove the two screws retaining brake release lever.

19. Remove the two screws retaining the hood release lever.

20. Remove the screw ant the steering column opening which retains the instrument panel to the instrument panel dash brace.

21. Disconnect the LH main wiring and RH main wiring bulkhead connectors from the main wiring harness.

22. Remove the three screws retaining the instrument panel to the cowl top.

23. Remove the two screws retaining the steering column mounting support to the instrument panel cowl brace.

24. On the LH cowl side, remove the two bolts retaining the instrument panel and loosen the captive bolt.

25. On the RH side, remove the nut and washer retaining instrument panel.

26. With the help of an assistant, remove the instrument panel from the vehicle.

**To install:**

27. With an assistant , place the instrument panel into the vehicle.

28. Install the three screws retaining instrument panel to the cowl top. Tighten to 18–26 in. lbs. (2–3 Nm)

➡**Do not overtighten nut. Damage to the instrument panel may result.**

29. On the RH cowl side, install the nut and washer retaining instrument panel to the body. Tighten to 89–123 ft. lbs. (10–14 Nm)

30. On the LH cowl side, install the two blots retaining the instrument panel to the body. Tighten the two retaining bolts and one captive bolt (to the right) to 13–16 ft. lb. (17–23 Nm).

31. Install the two screws retaining the steering column mounting support to the instrument panel cowl brace. Tighten the screws to 13–16 ft. lb. (17–23 Nm).

32. Connect the LH main wiring and RH main wiring bulkhead connectors to main wiring harness. Tighten the connector screws to 36–53 in. lbs. (4–6 Nm).

33. Install the screw at the steering column opening which retains the instrument panel to he instrument panel dash brace. Tighten the screws to 54–70 in. lbs. (6–8 Nm).

34. Install the hood and brake release levers.

35. Install the steering column.

36. Install the five screws retaining the instrument panel steering column opening cover reinforcement.

37. Install the three screws and instrument panel steering column cover.

38. On vehicles with traction control, connect the electrical connector for the traction control switch.

39. Install the RH and LH lower instrument panel insulator using pushpins.

40. Working through the glove compartment opening, connect the automatic temperature sensor hose (to the blower) and any other electrical connectors or vacuum lines connected to the A/C evaporator housing.

41. Re-install the glove compartment door damper. Press the sides of the glove compartment inward and close the glove compartment.

42. Install the defroster grille by connecting the two light sensors and snapping them into place.

43. Install or connect any other components removed or disconnected to remove the instrument panel.

44. Check all the instrument panel gauges and controls for proper operation. Check the air bag indicator operation.

### Mark VII

➡**Removal and installation of the instrument panel is best accomplished by two people.**

**WARNING**

**The electrical circuit necessary for air bag system deployment is powered directly from the battery and back-up power supply. To avoid accidental deployment and possible personal injury, the battery positive cable must be grounded for one minute after disconnecting it from the battery to de-energize the back-up power supply prior to servicing or replacing any air bag system components.**

1. Disconnect the positive battery cable. Ground the positive battery cable for one minute to de-energize the air bag system back-up power supply.

2. Disconnect all the underhood electrical connectors of the main wiring harness. Disengage the rubber grommet from the dash panel. Remove the RH and LH sound insulator assemblies from under the instrument panel and remove the bulb and socket assemblies from each insulator.

3. Remove the four screws retaining steering column opening trim cover and remove the cover.

4. Remove the steering column opening lower steel reinforcement.

5. Remove the four trim screws and remove the steering column shrouds.

6. Disconnect all the electrical connections from the steering column switches.

7. Remove the four nuts retaining the steering column to the support. Lower the steering column to rest on the seat cushion.

8. Remove the defroster opening grille panel.

➡**The grille has one retaining tab holding it in position.**

9. Remove the screws retaining floor console to the instrument panel and floor. Move the console rearward. Remove the two screws retaining the instrument panel to the floor. Remove the three screws retaining the instrument panel to the cowls. Remove the bolt attaching the instrument panel to the parking brake support plate.

10. Disconnect the main harness behind the instrument panel and on the RH side of the steering column support, at the blower motor, and at the RH and LH cowl panels.

11. Disconnect the radio antenna lead from the radio.

12. Disconnect any vacuum hoses attached to the instrument panel.

13. Remove the RH and LH A-pillar garnish moldings.

14. Remove the three screws retaining the instrument panel to the dash panel and pull/push the wiring harness and connectors into the passenger compartment.

15. If the instrument panel is being replaced, transfer ass the necessary components, including the wiring and retaining hardware to the new instrument panel.

**To install:**

16. Installation is the reversal of the removal procedure.

17. Connect the negative battery cable.

18. After installing the instrument panel defroster-opening grille, check all the components to ensure proper operation.

### Mark VIII

➡**Removal and installation of the instrument panel is best accomplished by two people.**

**WARNING**

**The electrical circuit necessary for air bag system deployment is powered directly from the battery and back-up power supply. To avoid accidental deployment and possible**

**personal injury, the battery positive cable must be grounded for one minute after disconnecting it from the battery to de-energize the back-up power supply prior to servicing or replacing any air bag system components.**

1. Disconnect the positive battery cable. Ground the positive battery cable for one minute to de-energize the air bag system back-up power supply.
2. Loosen the main wire harness connector bolt in the engine compartment at the LH side of the dash panel.

**➡Do not remove the front safety belt retaining bolts.**

3. Remove the three screws retaining the LH and RH front door scuff plates. Lift the front door scuff plates and remove the front door weather-strip from the body flanges.
4. Remove the instrument panel defroster-opening grille by lifting the rear edge upward to unsnap eight retainers and two retainers at each front corner. Disconnect the light sensor amplifier at the connector Remove the instrument panel and defroster-opening grille.
5. Remove the screws retaining the LH and RH instrument panel lower insulator located under the instrument panel.
6. Rotate the lamp from the instrument panel insulator and remove the instrument panel insulator.
7. Remove the LH cowl side trim panel and the RH cowl side trim panel.
8. Remove the console panel.
9. Remove the A/C evaporator register duct from the instrument panel to the console panel.
10. Remove the ignition/shifter interlock cable from the console panel. Release the ignition/shifter interlock cable from the pawl. Pull out on the center tab to release detent on the clip. Push the ignition/shifter interlock cable clip toward the rear while rotating the clip to the passenger side to remove.
11. Remove the two screws retaining the bottom of the instrument panel steering column cover. Pull on the lower edge of the instrument panel steering column cover to disengage the two push clips on the upper area of the instrument panel steering column cover and remove the instrument panel steering column cover.
12. Remove the two screws retaining the instrument panel reinforcement and remove the instrument panel reinforcement.
13. Remove the A/C recirculating air duct.
14. Cover the seats to protect from damage. Remove the four nuts retaining the steering column tube to the steering column bracket insulator. Lower the steering column bracket insulator. Lower the steering column tube to rest on the seat cushion.
15. Remove the steering column shroud.
16. Disconnect all the electrical connections from the steering column switches.
17. Loosen the screw and disconnect the main wiring harness at the connector located to the left of the steering column tube.
18. Disconnect the engine control sensor wiring from the instrument panel at the connectors.
19. Open the glove compartment door and disconnect the glove compartment door check form the RH side. Push the sides of the glove compartment inward to release the stops and lower the glove compartment door downward.

**➡The glove compartment door check will retract when removed from the glove compartment side.**

20. Disconnect the radio antenna lead in cable from the radio chassis. Disconnect any vacuum hoses attached to the instrument panel.
21. Disconnect the automatic temperature control sensor and wiring harness from the instrument panel A/C evaporator housing area.
22. Remove the two nuts retaining the center of the instrument panel to the floor tunnel mounting bracket.
23. Remove one nut retaining the lower RH instrument panel to the cowl.
24. Remove the one nut retaining the lower LH instrument panel to the cowl and the one retaining the parking brake to the half car beam.
25. Remove the six bolts retaining the top front of the instrument panel.

**➡Two technicians are required for removal of the instrument panel from the vehicle.**

26. Carefully pull the instrument panel away from the windshield glass, disengage the nine retainers at the top edge of the instrument panel, and remove the instrument panel.

**➡When installing the steering column tube to the steering column bracket insulator bracket, tighten the four retaining nuts to 16–20 ft. lb. (21–28 Nm).**

**To install:**

27. If the instrument panel is being replaced, transfer all the components, wiring and retaining hardware to the new instrument panel, as necessary.
28. Installation is the reversal of the removal procedure. After installing the instrument panel defroster-opening grille, check all the components to ensure proper operation.

## Center Console

### REMOVAL & INSTALLATION

#### Mark VII

1. Remove the glove compartment door-look bezel.
   a. Pull the rear of the front finish panel up and rearward to disengage from the two front locating clips. Disconnect the cigar lighter and lamp connectors.
2. Remove the two nuts retaining the front bracket of the console to the instrument panel. Remove the two console to the instrument panel. Remove the two screws retaining the front bracket to the floor bracket.
3. Pull back on the carpet at the two front edges of the console. Disengage the Velcro fasteners to gain access to the two console-to-instrument panel retaining screws. Remove the screws.
4. Remove the four screws retaining switch-mounting plate to the console base. Disconnect all the necessary electrical connectors, including the lamp for gear shift (PRNDL) illumination.
5. Open the lower console door and remove the cover in the bottom of the tray (snaps out), to gain access to the two console-to-rear floor bracket retaining screws. Remove the screws.
6. Slide the console rearward and up.

**To install:**

7. Installation is the reversal of the removal procedure.

#### Mark VIII

1. Remove the gear selector handle.
2. Pull the front finish panel up to disengage from the two locating clip. Disconnect the cigar lighter and lamp connectors. Remove the gear selector trim panel.
3. Remove the two screws retaining the front finish panel of the console to the front bracket of the console.
4. Open the console door and remove the cover in the bottom of the tray to gain access to the two console-to-rear floor bracket retaining screws. Remove the screws.
5. Slide the console rearward and up.

**To install:**

6. Installation is the reversal of the removal procedure.

#### Continental 1988–94

1. Remove the filler assembly by lifting up and then pulling rearward.
2. Remove the cupholder.
3. Remove the console top finish panel screw.
4. Remove the console top finish panel by lifting up near the rear (under the armrests).
5. Remove the base to A/C plenum hex flanged tap screw.
6. Remove the two base to front bracket retaining screws.
7. Remove the two base to center bracket retaining screws.
8. Remove the mat from the rear storage bin and remove the two base to rear bracket retaining screws.

**➡while lifting console base out, it may be necessary to disconnect the wiring connector to the shift control selector lever and housing.**

9. Remove the console base.

**To install:**

10. Installation is the reversal of the removal procedure.

#### Continental 1995–00

1. Close the beverage holders.
2. Remove the console glove compartment and glove compartment door. Pull glove compartment straight up and out of the console by hand.
3. Remove the console front finish pane. Using a small pry tool.
4. Removeee the console panel by unsnapping it from the console.
5. Remove the console to bracket retaining screws through the glove compartment opening.
6. Remove the two console to instrument panel screws.

**➡While lifting console base out, it may be necessary to disconnect the wiring connector to the gearshift lever. Remove the console base.**

**To install:**

7. Installation is the reversal of the removal procedure.

## Overhead Console

### REMOVAL & INSTALLATION

#### Town Car

1. Insert a small screwdriver in the slot at the rear of one reading lamp lens assembly. Push the screwdriver rearward and pull down on the lens. Remove the lens assembly, Repeat the procedure for the other reading lamp lens.
2. Remove the two-center finish panel retaining screws. Pull the finish panel down and disconnect all the electrical connectors.
3. Remove the center finish panel.

**To install:**

4. Connect all the electrical connectors.
5. Place the finish panel into position and install the two retaining screws.
6. Snap the reading lamp lens assemblies into place.

#### Continental 1988–94

1. Remove the two console retaining screws (located in the front under cover of the sun visor blade).
2. Remove the console by pulling down on the front of the console and disengage it from the rear hooks.
3. Disconnect the electrical connections.

**To install:**

4. Connect all the electrical connectors.
5. Installation is the reversal of the removal procedure.

#### Continental 1995–00

1. Open the front and rear panels of the roof console .
2. Remove the four screws retaining the roof console to the roof trim panel.
3. Disconnect the electrical connector and remove the roof console.

**To install:**

4. Connect all the electrical connectors.
5. Installation is the reversal of the removal procedure.

## Door Panels

### REMOVAL & INSTALLATION

#### Town Car 1988–91

See Figures 27 thru 41

1. If work has to be done inside the door panel, raise the glass to the closed position.
2. Disconnect the negative battery cable.
3. If removing the driver's door panel, remove the retaining screw and the remote mirror bezel nut from the power window regulator housing switch plate. Raise the plate to expose the window switch and power door lock switch and disconnect the switches.
4. Remove the retaining screws from the door inside handle cup.
5. Working through the pull cup opening, disconnect the remote lock rod from the lock knob.
6. Remove the retaining screws from the armrest finish panel. Remove the retaining screws from the armrest and remove the armrest.
7. Using a suitable trim pad removal tool, carefully pry the trim panel plastic pushpin retainers from the door inner panel.
8. Pull the door panel away from the door slightly and detach the bulb and wiring assembly from the door panel by giving it a half twist to disengage it from the reflector housing.

**➡Do not use the trim panel to pry the clips from the door inner panel. Replace any bent, damaged or missing pushpins.**

9. Disconnect the radio speaker wiring, if equipped. Remove the trim panel and water shield.

**To install:**

10. If the door panel is to be replaced, transfer the plastic pushpins to the new panel. Make sure that the watershield is positioned correctly to the door sheet metal. Remove the door pull handle from the old panel and transfer to the new one, if necessary. Install the bulb and wiring assembly. Install the lamp lens, if equipped, and the pull cup.
11. Align the plastic push pins on the door panel to the holes in the door sheet metal and press the pins into place.
12. Install the armrest and route the window

93140P54

**Fig. 27 Unscrew the remote mirror bezel nut**

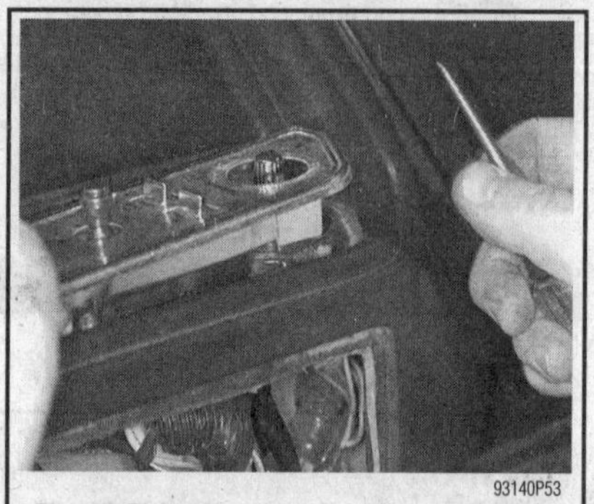

93140P53

**Fig. 28 Raise the plate by lifting the front part up then slide it forward to release the clip from the rear**

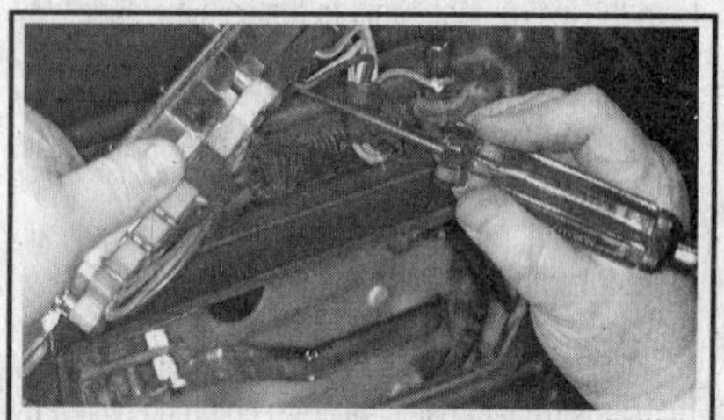

93140P51

**Fig. 29 You can check for power distribution once the control panel has been removed. Use a wiring diagram to determine which wires feed the different circuits. Here we found a broken wire to the seat adjuster**

93140P50

**Fig. 30 On the other door panels, it is necessary to remove the chrome screw in the ashtray to lift the control panel and slide it forward**

93140P49

**Fig. 31 Removal of the armrest panel and the door handle cup will allow access to the two hidden mounting screws**

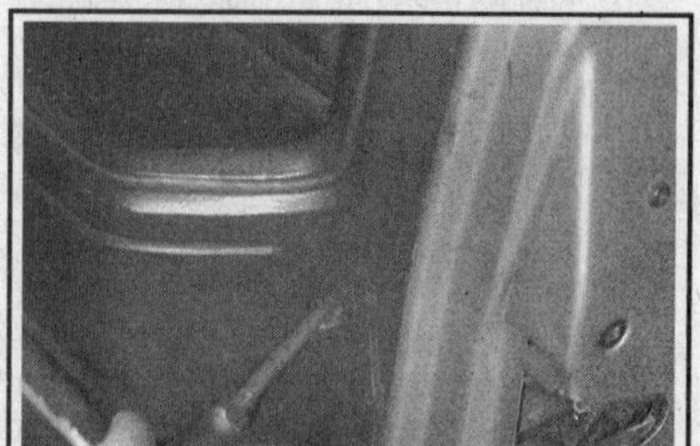

93140P47

**Fig. 32 Remove the screw at the aft part of the door at the level of the latch. There is also one in the front section of the door (not shown) above latch height**

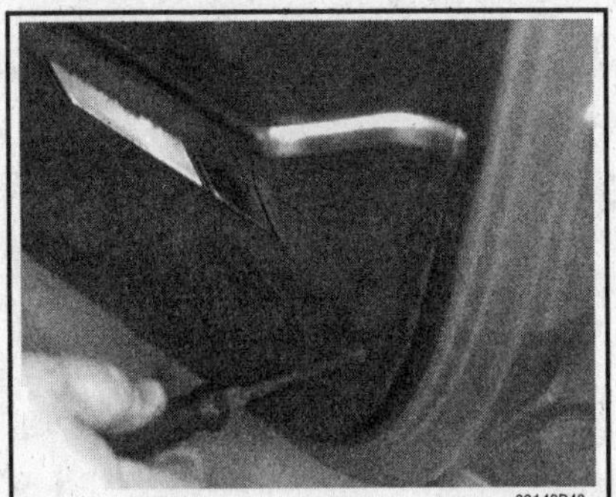


**Fig. 33 Remove the screw at the lower part of the door near the door exit lamp**

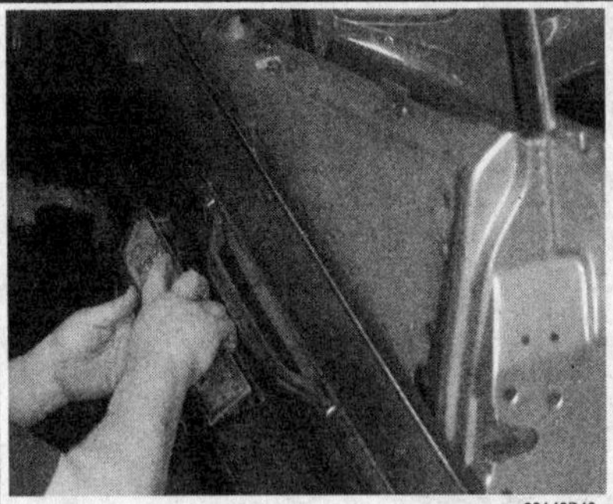


**Fig. 34 Using a pry tool for the plastic snaps pry the door panel away from the door**

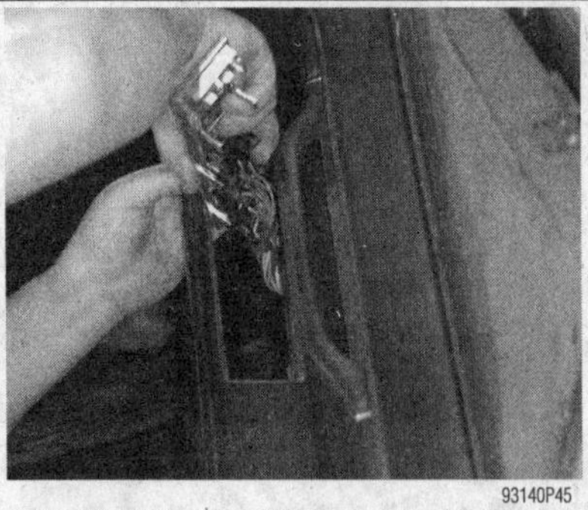


**Fig. 35 Slide the control panel connectors through the opening in the door handle to ease in removal of the panel**

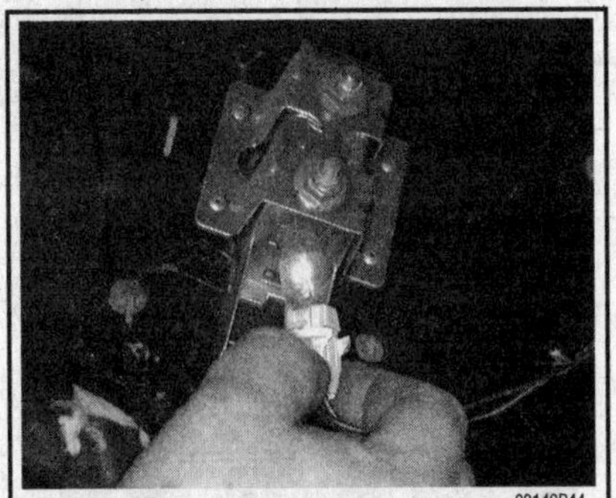


**Fig. 36 Don't forget to unplug the exit lamp from the back of the housing connected to the inside of the door panel**

**Fig. 37 Removing the door panel gives access to the weather-sheet. A torn weather-sheet can be repaired with duct tape**

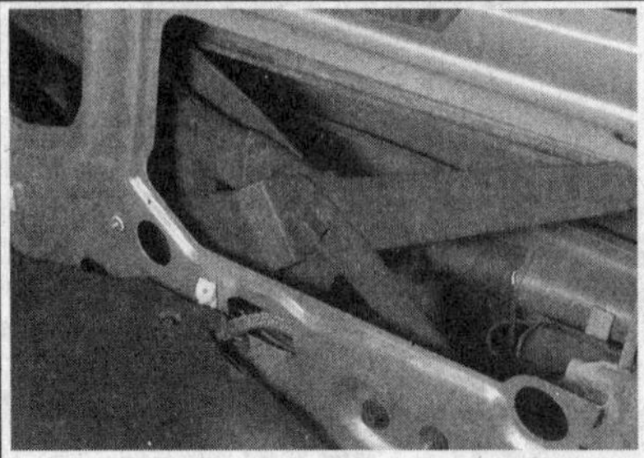


**Fig. 38 A missing or destroyed weather-sheet can be repaired or replaced using a sheet of plastic. A large trash bag cut to size works well in keeping the interior dry**

**Fig. 39 Pulling the weather-sheet away from door allows access to the window regulator and other internal components inside the door**

regulator, remote mirror and power lock harness through the access hole. Install the armrest finish panel.

13. Install the power window regulator switch plate housing to the armrest connecting the power window switch, power door lock switch and remote mirror bezel nut, if equipped, prior to securing the retainer screw.

14. Connect the lock remote rod to the lock knob retainer boss.

**➡Make sure that the remote rod is fully seated into the retainer boss, then function manually or with the power switch to ensure smooth operation of the lock knob.**

15. Connect the negative battery cable.

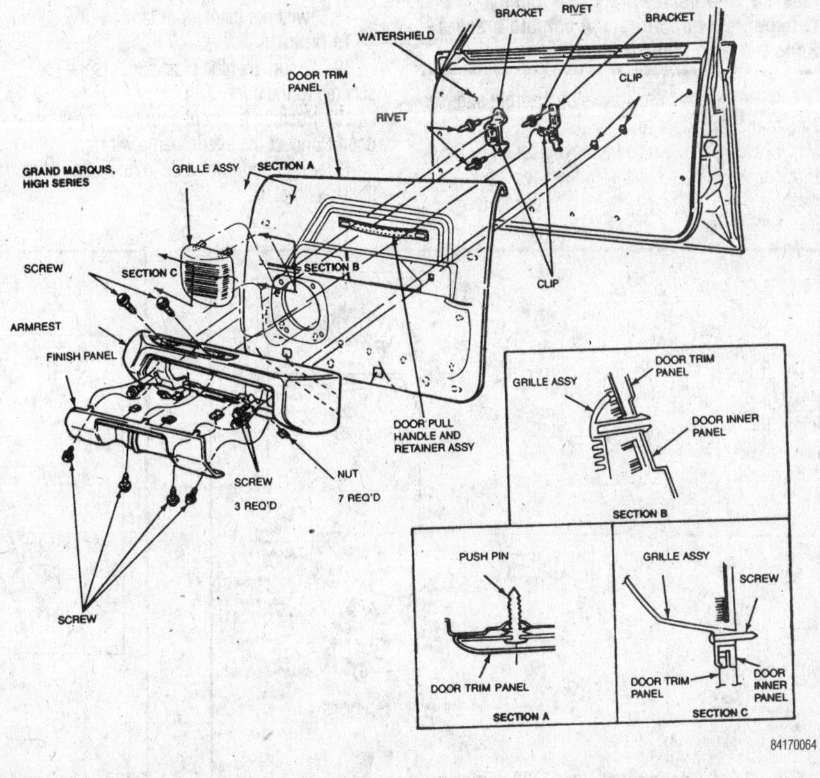


**Fig. 40 Front door panel—1988–91 vehicles**

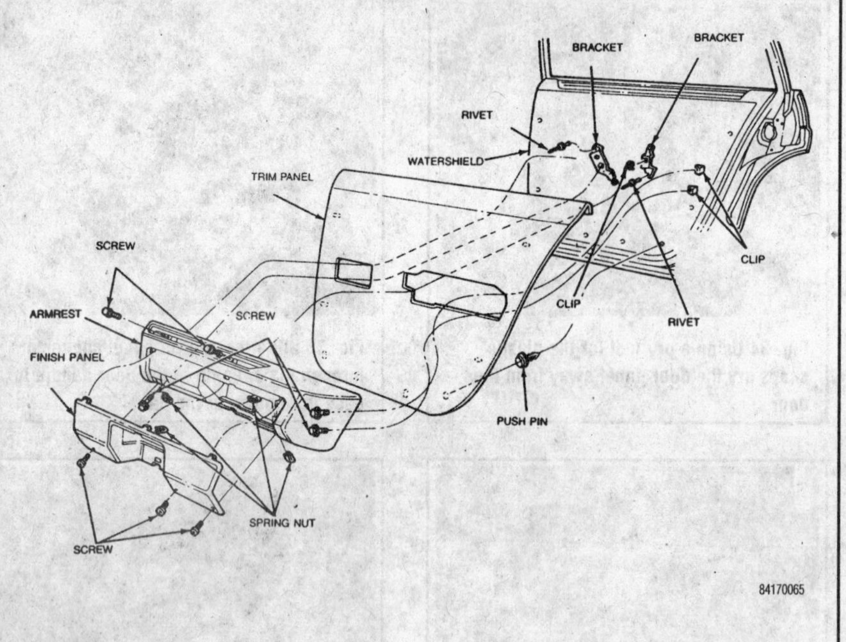


**Fig. 41 Rear door panel—1988–91 vehicles**

### Town Car 1992–00

➧ See Figures 42 and 43

1. Disconnect the negative battery cable.
2. Snap out the two door pull strap retaining screw covers. Remove the screws.

**CAUTION**

**To avoid breakage of the door pull covers, insert a small screwdriver diagonally between the pull strap and chrome bracket. Snap out both sides then remove.**

3. Remove the two screws on the front and rear side of the front door trim panel.
4. Using the trim pad removing tool, pry the trim panel retaining clips from the door inner panel.

**➡Do not use the front door trim panel to remove the trim clips from the door inner panel. Replace any bent, damaged or missing push pins.**

6. Remove the window regulator switch housing from the back of the front door trim panel. Lift up the housing and disconnect all connectors from the switch housing.
7. Disconnect the driver seat regulator control processor switch if equipped.
8. Twist out the interior lamp wire assembly.

**To install:**

9. Ensure that the plastic watershield is secured to the door .
10. Position the front door trim panel to the door. Connect the interior lamp wiring.
11. Align door lock side to its mating slide on the sheet metal.
12. Snap in the front door trim panel. Ensure all retainers fit properly.

Install the two retaining screws on the front and rear side of the front door trim panel.

13. Connect the driver seat regulator control processor, if equipped.
14. Position the window regulator control switch housing and connect the switch connectors. Install it to the front door trim panel by snapping it in, or by installing the screw at the rear.
15. Install the two retaining screws and pull strap covers.
16. Connect the negative battery cable.

### Continental 1988–94

➧ See Figures 44 thru 51

1. Remove the front door window regulator switch housing.
2. Remove all the screws retaining front door trim panel to the door. Using the trim pad removing tool, pry the front door trim panel from the door inner panel.
3. Remove the front door trim panel opening cover.

**To install:**

4. Connect all the electrical connectors.
5. Installation is the reversal of the removal procedure.

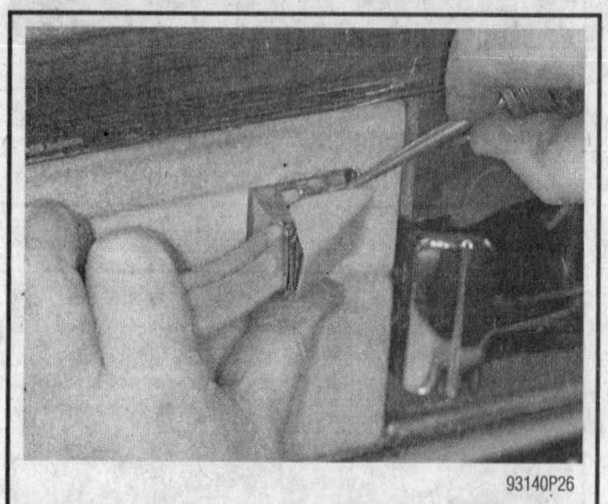


**Fig. 44 Using a sharp seal pick, release the screw cover from the snap**

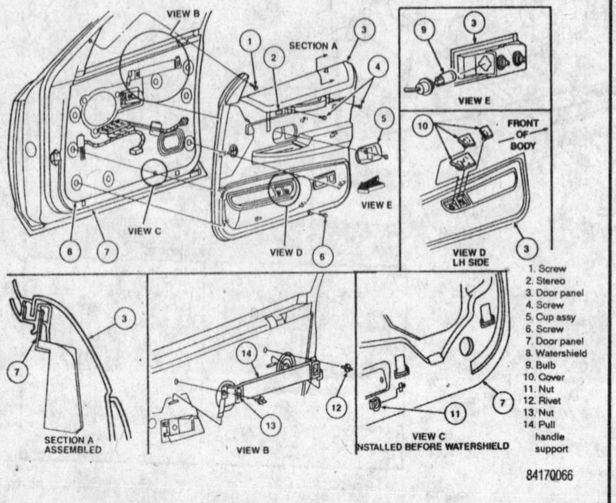


**Fig. 42 Front door panel—1992–00 vehicles**

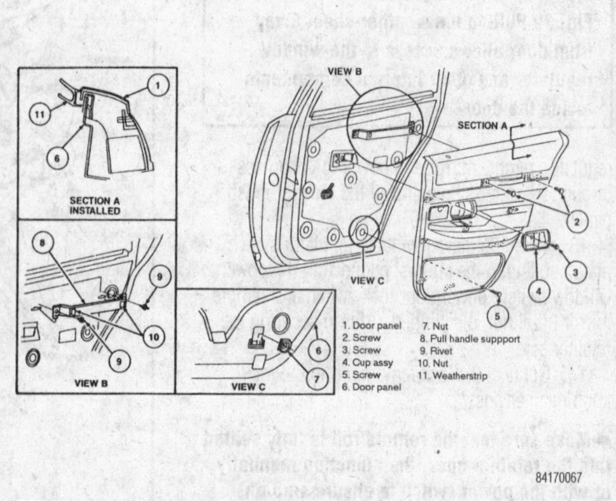


**Fig. 43 Rear door panel—1992–00 vehicles**

93140P25

**Fig. 45 Removing the cover exposes the pull handle retaining screws**

93140P24

**Fig. 46 The two pull handle screws must be removed to remove the door panel**

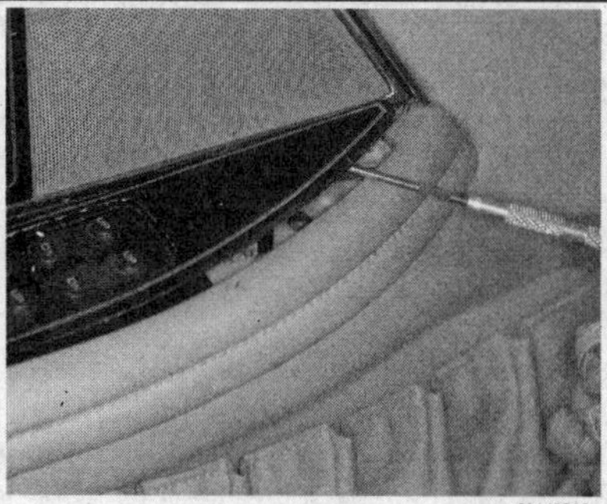

93140P32

**Fig. 47 Pry up on the front edge of the armrest control panel first to release it from retainer snap**

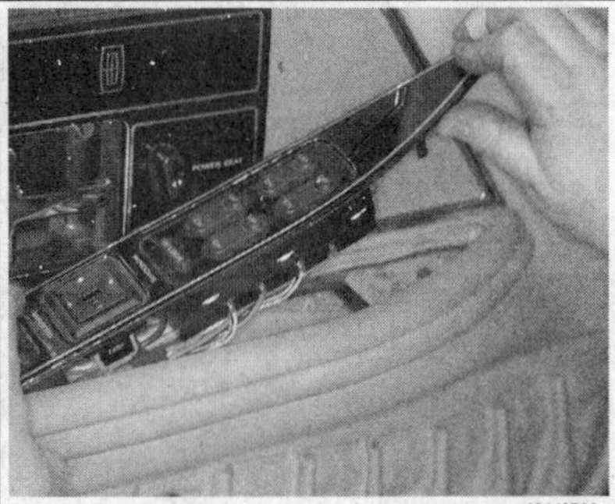

93140P30

**Fig. 48 Lift the panel up and slide it forward to remove it**

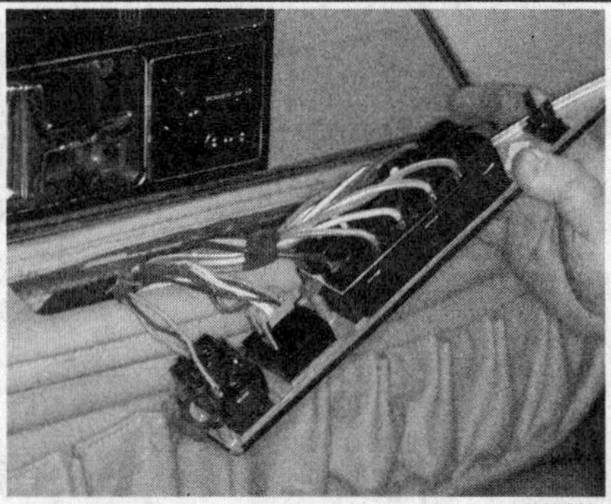

93140P31

**Fig. 49 The control connectors are screwed into the armrest control panel from the underside**

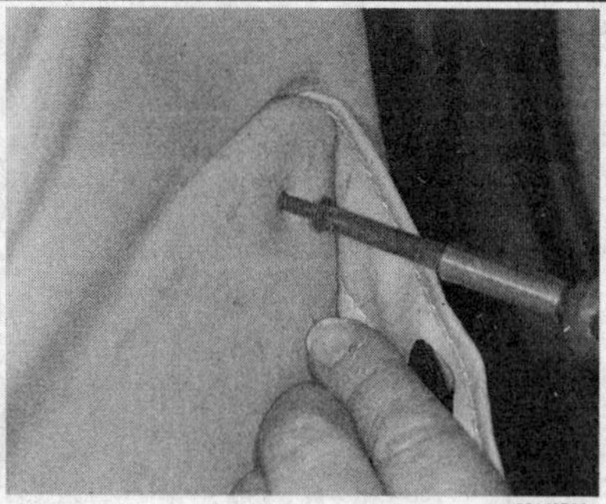

93140P16

**Fig. 50 Remove the screws hidden inside the map pocket before trying to remove the panel**

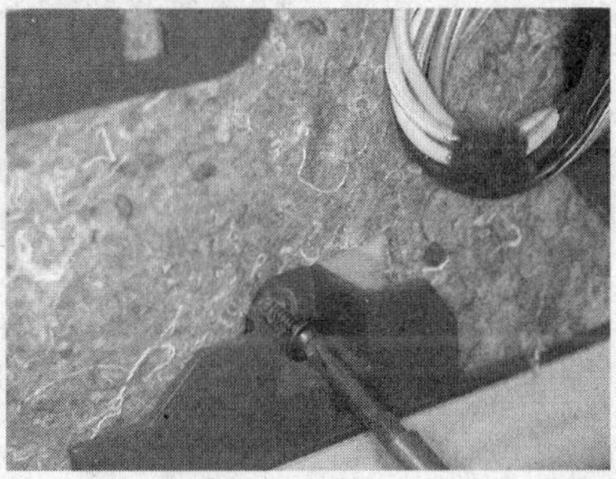

93140P27

**Fig. 51 After removing the two screws inside the map pocket, tilt it out from the top. Be careful with the snaps. When the map pocket is removed, it will allow access to the concealed screws that must be removed to remove the door panel**

#### Continental 1995–00

1. Using a small screwdriver, remove the screw cover from the armrest of the front door trim panel.
2. Remove the two retaining screws.
3. Using the trim pad removing tool , remove the front door trim panel
4. Disconnect the electrical connectors.
5. Remove the front door window regulator switch housing.

**To install:**

6. Position the front door trim panel on the door, align the two locators on the front door trim panel with the door and reverse the removal procedure.

#### Mark VII

1. Remove the retaining screws from the armrest assembly.
2. Remove the screws retaining the switches to the housing and remove the cover assembly.
3. Remove the door trim panel retaining screws.
4. Using the trim pad removing tool, pry the trim panel retaining clips from the door inner panel.
5. Disconnect all the wiring, if so equipped, and remove the trim panel.

**To install:**

6. Position the trim panel to the door inner panel and connect the wiring, if so equipped.
7. Push the trim panel and retaining clips into the inner door panel holes and install the retaining screws. Install the screws retaining the switches to the housing.
8. Position the armrest to the trim panel, and install the retaining screws.

#### Mark VIII

1. Remove the rear view mirror mounting hole cover.
2. Remove the inside door handle cup.
3. Remove the door lock control bezel.
4. Remove the window regulator switch plate.
5. Remove the interior lamp lens.
6. Remove the screw from the interior lamp opening .
7. Remove the screw from the window regulator switch plate opening.
8. Disconnect the window regulator jumper wire from the outside rear view mirror control , the seat regulator control, and the front door lock switch.
9. Disconnect the window regulator jumper wire form the luggage ocmp0aartnent remote control lockswitch.
10. Lift the front door trim panel vertically, out of the weather-strip and over the door latch control rod knob.
11. Disconnect the interior lamp form the window regulato0r jumper wire.
12. Remove the front door trim retention hooks into the door inner panel.
13. Remove the front door trim panel.

**To install:**

14. Reverse the removal procedure, paying special attention when inserting the front door trim panel into the weather-strip. Rock the front door trim panel into the weather-strip and push downward until the lower trim belt character ditch lines up with the score mark on the inner door panel.

## Door Locks

### REMOVAL & INSTALLATION

#### Front Door Latch

**See Figures 52 thru 58**

1. Remove the door trim panel and the watershield.
2. Mark the location of the rear glass run lower retaining bolt and remove the bolt.
3. Disconnect the outside release rod.

93140P28

**Fig. 52 Remove the access panel by prying it across the top and then lifting it up to clear the retaining tabs**

93140P29

**Fig. 53 If the inside door handle seems to stick out too far, it's probably broken. It is not necessary to remove the entire door panel to repair the handle. Unfasten the retaining screw**

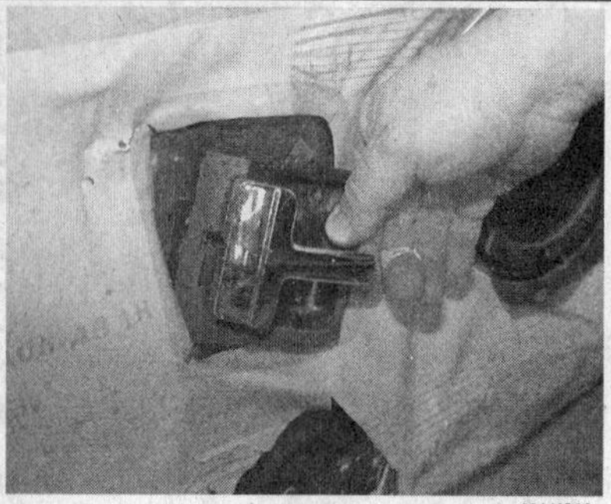

93140P20

**Fig. 54 We have removed the door panel for photo clarification. Pull the door handle forward and out of its seat**

93140P17

**Fig. 55 Slide the door handle off the connecting rod . . .**

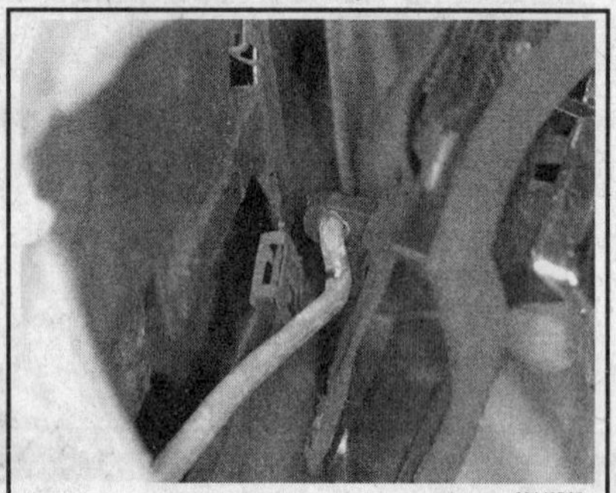

93140P22

**Fig. 56 . . . being careful not to allow the rod . . .**

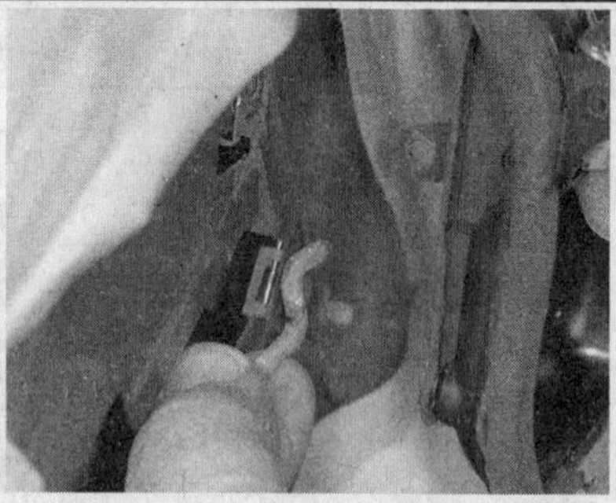

93140P19

**Fig. 57 . . . to snap out of your hand and drop inside the door**

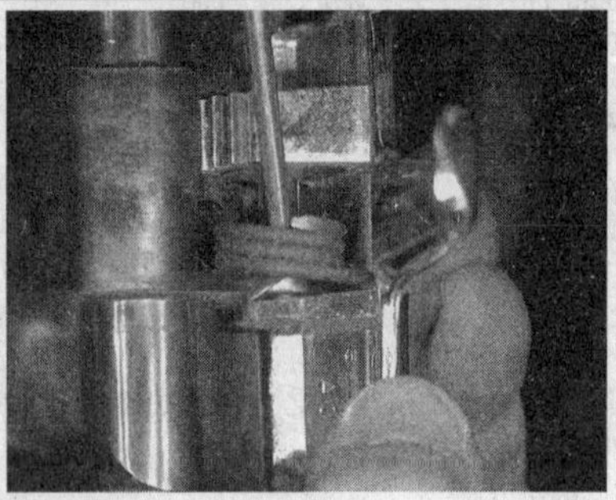

93140P15

**Fig. 58 This door handle has a broken return spring and needs to be replaced**

4. Check all rod connections. Correct any disconnected or loose connections and check operation before replacing parts.
5. Disconnect the rods from the latch. The remote link and the latch-to-lock cylinder rod cannot be removed because of the rod's end configuration.
6. Remove the lock cylinder rod from the lock cylinder lever.
7. Remove the power actuator, power rod, and clip, if equipped.
8. Remove the door latch remote control.
9. Remove the latch assembly retaining screws. Disconnect the door indicator switch wire, if equipped, and remove the latch from the door.
10. Remove the anti-theft shield from the latch.
11. Remove the remote link, the latch-to-lock cylinder rods, and the door indicator switch from the latch where applicable.

**To install:**

12. Install new rod retaining clips and grommets in the new latch assembly, using the removed latch as a guide.
13. Position the door indicator switch to the latch and install the attaching screw. Install the anti-theft shield to the latch.
14. Install the remote link and the latch-to-lock cylinder rod.
15. Position the latch in the door and connect the wire to the door indicator switch. Install the latch and retaining screws with the anti-theft shield. Tighten to 3–6 ft. lbs. (4–8 Nm).
16. Install the door latch remote control.
17. Connect the latch-to-lock cylinder rod to the lock cylinder lever, manual lock rod and power lock rod, if equipped.
18. Connect the outside release rod to the latch and check latch operation.
19. Install the rear glass run lower attaching bolt in the original position.
20. Install the door trim panel and watershield.

## Rear Door Latch

**➧ See Figures 59 and 60**

1. Remove the door trim panel and watershield.
2. Disconnect the door latch-actuating rod from the latch assembly.
3. Remove the rear door latch bellcrank.
4. Remove the door latch remote control.
5. Disconnect the power lock rod, if equipped.
6. Remove the three latch assembly retaining screws.
7. Disconnect the wire from the door indicator switch, if equipped, and remove the latch assembly from the door.
8. Remove the door indicator switch from the latch assembly and remove the 2 link assemblies from the latch.

**To install:**

9. Install new clips and grommets in the new latch assembly, using the removed latch as a guide.
10. Install the door indicator switch on the latch assembly.
11. Install the 2 link assemblies into the lower lever grommets.
12. Connect the power lock rod, if equipped.
13. Position the latch assembly on the door and connect the wire to the door indicator switch, if equipped.
14. Install the 3 retaining screws.
15. Connect the door latch-actuating rod to the latch assembly.
16. Install the door latch bellcrank and remote control.
17. Check latch operation, then install the door panel and watershield.

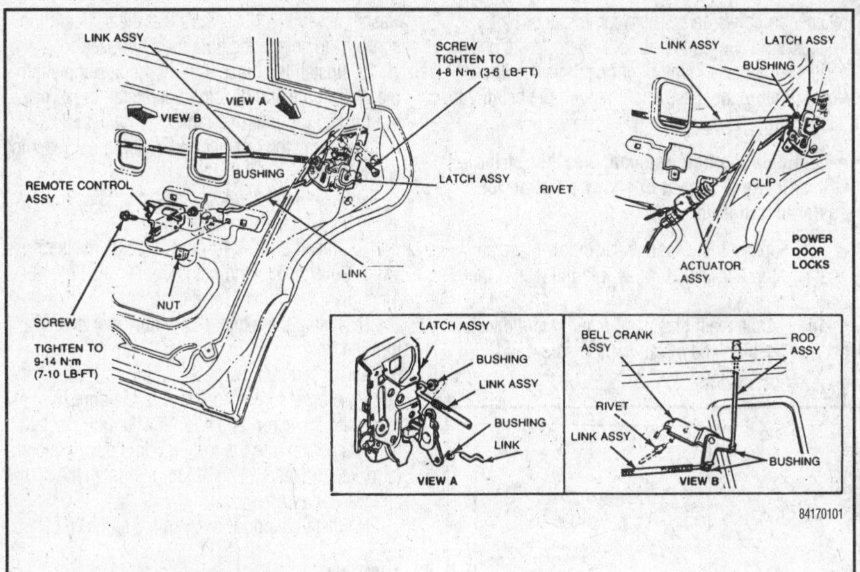


Fig. 59 Rear door—1988-91 typical

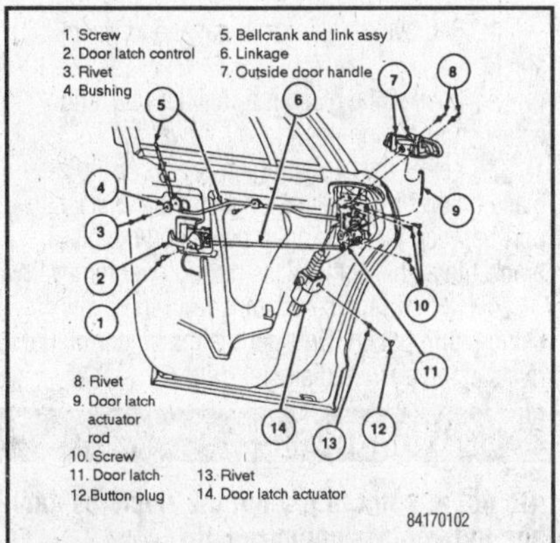


Fig. 60 Rear door—1992-00 typical

## Door Glass and Regulator

REMOVAL & INSTALLATION

### 1988-91

#### *FRONT DOOR*

▸ See Figure 61

1. Remove the door trim panel and watershield. Remove the inside door belt weather-strip.
2. Raise or lower the glass to gain access to the glass bracket retaining rivets. Loosen the nut and washer assemblies retaining the door glass stabilizer. Position a suitable block support between the door outer panel and the glass bracket to stabilize the glass during rivet removal.
3. Remove the center pin of each rivet with a drift punch. Drill out the remainder of the rivet with a ¼ in. diameter drill, being careful not to enlarge the rivet attachment.

**⁂ WARNING**

**Do not attempt to pry the rivets out as damage to the glass bracket and glass spacer retainer could result.**

4. Remove the glass by tipping it forward then removing it from the outboard side of the door.

**To install:**

5. Install the spacer and retainer assemblies into the glass retention holes. Make sure each assembly is securely fastened.
6. Insert the glass into the door between the door belt weather-strips.
7. Position the regulator arm slide assembly into the C-channel of the glass bracket.
8. Position the glass to the glass bracket and install three ¼ in. blind rivets. Three ¼ in.-20 bolt, washer and nut assemblies can also be used to attach the glass to the glass bracket. Tighten the bolt and nut to 3-5 ft. lbs. (4-7 Nm).
9. If necessary, loosen the upper and lower retaining screws on the run and bracket assembly to position the glass in the doorframe.
10. Install the door belt weather-strip, trim panel and watershield.

#### *REAR DOOR*

▸ See Figures 62 and 63

1. Remove the door trim panel and watershield.
2. Remove the glass-to-glass bracket retaining rivets. Remove the center pin from the rivets with a drift punch and drill the head from each rivet with a ¼ in. diameter drill. Lower the glass approximately 6 in. and let it rest in the door well.
3. Remove the door window glass inner stabilizer retaining screw and remove the stabilizer assembly.
4. Remove the retainer and division bar glass run attaching screw and washer assembly at the bottom.
5. Remove the screw and washer assembly at the top of the division bar at the doorframe. Tilt the division bar and main glass forward and remove the weather-strip from the top of the doorframe.
6. Remove the stationary vent glass and weather-strip from the doorframe.
7. Position the retainer, division bar and main glass in the upright position. Pull the main glass and division bar above and outside the doorframe. Swing the glass and division bar assemblies' 90 degrees from the doorframe and work the glass and division bar upward and out of the door channel between the belt moldings.

**To install:**

**➡The rear door glass, rear door window glass channel, division bar glass run, and retainer and division bar mechanism are assembled prior to installation.**

8. Install the glass channel to the glass using glass Everseal tape or equivalent, 0.065 in. (1.65mm) thick x 1¾ in. (44.45mm) wide x 17 ¾ in. (450.85mm) long. Be sure to align the notches in the glass to the cutouts within the glass channel. Clear tape from channel for installing glass guides.

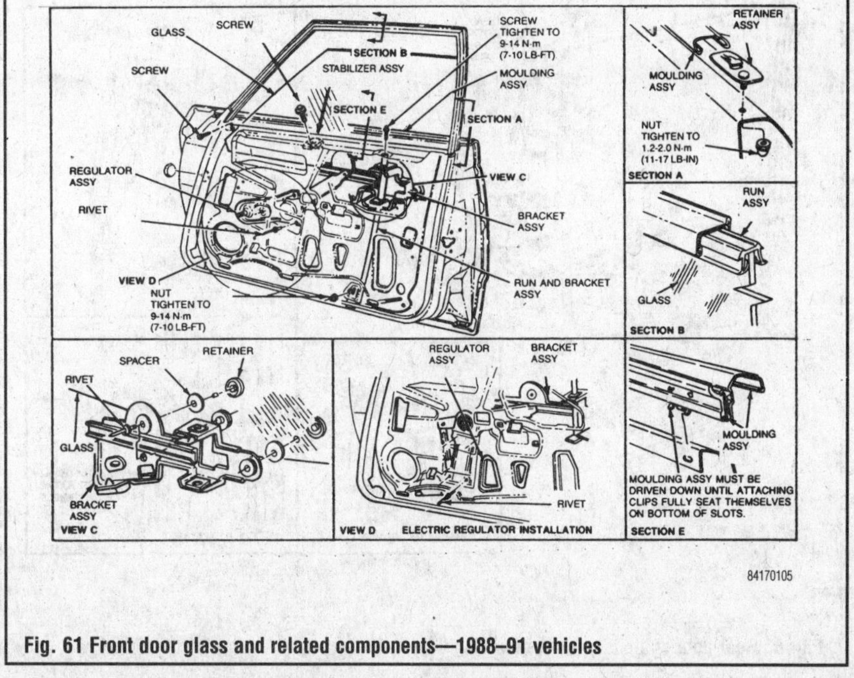


Fig. 61 Front door glass and related components—1988-91 vehicles

9. Install 2 nylon guides into the glass channel slots and snap the Mylar flocked glass run over the glass channel.

10. Lubricate the inside section of the retainer and division bar assembly with silicone lubricant. Place the retainer and division bar assembly over the nylon guides and slide over the glass channel.

11. Install the run assembly into the doorframe (front and top of door). Leave the last 6 in. (152mm) of run assembly next to the division bar hanging loose out of the door frame.

12. While holding the rear door glass, retainer, and division bar 90° from the door, insert the retainer and division bar between the door belt weather-strip. Swing the glass inboard to the belt and install loosely in the door channel. The upper front corner of the glass should touch the beltline in this position.

➡**Lubricate the belt and vent weather-strips with silicone lubricant or soapy solution for easier installation.**

13. Subassemble fixed rear window glass and weather-strip and install firmly into the rear of the door frame.

14. Set the main glass and retainer and division bar into position and install the top screw and washer assembly. Make sure that the sealer at the screw head covers the hole for a tight seal.

15. Install the loose 6 in. of run assembly into the door frame and division bar. Install the remaining flocked run into the frame.

16. Install the retainer and division bar retaining screw.

17. Install the window glass inner stabilizer assembly with the retaining screw.

18. Install 2 glass-to-glass bracket rivets or use ¼ in.-20 x 1 bolts and nuts. Tighten the bolts to no more than 3–5 ft. lbs. (4–7 Nm).

19. Install the retainer assembly rear door glass. Run the front lower (front guide) with the upper bracket locked into the frame and loosely attach the bottom bracket to the front face of the door (hinge face) with the screw and washer assembly. Install the flocked run into the front guide. Lower the glass to make sure there is no binding. Tighten the screw and washer assembly.

20. Install the door watershield and trim panel.

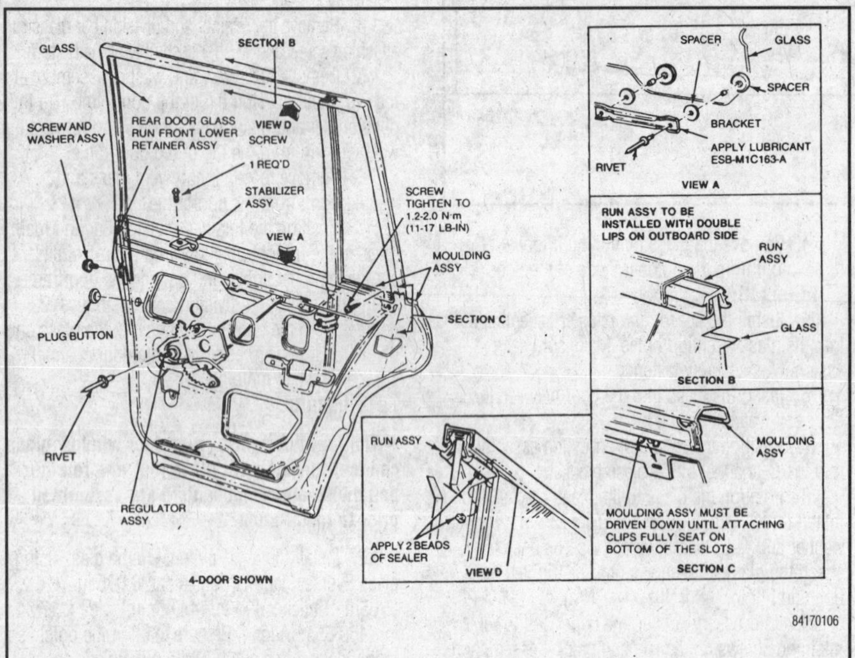


Fig. 62 Rear door glass mounting—typical

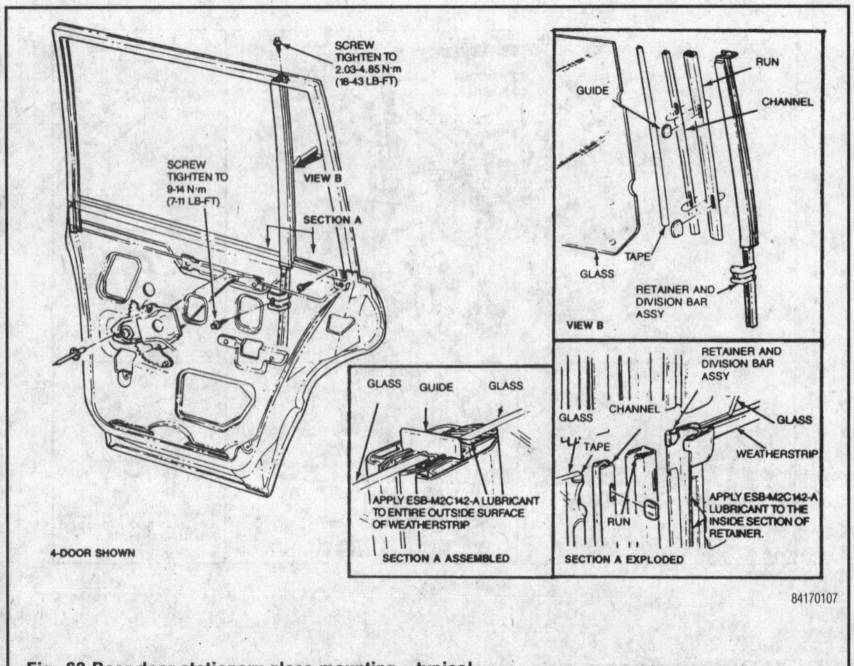


Fig. 63 Rear door stationary glass mounting—typical

## 1992–00

➧ See Figure 64

1. Remove the door trim panel and watershield.

2. Loosen the glass run retainer retaining screw and position the retainer forward.

3. Lower the glass to gain access to the 2 glass bracket rivets. Position a suitable block support between the door outer panel and the glass bracket to stabilize the glass during rivet removal.

4. Remove the center pins from the rivets using a drift punch. Drill out the remainder of the rivets using a ¼ in. diameter drill.

**WARNING**

**Do not attempt to pry out the rivets as damage to the glass could result.**

5. Remove the glass.

**To install:**

6. Insert the glass into the door between the outer belt weather-strip and inner panel.

7. Position the glass into the doorframe and lower the window to align with the regulator bracket.

8. Install two ¼ in. blind rivets. Two ¼-20 x 1 in. screw, washer and nut assemblies can also be used. Tighten the screws to no more than 7–10 ft. lbs. (9–14 Nm).

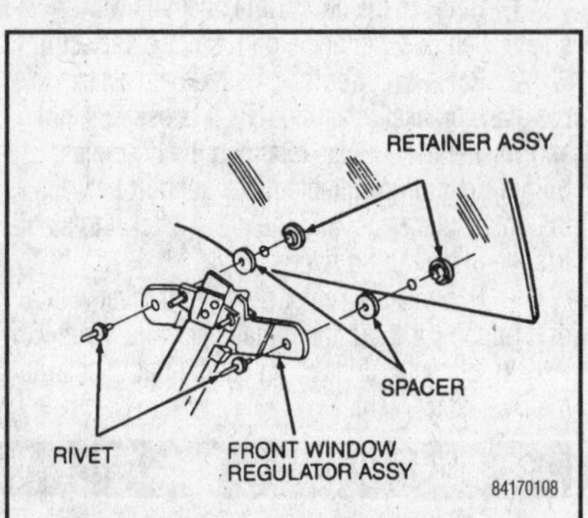


Fig. 64 Front door glass installation—1992–00

9. Adjust the door glass as follows:
a. Loosen, but do not remove, the upper regulator retaining nuts.
b. Raise the glass to the full-up position and tighten the nuts to 7–10 ft. lbs. (9–14 Nm).
c. Loosen, but do not remove, the front glass run retainer bolt.
d. Lower the glass to the full down position and tighten the run retainer bolt to 7–10 ft. lbs. (9–14 Nm).
10. Install the door trim panel and watershield.

## Door Window Regulator

### REMOVAL & INSTALLATION

#### 1988–91 Vehicles

***FRONT DOOR***

1. Remove the door trim panel and watershield.
2. Support the glass in the full-up position.
3. Detach the power window motor wiring connector, if equipped.
4. Remove the center pin from the regulator retaining rivets with a drift punch. Using a ¼ in. diameter drill, drill out the remainder of the rivet, being careful not to enlarge the sheet metal retaining holes.

**CAUTION**

**If the regulator counterbalance spring must be removed or replaced for any reason, make sure that the regulator arms are in a fixed position prior to removal to prevent possible injury during C-spring unwind.**

5. Disengage the regulator arm slides from the glass brackets C-channel and remove the regulator from the door.

**To install:**

6. Position the regulator in the door and insert the square slides into the glass brackets C-channel.
7. Position the regulator to the retaining holes in the door inner panel. Install the ¼ in. blind rivets. ¼ in.-20 **x** ½ in. screw and washer assemblies and ¼ in.-20 nut and washer assemblies can also be used.
8. Attach the power window wiring connector, if equipped.
9. Cycle the regulator to check for proper operation.
10. Install the door trim panel and watershield.

***REAR DOOR***

1. Remove the door trim panel and watershield.
2. Remove the retaining rivets . Remove the center pin from the rivets with a drift punch. Drill out the head of the rivet using a ¼ in. diameter drill. Be careful not to enlarge the sheet metal holes during drilling.
3. Remove the regulator arm roller from the glass bracket channel and remove the regulator from the door.

**To install:**

4. Lubricate the window regulator rollers, shafts and the entire length of the roller guides with multi-purpose grease.
5. Install the regulator into the access hole in the inner panel.
6. Position the regulator arm roller into the glass bracket channel.
7. Install the rivets attaching the regulator to the door inner panel. ¼ in.-20 **x** ½ in. screw and washer assemblies and ¼ in.-20 nut and washer assemblies can also be used.
8. Install the watershield and door trim panel.

#### 1992–00 Vehicles

See Figure 65

***OPERATIONAL WINDOW***

1. Remove the door trim panel and watershield.
2. Remove the door glass.
3. Detach the power window motor wiring connector.
4. Remove the two ¼ in. rivets attaching the lower bracket of the regulator to the inner panel. Use a drift punch to knock out the center pins, then drill out the remainder of the rivet with a ¼ in. diameter drill. Be careful not to enlarge the sheet metal holes in the door inner panel.
5. Remove the 3 motor retaining screws from inside the door to remove the motor from the bracket assembly.
6. Remove the 2 upper regulator retaining nuts and remove the regulator from the door.

**To install:**

7. Apply an even coating of multi-purpose grease to the window regulator rollers, shafts and the entire length of the roller guides.
8. Install the regulator into the access hole in the inner panel.
9. Position the regulator using the upper regulator studs and tabs on the motor mounting bracket.
10. Install the rivets attaching the regulator to the door inner panel. Two ¼ in.-20 **x** ½ in. screw and washer assemblies and ¼ in.-20 nut and washer assemblies can also be used.
11. Install the 2 upper regulator retaining nuts. Install the motor, being careful not to overtighten the screws.
12. Install and adjust the door glass.
13. Install the watershield and door trim panel.

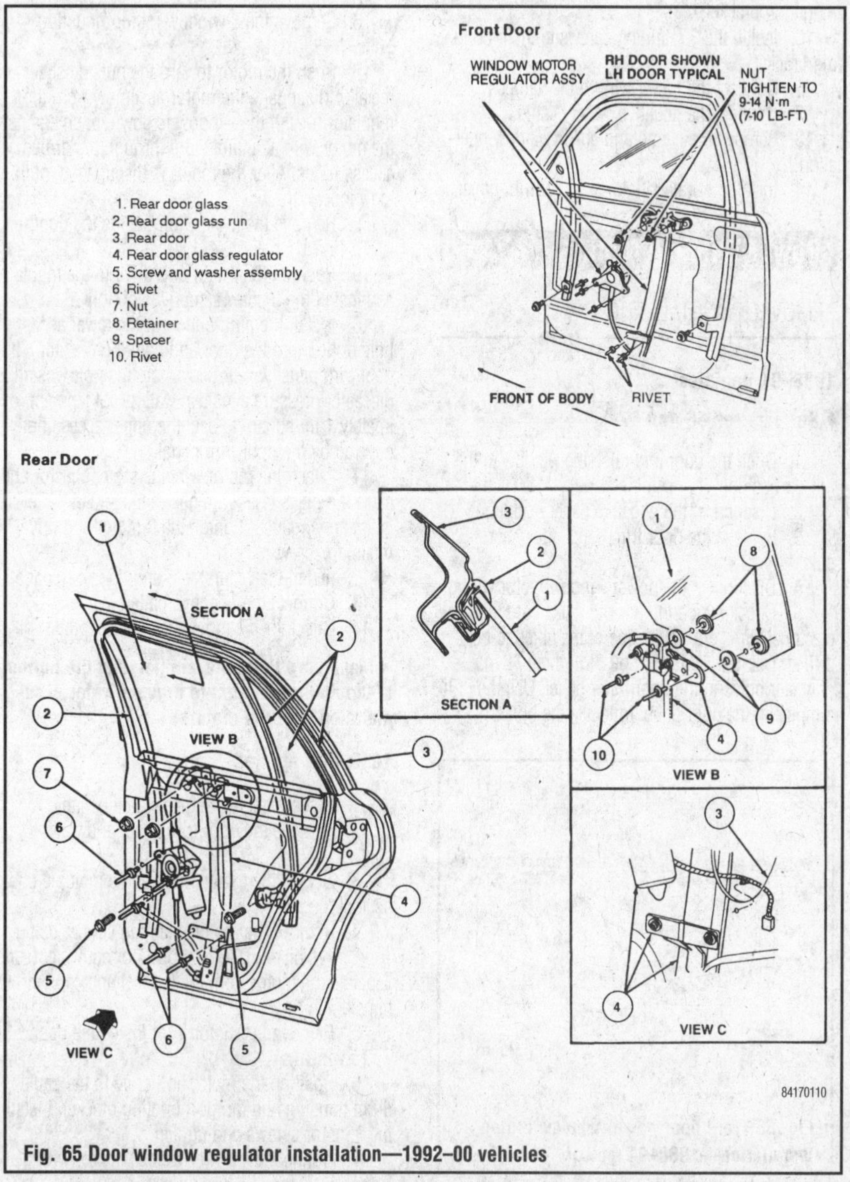


Fig. 65 Door window regulator installation—1992–00 vehicles

***DOWN AND INOPERABLE WINDOW***

1. Disconnect the negative battery cable.
2. Remove the door trim panel and watershield.
3. Remove the motor retaining screws through the holes.

**WARNING**

**Be careful not to strike or scratch the glass, as it could break.**

4. Remove the motor assembly from the drum housing.
5. Raise the glass to the full-up position by hand and secure with a clamp.
6. Remove the regulator as outlined in the previous procedure.

**To install:**

7. Install the regulator as described in the previous procedure.
8. Assemble the motor drive assembly to the drum housing. Align the mounting holes in the motor with the holes in the drum housing.
9. Align the motor drive assembly to the mounting bracket.
10. Install the 3 retaining screws to the mounting bracket.
11. Connect the motor wire to the harness.
12. Connect the negative battery cable.
13. Remove the clamp and check window operation.
14. Install the watershield and door trim panel.

## Power Window Motor

### REMOVAL & INSTALLATION

**1988–91 Vehicles**

**See Figures 66 and 67**

1. Open the door and raise the window to the full-up position, if possible.
2. Disconnect the negative battery cable.
3. Remove the door trim panel and watershield.
4. Disconnect the power window motor wiring.
5. Check inside the door to make sure those electrical wires are not in-line of the holes to be drilled. Using a ½ in. drill bit, drill three ½ in. diameter holes in the door inner panel. Use the drill dimples in the door panel to locate the holes.

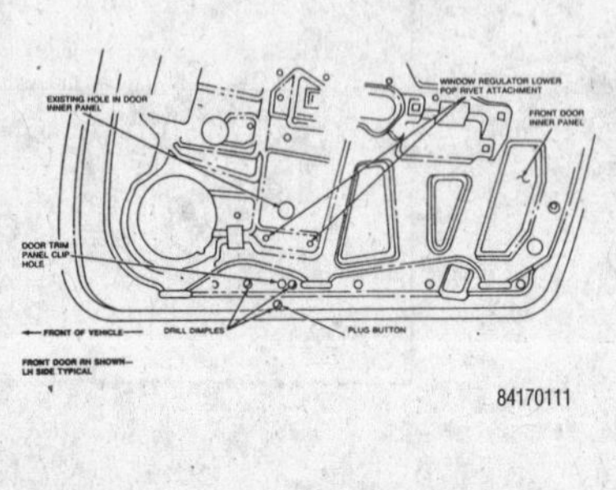


**Fig. 66 Front door power window motor installation—1988–91 typical**

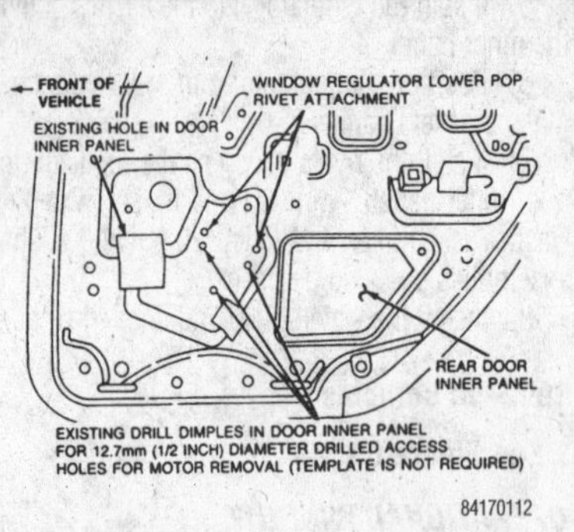


**Fig. 67 Rear door power window motor installation—1988–91 typical**

**CAUTION**

**Prior to motor assembly removal, make sure that the regulator arm is in a fixed position to prevent counterbalance spring unwind.**

6. Remove the 3 window motor mounting bolts.
7. Push the motor toward the outside sheet metal to disengage the motor assembly from the regulator gear. If the window is down, push against the motor with a suitable tool through the drilled access holes. After the motor is disengaged, pull the window up.
8. Remove the motor from inside the door.

**To install:**

9. Position the motor and drive to the regulator and install the 3 screws snug—not tight.
10. Install the plug button in the lower access hole drilled into the door and paint body color. The door trim panel will not cover up this hole. Install 2 pieces of pressure sensitive waterproof tape approximately 1 in. square to seal the upper access holes covered by the door trim panel.
11. Attach the motor wires at the connector and cycle the glass to ensure gear engagement. After the gears are engaged, tighten the 3 motor and drive retaining screws.
12. Install the watershield and door trim panel.
13. Connect the negative battery cable.
14. Check the window for proper operation.

**➡Make sure that all drain holes at the bottom of the doors are open to prevent water accumulation over the motors.**

**1992–00 Vehicles**

1. Disconnect the negative battery cable.
2. Remove the door trim panel and watershield.
3. Detach the motor wires at the multiple connector.
4. Remove the motor retaining screws using Torx® drive bit set D79P–2100–T or equivalent, and separate the motor from the bracket and cable drum housing.
5. Remove the motor from inside the door.

**To install:**

6. Position the motor and drive to the cable drum housing and motor mounting bracket. Install the 3 motor screws and tighten.
7. Connect the power window motor wiring.
8. Connect the negative battery cable.
9. Check window operation.
10. Install the watershield and door trim panel.

## Inside Rear View Mirror

### REMOVAL & INSTALLATION

**Mirror**

***1988–91 VEHICLES***

**See Figure 68**

1. Loosen the mirror-to-mounting bracket setscrew.
2. Remove the mirror by sliding upward and away from the mounting bracket.
3. Installation is the reverse of the removal procedure.

**➡If the vehicle is equipped with an electronic day/night mirror, the automatic dimmer sensor and mirror must be unplugged and the screw and washer must be removed to gain access to the mounting bracket set screw.**

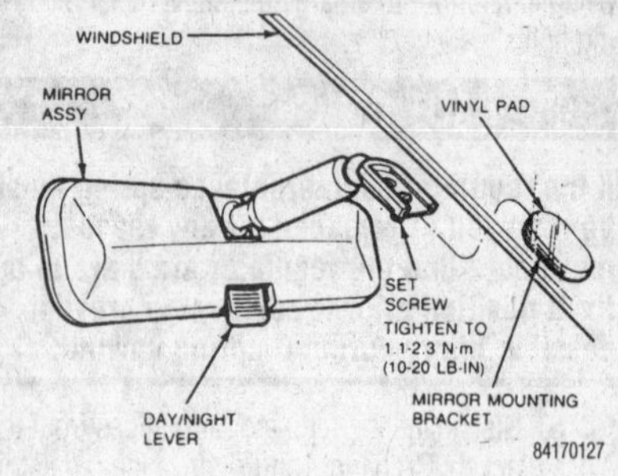


**Fig. 68 Inside rear view mirror installation—1988–91 vehicles**

***1992–00 VEHICLES***

**See Figure 69**

1. While firmly holding the mirror, insert inside mirror removal tool T91T–17700–A or equivalent, into the slot until the button is contacted.

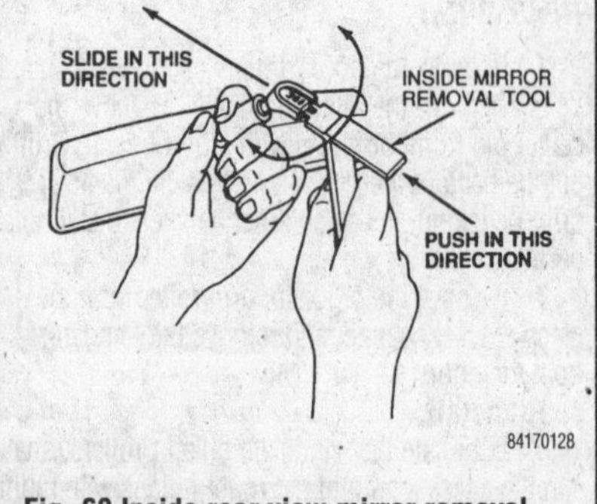


**Fig. 69 Inside rear view mirror removal—1992–00 vehicles**

2. Remove the mirror by pushing the mirror upward and away from the mounting bracket.
3. Installation is the reverse of the removal procedure.

## Seats

### REMOVAL & INSTALLATION

**Power Front Seat**

1. Disconnect the negative battery cable.
2. Remove the access covers from the lower shields, if equipped, or insulators, if equipped, to expose the nuts and washers and/or bolts.
3. Remove the nuts and washers and/or bolts retaining the seat track to the floorpan.
4. Lift the seat up enough to disconnect the seat harness connector and disconnect the connector.
5. On certain models, remove the bolt(s) attaching the seat belts to the floor.
6. Remove the seat and track assembly from the vehicle.
7. Installation is the reverse of the removal procedure.

**Rear Seat**

**➧ See Figures 70 and 71**

1. Apply knee pressure to the lower front portion of the rear seat cushion. Push rearward to disengage the seat cushion from the retainer brackets.

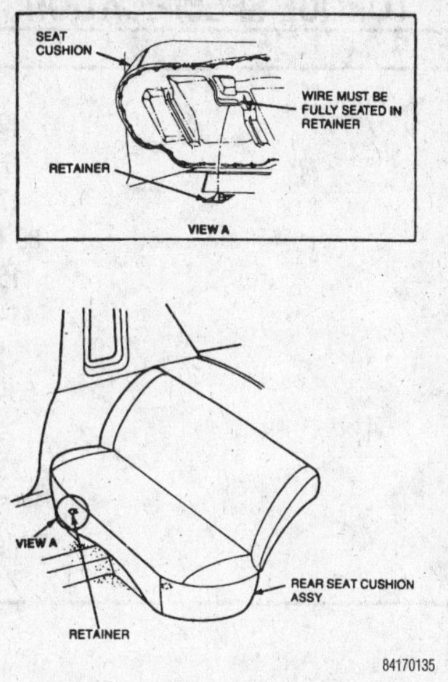


**Fig. 70 Rear seat cushion installation—typical**

2. Remove the outer seat belt and seat back lower retaining screws.
3. Grasp the seat back at the bottom and lift up to disengage the hanger wire from the retainer brackets.
4. Remove the seat back from the vehicle.

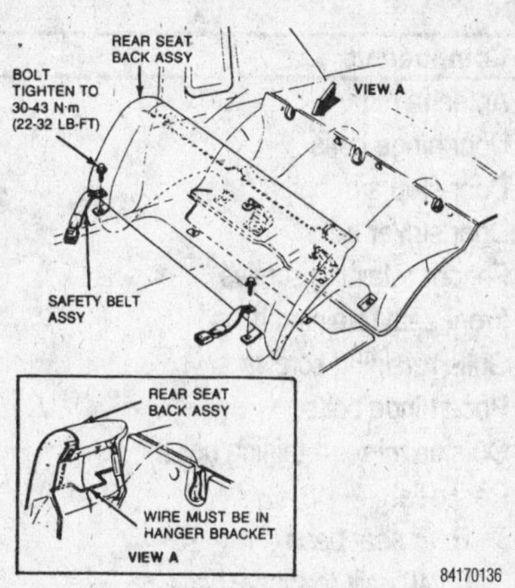


**Fig. 71 Rear seat back installation—typical**

**To install:**

5. Position the seat back into the vehicle so that the hanger wire is engaged with the retaining brackets.
6. Install the outer seat belt and seat back lower retainer screws. Tighten to 22–32 ft. lbs. (30–43 Nm).
7. Position the seat cushion into the vehicle. Apply knee pressure to the lower portion of the seat cushion, pushing rearward and down to lock the cushion into position.
8. Check the rear seat cushion to make sure it is secured into the floor retainer.

## TORQUE SPECIFICATIONS

| Components | English | Metric |
|---|---|---|
| Antenna nut | 31-44 inch lbs. | 4-5 Nm |
| Door hinge bolts | 19-25 ft. lbs. | 25-35 Nm |
| Door stop arm bolts | 89 inch lbs. | 10 Nm |
| Door striker bolts | 17-20 ft. lbs. | 22-28 Nm |
| Fender retaining screws | 89-124 inch lbs. | 10-14 Nm |
| Front seat retaining bolts | 15-19 ft. lbs. | 20-26 Nm |
| Grille retaining screws | 11-16 inch lbs. | 1-2 Nm |
| Hood hinge bolts | 18 ft. lbs. | 24 Nm |
| Outside mirror retaining bolts | 53-71 inch lbs. | 6-8 Nm |
| Rear seat | | |
| Rear seat back | 23-35 ft. lbs. | 31-48 Nm |
| 60/40 split rear seat back | 15-19 ft. lbs. | 20-26 Nm |
| Trunk lid hinge bolts | 89 inch lbs. | 10 Nm |
| Window regulator-to-door glass retaining bolts | 71 inch lbs. | 8 Nm |

93140C01

# 11 TROUBLESHOOTING

TROUBLESHOOTING INDEX 11-2
DIAGNOSTIC PROCEDURES 11-7

**TROUBLESHOOTING INDEX 11-2**
SECTION 1: ENGINE 11-2
SECTION 2: DRIVE TRAIN 11-3
SECTION 3: BRAKE SYSTEM 11-4
SECTION 4: WHEELS, TIRES, STEERING AND SUSPENSION 11-4
SECTION 5: ELECTRICAL ACCESSORIES 11-5
SECTION 6: INSTRUMENTS AND GAUGES 11-6
SECTION 7: CLIMATE CONTROL 11-6
**DIAGNOSTIC PROCEDURES 11-7**
SECTION 1: ENGINE 11-7
ENGINE STARTING PROBLEMS 11-7
ENGINE RUNNING CONDITIONS 11-8
ENGINE NOISES, ODORS AND VIBRATIONS 11-10
ENGINE ELECTRICAL SYSTEM 11-11
ENGINE COOLING SYSTEM 11-12
ENGINE EXHAUST SYSTEM 11-12
SECTION 2: DRIVE TRAIN 11-13
AUTOMATIC TRANSMISSION 11-13
MANUAL TRANSMISSION 11-13
CLUTCH 11-14
DIFFERENTIAL AND FINAL DRIVE 11-14
TRANSFER ASSEMBLY 11-15
DRIVESHAFT 11-15
AXLES 11-15
OTHER DRIVE TRAIN CONDITIONS 11-15
SECTION 3: BRAKE SYSTEM 11-16
BRAKE SYSTEM TROUBLESHOOTING 11-16
SECTION 4: WHEELS, TIRES, STEERING AND SUSPENSION 11-17
WHEELS AND WHEEL BEARINGS 11-17
TIRES 11-17
STEERING 11-18
SUSPENSION 11-18
DRIVING NOISES AND VIBRATIONS 11-18
SECTION 5: ELECTRICAL ACCESSORIES 11-19
HEADLIGHTS 11-19
TAIL, RUNNING AND SIDE MARKER LIGHTS 11-19
INTERIOR LIGHTS 11-20
BRAKE LIGHTS 11-20
WARNING LIGHTS 11-20
TURN SIGNAL AND 4-WAY HAZARD LIGHTS 11-22
HORN 11-22
WINDSHIELD WIPERS 11-22
SECTION 6: INSTRUMENTS AND GAUGES 11-23
SPEEDOMETER (CABLE OPERATED) 11-23
SPEEDOMETER (ELECTRONICALLY OPERATED) 11-23
FUEL, TEMPERATURE AND OIL PRESSURE GAUGES 11-23
SECTION 7: CLIMATE CONTROL 11-23
AIR CONDITIONER 11-23
HEATER 11-24

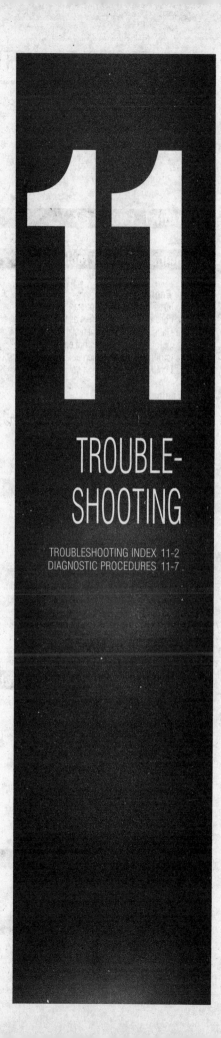

| Condition | Section/Item Number |
|---|---|

The following troubleshooting charts are divided into 7 sections covering engine, drive train, brakes, wheels/tires/steering/suspension, electrical accessories, instruments and gauges, and climate control. The first portion (or index) consists of a list of symptoms, along with section and item numbers. After selecting the appropriate condition, refer to the corresponding diagnostic procedure in the second portion's specified location.

## *INDEX*

## SECTION 1. ENGINE

### A. Engine Starting Problems

**Gasoline Engines**

| | |
|---|---|
| Engine turns over, but will not start | 1-A, 1 |
| Engine does not turn over when attempting to start | 1-A, 2 |
| Engine stalls immediately when started | 1-A, 3 |
| Starter motor spins, but does not engage | 1-A, 4 |
| Engine is difficult to start when cold | 1-A, 5 |
| Engine is difficult to start when hot | 1-A, 6 |

**Diesel Engines**

| | |
|---|---|
| Engine turns over but won't start | 1-A, 1 |
| Engine does not turn over when attempting to start | 1-A, 2 |
| Engine stalls after starting | 1-A, 3 |
| Starter motor spins, but does not engage | 1-A, 4 |
| Engine is difficult to start | 1-A, 5 |

### B. Engine Running Conditions

**Gasoline Engines**

| | |
|---|---|
| Engine runs poorly, hesitates | 1-B, 1 |
| Engine lacks power | 1-B, 2 |
| Engine has poor fuel economy | 1-B, 3 |
| Engine runs on (diesels) when turned off | 1-B, 4 |
| Engine knocks and pings during heavy acceleration, and on steep hills | 1-B, 5 |
| Engine accelerates but vehicle does not gain speed | 1-B, 6 |

**Diesel Engines**

| | |
|---|---|
| Engine runs poorly | 1-B, 1 |
| Engine lacks power | 1-B, 2 |

### C. Engine Noises, Odors and Vibrations

| | |
|---|---|
| Engine makes a knocking or pinging noise when accelerating | I-C, 1 |
| Starter motor grinds when used | 1-C, 2 |
| Engine makes a screeching noise | 1-C, 3 |
| Engine makes a growling noise | 1-C, 4 |
| Engine makes a ticking or tapping noise | 1-C, 5 |
| Engine makes a heavy knocking noise | 1-C, 6 |
| Vehicle has a fuel odor when driven | 1-C, 7 |
| Vehicle has a rotten egg odor when driven | 1-C, 8 |
| Vehicle has a sweet odor when driven | 1-C, 9 |
| Engine vibrates when idling | 1-C, 10 |
| Engine vibrates during acceleration | 1-C, 11 |

### D. Engine Electrical System

| | |
|---|---|
| Battery goes dead while driving | 1-D, 1 |
| Battery goes dead overnight | 1-D, 2 |

### E. Engine Cooling System

| | |
|---|---|
| Engine overheats | 1-E, 1 |
| Engine loses coolant | 1-E, 2 |
| Engine temperature remains cold when driving | 1-E, 3 |
| Engine runs hot | 1-E, 4 |

| Condition | Section/Item Number |
|---|---|
| **SECTION 1. ENGINE (continued)** | |
| **F. Engine Exhaust System** | |
| Exhaust rattles at idle speed | 1-F, 1 |
| Exhaust system vibrates when driving | 1-F, 2 |
| Exhaust system seems too low | 1-F, 3 |
| Exhaust seems loud | 1-F, 4 |
| **SECTION 2. DRIVE TRAIN** | |
| **A. Automatic Transmission** | |
| Transmission shifts erratically | 2-A, 1 |
| Transmission will not engage | 2-A, 2 |
| Transmission will not downshift during heavy acceleration | 2-A, 3 |
| **B. Manual Transmission** | |
| Transmission grinds going into forward gears while driving | 2-B, 1; 2-C, 2 |
| Transmission jumps out of gear | 2-B, 2 |
| Transmission difficult to shift | 2-B, 3; 2-C, 2 |
| Transmission leaks fluid | 2-B, 4 |
| **C. Clutch** | |
| Clutch slips on hills or during sudden acceleration | 2-C, 1 |
| Clutch will not disengage, difficult to shift | 2-C, 2 |
| Clutch is noisy when the clutch pedal is pressed | 2-C, 3 |
| Clutch pedal extremely difficult to press | 2-C, 4 |
| Clutch pedal remains down when pressed | 2-C, 5 |
| Clutch chatters when engaging | 2-C, 6 |
| **D. Differential and Final Drive** | |
| Differential makes a low pitched rumbling noise | 2-D, 1 |
| Differential makes a howling noise | 2-D, 2 |
| **E. Transfer Assembly** | |
| **All Wheel and Four Wheel Drive Vehicles** | |
| Leaks fluid from seals or vent after being driven | 2-E, 1 |
| Makes excessive noise while driving | 2-E, 2 |
| Jumps out of gear | 2-E, 3 |
| **F. Driveshaft** | |
| **Rear Wheel, All Wheel and Four Wheel Drive Vehicles** | |
| Clunking noise from center of vehicle shifting from forward to reverse | 2-F, 1 |
| Excessive vibration from center of vehicle when accelerating | 2-F, 2 |
| **G. Axles** | |
| **All Wheel and Four Wheel Drive Vehicles** | |
| Front or rear wheel makes a clicking noise | 2-G, 1 |
| Front or Rear wheel vibrates with increased speed | 2-G, 2 |
| **Front Wheel Drive Vehicles** | |
| Front wheel makes a clicking noise | 2-G, 3 |
| Rear wheel makes a clicking noise | 2-G, 4 |

| Condition | Section/Item Number |
|---|---|
| **SECTION 2. DRIVE TRAIN (continued)** | |
| **Rear Wheel Drive Vehicles** | |
| Front or rear wheel makes a clicking noise | 2-G, 5 |
| Rear wheel shudders or vibrates | 2-G, 6 |
| **H. Other Drive Train Conditions** | |
| Burning odor from center of vehicle when accelerating | 2-H, 1; 2-C, 1; 3-A, 9 |
| Engine accelerates, but vehicle does not gain speed | 2-H, 2; 2-C, 1; 3-A, 9 |
| **SECTION 3. BRAKE SYSTEM** | |
| Brakes pedal pulsates or shimmies when pressed | 3-A, 1 |
| Brakes make a squealing noise | 3-A, 2 |
| Brakes make a grinding noise | 3-A, 3 |
| Vehicle pulls to one side during braking | 3-A, 4 |
| Brake pedal feels spongy or has excessive brake pedal travel | 3-A, 5 |
| Brake pedal feel is firm, but brakes lack sufficient stopping power or fade | 3-A, 6 |
| Vehicle has excessive front end dive or locks rear brakes too easily | 3-A, 7 |
| Brake pedal goes to floor when pressed and will not pump up | 3-A, 8 |
| Brakes make a burning odor | 3-A, 9 |
| **SECTION 4. WHEELS, TIRES, STEERING AND SUSPENSION** | |
| **A. Wheels and Wheel Bearings** | |
| **All Wheel and Four Wheel Drive Vehicles** | |
| Front wheel or wheel bearing loose | 4-A, 1 |
| Rear wheel or wheel bearing loose | 4-A, 2 |
| **Front Wheel Drive Vehicles** | |
| Front wheel or wheel bearing loose | 4-A, 1 |
| Rear wheel or wheel bearing loose | 4-A, 2 |
| **Rear Wheel Drive Vehicles** | |
| Front wheel or wheel bearing loose | 4-A, 1 |
| Rear wheel or wheel bearing loose | 4-A, 2 |
| **B. Tires** | |
| Tires worn on inside tread | 4-B, 1 |
| Tires worn on outside tread | 4-B, 2 |
| Tires worn unevenly | 4-B, 3 |
| **C. Steering** | |
| Excessive play in steering wheel | 4-C, 1 |
| Steering wheel shakes at cruising speeds | 4-C, 2 |
| Steering wheel shakes when braking | 3-A, 1 |
| Steering wheel becomes stiff when turned | 4-C, 4 |
| **D. Suspension** | |
| Vehicle pulls to one side | 4-D, 1 |
| Vehicle is very bouncy over bumps | 4-D, 2 |
| Vehicle seems to lean excessively in turns | 4-D, 3 |
| Vehicle ride quality seems excessively harsh | 4-D, 4 |
| Vehicle seems low or leans to one side | 4-D, 5 |

| Condition | Section/Item Number |
|---|---|

## SECTION 4. WHEELS, TIRES, STEERING AND SUSPENSION (continued)

### E. Driving Noises and Vibrations

**Noises**

| | |
|---|---|
| Vehicle makes a clicking noise when driven | 4-E, 1 |
| Vehicle makes a clunking or knocking noise over bumps | 4-E, 2 |
| Vehicle makes a low pitched rumbling noise when driven | 4-E, 3 |
| Vehicle makes a squeaking noise over bumps | 4-E, 4 |

**Vibrations**

| | |
|---|---|
| Vehicle vibrates when driven | 4-E, 5 |

## SECTION 5. ELECTRICAL ACCESSORIES

### A. Headlights

| | |
|---|---|
| One headlight only works on high or low beam | 5-A, 1 |
| Headlight does not work on high or low beam | 5-A, 2 |
| Headlight(s) very dim | 5-A, 3 |

### B. Tail, Running and Side Marker Lights

| | |
|---|---|
| Tail light, running light or side marker light inoperative | 5-B, 1 |
| Tail light, running light or side marker light works intermittently | 5-B, 2 |
| Tail light, running light or side marker light very dim | 5-B, 3 |

### C. Interior Lights

| | |
|---|---|
| Interior light inoperative | 5-C, 1 |
| Interior light works intermittently | 5-C, 2 |
| Interior light very dim | 5-C, 3 |

### D. Brake Lights

| | |
|---|---|
| One brake light inoperative | 5-D, 1 |
| Both brake lights inoperative | 5-D, 2 |
| One or both brake lights very dim | 5-D, 3 |

### E. Warning Lights

**Ignition, Battery and Alternator Warning Lights, Check Engine Light, Anti-Lock Braking System (ABS) Light, Brake Warning Light, Oil Pressure Warning Light, and Parking Brake Warning Light**

| | |
|---|---|
| Warning light(s) remains on after the engine is started | 5-E, 1 |
| Warning light(s) flickers on and off when driving | 5-E, 2 |
| Warning light(s) inoperative with ignition on, and engine not started | 5-E, 3 |

### F. Turn Signal and 4-Way Hazard Lights

| | |
|---|---|
| Turn signals or hazard lights come on, but do not flash | 5-F, 1 |
| Turn signals or hazard lights do not function on either side | 5-F, 2 |
| Turn signals or hazard lights only work on one side | 5-F, 3 |
| One signal light does not work | 5-F, 4 |
| Turn signals flash too slowly | 5-F, 5 |
| Turn signals flash too fast | 5-F, 6 |
| Four-way hazard flasher indicator light inoperative | 5-F, 7 |
| Turn signal indicator light(s) do not work in either direction | 5-F, 8 |
| One turn signal indicator light does not work | 5-F, 9 |

| Condition | Section/Item Number |
|---|---|

## SECTION 5. ELECTRICAL ACCESSORIES (continued)

### G. Horn

| | |
|---|---|
| Horn does not operate | 5-G, 1 |
| Horn has an unusual tone | 5-G, 2 |

### H. Windshield Wipers

| | |
|---|---|
| Windshield wipers do not operate | 5-H, 1 |
| Windshield wiper motor makes a humming noise, gets hot or blows fuses | 5-H, 2 |
| Windshield wiper motor operates but one or both wipers fail to move | 5-H, 3 |
| Windshield wipers will not park | 5-H, 4 |

## SECTION 6. INSTRUMENTS AND GAUGES

### A. Speedometer (Cable Operated)

| | |
|---|---|
| Speedometer does not work | 6-A, 1 |
| Speedometer needle fluctuates when driving at steady speeds | 6-A, 2 |
| Speedometer works intermittently | 6-A, 3 |

### B. Speedometer (Electronically Operated)

| | |
|---|---|
| Speedometer does not work | 6-B, 1 |
| Speedometer works intermittently | 6-B, 2 |

### C. Fuel, Temperature and Oil Pressure Gauges

| | |
|---|---|
| Gauge does not register | 6-C, 1 |
| Gauge operates erratically | 6-C, 2 |
| Gauge operates fully pegged | 6-C, 3 |

## SECTION 7. CLIMATE CONTROL

### A. Air Conditioner

| | |
|---|---|
| No air coming from air conditioner vents | 7-A, 1 |
| Air conditioner blows warm air | 7-A, 2 |
| Water collects on the interior floor when the air conditioner is used | 7-A, 3 |
| Air conditioner has a moldy odor when used | 7-A, 4 |

### B. Heater

| | |
|---|---|
| Blower motor does not operate | 7-B, 1 |
| Heater blows cool air | 7-B, 2 |
| Heater steams the windshield when used | 7-B, 3 |

# DIAGNOSTIC PROCEDURES

## 1. ENGINE

### 1-A. Engine Starting Problems

**Gasoline Engines**

***1. Engine turns over, but will not start***

a. Check fuel level in fuel tank, add fuel if empty.
b. Check battery condition and state of charge. If voltage and load test below specification, charge or replace battery.
c. Check battery terminal and cable condition and tightness. Clean terminals and replace damaged, worn or corroded cables.
d. Check fuel delivery system. If fuel is not reaching the fuel injectors, check for a loose electrical connector or defective fuse, relay or fuel pump and replace as necessary.
e. Engine may have excessive wear or mechanical damage such as low cylinder cranking pressure, a broken camshaft drive system, insufficient valve clearance or bent valves.
f. Check for fuel contamination such as water in the fuel. During winter months, the water may freeze and cause a fuel restriction. Adding a fuel additive may help, however the fuel system may require draining and purging with fresh fuel.
g. Check for ignition system failure. Check for loose or shorted wires or damaged ignition system components. Check the spark plugs for excessive wear or incorrect electrode gap. If the problem is worse in wet weather, check for shorts between the spark plugs and the ignition coils.
h. Check the engine management system for a failed sensor or control module.

***2. Engine does not turn over when attempting to start***

a. Check the battery state of charge and condition. If the dash lights are not visible or very dim when turning the ignition key on, the battery has either failed internally or discharged, the battery cables are loose, excessively corroded or damaged, or the alternator has failed or internally shorted, discharging the battery. Charge or replace the battery, clean or replace the battery cables, and check the alternator output.
b. Check the operation of the neutral safety switch. On automatic transmission vehicles, try starting the vehicle in both Park and Neutral. On manual transmission vehicles, depress the clutch pedal and attempt to start. On some vehicles, these switches can be adjusted. Make sure the switches or wire connectors are not loose or damaged. Replace or adjust the switches as necessary.
c. Check the starter motor, starter solenoid or relay, and starter motor cables and wires. Check the ground from the engine to the chassis. Make sure the wires are not loose, damaged, or corroded. If battery voltage is present at the starter relay, try using a remote starter to start the vehicle for test purposes only. Replace any damaged or corroded cables, in addition to replacing any failed components.
d. Check the engine for seizure. If the engine has not been started for a long period of time, internal parts such as the rings may have rusted to the cylinder walls. The engine may have suffered internal damage, or could be hydro-locked from ingesting water. Remove the spark plugs and carefully attempt to rotate the engine using a suitable breaker bar and socket on the crankshaft pulley. If the engine is resistant to moving, or moves slightly and then binds, do not force the engine any further before determining the problem.

***3. Engine stalls immediately when started***

a. Check the ignition switch condition and operation. The electrical contacts in the run position may be worn or damaged. Try restarting the engine with all electrical accessories in the off position. Sometimes turning the key on an off will help in emergency situations, however once the switch has shown signs of failure, it should be replaced as soon as possible.
b. Check for loose, corroded, damaged or shorted wires for the ignition system and repair or replace.
c. Check for manifold vacuum leaks or vacuum hose leakage and repair or replace parts as necessary.
d. Measure the fuel pump delivery volume and pressure. Low fuel pump pressure can also be noticed as a lack of power when accelerating. Make sure the fuel pump lines are not restricted. The fuel pump output is not adjustable and requires fuel pump replacement to repair.
e. Check the engine fuel and ignition management system. Inspect the sensor wiring and electrical connectors. A dirty, loose or damaged sensor or control module wire can simulate a failed component.
f. Check the exhaust system for internal restrictions.

***4. Starter motor spins, but does not engage***

a. Check the starter motor for a seized or binding pinion gear.
b. Remove the flywheel inspection plate and check for a damaged ring gear.

***5. Engine is difficult to start when cold***

a. Check the battery condition, battery state of charge and starter motor current draw. Replace the battery if marginal and the starter motor if the current draw is beyond specification.
b. Check the battery cable condition. Clean the battery terminals and replace corroded or damaged cables.
c. Check the fuel system for proper operation. A fuel pump with insufficient fuel pressure or clogged injectors should be replaced.
d. Check the engine's tune-up status. Note the tune-up specifications and check for items such as severely worn spark plugs; adjust or replace as needed. On vehicles with manually adjusted valve clearances, check for tight valves and adjust to specification.
e. Check for a failed coolant temperature sensor, and replace if out of specification.
f. Check the operation of the engine management systems for fuel and ignition; repair or replace failed components as necessary.

***6. Engine is difficult to start when hot***

a. Check the air filter and air intake system. Replace the air filter if it is dirty or contaminated. Check the fresh air intake system for restrictions or blockage.
b. Check for loose or deteriorated engine grounds and clean, tighten or replace as needed.
c. Check for needed maintenance. Inspect tune-up and service related items such as spark plugs and engine oil condition, and check the operation of the engine fuel and ignition management system.

**Diesel Engines**

***1. Engine turns over but won't start***

a. Check engine starting procedure and restart engine.
b. Check the glow plug operation and repair or replace as necessary.
c. Check for air in the fuel system or fuel filter and bleed the air as necessary.
d. Check the fuel delivery system and repair or replace as necessary.
e. Check fuel level and add fuel as needed.
f. Check fuel quality. If the fuel is contaminated, drain and flush the fuel tank.
g. Check engine compression. If compression is below specification, the engine may need to be renewed or replaced.
h. Check the injection pump timing and set to specification.
i. Check the injection pump condition and replace as necessary.
j. Check the fuel nozzle operation and condition or replace as necess-ary.

***2. Engine does not turn over when attempting to start***

a. Check the battery state of charge and condition. If the dash lights are not visible or very dim when turning the ignition key on, the battery has either failed internally or discharged, the battery cables are loose, excessively corroded or damaged, or the alternator has failed or internally shorted, discharging the battery. Charge or replace the battery, clean or replace the battery cables, and check the alternator output.
b. Check the operation of the neutral safety switch. On automatic transmission vehicles, try starting the vehicle in both Park and Neutral. On manual transmission vehicles, depress the clutch pedal and attempt to start. On some vehicles, these switches can be adjusted. Make sure the switches or wire connectors are not loose or damaged. Replace or adjust the switches as necessary.
c. Check the starter motor, starter solenoid or relay, and starter motor cables and wires. Check the ground from the engine to the chassis. Make sure the wires are not loose, damaged, or corroded. If battery voltage is present at the starter relay, try using a remote starter to start the vehicle for test purposes only. Replace any damaged or corroded cables, in addition to replacing any failed components.
d. Check the engine for seizure. If the engine has not been started for a long period of time, internal parts such as the rings may have rusted to the cylinder walls. The engine may have suffered internal damage, or could be hydro-locked from ingesting water. Remove the injectors and carefully attempt to rotate the engine using a suitable breaker bar and socket on the crankshaft pulley. If the engine is resistant to moving, or moves slightly and then binds, do not force the engine any further before determining the cause of the problem.

***3. Engine stalls after starting***

a. Check for a restriction in the fuel return line or the return line check valve and repair as necessary.
b. Check the glow plug operation for turning the glow plugs off too soon and repair as necessary.
c. Check for incorrect injection pump timing and reset to specification.
d. Test the engine fuel pump and replace if the output is below specification.
e. Check for contaminated or incorrect fuel. Completely flush the fuel system and replace with fresh fuel.
f. Test the engine's compression for low compression. If below specification, mechanical repairs are necessary to repair.
g. Check for air in the fuel. Check fuel tank fuel and fill as needed.
h. Check for a failed injection pump. Replace the pump, making sure to properly set the pump timing.

***4. Starter motor spins, but does not engage***

a. Check the starter motor for a seized or binding pinion gear.
b. Remove the flywheel inspection plate and check for a damaged ring gear.

## 1-B. Engine Running Conditions

**Gasoline Engines**

***1. Engine runs poorly, hesitates***

a. Check the engine ignition system operation and adjust if possible, or replace defective parts.
b. Check for restricted fuel injectors and replace as necessary.
c. Check the fuel pump output and delivery. Inspect fuel lines for restrictions. If the fuel pump pressure is below specification, replace the fuel pump.
d. Check the operation of the engine management system and repair as necessary.

***2. Engine lacks power***

a. Check the engine's tune-up status. Note the tune-up specifications and check for items such as severely worn spark plugs; adjust or replace as needed. On vehicles with manually adjusted valve clearances, check for tight valves and adjust to specification.
b. Check the air filter and air intake system. Replace the air filter if it is dirty or contaminated. Check the fresh air intake system for restrictions or blockage.
c. Check the operation of the engine fuel and ignition management systems. Check the sensor operation and wiring. Check for low fuel pump pressure and repair or replace components as necessary.
d. Check the throttle linkage adjustments. Check to make sure the linkage is fully opening the throttle. Replace any worn or defective bushings or linkages.

e. Check for a restricted exhaust system. Check for bent or crimped exhaust pipes, or internally restricted mufflers or catalytic converters. Compare inlet and outlet temperatures for the converter or muffler. If the inlet is hot, but outlet cold, the component is restricted.
f. Check for a loose or defective knock sensor. A loose, improperly torqued or defective knock sensor will decrease spark advance and reduce power. Replace defective knock sensors and install using the recommended torque specification.
g. Check for engine mechanical conditions such as low compression, worn piston rings, worn valves, worn camshafts and related parts. An engine which has severe mechanical wear, or has suffered internal mechanical damage must be rebuilt or replaced to restore lost power.
h. Check the engine oil level for being overfilled. Adjust the engine's oil level, or change the engine oil and filter, and top off to the correct level.
i. Check for an intake manifold or vacuum hose leak. Replace leaking gaskets or worn vacuum hoses.
j. Check for dragging brakes and replace or repair as necessary.
k. Check tire air pressure and tire wear. Adjust the pressure to the recommended settings. Check the tire wear for possible alignment problems causing increased rolling resistance, decreased acceleration and increased fuel usage.
l. Check the octane rating of the fuel used during refilling, and use a higher octane rated fuel.

### *3. Poor fuel economy*

a. Inspect the air filter and check for any air restrictions going into the air filter housing. Replace the air filter if it is dirty or contaminated.
b. Check the engine for tune-up and related adjustments. Replace worn ignition parts, check the engine ignition timing and fuel mixture, and set to specifications if possible.
c. Check the tire size, tire wear, alignment and tire pressure. Large tires create more rolling resistance, smaller tires require more engine speed to maintain a vehicle's road speed. Excessive tire wear can be caused by incorrect tire pressure, incorrect wheel alignment or a suspension problem. All of these conditions create increased rolling resistance, causing the engine to work harder to accelerate and maintain a vehicle's speed.
d. Inspect the brakes for binding or excessive drag. A sticking brake caliper, overly adjusted brake shoe, broken brake shoe return spring, or binding parking brake cable or linkage can create a significant drag, brake wear and loss of fuel economy. Check the brake system operation and repair as necessary.

### *4. Engine runs on (diesels) when turned off*

a. Check for idle speed set too high and readjust to specification.
b. Check the operation of the idle control valve, and replace if defective.
c. Check the ignition timing and adjust to recommended settings. Check for defective sensors or related components and replace if defective.
d. Check for a vacuum leak at the intake manifold or vacuum hose and replace defective gaskets or hoses.
e. Check the engine for excessive carbon build-up in the combustion chamber. Use a recommended decarbonizing fuel additive or disassemble the cylinder head to remove the carbon.
f. Check the operation of the engine fuel management system and replace defective sensors or control units.
g. Check the engine operating temperature for overheating and repair as necessary.

### *5. Engine knocks and pings during heavy acceleration, and on steep hills*

a. Check the octane rating of the fuel used during refilling, and use a higher octane rated fuel.
b. Check the ignition timing and adjust to recommended settings. Check for defective sensors or related components and replace if defective.
c. Check the engine for excessive carbon build-up in the combustion chamber. Use a recommended decarbonizing fuel additive or disassemble the cylinder head to remove the carbon.
d. Check the spark plugs for the correct type, electrode gap and heat range. Replace worn or damaged spark plugs. For severe or continuous high speed use, install a spark plug that is one heat range colder.
e. Check the operation of the engine fuel management system and replace defective sensors or control units.
f. Check for a restricted exhaust system. Check for bent or crimped exhaust pipes, or internally restricted mufflers or catalytic converters. Compare inlet and outlet temperatures for the converter or muffler. If the inlet is hot, but outlet cold, the component is restricted.

### *6. Engine accelerates, but vehicle does not gain speed*

a. On manual transmission vehicles, check for causes of a slipping clutch. Refer to the clutch troubleshooting section for additional information.
b. On automatic transmission vehicles, check for a slipping transmission. Check the transmission fluid level and condition. If the fluid level is too high, adjust to the correct level. If the fluid level is low, top off using the recommended fluid type. If the fluid exhibits a burning odor, the transmission has been slipping internally. Changing the fluid and filter may help temporarily, however in this situation a transmission may require overhauling to ensure long-term reliability.

## Diesel Engines

### *1. Engine runs poorly*

a. Check the injection pump timing and adjust to specification.
b. Check for air in the fuel lines or leaks, and bleed the air from the fuel system.
c. Check the fuel filter, fuel feed and return lines for a restriction and repair as necessary.
d. Check the fuel for contamination, drain and flush the fuel tank and replenish with fresh fuel.

### *2. Engine lacks power*

a. Inspect the air intake system and air filter for restrictions and, if necessary, replace the air filter.
b. Verify the injection pump timing and reset if out of specification.

c. Check the exhaust for an internal restriction and replace failed parts.
d. Check for a restricted fuel filter and, if restricted, replace the filter.
e. Inspect the fuel filler cap vent . When removing the filler cap, listen for excessive hissing noises indicating a blockage in the fuel filler cap vents. If the filler cap vents are blocked, replace the cap.
f. Check the fuel system for restrictions and repair as necessary.
g. Check for low engine compression and inspect for external leakage at the glow plugs or nozzles. If no external leakage is noted, repair or replace the engine.

### *ENGINE PERFORMANCE TROUBLESHOOTING HINTS*

When troubleshooting an engine running or performance condition, the mechanical condition of the engine should be determined *before* lengthy troubleshooting procedures are performed.

The engine fuel management systems in fuel injected vehicles rely on electronic sensors to provide information to the engine control unit for precise fuel metering. Unlike carburetors, which use the incoming air speed to draw fuel through the fuel metering jets in order to provide a proper fuel-to-air ratio, a fuel injection system provides a specific amount of fuel which is introduced by the fuel injectors into the intake manifold or intake port, based on the information provided by electronic sensors.

The sensors monitor the engine's operating temperature, ambient temperature and the amount of air entering the engine, engine speed and throttle position to provide information to the engine control unit, which, in turn, operates the fuel injectors by electrical pulses. The sensors provide information to the engine control unit using low voltage electrical signals. As a result, an unplugged sensor or a poor electrical contact could cause a poor running condition similar to a failed sensor.

When troubleshooting a fuel related engine condition on fuel injected vehicles, carefully inspect the wiring and electrical connectors to the related components. Make sure the electrical connectors are fully connected, clean and not physically damaged. If necessary, clean the electrical contacts using electrical contact cleaner. The use of cleaning agents not specifically designed for electrical contacts should not be used, as they could leave a surface film or damage the insulation of the wiring.

The engine electrical system provides the necessary electrical power to operate the vehicle's electrical accessories, electronic control units and sensors. Because engine management systems are sensitive to voltage changes, an alternator which over or undercharges could cause engine running problems or component failure. Most alternators utilize internal voltage regulators which cannot be adjusted and must be replaced individually or as a unit with the alternator.

Ignition systems may be controlled by, or linked to, the engine fuel management system. Similar to the fuel injection system, these ignition systems rely on electronic sensors for information to determine the optimum ignition timing for a given engine speed and load. Some ignition systems no longer allow the ignition timing to be adjusted. Feedback from low voltage electrical sensors provide information to the control unit to determine the amount of ignition advance. On these systems, if a failure occurs the failed component must be replaced. Before replacing suspected failed electrical components, carefully inspect the wiring and electrical connectors to the related components. Make sure the electrical connectors are fully connected, clean and not physically damaged. If necessary, clean the electrical contacts using electrical contact cleaner. The use of cleaning agents not specifically designed for electrical contacts should be avoided, as they could leave a surface film or damage the insulation of the wiring.

## 1-C. Engine Noises, Odors and Vibrations

### *1. Engine makes a knocking or pinging noise when accelerating*

a. Check the octane rating of the fuel being used. Depending on the type of driving or driving conditions, it may be necessary to use a higher octane fuel.
b. Verify the ignition system settings and operation. Improperly adjusted ignition timing or a failed component, such as a knock sensor, may cause the ignition timing to advance excessively or prematurely. Check the ignition system operation and adjust, or replace components as needed.
c. Check the spark plug gap, heat range and condition. If the vehicle is operated in severe operating conditions or at continuous high speeds, use a colder heat range spark plug. Adjust the spark plug gap to the manufacturer's recommended specification and replace worn or damaged spark plugs.

### *2. Starter motor grinds when used*

a. Examine the starter pinion gear and the engine ring gear for damage, and replace damaged parts.
b. Check the starter mounting bolts and housing. If the housing is cracked or damaged replace the starter motor and check the mounting bolts for tightness.

### *3. Engine makes a screeching noise*

a. Check the accessory drive belts for looseness and adjust as necessary.
b. Check the accessory drive belt tensioners for seizing or excessive bearing noises and replace if loose, binding, or excessively noisy.
c. Check for a seizing water pump. The pump may not be leaking; however, the bearing may be faulty or the impeller loose and jammed. Replace the water pump.

### *4. Engine makes a growling noise*

a. Check for a loose or failing water pump. Replace the pump and engine coolant.
b. Check the accessory drive belt tensioners for excessive bearing noises and replace if loose or excessively noisy.

### *5. Engine makes a ticking or tapping noise*

a. On vehicles with hydraulic lash adjusters, check for low or dirty engine oil and top off or replace the engine oil and filter.
b. On vehicles with hydraulic lash adjusters, check for collapsed lifters and replace failed components.
c. On vehicles with hydraulic lash adjusters, check for low oil pressure caused by a restricted oil filter, worn engine oil pump, or oil pressure relief valve.

d. On vehicles with manually adjusted valves, check for excessive valve clearance or worn valve train parts. Adjust the valves to specification or replace worn and defective parts.
e. Check for a loose or improperly tensioned timing belt or timing chain and adjust or replace parts as necessary.
f. Check for a bent or sticking exhaust or intake valve. Remove the engine cylinder head to access and replace.

***6. Engine makes a heavy knocking noise***

a. Check for a loose crankshaft pulley or flywheel; replace and torque the mounting bolt(s) to specification.
b. Check for a bent connecting rod caused by a hydro-lock condition. Engine disassembly is necessary to inspect for damaged and needed replacement parts.
c. Check for excessive engine rod bearing wear or damage. This condition is also associated with low engine oil pressure and will require engine disassembly to inspect for damaged and needed replacement parts.

***7. Vehicle has a fuel odor when driven***

a. Check the fuel gauge level. If the fuel gauge registers full, it is possible that the odor is caused by being filled beyond capacity, or some spillage occurred during refueling. The odor should clear after driving an hour, or twenty miles, allowing the vapor canister to purge.
b. Check the fuel filler cap for looseness or seepage. Check the cap tightness and, if loose, properly secure. If seepage is noted, replace the filler cap.
c. Check for loose hose clamps, cracked or damaged fuel delivery and return lines, or leaking components or seals, and replace or repair as necessary.
d. Check the vehicle's fuel economy. If fuel consumption has increased due to a failed component, or if the fuel is not properly ignited due to an ignition related failure, the catalytic converter may become contaminated. This condition may also trigger the check engine warning light. Check the spark plugs for a dark, rich condition or verify the condition by testing the vehicle's emissions. Replace fuel fouled spark plugs, and test and replace failed components as necessary.

***8. Vehicle has a rotten egg odor when driven***

a. Check for a leaking intake gasket or vacuum leak causing a lean running condition. A lean mixture may result in increased exhaust temperatures, causing the catalytic converter to run hotter than normal. This condition may also trigger the check engine warning light. Check and repair the vacuum leaks as necessary.
b. Check the vehicle's alternator and battery condition. If the alternator is overcharging, the battery electrolyte can be boiled from the battery, and the battery casing may begin to crack, swell or bulge, damaging or shorting the battery internally. If this has occurred, neutralize the battery mounting area with a suitable baking soda and water mixture or equivalent, and replace the alternator or voltage regulator. Inspect, service, and load test the battery, and replace if necessary.

***9. Vehicle has a sweet odor when driven***

a. Check for an engine coolant leak caused by a seeping radiator cap, loose hose clamp, weeping cooling system seal, gasket or cooling system hose and replace or repair as needed.
b. Check for a coolant leak from the radiator, coolant reservoir, heater control valve or under the dashboard from the heater core, and replace the failed part as necessary.
c. Check the engine's exhaust for white smoke in addition to a sweet odor. The presence of white, steamy smoke with a sweet odor indicates coolant leaking into the combustion chamber. Possible causes include a failed head gasket, cracked engine block or cylinder head. Other symptoms of this condition include a white paste build-up on the inside of the oil filler cap, and softened, deformed or bulging radiator hoses.

***10. Engine vibrates when idling***

a. Check for loose, collapsed, or damaged engine or transmission mounts and repair or replace as necessary.
b. Check for loose or damaged engine covers or shields and secure or replace as necessary.

***11. Engine vibrates during acceleration***

a. Check for missing, loose or damaged exhaust system hangers and mounts; replace or repair as necessary.
b. Check the exhaust system routing and fit for adequate clearance or potential rubbing; repair or adjust as necessary.

## 1-D. Engine Electrical System

***1. Battery goes dead while driving***

a. Check the battery condition. Replace the battery if the battery will not hold a charge or fails a battery load test. If the battery loses fluid while driving, check for an overcharging condition. If the alternator is overcharging, replace the alternator or voltage regulator. (A voltage regulator is typically built into the alternator, necessitating alternator replacement or overhaul.)
b. Check the battery cable condition. Clean or replace corroded cables and clean the battery terminals.
c. Check the alternator and voltage regulator operation. If the charging system is over or undercharging, replace the alternator or voltage regulator, or both.
d. Inspect the wiring and wire connectors at the alternator for looseness, a missing ground or defective terminal, and repair as necessary.
e. Inspect the alternator drive belt tension, tensioners and condition. Properly tension the drive belt, replace weak or broken tensioners, and replace the drive belt if worn or cracked.

***2. Battery goes dead overnight***

a. Check the battery condition. Replace the battery if the battery will not hold a charge or fails a battery load test.
b. Check for a voltage draw, such as a trunk light, interior light or glove box light staying on. Check light switch position and operation, and replace if defective.
c. Check the alternator for an internally failed diode, and replace the alternator if defective.

## 1-E. Engine Cooling System

### 1. *Engine overheats*

a. Check the coolant level. Set the heater temperature to full hot and check for internal air pockets, bleed the cooling system and inspect for leakage. Top off the cooling system with the correct coolant mixture.
b. Pressure test the cooling system and radiator cap for leaks. Check for seepage caused by loose hose clamps, failed coolant hoses, and cooling system components such as the heater control valve, heater core, radiator, radiator cap, and water pump. Replace defective parts and fill the cooling system with the recommended coolant mixture.
c. On vehicles with electrically controlled cooling fans, check the cooling fan operation. Check for blown fuses or defective fan motors, temperature sensors and relays, and replace failed components.
d. Check for a coolant leak caused by a failed head gasket, or a porous water jacket casting in the cylinder head or engine block. Replace defective parts as necessary.
e. Check for an internally restricted radiator. Flush the radiator or replace if the blockage is too severe for flushing.
f. Check for a damaged water pump. If coolant circulation is poor, check for a loose water pump impeller. If the impeller is loose, replace the water pump.

### 2. *Engine loses coolant*

a. Pressure test the cooling system and radiator cap for leaks. Check for seepage caused by loose hose clamps, failed coolant hoses, and cooling system components such as the heater control valve, heater core, radiator, radiator cap, and water pump. Replace defective parts and fill the cooling system with the recommended coolant mixture.
b. Check for a coolant leak caused by a failed head gasket, or a porous water jacket casting in the cylinder head or engine block. Replace defective parts as necessary.

### 3. *Engine temperature remains cold when driving*

a. Check the thermostat operation. Replace the thermostat if it sticks in the open position.
b. On vehicles with electrically controlled cooling fans, check the cooling fan operation. Check for defective temperature sensors and stuck relays, and replace failed components.
c. Check temperature gauge operation if equipped to verify proper operation of the gauge. Check the sensors and wiring for defects, and repair or replace defective components.

### 4. *Engine runs hot*

a. Check for an internally restricted radiator. Flush the radiator or replace if the blockage is too severe for flushing.
b. Check for a loose or slipping water pump drive belt. Inspect the drive belt condition. Replace the belt if brittle, cracked or damaged. Check the pulley condition and properly tension the belt.
c. Check the cooling fan operation. Replace defective fan motors, sensors or relays as necessary.
d. Check temperature gauge operation if equipped to verify proper operation of the gauge. Check the sensors and wiring for defects, and repair or replace defective components.
e. Check the coolant level. Set the heater temperature to full hot, check for internal air pockets, bleed the cooling system and inspect for leakage. Top off the cooling system with the correct coolant mixture. Once the engine is cool, recheck the fluid level and top off as needed.

**NOTE: The engine cooling system can also be affected by an engine's mechanical condition. A failed head gasket or a porous casting in the engine block or cylinder head could cause a loss of coolant and result in engine overheating.**

Some cooling systems rely on electrically driven cooling fans to cool the radiator and use electrical temperature sensors and relays to operate the cooling fan. When diagnosing these systems, check for blown fuses, damaged wires and verify that the electrical connections are fully connected, clean and not physically damaged. If necessary, clean the electrical contacts using electrical contact cleaner. The use of cleaning agents not specifically designed for electrical contacts could leave a film or damage the insulation of the wiring.

## 1-F. Engine Exhaust System

### 1. *Exhaust rattles at idle speed*

a. Check the engine and transmission mounts and replace mounts showing signs of damage or wear.
b. Check the exhaust hangers, brackets and mounts. Replace broken, missing or damaged mounts.
c. Check for internal damage to mufflers and catalytic converters. The broken pieces from the defective component may travel in the direction of the exhaust flow and collect and/or create a blockage in a component other than the one which failed, causing engine running and stalling problems. Another symptom of a restricted exhaust is low engine manifold vacuum. Remove the exhaust system and carefully remove any loose or broken pieces, then replace any failed or damaged parts as necessary.
d. Check the exhaust system clearance, routing and alignment. If the exhaust is making contact with the vehicle in any manner, loosen and reposition the exhaust system.

### 2. *Exhaust system vibrates when driving*

a. Check the exhaust hangers, brackets and mounts. Replace broken, missing or damaged mounts.
b. Check the exhaust system clearance, routing and alignment. If the exhaust is making contact with the vehicle in any manner, check for bent or damaged components and replace, then loosen and reposition the exhaust system.
c. Check for internal damage to mufflers and catalytic converters. The broken pieces from the defective component may travel in the direction of the exhaust flow and collect and/or create a blockage in a component other than the one which failed, causing engine running and stalling problems. Another symptom of a restricted exhaust is low engine manifold vacuum. Remove the exhaust system and carefully remove any loose or broken pieces, then replace any failed or damaged parts as necessary.

***3. Exhaust system hangs too low***

a. Check the exhaust hangers, brackets and mounts. Replace broken, missing or damaged mounts.
b. Check the exhaust routing and alignment. Check and replace bent or damaged components. If the exhaust is not routed properly, loosen and reposition the exhaust system.

***4. Exhaust sounds loud***

a. Check the system for looseness and leaks. Check the exhaust pipes, clamps, flange bolts and manifold fasteners for tightness. Check and replace any failed gaskets.
b. Check and replace exhaust silencers that have a loss of efficiency due to internally broken baffles or worn packing material.
c. Check for missing mufflers and silencers that have been replaced with straight pipes or with non-original equipment silencers.

**NOTE: Exhaust system rattles, vibration and proper alignment should not be overlooked. Excessive vibration caused by collapsed engine mounts, damaged or missing exhaust hangers and misalignment may cause surface cracks and broken welds, creating exhaust leaks or internal damage to exhaust components such as the catalytic converter, creating a restriction to exhaust flow and loss of power.**

## 2. DRIVE TRAIN

### 2-A. Automatic Transmission

***1. Transmission shifts erratically***

a. Check and if not within the recommended range, add or remove transmission fluid to obtain the correct fluid level. Always use the recommended fluid type when adding transmission fluid.
b. Check the fluid level condition. If the fluid has become contaminated, fatigued from excessive heat or exhibits a burning odor, change the transmission fluid and filter using the recommended type and amount of fluid. A fluid which exhibits a burning odor indicates that the transmission has been slipping internally and may require future repairs.
c. Check for an improperly installed transmission filter, or missing filter gasket, and repair as necessary.
d. Check for loose or leaking gaskets, pressure lines and fittings, and repair or replace as necessary.
e. Check for loose or disconnected shift and throttle linkages or vacuum hoses, and repair as necessary.

***2. Transmission will not engage***

a. Check the shift linkage for looseness, wear and proper adjustment, and repair as necessary.
b. Check for a loss of transmission fluid and top off as needed with the recommended fluid.
c. If the transmission does not engage with the shift linkage correctly installed and the proper fluid level, internal damage has likely occurred, requiring transmission removal and disassembly.

***3. Transmission will not downshift during heavy acceleration***

a. On computer controlled transmissions, check for failed sensors or control units and repair or replace defective components.
b. On vehicles with kickdown linkages or vacuum servos, check for proper linkage adjustment or leaking vacuum hoses or servo units.

**NOTE: Many automatic transmissions use an electronic control module, electrical sensors and solenoids to control transmission shifting. When troubleshooting a vehicle with this type of system, be sure the electrical connectors are fully connected, clean and not physically damaged. If necessary, clean the electrical contacts using electrical contact cleaner. The use of cleaning agents not specifically designed for electrical contacts could leave a film or damage the insulation of the wiring.**

### 2-B. Manual Transmission

***1. Transmission grinds going into forward gears while driving***

a. Check the clutch release system. On clutches with a mechanical or cable linkage, check the adjustment. Adjust the clutch pedal to have 1 inch (25mm) of free-play at the pedal.
b. If the clutch release system is hydraulically operated, check the fluid level and, if low, top off using the recommended type and amount of fluid.
c. Synchronizers worn. Remove transmission and replace synchronizers.
d. Synchronizer sliding sleeve worn. Remove transmission and replace sliding sleeve.
e. Gear engagement dogs worn or damaged. Remove transmission and replace gear.

***2. Transmission jumps out of gear***

a. Shift shaft detent springs worn. Replace shift detent springs.
b. Synchronizer sliding sleeve worn. Remove transmission and replace sliding sleeve.
c. Gear engagement dogs worn or damaged. Remove transmission and replace gear.
d. Crankshaft thrust bearings worn. Remove engine and crankshaft, and repair as necessary.

***3. Transmission difficult to shift***

a. Verify the clutch adjustment and, if not properly adjusted, adjust to specification.
b. Synchronizers worn. Remove transmission and replace synchronizers.
c. Pilot bearing seized. Remove transmission and replace pilot bearing.
d. Shift linkage or bushing seized. Disassemble the shift linkage, replace worn or damaged bushings, lubricate and reinstall.

***4. Transmission leaks fluid***

a. Check the fluid level for an overfilled condition. Adjust the fluid level to specification.

b. Check for a restricted transmission vent or breather tube. Clear the blockage as necessary and check the fluid level. If necessary, top off with the recommended lubricant.

c. Check for a porous casting, leaking seal or gasket. Replace defective parts and top off the fluid level with the recommended lubricant.

## 2-C. Clutch

***1. Clutch slips on hills or during sudden acceleration***

a. Check for insufficient clutch pedal free-play. Adjust clutch linkage or cable to allow about 1 inch (25mm) of pedal free-play.

b. Clutch disc worn or severely damaged. Remove engine or transmission and replace clutch disc.

c. Clutch pressure plate is weak. Remove engine or transmission and replace the clutch pressure plate and clutch disc.

d. Clutch pressure plate and/or flywheel incorrectly machined. If the clutch system has been recently replaced and rebuilt, or refurbished parts have been used, it is possible that the machined surfaces decreased the clutch clamping force. Replace defective parts with new replacement parts.

***2. Clutch will not disengage, difficult to shift***

a. Check the clutch release mechanism. Check for stretched cables, worn linkages or failed clutch hydraulics and replace defective parts. On hydraulically operated clutch release mechanisms, check for air in the hydraulic system and bleed as necessary.

b. Check for a broken, cracked or fatigued clutch release arm or release arm pivot. Replace defective parts and properly lubricate upon assembly.

c. Check for a damaged clutch hub damper or damper spring. The broken parts tend to become lodged between the clutch disc and the pressure plate. Disassemble clutch system and replace failed parts.

d. Check for a seized clutch pilot bearing. Disassemble the clutch assembly and replace the defective parts.

e. Check for a defective clutch disc. Check for warpage or lining thicknesses larger than original equipment.

***3. Clutch is noisy when the clutch pedal is pressed***

a. Check the clutch pedal stop and pedal free-play adjustment for excessive movement and adjust as necessary.

b. Check for a worn or damaged release bearing. If the noise ceases when the pedal is released, the release bearing should be replaced.

c. Check the engine crankshaft axial play. If the crankshaft thrust bearings are worn or damaged, the crankshaft will move when pressing the clutch pedal. The engine must be disassembled to replace the crankshaft thrust bearings.

***4. Clutch pedal extremely difficult to press***

a. Check the clutch pedal pivots and linkages for binding. Clean and lubricate linkages.

b. On cable actuated clutch systems, check the cable routing and condition. Replace kinked, frayed, damaged or corroded cables and check cable routing to avoid sharp bends. Check the engine ground strap for poor conductivity. If the ground strap is marginal, the engine could try to ground itself via the clutch cable, causing premature failure.

c. On mechanical linkage clutches, check the linkage for binding or misalignment. Lubricate pivots or linkages and repair as necessary.

d. Check the release bearing guide tube and release fork for a lack of lubrication. Install a smooth coating of high temperature grease to allow smooth movement of the release bearing over the guide tube.

***5. Clutch pedal remains down when pressed***

a. On mechanical linkage or cable actuated clutches, check for a loose or disconnected link.

b. On hydraulically actuated clutches, check the fluid level and check for a hydraulic leak at the clutch slave or master cylinder, or hydraulic line. Replace failed parts and bleed clutch hydraulic system. If no leakage is noted, the clutch master cylinder may have failed internally. Replace the clutch master cylinder and bleed the clutch hydraulic system.

***6. Clutch chatters when engaging***

a. Check the engine flywheel for warpage or surface variations and replace or repair as necessary.

b. Check for a warped clutch disc or damaged clutch damper hub. Remove the clutch disc and replace.

c. Check for a loose or damaged clutch pressure plate and replace defective components.

**NOTE: The clutch is actuated either by a mechanical linkage, cable or a clutch hydraulic system. The mechanical linkage and cable systems may require the clutch pedal free-play to be adjusted as the clutch disc wears. A hydraulic clutch system automatically adjusts as the clutch wears and, with the exception of the clutch pedal height, no adjustment is possible.**

## 2-D. Differential and Final Drive

***1. Differential makes a low pitched rumbling noise***

a. Check fluid level type and amount. Replace the fluid with the recommended type and amount of lubricant.

b. Check the differential bearings for wear or damage. Remove the bearings, inspect the drive and driven gears for wear or damage, and replace components as necessary.

***2. Differential makes a howling noise***

a. Check fluid level type and amount. Replace the fluid with the recommended type and amount of lubricant.

b. Check the differential drive and driven gears for wear or damage, and replace components as necessary.

## 2-E. Transfer Assembly

### All Wheel and Four Wheel Drive Vehicles

***1. Leaks fluid from seals or vent after being driven***

a. Fluid level overfilled. Check and adjust transfer case fluid level.
b. Check for a restricted breather or breather tube, clear and check the fluid level and top off as needed.
c. Check seal condition and replace worn, damaged, or defective seals. Check the fluid level and top off as necessary.

***2. Makes excessive noise while driving***

a. Check the fluid for the correct type of lubricant. Drain and refill using the recommended type and amount of lubricant.
b. Check the fluid level. Top off the fluid using the recommended type and amount of lubricant.
c. If the fluid level and type of lubricant meet specifications, check for internal wear or damage. Remove assembly and disassemble to inspect for worn, damaged, or defective components.

***3. Jumps out of gear***

a. Stop vehicle and make sure the unit is fully engaged.
b. Check for worn, loose or an improperly adjusted linkage. Replace and/or adjust linkage as necessary.
c. Check for internal wear or damage. Remove assembly and disassemble to inspect for worn, damaged, or defective components.

## 2-F. Driveshaft

### Rear Wheel, All Wheel and Four Wheel Drive Vehicles

***1. Clunking noise from center of vehicle shifting from forward to reverse***

a. Worn universal joint. Remove driveshaft and replace universal joint.

***2. Excessive vibration from center of vehicle when accelerating***

a. Worn universal joint. Remove driveshaft and replace universal joint.
b. Driveshaft misaligned. Check for collapsed or damaged engine and transmission mounts, and replace as necessary.
c. Driveshaft bent or out of balance. Replace damaged components and reinstall.
d. Driveshaft out of balance. Remove the driveshaft and have it balanced by a competent professional, or replace the driveshaft assembly.

**NOTE: Most driveshafts are linked together by universal joints; however, some manufacturers use Constant Velocity (CV) joints or rubber flex couplers.**

## 2-G. Axles

### All Wheel and Four Wheel Drive Vehicles

***1. Front or rear wheel makes a clicking noise***

a. Check for debris such as a pebble, nail or glass in the tire or tire tread. Carefully remove the debris. Small rocks and pebbles rarely cause a puncture; however, a sharp object should be removed carefully at a facility capable of performing tire repairs.
b. Check for a loose, damaged or worn Constant Velocity (CV) joint and replace if defective.

***2. Front or rear wheel vibrates with increased speed***

a. Check for a bent rim and replace, if damaged.
b. Check the tires for balance or internal damage and replace if defective.
c. Check for a loose, worn or damaged wheel bearing and replace if defective.
d. Check for a loose, damaged or worn Constant Velocity (CV) joint and replace if defective.

### Front Wheel Drive Vehicles

***3. Front wheel makes a clicking noise***

a. Check for debris such as a pebble, nail or glass in the tire or tire tread. Carefully remove the debris. Small rocks and pebbles rarely cause a puncture; however, a sharp object should be removed carefully at a facility capable of performing tire repairs.
b. Check for a loose, damaged or worn Constant Velocity (CV) joint and replace if defective.

***4. Rear wheel makes a clicking noise***

a. Check for debris such as a pebble, nail or glass in the tire or tire tread. Carefully remove the debris. Small rocks and pebbles rarely cause a puncture; however, a sharp object should be removed carefully at a facility capable of performing tire repairs.

### Rear Wheel Drive Vehicles

***5. Front or rear wheel makes a clicking noise***

a. Check for debris such as a pebble, nail or glass in the tire or tire tread. Carefully remove the debris. Small rocks and pebbles rarely cause a puncture; however, a sharp object should be removed carefully at a facility capable of performing tire repairs.

***6. Rear wheel shudders or vibrates***

a. Check for a bent rear wheel or axle assembly and replace defective components.
b. Check for a loose, damaged or worn rear wheel bearing and replace as necessary.

## 2-H. Other Drive Train Conditions

***1. Burning odor from center of vehicle when accelerating***

a. Check for a seizing brake hydraulic component such as a brake caliper. Check the caliper piston for surface damage such as rust, and measure for out-of-round wear and caliper-to-piston clearance. For additional information on brake related odors, refer to section 3-A, condition number 9.
b. On vehicles with a manual transmission, check for a slipping clutch. For possible causes and additional information, refer to section 2-C, condition number 1.

c. On vehicles with an automatic transmission, check the fluid level and condition. Top off or change the fluid and filter using the recommended replacement parts, lubricant type and amount. If the odor persists, transmission removal and disassembly will be necessary.

### *2. Engine accelerates, but vehicle does not gain speed*

a. On vehicles with a manual transmission, check for a slipping or damaged clutch. For possible causes and additional information refer to section 2-C, condition number 1.
b. On vehicles with an automatic transmission, check the fluid level and condition. Top off or change the fluid and filter using the recommended replacement parts, lubricant type and amount. If the slipping continues, transmission removal and disassembly will be necessary.

## 3. BRAKE SYSTEM

## 3-A. Brake System Troubleshooting

### *1. Brake pedal pulsates or shimmies when pressed*

a. Check wheel lug nut torque and tighten evenly to specification.
b. Check the brake rotor for trueness and thickness variations. Replace the rotor if it is too thin, warped, or if the thickness varies beyond specification. Some rotors can be machined; consult the manufacturer's specifications and recommendations before using a machined brake rotor.
c. Check the brake caliper or caliper bracket mounting bolt torque and inspect for looseness. Torque the mounting bolts and inspect for wear or any looseness, including worn mounting brackets, bushings and sliding pins.
d. Check the wheel bearing for looseness. If the bearing is loose, adjust if possible, otherwise replace the bearing.

### *2. Brakes make a squealing noise*

a. Check the brake rotor for the presence of a ridge on the outer edge; if present, remove the ridge or replace the brake rotor and brake pads.
b. Check for debris in the brake lining material, clean and reinstall.
c. Check the brake linings for wear and replace the brake linings if wear is approaching the lining wear limit.
d. Check the brake linings for glazing. Inspect the brake drum or rotor surface and replace, along with the brake linings, if the surface is not smooth or even.
e. Check the brake pad or shoe mounting areas for a lack of lubricant or the presence of surface rust. Clean and lubricate with a recommended high temperature brake grease.

### *3. Brakes make a grinding noise*

a. Check the brake linings and brake surface areas for severe wear or damage. Replace worn or damaged parts.
b. Check for a seized or partially seized brake causing premature or uneven brake wear, excessive heat and brake rotor or drum damage. Replace defective parts and inspect the wheel bearing condition, which could have been damaged due to excessive heat.

### *4. Vehicle pulls to one side during braking*

a. Check for air in the brake hydraulic system. Inspect the brake hydraulic seals, fluid lines and related components for fluid leaks. Remove the air from the brake system by bleeding the brakes. Be sure to use fresh brake fluid that meets the manufacturer's recommended standards.
b. Check for an internally restricted flexible brake hydraulic hose. Replace the hose and flush the brake system.
c. Check for a seizing brake hydraulic component such as a brake caliper. Check the caliper piston for surface damage such as rust, and measure for out-of-round wear and caliper-to-piston clearance. Overhaul or replace failed parts and flush the brake system.
d. Check the vehicle's alignment and inspect for suspension wear. Replace worn bushings, ball joints and set alignment to the manufacturer's specifications.
e. If the brake system uses drum brakes front or rear, check the brake adjustment. Inspect for seized adjusters and clean or replace, then properly adjust.

### *5. Brake pedal feels spongy or has excessive travel*

a. Check the brake fluid level and condition. If the fluid is contaminated or has not been flushed every two years, clean the master cylinder reservoir, and bleed and flush the brakes using fresh brake fluid that meets the manufacturer's recommended standards.
b. Check for a weak or damaged flexible brake hydraulic hose. Replace the hose and flush the brake system.
c. If the brake system uses drum brakes front or rear, check the brake adjustment. Inspect for seized adjusters and clean or replace, then properly adjust.

### *6. Brake pedal feel is firm, but brakes lack sufficient stopping power or fade*

a. Check the operation of the brake booster and brake booster check valve. Replace worn or failed parts.
b. Check brake linings and brake surface areas for glazing and replace worn or damaged parts.
c. Check for seized hydraulic parts and linkages, and clean or replace as needed.

### *7. Vehicle has excessive front end dive or locks rear brakes too easily*

a. Check for worn, failed or seized brake proportioning valve and replace the valve.
b. Check for a seized, disconnected or missing spring or linkage for the brake proportioning valve. Replace missing parts or repair as necessary.

### *8. Brake pedal goes to floor when pressed and will not pump up*

a. Check the brake hydraulic fluid level and inspect the fluid lines and seals for leakage. Repair or replace leaking components, then bleed and flush the brake system using fresh brake fluid that meets the manufacturer's recommended standards.

b. Check the brake fluid level. Inspect the brake fluid level and brake hydraulic seals. If the fluid level is ok, and the brake hydraulic system is free of hydraulic leaks, replace the brake master cylinder, then bleed and flush the brake system using fresh brake fluid that meets the manufacturer's recommended standards.

***9. Brakes produce a burning odor***

a. Check for a seizing brake hydraulic component such as a brake caliper. Check the caliper piston for surface damage such as rust, and measure for out-of-round wear and caliper-to-piston clearance. Overhaul or replace failed parts and flush the brake system.
b. Check for an internally restricted flexible brake hydraulic hose. Replace the hose and flush the brake system.
c. Check the parking brake release mechanism, seized linkage or cable, and repair as necessary.

### *BRAKE PERFORMANCE TROUBLESHOOTING HINTS*

Brake vibrations or pulsation can often be diagnosed on a safe and careful test drive. A brake vibration which is felt through the brake pedal while braking, but not felt in the steering wheel, is most likely caused by brake surface variations in the rear brakes. If both the brake pedal and steering wheel vibrate during braking, a surface variation in the front brakes, or both front and rear brakes, is very likely.

A brake pedal that pumps up with repeated use can be caused by air in the brake hydraulic system or, if the vehicle is equipped with rear drum brakes, the brake adjusters may be seized or out of adjustment. A quick test for brake adjustment on vehicles with rear drum brakes is to pump the brake pedal several times with the vehicle's engine not running and the parking brake released. Pump the brake pedal several times and continue to apply pressure to the brake pedal. With pressure being applied to the brake pedal, engage the parking brake. Release the brake pedal and quickly press the brake pedal again. If the brake pedal pumped up, the rear brakes are in need of adjustment. Do not compensate for the rear brake adjustment by adjusting the parking brake, this will cause premature brake lining wear.

To test a vacuum brake booster, pump the brake pedal several times with the vehicle's engine off. Apply pressure to the brake pedal and then start the engine. The brake pedal should move downward about one inch (25mm).

## 4. WHEELS, TIRES, STEERING AND SUSPENSION

### 4-A. Wheels and Wheel Bearings

***1. Front wheel or wheel bearing loose***

**All Wheel and Four Wheel Drive Vehicles**

a. Torque lug nuts and axle nuts to specification and recheck for looseness.
b. Wheel bearing worn or damaged. Replace wheel bearing.

**Front Wheel Drive Vehicles**

a. Torque lug nuts and axle nuts to specification and recheck for looseness.
b. Wheel bearing worn or damaged. Replace wheel bearing.
c. Wheel bearing out of adjustment. Adjust wheel bearing to specification; if still loose, replace.

**Rear Wheel Drive Vehicles**

a. Wheel bearing out of adjustment. Adjust wheel bearing to specification; if still loose, replace.
b. Torque lug nuts to specification and recheck for looseness.
c. Wheel bearing worn or damaged. Replace wheel bearing.

***2. Rear wheel or wheel bearing loose***

**All Wheel and Four Wheel Drive Vehicles**

a. Torque lug nuts and axle nuts to specification and recheck for looseness.
b. Wheel bearing worn or damaged. Replace wheel bearing.

**Front Wheel Drive Vehicles**

a. Wheel bearing out of adjustment. Adjust wheel bearing to specification; if still loose, replace.
b. Torque lug nuts to specification and recheck for looseness.
c. Wheel bearing worn or damaged. Replace wheel bearing.

**Rear Wheel Drive Vehicles**

a. Torque lug nuts to specification and recheck for looseness.
b. Wheel bearing worn or damaged. Replace wheel bearing.

### 4-B. Tires

***1. Tires worn on inside tread***

a. Check alignment for a toed-out condition. Check and set tire pressures and properly adjust the toe.
b. Check for worn, damaged or defective suspension components. Replace defective parts and adjust the alignment.

***2. Tires worn on outside tread***

a. Check alignment for a toed-in condition. Check and set tire pressures and properly adjust the toe.
b. Check for worn, damaged or defective suspension components. Replace defective parts and adjust the alignment.

***3. Tires worn unevenly***

a. Check the tire pressure and tire balance. Replace worn or defective tires and check the alignment; adjust if necessary.
b. Check for worn shock absorbers. Replaced failed components, worn or defective tires and check the alignment; adjust if necessary.
c. Check the alignment settings. Check and set tire pressures and properly adjust the alignment to specification.
d. Check for worn, damaged or defective suspension components. Replace defective parts and adjust the alignment to specification.

## 4-C. Steering

**1. Excessive play in steering wheel**

a. Check the steering gear free-play adjustment and properly adjust to remove excessive play.
b. Check the steering linkage for worn, damaged or defective parts. Replace failed components and perform a front end alignment.
c. Check for a worn, damaged, or defective steering box, replace the steering gear and check the front end alignment.

**2. Steering wheel shakes at cruising speeds**

a. Check for a bent front wheel. Replace a damaged wheel and check the tire for possible internal damage.
b. Check for an unevenly worn front tire. Replace the tire, adjust tire pressure and balance.
c. Check the front tires for hidden internal damage. Tires which have encountered large pot holes or suffered other hard blows may have sustained internal damage and should be replaced immediately.
d. Check the front tires for an out-of-balance condition. Remove, spin balance and reinstall. Torque all the wheel bolts or lug nuts to the recommended specification.
e. Check for a loose wheel bearing. If possible, adjust the bearing, or replace the bearing if it is a non-adjustable bearing.

**3. Steering wheel shakes when braking**

a. Refer to section 3-A, condition number 1.

**4. Steering wheel becomes stiff when turned**

a. Check the steering wheel free-play adjustment and reset as needed.
b. Check for a damaged steering gear assembly. Replace the steering gear and perform a front end alignment.
c. Check for damaged or seized suspension components. Replace defective components and perform a front end alignment.

## 4-D. Suspension

**1. Vehicle pulls to one side**

a. Tire pressure uneven. Adjust tire pressure to recommended settings.
b. Tires worn unevenly. Replace tires and check alignment settings.
c. Alignment out of specification. Align front end and check thrust angle.
d. Check for a dragging brake and repair or replace as necessary.

**2. Vehicle is very bouncy over bumps**

a. Check for worn or leaking shock absorbers or strut assemblies and replace as necessary.
b. Check for seized shock absorbers or strut assemblies and replace as necessary.

**NOTE: When one shock fails, it is recommended to replace front or rear units as pairs.**

**3. Vehicle leans excessively in turns**

a. Check for worn or leaking shock absorbers or strut assemblies and replace as necessary.
b. Check for missing, damaged, or worn stabilizer links or bushings, and replace or install as necessary.

**4. Vehicle ride quality seems excessively harsh**

a. Check for seized shock absorbers or strut assemblies and replace as necessary.
b. Check for excessively high tire pressures and adjust pressures to vehicle recommendations.

**5. Vehicle seems low or leans to one side**

a. Check for a damaged, broken or weak spring. Replace defective parts and check for a needed alignment.
b. Check for seized shock absorbers or strut assemblies and replace as necessary.
c. Check for worn or leaking shock absorbers or strut assemblies and replace as necessary.

## 4-E. Driving Noises and Vibrations

### Noises

**1. Vehicle makes a clicking noises when driven**

a. Check the noise to see if it varies with road speed. Verify if the noise is present when coasting or with steering or throttle input. If the clicking noise frequency changes with road speed and is not affected by steering or throttle input, check the tire treads for a stone, piece of glass, nail or another hard object imbedded into the tire or tire tread. Stones rarely cause a tire puncture and are easily removed. Other objects may create an air leak when removed. Consider having these objects removed immediately at a facility equipped to repair tire punctures.
b. If the clicking noise varies with throttle input and steering, check for a worn Constant Velocity (CV-joint) joint, universal (U- joint) or flex joint.

**2. Vehicle makes a clunking or knocking noise over bumps**

a. A clunking noise over bumps is most often caused by excessive movement or clearance in a suspension component. Check the suspension for soft, cracked, damaged or worn bushings. Replace the bushings and check the vehicle's alignment.
b. Check for loose suspension mounting bolts. Check the tightness on subframe bolts, pivot bolts and suspension mounting bolts, and torque to specification.
c. Check the vehicle for a loose wheel bearing. Some wheel bearings can be adjusted for looseness, while others must be replaced if loose. Adjust or replace the bearings as recommended by the manufacturer.
d. Check the door latch adjustment. If the door is slightly loose, or the latch adjustment is not centered, the door assembly may create noises over bumps and rough surfaces. Properly adjust the door latches to secure the door.

### 3. Vehicle makes a low pitched rumbling noise when driven

a. A low pitched rumbling noise is usually caused by a drive train related bearing and is most often associated with a wheel bearing which has been damaged or worn. The damage can be caused by excessive brake temperatures or physical contact with a pot hole or curb. Sometimes the noise will vary when turning. Left hand turns increase the load on the vehicle's right side, and right turns load the left side. A failed front wheel bearing may also cause a slight steering wheel vibration when turning. A bearing which exhibits noise must be replaced.

b. Check the tire condition and balance. An internally damaged tire may cause failure symptoms similar to failed suspension parts. For diagnostic purposes, try a known good set of tires and replace defective tires.

### 4. Vehicle makes a squeaking noise over bumps

a. Check the vehicle's ball joints for wear, damaged or leaking boots. Replace a ball joint if it is loose, the boot is damaged and leaking, or the ball joint is binding. When replacing suspension parts, check the vehicle for alignment.

b. Check for seized or deteriorated bushings. Replace bushings that are worn or damaged and check the vehicle for alignment.

c. Check for the presence of sway bar or stabilizer bar bushings which wrap around the bar. Inspect the condition of the bushings and replace if worn or damaged. Remove the bushing bracket and apply a thin layer of suspension grease to the area where the bushings wrap around the bar and reinstall the bushing brackets.

## Vibrations

### 5. Vehicle vibrates when driven

a. Check the road surface. Roads which have rough or uneven surfaces may cause unusual vibrations.

b. Check the tire condition and balance. An internally damaged tire may cause failure symptoms similar to failed suspension parts. For diagnostic purposes, try a known good set of tires and replace defective tires immediately.

c. Check for a worn Constant Velocity (CV-joint) joint, universal (U- joint) or flex joint and replace if loose, damaged or binding.

d. Check for a loose, bent, or out-of-balance axle or drive shaft. Replace damaged or failed components.

**NOTE: Diagnosing failures related to wheels, tires, steering and the suspension system can often times be accomplished with a careful and thorough test drive. Bearing noises are isolated by noting whether the noises or symptoms vary when turning left or right, or occur while driving a straight line. During a left hand turn, the vehicle's weight shifts to the right, placing more force on the right side bearings, such that if a right side wheel bearing is worn or damaged, the noise or vibration should increase during light-to-heavy acceleration. Conversely, on right hand turns, the vehicle tends to lean to the left, loading the left side bearings.**

Knocking noises in the suspension when the vehicle is driven over rough roads, railroad tracks and speed bumps indicate worn suspension components such as bushings, ball joints or tie rod ends, or a worn steering system.

# 5. ELECTRICAL ACCESSORIES

## 5-A. Headlights

### 1. One headlight only works on high or low beam

a. Check for battery voltage at headlight electrical connector. If battery voltage is present, replace the headlight assembly or bulb if available separately. If battery voltage is not present, refer to the headlight wiring diagram to troubleshoot.

### 2. Headlight does not work on high or low beam

a. Check for battery voltage and ground at headlight electrical connector. If battery voltage is present, check the headlight connector ground terminal for a proper ground. If battery voltage and ground are present at the headlight connector, replace the headlight assembly or bulb if available separately. If battery voltage or ground is not present, refer to the headlight wiring diagram to troubleshoot.

b. Check the headlight switch operation. Replace the switch if the switch is defective or operates intermittently.

### 3. Headlight(s) very dim

a. Check for battery voltage and ground at headlight electrical connector. If battery voltage is present, trace the ground circuit for the headlamp electrical connector, then clean and repair as necessary.

If the voltage at the headlight electrical connector is significantly less than the voltage at the battery, refer to the headlight wiring diagram to troubleshoot and locate the voltage drop.

## 5-B. Tail, Running and Side Marker Lights

### 1. Tail light, running light or side marker light inoperative

a. Check for battery voltage and ground at light's electrical connector. If battery voltage is present, check the bulb socket and electrical connector ground terminal for a proper ground. If battery voltage and ground are present at the light connector, but not in the socket, clean the socket and the ground terminal connector. If battery voltage and ground are present in the bulb socket, replace the bulb. If battery voltage or ground is not present, refer to the wiring diagram to troubleshoot for an open circuit.

b. Check the light switch operation and replace if necessary.

### 2. Tail light, running light or side marker light works intermittently

a. Check the bulb for a damaged filament, and replace if damaged.

b Check the bulb and bulb socket for corrosion, and clean or replace the bulb and socket.

c. Check for loose, damaged or corroded wires and electrical terminals, and repair as necessary.
d. Check the light switch operation and replace if necessary.

***3. Tail light, running light or side marker light very dim***

a. Check the bulb and bulb socket for corrosion and clean or replace the bulb and socket.
b. Check for low voltage at the bulb socket positive terminal or a poor ground. If voltage is low, or the ground marginal, trace the wiring to, and check for loose, damaged or corroded wires and electrical terminals; repair as necessary.
c. Check the light switch operation and replace if necessary.

## 5-C. Interior Lights

***1. Interior light inoperative***

a. Verify the interior light switch location and position(s), and set the switch in the correct position.
b. Check for battery voltage and ground at the interior light bulb socket. If battery voltage and ground are present, replace the bulb. If voltage is not present, check the interior light fuse for battery voltage. If the fuse is missing, replace the fuse. If the fuse has blown, or if battery voltage is present, refer to the wiring diagram to troubleshoot the cause for an open or shorted circuit. If ground is not present, check the door switch contacts and clean or repair as necessary.

***2. Interior light works intermittently***

a. Check the bulb for a damaged filament, and replace if damaged.
b. Check the bulb and bulb socket for corrosion, and clean or replace the bulb and socket.
c. Check for loose, damaged or corroded wires and electrical terminals; repair as necessary.
d. Check the door and light switch operation, and replace if necessary.

***3. Interior light very dim***

a. Check the bulb and bulb socket for corrosion, and clean or replace the bulb and socket.
b. Check for low voltage at the bulb socket positive terminal or a poor ground. If voltage is low, or the ground marginal, trace the wiring to, and check for loose, damaged or corroded wires and electrical terminals; repair as necessary.
c. Check the door and light switch operation, and replace if necessary.

## 5-D. Brake Lights

***1. One brake light inoperative***

a. Press the brake pedal and check for battery voltage and ground at the brake light bulb socket. If present, replace the bulb. If either battery voltage or ground is not present, refer to the wiring diagram to troubleshoot.

***2. Both brake lights inoperative***

a. Press the brake pedal and check for battery voltage and ground at the brake light bulb socket. If present, replace both bulbs. If battery voltage is not present, check the brake light switch adjustment and adjust as necessary. If the brake light switch is properly adjusted, and battery voltage or the ground is not present at the bulb sockets, or at the bulb electrical connector with the brake pedal pressed, refer to the wiring diagram to troubleshoot the cause of an open circuit.

***3. One or both brake lights very dim***

a. Press the brake pedal and measure the voltage at the brake light bulb socket. If the measured voltage is close to the battery voltage, check for a poor ground caused by a loose, damaged, or corroded wire, terminal, bulb or bulb socket. If the ground is bolted to a painted surface, it may be necessary to remove the electrical connector and clean the mounting surface, so the connector mounts on bare metal. If battery voltage is low, check for a poor connection caused by either a faulty brake light switch, a loose, damaged, or corroded wire, terminal or electrical connector. Refer to the wiring diagram to troubleshoot the cause of a voltage drop.

## 5-E. Warning Lights

***1. Warning light(s) stay on when the engine is started***

**Ignition, Battery or Alternator Warning Light**

a. Check the alternator output and voltage regulator operation, and replace as necessary.
b. Check the warning light wiring for a shorted wire.

**Check Engine Light**

a. Check the engine for routine maintenance and tune-up status. Note the engine tune-up specifications and verify the spark plug, air filter and engine oil condition; replace and/or adjust items as necessary.
b. Check the fuel tank for low fuel level, causing an intermittent lean fuel mixture. Top off fuel tank and reset check engine light.
c. Check for a failed or disconnected engine fuel or ignition component, sensor or control unit and repair or replace as necessary.
d. Check the intake manifold and vacuum hoses for air leaks and repair as necessary.
e. Check the engine's mechanical condition for excessive oil consumption.

**Anti-Lock Braking System (ABS) Light**

a. Check the wheel sensors and sensor rings for debris, and clean as necessary.
b. Check the brake master cylinder for fluid leakage or seal failure and replace as necessary.
c. Check the ABS control unit, pump and proportioning valves for proper operation; replace as necessary.
d. Check the sensor wiring at the wheel sensors and the ABS control unit for a loose or shorted wire, and repair as necessary.

**Brake Warning Light**

a. Check the brake fluid level and check for possible leakage from the hydraulic lines and seals. Top off brake fluid and repair leakage as necessary.

b. Check the brake linings for wear and replace as necessary.
c. Check for a loose or shorted brake warning light sensor or wire, and replace or repair as necessary.

**Oil Pressure Warning Light**

a. Stop the engine immediately. Check the engine oil level and oil filter condition, and top off or change the oil as necessary.
b. Check the oil pressure sensor wire for being shorted to ground. Disconnect the wire from the oil pressure sensor and with the ignition in the ON position, but not running, the oil pressure light should not be working. If the light works with the wire disconnected, check the sensor wire for being shorted to ground. Check the wire routing to make sure the wire is not pinched and check for insulation damage. Repair or replace the wire as necessary and recheck before starting the engine.
c. Remove the oil pan and check for a clogged oil pick-up tube screen.
d. Check the oil pressure sensor operation by substituting a known good sensor.
e. Check the oil filter for internal restrictions or leaks, and replace as necessary.

**WARNING: If the engine is operated with oil pressure below the manufacturer's specification, severe (and costly) engine damage could occur. Low oil pressure can be caused by excessive internal wear or damage to the engine bearings, oil pressure relief valve, oil pump or oil pump drive mechanism.**

Before starting the engine, check for possible causes of rapid oil loss, such as leaking oil lines or a loose, damaged, restricted, or leaking oil filter or oil pressure sensor. If the engine oil level and condition are acceptable, measure the engine's oil pressure using a pressure gauge, or determine the cause for the oil pressure warning light to function when the engine is running, before operating the engine for an extended period of time. Another symptom of operating an engine with low oil pressure is the presence of severe knocking and tapping noises.

**Parking Brake Warning Light**

a. Check the brake release mechanism and verify the parking brake has been fully released.
b. Check the parking brake light switch for looseness or misalignment.
c. Check for a damaged switch or a loose or shorted brake light switch wire, and replace or repair as necessary.

### *2. Warning light(s) flickers on and off when driving*

**Ignition, Battery or Alternator Warning Light**

a. Check the alternator output and voltage regulator operation. An intermittent condition may indicate worn brushes, an internal short, or a defective voltage regulator. Replace the alternator or failed component.
b. Check the warning light wiring for a shorted, pinched or damaged wire and repair as necessary.

**Check Engine Light**

a. Check the engine for required maintenance and tune-up status. Verify engine tune-up specifications, as well as spark plug, air filter and engine oil condition; replace and/or adjust items as necessary.
b. Check the fuel tank for low fuel level causing an intermittent lean fuel mixture. Top off fuel tank and reset check engine light.
c. Check for an intermittent failure or partially disconnected engine fuel and ignition component, sensor or control unit; repair or replace as necessary.
d. Check the intake manifold and vacuum hoses for air leaks, and repair as necessary.
e. Check the warning light wiring for a shorted, pinched or damaged wire and repair as necessary.

**Anti-Lock Braking System (ABS) Light**

a. Check the wheel sensors and sensor rings for debris, and clean as necessary.
b. Check the brake master cylinder for fluid leakage or seal failure and replace as necessary.
c. Check the ABS control unit, pump and proportioning valves for proper operation, and replace as necessary.
d. Check the sensor wiring at the wheel sensors and the ABS control unit for a loose or shorted wire and repair as necessary.

**Brake Warning Light**

a. Check the brake fluid level and check for possible leakage from the hydraulic lines and seals. Top off brake fluid and repair leakage as necessary.
b. Check the brake linings for wear and replace as necessary.
c. Check for a loose or shorted brake warning light sensor or wire, and replace or repair as necessary.

**Oil Pressure Warning Light**

a. Stop the engine immediately. Check the engine oil level and check for a sudden and rapid oil loss, such as a leaking oil line or oil pressure sensor, and repair or replace as necessary.
b. Check the oil pressure sensor operation by substituting a known good sensor.
c. Check the oil pressure sensor wire for being shorted to ground. Disconnect the wire from the oil pressure sensor and with the ignition in the ON position, but not running, the oil pressure light should not be working. If the light works with the wire disconnected, check the sensor wire for being shorted to ground. Check the wire routing to make sure the wire is not pinched and check for insulation damage. Repair or replace the wire as necessary and recheck before starting the engine.
d. Remove the oil pan and check for a clogged oil pick-up tube screen.

**Parking Brake Warning Light**

a. Check the brake release mechanism and verify the parking brake has been fully released.
b. Check the parking brake light switch for looseness or misalignment.
c. Check for a damaged switch or a loose or shorted brake light switch wire, and replace or repair as necessary.

***3. Warning light(s) inoperative with ignition on, and engine not started***

a. Check for a defective bulb by installing a known good bulb.
b. Check for a defective wire using the appropriate wiring diagram(s).
c. Check for a defective sending unit by removing and then grounding the wire at the sending unit. If the light comes on with the ignition on when grounding the wire, replace the sending unit.

## 5-F. Turn Signal and 4-Way Hazard Lights

***1. Turn signals or hazard lights come on, but do not flash***

a. Check for a defective flasher unit and replace as necessary.

***2. Turn signals or hazard lights do not function on either side***

a. Check the fuse and replace, if defective.
b. Check the flasher unit by substituting a known good flasher unit.
c. Check the turn signal electrical system for a defective component, open circuit, short circuit or poor ground.

***3. Turn signals or hazard lights only work on one side***

a. Check for failed bulbs and replace as necessary.
b. Check for poor grounds in both housings and repair as necessary.

***4. One signal light does not work***

a. Check for a failed bulb and replace as necessary.
b. Check for corrosion in the bulb socket, and clean and repair as necessary.
c. Check for a poor ground at the bulb socket, and clean and repair as necessary.

***5. Turn signals flash too slowly***

a. Check signal bulb(s) wattage and replace with lower wattage bulb(s).

***6. Turn signals flash too fast***

a. Check signal bulb(s) wattage and replace with higher wattage bulb(s).
b. Check for installation of the correct flasher unit and replace if incorrect.

***7. Four-way hazard flasher indicator light inoperative***

a. Verify that the exterior lights are functioning and, if so, replace indicator bulb.
b. Check the operation of the warning flasher switch and replace if defective.

***8. Turn signal indicator light(s) do not work in either direction***

a. Verify that the exterior lights are functioning and, if so, replace indicator bulb(s).
b. Check for a defective flasher unit by substituting a known good unit.

***9. One turn signal indicator light does not work***

a. Check for a defective bulb and replace as necessary.
b. Check for a defective flasher unit by substituting a known good unit.

## 5-G. Horn

***1. Horn does not operate***

a. Check for a defective fuse and replace as necessary.
b. Check for battery voltage and ground at horn electrical connections when pressing the horn switch. If voltage is present, replace the horn assembly. If voltage or ground is not present, refer to Chassis Electrical coverage for additional troubleshooting techniques and circuit information.

***2. Horn has an unusual tone***

a. On single horn systems, replace the horn.
b. On dual horn systems, check the operation of the second horn. Dual horn systems have a high and low pitched horn. Unplug one horn at a time and recheck operation. Replace the horn which does not function.
c. Check for debris or condensation build-up in horn and verify the horn positioning. If the horn has a single opening, adjust the opening downward to allow for adequate drainage and to prevent debris build-up.

## 5-H. Windshield Wipers

***1. Windshield wipers do not operate***

a. Check fuse and replace as necessary.
b. Check switch operation and repair or replace as necessary.
c. Check for corroded, loose, disconnected or broken wires and clean or repair as necessary.
d. Check the ground circuit for the wiper switch or motor and repair as necessary.

***2. Windshield wiper motor makes a humming noise, gets hot or blows fuses***

a. Wiper motor damaged internally; replace the wiper motor.
b. Wiper linkage bent, damaged or seized. Repair or replace wiper linkage as necessary.

***3. Windshield wiper motor operates, but one or both wipers fail to move***

a. Windshield wiper motor linkage loose or disconnected. Repair or replace linkage as necessary.
b. Windshield wiper arms loose on wiper pivots. Secure wiper arm to pivot or replace both the wiper arm and pivot assembly.

***4. Windshield wipers will not park***

a. Check the wiper switch operation and verify that the switch properly interrupts the power supplied to the wiper motor.
b. If the wiper switch is functioning properly, the wiper motor parking circuit has failed. Replace the wiper motor assembly. Operate the wiper motor at least one time before installing the arms and blades to ensure correct positioning, then recheck using the highest wiper speed on a wet windshield to make sure the arms and blades do not contact the windshield trim.

## 6. INSTRUMENTS AND GAUGES

### 6-A. Speedometer (Cable Operated)

***1. Speedometer does not work***

a. Check and verify that the speedometer cable is properly seated into the speedometer assembly and the speedometer drive gear.
b. Check the speedometer cable for breakage or rounded-off cable ends where the cable seats into the speedometer drive gear and into the speedometer assembly. If damaged, broken or the cable ends are rounded off, replace the cable.
c. Check speedometer drive gear condition and replace as necessary.
d. Install a known good speedometer to test for proper operation. If the substituted speedometer functions properly, replace the speedometer assembly.

***2. Speedometer needle fluctuates when driving at steady speeds.***

a. Check speedometer cable routing or sheathing for sharp bends or kinks. Route cable to minimize sharp bends or kinks. If the sheathing has been damaged, replace the cable assembly.
b. Check the speedometer cable for adequate lubrication. Remove the cable, inspect for damage, clean, lubricate and reinstall. If the cable has been damaged, replace the cable.

***3. Speedometer works intermittently***

a. Check the cable and verify that the cable is fully installed and the fasteners are secure.
b. Check the cable ends for wear and rounding, and replace as necessary.

### 6-B. Speedometer (Electronically Operated)

***1. Speedometer does not work***

a. Check the speed sensor pickup and replace as necessary.
b. Check the wiring between the speed sensor and the speedometer for corroded terminals, loose connections or broken wires and clean or repair as necessary.
c. Install a known good speedometer to test for proper operation. If the substituted speedometer functions properly, replace the speedometer assembly.

***2. Speedometer works intermittently***

a. Check the wiring between the speed sensor and the speedometer for corroded terminals, loose connections or broken wires and clean or repair as necessary.
b. Check the speed sensor pickup and replace as necessary.

### 6-C. Fuel, Temperature and Oil Pressure Gauges

***1. Gauge does not register***

a. Check for a missing or blown fuse and replace as necessary.
b. Check for an open circuit in the gauge wiring. Repair wiring as necessary.
c. Gauge sending unit defective. Replace gauge sending unit.
d. Gauge or sending unit improperly installed. Verify installation and wiring, and repair as necessary.

***2. Gauge operates erratically***

a. Check for loose, shorted, damaged or corroded electrical connections or wiring and repair as necessary.
b. Check gauge sending units and replace as necessary.

***3. Gauge operates fully pegged***

a. Sending unit-to-gauge wire shorted to ground.
b. Sending unit defective; replace sending unit.
c. Gauge or sending unit not properly grounded.
d. Gauge or sending unit improperly installed. Verify installation and wiring, and repair as necessary.

## 7. CLIMATE CONTROL

### 7-A. Air Conditioner

***1. No air coming from air conditioner vents***

a. Check the air conditioner fuse and replace as necessary.
b. Air conditioner system discharged. Have the system evacuated, charged and leak tested by an MVAC certified technician, utilizing approved recovery/recycling equipment. Repair as necessary.
c. Air conditioner low pressure switch defective. Replace switch.
d. Air conditioner fan resistor pack defective. Replace resistor pack.
e. Loose connection, broken wiring or defective air conditioner relay in air conditioning electrical circuit. Repair wiring or replace relay as necessary.

***2. Air conditioner blows warm air***

a. Air conditioner system is discharged. Have the system evacuated, charged and leak tested by an MVAC certified technician, utilizing approved recovery/recycling equipment. Repair as necessary.
b. Air conditioner compressor clutch not engaging. Check compressor clutch wiring, electrical connections and compressor clutch, and repair or replace as necessary.

***3. Water collects on the interior floor when the air conditioner is used***

a. Air conditioner evaporator drain hose is blocked. Clear the drain hose where it exits the passenger compartment.
b. Air conditioner evaporator drain hose is disconnected. Secure the drain hose to the evaporator drainage tray under the dashboard.

***4. Air conditioner has a moldy odor when used***

a. The air conditioner evaporator drain hose is blocked or partially re-stricted, allowing condensation to build up around the evaporator and drainage tray. Clear the drain hose where it exits the passenger compartment.

## 7-B. Heater

### *1. Blower motor does not operate*

a. Check blower motor fuse and replace as necessary.
b. Check blower motor wiring for loose, damaged or corroded contacts and repair as necessary.
c. Check blower motor switch and resistor pack for open circuits, and repair or replace as necessary.
d. Check blower motor for internal damage and repair or replace as necessary.

### *2. Heater blows cool air*

a. Check the engine coolant level. If the coolant level is low, top off and bleed the air from the cooling system as necessary and check for coolant leaks.
b. Check engine coolant operating temperature. If coolant temperature is below specification, check for a damaged or stuck thermostat.
c. Check the heater control valve operation. Check the heater control valve cable or vacuum hose for proper installation. Move the heater temperature control from hot to cold several times and verify the operation of the heater control valve. With the engine at normal operating temperature and the heater temperature control in the full hot position, carefully feel the heater hose going into and exiting the control valve. If one heater hose is hot and the other is much cooler, replace the control valve.

### *3. Heater steams the windshield when used*

a. Check for a loose cooling system hose clamp or leaking coolant hose near the engine firewall or under the dash area, and repair as necessary.
b. Check for the existence of a sweet odor and fluid dripping from the heater floor vents, indicating a failed or damaged heater core. Pressure test the cooling system with the heater set to the fully warm position and check for fluid leakage from the floor vents. If leakage is verified, remove and replace the heater core assembly.

**NOTE: On some vehicles, the dashboard must be disassembled and removed to access the heater core.**

## GLOSSARY

**AIR/FUEL RATIO:** The ratio of air-to-gasoline by weight in the fuel mixture drawn into the engine.

**AIR INJECTION:** One method of reducing harmful exhaust emissions by injecting air into each of the exhaust ports of an engine. The fresh air entering the hot exhaust manifold causes any remaining fuel to be burned before it can exit the tailpipe.

**ALTERNATOR:** A device used for converting mechanical energy into electrical energy.

**AMMETER:** An instrument, calibrated in amperes, used to measure the flow of an electrical current in a circuit. Ammeters are always connected in series with the circuit being tested.

**AMPERE:** The rate of flow of electrical current present when one volt of electrical pressure is applied against one ohm of electrical resistance.

**ANALOG COMPUTER:** Any microprocessor that uses similar (analogous) electrical signals to make its calculations.

**ARMATURE:** A laminated, soft iron core wrapped by a wire that converts electrical energy to mechanical energy as in a motor or relay. When rotated in a magnetic field, it changes mechanical energy into electrical energy as in a generator.

**ATMOSPHERIC PRESSURE:** The pressure on the Earth's surface caused by the weight of the air in the atmosphere. At sea level, this pressure is 14.7 psi at 32°F (101 kPa at 0°C).

**ATOMIZATION:** The breaking down of a liquid into a fine mist that can be suspended in air.

**AXIAL PLAY:** Movement parallel to a shaft or bearing bore.

**BACKFIRE:** The sudden combustion of gases in the intake or exhaust system that results in a loud explosion.

**BACKLASH:** The clearance or play between two parts, such as meshed gears.

**BACKPRESSURE:** Restrictions in the exhaust system that slow the exit of exhaust gases from the combustion chamber.

**BAKELITE:** A heat resistant, plastic insulator material commonly used in printed circuit boards and transistorized components.

**BALL BEARING:** A bearing made up of hardened inner and outer races between which hardened steel balls roll.

**BALLAST RESISTOR:** A resistor in the primary ignition circuit that lowers voltage after the engine is started to reduce wear on ignition components.

**BEARING:** A friction reducing, supportive device usually located between a stationary part and a moving part.

**BIMETAL TEMPERATURE SENSOR:** Any sensor or switch made of two dissimilar types of metal that bend when heated or cooled due to the different expansion rates of the alloys. These types of sensors usually function as an on/off switch.

**BLOWBY:** Combustion gases, composed of water vapor and unburned fuel, that leak past the piston rings into the crankcase during normal engine operation. These gases are removed by the PCV system to prevent the buildup of harmful acids in the crankcase.

**BRAKE PAD:** A brake shoe and lining assembly used with disc brakes.

**BRAKE SHOE:** The backing for the brake lining. The term is, however, usually applied to the assembly of the brake backing and lining.

**BUSHING:** A liner, usually removable, for a bearing; an anti-friction liner used in place of a bearing.

**CALIPER:** A hydraulically activated device in a disc brake system, which is mounted straddling the brake rotor (disc). The caliper contains at least one piston and two brake pads. Hydraulic pressure on the piston(s) forces the pads against the rotor.

**CAMSHAFT:** A shaft in the engine on which are the lobes (cams) which operate the valves. The camshaft is driven by the crankshaft, via a belt, chain or gears, at one half the crankshaft speed.

**CAPACITOR:** A device which stores an electrical charge.

**CARBON MONOXIDE (CO):** A colorless, odorless gas given off as a normal byproduct of combustion. It is poisonous and extremely dangerous in confined areas, building up slowly to toxic levels without warning if adequate ventilation is not available.

**CARBURETOR:** A device, usually mounted on the intake manifold of an engine, which mixes the air and fuel in the proper proportion to allow even combustion.

**CATALYTIC CONVERTER:** A device installed in the exhaust system, like a muffler, that converts harmful byproducts of combustion into carbon dioxide and water vapor by means of a heat-producing chemical reaction.

**CENTRIFUGAL ADVANCE:** A mechanical method of advancing the spark timing by using flyweights in the distributor that react to centrifugal force generated by the distributor shaft rotation.

**CHECK VALVE:** Any one-way valve installed to permit the flow of air, fuel or vacuum in one direction only.

**CHOKE:** A device, usually a moveable valve, placed in the intake path of a carburetor to restrict the flow of air.

**CIRCUIT:** Any unbroken path through which an electrical current can flow. Also used to describe fuel flow in some instances.

**CIRCUIT BREAKER:** A switch which protects an electrical circuit from overload by opening the circuit when the current flow exceeds a predetermined level. Some circuit breakers must be reset manually, while most reset automatically.

**COIL (IGNITION):** A transformer in the ignition circuit which steps up the voltage provided to the spark plugs.

**COMBINATION MANIFOLD:** An assembly which includes both the intake and exhaust manifolds in one casting.

**COMBINATION VALVE:** A device used in some fuel systems that routes fuel vapors to a charcoal storage canister instead of venting them into the atmosphere. The valve relieves fuel tank pressure and allows fresh air into the tank as the fuel level drops to prevent a vapor lock situation.

**COMPRESSION RATIO:** The comparison of the total volume of the cylinder and combustion chamber with the piston at BDC and the piston at TDC.

**CONDENSER:** 1. An electrical device which acts to store an electrical charge, preventing voltage surges. 2. A radiator-like device in the air conditioning system in which refrigerant gas condenses into a liquid, giving off heat.

**CONDUCTOR:** Any material through which an electrical current can be transmitted easily.

**CONTINUITY:** Continuous or complete circuit. Can be checked with an ohmmeter.

**COUNTERSHAFT:** An intermediate shaft which is rotated by a mainshaft and transmits, in turn, that rotation to a working part.

**CRANKCASE:** The lower part of an engine in which the crankshaft and related parts operate.

**CRANKSHAFT:** The main driving shaft of an engine which receives reciprocating motion from the pistons and converts it to rotary motion.

**CYLINDER:** In an engine, the round hole in the engine block in which the piston(s) ride.

**CYLINDER BLOCK:** The main structural member of an engine in which is found the cylinders, crankshaft and other principal parts.

**CYLINDER HEAD:** The detachable portion of the engine, usually fastened to the top of the cylinder block and containing all or most of the combustion chambers. On overhead valve engines, it contains the valves and their operating parts. On overhead cam engines, it contains the camshaft as well.

**DEAD CENTER:** The extreme top or bottom of the piston stroke.

**DETONATION:** An unwanted explosion of the air/fuel mixture in the combustion chamber caused by excess heat and compression, advanced timing, or an overly lean mixture. Also referred to as "ping".

**DIAPHRAGM:** A thin, flexible wall separating two cavities, such as in a vacuum advance unit.

**DIESELING:** A condition in which hot spots in the combustion chamber cause the engine to run on after the key is turned off.

**DIFFERENTIAL:** A geared assembly which allows the transmission of motion between drive axles, giving one axle the ability to turn faster than the other.

**DIODE:** An electrical device that will allow current to flow in one direction only.

**DISC BRAKE:** A hydraulic braking assembly consisting of a brake disc, or rotor, mounted on an axle, and a caliper assembly containing, usually two brake pads which are activated by hydraulic pressure. The pads are forced against the sides of the disc, creating friction which slows the vehicle.

**DISTRIBUTOR:** A mechanically driven device on an engine which is responsible for electrically firing the spark plug at a predetermined point of the piston stroke.

**DOWEL PIN:** A pin, inserted in mating holes in two different parts allowing those parts to maintain a fixed relationship.

**DRUM BRAKE:** A braking system which consists of two brake shoes and one or two wheel cylinders, mounted on a fixed backing plate, and a brake drum, mounted on an axle, which revolves around the assembly.

**DWELL:** The rate, measured in degrees of shaft rotation, at which an electrical circuit cycles on and off.

**ELECTRONIC CONTROL UNIT (ECU):** Ignition module, module, amplifier or igniter. See Module for definition.

**ELECTRONIC IGNITION:** A system in which the timing and firing of the spark plugs is controlled by an electronic control unit, usually called a module. These systems have no points or condenser.

**END-PLAY:** The measured amount of axial movement in a shaft.

**ENGINE:** A device that converts heat into mechanical energy.

**EXHAUST MANIFOLD:** A set of cast passages or pipes which conduct exhaust gases from the engine.

**FEELER GAUGE:** A blade, usually metal, or precisely predetermined thickness, used to measure the clearance between two parts.

**FIRING ORDER:** The order in which combustion occurs in the cylinders of an engine. Also the order in which spark is distributed to the plugs by the distributor.

**FLOODING:** The presence of too much fuel in the intake manifold and combustion chamber which prevents the air/fuel mixture from firing, thereby causing a no-start situation.

**FLYWHEEL:** A disc shaped part bolted to the rear end of the crankshaft. Around the outer perimeter is affixed the ring gear. The starter drive engages the ring gear, turning the flywheel, which rotates the crankshaft, imparting the initial starting motion to the engine.

**FOOT POUND (ft. lbs. or sometimes, ft.lb.):** The amount of energy or work needed to raise an item weighing one pound, a distance of one foot.

**FUSE:** A protective device in a circuit which prevents circuit overload by breaking the circuit when a specific amperage is present. The device is constructed around a strip or wire of a lower amperage rating than the circuit it is designed to protect. When an amperage higher than that stamped on the fuse is present in the circuit, the strip or wire melts, opening the circuit.

**GEAR RATIO:** The ratio between the number of teeth on meshing gears.

**GENERATOR:** A device which converts mechanical energy into electrical energy.

**HEAT RANGE:** The measure of a spark plug's ability to dissipate heat from its firing end. The higher the heat range, the hotter the plug fires.

**HUB:** The center part of a wheel or gear.

**HYDROCARBON (HC):** Any chemical compound made up of hydrogen and carbon. A major pollutant formed by the engine as a byproduct of combustion.

**HYDROMETER:** An instrument used to measure the specific gravity of a solution.

**INCH POUND (inch lbs.; sometimes in.lb. or in. lbs.):** One twelfth of a foot pound.

**INDUCTION:** A means of transferring electrical energy in the form of a magnetic field. Principle used in the ignition coil to increase voltage.

**INJECTOR:** A device which receives metered fuel under relatively low pressure and is activated to inject the fuel into the engine under relatively high pressure at a predetermined time.

**INPUT SHAFT:** The shaft to which torque is applied, usually carrying the driving gear or gears.

**INTAKE MANIFOLD:** A casting of passages or pipes used to conduct air or a fuel/air mixture to the cylinders.

**JOURNAL:** The bearing surface within which a shaft operates.

**KEY:** A small block usually fitted in a notch between a shaft and a hub to prevent slippage of the two parts.

**MANIFOLD:** A casting of passages or set of pipes which connect the cylinders to an inlet or outlet source.

**MANIFOLD VACUUM:** Low pressure in an engine intake manifold formed just below the throttle plates. Manifold vacuum is highest at idle and drops under acceleration.

**MASTER CYLINDER:** The primary fluid pressurizing device in a hydraulic system. In automotive use, it is found in brake and hydraulic clutch systems and is pedal activated, either directly or, in a power brake system, through the power booster.

**MODULE:** Electronic control unit, amplifier or igniter of solid state or integrated design which controls the current flow in the ignition primary circuit based on input from the pick-up coil. When the module opens the primary circuit, high secondary voltage is induced in the coil.

**NEEDLE BEARING:** A bearing which consists of a number (usually a large number) of long, thin rollers.

**OHM:** (Ω) The unit used to measure the resistance of conductor-to-electrical flow. One ohm is the amount of resistance that limits current flow to one ampere in a circuit with one volt of pressure.

**OHMMETER:** An instrument used for measuring the resistance, in ohms, in an electrical circuit.

**OUTPUT SHAFT:** The shaft which transmits torque from a device, such as a transmission.

**OVERDRIVE:** A gear assembly which produces more shaft revolutions than that transmitted to it.

**OVERHEAD CAMSHAFT (OHC):** An engine configuration in which the camshaft is mounted on top of the cylinder head and operates the valve either directly or by means of rocker arms.

**OVERHEAD VALVE (OHV):** An engine configuration in which all of the valves are located in the cylinder head and the camshaft is located in the cylinder block. The camshaft operates the valves via lifters and pushrods.

**OXIDES OF NITROGEN (NOx):** Chemical compounds of nitrogen produced as a byproduct of combustion. They combine with hydrocarbons to produce smog.

**OXYGEN SENSOR:** Use with the feedback system to sense the presence of oxygen in the exhaust gas and signal the computer which can reference the voltage signal to an air/fuel ratio.

**PINION:** The smaller of two meshing gears.

**PISTON RING:** An open-ended ring with fits into a groove on the outer diameter of the piston. Its chief function is to form a seal between the piston and cylinder wall. Most automotive pistons have three rings: two for compression sealing; one for oil sealing.

**PRELOAD:** A predetermined load placed on a bearing during assembly or by adjustment.

**PRIMARY CIRCUIT:** the low voltage side of the ignition system which consists of the ignition switch, ballast resistor or resistance wire, bypass, coil, electronic control unit and pick-up coil as well as the connecting wires and harnesses.

**PRESS FIT:** The mating of two parts under pressure, due to the inner diameter of one being smaller than the outer diameter of the other, or vice versa; an interference fit.

**RACE:** The surface on the inner or outer ring of a bearing on which the balls, needles or rollers move.

**REGULATOR:** A device which maintains the amperage and/or voltage levels of a circuit at predetermined values.

**RELAY:** A switch which automatically opens and/or closes a circuit.

**RESISTANCE:** The opposition to the flow of current through a circuit or electrical device, and is measured in ohms. Resistance is equal to the voltage divided by the amperage.

**RESISTOR:** A device, usually made of wire, which offers a preset amount of resistance in an electrical circuit.

**RING GEAR:** The name given to a ring-shaped gear attached to a differential case, or affixed to a flywheel or as part of a planetary gear set.

**ROLLER BEARING:** A bearing made up of hardened inner and outer races between which hardened steel rollers move.

**ROTOR:** 1. The disc-shaped part of a disc brake assembly, upon which the brake pads bear; also called, brake disc. 2. The device mounted atop the distributor shaft, which passes current to the distributor cap tower contacts.

**SECONDARY CIRCUIT:** The high voltage side of the ignition system, usually above 20,000 volts. The secondary includes the ignition coil, coil wire, distributor cap and rotor, spark plug wires and spark plugs.

**SENDING UNIT:** A mechanical, electrical, hydraulic or electro-magnetic device which transmits information to a gauge.

**SENSOR:** Any device designed to measure engine operating conditions or ambient pressures and temperatures. Usually electronic in nature and designed to send a voltage signal to an on-board computer, some sensors may operate as a simple on/off switch or they may provide a variable voltage signal (like a potentiometer) as conditions or measured parameters change.

**SHIM:** Spacers of precise, predetermined thickness used between parts to establish a proper working relationship.

**SLAVE CYLINDER:** In automotive use, a device in the hydraulic clutch system which is activated by hydraulic force, disengaging the clutch.

**SOLENOID:** A coil used to produce a magnetic field, the effect of which is to produce work.

**SPARK PLUG:** A device screwed into the combustion chamber of a spark ignition engine. The basic construction is a conductive core inside of a ceramic insulator, mounted in an outer conductive base. An electrical charge from the spark plug wire travels along the conductive core and jumps a preset air gap to a grounding point or points at the end of the conductive base. The resultant spark ignites the fuel/air mixture in the combustion chamber.

**SPLINES:** Ridges machined or cast onto the outer diameter of a shaft or inner diameter of a bore to enable parts to mate without rotation.

**TACHOMETER:** A device used to measure the rotary speed of an engine, shaft, gear, etc., usually in rotations per minute.

**THERMOSTAT:** A valve, located in the cooling system of an engine, which is closed when cold and opens gradually in response to engine heating, controlling the temperature of the coolant and rate of coolant flow.

**TOP DEAD CENTER (TDC):** The point at which the piston reaches the top of its travel on the compression stroke.

**TORQUE:** The twisting force applied to an object.

**TORQUE CONVERTER:** A turbine used to transmit power from a driving member to a driven member via hydraulic action, providing changes in drive ratio and torque. In automotive use, it links the driveplate at the rear of the engine to the automatic transmission.

**TRANSDUCER:** A device used to change a force into an electrical signal.

**TRANSISTOR:** A semi-conductor component which can be actuated by a small voltage to perform an electrical switching function.

**TUNE-UP:** A regular maintenance function, usually associated with the replacement and adjustment of parts and components in the electrical and fuel systems of a vehicle for the purpose of attaining optimum performance.

**TURBOCHARGER:** An exhaust driven pump which compresses intake air and forces it into the combustion chambers at higher than atmospheric pressures. The increased air pressure allows more fuel to be burned and results in increased horsepower being produced.

**VACUUM ADVANCE:** A device which advances the ignition timing in response to increased engine vacuum.

**VACUUM GAUGE:** An instrument used to measure the presence of vacuum in a chamber.

**VALVE:** A device which control the pressure, direction of flow or rate of flow of a liquid or gas.

**VALVE CLEARANCE:** The measured gap between the end of the valve stem and the rocker arm, cam lobe or follower that activates the valve.

**VISCOSITY:** The rating of a liquid's internal resistance to flow.

**VOLTMETER:** An instrument used for measuring electrical force in units called volts. Voltmeters are always connected parallel with the circuit being tested.

**WHEEL CYLINDER:** Found in the automotive drum brake assembly, it is a device, actuated by hydraulic pressure, which, through internal pistons, pushes the brake shoes outward against the drums.

# MASTER INDEX


ABS MODULE 9-16
    REMOVAL & INSTALLATION 9-16
ADJUSTMENTS (AUTOMATIC TRANSAXLE) 7-4
    SHIFT LINKAGE 7-4
    THROTTLE CABLE 7-4
    THROTTLE VALVE CONTROL LINKAGE 7-4
ADJUSTMENTS (DISTRIBUTOR IGNITION) 2-3
ADJUSTMENTS (DISTRIBUTORLESS IGNITION SYSTEM) 2-6
**AIR BAG (SUPPLEMENTAL RESTRAINT SYSTEM) 6-7**
AIR CLEANER 1-16
    REMOVAL & INSTALLATION 1-16
AIR CONDITIONING COMPONENTS 6-15
    REMOVAL & INSTALLATION 6-15
AIR CONDITIONING SYSTEM 1-29
    PREVENTIVE MAINTENANCE 1-30
    SYSTEM INSPECTION 1-30
    SYSTEM SERVICE & REPAIR 1-29
AIR SPRINGS 8-14
    REMOVAL & INSTALLATION 8-14
ALTERNATOR 2-8
    REMOVAL & INSTALLATION 2-9
    TESTING 2-8
ALTERNATOR PRECAUTIONS 2-8
ANTENNA 10-4
    REPLACEMENT 10-4
**ANTI-LOCK BRAKE SYSTEM 9-16**
AODE TORQUE SPECIFICATIONS 7-14
**AUTOMATIC TRANSAXLE (DRIVE TRAIN) 7-4**
AUTOMATIC TRANSAXLE (FLUIDS AND LUBRICANTS) 1-36
    FLUID RECOMMENDATIONS 1-36
    LEVEL CHECK 1-37
**AUTOMATIC TRANSMISSION 7-2**
AUTOMATIC TRANSMISSION ASSEMBLY 7-3
    REMOVAL & INSTALLATION 7-3
AUTOMATIC TRANSMISSIONS 1-37
    FLUID RECOMMENDATIONS 1-37
    PAN & FILTER SERVICE 1-37
AVOIDING THE MOST COMMON MISTAKES 1-2
AVOIDING TROUBLE 1-2
AX4N TORQUE SPECIFICATIONS 7-14
AXLE HOUSING 7-12
    REMOVAL & INSTALLATION 7-12
AXLE SHAFT, BEARING AND SEAL 7-10
    REMOVAL & INSTALLATION 7-10
AXODE (AX4S) TORQUE SPECIFICATIONS 7-13
BALANCE SHAFT 3-40
    REMOVAL & INSTALLATION 3-40
BASIC ELECTRICAL THEORY 6-2
    HOW DOES ELECTRICITY WORK: THE WATER ANALOGY 6-2
    OHM'S LAW 6-2
**BASIC FUEL SYSTEM DIAGNOSIS 5-2**
BASIC OPERATING PRINCIPLES 9-2
    DISC BRAKES 9-2
    DRUM BRAKES 9-2
    POWER BOOSTERS 9-3
BATTERY 1-18
    BATTERY FLUID 1-18
    CABLES 1-19
    CHARGING 1-20
    GENERAL MAINTENANCE 1-18
    PRECAUTIONS 1-18
    REPLACEMENT 1-20
**BATTERY CABLES 6-7**
BELTS 1-20
    ADJUSTING 1-20
    INSPECTION 1-20
    REMOVAL AND INSTALLATION 1-21
BLEEDING THE ABS SYSTEM 9-19
BLEEDING THE BRAKE SYSTEM 9-4
BLOWER MOTOR 6-9
    REMOVAL & INSTALLATION 6-9

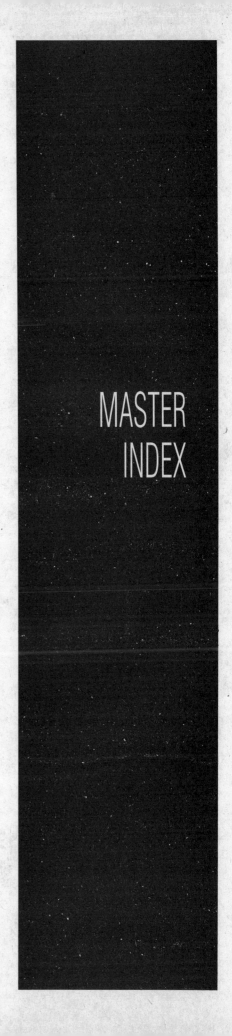

BOLTS, NUTS AND OTHER THREADED RETAINERS 1-7
BRAKE CALIPER 9-7
REMOVAL & INSTALLATION 9-7
BRAKE DISC (ROTOR) 9-8
INSPECTION 9-9
REMOVAL & INSTALLATION 9-8
BRAKE DRUMS 9-11
INSPECTION 9-11
REMOVAL & INSTALLATION 9-11
BRAKE LIGHT SWITCH 9-3
REMOVAL & INSTALLATION 9-3
**BRAKE OPERATING SYSTEM 9-2**
BRAKE PADS 9-5
INSPECTION 9-7
REMOVAL & INSTALLATION 9-5
BRAKE PRESSURE CONTROL VALVE 9-4
REMOVAL & INSTALLATION 9-4
BRAKE SHOES 9-11
ADJUSTMENTS 9-14
INSPECTION 9-11
REMOVAL & INSTALLATION 9-11
BRAKE SHOES (PARKING) 9-15
REMOVAL & INSTALLATION 9-15
BRAKE SPECIFICATIONS 9-20
BUY OR REBUILD? 3-44
CAMSHAFT, BEARINGS AND LIFTERS 3-38
INSPECTION 3-39
REMOVAL & INSTALLATION 3-38
CAMSHAFT POSITION SENSOR 4-12
REMOVAL & INSTALLATION 4-12
TESTING 4-12
CAPACITIES 1-48
CENTER CONSOLE 10-9
REMOVAL & INSTALLATION 10-9
**CHARGING SYSTEM 2-8**
CHASSIS GREASING 1-43
CIRCUIT BREAKERS 6-31
**CIRCUIT PROTECTION 6-29**
CLEARING CODES (TROUBLE CODES—EEC-IV SYSTEM) 4-21
CONTINUOUS MEMORY CODES 4-21
KEEP ALIVE MEMORY 4-21
CLEARING CODES (TROUBLE CODES—EEC-V SYSTEM (OBD-II)) 4-22
CONTINUOUS MEMORY CODES 4-22
KEEP ALIVE MEMORY 4-22
COIL SPRINGS (FRONT SUSPENSION) 8-4
REMOVAL & INSTALLATION 8-4
COIL SPRINGS (REAR SUSPENSION) 8-12
REMOVAL & INSTALLATION 8-12
COMMON EMISSIONS AND ELECTRONIC ENGINE CONTROL COMPONENT LOCATIONS—3.8L ENGINE 4-14
COMMON EMISSIONS AND ELECTRONIC ENGINE CONTROL COMPONENT LOCATIONS—4.6L ENGINE 4-15
COMMON EMISSIONS AND ELECTRONIC ENGINE CONTROL COMPONENT LOCATIONS—5.0L ENGINE 4-16
**COMPONENT LOCATIONS**
COMMON EMISSIONS AND ELECTRONIC ENGINE CONTROL COMPONENT LOCATIONS—3.8L ENGINE 4-14
COMMON EMISSIONS AND ELECTRONIC ENGINE CONTROL COMPONENT LOCATIONS—4.6L ENGINE 4-15
COMMON EMISSIONS AND ELECTRONIC ENGINE CONTROL COMPONENT LOCATIONS—5.0L ENGINE 4-16
REAR DRUM BRAKE COMPONENTS 9-10
UNDERHOOD COMPONENT LOCATIONS—3.8L ENGINE 1-13
UNDERHOOD COMPONENT LOCATIONS—4.6L ENGINE 1-14
UNDERHOOD COMPONENT LOCATIONS—5.0L ENGINE 1-15
CONTROL ARMS 8-18
REMOVAL & INSTALLATION 8-18
COOLANT TEMPERATURE SENSOR 2-10
REMOVAL & INSTALLATION 2-10
TESTING 2-10
COOLING SYSTEM 1-40
DRAIN & REFILL 1-41
FLUID RECOMMENDATION 1-40
FLUSHING & CLEANING THE SYSTEM 1-42
LEVEL CHECK 1-40
TESTING FOR LEAKS 1-40
CRANKSHAFT AND CAMSHAFT POSITION SENSORS 2-8
CRANKSHAFT DAMPER 3-32
REMOVAL & INSTALLATION 3-32
CRANKSHAFT POSITION SENSOR 4-13
OPERATION 4-13
REMOVAL & INSTALLATION 4-13
TESTING 4-13
**CRUISE CONTROL 6-15**
CRUISE CONTROL TROUBLESHOOTING 6-15
CV-BOOTS 1-22
INSPECTION 1-22
CYLINDER HEAD (ENGINE MECHANICAL) 3-24
REMOVAL & INSTALLATION 3-24
CYLINDER HEAD (ENGINE RECONDITIONING) 3-46
ASSEMBLY 3-50
DISASSEMBLY 3-46
INSPECTION 3-48
REFINISHING & REPAIRING 3-49
DATA LINK CONNECTOR 4-22
ELECTRICAL TOOLS 4-22
DETERMINING ENGINE CONDITION 3-43
COMPRESSION TEST 3-43
DIAGNOSIS AND TESTING (DISTRIBUTOR IGNITION) 2-2
CYLINDER DROP TEST 2-3
SECONDARY SPARK TEST 2-2
DIAGNOSIS AND TESTING (DISTRIBUTORLESS IGNITION SYSTEM) 2-6
DIAGNOSTIC LINK CONNECTOR 4-17
ELECTRICAL TOOLS 4-17
HAND-HELD SCAN TOOLS 4-17
**DISC BRAKES 9-5**
DISCONNECTING THE CABLES 6-7
DISTRIBUTOR 2-5
REMOVAL & INSTALLATION 2-5
DISTRIBUTOR CAP AND ROTOR 1-27
INSPECTION 1-27
REMOVAL AND INSTALLATION 1-27
**DISTRIBUTOR IGNITION 2-2**
**DISTRIBUTORLESS IGNITION SYSTEM 2-6**
DO'S 1-6
DON'TS 1-6
DOOR GLASS AND REGULATOR 10-15
REMOVAL & INSTALLATION 10-15
DOOR LOCKS 10-13
REMOVAL & INSTALLATION 10-13
DOOR PANELS 10-10
REMOVAL & INSTALLATION 10-10
DOOR WINDOW REGULATOR 10-17
REMOVAL & INSTALLATION 10-17
DOORS 10-2
ADJUSTMENT 10-2
DRIVE AXLE (FLUIDS AND LUBRICANTS) 1-38
DRAIN AND REFILL 1-39
FLUID RECOMMENDATIONS 1-38
LEVEL CHECK 1-39
DRIVE AXLE (SERIAL NUMBER IDENTIFICATION) 1-11
**DRIVELINE 7-9**
DRIVESHAFT AND U-JOINTS 7-9
REMOVAL & INSTALLATION 7-9
U-JOINT REPLACEMENT 7-10

**DRUM BRAKES 9-10**
DUCKBILL CLIP FITTING 5-2
REMOVAL & INSTALLATION 5-2
EEC-V DIAGNOSTIC TROUBLE CODES (DTC'S) 4-22
ELECTRIC FAN SWITCH 2-12
REMOVAL & INSTALLATION 2-12
TESTING 2-12
ELECTRIC FUEL PUMP 5-11
REMOVAL & INSTALLATION 5-11
ELECTRICAL COMPONENTS 6-2
CONNECTORS 6-4
GROUND 6-3
LOAD 6-3
POWER SOURCE 6-2
PROTECTIVE DEVICES 6-3
SWITCHES & RELAYS 6-3
WIRING & HARNESSES 6-4
**ELECTRONIC ENGINE CONTROLS 4-6**
**EMISSION CONTROLS 4-2**
ENGINE (ENGINE MECHANICAL) 3-4
REMOVAL & INSTALLATION 3-4
ENGINE (FLUIDS AND LUBRICANTS) 1-33
CHANGING OIL & FILTER 1-34
OIL LEVEL CHECK 1-33
ENGINE BLOCK 3-51
ASSEMBLY 3-53
DISASSEMBLY 3-51
GENERAL INFORMATION 3-51
INSPECTION 3-52
REFINISHING 3-53
ENGINE COOLANT TEMPERATURE (ECT) SENSOR 4-8
OPERATION 4-8
REMOVAL & INSTALLATION 4-9
TESTING 4-8
ENGINE FAN 3-20
REMOVAL & INSTALLATION 3-20
ENGINE IDENTIFICATION AND SPECIFICATIONS 1-12
**ENGINE MECHANICAL 3-2**
ENGINE MECHANICAL SPECIFICATIONS 3-2
ENGINE NUMBER 1-11
ENGINE OVERHAUL TIPS 3-44
CLEANING 3-44
OVERHAUL TIPS 3-44
REPAIRING DAMAGED THREADS 3-45
TOOLS 3-44
ENGINE PREPARATION 3-46
**ENGINE RECONDITIONING 3-43**
ENGINE START-UP AND BREAK-IN 3-56
BREAKING IT IN 3-56
KEEP IT MAINTAINED 3-56
STARTING THE ENGINE 3-56
**ENTERTAINMENT SYSTEMS 6-16**
EVAPORATIVE CANISTER 1-18
SERVICING 1-18
EVAPORATIVE EMISSION CONTROLS 4-2
OPERATION 4-2
REMOVAL & INSTALLATION 4-3
EXHAUST GAS RECIRCULATION SYSTEM 4-3
COMPONENT TESTING 4-4
OPERATION 4-3
REMOVAL & INSTALLATION 4-4
EXHAUST MANIFOLD 3-16
REMOVAL & INSTALLATION 3-16
**EXHAUST SYSTEM 3-42**
EXTENSION HOUSING SEAL 7-3
REMOVAL & INSTALLATION 7-3
**EXTERIOR 10-2**
**FASTENERS, MEASUREMENTS AND CONVERSIONS 1-7**
**FIRING ORDERS 2-8**
FLASHERS 6-31
FLUID DISPOSAL 1-33
FLUID PAN 7-4
REMOVAL & INSTALLATION 7-4
FLUID PAN AND FILTER SERVICE 7-2
REMOVAL & INSTALLATION 7-2
**FLUIDS AND LUBRICANTS 1-33**
FLYWHEEL/FLEXPLATE 3-41
REMOVAL & INSTALLATION 3-41
**FRONT SUSPENSION 8-4**
FRONT WHEEL BEARINGS 8-11
REPLACEMENT 8-11
FUEL AND ENGINE OIL RECOMMENDATIONS 1-33
FUEL 1-33
OIL 1-33
FUEL FILTER 1-16
REMOVAL & INSTALLATION 1-16
**FUEL LINES AND FITTINGS 5-2**
FUEL PRESSURE REGULATOR 5-10
REMOVAL & INSTALLATION 5-10
FUEL PUMP 5-5
REMOVAL & INSTALLATION 5-5
TESTING 5-5
FUEL RAIL AND FUEL INJECTOR(S) 5-7
REMOVAL & INSTALLATION 5-7
TESTING 5-9
**FUEL TANK 5-11**
FUSES 6-29
REPLACEMENT 6-29
FUSIBLE LINKS 6-29
REPLACEMENT 6-30
GASOLINE ENGINE TUNE-UP SPECIFICATIONS 1-29
**GASOLINE FUEL INJECTION SYSTEM 5-4**
GAUGES 6-23
REMOVAL & INSTALLATION 6-23
GENERAL INFORMATION (AIR BAG) 6-7
ARMING THE SYSTEM 6-9
DISARMING THE SYSTEM 6-8
SERVICE PRECAUTIONS 6-7
GENERAL INFORMATION (ANTI-LOCK BRAKE SYSTEM) 9-16
SYSTEM COMPONENTS 9-16
GENERAL INFORMATION (DISTRIBUTOR IGNITION) 2-2
THICK FILM INTEGRATED (TFI-IV) IGNITION SYSTEM 2-2
GENERAL INFORMATION (DISTRIBUTORLESS IGNITION SYSTEM) 2-6
ELECTRONIC DISTRIBUTORLESS IGNITION SYSTEM (EDIS) 2-6
OBD II—EEC V 2-6
GENERAL INFORMATION (GASOLINE FUEL INJECTION SYSTEM) 5-4
FUEL SYSTEM SERVICE PRECAUTIONS 5-5
GENERAL INFORMATION (TROUBLE CODES—EEC-IV SYSTEM) 4-17
FAILURE MODE EFFECTS MANAGEMENT (FMEM) 4-17
HARDWARE LIMITED OPERATION STRATEGY (HLOS) 4-17
GENERAL INFORMATION (TROUBLE CODES—EEC-V SYSTEM) 4-21
HAIRPIN CLIP FITTING 5-2
REMOVAL & INSTALLATION 5-2
HALFSHAFTS 7-6
REMOVAL & INSTALLATION 7-7
HEADLIGHTS 6-23
AIMING THE HEADLIGHTS 6-24
REMOVAL & INSTALLATION 6-23
HEATER CORE 6-11
REMOVAL & INSTALLATION 6-11
**HEATING AND AIR CONDITIONING 6-9**

HOOD 10-2
REMOVAL & INSTALLATION 10-2
HOSES 1-21
INSPECTION 1-21
REMOVAL & INSTALLATION 1-22
**HOW TO USE THIS BOOK 1-2**
HYDRAULIC CONTROL UNIT 9-17
REMOVAL & INSTALLATION 9-17
IDLE AIR CONTROL VALVE 4-8
OPERATION 4-8
REMOVAL & INSTALLATION 4-8
TESTING 4-8
IDLE SPEED AND MIXTURE ADJUSTMENTS 1-28
ADJUSTMENT 1-28
IGNITION COIL 2-3
REMOVAL & INSTALLATION 2-4
TESTING 2-3
IGNITION COIL PACK 2-6
REMOVAL & INSTALLATION 2-6
TESTING 2-6
IGNITION LOCK CYLINDER 8-21
REMOVAL & INSTALLATION 8-21
IGNITION MODULE (DISTRIBUTOR IGNITION) 2-4
REMOVAL & INSTALLATION 2-4
IGNITION MODULE (DISTRIBUTORLESS IGNITION SYSTEM) 2-7
REMOVAL & INSTALLATION 2-7
IGNITION SWITCH 8-20
REMOVAL & INSTALLATION 8-20
IGNITION TIMING 1-27
INSPECTION &ADJUSTMENT 1-28
INSIDE REAR VIEW MIRROR 10-18
REMOVAL & INSTALLATION 10-18
INSPECTION 3-42
REPLACEMENT 3-42
INSTRUMENT CLUSTER 6-21
REMOVAL & INSTALLATION 6-21
INSTRUMENT PANEL AND PAD 10-6
REMOVAL & INSTALLATION 10-6
**INSTRUMENTS AND SWITCHES 6-21**
INTAKE AIR TEMPERATURE SENSOR 4-10
OPERATION 4-10
REMOVAL & INSTALLATION 4-10
TESTING 4-10
INTAKE MANIFOLD 3-11
REMOVAL & INSTALLATION 3-11
**INTERIOR 10-6**
**JACKING 1-46**
JACKING PRECAUTIONS 1-46
**JUMP STARTING A DEAD BATTERY 1-45**
JUMP STARTING PRECAUTIONS 1-45
JUMP STARTING PROCEDURE 1-45
**LIGHTING 6-23**
LINCOLN VEHICLE IDENTIFICATION CHART 1-11
LOW OIL LEVEL SENSOR 2-11
REMOVAL & INSTALLATION 2-11
TESTING 2-11
LOWER BALL JOINT 8-9
INSPECTION 8-9
REMOVAL & INSTALLATION 8-9
LOWER CONTROL ARM 8-10
CONTROL ARM BUSHING REPLACEMENT 8-11
REMOVAL & INSTALLATION 8-10
MACPHERSON STRUTS 8-5
REMOVAL & INSTALLATION 8-5
MAINTENANCE OR REPAIR? 1-2
MALFUNCTION INDICATOR LAMP 4-22
MANIFOLD AIR PRESSURE (MAP) SENSOR 4-11
OPERATION 4-11
REMOVAL & INSTALLATION 4-12
TESTING 4-11
MANUAL LEVER POSITION (MLP) SENSOR/TRANSMISSION RANGE (TR) SENSOR 7-2
ADJUSTMENT 7-2
REMOVAL & INSTALLATION 7-2
MANUFACTURER RECOMMENDED NORMAL MAINTENANCE INTERVALS 1-46
MANUFACTURER RECOMMENDED SEVERE MAINTENANCE INTERVALS 1-47
MASS AIRFLOW SENSOR 4-10
OPERATION 4-10
REMOVAL & INSTALLATION 4-11
TESTING 4-11
MASTER CYLINDER (BRAKE OPERATING SYSTEM) 9-3
REMOVAL & INSTALLATION 9-3
MASTER CYLINDER (FLUIDS AND LUBRICANTS) 1-42
FLUID LEVEL 1-42
FLUID RECOMMENDATION 1-42
METERING VALVE 9-4
REMOVAL & INSTALLATION 9-4
MULTI-FUNCTION/COMBINATION SWITCH 8-19
REMOVAL & INSTALLATION 8-19
NEUTRAL SAFETY SWITCH (AUTOMATIC TRANSAXLE) 7-4
REMOVAL & INSTALLATION 7-4
NEUTRAL SAFETY SWITCH (AUTOMATIC TRANSMISSION) 7-2
ADJUSTMENT 7-2
REMOVAL & INSTALLATION 7-2
OIL PAN 3-29
REMOVAL & INSTALLATION 3-29
OIL PRESSURE SENDER/SWITCH 2-11
REMOVAL & INSTALLATION 2-11
TESTING 2-11
OIL PUMP 3-31
REMOVAL & INSTALLATION 3-31
OUTSIDE MIRRORS 10-3
REMOVAL & INSTALLATION 10-3
OVERHEAD CONSOLE 10-10
REMOVAL & INSTALLATION 10-10
OXYGEN SENSOR 4-6
OPERATION 4-6
REMOVAL & INSTALLATION 4-7
TESTING 4-7
**PARKING BRAKE 9-15**
PCV VALVE 1-18
REMOVAL & INSTALLATION 1-18
PINION SEAL 7-12
REMOVAL & INSTALLATION 7-12
POSITIVE CRANKCASE VENTILATION SYSTEM 4-2
OPERATION 4-2
REMOVAL & INSTALLATION 4-2
TESTING 4-2
POWER RACK AND PINION STEERING GEAR 8-26
REMOVAL & INSTALLATION 8-26
POWER STEERING GEAR 8-24
REMOVAL & INSTALLATION 8-24
POWER STEERING PUMP (FLUIDS AND LUBRICANTS) 1-43
FLUID RECOMMENDATION 1-43
LEVEL CHECK 1-43
POWER STEERING PUMP (STEERING) 8-25
BLEEDING 8-25
REMOVAL & INSTALLATION 8-25
POWER WINDOW MOTOR 10-18
REMOVAL & INSTALLATION 10-18
POWERTRAIN CONTROL MODULE (PCM) 4-6
OPERATION 4-6
PRESSURE RELIEF VALVE 5-11
REMOVAL & INSTALLATION 5-11

RADIATOR 3-18
REMOVAL & INALLATION 3-18
RADIO RECEIVER/APLIFIER/TAPE PLAYER/CD PLAYER 6-16
REMOVAL & INALLATION 6-16
READING CODES (OUBLE CODES—EEC-IV SYSTEM) 4-18
ELECTRONIC TTING 4-18
VISUAL INSPECON 4-18
READING CODES (OUBLE CODES—EEC-V SYSTEM) 4-22
REAR DRUM BRAKCOMPONENTS 9-10
REAR MAIN SEAL 3-40
REMOVAL & INALLATION 3-40
**REAR SUSPENSN 8-12**
REGULATOR 2-9
REMOVAL & INTALLATION 2-9
RELIEVING FUEL STEM PRESSURE 5-5
ROCKER ARM (VAE) COVER 3-8
REMOVAL & ISTALLATION 3-8
ROCKER ARMS/RLLER FOLLOWERS 3-10
REMOVAL & ISTALLATION 3-10
**ROUTINE MAINENANCE 1-13**
SEATS 10-19
REMOVAL & STALLATION 10-19
SENDING UNITSND SENSORS 2-10
**SENDING UNIT AND SENSORS 2-10**
**SERIAL NUMBR IDENTIFICATION 1-11**
**SERVICING YOR VEHICLE SAFELY 1-6**
SHOCK ABSORERS (FRONT SUSPENSION) 8-5
REMOVAL &NSTALLATION 8-5
TESTING 5
SHOCK ABSORERS (REAR SUSPENSION) 8-17
REMOVAL INSTALLATION 8-17
TESTING -18
SIGNAL AND MRKER LIGHTS 6-25
REMOVAL INSTALLATION 6-25
SPARK PLUG IRES 1-26
REMOVAL INSTALLATION 1-26
TESTING 1-26
SPARK PLUG 1-22
INSPECTIN & GAPPING 1-24
REMOVAL& INSTALLATION 1-23
SPARK PIG HEAT RANGE 1-23
SPEAKERS -17
REMOVA& INSTALLATION 6-17
SPECIAL TOOS 1-4
**SPECIFICATN CHARTS**
BRAKE SPEIFICATIONS 9-20
CAPACITIE 1-48
ENGINE IDTIFICATION AND SPECIFICATIONS 1-12
ENGINE MEHANICAL SPECIFICATIONS 3-2
GASOLINENGINE TUNE-UP SPECIFICATIONS 1-29
LINCOLN VHICLE IDENTIFICATION CHART 1-11
MANUFACURER RECOMMENDED NORMAL MAINTENANCE INTERVAS 1-46
MANUFACURER RECOMMENDED SEVERE MAINTENANCE INTERVAS 1-47
TORQUE SECIFICATIONS (BODY AND TRIM) 10-20
TORQUE SECIFICATIONS (DRIVE TRAIN) 7-13
TORQUE SECIFICATIONS (ENGINE AND ENGINE OVERHAL) 3-57
TORQUE SECIFICATIONS (SUSPENSION AND STEERING) 8-28
SPEED SENORS 9-17
REMOVL & INSTALLATION 9-17
SPINDLE -11
REMOVL & INSTALLATION 8-11
SPRING LCK COUPLING 5-2
REMOVL & INSTALLATION 5-2
STABILIZE BAR (FRONT SUSPENSION) 8-9
REMOAL & INSTALLATION 8-9
STABILIZER BAR (REAR SUSPENSION) 8-18
REMOVAL & INSTALLATION 8-18
STANDARD AND METRIC MEASUREMENTS 1-10
STARTER 2-10
REMOVAL & INSTALLATION 2-10
SOLENOID/RELAY REPLACEMENT 2-10
TESTING 2-10
**STARTING SYSTEM 2-10**
**STEERING 8-18**
STEERING LINKAGE 8-22
REMOVAL & INSTALLATION 8-22
STEERING WHEEL 8-18
REMOVAL & INSTALLATION 8-18
TANK ASSEMBLY 5-11
REMOVAL & INSTALLATION 5-11
TEST EQUIPMENT 6-4
JUMPER WIRES 6-4
MULTIMETERS 6-5
TEST LIGHTS 6-5
TESTING 6-6
OPEN CIRCUITS 6-6
RESISTANCE 6-6
SHORT CIRCUITS 6-6
VOLTAGE 6-6
VOLTAGE DROP 6-6
THERMOSTAT 3-10
REMOVAL & INSTALLATION 3-10
THROTTLE BODY 5-5
REMOVAL & INSTALLATION 5-5
THROTTLE POSITION SENSOR 4-12
OPERATION 4-12
REMOVAL & INSTALLATION 4-12
TESTING 4-12
TIMING CHAIN AND GEARS 3-35
REMOVAL & INSTALLATION 3-35
TIMING CHAIN COVER 3-34
REMOVAL & INSTALLATION 3-34
REMOVAL & INSTALLATION 3-35
TIRES AND WHEELS 1-30
INFLATION & INSPECTION 1-31
TIRE DESIGN 1-31
TIRE ROTATION 1-31
TIRE STORAGE 1-31
**TOOLS AND EQUIPMENT 1-3**
TORQUE 1-7
TORQUE ANGLE METERS 1-10
TORQUE WRENCHES 1-8
TORQUE SPECIFICATIONS (BODY AND TRIM) 10-20
TORQUE SPECIFICATIONS (DRIVE TRAIN) 7-13
TORQUE SPECIFICATIONS (ENGINE AND ENGINE OVERHAUL) 3-57
TORQUE SPECIFICATIONS (SUSPENSION AND STEERING) 8-28
TRANSAXLE 7-5
REMOVAL & INSTALLATION 7-5
TRANSMISSION/TRANSAXLE NUMBER 1-11
**TROUBLE CODES—EEC-IV SYSTEM 4-17**
**TROUBLE CODES—EEC-V SYSTEM (OBD-II) 4-21**
**TROUBLESHOOTING CHART**
CRUISE CONTROL TROUBLESHOOTING 6-15
TROUBLESHOOTING ELECTRICAL SYSTEMS 6-5
TRUNK LID 10-3
ALIGNMENT 10-3
UNDERHOOD COMPONENT LOCATIONS—3.8L ENGINE 1-13
UNDERHOOD COMPONENT LOCATIONS—4.6L ENGINE 1-14
UNDERHOOD COMPONENT LOCATIONS—5.0L ENGINE 1-15
**UNDERSTANDING AND TROUBLESHOOTING ELECTRICAL SYSTEMS 6-2**
UPPER BALL JOINT 8-8

INSPECTION 8-8
REMOVAL & INSTALLATION 8-8
UPPER CONTROL ARM 8-9
CONTROL ARM BUSHING REPLACEMENT 8-10
REMOVAL & INSTALLATION 8-9
**VACUUM DIAGRAMS 4-27**
VALVE LASH 1-28
ADJUSTMENT 1-28
VEHICLE IDENTIFICATION PLATE 1-11
WATER PUMP 3-21
REMOVAL & INSTALLATION 3-21
WHEEL ALIGNMENT 8-12
CAMBER 8-12
CASTER 8-12
TOE 8-12
WHEEL BEARINGS 1-43
REPACKING 1-43
WHEEL CYLINDERS 9-14
INSPECTION 9-14
REMOVAL & INSTALLATION 9-14
WHEEL LUG STUDS 8-2
REMOVAL & INSTALLATION 8-2
**WHEELS 8-2**
WHEELS (WHEELS) 8-2
INSPECTION 8-2
REMOVAL & INSTALLATION 8-2
WHERE TO BEGIN 1-2
WINDSHIELD WIPER BLADE AND ARM 6-19
REMOVAL & INSTALLATION 6-19
WINDSHIELD WIPER MOTOR 6-20
REMOVAL & INSTALLATION 6-20
WINDSHIELD WIPER SWITCH 8-20
REMOVAL & INSTALLATION 8-20
WINDSHIELD WIPERS 1-30
ELEMENT (REFILL) CARE & REPLACEMENT 1-30
**WINDSHIELD WIPERS AND WASHERS 6-19**
WIRE AND CONNECTOR REPAIR 6-7
**WIRING DIAGRAMS 6-41**